Pravarasena's Setubandha

Pravarasena's

Setubandha

Original text in Prakrit
accompanied with Sanskrit rendering

English Translation with Extracts
from Unpublished Commentaries,
Critical Notes and an Introduction

by

Krishna Kanta Handiqui

Rashtriya Sanskrit Sansthan
Deemed University
Under M/o Human Resource Development
Govt. of India, New Delhi

D K PRINTWORLD
Publishers of Indian Traditions

Cataloging in Publication Data — DK
[Courtesy: D.K. Agencies (P) Ltd. <docinfo@dkagencies.com>]

Pravarasena, active 5th century.
[Setubanda. Polyglot]

Pravarasena's Setubandha: with original text in Prakrit accompanied with Sanskrit rendering /English translation with extracts from unpublished commentaries, critical notes and an introduction by Krishna Kanta Handiqui.
p. cm.
In Prakrit; translation in English and Sanskrit; commentary, critical notes and introductory matter in English.
Includes bibliographical references.
ISBN 13: 9788124607244

1. Rāma (Hindu deity) – Poetry. 2. Pravarasena, active 5th century. Setubanda I. Handiqui, Krishna Kanta. II. Title.

DDC 891.3 23

first published in 1976
Revised edition published in 2014
ISBN 13: 978-81-246-0724-4

Published by:
Rashtriya Sanskrit Sansthan
56-57, Institutional Area, Janakpuri,
New Delhi – 110 058
e-mail : rsks@nda.vsnl.net.in
Web : www.sanskrit.nic.in

and

D.K. Printworld (P) Ltd.
Regd. Office : *'Vedaśrī,'* F-395, Sudarshan Park,
New Delhi – 110 015
Phones : (011) 2545 3975, 2546 6019; *Fax* : 2546 5926
e-mail : indology@dkprintworld.com
Web : www.dkprintworld.com

Printed by: D.K. Printworld (P) Ltd., New Delhi

Foreword

LITERARY traditions in Sanskrit and Prakrit have gone hand-in-hand for more than two millennia in India. A unique bond existed between them leading to the rejuvenation of arts, cultures and literary creativity. Great poets of Sanskrit also wrote in Prakrit. If the lyrics of *Gāhāsatasai* made an everlasting impact on classical Sanskrit poetry, the great epics as well as Sanskrit Mahākāvyas formed models for the poets of Prakrit. *Setubandha* or *Rāvaṇavaho* by Pravarasena is an excellent example of this synchronization between diverse literary traditions of Sanskrit and Prakrit. Pravarasena was also a gifted Sanskrit poet as is evident from a number of *subhāṣitas* in old anthologies attributed to him.

The English translation of *Setubandha* with detailed "introduction" and notes by Prof. K.K. Handiqui has been one of the most monumental works of the past century in the field of Prakrit Mahākāvyas. This translation was published by Prakrit Text Society of Ahmedabad under the general editorship of Prof. H.C. Bhayani. The work was not easily available for so many years.

A number of editions of *Setubandha* are presently available. Besides the Kavyamālā edition printed with the commentary of Ramadāsabhūpati and Sanskrit College edition (1957) by Shri Radha Govind Vasak, there are editions with Hindi translations by Dr Asha Kumari and Dr Harishankar Pandey published from Varanasi. The need for an English translation of the poem with an authentic edition of the text was acutely felt in academic circles for a long time. Hence the present edition. The English translation by Prof. Handiqui is being printed here for the first time with the original poem and its Sanskrit rendering.

Marked with an amazing accuracy and analytical acumen, the study by Prof. Handiqui presents *Setubandha* in a holistic perspective. Bhayani had rightly termed Handiqui's rendition of *Setubandha* as a "critical translation", adding that "no recent work of Prakṛta literary scholarship matches the present work in richness of the exegetical materials culled after a meticulous scanning of numerous commentaries so as not to miss any significant detail".

With the maturity of an extraordinary scholar, Prof. Handiqui recovers and clarifies the original meanings, author's intentions and implications of poetic expressions in *Setubandha*. In doing so, he has copiously consulted the vast mass of Sanskrit commentaries, but has not let down the authority of his own.

In a very elaborate introduction Prof. Handiqui has comprehensively dealt with all the aspects of *Setubandha*, he has meticulously examined the issues of authorship, date and sources of the epic, has also taken into account the textual problems as well as the socio-cultural background of the poem.

I am extremely grateful to Mrs Ahalya Gogoi for having taken pains to make this work available to Rashtriya Sanskrit Sansthan (RSkS) and giving us permission to produce this new edition. I specially want to thank Shri Susheel Mittal and D.K. Printworld for collaborating with RSkS in bringing out this important treatise and for their meticulousness in carrying out the printing work. I am confident that the publication of this work will further stimulate the study of Prakrit literature.

Radhavallabh Tripathi
Vice-Chancellor
Rashtriya Sanskrit Sansthan, New Delhi

Preface

THE *Setubandha* is the only extant Prākṛta Mahākāvya that has come down to us from early times. The date of composition (*c.* fifth century CE) makes it a notable link in the evolution of the Mahākāvya in Prākṛta and Sanskrit. Further, as pointed out in the Introduction, the *Setubandha* has exercised unmistakable influence on Bhāravi and Māgha; and its importance lies in the fact that it represents a significant phase of the development of Kāvya poetry after Kālidāsa. Pravarasena's poem is often quoted in Alaṁkāra works, which points to the esteem in which it is held by Sanskrit writers on poetics.

The *Setubandha*, also called *Rāvaṇavaho*, was critically edited by S. Goldschmidt, and published for the first time in 1880 at Strassburg then in Germany. A German translation of the text followed in 1884 as the second volume of the work. The *Setubandha* was published in India by the Nirnaya Sagar Press, the second edition of which appeared in 1935. The only merit of this edition is that it contains the commentary of Rāmadāsa on the poem as well as the Sanskrit *chāyā*. Goldschmidt had utilized this commentary in manuscript, and had also access to an imperfect manuscript of the commentary of Kṛṣṇavipra.

It was on the basis of the above materials that I had commenced translating the *Setubandha* from Prākṛta. But after translating a few hundred verses, I realized the need to consult other commentaries besides that of Rāmadāsa; and at my request my lamented friend Dr P.K. Gode, Curator, Bhandarkar Oriental Research Institute, Poona, was kind enough to obtain for me transcripts of several unpublished commentaries from different manuscript libraries in India. The commentaries appeared to be of great value for a critical study of the poem, and it was thought advisable to include extracts from them as a supplement to the translation. The correction and revision of these extracts compiled from transcripts of imperfect manuscripts involved considerable time and labour; but a study of the commentaries encouraged me to undertake the translation anew with a better idea of Pravarasena's style and use of the Prākṛta language.

The translation generally follows Goldschmidt's edition based on the text of Rāmadāsa. It will however be seen that it does not always agree with the printed text of Goldschmidt, or that of the Nirnaya Sagar edition, because, except in a few cases, I have followed Rāmadāsa's readings only when they agreed with those of his predecessor Kulanātha. The relevant details have been explained in the opening section of the Introduction; and in all such cases of discrepancy, reference may be made to the Extracts where the readings of the principal commentators including Rāmadāsa have been clearly shown as far as they could be ascertained.

The extracts include substantial portions of the important commentaries of Kṛṣṇavipra, Mādhavayajvan and Kulanātha besides occasional excerpts from certain other commentaries. Details of all the commentaries utilized for this work and information about the original manuscripts will be found in the relevant section of the Introduction.

The book has been in the press for several years, and had to be printed at different places under difficult conditions. This stood in the way of continuous pagination necessitating the division of the volume into two parts.

In conclusion, I wish to pay homage to the memory of Dr P.K. Gode for his kindly help and co-operation which enabled me to continue working almost without interruption.

Dr A.N. Upadhye at whose suggestion I had undertaken this work passed away to my great sorrow shortly before the publication of the volume. Without his help and encouragement it would have been difficult for me to complete the task in my declining years marked by ill-health and bereavement. I express my sincere gratitude to him.

I am indebted to Shri D.D. Malvania, Secretary, Prakrit Text Society, for his unfailing courtesy and earnest efforts to expedite the publication of the volume.

Jorhat, Assam **K.K. Handiqui**
May, 1976

Contents

Abbreviations

Deva = Devarāṭa

Gaūḍa = *Gaūḍavaho*, ed. Pandit;

GOM = Master, *A Grammar of Old Marathi*. Oxford, 1964;

GS = *Gāthāsaptaśati* with the commentary of Gaṅgādhara, NS edn., 1889;

K = Kr̥ṣṇavipra

KM = *Kuvalayamālā;*

Kula = Kulanātha

Līlā = Līlāvaī;

Muda = Mudamalla

MY = Mādhavayajvan

OMR = Tulpule, *An Old Marathi Reader*, Poona, 1960.

R = Rāmadāsa

SC = *Setutattvacandrikā*

SK = *Sarasvatīkaṇṭhābharaṇa;*

Vasu = *Vāsudevahiṇḍī;*

Introduction

1. The Present Translation and the Text of the Setubandha

THE text of the *Setubandha* followed in the translation is that of the critical edition of Goldschmidt[1] which, on the whole, presents the Prākṛta original as explained by Rāma dāsa in his well-known commentary on the poem.

The different commentaries on the poem, utilized for the present work, revealed, however, a large number of variant readings, which could be classified into several interrelated groups. There is a considerable number of readings, for instance, in which Rāmadāsa of Rājasthān and Kulanātha of Bengal agree, differing herein from the south Indian commentators represented by Kṛṣṇavipra and others. There is, however, another group of readings in which Kulanātha, who is earlier than Rāmadāsa, agrees not with him, but with the southern commentators, and nearly always the readings of this group yield a better meaning than those of Rāmadāsa. We shall presently speak about the recension followed by Rāmadāsa and its relation to the other recensions of the *Setubandha*; but so far as the translation is concerned, we have, in the interest of clarity and intelligibility, consistently followed Rāmadāsa's readings only where he agrees with Kulanātha, and in most other cases preferred those which Kulanātha has in common with the south Indian commentators.

There are a few exceptions to what has been stated above. In one or two cases, e.g. setu 3.8,[2] Rāmadāsa's readings have been followed, as they appeared to be the best. Besides, there is a small number of

---

[1] Rāvaṇavaha oder Setubandha Prākṛta und Deutsch herausgegeben von Siegfried Goldschmidt. 1. Lieferung: Text, Index. Strassburg, 1880.

[2] It now appears that Rāmadāsa's reading in this verse also found in the commentary of Laṭakanamiśra.

readings in which the commentators differ from each other, and even the south Indians disagree among themselves. In such cases, too, unless otherwise stated, Rāmadāsa's readings have been followed *faute de mieux.*

In a translation based on different commentaries containing many alternative explanations, it is not always easy to hit upon the right meaning of a word or a phrase, especially on account of the vagueness of Prākr̥ta as a medium of expression; and there will always be room for improvement in the rendering of particular verses. In setu 1.22, for instance, it would be better to take *velā* in the sense of *samudrajalavr̥ddhi*, as suggested in Kr̥ṣṇavipra's alternative explanation, so that the rendering might be: "the pure-rayed pearls, the stars, . . . shone in the ocean of the firmament, adhering to its floodtide, the night". It is needless to give other example. The extracts from the commentaries appended to the translation contain adequate material for an evaluation of the different interpretations and variant readings.

2. The Setubandha: An Outline

The *Setubandha* of Pravarasena deals with a portion of the story of Rāma from the return of Hanumat from Laṅkā with the tidings of Sītā to the death of Rāvaṇa, with special emphasis on the construction of the great causeway between the mainland and the island. The poem, though written in Prākr̥ta, is well known to students of Sanskrit literature from the eulogistic references in Daṇḍin's *Kāvyādarśa* and Bāṇa's *Harṣacarita*. The reference to Pravarasena and his *Setubandha* in one of the introductory verses of the *Harṣacarita*[3] shows that the poems is earlier than the seventh century CE; and it is, in fact, believed to be about two centuries earlier than Bāṇa. Before we go into the question, it will be convenient to give an outline of the contents of the poem:

Canto I: Description of the autumn. Hanumat returns from Laṅkā with news of Sītā. The martial hosts of the *vānara*s led by Sugrīva march to the shore of the southern sea, accompanied by Rāma, on their way to the *rākṣasa* capital where Sītā is held captive.

---

[3] *kīrtiḥ pravarasenasya prayātā kumudojjvalā* । *sāgarasya paraṁ pāraṁ kapiseneva setunā* ॥

Canto II: The *vānara* host is paralysed with fear at the sight of the ocean which is elaborately described.

Canto III: Sugrīva in a warlike speech tries to stir up the valour of his followers. He exhorts them to exert themselves and traverse the ocean to destroy the enemy and rescue Sītā. He appeals to their sense of responsibility and praises the value of the silent performance of one's duties.

> This responsibility is yours. The master' authority is restricted to command. The lotus beds in the pools burst into bloom by themselves. The sun only adds to their lustre. —v. 6
>
> Rare are the honest persons that silently achieve their tasks. Few also are the trees that yield fruit without their flowering being noticed. —v. 9

Sugrīva stresses the role of prestige and martial reputation, and dwells on the character of the valiant warrior.

> It is unthinkable that one's prestige, never lowered before, should be humiliated by others, the prestige that hath been built up with a sense of pride, and maintained from one generation to another.
>
> Martial reputation radiates enthusiasm, and its value cannot be appreciated by those who lack ardour for war. It is hard to regain, once it departs, tarnished by disgrace.
>
> The valiant, who welcome the advent of war, and preserve their equanimity in weal and woe, remain steadfast even in danger, faces with a calamity brought by fate. —vv. 18-20

Death is preferable to the loss of self-respect.

> Death, not long life, is preferable for one that hath lost his pride, even if he takes possession of the enemy's wealth, maintains the renown of his family, and upholds the moral law. –v. 45

He tries to evoke the sympathies of the *vānara*s by an impassioned appeal in which he gives utterance to his loyalty and devotion to Rāma.

> While Rāma's heart is full of sorrow, and afflicted with delusion, and is like the moon, the mainstay of the night, when obscured by the clouds; . . . let none pity the lot of Sītā, suffering like a day lotus plant wilted by cold-rayed moon! While Rāma's heart, pining with love, is distraught with grief, what craving can one have for one's fading life? —vv. 47, 48

Sugrīva is vexed at the failure of his speech to produce any visible effect on the *vānara*s who remain as stolid as ever. He now changes his tone, and breaks out into a wild exaggeration of his own powers, declaring that he will alone traverse the ocean and ravage Laṅkā and slay Rāvaṇa with-out waiting for assistance from such unreliable followers.

Canto IV: The *vānara*s are warmed up by Sugrīva's provocative speech. He is criticized by Jāmavant, who begins his speech with a colourful reference to his miraculous longevity going back to primordial times. He counsels patience, and cautions Sugrīva against rash and precipitate action and reckless initiative, and reminds him of his responsibility as the leader of the army. Rāma, however, reiterates his confidence in Sugrīva; and Jāmavant suggests that they should request the ocean to provide a passage to the other shore. Meanwhile Vibhīṣaṇa arrives by air with his followers, and is presented to Rāma, who extols him for his virtuous conduct in sharp contrast to his *rākṣasa* origin, and then consecrates him as the future ruler of Laṅkā.

Canto V: Rāma undertakes a religious fast under the moonlit sky to induce the ocean to facilitate the crossing. But, in the morning, incensed at the unresponsive attitude of the ocean, he gives vent to his wrath by discharging his fiery arrows whose flames envelop the seething waters in a vast conflagration.

Canto VI: The ocean emerges grievously wounded by Rāma's arrows. He is supported by his consort Gaṅgā, and utters words that are "cogent though soft in tone, deeply significant though brief, dignified though polite, and outspoken though accompanied with praise". He regrets that he has incurred Rāma's displeasure by trying to maintain his pre-ordained stability and untraversable character, but tells him plainly that he has grievously suffered on many such occasions on account of Rāma's exploits during his career as Viṣṇu. Nevertheless he declares that the unhappiness caused to Rāma by his resistance grieves him more than the physical suffering inflicted upon him by the conflagration. He appeals to Rāma to save the waters which have to be stored up for the deluge; and points out that even if the waters are dried up by any means, the sodden seafloor will be as impassable as ever. The only way to reach Laṅkā is by a bridge of mountains to be built across the ocean (vv. 9-17). Rāma approves the idea; and at his command the *vānara*s, who are represented as giants endowed with supernatural strength, set about uprooting the mountains all over the mainland, and fly to the seashore, loaded with mountains poised on their shoulders.

Canto VII: The *vānara*s proceed to build the causeway "that was to be the touchstone of their valour; the precursor of the overthrow of Rāvaṇa's might; the abiding symbol of Rāma's fame". Heaps of mountains are vehemently dropped into the waters, convulsing the ocean and rocking the earth, but this does not produce the desired result.

> Formed by the mountains that were continuously released, and came in a long unbroken series, the causeway appeared to be built in the sky, but vanished as it plunged into the sea. — v. 70

Canto VIII: The remaining mountains are placed on the shore, and the sea becomes calm. The *vānara*s are worn out with toil, but the situation is saved by the genius of Nala, who at the request of Sugrīva applies his skill to the construction of the bridge. He methodically fits the mountains together as they are dropped in, and succeeds in building a causeway linking the Malaya mountain on the mainland with the plateau of the Suvela on the island of Laṅkā.

> Soaked in water, and clinging together, the mountains, with the join imperceptible, were not parted from each other, even though battered by the raging sea. — v. 32

The causeway is named after the great *vānara* architect.

> Did Nala's way drop on the sea, fashioned in the sky? Built long ago, was it hauled from the Malaya range? Did it come into being in the waters of the sea? Did it emerge from the nether regions, complete in structure? — v. 57

> The deer (on the mountains of the causeway) looked at the ocean, and the people at Nala, all together, with eyes full of fear lest the mountains should topple down and the waters of the mountain streams that cascaded far into the sea rose aloft as they dashed (against the waves) to the music provided by the jubilation of the apes. — v. 65

Some characteristic features of the bridge of mountains are mentioned.

> Portions of the causeway, built of crystal rocks, and interspersed between the mountains, seemed at places to be rent in the middle, being similar in colour to the tranquil sea.[4] —v. 91

> Peaks of the Himālaya, covered with snow, and those of the Malaya, fragrant with the broken sandal trees, could be clearly recognized, even though built into Nala's way. —v. 92

On completion of the causeway, the *vānara*s cross over to Laṅkā unopposed, with the result that the demons become remiss in carrying out the orders of their master Rāvaṇa.

Canto IX: The *vānara*s reach the Suvela mountain which is elaborately described.

Canto X: The sun sets as the *vānara*s occupy the Suvela. The canto opens with a long description of the evening scenery followed by an account of the gaieties of love of the young women of Laṅkā under the shadow of the impending disaster.

Canto XI. The evening has not proved as delightful to Rāvaṇa as to his subjects. He pines for Sītā amid the reproaches of his wives, who, after observing his condition, "did laugh at him; but having laughed, could not help pitying him". Musing for a while on how to gain Sītā's favour, Rāvaṇa concludes that she might perhaps yield if she saw the severed head of Rāma, because

> People dare violate their cherished principle out of fear, when they are helpless and humble for lack of friends, and see no cause for shame, with all hope gone owing to the loss of protection. —v. 29

Ordered by Rāvaṇa, the demons produce a severed head of Rāma by magic, exactly like the real one, and proceed to the pleasure garden where Sītā is held captive. Her pitiful condition is described in a number of verses (39-50). The demons are moved to pity, but leave the head before her, as ordered by Rāvaṇa.

> Sitā was seized with grief when she espied it, and began to tremble as the demons brought it near, and fainted when they said it was Rāma's head. —v. 53

---

[4] I.e., the transparent rocks looked like branches through which the waters of the sea seemed to flow.

> She shed no tears nor could even look at Rāma's head. Having fainted, she only sank to the ground, helpless like one dead. — v. 56
>
> With eyes closed as she swooned, she felt only bliss free from the pangs of separation, with the sorrow caused by Rāma's death forgotten for the moment. — v. 58

Coming to herself, she bemoans her fate.

> During separation from thee, I kept somehow alive in the hope of seeing thee, and thus have I seen thee. My hopes, although they were coming to fruition, were not fulfilled.
>
> The Earth will have another lord, and Royal Fortune pass to many an eminent man. How is it that this uncommon widowhood hath befallen me alone ? — vv. 77-78

She feels ashamed that she is alive after witnessing the severed head, and fears that she will be remembered as a woman that lacked the courage to die.

Trijaṭā, a *rākṣasa* woman who had befriended Sītā, tries to console her in her grief. She lays stress on the divine character of Rāma, and asks her not to judge him to be on a par with other men. How could she believe that the earth could hold Rāma's severed head without convulsions like the overturning of the earth and the commingling of the oceans, or the collapse of the mountains? The wind still breaks the branches of the trees in Rāvaṇa's palace garden, and the lotus blossoms there still close in contact with the rays of the moon, showing that Rāma is alive, and the forces of nature continue to function under his protection (vv. 90, 91).

Rāma will come to her before long.

> Soon wilt thou see Rāma happy with this bow unstrung, and serene and free from wrath, his face worn and pallid on account of separation from thee. — v. 93

Trijaṭā points to the pleasure garden, laid waste by Hanumat who was but a servant of Rāma, a symbol of the humiliation of Rāvaṇa's pride (v. 95). Then she says —

> Fainting and sinking to the ground, languid and drooping, thou art under such a delusion that even knowing it clearly to be a deception of the demons, I am likewise stricken with grief.

> Why hast thou no confidence in Rāma even now? He hath built a causeway between the Suvela and the Malaya before the eyes of the united demons, and stormed the peaks of the Suvela. —vv. 97, 98

Paying no heed to the admonition of Trijaṭā, Sītā sinks down upon her bossom, and then suddenly recovering herself, speaks again —

> Tell me if I am the same that first saw this head and sank to the ground, and then recovering from the swoon, see it again, and cling to life
> —v. 103

> Thou hadst sped hither, O scion of Raghu, . . . to save my life worn by the sorrows of separation; but I destroyed thy life, myself remaining alive.
> —v. 106

She looks at the severed head once more; and begs Trijaṭā to suffer her to die (v. 113). But her death, she says, will be a shameless one, "despicable because of lack of love", since she "accepted widowhood with a cruel heart" instead of resolving to die on seeing the head (v.114).

> "This is the fate of all, but such an end is unbecoming to those who have an exalted sense of honour." As she uttered these words she threw herself on the ground, beating her breast. —v. 115

> No more did she wish to lament, nor smote her breast, like an enemy. She shed no tears, but checked their flow. Her heart was bent on death.
> —v. 117

Trijaṭā consoles her again. It is impossible even to imagine what Sītā has thought to be true. Referring to the burning of Laṅkā by Hanumat, she argues: a single ape made the wails of the people re-echo through the houses of the city; how could Rāma die with the demons unscathed (v. 122)?

> It is impossible. Rāma cannot be killed. The world will soon be without any demons. I say so because I have foreseen it clearly. Believe me. To whom is the destruction of his race dear? —v. 123

She is aggrieved at the change in Rāvaṇa's character that makes him stoop to such meanness while Rāma is alive (v. 127); and reminds Sītā of his heroic achievements.

> Think not that the power of Rāma's arms couns for little. Its efficacy was seen in the slaying of Vāli. On account of it, the ocean, driven by his arrows, hath granted a pathway across its waters. On account of it, Laṅkā is besieged. —v. 128

She relates her dreams presaging Sītā's glory and the death of Rāvaṇa; and asks her to take heart and cease from weeping. "Let the illusion vanish, ignored and futile, and empty because the truth is known" (v. 131).

Sītā is not consoled by Trijaṭā's words until she hears the yelling of the *vānara*s and Rāma's war-drum at dawn, heralding the preparations for the impending battle.

Canto XII: The canto opens with a description of the morning scenery (vv. 1-20). Rāma takes up his bow, and the *vānara*s arm themselves with mountains and trees. The demons, awakened by the roll of Rāvaṇa's war-drum, hastily take leave of their mistresses, and rise up in arms against the invaders.

> Even as their mistresses restrained the martial zeal of the warriors it grew more ardent because of the rancour harboured against the enemy, all the more because they were reminded of the possible humiliation of their master — v. 51

The leaders of the demons equip themselves with armour, which is described in detail (vv. 54-63). Meanwhile, the *vānara*s close in upon Laṅkā and completely encircle the city; they smash the moats and demolish the fortified gate.

> The moats of Laṅkā looked like the brooks streaming down the damaged Suvela mountain and meandering on all sides, because their bejewelled embankments were smashed down by the apes, and the waters poured into the neighbouring hollows. — v. 75

The army of the demons begins to move after the storming of the city by the *vānara*s (v. 81). The movement of the vast multitude through the gates of the city is described in a few verses.

> The army took a devious route, unable to make its exit all at once: it was impeded by the congestion of the chariots, and crammed into the space between the mansions, with the elephant corps crowded into the gateways of the city. — v. 89

> Thus impeded at the gates, the army of the demons moved out of the city, dispersed along a wide front, like unto a river issuing from a cave with a single entrance, and flowing wide over the plains. — v. 93

The *vānara*s rush forth, "like a forest fire driven by a violent gale", on seeing the demons emerge through the gates.

> The army of the demons swelled, the infantry ready to strike, and the cavalry advancing on the flanks; the elephants urged on by the goad, and the chariots driven at full speed. —v. 96

> The wrathful warriors assailed the enemy, and were assailed in turn. Full of exalted martial pride, they slew and were slain. Only they yielded not on account of their Zeal. —v. 98

Canto XIII: The fighting continues. The demons who are well provided with horses, elephants and chariots are worsted in their encounter with the mountain-hurling *vānara*s.

> The chariots were dashed on the ground as the apes swooped down on them. The elephants, thrown up by the apes as they sprang into the air, had their limbs broken. The captured horses ran away, and the demon warriors were slain by the pursuring apes. —v. 22

> The troops scattered, with the tangled mass of chariots broken by the elephants, and the horses trapped in the chariots, and the foot-soldiers stumbling over the horses, and the elephants tumbling over the former. —v. 71

> The horses stood motionless, pursued and seized by the tail by the impetuous apes; and the chariots, with the fighters killed and the drivers fallen, were whirled away by the horses, frightened by the apes. —v. 76

In spite of their reverses, the demons return to the fray.

> The demons resumed the burden of war abondoned by them, and summoned their fading courage; retrieved their lost renown, and became unconquerable by the martial hosts of apes. —v. 79

The concluding verses describe a series of single combats between the chosen leaders of the demons and the *vānara*s: Prajaṅgha and Sugrīva, Aśaniprabha and Dvivida, Varjramuṣṭi and Mainda, Vidyunmālin and Suṣeṇa, Tapana and Nala, Jambūmālin and Hanumat, and Indrajit and Aṅgada (vv. 80-99). The leaders of the demons are slain with the exception of Indrajit, who has a trial of strength with Aṅgada, marked by vicissitudes that alternately give hopes and fears to their followers.

> Thereafter when Indrajit's spirit was broken by Aṅgada by dint of martial zeal, the apes made merry thinking that he was slain; but the demons rejoiced, because they knew that he had vanished by magic. —v. 99

Canto XIV: Rāma actively participates in the fighting, and his arrows play havoc among the demons. At nightfall Indrajit, flying aloft from his chariot broken by Aṅgada, moves about invisible in the sky, and discharges the miraculous serpent arrows at Rāma and Lakṣmaṇa, which penetrate through their limbs, paralysing and binding them fast. Rāma, followed by Lakṣmaṇa, sinks to the ground.

> When Rāma fell, the world was stupefied as when the mental faculties fail. It was suddenly plunged into gloom as at the setting of the sun. It appeared to be bereft of life as when the (severed) head falls to the ground. — v. 34

The *vānaras*, anxious and bewildered, "keep still as in a picture, their eyes fixed on Rāma, and hearts smitten with grief". Sugrīva, whose eyes are sprinkled with consecrated water by Vibhīṣaṇa, sees the hitherto invisible Indrajit and chases him to the gates of Laṅkā.

Forgetting at the moment his grief for Sītā, Rāma bewails the fate of Lakṣmaṇa and bids farewell to Sugrīva.

> So lose not heart. Depart quickly by that very causeway, and see thy kinsfolk. Hard it is to know the working of fate. — v. 48.

Choking back his tears, and without answering Rāma, Sugrīva asks the *vānaras* to carry him and Lakṣmaṇa in comfort to the city of the apes. Then in an emotional outburst he declares his resolve to chastise and kill Rāvaṇa that very day.

> I will break his Candrahāsa sword with my hands even as it is plunged into my shoulder; while his weapons will tumble out of his chariot, grabbed, kicked and smashed by me. — v. 52

> With my hands I will part, pull and sever each of his groaning heads from the body, and dash it down; and with my nails tear out his heart, attached to Sītā in vain. — v. 54

Learning from Vibhīṣaṇa that the arrows are live serpents, Rāma meditates on the mystic formula sacred to Garuḍa, the serpent-destroying bird that carries Viṣṇu on its back. In an instant the mighty bird rushes in, raising a violent gale and stirring up the sea with its speed; and the serpents disappear as soon as Rāma embraces Garuḍa (vv. 56-61).

Hearing of the deliverance of Rāma by Garuḍa, Rāvaṇa entrusts Dhūmrākṣa with the conduct of the war. In the fatal encounter of the demons with the *vānara*s he attacks Hanumat with arrows and other weapons that prove ineffectual. The latter wrecks Dhūmrākṣa's chariot at one fell swoop, and after snatching his bow from him, mocks at the demon. He then strangles him to death (vv. 62-69).

Hanumat kills also Akampana, Dhūmrākṣa's successor, "tearing asunder his limbs one by one, and scattering them about", after which Prahasta takes the field (vv. 70, 71).

The remaining verses describe the combat between Prahasta and the *vānara* leader Nīla, who hurls at him mountains, trees and boulders that are swiftly riven by arrows of the demon. Ultimately Nīla springs high into the air, and hurls a massive rock, shattering Prahasta with the blow.

Canto XV: Shedding tears at the death of Prahasta, Rāvaṇa goes out to fight, and chases the host of *vānara*s out of the battlefield. They are rallied by their leader Nīla; and Rāvaṇa, hit by Rāma's arrows, beats a hasty retreat, the *vānara*s making fun of his chariot as he hurries back to Laṅkā.

Faced with ruin, Rāvaṇa wakes up the sleeping Kumbhakarṇa who sallies out after a hearty laugh at the trivial command to kill Rāma. At the sight of his stupendous figure the *vānara*s run away, dropping their mountains; but, after protracted fighting, his arms and then his lofty head are struck off by Rāma's arrows. Hearing of Kumbhakarṇa's death, Rāvaṇa is on the point of returning to the fray, but is held back by his son Meghanāda, who asks him to give him a chance to prove his worth; and promises to kill Rāma, or even outdo him in his feat of withering the ocean (vv. 25-29).

Meghanāda hastens to the battle and routs the *vānara*s, but is slain by Lakṣmaṇa as he proceeds to the shrine of Nikumbhilā to worship for victory. Smitten with grief and despair, Rāvaṇa attacks Lakṣmaṇa and pierces him in the chest with a lance. He is resuscitated by the plants of a mountain brought over by Hanumat, and fights with the demons as before (vv. 46-47).

Mātali, the charioteer of Indra, now descends from heaven in his master's chariot, and presents Rāma with the massive armour of Indra. As soon as Rāma mounts the chariot placed at his disposal, Lakṣmaṇa approaches him with Nīla and Sugrīva; and begs him to direct his wrath to something weightier than the killing of Rāvaṇa, and relegate the task to one of them. Rāma expresses his confidence in their capacity for success, but declines the request, asking them not to snatch Rāvaṇa from him, who has come face to face with him, like a wild elephant falling a prey to a lion's jaws (vv. 48-61).

Meanwhile Rāvaṇa sets about overwhelming the host of *vānara*s with his arrows, but the fight now resolves itself into an archery contest between Rāma and his adversary, "marked by equal valour, and momentous because of the certain death of one of them". At long last the cluster of Rāvaṇa's heads is severed all at once by Rāma with a single arrow (vv. 62-79).

Vibhīṣaṇa laments the death of Rāvaṇa (vv. 84ff).

> If I am pious, I who forsook thee, unforsaken by thy other kinsmen who shared thy joys and sorrows; then, O king, who should be counted first among the impious?
>
> Sorrowing over the killing of his kinsmen, Vibhīṣaṇa spoke to Rāma as he checked his oncoming tears with an effort more unbearable than death, like unto a mountain whose streams were dried by the heat of summer. — vv. 88, 89

He begs leave to fall at the feet of the dead Rāvaṇa and Kumbhakarṇa, and touch the head of "the child Meghanāda", his nephew. Moved to pity by his lament, Rāma orders Hanumat to perform the funeral rites for the lord of the demons.

Taking with him Sītā, purified in the fire like a bar of gold, Rāma returns to Ayodhyā "to crown Bharata's devotion to him with glory".

3. Pravarasena and the Setubandha

That Pravarsena, the author of the *Setubandha*, was a king is generally accepeted by our commentators, but they record different traditions about his identity. Kulanātha, in his gloss on *setu* 1.12, says that there is a tradition (*śruti*) that Anurāga is another name of the poet which he records in the concluding verse of each Canto. Anurāga is, in fact, one of the poets to whom a few verses of the *Gāthāsaptaśatī* are attributed by the commentators of that work; but there are also some verses ascribed to Pravarasena separately. There is no reason to assume that the same writer is quoted under two different names.

Kṛṣṇavipra's reference to the authorship of the *Setubandha* is more difficult to understand. He calls Pravarasena the Mahārāja of the Prākṛtas; and the phrase used by him is curiously like the peculiar expression employed in referring to the kings of the Vākāṭaka dynasty in their inscriptions. He says at the end of his gloss on Canto 1: *iti prākṛtānām mahārāja-śrī-pravarasenasya rājñaḥ skandhakākhye kāvye*, etc. followed by the remark: *prākṛtānāmiti nirdhāraṇe ṣaṣṭhi*.[5] Another commentator Kṛṣṇadāsa makes exactly the same remark except that he uses the word *madhye* after *prākṛtānāṁ*, making any grammatical observation unnecessary. Kṛṣṇavipra is a south Indian, and Kṛṣṇadāsa appears to be the same. It is difficult to say what they mean by *Prākṛta*. Besides, Kṛṣṇadāsa goes on to say that Vākappam is the name of Pravarasena's family (*pravarasenakulasya nāma*).

The colophon at the end of the *Setutattvacandrikā* commentary refers to Pravarasena as a "Cauhāna king". The statement is obviously wrong, as no king of that name is found in any of the branches of the Cauhāna dynasty, which, besides, belongs to a rather late period of Indian histroy.

Rāmadāsa who belongs to Rājasthān introduces an altogether new story about the authorship of the *Setubandha*. He says at the beginning of his commentary that the poem was composed by Kālidāsa for Mahārāja Pravarasena at the command of Mahārājādhirāja Vikramāditya. It may also be noted that the colophon at the end of the different Cantos in *some* of the *Setubandha* manuscripts belonging to the recension of Rāmadāsa refers to the poem as "composed by Pravarasena and made by Kālidāsa" (*śrī-*

---

[5] Kielhorn, while editing the Bālāghāṭ plates of Pṛthivīṣena II (*EI*, vol. IX, p. 267), remarks: "Here and in the congnate plates the Vākāṭaka kings have the title Mahārāja followed by the word *śrī* prefixed to their names, and before the title there stands in each case the genitive *vākāṭakānāṁ*, e.g. *vākāṭakānāṁ mahārāja-śrī-pravarasenasya*. . . . From the grammarian's point of view such a construction would be objectionable." It was probably to meet such an objection that Kṛṣṇavipra thought it necessary to explain the nature of the genitive in the expression recorded by him.

pravarasena-viraie kālidāsakae dahamuha-vahe mahākavve).[6] The report that the *Setubandha* was composed, or perhaps revised, by Kālidāsa is apparently based on a tradition current in Rajasthan, and not found in any of our commentators other than Rāmadāsa. Another such report seems to have been current at the time, as Rāmadāsa says in his gloss on *setu* 1.9 that, according to some, Pravarasena is Bhojadeva.[7] Apparently the famous Paramāra king and author of the first half of the eleventh century, an absurd date for the *Setubandha*. So far as Kālidāsa is concerned, considerations of style if not the date of composition militate against the attribution of the work to the famous poet, a point to which we shall presently return.

That Pravarasena, the author of the *Setubandha*, was a well-known king can be deduced from an inscription of the Cambodian king Yaśovarman, who reigned in the last decade of the ninth century CE. Verse 34 of this inscription says in praise of Yaśovarman:

> *yena pravarasenena dharma-setuṁ vivr̥ṇvatā* ।
> *paraḥ pravaraseno 'pi jitaḥ prākr̥tasetukr̥t* ॥[8]

Here, by a kind of word-play common in Kāvya poetry, the court panegyrist makes a comparison between Yaśovarman and Pravarasena. The former is also *pravarasena* "one that has an excellent army"; but while he built a bridge of piety (*dharmasetu*) consisting of his religious foundations, the other Pravarasena made only a *prākr̥tasetu*, which at first sight means *an ordinary bridge*, but really means *the Setukāvya composed in Prākr̥ta*. The fact that a distinguished king like Yaśovarman, the founder of Yośodharapura, the first captial of Cambodia,[9] is compared with Pravarasena shows the extent of the Indian king's fame as a poet in cultured circles in South-East Asia.

It is not very easy to determine the identity of Pravarsena, as several kings of that name are known to Indian history. Of these we may eliminate Pravarasena I and II of Kashmir whose reigns are

---

6 See NS edition. In Goldschmidt's edition the reference to Kālidāsa is found only at the end of three cantos.

7 *pravaraseno bhojadeva iti kecit.*

8 Majumdar ed., *Inscriptions of Kambuja*, p. 99, Calcutta: The Asiatic Society, 1953.

9 Coedès, *The Indianized States of Southeast Asia*, pp. 111ff., Honolulu, 1968.

included in Kalhaṇa's *Rājataraṅgiṇī*. The real name of the first was Śreṣṭhasena who was known also as Pravarsena and Juñjīna.[10] The second was his grandson and a much more important ruler whose career is treated at length in Kalhaṇa's Chronicle (3.106-378). He has been assigned to the second half of the sixth century CE; and is said to have introduced the art of constructing bridges of boats (*nausetu*) by having a great bridge of this type built over the Vitastā (3.354). The *Rājataraṅgiṇī*, however, does not attribute any literary activity to Pravarasena; and there appear to be no valid grounds for supposing, as is sometimes done, that he was the "author or patron" of the *Setubandha*.[11] It is well known that Kalhaṇa, while describing political events, occasionally gives valuable information about contemporary writers as well as the literary activities of particular kings. The *Setubandha* was a famous work for centuries before the completion of the *Rājataraṅgiṇī* in CE 1149-50; and is referred to by Kashmir writers on poetics from the ninth century onwards. If it were the work of Pravarasena of Kashmir, it would be difficult to explain why Kalhaṇa should have concealed the fact from his readers.

The other two kings to whom the authorship of the *Setubandha* could be attributed are Pravarasena II of the elder branch of the Vākāṭaka dynasty, and Pravarasena II of the younger branch of the same family of kings who ruled in Vidarbha, or the region comprising the former Central Provinces and Berar. The former has been assigned to the second quarter of the fifth century CE, and the latter to the early years of the same century.[12] Pravarasena II of the elder branch is preferred as the author of the poem, apparently because he had a longer reign, and is much better known from his inscriptions. As a matter of fact, all the inscriptions of the elder branch of the Vākāṭakas so far discovered, except a few, belong to the reign of Pravarasena II. He was a grandson of the famous Gupta emperor Candragupta II through his daughter Prabhāvatīguptā married to the Vākāṭaka king Rudrasena II. It is also conjectured that Kālidāsa, believed to have been the court-poet of Candragupta

---

[10] *Rājataraṅgiṇī* 3.97, ed. Stein.

[11] Keith, *A History of Sanskrit Literature*, p. 97.

[12] See Mirashi, "Inscriptions of the Vākāṭakas," *CII*, vol. V, 1963.

II, was probably deputed as a counsellor to the court of Pravarasena, and composed for him the *Setubandha*, as reported by Rāmadāsa.

As we have seen, Rāmadāsa's statement seems to be based on a late tradition current in Rajasthan; and whatever its value might be, it is impossible to accept the *Setubandha* as a composition of Kālidāsa on stylistic grounds. Keith is, on the whole, right when he says that the suggestion that Kālidāsa is responsible for the *Setubandha* "is excluded by the style, with its innumerable plays on words, alliterations, recondite similes, exaggeration, and its enormous compounds".[13]

The report that the *Setubandha* was composed by Kālidāsa seems to have been unknown to Bāṇa, who lived only 200 years after Pravarasena, and praises the achievements of the two poets in separate verses in the prelude to his *Harṣacarita*. Among later poets, Kr̥ṣṇakavi, of uncertain date, pays quite different kinds of tribute of Kālidāsa and Pravarasena at the beginning of his poem *Bharatacarita*.[14]

After describing Kālidāsa's diction as beautiful like a water-lily or a pearlstring, and charming as the beloved's presence (1.3), he praises the *Setubandha* as a famous poem "that does not go deep into the understanding of the dull-witted", by which he seems to mean that the poem is hard to understand for the ordinary reader.[15] This is no doubt a fair assessment of the poem.

---

[13] Keith, op. cit., p. 97.

[14] Trivandrum Sanskrit Series.

[15] Kr̥ṣṇakavi says: *jalāśayasyāntaragāḍhamārgamalabdhabandhaṁ giricauryavr̥ttyā* I *lokeṣvalaṁ kāntamapūrvasetuṁ babandha kīrttyā saha kuntaleśaḥ* II (1.4). The verse plays upon the word *setu* (bridge) and the epithets applied to it. The apparent sense is: a king of Kuntala built a marvellous bridge that was not planted in any repository of water (i.e. the ocean), nor was it erected by "stealing" the mountains, i.e. uprooting and carrying them away for building the bridge, as described by Pravarasena. The real meaning is that he produced the wonderful *Setukāvya* that was not fully understood by the dull-witted, nor was it composed by resorting to theft, i.e. plagiarism. The phrase *giricauryavr̥ttyā* should also be construed as *giri cauryavr̥ttyā*. Similarly, *jalāśaya* should also be taken as *jaḍāśaya* according to the dictum *ḍa-layoraikyam*. Cf. Bhoja (*SK*) 2.75. There is a similar play on *jalāśaya* in the *Avantīsundarī* of Daṇḍin in connection with the *Setubandha*. The citizens of Kusumapura in Magadha are described as *na jalāśayāḥ setubandhalagnāśca*. The apparent meaning →

As regards the authorship of the *Setubandha*, Kṛṣṇakavi says that it was composed by a king of Kuntala. It is a rather vague statement, as the name Kuntala is applied to various parts of Deccan and Mysore.[16] Kṛṣṇakavi's statement has, however, some relevance to the identification of Kuntala with Vidarbha by Rājaśekhara in one of his works. In the *Kāvyamīmāṁsā* he mentions Mahārāṣṭra, Vidarbha and Kuntala separately among the countries of southern India[17];

→ of the phrase is: "they are not tanks; yet have bridges fixed in them". The real meaning is: "they are not *jaḍāśaya* (dull), so are devoted to the study of the *Setubandha*". Trivandrum edn., p. 20.

[16] Pratiṣṭhāna (Paiṭhan) on the Godāvarī in the former Hyderabad state is twice mentioned as the capital of Kuntala in the *Udayasundarīkathā* of Soḍḍhala who lived in southern Gujarat and Koṅkaṇa in the first half of the eleventh century. — Mirashi, *Studies in Indology*, vol. IV, p. 129. The name was also applied to southern Mahārāṣṭra where an early Rāṣṭrakūṭa dynasty ruled with its capital at Mānapura, identified with Māṇ in Satārā district. An inscription found near Kolhapur describes the founder Mānāṅka as the ruler (*praśāsitā*) of the Kuntala country. — Ibid., pp. 124 ff. Certain parts of Karṇāṭaka are also called Kuntala, and sometimes the name is applied to the whole of Karṇāṭaka. The early Kadambas who ruled in north Mysore, Dhārwāṛ and Belgaum with their capital at Vanavāsī (Banavāsī in North kanara district) are described as ruling in Kuntala in *later* inscriptions. The Kadamba king Śāntivarman (*c.* CE 450-475) is, however, called the lord of the entire Karṇāṭa region in an inscription of his nephew Viṣṇuvarman. — Moraes, *Kadambakula*, p. 29: *The Vākāṭaka-Gupta Age*, p. 222. Similarly, Narasiṁha II (1220-35), the Hoysaḷa king of Mysore, is called the lord of Kuntala in the contemporary prose romance *Gadyakarṇāmṛta*. —Sastri, *The Colas*, 1955, p. 422; Introduction to *Alaṁkārasarvasva*, ed. Janki, p. 41, Delhi, 1965. An incription of CE 1385, engraved on a pillar in front of a Jaina temple at Vijayanagara (Hampī), locates the city in Kuntala which is called a district (*viṣaya*) of the wide Karṇāṭa country. — *South Indian Inscriptions*, vol. I, p. 155. On the other hand, the terms, Kuntala and Karṇāṭa are used as synonyms to designate the kingdom of the Cāḷukyas of Kalyāṇa in Bilhaṇa's *Vikramāṅkadevacarita* written in the last quarter of the eleventh century. — Bühler's introduction to his edition, p. 28. Earlier than this, Somadevasūri, in his *Yaśastilaka* (CE 959), mentions Vanavāsī, Karṇāṭa, and Kuntala separately in the same verse (1.211). The commentator here explains Vanavāsī as Girisopā (Gersoppa) and other town, i.e. the territory round Banavāsī. He explains Karṇāṭa as Vidara and other towns, an obvious reference to the territory of the Cāḷukyas of Kalyāṇa. He identifies Kuntala with Pūrvadeśa, probably Vidarbha, which is located in the south-east division in the *Bṛhatsaṁhitā* 14.8, and identified with Kuntala by Rājaśekhara (see below). In any case, if Kuntala is neither Vanavāsī nor Karṇāṭa, it can mean only some part of Maharashtra.

[17] Third edn., 1934. p. 93,

but in the *Bālarāmāyaṇa* he appears to identify Kuntala with Vidarbha and include the region in Mahārāṣṭra.[18] In the *Kāvyamīmāṁsā*[19] he locates the city of Vatsagulma Vindarbha; but in the *Karpūramāñjarī* he locates Vacchoma or Vatsagulma in Kuntala.[20] As pointed out by Sten Konow, the commentaries on the play call it the capital of Kuntala.[21] Vastagulma, identified with Bāsim in the Akolā district of Berar, was the capital of the younger branch of the Vākāṭakas. So if Kr̥ṣṇakavi's statement was based on an old tradition that the *Setubandha* was composed by a king of Kuntala, the reference would rather be to Pravarasena II of the younger branch ruling from Vatsagulma than to his namesake of the senior branch who ruled in northern Vidarbha. It is, however, difficult to say what a late writer like Kr̥ṣṇakavi had in his mind when he referred to Kuntala; and in any case the tradition that Vatsagulma was in Kuntala does not seem to go beyond the time of Rājaśekhara (ninth-tenth century). What is more important is that the Vākāṭakas do not call themselves rulers of Kuntala in their records. The references to Kuntala in their inscriptions show that it was outside the territory ruled by them.[22]

We may now turn to Pravarasena II of the elder branch, who has been assigned to the period *c.* CE 420-50. Nandivardhana, identified with Nandardhan or Nagardhan, was the capital of the

---

[18] In the third Act, the king of Krathakaiśika or Vidarbha is called "the lord of Kuntala" and "the best of men in Maharashtra". In the tenth Act, as soon as Sugrīva points out the country of Maharashtra to Rāma, the latter utters two verses, one of which extols the land of Vidarbha, and the other pays a compliment to the women of Kuntala (10.74, 75).

[19] P. 10.

[20] The jester, in the first Act, says that he had seen a beautiful maiden in the city of Vacchoma in the south; and at his request the magician makes her appear at the royal court where she introduces herself as the daughter of the king of the Kuntala country in the south.

[21] Harvard edn., p. 160.

[22] The wife of Narendrasena, the son and successor of Pravarasena II, is said to be the daughter of the king of Kuntala. Similarly, an inscription in Ajantā Cave XVI states that Vindhyasena of the younger branch of the Vākāṭakas defeated the king of Kuntala, which appears also among the countries overrun by his descendant Hariṣeṇa, the last known king of the dynasty.

— Mirashi, *Inscriptions of the Vākāṭakas*, pp. 81, 108

elder branch of the Vākāṭakas. It was about 3 miles from the sacred hill of Rāmṭek, a well-known centre of pilgrimage, 28 miles from Nagpur. Rāmṭek is no doubt Rāmagiri, immortalized by Kālidāsa in his *Meghadūta* and described as being marked with Rāma's footprints venerated by men.[23] Rāmagiri seems to have played a significant part in the cultural life of the Vākāṭakas. A land-grant of Prabhāvatīguptā, mother of Pravarasena II, was issued "from the feet of the lord of Rāmagiri",[24] which seems to be a reference to the shrine of Rāma at Rāmagiri, or perhaps his *pādukā*s which are still worshipped at Rāmṭek. The grant was made in the nineteenth year of Pravarasena's reign; and he, like his mother, no doubt venerated the shrine of Rāma in close vicinity to the capital. It was probably from Rāmagiri that Pravarsena drew his inspiration for writing a poem on the deeds of Rāma, laying stress on the building of the great causeway described by him as "the abiding symbol of Rāma's fame". Several early sculptures depicting scenes from the *Rāmāyaṇa* have also been discovered at Pavnār, a village 6 miles from Wardha, supposed to represent the site of the city of Pravarapura founded by Pravarasena. These panels possibly belonged to a temple of Rāma built at the new city.[25]

It is noteworthy that Rāma is presented in the *Setubandha* not as an incarnation of Viṣṇu, but as Viṣṇu himself, the latter's incarnations and functions being likewise attributed to him. The idea is clearly put forward in Brahmā's address to Rāma in the *Rāmāyaṇa* 6.105.12ff.; and Pravarasena has no doubt been influenced by the *Rāmāyaṇa* in his identification of Rāma with Viṣṇu. This is particularly in evidence in the Ocean's address to Rāma in *Setu* 6.10ff. Besides, Gaṅgā, the famous Viṣṇupadī, is described as having issued from the feet of Rāma, which are designated as "the feet of Hari"

---

[23] On Rāmagiri, see Mirashi, *Studies in Indology*, vol. 1, pp. 12ff; vol. IV, pp. 42ff.

[24] *rāmagirisvāminaḥ pādamūlāt*. — Mirashi, *Inscriptions of the Vākāṭakas*, p. 35. *Pādamūla* is a polite expression for *pāda*. It is frequently used in the early Prākṛt prose romance *Vasudevahiṇḍī*, e.g. *sāmissa pasādeṇa coraṁ sāmipādamūlaṁ uvaṇemi*, p. 39; *jiṇasāsaṇadhammaṁ soūṇa daḍhacittassa pāyamūle*, p. 49, etc. The word *mūla* is used alone to indicate nearness, e.g. *mama mūlaṁ dhāvamāṇo āgato*, p. 44; *visajjio me parijaṇo gharaṁ ammāe mūlaṁ*, p. 46 etc.

[25] Mirashi, op. cit., p. 23 and Introduction, chap. XI.

(6.8). The ocean is said to have served as Rāma's couch "at another epoch", and Lakṣmī mentioned as his "consort at the epoch of universal destruction" (2.38). Rāma is here identified with Viṣṇu resposing on the all-pervading ocean for the purpose of recreating the world after its total destruction, as related in the *Viṣṇu Purāṇa* I.2.60 and other texts. Further, in *Setu* 11.89, 96 Rāma is assumed to be the Supreme Being, and called the primal support of the three worlds (*tihuaṇamūlāhāra*), with which may be compared *Viṣṇu Purāṇa* II.13.2 (*viṣṇvādhāraṁ tathā caitat trailokyaṁ samavasthitam*). The emphasis with which Pravarasena glorifies Rāma in the *Setubandha* might indicate that he was influenced by the cult of Rāma at the familiar site of Rāmagiri.

The *Setubandha* throws further light on the religious tendencies of Pravarasena. As we have seen, he represents Rāma as Viṣṇu. Accordingly he devotes the first four of the invocatory verses of the *Setubandha* to Viṣṇu (1.1-4), but reserves the remaining four for the glorification of Śiva in the forms of Ardhanārīśvara and Naṭarāja. This is not surprising, as several of Pravarasena's inscriptions describe him as *parama māheśvara* or devoted worshipper of Śiva. As a matter of fact, the emotial fervour of the verses (1.5, 7, 8) in which he invokes Naṭarāja-Śiva might be an indication that, even though he venerated Viṣṇu as Rāma, his *iṣṭa devatā* was probably Maheśvara in his dancing form. His religious outlook appears to have been like that of Bhartṛhari, who says in his *Vairāgyaśataka* that he knows no difference between Maheśvara, the lord of the worlds, and Janārdana, the soul of the universe; nevertheless he adores the god crowned with the moon.[26] Such catholicity of views points to sectarian harmony in the early period; and there is nothing uncommon about a Śaiva of this type composing a poem in honour of Rāma. Kālidāsa's religious attitude is very similar. He invokes Śiva at the beginning of the *Raghuvaṁśa* and the *Abhijñānaśākuntala*, but glorifies Viṣṇu as the supreme arbiter of the universe in the hymn to that deity in the former work (10.16ff.).

The verses invoking Naṭarāja-Śiva in our poem contain probably the most eloquent description in old Indian poetry of the god's mystic dance. The all-pervading energy and ever-ebullient spirit of

[26] I.e., Śiva, verse 84, NS edn., 1957.

the Creative Power viewed as the Great Dancer find here terse but animated expression. Kālidāsa's mythological reference to Śiva's evening dance in the *Meghadūta* is picturesque, but not as impressive as Pravarasena's spirited vision of the dance as a cosmic phenomenon divested of mythological associations.

The dance of Śiva is believed to symbolize the endless, ever-recurring process of creation, maintenance and destruction; and one or other aspect of these functions of the deity is usually mentioned in his glorification as the Supreme Dancer.[27] A benedictory verse cited in Bharata's *Nāṭyaśāstra* 5.132,[28] for instance, describe Śiva's *tāṇḍava* dance at the end of the universal destruction, in the course of which the oceans are convulsed and the mountains overthrown by the impact of his feet. The creative aspect is emphasized in an elaborate verse quoted by Abhinavagupta,[29] in which the god is invoked as the architect of the universe (*trailokyasthapati*), initiating the manifold process of creation as he dances in marvellous poses on the stage of the sky, in the evening twilight, at the end of the night of destruction. The author of the *Mahimnastava* (v. 16) is puzzled by the mystery of Śiva's dance: its purpose is to sustain the world, but, while he dances, the earth is imperilled by the stamping of his feet, the stars are bruised by the movements of his hands, and the heavens lashed by the loosed hair.[30] On the other hand, one of the invocatory verses at the beginning of the *Mudrārākṣasa* postulates the idea that the deity dances with toil and trouble, because he has to slow down his steps and contract his arms and deflect the fiery glances from all that is visible to avoid injury to the universe, the scene of his dance. The *Setubandha* verses in praise of Naṭarāja lay stress on ecstatic joy as the inspiration of

[27] The functions of Śiva are explained as *sṛṣṭi, sthiti, saṁhāra, tirobhāva* and *anugraha*. — See *Śiva Purāṇa, Videśvara-Saṁhitā*, chap. 8.

[28] GOS, vol. I.

[29] See his commentary on *Nāṭyaśastra* 4.260ff., GOS, vol. 1, p. 169.

[30] Arthur Avalon remarks on the verse: "Such is the nature of things that it is not possible to do good without some accompanying evil. When we look at the whole *sub specie aeternitatis*, what we thought to be evil when considered as a fact detached from its surroundings is no longer seen to be such when taken as part of a whole which is working for good. So with the dance of Śiva." — *Mahimnastava* of Puṣpadanta, trn. with comm. by Arthur Avalon, Madras, 1953.

the dance. A similar view is recorded in the *Liṅga Purāṇa*,[31] which, after narrating the legendary origin of the dance of Śiva, tells us that, according to some, the Lord's *tāṇḍava* is occasioned by rapture born of yogic contemplation (*yogānanda*).

It may be noted that in the age of Pravarasena and thereabouts Śaivism had made considerable progress in the Tamil country; and Śaiva doctrine was formulated in a definitive form by the saint theologian Tirumūlar, who has been assigned to the sixth century or thereabouts. The cult of Naṭarāja was widespread in the south; and the mystic interpretation of the external symbols of the image of Naṭarāja as worshipped at Cidambaram already appears in Tirumūlar's poetical treatise *Tirumandiram*, which also enumerates different categories of the dance of Śiva.[32] The glorification of the deity by Pravarasena independent of these developments might represent an earlier phase of the purely devotional aspect of the cult of Naṭarāja in Deccan.[33] A noteworthy feature of south Indian Śaivism, on the other hand, was that here the dance of Śiva became the symbol of a deep spiritual experience, and was invested with a new meaning, based on the idea that "Cidambaram is everywheres

---

[31] 106.28 (*pūrvabhāga*), Calcutta, 1885. The date of the *Liṅga Purāṇa* is uncertain, but it seems to contain old materials. A *Liṅga Purāṇa* was known to the Tamil Śaiva saint and theologian Tirumūḷar. — See Ayyar, *Origin and Early History of Saivism in South India*, pp. 209ff., Madras, 1936.

[32] Ayyar, op. cit., pp. 229, 361ff.

[33] The cult of Naṭarāja was popular in Deccan; and the sculptural representation of the deity appears to have been fully developed by the sixth century. The colossal figure of Naṭarāja with sixteen hands in one of the caves at Bādāmī presupposes a fairly long period of development. These caves are assigned to the sixth century on the basis of an inscription of CE 578 in the Vaiṣṇava Cave. 3. — See Banerji, *Bas-reliefs of Badami*, Calcutta, 1928. There are statues of Naṭarāja in all the Brāhmanical caves at Ellorā, of which the most remarkable is that in the Rāmeśvara cave assigned to the sixth century. Other notable examples exist at Aihole, Elephaṇṭā and Paṭṭaḍakaḷ. — Jouveau-Dubreuil, *Iconography of Southern India*, pp. 29, 118, Paris, 1937; Burgess, *A Guide to Elura Cave Temples* p. 43; Gupte, *The Art and Architeture of Aihole*, pp. 37, 77, 85, 109, Bombay, 1967; *Journal of Indian History*, vol. XLIII, pp. 513ff.; Cousens, *The Cāḷukayan Architecture of the Kanarese Districts*, pp. 63ff.; *A Guide to the Pattadakal Temples*, Kannada Research Institute, Dharwar, 1961. In south India the beginnings of the famous temple of Naṭarāja at Cidambaram are roughly traced to the sixth century CE. As regards sculpture, the figure →

and everywhere is His dance".[34] As Coomaraswamy says the deepest significance of the dance "is felt when it is realized that it takes place within the heart and the self. Everywhere is the heart."[35]

Of the verses in praise of Viṣṇu, the first is a thoughtful representation of the deity in the abstract. He is lofty without being heightened, extensive without being broadened, deep without subsiding, minute yet vast, manifest yet inscrutable (1.1). The reference to what may be called apparent contradictions in the nature of Viṣṇu appears in greater detail in Kālidāsa's *Raghuvaṁśa* 10.16ff.; and he, like Pravarasena, concludes that no one knows the truth about the deity.[36] These ideas can be traced to the *Viṣṇu Purāṇa* to which both Kālidāsa and Pravarasena seem to be indebted for their conception of the character of Viṣṇu. The Purāṇa, for instance, describes Viṣṇu as single and manifold, corporeal and subtle, perceptible and imperceptible, etc.[37] He is the support of all things, yet the smallest of the small.[38] In his perceptible form he is the world, but he is also primary matter (*mūla-prakṛti*), known as *pradhāna*, or the *avyakta* (imperceptible cause).[39] His shape is all visible things, but he is without shape or form.[40] He assumes all forms, but is not a substance.[41] The mysticism underlying these tenets is reflected in Pravarasena's statement that Viṣṇu is manifest, but the truth about him is unknown.

Pravarasena compares the ocean to Viṣṇu in *Setu* 2.15: it moves

→ of Naṭarāja on a pilaster of the cave-temple built by Mahendravarman (*c.* CE 580-630) at Śiyamaṅgalam in North Arcot district is "perhaps the earliest extant representation of such a form in the south". — Krishna Sastri, *South-Indian Images of Gods and Goddesses*, p. 88, Madras, 1916; Srinivasan, *Cave-Temples of the Pallavas*, p. 92, ASI, 1964.

[34] See Tirumūḷar cited in Coomaraswamy, *The Dance of Shiva*, p. 88, Bombay, 1948.

[35] Ibid., p. 89.

[36] *avijñātaḥ* (10.20); *yāthārthyaṁ veda kastava* (10.24). Pravarasena says *aṇāa-paramattha* (1.1).

[37] I.2.3.

[38] I.2.5.

[39] II.7.42; I.2.19.

[40] I.22.80.

[41] II.12.38.

back and forth within itself, even as Viṣṇu comes and goes (in the form of incarnations) in the universe that is his self. As the *Viṣṇu Purāṇa*[42] says, he, the mighty one, is the seven worlds, and his form is composed of all the worlds (*lokātmamūrti*). The idea of comparing the ocean to the god seems, however, to have come from Kālidāsa, who is *Raghuvaṁśa* 13.5 describes the character of the ocean as indefinable like that of Viṣṇu; and likens the various moods of the ocean to the different phases of Viṣṇu's activity, i.e. creation, maintenance and destruction as explained in the *Viṣṇu Purāṇa* I.2.57ff.[43]

The remaining verses in praise of Viṣṇu (1.2-4) extol the Man-Lion and Kṛṣṇa incarnations; and of the latter's exploits and poet mentions only the killing of the Bull demon and the Pārijāta episode. Two other incarnations are mentioned, the Boar and the Dwarf, the former being more frequently mentioned than any other incarnation of Viṣṇu.[44]

The Dwarf incarnation is mentioned in *Setu* 2.9, and the Trivikrama aspect of it in 9.7, 51 and probably also in 9.91. In the latter verse the three worlds are described as lying round the Suvela mountain like the three bracelets encircling "the massive and lofty arm of Hari". The commentators Rāmadāsa and Mādhavayajvan find here a reference to Trivikrama. No such details, however, occur in the principal Purāṇic accounts of the Dwarf incarnation;[45] and it is difficult to say whether Pravarasena's allusion to the three bracelets is based on poetic fancy or any mythological source. In sculptural representation the image of Trivikrama usually shows two bracelets; but images with three bracelets are known, of which perhaps the most remarkable is the eight-armed figure of Trivikrama in a panel of the Varāhamaṇḍapam cave-temple at Mahābalipuram, exhibiting three bracelets on each of the hands excepting the one grasping a

---

[42] I.22.78, 79.

[43] Kālidāsa and the *Viṣṇu Purāṇa* both use the word *avasthā: tāṁ tāmavasthāṁ pratipadyamānaṁ — Raghu; brahmādyavasthā-bhiraśeṣamūrtiḥ — V P* I.2.66.

[44] *Setu* 4.22; 5.44; 6.2, 13; 7.2, 40; 8.54; 9.5, 29.

[45] *Harivaṁśa* (Bhaviṣyaparva), chap. 70 ff.; *Matsya Purāṇa*, chap. 245-46; *Bhāgavata* 8.18 ff: *Viṣṇudharmottara Purāṇa*, Part I, chap. 21, 55; *Vāmana Purāṇa*, chap. 65, etc.

sword.[46] The image belongs to about the middle of the seventh century CE, and so is much later than the age of Pravarasena. The existence of such images might, however, point to an old tradition about the three bracelets symbolizing probably the three worlds covered by Trivikrama's strides.

4. The Setubandha and the Rāmāyaṇa

(A) Pravarasena is one of the earliest writers to have composed a *kāvya* exclusively on the subject of Rāma in conformity with the *Vālmīki-Rāmāyaṇa*. Apart from the little known *Rāvaṇavijaya*, there seem to have been certain other poems in Prākṛta on the subject, but we know nothing about their structure. The *Svayambhūcchandas* cites a verse each from Nāgaha and Kṛṣṇadatta who seem to have written poems dealing with the story of Rāma. The verse from Nāgaha describes the army of Rāvaṇa, "dark as the water-filled, towering clouds", rushing at the apes. The verse cited from Kṛṣṇadatta is spoken by someone urging Rāvaṇa to return Sītā and appease Rāma. A narrative poem on the legend of Rāma was also written by the Apabhraṁśa poet Caturmukha, who is cited by Svayambhū, and wrote also other works. It is not clear whether these writers followed Vālmīki or the *Jaina Rāmāyaṇa*; but Caturmukha is known to have been a Brāhmanical writer, and no doubt followed Vālmīki[47] like Pravarasena. Svayambhū's date (eighth-ninth century) offers a clue to the dates of these writers, but none of them is probably earlier than Pravarasena. The oldest Sanskrit writer to compose an independent *kāvya* on the early career of Rāma was probably the author of the *Bhaṭṭikāvya*, who, as we shall see, was influenced by Pravarasena. The *Bhaṭṭikāvya* is at least a century later than the *Setubandha*.

Generally speaking, the *Setubandha* consistently follows the story of Rāma as related in the *Rāmāyaṇa*; and it is necessary to point out only a few minor variations in some of the episodes. There is nothing, for instance, in the *Rāmāyaṇa* corresponding to the contents of the

---

[46] Srinivasan, op. cit., p. 147, pl. XLIV, Cf. Kramrisch, *The Art of India*, p. 206, pl. 85, Phaidon Press, 1955. See also Yasoda Devi, "Vāmana Trivikrama" in *Journal of Indian History*, vol. 43, pp. 833 ff.

[47] See Bhayani's paper on Caturmukha in *JOI*, vol. VII, p. 214.

third and fourth Cantos of the *Setubandha*: the consternation of the *vānara*s at the sight of the ocean, Sugrīva's effort to inspire them with courage, his vexation at their unresponsive attitude and the consequent threat to destroy Laṅkā without their co-operation, followed by Jāmavant's criticism of what he considers to be Sugrīva's haste, obstinacy and lack of judgement. In the *Rāmāyaṇa*, the army of *vānara*s arrives at the seashore full of enthusiasm; and Rāma declares that it is time for them to take counsel together on the problem of crossing the ocean.[48] The proposed deliberation, however, does not take place; and Pravarasena fills the gap with the elaborate discourses of Sugrīva and Jāmavant in his poem. But in doing so he draws materials from a similar episode in the Kiṣkindhākāṇḍa (Cantos 63, 64). Here the *vānara*s who had gone south in search of Sītā are seized with fear on seeing the ocean. They are dumbfounded, and look on in amazement; while their leader Aṅgada, like Sugrīva in our poem, inveighs against despondency, and tries to restore their confidence by exalting their might and distinguished lineage.[49] Jāmavant is with them; and, as in our poem, reminds his companions of his great age by mentioning events witnessed by him in primordial times just to prove that age brings wisdom. Further, in the *Rāmāyaṇa* episode, when Aṅgada offers to fly over to Laṅkā, Jāmavant objects on the ground that the master whose function is to commission others must not be commissioned to do any job.[50] Similar views on the relationship of a commander and his followers are found in Jāmavant's discourse in the *Setubandha* 4.33, 34.

In the *Rāmāyaṇa* the suggestion that Rāma should supplicate the Ocean to facilitate the crossing is made by Vibhīṣaṇa (6.13.13); in the *Setubandha* it comes from Jāmavant (4.48). The obstinacy of the Ocean leads to his chastisement by Rāma with his fiery arrows. The *Rāmāyaṇa* narrative here is brief and restrained,[51] and comparable to one of the most beautiful eposides in the *Iliad* (21.342ff.), the fight between

[48] 6.4.70 ff. Unless otherwise stated all Rāmāyaṇa references are to the critical edition.

[49] *vyapadeśyakule jātāḥ* — *Rāmāyaṇa* 4.63.22. Cf. *kula-vavaesa-kkhamaṁ vahantāṇa jasaṁ* — *Setu* 3.26.

[50] 4.64.22.

[51] See the critical edition.

the river god and Helphaestus, the god of fire. The *Rāmāyaṇa* speaks of the waves enveloped in smoke, and the billows towering up like the Vindhya and Mandara mountains, and the distressed animals flung about by the waves.[52] Pravarasena, on the other hand, devotes an entire Canto to a grotesque and wearisome description of a huge conflagration of the ocean let loose by Rāma's arrows.

In the *Rāmāyaṇa* 6.15 the Ocean appears before Rāma, wearing scarlet robes and garlands and ornaments of gold.[53] In the southern and north-western recensions[54] he comes surrounded by the great rivers led by Gaṅgā and Sindhu. In the Bengal recension he is accompaied by his ministers.[55] In the *Setubandha* 6.1ff. The Ocean emerges, grievously wounded, supporting his arm on his consort Gaṅgā. So far the picture is Pravarasena's own, but he goes on to say that the Ocean was wearing a pearlstring which was so charming that it alleviated his sorrow at the loss of the *kaustubha* gem.[56] A verse corresponding to this occurs in some manuscripts of the *Rāmāyaṇa*, and is given in a footnote in the critical edition under 6.15.2.[57] It is probable that the verse in question formed part of the text of the *Rāmāyaṇa* used by Pravarasena. It also throws light on the expression *ekkāvali-raaṇa* which has been misunderstood by the commentators, who explain it as *ekāvalīratna*, a pearlstring of surpassing beauty.[58] It is, however, clear from the *Rāmāyaṇa* verse that the reference is to a gem set in a pearlstring.[59]

---

52 6.14.16ff.

53 In the Rāma story in *Mahābhārata* the Ocean appears in a dream and suggests the building of a causeway; and Rāma does not carry out his threat to chastise the Ocean.

54 6.22.22, NS edn.; 5.96.19, Lahore edn.

55 5.96.3, Calcutta edn. with the commentary of Lokanātha, 1941.

56 *lahuia-kotthuha-virahaṁ mandara-girl-mahaṇa-saṁbhameviamukkaṁ* । *tārekkāvaliraaṇaṁ sasi-mairāmaa-sahoaraṁ vahamāṇo* ॥ — *Setu* 6.4.

57 एकवलीमध्यगतं तरलं पाटलप्रभम् ।
विपुलेनोरसा बिभ्रत् कौस्तुभस्य सहोदरम् ॥

It will be seen that Pravarasena takes over the word *sahodara* from the Sanskrit verse, though he uses it in a different context.

58 See extracts 6.4.

59 Translation requires emendation.

In the *Rāmāyaṇa* 6.15 the causeway is built by Nala, as suggested by the Ocean, the material used being the trees, bamboos, rocks and mountains brought in by the *vānara*s. Pravarasena's account is different in two respects. First, his bridge is entirely built of mountains, skilfully fitted together with transparent crystal rocks interspersed in the structure. Aa suggested by the Ocean in our poem (6.17), it is primarily a causeway of mountains, *giri-setubandha*. The north-western recension of the *Rāmāyaṇa*, which has a longer description of the *Setu* than the other recensions, seems to put some emphasis on the shower of mountains (*parvatavr̥ṣṭi*) on the sea;[60] but it also mentions the other materials used for the purpose.[61] Secondly, in the *Setubandha* Nala appears at a larger stage of the project after the complete failure of the initial attempt. The *vānara*s uproot the mountains and carry them in an aerial procession to the seashore, but all their efforts are wasted, as the mountains, thrown pell-mell into the sea, disappear in the waters. Sugrīva then appeals to Nala to build the causeway, and the latter accepts the responsibility. He methodically arranges the mountains, and succeeds in joining them closely together in a compact concatenation. Nala's achievement is a triumph of method and planning. Pravarasena gives a new meaning to the ancient legend.

---

[60] 5.98, Lahore edn.

[61] In sculptural representation of *Rāmāyaṇa* scenes stones are usually shown as being used for the building of the causeway. The most famous of these are in a large Śiva Temple forming part of a vast complex of shrines at Prambanan in Central Java. The majestic monument, assigned to the reign of Dakṣa in the second decade of the tenth century, has galleries of reliefs illustrating the story of Rāma up to the arrival of him army in Laṅkā. Here we see robust, stocky apes carrying roundish boulders on their heads and shoulders, and in the hands, to the seashore. Another series of reliefs depicting a part of the story can be seen in a temple at Panataran in East Java dating from the fourteenth century. Here the style is entirely different; and the figures of the apes, the face resembling that of a human being, appear to be slimmer and taller than at Prambanan. They carry large blocks of stone on their shoulders; and two of them are about to cast the rocks into the sea. Smaller stones are carried in bamboo frames suspended from yokes, or moved along with a crowbar. — See Stutterheim, *Rāma-Legenden und Rāma-Reliefs in Indonesien,* Text and Plates in separate volumes, Munich, 1925. Cf. Hall, *A History of South-East Asia,* p. 65, 1968.

It may be noted here that, in a footnote under 6.15.21, the critical edition of the *Rāmāyaṇa* gives an additional verse closely resembling the *Setu* 8.43, which describes how Nala planted in the sea the mountains brought by Hanumat. It is probable that the verse was known to Pravarasena who puts the idea in a more elaborate form.[62]

The *Bhaṭṭikāvya* (canto 13) which deals with the building of the causeway follows Pravarasena closely in summarizing the events outlined in cantos 6-8 of our poem. As is well known, this canto is mostly written in Prākṛta in the same metre as the *Setubandha*. The coincidences are as follows. The Ocean appears, supporting his arm on Gaṅgā. He appeals to Rāma to save the waters that serve as a resting place for him as Viṣṇu; and points out that even if the sea dried up, the slimy bottom would be impassable for the *vānaras*. The *vānaras* rush through the air and uproot the mountains and return with loads of them. The causeway, built entirely of mountains, is called *giri-* or *adri-bandha*. As in our poem, the narrative is followed by a description of Mount Suvela, the southern terminus of the causeway.[63]

The episode of the magic head of Rāma is a good example of Pravarasena's masterly condensation of materials found in different parts of the *Rāmāyaṇa*. In the *Setubandha* (Canto 11) Sītā laments at the sight of the severed head of Rāma; and Trijaṭā, one of the *rākṣasa* women appointed to watch over her, consoles her in her grief. In the *Rāmāyaṇa* the aged Trijaṭā first appears in the Sundarakāṇḍa,

---

[62] सहेलं हनुमाञ्शैलं यं यं विपुलमाक्षिपत्।
तं तं करेण वामेन सलीलं जगृहे नलः॥ — p. 89 (crit. edn.)

jaṁ jaṁ āṇei giriṁ rai-raha-cakkapari-maṭṭha-siharaṁ haṇumā ।
taṁ taṁ līlāi ṇalo vāma-karutthaṁghiaṁ raei samudde ॥ — *Setu* 8.43

[63] Another Sanskrit poet Kumāradāsa (earlier than the tenth century) follows the general outline of Pravarasena's account in describing the building of the causeway in his *Jānakīharaṇa* (canto 14). But he amplifies and greatly exaggerates a statement of Pravarasena in *Setu* 7.8 that a mountain thrown into the sea by the apes was swallowed by whale-devouring monster (*timiṁgila*). In Kumāradāsa's poem Rāma asks the apes to give up the hope of building the causeway, because the *timiṁgila*s were swallowing the mountains mistaking them for whales (14.46). Bragging like Sugrīva in *Setu* 3.58 ff., Rāma declares that the Ocean, spurred by his arrows, will transport the troops to the other shore as they ride on the lofty backs of the whales forming a bridge across the waters. Thereupon, Nala, already commissioned to →

Canto 25, where she chides her companions for being harsh to Sītā, and warns them of the coming danger by relating certain dreams in which she has seen Sītā's glorious reunion with Rāma and the destruction of Rāvaṇa and Laṅkā. After the landing of Rāma's army Rāvaṇa makes a concerted attempt to force Sītā into submission by showing her the severed head of Rāma and his bow, produced by magic by a demon named Vidyujjihva. Sītā laments Rāma's death; and Rāvaṇa is called away to an urgent session of his council. Saramā, a *rākṣasa* woman, "an affectionate friend" of Sītā, appears on the scene and tells her that Rāma has crossed over to Laṅkā, and that the severed head was a magical trick. She declares her willingness to sacrifice her life for Sītā, and offers to carry a message to Rāma; but instead, at the request of Sītā, goes and overhears the deliberations of Rāvaṇa with his ministers, and returns to report his decision to fight to death.[64] The episode of the severed head ends here in the *Rāmāyaṇa*. In the fighting that ensues, Sītā is brought by Trijaṭā in the aerial car Puṣpaka under the orders of Rāvaṇa to witness Rāma and Lakṣmaṇa lying on the battlefield apparently dead, pierced by the serpent arrows of Indrajit. For the second time Sītā bewails the death of Rāma; and Trijaṭā consoles her by explaining the signs indicating that they are alive.[65]

Pravarasena makes a few modifications in the *Rāmāyaṇa* narrative, and reshapes the materials into a coherent picture of the deception of Rāvaṇa, Sītā's grief and Trijaṭā's consolation to her. The course of events that had led Trijaṭā to reveal her dreams in the Sundarakāṇḍa

→ build the bridge, starts his work by planting the first mountains in the caves of the Malaya range. Kumāradāsa's description looks like a clumsy attempt at variation on the theme as treated by Pravarasena. As regards the *timiṁgila* episode, similar details are found in some later versions of the Rāma story in art and literature. The Prambanan reliefs, for instance, show some of the stones thrown by the apes as being swallowed by the sea fish. It has been pointed out that this agrees with the Malaya version of the Rāma legend (*Hikāyat Serī Rāma*), which is, however, believed to be later than the Prambanan sculpures. According to the *Hikāyat*, Rāvaṇa ordered a demon to destroy the bridge before its completion, and at the latter's bidding the fish set about the task until they were devoured by the apes. — Stutterheim, op. cit., text, p. 173; *Zieseniss Die Rama-Sage bei den Malaien*, pp. 42, 112, Hamburg, 1928.

[64] *Rāmāyaṇa* 6.22-25.

[65] Ibid., 6.37-38.

is outside the scope of the *Setubandha*, but the gist of the dreams appears in her comforting words to Sītā in our poem (11.129, 130). In the *Rāmāyaṇa* Rāvaṇa goes to the Aśoka grove and tells Sītā a concocted story of Rāma having been killed in his sleep in a night attack on his camp, and asks Vidyujjihvā to show the severed head, which he says has just been brought from the scene of fighting; while he himself throws before Sītā the famous bow of Rāma. In the *Setubandha* the magic head is quietly taken to the grove by the demons and left in front of Sītā who is shocked at its sudden appearance. More conspicuous is the absence of Saramā and her kindly services. In the *Seubandha* her place is taken by the more familiar Trijaṭā. Pravarasena does not mention her in his brief reference to Sītā's visit to the battlefield in Canto 14 of *Setubandha*; but the part played by Trijaṭā on that occasion in the *Rāmāyaṇa* serves as a model for the role assigned to her in the episode of the magic head in our poem.

It is noteworthy that Kālidāsa also mentions Trijaṭā in connection with the magic head in a passing reference to the episode in the *Raghuvaṁśa* 12.74. It is probable that the poets here follow a tradition slightly different from that found in the *Rāmāyaṇa*.[66] Pravarasena deals with the topic in his own manner, and gives an appealing picture of Trijaṭā's friendship and affection for Sītā. Particularly touching is his reference to the mingling tears of the two women as Sītā in her grief reclines on Trijaṭā's bossom (11.101).[67] Love for Sītā is at the root of the patient humility that finds expression in Trijaṭā's words of consolation. She asks Sītā not to disregard her affectionate words because she is a *rākṣasa* woman. Fragrant flowers, she says, are welcome whether they grow in a pleasure garden or in a wood (11.119). No less remarkable is her candour which prompts her to tell Sītā that she is not so much aggrieved on her account as at the change in Rāvaṇa's character, as seen in the mean trick played by him while Rāma is alive (11.127). A noteworthy trait of Pravarasena's Trijaṭā is that he makes her a mouthpiece of his religious views. Her argument that Rāma cannot die is based on the clearly expressed

[66] Trijaṭā appears also in the Rāma story in the *Mahābhārata* which does not, however, refer to the episode of the magic head.

[67] See Extracts 11.101.

idea that he is the Supreme Being, the mainstay of the universe, on whom depends the functioning of the forces of nature (11.89-91). In the corresponding scene in the *Rāmāyaṇa* Saramā calls him only a powerful hero, who will vanquish the demons with the help of Lakṣmaṇa, even as Indra does his enemies with the help of Viṣṇu (6.24.29). It may be said on the whole that Saramā is depicted in the *Rāmāyaṇa* as a younger woman who loves Sītā, and is active on her behalf. Pravarasena represents Trijaṭā as a woman of mature judgement, capable of subtle reasoning, who tries to convince her young friend that Rāma could not be dead. Her finer sentiments are revealed in her affectionate disposition and in her exaltation of Rāma's love for Sītā.

A study of Sītā's laments in the *Setubandha* and in the relevant portions of the *Rāmāyaṇa* reveals certain differences in the sentiments expressed and in the outlook on life as presented in the two works. The laments as such are deeply moving in both works; but in the *Setubandha* Sītā's utterances are those of a sophisticated woman who is obsessed by the idea of self-immolation, and feels ashamed that she "accepted widowhood with a cruel heart" instead of dying at the sight of the severed head of Rāma. Rāma, she says, will be praised as valiant, because, as she thinks, he died in battle, but she grieves that she will be passed over in silence as a woman who lacked the courage to die (11.84). In her last words she brings in the concept of honour, dear to her as a woman of noble birth: "This is the fate of all, but such an end is unbecoming to those who have an exalted sense of honour (11.115)."[68] Another idea that appears more than once in Sītā's words in the *Setubandha* is that of revenge. The frustration of her hope of seeing Rāvaṇa killed by Rāma adds to the poignacy of her grief.

Compared with Sītā's utterances in the *Setubandha*, the laments in the *Rāmāyaṇa* 6.23 and 6.38 are homely, naïve and unpretentious,

---

[68] The expression *māṇuṇṇaa* (*mānonnata*) used in the verse is same as *māna prāṁśu* in Bhāravi 11.63. The reference is to what appears to be a humiliating death for Rāma at the hands of the demons. According to the south Indian reading (*mānonnata-jāti*, etc.), the reference is to Sītā herself, the idea being that it is disgraceful for a woman belonging to a race that has a high sense of honour, i.e. a kṣatriya woman, to accept widowhood in lieu of self-immolation. — See Kṛṣṇa's gloss on the verse in Extracts 11.115.

and such that an Indian woman of a cultured family, devoted to the ancient ideals and conversant with the popular traditions and beliefs, might be expected to utter in a similar predicament. In the *Rāmāyaṇa* Sītā refers to the palmists and soothsayers who had told her fortune, and laments that all their statements, based on the auspicious marks on her body, have proved incorrect and false. Her thoughts go back to her sorrowing mother-in-law whom she visualizes as dying broken-hearted on learning that Rāma is dead and herself held captive by the demon. There is no rancour nor any thought of revenge in her words. On the other hand, she re-calls Rāma's virtues such as forbearance, self-control, charity and *ahiṁsā*; and appeals to Rāvaṇa to slay her and unite her with Rāma in death. Nothing in Sītā's lament in the *Setubandha* is so affecting as her reference to her early marriage with Rāma in the *Rāmāyaṇa* 6.23.20:

kiṁ māṁ na prekṣase rājan kiṁ māṁ na pratibhāṣase ।
bālāṁ bālena saṁprāptāṁ bhāryāṁ māṁ sahacāriṇīṁ ॥

Pravarasena represents Sugrīva as an impulsive leader, who in his emotional outbursts is apt to exaggerate his own powers and abilities. Vexed at the inactivity of the *vānara*s on the seashore, he threatens to dispense with their services; and, after announcing his resolve to carry out certain impossible exploits, he declares that, "mad with love for Rāma", he will kill Rāvaṇa, and pull down Laṅkā with Sītā as the only survivor (3.62, 63). Similarly, when Rāma and Lakṣmaṇa are paralysed by the serpent arrows he describes in magniloquent verses the chastisement he will inflict on Rāvaṇa, hewing down his heads and tearing out his heart attached to Sītā in vain. Even in the *Rāmāyaṇa* Sugrīva says on that occassion that he will slay Rāvaṇa with his kinsmen, and bring back Sītā (6.40.25). But the north-western and Bengal recensions (6.26.29ff.; 6.25.26ff.) have here a number of additional verses known as *Sugrīva-garjana*, which greatly amplify the original statement, and are similar in tone to Sugrīva's *garjana* in our poem. Such, for instance, is the declaration that, unaided, he will reduce Laṅkā to ashes and destroy Rāvaṇa, and that the world will that day witness his might and steadfast devotion to Rāma. It is probable that Pravarasena's conception of Sugrīva's character is based on declamations of this type which seem to have formed part of the *Rāmāyaṇa* text known to him.

The *Setubandha* (15.55ff.) has an episode involving Rāma and Lakṣmaṇa, which does not occur in the *Rāmāyaṇa*. After the presentation of Indra's chariot to Rāma by Mātali, Lakṣmaṇa, accompanied by Sugrīva and Nīla, approaches Rāma with the request that the easy task of slaying Rāvaṇa may be entrusted to one of them; but Rāma politely refuses to comply. It is difficult to say whether this episode is an invention of Pravarasena, or taken from some other source. The timing of the incident is, however, incompatible with the sequence of events in the *Rāmāyaṇa* narrative. According to the *Rāmāyaṇa* 6.89.29ff. Lakṣmaṇa on recovering from the effect of the Śakti missile, urges Rāma to kill Rāvaṇa that very day, before sunset, as promised by him. Rāma immediately goes forth to battle; and soon after Mātali brings for him Indra's chariot and armour, and the *dvairatha* combat begins (6.90). Having urged Rāma to slay Rāvaṇa only a short while before, it would be rather incongruous for Lakṣmaṇa to request permission for himself or any of his companions to carry out the job undertaken by Rāma.

The lament of Vibhīṣaṇa in the *Setubandha* (15.85-90) throws further light on the text of the *Rāmāyaṇa* known to Pravarasena. In our poem Vibhīṣaṇa piteously mourns the death of Rāvaṇa, and begs leave of Rāma to pay homage to his brother; and Rāma, moved to pity by his tears, orders Hanumat to perform the funeral rites for Rāvaṇa. The different recensions of the *Rāmāyaṇa* have a special canto containing Vibhīṣaṇa's lament, his request for permission to perform the last rites, and Rāma's compliance with his wishes,[69] but a subsequent canto of the *Rāmāyaṇa* has another account, in which[70] Vibhīṣaṇa refuses to perform the obsequies on account of Rāvaṇa's impiety; and Rāma has to persuade him to do so by emphasizing Rāvaṇa's greatness as a warrior. The verse containing Rāma's words, "hostilities end with death" (or,"victory", according to another reading), occurs in both the accounts; and obviously the two versions are inconsistent with each other. The critical edition of the *Rāmāyaṇa* (6.99.31ff.) adopts the latter account and gives the lament of Vibhīṣaṇa in an Appendix. So far as Pravarasena is concerned, he seems to follow

---

[69] NS edn. 6.109; Cal. edn. 6.94; Lahore edn. gives the canto in a footnote from one of the manuscripts at the end of 6.90.

[70] NS edn. 111.92 ff; Cal. edn. 6.96.45 ff; Lahore edn. 6.92.39 ff.

the *Vibhīṣaṇa-vilāpa* as given in the different recensions of the *Rāmāyaṇa*; and was not probably acquainted with the verses describing Vibhīṣaṇa's refusal to undertake the funeral rites. In any case Pravarasena is consistent in his portrayal of Vibhīṣaṇa; and the lament attributed to him is in keeping with his character as conceived by the poet in the *Setubandha*. In the *Rāmāyaṇa* Vibhīṣaṇa takes an active part in the battle and fights with Rāvaṇa together with Lakṣmaṇa (6.88.17ff.). In the *Setubandha* he is more or less a silent spectator; and even his role as a counsellor is reduced to a minimum;[71] and what is more, Rāvaṇa is filled with pity for him when he sees him on the battlefield. As the poet says, his arrow wobbles, because Vibhīṣaṇa is humble, and because he is his brother (15.45). In the *Setubandha* the natural feelings of the brothers do not appear to be obliterated to the same extent as in the *Rāmāyaṇa*; and the lament of Vibhīṣaṇa in our poem is no doubt appropriate to such a conception of their relations.

Pravarasena differs from the *Rāmāyaṇa* in describing the manner of Rāvaṇa's death. According to the *Rāmāyaṇa* 6.97, an arrow formerly fashioned by Brahmā, for Indra is discharged by Rāma, hitting Rāvaṇa in the chest. Pravarasena seems to follow Kālidāsa (*Raghu* 12.97ff.) when he says that Rāvaṇa's heads were severed by Rāma's arrow all at once (15.79). In the story of Rāma in the *Mahābhārata*,[72] Rāvaṇa is consumed by the flames issuing from the consecrated arrow without leaving any trace of the ashes.

Pravarasena follows on the whole the course of events as related in the Yuddhakāṇḍa of the *Rāmāyaṇa*, but his main purpose is to describe the construction of the great causeway as the central point in the narrative. The first eight Cantos of the poem recount the events from the march to the sea to the building of the causeway. The ninth and tenth Cantos contain descriptions usual in *kāvya* poetry. Most of the eleventh Canto deals with the episode of the magic head of Rāma, to which the *Setubandha* seems to give greater prominence than any other version of the Rāma story. The last four Cantos give an outline of the remaining portion of the story up to the death of

---

[71] Cf. *Setu* 14.56; 15.36.

[72] 3.274, 31. crit. edn.

Rāvaṇa and the recovery of Sītā; and we miss in them many colourful details found in this part of the *Rāmāyaṇa*. On the other hand, even in these crowded Cantos Pravarasena makes room for conventional *kāvya* themes such as the description of morning secenery (12.1ff.) and that of the swirling dust of the battlefield (130.49ff.). Thus while preserving the general outline and sequence of the principal events described in the Yuddhakāṇḍa, Pravarasena concentrates on selected episodes, and writes an independent *kāvya* on the early career of Rāma. Nevertheless his close dependence upon the *Rāmāyaṇa* is manifest in the treatment of many of the leading topics in the *Setubandha*. A striking example of this is provided by the ullerances of Rāma as he lies on the baltlefield, pierced by the arrows of Meghanāda. In the *Setubandha* the plaint is particularly impressive because of its brevity and deep pathos (14.43-48); but it looks like a condensation of some of the most affecting lines in the comprehensive lament of Rāma in the corresponding portion of the *Rāmāyaṇa* (6.39).

It may also be noted that the word *anurāga* used in the concluding verse of each Canto of the *Setubandha* seems to be suggested by the *Rāmāyaṇa*. Pravarasena uses it in a variety of allied senses such as devotion, loyalty, affection, also enthusiasm (7.71; 12.98; 13.99; 14.84). The word is frequently used in the *Rāmāyaṇa* which, for instance, speaks of the valour and devotion of Lakṣmaṇa (6.100.3); and declares that the servant who carries out an arduous task set by the master out of loyalty or devotion to him is the best of men (6.1.7).[73]

(B) Pravarasena is familiar with the southern mountain system referred to in the *Rāmāyaṇa*. In this connection his mention of the Vindhya range in *Setu* 1.54 needs comment. In the *Rāmāyaṇa* Rāma's expedition starts from Kiṣkindhā, which is identified by Pargiter with the region around Bellary, with the Tungabhadrā and Vedavatī for its chief rivers.[74] In our poem, on the other hand, the *vānara* hosts marching to the sea first cross the Vindhya range, after which they pass on to the Sahya range, and then reach the Malaya hills and thereafter the seashore. In the *Rāmāyaṇa* (6.4.34ff.) they first cross the Sahya and the Malaya, and then reach the Mahendra hill from

[73] Also ibid 5.33. 21; 63. 3, etc.

[74] Pargiter, "The Geography of Rāma's Exile", *JRAS*, 1894, p. 257.

the peak of which Rāma looks at the ocean. They then descend to the magnificent forest on the seashore (*velāvanamanuttamam*) and establish their camp there. It is noteworthy that the Bengal and north-western recensions of the *Rāmāyaṇa* read here Vindhya for Sahya.[75] Pargiter, basing his conclusions on the Bengal recension edited by Gorresio, identifies this Vindhya with the hills and plateau of south Mysore. "These stretch across from the Western to the Eastern Ghāṭs, and form a dividing ridge in the south, somewhat like the Vindhya range in the north, so that the same name may not inaptly be applied to them." He points out that "it cannot be supposed that Rāma, after reaching Kiṣkindhā, which was certainly far south of the Godāvarī, and forming the alliance with Sugrīva, would have retraced his steps to the north of the modern Vindhya, and separated himself from Sugrīva by that immense distance".[76]

It may be added in support of Pargiter's conjecture that the *Rāmāyaṇa* has a verse which says that the mountains Vindhya, Kṛṣṇagiri and Sahya are the constant haunt of a *vānara* chief variously called Rambha or Parvata,[77] which shows that these were located not far from each other. Kṛṣṇagiri seems to refer to the hills near modern Kṛṣṇagiri in Salem district of Tamil Nadu; and Vindhya might very well be the hills of south Mysore and the southern portion of the Eastern Ghāṭs. This helps us to understand Pravarasena's statement that the *vānara* hosts crossed the Vindhya range before passing on to the Sahya, which is the name given to the northern portion of the Western Ghāṭs from the Tāptī to the Nīlagiris.[78]

Of the remaining hills Pravarasena mentions only the Malaya in connection with the route followed by Rāma's army. It is the famous range of hills in Kerala, being the southern portion of the Western Ghāṭs terminating near Cape Comorin. South of the Pālghāṭ gap it

---

[75] 5.74.46; 5.75.1, 2, 13 Cal. edn.; 5.72, 5, 6, 7, 14 Lahore edn.

[76] Pargiter, op. cit., pp. 259, 261.

[77] 6.17.26 crit. edn.

[78] Cf. Pargiter, *The Mārkaṇḍeya Purāṇa*, p. 285. It appears from certain references in the Kiṣkindhākāṇḍa that the name Vindhya was also applied to the hills beyond the southern end of the Eastern Ghāṭs. The *vānara*s who went south to search for Sītā are described as halting after their vain efforts on the slope of the Vindhya (4.52.16). Sampāti meets them there, and tells them how he fell on the peak of that mountain after his wings had been scorched by the →

consists of a series of hill ranges with a variety of names: the Ānaimalai, the Elāmalai known as the Cardamom hills,[79] Pīrmed and the Agastyamalai peak in the south.[80] Malai is the Dravidian word for hill, and Malaya is apparently the collective name of all these hill ranges. The *Setubandha* has many other references to the Malaya range, represented as a coastal mountain in contact with the sea.[81] There may be a slight poetical exaggeration in this, or perhaps the sea may have receded somewhat in the course of the centuries.[82] It may, however, be noted that the *Līlāvai* of Koūhala, written about four centuries later, also refers to the caves of the Malaya as being filled with the waters of the ocean (v. 339).[83]

→ sun, and concluded that it was the Vindhya on the coast of the southern sea after observing the surroundings (4.59.4 ff.). He reports that Laṅkā was at a distance of full 100 *yojana*s from there (4.57.20). It can also be gathered from his words that the Mahendra hill, which was very close to the sea (see below), was not far from the Vindhya, as he once had occasion to rebuke his son Supārśva for tarrying on that hill where he had gone in quest of food for his father (4.58.10 ff.). After Sampāti's departure, the *vānara*s, encouraged by his words, proceed in a southerly direction (4.62.15) and reach the seashore. The references to the Vindhya in Kiṣkindhākāṇḍa would lead one to suppose that it was located near the southern ocean, though not as close to the sea as the Mahendra hill. The southern Vindhya of the *Rāmāyaṇa* would thus seem to comprise the southern portion of the Eastern Ghāṭs and the hilly country at the foot of the Ghāṭs as far as the Tirunelveli hills in the neighourhood of the sea. In *Setu* 1.54 the sea skirting the (south-east) coast is compared to a bow, and the Vindhya range fancied as the string attached to both ends of the bow, the rivers being the arrows joined to the bowstring. The commentators do not explain whether the reference is to the northern or the southern Vindhya. The footnote to the translation explaining the verse requires emendation.

79 Cf. *elālatāliṅgitacandanāsu malayasthalīṣu* — *Raghu* 6.64. The Elāmalai has a number of cardamom plantations. — *The Gazetteer of India*, vol. 1, p. 46, 1965.

80 Thurston, *The Madras Presidency*, p. 18, Cambridge, 1913.

81 *Setu* 5.70; 6.21; 7.41.

82 "From the main range of the Ghāṭs rocky spurs run out towards the west, in some cases to within a short distance of the sea. From Quilon southwards these secondary ranges soften down into undulating slopes, intersected by glens and valleys, which grow wider as the elevation of the hills decreases. . . ." — *Imperial Gazetteer of India*, vol. 24, p. 3. "The southernmost hills of the Western Ghāṭs serve as a natural barrier between the west side of the Tinnevelly district and the State of Travancore up to within a few miles of Cape Comorin." — Ibid., vol. 23, p. 362.

83 Cf. *Setu* 7.41; *Vikramāṅkadevacarita* 4.9.

There are numerous references to the Malaya range in old Indian poetry, but Pravarasena is perhaps the only poet who speaks of the climatic conditions on the hills. He twice refers to the prevailing cloudy weather (*saī-duddiṇa*) on the Malaya range (1.59; 6.22); and his statement is in accord with modern observations of meteorological phenomena in the hills of Kerala.[84]

Pravarasena makes the Malaya range the northern terminus of the causeway which stretches across the sea to Mount Suvela in Laṅkā (8.83, 85).[85] He locates Mount Mahendra close to the Malaya on the seashore; and speaks of the Malaya and Mahendra as the breasts of the earth (2.8). Landslide masses from the Malaya and the Mahendra are described as being carried by the waves to each other's slope (8.10). Bāṇa likewise says that the Mahendra joins the Malaya.[86]

In the *Rāmāyaṇa* (4.66.34ff.) Hanumat jumps across to Laṅkā from Mount Mahendra; and Sampāti tells the *vānara*s how on one occasion his son Supārśva, while standing guard on the hill, barring the way to all creatures that were flying over to the sea, allowed Rāvaṇa to continue his flight with Sītā when he begged him for passage (4.58.13ff.). The Mahendra hill mentioned in the *Rāmāyaṇa* and the *Setubandha* is thus different from the hill of that name in the Gañjam district of Orissa. The *Vāmana Purāṇa*, in fact, mentions the northern and the southern Mahendra separately.[87] The *Arthaśāstra* 2.11 refers

[84] "The rainfall is heavy. The greatest quantity, brought by the south-west monsoon, falls between May and August. Towards the end of October the north-east monsoon asserts itself, but the rain it brings is lighter on the low country than on the hills in the north-east, where it descends in sudden and very heavy showers." — Ibid., vol. 24, p. 5. The Agastyamalai peak is "often for weeks together wreathed in clouds, enjoying as it does the full benefit of both monsoons". — *Gazetteer of the Tinnevelly District*, vol. 1, p. 4, 1917.

[85] Cf. *nalena sukṛtaścāsau seturmandara-saṁnibhaḥ* ।
malayāttu samārabdho laṅkāmūle pratiṣṭhitaḥ ॥
— *Rāmāyaṇa* 5.98.22. (Lahore edn.)

[86] *malayalagna eva ca mahendraḥ*. — *Harṣacarita*, chap. 7.

[87] 57.10, 11, 12; 63.10, 11. Critical edn., Varanasi, 1967. The verse 57.11 is more correctly given in the 1968. ed. with English trans. Ardhanārīśvara is stated to be the presiding deity at Dakṣiṇa Mahendra, and Somapīthin or Somapāyin Gopāla at Uttara Mahendra. The Mahendra is also mentioned in the *Bṛhat Saṁhitā* 14.11 where it is included in the list of southern mountains along with the Malaya.

to Mahendra pearls, i.e. those found in the streams of Mount Mahendra, situated on the seashore, as explained in the *Cāṇakyaṭīkā* of Prabhāmati (earlier than the middle of the twelfth century).[88] The southern Mahendra is also described in the *Bhaṭṭikāvya* (10.44ff.) which refers to its contiguity to the sea (v. 49).[89]

The Mahendra hill mentioned above is identified with the Mahendragiri peak, 14 miles from Nānguneri, in the Tirunelveli district of Tamil Nadu.[90]

As we have seen, in the *Rāmāyaṇa*, the magnificent forest on the seashore in which Rāma's army stationed itself is located at the foot of the Mahendra hill. In our poem the *vānara*s reach the Malaya range and then the seashore (*velā*) covered with *vakula* and *tamāla* trees and blossoming cardamom groves (1.62ff.). The *Rāmāyaṇa* also makes a general remark that the *vānara*s reached the roaring ocean after crossing the Sahya and the Malaya range (6.4.65). The forest on the seashore (*velāvana*) mentioned in this connection in the *Rāmāyaṇa* appears to be the same as the wooded seashore described by Pravarasena, being the littoral tract near the twin hills Malaya and Mahendra.[91]

---

88 *Cāṇakyaṭīkā*, ed. G.H. Sastri, p. 139. See Supplement to *JOR*, vol. 28 and Introd. to *Jayamaṅgalā* in Suppl. to vol. 26.

89 In a description of the sea in Haribhadra's *Samarāiccakahā*, chap. 4, p. 202, the elephants of the Mahendra hill are spoken of as trampling down the shore.

90 *Imperial Gazetteer of India*, vol. 23, p. 362. South of the Agastyamalai peak, "half in Tinnevelly and half Travancore". "the watershed turns south-east as far as Nānguneri, which marks the point from which the Ghāṭs again march southwards, dropping slightly to the Mahendragiri range, which ends abruptly in a magnificent scarp of bare precipitious rock. This is the last of the Tinnevelly Ghāṭs." It is not precisely on the seashore, but after some distance the mountains rise once more to half their height; and "their final effort is a comparatively low detached hill, whose southern base is two or three miles from the sea slightly west of Cape Comorin."

— *Gazetteer of the Tinnevelly District*, p. 4.

91 The southern Mahendra seems to be mentioned in the Mandasaur Stone Pillar Inscription of Yaśodharman who reigned in the second quarter of the sixth century CE. His dominions "are described as including the whole of the northern part of India, from the river Lauhitya; or the Brahmaputra, to the Western Ocean, and from the Himālayas to the mountain Mahendra"; आ लौहित्योपकण्ठात् तलवनगहनोपत्यकादा महेन्द्रात्, आ गङ्गाश्लिष्टसानोस्तुहिनशिखरिण: पश्चिमादा पयोधे: —See Fleet, *Inscriptions* →

5. The Setubandha as a Mahākāvya

(A) A *mahākāvya* is a fairly long poem divided into *sargas* (cantos), and composed in *kāvya* style. The importance of the *Setubandha* lies in the fact that it is the only extant *mahākāvya* written in Prākr̥ta. Bhoja in his *Śr̥ṅgāraprakāśa* and Hemacandra in his *Kāvyānuśāsana* speak of three Prākr̥ta *mahākāvyas* current in their time: *Harivijaya, Rāvaṇavijaya* and *Setubandha*. Of these the first two appear to be completely lost. Very little is known about the *Rāvaṇavijaya*, but the *Harivijaya* of Sarvasena is appreciated by Sanskrit writers on poetics like Ānandavardhana, Kuntaka and Bhoja.[92] Daṇḍin mentions the *Harivijaya* in a mutilated verse at the beginning of his *Avantīsundarī*, and refers to Sarvasena as a king, probably identical with Sarvasena, the founder of the younger branch of the Vākāṭakas. If so, the *Harivijaya* was composed in the first half of the fourth century CE, about 100 years earlier than the *Setubandha*. The reason why the *Rāvaṇavijaya* and the *Harivijaya* went out of vogue was probably that they failed to hold their own in a branch of literature dominated by the works of Kālidāsa, Bhāravi and Māgha. The *Setubandha*, on the other hand, was extolled by Daṇḍin and Bāṇa two centuries before the *Harivijaya* was appreciated by Ānandavardhana; and it was evidently regarded as the best of the *mahākāvyas* written in Prākr̥ta. As we have seen, it was well known in literary circles in Cambodia in the ninth century CE. The different recensions of the poem and the numerous commentaries written in Sanskrit show that the *Setubandha* was studied in almost all parts of India, and occupied an important place in the literary curriculum of a bygone age.

There is an interesting reference to "the five *mahākāvyas*" in Svayambhū's Apabhraṁśa poem *Paūmacariū* 1.3.7.[93] According to the old gloss, the poems included in the reference are *Kumārasambhava, Raghuvaṁśa, Meghadūta* and the two poems of Bhāravi and Māgha. The explanation is obviously wrong in respect of the *Meghadūta*. At

→ *of the Early Gupta Kings* (CII), p. 145.

Fleet, however, says that it is doubtful whether Mahendra denoted in the inscription of Mahendragiri in the Gañjam district, or another mountain of the same name, which must be located somewhere in the Western Ghāṭs.

[92] See below. Cf. Raghavan, Bhoja's *Sr̥ṅgāraprakāśa*, p. 824, Madras, 1963.

[93] Ed. Bhayani, Singhi Jain Series.

the time when Svayambhū wrote (eighth or ninth century) the only other *mahākāvya* that could be placed by the side of the masterpieces of Kālidāsa, Bhāravi and Māgha was apparently the *Setubandha* of Pravarasena. That it was included in Svayambhū's reference to the *mahākāvyas* is rendered probable by the fact that he quotes a verse from the *Setubandha* to illustrate the Skandhaka metre in his manual of Prākṛta prosody known as *Svayambhūcchandas*.[94] Skandhaka is the prevailing metre of a Prākṛta *mahākāvya*; and Svayambhū seems to have taken his illustration from the best known of the Prākṛta *mahākāvyas* current in his time.

A manuscript of the *Setubandha*, preserved in the India Office Library, styles the first canto *sarga*, and the remaining cantos *niśreṇikā*.[95] The nomenclature is very unusal. A canto of a Prākṛta *mahākāvya* is usually known as *āśvāsa*.[96]

Generally speaking, a *mahākāvya* recounts the triumphant career of the hero, and contains a number of descriptive cantos on a variety of themes. The *mahākāvya* is, on the whole, descriptive rather than narrtive in character.

A clear idea of the *Setubandha* as a *mahākāvya* may be had from a comparison of its structure with that of the Sanskrit poems of the same category composed immediately before and after. Kālidāsa's *Raghuvaṁśa*, written probably half a century earlier, has exercised its influence on the *Setubandha*, but the two works are different in some of their essential characteristics. In the first place, the subject matter of the *Raghuvaṁśa* is far more extensive than that of the *Setubandha*. It recounts the careers of many kings of a dynasty including the entire story of Rāma. As Śāradātanaya says, the *Raghuvaṁśa* is a Saṁhitā poem, in which diverse isolated narratives are grouped together.[97] Compared with this, the theme of the *Setubandha* is extremely limited;

---

94 See Section 7 on Metres.

95 *Catalogue of the Sanskrit and Prākṛt Manuscripts*, vol. II, part II, p. 1066, Oxford, 1935.

96 The cantos of the lost Sanskrit poem *Hariprabodha*, a *yamakakāvya*, are known to have been styled *āśvāsas*. It is quoted in Vāmana's *Kāvyālaṁkārasūtravṛtti* 4.1.2. — See Hemacandra, *Kāvyānuśāsana* 8.6. vol. 1, p. 461, Bombay, 1938.

97 वृतान्ता विप्रकीर्णाः स्यु संहिता यत्र कोविदैः ।
सा संहितेत्यभिहिता रघुवंशी यथा कृतः ।। —*Bhāvaprakāśana*, chap. 9

it deals only with a portion of the early career of Rāma. Secondly, the descriptions that are an essential feature of a *mahākāvya* are strictly subordinated to the narrative in Kālidāsa's poem. In the *Setubandha* they play a much more extensive role, and are aften carried beyond the requirement of the narrative. The description of the ocean, for instance, occupies nearly a canto; and an entire canto of much greater length is devoted to that of Mount Suvela. Kālidāsa, on the contrary, describes the ocean in sixteen verses in the *Raghuvaṁśa* (canto 13), and assigns about the same number of verses to the description of the Himalaya in the *Kumārasambhava*. Apart from these conventional descriptions, the minute delineation of incidents such as we find in the *Setubandha* (cantos 5-8) in connection with the building of the causeway is a characteristic alien to the poetic art of Kālidāsa. It may be noted that Kālidāsa devotes only a verse to this topic in the *Raghuvaṁśa* (12.70). Further, in the *Setubandha* (canto 10) Pravarasena introduces a new category of description: elaborate pictures of the evening scenery and the moonlit landscape, and the joys of wine and love with the *abhisārikā*s playing their customary role. Nothing like this sequence of descriptions is found in Kālidāsa.

As regards the *mahākāvya*s later than Pravarasena, Bhāravi's *Kirātārjunīya* and Māgha's *Śiśupālavadha* deal with brief episodes; and their subject matter is in any case much more limited than that of the *Setubandha*. Nevertheless the Sanskrit poems are more extensive than the Prākṛta work because of the greater emphasis on elaborate and often long-winded descriptions. Bhāravi's description of the fight between Arjuna and the Kirāta, for instance, occupies more than three cantos of his poem (15-18). Māgha, like Pravarasena, devotes an entire canto to the portrayal of a mountain; but most of the conventional descriptions in his poem are much more elaborate than those in the *Setubandha*. To sum up, the *Raghuvaṁśa* treats a very wide subject within a relatively narrow compass (nineteeṅ cantos). The *Setubandha*, though much more limited in scope, has as many as fifteen; while the *mahākāvya*s of Bhāravi and Māgha, in spite of the greater brevity of their themes, have eighteen and twenty cantos respectively. In the evolution of the *mahākāvya* the *Setubandha* thus marks the stage at which the descriptions begin to preponderate at the expense of the narrative, and illustrates the transition from Kālidāsa to the poems of Bhāravi and Māgha.

The topics introduced by Pravarasena into the tenth canto of his poem appear in toto in Bhāravi's *Kirātārjunīya* (canto 9) in the same sequence as in the *Setubandha*. They were taken over by Māgha from Bhāravi, and expanded into two cantos of the *Śiśupālavadha* (9-10), and soon became stereotyped in the Sanskrit *mahākāvya*. Bhāravi treats of these topics in his own manner, but sometimes betrays close acquaintance with particular verses of Pravarasena. For example,

> शङ्किताय कृतबाष्पनिपातामीर्ष्यया विमुखितां दयिताय।
> मानिनीमभिमुखाहितचित्तां शंसति स्म घनरोमविभेदः॥
> — Bhāravi 9.46
>
> *śaṅkitāya kṛtabāṣpanipātāmīrṣayayā vimukhitāṁ dayitāya*।
> *māninīmabhimukhāhitacittāṁ śaṁsati sma*
> *ghanaromavibhedaḥ*॥
>
> *sāi vimukka-māṇo bahalubbhiṇṇa-pulauggameṇa piāṇaṁ*।
> *purao-hutta-ṇisaṇṇo gaoṇiatta-hiao vilāsiṇi-sattho*॥
> — *Setu 10.77*

Bhāravi's beautiful verse

> चित्तनिर्वृतिविधायि विविक्तं मन्मथो मधुमदः शशिभास्रः।
> संगमश्च दयितैः स्म नयन्ति प्रेम कामपि भुवं प्रमदानाम्॥
> — 9.71
>
> *cittanirvṛtividhāyi viviktaṁ manmatho madhumadaḥ śaśibhāsraḥ*।
> *saṁgamaśca dayitaiḥ sma nayanti prema kāmapi bhuvaṁ*
> *pramadānām*॥

is based on *Setu* 10.82:

> *canda-areṇa paose ṇijjai māṇeṇa mahu-maeṇa a samāṁ*।
> *dūraṁ dūrārūḍho juvaīṇa piesu bahu-raso aṇurāo*॥

Bhāravi 9.42 and Pravarasena 10.73 both refer in the same strain to the relative strength of passion and wine in overcoming maidenly bashfulness.

Occasionally Bhāravi borrows also ideas from other parts of the *Setubandha*. His picture of Arjuna fighting the Kirāta with boulders and trees which are cut up by the latter's arrows is suggested by similar combats described in the *Setubandha*.[98] Similarly, the fanciful

---

[98] Bhāravi 17.60-62. Cf. *Setu* 13.89, 94; 14.74, 77, 78, etc.

encounter of the elephants of the woods with the "water elephants" emerging from the Himalayan Gaṅgā, described by Bhāravi (6.14), is borrowed from the *Setubandha*, which presents such incidents in greater detail in connection with the sea.[99]

Pravarasena follows Kālidāsa closely in several items in the description of battle scenes. The *Raghuvaṁśa* briefly describes the dust enshrouding a battlefield (7.39-43), a topic to which Pravarasena assigns more than double the number of verses (13.49-61). Māgha's description of the phenomenon (17.52-69) is still more elaborate and full of exaggerated notions; and with him the topic becomes stereotyped in the later *kāvya*.

Kālidāsa describes in *Raghu* 7.50 how, after the carnage, a jackal snatches the half-consumed arm of a dead warrior from the birds of prey, but discards it when pierced in the palate by the sharp ends of the armlet.[100] Variations of this topic are found in two verses of the *Setubandha* (13.39, 65). Māgha also describes such scenes (18.73-78), but some of his pictures are marred by a curious superstition that flames issue from the mouths of the howling jackals.

Kālidāsa refers to the belief that a warrior who dies on the battlefield *betakes* himself to heāven and wins a nymph.[101] In *Raghu* 7.51, for instance, we have the picture of a warrior, metamorphosed into a god and united with his celestial bride, watching his headless corpse "dancing" on the battlefield.[102] In *Setu* 12.67, while the warriors put on their armour on the eve of the battle, the nymphs adorn themselves in their celestial cars to receive their prospective lovers.[103]

---

[99] *Setu* 7.54; 8.8, 63.

[100] Cf. Vākpati 435.

[101] The *Parāśara Smṛti*. chap. 3 deals with the merit of dying on the battlefield, and speaks of the rush of thousands of celestial damsels to marry the heroes killed in battle. The *Harivaṁśa* 2.31.24 (Cal. edn.) says that it is better for a woman to go without a husband than to have a hero for a husband, because the heroes are beloved of the nymphs, and they too are fond of them.

[102] The main idea of Kālidāsa's verse is based on the *Harivaṁśa* which says in connection with a great battle fought at Puṣkara: यमराष्ट्रं गताः केचित् केचित् स्वर्गं समाययुः । अप्सरोभिः सभासेदुः पश्यन्तुः स्वकलेवरम् ॥ 3-122.14, 15. Kālidāsa gives another picture of heroes and nymphs in *Raghu* 7.53.

[103] See also *Setu* 13.17, 20, 21.

In Māgha 17.34 they do so on hearing the beat of the war drum, ready to accept those killed in the fighting.[104] Pravarasena says that as the battle raged nymphs were won at the cost of one's life, and heads bartered for fame (13.47). Māgha tells us that fame came to a dead warrior in this world, and a nymph in the next, both ever new and pleasing and ensuring eternal life in heaven (18.62).[105] While diverse poets give playful versions of this ancient belief, it is Kālidāsa who seems to have introduced it as an item of description in the *mahākāvya* under the influence of the ethico-religious literature current in his age.

The dance of the *kabandha*[106] is another item in the description of battle scenes. It is mentioned by Kālidāsa in *Raghu* 7.51; and the idea often appears in an exaggerated form in the later poets. Pravarasena speaks of the headless *kabandha* rushing forward as it squirts streams of blood (13.40); while Māgha describes *kabandhas* that dance with sword in hand, or to the strains of martial music (18.53, 54). The statements of the poets appear to be based on an ancient belief connected with the holocaust in a battle. Pravarasena (13.64) and Māgha (19.51), for instance, mention the dance of the *sahasrapūraṇa kabandha*, i.e. the headless corpse of the thousandth warrior killed in the fighting. The commentators here refer to a belief that a *kabandha* dances when 1,000 men have fallen in battle. It is noteworthy that a similar belief is recorded in early texts like the *Harivaṁśa* and the *Milindapañha*.[107]

The affinity of the *Setubandha* to the Sanskrit *mahākāvyas* is no

---

104 See also Māgha 18.58-62.

105 Cf. अव्वो दुहा वि लाहो रणंगणे सूरवीरपुरिसाण ।
जइ भरइ अच्छराओ अह जीवइ तो सिरी प्रहइ ॥ — *Kuvalayamālā*, p. 51

106 A headless corpse, especially of a soldier just killed in battle.

107 The *Harivaṁśa* 2.36.9 says in the account of a fierce battle that numerous *kabandhas* stood up on all sides. The commentator Nīlakaṇṭha remarks that a *kabandha* rises when a hundred thousand men are killed. Similarly, the *Milindapañha* (ed. Trenckner, p. 292) says in connection with a battle that eighty *kabandhas* rose, and that one *kabandha* is said to rise when there is a complete heap of heads (*ekasmiṁ kira sīsa-kalande paripuṇṇe ekaṁ kavandha-rūpaṁ uṭṭhahati*). See *Pāli-English Dictionary* (PTS) under *kalanda* rendered as *heap, stack*. Rhys Davids gives a free translation of the passage, expanded in accordance with the Siṁhalese interpretation, which gives fantastic numbers for those killed. — *The Questions of King Milinda*, part 2 (SBE), p. 147

doubt one of the causes of its popularity through the centuries. It is, however, difficult to assess its position in relation to the Prākr̥ta *kāvyas* of the same category that are no longer extant. Of these Sarvasena's *Harivijaya* appears to have been the best known; and, as noted above, there are a few references to it in Sanskrit works on poetics. But nothing seems to be known about the extent and structure of the poem. Hemacandra refers to it in connection with the various descriptions found in the different *mahākāvyas*, and mentions several topics described in Sarvasena's work;[108] but he criticizes the author for inserting in his poem an irrelevant description of the ocean, "a superfluous excrescence", as he calls it.[109] The subject of the poem is the forcible removal of the Pārijāta tree from heaven by Kr̥ṣṇa. Ānandavardhana praises Sarvasena for introducing an element of *rasa* into the insipid mythological theme by representing Kr̥ṣṇa's action as motivated by a desire to appease his wife Satyabhāmā.[110] But, in the absence of the text, it is difficult to determine how far Kr̥ṣṇa's action in going to war with Indra for the purpose of placating his wife's jealousy lent dignity to the subject, or contributed to the success of the poem as a work of art. Sarvasena is also praised by Kuntaka for following the *Sukumāramārga* corresponding to the old Vaidarbhī style;[111] but to judge from Hemacandra's criticism, it may be doubted if the *Harivijaya* was a mature effort in the field of the *mahākāvya*, comparable to the *Setubandha*. In any case it failed to maintain its popularity as a major work of the early *kāvya* literature.

At the beginning of the *Setubandha* just after the invocatory verses, Pravarasena recounts the advantages to be derived from the study of poetry (1.10); and speaks of the difficulty in successfully completing a poem undertaken in the first flush of enthusiasm, and, above all, in combining beauty of composition (*bandhacchāya*)

---

108 *Kāvyānuśāsana*, vol. 1, p. 458.

109 See section 7 on Metres.

110 *Dhvanyāloka* (NS), p. 148. The *Locano* says हरिविजये कान्तानुनयनाङ्गत्वेन परिजातहरणादि निरूपितमितिहासेषु अदृष्टमपि. See also Vaidya's Introd. to *Rāmāyaṇa*, Yuddhakāṇḍa, p. XXXV.

111 एवं सहजसौकुमार्यसुभगानि कालिदाससर्वसेनादीनां काव्यानि दृश्यन्ते, तत्र सुकुमारमार्गस्वरूपं चर्चनीयम् — *Vakroktijīvita*, p. 71, ed. De, Calcutta, 1961.

with a new range of meaning (*ahiṇavā atthagaī*), i.e. the novelty of ideas (1.9, 11). It is noteworthy that the expression *bandhacchāyā* is frequently used by writers like Ānandavardhana and Kuntaka in expounding their poetical theories.[112] Ānandavardhana in particular refers to the objectives mentioned by Pravarasena in almost identical language, and gives a recipe for attaining the desired result in conformity with his own view of poetry.[113] Pravarasena appears to be one of the earliest writers to use the expression *bandhacchāyā*, and it is probable that Ānandavardhana was influenced by the use of the word in the *Setubandha* in connection with a fundamental problem of poetry. Vākpati, apparently taking his cue from Pravarasena, also speaks of new ideas and beauties of composition; but he does not bother about the difficulty mentioned by his predecessor, and claims rather light-heartedly that these qualities have been common only in Prākṛta poetry "since the creation of the world".[114]

Pravarasena's remarks on poetry are interesting, because similar observations are not usual in the Sanskrit *mahākāvya*s. Hemacandra quotes a verse in praise of the insight of poets from the Prākṛta *Rāvaṇavijaya*[115] but it is difficult to say whether it was usual to commence a Prākṛta *mahākāvya* with similar observations on poetry.

The *Setubandha* contains a considerable number of verses of ethical import; but we miss in it the many pithy sayings found in the Sanskrit *mahākāvya*s, usually, at the end of a verse that are formally called

---

[112] *Bandha* is poetic composition. Vāmana sayes बन्धः पदरचना — *Kāvyālaṁkārasūtravṛtti* 3.1.4. Kuntaka calls it *vākyavinyāsa* and gives definition of the term: वाच्यवाचकसौभाग्यलावण्यपरिपोषकः । व्यापारशाली वाक्यस्य विन्यासो बन्ध उच्यते ॥

Vakroktijīvita, ed. De, pp. 11, 54, 43. Kuntaka explains बन्धछाया as संनिवेशकान्ति, pp. 70, 109; he speaks also of *bandha-saundarya*. Vidyācakravartin explains *bandhacchāyā* as *grathana-vaicitrya* in his commentary on *Alaṁkārasarvasva* (ed. Janki, p. 63). The lack of the *kāntiguṇa* in composition, a defect described by Vāmana 3.1.25 as *purāṇacchāyā* "faded lustre", i.e. lack of colour, is explained by Hemacandra as *purāṇī bandhacchāyā* — *Kāvyānuśāsana*, vol. 1, p. 286.

[113] अङ्गिभूतरसाद्याश्रयेण काव्ये क्रियमाणे नवनवार्थलाभो भवति बन्धच्छाया च महतो संपद्यते इति — p. 239. For other uses of the term see *Dhvanyāloka*, pp. 154, 218, 240, 246, NS edn.

[114] णवमत्थदेसणं संनिवेससिसिराओ बन्धरिद्धीओ ।
अविरलमिणमो आभुषणबन्धमिह णावर पययम्मि ॥ — 92

arthāntaranyāsa. Likewise the absence of any reference to philosophical or other tenets relating to the different branches of learning is another feature that differentiates the poem from the Sanskrit *mahākāvyas*.

Among mythological allusions the clipping of the wings of the mountains by Indra is frequently mentioned.[116] There is a reference to the fight between Garuḍa and Indra for nectar (14.59) as related in the *Mahābhārata*.[117] Pravarasena mentions several legends found in the Uttarakāṇḍa of the *Rāmāyaṇa*, e.g. the victory of Rāvaṇa over Yama (15.86);[118] the boon of immortality granted to Vibhīṣaṇa (15.85); Rāvaṇa's attempt to uproot the Kailāsa mountain (15.28); and the story that he had cut-off nine of his heads and was about to get rid of the tenth when he was stopped by Brahmā (6.17).[119] An allusion to the *yoga-nidrā* of Viṣṇu occurs in *Setu* 1.21 where the god is described as having awaked in the autumn, though he had not been really asleep.[120] The Lokāloka mountain is mentioned in 8.106.[121]

The *Setubandha* is rather poor in literary and social data. Some of the incidental topics referred to in the poem are the eight intellectual qualities 4.62;[122] the northern and southern courses of the sun (4.30,

---

115 *Kāvyānuśasana*, vol. 1, p. 456.

116 *Setu* 5.37, 51; 7.53, etc. See *Rāmāyaṇa* 5.1.108 ff. The wings were clipped because the flying mountains were a terror to the world. Another version of the story is that once the mountains flew away, abandoning their task of supporting the earth. As a consequence, the earth wobbled, and the waters of the ocean inundated the city of the demons, whereupon their leader Hiraṇyākṣa, scenting danger, declared war against the gods, but was killed by Viṣṇu incarnate as Nṛ-Varāha. Subsequently the wings of the mountains were clipped by Indra as a punishment for their misdemeanour. — *Viṣṇudharmottara Purāṇa*, Part I, chap. 53. Pravarasena in *Setu* 4.46 seems to have this episode in mind when he compares the failure of an enterprise for lack of able supporters to the subsidence of the earth abandoned by the mountains (*mahihara-mukka vva mahī*). The Purāṇa has *dharādharaparityaktā dharā*.

117 See Ādiparva (Āstikaparva). Cf. Māgha 20.73.

118 *Rāmāyaṇa* 7.21, 22; also 6.7.12, 13.

119 Ibid. 7.10, 16.

120 Pravarasena says *asuvanto vi vibuddho*. Cf. *Raghu* 10.24: स्वपतो जागरूकस्य याथार्थ्यं वेद कस्तव and Māgha 20.36: उचितस्वपनोऽपि न नीरराशौ . . . भुवनत्रयकार्यजागरूक . . .

121 See fn. to trans. Cf. Bhāravi 12.22; Māgha 16.83.

122 Pravarasena speaks of the intellectual qualities (*matiguṇa*) by means of which →

9.83);[123] the custom of *anumaraṇa* (14.55);[124] conch bangles (5.63);[125] poison-destroying plants avoided by serpents;[126] Madana trees, of which the slap has a toxic effect on fish (7.66);[127] cardamom plants growing on the seashore (1.62, 63);[128] and the flavouring of wine

→ able men, worthy of being kings, determine their course of action. These are called *projñāguṇa* in *Arthaśāstra* 6.1: viz. *śuśrūṣā* (the desire to learn), *śravaṇa* (the effort to learn), *grahaṇa* (comprehension), *dhāraṇā* (retention), *vijñāna* (detailed knowledge), *ūha* (conjecture based on reasoning), *apoha* (elimination), *tattvābhiniveśa* (adherence to the truth). The *Arthaśāstra* mentions the *prajñāguṇas* along with diverse other qualities that constitute the merit of the king. Cf. *Kāmandakīya Nītisāra* 4.21 where they are called *dhīguṇa*. See Poona edn. 1958.

123 Cf. *Raghu* 4.49; 16.44; 17.2.

124 One of the early literary references to the custom. Cf. *Kāmasūtra* 6.2.53; *Raghu* 17.6; *Gāthāsaptaśatī*; 5.49; 7.33 (NS edn., 1889). The Eraṇ Stone Pillar Inscription of a chieftain or noble named Goparāja, an ally of Bhānugupta dated in CE 510-11, records the self-immolation of his wife after his death in a battle. — Fleet, *Inscription of the Early Gupta Kings*, pp. 221ff., vol. 3.

125 There are many references to conch bangles in Indian literature. Cf. *Mahābhārata*, Virāṭaparva (vulgate) 2.27; *Drāhyāyaṇa Gṛhyasūtra* 4.3.6 and Rudraskanda's commentary thereon; *Kāmasūtra* 6.2.44, *Sāṁkhyasūtra* 4.9; *Kādambarī* (Pūvabhāga), ed. Kale, p. 70; Māgha 7.30, 10.43, 13.41; Kumāradāsa 3.41; *Haravijaya* 4.29; 17.8; 27.15, etc.; *Udayasundarīkathā*, pp. 41, 101; *Naiṣadhacarita* 12.35; 15.45; *Kavalayamālā*, ed. Upadhye, p. 8: *gāma-juvaīo iva rīriya-saṁkhavalaya-kāya-maṇiya-sohāo.*

126 See fn. to trans. 4.63.

127 The *madana* plant is mentioned in works like the *Dhanvantarīyanighaṇṭu* and *Rājanighaṇṭu* (Āanadāśrama edn., p. 39), *Madanapālanighaṇṭu* (Cal. edn., p. 49), and Hemcandra's *Nighaṇṭuśeṣa*, vv. 126-27 (Ahmedabad, 1968). *Phala* is one of the many names of the tree; and it is called *madanphal* or *maynāphal* in Bengali, and *mainphal* in Hindi. It is a small thorny tree with various medicinal properties, the ripe fruit being used as an emetic — Biswās, *Bhāratiya Vanauṣadhi* (in Bengali), vol. 2, p. 273, Calcutta University, 1951; Dutt, *The Materia Medica of the Hindus*, pp. 178, 309, Calcutta, 1922. Roxiburgh adds: "The fruit when ripe looks like a small yellow apple; if bruised and thrown into ponds where there are fish, they are soons intoxicated, and seen floating. If this is done during the hot season, it is said, the fish generally die, but if during the wet or cold season they recover. Fishermen sometimes follow this mode to enable them to take the fish with more ease." — *Flora Indica*, p. 240, rpt., Calcutta, 1874. Hemacandra (op. cit.) gives *mastsyāntakaphala* as one of the names of the *madana* tree. Pravarasena, however, says in *Setu* 7.66 that the fish were tossing about helplessly, being intoxicated by the sap of the broken Madana trees thrown into the sea. The information given by him seems to be based on a slightly different tradition, or perhaps on personal observation.

128 Cf. Vākpati 417: *elā-surahimmi jalahi-velā-vaṇantammi.*

with lotus blossoms (12.14).[129]

The process of tempering iron by dipping it red hot into cold water is referred to in *Setu* 14.19.[130] Quicksilver is mentioned in 9.68 and realgar in 7.59 and 12.5. There might be a reference to mica (*abhraka*) in 10.49, but this reading found in Rāmadāsa is not followed by other commentators.

(B) Generally speaking, the *Setubandha* is written in a style that lacks the lucidity of Kālidāsa, and has greater affinity to Bhāravi's style in the *Kirātārjunīya*. A comparison of the *Setu* 1.13 and *Raghu* 11.20 illustrates the contrast between Pravarasena and Kālidāsa in the use of the conceits of *kāvya* poetry. Both poets figure Rāma as Manmatha or the god of love. Referring to the killing of Tāḍakā by Rāma, Kālidāsa says that the demoness, hit in the heart by the arrow of Rāma-Manmatha, went to the abode of "the lord of her life" (*jīviteśa*), meaning *consort* as well as *the god of death*. The imagery is complex enough in Kālidāsa, but it is more complicated in Pravarasena, who describes the killing of Vāli by Rāma and Sugrīva's succession to the throne by saying that the goddess of royal sovereignty, pierced in her Vāli-heart by the arrow of Rāghava-Manmatha, accepted Sugrīva as her lover. The verse is a good example of the intricacy which at times characterizes the style of the *Setubandha*; but it is by no means typical of the usual manner of Pravarasena. The *Setubandha* contains other elaborately constructed *rūpaka*s that are vivid and

---

[129] Cf. Bhāravi 9.51, 56; *Bṛhat Saṁhitā* 76.1 (*sotpalaṁ madhu*).

[130] Pravarasena calls such iron *ṇiddhoa* (*nirdhauta*), explained by Rāmadāsa as *nirdhautaṁ dāhottaraṁ jale kṣiptam*. This method of tempering iron is mentioned in the Ardhamāgadhī canon, being called *pajjaṇa* (*pāyana*). Abhayadeva in his commentary on *Nāyādhammakahāo*, chap. 7 (*tikkhehiṁ nava-pajjaṇaehim asiehiṁ luṇanti*) remarks: नवं प्रत्यग्रं पायनं लोहकारेणातापितं कुट्टितं तीक्ष्णधारीकृतं पुनस्तापितानाँ जले निबोलनं येषां तानि तैः — *Nāyādhamma*, ed. Vaidya, p. 86, Poona, 1940; *Jñātādharmakathāṅgam*, pt 1, p. 126, ed. Candrasāgar, Bombay, 1951. The reference is to sharp, newly-tempered sickles; i.e. these were heated and plunged in water to get the required degree of hardness. Homer likewise speaks of a big axe or an adze hissing as it is dipped red-hot in water to temper it. (*Odyssey*, IX 391 ff.). Homer uses the verb *pharmassein* in this sense, but the process is called also *baphe* (dipping) with which may be compared *pajjaṇa=pāyana* (causing or giving to drink) *DN* 6.11 gives *pajjaṇa*, in the sense of drinking.

interesting (e.g. 1.14, 16, 18, 22, 24, 29; 7.1). Of these two are given as examples of different kinds if *rūpaka*s in the *Sarasvatīkaṇṭhābharaṇa* of Bhoja.[131]

A conspicuous feature of the style of the *Setubandha* is the use of numerous long compounds in the poem. There are at least sixty-four verses, in which both the halves are composed of single compounds so that each verse is no more than a pair of sesquipedalian compounds.[132] These are usually descriptive verses often presented in groups, and nearly half of them occurs in connection with the Suvela range and the battle scenes described in cantos 9 and 13 respectively. Apart from this, there are some sixty compounds, each of which constitutes the entire half of a verse; and nearly 124 others shorter only by a word or two, besides a large number of compounds of medium length. Such methodical use of long compounds is not usual in the Sanskrit *mahākāvyas*.[133] This seems, however, to be a characteristic of some of the longer poems of Prākṛta literature. Even a popular work like the *Gāthāsaptaśatī* contains more than fifteen verses,[134] in which one half of each verse, usually the first, consists of a single compound. In any case Pravarasena is one of the earliest writers to have made such an extensive use of this stylistic device. Among later Prākṛta poets Vākpati freely uses single compounds constituting the entire half of a verse, but he has only a few verses (e.g. 202-206) which show this characteristic in both the halves. The other outstanding poetical works of the eighth century or thereabouts, Koūhala's *Līlāvaī*, Haribhadra's *Śamarāiccakahā* and Uddyotana's *Kuvalayamālā* (the latter two in the verse portions) follow, on the whole, the same pattern as the *Setubandha* in the use of long and elaborarte compounds. In *Līlāvaī*,

---

131 *Setu* 1.14 as an example of *paramparārūpaka* and 1.22 as that of *ādhāravat rūpaka*. See *SK* 4.29, 41, NS edn. 1925.

132 See cantos 2, 5, 7, 8, 9, 11, 13, 14, 15.

133 Kālidāsa avoids long compounds. Bhāravi has really long compounds only in a few verses (e.g., 12.41, 45; 13.18; 18.4), Māgha uses them frequently, and has besides more than sixty compounds which constitute or nearly constitute the half of a verse; but he seems to have only one verse (7.34) in which both the halves consist of single compounds.

134 1.62; 2.2, 46, 48, 70; 3.44; 4.34, etc. NS edn.

for instance, the concatenations of compounds are mostly arranged in groups of three, and sometimes four, or even six verses.[135]

A considerable number of verses is quoted from the *Setubandha* in the *Sarasvatīkaṇṭhābharaṇa* of Bhoja to illustrate different figures of speech with explanatory remarks. The *Setu* 3.31.17 and 5.50 are quoted as examples of different kinds of *dṛṣṭāntokti*, a variety of *sāmya*.[136] As examples of various kinds of *saṁkīrṇa-rūpaka* Bhoja quotes *Setu* 1.17, 19, 24, being combinations of *rūpaka* with *upamā*, *utprekṣā* and *śleṣa* respectively.[137] A number of verses (*Setu* 4.57, 11.54, 6.81, 4.23, 5.10) is cited as illustrations of different varieties of *parikara*.[138] *Sahokti* is illustrated with *Setu* 5.7 and 2.14,[139] *vibhāvanā* with 1.1,[140] *kāraṇamālā* with 1.3,[141] *atiśayokti* with 1.42 and 9.7,[142] and *mālopamā* with 1.48.[143] The difference between *ākṣepa* and *rodha* is explained by citing *Setu* 4.36 and 1.15.[144] *Setu* 3.9 is cited as an example of *ubhayanyāsa*, a form of *arthāntaranyāsa*,[145] and *Setu* 1.56 as that of *ojasvinī vṛtti*.[146]

Among other writers on poetics Abhinavagupta in his *Locana* on the *Dhvanyāloka* quotes *Setu* 4.20 to illustrate a variety of *aprastutapraśaṁsā*.[147] Bhoja cites the verse as an example of one of the varieties of *abhāva*.[148] Jayaratha in his commentary on the *Alaṁkārasarvasva*[149] cites *Setu* 4.6 as an instance of *śliṣṭarūpaka*. Citations from the *Setubandha* occur also in Hemacandra's *Kāvyānuśāsana* and

[135] Vv. 287-90, 353-55, 594-96, 741-43, 1026-31, etc.

[136] *SK* 4.50, 52, 53. The verse numbers are those of the citations.

[137] Ibid., 4.45, 47, 48.

[138] Ibid., 4.171, 172, 173, 174, 182.

[139] Ibid., 4.132, 133.

[140] Ibid., 3.16.

[141] Ibid., 3.49.

[142] Ibid., 4.223, 224.

[143] Ibid., 4.19.

[144] Ibid., 4.152, 157.

[145] Ibid., 4.162.

[146] Ibid., 2.191.

[147] NS edn., p. 43.

[148] *SK* 3.177.

[149] NS edn., 1939, p. 48.

the anonymous *Sāhityamīmāṁsā*.[150] Mahimabhaṭṭa criticizes the use of the particle *va* (*iva*) after the adjective instead of after the *upamāna* in *Setu* 2.11 *ukkhādumaṁ va selaṁ*), and remarks that the words should be read as *selam va ukkha'* to avoid ambiguity.[151]

The citations from the *Setubandha* in Alaṁkāra works give some idea of the style of the poem. The most commonly used figures of speech are, however, the *upamā* and the *utprekṣā*: and, generally speaking, the *utprekṣā*s provide the more interesting examples. In *Setu* 2.1 the ocean, for instance, is fancied as the youth of Rāma's enterprise. This has led to a variety of explanations, but the idea is sufficiently clear. Youth with its ethical problems is the most difficult period of life, and the ocean likewise was a formidable obstacle to the success of Rāma's expedition. In *Setu* 10.39 the earth with the mountains standing and the rivers flowing as before is fancied as being carved anew by the moon out of the accumulated mass of darkness.[152] The imagery is obviously based on the general pattern of the rock-cut architecture of Deccan that was familiar to Pravarasena. Ajantā was, in fact, in the dominion of the younger branch of the Vākāṭakas. The *utprekṣā* in *Setu* 9.53 is based on a fanciful incident of family life applied to the lashing of the Suvela mountain by the waves of the sea. The mountain is represented as enduring the chastisement for the sake of its daughters, the streams, married to the Ocean, raging furious at the reluctance of the brides to leave their paternal home.

Pravarasena makes effective use of alliterative devices to embellish his verses. This at times involves the repetition of words without any difference of meaning, and two examples of this are cited from our poem in the *Sarasvatīkaṇṭhābharaṇa*, chapter 2: *Setu* 4.43 under *lāṭānuprāsa;*[153] and *Setu* 5.19 under a variety of *padānuprāsa*. In the latter verse the alliterative effect is produced by the use of cognate forms

---

[150] TSS, 1934, *Setu* 11.56 and 65 are quoted on p. 56 as examples of *pralaya* (stuporcaused by grief). Cf. 5.145, *Setu* 1.7 is quoted on p. 122. There are a few more citations from our poem.

[151] *Vyaktiviveka*, p. 284, KSS.

[152] *khantūṇa va ukkiṇṇaṁ sasiṇā tamasaṁcaaṁ puṇo vi mahialaṁ*. Translation requires modification. Khantūṇa should be rendered as *hewing* to go with *ukkiṇṇaṁ*. Rāmadāsa rightly says यथा काष्ठादिकं खनित्वा प्रतिमादिकं क्रियते.

[153] *uahissa jaseṇa jasaṁ dhīraṁ dhīreṇa*, etc.

of the same words. There is another example of this in our poem.[154] Similarly, the verb *valaī* and its derivatives are often used more than once in the same verse, and sometimes even thrice.[155] Certain other words are used three or four times in the same verse.[156] The word *khaṇa* is used five timer in 12.85; *ṇu* appears four times in 8.57 and thrice in 10.81 and 13.51. Bhāravi seems to imitate Pravarsena in the similar repetition of this particle in the *Kirātārjunīya*.[157]

Another alliterative device used by Pravarasena consists in repetition of the last word of a compound at the begining of the next and so on till the end of the verse.[158] Rāmadāsa calls it *śr̥ṅkhalābandha* in his gloss on *Setu* 10.27. It resembles the *saṁdaṣṭayamaka* illustrated by Daṇḍin and employed in the *Bhaṭṭikāvya* 10.8,[159] but it is essentially different from a *yamaka*, in which the repeated syllables in spite of their verbal similarity are intended to convey different meanings.

The *śr̥ṅkhalābandha* is an old device frequently used in Prākr̥ta poetry, and sometimes also in prose, and has been traced by Jacobi to the *Sūtrakr̥tāṅga* 1.15 of the Ardhamāgadhī canon.[160] It appears to have two varieties in Prākr̥ta poetical literature. The first is the one used in the *Setubandha* as stated above; and at least three examples of this are found in Uddyotana's *Kuvalayamālā* where it appears in

---

154 जलइ-जलन्त-जलअरं भमइ भमन्त-मणि-विद्दुम-लआजालं ।
रसइ रसन्तावत्तं भिज्जइ भिज्जन्त–पव्वअं उअहि–जलं ॥ —5.65. Cf. 6.35; 12.87

155 वलन्ति वलमाण-जुअ-वलन्त-क्खन्धा (9.74); and likewise *valia, valanta, valanta* in 6.46 and 7.29.

156 *dara* 6.64, 10.37; *addhe addha*⁰ 6.66; *addha* 8.52; *dūra* 9.4; *thoa* 9.62; *putta* 15.26; *saī* 15.68.

157 Bhāravi uses *nu* five times in 9.15 and thrice in 9.7 and more than once in verses 42, 54 and 69 of the same Canto. Cf. Māgha 10.14.

158 घण-विडवट्ठिअ-तिमिरा तिमिरालिद्ध-मइलन्त मुद्ध-किसलआ ।
किसलअ-णिसण्ण कुसुमा-कुसुमामोएण णवर णज्जन्ति दुमा ॥ 10-27
There are four other verses with a similar arrangement: 8.4, 11.50, 13.71 and 5.68, the latter with a slight inconsistency.

159 The commentators call it *Kāñcīyamaka*, but Bharata in his gloss on the verse points out that it is the same as the *Saṁdaṣṭayamaka* defined by Daṇḍin in *Kāvyādarśa* 3.51, 52.

160 Introduction to *Samarāiccakahā*, p. xxii.

groups of two or more verses, the repetition of the words being continued from one verse to another.[161] The other variety appears in groups of verses usually composed of long compounds, in which the last word of the first line is repeated at the beginning of the second line, and the last word of the second line at the beginning of the next verse and so on to the end of the group.[162]

The use of verbs in more or less close succession sometimes gives a certain picturesqueness to a verse, as in *Setu* 5.70; 10.59; 11.38; 13.48.[163]

Pravarasena makes limited use of *śleṣa*. It is also noteworthy that the *Setubandha* does not contain any example of *citrakāvya*.

6. Pravarasena as a Poet

The *Setubandha* is one of the few *mahākāvyas* that may be said to have a central thought behind the events described in the narrative. Underlying its main topic, the building of the great causeway, is the idea of the supreme value of right method and its application, without which neither united effort nor even superhuman energy is adequate for success in a prodigious enterprise.[164] Except for a solitary hint, Pravarasena nowhere gives a clear expression to this idea, but it slowly emerges from his description of the undertaking. He is a poet who inculcates an idea without appearing to do so; and there is no doubt that he invests the mythological theme with a human interest of great value.

Pravarasena has occasion to speak a good deal about the manly virtues; and gives his ideas of the able, the valiant and the good in impressive verses. The able (*samatthā*), for instance, makes even a failing enterprise thrive with a success unattainable by others, even as the Sun drives his tottering one-wheeled chariot through the sky (3.14). The unremitting zeal of valiant warriors is heightened when thwarted by obstacles, even as the everflowing water of great rivers

---

[161] See *Kuvalayamālā*, ed. Upadhye, pp. 14, 18, 171.

[162] *Kuvalayamālā*, pp. 60, 96, 112, 118, 134; *Saṁarāiccakahā*. pp. 79, 423-24, 449, 498-99; *Lilāvaī*, vv. 353-55, 1323-26. ed. Upadhye.

[163] E.g., धूमाइ जलइ विहडइ ठाणं सिढिलेइ मलइ मलउच्छङ्ग (5-70)

[164] See Section 4, p. 30.

surges up when obstructed in its course (3.17). Pravarasena frequently uses the word *sappurisa* or *sūrisa* to indicate different types of good men such as the few who accomplish a work silently (3.9); persons who cannot be induced to retrace their steps without having achieved their task (3.24); those who achieve a task, however arduous, by maintaining their fortitude, even as the rays of the sun scorch the universe by adhering to the solar orb (3.39). The term is also applied to those who take the lead in the fighting, and gain control over their own forces before vanquishing the enemy (3.40). Bravery in war is here conceived as an aspect of goodness; and the idea behind Pravarasena's statement seems to be that the good man is proved in war. It may be noted that the idea of affinity of bravery to goodness appears even more explicitly in the evolution of ethical thought in Greek literature.[165]

There is a number of verses in canto 13 in which Pravarasena speaks of the ideals and aspirations that inspire the warrior on the battlefield. Such verses are not usual in the description of battle scenes in the Sanskrit *mahākāvya*s. The warrior, for instance, preserves his *māna* like a flower (v. 44), and his *abhimāna* at the cost of his life (v. 35). Both the words are used in the sense of *honour* as in Bhāravi's *Kirātārjunīya*.[166] Bhāravi uses them also in the sense of self-conceit[167] with which Pravarasena is not concerned. The latter refers to *māna* in another connection in *Setu* 4.62 when he speaks of persons of character that take their stand upon family tradition and *self-respect*.[168] Further, he tells us in *Setu* 13.16 that the warriors remembered shame (*lajjā*) even in face of danger. *Lajjā* means here shame in a good sense, which makes a man shun disgraceful deeds, i.e. honour. This use of

---

[165] Words like *aretē* (goodness, virtue), *areiōn* (better) and *artistos* (best) come from the same root as *arēs*, the god of war, "the first notion of goodness being that of manhood, bravery in war". — Liddell and Scott, *Greek-English Lexicon* under Arēs. Abridged edn., Oxford, 1963. Similarly, *agathos* (good) means also brave, valiant in the Iliad and Herodotus. — Liddell and Scott, new edn. by Jones *sub voce*.

[166] 11-59, 61; 2.13, 19. *Abhimāna* is rendered as "self-respect" by Stein in his translation of *Rājataraṅgiṇī* 1.226.

[167] 2.48, 49.

[168] Cf. आर्यकेणार्यवृत्तेन कुलं मानं च रक्षता — *Mṛcchakaṭika* 10.50, NS edn., 1922. Pravarasena says कुल–माण–ववट्ठम्भा . . . सप्पुरिसा.

the word is exactly like that of Greek aischune *shame, dishonour*; also, *sense of shame, honour*.[169] Broadly speaking, Pravarasena here gives weighty expression to some fundamental ideas underlying the old Indian code of honour.

We are told in *Setu* 13.35 that the warriors maintained their valour with manly effort, and their *chāyā* by striking hard. *Chāyā* lustre seems to mean here *prestige* as in *Gāthāsaptaśatī* 1.38.[170] The word appears to have the same meaning in *Setu* 3.18 where Sugrīva speaks of one's prestige built up with a sense of pride, and maintained from one generation to another.

A desire for ever increasing fame and the hope of glory after death impel the warrior to valiant efforts (13.35, 44, 47); and gratitude for the master's kindness also serves as an inspiration (12.66; 13. 16). Ingratitude is hateful, and strongly condemned in Sugrīva's address to his followers: "when a person desists from daring deeds, it is surely because he wants to preserve his dear life. But whosoever fails to repay a kindness is counted in the world as dead even while alive" (3.12).

Sītā'a lament at the sight of the severed head of Rāma (11.57ff.) reveals another aspect of Pravarasena's genius. Her grief and stupefaction are described in a number of verses; but the lament itself is commendably brief, and its continuity is broken by Trijaṭā's beautiful words of consolation. With a rare artistic sense Pravarasena

---

[169] See Jones op. cit. *sub voce*. Aeschylus uses the word in the latter sense in his portrayal of a Theban champion as one who reveres the throne of Honour: ton Aischunēs thronon timōnta *The Seven Against Thebes* 409-10.

[170] NS edn., 1889. In the verse in question the wife of a poor man proud of his high birth is annoyed when her relatives bring her pecuniary help, because she wants to maintain the prestige (*chāhī=chāyā*) of her husband. Cf. *Samarāiccakahā*, p. 442. अत्थो नाम महन्तं देवारूवं । एसो खु पुरिस्स बहुमाणं वद्धावेइ गौरवं जणेइ, सोहग्गं करेइ, छायामावहइ, etc.

In a story in the *Kuvalayamālā* (sec. 102, p. 52) Mānabhaṭa offends his young wife by declaring in a song his longing for another girl in a village festival. Taunted and pitied the village belles, she sadly thinks that he did not care about her prestige even in the presence of her companions (*ṇa cchāyā-vakkhaṇaṁ kayaṁ*) Pravarasena has *chāā . . . rakkhijjai*. The expression *chāyābhaṁga* is likewise used to denote "loss of prestige", "dishonour", "disgrace". — See *Bhavisayattakahā* of Dhanapāla 10.7,12, pp. 72, 74 (Gune's edition GOS, 1923).

gives the utterances of the two women in the form of a dialogue, which avoids monotony, and makes the sequence of lament and consolation a master-piece of poetic intensity. Trijaṭā's concluding words are profoundly moving: "Had it been Rāma's head, it would have returned to life even in such a plight, having obtained the familiar touch of thy hands, sweet as nectar" (11.132). Her grief is strung to a still higher pitch at this mention of Rāma's love for her. A new burst of grief overpowers her; and "she wept aloud in a different manner, remembering the past, even though she was intent on death (v. 133)". Pravarasena's delineation of the inherent pathos of the scene is praised by Anandavardhana as the work of a poet of genius.[171]

The conventional descriptions in the *Setubandha*, though often characterized by artifical conceits, have a considerable number of verses that give excellent pictures of the scenes described, and reveal a sensitive appreciation of natural beauty. A few examples may be given. The succession of moonlit nights and brilliant days in the autumn is likened to a necklace of pearls interspersed with jewels (1.27). Flowers and birds typical of the autumn are mentioned with deep feeling: "The scent of the *saptaparṇa* blossoms appealed to the heart, but the fragrance of the *kadamba* flowers pleased no more. The sweet note of the swans lingered in the heart, but not the cry of the peacock, because its time was past (1.23)." The description of the sea in canto 2 has many mythological associations, but is not without vivid touches. "The palm groves on the shore rustled as they were hit by sea spray blown by the wind; and the expanse of the beach was lashed by the waters, swollen by the streams of rays from the mountain that was the moon (2.34)." The gravitational effect of the moon on the sea is described with the aid of an abstract simile:

> The sea surged when the moonlight came, bringing joy by its cherished presence, and calmed down when it was gone; just as passion is strong at the advent of youth, delightful with the company of the beloved, and loss its turbulence when youth has passed. — 2.20

Sunset, the oncoming darkness and moonrise form the subject of a large number of verses in canto 10. The play of moonlight on the shifting shadows is described with an observing eye.

[171] *Dhvanyāloka* (NS), p. 87.

> With the darkness vanishing like a rainy day, the partly distinct woods, with lovely foliage, seemed to be dripping as the moonbeams came scattered through the branches. —10.44
>
> The trees, hemmed in by the lunar rays, and rocked at the top by the wind, with the shadows wavering on account of the branches moving to and fro, seemed to swim as they swayed in the current of moonlight. —10.51

The mournful plight of a pair of *cakravāka* birds supposed to separate in the evening is feelingly portrayed in *Setu* 10.24, and their reunion in the description of the morning scene at the beginning of canto 12 (v. 9). This is a recurrent theme in later *kāvya* poetry.

The lengthy description of the Suvela mountain in canto 9 is often marred by exaggerated conceits and fanciful imagery. From a literary point of view, there could be no greater contrast than between Kālidāsa's picture of the Himālaya in the *Kumārasambhava* and Pravarasena's portrayal of the Suvela in the *Setubandha*. It redounds to the credit of Kālidāsa that he steered clear of the artificialities that had begun to appear in the literature of the age. Nevertheless Pravarasena's description of the Suvela has a number of good verses, based on the proximity of the mountain to the sea, and containing vivid glimpses of animal life in which the poet is particularly interested.

> The colour of the young foliage of the trees faded slightly in contact with the briny sea spray; and the deer ran away, scared by the roar of lions, but stopped short, bending a leg, and pricking up their ears. —9.16
>
> The slopes, rich in gems, seemed to bristle with thorns, like nettles, on account of the incessant sea spray; and the lion roared, riding on the elephant's head, with the pearls[172] stuck in its claws. —9.24
>
> The roar of lions filled the caves, making the elephants in the woods prick up their ears; while the direction from which the sound came being unknown, the deer fled straight on, but turned back, scared by the echoes. —9.30
>
> The deer fainted on account of the smell of the yellow orpiment heated by the fierce midday sun; and the buffaloes licked the rocks for the taste of the salt crust formed by sea spray. —9.41

[172] Supposed to be in the head of an elephant.

Another verse gives the picture of a boar eluding an attacking lion by slinking back to its miry retreat (9.48).

The descriptions in the *Setubandha* in connection with its special topics such as uprooting the mountains and dropping them on the sea contain much that is grotesque and fanciful; but once we accept the mythological background, we have no difficulty in appreciating the ingenuity with which the details of some of the unusual scenes have been worked out. Some of the verses reveal a genuine feeling for nature and considerable powers of graphic description.

> (During the uprooting of a mountain) a pair of bees with the wings heavy-laden with the honey of flowers, could not leave a cluster of blossoms shed by a leaning sylvan creeper, even though they had partaken of the honey. — 6.47

> The ever-flowing brooks, swaying as the mountains swayed, and turbid with the mud that was stirred up, swelled for a moment as they ran into one another and became large streams. — 6.50

> While the sylvan deities fled from the creepers in fear when a mountain was violently uprooted, even their fresh blossoms dropped, and the young shoots withered, even though the stems were unhurt. — 6.52

> While the mountains, their home, were carried away, the hinds started to run, but turned back, distraught with fear; and the woods were charming when they turned round and looked up in bewilderment for a while. — 6.80

The plight of the animals on the disturbed mountains often adds to the interest of the description. We have pictures of elephants worn out with fatigue (6.61); cow elephants weeping for the missing leader of the herd (6.68); buffaloes disappearing as they turn round in a whirlpool (7.23); and deer carried away by the waves, meeting and parting again (7.24). Another verse (7.50) depicts a herd of elephants in a whirlpool, trunks raised, and holding up a distressed cub, while the leader of the herd keeps a prowling sea lion off. There is also a reference to elephants, half submerged in the waters, tearing the serpents clinging to their feet, like ropes, stretching and pulling them with their trunks (8.48). Motifs similar to those in the last two verses are found in a painting in Ajantā Cave X, in which a python coiling round the trunk of a tree is shown as having caught one of the hind legs of an elephant; while several other elephants with their trunks raised are seen coming to rescue their companion.[173] Similarly, the *Setu* 9.23 describes the encounter of an elephant with a tiger in which the tiger, pierced and tossed by the elephant's tusks, pounces on the latter's temples. Usually the lion is represented as the enemy of the elephant, and references to the tiger in this connection appear to be rare in *kāvya* poetry. A sculptured frieze in a corridor of the upper story of Ajantā Cave VI has, however, some animated figures of elephants, one of whom is shown as killing a tiger.[174] Such similarities between motifs in the art of Ajantā and themes treated in Pravarasena's descriptions, though rare, bear witness to his close observation of animal life. It is noteworthy that camels are not mentioned in the *Setubandha* in sharp contrast to the Yuddhakāṇḍa of the *Rāmāyaṇa* on which the poem is based.[175] It is probable that camels were rare in ancient Deccan, and Pravarasena was not familiar with that animal.

As we have pointed out, the description of the evening scene in *Setu* Canto 10 is followed by a portrayal of the amorous activities of the *nāyikā*s aided by their maiden messengers, a theme introduced by Pravarasena, probably for the first time, in the structure of a *mahākāvya*. As a matter of fact, he brings in the spirit of the *Gāthāsaptaśatī* in this Canto, and for this purpose seems to draw on the rich fund of Prākṛta erotic poetry from which the *Gāthāsaptaśatī* itself was compiled. In any case there are some striking resemblances between certain verses of the *Gāthāsaptaśatī* and *Setu* Canto 10 in the treatment of these topics. For example, *GS* 2.98[176] is practically a variation in direct speech of the *Setu* 10.67.[177] Similarly, *GS* 1.87 expresses in direct speech exactly the same idea as that conveyed in

[173] Yazdani, *Ajanta*, pt. III, p. 33, Text.

[174] Ibid., p. 6.

[175] Cf. *Rāmāyaṇa* 6.47.23; 48.38; 58.28, etc.

[176] See NS edn. with commentary of Gaṅgādhara, 1889.

[177] In the *GS* verse the *dūtī* speaks to the *nāyaka* about the *nāyikā*:

बहुसो वि कहिज्जन्तं तुह वअणं मज्झ हत्थसंदिट्ठं ।
ण सुअं त्ति जम्पमाणा पुणरुत्तसअं कुणइ अज्जा ।।

Pravarasena says: "what the messenger girls reported openly, returning after meeting the lovers, the young women caused to be repeated again and again. . . ."

Setu 10.77.[178] The picture of the *navavadhū* in *GS* 7.47 finds elaboration in *Setu* 10.76. In 10.72 Pravarasena refers to the *māna* or sulky wrath of the *nāyikās*, or rather an aspect of it, because it is a many-sided topic that appears frequently in the *kāvyas* and works on poetics. The gist of the verse is that the *nāyikās* hastened to greet the *nāyakas* unreservedly whereupon their maiden friends stared them out of countenance for neglecting their advice to practise *māna*. The background of all this can be clearly understood by referring to the *Gāthāsaptaśatī* which has a considerable number of verses on the various aspects of *māna*.[179] The interrelation of the *GS* and the *Setubandha* in the treatment of these topics seems to show the influence of popular poetry on the evolution of the Prākṛta *mahākāvya*. As we have said above, the Sanskrit *mahākāvyas* like those of Bhāravi and Māgha follow in this respect the lead of the *Setubandha*.

7. Metres

Not much was adequately known about ancient Prākṛta metres until the publication of Virahāṅka's *Vṛttajātisamuccaya* and the *Svaymbhūcchandas*, both edited and elucidated by H.D. Velankar,[180] and his critical edition of Hemacandra's *Chandonuśāsana* with valuable indices.[181] A metrical analysis of the *Setubandha* is beyond the scope

---

[178] *GS* has:

अवलम्बिअमाणपरंमुहीए एन्तस्स माणिणि पिअस्स ।
पुट्ठपुलउग्गमो तुह कहेई संमुहठिअं हिअअं ॥

Pravarasena says: "The constant thrills of the young women assured their beloved that their anger was appeased, and their hearts favourably inclined as they sat looking straight ahead." The south Indian reading *parao-hutta-ṇisaṇṇo*, i.e. *parāṁmukhaṁ niṣaṇṇaḥ* for *parao-hutta* — brings the *Setu* verse into even greater harmony with the *GS* which has *paraṁmuhī*. The commentator Mādhava seems to have been aware of the parallelism of the two verses, as he uses the expression *pṛṣṭhapulaka* corresponding to *puṭṭha-pulaa* of the *GS* verse.

[179] E.g., the *sakhī* recounts the pleasures of *māna* denied to a *nāyikā* who is elated at the very sight of the *nāyaka* (5.65); sometimes she administers a mild rebuke to a *nāyikā* who is unable to practise *māna* (7.59); a *nāyikā* declares that the *māna* induced by her friends disappeared, like a paramour, at the sight of the beloved (2.44). Māna is viewed also from other standpoints.

[180] Revised edition in *Rajasthan Purātana Granthamālā*, 1962.

[181] Singhī Jain Series, 1961.

of this essay. We shall confine ourselves to a few general remarks about the metres used in the poem. The prevailing metre in the *skandhaka* consisting of two equal halves of thirty-two (12+20) *mātrās*. Its older name is *aryāgīti*.[182] Svayambhū 1.1.3[183] says that there are eight *caturmātras* in each half of a *skandhaka* subject to the rule that at the sixth place they should have a *dvimātrā* in the middle, i.e. be either *madhyaguru* or *sarvalaghu*; but a *madhyaguru* should not be used at the odd places, i.e. the first, third, fifth and the seventh. Svayambhū cites *Setu* 3.9 as an example of a *skandhaka*:

> ते विरला सप्पुरिसा जे अभणन्ता घडेन्ति कज्जालावे।
> थोअच्चिअ ते वि दुमा जे अमुणिअ-कुसुम-णिग्गमा देन्ति फलं।।[184]
>
> *te viralā sappurisā je abhaṇantā ghaḍenti kajjālāve*।
> *thoaccia te vi dumā je amuṇia-kusuma-ṇiggamā denti phalaṁ*।।

An interesting feature of the *Setubandha* is that it has about forty verses known as *galitaka*, composed in different varieties of a metre of that name. Examples of *galitaka* verses are extremely rare in extant Prākṛta literature; and Pravarasena's *kāvya* appears to be one of the earliest in which they occur. The commentaries on the *Setubandha* give very little information about these metres, but most of them can be identified with the help of the definitions given by Hemacandra, Virahāṅka and Svayambhū in their manuals of Prākṛta prosody. Virahāṅka 4.89ff. describes fourteen such metres, and Hemacandra 4.25ff. twenty-four. The section of Svayambhū's work dealing with the *galitaka* metres is incomplete and mutilated in the existing text, but he quotes three illustrative verses from little known Prākṛta poets. Virahāṅka does not quote any examples; while Hemacandra gives examples composed by himself. Mudamalla in his commentary on the *Setubandha* quotes the definitions of two *galitaka* metres apparently in the form of *sūtras* in Prākṛta, but we are unable to state the source utilized by him. Among our authorities Virahāṅka and Svayambhū composed their works in Prākṛta verse; while Hemacandra's definitions are given in Sanskrit in the form of *sūtras*.

---

182 आर्यागीतिरित्यहीन्द्रः — *Chandonuśāsana* 4.13.

183 See also pp. 762-65.

184 Printed text of Svayambhū has *ghaḍanti* in the first line and *a* for *vi* in the second.

Little is known about the meaning of the word *galitaka*.[185] Virahaṅka uses the term *galiā* (*galitā*), but *galia* and *galiā* (*galitaka*) appear in Svayambhū; while Hemacandra employs the Sanskrit name. That the older expression was *galiā* or perhaps *galita* is shown by the fact that the former term occurs in Virahāṅka (about the seventh century CE), and the later in the *Jānāśrayī*, written towards the end of the sixth century CE, which defines and illustrates the *galita* metre (5.45) in Sanskrit.[186]

An essential feature of the *galitaka* verses is that they are always rhymed, i.e. provided with *antyayamakas*. Hemacandra 4.48.1 says that, according to some, *galitakas* are metres other than the *daṇḍaka*, the *āryā* and the like, and provided with *yamakas*. Svayambhū 1.24 says that leaving aside the *daṇḍakas* and the metres of the *skandhaka* class, all other metres accompanied by *yamakas* are known as *galitas*. By metres of the *skandhaka* class he means those of the *gāthā* group which he derives from the *skandhaka*.[187] Broadly speaking, the Prākṛta prosodists down to the time of Hemacandra recognize an independent group of metres variously called *galitā*, *galita* or *galitaka* with rhyme as their special characteristic. On the other hand, the *Kavidarpaṇa*,[188] a comprehensive Prākṛta work on metres written in the thirteenth century, defines and illustratres only one such metre (2.23), which may be contrasted with the rich variety of the *galitaka* metres treated by Virahāṅka and others. This seems to be an indication that these metres had fallen into desuetude by the time of the *Kavidarpaṇa*, and that they belong to a rather early period of Prākṛta poetry. Virahāṅka 4.106 tells us how the leading poets (*kaī-vasahā*) adjust the *yamakas* to the *galiās* employed by them; and Pravarasena's lavish use of them may be said to illustrate the practice of the early poets. The lost *Harivijaya* of Sarvasena likewise contained a number of *galitakas* as he is criticized by Hemacandra for inserting

[185] The word in its masculine form appears in a stage direction in the *Vikramorvaśīya*, Act 4, after v. 56, and is explained by Raṅganātha as *nāṭyaviśeṣa*. The *galitaka* of prosody is usually neuter.

[186] The section of the *Jānāśrayī* dealing with the Prākṛt metres is edited and discussed by Velankar in *JAS*, Bombay, 1959.

[187] *Svayambhūcchandas*, ed. Velankar, Introduction, p. v.

[188] Ed. Velankar, *Rajasthan Purātana Granthamālā*, 1962.

in the poem an irrelevant description of the ocean for the sole purpose of composing verses in the *galitaka* metres.[189] The Sanskrit verse illustrating the *galita* metre in an early work like the *Jānāśrayī* is no doubt based on Prākṛta models[190] and shows the popularity of the metre even among the votaries of Sanskrit poetry. *galita* heads the list of the Prākṛta metres treated in the *Jānāśrayī*; and it is noteworthy that the author describes them as being current among the people.[191]

Hemacandra records the opinion of certain critics that the Prākṛta poems *Rāvaṇavijaya*, *Harivijaya* and *Setubandha* are composed in a single metre, i.e. the *skandhaka*, from the beginning to the end, and that the *galitaka*s are later interpolations.[192] Bhoja likewise mentions this view in the *Śṛṅgārprakāśa*, but he records also a counter-argument that the *galitaka*s are only one of the many varieties of the *skandhaka* metre.[193] This view fails to grasp the essential difference between the two metres, but nevertheless shows that the interpolation theory was not accepted by all. Hemacandra does not offer any comment on the topic, but so far as the *Harivijaya* is concerned, he assumes the author of the poem to have composed also the *galitaka*s, because he criticizes him for using them in an irrelevant description of the ocean. We are on surer ground with regard to the *Setubandha*. None of our commentators except one mention the story of the *galitaka*s being interpolations;[194] they explain

189 तथा हि हरिविजये ईर्ष्याकुपितसत्यभामानुनयनप्रवृत्तस्य हरेः परिजातहरणव्यापारेणो-पक्रान्तविप्रलम्भस्य वर्णनप्रस्तावे गलितकनिबन्धनरसिकतया कविना समुद्रवर्णनमन्तरा गडुस्थानीयं विस्तृतम् — *Kāvyānuśāsana*, vol. 1, p. 171.

190 The *galita* of the *Jānāśrayī* corresponds to the *lalitā* metre of 22 *mātrā*s defined by Virahāṅka 4.60. Though it is not included in Virahāṅka's group of *galitā* metres (4.89-105), it is provided with *antyayamaka*s like them, and was probably regarded by some as a *galita* or *galitaka* metre.

191 लोके प्रचरन्त्यः ।

192 रावणविजयहरिविजयसेतुबन्धेष्वादितः समाप्तिपर्यन्तमेकमेव छन्दो भवतीति । गलितकानि तु तत्र कैरपि विदग्धमानिभिः क्षिप्तानीति तद्विदो भाषन्ते ।। — op. cit., p. 461.

193 See Raghavan, *Bhoja's Śṛṅgāraprakāśa*, p. 802, Madras, 1963.

194 Kṛṣṇadāsa merely reports the view mentioned by Hemcandra and Bhoja, and says;

स्कन्धककाव्यमिति एकरूपेण वृत्तेन कृतं काव्यं वदन्ति ।
अतएव गलितका नास्येति वदन्ति।।

them with as much care as the *skandhakas*. The fact is that the *galitakas* have a special relevance to the structure of our poem. They not only relieve the monotony of the ubiquitous *skandhaka* but enliven the longer descriptions. That is why most of them are found in cantos 2, 6, 7, 8 and 9. The only other *galitakas* in our poem are employed to heighten the effect of certain impassioned utterances of Sugrīva in his address to his followers (3.45-48). The *Setubandha* would lose much of its freshness and variety if we were to exclude the ingeniously constructed *galitakas* with their lyric tone and animated imagery. It is difficult to believe that anyone other than the poet himself could weave these verses into the text without disturbing the current of thought and ideas. The view that the *galitakas* were interpolations seems to have been current in some literary circles in western India in the eleventh and twelfth centuries. An authoritative writer like Viśvanātha (fourteenth century) says that a Prākr̥ta *mahākāvya* is composed in the *skandhaka* metre, and at places in *galitaka* metres as well.[195] He gives the *Setubandha* as an example of this, which shows that the view that the *galitakas* were interpolations was not prevalent in eastern India.

We may now give an account of the *galitaka* metres used in the *Setubanda* as far as we have been able to identify them. All of them are *catuṣpadīs*.

Galitaka

Hemacandra's treatment of the *galitaka* group of metres begins with the so-called *galitaka* metre (4.25), which corresponds to the *saṁpiṇḍitā galitā* metre described by Virahāṅka 4.89. Each *pāda* has 21 *mātrās* (5, 5, 4, 4, 3). Hemacandra 4.26 says that when the third and sixth *mātrās* are short the metre is called *upagalitaka*. Mudamalla points out in his commentary that *Setu* 2.27, 31 and 33 are *upagalitakas*; but as a matter of fact, most of the examples of the *galitaka* metre in the *Setubandha* are *upagalitakas*. Other examples are *Setu* 2.24; 6.62; 7.43; 9.18, 40, 42, 46.

Three other examples of the *galitaka* metre in our poem require comment. In *Setu* 7.41 the first *pāda* has 22 *mātrās*: *malaa-candaṇa-laā-hare*

195 प्राकृतैर्निमिते तस्मिन् सर्गा आश्वाससंज्ञका: ।
छन्दसा स्कन्धकेनैतत् क्वचिद् गलित कैरपि ।।
— *Sāhityadarpaṇa* 6.305, Lahore, 1938.

saṁbharamāṇao. The line as read in the south Indian and Bengal recensions of the poem has, however, 21 *mātrās*, and presents no metrical difficulty: *malaa-candaṇa-laā-haresu bharamāṇao*. In *Setu* 9.49 the sequence of the *mātrāgaṇas* is irregular in the third *pāda*; and in 9.72 the *trimātrā* at the end of the first *pāda* is short of 1 *mātrā*.

It may be added that Mudamalla in his gloss on *Setu* 2.27 quotes a definition of the *upagalitaka* metre in Prākr̥ta, which is imperfect in our copy; but the three words that are clearly legible (*taïa-cchaṭṭha . . . mupagaliaṁ*) seem to show that it corresponds to Hemacandra's Sanskrit definition of the metre.

Lambitā

The *lambitā* metre consists of 22 *mātrās*. According to Virahāṅka 4.96, each *pāda* should contain an initial *dvimātrā* followed by five *caturmātrās* of which the second and the fourth should be *madhyaguru*. According to a general rule laid down by Virahāṅka 4.107, it is permissible to use a *sarvalaghu* in place of a *madhyaguru* wherever it is prescribed. There are several perfect examples of this metre in the *Setubandha*: 6.48, 53, 56; 7.45, 47, 49, 51, 60; 8.65; 9.88. Two other examples (8.61, 63) contain slight irregularities.

Kumudinī

The *kumudinī* metre, described by Virahāṅka 4.98, is similar to the *lambitā*, with 22 *mātrās* consisting of five *caturmātrāṣ* and a long letter at the end of a *pāda* instead of a *dvimātrā* at the beginning. The fourth *caturmātrā* should be *madhyaguru*. *Setu* 6.68 is a complete example of *kumudinī*, which seems also to be employed in 6.59; but in the latter verse the fourth *caturmātrā* is *madhyaguru* in the first and second *pādas* only.

Lalitā

The *lalitā* metre, described by Virahāṅka 4.93, has 24 *mātrās* in each *pāda* distributed in the following order: two *caturmātrās*, one *pañcamātrā* (*madhyalaghu*), another *caturmātrā*, another *pañcamātrā* like the previous one, and a long letter at the end of the *pāda*. Mudamalla says in his commentary on *Setu* 3.46 that this and the preceding verse form a *saṁdānitaka*, and the metre is *lalitā*. He quotes a definition of the metre in Prākr̥ta which is imperfect in our copy, but the following words are legible: *vicchittiā ccia lalitā (ā?) . . . hīṇā*. It is noteworthy that Hemacandra 4.43 defines a *galitaka* metre called *vicchitti* which has 25 *mātrā*s; while the *lalitā* has one *mātrā* less. This seems to be referred to in the definition cited by Mudamalla.

Setu 3.45 and 3.46 are perfect examples of the *lalitā* metre. *Setu* 3.48 illustrates the *viṣamā galitaka* defined by Hemacandra 4.45, being a combination of *lalitā* and *vicchitti*. The first two *pāda*s of the verse have 25 *mātrā*s each corresponding to *vicchitti* in which the sequence of the *mātrāgaṇa*s is 5, 4, 5, 4, 5, 2; while the last two *pāda*s have 24 *mātrā*s each corresponding to *lalitā* in which the sequence is 4, 4, 5, 4,5 2.

Ugragalitaka

The *ugragalitaka*, described by Svayambhū 1.2.3 and Hemacandra 4.35, has in each *pāda* 30 *mātrā*s consisting of an initial group of 6 *mātrā*s followed by 6 *caturmātrā*s, subject to the general rule that the *caturmātrā*s at the odd places should not be *madhyaguru*, and those at the even places should be either *madhyaguru* or *sarvalaghu*.[196]

Setu 6.65 provides a complete example of the *ugragalitaka*. The only other early example of this metre known to us is quoted by Svayambhū from a little known poet named Vṛddhamitra. It is in a mixed dialect with some Sanskrit words spoken by someone desiring a treaty with Rāma.

Mālāgalitaka

The *mālāgalitaka*, described by Hemacandra 4.33, has in each *pāda* 46 *mātrā*s consisting of an initial group of 6 *mātrā*s followed by 10 *caturmātrā gaṇa*s, subject to the *madhyaguru* rule mentioned in connection with the *ugragalitaka* (see above).

Setu verses 7.59, 61 are examples of the *mālāgalitaka*. It may be noted that in the verse 7.61 the second *pāda* has 47 *mātrā*s in Rāmadāsa's text. The reading of ms. C of Goldschmidt *mahiharāhao* for *mahiharāhihao* avoids the metrical difficulty. The other verse 7.59 has two cases of overlapping of *caturmātrā*s. The sixth and seventh *caturmātrā*s in the second *pāda*, and the first and second in the third *pāda* do not divide into equal groups, the division of the *mātrā*s being

---

[196] See *Svayambhūcchanda*s, ed. Velankar, p. 163.

5, 3 owing to the presence of a long letter at the junction of the two *caturmātrā*s in both *pāda*s.

Sundarā

The *sundarā* metre, defined by Hemacandra 4.36, has 13 *mātrā*s in each *pāda*, the order of the *gaṇa*s being 5, 5, 3. It is the metre of *Setu* 9.43, 44, 47, 50. In 9.47 we have to treat the conjunct *gga* in *ggaha* as unstressed (*atīvraprayatna*) to maintain the regularity of the *mātrāgaṇa*s. Rāmadāsa in his gloss on *Setu* 9.47 calls the metre *sundarī*, but says nothing about its characteristics. It may be added that the *yamaka*s in the four verses mentioned above go beyond the prosodical requirement, and extend to the *pāda*s as a whole, the first *pāda* agreeing with the second, and the third with the fourth. For example,

> असुरवन्दिसाहारणं असुरवं दिसाहारणं।
> सूरअं तमणिवालअं सूरअन्तमणिवालअं।। – 9.50
>
> *asuravandisāhāraṇaṁ asuravaṁ disāhāraṇaṁ* ।
> *sūraaṁ tamaṇivālaaṁ sūrantamaṇivalaaṁ* ।।

8. Commentaries on the Setubandha

We shall now give an account of the Sanskrit commentaries on the *Setubandha* utilized for this work. Only two of them have so far been published, that of Rāmadāsa and the anonymous *Setutattvacandrikā*, hereinafter referred to as *SC*. Some of the unpublished commentaries are incomplete and fragmentary; while quotations from a few others, otherwise unknown, are found in *SC*. As the titles of the commentaries are in some cases similar, they are here mentioned by the names of their respective authors.

Kṛṣṇavipra

The extracts from Kṛṣṇavipra's commentary are given from a beautiful transcript of a Devanāgarī manuscript (R. 3226) preserved in the Government Oriental Manuscripts Library, Madras. The curator informs us.[197] that the manuscript along with those of the commentaries of Mādhavayajvan and Devarāṭa was copied during the years 1918-26 from the originals belonging to a resident of Nareri, Pālghāṭ district, Kerala; but that there is nothing on record to

[197] In his letter D.O. No. 47/AL/68, dated 14-03-1968.

indicate the script of the originals. The name of the scribe is given as Paśupati at the end. Apart from a few mistakes, the manuscript is generally correct and reliable. Unfortunately it is incomplete, as the gloss on canto 14 is missing, and that on canto 13 breaks off at verse 30. The division of the poem into cantos in the south Indian recension will be dealt with later; here we give the numbers of the cantos according to the generally accepted text.

The Oriental Manuscripts Library, Madras, has another manuscript of Kṛṣṇavipra's commentary on the *Setubandha* in Grantha characters,[198] of which a Devanāgarī transcript was obtained later for comparison with our copy of the manuscript described above. Apart from the removal of a few inaccuracies from the extracts, it has not been very helpful for our purpose. It breaks off towards the end of canto 10, and contains numerous mistakes besides lacunae and jumbling of verses.

A Devanāgarī transcript of another manuscript of Kṛṣṇa's commentary, preserved in the Oriental Research Institute and Manuscripts Library, Trivandrum, could be obtained after the major portion of the extracts was in the press. It is, on the whole, a good manuscript, and has been utilized for the purpose of this Introduction and some of the verses of the later cantos.[199]

Unfortunately it breaks off at verse 63 of canto 12.

It may be noted that Goldschmidt in his edition of the *Setubandha* gives many of the readings of Kṛṣṇavipra in footnotes from what appears to be a complete manuscript of the commentary. However, in the Introduction to his edition (p. xi), he states that this manuscript, written in Telugu script, is very carelessly copied, and fragmentary at places. Nevertheless we have depended on the readings recorded by him in the portion of the text not covered by the manuscripts mentioned above.

It is difficult to determine the date of Kṛṣṇavipra accurately. He

---

198 The manuscript is referred to in the Extracts as B of K. In the Extracts from Kṛṣṇa (3.61) भ्रामितौ निवर्तितौ should be. . . विवर्तितौ which is the reading of B.

199 In the Extracts from Kṛṣṇa (2.9) the explanation of *sthitiprabhūtam* is incomplete. It is given in full in the Trivandrum manuscript: *sthitau maryādāyāṁ prabhūtaṁ paryāptam.*

frequently quotes the *Vaijayantī* of Yādavaprakāśa who is identified with Rāmānuja's early teacher of that name; and the lexicon may therefore be assigned to the second half of the eleventh century.[200] This gives the upper limit of Kṛṣṇa's date. The lower limit is uncertain, and we shall consider it in connection with the date of his successor Mādhavayajvan.

Kṛṣṇavipra's commentary seems to have been popular in Kerala. He refers to the Sahya as a mountain on the border of Kerala in his gloss on *Setu* 1.56, and mentions a north Indian custom in that on 1.2.

Unlike most other commentaries on the *Setubandha*, Kṛṣṇavipra's work contains a number of quotations from Sanskrit texts, almost all of which will be found in the extracts. Among lexicons he quotes, besides the *Vaijayantī*, Halāyudha's *Abhidhānaratnamālā* several times as well as Amarasiṁha and the *Amaraśeṣa*. The latter work is obviously a supplement to the *Amarakośa* like the *Trikāṇḍaśeṣa* of Puruṣottama. Aufrecht says that *Amaraśeṣa* is another name of the *Trikāṇḍaśeṣa*;[201] but our quotation[202] does not tally with the corresponding statement in the *Trikāṇḍaśeṣa*.[203] It is therefore probable that the *Amaraśeṣa* quoted by Kṛṣṇavipra is different from the work of Puruṣottama.

There is another quotation in Kṛṣṇavipra's gloss on *Setu* 2.9 which purports to give the different meanings of *praṇayana*. The Devanāgarī manuscript gives the source of the citation as Śeva; while the Grantha manuscript gives it as Ākhyāna. The Trivandrum manuscript has Khyāta. The correct reading is probable Ākhyāta, a work cited by Kṛṣṇa in his gloss on *Setu* 8.8.[204] It appears to be a work on verbs and their meanings.[205]

---

200 See Oppert's edition, Madras, 1893; and Introduction to *Kalpadrukośa* (GOS), p. XXVI.

201 Cat. Cat. I *sub voce*.

202 See Extracts 8.102.

203 Kṛṣṇa says तुषारः शीकरेऽपि चेत्यमरशेषे. The printed text of *Trikāṇḍaśeṣa* has तुषारः शीकरे हिमे (3.354). This appears also in a well-preserved manuscript of Puruṣottama's work in the Madras Oriental Manuscripts Library (D 1600).

204 See Extracts 8.8.

205 The quotation mentioned above is imperfectly reporoduced in Extracts 2.9 from the Devanāgarī manuscript. It seems to be correctly given in the Trivandrum manuscript: प्रणयनं याच्ञा। 'निर्माणमैत्रीयाच्ञासु प्रणये चाग्निसंस्कृतौ' इति (आ)ख्याते.

Among works on poetics, apart from the *Kāvyādarśa* of Daṇḍin and Bhoja's *SK*, Kr̥ṣṇavipra quotes a little known work called *Bhāvaviveka*, of which an incomplete manuscript is preserved in the Oriental Manuscripts Library, Madras. The curator informs us that it is a paper manuscript transcribed from the original belonging to a resident of Kannur Mana, Ottapalam, Pālghāṭ district (Kerala). A Devanāgarī transcript obtained from the Library shows that it is a fragment of a little more than 100 verses, being the concluding portion of a work dealing with the different *bhāva*s. It is difficult to say how far it is an independent compilation, as no less than twenty-eight verses are reproduced from the *Nāṭyaśāstra*[206] without acknowledgement. Of the two verses quoted by Kr̥ṣṇavipra from *Bhāvaviveka* in his gloss on *Setu* 1.6, the first containing a definition of *praṇaya* is missing in our copy of the fragment; while a definition of *anukampā* is quoted from the same work twice under *Setu* 5.24 and 11.21.[207]

Among other works Kr̥ṣṇavipra refers to the *Viṣṇu Purāṇa*[208] and quotes several verses from the *mahākāvya*s of Kālidāsa, Bhāravi and Māgha, besides a verse from the *Vikramorvaśīya* in his gloss on *Setu* 11.40. He states at the beginning of his work that many scholars had written commentaries on Pravarasena's poem but were unable to bring out the meanings clearly; and he expresses his own diffidence in trying to expound the poets's difficult ideas.[209]

Mādhavayajvan

The extracts from Mādhava's commentary on the *Setubandha* are given from Devanāgarī transcripts of the manuscripts mentioned below:

A. A Devanāgarī manuscript preserved in the Government Oriental Manuscripts Library, Madras (R. 2772), copied from

---

[206] See chapters 23 and 24, especially the latter, in the edition of M. Ghosh, vol. 1, Calcutta, 1967.

[207] See Extracts.

[208] See Extracts 4.30.

[209] सूरयो बहवो ह्यस्य व्याख्यानानि प्रचक्रिरे ।
न तैरप्यखिलैरस्य सम्यगर्थः प्रकाशितः ।।
भावः प्रवरसेनस्य निगूढो (गहनो B) न हि शक्यते ।
प्राज्ञैरपि परिज्ञातुं मन्दैः किमुत मादृशैः ।।

the original belonging to the same owner as the manuscript of Kṛṣṇavipra's commentary (R.3226) described above. Cantos 11 and 12 are missing; while canto 13 begins with verse 12, some of the missing verses being tagged on to canto 10.

B. A manuscript in Malayalam script preserved in the Oriental Insitute, Baroda. The director of the institute informs us that it was acquired from Pandit V. Vekatarama Sharma 'Vidyābhūṣaṇā', Kizhakkanada, Chenganur, of the former Travoncore State in 1923. Apart from a few verses of canto 5, the manuscript contains the commentary from canto 6 to the end. Both the manuscripts are fairly correct, but groups of verses belonging to cantos 6, 7 and 8 are jumbled together in manuscript B.[210]

Mādhava's work is not a running commentary on the poem, but explains selected words and phrases, and often gives the gist of a verse, or expounds a leading idea. It is rightly called *Setutātparyaṭīkā* in the manuscripts. What makes his commentary particularly valuable is that he often cites the Prākṛta words in the original with their Sanskrit equivalents which are of great use in determining the readings of the south Indian recension of the poem. The number of quotations in his work is very small. Apart from a few references to Bhoja,[211] most of the quotations are anonymous. The definition of Vibhāvanā with the example, cited in the beginning of the commentary, is from Daṇḍin's *Kāvyādarśa*. Two verses are cited from the *Daśarūpaka*[212] in the gloss on *Setu* 4.3. Two other anonymous quotations are found in the gloss on 10.75[213] and 12.50.[214]

---

210 In his letter dated 19 March 1968.

211 परगुणसंभावनासहिष्णुता मात्सर्यमिति भोजः in the gloss on *Setu* 11.16. See also Extracts 10.64.

212 स्वादः काव्यार्थसंभेदादात्मानन्दसमुद्भवः ।
विकाशविस्तरक्षोभविक्षेपैः स चतुर्विधः ॥ — 4.43
वीरः प्रतापविनयाध्यवसायसत्त्वामोहाविषादनयविस्मयविक्रमाद्यैः ।
उत्साहभूः स च दयारणदानयोगात् त्रेधा किलात्र मतिगर्वधृतिप्रहर्षाः ॥ — 4.72

The verses are imperfectly reproduced in Extracts 4.3 from our copy of manuscript A.

213 See Extracts 10.75.

214 लज्जा सखीभ्यस्तद्वाक्यं विपक्षेणानुकम्पनम् ।

→

Mādhavayajvan appears also to have composed a commentary on the *Gāthāsaptaśatī*. Two manuscripts of this commentary called *Tātparyadīpikā* are reported to be in the Punjab University Library, now in Pakistan.[215]

There is no doubt that our Mādhavayajvan is identical with the author of that name who wrote the *Nayacandrikā* commentary on the *Arthaśāstra*. A portion of this commentary, edited by Udayavīra Śāstrī from an incomplete manuscript, was included in the second volume of the *Arthaśāstra* edited by Jolly and Schmidt.[216] The colophon at the end of each chapter of the *Nayacandrikā* gives the name of the author as Vādikavicūḍāmaṇi Mahopādhyāya Śrīmat Mādhavayajvamiśra, which is also found in his commentary on the *Setubandha*, at the end of the first canto in manuscript A, and at the end of the last canto in manuscript B. The colophon at the end of the commentary and that at the end of canto 6 in manuscript A has Vaidika and Vaidikakavi respectively for Vādikavi; but there is no doubt that the correct designation is Vādikavi, found both in the *Nayacandrikā* and the *Setutātparyaṭīkā*.

The *Nayacandrikā* belongs to the same type of commentary as the *Setutātparyaṭīkā* described above. Shamasastry says in the preface to the second edition of his translation of the *Arthaśāstra* that the *Nayacandrikā* "is neither a word for word commentary like Bhaṭṭasvāmi's, nor a paraphrase like the Tamil-Malayalam commentary. Mādhavayajvan, its author, satisfies himself by supplying some connecting links between successive chapters and successive paragraphs in each chapter." The *Nayacandrikā* is thus not a running commentary. Apart from the meanings of selected words and phrases, it gives, as a rule, only the gist of particular passages, like the same author's commentary on the *Setubandha*, It is also noteworthy that the original manuscripts of the commentaries of

---

→ मानस्योद्दीपनान्याह द्वादशैतानि तद्विदः ॥

The quotation is not very well-preserved, and ends with the above verse.

215 See Pītāmbara's *Gāthāsaptaśatīprakāśikā*, ed. Jagdish Lal, Introduction, p. 15, Lahore, 1942.

216 Lahore, 1924.

Mādhavayajvan on both the *Setubandha* and the *Arthaśāstra* as far as they are known to us belong to Kerala.[217]

Mādhavayajvan is later than Kṛṣṇavipra. In his gloss on *Setu* 3.61 he reproduces verbatim Kṛṣṇa's gist of the verse as an alternative explanation.[218] He refers to his predecessor's interpretation in his gloss on *Setu* 8.100, and criticizes him in that on 10.40.[219]

Mādhavayajvan might be earlier than Rāmadāsa who wrote his commentary on the *Setubandha* in CE 1595. Rāmadāsa, in his gloss on *Setu* 1.55, says that the expression *helā-vāa* is explained by some as *helayā vātaḥ*. This rather peculiar explanation seems to occur only in Mādhava among our commentators.[220] If, by *kaścit*, Rāmadāsa means Mādhavayajvan, the latter must be at least a few decades earlier than the former.

As pointed out above, the *Vaijayantī* lexicon may have become an authoritative work by the end of the eleventh century. Kṛṣṇavipra who quotes it frequently could not therefore have lived before the first quarter of the twelfth century. He was probably much later, as he says that there were many commentaries on the *Setubandha* written before his time. Mādhavayajvan who quotes and criticizes Kṛṣṇavipra may have lived a few decades later; and if we are right in thinking that Rāmadāsa refers to Mādhava, the latter's literary activity may be dated earlier than about CE 1550.

Mudamallabhaṭṭa

The extracts from the commentary of Mudamallabhaṭṭa known as *Setucandrikā* are given from a transcript of an incomplete Devanāgarī manuscript preserved in the Oriental Institute, Baroda. The director informs us that the manuscript was acquired from Vasudeva Sastri Telang, Kadam Ghat, Saugar, in 1922. The name of the commentator sometimes appears also as Mudamalla.

---

217 The Madras manuscript, on which the Lahore edition of the *Nayacandrikā* is based, was transcribed from the original in the possession of a resident of Chelapuram, Calicut. See Sanskrit Introduction to *Nayacandrikā*, p. 6 and Gode, *Studies in Indian Literary History*, vol. 1, p. 147, Bombay, 1953.

218 अथवा 'मलयसुवेलयोरन्तराले . . . घटितच्छेदमार्ग (समुद्रं) करोमी'त्यर्थः . . .
— See Extracts 3.61.

219 See Extracts 8.100; 10.40.

220 See Extracts 1.55.

Apart from the last three verses of canto 1, the manuscript contains only the commentary on 2 cantos 2, 3, 4 and 5, breaking off at 5.59 After this there is a long gap, at the end of which appears the gloss on the verse 12.97 and the first four verses of canto 13. The *Setucandrikā* is a good commentary; and it is a pity that only a small portion of it is available to us.

Mudamalla frequently quotes Hemacandra's Prākṛta grammar and his *Deśīnāmamālā*. He quotes also the *Viśvaprakāśa*.[221] In his gloss on *Setu* 5.35 he seems to refer to Kṛṣṇavipra's explanation of the verse. The word *ṭaṅka* in that verse is explained by Kṛṣṇa as *arrow*; and this explanation is found only in him among our commentators. Mudamalla mentions it as the opinion of *kaścit*, and confines himself to elucidating the purport of Kṛṣṇavipra's interpretation.[222] That he is the purport of Kṛṣṇavipra seems certain; but there is no definite clue to his date. He seems to be referred to by Laṭakanamiśra whom we have placed about CE 1625 (see below).

Kṛṣṇadāsa

An incomplete palm-leaf manuscript of the commentary of Kṛṣṇadāsa on the *Setubandha* in Malayalam script is preserved in the Oriental Research Institute and Manuscripts Library, Trivandrum. A Devanāgarī transcript of this manuscript was available for study long after the extracts from the commentaries were in the press. It covers only the first seven cantos and four verses of canto 8 (13-16), breaking off at the beginning of the gloss on v. 17. The manuscript is not very well preserved, and contains numerous mistakes and omissions, especially in the Sanskrit *chāyā* of the Prākṛta verses.

The commentary is brief and contains some interesting explanations, but it does not explain all the difficulties, often confining itself to general remarks. There are many verses of which it gives only the *chāyā* without any gloss. With regard to readings, Kṛṣṇadāsa consistently follows the south Indian recension; and his text is, therefore, practically the same as that of Kṛṣṇavipra and Mādhavayajvan. It is noteworthy that ten of the thirteen verses

---

221 See Extracts 4.47.

222 See Extracts 5.35. Kṛṣṇa says *ṭaṅka(ccheda)śabdena śarābhighāta ucyate.*

peculiar to the south Indian recension are found in the available portion of his commentary.

In the Prākṛta colophon at the end of each canto explained in the commentary. Kaṇhadāsa calls himself "the eighth Raṭṭha of the Śrīkumāras", also called the Kulakumāras, a phrase not intelligible to us. There is no other clue to his date as he does not refer to or quote any previous author or work.

Kṛṣṇadāsa seems to be referred to in another commentary on the *Setubandha*, the *Setutattvacandrikā* compiled in Bengal. In *Setu* 2.1 the ocean is described as the youth of Rāma's expedition; and this has led to a variety of interpretations. Criticizing one of them, *SC* says that "according to some, the childhood of the enterprise is the slaying of Vāli, the youth the crossing of the ocean, and the old age the slaying of Rāvaṇa. This explanation is wrong, because a resemblance is sought to be established between the ocean and youth by representing the crossing of the ocean as the youth of the undertaking". It is noteworthy that Kṛṣṇadāsa in his gloss on the verse speaks of the childhood and youth of Rāma's expedition. He says that the period from the alliance with Sugrīva to the ascertainment of Sītā's whereabouts, is, as it were, the childhood of the undertaking; while the period from Rāma's arrival at the seashore to her recovery represents its youth. If the criticism mentioned above is aimed at Kṛṣṇadāsa, the latter might be supposed to have written his commentary before the middle of the seventeenth century, which is the approximate date of the *Setuttatvacandrikā* (see below).[223]

Devarāṭa

The extracts from the commentary of Devarāṭa alias Subrahmaṇya are given from a transcript of an incomplete Devanāgarī manuscript preserved in the Oriental Manuscripts Library, Madras. As far as can be judged from the colophon at the end of cantos 1 and 2, the commentary, called *Setudīpa*, was composed at the request of one Śrīdāsa,who seems to have been the chief of a village named Ravivara.

---

[223] The statement in Extracts 2.1 that Mudamalla is criticized in *SC* was made before we had access to Kṛṣṇadāsa's commentary. It now appears that the criticism is levelled at Kṛṣṇadāsa rather than Mudamalla.

The manuscript covers only cantos 1, 2, 3, 4 (up to verse 39), 7 and 8. This is followed by cantos 9, 10 and 11 (up to verse 113), of which only the Sanskrit *chāyā* is given without any gloss except in the case of four or five verses. The available portion of the manuscript is fairly correct, but has a number of lacunae.

Devarāṭa belongs to the southern school of commentators, and sometimes follows Kṛṣṇavipra closely. There is nothing remarkable in his commentary, but he seems to reproduce a number of alternative interpretations from other commentaries on the *Setubandha*. In his gloss on *Setu* 11.1, for instance, he reproduces that of Mādhavayajvan *in toto* as an alternative explanation. But more conspicuous are the long anonymous excerpts from the commentary of Kṛṣṇadāsa. There are usually introduced by the word *athavā*; but at least in one case, in Devarāṭa's gloss on *Setu* 4.26, the long quotation from Kṛṣṇadāsa is preceded by the words *anye tvāhuḥ*. Smaller citations from Kṛṣṇadāsa are, however, quietly incorporated in his own gloss without any prefatory remark (e.g. under *Setu* 3.37, 4.23, 7.50, etc.).

It is necessary to point out that some of the passages quoted from Devarāṭa in our extracts are really citations from the commentary of Kṛṣṇadāsa. In extracts 2.15 the entire passage beginning with the words *svāṁśabhūte trailokye madhumathanamiva*, attributed to Devarāṭa, is a quotation from Kṛṣṇadāsa; so also the passage cited in extracts 2.16. The citation from Devarāṭa in extracts 3.37 likewise belongs to Kṛṣṇadāsa. Here the misleading expression *samaramukha-vyāvṛtta* should be replaced by *samaramukhavyāpṛta* found in Kṛṣṇadāsa. It may, however, be noted that the citations in Devarāṭa often help correct mistakes in the Trivandrum manuscript of Kṛṣṇadāsa's commentary.

Rāmadṛṣti

This is a curious fragment in Devanāgarī preserved in the Oriental Manuscripts Library, Madras. The author who remains anonymous offers obeisance to his teacher Govinda, and explains the first verse of the *Setubandha* with special reference to Viṣṇutattva. After remarking that there are difficulties everywhere in *Setukāvya*, he contents himself with explaining verses 7-12 of canto 3. The only noteworthy feature of the fragment is that it mentions Mādhavayajvan in the gloss on *Setu* 1.1, and gives an extract from his commentary on the verse.

Kulanātha

The extracts from Kulanātha's commentary on the *Setubandha* are given from a Bengali transcript of an old palm-leaf manuscript in Bengali characters preserved in the Asiatic Society of Bengal,[224] and dated in the Śaka year 1457 (CE 1535). Kulanātha is referred to as Upādhyāya in the colophon; and it is also stated that the *pustaka* belonged to Śrī Raghunātha Vidyālaṅkārācārya. The commentary is called *Rāvaṇavadhaṭīkā*, but the title *Rāvaṇavadhapañjikā* appears at the end of canto 7.

The manuscript, although described as correct by R.L. Mitra, contains a large number of mistakes and lacunae, besides a considerable jumbling of verses belonging to different cantos. After canto 5 comes canto 6 ending with verse 67 (incomplete), followed by 8.17 (minus the first sentence) to the end of canto 8. After this comes canto 9 ending with verse 43 (incomplete), followed by the remaining portion of 6.67 to the end of canto 6. Then comes canto 7, after which appear the first sixteen verses of canto 8 and the first sentence of 8.17, followed by the remainder of 9.43 to the end of canto 9. Fortunately the sequence of the remaining cantos is not broken by any such confusion. The manuscript is, on the whole, carelessly written, but the *Setutattvacandrikā*, mentioned above, has been of great use in preparing the extracts from the commentary of Kulanātha.

Kulanātha, like Kṛṣṇavipra, is an important commentator, and is known to have written also a commentary on the *Gāthāsaptaśatī*.[225] There is reason to believe that the old commentary of Kulanātha on the *Setubandha* had gone out of use; and a systematic effort was made in Bengal to compile a new commentary, primarily based on his work. The *Setutattvacandrikā* appears to have been the result of this

[224] *A Descriptive Catalogue of the Sanskrit Manuscripts in the Collections of the Asiatic Society of Bengal*, vol. VII, 1934, p. 630, no. 1850; R.L. Mitra, *Notices of Sanskrit Manuscripts*, vol. V, 1880, no. 1978.

[225] Cf. Pītāmbara's *Gāthāsaptaśatīprakāśikā*, ed. Jagdish Lal, Introduction, p. 15.

undertaking. It is compiled from different sources, but mainly from Kulanātha, probably by more than one scholar interested in Prākṛta studies. The study of Prākṛta poetry and specially the *Setubadha* seems to have been popular in Bengal, as can be seen from the making of commentaries on the work and the existence of a manuscript of the text in old Bengali characters, dated in Lakṣmaṇasena Saṁvat 102 corresponding to CE 1222.[226]

Kulanātha refers to two earlier commentators of the *Setubandha*. In his gloss on *Setu* 6.63 he quotes a remark of Śrīharṣa to elucidate the purport of the verse;[227] and the same is found also in the *Setutattvacandrikā* where Kulanātha's gloss on the verse is anonymously reproduced. Nothing is known about this Śrīharṣa, and it is difficult to say if he is identical with the commentator Harṣapāla, quoted several times in *SC*.

In his gloss on *Setu* 10.35 Kulanātha remarks that the expression *suragaja* used in the verse is explained by some as *Gaṇapati*.[228] His gloss on the verse is multilated in our copy, but seems to be reproduced in full in *SC* where the rather peculiar explanation of the word is attributed of Śrīnivāsa, whom we have placed between CE 1150 and 1440 (see below). It is probable that Kulanātha had Śrīnivāsa in mind when he referred to the explantation mentioned above as that of *kecit*. He is thus later than Śrīnivāsa, but cannot possibly be placed later than the early years of the sixteenth century.

Kulanātha cites a *deśī* lexicon different from the *Deśīnāmamālā* of Hemacandra. In his gloss on *Setu* 6.8[229] he cites a *deśī* lexicon which explains *hittha* as *ashamed* and *affrighted.* Hemacandra (*DN* 8.67) quotes in his connection Gopāla, one of his predecessors in the field of *deśī* lexicography, who records these meanings of the word. The wording of Kulanātha's quotation is, however, somewhat different; and he seems to cite a lexicon other than that of Gopāla. Another reference to *deśī* lexicon seems to occur in Kulanātha's gloss on *Setu* 6.38.[230] In

[226] *Descriptive Catalogue*, pp. x, 630.

[227] See Extracts 6.63.

[228] सुरश्चासौ गजश्चेति सुरगजोऽत्र गणपतिरिति केचित्.

[229] See Extracts.

[230] See Extracts.

his gloss on 3.61[231] the *deśīkoṣa* quoted by him explains the word *addhanta* as *eskadeśa*, while the meaning assigned to it by Hemacandra is *paryanta* (*DN* 10.8).

On grammatical topics Kulanātha follows Vararuci, and sometimes ignores Hemacandra. In his gloss on *Setu* 6.53, for instance, he objects to *samatta* being explained as *samsta*, because, according to Vararuci 3.12, *samasta* becomes *samattha*, and not *samatta*, as allowed by Hemacandra 2.45. It may be noted that Kr̥ṣṇavipra, who usually follows Vararuci, seems in this case to follow Hemacandra as he cxplains *samatta* as *samasta*.[232] Kulanātha's criticism might be directed at him, but we cannot be sure on the point.

Setutattvacandrikā

The *Setutattvacandrikā*, mentioned in connection with Kulanātha, marks an interesting phase of the progress of Prākr̥ta studies in Bengal. It has been edited from a fairly well-preserved manuscript written in Bengali characters in CE 1646.[233] Unlike most of the other manuscript utilized by us, this one gives the Prākr̥ta text as well as the *chāyā* and the commentary. Besides, the scribe Viśvanātha seems to have been well acquainted with the Prākr̥ta language.

The *SC* is an anonymous work. It is significant that the intial *maṅgala* is absent. The commentary is, in fact, a compilation from other commentaries; and as we have already said, it is largely based on that of Kulanātha. The latter's gloss on numerous verses is anonymously reproduced, and occasionally supplemented by citations from other commentaries. There is also specific quotations from Kulanātha mentioned by name, more numerous than those from any other commentator cited in *SC*. Some of quotations are mutilated, and contain mistakes, omissions and inaccuracies, which can be rectified with the help of the manuscript of Kulanātha's commentary described above.

SC has a large number of quotation assigned to *anye*, *kecit*, etc.; and even among these there are not a few that are taken from

---

231 See Extracts.

232 See Extracts 6.53.

233 See *Rāvaṇavaha-mahākāvyam*, ed. Basak Calcutta, 1959.

Kulanātha, e.g. under *Setu* 1.26, 2.8 (12 *SC*), 4.31, 11.41, 12.86 (85 *SC*), 13.71, 14.1, etc. In the gloss on *Setu* 4.33, after reproducing Kulanātha anonymously, *SC* gives a further quotation from him, which is, however, stated to be from *anye*. Under *Setu* 13.47 the quotation stated to be from Kulanātha is not found in him; it is the longer quotation from *kecit* that is actually found in Kulanātha's gloss on the verse. These and other peculiarities may be explained by supposing that perhaps more than one hand was at work in compiling the new commentary. The first compilation based on Kulanātha may have been made early in the seventeeth century, and further quotations from him and others seem to have been added from time to time. Viśvanātha's work probably represents the final redaction made about the middle of the century.

There are other instances of the heterogeneous character of the compilation. The *Setu* 12.26 occurs twice in *SC*, first as 4.42, and again as 12.25, each time with a different gloss. A quotation from Kulanātha occurs at the latter place, but it is difficult to see how the repetition could have been made by one and the same compiler.

The relation of *SC* to Rāmadāsa's commentary on the *Setubandha* points to a similar conclusion. *SC* remarks that the *Setu* 15.16, 17 (15, 16 *SC*) are not included in the text by any other commentator. This is true of the south Indian and Bengal recensions of the poem, but the verses in question are found in Rāmadāsa and explained by him. This would lead one to suppose that *SC* was not acquainted with the work of Rāmadāsa written towards the end of the sixteenth century. But there is other evidence which seems to indicate that *SC* was familiar with Rāmadāsa's interpretations, the relevant citations being found among those attributed to *kecit*, *kaścit* and *anye*. For example,

1.58 महापथपदस्य श्मशानवाचकत्वेऽपि प्रहतपदसमभिव्याहारान्न दोष इति कश्चित् *SC* महापथशब्दस्य तु श्मशानवाचकत्वं न शङ्कनीयम्। प्रहतपदसंनिधानात् Rāmadāsa.

8.94 (95 *SC*) शैलाकर्षणात् पतिता इति केचित् *SC*; शैलस्यातिक्रमेणाकर्षणेन पतिता: R.

9.35 (34 *SC*) मृगतृष्णा मरीचिका तया वेष्टितान् इति केचित् *SC*; मृगतृष्णया आवेष्टितान्। मृगतृष्णा मरीचिका R.

10.5 दशवदनेति युक्तपदं यतो न कुत्राप्यवस्थाने दृष्टिपातः परिहृतो भवतीति केचित् *SC*; दशमुखत्वात् क्वाप्यवस्थाने दृष्टिपातः परिहृतो न स्यादिति R.

12.40 (39 *SC*) विजृम्भितानन (*i.e. viambhiāṇaṇa*) इति केचित् *SC*. The reading is against the metre, but found in Rāmadāsa.[234]

12.69 (68 *SC*) शोभाया विशेषतो निदर्शनं दृष्टान्तमिति केचित् *SC*; शोभाया विशेषतो निदर्शनं दृष्टान्तभूतां R.

13.42 सर्वत्र सहोपमेति केचित् *SC*; सर्वत्र सहोपमा R.

13.63 पतन्ति म्रियन्त इति केचित् *SC*; पतन्ति म्रियन्ते R.

13.79 शिथिलिता त्यक्ता इति केचित् *SC*; शिथिलिता त्यक्ता R.

14.6 शरेणाभिसंहितो वञ्चित इति केचित् *SC*; ditto R.

There is at least one instance where *SC* seems to criticize Rāmadāsa. The word *vimharāia* or *vimharāvia* in *Setu* 9.41 is explained by all our commentators as *mūrcchita* or in a similar sense; but Rāmadāsa, in an alternative explanation, explains it as *vismāpita*. *SC* objects to this interpretation, and cites a *deśī* lexicon to show that the correct meaning of the word is *mūrcchita*.[235]

The conflicting character of the two sets of evidence mentioned above seems to suggest that the commentary of Rāmadāsa was not known to the compilers of *SC* at the first phase of the compilation, but that references to his interpretations were added later when his work became available to scholars in Bengal.

Rāmadāsa

The *Rāmasetupradīpa* of Rāmadāda is the best known commentary on the *Setubandha*, largely because it is not only complete and well preserved, but was the first commentary on the poem to be published along with the text.[236]

---

[234] See Extracts 12.40.

[235] See Extracts 9.41. The initial portion of *SC*'s gloss on the verse is anonymously reproduced from Kulanātha, but the word *vismāpita* found there is a mistake for *vismārita*, which is Kulanātha's rendering of the Prākṛta word.

[236] Second edition, NS Press, 1935. The editors do not give any information about the manuscript material used by them; and the text of the poem seems to have been reproduced as it is from the manuscript available to them. Nevertheless, apart from mistakes and minor variations, it generally →

Rāmadāsa gives some interesting information about himself and his environment in the introductory and concluding verses of his commentary. He was a Rājpūt prince, patronized by Akbar, and belonged to the Kacchavāha clan, like Rājā Mān Singh of Amber, to whom he refers. The editors of the NS edition of the *Setubandha* state that he was the chief of a place named Volī in the former Jaipur State. He says that he composed his commentary in Saṁvat 1652 (CE 1595) in the fortieth year of the reign of Jallāladīndra (Jalāluddīn Muhammad Akbar), to whom he expresses his devotion in eloquent terms. He reports that Akbar protected the cow, and abolished the pilgrim tax and what appears to be a tax on commercial transactions.[237] He tells us further that the emperor listened to the recitation of the Purāṇas, and adored the Sun and practised Yoga; but probably exaggerates when he says that Akbar drank no other water than that of the Gaṅgā. More interesting is his statement that he composed the *Rāmasetupradīpa* "at the command of King Jallāladīndra" to facilitate the expounding of the poem in a learned assembly (*pariṣadī*), probably patronized by the emperor. Akbar's great interest in Sanskrit literature is well known; and works like the *Mahābhārata* and the *Rāmāyaṇa* were translated into Persian at his command. Rāmadāsa's statement shows that he encouraged also the study of Prākr̥ta literature.

Apart from his literary activity, Rāmadāsa appears to have played at least on one occasion an important part in contemporary politics. During Akbar's fatal illness in October 1605 he supported Salīm against the intrigues of Azīz and Mān Singh; and his action in posting an adequate guard of faithful Rājpūts over the treasury was a decisive step in the interests of Prince Salīm.[238]

The *Rāmasetupradīpa* is a useful but somewhat verbose

→ agrees with the text of Goldschmidt. The latter gives a critical text based on four manuscripts of Rāmadāsa's commentary containing the text and the *chāyā*; but in a few cases adopts readings from his manuscript C written in CE 1596, Kr̥ṣṇavipra's and Hemcandra's Prākr̥t Grammar. For instance, in *Setu* 7.21 he rejects Rāmadāsa's reading *paiṇṇa* (see NS edn.), and adopts the reading *paalla* from manuscript C. Trans. follows Goldschmidt, but Rāmadāsa's reading is well supported. See section 9.

237 'दूरे गा पाति मृत्योरपि करममुचत् तीर्थवाणिज्यवृत्योः'

238 Smith, *Akbar*, p. 322, Oxford, 1926.

commentary; and in the point of lucidity and insight Rāmadāsa cannot rank with commentators like Kṛṣṇavipra and Kulanātha. He has utilized the work of previous commentators as shown by his many references to the views of *kecit, kaścit,* etc. Occasionally he refers to *sampradāya* or the traditional interpretation, but his effort to improve upon it, sometimes called by him *madunnītaḥ panthāḥ,* is not always successful.[239] Neither of his explanations of the word *nibaddha* in *Setu* 14.9, for instance, is satisfactory; the traditional interpretation mentioned by him is better, and found also in *SC*.[240]

Rāmadāsa's commentary seems to have been unfavourably criticized by contemporary scholars; and he has a fling at "villains that soil the spotless texture of a commentary with the ink of fault-finding". He appeals to the learned public not to neglect his work because he was a prince devoted to the practice of arms, and declares that, in his family, i.e. the dynasty of the Sun, there appeared Manu, great savant and universal monarch, versed in arms.

Rāmadāsa in his gloss on *Setu* 8.44 quotes a Sanskrit prose writer named Badhira-kavirāja. The *Raghuvaṁśa* (12.71) is quoted under *Setu* 12.78, and the *Naiṣadhacarita* (12.22) under 1.25, and a *Saṅgītasāra* under 5.8. Among lexicons he quotes the *Viśvaprakāśa* frequently; and a few citations are also made from Śāśvata, Dharaṇī and the Hārāvalī[241]

Some of the explanations of Prākṛta words and forms by Rāmadāsa are inaccurate. In *Setu* 15.58 he renders *suvvaī* (or *suvvasi* according to some manuscripts)[242] as *śṛṇoṣi.* In 4.53 his explanation of *ahileuṁ* as *abhilavituṁ chettuṁ* cannot be right.[243] His rendering of

---

239 See R on *Setu* 1.15, 48; 6.79; 8.45; 9.42, 78, 85, 88, 89; 10.29, 73, 75; 11.42; 13.80; 14.9 etc.

240 Mādhava's explanation of the word as *avicchinna* is the best. Cf. Pāli *nibaddhaṁ* constantly, continually PTS Dictionary *sub voce.*

241 See R on *Setu* 1.45; 9.43, 80; 6.4; 10.52.

242 See Goldschmidt's footnote.

243 See Extracts 4.53, to which may be added Laṭakanamiśra's explanation of *ahileuṁ* as *abhiletuṁ āskandituṁ*. His alternative explanation *abhileḍhuṁ* is, however, unacceptable. Rāmadāsa in his gloss on *Setu* 5.50 correctly explains *ahileï* as *abhilīyate milati* which is found also in LM. Cf. Vākpati 178: *ahileï* explanation in the commentary as *abhilīyate vyāpnoti*; also 930 and 511. Hāla 4.66 has अहिलेन्ति . . . भमरा . . . मुहं तिस्सा where the idea is that of bees swarming round flowers.

saṁghāia as *saṁghaṭita* (13.61) is obviously wrong, and that of *asaṁpaḍanta* as *asaṁpadyamāna* (14.1) doubtful;[244] while the meaning *vilipta* assigned to *vellavia* or *velavia* in 1.26 appears to be guesswork, though also found in Devarāṭa.[245]

Some of the explanations of Rāmadāsa are however important and noteworthy. The expression *gharamaṇi* in *Setu* 10.52 is explained by Rāmadāsa as "lamp", citing in this connection the *Hārāvalī* which includes *gr̥hamaṇi* among the words used in that sense. The citation is found also in *SC*. Commentators like Kr̥ṣṇavipra, Mādhava and Kulanātha take the compound literally; and it is difficult to say if the Prākr̥ta word as used by an ancient writer like Pravarasena has the same meaning as *gr̥hamaṇi*. The expression *gharamaṇi*, however, occurs also in *Līlāvaī* 56 in a similar context, and is explained in the commentary as "lamp" or "walls studded with jewels". Similarly, the expression *chiṇṇa-kaḍaa* in *Setu* 9.39 is explained by Kulanātha literally; while Kr̥ṣṇavipra and Mādhava read *bhiṇṇa* for *chiṇṇa*. Rāmadāsa here quotes an unspecified Sanskrit verse which defines *chinnakaṭaka* as a kind of particularly steep and precipitous mountain peak. It is noteworthy that *chiṇṇakaḍaa* is an old word occurring more than once in the early Jaina Mahārāṣṭrī text *Vasudevahiṇḍī*, pp. 248, 250.[246]

Laṭakanamiśra

No extracts could be given from the *Bhāvaprakāśikā* of Laṭakanamiśra, as a photostat copy of a manuscript of the commentary preserved in the Bombay University Library was avilable for study long after

---

[244] See Extracts 13.61 and 14.1. Kr̥ṣṇavipra rightly takes *asaṁpaḍanta* as *asaṁpatat*, *saṁpadaï* is, however, often rendered in the commentaries as *saṁpadyate* according to the sense, e.g. Gaṅgādhara on Hāla 4.78. See also Līlāvaī (commentary on 210, 880). On the other hand, *saṁpaḍia* ocurring in an Apabhraṁśa verse cited by Hemcandra and Trivikrama in their Prākr̥t grammars is accurately rendered as *saṁpatita* in the *chāyā*. See *HC* 4.423 and Tr. 3.3.57(92).

[245] See Extracts 1.26 and 10.68.

[246] Cf. *pavvayaṁ ubhaopāsa-chiṇṇakaḍayaṁ aikkaṁtā*, ibid, p. 149. The Jaina work sometimes writes *kaḍaga* for *kaḍaa*. Cf. also *chinna-sela* used in *Vivāgasuya* 58, ed. Vaidya, and explained by Abhayadeva as a beetling crag (छिन्नो विभक्त: अवयवान्तरापेक्षया य: शैल:).

the extracts were sent to the press. The manuscript is incomplete, and covers only cantos 2 to 5, besides containing considerable portions of cantos 1, 6, 10 and 11. It is fairly correct and written in clear Devanāgarī, and contains not only the commentary but also the Prākṛta text and Sanskrit *chāyā*.

The name of the author is given as Laṭakanamiśra in the colophon at the end of the first canto. It appears from a verse repeated at the end of each canto that his original name was Hemanta, Amareśvara being his father's name. He seems to belong to north, or perhaps north-east, India.

The *Bhāvaprakāśikā* is a fairly clear and concise commentary. There is no clue to its date, but there are certain indications that the author was probably acquainted with Rāmadāsa's commentary. For example, the word *vikkhambha* in *Setu* 3.14, variously explained by the commentators, is taken by Rāmadāsa as a *deśī* word meaning *vivara*. Laṭakana, who explains it as *avakāśa*, remarks: *deśī vivaramiti kvacit*, which seems to be a reference to Rāmadāsa's explanation of the word.[247] Similarly, in *Setu* 3.44 (first line), Rāmadāsa reads *aṇāhia* (*anādhi*), while others read *aṇāḍhia* (*anādṛta*).[248] Here, Laṭakana has the majority reading *anādṛta*,[249] but mentions also the reading *anādhi*, which seems to occur only in Rāmadāsa among our commentators.

The *Setutattvacandrikā*, compiled about the middle of the seventeenth century has at least two citations which seem to be from Laṭakanamiśra's commentary. The expression *chāā-vahaṇa* in *Setu* 3.6 is rendered by Kulanātha as *chāyā-vahana*, taking *chāyā* in the sense fo *lustre*; and he also construes it as *chāyāmapahantīti* (i.e., as *chāyāpaghna*), taking *chāyā* in the sense fo *shadow*.[250] *SC* which reproduces Kulanātha's gloss on the verse remarks that some here take *chāyā* in the sense of *darkness*.[251] It is interesting to find that this interpretation is found in Laṭakana, who renders *chāā-vahaṇa* as

---

247 Rāmadāsa's remark विष्कम्भो विवरे देश्याम् is wrongly shown in the NS edn. as part of an anonymous citation found in the *Viśvaprakāśa*.

248 See Extracts 3.44 and 3.20.

249 Laṭakana (text) has *aṇādi* which is a mistake for *aṇāḍhia*.

250 See Extracts 3.6.

251 'केचित्तु–. . . . तिमिरात्मकं छायामात्रमपहन्ति' *SC* 3.7.

chāyāpaghna and explains it as *timirāpahāriṇ*. Similarly, in explaining the double meaning of the word *vihāṇa* in *Setu* 3.31, it is usual to take it first as equivalent to *vidhāna*.[252] *SC* on this verse remarks that some take *vihāṇa* as *vibhāna* mening *asadbhāna*. It is noteworthy that the rendering *vibhāna* is found in Laṭakana, who explains it as *pramāda*, which means the same thing as *asadbhāna*. If we assume Laṭakanamiśra to be later than Rāmadāsa and earlier than *SC*, he may be placed about CE 1625.

Laṭakanamiśra seems to refer to Mudamalla's interpretation of *Setu* 2.1 where the ocean is described as the youth of Rāma's expedition. Mudamalla says that Rāma's enterprise has three stages (*avasthā*), the events from the arrival at the seashore to the crossing of the ocean being the middle stage, which is, as it were, the youthful period of the undertaking; and the ocean is therefore fancied as the youth of Rāma's enterprise.[253] This is not a cogent explanation, and differs from that of commentators like Kṛṣṇavipra and Kulanātha. Laṭakanamiśra records both the interpretations, but gives priority to that of Mudamalla, reproducing some of the expressions used by him.[254] If he was acquainted with the commentary of Mudamalla, the latter might be assumed to have written it before CE 1625.

Śrīnivāsa

In addition to Kulanātha, four other commentators are quoted by name in the *Setutattvacandrikā*. They are Śrīnivāsa, Lokanātha, Sāhasāṅka and Harṣapāla.

Śrīnivāsa appears to be referred to by Kulanātha, as stated above. A copy of his commentary called *Setudarpaṇa* is known to have been made in CE 1440 by a scribe named Ratneśvara during the reign of

---

[252] See Extracts 3.31.

[253] Mādhavayajvan has a similar explanation, but it is not so explicit as that of Mudamalla. Mādhava says पुरुषस्येवोपजातस्य रावणवधपरिणतिं यावद्वर्धमानकार्यशरीरस्यारम्भस्य मध्ये वर्तमानं समुद्रं यौवनाख्यमवस्थाविशेषमिव ऊक्तसाधर्म्ययोगात् अपश्यदित्यर्थः.

[254] Laṭakana says कार्यारम्भस्य अवस्थात्रयमुपक्रमो मध्यः समाप्तिश्चेति। तत्र मध्यावस्था समुद्रतीरप्राप्तिः, मध्यावस्थात्वेन यौवनपदेनोपन्यासः। For Mudamalla's interpretation see Extracts 2.1.

Dhīrasiṁha of Mithilā.[255] On the other hand, Śrīnivāsa, quoted in *SC* on *Setu* 14.2, quotes the *Viśvaprakāśa*[256] in support of his explanation of *sara* as *svara* in the sense of *breath* or *sighs*. As the *Viśvaprakāśa* was composed in CE 1111, he may be placed between 1150 and 1440, the date of the manuscript copied by Ratneśvara, or thereabouts.

Lokanātha

Next to Kulanātha, the largest number of passages quoted in the *Setutattvacandrikā* is from the commentary of Lokanātha. In the extract given in *SC* on *Setu* 7.15, Lokanātha quotes the *Medinī*, which has been assigned to a date between CE 1200 and 1275.[257]

Lokanātha, like Kulanātha, might be a Bengali; but we are unable to say whether he is identical with Lokanātha-cakravartin, who wrote a commentary on the Bengal recension of the *Rāmāyaṇa*.[258] This commentary contains numerous quotations from the *Bhūriprayoga* lexicon of Padmanābhadatta, who wrote his *Pṛṣodarādivṛtti* in CE 1375.[259] Lokanātha-cakravartin could not, therefore, have written his commentary on the *Rāmāyaṇa* earlier than about CE 1400. If he is identical with Lokanātha, quoted in *SC*, the latter may be placed between CE 1400 and 1600.

Sāhasāṅka

There are only three quotations from Sāhasāṅka in *SC*. In the extract from his commentary given in *SC* on *Setu* 12.73 (*SC* 72), Sāhasāṅka quotes the *Prākṛta Paiṅgala* 1.5.[260] The quotation in *SC* is not well preserved, but Sāhasāṅka's meaning seems to be clear. He suggests that the reading *pāārantarie* would be more appropriate than *pāārantaria*

---

255 H.P. Sastri's Report (p. 19) on the search of Sanskrit Manuscripts (1895–1900), cited in Introduction to *Rāvaṇavaha-mahākāvyam*, ed. Basak, p. XVII.

256 See Benares edn., 1911, p. 125.

257 Gode, *Studies in Indian Literary History*, vol. 1, pp. 281 ff.

258 Calcutta Sanskrit Series. We had access only to the Sundarakāṇḍa and the Yuddhakāṇḍa, 1941. Lokanātha refers to *Rāmāyaṇa* manuscripts belonging to Kāmarūpa or Lower Assam. He remarks in his gloss on Sundarakāṇḍa 32.45: पद्यमिदं कामरूपीयपुस्तके वर्तत इति व्याख्यातम्.

259 See Introduction to *Kalpadrukośa* (GOS), p. X.

260 BI edn., p. 7.

in the verse in question; but as it violates the metre, he cites the *Prākṛta Paiṅgala* to show that an *ekāra* may sometimes be treated as short.

It is well known that the *Prākṛta Paiṅgala* mentions Hammīra in some of the illustrative verses. Composed in late Apabhraṁśa to celebrate the military exploits of Hammīra, these verses seem to have been current after the fall of Raṇathambhor in CE 1301;[261] and the *Prākṛta Paiṅgala* could not possibly have been written earlier than about the middle of the fourteenth century. In that case, Sāhasāṅka, who quotes it, and is quoted in *SC*, may be placed in the fifteenth or sixteenth century.

Harṣapāla

A few quotations from the commentary of Harṣapāla occur in *SC*, but there is hardly any clue to his date, except that he is earlier than the second quarter of the seventeenth century. If, however, Harṣapāla is identical with the commentator Śrīharṣa quoted by Kulanātha (see above), he must be earlier than the sixteenth century.

9. The Commentaries and the Recensions of the Setubandha

The commentaries throw considerable light on the recensions of the *Setubandha* followed by them. So far we can speak of three different recensions of the poem, south Indian, north Indian and Bengali. A western recension appears to have existed; but our knowledge of it is at present derived from sources other than commentaries. The south Indian recension is represented by two important commentators, Kṛṣṇavipra and Mādhava, and by Kṛṣṇadāsa, Devarāṭa and probably Mudamalla. In the fragment of Mudamalla's commentary that was available to us, he, as a rule, agrees with Kṛṣṇavipra in his readings, and follows the peculiar arrangement of cantos 12-15 found in the southern recension, as explained below.

Kulanātha is the chief representative of the Bengal recension, and many of his readings are found in the text accompanying the *Setutattvacandrikā*. The latter work, however, being a compilation from

[261] Sharma, *Early Cauhān Dynasties*, pp. 114ff., Delhi, 1959.

different commentaries, does not wholly conform to any particular recension of the poem.

The commentary of Rāmadāsa provides the only specimen of the northern, or rather the north-western, recension that has come down to us in a complete form. The available portion of the commentary of Laṭakanamiśra and the extracts from Śrīnivāsa in *SC* show that they follow recensions of the poem, current in other parts of north India, that do not wholly agree with the recension followed by Rāmadāsa.

As pointed out by Goldschmidt long ago, a curious feature of the south Indian recension is that it has sixteen instead of fifteen cantos, the extra canto being made up by dividing canto 13 into two unequal halves. In other words, the first sixty-seven verses form canto 13 proper, and the remainder canto 14. The arrangement is completely gratuitous, and has led to a further complication. As the word *aṇurāa* occurs in the concluding verse of each canto of the poem, the last verse of canto 12 has been transferred to the newly-formed canto 13 to mark its termination; but as this strips canto 12 of the usual concluding verse, the preceding verse, i.e. 12.97, has been adapted for the purpose by inserting in it the word *aṇurāa*.[262]

As will be seen from the extracts, the order of verses in the southern recension is in a few cases different from that of the other recensions. It may also be noted that the verse 3.61 appears in the southern recension in canto 8 after verse 23;[263] while the verse 10.3 occurs in canto 12 after verse 29.

There are some cases of verses occurring in one recension and missing in another. A good example is provided by Goldschmidt's Anhang showing fourteen verses not explained by Rāmadāsa. Almost all of them (1-13) belong to the south Indian recension, being included in the commentaries of Kr̥ṣṇavipra and Mādhava and those of Kr̥ṣṇadāsa, Mudamalla and Devarāṭa as far as they are available to us. It is noteworthy that at least four of these verses occur also in the Bengal recension represented by Kulanātha; and they are, in

[262] See Extracts 12.97, 98.

[263] The arrangement is slightly different in Devarāṭa.

fact, included in the text accompanying the *Setutattvacandrikā*.[264] One of these verses forming part of Sugrīva's speech in canto 3 is reproduced below.

> गरुए वि[265] समरकज्जे विअसन्ते च्चिअ रसं लहन्ति समत्था।
> बद्धप्फलम्मि कुसुमे वोलीणो होइ महुअराण अवसरो।। – 3.6
>
> *gasue vi samarakajje viasante ccia rasaṁ lahanti samatthā*।
> *baddhapphalammi kusume volīṇo hoi mahuarāṇaavasaro*।।
>
> The valiant rejoice when an arduous martial enterprise is in full swing.
> The time for bees is past when flowers culminate in fruit.[266]

The last vcerse in Goldschmidt's Anhang, cited in an imperfect form from his manuscript C, is variously read, and has not found general acceptance. It is not explained by the south Indian commentators, nor by Kulanātha and Rāmadāsa. It is, however, included in *SC* 15.66.[267] with the remark that it is omitted by Sāhasāṅka and Kulanātha, leading one to suppose that it was probably explained by Lokanātha and Śrīnivāsa, the two other commentators quoted by name in *SC*. The verse is also cited in a mutilated form in Bhoja's *Sarasvatīkaṇṭhābharaṇa* 5.13[268] and Narendraprabha' *Alaṁkāramahodadhi*[269] as an example of *rasābhāsa*. But not a few commentators from different parts of India seem to have rejected it because of the unpleasant idea involving Sītā in the description.

A general record of the diverse readings followed in the commentaries will be found in the extracts. We shall here confine ourselves to a few large groups of readings belonging to the different recensions of the poem. Of these the south Indian readings form a distinct group as against a corresponding group of readings consistently followed by Rāmadāsa and Kulanātha, representing the north-western region and Bengal respectively. For example,

---

264 See Calcutta edition of *Rāvaṇavaha-mahākāvyam*, 3.6; 5.49, 72; 8.58.

265 Kṛṣṇavipra reads *guruammi*.

266 Sugrīva urges his followers to take an active part in Rāma's expedition before it attains its objective without their co-operation.

267 पुलअं जणेन्ति दाकन्धरस्स रांहक्खरा सरीरअडन्ता।
जणअतणआपओहरफंसमहग्घविअकरजुअलणिव्वूढा।।

268 NS edn.

269 Page 97, GOS.

	South Indians	Rāmadāsa and Kulanātha
1.1	*avisāria*	*avasāria*
1.10	*visappanti*	*viḍhappanti*
2.23	*ohāmia*[270]	*ohāsia*
4.23	*khaveī*	*ṭhaveī*
5.75	*viambhia*	*vilambia*
5.85	*uddhāanta*	*rundāvatta*
6.12	*khaa-dukkālāṇ-uaraṁ*	*khaa-kālāṇala-khaviaṁ*
6.37	*vihuvvantā*	*viijjantā*
7.21	*vilagga*	*païṇṇa*[271]
7.37	*milijjantā*	*maïjjantā*
8.3	*ukkampā*	*uppīḍā*
8.40	*thāma* (also in 15.19)	*thāha*[272]
8.104	*galia-paāva-khuhio*	*pelavāṇattiaro*
9.85	°*kkhambhālia*	°*kkhambha-ṇialia*[273]
11.95	*uppāa*	*upphāla*

[270] Explained by Kṛṣṇavipra as *abhibhūta*. Cf. *ohāmiya-surasundarī-rūvāisayaṁ* — *Samarāiccakahā*, p. 313. The commemtary of *Līlāvaī* (204): *vaya-pariṇāmohāmiya-lāyaṇṇa* renders the word as *sthagita*. The original meaning seems to be "slighted", "humiliated" as in *jeṇaṁ vo samaṇeṇaṁ mahājaṇamajjhe ohāmiyā taṁ pacchannaṁ jīviyāo vavaroveha* — *Vasudevahiṇḍī*, p. 88. Cf. *lahuiaṁ ohāmiaṁ* — *Pāiyalacchī* 539, Pāṭaṇa edn. 15.

[271] This is also the reading of Lokanātha. See Extracts 7.21.

[272] In 15.19 Rāmadāsa reads *thāma* like the south Indians.

[273] Goldschmidt (see his footnote on 9.85) rejects Rāmadāsa's reading *kkhambha-ṇīalia* on the ground that it is against the metre, but there is no metrical difficulty in the line as read in *SC* (9.84) which follows Kulanātha. Goldschmidt's reading °*kkhambhallia* is conjecture based on *stambhālīna* found in Kṛṣṇa's *chāyā*. The south Indian reading as recorded by Mādhava is, however °*kkhambhālia* which appears to be rendered by Kṛṣṇa as *stambhālīna*. See also Extracts 9.85.

14.51	*āāria*	*āsāia*
15.31	*sumbhanta*	*muccanta*
15.46	*paḍhama-ppahāra-mahio*	*visahia-paḍhama-ppaharo*

While Rāmadāsa and Kulanātha agree in many of their readings as against the south Indians, there is a considerable number of readings in which they differ from each other; and in such cases Kulanātha usually follows the south Indian readings, leaving Rāmadāsa practically isolated. For example,

	Rāmadāsa	South Indian and Kulanātha
2.12	*ṇipphaṇṇa*	*ṇivvaḍia*
3.20	*āhia*	*āḍhia*
3.33	*dūranta*	*tūranta*
3.44	*aṇāhio*	*aṇāḍhio*[274]
4.32	*ṇivvalia-guṇo*	*ṇivvūḍha-bharo*
5.45	*ṇaha-ṇirālambe*	*ṇirāa-valambo* (*valambe* Kula)
5.62	*thavaa*	*theva*[275]
	(also in 1.40; 12.21; 15.43, 78, 84)	
5.87	*govia*	*ṇūmia*
6.53	*paüṇaṁ*	*paḍaṇaṁ*
6.57	*pavitta*	*parinta*[276]
	(also in 7.50; 9.68, 88)	

[274] I.e., *anādr̥taḥ*. See also Extracts, 3.20, 44. Cf. *evaṁ so aṇāḍhio kaha vi jīvio — Vasudevahiṇḍī*, p. 113. In *Setu* 3.44 the word is used in active sense as in Bhāravi 14.10 अनादृतस्यामरसायकेषु.

[275] Kulanātha on 15.78 has *stabaka* like Rāmadāsa.

[276] Rendered as *pariyat*. Cf. Extracts, 6.57 where *pariyata* is a misprint for *pariyat*. See also Extracts 7.50. The verbal forms *palei*, *palenti* with *la* for *ra* occur in *Uttarādhyayanasūtra* 14.34, 36, and are explained by Nemicandra as *paryeti* and *pariyanti*. Cf. *HC* 4.161: *parīi bhamai*. *Setu* 7.61 has *parīi* rendered as *paryeti*, *Vasudevahiṇḍī*, has *sā vi ṇaṁ savvao parīi*, p. 136; also *jīvo kasāyavasago jahā parīti*, p. 271.

8.2	*uvvatta*	*uvvāa*
11.60	*aṇuvajjha*	*bajjhanta*
11.70	*sāṇusaa*	*sāṇuṇaa*
11.128	*laṅkā-valaa*	*laṅkā-malaa*[277]
12.26	*vāma*	*ṇiaa*
12.29	*maïa*	*maliṇa* or *maïla*
12.40	*viambhia*	*vimhia*
12.97	*mahiala*	*ṇasahia*
14.37	*saṁlāva*	*mābhāi*
15.25	*ugghāḍia*	*ujjāaa* or *ujjāgaa*
15.45	*pāsa*	*pantha*
15.47	*jīabbhahia*	*jīabbhuaa*

In 14.48 Rāmadāsa reads *pariṇāmaṁ*, and the others, *pariṇāmo* which gives a much better meaning. See below (section 10).

Perhaps the most striking in the above group of readings are those in *Setu* 12.26 where Rāmadāsa reads *vāma*, and the others *ṇiaa*. Rāmadāsa's reading would mean that the twitching of Rāma's left arm presaged his early reunion with Sītā, a notion contrary to the prevailing Indian belief that the twitching of a left limb brought luck only to a woman.[278] Kulanātha and Kr̥ṣṇavipra, on the other hand, take *ṇiaa* as referring to the right arm[279] in conformity with similar

[277] The expression is misunderstood by Kulanātha, but correctly explained by Kr̥ṣṇavipra and Mādhava as referring to the Malaya mountain of Laṅkā, mentioned in the *Rāmāyaṇa* 5.1.183; 5.66.27; 6.55.48 (crit. edn.). It is also mentioned in the *Mahāvaṁsa* 7.68, being the central mountain region in the interior of Ceylon (Geiger, Trans., p. 60). Cf. *Laṅkāvatārasūtra*, ed. Nanjio, chap. 1; *laṅkāpurīmalayaśikhare; laṅkāmalayaparvatam*, etc.

[278] See Mallinātha on *Meghadūta*, vv. 100. 101 (ed. Pathak, Poona, 1916). Maheśvara says in his *Nāṇapañcamīkahā* written about the middle of the tenth century: पुरिसस्स दहिणंगं फुरियं इट्ठस्स सुयगं होइ। वामं च इत्थियाए एयं खलु जाणए सब्बो।।
— 6.68 (Singhi Jaina Series). Cf. *Kuvalayamālā*, p. 157, ll. 17ff.

[279] See Extracts 12.26.

references in our poem and elsewhere.[280] It is difficult to explain how such an inconsistent reading crept into the recension followed by Rāmadāsa; in any case it is the most dubious of the readings peculiar to him.

It may be noted that Rāmadāsa mentions the majority reading as a variant in a few cases. For instance, in *Setu* 10.22 he reads *saṁvatta*, but mentions the usual reading *savvattha* as a variant.[281] *Saṁvatta* (*saṁvarta*) is, however, an old reading (see below); and the word appears in Prākṛta as early as Aśoka's Girnar Edicts IV and V.

As we have already stated, Rāmadāsa often refers to *sampradāya* in his commentary; and he seems to have followed a recension of the poem current in his part of the country. The extracts from Śrīnivāsa in the *Setutattvacandrikā* and specially the available portion of the commentary of Laṭakanamiśra have enough material to show that there were probably several recensions in north India as a whole, which were akin to that of Rāmadāsa in some respects, but divergent in others. Some of the readings of Rāmadāsa found neither in Kulanātha nor in the south Indians occur, for instance, in Śrīnivāsa: *saṁvatta* 10.22; *sāṇusaa* 11.70; *ohīanta* or *ohijjanta*[282] 12.42; *vihatta* 12.79. Again, in 9.25 Rāmadāsa reads *ovaṭṭa*,[283] explained by him as *avavarṣa*, *vṛṣṭi* for *oaṭṭha* or *ovaṭṭha* (*apa-* or *avavṛṣṭa*) found in other commentators. Here, too, Rāmadāsa agrees with Śrīnivāsa who reads *ovaṭṭa* and explains it as a *deśī* word meaning *meghajalaseka*.[284] Similarly, in 11.1 Rāmadāsa's reading *cittavia* is found also in Śrīnivāsa; it is an old reading noticed also by the south Indians.[285] The materials at our

---

[280] Cf. *Setu* 15.76 *Gāthāsaptaśatī* 2.37 (NS, 1889); *Rāmāyaṇa* (crit. edn.) 3.22.16, 57.4; 5.25 and 27; 6.43.7, 53.43, 83.34; *Raghu* 6.68; 12.90; 14.49; Bhaṭṭi 14.83; 15.27, etc. Except for the context, the reference in *Setu* 12.26 is exactly the same as that in *Raghu* 12.90.

[281] See also Extracts 3.59; 10.49; 11.48.

[282] The reading is found in this form in the extract from Śrīnivāsa in *SC*.

[283] See Goldschmidt's footnote, but the more familiar *ovaṭṭha* appears in both G and NS editions.

[284] *SC* text has *ovaṭṭa*, obviously following Śrīnivāsa. In *SC* the verse number is 24, DNI.152 has *ovaṭṭha* explained as *meghajalaseka*.

[285] See Extracts 11.1. *DN* 3.12 has *cittaṭhia* (*v.r. cittavia*) in the sense of *paritoṣita*. The *Ṣaḍbhāṣācandrikā* of Lakṣmidhara (p. 178) gives *cittaviaa* among irregular forms in the same sense.

disposal are, however, too scanty to give an adequate idea of Śrīnivāsa's text. He is earlier than Rāmadāsa, and seems to follow an older recension with independent features. Even in the meagre fragments of his interpretations available to us, it is not difficult to detect readings that do not appear in our commentators; e.g. *kaleūṇa* (Lokanātha also) for *tuleūṇa* 5.20, *paricala* for *parimala* 9.68, and *vajjanta* for *majjhammi* or *bhajjanta* 14.81. In 15.4 he reads *sahā* like the others for *mahā* found in Rāmadāsa; and in 15.74 reads *pakkhante* for the latter's reading *panthaddhe*.

We are better informed about Laṭakanamiśra's text. The recension followed by him is in certain respects somewhat closely related to that of Rāmadāsa. In the first place, there is a considerable number of readings in which he agrees with Rāmadāsa and Kulanātha as against the south Indians. In the second place, some of the readings of Rāmadāsa not found in the other commentators appear in his work. For example,

Laṭakana and Rāmadāsa		Others
1.50	*pariṇāha*	*parimāṇa*
2.12	*ṇipphaṇṇa*	*nivvaḍia*
3.8	*ṇialuṇṇamanta*[286]	*ṇialoṇamanta*
3.20	*āhia*	*āḍhia*
3.33	*dūranta*	*tūranta*
5.62	*thavaa* (also in 1.40)	*theva*
6.57	*pavitta*	*parinta*
11.62	*bhajjanta*	*tajjanta*
11.70	*sāṇusaa*	*sāṇuṇaa*

[286] Laṭakana (Text) has *ṇialoṇamanta*, but his reading is clear from the *chāyā* and the commentary : धुतावामाननिगलोन्नमन्मुखानां अपसारितापमाननिगडेन शृंखलेन उन्नमन्मुखानां.

Similarly, in 216 Laṭakana reads *aṇuṇijjamāṇa-(maggaṁ)* like Rāmadāsa,[287] while others have *aṇuijjamāṇa*.[288]

Notwithstanding the affinities mentioned above, there are certain conspicuous differences between the texts followed by Rāmadāsa and Laṭakanamiśra. In a conserable number of readings the latter agrees not with Rāmadāsa, but with the south Indians or Kulanātha or both. For example, he has the south Indian readings *ohāmia* (for *ohāsia*) 2.23, *se* (for *je*) 4.36, *viambhia* (for *vilambia*) 5.75. Occasionally he agrees with Kulanātha, but in many other cases he has the readings followed by the south Indians and Kulanātha as against those of Rāmadāsa. For example,

	Laṭakana , Kulanātha and South Indians	Rāmadāsa
1.47	*saṁcāra*	*vikkheva*
2.19	*salila*	*uara*
3.56	*ṇivvutta*	*ṇivvūḍha*
4.32	*ṇivvūḍha-bharo*	*ṇivvalia-guṇo*
4.39	*mujjhijjai*	*vimuhijjai*
5.64	*vitthārā*	*pabbhārā*
5.87	*ṇūmia*	*govia*
6.44	*paḍisāi*	*paḍisamai*
10.44	*paalantï*	*paaḍantï*
10.49	*accha*	*abbha*
11.27	*bhaaṁ*	*vahaṁ*
11.58	*viaḍia*	*visaria*
11.85	*paḍiaṁ*	*ṇihaaṁ*

287 Rāmadāsa explains *aṇuṇijjamāṇa* as *anugamyamāna*, apparently deriving it from *ṇī* (*HC* 4.162). Laṭakana's explanation is ambiguous. He has *anunīyamāna* in the *chāyā* and *anvīyamāna* in the gloss, explained as *anugamyamāna*.

288 Explained as *anvīyamāna*. See Extracts 2.16 and *SC* text. Cf. *annijjamāṇa-magga*, often found in AMg texts (*Vivāgasuya* 9; 130, ed. P. Vaidya; *Nāyādhamma* 16.113, 117, ed. N. Vaidya). Abhyadeva on *Vivāga* explains it as *anvīyamāna anugamyamāna*.

Similarly, the verse *garue vi samarkajje*, which, as stated above, occurs in the south Indian and Bengal recensions, but not in Rāmadāsa, is found in Laṭakanamiśra's text after the verse 3.5 with slight variations.

A few examples of Laṭakanamiśra's readings not found in the other commentators may be given: *viiṇṇa-vāhu-laiāiṁ* 3.50; *jattha ahaṁ paliuttho*[289] = *yatrāhaṁ pratyutthitaḥ* explained as *pratikupitaḥ* 4.50; *saṁṭhavia* for *saccavia* 5.25; *uvvāsio* for *uddhāio* 5.34; *pūria* for *vihaḍia* 5.38; *māṇa* explained as *mlāna kṣīṇa* for *vāa* 5.57; *pulaiaṁ* for *palattaṁ* 11.79. Some of his readings appear to be doubtful. In 10.65 he reads *ṇivalia* for *paḍihaa*, and explains it as *bhīta*. In 11.38 (first half) his readings are different from those of others, but do not yield a probable meaning.[290] In 10.57 he reads *ahikaṁkhanti* (*abhikāṁkṣanti*) which is an easier reading for *ahilaṁghanti* in the same sense found in Kulanātha and the south Indians (cf. *HC* 4.192). It is also noteworthy that in 11.80 the idiomatic Prākr̥ta conditional formed with the present participle is replaced by the simpler form with *jja*; that is, he reads *hoejja* (*hojja*?) and *vialejja* for *hontaṁ* and *vialantaṁ* respectively.

An adequate account of the Bengal recension of the *Setubandha* cannot possibly be given without examining the thirteenth-century manuscript of the text preserved in the Asiatic Society of Bengal. There is, however, no doubt that Kulanātha follows a recension of the poem that must have been current in Bengal since before the sixteenth century. As we have seen, he sometimes agrees with Rāmadāsa, and sometimes with the south Indians; and has comparatively few independent readings not found in the other commentators. In *Setu* 1.64 he reads *parivuttha* for *parihutta*, but this reading is also found in Lokanātha. He reads *ghaṭṭavia* for *ṇiṭṭhavia* in 9.1 *dāḍhāhoaṁ* for *dārāhoaṁ* in 12.79, and *pakkha* for *cakkhu* in 13.78. A few other examples need comment. In *Setu* 13.83 he reads *āattha-diṭṭhi* for *āhittha-*,*āattha* being *āyasta*, explained by Kulanātha as *krodhadīpta*. Derived from *yasu prayatne*, the word is somewhat vague and used with different shades of meaning in classical Sanskrit;

---

[289] I.e. *paḍiuttho*. Laṭakanamiśra invariably writes *la* for *da*, e.g., *phula* for *phuḍa* 4.40; *pāala* for *pāaḍa* 4.42; *ubbhala* for *ubbhaḍa* 5.9, etc.

[290] See Extracts 11.38.

while it has the meaning *be heated* in the Vedic language.[291] There is, however, no doubt that it has also the meaning assigned to it by Kulanātha; for instance, in *Rāmāyaṇa* 6.46.40.[292]

In *Setu* 15.38 Kulanātha reads *taila* (probably *ṇeha*) for *tuppa* (*ghee*).[293] The verse is not found in the south Indian recension. Rāmadāsa's reading is *ghaa* or *ghia*, as pointed out by Goldschmidt, who, however, reads *tuppa* found in his manuscript C. The NS edition also has the same reading probably from some other source. *Tuppa* is extant in old and new Kannaḍa, and is the usual word for *ghee* in that language. It was borrowed by Mahārāṣṭrī, and survives in Marathi *tūp*. *Tuppa* and its derivative *tuppalia* occur also in the *Gāthāsaptaśatī*;[294] and its use in an early Mahārāṣṭrī work like the *Setubandha* in connection with the lighting of lamps is quite normal. The word seems to have been replaced by the more familiar *ghaa* or *ghia* in the recension of Rāmadāsa; but it is difficult to explain how a word for *oil* could be substituted for it in the recension of Kulanātha, specially as the use of *ghee* for lighting purposes was popular in Bengal as elsewhere in India.[295] It is, however, possible that the Bengal recension was here influenced by a verse of the *Rāmāyaṇa*, of which the *Setu* 15.38 is a close imitation. Describing Rāvaṇa's wrath and grief at the death of Indrajit, the *Rāmāyaṇa* says

> तस्य क्रुद्धस्य नेत्राभ्यां प्रापतन्नस्रबिन्दवः।
> दीप्ताभ्यामिव दीपाभ्यां सार्चिषः स्नेहबिन्दवः॥ – 6.80.18 (crit. edn.)

---

[291] Cf. Whitney, *The Roots, Verb-forms, etc. of the Sanskrit Language*, p. 130, Leipzing, 1885.

[292] आजघान तदा नीलं ललाटे मुसलेन सः । प्रहस्तः परमायस्तः (v.r. परमः क्रुद्धः . . . crit. edn., p. 298. The word is also explained as उत्सुक (Bhāravi 7.32, cf. Māgha 5.6); खिन्न (Bhāravi 15.7, cf. *Rāmāyaṇa* 4.55.6). For other uses see Abhinavagupta on *Nāṭyaśāstra* 21.106; *Veṇīsaṁhāra* 1.2; 6.9; Bhāravi 16.50; *Kāvyālaṁkāra* of Rudraṭa 11.30; *Amaruśataka*, verse 63, Poona. 1959, etc.

[293] See Extracts 15.38.

[294] See commentary of Gaṅgādhara on 3.89; 6.28. *Tuppia* same as *tuppalia* "besmeared", is found in AMg texts, e.g. *nehatuppiyagattaṁ* — *Vivāgasuya* 37, ed. Vaidya. Cf. न य लोणं लोणिज्जइ ण य तुप्पिज्जइ धयं व तेल्लं वा cited in Śīlāṅka's commentary on *Sūtrakṛtāṅga* 1.4.1.18, Śrīgoḍī Parśva-Jainagranthamālā, 1950.

[295] Murārīgupta, a Bengali Vaiṣṇava poet of the sixteenth century, says in one of his songs: *ghṛta diyā eka rati jvali āilā yugabāti se kemane rahe ayogāne.* See Sen, *A History of Brajabuli Literature*, p. 31, Calcutta, 1935.

tasya kruddhasya netrābhyaṁ prāpatannasrabindavaḥ ।
dīptābhyāmiva dīpābhyāṁ sārciṣaḥ snehabindavaḥ ॥

The *Setubandha* says in the same context:

सोऊण इन्दवहं मुअइ सरोसं दसाणणो बाहजलं।
अब्भुत्तिअदीवाणं णिवडइ तुप्पं व तक्खणं सहुआसं।। — 15.38

soūṇa indavahaṁ muai sarosaṁ dasāṇaṇo bāhajalaṁ ।
abbhuttiadīvāṇaṁ ṇivaḍai tuppaṁ va takkhaṇaṁ sahuāsaṁ ॥

It will be seen that the *Rāmāyaṇa* compares Rāvaṇa's tears to fiery drops of oil shed by lighted lamps; and Pravarasena says the same thing except that he speaks of "fiery" or molten *ghee* dripping from such lamps. If *tuppa* was the original reading, it is probable that the unfamiliar southern vocable was replaced in the Bengal recension by a word for *oil* as recorded in the *Rāmāyaṇa*.

In the last verse of the *Setubandha* (15.95) Kulanātha reads in the second line *sakarṇa* (*saaṇṇa*) for *samattha* which is the reading of Rāmadāsa. Kṛṣṇavipra reads *satṛṣna* (*saaṇha*).[296] Mādhava has *śrotravat*. Probably he reads *saaṇṇa* like Kulanātha. Of these readings *sakaṇṇa* or *saaṇṇa* is the most interesting. It is an idiomatic expression meaning *expert*, *proficient*,[297] and refers here to those who are capable of appreciating poetry.

No commentary on the *Setubandha* composed in western India seems to have been discovered so far; but the considerable number of quotations from it in works like Bhoja's *Sarasvatīkaṇṭhābharaṇa* and *Śṛṅgāraprakāśa* and Hemacandra's Prākṛta grammar point to the existence of a western recension of the poem. There are thirty-seven quotations from it in the *Sarasvatīkaṇṭhābharaṇa*, of which all except one are found in Rāmadāsa's text. About half of these verses do not contain any important variants. The remaining verses generally agree with Rāmadāsa and Kulanātha as against the south Indians. However, in *Setu* 1.1 Bhoja reads *avisāria*[298] like Kṛṣṇavipra for *avasāria* (R and Kula); in 11.58 *vialia-vioa-viaṇam*[299] like the south Indians and Kulanātha for *visaria-*

---

[296] This is also the reading of *SC* text.

[297] Cf. *tumaṁ jovvaṇavatī kalāsu ya sakaṇṇā — Vasudevahiṇḍī*, p. 362.

[298] *SK*, p. 273 (NS).

[299] *SK*, p. 561.

vioa-dukkhaṁ (R); and in 1.56 *ṇimmahia*[300] like the south Indians for *ṇikkanta* (R). In *Setu* 5.50 he reads *sāmalaijjai*[301] for *kajjalaījjai* of the commentators; and in 11.75 *ṇāha jiantīa mae diṭṭhaṁ sahiaṁ a tuha imaṁ avasāṇaṁ*[302] for *jaṁ mahilā-vīhacchaṁ diṭṭhaṁ sahiaṁ ca tuha mae avasāṇam*, which is the reading of the commentators with slight variations.

A few quotations from the poem occur also in the published portions of Bhoja's *Śṛṅgāraprakāśa*. In *Setu* 12.13, for instance, his reading *pattaṭṭha*[303] is different from that of Rāmadāsa and the south Indians, but agrees with that of Kulanātha.[304] In *Setu* 11.27 he reads *bhaaṁ* and in 12.12 *pia*[305] like Kulanātha and the south Indians for *vahaṁ* and *pai* respectively found in Rāmadāsa. Bhoja's readings are of considerable interest, as they give us an idea, however inadequate, of the text of the *Setubandha* as it existed in western India.

Hemacandra's citations from the poem are confined to phrases and sentences; but the reading *vaṇe* in the line quoted from *Setu* 14.43 in his grammar (2.206) needs comment. This reading has been adopted by Goldschmidt in his edition, but it is not found in any of our commentators.[306] Kulanātha, however, reads *manye*, that is, *maṇe*,[307] which occurs also in *Gāthāsaptaśatī* 2.11, 54.[308] It is interesting to find that Bhuvanapāla in his commentary on *GS* reads *vaṇe* for *maṇe* in the corresponding verses.[309] His explanation of *vaṇe* as a form of

---

300 *SK*, p. 205.

301 *SK*, p. 369.

302 *SK*, p. 556.

303 See *Śṛṅgāraprakāśa* 22.25, ed. Yatirājasvāmin, Madras, 1926.

304 See Extracts 12.13. The word *pattaṭṭha* occurs several times in Līlāvaī (see Index to Upadhye's edition), and is explained in the commentary as *nipuṇa, kuśala,* etc.

305 SP 22.78, 94.

306 See Extracts 14.43.

307 Cf. *Setu* 5.20, where the commentators take *maṇe* as *manye*. Rāmadāsa takes it also as *manasi*.

308 NS edn. with commentary of Gaṅgādhara has *maṇṇe* in 2.54, but Weber reads *maṇe*. The form *maṇṇe* appears in GS 7.99 (NS; Weber 702) and in *Setu* 11.27, 49.

309 See *GS* 2.11, 54; 7.99 (NS), and Weber: "Über Bhuvanapāla's Commenatar zu Hāla's Saptaśatakam", *Indische Studien*, vol. 16, pp. 7, 63, 107, 125.

address (*sakhi* or even *sakhe*) is, however, misleading, and even self-contradictory in one case. Weber, therefore, suggests that *vaṇe* is most simply taken as coming from *maṇe*.[310] Bhuvanapāla, according to Weber, was probably a native of Gujarat, and lived in the first half of the fourteenth century. In that case he may have found *vaṇe* for *maṇe* in the text of the *Gāthāsaptaśatī* current in his part of the country. On similar grounds it may be surmised that the reading *vaṇe* probably belonged to the recension of the *Setubandha* current in western India, from which Hemacandra quoted the line in his grammar. It may be noted that the word appears to be rare, but occurs more than once in Uddyotana's *Kuvalayamālā* composed in CE 779 at Jābālipura (Jalor) in Rājasthān.[311]

The above account of the recensions of the *Setubandha*, based mainly on the commentaries, is necessarily tentative, as old and independent manuscripts of the text as far as they are available are expected to throw further light on the subject. We are fairly well informed about the south Indian recension because of the commentaries of its distinguished representatives Kṛṣṇavipra and Mādhavayajvan. There is no doubt that the poem has undergone some amount of revision in the south, but the fact that the south Indian recension has a considerable number of readings in common with Kulanātha, and even with Laṭakanamiśra to a lesser extent, shows that it probably goes back to a text that was current in a large part of the country comprising south India and beyond.

Compared with the south Indian recension, our knowledge of the recensions current in different parts of north India is extremely limited. The commentary of Rāmadāsa seems to follow a text long in use in Rājasthān, and represents what we may call the north-western recension. The relation of this to other north Indian recensions cannot be fully determined, as no other complete

---

310 According to Hemacandra, the indecl. *vaṇe* expresses *saṁbhāvana*, while *maṇe* conveys the sense of *vimarśa* (2.207). But he points out that *maṇe* is explained by others as *manye*.

311 ईय जं जं किंचि वणे सुन्दररूवं जणम्मि सयलम्मि।
अक्खिविऊणं तं चिय सो च्चिय णूणं विणम्मविओ।। — p. 29
बालो दंसणसुहवो परिवड्ढंतो तवेइ कह सूरो।
सव्वो च्चिय णूण वणे जोब्वणसमयम्मि दुप्पेच्छो।। — p. 61
णयणाइँ इमस्स वणे णिवडेज्जंगेसु किं मज्झं — p. 163

commentary on the *Setubandha*, composed in north India, has so far been discovered. While Rāmadāsa's recension has much in common with the Bengal recension and another north Indian recension, partly known to us, there is a considerable number of readings peculiar to Rāmadāsa, which are not found in the other commentaries and fragments accessible to us.

None of the commentaries utilized for this work seem to have been written in Orissan,[312] and very little is known about the text of the *Setubandha* current in that part of the country. It is, however, noteworthy that more than twenty citations from the poem have been traced in the *Prākṛtasarvasva* of Mārkaṇḍeya, who wrote his grammar during the reign of Mukundadeva, the last independent ruler of Orissa (1559-68).[313] Some of the readings found in these citations give an idea, however imperfect, of the recension prevalent in the region.

(i) The phrase *baddha-pphalammi kusume* cited in *PS* 3.76 is from the *Setu* verse *garue vi samara-kajje* 3.6, cited above, which is not found in Rāmadāsa, but occurs in the south Indian and Bengal recensions.

(ii) The line *kiṁ sīsau jaṁ ṭhaveï vaa-pariṇāmo*, cited under *PS* 5.69, is from *Setu* 4.23. Here *ṭhaveï* belongs to the Rāmadāsa-Kulanātha group of readings. The south Indian reading is different (see above).

(iii) In the phrase *ia pahasia-kusuma-sare*, cited from *Setu* 1.34 under *PS* 1.17, all our commentators read *kumua* for *kusuma* which, however, occurs in manuscript C of Goldschmidt written in CE 1596.

(iv) In the sentence *chiviosariehi pellavantaṁ va mahiṁ*, cited under *PS* 6.46 from *Setu* 2.8, the reading *pellavantaṁ* (*prerayantam*) is found only in Mārkaṇḍeya. All our commentators read *velavantam*.

(v) The phrase *aṇurāa-paḍhuma-iṁdhaṁ* cited under *PS* 3.47 has

[312] We do not know, however, the native place of Laṭakanamiśra whom we have tentatively called a north Indian.

[313] Introduction to *Prākṛtasarvasva*, ed. K.C. Acharya, pp. 25ff., PTS, 1968.

> been traced by the editor to *Setu* 1.24 (*sohagga-paḍhama-iṇhaṁ*). This seems to be doubtful. If, however, *aṇurāa* is the reading for *sohagga*, it must be regarded as an aberration not found in any of the recensions of the poem known to us, because the word *sohagga* as used in the verse conveys two meanings *beauty* and *love*, a function which *aṇurāa* cannot fulfil.[314]

The materials available in the above citations are too scanty for determining the relation of Mārkaṇḍeya's text of the *Setubandha* to the other recensions, but there is no doubt that it had certain independent features of its own.

10. Linguistic Features of the Setubandha[315]

In a well-known verse of the *Kāvyādarśa,* Daṇḍin tells us that the language of Maharashtra, i.e. Mahārāṣṭrī, is called the best of Prākṛtas in which works like the *Setubandha* are written.[316] Bhoja in his *Śṛṅgāraprakāśa*, chapter 3,[317] speaks of six varieties of Prākṛta:[318] Saṁskṛta-sama, Deśya, Mahārāṣṭra, Śaurasena, Paiśāca, and Māgadha. Of these he illustrates the Mahārāṣṭra Prākṛta by quoting the first verse of the *Setubandha*. Rāmadāsa refers to Mahārāṣṭra-bhāṣā more than once while explaining points of grammar in his commentary on the poem (6.19, 59; 8.36).

Mārkaṇḍeya quotes the *Setubandha* frequently to illustrate

---

[314] See Extracts 1.24. Laṭakanamiśra brings out the meaning of *sohagga* clearly : इन्द्रधनुः प्रम्लायति। किंभूतं धनुः–दिशामाशानां सरसनखपदं अभिनवनखक्षतमिव। इन्द्रधनुषो दिग्नखापदत्वेन रूपणादनुत्तमपि दिशां नायिकात्वं लभ्यते। विपुलजलधरलग्नं, प्रवसज्जलदसमयवितीर्णं अपगच्छता मेघकालेन विरचितं सौभाग्यप्रथमचिह्नं सौभाग्यस्य रामणीयकताया आदिभूतं लक्षणम्। नखपदमपि पीनपयोधरलग्नं यियासता पुरुषेण दत्तं सौभाग्यस्य प्रियानुरागस्य प्रथमचिह्नम्.

[315] Abbreviations: *GS=Gāthāsaptaśati* with the commentary of Gaṅgādhara, NS edn., 1889; *Gaūḍa=Gaūḍavaho*, ed. Pandit; *KM=Kuvalayamālā*; *Līlā*=Līlāvaī; *SC=Setutattvacandrikā*; *SK=Sarasvatīkaṇṭhābharaṇa*; *Vasu=Vasudevahiṇḍī*; *GOM*= Master, *A Grammar of Old Marathi*. Oxford., 1964; *OMR*= Tulpule, *An Old Marathi Reader*, Poona, 1960.

[316] महाराष्ट्राश्रयां भाषां प्रकृष्टं प्राकृतं विदुः ।
सागरः सूक्तिरत्नानां सेतुबन्धादि यन्मयम् ॥ 1.34

[317] Josyer ed., p. 102, Mysore, 1955.

[318] Three main varieties (*sahaja, lakṣita* and *śliṣṭa*) with two sub- varieties each. Mahārāṣṭra and Śaurasena come under *lakṣita*.

grammatical rules in the Mahārāṣṭrī section of his *Prākṛtasarvasva*. Hemacandra does the same in his Prākṛta grammar, but he calls the language treated therein by the generic name Prākṛta instead of Mahārāṣṭrī. He deals with six varieties of Prākṛta in his work: Prākṛta proper (i.e. Mahārāṣṭrī), Śaurasenī, Māgadhī, Paiśācī, Cūlikā-Paiśācī and Apabhraṁśa.[319] He quotes from the *Setubandha* as well as the *Gaüḍavaho* to illustrate the rules of what he calls Prākṛta. Some of his remarks are interesting. He says, for instance, that the form *dāṇiṁ* is used in Śaurasenī, but found also in Prākṛta (i.e. Mahārāṣṭrī) contrary to the usual rule (4.277). The form in fact appears as *ādṇi* (*idānīm*) in *Setu* 11.121. Similarly, he observes that dialectal words like *āhitta* current in countries like Maharashtra and Vidarbha should be learnt from popular usage (*lokataḥ*), i.e. from the colloquial speech of the people of those countries (*HC* 2.174). It may be noted that *āhittha* is used in *Setu* 13.75, 83, and there is a number of such words in the poem usually known as *deśī*.

In his *Kāvyānuśāsana* also Hemacandra means Mahārāṣṭrī when he speaks of Prākṛta. He says, for instance, that a *kathā* is composed in all languages, in Sanskrit, Prākṛta, Māgadhī, Śaurasenī, Paiśācī and Apabhraṁśa. Similarly, he refers to poems like the *Setubandha* composed in Prākṛta-bhāṣā in cantos called Āśvāsa.[320]

Mahārāṣṭrī as the name of a Prākṛta dialect seems to have become popular at a date later than Hemacandra. As we have seen, Daṇḍin and Bhoja describe the Prākṛta of Mahārāṣṭra as the language of the *Setubandha*. Very often, however, Prākṛta means the Prākṛta of Mahārāṣṭra, i.e. Mahārāṣṭrī, even without any reference to its geographical extent, because it was regarded as the Prākṛta *par excellence*. Earlier than Hemacandra, Rudraṭa and Bhoja, for instance, refer to a six-fold division of languages comprising Sanskrit, Prākṛta, Māgadhī, Śaurasenī, Paiśācī and Apadhraṁśa, where Prākṛta obviously stands for the Prākṛta of Mahārāṣṭra, i.e. Mahārāṣṭrī.[321]

---

[319] Hemacandra's classification of Prākṛtas is found also in the *Śadabhāṣācandrikā* of Lakṣmīdhara who defines Prākṛt as the Prākṛt of Mahārāṣṭra: तत्र तु प्राकृतं नाम महाराष्ट्रोद्भवं विदुः See introductory verses, p. 4.

[320] Vol. 1, pp. 461, 463.

[321] *Kāvyālaṁkāra* with the commentary of Namisādhu 4.10 ff.; *SK* 2.16 ff.

This is made clear by Rudraṭa's illustrations of the literary device known as Bhāṣāśleṣa, which consists in employing in a verse more than one language, e.g. Sanskrit and Prākṛta, or Sanskrit and Śaurasenī, simultaneously in the same sense, or with different meanings.[322] Bhoja likewise illustrates what he calls pure Prākṛta (*prākṛtajātiḥ śuddhā*) with a verse from Kālidāsa's *Śākuntalam*, Act 3: *tujjha ṇa āṇe hiaaṁ*, which Mārkaṇḍeya 9.86 specifically mentions as composed in Mahārāṣṭrī because of the form *tujjha*. The *Sāhityamīmāṁsā* of Ruyyaka reproduces the above statement of Bhoja about pure Prākṛta along with the example, but calls the language Mahārāṣṭra-Prākṛta,[323] probably for the sake of clarity. A reference to the Prākṛta of Mahārāṣṭra occurs also in Jayamaṅgala's commentary on canto 13 of the *Bhaṭṭikāvya* composed in *tatsama* Prākṛta.[324] Such references are, however, rare, and it is usual to employ the term Prākṛta for Mahārāṣṭrī without any teritorial association.[325]

Prākṛta writers sometimes refer to Mahārāṣṭrī as the native or regional language of Mahārāṣṭra (*marahaṭṭha-desī-bhāṣā*), or simply as the language of Mahārāṣṭra (*marahaṭṭhayabhāṣā*). The author of the *Līlāvaī* (c. CE 800) says that the poem is composed in *marahaṭṭha-desī-bhāṣā* (v. 1330), which turns out to be post-classicial Mahārāṣṭrī influenced by Apabhraṁśa and the spoken language of Mahārāṣṭra.[326] The generic term *Prākṛta* also occurs in an earlier verse which says that the story is being narrated in the Prākṛta language using very few *deśī* words.[327] Uddyotana says the same thing in a different way in a verse of his *Kuvalayamāla* (CE 779), which tells us

---

[322] The illustration of the *śleṣa* of Sanskrit and Prākṛta in Rudraṭa 4.11 reads in Prākṛt as follows: सर-सबलं सहि सूरो संगामे माण-बन्धुर-सहावं। मित्तमसीसर-दव-रं ससरणमुद्धरइ मन्द–बलं।।

[323] P. 92 (TSS).

[324] रीणमित्यप्रयोग: प्राकृते महाराष्ट्रे तस्याप्रयोगात्।

[325] Maheśvara who wrote his *Nāṇapañcamīkahāo* (Singhi Jain Series), about the middle of the tenth century CE says at the beginning of his work that he has composed it in simple Prākṛt easily intelligible to all; actually it is written in Jaina Mahārāṣṭrī.

[326] See Introduction to Upadhye's edition, pp. 75ff.

[327] . . . पाययाए भासाए। पविरल–देसि–सुलक्खं कहसु कहं . . .।। — v. 41

that the romance is "composed in the Prākṛta language, and furnished with descriptions of the type current in Mahārāṣṭra".[328] The language employed in the work may be described as post-classical Mahārāṣṭrī with Apabhraṁśa and Jaina features. It is written in a fluent style, and occasionally borrows a phrase from the *Setubandha.*[329] Another reference to"the language of Mahārāṣṭra" (*marahaṭṭhayabhāṣā*) is found in a verse praising it in the course of a natural description in the *Dharmopadeśamālā-vivaraṇa* of Jayasiṁhasūri, composed in CE 858 in Jaina Mahārāṣṭrī.[330] The expression *marahaṭṭhayabhāṣā* appears in its Sanskrit form in Bhoja's *Śṛṅgāraprakāśa*, which tells us that certain small romances (*kṣudrakathā*), like the lost *Gorocanā* and *Anaṅgavatī*, belonging to a type known as Manthullī, are composed in Mahārāṣṭra-bhāṣā or "the language of Mahārāṣṭra".[331] This appellation seems to be earlier than the name Mahārāṣṭrī popularized by writers like Viśvanātha[332] and Mārkaṇḍeya (fourteenth-sixteenth centuries).

Vararuci's *Prākṛtaprakāśa* does not refer to Mahārāṣṭrī except in the last chapter which is considered an interpolation. But the *Subodhinī* commentary, which, like the *Saṁjīvanī*, omits the last three chapters dealing with Paiśācī, Māgadhī and Śaurasenī, starts with the remark that the language described in the work is Mahārāṣṭrī. A citation from the *Setubandha* occurs in Bhāmaha's commentary on Vararuci, 1.14, where one of the examples *pio tti* is taken from *Setu* 15.9.

It may generally be said that the language of the *Setubandha* is in conformity with the Prākṛta described by Vararuci and Hemacandra except that in one respect, the change of *t* to *d*, Pravarasena tends to

---

328 पाइय-भासा-रइया मरहट्ठय-वण्णय-णिबद्धा — p. 4.

329 Cf. सोहग्ग-पढम-इण्हं *Setu* 1.24=सोहग्ग-पढम-इंधं — *KM* p. 22, l. 14. The expression पमुह-रसिअ *Setu* 1.9 is used in *KM* p. 6, l. 5 (विसु पमुह-रसिउ जीयंतकरो वि). The verse in *KM* p.13: जाव य ण देंति हिययं पुरिसा कज्जाइँ ताव विहड़ंति। अह दिण्णं चिय हिययं गुरुं पि कज्जं परिसमत्तं॥ expands the idea in *Setu* 3.56: जाव ण दिज्जइ दिट्ठी काअव्वं दाव होइ चिर-णिव्वूढ.

330 सललिय-पय-संचारा पयडिय-मयणा सुवण्ण-रयणेल्ला।
मरहट्ठय-भासा कामिणी य अडवी य रेहंति॥ — p. 4. (Singhi Jain Series)

331 Raghavan, *Bhoja's Śṛṅgāraprakāśa*, p. 623.

332 *Śāhityadarpaṇa*, chapter 6 (Bhāṣāvibhāga).

agree with Vararuci rather than Hemacandra as shown below. As an elaborate specimen of early Mahārāṣṭrī, the *Setubandha* shows few deviations from the established norm; and we shall here confine ourselves to a few characteristic features and certain peculiar forms found in the text of Rāmadāsa, representing the best known recension of the poem. Goldschmidt's Index gives a comprehensive picture of the lexical material and grammatical forms found in the work.

The Change of medial *t* to *d* occurs in a few words and terminations in the *Setubandha*. This is normal in Śaurasenī, and its occurrence in Mahārāṣṭrī text has attracted the notice of scholars. The forms are *udu* 1.18, 3.29, 6.11, 9.85; *maïladā* 3.31; *uivaṇṇadā* 8.87; *dā* = *tā* (*tāvat*) 3.10, 27; *dāva* 3.26, 29, 56; 4.32; *de* 4.31, 33; 11.83, 92, 126; *rāmādo* 8.87. These are readings found in Rāmadāsa's recension. The south Indian recension seems to have read *sarada* for *saraa* (*śarad*) 1.16, as can be seen from Kṛṣṇavipra's commentary on the verse.[333] Further, the south Indians have *dayālutā* for *rasantara* in 5.24, and their reading seems to have been *daāidā* (*dāāludā*).[334] *SC* text reads *raada* for *raaa* 9.42. But it has *maïlaā* for *maïladā* 3.31,[335] while Laṭakanamiśra reads *maïliā*. The reading *maïladā* appears, however, in the verse as quoted in *SK*.[336] Another *Setubandha* verse 1.56 quoted in *SK*[337] has *pahasida* for *pahasia*. Laṭakanamiśra reads *uvaṇīdā* for *uvaṇiā* in 4.63 and *soijjadu* in 3.47. While there are divergences in the readings of the commentators, it may be stated on the whole that the change of medial *t* to *d* in certain words and forms is a feature of the language of the *Setubandha*. On the other hand, examples of retention of *d* are rare in our text; it has *ṇadī* 6.65; *udanta* 4.55 of which there is a variant *uanta* in the manuscript C of Goldschmidt.

From a grammatical point of view there is nothing very abnormal in Pravarasena's use of forms with *d* for *t*. It is true that Hemacandra regards the change of medial *t* to *d* as an exclusive feature of

333 See Extracts 1.16.

334 See Extracts 5.24.

335 *SC* text is not always consistent. It has *vivaṇṇaā* for °*dā*, but *rāmādo* in 8.87 (*SC* 88). Here as elsewhere the number of verses often various in *SC*.

336 Chapter 4, quotation no. 50, NS edn., 1925.

337 Chapter 2, quotation no. 191.

Śaurasenī, and objects to its use in Prākṛta, i.e. Mahārāṣṭrī.[338] His criticism is directed at Vararuci who allows this change in words like *ṛtu, rajata, śarad,* etc., and recognizes forms like those used by Pravarasena: *mailadā, rāmādo, de,* etc.[339] Vararuci evidently draws his materials from an earlier phase of Mahārāṣṭrī, while Hemcandra's objections are based on a later phase when the process of vocalization of the consonants had become complete. He seems to have drawn his conclusion from works like the *Gaüḍavaho* and the *Līlāvaī* where the change of *t* to *d* is conspicuous by its absence.[340] Accordingly he reads *uu* for *udu* in the *Setu* 6.11 quoted in his *Kāvyānuśāsana*.[341]

It may be noted that examples of *d* for *t*, some of them admitted by Vararuci,[342] are found also in the *Gāthāsaptaśatī*, especially in the NS edition with the commentry of Gaṅgādhara: *de* 1.15; 6.53: 7.7, 53; *āada* 4.1; *ṇiggadā* 6.5; *dāva* 1.90; 2.68; *ṇivvudi* 1.85; 3.29, 42; 42; *devadā* 2.94; *ṇecchadi* 3.5; *visada* 4.43, etc. Weber adopts some of these forms: *de, dāva, ṇivvudi* 5.21; while he reads *parido* not found in the NS edition (5.54). In some cases Weber gives the forms with *d* as variants. It may be added that similar forms are also found occasionally in certain Mahārāṣṭrī verses in Kālidāsa's dramas.[343]

The occurrence of forms like those mentioned above in the *Setubandha* and the *Gāthāsaptaśatī* points to the fact that non-tinitial *t* occasionally becomes *d* in early Mahārāṣṭrī in certain words and terminations.[344] On the other hand, the change of *t* to *d* does not

---

338 अत्र केचिद् ऋत्वादिषु द (cf. Vararuci 2.7) इत्यारब्धवन्तः स तु शौरसेनीमागधीविषय एव दृश्यते इति नोच्यते। प्राकृते हि ऋतुः रिऊ उऊ, etc. — *HC* 1.209; पीनता इत्यस्य प्राकृते पीणया इति भवति । पीणदा इति तु भाषान्तरे। तेनेह तलो दा न क्रियते — ibid. 2.154.

339 Cf. Vararuci 2.7; 4.10, 22; 5.6; 6.32, etc.

340 Cf. Upadhye, *Līlāvaī*, Introduction, p. 83.

341 Vol. 1, Bombay, 1938, p. 361, quotation no. 550.

342 Cf. Vararuci 2.7; 6.32.

343 *udu-maṅgalaaṁ* — *Śakuntalā*, ed. Cappeller, v. 124; *ṇandaṇa-vaṇa-vāḍā* — *Vikramorvaśīyam* 2.13, ed. Pandit.

344 A few examples of this are also found in the early Jaina Mahārāṣṭrī text *Vasudevahiṇḍī*. It has usually *saraya* and *uu*, but also *sarada* and *udu* occasionally (pp. 129, 130, 234, 238, 140). A few other *d*-forms are *diyādi* p. 210, *namida* p. 230, *saṁvarida* p. 226 (also *saṁvariya*), *vaḍḍhāvida* p. 152; also *padi* in *nāma-metta-padiṇā* p. 70. But as is usual in Jaina Mahārāṣṭrī, *Vasu* often retains *d*: *madaṇa, sādara, nadī*, etc.

appear to have been a rigid characteristic of Śaurasenī in its early phase. The Dhruvā songs in the *Nāṭyaśāstra*, which are composed in Śaurasenī,[345] have not a few examples in which medial *t* does not change to *d*, but is vocalized as in Mahārāṣṭrī. It seems therefore that the vocalization of consonants and the change of medial *t* to *d* have grown up as distinctive features of Mahārāṣṭrī and Śaurasenī respectively in the gradual process of development of each language.

A peculiar form *dūsaha* (for *tūsaha=tuṣyata*) occurs in *Setu* 15.61. Mādhava reads *tūsaha*, but *SC* text has *dūsaha* like Rāmadāsa.[346] The change of initial *t* to *d* in a word not forming part of a compound is extremely rare. Reference may be made in this connection to *dose* for *tose* (*toṣaḥ*) in the Kalsi version of Aśoka's sixth Rock Edict. The *d*, however, does not appear in any other version of the Edict. The expression *disai* in a verse quoted in the *prākr̥tapaiṅgalam* 2.193 is explained as *tviṣaḥ api* in one of the commentaries.[347] *Dala* for *tala* appears in compounds like *gaaṇadala* in Śaurasenī;[348] and one such example is noticed even in a Mahārāṣṭrī text like the *Gaüḍavaho* (v.815).[349]

The treatment of *kṣ* in *Setu* is in conformity with the practice generally followed in Mahārāṣṭrī works. According to the grammarians *kṣ* becomes *kh* except in a limited number of words in which it changes to *ch*. Mahārāṣṭrī writers do not, however, follow a hard and fast rule in the use of *kh* and *ch* for *kṣ*.[350] Pravarasena, for instance, writes *peccha* in all the derivative forms, but writes also *aṇavepkhia* (*anapekṣita*) 10.80 and *paḍikkhanti* (*pratīkṣante*) 13.19. *Gaüḍa* likewise has *peccha* throughout, but uses *kh* in the expression *vīyāvekkhī*[351] (v. 80). *GS* has *pecchanta* 4.73, *pecchaa* 5.98; but also *uvekhia* 5.20, *uppekkhāmi* 5.45. *Gaüḍa* has both *chīra* and *khīroa* (810, 1039). It has

---

[345] *Nāṭyaśāstra* 32.440, ed. Ghosh (BI) = GOS edn., 32.383.

[346] The printed text of *SC* has *tūsaha*, but the editor's footnote shows that the manuscript has *dūsaha*.

[347] BI edn., p. 541.

[348] See *Nāṭyaśāstra* 32.214, 216, ed. Ghosh (BI).

[349] रविणा स-मऊह-दाविय-दलेण=स्वमयूखदर्शिततलेन Commentary.

[350] Rāmadāsa reads पेक्खइ, पेक्खसु पेक्खिज्जन्त respectively in *Setu* 2.40, 8.21 and 15.63; but there are variants with *cch*. See Extracts 8.21 and *SC* text.

[351] =द्वितीयापेक्षी। .

vikkhitta, ukkhitta, etc., with *kh;*[352] in such cases *Setu* has both *ch* and *kh*: *vikkhipanta* 6.35 and *ucchippanta* 14.57; *ukkhitta* and *ucchitta*. Both the forms occur in *Līlā*.[353] *Ukkhitta* is used much more frequently in *Setu*, but, as pointed out by Goldschmidt in the Index, *ucchitta* often appears as a variant. Mārkaṇḍeya in fact allows both *ukkhitta* and *ucchitta* in Mahārāṣṭrī (3.42).

Reference may be made in this connection to the word *rukkha* found in *Setu* 7.36; 10.51. The *kṣ* of *vṛkṣa* appears in Prākṛta as *ch* in *vaccha* and as *kh* in *rukkha*. According to Mārkaṇḍeya 9.17, *rukkha* alone is used in Śaurasenī, not *vaccha*. But as he gives *rukkha* and *vaccha* as alternative forms of *vṛkṣa* in the Mahārāṣṭrī section of his grammar (3.42), the obvious implication is that both the forms are allowed in Mahārāṣṭrī.[354] Accordingly we find *rukka* used in outstanding Mahārāṣṭrī texts like the *Setubandha* and the *Līlāvaī*.[355] It seems therefore that while *kh* for *kṣ* is normal in Śaurasenī, Mahārāṣṭrī writers show a tendency to use *ch* as well as *kh* as a substitute for *kṣ*. So it is futile to claim that the *Setubandha* is composed in Śaurasenī, because it happens to record forms with *kh* more frequently than those with *ch*.[356] It may also be noted that *kṣ* often becomes *kh* in Old Marāṭhī, e.g. *pākhālī* (*prakṣālita*), *pākhiru*, *khuṇāvaṇe* (*kṣuṇatti*), *sārikhā* (*sadṛkṣa*), etc.[357]

A reference may be made to the suffix *-alla* in words like *mūallia*[358] and *galatthallia*[359] found in *Setu* 5.41, 43, 8.61[360] This suffix added in various forms to adjectives and especially past participles may be

---

352 See Index to *Gaūḍavaho*.

353 See Index to *Līlāvaī*, ed. Upadhye.

354 The word *rukkha* is also used by Mārkaṇḍeya to illustrate the declension of nouns in Mahārāṣṭrī (chapter 5).

355 vv. 4.49, 677.

356 The point is dealt with in Introduction to *Prākṛtasarvasva*, ed. Acharya, p. 82.

357 *OMR*, pp. 28, 43; *GOM*, p. 154.

358 This is the reading of most of the commentators other than Rāmadāsa who reads *mūallaïa* (*muhalā*). *SC* text reads *mūllia-*(*pamuhalā*), and Laṭakanamiśra *mūallia-*(*mūhaliā*)=*mūkāyita-*(*mukharitāḥ*). Cf. Extracts 5.41. *Gaūḍa* 1206 has *mūyallia*.

359 An expanded form of *galatthia* (*galahastita*) which also occurs in *Setu* 11.128 and 12.11.

360 Another formation of this kind: *pāsallaïa* (पार्श्वायित) occurs in *Setu* 9.77 *Gaūḍa* 266 has *pāsalliya* (पार्श्वीकृत).

said to be a characteristic feature of the Mahārāṣṭrī language. Numerous examples of such expanded past participles are found in Mahārāṣṭrī prose in works like the *Vasudevahiṇḍī* and the *Kuvalayamālā*, especially the latter. The *Vasudevahiṇḍī* has, for instance, forms like *āṇielliya* (p. 57. l. 21), *hāelliya* (p. 56, l. 11): and *diṇṇellaya* (p. 30, l. 25).[361] The latter form is of particular interest, because the *Kuvalayamālā* represents the Marahaṭṭhas as using the expressions *diṇṇalle* and *gahiyalle* (*given* and *taken*) in their conversation at the market place of a big city, in desription in which the author gives specimens of the dialects spoken by the merchants from different parts of India.[362] Uddyotana's statement is corroborated by the fact that the form *diṇṇalle* said to be current among the Marahaṭṭhas appears in Old Marāṭhī (OM) as *dīnhalā*, *dīnhale*, etc. in the same sense.[363] It is probable that *diṇṇalle* is a colloquial form of *diṇṇelleya* used in *Vasudevahiṇḍī* and the past participles in *alla* (often extended), which appear in literary Mahārāṣṭrī are probably based on the spoken language of Mahārāṣṭra.

The 2nd pers. pl. of the Present indicative of the root *as* (*ttha*) found in *Setu* 3.3 was considered a very rare form by Pischel (498); but as pointed out by Alsdorf, it occurs more than forty times in the *Vasudevahiṇḍī*.[364] The frequent use of this form which later became obsolete in Prākr̥ta has been considered one of the signs of the antiquity of the Jaina romance;[365] and its occurrence in our poem seems to indicate that the form was still current when the *Setubandha* was written.

The absolutive in *ūṇa*, a prevailing characteristic of Mahārāṣṭrī, is uniformly used in *Setu* except in some doubtful cases. It is

---

361 'तस्स य इक्केण धम्ममइणा गिहिणा खेत्तनियत्तणं दिण्णेल्लयं' (i.e. दिण्णं). KM has forms like जायल्लिय p. 6. l. 2 मयल्लय p. 48. l. 14, मिलिएल्लय p. 55. l. 13, कयल्लिय p. 84, l. 14, धरियल्लओ l. 10, मारिएल्लय p. 112, l. 11, छाइएल्लय l. 10, जिमियल्लय p . 151, l. 19, etc.

362 दिण्णल्ले गहियल्ले उल्लविरे तत्थ मरहट्ठे — *KM*, p. 153.

363 *OMR*, pp. 77, 88, 162; Upadhye, *The Kuvalayamālā*, Introduction, notes, etc., p. 145, 1969.

364 See Alsdorf, "The Vasudevahiṇḍī: A Specimen of Archaic Jain Mahārāṣṭrī" in *BSOS*, vol. VIII, 1936.

365 Alsdorf assigns the work to a date much earlier than the sixth century CE.

noteworthy that it is also found in Old Marāṭhī where the suffix is *ūni*, *ūna*, etc.[366] *Setu* has a few examples in *ia*, which is the recognized absolutive suffix in Śaurasenī, but they are not taken as absolutives by all the commentators. *Vīsajjia* 6.77 is *visṛjya* according to Kṛṣṇa, but *visṛṣṭa* according to Rāmadāsa. *Ahilīa* 2.16 is usually taken as an absolutive, but there is a variant reading *ahilīṇa*. *Aṇuhūa* 4.24 is taken only by the south Indians as *anubhūya*, but this is unacceptable. In *Setu* 11.133 *saṁbharia* is taken by several commentators as *saṁsmṛtya*, but Mdhava disagrees and takes it as a past participle.[367] In 11.92 the same word is construed by Kṛṣṇa as *saṁsmṛta*, while Rāmadāsa takes it as an absolutive. It may be said on the whole that *Setu*, like *Gaüḍa*, avoids the absolutive in *ia*. *Līla* (v. 1328) has *vandiya* (*vanditvā*), but such forms are rare in that work. Absolutives in *ia* are found in some of the Mahārāṣṭrī verses quoted by Svayambhu.[368] Even *GS* 2.37 has *saṁmīlīa* (*saṁmīlya*). Nevertheless *ūṇa* is the recognized absolutive suffix in Mahārāṣṭrī. Some of the forms in *Setu* are *dāūṇa* 12.28, *uppaiūṇa* 8.37, *nāūṇa* 11.21, *ukkariseūṇa* 15.75, *uaūheūṇa* 11.92, *āsāeūṇa* 11.132, *ahileūṇa* 14.39, *voḍhūṇa* 9.75, *niameūṇa* 4.55, *jeūṇa* 3.27, etc.

Some of the gerundives used in *Setu* are *samāsasiavva* 11.95 *rottavva* 11.92, *māavva* 9.3, *uaivva=upajīvya* 1.31, *muṇeavva* 4.24, *soavva* 2.10, *bhareavva* 9.3, *lāiavva* 15.75, *ovatteavva* 10.50, *okkhaṇḍeavva* 10.29, *gejjha* 10.43, etc.

Gerundives are sometimes used as nouns: *visammiavva* 9.2 (विश्रमित्वय=विश्राम), — *hareavva* 9.3 (धर्तव्य=धारण), *bhareavva* 9.3 (भर्तव्य=पूरण), *māavva* 9.3 (मातव्य=मान), *rumbhiavva* 9.3 (रोद्धव्य=रोधन), *uppaiavva* 6.78 (उत्पतितव्य=उत्पतन), *mariavva* 11.117 (मर्तव्य=मरण), *saṁcariavva* 14.28 (संचरण). Similar examples are found in *GS*: *pāmpiavva* 5.50 (प्रजल्पितव्य=वचन), *ramiavva* 5.61 (रन्तव्यक=रत), *cumbiavva* 5.65, *rūsiavva* 5.66 (रोष), *roiavva* 4.48, etc. *Gaüḍa* 58 uses *vīsūriyavva* as a noun.[369]

Gerundives in *aṇijja* are *vimhaaṇijja* 4.39 *lajjaṇijja* 11.29, *vaaṇijja* 4.13, *tavaṇijja* 15.13, etc. But *saaṇīa* occurs in 12.25. The forms in *aṇīa* properly belong to Śaurasenī, but sometimes occur in Mahārāṣṭrī texts. *Gaüḍa*

[366] E.g., *karūni*, *gheūni*, *gheūna*, *leūni*, *hoūni*, *hoūna*, etc. — *OMR*, p. 80; *GOM*, p. 142.

[367] See Extracts 11,133.

[368] *Svayambhūcchandas*, p. 20, v. 45; p. 21, v. 48, etc.

[369] Cf. Vasu: *dāyavva* p. 2, *saṁsariyavva*, p. 24, *mariyavva*, p. 34, *acchiyavva* p. 66, etc. used as nouns.

has both *ramaṇijja* and *ramaṇīya* (602). *Līla* has *ramaṇīya, sayaṇīya, asoyaṇīya* (311) with *ṇījja* as a variant. *GS* 4.63 has *dūsahaṇīa*.

Apart from special forms, the passive is invariably formed with *ijja*: e.g. *lakkhijjai* 6.95, *cintijjaü* 3.26 *saṁkhohijjai* 6.69 *cakkalaijjanta* 13.74, *āāmijjanta* 10.7, *sūijjai* 11.59, *pahāmijjanta*[370] 7.69, *khavijjai* 3.25, *muṇijjai* 6.58, *lāijjai*[371] 4.35, *raijjanta*[372] 8.87, *ṇimmāvijjai*[373] 8.79, *ṇivvavijjaü*[374] 11.76, *viijjanta*[375] 6.37, *dohāijjai*[376] 5.35, etc.

The passive in *ia*, usual in Śaurasenī, seems to be absent in both *Setu* and *Gaüḍa*; while *Līlā* (800) has an isolated form *pariṇīyasi*. It may also be noted that the suffix *ija* with which the passive is formed in Old Marāṭhī[377] is considered the successor of Prākr̥ta *ijja*.[378]

Some of the special forms of the passive are *viḍhappanti* 1.10, *gheppai* 1.30 (OM *ghepe*), *dīsai* (OM *dise*[379]), *ṇihammai* 11.123, *tīrai* 3.18, *ukkhammanti* 6.33, *libbhanta* 9.41, *kīrai* 3.12, *hīrai* 6.11 *sīsai*[380] 10.77 (majority reading for *sāsai*), *sīsaü*[381] 4.23, *ṇivvubbhai* 4.41, *samappai* 5.10, *ālokkanta* 1.25, *ṇisubbhanti*[382] 7.61, *dhuvvamāṇa* 14.57, *vihuvvanta* 6.85, *suvvai* 1.10, *ṇihippanta*[383] 8.97, *rubbhai* 12.51, *aīsanta*[384] 1.35, *mijjanta*[385] 7.69, *jhijjai* 1.35, *ṇajjai* 2.37, *vihijjanta*[386] (*SC* text) for *vihuvvanta*[387] 8.86, etc.

370 प्रभ्राम्यमाण।

371 लाग्यते।

372 रच्यमान ।

373 निंमीयते।

374 निवाप्यताम्।

375 वीज्यमान; better विकीर्यमाण (cf. *Gaūḍa* 334).

376 द्विधा क्रियते।

377 E.g., *jāṇije, pāhije* (3rd. sg.); *pāvijati* (pl.); *gilijatu, sevijatu* (pres. part.).

378 *GOM*, p. 134; *OMR*, 70.

379 *OMR*, Extract 20,5.

380 शिष्यते; शस्यते (कथ्यते)।

381 शिष्यतां (कथ्यताम्)।

382 निपात्यन्ते।

383 निधीयमान।

384 अदृश्यमान, cf. *GS* 3.24; 4.38.

385 मीयमान।

386 विमिद्यमान।

387 विधूयमान।

There is a number of examples which are active in form, but passive in sense, e.g. *bharai*[388] 7.60; 8.62, *bharanta*[389] 1.58, *ārambhanta*[390] 8.82, *uvvellai*[391] 6.41, *pūrai*[392] 8.54, *osumbhanta*[393] 4.54 from *osumbhai*[394] 14.71, *ṇisumbhanta*[395] 5.69 from *ṇisumbhai* 15.57, *rumbhai*[396] 8.62; 11.112, *ṇivvaṇṇanta*[397] 1.45, *ohuppanta*[398] 3.18 as against *pahuppai*[399] 7.63; 11.31, *pahuppanta*[400] 7.27; 10.56, etc.

A number of passives appear to be used in active sense. *Ṇisuḍhijjanta* 3.58 is taken by Rāmadāsa as *nipātyamāna*, but Kṛṣṇa explains it as *bharāvanamat*, deriving it from *ṇisuḍhai* recorded by *HC* 4.158 in the sense of *bhārākrānto namati*. *Muhijjantī* 11.100 is taken by the commentators as *muhyantī*. In 5.50 *kajjalaijjai* is taken by most of the commentators as active (*kajjalayati*). Kṛṣṇa takes it as passive (*kajjalīkriyate*), but his construction is somewhat artificial. In 5.8 *dharijjai* is taken by Rāmadāsa as active (*dhriyate jīvati*)[401] which gives a better meaning than *dhāryate* found in other commentators. Similar instances of passives used in active sense are found elsewhere. In *GS* 7.77[402] *pucchijjantī* stands for *pṛcchantī*; and in 7.76 *pijjai* for *pibati*, as pointed out by Gaṅgādhara.[403]

---

388 भ्रियते।

389 भ्रियमाण।

390 आरभ्यमाण।

391 उद्वेष्ट्यते, cf. *HC* 4.223.

392 पूर्यते।

393 अवपात्यमान।

394 अवपातयति।

395 निपात्यमान।

396 रुध्यते।

397 निर्वर्ण्यमान।

398 आक्रम्यमाण; अभिभूयमान।

399 प्रभवति।

400 प्रभवत्।

401 'धृङ् अवस्थाने'

402 पुच्छिज्जन्ती पिअस्स चरिआइं।

403 *HC*'s mention of *pijjaï* (4-10) as an active verb appears to be based on current usage.

Another example of a passive used in active sense occurs in *Setu* 15.86: जो च्चिअ जेऊण जर्म दिट्ठो . . . तुमे जमलोओ । दीसिहिसि कह णु . . . इण्हिं तं सेस–जण–सामण्ण ॥ Here *dīsihisi* (*drakṣyase*) is used for *drakṣyasi*. The forms *dīsahasi* and *dīsihasi* occur in *Līlā* 695, 708 where they are used in the regular sense. *Setu* 3.33 has likewise *dīsihai* (*drakṣyate*), (cf. *GS* 7.17). It is therefore surprising to find *dīsihisi* used in the same work in active sense; and the variant *dacchihisi* shows that this irregular form is not found in all the recensions. It may, however, be pointed out that *dīsai* (*dṛśyate*) is sometimes used in active sense in Apabhraṁśa, and more than one instance of this occurs in Svayambhū's *Paümacariu*.[404] The occurrence of *dīsihisi* in active sense in *Setu* 15.86 might be due to the influence of Apabhraṁśa of which there are other indications in the text followed by Rāmadāsa.

Some of the infinitives used in *Setu* are *ghettuṁ* 10.40, *ahileuṁ* 4.53, *loheuṁ* 11.27, *laṅgheuṁ* 12.80, ṇiatteuṁ 3.24, *ṇivvoḍhuṁ* 1.9,[405] *kāuṁ* 4.36, *appāheuṁ* 11.31, etc. Some infinitives are formed by adding the suffix to passive verbs; e.g., आढत्ता दीसिउं णिसिअरच्छाआ 4.51; दीसिउं पउत्तं . . . . सेउबन्धस्स मुहं 8.30; घेप्पिउ पउत्ता . . . .परिस्समेण पवंगा 7.71. आहम्मिउं पअत्तं . . . . दसाणणतूरं 12.45. These infinitives of passive verbs are usually followed by the past participle of a verb meaning "to begin" to mark the commencement of the action denoted by the infinitive.[406]

There are two examples in *Setu* of infinitives used in certain idiomatic statements in which neuter adjectives like *dukhaṁ* and *dukkaraṁ* in the sense of *hard, difficult* qualify nouns of a different gender: *ṇivvoḍhuṁ hoi dukkaraṁ kavva-kahā* 1.9; *dukkhaṁ kālassa jāṇium pariṇāmo* 14.48.[407] This use of neuter adjectives that retain their form irrespective of the gender of the nouns they qualify represents a

---

404 वहिणि सहोयरि दससयणेत्तहो॥ किर सहुँ सहियहिँ ढुक्कइ सरवरु दीसइ ताम सयरु पिहिमीसरु॥ विद्धी कामसरेहिँ . . . 5.4.7 ff.; लच्छिभुत्ति तं लच्छीणयरु पईसई। ववहरन्तु जं सुन्दरु तं तं दीसई (v.r. दीसई)॥ — 45.4.1.

405 Cf. *GS* 1.71.

406 Cf. आलावा सुव्विउं पयत्ता — *KM*, p. 25; किं च कीरिउं समाढत्तं — ibid., p. 199; खज्जभोज्जपेज्जं दिज्जउमाढत्ता — *Vasu*, p. 64.

407 We have adopted here and in the translation the reading *pariṇāmo* of the Southern and Bengal recensions. Rāmadāsa's reading *pariṇāmaṁ* gives a different meaning. See Extracts 14.48.

Prākr̥ta idiom found also in other early texts.[408] For example, रमणीओ अयं पएसो दुक्खं परिचइउं *Vasu* p. 136, l. 13; जहा भुयाहिं तरिउं दुक्करं रयणायरो *Uttarādhyayanasūtra* 19.42. Examples like एण्हिं एत्थम्ह गामे सुलहवसही दुक्करं पंथिआणं[409] without the infinitive seem to be rare.

Most of the imperatives (2nd pers. sing.) end in *su*: *uṭṭhesu* 11.124, *muasu* 11.124, *sāhasu* 11.76, *pusasu* 11.92, etc. Plural forms are *avamaṇṇaha* 4.24 *parumhāha* 3.4, etc. Other forms (2nd pers. sing.) are *pusa* 11.124; *pattihi* (*pratīhi*) 11.94, also *pattia* 11.123. Cf. *pattiai* (*pratyeti*) 13.44, *pattiasi* 11.90. The form *pattia* is used in *GS* 3.16, 45; 4.76, etc., and many times in Svayambhū's *Paümacariu* 35.8; 36.13, etc.

Besides *dīsihai* and *dīsihisi* mentioned above, examples of the Future are *hohii* 11.26, etc, *ehii* 10.79 *kāhii* 4.41, *galihii* 5.4, *aṇumarihii* 14.55, *vasihii* 4.50, *uggāhii* 11.84, *ṇiattihii* (*nivartayiṣyati*) 11.84, *samappihii* (*samāpsyate*) 5.4. Cf. *samappai* (*samāpyate*) 5.10, 9.83, 15.95.

Other examples of the Future are *dacchāmi*, *dacchimi* (*drakṣyāmi*) 11.77, 85; and *dacchāma* (pl.) 3.50. *Decchiha* (*drakṣyatha*) 3.23 is a rare form. The initial *e* appears to be due to the influence of *peccha*, just as the Aśokan form *dekhati* is supposed to have evolved through contract with *pekkh* (*prekṣ*).[410]

Three other examples *dacchihi* (*drakṣyasi*) 11.93; *dacchihi* (*drakṣyati*) 14.55, and *mocchihi* (*mokṣyati*) 3.30, 4.49, 11.126 need comment.

a) *dacchihi* (*drakṣyasi*) for *dacchihisi* or *dacchisi*:

The Future 2nd pers. sing. ends in *esahi* in Apabhraṁśa, sometimes without the *e*[411]; e.g., *hosahi, lahesahi, pāvesahi, jāisihi* or *jāesahi*, etc.[412] In the Present Indicative also the 2nd pers. sing. ends in *si* or *hi* in

---

408 Such use in Sanskrit is explained in *Vāmana-kāvyālaṁkārasūtravr̥tti* 5.2.23, Poona, 1927.

409 Quoted in *Svayambhūcchandas*, ed. Velankar, verse 54, p. 23. Cf. जह परिययम्मि लोओ तह भुज्जन्तो वि दुक्करं को वि — *Gaūḍa* 957.

410 Bloch, *Les Inscriptios d'Asoka*, p. 91, fn 11, Paris, 1950.

411 Cf. Introduction to *Bhavisattakahā*, ed. Jacobi (p. 41, para 36) München, 1918; Introduction to *Nāyakumāracariu*, p. LV, ed. H. Jain, Karanja, 1933.

412 Cf. *Bhavisattayakahā* 6.8, p. 41; 7.14, p. 53, ed. Gune; GOS; *Paümacariu* 19.7.5 ed. Bhayani; *Yogasāra*, v. 70, in *Paramātmaprakāśa* and *Yogasāra*, ed. Upadhye, p. 386.

Apabhraṁśa, e.g., *karasi, karahi*. In *dacchihi* the *hi* might be due to Apabhraṁśa influence. In that case *dacchihi* stands for *dacchisi*.[413]

b) *dacchihi* (*drakṣyati*) for *dacchihii*:

The Future ending *hii* in 3rd pers. sing. is often contracted to *hi* in Apabhraṁśa, giving rise to forms like *hohī, kāhī, gamihī*, etc. Such forms are also frequently found in Jaina Mahārāṣṭrī, and sometimes in later Mahārāṣṭrī texts like the *Līlāvaī*.[414] This *hī* appears also in a short form *hi* in Apabhraṁśa, e.g. *hohi*,[415] *jāihi*,[416] *jahi*, etc.[417]The *hi* form occurs also in Jaina Mahārāṣṭrī. The fact that Jaina Mahārāṣṭrī is closer to the spoken language explains the presence of a considerable number of such forms in texts like the *Kuvalayamālā* and the*Vasudevahiṇḍī* where it is often followed by *tti* usual after verbs.[418]

Forms like those mentioned above are rare in classical Mahārāṣṭrī. *GS* has however, *pavasiihi* (*pravatsyati*) 1.46 and *hoihi* (*bhaviṣyati*) 2.87[419];

---

413 Dacchihi seems also to stand for *dacchisi* or *dacchihisi* in *Vasu*, p. 135. चारुसामि एरिसं मे न दिट्ठपुव्वं, जइ त्थ दट्ठुकामा इहमागया दच्छिहि त्ति. Here the person addressed (i.e. the merchant Cārudatta) is put in the plural, but the principal verb *dacchihi* is in singular. It may be noted that the verb does not always agree with the subject in number in this archaic text, e.g. अम्हे दुवे ज़णीओ तुमं वट्टावेहामि त्ति p. 144, l. 29; अहं पुण एवं बाहमाणं अणुवत्तामहे गुरुंति चिन्तमाणो — p. 206, l. 18; उट्ठिओ मि कत्थ मण्णे वत्तामहे त्ति चिन्तयन्तो — p. 144, l. 7. Here, in the first sentence the subject is in pl. and the verb in sing.; and in the next two the subject is in sing., but the verb in pl. Similarly, in हरे पाणा अवसरह सिग्घं, मा हत्थिणा चमढिज्जिहि त्ति — p. 98, l. 27 चमढिज्जिहि seems to stand for चमढिज्जिहिसि, although the subject is in plural. The variant अवमद्दिज्जिहिह provides a grammatically correct reading.

414 *Hohī, lahihī, kāhī, ehī, pesihī* (vv. 158, 41I, 225, 862), etc.

415 Alsdorf, *Kumārapālapratibodha*, p. 100 and Glossary under *hoi*. Hamburg, 1928.

416 *Prākṛta-Paiṅgalam* (BI) 2.144. *Jāihi* is explained in the commemtary as *yāsyati*.

417 Cf. *tā kimittu vi turau jāhi tti cinteviṇu*, *Sanatkumāracaritam* 569. Ed. Jacobi, München, 1921. See also Introduction (p. 17) to the Text.

418 E.g., दंसणेण चेय तीए सव्वं सुंदरं होहि — *KM* p. 14; एसा का वि रायपुत्तस्स पिययमा होहि त्ति — ibid., p. 17; जो एयं पायं पूरेहिइ सो मं परिणेहि त्ति — ibid., p. 153; वासुदेवो य किर सिसुपालजरासंधे वहेहि त्ति वाओ पवत्तई त्ति — *Vasu*, p. 30; एस जड्डो किं एस सिक्खिहि त्ति — ibid, p. 127.

419 See NS edn. with the commentary of Gaṅgādhara. Weber adopts the regular forms. The form *hoihi* occurs also in *Vasu*: किह मम तव सरिसो पुत्तो होइहि त्ति — p. 97, l. 20.

and *Gaüḍa* 997 has *saṁṭhavehi* (*saṁsthāpayiṣyati*). It may be noted that, unlike *HC* 3.172, Trivikrama allows alternaive forms like *mocchihi, mocchihii; socchihi, socchihii; rocchihi, rocchihii,* etc.[420] but the occurrence of such forms in classical Mahārāṣṭrī texts seems to be due to the infiltration of Apabhraṁśa traits.

It is necessary to point out that some of the irregular forms mentioned above have variants, and it is not always possible to determine the readings of all the commentators in the absence of the texts followed by them. Some of them occasionally record the regular forms, e.g. *dacchihisi* for *dacchihi*.[421] Mādhava agrees with Rāmadāsa in reading *dacchihi* (*drakṣyati*) in 14.55, but not elsewhere. In 4.49 Laṭakanamiśra reads, *mocchihi* (*mokṣyati*) like Rāmadāsa, but in 3.30 he has *mocchii* in the same sense (cf. *HC* 3.172). The forms in *hi* are thus consistently found only in Rāmadāsa; and it is therefore probable that the recension of the *Setubandha* followed by him has been affected to some extent by the influence of Apabhraṁśa.

Examples of the Optative are *ṇejjāmi* 3.55; *dharejja* 5.4; *jivejja* 5.5; *paavejja* 4.28; *virahejja* (*virahayet tyājayet*) 5.4; *ṇamejja* 8.14.

There are several examples of the Conditional formed with present participles.[422]

फुट्टन्तं जइ होन्तं . . . रामसिरं 11.94 जह संभावेसि तह इमं जइ होन्तं 11.121; होन्तं जइ रामसिरं एआवत्थं पि तो समूससमाणं 11.132. See also 11.80.

Similar examples are found in *GS* 1.26; 3.16. The use of the present participle for the Conditional is also found in Apabhraṁśa,[423] and may have derived from the spoken language. Many examples of this in prose are found in the *Vasudevahiṇḍī*.[424]

Reference may be made to a few words which occur in our text, at least in Rāmadāsa's recension, in a form unusual in classical

---

[420] *Prakrit Grammar of Trivikrama* 2.4.30, ed. Vaidya, Sholapur, 1954.

[421] See Extracts 11.93.

[422] Cf. *HC* 3.179, 180 and Mārkaṇḍeya 6.18, 36.

[423] See the verses cited in *HC* 4.351, 1; 4.395, 1 and Jacobi's Introductions to *Sanatkumāracaritam*, p. 16 and *Bhavisattakahā* p. 41.

[424] E.g. जइ य पुरोहितो अप्पणो अवराहेण निव्वासिओ मि त्ति पयणुकामरिसो होंतो तो बहु कालं सारीरमाणसाणि दुक्खाणि णाणुहवेंतो — p. 263.

Mahārāṣṭrī, but current in Apabhraṁśa. In *Setu* 5.40, 42 Rāmadāsa reads *uvahi* for *uahi* (*udadhi*). The *va-śruti* of which *uvahi* is an example is a prominent feature of Apabhraṁśa.[425] The form *uvahi*, for instance, is used throughout the sea romance *Bhavisattakahā* of Dhanapāla. It is also occasionally found in Jaina Mahārāṣṭrī,[426] and used several times in the *Līlāvaī*,[427] the language of which has undergone considerable Apabhraṁśa influence. We have no information about the reading recorded by the commentators other than Rāmadāsa, but *SC* text and Laṭakanamiśra read *uahi* for *uvahi*. On the other hand, the latter reads *uvara* for *uara* in *Setu* 10.45, *uvara* being the equivalent of *udara* in Apabhraṁśa.

Lāvijjanta (*lāgyamāna*) for *lāvijjanta* in *Setu* 13.13 provides another example of *va-śruti* in our text (Rāmadāsa's recension). The verbal form *lāijjai* (*lāgyate*) occurs in *Setu* 4.35.[428] Mādhava and *SC* text in fact read *lāijjanta* for *lāvijjanta* in *Setu* 13.13. It may be noted that the root *lag* causative, rarely used in Sanskrit, gives rise to forms that are very much in evidence in Prākṛta and specially Apabhraṁśa texts, often with the *va-śruti*: e.g., *lāyai*, *lāvai* (cf. *joai*, *jovai see*),[429] *lāvahi* (imper.),[430] *lāijjaü*,[431] *lāia*,[432] etc.

A peculiar form *doṇha* occurs in *Setu* 15.18.[433] It is the genitive plural of *do*, but appears here in the nominative: *doṇha bhuā* "two arms". *Doṇha* as

---

425 Introduction (p. 25) to *Bhavisattakahā*, ed. Jacobi.

426 *KM*, pp. 14, l. 14; 26, l. 33; 34, l. 9; 35, l. 9; 56, l. 3; 60, l. 29; 91, l. 4; 217, l. 24, etc. *Gaüppannamahāpurisacariya* (PTS), p. 9, verse 27; *Nāṇapañcamīkahāo* (Singhi Jain series) 1.110, 454; 10.5, 61, etc.

427 See Glossary in Upadhye's edition.

428 Cf. अंगेसु लाइज्जइ चन्दणपंको — *KM*, p. 112, l. 30.

429 णउ लायइ कुंकुमु *Jasaharacariu* 1.22.2; एउ सेण्णु खरदूसणकेरउ . . . लायमि सम्बुकुमारहो पन्थें — *Paümacariu* 40.5.3; सीय तुहारए करयले लावमि — ibid. 45.15.3; णियगोत्ते कलंकउ लावमि — ibid 49.20.3.

430 दिणयरमण्डले दीवउ लावहि — ibid. 55.2.5.

431 रामहो गम्पि करे लाइज्जउ जणयसुय — ibid. 54.13.10.

432 सरधोरणि लाइय हणुव-धयवडे — ibid. 46.5.1; लाइउ केण हुवासणु — ibid. 47.6.8; अंकुसु लाइउ (v.r. लाविउ) — ibid. 11.7.5; लाइओ जलणो — *KM*, p. 108. l. 27; तिण्णि सायगा कुम्भीभागम्मि लाइया — *Vasu*, p. 44. l. 26; In *Setu* 2.26 (महि–लाइअं) *lāia* is rendered as *lāgita yojita* by Rāmadāsa in an alternative explanation.

433 This is the reading of Goldschmidt and *SC* Text. NS edn. has *doeha* which is an error and against metre.

an equivalent of *dvau* occurs also in *GS* 7.25.[434] Mādhava, on the other hand, reads *doṇṇa*, for *doṇha*. The form *doṇha* appears in Jaina Mahārāṣṭrī as *donna* with *donni* as a variant.[435] *Doṇha* and *doṇṇa* appear to be collateral forms going back to Prākṛta. *doṇṇi*, and seem to be taken from the colloquial language. Cf. Marāṭhī *don two* and OM *doni* expanded into *donhī*.[436]

A reference may be made to the particle *je* used in *Setu* 4.36: किं इच्छसि काउं जे पिअं ति विप्पिअं रहुवइणो. According to *HC* 2.217 it is used for *pādapūraṇa*.[437] *Je* is also found in Ardhamāgadhī, and it is nearly always used after an infinitive as in our poem.[438] The use of *je* seems to be an old idiom probably taken from the colloquial language. In fact, it is in Apabhraṁśa that we find it freely used, often for emphasis.[439] The cognate form *ji* likewise frequently occurs in Apabhraṁśa texts.[440]

434 तह तेण वि सा दिट्ठा तीअ वि तह तस्स पेसिआ दिट्ठी। जह दोण्ह वि समअं चिअ णिव्वुत्तरआइ जाआइ।। The *chāyā* has यथा द्वावपि सममेव र्निवृत्तरतौ जातौ.

435 Cf. दोन्न वि झाडिन्ति असिं दोन्न वि भिन्दन्ति महिवीढं — *Nāṇapañcamī* 1.174. In the preceding verse *donni* appears with donna as a variant. See the editor's footnotes.

436 *GOM*, p. 102.

437 Nemicandra says the same thing in his commentary on *Uttarādhyayanasūtra* 20.31.

438 E.g. जहा दुक्खं भरेउं जे होइ वायस्स कोत्थलो। तहा दुक्खं करेउं जे कीवेणं समत्तणं।। — *Uttarādhya*, 19.40; ibid. 19.39, 20.31, 22.21; *Nāyādhammakahāo* 9.90. 7, etc.

439 E.g. एक्कहो जे दुक्खु एक्कहो जे सुक्खु एक्कहो जे बन्धु एक्कहो जे मोक्खु।। एक्कहो जे पाउ एक्कहो जे धम्मु एक्कहो जे मरणु एक्कहो जे जम्मु।। — *Paümacariu* 54.7.8.9. *Je* is occasionally used in Jaina Mahārāṣṭrī, e.g. एवंविहम्मि कज्जे किं जुत्तं मज्झ एत्थ काउं जे *Nāṇapañcamī* 1.79. It occurs frequently in *KM* both in prose and verse, usually after an infinitive (pp. 2, 15, 34, 46, 48, 82, 90, 103, 108, etc.), but also independently as in Apabhraṁśa (see p. 31, ll. 26ff.).

440 Cf. *HC* 4.420 and *Apabhraṁśakāvyatrayī* (GOS), pp. 17, 68.

Setubandha

Text in Prakrit, Chāyā in Sanskrit,
English Translation and
Critical Notes

प्रथम आश्वासः
First Āśvāsakaḥ

1. णमह अवड्ढिअतुङ्गं अवसारिअवित्थअं अणोणअगहिरम्।
अप्पलहुअपरिसह्णं अणाअपरमत्थपाअडं महुमहणम्।।

[नमतावर्धिततुङ्गमप्रसारितविस्तृतमनवनतगभीरम्।
अप्रलघुकपरिश्लिक्ष्णमज्ञातपरमार्थप्रकटं मधुमथनम्।।]

Bow down to Viṣṇu, who is high without being heightened, pervasive without being stretched, deep without being low, infinitesimal without being light, and manifest, even though his true nature is unknown.

K reads अविसारित for *aavasāria* अप्रसारित (R and Kula).

K says अर्वार्धततुङ्गं केनचित् अर्वार्धतमपि तुङ्गम्। स्वभावेनैव तुङ्गं सर्वोन्नतम्। अनेन विश्वव्यापको विराट्स्वरूपो विष्णुरुच्यते। अविसारितविस्तृतं कैश्चिदविसारितमपि विस्तृतम्। अनवतगभीरम् अनवनतत्वेऽपि अनिम्नत्वेऽपि स्वत एव गभीरभगाधम्[1]। अप्रलघुकपरिश्लिक्ष्णं, प्रलघुरेव प्रलघुकः, अप्रलघुत्वेऽपि परिश्लिक्ष्णमतिसूक्ष्मं, सूक्ष्मलेशलवश्लक्ष्णक्षुद्रदभ्रकणाणवः इति हलायुधः। अज्ञातपरमार्थप्रकटम् – कैश्चिदपि अविज्ञातः परमार्थः यथार्थ्यं यस्य स तथोक्तः। अज्ञातपरमार्थत्वेऽपि प्रकटम् अतिप्रकाशम्। अथवा आकाशवायुवह्निजलभूमीनां परमात्मनः समुतपत्तिक्रमो वेदेन सर्मार्थतः। आत्मन आकाशः संभूत इत्यादिभिः वाक्यैः। परमात्मा हि पुरुषोत्तमः। तत्र आकाश ईश्वरेण वर्धित एवोत्तुङ्गो दृश्यते। तेनैव विस्तारिता पृथिवी विस्तृता। तेन निम्नीकृतमेव जलं गम्भीरं भवति। अतिलघुरेव सृष्टो वायुः सुसूक्ष्मः। ज्ञातस्वरूप एवाग्निः प्रकटो भवति। एतेभ्यो मधुमथनस्वरूपस्य व्यतिरेक उक्त इति स्वाभाविकविभावनाख्यश्चायमलङ्कार। तथा सरस्वतीकण्ठाभरणे समर्थितम्। वृत्तमार्यागीतिः।

MY says अथवावृद्धतुङ्गमित्यनेन उज्ज्वलनस्वभावतेजोरूपत्वमुच्यते। द्वितीयेन विशेषणेन पृथिवीमयत्वम्। तृतीयेन तोयात्मकत्वम्। चतुर्थेन वायुरूपत्वम्। पञ्चमेन आकाशमूर्तित्वमिति भगवतः सर्वात्मकत्वमुक्तं स्यादिति।

---

[1] SC says अनवखातगभीरम् . . . *oṇaa* – शब्दः अवखातशब्दोद्भवः। अवखाते देशीय इति केचित्। Rāmadṛṣṭi says न केनाप्यवनमितं अगाधतां न नीतं सगरसुतादिभिः समुद्रादिमिव तथाति गभीरमगाधम्।

MY remarks परिसूक्ष्ममिति केचित। This explanation is found in Kula who says प्रकृष्टो लघूः प्रलघुः स्वार्थे कन्। न तथा प्रलघुः। तथाविधमपि परि समन्तात् सूक्ष्मम्। अज्ञातपरमार्थमपि प्रकटं जगदुत्पत्तिस्थितिप्रलयहेतुं विष्णुम्। विष्णुरिति प्रकटस्याप्यस्य यत् परमार्थं, तन्न कोऽपि वेत्तीत्यर्थः। एतेन एतदुक्तं त्रैलोक्ये यत् किंचित . . . स्थूलसूक्ष्मादिवस्तुजातं तत् सर्वं विश्वमूर्तेः विष्णोः स्वाभाविकरूपम्। अतो वर्धनप्रसारणादेः लोके सिद्धहेतोरनवसर (?) एवेति। R has परिश्लिक्ष्ण – अप्रलघुको महांश्चासौ परिश्लक्ष्णः कृशश्चेति तथा। Kula also says किञ्चात्र . . . पञ्चमहाभूतात्मकहरिनमस्कारोऽपि . . . लक्ष्यते । तथाहि प्रथमेन पादेन आकाशम्। द्वितीयेन पृथिवी। तृतीयेन जलम्। चतुर्थेन पवनः तस्य महाबलपराक्रम . . . इन्द्रियाविषयत्वात परिसूक्ष्मता च। त्वगिन्द्रियेण स्पर्शमात्रं गृह्यते न वायुरिति न्यायमतम्। पञ्चमेन तेजः। तथा च वह्निरिति प्रकटोऽपि किमयं देवतारुपः, किं वा तेजोद्रव्य (रूपः) . . .।

2. दणुएन्दरुहिरलग्गे जस्स फुरन्ते णहप्पहाविच्छड्डे।
गुप्पन्ती विवलाआ गलिअ व्व थणंसुए महासुरलच्छी।।

[दनुजेन्द्ररुधिरलग्ने यस्य स्फुरति नखप्रभाविच्छर्दे।
व्याकुला विपलायिता गलित इव स्तनांशुके महासुरलक्ष्मीः।।]

When the radiant lusture of his nails disappeared[2] in the blood of Hiraṇyakaśipu, the Fortune of the great demon slunk away bewildered, as if her scarf had slipped off her bosom.[3]

K says दनुजेन्द्रो हिरण्यकशिपुः। तस्य वक्षःस्थलविदलने प्रवृत्तस्य यस्य स्फुरति प्रथमं वक्षसि स्तनांशुकवत् प्रकाशमाने नखप्रभासमूहे पश्चात् तस्य भिन्नवक्षसो रुधिरलग्ने रुधिरेषु निमग्ने सति महासुरस्य तस्यैव लक्ष्मीः स्तनांशुके गलिते इव गुप्यन्ती व्याकुलीभवन्ती विपलायिता। तं प्रणमतेति पूर्वेण संबन्धः। अयमर्थः-महासुरवक्षःस्थलनिवासिनी दानवश्रीः प्रथमं निजस्तनांशुकवत् प्रकाशमाने नरसिंहस्य नखप्रभाविताने सद्य एव भिन्नहृदयस्य दैत्यस्य वक्षोरुधिरनिमग्ने सति अपहृतस्तनांशुकेव पर्याकुलीभवन्ती देवस्य पुरः स्थातुमसमर्था लज्जातिरेकात् म्रियमाणं भर्तारमपि परित्यज्य शीघ्रं प्रयातेति। उत्तरभूमौ हि स्त्रियः परिधानीयमिव स्तनाशुकं संततं धारयन्तीति प्रसिद्धम्।

---

2 Lit. got stuck.

3 The reference is to the Man–Lion incarnation of Viṣṇu and the slaying of Hiraṇyakaśipu by him. The lustre of the claws of the deity is likened to that of the scarf covering the bosom of the goddess of fortune attending upon the great demon. It is also fancied that when the dazzling claws of Narasiṁha suddenly disappeared, having penetrated the victim's bosom, she ran away in confusion, thinking that her scarf had slipped off her breast.

3. पीणत्तणदुग्गेज्झं जस्स भुआअन्तणिट्ठुरपरिग्गहिअम्।
रिट्ठस्स विसमवलिअं कण्ठं दुःखेण जीविअं बोलीणम्।।

[पीनत्वदुर्ग्राह्यं यस्य भुजान्तनिष्ठुरपरिगृहीतम्।
अरिष्टस्य विषमवलितं कण्ठं दुःखेन जीवितं व्यतिक्रान्तम्।।]

Life departed with toil and trouble from the severely twisted neck of the bull demon Ariṣṭa, hard to grasp because of its massive size, when it was cruelly gripped by his encircling arms.[4]

K says अरिष्टो नाम वृषभाकृतिः कंसामात्यो महासुरः। अरिष्टशब्दस्य आद्यक्षरलीपः। पीनत्वात् दुर्ग्रहम् अतिमेदुरत्वादन्यैः ग्रहीतुमशक्यं, यस्य कृष्णस्य भुजायन्त्रेण भुजद्वयमण्डलेन निष्टुरमतिदृढं परिगृहीतं, विषमवलितं भृशं विवर्तितम् अरिष्टस्य कण्ठं जीवितं तस्य जीवं दुःखेन अतिकृच्छ्रात अतिक्रान्तमतीत्य गतम्। वस्त्रवत् कण्ठनिष्पीडनात् वक्रीकृतेन कण्ठनालेन कथञ्चित् निर्गतमित्यर्थः। MY remarks विषमवलितत्वं जीवितस्य दुःखेनातिक्रमणहेतुः। Kula says कण्ठं कर्मभूतं जीवितं कर्तृ। The verse is quoted in *Sarasvatīkaṇṭhābharaṇa* 3.49 with the remark: अत्र जीवितदुःखातिक्रमणे कण्ठस्य वलनं, वलनस्य निष्ठुरग्रहणं, निष्ठुरग्रहणस्यापि पीनत्वेन दुर्ग्राह्यत्वं हेतुरिति प्रतीयमानकारणत्वं कारणमालेति अहेतुभेदः।

4. ओआहिअमहिवेढो जेण परूढगुणमूललद्धत्थामो।
उम्मूलन्तेण दुमं पारोहो व्व खुडिओ महेन्दस्स जसो।।
(आइकुलअम्)

[अवगाहितमहीवेष्टं येन प्ररूढगुणमूललब्धस्थाम।
उन्मूलयता द्रुमं प्ररोह इव खण्डितं महेन्द्रस्य यशः।।]
(आदिकुलकम्)

When he uprooted the *pārijāta* tree (from heaven), Indra's fame pervading the earth, and deep-rooted because of his eminent qualities, was destroyed by him, like the branch-root of a tree[5] that goes deep into the earth, and is firmly established on account of the roots and rootlets growing into the soil.

---

[4] This and the next verse refer to the Kṛṣṇa incaranation of Viṣṇu.

[5] E.g. the banyan tree "from whose branches grow shoots that take root and become new trunks".

K and MY *pratīka* has *ovāhia* (अवमाढ़ MY) for *oāhia* (R). Kula is uncertain, but he has अवागाढ़[6]

K says द्रुमः पारिजातः। पारिजातयशसोः साम्यमुच्यते। यशःशब्दस्य 'नसान्तप्रावृट्शरदः पुंसीति' (Vararuki 4.18) पुंलिङ्गता। अपगाढमहीवेष्टं व्याप्तमहीमण्डलम्। प्ररोहपक्षे अन्तर्व्याप्तमहीतलः। प्ररूढगुणमूललब्धस्थाम प्ररूढा प्रसिद्धाः गुणा एव मूलं कारणं तेन लब्धस्थाम लब्धस्थैर्यम्। अथवा प्ररूढगुणमूलत्वात लब्धस्थाम। अन्यत्र मूलं शिफा, गुणाः क्षुद्रशिफाः। अधःप्रसृतगुणमूलत्वात् लब्धस्थामा। एवंभूतं महेन्द्रस्य यशः द्रुममुन्मूलयता नन्दनवनादुद्धरता येन त्रुटितमुच्छिन्नम्। किमिव – प्ररोह इव। प्ररोहो नाम प्लक्षन्यग्रोधादीनां शाखामुखाधस्तात् प्रसृताः पादाः। तत् कल्पवृक्षस्यापि संभवतीति एवमुक्तम्। प्ररोहशब्दस्य समृद्धयादिगणत्वादाकारः।

Kula says येन कृष्णावतारे सत्यभामायाः प्रसादनार्थं द्वारवत्यामानेतुं द्रुमं पारिजातमुन्मूलयता प्ररोह इव शाखाशिफेव महेन्द्रस्य यशः खण्डितं तं नमतेति। . . . प्ररोहस्तु प्ररूढा गुणाः तन्तवो यस्य मूलस्य तेन लब्धस्थामा।

5. णमह अ जस्स फुडरवं कण्ठच्छाआघडन्तणअणग्गिसिहम्।
फुरइ फुरिअट्टहासं उद्धपडित्ततिमिरं विअ दिसाअक्कम्।।

[नमत च यस्य स्फुट रवं कण्ठच्छायाघटमाननयनाग्निशिखम्।
स्फुरति स्फुरिताट्टहासमूर्धप्रदीप्ततिमिरमिव दिक्चक्रम्।।]

Bow down to him[7] (during whose evening dance[8]), the regions of the sky, resounding with his loud laughter, glimmer as the flame of his eyes blends with the lustre of his (deep blue) neck, and seem to be enveloped in darkness surmounted by flames.[9]

K says यस्य नृत्यतो महेश्वरस्य परितो दिक्चक्रमेवं प्रतिभाति। तं च नमतेति सम्बन्धः। कीदृग्भूतम – स्फुरिताट्टहासं प्रतिफलिताट्टहासम्, अत एव स्फुटरवं, कण्ठच्छायाघटमाननयनाग्निशिखं चक्रनृत्ते क्रियमाणे देवस्य कण्ठप्रभया संयुज्यमाननयनाग्निज्वालं, परितः प्रसरन्त्या कण्ठविषत्विषा घटमाननयनाग्नेः शिखा यस्य तत्तथाभूतम्। तदानीमूर्ध्वप्रदीप्ततिमिरमिव ऊर्ध्वमुपरिभागे प्रज्वलितं तिमिरं यस्य तत्तथा। प्रदीपादयो हि अधःप्रसृततिमिरा भवन्ति। दिक्चक्रमपि तद्वदूर्ध्वप्रज्वलिततिमिरमिव स्फुरतीति। ज्वलनक्रिया च ध्वनिमती भवतीति स्फुटरवमित्युक्तम्। MY says दिक्चक्रमूर्ध्वप्रदीप्ततिमिरमिव प्रतिभाति। यत्र काष्ठादिवत् तिमिरं दह्यमानोर्ध्वप्रदेशमिव दृश्यते तत्तथोक्तम्।

---

6 Hemacandra 4.205 gives *ovāhai* as equivalent of *ogāhai*.

7 Refer to Śiva who is described in verses 5-8.

8 Cf. *Naiṣadhacarita* 22.7, 8.

9 Lit. darkness set on fire at the top.

6. वेवइ जस्स सविडिअं वलिउं महइ पुलआइअत्थणअलसम्।
पेम्मसहावविमुहिअं वीआवासगमणूसुअं वामद्धम्।।

[वेपते यस्य सव्रीडं वलितुं महति पुलकाचितस्तनकलशम्।
प्रेमस्वभावविमुषितं द्वितीयावकाशगमनोत्सुकं वामार्धम्।।]

His left half,[10] overpowered by love, with the ample bosom thrilling with rapture, quivers bashfully as it yearns to turn round in its eagerness to encompass the other half.

K has पुलकाञ्चित for pulaāia पुलकाचित। He says यस्य वामार्घमेवंभवति तं नमतेति। मिलिताङ्गत्वेऽपि गाढोपगूहनमुखकान्तिदर्शनचुम्बनादीनां शरीरपृथग्भाव-सुलभानाम् अननुभवात् विप्रयोग इव कामातुरं भवतीति भावः। प्रथमं सव्रीलितं वेपते। व्रीलैव व्रीलितम्। भावे निष्ठाप्रत्ययः। पत्युरतिसन्निकर्षात् सव्रीलं भूत्वा साध्वसाद्वेपते। अयमभिप्रायः – आलम्बनविभावभूतस्य देवस्य सन्निधानादवतरता रत्याख्येन स्थायिभावेनैवम् आकुलीभवतीति। अनन्तरमनुभावैः सात्त्विकैश्च पुलकाञ्चितस्तनकलशं पुलकपूरितस्तनकलशं भूत्वा वलितुमिच्छति। इच्छतेः महशब्दादेशः। चलितुमिच्छति भावपरिणामानुरूपं किंचित् चेष्टितुमिच्छतीत्यर्थः। अनन्तरक्षणे व्यभिचारिभिः त्रयस्त्रिंशता रसत्वेन परिणमता भावेन प्रेमस्वभावविमोहितम्। प्रेम प्रणयोत्कर्षः। यथोक्तं भावविवेके –

इतरेतरसंयोगप्ररूढमदबृंहितम्।
यद् गात्राणां सुखकरं प्रणयः स निगद्यते।।

स एव प्रचयाद्वस्तुप्रयुक्तो विवशं नरम्।
संततं तत्समीपे तु क्षिपन् प्रेमतयोदितः।।"

इति। तत्समीपे पत्युः समीपे प्रेरयन्नित्यर्थः। एवंलक्षणस्य प्रेम्णः स्वभावेन मोहितं कृत्याकृत्यविवेकरहितं भूत्वा द्वितीयपार्श्वगमनोत्सुकम् अर्धात्मना पृथग्भाव-मसहमानमीश्वरभागमपि व्याप्तुमुत्सुकं भवतीति।

MY says गतभूयिष्ठत्वेऽपि लज्जायाः सविशेषतया वलितुं परावृत्य अवस्थातुमिच्छति। अथवा प्रेमवशात् क्षणार्धमपि व्याप्यावस्थातुमभिलषतीत्यर्थः।

Kula says अर्धनारिश्वररूपमाह। यस्य वामार्धं स्त्र्यात्मकं द्वितीयावकाशे पुरुषात्मकदक्षिणार्धे गमनोत्सुकं यत् वलितुं वाञ्छति तं नमत। स्वयमभिगमनेच्छया सव्रीडं कलङ्कसाध्वसवशाच्च वेपते। भाववशात् पुलकाचितस्तनकलशं . . . । स्त्रीणां स्नेहधर्म एवायं यदनुरागेऽपि वाम्योपदर्शनम्। एतेन सुभगत्वस्तुतिरियं देवस्य।

7. जस्स विलग्गन्ति णहं फुडपडिसद्दा दिसाअलपडिक्खलिआ।
जोण्हाकल्लोला विअ ससिधवलासु रअणीसु हसिअच्छेआ।।

---

[10] I.e. the female half, a reference to the Ardhanārīśvara form of Śiva.

[यस्य विलगन्ति नभः स्फुटप्रतिशब्दा दिक्तलप्रतिस्खलिताः।
ज्योत्स्नाकल्लोला इव शशिधवलासु रजनीषु हसितच्छेदाः॥]

On moonlit nights, the resonant outbursts of his laughter (while dancing), reverberating in the regions of the sky, reach the heavens, like ripples of moonbeams.[11]

K, MY and Kula read दिक्तट (*disā-aḍa*) for *disā-ala* दिक्तल (R)।

K says नृत्यतो यस्य हसितच्छेदाः अट्टहासविभागाः एवं भवन्ति। तं नमतेति सम्बन्धः। कथंभूताः – दिशां पर्यन्ता दिक्तटाः तेषु प्रतिस्खलिताः अण्डकटाहभित्तौ प्रतिहता इति यावत्। अत एव स्फुटप्रतिशब्दाः विजृम्भितप्रतिध्वनयः शशिधवलासु रजनीषु ज्योत्स्नामयाः कल्लोला इव। हासस्य दन्तप्रभामयत्वात् एवमुक्तम्। नभो विलगन्ति आरोहन्ति। लगतिरत्र सकर्मकः। सन्ध्यासु नृत्यतो यस्य एवंरूपा हासविभागा ज्योत्स्नालहर्य इव नभः पूरयन्तीति। अथवा शशिधवलासु रजनीषु ज्योत्स्नाकल्लोला यथा दिगन्तान् पूरयित्वा नभः पूरयन्ति तद्वदिहापि यस्याट्टहासाः नभः पूरयन्तीति योज्यम्।

MY says यस्य वा धवलतरा हसितच्छेदा दिक्तटप्र(ति)स्खलिततया स्फुटप्रतिशब्दतया च ज्योत्स्नायां कल्लोलवत् प्रतिभासमाना वृद्धिवशात् नभो विलगन्तीत्यर्थः।

Kula reads *valagganti* आरोहन्ति (Hemacandra 4.206) for *vilagganti*. He remarks तटप्रतिस्खलनं.... नभोलङ्घनं च कल्लोलसाधर्म्यं हसितच्छेदानामुक्तम्।

8. णट्टारम्भक्खुहिआ जस्स भडब्भन्तमच्छपहअजलरआ।
होन्ति सलिलुद्धुमाइअधूमाअन्तवडवामुहा मअरहरा॥
(आइकुलअम्)

[नृत्यारम्भक्षुभिता यस्य भयोद्भ्रान्तमत्स्यप्रहतजलरयाः।
भवन्ति सलिलोद्ध्मापितधूमायमानवडवामुखा मकरगृहाः॥]
(आदिकुलकम्)

The oceans are convulsed when begins to dance,[12] with the swirling water struck by the fish, crazed with fear, and the submarine fire belching forth smoke, being submerged by the waves.

K reads उद्वृत्त (*uvvatta*) for *ubbhanta* उद्भ्रान्त (R), and *jalaharā* for *jala-raā* – रयाः (R),– रवाः (Kula)।

---

[11] In *kāvya* poetry a laugh is always described as white.

[12] I.e. as a result of the earthquake caused by the movement of Śiva's feet.

K says यस्य नृत्तारम्भेण क्षुभिता: पादाभिघातचलितमहीतलया क्षुभिता:, भयोद्वृत्तै: भयादूर्ध्वमुच्चलितै: मत्स्यै: प्रहतमेघा: मकरगृहा: समुद्रा: सलिलेनातिवृद्धेन उत्थापितत्वात् (*chāyā* has सलिलोत्थापित) पूरितत्वात् धूमायमानवडवामुखा भवन्ति। तं नमतेति योजना।

Kula says भयेनोद्भूतै: (?) मत्स्यै: तिमिप्रभृतिभि: प्रहतजलरवा: . . . सलिलै: ध्मातत्वात् धूमायामान, etc. He seems to read *saliladdhumāia* for *salilu*, — like manuscript C of Goldschmidt. *SC* says सलिलेनाध्माता आपूरिता: सन्तो धूमायमाना वडवामुखा वडवानला येषु।

9. अहिणवराआरद्धा चुक्कक्खलिएषु विहडिअपरिट्ठविआ।
मेत्ति व्व पमुहरसिआ णिव्वोढुं होइ दुक्करं कव्वकहा।।

[अभिनवराजारब्धा च्युतस्खलितेषु विघटितपरिस्थापिता।
मैत्रीव प्रमुखरसिका निर्वोढुं भवति दुष्करं काव्यकथा।।]

Begun with fresh ardour, and amended when marred by flaws due to inattention, a poetical composition is delightful in the beginning, but hard to complete with success, even like friendship, which too, begins when affection is fresh, and is restored when disrupted by faults and mistakes.

K, MY and Kula read प्रतिष्ठापिता for परि – (R)।

K says पूर्वमभिनवेन रागेण अभिनिवेशेन आरब्धा, तत: प्रमादस्खलितेषु अनवधानात् शब्देषु अर्थेषु वा स्खलितेषु विघटिता शिथिला पुन: प्रतिष्ठापिता समाहिता, प्रमुखे आरम्भावस्थायां रसिका सरसा काव्यकथा काव्यस्य कथनं रचना निर्वोढुं निर्धर्तयितुं दुष्करं यथा स्यात् तथा भवति। अविच्छेदेन निर्वर्तयितुमशक्येत्यर्थ:। किमिव – मैत्रीव। (सा) च कयोश्चति पूर्वमभिनवेन स्नेहेन प्रारब्धा प्रामादापराधेषु विघटिता पुन: स्थापिता प्रमुखे सरसा निर्वोढुं दुष्करा भवतीति। दुष्करमिति सामान्यनिर्देशात् नपुंसकम्। Kula says काव्यकथा मैत्री च दु:खेन समाप्तिं नीयत इत्यर्थ:।

MY says रागस्य अभिनवत्वमतिशयवत्वम्। *paḍiṭṭhaviā* प्रतिष्ठिापिता . . . निवेशितरूपान्तरा। *pamuha-rasiā* प्रमुखरसा काव्यकथा काव्यरूढा कथेत्यर्थ:। R says *cukka-* शब्द: प्रमादे देशी इति केचित्।

10. परिवड्ढइ विण्णाणं संभाविज्जइ जसो विढप्पन्ति गुणा।
सुव्वइ सुउरिसचरिअं किं तं जेण ण हरन्ति कव्वालावा।।

[परिवर्धते विज्ञानं संभाव्यते यशोऽर्ज्यन्ते गुणा:।
श्रूयते सुपुरुषचरितं किं तद्येन न हरन्ति काव्यालापा:।।]

Is there a way in which poetical compositions do not delight the heart? Through them knowledge increases, fame is won, virtues are acquired, and the life-history of good men is known.

K read विसर्पन्ति for *viḍhappanti* अर्ज्यन्ते (R and Kula)।

K says काव्यस्व श्रोतृणां प्रथमं विज्ञानं परिवर्धते शब्दार्थविमर्शसंस्कारेण विज्ञानं भूयो वर्धते। यशः संभाव्यते जनैः। तथा गुणाः शिक्षागुणाः विसर्पन्ति लोके प्रसरन्ति। सुपुरुषस्य कथानायकस्य चरितं श्रूयते। एवं काव्यालापाः काव्यकथा येन वस्तुना न हरन्ति मनो न हरन्ति तत् किं न किंचिदित्यर्थः।

Kula says धर्मार्थकामशास्त्रार्थज्ञानं तस्याङ्गत्वेन निबद्धं, तदध्येतृणां विज्ञानबुद्धिर्भवतीति भावः। संभाव्यते यशः काव्याभ्यासेन कवित्वलाभात् काव्य . . . लभ्यते। गुणाः शौर्यादयो लभ्यन्ते काव्ये शौर्यादिगुणस्तुतिदर्शनात् तदुपार्जनरसः . . . भवतीति भावः। . . . काव्यालापाः काव्यमिव आलप्यन्त इति काव्यशब्दवाच्यप्रबन्धा इत्यर्थः।

MY says न हरन्ति नाकर्षन्ति न स्वश्रवणे प्रवर्तयन्ति। तदनर्थहेतुत्वरूपं वा निमितं किं, न किंचिदित्यर्थः।

11. इच्छाइ व धणरिद्धी जोव्वणलद्ध व्व आहिआईअ सिरी।
दुःखं संभाविज्जइ बन्धच्छाआइ अहिणवा अत्थगई।।

[इच्छयेव धनऋद्धिर्यौवनलब्धेवाभिजात्या श्रीः।
दुःखं संभाव्यते बन्धच्छाययाभिनवार्थगतिः।।]

It is hard to combine new ideas[13] with beauty of composition, just as it is hard to combine riches, acquired in one's youth, with decorous conduct, or to make the acquisition of wealth conform to one's desire.

K reads संपाद्यते for *saṁbhāvijjai* संभाव्यते (R and Kula)।

K says अभिनवा पूर्वैरनुक्ता अर्थगतिः अभिधेयपद्धतिः बन्धच्छायया संदर्भशोभया दुःखं कृच्छ्रात संपाद्यते। आनुकूल्यं संपादः। समुद्रसदृशस्य काव्यस्यार्थसमृद्ध्या संपादः कदाचिदपि न भवति। अभिनवः अर्थविशेषो लब्धश्चेत् शब्दरचनागुणेन सम्यगवधारयितुं न शक्यत इत्यर्थः। किमिव – इच्छया आशाया धनसमृद्धिरिव। अर्थविभूतिराशया संपादयितुं यथा न शक्यते। तथा यौवने लब्धा श्रीः अभिजात्येव। अभिजातिः अभिजः वंशगुणः। अनेन विनयादये उच्यन्ते। MY says धनर्द्ध्यादयः इच्छादिभिः सह दुःखं क्लेशेन अविरोधमापाद्यन्ते पुरुषेणेति वाक्यार्थः।

[13] Lit. a new range of meaning.

Kula says अपूर्ववस्तुपादानात् अभिनवानामर्थानां प्रमेयाणां गतिः प्रस्थानं बन्धानां मृदुस्फुटोन्मिश्रधर्मप्रभवतया द्विविधानां छायया शोभाया दुःखं यथा स्यात् तथा संभाव्यते योज्यते। तथा धनऋद्धिः (इव) इच्छया। इच्छानुरूपो हि विभवो दुर्लभः। यौवनमेव तावत् मदहेतुः, तेन लब्धा तु श्रीः सुतरामेव। अतः सा यथा अभिजात्या कुलीनतया(?) (तदा)त्मनाचारेण दुःखं योज्यत[14] इत्यर्थः R says संभाव्यते संबध्यते।

12. तं तिअसबन्दिमोक्खं समत्थतेल्लोक्कहिअअसल्लुद्धरणम्।
सुणह अणुराअइण्हं सीआदुक्खक्खअं दहमुहस्स वहम्।।

[तं त्रिदशबन्दिमोक्षं समस्तत्रैलोक्यहृदयशल्योद्धरणम्।
शृणुतानुरागचिह्नं सीतादुःखक्षयं दशमुखस्य वधम्।।]

Hearken to the story of the slaying of Rāvaṇa, which brought Sītā's sufferings to an end, and the declared Rāma's love for her,[15] and led to the release of the captive nymphs, and removed, as it were, a dart from the hearts of the people of the entire universe.

K says चिह्ने न्ध इति न्धादेशः (Vararuci 3.34) which shows that he reads *aṇurāa — cindhaṁ* or *indhaṁ* for — *iṇhaṁ*.

MY says आयुर्घृतमितिवत् रावणवधस्य तत्साधनतयोपचारात् त्रिदशवन्दीमोक्षादिरूपत्वे विवक्षिते तद्भिधाय तस्यास्य काव्यस्यापि तत्तद्विशेषणसामानाधिकरण्य-मुपपन्नमित्यवसेयम्।

13–14. अह पडिवण्णविरोहे राहववम्महसरेण माणब्भहिए।
विद्धाइ वालिहिअए राअसिरीअ अहिसारिए सुग्गीवे।।१३।।

ववसाअरइपओसो रोसगइन्ददिढसिङ्खलापडिबन्धो।
कह कह वि दासरहिणो जअकेसरिपञ्जरो गओ घणसमओ।।१४।।
(जुग्गअम्)

[अथ प्रतिपन्नविरोधे राघवमन्मथशरेण मानाभ्यधिके।
विद्धया वालिहृदये राजश्रियाभिसारिते सुग्रीवे।।

व्यवसायरविप्रदोषो रोषगजेन्द्रदृढशृङ्खलाप्रतिबन्धः।
कथंकथमपि दाशरथेर्जयकेसरिपञ्जरो गतो घनसमयः।।]
(युग्मकम्)

---

[14] Our copy has मुह्यते।

[15] Also: "marked by the word *anurāga*" at the end of each canto.

When Royal Fortune accepted Sugrīva for her consort, after her proud and hostile heart, namely, Vāli, had been pierced[16] by Rāma's arrow, Cupid's dart as it were[17] (at that time); Rāma had somehow passed the rainy season that was, as it were, nightfall to the sun of his endeavour; a strong chain restraining the mighty elephant, his wrath; and a cage imprisoning the lion, his victory (in the coming war).[18]

K says अथशब्दो वालिवधस्य आनन्तर्यमाह। अत्र सुग्रीवो नायकत्वेन कल्पित: राजश्रीश्च नायिकात्वेन। तस्या अभिसारणधर्मा उच्यन्ते। वाल्येव हृदयं वालिहृदयं, प्रतिपन्नविरोधे सुग्रीवं प्रति बद्धविरोधे, मानाभ्यधिके वालिमयहृदये राघवमन्मथशरेण विद्धया राजश्रिया सुग्रीवे अभिसारिते सति। मानिनीहृदयं च भर्तरि प्राप्तविरोधं मानाभ्यधिकं च भवतीत्युत्तरत्न सम्बन्ध:।

Kula says राघवो मन्मथ इव, तस्य शरेण प्रहृतत्वात्(?) वाली हृदयमिव, तस्मिन् विद्धया राजश्रिया सुग्रीवे अभिसारिते कृताभिषेके सति। . . . प्रतिपन्नविरोधे इत्याभिसारिकाहृदयस्य वालिना तुल्यं विशेषणम्।

K says घनसमयो वर्षाकालो दाशरथे: कथं कथमपि गत: अतिकृच्छ्रादतीत:। कथंभूत: – व्यवसायरवे: रामस्य कार्यव्यवसायसूर्यस्य प्रदोषभूत: etc. *SC* says व्यवसाय: कार्योद्यम:।

15. गमिआ कलम्बवाआ दिट्ठं मेहन्धआरिअं गअणअलम्।
सहिओ गज्जिअसद्दो तह वि हु से णत्थि जीविए आसङ्घो।।

[गमिता: कदम्बवाता दृष्टं मेघान्धकारितं गगनतलम्।
सोढो गर्जितशब्दस्तथापि खल्वस्या नास्ति जीवितेऽध्यवसाय: (आसङ्ग:)।।]

He had lived through the breezes of the *kadamba* groves, seen the sky obscured by the clouds, and endured the rumble of thunder, yet verily, he had no confidence in his life.[19]

K says ये कदम्बवातादयो विरहिणां महान्ति प्रमादस्थानानि रामेण तु धैर्यातिशयात्

---

16 Lit. Royal Fortune who was pierced in her heart that was Vāli.

17 I.e. when Sugrīva was placed on the throne by Rāma after killing Vāli. The latter is fancied as the proud heart of the goddess of royal fortune, represented as a *nāyikā* hostile to Sugrīva. Rāma's arrow, fancied as Cupid's dart, pierces her heart, i.e. Vāli, inclining her to accept her new lover.

18 The rainy season is so described, because it halted Rāma's warlike preparations for the recovery of Sītā.

19 I.e. Rāma had somehow passed the rainy season believed to be unbearable to separated lovers, but the advent of the autumn filled him with despair.

कथंचित् अतिक्रान्ताः। तथाप्यागच्छतः शरत्कालस्य असह्यत्वात् जीवितं प्रति विश्वासो नासीत्। आसंघशब्दो देशीति विशासपर्यायः।

MY explains the word as आशंसा–निश्चय इत्यर्थः। विरहानलसंधुक्षणानां कदम्बवातादीनां गमितवेऽपि नास्य जीविते निश्चयः विरहाग्नेः पूर्वतो निर्विशेषत्वात्। Kula says रागस्य तीव्रतमत्वात् तत्प्रशमहेतोः सीतालाभस्य रावणवधस्य च सन्दिग्धत्वात्।

16. तो हरिवइजसवन्थो राहवजीअस्स पढमहत्थालम्बो।
सीआबाहविहाओ दहमुहवज्झदिअहो उवगओ सरओ।।

[ततो हरिपतियशःपथो राघवजीवस्य प्रथमहस्तालम्बः।
सीताबाष्पविघातो दशमुखवध्यदिवस उपगता शरत्।।]

Then came the autumn, the pathway to Sugrīva's fame, the initial succour to Rāma's life, the hindrance to Sītā's tears, the day of Rāvaṇa's doom.[20]

K says हरिपतेः सुग्रीवस्य यशःपथः रामकार्यप्रवृत्तस्य सुग्रीवस्य यशःप्रसारणमार्गो यात्राकालत्वात्। राघवजीवस्य प्रथमो हस्तालम्बः, सीतायाः वाष्पविच्छेदकारी, दशमुखस्य वध्यदिवसो वधार्हदिवसः। अर्हे कृत्यतृचश्चेत्यर्हार्थे यप्रत्ययः। एवंरूपिता शरदुपागता। शरदो द इति दकारादेशः। It will be seen that K reads *sarado* for *sarao* following Vararuci 4.10.

Kula says राघवजीवस्य प्रथमो हस्तावलम्बः, कार्यानुगुणत्वात् शरत्कालस्य तमालम्ब्य स्थैर्यलाभात्। सीताबाष्पविघातः, विहन्यते अनेनेति विघातः।

17. रइअरकेसरणिवहं सोहइ धवलब्भदलसहस्सपरिगअम्।
महुमहदंसणजोग्गं पिआमहुप्पत्तिपङ्कअं व णहअलम्।।

[रविकरकेसरनिवहं शोभते धवलाभ्रदलसहस्रपरिगतम्।
मधुमथनदर्शनयोग्यं पितामहोत्पत्तिपङ्कजमिव नभस्तलम्।।]

The sky, a worthy sight for Viṣṇu, looked beautiful like the lotus whence Brahmā was born.[21] It was covered with banks of white clouds, thousands of petals, as it were; while the rays of the sun were the mass of filaments.

---

[20] The autumn, the season of military expeditions, is described as heralding the fulfilment of Rāma's hopes and the success of his ally Sugrīva and the destruction of Rāvaṇa.

[21] I.e. the autumn sky was fit to be seen by Viṣṇu at the end of his sleep during the rainy season. The lotus in question grew out of his navel.

K says प्राकृतेषु लडन्तानि पदानि भूतार्थानि द्रष्टव्यानि। नभस्तलमशोभत। किमिव – पितामहोत्पत्तिपङ्कजमिव नारायणनाभिकमलमिव। कीदृग्भूतम् – रविकरकेसरनिवहं रविकिरणमयकेसरनिवहयुक्त म्। रविरेव कर्णिकात्वे कविना कल्पित इति बोद्धव्यम्। धवलानि अभ्रदलानि मेघशकलान्येव दलसहस्रं तेन परिगतम्। नाभिसमुत्पन्नत्वात् मधुमथनदर्शनस्य योग्यं पितामहोत्पत्तिकमलं भवति। नभस्तलमपि तदानीं शरदि योगनिद्राविरामात् मधुमथनस्य दर्शनयोग्यं भवतीति।

MY says रविकराणां केसरत्ववर्णनात् तद्बिम्बं कर्णिकात्वेन सिध्यति नभसो मधुमथनदर्शनयोग्यत्वं तस्य तदानीं प्रबोधात्। पङ्कजस्य तु तथात्वमाभिमुख्येन नाभ्यामवस्थानात्। Kula says अधोमुखपद्माकारत्वेन प्रतीयमानत्वात् प्रसिद्धविबोधस्य मधुमथनस्य दर्शनयोगयम्। सुप्तोत्थितानां हि महतां शङ्खादर्शपद्मादिप्रशस्तदर्शनमुचितम्। . . . महत्त्वात् पितामहोत्पत्तिपङ्कजमिव गगनतले राजते।

18. दिणमणिमोहप्फुरिअं गलिअं घणलच्छिरअणरसणादामम्।
उदुमअणबाणवत्तं णहमन्दारणवकेसरं इन्दधणुम्।।

[दिनमणिमयूखस्फुरितं गलितं धनलक्ष्मीरत्नरशनादाम।
ऋतुमदनबाणवक्त्रं नभोमन्दारनवकेसरमिन्द्रधनुः।।]

The rainbow, a flash from the rays of the sun, departed from the sky: it was, as it were, the bejewelled girdle of the beauty of the clouds; a quiver for the arrows of the god of love in the shape of the season of rains;[22] a fresh filament, as it were, of a flower of the *mandara* tree that was the sky.

K says दिनमणिमयूखैः स्फुरितं जलशीकरमिश्रैः दिनकररश्मिभिः उद्भूतं, धनलक्ष्मया मेघश्रियो रत्नरशनादाम, ऋतुरेव मदनः तस्य बाणपात्रं तूणीरं, नभोमन्दारवृक्षस्य नवकेसरमिन्द्रधनुः गलितं मेघेभ्य इति शेषः।

MY says *moha* मयूख। रविकिरणस्फुरणात् घनेषु आविर्भूतम्। अथवा दिनमेव मणितस्य मयूखस्फुरणम्। ऋतुरेव मदनबाणस्तस्य पत्रं निर्वाहकमित्यर्थः। Kula says दिनमणेः सूर्यस्य मयूखानां स्फुरितं रविरश्मेर्विकास एवेन्द्रधनुरित्यर्थः। नायिकाया इव धनलक्ष्म्या नानारत्नमयं काञ्चीदामेव। ऋतुर्वर्षाख्यो मदन इव तस्य बाणानां पात्रं सन्धानयोग्यम्।

19. धुअमेहमहुअराओ घणसमआअड्ढिओणअविमुक्काओ।
णहपाअवसाहाओ णिअअट्ठाणं व पडिगआओ दिसाओ।।

[धुतमेघमधुकरा घनसमयाकृष्टावनतविमुक्ताः।
नभःपादपशाखा निजकस्थानमिव प्रतिगता दिशः।।]

---

[22] The rainy season is intimately associated with love in *kāvya* poetry.

The regions of the sky, branches, as it were, of the tree was the firmament, drawn down by the rainy season, and then released, seemed to have returned to their respective places, shaking off the bees in the shape of the clouds.[23]

K says घनसमय इति कश्चित् पुरुष उच्यते। नभोमयस्य पादपस्य शाखाभूता दिशो घनसमयेन आकृष्टाः संकोचिताः अतः एव अवनताः मेघाच्छन्नात्वादानताः ततः शरदि विमुक्ताः,घुतमेघमधुकराः विधुतमेघाख्यभ्रमराः भूत्वा निजं स्थानमाकर्षणात् पूर्वावस्थानं प्रतिगतत्वात् अप्रकाशाः शरदि मेघापायात् प्रकाशा दिशः कविनैवमुत्प्रेक्षिताः।

Kula says नभसः पादपस्येव शाखा इव दिशः घनसमयेनाकृष्टाः सद्योऽवनता इव संनिहिताः कृताः पश्चात् विमुक्ताः। अतो निजस्थानं पूर्वस्थानं प्रतिगता इव मेघावरणापगमात् दूरे तासां प्रतीयमानत्वात्। वेगेन गमनात् धुता मेघा मधुकरा (इव) यासां तास्तथा।

The verse is quoted in *Sarasvatīkaṇṭhābharaṇa* 4.47 with the remark: अत्र पादपरूपेण रूपितस्य नभसो यदेतत् दिशां शाखारूपेण रूपणं मेघानां च मधुकरप्रकरेण तदुभय मप्यन्यपदार्थषष्ठीसमासयोरभिधीयमानेन सावयवं निरवयवं चेत्युत्प्रेक्षया च संकीर्यमाणमुभयसंकीर्णरूपकव्यपदेशं लभते।

20. अहिणवणिद्धालोआ उद्देसासारदीसमाणजललवा।
णिम्माअमज्जणसुहा दरवसुआअच्छविं वहन्ति व दिअहा।।

[अभिनवस्निग्धालोका उद्देशासारदृश्यमानजललवाः।
निर्मितमज्जनसुखा दरशुष्कच्छविं वहन्तीव दिवसाः।।]

Fresh and serene, the days, with pools visible at places after showers, assumed a partly dry aspect, as if they had enjoyed a dip in the waters.

K says दरशब्दः ईषदर्थः। निर्मितमज्जनसुखाः वर्षजलेन कृतस्नानसुखाः, अत एव अभिनवस्निग्धालोकाः अभिनवसुकुमारच्छव्यः। आसारो वर्षम्। अतीतेन आसारेण उद्देशेषु दृश्यमानजलशकलाः। स्नातानामपि अङ्गेषु क्वचित् जलबिन्दवो दृश्यन्ते। एवंभूता दिवसा इदानीमातपयोगात् ईषच्छोषणच्छविमवहन् इव। शुष्यतिधातोः वसुआदेशः।

Kula says अभिनवस्निग्धालोकाः प्रत्यग्रचिक्कणाः, . . . उद्देशेषु एकदेशेषु आसारस्य वेगवर्षस्य दृश्यमानजललवाः, . . . एतेन कृतस्नानस्य स्निग्धदयुतेः हृदयादिप्रदेशे दृश्यमानजलकणस्य पुरुषस्य धर्मा दिवसेषु समाहिताः।

---

[23] The regions of the sky, which seemed to be weighed down by the clouds during the monsoon, are described as clearing up in the autumn. The sky is fancied as a tree whose branches, bent down by the rainy season, spring back when released at the advent of the autumn, scattering the clouds in the process.

21. सुहसंमाणिअणिद्दो विरहालुङ्खिअसमुद्ददिण्णुक्कण्ठो।
असुवन्तो वि विबुद्धो पढमविबुद्धसिरिसेविओ महुमहणो।।

[सुखसंमानितनिद्रो विरहस्पृष्टसमुद्रदत्तोत्कण्ठः।
अस्वपन्नपि विबुद्धः प्रथमविबुद्धश्रीसेवितो मधुमथनः।।]

Having gone through the process of (yogic) sleep with joy, Viṣṇu, even though he had not slept, woke up, attended by his consort, the goddess of wealth, who had woken first; and brought anxiety to the ocean, saddened by his impending departure.[24]

K says यथासुखं संमानितयोगनिद्रः, निद्रायमाणस्यात्मनो विरहेण स्पृष्टस्य समुद्रस्य कृतोत्कण्ठः। प्रथममेव विबुद्धया श्रिया देव्या सेवितः। स्त्रीणां पत्युश्चरमं स्वापः प्रथममेव प्रबोध इत्याचारः। मधुमथनः अस्वपन्नपि योगनिद्राया जगत्कार्यचिन्तावशात् अस्वपन्नपि विबुद्धः निद्रामुद्रामत्यजदित्यर्थः। MY says अस्वपन्नपीति योगमयनिद्रोऽपीत्यर्थः।

Kula says निमिषहेतुना योगसुलभेन सुखेन संमानिता निद्रा स्वनेत्रस्था[25] चण्डीरूपाक्षशक्तिर्येन। SC says निद्रा स्वशक्तिरूपा योगनिद्रा।

22. सोहइ विसुद्धकिरणो गअणसमुद्दम्मि रअणिवेलालग्गो।
तारामुत्तावअरो फुडविहडिअमेहसिप्पिसंपुडमुक्को।।

[शोभते विशुद्धकिरणो गगनसमुद्रे रजनिवेलालग्नः।
तारामुक्ताप्रकरः स्फुटविघटितमेघशुक्तिसंपुटमुक्तः।।]

The pure-rayed pearls, the stars, released from the split oyster shells, the torn clouds, shone in the ocean of firmament, adhering to its coast, the night.

K says गगनमयसमुद्रे रजनिरेव वेला तीरं तत्र लग्नः, रजनिसमयलग्न इति च ध्वनति। विशुद्धकिरणः, स्फुटविघटितैः स्फुटभिन्नैः मेघशुक्तिमुखैः मुक्तः तारामौक्तिकप्रकरः शोभते स्म। Kula says स्फुटविघटितैः व्यक्तिमुपगतैः स्फुटितमुखैः शुक्तिसंपुटैरिव(मेघैः)मुक्तः।

23. सत्तच्छआणँ गन्धो लग्गइ हिअए खलइ कलम्बामोओ।
कलहंसाणँ कलरओ ठाइ ण संठाइ परिणअं सिहिविरुअम्।।

[24] Viṣṇu "sleeps" in the waters of the ocean during the rains, absorbed in yogic meditation for the good of the world, and wakes up at the advent of the autumn.

[25] Our copy has निद्रासु नेत्रस्था।

[सप्तच्छदानां गन्धो लगति हृदये स्खलति कदम्बामोदः।
कलहंसानां कलरवस्तिष्ठति न संतिष्ठते परिणतं शिखिविरुतम्।।]

The scent of the *saptaparṇa* blossoms appealed to the heart, but the fragrance of the *kadamba* flowers pleased no more. The sweet note of the swans lingered in the heart, but not the cry of the peacock, because its time was past.[26]

K (*chāyā*) has लगति स्खलति हृदये। He says सप्तच्छदकुसुमानां गन्धः अभिनवत्वात् हृदये लगति स्म हृद्योऽभवदित्यर्थः। कदम्बामोदस्तु चिरपरिचितत्वात् स्खलति स्म। कलहंसानां कलरवो हृदये तिष्ठति स्म। परिणतत्वात् शिखिनां मयूराणां विरुतं हृदये नातिष्ठत। Kula says स्खलति कदम्बामोदः परिणत इति योज्यम्। न तिष्ठति परिणतं शिखिविरुतम्। परिणतो हि प्रवाणतां गतो न मनो हरतीत्यर्थः। MY says *saṁṭhāi* संतिष्ठते। उपसर्गोऽनर्थकः।

24. पीणपओहरलग्गं दिसाणँ पवसन्तजलअसमअविइण्णम्।
सोहग्गपढमइण्हं पम्माअइ सरसणहवअं इन्दधणुम्।।२४।।

[पीनपयोधरलग्नं दिशां प्रवसज्जलदसमयवितीर्णम्।
सौभाग्यप्रथमचिह्नं प्रम्लायति सरसनखपदमिन्द्रधनुः।।]

The rainbow whose place was in the sky, drenched with rain, faded away: it was, as it were, a fresh nail mark given by the departing season of rains on the ample bosom of the regions of sky, namely, the massive clouds, as a supreme emblem of beauty.[27]

K says वर्षविगमादिन्द्रधनुः प्रग्लायति स्म। कीदृग्भूतम् – दिशां पीनेषु पयोधरेषु मेघेषु लग्नं, प्रवसता अपगच्छता जलदसमयेन वितीर्णं, सौभाग्यस्य कान्तिविशेषस्य प्रथमचिह्नं, सरसनभःपदं सरसे सवर्षे नभसि पदं स्थानं यस्य तत्तथा। अत्र प्रवासं कुर्वता दयितेन प्रयसीनां स्तनेषु कृतं नखपदं च स्फुरति। तथाहि दिगङ्गनानां पीनेषु स्तनेषु लग्नं सौभाग्यस्य प्रथमचिह्नं सरसं नखव्रणमिति। R says सौभाग्यस्यानुरागस्य प्रथमं ज्ञापकम्।

The verse is quoted in *Sarasvatīkaṇṭhābharaṇa* 4.48 with the remark: अत्र सरसनखपदाकारस्य इन्द्रधनुष उत्पन्नसादृश्यादभेदोपचारेण रूपणे

[26] *Kadamba* flowers and the call of the peacock are associated with the rainy season. The time indicated in this and the preceding verses is the passing of the monsoon and the gradual advent of the autumn. Cf. the next verse.

[27] Means also "luck": here affection. The imagery is that of a departing husband, leaving a nail mark on the bosom of his wife as a memento of their love. Paohara means both "cloud" and "a woman's breasts".

योऽयं सरसे नभसि पदमस्येति व्युत्पत्त्या श्लिष्टरूपेण तद्विशेषणप्रकारो यश्च शोभायाः प्रथमम्यग्रं चिह्नं सौभाग्यस्य च प्रथमं चिह्नं पीनपयोधरे मेघे स्तने वा लग्नमित्यादिविशेषणविशेष्यभावः तेनेदंश्लेषेणोपधीयत इति श्लेषोपहितं नाम संकीर्णरूपकेषूभयभूयिष्ठरूपकभेदः।

25. पज्जत्तसलिलधोए दूरालोक्कन्तणिम्मले गअणअले।
अच्चासण्णं व ठिअं विमुक्कपरभाअपाअडं ससिबिम्बम्।।

[पर्याप्तसलिलधौते दूरालोक्यमाननिर्मले गगनतले।
अत्यासन्नमिव स्थितं विमुक्तपरभागप्रकटं शशिबिम्बम्।।]

In the thoroughly washed sky, spotless and visible far and wide, the orb of the moon seemed to be close at hand, isolated and clear.

K and probably MY read *amukka* for *vimukka* (R and Kula) — K says पर्याप्तेन सलिलेन धौते, दूरमालोक्यमानावस्थायां निर्मले गगनतले अमुक्त परभागत्वात प्रकटम् अमुक्तः परभागो वर्णगुणोत्कर्षो यस्य, आकाशस्य नीलिम्ना स्वेन धवलत्वेन च प्रकटं शशिबिम्बम् अत्यासन्नमिव स्थितं हस्तप्राप्यमिवातिष्ठत्। MY says पर्याप्तनिर्मलतया नभसश्च भूपथादुपरि अपि अतिदूरमालोक्यमानत्वात् शशिबिम्बमात्मनः परभागलाभेन प्रकटत्वात् च आसन्नमिवालक्ष्यतेत्यर्थः।

Kula says वर्षासु यथेष्टधौतत्वात् निर्मलं दूरमालोक्यमानं च यत् तस्मिन् गगनतले विमुक्तपरभागमिव उपरिप्रदेशं (विमुच्य?) लम्बितमिव प्रकटं व्यक्तम्, अथवा मेघनीहाराद्यावरणाभावे अतिविस्पष्टपरभागं प्रकटितशोभातिशयम्, अतः(?) प्रकटं शशिबिम्बम् अत्यासन्नामिव[28] स्थितम्। R says विमुक्तः परभागोऽन्यभागो मेघादिसंम्बन्धस्तेन प्रकटमतिव्यक्तम्।

26. चिरआलपडिणिउत्तं दिसासु घोलन्तकुमुअरअवेल्लविअम्।
भमइ अलद्धासाअं कमलाअरदंसणूसुअं हंसउलम्।।

[चिरकालप्रतिनिवृत्तं दिक्षु घूर्णमानकुमुदरजोविलिप्तम्।
भ्रमत्यलब्धास्वादं कमलाकरदर्शनोत्सुकं हंसकुलम्।।]

Returning after a long lapse of time, the swans[29] were confused by the swirling pollen of the flowers.[30] Dissatisfied, they flew about on all sides, eager to see the day lotus pools.[31]

[28] Our copy has अष्टसिद्धमिव।

[29] The birds are supposed to migrate to the Mānasa Lake during the rainy season, and return in the autumn.

[30] "Night lotus blossoms" according to Rāmadāsa's reading.

[31] I.e. their favourite old haunts.

K and MY read कमुस for *kumua* (R). Kula has कमल।

K says मानससर:प्रदेशात् चिरकालात् प्रतिनिवृत्तं, दिक्षु घूर्णमानेन वायुवशात् प्रसरता कुसुमरजसा व्याकुलीकृतं कमलपरागशङ्कया व्याकुलितं, कमलाकरत्य दर्शनोत्सुकं हंसकुलमभ्रमदिति।

MY reads *velaiaṁ* (explained as वञ्चितं व्याकुलितमिति वा) for *vellaviaṁ* (R). He says पूर्वदृष्टकमलाकराणां चिरविस्मृतप्रदेशतया रजोलिङ्गेन उन्नेतुकामा हंसाः तदन्यकुसुमरजोभिः वञ्च्यमानाः तदन्वेषणपरा बभूवुरित्यर्थः।

Kula reads *a* (च) *laddha* for *aladdha*. He says कमलरजसा *velaviaṁ* प्रभावितं प्रलोभ्याभिमुखं कृतमित्यर्थः। लब्धास्वादं पूर्वमुपभुक्तरसत्वात् सतृष्णं, चिरकालनिवृत्तत्वेन प्रस्मृतपूर्वानु भूतकमलाकरस्थानत्वात् तदनुसारार्थ कमलाकरदर्शनोत्सुकं भ्रमरकुलं च भ्रमति। चकारः समुच्चये। Kula seems to read भ्रमर for हंस, but it might be a mistake.

27. चन्दाअवधवलाओ फुरन्तदिअसरअणन्तरिअसोहाओ।
सोम्मे सरअस्स उसे मुत्तावलिविब्भमं वहन्ति णिसाओ।।

[चन्द्रातपधवलाः स्फुरद्दिवसरत्नान्तरितशोभाः।
सौम्ये शरद उरसि मुक्तावलिविभ्रमं वहन्ति निशाः।।]

The moonlit nights, their splendour alternating with that of the brilliant jewels, the days, assumed the beauty of a necklace on the serene bosom of the autumn.[32]

K and Kula read अन्तरितरूपाः for*sohāo* (शोभाः) found in R .

K says चन्द्रातपेन धवलाः चन्द्रातपवत् धवला इति च। स्फुरद्भिः दिवसरत्नैः अन्तरितरूपाः व्यवहितरूपा निशाः सौम्ये सुन्दरे शरद उरसि मध्यप्रदेशे मुक्तावलिशोभां वहन्तीति(?)।

Kula says सौम्ये मनोहरे शरदो नायिकाया इव उरसि मध्यभागे चन्द्रातपेन ज्योत्स्नया धवला निशाः स्फुरन्तो रविकिरणयोगात् प्रकाशमाना दिवसा रत्नानीव तैरन्तरितरूपा एकान्तरग्रथितमुक्त ावलीविभ्रमं वहन्तीवेत्यर्थः।

28. भमररुअदिण्णसण्णं घणरोहविमुक्कदिणअरअरालिट्टम्।
फरिससुहाअन्तं विअ पडिबुज्झइ जलणिहित्तणालं णलिणम्।।

[भ्रमररुतदत्तसंज्ञं घनरोधविमुक्तदिनकरकराश्लिष्टम्।
स्पर्शसुखायमानमिव प्रतिबुध्यते जलनिहितनालं नलिनम्।।]

---

32 The succession of moonlit nights and brilliant days is likened to a necklace of pearls interspersed with jewels.

Warned by the hum of the bees, the lotus, with its stalk hidden in the water, work up[33] in contact with the rays of the sun bursting through the clouds, as if it took delight in the touch.

K and MY read कर्णं for *saṇṇaṁ*–संज्ञं (R and Kula).

K says अत्र समाध्यलङ्कार: कविना विवक्षित:। नलिनं प्रत्यबुध्यत विकसति स्म। कश्चित प्रभु: निद्रां मुमोचेति च स्फुरति। भ्रमररुताय दत्तकर्णं, वैतालिकगीताय दत्तकर्णमिति च। पद्मे कर्णशब्दप्रयोग: पुरुषसमाधिवशात् कृत: घनरोधविमुक्तस्य दिनकरस्य करै: स्पृष्टं, कुतश्चित् निरोधात् विमुक्तस्य पुंस: करेण प्रणयात् स्पृष्टमिति च। जलनिहितनालं जले मग्ननालदण्डम्। कस्यचिदुत्सङ्गे निहितचरणमिति च। स्पर्शे सुखायमानमिव करस्पर्शेन सुखमनुभवदिव प्रत्यबुध्यत। अनेनैव विशेषणेन समाधि: स्फुटीकृत:।

MY says आप्तजनकरस्पृष्ट: तत्स्पर्शसुखमनुभवन् पादपीठनिहितचरणो यथा राजा प्रभाते प्रतिबुध्यते तथा।

Kula says भ्रमररुतेन उत्तिष्ठेति दत्ता संज्ञा यस्य तत् नलिनं प्रतिबुध्यते। स्निग्धजनकरतलविबुध्यमानस्य करस्पर्शसुखमनुभवतो दत्तसंज्ञस्य पुरुषस्य धर्मा: कमले समाहिता:।

29. मम्महधणुणिग्घोसो कमलवणक्खलिअलच्छिणेउरसद्दो।
सुव्वइ कलहंसरओ महुअरिवाहित्तणलिणिपडिसंलाओ।।

[मन्मथधनुर्निर्घोष: कमलवनस्खलितलक्ष्मीनूपुरशब्द:।
श्रूयते कलहंसरवो मधुकरीव्याहृतनलिनीप्रतिसंलाप:।।]

The call of the swans could be heard: it was, as it were, the sound of the bow of the god of love; the jingle of the anklets of the goddess of beauty stepping across the lotus beds; the answer of the lilies addressed by the bees.

K says कमलवनप्रविष्टानां कलहंसानां हंसविशेषाणां कलरव: श्रूयते स्म। कीदृश: – मन्मथस्य स्ववशे भवनं कर्तुमुद्यतस्य धनु:शब्दभूत:। हंसरवस्य मदनोद्दीपनत्वादेवमुक्तम्। कमलवनेषु स्खलन्त्या: सविभ्रमं चलन्त्या लक्ष्म्या: नूपुरशब्दभूतो, मधुकरीव्याहृतनलिनीप्रतिसंलाप:। नलिनी पद्मस्तम्बम्। नलिन्या मधुकरीमुखेन व्याहृत: प्रतिसंलाप: प्रतिवचनं यस्य स तथा।

MY says मधुकर्या व्याहृताया नलिन्या: स्वागतप्रश्नादिरूपप्रतिसल्लाप:। अथवा चिरप्रोषितसंगतानां हंसानां मधुकरीसखीमुखेन नलिनीभि: स्वागतादिप्रश्ने कृते तदुत्तररूपो हंसकृत: प्रतिसल्लाप इत्यर्थ:। तदानीं व्याहृतेति कर्तरि क्त इति द्रष्टव्यम्।

[33] I.e. burst into bloom.

30. खुडिडप्पइअमुणालं दट्ठूण पिअं व सिढिलवलअं णलिणिम्।
महुअरिमहुरुल्लावं महुमअतम्बं मुहं व घेप्पइ कमलम्।।

[खण्डितोत्पाटितमृणालां दृष्ट्वा प्रियामिव शिथिलवलयां नलिनीम्।
मधुकरीमधुरोल्लापं मधुमयाताम्रं मुखमिव गृह्यते कमलम्।।]

(Wayfarers), after watching the lotus plant with its stalk torn up (by the birds), as if it were their beloved, with her bangles loose, took the lotus blossom, rosy and full of honey and the sweet hum of bees, for her face, flushed with wine, and uttering words sweet as the hum of bees.

K reads *mahuara* for *mahuari*. He says जलपक्षिभिः खण्डितोत्पतितमृणालां नलिनीं शिथिलवलयां प्रियामिव दृष्ट्वा रामेण मधुकरमधुरोल्लापं मधुकराणां मधुरः उल्लापः शब्दो यस्य तत् कमलं स्वत एव ताम्रं कमलं मधुमदाताम्रं मुखमिव प्रियाया मुखमिव अगृह्यत ज्ञायते स्म। गृह्यत इत्यनेन पीयत इति च स्फुरति। मुखमपि मधुरालापं भवति।

MY says हंसादिभिः त्रुटितोत्प्लावितमृणालां नलिनीं प्रियतम दर्शनालिङ्गनजनित-कुतूहलरभसबृंहितशरीरावयवतया तत्क्षणस्फुटितशङ्खवलयां प्रियामिव दृष्ट्वा तस्या मधुकरीविरुतमुखरं कमलं, मधुकररुतानुकारिमणितगर्भमधुमदताम्रमुखं यथा गृह्यते चुम्ब्यते प्रियेण इत्येकत्र, अन्यत्र ज्ञायते जनैरित्यर्थः अनुसंधेयः।

Kula says हंसादिना खण्डितमुत्पाटितं मृणालं यस्याः तां नलिनीं प्रशिथिलवलयां प्रियामिव दृष्ट्वा तस्या लोहितकमलं मधुमदाताम्रं मुखमिव गृह्यते अर्थवशात् पथिकैः स्मर्यते। मधुकर्या मधुर उल्लापो यत्र। प्रियामुखमपि मधुरालापं भवति।

31. पज्जत्तकमलगन्धो महुतण्णाओसरन्तणवकुमुअरओ।
भमिरभमरोअइव्वो संचरइ सदाणसीअरो वणवाओ।।३१।।

[पर्याप्तकमलगन्धो मध्वार्द्रापसरन्नवकुमुदरजाः।
भ्रमद्भ्रमरोपजीव्यः संचरति सदानशीकरो वनवातः।।]

The woodland breeze blew, rich in the fragrance of the day lotus blossoms, and laden with the swirling fresh pollen of the flowers moist with honey. Wafting spray from the ichor of the rutting elephants, it afforded enjoyment to the vagrant bees.

K and Kula read *pasaranta* for *osaranta* अपसरत् (R), and कुसुम for *kumua* (R).

K says परिपूर्णकमलगन्धः, मध्वार्द्रैः प्रसरद्भिः नवकुसुमरजोभिः उपेतः, भ्रमणशीलैः भ्रमरैः आस्वाद्यः तदानीं मत्तानां गजानां दानशीकरैः सहितः वनवातः संचरति स्म। Kula says पर्याप्तः यथेष्टः।

32. कण्टइअणूमिअङ्गी थोअत्थोओसरन्तमुद्धसहावा।
रइअरचुम्बिज्जन्तं ण णिअत्तेइ णलिणी मुहं विअ कमलम्॥

[कण्ठकितगोपिताङ्गी स्तोकस्तोकापसरन्मुग्धस्वभावा।
रविकरचुम्ब्यमानं न निवर्तयति नलिनी मुखमिव कमलम्॥]

The lotus plant that outgrew its immaturity little by little, with its thorny stalk hidden (in the water), did not turn away its blossom, while being kissed by the rays of the sun, even as a maiden, thrilling with rapture, and discarding her bashfulness by degrees, is loth to withdraw her face, while being kissed by her lover.

K says मुग्धवधूसमाधिः नलिन्यामाहितः। कण्टकितगोपिताङ्गी कण्टकितं जले गोपितं चाङ्गं यस्याः सा तथा। पुलकितच्छादिताङ्गीति च स्फुरति। स्तोकस्तोकेन शनैः शनैः अपसरन्मुग्धस्वभावा, कमलस्य मौग्ध्यं मुकुलभावः, एवंभूता नलिनी रविकरेण चुम्ब्यमानं स्पृश्यमानं कमलं मुखमिव न निवर्तयति स्म। यथा नववधूः मौढ्यस्य शनैर्विगमात् प्रियेण चुम्ब्यमानं मुखं न निवर्तयति तद्वदिति। R says उत्प्रेक्षते – मुखमिव। यथा पद्मिनी नायिका रतिकरो नायकस्तेन चुम्ब्यमानं, etc. MY says *ṇūmiaṁgī* गुप्ताङ्गी जलांशुकेनेति शेषः। नववधूरिव मुखं नलिनी नलिनं न निवर्तयति। Kula says न विवर्तयति प्रत्युत सविकाशमर्पयति।

33. परिघोलन्तक्खलिअं सत्तच्छअकुसुमधवलरेणुक्खइअम्।
उप्पुसइ दाणवङ्कं मुहुत्तगअकण्णचामरं भमरउलम्॥

[परिघूर्णमानस्खलितं सप्तच्छदकुसुमधवलरेणूत्खचितम्।
उत्प्रोञ्छति दानपङ्कं मुहूर्तगजकर्णचामरं भ्रमरकुलम्॥]

The roving unsteady bees, whitened by the pollen of the *saptaparṇa* flowers, wiped off the thick ichor of the elephants as they served for a moment as the *cāmara* whisks decorating their ears.[34]

K says भ्रमरकुलं गजस्य दानपङ्कमुन्ममार्ज। कीदृग्भूतम् – मुहूर्तं गजस्य कर्णचामरभृतम्। कथम् – परिघूर्णमानम् इतस्ततः परिभ्रमत् अत एव

[34] I.e. the bees, covered with the white pollen of the flowers, settled for a moment on the moist ears of the elephants, looking like the decorative whisks.

स्खलितमनवस्थितं, सप्तच्छदकुसुमानां धवलै रजोभिर्मिश्रितम् धवलीकृतम्। तस्मात् कर्णचामरभृतम्। एवंभूतं भ्रमरपटलं गजस्य दानपङ्कं ममार्जेति।

MY has *khasia* explained as खचित। रूषितमिति यावत् for *khaia*, cf. Hemacandra 1.193.

Kula says गजकर्णचामरमिव, तच्च मुहूर्तं, न चिरं, क्षणान्तरेण मदमलिनत्वात्। He remarks on the verse: एतेन विजिगीषुजनोत्साहहेतुगजमदोदयजनकत्वं शरदः कथितम्।

34–35. इअ पहसिअकुमुअसरे भडिमुहपङ्कअविरुद्धचन्दालोए।
जाए फुरन्ततारे लच्छिसअंगाहणवपओसे सरए।।

छिज्जइ झिण्णावि तणू अट्ठिअवाहं पुणो परुण्णं व मुहम्।
रामस्स अईसन्ते आसाबन्धे व्व चिरगए हणुमन्ते।।

(जुग्गअम्)

[इति प्रहसितकुमुदसरसि भटीमुखपङ्कजविरुद्धचन्द्रालोकायाम्।
जातायां स्फुरत्तारायां लक्ष्मीस्वयंग्राहनवप्रदोषे शरदि।।

क्षीयते क्षीणापि तनुरास्थितबाष्पं पुनः प्ररुदितमिव मुखम्।
रामस्यादृश्यमाने आशाबन्ध इव चिरगते हनूमति।।]

(युग्मकम्)

When thus the autumn came with the night lotus pools in bloom, and the stars glittering in the sky, and the moonbeams sadden-ing[35] the lotus faces of the soldiers' wives;[36] the autumn that was, as it were, the early evening for the goddess of fortune to choose her lover[37] (at that time); Rāma's worn body was worn still more; and his eyes,[38] streaming with tears, seemed to fill with tears again, because Hanumat, who had departed long ago,[39] was still out of sight, even like the hope (of recovering Sītā).

---

35 Lit. hostile to. . . .

36 The light of the moon is unbearable to separated lovers, and supposed to close the petals of the day lotus. Here, the reference is to the women pining for their husbands, absent on the military campaigns usual in the autumn.

37 I.e. the victor in the wars of the season. The goddess of fortune is figured as an *abhisārikā* who goes out in the evening to meet her lover.

38 Lit. face.

39 To obtain news of Sītā.

K says हसितकुमुदसरसि विकसितकुमुदं सरः यत्र तत्र। भटीमुखपङ्कजानां विरुद्धचन्द्रालोकेः। शरतसमये भटानां युद्धोद्योगो भवति, अतस्तेषां स्त्रीणां मुखपङ्कजानां चन्द्रलोकः चन्द्रस्य दर्शनं, शरदि हि चन्द्रः प्रकाशते, पङ्कजानां च चन्द्रालोकः चन्द्रप्रकाशो विरुद्ध इति। स्फुरत्तारे। राघवं प्रति लक्ष्म्या जयलक्ष्म्याः स्वयंग्रहाय अभिसारणाय नवप्रदोषे शरदि जाते जातायामित्यर्थः। शरदः पुंस्त्वं प्रागेवोक्तम्। प्रदोषो हि चन्द्रालोक नक्षत्रस्फुरणयुक्तो भवति। उत्तरत्र सम्बन्धः।

Kula says इत्येवमुक्तप्रकारायां शरदि जयलक्ष्मीसुसंग्रहाय[40] नवप्रदोषायाम्। नवप्रदोषशरत्कालयोः साम्यमह। प्रहसितं कुमुदसरो यत्र . . . प्रोषितभर्तृकत्वात भटीमुखानां पङ्कजानामिव विरुद्धः प्रत्यनीकः चन्द्रालोको यत्र तस्यां शरदि वातायाम्। Deva says लक्ष्मीस्वयंग्राहनवप्रदोषे प्रदोषे हि नार्यः अभिसरणेन स्वयं गृह्णन्तीति लक्ष्म्याः स्वयंग्राहदर्शनात् शरदः प्रदोषत्वारोपः[41]।

K says सीतां प्रति आशाबन्ध इव चिरगते चिराय गते हनुमति अदृश्यमाने, etc. Kula says कार्यसाधनार्हः अयमिति प्रत्याशा यत्रोपाये बध्यते स आशाबन्धः। MY says आस्थितबाष्पम् अनुपरतबाष्पमित्यर्थः। K seems to have अस्थितबाष्पं निपतद्बाष्पम्। Kula says अस्थितबाष्पमविश्रान्तश्रुजलमपि पुनः रुदितमिव रोदितुमारब्धं मुखम्। विषादभरेणाधिक्यदर्शनात् उत्प्रेक्षेयम्।

36. णवरि अ जहासमत्थिअणिव्वत्तिअकज्जणिव्वलन्तच्छाअम्।
पेच्छइ मारुअतणअं मणोरहं चेअ चिन्तिअसुहोवणअम्।।

[अनन्तरं च यथासमर्थितनिर्वर्तितकार्यनिर्वलच्छायम्।
प्रेक्षते मारुततनयं मनोरथमेव चिन्तितसुखोपनतम्।।]

He then espied Hanumat, who had a halo of glory,[42] having achi-eved his task as determined before. He was, as it were, the fulfilment of Rāma's hope that readily arrived as he thought of him.

K says अथ रामो यथासमर्थितं गमनसमये समर्थितं यत् संकल्पितं तस्यानतिक्रमेण तदनुरूपमेव निर्वर्तितकार्यत्वात् निर्व्यज्यमानच्छायं प्रकाशमानशोभं मारूततनयं प्रैक्षत। कथंभूतम् – चिन्तितमात्रे सुखोपनतम् अकृच्छ्रागतं मनोरथमेव भूतम्। रामस्य हनुमदागमनमेव तदानीं मनोरथत्वेन स्थितम्। तस्मात् तदागमनेन मनोरथः पूर्णोऽभूदिति।

37. पढमं विअ मारुइणा हरिसभरिज्जन्तलोअणेण मुहेण।
जणअतणआपउत्ती पच्छा वाआइ णिरवसेसं सिट्ठा।।

---

[40] Our copy has जलदलक्ष्मी . . . . Further, सुसंग्रहाय seems to be a mistake for स्वयंग्रहाय।

[41] SC says स्वयंग्राहस्य अभिसारस्य (नव)प्रदोषे। . . . प्रदोषे यथा कान्ताभिसरति तथा लक्ष्मीरपि शरदीति प्रदोषत्वेन शरदो निरूपणम्।

[42] Lit. a distinct lustre.

[प्रथममेव मारुतिना हर्षभ्रियमाणलोचनेन मुखेन।
जनकतनयाप्रवृत्तिः पश्चाद्वाचा निरवशेषं शिष्टा।।]

Hanumat first conveyed the news about Sītā with the expression of his face, revealed by his joyful eyes, and then, in its entirety, in words.

Kula says यथा समर्थितं संप्रधारितं तथैव निर्वर्तितं यत् कार्यं तेन निष्पाद्यमाना छाया शोभा यस्य तम्। MY says *ṇivvaḍanta*[43] पृथग्भवत्। यथा मन्त्रसमये निरूपितं तथा निर्वर्तितेन कार्येण पूर्वविलक्षणोपजातोल्लासमित्यर्थः। कदा नु कृतकार्योऽनघश्चासौ आगमिष्यतीति एवंरूपवाञ्छाविषयरूपः सन् मारुतिरेव तदानीं मनोरथो रामस्य। मनोहरश्च अचिन्तितसुखोपस्थितो लोके सर्वप्रीतिहेतूनामुपरि गण्यते। तं मनोरथभूतं मारुतिम् अचिन्तितोपस्थितमपश्यदिति प्रीत्यतिशयसूचनार्थमुक्तम्।

38. दिट्ठ त्ति ण सद्दहिअं झीण त्ति सबाहमन्थरं णीससिअम्।
सोअइ तुमं ति रुण्णं पहुणा जिअइ त्ति मारुई उवऊढो।।

[दृष्टेति न श्रद्धितं क्षीणेति सबाष्पमन्थरं निःश्वसितम्।
शोचति त्वामिति रुदितं प्रभुणा जीवतीति मारुतिरुपगूढः।।]

The mighty Rāma did not believe, when Hanumat said that he had seen her; heaved a weary sigh with tears on hearing that she was pining away; wept when told "She grieves for thee"; and embraced him, when he said she was alive.

Kula says शोचति त्वामित्युक्ते तस्यामप्यवस्थायां मामेव शोचति नात्मानमिति जातनिर्वेदेन रुदितम्।

39. चिन्ताहअप्पहं मिव तं च करे खेअणीसहं व णिसण्णम्।
वेणीबन्धणमइलं सोअकिलन्तं व से पणामेइ मणिम्।।

[चिन्ताहतप्रभमिव तं च करे खेदनिःसहमिव निषण्णम्।
वेणीबन्धमलिनं शोकक्लाम्यन्तमिवास्य प्रणयति मणिम्।।]

He placed in Rāma's hand the jewel (sent by Sītā): it was tarnished from being fastened in her unkempt lock of hair, and seemed to be pale from anxiety, and weary with toil, and weighed down with grief.

---

[43] R has *ṇivvalanta*. Hemacandra 4.62 and 128 gives *ṇivvaḍai* पृथक्स्पष्टो वा भवति; and *nivvalai* निष्पद्यते (cf. Kula's gloss). R says निर्वलन्ती इतरवानरापेक्षया पृथग्भवन्ती छाया मुखादिकान्तिर्यस्य तम्।

K says सीतया प्रेषितं तं मणिं च तस्य करे समर्पयामास। कथं भूतम – वेणीबन्धनमलिनम्। विरहे स्त्रीणां त्रिगुणबन्धो दीर्घः केशनिवेशो वेणी। धूसरायां वेण्यां बन्धनेन मलिनम्। तदानीं चिन्ताहतप्रभमिव कदा नु खलु देव्या रामेण सह संगतिः स्यादिति चिन्तया नष्टप्रभमिव, खेदनिःसहं निषण्णमिव निःस्पन्दत्वात् खेदेन निःसहमतिदुर्बलं भूत्वा स्थितमिव, तथा शोकेन क्लान्तमिव इत्युत्प्रेक्षते। MY says *ṇisaṇṇaṁ* निःसंज्ञम्। Kula says शोकेनाक्रान्तमिव। He seems to read *soakkantaṁ* for *soa-kilintaṁ.*

40. सो करअलञ्जलिगओ वाहत्थबअपहओसिहन्तमऊहो।
णअणेहिँ दासरहिणा दिट्ठो पीओ णु पुच्छिओ णु पउत्तिम्।।

[स करतलाञ्जलिगतो बाष्पस्तबकप्रहतावसीदन्मयूखः।
नयनाभ्यां दाशरथिना दृष्टः पीतो नु पृष्टो नु प्रवृत्तिम्।।]

Held in his folded hands, and watched by him, with its lustre dimmed by his tears — was it absorbed by his eyes? Was it questioned for news?

K says तस्य करतलाञ्जलिगतः, बाष्पबिन्दुप्रहतत्वात् अवसीदन्मयूखः दाशरथेः नयनाभ्यां दृष्टो नु। अथवा स्नेहातिशयात् पीतो नु। कवलितः सन् सीतायाः प्रवृत्तिं पृष्टौ नु। अयमुत्प्रेक्षान्वितः संशयोऽलंकारः। तथा च किरातार्जुनीये–अनुवृत्त (अनुयुक्त?) इव स्ववार्तमुच्चैः परिरेभे नु भृशं विलोचनाभ्याम् (13.34) इति। It will be seen that K reads दाशरथेः for *dāsarahiṇā*. Kula's reading is the same.

MY reads *osianta* (अवसीदत्) for *osihanta*; and *theva* (explained as पूर) for *thavaa* स्तबक (R). K has बिन्दु (see above), and his reading is same as MY's *Deśīnāmamālā* 5.29 gives *theva* in the sense of बिन्दु। Kula's reading is uncertain, but see 5.62, 14.75 and 15.43 below.

MY says नयनाभ्यां दृष्टो मणिः पीत इव, पृष्ट इव आलक्ष्यत इत्यर्थः।

41. सोअइ अ णं रहुवई विरलङ्गुलिगलिअकिरणधारावअरम्।
वअणे विमलुज्जोअं दररोत्तूण सलिलञ्जलिं व णिमेन्तो।।

[शोचति चैनं रघुपतिर्विरलाङ्गुलिगलितकिरणधाराप्रकरम्।
वदने विमलोद्द्योतं दररुदित्वा सलिलाञ्जलिमिव नियोजयन्।।]

Rāma grieved over the radiant jewel, which sent forth jets of rays through the gaps between his fingers, as he, after weeping for a while, laid it on his face, like a palmful of water.[44]

K says रघुपतिः विरलाभिरङ्गुलीभिः अङ्गुलीरन्ध्रैः गलितकिरणमयधाराप्रकरं, विमलोद्द्योतं विमलप्रकाशप्रकरम्, स्मृताः प्रकाश आलोक उद्द्योतश्च समास्त्रय इति हलायुधः, तं मणिम् ईषत् रुदित्वा पश्चात् सलिलाञ्जलिमिव वदने निक्षिपन् (निमिन्वन् *chāyā*) शोचति स्म। अहो त्वमेवंभूतोऽसीति तं मणिम् अशोचत् चेति। Kula says वदने सलिलाञ्जलिमिव निर्मुञ्चन्।

42. तं दइआहिण्णाणं जम्मि वि अङ्गम्मि राहवेण ण णिमिअम्।
सीआपरिमट्ठेण व वूढो तेण वि णिरन्तरं रोमञ्चो।।

[तद्दयिताभिज्ञानं यस्मिन्नप्यङ्गे राघवेण न नियोजितम्।
सीतापरिमृष्टेनेव व्यूढस्तेनापि निरन्तरं रोमाञ्चः।।]

On whatever limb that token[45] of his beloved was placed by him, an incessant thrill passed through it, as if it had been touched by Sītā.

K says तत् दयिताया अभिज्ञानं राघवेण यस्मिन् अप्यङ्गे न निक्षिप्तं (विन्यस्तं Kula) तेनाप्यङ्गेन सीतया स्पृष्टेनेव रोमाञ्च ऊढः।

43. बाहमइलं पि तो से दहमुहचिन्ताविअम्भमाणामरिसम्।
जाअं दुक्खालोअं जरढाअन्तरविमण्डलं मिव वअणम्।।

[बाष्पमलिनमपि ततोऽस्य दशमुखचिन्ताविजृम्भमाणामर्षम्।
जातं दुःखालोकं जरठायमानरविमण्डलमिव वदनम्।।]

Inflamed with wrath at the thought of Rāvaṇa, his face, though soiled with tears, thereupon looked formidable like the orb of the fierce midday sun.

K says ततः दशमुखचिन्तया दशमुखस्मरणेन विजृम्भमाणामर्ष तस्य वदनं बाष्पमलिनमपि जरठायमानरविमण्डलमिव मध्याह्ने तीव्रायमाणरविमण्डलमिव दुःखालोकं दुःखेन अतिकृच्छ्रेण आलोको दर्शनं यस्य तत् तथा जातम्।

44. तो से चिरमज्झत्थे कुविअकअन्तभुमआलआपडिरूए।
दिट्ठी दिट्ठत्थामे कज्जधुरव्व णिअए धणुम्मि णिसण्णा।।

[44] As if to wash his tear-stained face. The jewel is likened to a palmful of water.

[45] I.e. the jewel.

[ततोऽस्य चिरमध्यस्थे कुपितकृतान्तभ्रूलताप्रतिरूपे।
दृष्टिर्दृष्टस्थाम्नि कार्यधुरेव निजके धनुषि निषण्णा।।]

His gaze, even like the burden of the task before him, rested on his powerful bow, long inactive, but a true image of the eyebrows of the angry god of death.[46]

K and MY read निभृत (*ṇihua*) for *kuvia* कुपित (R and Kula). K reads निहिता (*ṇihittā*) for *ṇisaṇṇā* (R and Kula).

K says चिरमध्यस्थे युद्धाभावात् चिरं मध्यस्थे उदासीने निर्व्यापारे, तदानीं निभृतायाः प्रजासंहारसंनाहाभावात् निष्पन्दायाः कृतान्तभ्रूलताया यमस्य भ्रूलतायाः प्रतिरूपे सदृशे, दृष्टस्थाम्नि पूर्वमेव दृष्टस्थैर्ये धनुषि (तस्य दृष्टिः) निहिता। कार्यधुरेव कार्यनिर्वाह इव। कार्यस्यापि तदायत्तत्वात्। *kajja-dhureva hiae* इति च पाठः। Kula says निजके धनुषि कार्यधुरेव निषण्णा धनुषैव वोढव्यत्वात्। कार्यधुरापि धनुषि समासक्ता।

45. खणमूलाबद्धाए णिव्वण्णन्तमसिणं समारूढाए।
सज्जीअं मिव जाअं अणोणमन्तं पि रामदिट्ठीअ धणुम्।।

[क्षणमूलाबद्धया निर्वर्ण्यमानमसृणं समारूढया।
सजीवमिव जातमनवनतमपि रामदृष्ट्या धनुः।।]

The bow, though unbent, seemed to be equipped with the string as Rāma's gaze, fixed for a moment at the lower end, slowly moved upwards, surveying the weapon.[47]

K says क्षणं धनुषो मूले आबद्धया, पश्चात् निर्वर्णयत् धनुःस्वरूपं वीक्षमाणं यथा तथा मसृणं मन्दं समारूढया रामदृष्ट्या धनुः अनवनमदपि अनम्रमपि सज्यमिव जातम्। धनुर्मूलादारभ्य यावद्धनुष्कोटिपर्यन्तं नयनरश्मिव्याप्तत्वात् सज्यमिव आसीदिति। K quotes Vararuci 3.66 – ज्यायामीदिति ईकारादेशः *SC* explains *aṇoṇamantaṁ* as अनवनम्यमानम्।

MY says *ṇivvaṇṇanta-masaṇaṁ* निर्वर्णयन्ती च मसृणा च यथा स्यात् तथेति क्रियाविशेषणम्। Kula says क्षणं मूले अधोऽटन्याम् आबद्धया, निर्वर्णयन्ती निरूपयन्ती च सा मसृणं शनैः समारूढा मुखाटनीं गता चेति तथा तया रामदृष्ट्या . . . धनुः सज्यमिव गुणसहितमिव गृहीतबलारम्भमिव जातम्। R says निर्वर्ण्यमाने सति धनुर्गुणकार्यविचारे सति मसृणं मन्द यथा स्यादेवं परामटनिमारूढया रामदृष्ट्या।

[46] I.e. when Yama knits the brows in wrath.

[47] Rāma's gaze moving from one end of the bow to the other is fancied as the bowstring.

SC says परनिपातात् मसृणनिर्वर्ण्यमानं यथा स्यादिति श्रीनिवासः, तच्चिन्त्यम्। The परनिपात makes the construction regular, but spoils the meaning.

46. सुग्गीअस्स वि हिअअं राहवसुकअपडिमोअणासत्तण्हम्।
अगणिअदहमुहदप्पं णिव्वूढभरं व तक्खणं ऊससिअम्।।

[सुग्रीवस्यापि हृदयं राघवसुकृतप्रतिमोचनासतृष्णम्।
अगणितदशमुखदर्पं निर्व्यूढभरमिव तत्क्षणमुच्छ्वसितम्।।]

And, Sugrīva's heart, yearning to re-quite the kindness of Rāma, was at that moment filled with elation, regardless of Rāvaṇa's pride, as if the heavy task imposed upon him had already been achieved.[48]

K says तदानीं सुग्रीवस्य हृदयमपि समुच्छ्वसितम् आश्वस्तम्। कथम् – शरत्कालानुकूल्यात् राघवसुकृतस्य रामेण कृतस्योपकारस्य प्रतिमोचने प्रतिक्रियायां सतृष्णम्, अगणितदशमुखदर्पं, तत्क्षणमेव निर्व्यूढभरमिव निर्वर्तितकार्यगौरवमिव आश्वस्तमिति।

MY has *paḍimuñcaṇā* for *paḍimoaṇā* and says प्रतिमोचनं प्रत्युपकारणम्। Kula says राघवसुकृतात् रामकृतराज्यदानोपकारात् आत्मनः प्रत्युपकारेण प्रतिमोचनायां सतृष्णम्, . . . निर्व्यूढभरमिव निर्वर्तित सीतानयनरूपकार्यभरमिव।

47. चिन्तितअलद्धत्थं मिव भुमआविक्खेवसूइआमरिसरसम्।
गमणं राहवहिअए रक्खसजीविअहरं विसं व णिहित्तम्।।

[चिन्तितलब्धार्थमिव भ्रूविक्षेपसूचितामर्षरसम्।
गमनं राघवहृदये राक्षसजीवितहरं विषमिव निहितम्।।]

The resolve to march (to Laṅkā) was implanted in Rāma's heart, like a poison that was to bring destruction to the demons: it seemed to promise fulfilment of his cherished purpose; while the knitting of the brows revealed his wrath.

K and Kula read संचार for *vikkheva* विक्षेप (R). K reads लब्धार्थे and रसे for *laddhatthaṁ* and रसं (R and Kula).

K says धनुरालोकनानन्तरमेव राघवहृदये गमनं निहितम्। गमनस्य व्यवसायो निहित इत्यर्थः। कथंभूते – चिन्तितलब्धार्थ इव चिन्तितमात्र एव लब्धः अर्थः प्रयोजनं रावणवधस्वरूपं यत्र तत्तथाभूत इव वर्तमाने, भ्रूलतासंचारेण सूचितामर्षातिशये।

[48] I.e. Sugrīva cheered up at the prospect of vanquishing Rāvaṇa and requiting his obligation to Rāma.

विषमिव राक्षसजीवितहरं गमनं निहितमिति गन्तुमुद्यतो रामः सुग्रीवादीन् तदनुरूपमालोकयामास इत्याह (see next verse)।

Kula says कथं रावणं हत्वा सीतामानयामीति चिन्तितः अर्थः लब्ध इव यस्मिन् गमने तत् चिन्तितलब्धार्थमिव। एतेन सोत्साहत्वमुक्तम्। भ्रूसंचारेण भ्रुकुटिरचनया सूचितामर्षरसं गमनं रामहृदये . . . विषमिव निहितं रामेण हृदि कृतमित्यर्थः।

48. सोह व्व लक्खणमुहं वणमाल व्व विअडं हरिवइस्स उरम्।
किति व्व पवणतणअं आण व्व बलाइँ से विलग्गइ दिट्ठी।।

[शोभेव लक्ष्मणमुखं वनमालेव विकटं हरिपतेरुरः।
कीर्तिरिव पवनतनयमाज्ञेव बलान्यस्य विलगति दृष्टिः।।]

His gaze rested on Lakṣmaṇa's face like an adornment;[49] on Sugrīva's broad chest,[50] like his garland of sylvan flowers; on Hanumat, like his fame;[51] and like a command, on the host of apes.

K says तदानीं तस्य रामालोकनस्य भावविशेषाः केचिदभूवन्। कथम् – तस्य दृष्टिः लक्ष्मणमुखं शोभेव प्राप। अतिवात्सल्यात् स्निग्धा दृष्टिः शोभेव आरोहति स्म। तया दृष्ट्या लक्ष्मणमुखं प्रसन्नमशोभतेत्यर्थः। हरिपतेः सुग्रीवस्य विकटमुरः वनमालेव प्राप। साहाय्यकं करिष्यतस्तस्य वक्षःस्थलं वनमालेव अलंचकारेत्यर्थः। वीरपुरुषस्य वक्ष एव भरसहमिति वक्षःस्थलं संभावयामास। वनमाला नाम कुसुमवान् वीरुद्विशेषः। पवनतनयं कीर्तिरिव प्राप। कृतकार्यमिव आगतं हनूमन्तं कीर्तिरिव भूत्वा व्याप्नोदित्यर्थः। बलानि वानरसैन्यानि आज्ञेव गमनाज्ञेव प्रापत्। सा दृष्टिरेव सैन्यानि गन्तुमाज्ञापयामासेत्यर्थः। एवमालोकनानन्तरमेव तैरिङ्गितज्ञैः सह रामः प्रयाणमकरोदित्याह (see next verse). MY says एकापि दृष्टिः तद्विषयरूपभेदेन अनेकरूपेव व्यलगदित्यर्थः।

Kula says रामस्य दृष्टिः लक्ष्मणमुखं *valaggai* (for *vilaggai*) आरोहति। लक्ष्मणमुखमनेन अवलोकितमित्यर्थः। लक्ष्मणस्य च गमनोत्साहवतः प्रथमं दृष्ट्या संभावितस्य मुखप्रसादोदयात् दृष्टिः शोभेव भवति। ततोऽभिमतानुवचनात् सानुरागा दृष्टिः वनमालेव . . . सुग्रीवस्य विकटं सौहार्दायतनम् उरो(व्याप्नोति?)। सा च तस्य वनमालेव हृदयोल्लासहेतुत्वात्[52]। कार्यमिदमनेन कृतं करिष्यते चेति प्रसादविशदा

[49] I.e. added to the lustre of his face by cheering him up.

[50] I.e. in token of admiration for his valour.

[51] I.e. heightened the glory of Hanumat, already famous for his exploits.

[52] Jagaddhara in his commentary on *Sarasvatīkaṇṭhābharaṇa* 4.19 where this verse is quoted says सुग्रीवस्य विस्तीर्णमुरः सा विलगति वनमालेव पौरुषाध्यवसायनिमित्तम्, . . . वनमालेव प्रमाणावसरे प्रभुणा सुग्रीवाय प्रसादीकृतेति भावः। 'आपादप्रवणां मालां वनमालेति तां विदुः' इति शाश्वतः।

गुणोत्कर्षं ख्यापयन्ती कीर्तिरिव पवनतनयम्। सज्जीभवेति आज्ञेव (बलानि), दृष्टिपातदर्शना(नन्तर) मेव तेषां गमनोद्यमदर्शनात्।

49. संखोहिअमहिवेढो तो सो कइसेण्णविलुलिअवणाहोओ।
खुहिअसमुद्दाहिमुहो महणारम्भम्मि मन्दरो विअ चलिओ।।

[संक्षोभितमहीवेष्टस्ततः स कपिसैन्यविलुलितवनाभोगः।
क्षुभितसमुद्राभिमुखो मथनारम्भे मन्दर इव चलितः।।]

He, then, set out on his march towards the surging sea, convulsing the earth, with the woods trampled down by the host of apes; even as the Mandara mountain journeyed to the sea on the eve of the churning of the ocean.[53]

K says ततः स रामः क्षुभितसमुद्राभिमुखो विचलितः। कपिसैन्यैराकुलितवनविस्तारः, अत एव संक्षोभितमहीमण्डलः मथनारम्भे मन्दर इव चलितः। देवतात्मा मन्दरो मथनारम्भे यथा क्षोभितमहीमण्डलो भूत्वा समुद्राभिमुखं प्रचलितः तद्वदिति। K *chāyā* has मन्दर इव विचलितः। He seems to read *mandarovva vicalio* for *via calio*.

50. चलिअं च वाणरवलं चलिए तम्मि चलकेसरसडुज्जोअम्।
गहिअदिसापरिणाहं मऊहजालं व दिणअरस्स फुरन्तम्।।

[चलितं च वानरबलं चलिते तस्मिंश्चलकेसरसटोद्द्योतम्।
गृहीतदिक्परिणाहं मयूखजालमिव दिनकरस्य स्फुरत्।।]

When he moved, the host of apes, too, began to move, bright with their flowing mane, and flashing like the rays of the sun as they spread out on all sides.

K *pratīka* has *caliaṁ a* (for च)। K reads सटोद्घातं for *saḍujjoaṁ* (R and Kula). K, MY and Kula read परिमाणं for परिणाहं (R). K and MY read दिनकरे for *diṇaarassa* (R and Kula)।

K says तस्मिन् रामे चलति वानरबलं चलितम्। कथंभूतम् – चलकेसरसटोद्घातम्। केसराः शिरसिजाः, सटाः श्मश्रूरोमाणि, उद्घातः संघातः। गमनरभसात् चञ्चलकेसरसटोद्घातं, गृहीतदिक्परिमाणं व्याप्तदिगन्तं, दिनकरे चलिते स्फुरत मयूखजालमिव। तदपि गृहीतदिक्परिमाणं भवति। MY says दिशां परिमाणं गृहीतं येन तत्तथा। सर्वदिग्व्यापकमित्यर्थः।

---

[53] One of the frequent references in the poem to the churning of the ocean by the gods and demons with the Mandara mountain as the churn-staff.

Kula says चलो विलसन् केसरसटायाः स्कन्धरोमस्तबकस्य उद्द्योतो यस्य तत्। तथा विस्तारेण गृहीतो दिशां परिमाणं पर्यन्तो येन तत्। तथा दिनकरस्य मयूखजालमिव स्फुरत। एकमुतसाहशक्त्या, अन्यत् शुभाशुभरूपत्वेन।

51. वेरारणिपज्जलिओ तो सो रोसपवणाहउद्धअमुहलो।
वड्ढइ मग्गाणुगओ लङ्कावणराइवणदओ कइलोओ।।

[वैरारणिप्रज्वलितस्ततः स रोषपवनाहतोद्धतमुखरः।
वर्धते मार्गानुगतो लङ्कावनराजिवनदवः कपिलोकः।।]

The multitude of apes swelled as they followed close one on the other. Kindled by the fuel[54] of hatred, and stirred by the gale of wrath, and roaring, it was a forest fire to consume Laṅkā for a woodland.

K says ततः स कपिलोकः वर्धते स्म भूयो भूयः प्रवृद्धः अभूत्। कथंभूतः – लङ्कारूपाया वनराजेः वनदवः वनवह्निः। . . . मार्गानुगतः अन्योन्येषां गमनमार्गमनुगतः, पूर्वं गच्छतां मार्गाविच्छेदेन अनुगच्छन्नित्यर्थः। अग्निरपि तथाविधः प्रसरति। एवं भूत्वा वर्धते स्म। MY says मार्गो लङ्काप्राप्त्यनुगुणः। तमनुगत इत्यर्थः।

52. वच्चइ अ चडुलकेसरसडुज्जलालोअवाणरपरिक्खित्तो।
सव्वदिसाआअड्ढिअपलअपलित्तगिरिसंकुलो व्व समुद्दो।।

[व्रजति च चटुलकेसरसटोज्ज्वलालोकवानरपरिक्षिप्तः।
सर्वदिगाकृष्टप्रलयप्रदीप्तगिरिसंकुल इव समुद्रः।।]

Surrounded by the apes, resplendent with their agile mane, Rāma advanced like the ocean (of the epoch of destruction), thronged with mountains blown over (by gales) from all sides, and lit up by the fire of universal ruin.[55]

K, MY and Kula read *sāaḍḍhia* for *āaḍḍhia* आकृष्ट (R). Hemacandra 4.187 gives *sāaḍḍhai* in the sense of कर्षति K says स रामो व्रजति च। कीदृग्भूतः – चटुलाभिः केसरसटाभिः उज्ज्वलालोकैः वानरैः परिक्षिप्तः, सर्वदिग्भ्यः स्वाकृष्टैः प्रलयवायुना। सुष्ठु आकृष्टैः प्रलयप्रदीप्तैः प्रलयानलप्रदीप्तैः गिरिभिः संकुलः समुद्र इव। युगान्ते महावेगेन प्रलयवायुना ततस्तत उन्मूल्य समाकृष्टैः प्रलयपावकप्रदीप्तैः गिरिभिः व्याप्तः प्रचलन समुद्र इवेत्यर्थः। वानाराः सर्वे स्वर्णवर्णाः पर्वतवदुत्तुङ्गाश्च। ततस्तदेवमुपमितम्।

---

[54] Lit. fire-sticks (the two pieces of wood used for producing fire by friction).

[55] The apes who are represented as giants throughout the poem are likened to the mountains, and their ruddy mane to the blazing fire.

MY says *sāaḍḍhia* समाकृष्ट। लङ्कााया नाशहेतुत्वात् गम्भीरत्वाच्च रामः प्रलयसमुद्र इवेति। महत्त्वात् वानराः तत्प्रेर्यत्वाच्च गिरय इव चेत्युक्तम्। प्रलये वृद्धिमतः समुद्रस्य महापृथुलिमाक्राम(क)त्वक्रमेण व्रजनमपि . . . भवतीति दृष्टान्तत्वोपपत्तिः।

Kula says परिक्षिप्तः परिवृतः। सर्वाभ्यो दिग्भ्यः समाकृष्टाः प्रलय-प्रदीप्ता ये गिरयः तैः संकुलो व्याप्तः समुद्र इव व्रजति च। पिङ्गलोज्ज्वलसटोद्द्योतः प्रलयाग्निरिव, वानरा गिरय इव, रामः समुद्र इवेत्यर्थः।

53. घोलन्ति णिम्मलाओ फुरन्तदिअसअरपाअडिअरूआओ।
दाविअमग्गम्मि वि से हिअए सोअन्धआरिअम्मि दिसाओ।।

[घूर्णन्ते निर्मलाः स्फुरद्दिवसकरप्रकटितरूपाः।
दर्शितमार्ग इव यस्य हृदये शोकान्धकारिते दिशः।।]

The spotless regions of the sky, revealed by the brilliant sun, reeled in his mind, clouded with grief, even though the path ahead was manifest to it.

K says दिशः स्फुरद्दिवसकरप्रकटितरूपा, अत एव निर्मलाः, तस्य रामस्य दर्शितमार्गेऽपि शरत्कालेन दर्शितो मार्गः कार्यपथो यस्य तस्मिन् तथाभूतेऽपि हृदये शोकान्धकारिते सति घूर्णन्ति भ्रमन्ति स्म। शोकान्धकारितहृदयत्वात् रामस्य दिशो यथायथं न प्रकाशन्त इत्यर्थः।

MY says घूर्णनं विशेषतो नाकलनम्। प्राच्यादयो दिशो रामेण न व्यज्ञायन्त। Kula says दिशः दर्शितमार्गेऽपि उपदिष्टदिग्विभागेऽपि तस्य रामस्य हृदये घूर्णन्ते भ्रान्तिं कुर्वन्ति। हेतुमाह। शोकान्धकारित इति। सीताविरहशोकाकुलत्वात् तस्य दिङ्मोह इत्यर्थः।

54. आलोएइ अ विञ्झं धणुसंठाणस्स साअरस्स भरसहम्।
संधिअणइसोत्तसरं अवहोवासघडिअं व जीआबन्धम्।।

[आलोकते च विन्ध्यं धनुःसंस्थानस्य सागरस्य भरसहम्।
संहितनदीस्रोतःशरमुभयावकाशघटितमिव जीवाबन्धम्।।]

He saw the Vindhya, capable of standing the pressure of the bow-shaped sea, as if it were the powerful string of the bow attached to both ends, with the rivers joined to it as arrows.[56]

K and MY *pratīka* has *āloanti* (अलोकयन्ति)for *āloei* अलोकते (R and Kula).

[56] The southern sea is fancied as meeting the mountain at the eastern and the western end, like the arch of a bow, and the mountain as the string attached to both ends of the bow.

K says ते गत्वा विन्ध्यमालोकयन्। किंभूतम् – धनुःसंस्थानस्य सागरस्य भरसहम्। धनुराकारस्य सागरस्य दक्षिणस्योभयपार्श्वघटितं ज्याबन्धमिव स्थितम्। विन्ध्यपर्वतो हि पूर्वापरसमुद्राववगाह्य तिष्ठति। कथंभूतं ज्याबन्धम् – भरसहं शराकर्षणभरसहम्। विन्ध्यः भूधारणभरसहः। संहितनदीस्रोतांस्येव शरायस्य तत्तथाभूतम्। ज्यास्थानीये विन्ध्ये संहितनदीस्रोतःशरमित्यर्थः।

MY says धनुष इव संनिवेशः अस्येति धनुःसंस्थानः (तस्य)। सागरभरस्य धारकं समुद्रावगाढोपान्तं विन्ध्यमालोकयन् इत्यर्थः। Kula says वक्रत्वेन धनुःसंस्थानस्य सागरस्य भरसहं पीडासहम्। उभयपार्श्वघटितं पूर्वपश्चिमसमुद्रपर्यन्तयोः अटनीद्वये योजितं जीवाबन्धमिव। संहितानि नदीस्रोतांसि शरा इव यत्र तं विन्ध्यमालोकते च।

55. मसिणिअसिहरुच्छङ्गो विहुअणिअम्बवणपाअडिअतुङ्गअडो।
विञ्झेण भरिअकुहरो हेलावाओ वि वाणराणँ ण सहिओ।।

[मसृणितशिखरोत्सङ्गो विधुतनितम्बवनप्रकटिततुङ्गतटः।
विन्ध्येन भृतकुहरो हेलापातोऽपि वाणराणां न सोढः।।]

The Vindhya could not endure even the leisurely march of the apes, which levelled the expanse of its peaks, and laid bare its lofty sides by destroying the woods on the slopes, and filled the caves (with the broken trees).

K *pratīka* has *masaṇia*. He reads विवर for कुहर (R and Kula). R says वानराणां हेलयाऽनास्थयापि पातो गमनम्, . . . उत्फालादवपतनं वा।

K says विन्ध्येन वानराणां हेलापातोऽपि, लीलाविशेषो हेला, हेलया पातो हेलापातः सोऽपि न सोढः। कथंभूतः – मसृणितशिखरोत्सङ्गः क्षोदितशिखराग्रप्रदेशः। विधुतनितम्बवनत्वात् निरस्तनितम्बवनत्वात् प्रकाशिततुङ्गतटः।

Kula says भग्नशिलातरुलतादिभिः भृतानि कुहराणि येन स वानराणां हेलापातोऽपि सागरभरसहेनापि विन्ध्येन न सोढः पूर्वरूपापगमात्। MY says हेलया वातोऽपि न पुनः अवस्कन्दनबुद्ध्या इत्याशयः। R says हेलावातो हेलया वातः पवनो जङ्घादिसमुत्थो न सोढः . . . इत्यपि कश्चित्।

56. पत्ता अ सीभराहअधाउसिलाअलणिसण्णराइअजलअम्।
सज्झं ओज्झरपहसिअदरिमुहणिक्कन्तबउलमइरामोअम्।।

[प्राप्ताश्च शीकराहतधातुशिलातलनिषण्णराजितजलदम्।
सह्यं निर्झरप्रहसितदरीमुखनिष्क्रान्तबकुलमदिरामोदम्।।]

They reached the Sahya, with the clouds tinged with diverse hues as they rested upon its mineral rocks drenched with their spray; with the wine-like fragrance of *bakula* flowers issuing from the mouths of the caves, laughing with the brooks.

K says शीकरैः मेघस्यैव जलशीकरैराहते धातुशिलातले निषण्णाः धातुरागेण रञ्जिताः जलदा यत्र। निर्झरेण प्रहसितात् निर्झरस्य धावल्येन ध्वनिना च प्रहसितात् दरीमुखात् निर्वान्तो वकुलकुसुमानां मदिरामोदो यत्र तम्। दरीषु बधूधर्मः अध्यस्तः। यथा प्रहसितात् वधूमुखात वकुलकुसुमगन्धसदृशो मदिरामोदो निर्गच्छति तद्वदिति। एवंभूतं सह्यं च पर्वतं प्राप्ता वानरा इति। केरलविषयस्य सीमापर्वतः सह्यः। स विन्ध्यात् दक्षिणतः प्राचीनः प्रसृतो दृश्यते।

K seems to read *rāvia* (रञ्जित) for *rāia* (रजित)। Cf Hemacandra 4.49 — *rāvei rañjei*. MY, however, says *rāia* रञ्जित। Further, he has *ṇivvahia* (*ṇimmahia* ?) निर्गत for *ṇikkanta* (निष्क्रान्त)। K has निर्वान्त।

Kula says वकुलकुसुमानां मदिराया इव आमोदो यत्र तम्।

57. बोलन्ति अ पेच्छन्ता पडिमासंकन्तधवलघणसंघाए।
फुडफडिहसिलासंकुलखलिओवरिपत्थिए विअ णइप्पवहे।।

[व्यतिक्रामन्ति च पश्यन्तः प्रतिमासंक्रान्तधवलघनसंघातान्।
स्फुटस्फटिकशिलासंकुलस्खलितोपरिप्रस्थितानिव नदीप्रवाहान्।।]

They passed on as they looked at the rivers, which, with the white clouds reflected in the waters, seemed to dash over rugged masses of clear crystal rocks.

K and Kula read संकट for संकुल (R). K says ते सह्यमतिक्रामन्ति स्म। किं कुर्वाणाः – प्रतिमारूपेण संक्रान्तधवलघनसंघातान्, तदानीं स्फुटस्फटिकशिलासंकटेन स्फटिकशिलासंमर्देन स्खलितत्वात् प्रतिबद्धत्वात् स्फटिकशिलासंकटस्योपरि प्रस्थितानिव नदीप्रवाहान् पश्यन्तः।

Kula says प्रतिमया संक्रान्तो धवलो घनसंघातो येषु तान् गिरिनदीप्रवाहान् स्फुटं व्यक्तं स्फटिकशिलानां संकटेषु गहनेषु स्खलितान् उपरिप्रस्थितान् प्रेक्षमाणा व्यतिक्रामन्ति च। प्रतबिम्बितधवलमेघसमूहस्य स्फटिकशिलानिवह – साम्यमनेन दर्शितम्। It will be seen that Kula reads गिरि for *via* (इव)।

58. तडपब्भारभरन्ता दलन्तपाआलगलिअजलपइरिक्का।
आवाए च्चिअ जाआ पहअमहावहणिहा महाणइसोत्ता।।

[तटप्राग्भारध्रियमाणानि दलत्पातालगलितजलप्रतिरिक्तानि।
आपात एव जातानि प्रहतमहापथनिभानि महानदीस्त्रोतांसि।।]

Large streams looked like broad well-beaten paths at the heavy tread (of the multitude), because they filled up with the massive banks (crumbling under the weight), and were emptied of the waters, which poured into the cracking low lands.

K has व्यतिरिक्त (*vairikka*) for *pairikka* प्रतिरिक्त (R). Cf. 2.15.

K says वानराणां धावताम् आपात एव आक्रमण एव महानदीस्रोतांसि जलप्रवाहा: एवमभवन्। कथम् – दलत्पातालगलज्जलव्यतिरक्ता: पादाघातै: दलति पाताले अध:स्थले गलता जलेन रिक्ता इत्यर्थ:। भग्नै: तटप्राग्भारै: तटविस्तारै: पूर्यमाणानि एवंभूतानि महानदीस्रोतांसि प्रहतानाम् अतिचिरप्रचारेण क्षुण्णानां महापथानां सदृशानि जातानि।

Kula says आपात एव कपीनामापतनमात्र एव आक्रमणभरविशीर्णै: तटप्राग्भारै: तटोच्चदेशै: भ्रियमाणानि, दलता भिदां गच्छता पातालेन नितम्बभागाधोभागेन गलितै: जलै: प्रविविक्तानि[57] तुच्छानि, अथवा गलितजलत्वात् विशीर्णानि, प्रहत: क्षुण्णो यो महान् विशाल: पन्था: तन्निभानि महानदीनां स्रोतांसि जातानि।

59. जलहरणिद्दाअन्तं पाअवगहणेसु सिसिरणिद्दाअन्तम्।
सइ दुद्दिणसामलअं पत्ता भग्गधुअचन्दणरसा मलअम्।।

[जलधरनिर्दावान्तं पादपगहनेषु शिशिरनिद्रायन्तम्।
सदा दुर्दिन श्यामलतं प्राप्ता भग्नधुतचन्दनरसा मलयम्।।]

They reached the Malaya as they smashed the sandal trees and made the ground tremble.[58] Cool amidst the thickets, it appeared to be asleep, with the creepers green on account of constant rain, and the region free from forest fires because of the clouds.

K says जलधरै: निर्दावान्तम् निर्दाव: अन्त: प्रदेशो यस्य तम्। पादपकुञ्जेषु शिशिरं यथा निद्रायमाणं निद्रायमाणमिव। सदादुर्दिनत्वात् श्यामीभूतलतं मलयं प्राप्ता:। भग्नधुतचन्दनरसा:, रसा हि भूमि:, भग्नधुतचन्दनभूमय: प्राप्ता इति। पादान्तयमकमेतत्। शिशिरनिद्रायन्त्रमिति बा पाठ:। रज्जुभिरूर्ध्वबद्धा खट्वा निद्रायन्त्रम्। My says पादपगहनेषु शिशिरनिद्रायन्त्रम्। अनेन निद्राजनकम्।

Kula says जलधरै: निर्दाव: वनाग्निशून्य: अन्तो यस्य। पादपानां गहनेषु शिशिर: शीतल:, अत (?) एव निद्रावन्तम्। सदादुर्दिनत्वेन श्यामलकं स्वार्थे कन्। भग्नाश्चन्दना धुता रसा भूमिश्च यैस्ते भग्नधुतचन्दनरसा मलयं प्राप्ता:।

---

[57] This seems to be a mistake. *SC* which reproduces Kula's gloss on this verse almost verbatim has प्रतिरिक्तानि।

[58] Cf. Kulanātha in Extracts.

60. चन्दणपाअवलग्गे खुडिउव्वेलिअलआपरिमलच्छाए।
संदाणिअणिम्मोए पेच्छन्ति महाभुअङ्गवेढणमग्गे।।६०।।

[चन्दनपादपलग्नान्खण्डितोद्वेल्लितलतापरिमलच्छायान्।
संदानितनिर्मोकान्पश्यन्ति महाभुजंगवेष्टनमार्गान्।।]

They beheld the marks left by the coils of huge serpents on the sandal trees, with their slough clinging to them; marks that looked like the imprint of creepers, torn off and untwined.

K says ते वानरा मलयपर्वते चन्दनपादपलग्नान् चन्दनपादपेषु निमग्नान्, महाभुजङ्गानां वेष्टनमार्गान् सुचिरं चन्दनेषु लीनानां पश्चादपगतानां महाभुजङ्गानां भोगवेष्टनमार्गान् पश्यन्ति स्म। कीदृशान् – त्रुटितोद्वेष्टितानां त्रुटितस्रंसितानां लतानां परिमलच्छायान् परिमर्दसदृशान्। संबद्धनिर्मोकान्। परिमर्देऽपि परिमल इति वैजयन्ती।

Kula says महाभुजङ्गमानां वेष्टनमार्गान्। खण्डिताः सत्य उद्वेष्टिता उन्मोचिता या लताः तासां परिमलस्य विमर्दस्थानस्य छाया शोभा येषां तान्।

R read *uvvelia* (उद्वेल्लित)। The reading of K and Kula might be *uvvellia* (उद्वेष्टित). Hemacandra 4.223 has *uvvellai uvveḍhai*. R says उद्वेल्लिता उद्घाटिता स्फोटितेति यावत् एवंभूता या लता।

61. सेवन्ति तीरवड्ढिअणिअअभरोव्वत्तचन्दणलआलिद्धे।
रम्मत्तणदिप्पवहे वणगअदानकडुए गिरिणईप्पवहे।।

[सेवन्ते तीरवर्धितनिजकभरापवृत्तचन्दनलतालीढान्।
रन्यतृणदीप्रपथान्वनगजदानकटून्गिरिनदीप्रवाहान्।।]

They resorted to the mountain streams, touched by the sandal tree branches, growing luxuriant on the banks, and bowed down with their own weight; (streams) redolent with the ichor of wild elephants (sporting in the waters), and bordered by paths glistening with lovely grass.

K reads कुसुम for *ṇiaa* निजक (R and Kula). K and MY read *rammattaṇa-dappa-vahe* for *ramma-ttaṇa-dippa-vahe* रम्यतृणदीप्रपथान् (R and probably Kula who have दीप्त)।

K says ते गिरिनदीप्रवाहान् असेवन्त। कथंभूतान् – तीरवर्धिताभिः कुसुमभरेण अपवृत्ताभिः चन्दनलताभिः चन्दनशाखाभिः स्पृष्टान्। चन्दनवृक्षस्य कुसुमानि न सन्तीति लोकवादः अत्र विपरीतो दृष्टः। अथवा तीरवर्धितकुसुमभरापवृत्त-चम्पकलतास्पृष्टानिति पाठः। रम्यत्वेन दर्पवहान् वयमेव रम्या इति दर्पधरान्।

वनगजदानैः कटुकान् सुरभीन्। कटुतिक्तकषायस्तु सौरभ्येऽपि प्रकीर्तिता इति हलायुधः। Kula says याः चन्दनलताः ताभिराश्लिष्टान्। पन्था अवतरणमार्गः।

62. तो तरुणसिप्पिसंपुडदरदाविअजलणिहित्तमुत्तावअरम्।
पत्ता पत्तलवउलं गअदाणसुअन्धिरअणवेलं वेलम्।।

[ततस्तरुणशुक्तिसंपुटदरदर्शितजलनिहितमुक्ताप्रकराम्।
प्राप्ता पत्रलबकुलां गजदानसुगन्धिरजोनवैलां वेलाम्।।]

They, then, reached the seashore, with the leafy *bakula* trees, and the fresh cardamom plants with pollen fragrant like the ichor of elephants, and the pearls, partly released[59] by the immature oyster shells, and hidden in the waters.

K reads *suandhiara* for *suandhi-raa* (R and Kula). Kula reads दर for जल।

K says ततस्ते तरुणैः शुक्तिसंपुटैः ईषद्दर्शितः जले निहितः मुक्ताप्रकरः यस्यां ताम्। पत्रबहुलवकुलां, गजदानवत् सुगन्धितरा नवाः एलाः यत्र तां वेलां समुद्रतीरं प्राप्ताः। एलाफलानि गजमदसदृशगन्धीनि इति प्रसिद्धिः।

Kula says तरुणैः शुक्तिसंपुटैः तरुणत्वेन निविडाङ्गसन्धित्वात् सहसा निःशेषं मुक्तजालममुञ्चद्भिः दरदर्शितः दरनिहितः मुक्ताप्रकारो[60] यस्याम्। गजदानवत् सुगन्धिरजसो नवा एला यत्र तां वेलाम्। Muda fragment has (सु)गन्धरजाः नवा एला च द्रवालाख्यो गन्धवृक्षो यस्यां ताम्।

63. विअसिअतमालणीलं पुणो पुणो चलतरङ्गकरपरिमट्ठम्।
फुल्लेलावणसुरहिं उअहिगइन्दस्स दाणलेहं व ठिअम्।।

[विकसिततमालनीलां पुनः पुनश्चलतरङ्गकरपरिमृष्टाम्।
फुल्लैलावनसुरभिमुदधिगजेन्द्रस्य दानलेखामिव स्थिताम्।।]

Blue with blossoming *tamāla* trees, and fragrant with groves of cardamom plants in full bloom, the seashore seemed to be a streak of ichor of the mighty elephant, the ocean,[61] touched ever and anon by its agile trunk, the waves.

---

[59] Lit. shown.

[60] The words निविडाङ्ग are restored from *SC* which anonymously reproduces Kula's gloss on the verse. *SC*, however, says तरुणत्वेन कर्कशसन्धितया ईषद्दर्शित ईषन्निहित इति कुलनाथः। This may be a clarification of Kula's meaning.

[61] The ichor of an elephant is supposed to have a smell like that of cardamom. See the preceding verse.

K says फुल्लैलावनैः सुरभिम्, अन्यत्र फुल्लैलावनवत् सुरभिं गजेन्द्र – दानधारारेखामिव स्थितां प्राप्ताः इति पूर्वत्र संबन्धः। Kula says विकसितैः तमालैः, विकसिततमालवच्च नीलाम्। Muda says परिमृष्टां स्पृष्टाम्।

64. फेणविसमङ्गराअं विद्दुमदन्तव्वणाणिअमुहच्छाअम्।
मलिअवणकेसकुसुमं परिहुत्तसमुद्दपरिमलं व वहन्तिम्।।

[फेनविषमाङ्गरागां विद्रुमदन्तव्रणानीतमुखच्छायाम्।
मृदितवनकेशकुसुमां परिभुक्तसमुद्रपरिमलमिव वहन्तीम्।।]

The shore, the mistress of the sea, seemed to bear the imprint left by him when he enjoyed with her the pleasures of love. The foam was the ornamental paint of the limbs rubbed off at places; the corals were the bites (tinged with red) that lent charm to the face; and the flowers of the woods, crushed (by the waves), were the flowers of her ruffled hair.[62]

K says फेनमेव विषमः प्रभूतः अङ्गरागो यस्यास्ताम्। विद्रुममयेन दन्तव्रणेन आनीतमुखशोभाम्। मुखशब्देन वेलायाः समुद्रसंनिकर्षस्थानमुच्यते। एवंभूतत्वात् परिभुक्तस्य कृतसंभोगस्य समुद्रस्य परिमलं सुरतसंमर्द वहन्तीमिव। MY says *paribhutta* कर्तरि क्तः। अथवा स्त्रीणामपि क्वचित् रागातिशयविवक्षया वा भोक्तृत्वे सति पुरुषस्य भोक्तृत्वमपि स्यात् इति समुद्रस्य वेलापरिभुक्तत्वापत्तिः।

Kula says स्थानेषु स्थानेषु स्थितः फेन एव विषमः[63] अङ्गरागो यस्यास्ताम्। विद्रुमैः प्रवालमणिभिः दन्तव्रणैरिव आनीता मुखच्छाया यस्याः। मृदितं वनस्य केशस्येव कुसुमं यस्याः। एतेनोपभुक्तनायिकाया धर्मा वेलायां समाहिताः। Kula reads पर्युषित (*parivuttha*, cf. *SC* text)for *parihutta* (परिभुक्त). So he says पर्युषितः सम्भोगाय रात्राववस्थितो यः समुद्रो नायकस्तस्य परिमलं सुरतविमर्दमिव वहन्तीम्।

65. सिप्पिउडमउलिअच्छिं लआहरब्भन्तरेसु परिवड्ढन्तम्।
अणुराअपरिट्ठविअं आअण्णन्ति व किंणरुग्गीअरवम्।।

[शुक्तिपुटमुकुलिताक्षीं लतागृहाभ्यन्तरेषु परिवर्धमानम्।
अनुरागपरिस्थापितमाकर्णयन्तीमिव किंनरोद्गीतरवम्।।]

With closed eyes in the shape of the oyster shells, the shore seemed to be listening to the melody of the songs of the

---

[62] The imagery is based on *velā* (seashore) being a feminine noun.

[63] R says विषमः परिरम्भणादिना क्वचित् क्वचित् विलुलितः।

kinnaras, conforming to diverse musical modes, as it echoed through the groves of creepers.

K says लतागृहाभ्यन्तरेषु परिवर्धमानम्, अनुरागेण अन्योन्यानुरागेण प्रतिष्ठापितं गान्धर्वशास्त्रविधिना कृतप्रतिष्ठं किन्नराणां चोद्‌गीतरवम् आकर्णयन्तीमिव। शुक्तिपुटमेव मुकुलितमक्षि यस्यास्तां वेलामपश्यन्निति।

Muda says अनुरागेति रागे रागे प्रतिष्ठापितम्, अनुरागेण वा।

R and Kula have परिस्थापितम्[64]।

इअ सिरिपवरसेणविरइए दसमुहवहे महाकव्वे
पढुमो आसासओ समत्तो।।

[इति श्रीप्रवरसेनविरचिते दशमुखवधे महाकाव्ये
प्रथम आश्वासकः समाप्तः।]

[64] Our copy of Kula has परिष्ठा-। *Cf. Kāśikā* on *Pāṇini* 8.3.65.

द्वितीय आश्वासकः
Second Āśvāsakaḥ

1. अह पेच्छइ रहुतणओ चडुलं दोससअदुक्खबोलेअव्वम्।
अमअरससारगरुअं कज्जारम्भस्स जोव्वणं व समुद्दम्।।

[अथ पश्यति रघुतनयश्चटुलं दोषशतदुःखव्यतिक्रमणीयम्।
अमृतरससारगुरुकं कार्यारम्भस्य यौवनमिव समुद्रम्।।]

Then did Rāma behold the restless sea, esteemed as the (source) of the precious nectar, but hard to traverse on account of many a hazard; as if it were the youth of his enterprise (the age), that is valued for the bliss of the sweet emotion (of love), but fickle, and must be passed with worries because of its numerous flaws.[1]

K says अथ रघुतनयः समुद्रं पश्यति स्म। कथंभूतम् – चटुलं चञ्चलम्। दोषाः मकरादयः तेषां शतैः दुःखेन लङ्घनीयम्। अमृतमयेन सारेण अन्तर्वर्तिना अमृतरसमयेन सारेण गुरुम्। कार्यरम्भस्य रावणवधरूपस्य यौवनमिव प्रतिबन्धहेतुमित्यर्थः। यौवनमपि चटुलं चलस्वभावं दोषशतैः परकलत्राभिलाषादिभिरेव दुःखेन अतिलङ्घयितव्यम्। अमृतरसशब्देन श्रृङ्गररसो लक्ष्यते। स एव सारः तेन गुरुकम्। एवंभूतत्वात् कार्यारम्भस्य यौवनमिव निःश्रेयसकर्मारम्भस्य प्रतिबन्धकमिति।

Kula says कार्यारम्भस्य (यौवनमिव)। यथा यौवनं कामक्रोधादिदोषसंकुलत्वेन दुस्तरत्वात् पुरुषार्थसिद्धेरन्तरायः स्यात्, एवं त्रैलोक्यकल्याणहेतुरावणवधारम्भस्य दुर्लङ्घ्यत्वात् समुद्रोऽपि अन्तराय इत्यर्थच्छलम्। . . . अमृतं जलं तस्य रसो वीर्यं तस्य सारः सुरासुधांशुकौस्तुभादयः तैः गुरुकम्। यौवनपक्षे अमृतमिव यो रससारः शृङ्गाररससारः तेन (गुरुकम्)। अथवा अमृतस्य रसो माधुर्यं स एवोत्कृष्टत्वात् सारः तेन गुरुकम्। यौवनं हि विरूपादीनपि विषयान् मधुरीकरोतीति मधुरमित्याशयः।

Muda says कार्यशरीरस्यापि तिस्रः अवस्थाः। तत्र समुद्र प्राप्तिप्रभृतितरणान्ता मध्यमावस्था यौवनस्थानीयेति यौवनमिव इत्युक्तम्। This explantion is criticized by *SC*–केचित्तु कार्यारम्भस्य . . . यौवनं समुद्रतरणं . . . इति व्याचक्षते, तन्न समुद्रतरणस्य हि यौवनत्वेन समुद्रयौवनयोः साग्यमाह। R says कार्यारम्भस्य . . . यौवनं मध्यभागमिव। कार्ये आद्यन्तभागौ सुकरौ, मध्यभागस्य परं दुष्करत्वमित्यर्थः।

---

[1] The sea is represented as the great obstacle to Rāma's undertaking, and fancied as its youth, because that period of a man's life is beset with difficulties on account of temptations and follies.

2. गअणस्स व पडिबिम्बं धरणीअ व णिग्गमं दिसाण व णिलअम्।
भुअणस्स व मणितडिमं पलअस्स व सावसेसजलविच्छड्डम्।।

[गगनस्येव प्रतिबिम्बं धरण्या इव निर्गमं दिशामिव निलयम्।
भुवनस्येव मणितडिमं प्रलयस्येव सावशेषजलविच्छर्दम्।।]

It seemed to be the reflection of the sky; the opening through which the earth emerged; the home of the regions of the sky; the bejewelled floor of the world; the mass of waters that remained after the deluge.

K (*chāyā*) has मणितलिमं।

K says स्वच्छत्वसूक्ष्मत्वविशालत्वादिभिः गगनस्य प्रतिबिम्बमिव प्रतिनिधिमिव। धरण्या निर्गमस्थानमिव समुद्रेण वेष्टितस्य भूमण्डलस्य निर्गमस्थानमिव। तत्रैव दिङ्मण्डलस्य विस्तारदर्शनात् दिशां निलयमिव आलयमिव। भुवनस्य त्रिभुवनस्य विहारार्थं मणिकुट्टिममिव इन्द्रनीलमणिस्थलमिव। तलिमं कुट्टिमे तल्प इति वैजयन्ती। प्रलयशब्देन एकार्णव उच्यते। तस्य जलसमूहम् अवशेषेण सहितमिव। जगत्प्लावनोपयोगस्य अवशिष्टेन जलेन सहितं प्रलयार्णवजलमिव इत्यर्थः।

MY says प्रतिबिम्बशब्देनात्र प्रतिबिम्बस्थानं लक्ष्यते। तेन समवृत्ततया यन्मुद्रादिसंक्रान्तिस्थानं तद्वदित्यर्थः। मुद्रादेरपि तत्संक्रमणस्थानमधिकपरिमाणं दृष्टम्। एवं च पृथिव्यादिभ्यः तन्निर्गमादीनां विवक्षितमाधिक्यमत्रापि निर्व्यूढं स्यादिति न रीतिभङ्गः। सिन्धोः संक्रान्तिस्थानादिभिः सह सादृश्यं गगनादितश्च आधिक्यमित्युभयमपि अनुसंधेयम्।

Kula says गगनस्य प्रतिबिम्बमिव यद्दर्शनात् गगनबुद्धिर्भवति। निर्गच्छति अस्मादिति निर्गमः। विस्तारातिशयात् धरण्या निर्गममिव। . . . भुवनस्य भुवनन्विासिसकलजनस्य युगपच्चंक्रमणोचितं मणितलिनमिव मणिकुट्टिममिव। प्रलयस्य सावशेषं समग्रं जलनिवहमिव।

Muda quotes *Deśīnāmamālā* 5.20, and says तलिमेति शय्या वासगृहं वा। D.N. mentions कुट्टिम also as one of the meanings of तलिम।

3. भगिरुव्भडकल्लोलं थोरकराहअदिसामुहोत्थअसलिलम्।
सासअमएण बहुसो खोहिज्जन्तं दिसागएण व ससिणा।।

[भ्रमणशीलोद्भटकल्लोलं स्थूलकराहतदिङ्मुखावस्तृतसलिलम्।
स्वाश्रयमृगेण (पक्षे-शाश्वतमदेन) बहुशः क्षोभ्यमाणं दिग्गजेनेव शशिना।।]

With the rolling formidable waves, and the waters smitten by the massive moonbeams, and spreading on all sides, the sea was violently stirred by the moon that shelters a deer, even as it is stirred by an ever-rutting elephant of the quarters[2] (with its massive trunk).

K says भ्रमद्भयङ्करकल्लोलं, चन्द्रस्य स्थूलैः करैः रश्मिभिः आहतत्वात् दिङ्मुखेषु विस्तारितसलिलम् (अवस्तृत *chāyā*)। शाश्वतमृगेण शशिना शाश्वतमदेन दिग्गजेनेव क्षोभ्यमाणम्। करशब्दो दिग्गजेऽपि योज्यः। पश्यतीति सम्बन्धः।

Kula first says दिङ्मुखेषु विस्तृतं (अवस्तृतं?) विततं, and then says दिङ्मुखानि अवस्थगयतीति दिङ्मुखावस्थगं सलितं यस्य तम्। He explains *sāsaa* in the case of the moon as साश्रयः लब्धवसतिः मृगो यत्र तेन शशिना। R has स्वाश्रयमृगेण। My says *sāsaamaeṇa* साशयमृगेण शाश्वतमदेन च।

4. अप्फुण्णविद्दुमवणे गुप्पन्तपडित्थिरे सलिलकल्लोले।
मन्दरगूढप्पहरे अज्जिव संखाअलोहिए व्व वहन्तम्।।

[आक्रान्तविद्रुमवनान्व्याकुलपरिस्थिरान्सलिलकल्लोलान्।
मन्दरगूढप्रहारानद्यापि संस्त्यानलोहितानिव वहन्तम्।।]

It bore waves, now restless, now still, that overran the coral-reefs and seemed to be the bruises inflicted by the Mandara mountain, with the clotted gore still in them.[3]

K and MY read *appuṇṇa* (आपूर्ण K and Deva; आक्रान्त MY) for *apphuṇṇa* आक्रान्त found in R and Muda who refer to Hemacandra 4.258. Kula has आक्रान्त। *SC* text agrees with R.

K has प्रतिष्ठतान् for *paḍitthire* परिस्थिरान् (R)। For Kula's reading see below. K and MY read संघात for *saṁkhāa* संस्त्यान found in R, Kula and Muda. Cf. Hemacandra 4.15. K, MY and kula read मूढ for गूढ (R and Muda)।

K says आपूर्णविद्रुमवनान्, अद्यापि संघातलोहितानिव घनीभूतरुधिरान् मन्दरस्य मन्थनसमये मूढप्रहारानिव, अदर्शितव्रणः प्रहारो मूढप्रहारः, एवं दृश्यमानान् व्याकुलप्रतिष्ठितान् जलकल्लोलान् वहन्तम्।

MY says *saṁghāa* संस्त्यान। Kula says मूढप्रहारः अस्फुटितो घातः। He seems to read प्रविस्तृतान् (*pavitthie*, *SC* text), and says आक्रान्तं विद्रुमवनं यैस्तान्, विद्रुमवनस्खलनात् गुप्यमानप्रविस्तृतान् व्याकुलीभवत्प्रविततान्,

---

[2] One of the elephants supposed to support the earth.

[3] The waves are fancied as the bruises received by the sea when it was churned with the Mandara mountain by the gods and demons, the coral-reefs being the clotted blood.

विस्तृतत्वेन स्वच्छतायां सत्यां प्रकटविद्रुमालोकत्वात् संस्त्यानलोहितान् पिण्डितरुधिरान् (partly corrected from *SC*)।

5. मुहलघणविप्पइण्णं जलणिवहं भरिअसअलणहमहिविवरम्।
णइमुहपह्लत्थन्तं अप्पाण विणिग्गअं जसं व पिअन्तम्।।

[मुखरघनविप्रकीर्णे जलनिवहं भृतसकलनभोमहीविवरम्।
नदीमुखपर्यस्यन्तमात्मनो विनिर्गतं यश इव पिबन्तम्।।]

It was absorbing its own water, scattered by the rumbling clouds, and pervading the interval between the sky and the earth, and cascading through the mouths of the rivers; as if it were its own fame, constantly spread abroad by the minstrels, and expanding through (the praises of) suppliants, and permeating the entire heavens, the earth and the nether regions.

K says आत्मविनिर्गतं पूर्वमात्मनो विनिर्गतं जलनिवहं यश इव पिबन्तम्। कथमिति – मुखरैः घननिवहैः तत एव गृहीत्वा विप्रकीर्णमभिवृष्टं, पूरितसकलनभोमहीविवरं, प्रवृद्धनदीमुखैः पर्यस्यमानम् आत्मन्येव पात्यमानम्। यशोऽपि मुखरैः प्रशंसापरैः पुरुषैः घनं विप्रकीर्णं लोके ख्यापितं, भरितसकलमहीविवरं, पुनः केषांचित् याचकानां मुखैः पर्यस्यमानं पुरतः प्रकाश्यमानं यशस्विना पीयत इति। R says नतिमुखेन याचकेन पर्यस्यत् दिशि दिशि गच्छत् (यशः), and नदीमुखेन नदीप्रवेशस्थानेन पर्यस्यन्तमितस्ततो गच्छन्तं (जलनिवहम्)। समुद्रतरङ्गाभिघातादिति भावः। He also says व्याप्ताकाशमहीपातालं (यशः)। विवरं पातालम्।

My says अत्रोदाररसिकराजसमाधिः। अपश्लोकनपरैः कविभिः विस्तारितमशेषलोकव्याप्तमात्मीयमौदार्यादिगुणनिमित्तं यशो वारस्त्रीभिः गीयमानं यथा राजा श्रृणोति तद्वदित्यर्थः। Kula says पर्यस्यत् आपतत्। Muda says पर्यस्यमानं क्षिप्यमाणम्। नतिमुखैः याचकैः।

6. जोह्लाए व्व मिअङ्कं कित्तीअ व सुउरिसं पहाए व्व रविम्।
सेलं महाणईअ व सिरीअ चिरणिग्गआइ वि अमुञ्चन्तम।।

[ज्योत्स्नयेव मृगाङ्कं कीर्त्येव सुपुरुषं प्रभयेव रविम्।
शैलं महानद्येव श्रिया चिरनिर्गतयाप्यमुच्यमानम्।।]

The goddess of wealth, even though she emerged from it long ago,[4] still adhered to it, as does moonlight to the moon,

[4] I.e. during the churning, cf. verse 11.

or fame to a good man, or sunshine to the sun, or a great river to a mountain.

K says चिरनिर्गतयापि अमृतमथनवेलायामेव निर्गतयापि श्रिया इदानीममुच्यमानम्। श्रीशब्दो लक्ष्म्यां च विभूत्यां च वर्तते। परया विभूत्या युक्तमिति परमार्थः। शोभाविभूत्यादयोऽपि लक्ष्मीस्वरूपाणीत्येवमुक्तम्। कथमिवज्योत्स्नया चिरनिर्गतयापि मृगाङ्कमिव। ज्योत्स्नादिभिः मृगाङ्कादयः शश्वदमुच्यमाना एव भवन्ति। Kula says श्रिया चिरनिर्गतयापि अमुच्यमानम् अद्यापि नानारत्नसम्पत्तेरविच्छेददर्शनात्।

7. कालन्तरजीअहरं गओणिअत्तन्तपवणरअघट्टिज्जन्तम्।
सल्लं व देहलग्गं विअडं वडवामुहाणलं वहमाणम्।।

[कालान्तरजीवहरं गतापनिवर्तमानपवनरयघट्यमानम्।
शल्यमिव देहलग्नं विकटं वडवामुखानलं वहमानम्।।]

It bore the vast submarine fire, clinging to its bosom, that consumed its waters at the epoch of destruction, being stirred by the winds sweeping back and forth, as if it were a massive spear, embedded in the body, and shaken by the recurrent breathings that destroyed life at the end.

K says शल्यमिव वडवामुखाग्निं वहन्तम्। कथंभूतम् – कालान्तरे युगान्ते जीवहरं जलस्य दाहकम्। कालान्तरे प्राणहरमिति च। गतेन पुनरपि निवर्तमानेन पवनेन घट्ट्यमानम् आहन्यमानम्। शल्यमपि गतागतं कुर्वता प्राणवायुना घट्ट्यते। देहलग्नं जलमये देहे लग्नम्। अन्यत्र देहे मर्मस्पृशि लग्नम्। विकटम् अतिस्फुटम्।

Kula says कालान्तरे प्रलये जीवन् प्राणिनः, अथवा जीवं जीवनं हरतीति तम्, पक्षे मरणकाले प्राणहरं, गतापनिवृत्ताभ्यां गमनागमनाभ्यां पवनेन वायुना श्वासवायुना च घट्ट्यमानं चाल्यमानं शल्यमिव देहे पाताले शरीरे च लग्नं विकटं विशालं वडवामुखानलं वहमानम्। Muda says जीवो जलं प्राणश्च। घट्ट चलने।

8. धुअवणराइकरअलं मलअमहिन्दत्थणोरसोल्लणसुहिअम्।
वेलालिङ्गणमुक्कं छिविओसरिएहि वेलवन्तं व महिम्।।

[धुतवनराजिकरतलां मलयमहेन्द्रस्तनोर आर्द्रीकरणसुखिताम् (पक्षे–सुहिताम्)।
वेलालिङ्गनमुक्तां स्पृष्टापसृतकैर्वेपयन्तमिव (पक्षे–व्याकुलयन्तमिव) महीम्।।]

It seemed to be teasing the earth by touching and withdrawing (by turns), while she, released after being embraced by the flood-tide,[5] shook her hands, the woods

[5] Cf. Kulanātha in Extracts.

(on the shore); with her breasts, the Malaya and the Mahendra mountain, refreshed by sea spray.[6]

R reads *malaa-mahinda-tthaṇora-sollaṇa-suhiaṁ* which he construes as मलयमहेन्द्रस्तनोरआर्द्रीकरणसुखिताम् (पक्षे सुहिताम्)। Kula's reading is same, but his interpretation is different. See below. K, MY and Muda read — *tthaṇiṁ*(-स्तनीं) separately followed by रस। K reads रसार्द्रित, i.e. *rasollia. Ollia* is used several times in the poem (88, 90, etc.). Muda reads *rasollaṇa* explained as रसेनार्द्रीकरणम्। K reads आलिङ्गित for *āliṁgaṇa.*

K says समुद्रस्य वेला च मही च नायिकात्वनोपात्ते। तत्र संनिकृष्टया वेलया समालिङ्गितत्वात् समुद्रेण मुक्तां महीं स्पृष्टापसृतैः वृद्धिक्षययोः क्रमेण स्पर्शनैरपसरणैश्च व्याकुलयन्तमिव। कथंभूताम् – धुतवनराजिकरतलां स्पर्शसमये धुतवनराजिकरतलां, मलयमहेन्द्राख्यस्तनीं, रसेन जलेन आर्द्रितत्वात् सुखितां कन्दलितवीरुधमित्यर्थः। अन्यत्र रसेन रागेण आर्द्रां सुखितां च। वेलामालिङ्ग्य स्पर्शसज्जनक्रिया तस्य परिहास इति मन्तव्यम्। अत एवमपि व्याकुलता भवति।

MY reads लङ्घित for (आ)लिङ्गित। He says रसः शृङ्गारो जलं च। *suhiaṁ* सुखितामिति स्त्रीपक्षे। जातसौहित्यामिति महीपक्षे। स्पृष्टावसृतैः वञ्चयन्तमिव व्याकुलयन्तमिवेति वा। वेलायाम् अवसरलाभे सति आदरचुम्बनादिना लङ्घितां पुनरसहनतया विमुक्तामिति। अन्यत्र वेलायां तीरदेशे लङ्घितां पुनर्विमुक्तामिति। आलिङ्गनाद्यसहनायामपि अन्तरूप जातरसायां स्त्रियां कामिनः तदावर्जनसमाधिरत्रानुसंधेयः।

Kula says महीसागरयोः नायकनायिकाधर्मान् समादधदाह। महीं कुपितनायिकामिव स्पृष्टापसृतैः(?) व्याकुलयन्तमिव प्रलोभ्य आवर्जयन्तमिवेत्यर्थः। स्त्रीस्वभावेन वाम्योपदर्शनार्थं धुतवनराजिकरतलां, रागजननार्थं वेला अम्बुविकृतिः तया . . . यदालिङ्गनं तेन मुक्ताम्। रागवृद्धिं सूचयन्नाह। मलयमहेन्द्रौ स्तनाविव, आभ्याम् उरसि *sollaṇeṇa*(?) सुखितं समुद्रं सुखितां महीं वा। *SC* renders *sollaṇa* as आर्द्रीकरण, but Hemacandra 4.90, 143 gives *sollaī* in the sense of पचति and क्षिपति।

Deva says *malaa-mahinda-tthaṇorasollaṇa-suhiaṁ* इति केचित्, i.e. मलयमहेन्द्रस्तनालिङ्गनसुखितं (सुखितां?)। The last word is not clear. Then he says *ura-solaṇaṁ*(*-lla-*?) आश्लेषः। Deva seems to refer to Kula's reading.

---

[6] Lit. delighted at the drenching of her bosom that had the Malaya and the Mahendra for breasts. The earth is fancied as a *nāyikā*, and the sea as a *nāyaka*; and the ebb and flow of the sea as a series of embraces and withdrawals.

R says मलयमहेन्द्रावेव स्तनौ यत्र तादृशं यदुरः स्वमध्यदेशः तरङ्गेण तदार्द्रीकरणेन सुखितां शैत्यमासादयन्तीम्।

9. ठाणे वि ठिइपहुत्तं पलए महिमण्डलम्मि वि अमाअन्तम्।
पणअन्तवामणतणुं कमन्तदेहभरभरिअलोअं व हरिम्।।

[स्थानेऽपि स्थितिप्रभूतं प्रलये महीमण्डलेऽप्यमान्तम्।
प्रणयद्वामनतनुं क्रममाणदेहभरभृतलोकमिव हरिम्।।]

It had ample room in its appointed place, because it kept within bounds, but had not enough space even on the entire earth during the deluge. It was like Viṣṇu that assumed the form of a suppliant dwarf, but (later) filled the universe with the bulk of his striding figure.[7]

K says स्थाने निभृतावस्थापनेऽपि स्थितिप्रभूतं पर्याप्तम्। स्थानमर्यादयोः स्थितिरिति वैजयन्ती। प्रलये भूमण्डलेऽपि अपर्याप्नुवन्तम्। तदानीं प्रणयद्वामनतनुम्। प्रणयनं याच्ञा निर्माणं मैत्री। याच्ञासु प्रणये चाग्निसंस्कृताविति शेवः(?)। प्रणयनावस्थायां वामनतनुं पश्चात् क्रामता देहभरेण पूरितलोकं हरिमिव। MY says *paṇaanta* प्रार्थयमान। इदानीं दृश्यमानं महत्त्वमपि हरेः वामनतनुत्ववत् लघुतरमेवास्य भाविविजृम्भणापेक्षया इत्याशयः।

Kula says स्थानेऽपि प्रतिनियतनिजदेशेऽपि स्थित्या मर्यादया प्रभूतं, प्रलये महीमण्डलेऽपि असंमान्तम्। अर्थिभ्यो दातुं प्रतिज्ञातः अर्थः पणः। पणाय पणग्रहणाय कान्ता मनोहरा वामनतनुर्यस्य तम्। अथवा प्रणयन्ती प्रतिग्रहार्थम् उपसर्पन्ती वामनतनुर्यस्य तं . . . हरिमिव।

Muda says स्थाने स्थितिवेलायां स्थित्या मर्यादया *vahuttaṁ* पर्याप्तं परिच्छिन्नमपि कल्पान्ते सर्वस्मिन्नपि भूमण्डले *amāantaṁ* अधिकीभवन्तम्।

10. दीसन्तं अहिरामं सुव्वन्तं पि अविइह्णसोअव्वगुणम्।
सुकअस्स व परिणामं उअहुज्जन्तं पि सासअसुहप्फलअम्।।

[दृश्यमानमभिरामं श्रूयमाणमप्यवितृष्णश्रोतव्यगुणम्।
सुकृतस्येव परिणाममुपभुज्यमानमपि स्वाश्रयशुभ (पक्षे–शाश्वतसुख) फलदम्।।]

It gave delight as one beheld it. One had to listen eagerly to the recital of its virtues, even though one heard about it (often). Although its gifts were enjoyed (in profusion), it (freely) yielded its products that brought abiding joy; just as

[7] A reference to the three great strides of the Dwarf incarnation of Viṣṇu.

the fruit of one's religious merit, although enjoyed (in this life), conferred everlasting bliss.

K, Kula and Muda read परिभुज्यमानम् for *ua-* (उप) found in R.

K says दृश्यमानावस्थायाम् अभिरामम्। श्रूयमाणमपि महिमातिशयात् अवितृष्णं यथा अविगततृष्णं यथा भवति तथा श्रोतव्यगुणम्। परिभुज्यमानमपि पुंसां महारत्नप्रदानैः शाश्वतसुखफलदम्। सुकृतस्य परिणाममिव पुण्यस्य महतः परिणाममिव। स च परिभुज्यमानोऽपि सुकृतस्य अतिमहत्तया शाश्वतसुखरूपं फलं ददाति। MY says सुकृतस्य परिणामो जात्यायुर्भोगरूपो विपाकः। Kula says सुकृतस्य यागादिकर्मणः परिणाममिव फलनिष्पत्तिमिव। शाश्वतम् अविच्छिन्नं शुभफलं मणिमुक्तादिकं यस्य। पक्षे शुभफलं ददातीति तथा तम्।

11. उक्खअदुमं व सेलं हिमहअकमलाअरं व लच्छिविमुक्कम्।
पीअमइरं व चसअं बहुलपओसं व मुद्धचन्दविरहिअम्।।

[उत्खातद्रुममिव शैलं हिमहतकमलाकरमिव लक्ष्मीविमुक्तम्।
पीतमदिरमिव चषकं बहुलप्रदोषमिव मुग्धचन्द्रविरहितम्।।]

[उत्खातद्रुमं वशेलं हिमहयकमलाकरं बलच्छिद्विमुक्तम्।
पीतमदिरं वचाशयं बहुलप्रदोषं वमुग्धचन्द्रविरहितम्।।]

It was like a mountain with its (best) tree uprooted. Abandoned by the goddess of wealth, it was like a lotus pool with the flowers blasted by frost. It was like a wine-bowl, emptied of the wine. Bereft of the young moon, it was like an evening of the dark half of the month.[8]

K says उत्खातद्रुमं मथने देवैः स्वयमेवोद्धृतवृक्षम् उद्गृहीतपारिजातं, तदा शैलमिव। शैलोऽपि जनैः दारुक्रियार्थमुच्छिन्नोद्रुमो भवति। तथा लक्ष्मीविमुक्तं नारायणगृहीतया लक्ष्म्या विमुक्तम्। तदानीं हिमहतकमलाकरमिव। हिमोपहतस्य पद्माकरस्य नहि लक्ष्मीः न शोभास्ति। तथा दैतेयैः पीतमदिरम्, मदिरा मथनोत्थिता वरुणस्य आत्मजा, चषकमिव। चषकमपि स्त्रीभिः पीतमद्यं भवति। बहुलपक्षप्रदोषमिव मुग्धचन्द्रेण परमेश्वराय अर्पितेन चन्द्रेण विरहितम् (मुग्धेन मनोहरेण कलामात्राशेषेण चन्द्रेण विरहितं बहुलप्रदोषमिव कृष्णपक्षरजनीमिव Kula)। दुर्वाससः शापेनोपहतानां देवानामेवमात्मसंभवैः पारिजातलक्ष्मीमदिराचन्द्रकौस्तुभामृतप्रभृतिभिः द्रव्यैः स्वास्थ्यं कृतवन्तमित्यर्थः। इदमौदार्यलक्षणमुक्तमाचार्यदण्डिना – न स्तूयसे नरेन्द्र त्वं ददासीति कदाचन। स्वमेव मत्वा गृह्णन्ति यतस्त्वद्धनमर्थिनः।। इति।

---

[8] The *pārijāta* tree, the goddess of wealth, wine and the moon were taken out of the ocean during the churning.

अत्र केचिदन्यथापि व्याचक्षते। तद् यथा उत्खातद्रुमम्। वशेलं वशा स्ववशा इला भूर्मियस्य तम्। हिमहयकमलाकरम्। हिमशब्देन चन्द्र उच्यते। हय उच्चैःश्रवाः। कमला श्रीः तेषामाकरमुत्पत्तिस्थानम्। बलच्छिद्विमुक्तं बलच्छित् देवेन्द्रः तेन विमुक्तम्। पर्वतपक्षच्छेदसमये पर्वताः सपक्षाः केचित् समुद्रं प्रविष्टाः। तदा तेन देवेन्द्रेण परिहृतः समुद्र इति। पीतमदिरमिति च। स्वयं पीतमदिरमिव चञ्चलत्वादेवमुक्तम्। बहुलप्रदोषं बहुलाः प्रकृष्टाः दोषाः तिमिङ्गिलादयो यस्य तम्। वमोद्धृतं वमनं वमः, अगस्त्येन पीतस्य पुनर्वमनात् उद्धृतमित्यर्थः। दविरहितम्। दु उपताप इति धातुः। दवनशीलाः दविराः दानवाः तेषाम् आवासतया हितम्। अयमर्थः परिक्लिष्टत्वात् नातिसमञ्जसः। पूर्वोक्त एवार्थः साधीयान्।

It will be seen that in the artificial interpretation of the verse K reads *vamuddhaaṁ* (वमोद्धृतं) *davira*, etc. which shows that in the normal interpretation he reads *anda* for *canda*. The explanation of *vaca-saaṁ* in the artificial interpretation is missing in K. R says वचा पृथिवी तत्र शेते यस्तम्, i.e. वचाशयम्।

12. णिप्फण्णसुहालोअं विमलजलब्भन्तरट्ठिअं वहमाणम्।
दरकड्ढिअं व रइणा करावलम्बिअकरं रअणसंघाअम्।।

[निष्पन्नसुखालोकं विमलजलाभ्यन्तरस्थितं वहमानम्।
दरकृष्टमिव रविणा करावलम्बितकरं रत्नसंघातम्।।]

It had masses of jewels, lying in the depth of its limpid waters, that, with their pleasant lustre clearly visible, seemed to be partly drawn up by the sun, taking hold of their rays with its own rays.[9]

K, MY, Muda and probably Kula read *ṇivvaḍia* for *ṇipphaṇṇa* निष्पन्न found in R.

K says निर्व्यक्तः जलात् पृथक् प्रकाशमानः सुखो दृष्टिप्रियङ्कर आलोकः किरणप्रकाशो यस्य तम्। विमलस्य जलस्याभ्यन्तरस्थलेषु स्थितं, करावलम्बितकरम् आदित्यस्य करैः अवलम्बितरश्मिसमूहम्। करशब्देन हस्तश्च विवक्षितः। रविणा किंचिदाकृष्टमिव दृश्यमानं रत्नसंघातं वहन्तम्। Kula says निकटमिव उपलक्ष्यमाणत्वात् दराकृष्टमिव रविणा करैरवलम्बिताः करा यस्य तं रत्नसंपातं (संघातं?)वहमानम्।

MY says *ṇivvaḍia* पृथग्भूत (Kula also). Muda refers to

[9] *Kara* means both "hands" and "rays". The imagery is that of someone pulling a person out of deep water by catching hold of his hands. The idea is, the jewels glittering in the waters seemed to be quite close to the sunlit surface of the sea.

Hemacandra 4.62 (*ṇivvaḍai* पृथक् स्पष्टो वा भवतीत्यर्थ:)। Muda (*chāyā*) has स्पष्टसुखालोकं।

K, MY, Muda and Kula read verses 9-12 after verse 2.

13. महणासाअविमुक्कं उच्छित्तामअविसङ्खलाणलणिवहम्।
वासुइमुहणीसन्दं वडवामुहकुहरपुञ्जिअं वहमाणम्।।

[मथनायासविमुक्तमुत्क्षिप्तामृतविशृङ्खलानलनिवहम्।
वासुकिमुखनि:स्यन्दं वडवामुखकुहरपुञ्जितं वहमानम्।।]

It seemed to carry the venom, ejected from the mouth of Vāsuki during the toil of churning the ocean, and accumulated in the cavern of the submarine fire, and enveloped in raging flames, because the nectar had been taken out of the waters.[10]

K, MY Muda and Kula read *va vahantaṁ* for *vahamāṇaṁ* (R).

K says मथनायासेन आत्मानो मथनक्लेशेन विमुक्तमुद्गीर्णम् उद्धृतामृतत्वात् विषप्रतिबन्धभूतस्य अमृतस्योद्धारात् विशृङ्खलाग्निनिवहं, वडवाया मुखकुहरे पुञ्जितं वासुकेर्मुखनिष्यन्दं वहन्तमिव। वडवामुखे पुञ्जित: अग्नि: न तत्संभव:, किं पुनर्वासुकिविषनिष्यन्द: तत्र पुञ्जित इत्युतप्रेक्षितम्। MY says उद्धृतामृतरसतया स्वैरज्वलितदहनं वासुकिविषं सर्वत्र व्याप्य स्थितमपि वडवाकुहरे पुञ्जीभूतमिव लक्ष्यमाणंवहन्तम्। अथवा वडवाग्निमध्यस्थितमिव ज्वलग्निजज्वालापरीतं वासुकिविषं वहन्तमित्यर्थ:।

Kula says मथनकृतेन आयासेन विमुक्तमुद्गीर्णं, समुद्रस्य उद्धृतामृतत्वात् विशृङ्खल: अनलनिवहो विषाग्निसमूहो यस्य तं, मथनरज्जूकृतस्य वासुके: मुखनिष्यन्दं मुखप्रच्युतविषं वडवामुखकुहरे पुञ्जितमिव वहन्तं वाडवाग्निव्याजात् वासुकिविषकूटमिव वहन्तमित्युत्प्रेक्षा।

14. धीरं व जलसमूहं तिमिणिवहं मिव सपक्खपव्वअलोअम्।
णइसोत्ते व्व तरङ्गे रअणाइ व गरुअगुणसआइँ वहन्तम्।।

[धैर्यमिव जलसमूहं तिमिनिवहमिव सपक्षपर्वतलोकम्।
नदीस्रोतांसीव तरङ्गान्रत्नानीव गुरुकगुणशतानि वहन्तम्।।]

[10] The serpent Vāsuki was used as a rope coiled round the Mandara mountain, with which the ocean was churned. Here, the submarine fire is fancied as his fiery venom, enveloped in flames that remained unquenched, because the nectar, which could have counteracted the poison, was taken away by the gods when it emerged durning the churning.

It had the mass of waters just as it had fortitude. It had the winged mountains[11] as it had shoals of whales. It had the waves as it had the incoming rivers, and numerous substantial qualities as it had gems.

K and Muda read जालम् for *loaṁ* लोकम् (R and Kula)।

K says तिमिः महामत्स्यः। तिमिनिवहमिव सपक्षं पर्वतजालं वहन्तम्। समुद्रस्थाः तिमयः सपक्षपर्वतसदृशा इत्यर्थः। MY says अत्र इवशब्दाः सहार्थाः सादृश्यार्थाश्च।

15. पाआलोअरगहिरे महिपइरिक्कविअडे णहणिरालम्बे।
तेल्लोक्के व्व महुमहं अप्पाण च्चिअ गआगआइँ करेन्तम्।।

[पातालोदरगभीरे महीप्रतिरिक्तविकटे नभोनिरालम्बे।
त्रैलोक्य इव मधुमथनमात्मन्येव गतागतानि कुर्वन्तम्।।]

It moved back and forth in itself, deep like the cavity of the nether regions, and vast without including the earth, and independent like the sky; even as Viṣṇu comes and goes[12] in his own self, the universe, deep in the nether regions, far more extensive than the earth, and unsupported in the sky.

Pairikka is rendered by R as प्रतिरिक्त। Muda reads it as *vairikka* and quotes *Deśīnāmamālā* 6.71 which gives *pairikka* in the sense of विशाल, एकान्त and शून्य। The world is taken also as व्यतिरिक्त। Cf. 1.58.

K says त्रैलोक्यस्य च समुद्ररूपस्य च साम्यमुच्यते। पातालोदरैः पातालान्तरालैः गम्भीरे। समुद्रपक्षे पातालोदरवत् गम्भीरे। महीव्यतिरिक्तविकटे महीमण्डलात् विशेषेण अतिरिक्तविशाले अधिकविपुले[13]। महीवलयसंवेशात् अन्तरिक्षं विशालं भवति। ततः स्वर्गो विशालः ततो महर्लोकादयः। यथाह श्रुतिः – उरवो ह वे नामैते लोकाः ये परेणादित्यम्। अथ हैते वरीयांसो लोकाः ये परेणादित्यमिति। परेण परस्तादित्यर्थः। समुद्रोऽपि महीमण्डलात् विशाल एव दृश्यते। नभसि निरालम्बे। नभसः शून्यत्वात् तत्र कस्यचिदालम्बनं न स्यादिति। अमरावतीविमानादयः तपःप्रभावेन ध्रियन्ते। उभयत्र समानमेतत्। एवंभूते त्रैलोक्ये मधुमथनो यथा गतागतानि अवतारैः करोति तद्वत् एवंभूते स्वात्मन्येव गमनं गमनक्रियां कुर्वन्तम्।

---

[11] Those of the mountains which had jumped into the ocean to save their wings when these were being clipped by Indra.

[12] I.e. appears and disappears in the course of his incarnations.

[13] R says महीप्रतिरिक्ते भूमिशून्ये खाते विकटे भयानके। . . . कीदृशि त्रैलोक्य–महीप्रतिरिक्ते मह्या व्यतिरिक्ते कन्दरादौ विकटे शून्ये।

MY says पातालोदरवत् गम्भीरे, महीतलवत् केवलविकटे, नभोवत् निरालम्बे इति आत्मन्येवेति समुद्रविशेषणतायां। योज्यम्। त्रैलोक्यविशेषणत्वे तु पातालोदरे गभीर इत्यादिरूपेण सप्तमीसमासः। *pairikka-viaḍe* केवलविकटे। अत्र गतागते त्रैलोक्यात्मानो भगवत आविर्भावतिरोभावौ।

Muda says *pāāloara-gahire* – समुद्रस्तावत् पातालोदरवत् गभीरः तथा *mahi-vairikka-viaḍe* महीशून्ये विकटे च। तथा *ṇaha-ṇirālambe* नभोवत् निरालम्बे। त्रैलोक्यमपि पातालोदरे गम्भीरं मह्यां विशालं विकटं (च) यद्वा महीव्यतिरिक्तं विकटम्। नभसि निरालम्बम्। विष्णुरपि पातालोदरवत् तलस्पर्शविरहात् गभीरः। तथा महीव्यक्तिरिक्तः प्रपञ्चबहिर्भूतत्वात्। नभोवत् निरालम्बश्च। उक्तं च – सर्वाधारमनाधारमिति। Muda remarks त्रैलोक्यस्य विष्णोः समुद्रस्य च श्लिष्टाणि विशेषणानि।

Deva says स च सकलजगत्स्वरूपी भगवान् त्रैलोक्ये सर्गप्रलयाद्याविर्भावतिरोभावरूपगतागतानि करोति। . . . स्वांशभूते त्रैलोक्ये मधुमथनमिव[14] आत्मन्येव गतागतानि कुर्वाणं समुद्रमिति। समुद्रस्य च त्रैलोक्यस्य च श्लेषः। समुद्रोऽपि पातालोदरवत् गभीरः, महीशून्यत्वात् विशालो, नभ इव निर्मलः। त्रैलोक्यमपि पातालोदरेण गम्भीरं, मह्यादिभ्यो व्यतिरिक्तं विशालं विशेषेण विशालं, नभसि निवारणम् (निरावरणम्?) इति। Kula's gloss on this verse is missing in our copy.

16. अहिलीअ परमुहीहिं छिविओसरिएहिँ अणुसअविलोलाहिं।
अणुणिज्जमाणमग्गं वेवन्तणिअत्तपत्थिआहिँ णईहिं।।

[अभिलीय पराङ्भुखीभिः स्पृष्टापसृताभिरनुशयविलोलाभिः।
अनुगम्य(नीय)मानमार्गं वेपमाननिवृत्तप्रस्थिताभिर्नदीभिः।।]

Approaching and retreating, the rivers (first) appeared to withdraw on being caressed by the sea, and then followed in its wake, as if they were smitten with remorse, quivering as they advanced and retraced their steps.[15]

R reads *ahilīa paramuhīhiṁ* अभिलीय पराङ्मुखीभिः। K says the same thing, but his *pratīka* is *abhilia*, which show that he reads *paraṁmuhīhiṁ*. MY and Muda have *ahilia*, but they explain it as

---

[14] R says यथा मधुमथनः त्रैलोक्ये गतागतान्यात्मन्येव करोति।

[15] The rivers, advancing and receding as they encounter the waves, and then falling into the sea, are fancied as *nāyikās*, who repent having rejected the advances of their lovers, and subsequently go out to meet them. The readings followed are *ahilia* and *osariāhi*. See Extracts, especially the interpretation of Kulanātha.

अभिलीन, which is found also in Kula and Deva. *SC* text has *ahiliṇa*. K and Kula read अपसृताभिः (*osariāhi*) for *osariehi* अपसृतैः (R, MY and Muda)।

K says पूर्वं समुद्रमभिलीय आलिङ्ग्य जलवृद्धिसमये पराङ्मुखीभिः, तदानीमनुपतता समुद्रेण स्पृष्टापसृताभिः, पुनः समुद्रजले प्रकृतिं भजति सति अनुशयात् विलोलाभिः, अत एव वेपमाननिवृत्तप्रस्थिताभिः नदीभिः दायिताभिरन्वीयमानमार्गम्। समुद्रस्य हि नद्यः पत्न्यः तस्मात् नायिकाधर्मा नदीष्वेव दर्शिताः।

MY says अभिलीनपराङ्मुखीभिः पत्युः समुद्रस्य रभसोपगमेन प्रतिपथं गताभिः, पुनः स्पृष्टापसृताभ्यां निवृत्ते तस्मिन् अनुशयादिव विलोलाभिरत एव वेपमानाभिः निवृत्तप्रस्थिताभिः नदीभिः प्रियाभिः अन्वीयमानमार्गमिति (Muda also)।

Muda says स्त्रियो हि पुरुषेणाभियुज्यमानाः प्रथमं पराङ्मुख्यो भवन्ति। तस्मिन् उपेक्ष्य गते पश्चात्तप्ता भवन्ति। ततो दुर्वारस्मरपीडिताः तद्गृहं यान्तीति स्थितिः। तदेतत् समुद्रपतित्वेन नदीषु आरोप्यते।

Kula says प्रथमं वेगात् नदीभिः स्त्रीभिः रागादभिलीनाभिः पश्चात् समुद्राम्बुप्रतीघातात् स्वयमभिगभव्रोडया च पराङ्मुखीभिः, स्पृष्टाश्च ता अपसृताश्चेति तथा ताभिः, वेपमानाश्च निवृत्ताश्च प्रस्थिताश्चेति तथोक्ताः ताभिः, अतो दयितावधीरणात् अनुशयेन पश्चात्तापेन विलोलाभिः पुनरागमनकांक्षिणीभिः नदीभिः अन्वीयमानमार्गम्। एतेन कलहान्तरितानायिका लक्ष्यते। तथोक्तम् – चाटुकारमपि जीवितनाथं, कोपतः समवधीर्य गता या। तप्यतेऽनुशयवह्निवितानैः, कथ्यतेऽत्र कलहान्तरिता सा।। इति। *SC* reproduces all this with a slight difference in the quotation, and remarks नदीनामेष स्वभावो यत् समुद्रे निपतन्त्यो वर्धमानतदम्बुभिः प्रतीघातात् प्रतीपगामिन्यो भवन्ति, पुनश्च निवर्तमाने समुद्राम्बुनि वेगवशात् वेपमानाः तत्र निपतन्ति।

Deva reads *ahilia* (अभिलीन) and says – *chiviosariehi* प्राप्त्यपसरणाभ्यां हेतुभूताभ्यामात्मनः अभिव्रीलितपराङ्मुखीभिः। व्रीलितमहेलासमुचितपराङ्मुखत्वदर्शनात् नदीनामपि व्रीलितत्वारोपः। Here he takes अभिलीन or *ahilia* in the sense of अभिव्रीडित। The word is recorded in *Deśīnāmamālā* 1.57, but with the meanings अभिभव and कोप। In an alternative explanation Deva explains अभिलीन as अभिगत।

Deva (*chāyā*) reads स्पृष्ट्वापसृतमिव, i.e. *chiviosariaṁ va*, taking *chivia* as an absolutive. Explaining the verse according to this reading, he says अभिलीनपराङ्मुखीभिरिति . . . (प्रति)हतत्वात् प्रतिनिवृत्तगताभिः तस्मिन् अन्तः प्रविष्टे त्वरितनिवृत्ताभिः नदीभिः पुनः प्रविश्यमानं समुद्रमिति। स्त्रियो हि झटिति पुरुषेण (अभिगम्य)-मानाः स्वयं पराङ्मुख्यो भवन्ति। पश्चात् तस्मिन उपेक्ष्य गते अनुशयविलोलाः स्वगृहं (तद्गृहं ?) स्वयमेवाभिसरन्ति। एवं समुद्रेण यदाभिलीना अभिगताः तदा पराङ्मुख्योऽभूवन् नद्यः। स च (?) स्पृष्ट्वा तत्रालब्धसुखः

अपसृतः। तदनुशयविलोलाभिरेव वेपमाननिवृत्तप्रस्थिताभिः नदीभिः समुद्रः अन्वीयमानमार्ग इति।

R who reads *chiviosariehi* says स्पृष्टापसृतकरूपव्यापारैः अभिलीय मिलनं कृत्वा पराङ्मुखीभिः नदीभिरनुगम्यमानमार्गम्। R on verse 8 says स्पृष्टापसृतकैरालिङ्गनविशेषव्यापारैः।

17. जीअगरुईहि अज्ज वि इच्छापज्जत्तसुहरसाहि मएन्तम्।
धणरिद्धीअ सिरिअ अ सलिलुप्पण्णाइ वारुणीअ अ लोअम्।।

[जीवगुर्वीभिरद्यापीच्छापर्याप्तसुखरसाभिर्मदयन्तम्।
धनऋद्ध्या श्रिया च सलिलोत्पन्नया वारुण्या च लोकम्।।]

It still maddened the world with the splendour of its riches and the goddess of wealth and wine. All these had emerged during the churning,[16] and are esteemed more than one's life and afford enjoyment to one's heart's content.

K, MY, Muda and Kula read मथन (*mahaṇa*) for सलिल (R). K says मथनोत्पन्नया धनद्ध्यां। धनशब्देन कौस्तुभपारिजातादय उच्यन्ते। मथनोत्पन्नया च वारुण्या मदिरया च एताभिः जीववत् गुर्वीभिः, अथवा जीवितादपि गुर्वीभिः। इच्छापर्याप्तसुखरसाभिः इच्छायाः पर्याप्तः सुखरसो यासां, पुंसाम् आशापर्याप्तसुखप्रदायिनीभिः इत्यर्थः। अद्यापि लोकं मदयन्तं प्रीणयन्तम्। अमृतस्यापि उपलक्षणार्थो वारुणीशब्दप्रयोगः।

MY has *mayantaṁ*, i.e. *maantaṁ* (मदयन्तम्) for *maentaṁ*. Muda says विशेषणत्रयं तिसृषु प्रत्येकं योज्यम्।

18. चडुलं पि थिईअ थिरं तिअसुक्खित्तरअणं पि सारब्भहिअम्।
महिअं पि अणोलुग्गं असाउसलिलं पि अमअरसणीसन्दम्।।

[चटुलमपि स्थित्या स्थिरं त्रिदशोत्क्षिप्तरत्नमपि साराभ्यधिकम्।
मथितमप्यनवरुग्णमस्वादुसलिलमप्यमृतरसनिःस्यन्दम्।।]

Even though restless, it remained steadfast by respecting its limits. It abounded in riches, even though its treasures had been taken out by the gods (during the churning). It was unscathed, even though churned; and oozed nectar,[17] even though its waters had a briny taste.

---

[16] Cf. verse 11.

[17] Traces of nectar are probably meant, the ocean being the original home of nectar which was taken out during the churning.

K says त्रिदशैरुद्धृतरत्नमपि, रत्नं श्रेष्ठद्रव्यम्, रत्नं श्रेष्ठे मणावपि इति वैजयन्ती, साराभ्यधिकं सार: प्रशस्तवस्तुसमूह: तेनाभ्यधिकम्। मथितमपि अभग्नम् (अनवरुग्णम् *chāyā*)। Muda has अम्लानम्। He seems to read *aṇullaggaṁ* for *aṇoluggaṁ* (अनवरुग्णम्) as he says *ullagga* म्लान। This seems to be a *deśī* word. Cf. *ullukka* explained as त्रुटित in *Deśīnāmamālā* 1.92।

R says तरङ्गादिना चञ्चलमपि स्थित्या मर्यादया स्थिरं वेलानतिक्रामकम्।

19. पज्जत्तरअणगब्भे णहअरुपल्लत्थचन्दअरपारोहे।
उअरब्भन्तरसेले सुरवइडिम्बणिहिए णिहि व्व वहन्तम्।।१९।।

[पर्याप्तरत्नगर्भान्नमस्तरुपर्यस्तचन्द्रकरप्ररोहान्।
उदराभ्यन्तरशैलान्सुरपतिडिम्बनिहितान्निधीनिव वहन्तम्।।]

It had in its depths the mountains[18] abounding in jewels, as if they were treasure hidden in dread of Indra, and marked by branch-roots, the moonbeams, coming down from the tree that was the sky.[19]

K, Muda, Kula and Deva read सलिल for *uara* उदर (R)।

K says पर्याप्तं रत्नमय: गर्भो: येषां तान्। नभ एव तरु: नभस्तरु: तस्मात् पर्यस्ता: अध:प्रसृता: चन्द्रकरा उव प्ररोहा येषाम्। सलिलाभ्यन्तरे शैलान् वहन्तम्। किमिव – सुरपतिडिम्बनिहितान् निधीनिव। डिम्ब उपप्लव आपत्। डमरो डिम्बश्च विप्लव: कथित इति हलायुध:। सुरपतिना डिम्बे उपप्लवे सति निहितान्। अन्यत्र सुरपतिनिमित्तेन डिम्बेन पक्षच्छेदात्मना निहितानिति योजना। अप्रसिद्धप्ररोहाणां तरूणां प्ररोहोत्पत्ति: अधोनिहितं निधिं सूचयति इति प्रसिद्धम्। For प्ररोह "branch-root" see K and Kula on 1.4 and 7.18.

Kula says पर्याप्तानि प्रभूतानि रत्नानि गर्भे येषां शैलानां निधीनां च ते तथा तान्। नभ: तरुरिव तत: पर्यस्ता: पतिता: चन्द्रकरा: प्ररोहा इव येषु तान्। यत्र निधिस्तत्र तरुप्ररोहो लम्बते[20] इति श्रुते:। सलिलाभ्यन्तरस्थितान् शैलान् सुरपते: सकाशात् डिम्बेन विप्लवेन निहितान् निधीनिव वहन्तम्।

MY says डिम्ब: क्षोभ:। निधिगर्भे भूतले तदुपरि प्ररूढानां तरूणां (प्ररोहा:) प्रादुर्भवन्त: अधस्तनं भूतलमवगाहमाना: शिथिलसंस्थानं कुर्वन्ति। तद्वत् चन्द्रकरा:

[18] See verse 14.

[19] The verse refers to a belief that the presence of a tree with branch- roots indicates the location of buried treasure. Here, the mountains, which took shelter in the ocean to save their wings from Indra's thunder, are fancied as treasure buried in the sea. The sky is a tree, and the moonbeams disturbing the waters of the sea are the branch-roots cleaving the ground. See fn. 14 above.

[20] *SC* has लम्बते which gives the correct meaning. Our copy of Kula has लभ्यते।

अप्यवगाहमानाः समुद्रसलिलस्थितिशैथिल्यापादकतया प्ररोहत्वेन रूपिताः। न तु सूर्यकाराः तेषाम् अतथाभूतत्वादित्यवसेयम्। R, like MY, takes प्ररोह in the sense of ordinary roots. He says प्ररोहः शिफा, and remarks समुद्रो भूमिस्तदन्तर्गताः पर्वता निधयस्तदुपरि चिह्नवृक्षो गगनं तत्प्ररोहाः चन्द्रकरा इति भावः।

20. परिअम्भिअं उवगए बोलीणम्मिअ णिअत्तचडुलसहावम्।
णवजोव्वणे व्व कामं दइअसमागमसुहम्मि चन्दुज्जोए।।

[परिजृम्भितमुपगते व्यतिक्रान्ते निवृत्तचटुलस्वभावम्।
नवयौवन इव कामं दयितसमागमसुखे चन्द्रोद्द्योते।।]

The sea surged when the moonlight came, bringing joy by its cherished presence, and calmed down when it was gone; just as passion is strong at the advent of youth, delightful with the company of the beloved, and loses its turbulence when youth has passed.

K and MY read *praviambhiaṁ* (प्रविजृम्भितम्) for परि- (R and Kula). K and MY read आलोके for *ujjoe* उद्द्योते (R and Kula)।

Kula says उपगते चन्द्रोद्द्यीते परिजृम्भितं, व्यतिकान्ते च निवृत्तचटुलस्वभावं नवयौवन इव कामम्। दयितः स्पृहणीयः समागम एव सुखहेतुर्यस्य चन्द्रोद्द्योतस्य तस्मिन्। दयितस्य समागमेन सुखयतीति यथोक्ते नवयौवने। K says स्त्रीणां दयितैः समागमे सति सुखभूते चन्द्रालोके उपगते प्रविजृम्भितं प्रवृद्धम्। MY says दयितसमागमसुख इति चन्द्रालोकेन संयोगात् यत् सुखं जायते तत् समुद्रस्याभिमतमिति तथोक्तः चन्द्रालोकः। यौवने तु दयित इष्टजन इति मन्तव्यम्।

21. दरफुडिअसिप्पिसंपुडपलोट्टसङ्खमुहभरिअमुत्ताणिअरम्।
मारुअदूरुच्छालिअजलभरिअद्धवहपडिणिअत्तजलहरम्।।

[दरस्फुटितशुक्तिसंपुटप्रलुठितशङ्खमुखभृतमुक्तानिकरम्।
मारुतदूरोच्छालितजलभृतार्धपथप्रतिनिवृत्तजलधरम्।।]

The pearls, issuing from the partly split oyster shells, filled the mouths of the conches; and the clouds withdrew from half the way, because they were filled with water blown high by the wind.

K, MY and Kula read *bhiṇṇa* for *phuḍia* स्फुटित (R). K and Kula read प्रकर for *ṇiara* निकर (R). Ms. C of Goldschmidt has *mottā-vaaraṁ*. K read उच्चालित for उच्छा–।

K says दरभिन्नात् शुक्तिसंपुटात् प्रलुठितो विगलितः शङ्खानां मुखेन भृतः मुक्ताप्रकरो यत्र तम्। MY says शुक्तीनाम् ईषद्भिन्नतया क्रमेण एकमुखनिर्गताभिः मुक्ताभिः पूरितशङ्खमपि। अनेन शुक्तिगतं मुक्ताबाहुल्यं शङ्खादिबाहुल्यं चोभययुक्तं भवति। Kula agrees with K. R says परिणतमुक्ताभरात् ईषत्स्फुटिते शुक्तिसंपुटे मुक्ताबुभुक्षया प्रलुठितं यत् शङ्खमुखं तेन भृतो धृतो मुक्तानिकरो यत्र तम्। शुक्तिपुटात् शङ्खेनाकृष्टा मुक्तास्तदभ्यन्तरे प्रविशन्तीत्यर्थः।

22. मरगअमणिप्पहाहअहरिआअन्तजरढप्पवालकिसलअम्।
सुरगअगन्धुद्धाइअकरिमअरासण्णदिण्णमेहमुहवडम्।।

[मरकतमणिप्रभाहतहरितायमानजरठप्रवालकिसलयम्।
सुरगजगन्धोद्धावितकरिमकरासन्नदत्तमेघमुखपटम्।।]

The mature sprouts of the corals looked green in contact with the lustre of the emeralds; and the hovering clouds seemed to be veils, thrown over the faces of the sea elephants, as they rushed forward at the smell of the celestial elephants (that came to bathe in the sea).[21]

K has उत्थापित and Deva ऊर्ध्वायित for *uddhāia* taken as उद्धावित by R and Kula.

K says मरकतमणीनां प्रभाभिराहतत्वात् हरितायमानं श्यामायमानं जरठं परिणतं प्रवालकिसलयं यत्र तम्। सुरगजगन्धेन यदृच्छयागतस्य सुरगजस्य गन्धात् मदगन्धात् उत्थापितस्य उत्प्लुतस्य करिमकरस्य आसन्नदत्तमेघमयमुखपटम्। मुखपटनिवारणे सति गजः शान्तसंरम्भो भवतीति भावः। दत्तं निपतितमित्यर्थः।

MY says हरितायमानजरठेति हरितायमानतया जरठवत् प्रतिभा समानमित्यर्थः। Kula says . . . जरठः प्रौढ़ः प्रवालाङ्कुरः यत्र तम्। प्रौढत्वेन द्युतिमत्ता सूचिता। सुरगजस्य गन्धेन उद्धावितस्य करिमकरस्य आसन्ने मध्ये दत्तो मेघ एव मुखपटो येन तम्। Deva says क्रीडासमवनतसुरगजगन्धोत्थितजलगजवदननिकटवर्ती जलदः सुरगजयुद्धोद्यतस्य निजगजस्य दत्तो मुखपट इत्युत्प्रेक्षते। प्रतिगजाभिमुखं धावतः संनिकृष्यतो मदगजस्य मुखं निवारणार्थं पटेनाच्छाद्यते। एवं सुरगजं संनिकृष्यतो निजकरिमकरस्य दत्तमेघरूपमुखपटं समुद्रमिति।

R says जरठाः चिरन्तनाः प्रवालस्य विद्रुमस्य पल्लवा यत्र तम्।

23. मणिवालअं तीरलाआहरप्पहोहासिअरम्मणिवालअम्।
घणवारिअं वेलालिङ्गणेण चडुलं महिलङ्घणवारिअम्।।

[21] The eyes of a furious elephant were covered with a veil to prevent it from attacking other elephants. Here, the cloud are fancied as veils, with which the sea restrained its elephants from attacking the visiting elephants of the gods.

[मणिपालयं तीरलतागृहप्रभावभासितरम्यनृपालयम्।
घनवारिदं वेलालिङ्गनेन चटुलं महिलङ्घनवारितम्।।]

It was the custodian of gems. The groves of creepers on its shore outshone beautiful royal mansions. It gave water to the clouds. It was restless as it embraced the coast, but refrained[22] from overrunning the earth.[23]

K reads *ohāmia* (अभिभूत) for *ohāsia* (अवभासित R; अवहसित Kula). Deva has न्यक्कृत which shows that his reading is same as that of K. Our copy of MY has न्यकित which seems to stand for न्यक्कृत।

K says मणीन् पालयतीति मणिपालकम्। ओहामिअशब्दो धात्वादेश: अभिभवार्थ:। तीरलतागृहप्रभाभिभूतरम्यनृपालयम्। घनानां वारिप्रदम्। चटुलमपि वेलालिङ्गितेन (वेलालिङ्गनेन *chāyā*) महीलङ्घनात् वारितम्। MY says अत्र स्वस्त्रियामेव निरतस्य परस्त्रीप्रसङ्गविमुखस्य शीलवत: समाधिरनुसंधेय:।

Kula says तीरलतागृहप्रभया अवहसितो निर्भर्त्सितो रम्यो नृपालयो हर्म्यादिर्येन तम्। घना एव तावत् वारिदा:, तेभ्यो वारि ददातीति महामहिमेत्यर्थ:। चटुलं चञ्चलम् अतो वेलालिङ्गनेन जलोल्लासाश्लेषेण मह्या यत् लङ्घनम् आक्रमणं तेन (तस्मात्?) वारितं स्थितिकारिणा हरिणेति श्रुति:। अथवा वेलाया: तीरलेखाया: प्रियाया: आलिङ्गनेन महीलङ्घनवारितम्। *SC* has प्रियाया इवालिङ्गनेन।

24. ससिमऊहपडिपेल्लणपक्खुब्भन्तअं संचरन्तधरणीहरपक्खुब्भन्तअम्।
धीरअं सइमुहलघणपअविज्जन्तअं अट्ठिअं च वलवाणलपअविज्जन्तअम्।।

[शशिमयूखपरिप्रेरणप्रक्षुभ्यत्कं संचरद्धरणीधरप्रक्षोभ्यमाणम्।
धैर्यकं सदामुखरघनपीयमान मस्थितं च वडवानलप्रताप्यमानम्।।]

It was heaving under the pressure of the rays of the moon. Its waters were troubled by the moving wings of its mountains,[24] and constantly absorbed by the rumbling clouds. It was heated by the submarine fire, and was both unsteady and calm.

---

[22] Lit. was prevented, i.e. by the customary limit.

[23] Velā (seashore) is figured as the mistress of the sea (cf. 1.64), and the earth also plays the same role (cf. verse 8). It is implied that loyalty to one prevented the sea from paying attention to the other.

[24] See verse 14.

K, MY, Deva and Kula read धीरं (धीरकं Deva) सदा मुखरजलद – for *dhīraaṁ sai muhala-ghaṇa* – धैर्यकं (धीरकं वा) सदा मुखरघन – (R). K, MY and Deva have वडवामुखानल for *valavāṇala* (R and Kula).

The beginning of K's gloss on the verse is missing. (K *chāyā*) has शशिमयूखप्रतिपीडनप्रक्षुभ्यन्तं, संचरद्धरणिधरपक्षोद्भ्रान्तकम्। MY and Deva also have प्रतिपीडन। R has परिप्रेरण K says . . . पक्षैः उद्भ्रान्तजलं, धीरं सदामुखरजलदपीयमानपयसम्। अत्रेदमनुसंधेयम्। प्राकृतेषु समासानां पदप्रयोगो व्युत्क्रमेणापि घटत इति। एवमुत्तरत्रापि द्रष्टव्यम्। सदामुखरैः जलदैः पीयमानजलम्। अस्थितं चञ्चलं च। वडवामुखानलप्रताप्यमानम्।

My takes *paa* in the third line as *vaa*, and says जलदा एव वयांसि पक्षिणः। He takes *aṭṭhiaṁ* as आस्थितं, or अस्थितं, and says आस्थितम् अजस्रं चटुलमिति वा[25]। तदानीं धीरमपि चटुलमिति विरोधोऽभिप्रेतः। Kula says तरङ्गोल्लासप्रेरितानां शशिमयूखानां अतिप्रेरणेन (प्रति-?)प्रक्षोभ्यमाणम्। संचरमानानां धरणीधराणां पक्षैरुद्भ्रान्तमुद्गतं (कं) जलं यस्य तम्। मुखरैः गर्जितैः जलदैः सदा पीयमानम्। . . . वडवानलप्रताप्यमानं तथापि धैर्य (i.e. *dhīraṁ*, cf. 4.23) धैर्याधिकं महामाहात्म्यकमित्याशयः। R says धैर्यकं धैर्यस्वरूपम्।

25. णिअअविसाणलपअविअमुत्ताणिअरपरिघोलमाणविसहरम्।
मीणगइमग्गपाअडसेआलोमइलमणिसिलासंघाअम्।।

[निजकविषानलप्रतापितमुक्तानिकरपरिघूर्णमानविषधरम्।
मीनगतिमार्गप्रकटशेवालावमलिनमणिशिलासंघातम्।।]

The serpents, heated by the fire of their venom, crawled over the masses of pearls; and clusters of gems, tarnished by moss, were clearly visible along the tracks of the fish.

K reads उपरि for परि, and गत for *gai* (गति)। He says निजविषानलेन प्रतापितत्वात् मुक्तानिकरस्योपरि भ्रमद्भुजङ्गम्। मीनानां गतमार्गेण प्रकटः प्रकाशमानः शैवालैः अवमलिनः मणिशिलासंघातो यत्र तम्। MY says शैवालावमलिनानां मणीनां मीनगतिमार्गेषु घर्षणेन स्फुरणं जायत इति भावः। Kula says निजकेन विषानलेन प्रतप्ताः तापशान्तये मुक्तानिकरे परिघूर्णमाना विषधरा यत्र तम्। मीनानां गतिमार्गे प्रकटः शैवालावमलिनो मणिशिलासंघातो यत्र तम्।

26. सरिसंकुलं महुमहवल्लहाइ लच्छीअ सारसरिसं कुलम्।
महिलाइअं णइमुहपत्थिओणिअत्तिअवेलामहिलाइअम्।।

---

25 Kula explains अस्थितं as अनाहतं। *SC* has अनवरतं, which might be the correct reading.

[सरित्संकुलं मधुमथनवल्लभाया लक्ष्म्याः सारसदृशं कुलम्।
महीलालितं नदीमुखप्रस्थितापनिवृत्तवेलामहिलायितम्।।]

It was permeated by rivers. By virtue of its riches, it was the worthy paternal home of the goddess of wealth, the consort of Viṣṇu.[26] It was attached to the earth. The torrent of water, advancing and retreating through the mouths of the rivers,[27] behaved with it like a woman (bashfully approaching her lover).

K read *mahilālaaṁ* (महिलालयम् and महीलालकम्) for *mahilāiaṁ* (महीलागितम् and महिलायितम्)।

K says सरिद्भिः संकुलं, मधुमथनवल्लभाया लक्ष्म्याः सारस्य उत्कर्षस्य[28] सदृशं कुलं जन्मगृहम्। आवासोऽवसथो गृहं च भवनं स्थानं निशान्तं कुलम् इति हलायुधः। महिलानामङ्गनानाम अप्सरसामालयं पूर्वनिवासम्। नदीमुखैः प्रस्थितं वृद्धिसमये नदीमुखैः प्रयातं पश्चात् अपनिवर्तमानावस्थायां वेलामह्या वेलाभुवः लालकं संभावयितारम्।

Kula says सरिद्भिः संकुलं व्याप्तं . . . मह्यां लागितं जलस्कन्धकस्योपरि मह्याः स्थापितत्वात्। नदीमुखेन प्रस्थितया (अप)निवृत्तया वेलया अम्बुविकृत्या महिलायितं नायिकयेव आचरितं यत्र तम्। शब्दच्छलेन नदीति सखी सूच्यते। तन्मुखेन प्रस्थिता पश्चादपनिवृत्ता वेलेति वेलायां महिलासाधर्म्यम्। R says मह्यां लागितं योजितमर्थादीश्वरेण । एवं नदीमुखेन प्रस्थिता समुद्राभिमुखी अथापनिवृत्ता तत्तरङ्गाभिघातेन पश्चादभिमुखी वेला जलं महिलायित। महिलावदाचरन्ती यत्र तम्। MY says नदीमुखपस्थितापनिवर्तमानवेलामहिलायितम् . . . महिलावदाचरणं यस्य तमित्यर्थः। अथवा वेलाख्यया महिलया इतः प्राप्तः (तम्)।

Mudasaysमहीलागितंन्नदीमुखप्रस्थितापनिवर्तमानवेलामहिलाचितम् प्रस्थितापनिवर्तमाना गमागमौ कुर्वाणा वेलाख्या महिला स्त्री तया महिलया आचितं व्याप्तम्। यद्वा महिलया अयितम्। अयतेर्गत्यर्थात् कर्मणि क्तः। Deva says वेलामहिलाजितम्, and remarks कासुचित् कान्तासु स्वतन्त्रः कयापि कामिन्या बद्धः कोऽपि विवक्ष्यते।

27. णइसहस्सपडिउम्बणणाअरसन्तअं पलअमेहसमदूसहणाअरसन्तअम्।
पेलवेण पवणेण महुरसंचारिअं मउअमअखलन्तं व महुरसं चारिअम्।।२७।।

[26] Cf. verse 6.

[27] Retreating on account of being repelled by the waves of the sea. Cf. verse 16.

[28] R says सारो धनं तेन सदृशं योग्यम्।

[नदीसहस्त्रपरिचुम्बनज्ञातरसान्तरं प्रलयमेघसमदुःसहनादरसन्तम्।
पेलवेन पवनेन मधुरसंचारितं मृदुमदस्खलन्तमिव मधुरसं चारितम्।।

It reached the height of enjoyment as it kissed a thousand rivers; and its waters roared with a din unbearable like the rumbling of the clouds at the epoch of destruction. Gently rocked by soft breezes, it was like one regaled with wine, and reeling in mild inebriation.

K says नदीसहस्रस्य परिचुम्बनेन ज्ञातरसं, ततं विततम्। प्रलयमेघध्वनिसमदुःसहनादं यथा भवति तथा शब्दायमानजलम्। पेलवेन मृदुना पवनेन मधुरं संचारितं संचलितम्। तदानीं मधुरसं मद्यरसं चारितं भक्षितं पायितं, मधुमदेन स्खलन्तमिव पायितमधुत्वात् मधुमदेन स्खलन्तमिव संचलितमिति योजना। It will be seen that K reads मधुमद (Muda also) for *maua-maa* मृदुमद (R and Kula)।

Muda says ज्ञातो रसस्य अन्तः काष्ठा येन तम्। मधुरं यथा स्यात् तथा संचारितमान्दोलितम्। Kula says नदीसहस्रपरिचुम्बनेन ज्ञातः अनुभूतः रसस्य कृत्याकृत्यस्य च अन्तः पर्यन्तो येन तम्। . . . मृदुकेन मन्देन मदेन स्खलन्तं घूर्णमानं पुरुषमिव। सोऽपि दुःसहैः नादै रसति। बहुस्त्रीमुखचुम्बनरसं च जानाति, मृदुमदत्वात् घूर्णते।

28. कसणमणिच्छाआरसरज्जन्तोवरिपरिप्पवन्तप्फेणम्।
हरिणाहिपङ्कअक्खलिअसेसणीसासजणिअविअडावत्तम्।।२८।।

[कृष्णमणिच्छायारसरज्यमानोपरिपूवमानफेनम्।
हरिनाभिपङ्कजस्खलितशेषनिःश्वासजनितविकटावर्तम्।।]

The foam, floating on its surface, was tinged with the streaming lustre of the dark blue gems; and the breath of the serpent Ananta, on whose coils Viṣṇu slept, caused massive whirlpools as it hit the lotus growing out of his navel.[29]

K says कृष्णमणीनाम् इन्द्रनीलानां छायारसेन प्रभाप्रवाहेण रज्यमानाः उपरि परिप्लवमानाः फेना यस्य तम्। अन्तः शयानस्य हरेः नाभिपङ्कजे प्रतिहतैः शेषस्य मुखनिश्वासैः जनितविशालावर्तम्। MY has *parippaanta* परिपूवमान। Kula says कृष्णमणीनां छाया द्युतिः सैव रसौ नीलिकाद्रव इव तेन रज्यमान उपरि परिपूवमानः फेनो यत्र तम्। एतेन कृष्णमणिप्राचुर्यमुक्तम्।

---

[29] See 1.17, 21

29. सअरङ्गअं विद्दुमपल्लवप्पहाघोलिरसासअरङ्गअम्।
रविराइअं धरणिअलं व मन्दराअङ्ढणदूरविराइअम्।।

[सतरङ्गकं विद्रुमपल्लवप्रभाघूर्णमानशाश्वतरङ्गकम्।
रविराजितं धरणितलमिव मन्दराकर्षणदूरविराविकम्।।]

Rolling in waves, and brilliant with sunshine, the sea was the ever-undulating dance-floor for the gleam of the coral fronds. It resounded far and wide, when the Mandara mountain[30] was pulled about in its waters (during the churning); even as the earth groaned when the mountain was pulled up from its roots.[31]

K says सतरङ्गं, विद्रुमपल्लवप्रभाणां घूर्णनस्य भ्रमणस्य नर्तनस्य शाश्वतरङ्गं नृत्तस्थानम्। घरणितलमिव रविणा राजितं विराजितम्। मथनसमये मन्दराकर्षणे दूरं भृशं विरावितं ध्वनितम्। It will be seen that K reads घूर्णन (*gholaṇa*)for *gholira* (घूर्णनशील)। MY says विद्रुमप्रभाघूर्णनशीलशाश्वतरङ्गं विद्रुमप्रभाणां नर्तकीनामिव सदाडोलायमानरङ्गम्।

Kula says सतरङ्गं कं पानीयं यस्य तम्। सतरङ्गत्वादेव विद्रुमपल्लवप्रभया घूर्णनशीलः प्रसृमरः शाश्वतोऽनश्वरो रङ्गः रोगो यस्य तम्। रविणा रञ्जितं रश्मिनिकरेण विसारिणा भरितविवरं, मन्दरस्य आकर्षणेन तत्कोटरे दूरं विलायितम्। धरणीतलमिव . . . । विलीनसमानार्थो विवास्र (!) (*virāa-virāia*?) शब्दो देशीयः[32]। It will be seen that Kula explains *virāia* as विलायित। Cf. K and Kula on 9.45 below. Hemacandra 4.56 gives *virāi vilijjai* (विलीयिते)।

Muda renders *saaraṁgaaṁ* as शतरङ्गकम्। He reads *rāvia* for *rāia*, and says रविरञ्जितम्, रञ्जे रावादेशः (cf. Hemacandra 4.49), रविणो हंसादयः। दूरमत्यर्थं *virāviaṁ* शब्दायितम्। धरणीतलपक्षे सकराङ्गकम्। करो राजग्राह्यम्। विद्रुमाणां पल्लवप्रभावघूर्णन (शील)स्वाश्रयरङ्गकम्। मन्दराकर्षणदूरविरातितं (विरादितं ?) विशारितम्। This is explained more fully by R — सकराङ्गकं सह करेण राजग्राह्येण वर्ततेऽङ्गंशरीरं यस्य तत्। तथा भूमौ करसत्त्वात्। विशिष्टो द्रुमो विद्रुमः तत्पल्लवप्रभाभिः घूर्णमानः संबध्यमानः स्वाश्रयः स्वनिष्ठो

---

30 Cf. verse 4.

31 For using it as a staff for churing the ocean. Cf. 1.49. For other interpretations see Extracts.

32 *SC* says विरशब्दो देशीयः, which is a mistake for *virāa* or *virāia* rendered as विलीनायित in case of the earth – धरणीतलमिव मन्दरस्य आकर्षणेन उत्पाटनेन दूरं विलीनायितं निखातम्। This seems to be the missing sentence of Kula's gloss.

रङ्गो यत्र तत्। तल्लौहित्यसंक्रमात्। प्रशंसायां कन्। एवं रविणा राजितं दीपितम्। मन्दराकर्षणेन दूरं व्याप्य विदारितम्। तदुत्पाटनेन भूमेर्विदीर्णत्वादित्यर्थः।

Deva says कठिनतलधरणीसमाकर्षणेन यथा ध्वनिः तथा मथनेऽपीति विवक्षा।

30. मुत्तालअं तिअसविइण्णजीविअसुहामअजम्मुत्तालअम्।
वित्थिण्णअँ पलउव्वेलसलिलहेलामलिउव्वित्थिण्णअम्।।३०।।

[मुक्तालयं त्रिदशवितीर्णजीवितसुखामृतजन्मोत्तालकम्।
विस्तीर्णकं प्रलयोद्वेलसलिलहेलामृदितोर्वीस्त्यानकम्।।]

It was the home of pearls, and was preeminent, because from it emerged nectar that gave the gods the joy of life. It was vast, and its waters were turned into mire[33] by the earth, crushed with ease by the surging waters of the deluge.

K's gloss on the first line is missing in our copy. He says विस्तीर्ण, प्रलयोद्वेलसलिलैः हेलया लीलया मृदितायाम् उर्व्यामास्तीर्णं विततं कर्मकर्तरि। R says प्रलये उद्वेलमुच्छलितं यत् सलिलं तस्य हेलया संचारेण मृदितया उर्व्या स्त्यानं काठिन्यात् कर्दमीभूतम्। Kula and Muda have स्त्यानकं or स्त्यानं like R. Hemacandra 1.74 gives *thiṇṇa* as an equivalent of स्त्यान। Deva renders *thiṇṇa* as आस्तीर्ण like K. Kula says प्रलये उद्वेलैरुल्लसितैः सलिलैः हेलामृदितया उर्व्या स्त्यानं घनीभूतं कर्दमितं कं पानीयं यस्य तम्।

With regard to the first line, MY says त्रिदशेभ्यो दत्तजीवितसुखस्य अमृतस्योत्पत्त्या उद्धतम। Muda says उत्तालमुन्नतम्। Kula says उत्तालम् उद्भटं प्रख्यातमित्यर्थः।

31. चिरपरूढसेआलसिलाहरिअन्तअं पवणभिण्णरवदारुणणीहरिअन्तअम्।
महुमहस्स णिद्दासमए वीसामअं पलअडड्ढविज्झाअतलुव्वीसामअम्।।

[चिरप्ररूढशेवालशिलाहरितायितं पवनभिन्नरवदारुणनिर्ह्रदत्कम्।
मधुमथनस्य निद्रासमये विश्रामदं प्रलयदग्धविध्माततलोर्वीश्यामकम्।।]

It was green with rocks long overgrown with moss; and extensive, with a terrible roar re-echoed by the wind. It afforded repose to Viṣṇu in his season of sleep;[34] and was dark like the surface of the earth, when it had cooled after being scorched by the fire of universal ruin.

---

[33] Lit. thickened.

[34] See 1.21.

K, MY and Muda read आगमे for *samae* (R and Kula). *SC* text has *paaṇa* for *pavaṇa*, and *raa* for *rava*.

K and Muda render *ṇīhariantaaṁ* as निर्ह्लादमानम् – गर्जन्तम् (K). K says मधुमथनस्य निद्रागमे सति विश्रामप्रदम्। युगान्तदग्धं पश्चात् निर्वाणं शान्तं तलं यस्या उर्व्याः सा प्रलयदग्धनिर्वाणतलोर्वी यथा श्यामा भवति तद्वत् श्यामं कृष्णम्। Kula says मषीमलिनोर्वीतलसदृशमित्यर्थः।

Kula says चिरप्ररूढानि शैवालानि यासु शिलासु ताभिः हरितः अन्तः यस्य तम्। पवनेन भिन्नरवं विस्तारितध्वनि दारुणं दुःसहं निर्ह्लादितं यस्य तम्। ततं विस्तृतम्। मधुमथनस्य विष्णोः निद्रासमये विश्रामदम्। K says शिलाभिरन्तर्गताभिः हरितायमानं श्यामायमानम्। MY has हरितान्तम् and निर्ह्रदन्तम्। R says निर्ह्रदत् शब्दान्तरोत्पादिकं जलं यस्य तम्।

32. असुरोवडणविहट्टिअजलविवरुट्ठिअरसाअलुम्हाणिवहम्।
मह‌णवसभिण्णभामिअदीवन्तरलग्गमन्दरअडक्खण्डम्।।

[असुरावपतनविघटितजलविवरोत्थितरसातलोष्मनिवहम्।
मथनवशभिन्नभ्रामितद्वीपान्तरलग्नमन्दरतटखण्डम्।।]

Hot vapours from the nether regions rose through its waters as they parted when the demons plunged down; while portions of the Mandara slopes, torn down by the force of the churning, whirled about, and stuck fast to diverse isles.

K and MY *pratīka* has *ovaaṇo* for *ovaḍaṇa* (अवपतन). *SC* text has *vihāḍia* (विघाटित) for *vihaṭṭia* (विघटित)। Ms. C of Goldschmidt has *vihālia*.

K says पातालं प्रविशताम् असुराणामवपतनेन विघटितं जलविवरं तदुत्थितः रसातलसंबन्धी ऊष्मनिवहः नागविषोष्मनिवहो यत्र तम्। मथनवशेन मथनरभसेन भिन्नो भ्रमितः दूरतो निरस्तो द्वीपान्तरे लग्नः मन्दरतटस्य खण्डो यत्र तम्। Kula says विघटितस्य जलस्य विवरेण उत्थितः रसातलस्य, etc.

33. एस अमअरससंभवो त्ति संभाविअं णहणिहतमेण व चउद्दिसं भाविअम्।
गुणमहग्घसारं वसुहारक्खाणिअं णिअअजसणिहाणं मिव सअरक्खाणिअम्।।

[एषोऽमृतरससंभव इति संभावितं नभोनिभतमसेव चतुर्दिशं भावितम्।
गुणमहार्घसारं वसुधारक्षानीतं निजकयशोनिधानमिव सगरखानितम्।।]

It was esteemed as the source of nectar. Resembling the sky, it seemed to be tinged with darkness all round. Endowed with treasures, highly prized for their excellence, it was brought into being for the protection of the earth. King Sagara had it dug (by his sons), as if as a repository of his fame.

K says तमसा चतुर्दिशं चतसृषु दिक्षु भावितं रूषितम् (MY also) इव। रत्नादिगुणैः प्रभाविशेषैः महार्घः सारो यस्य स तथा तम्। अत एव वसुधारक्षार्थमानीतं रत्नप्रदानैः वसुधारक्षार्थं विधात्रा संपादितमित्यर्थः। MY says गुणैः श्लाघ्याः साराः चन्द्रादयो यस्य तम्। Muda says सारः स्थैर्यम्। Kula says एषोऽमृतरसस्य संभवः प्रभव इति संभावितं सादरं ख्यातम्। स्वच्छश्यामविततत्वात् नभोनिभम्, अत एव तमसेव चतुर्दिशं समन्ततो भावितं रञ्जितम्। निजयशोनिधानमिव सगरेण आश्वमेधिकतुरगानुसारिभिः पुत्रैः खानितम्।

34. पवणुग्गाहिअजललवणिवहपहम्मन्तमुहलतीरतलवणम्।
ससिसेलमऊहोज्झरपरिवड्ढिअसलिलमलिअपवणुच्छङ्गम्।।

[पवनोद्ग्राहितजललवनिवहप्रहन्यमानमुखरतीरतलवनम्।
शशिशैलमयूखनिर्झरपरिवर्धितसलिलमृदितपुलिनोत्सङ्गम्।।]

The palm groves on the shore rustled as they were hit by sea spray blown by the wind; and the expanse of the beach was lashed by the waters, swollen by streams of rays from the mountain that was the moon.

K, Muda and Deva read आभोगम् (*āhoaṁ*) for *ucchaṁgaṁ* उत्सङ्गम् (R and Kula).

K says पवनेन उद्गृहीतेन उत्क्षिप्तेन जललवनिवहेन प्रहन्यमानं मुखरं तीरतलवनं तीरस्थं तालवनं यस्य तम्। तृणराजः कथ्यते तलस्ताल इति हलायुधः। शशिमयशैलस्य मयूखनिर्झरैः परिवर्धितेन सलिलेन मृदितपुलिनविस्तारम्। MY says *uggāhiaṁ* उद्गृहीतम्। स्वार्थे णिच् उत्क्षिप्तमित्यर्थः। Muda says उद्ग्राहितमूर्ध्वं नीतमित्यर्थः। तलस्तालः (Kula also)।

35. मन्दरमेहक्खोहिअससिकलहंसपरिमुक्कसलिलुच्छङ्गम्।
मरगअसेवालोवरि णिसण्णतुह्निक्कमीणचक्काअजुअम्।।

[मन्दरमेघक्षोभितशशिकलहंसपरिमुक्तसलिलोत्सङ्गम्।
मरकतशेवालोपरि निषण्णतूष्णीकमीनचक्रवाकयुगम्।।]

Its waters were abandoned by yonder swan, the moon, scared by the raincloud in the shape of the Mandara mountain;

and pairs of fish, looking like red geese, lay still on the moss-like emeralds.[35]

K says मन्दराख्येन मेघेन क्षोभितेन शशिमयेन कलहंसेन मुक्तसलिलोपरिभागम्। Muda remarks कलहंसा हि मेघकलुषं जलं हित्वा मानससरो (यान्ति)। K says मरतकस्य शैवालस्य(च) उपरि निषण्णानि तृष्णिकानि मरतकशैवालयोरन्धकार-सदृशवर्णत्वात् रात्रिशङ्कया तूष्णींभूतानि संभोगमपास्य निर्व्यापाराणि मीनचक्रवाकयुगानि यत्र तम्।

MY says मन्दरमेघक्षोभितश्च शशिकलहंसमुक्तश्च जलोत्सङ्गो यस्य तम्। मरतकमेव शैवालं तस्योपरि निषण्णं प्रभाबलच्छन्नतया परस्परादृश्यमानत्वेन (?) . . . मीनचक्रवाकयोः युगं यत्र तम्। क्वचित् चक्रवाककुलमिति पाठः। अथवा मरतकशैवालयोरुपरि मीनात्मकयोः चक्रवाकयोः मिथुनं यस्य (तम्)। तयोः मरतकशैवालयोः श्यामतया रात्रिशङ्कया विरहभयेन तूष्णीकत्वमिति। Muda says मीनचक्रवाकयुगलमिति रूपकमिति केचित्।

Dva says मीनरूपचक्रवाकः कूजितुमशक्नुवन् मरतकवत् परिमृदितशैवाले तिष्ठति। अथवा मरतके शैवाले च निषण्णो मीनश्चक्रवाकश्च तत्प्रभारूषितत्वात् अन्योन्यमज्ञातौ तूष्णीमसात इति।

Kula says मरकताः शैवालानीव तेषामुपरि निषण्णानि तूष्णीकानि(?) मीनानां चक्रवाकानामिव युगानि मिथुनानि यत्र तम्। *SC* text has *seāla* for *sevāla*. R says मन्दरपरिघट्टनभिया तूष्णींभूय मीनाः पातालमूले स्थिताः, etc.

36. पुण्णणइसोत्तसंणिहजलमज्झमुणिज्जमाणचलतिमिणिवहम्।
वलआमुहमूलसमीसरन्तमसिरासिकज्जलिअपाआलम्।।३६।।
(आइकुलअम्)

[पुण्यनदीस्रोतःसंनिभजलमध्यज्ञायमानचलतिमिनिवहम्।
वडवामुखमूलसमवसरन्मषीराशिकज्जलितपातालम्।।]
(आदिकुलकम्)

The tracks of the moving whales, resembling currents of a flooded river, were discernible in the midst of the waters; and, the nether regions were blackened by the sooty ooze issuing from the base of the submarine fire.

---

35 The moon, which left the ocean while it was being churned with the Mandara mountain, is fancied as a swan migrating to the Mānasa Lake in the rainy season; and the fish, taking shelter on the emerald deposits at the bottom during the commotion, are likened to red geese huddling together on the mossy banks of streams. The second line is variously interpreted. See Extracts.

K and Muda read *magga* for *majjha* (R and Kula). K, Muda and Kula read *calia-timi-vahaṁ* for *cala-timi-ṇivahaṁ* found in R who says चलः चलितः तिमिनिवहो यत्र तम्। They read *visama-masi* for *masi-rasi* (R); and *kaddamia* for *kajjalia* (R).

K says पूर्णनदीस्रोतःसंनिभेन जलमार्गेण ज्ञायमानः अधः चलितस्य तिमेः पन्था यत्र तम्। वडवामुखमूलात् समपसरन्त्या अधः पतन्त्या विषमया प्रचुरया मष्या कर्दमितपातालम्। वडवामुखाग्नेः इन्धनीभूय दग्धस्य बहुलेन कज्जलेन जलमिश्रेण कर्दमितपातालम्। Muda also takes *puṇṇa* as पूर्ण like K.

Kula says पुण्यनद्या गङ्गायाः स्रोतःसंनिभो दीर्घविशालविशदत्वात् जलमध्ये ज्ञायमानः चलितानां तिमीनां पन्था यत्र तम्। वडवामुखमूलेन समपसरन्तीभिः विविधजलजन्तुदाहसंभवाभिः विषमाभिः गाढाभिः (मषीभिः) मषीराशिभिः कर्दमितं कज्जलितं वा पातालं येन तम्।

37. तो उग्घाडिअमूलो पवअबलक्कन्तमहिअलुद्धुच्छलिओ।
दिट्ठीअ दिट्ठसारो णज्जइ तुलिओ त्ति राहवेण समुद्दो।।

[तत उद्घाटितमूलः प्लवगबलाक्रान्तमहीतलोर्ध्वोच्छलितः।
दृष्ट्या दृष्टसारो ज्ञायते तुलित इति राघवेण समुद्रः।।]

Thereupon as the power of the sea was seen as it rose surging towards the sky, revealing its bottom, while the earth was trampled by the host of apes, it was apparent that Rāma had appraised its magnitude with his eyes.[36]

K has चलितः (उच्चलितः?)for *ucchalio* (उच्छलितः)। He says ततः प्लवगबलाक्रान्ते महीतले ऊर्ध्वचलितः, अत एवोद्घाटितमूलः प्रकाशितमूलः दृष्टसारश्च दृष्टगाम्भीर्यादिबलश्च समुद्रः दृष्ट्या तुलितः परिच्छिन्न इति ज्ञायते स्म। पार्श्वस्थैरिति शेषः। MY says तुलित इति लङ्घयितुं शक्यतया परिच्छिन्न इति राघवेण दृष्ट्या तुलित इति पार्श्वस्थैरज्ञायत। Kula says प्लवगबलाक्रान्तेन महीतलेन ऊर्ध्वोच्छलितः, अत एव उद्घाटितमूलः प्रकाशिततलः, अतः ज्ञातसारो दृष्टतद्बलः समुद्रो दृष्ट्या राघवेण तुलितः परिकलित इति ज्ञायते। इयानेवास्य सारः, सुलङ्घ्य एवायम् इत्येवं रामेण तुलित इति दृष्टिप्रसादेनैव ज्ञायते(?) इत्यर्थः। Muda says राघवेण समुद्रः तुलित इयत्तया परिच्छिन्नः अज्ञायतेत्यर्थः।

38. कालन्तरपरिहुत्तं दट्ठूण वि अप्पणो महोअहिसअणम्।
जणअसुआबद्धमणो रामो पलअघरिणिं ण संभरइ सिरिम्।।

---

36 The earth is fancied as trembling under the heavy tread of the apes and thereby convulsing the sea, which appeared to Rāma to be not as formidable as it was imagined to be.

[कालान्तरपरिभुक्तं दृष्ट्वाप्यात्मनो महोदधिशयनम्।
जनकसुताबद्धमना रामः प्रलयगृहिणीं न स्मरति श्रियम्।।]

Even at the sight of the ocean, his couch at another epoch, Rāma, with his mind rivetted on Sītā, did not remember the goddess of wealth, his companion at the epoch of universal ruin.[37]

K says कालान्तरे अवतारात् पूर्वस्मिन् काले परिभुक्तम् आत्मनो महोदधिमयं शयनं दृष्ट्वापि रामो जनकसुतायां बद्धमनस्कत्वात् प्रलयकाले गृहिणीं श्रियं न सस्मारेति। Kula says कालान्तरे संहारकाले। प्रलयगृहिणीमिव विपत्कालस्य अपरित्यक्तपरिचर्यां श्रियं न संस्मरति।

39. ईसिजलपेसिअच्छं विहसन्तविइण्णपवअवइसंलावम्।
अद्दिट्ठे व्व ण मुक्कं दिट्ठे उ अहिम्मि लक्खणेण वि धीरम्।।

[ईषज्जलप्रेक्षिताक्षं विहसद्वितीर्णप्लवगपतिसंलापम्।
अदृष्ट इव न मुक्तं दृष्टे उदधौ लक्ष्मणेनापि धैर्यम्।।]

Glancing at the waters, and laughing as he held converse with Sugrīva, Lakṣmaṇa remained calm even on seeing the ocean, as if he had not seen it.

K says ईषत् समुद्रजले प्रेषितांक्ष यथा, विहसदवस्थायां वितीर्णो दत्तः प्लवगपतौ सल्लापश्च यथा, लक्ष्मणेन उदधौ दृष्टेऽपि अदृष्ट इव धैर्यं न मुक्तम्। MY says सागरानादरेण विहसतानेन वितीर्णः प्लवगपतिना सार्धं सल्लापो यथा स्यात् तथेति क्रियाविशेषणम्। Kula says शक्य एवायं लङ्घितुमित्यवज्ञया ईषज्जलप्रेषितांक्ष यथा स्यात् तथा, विहसता वितीर्णः प्लवगपतेः संलापः अयमन्यैः सागरो दृष्टो योऽन्तराय इति श्रूयते इत्येवमादिव्यवहारो यत्र तद् धैर्यम् अदृष्टे उदधौ यथा न मुक्तं तथा दृष्टेऽपि न मुक्तं लक्ष्मणेनापि। न केवलं रामेण इत्यपिशब्दार्थः। R says विहसता अर्थात् स्वेन वितीर्णो दत्तः प्लवगपतये संलापः परस्परभाषणं यत्र तत् (धैर्यम्)। सस्मितं सुग्रीवेण सह कथां कुर्वाणेन . . . कदाचित् समुद्रोऽपि कटाक्षित इति, etc.

40. हरिसणिराउण्णामिअपीणअरालोअपाअडोवरिभाअम्।
पवआहिवो वि पेक्खइ अद्धुप्पइअं व रुम्भि(न्धि)ऊण सरीरम्।।

[हर्षनिरायतोन्नामितपीनतरालोकप्रकटोपरिभागम्।
प्लवगाधिपोऽपि प्रेक्षते अर्धोत्पतितमिव रुद्ध्वा शरीरम्।।]

[37] Rāma is presented as an incarnation of Viṣṇu, who periodically sleeps in the ocean with his consort Lakṣmī in attendance. Cf. 1.21.

Sugrīva, too, looked at the ocean, and seemed to restrain his body, half aloft in the air,[38] with the chest prominent and looking broader, being stuck out in joy.[39]

K and Muda read शोभते (*sohai*) for *pekkhai* (R and Kula).

K says हर्षेण निरायतं यथा उन्नमितत्वात् पीनतरालोकमतिपीनदर्शनं प्रकटोपरिभागं च प्रकाशोर:स्थलं च, अत एव अर्धोत्पतितमिव समुद्रलङ्घनार्थम् अर्धेन उत्पतितमिव स्थिरं शरीरं रुद्ध्वा प्रकृतिं गमयित्वा प्लवङ्गाधिपोऽपि अशोभत। समुद्रदर्शनहर्षात् उन्नामितनिरायतपीनतर- दर्शनप्रकटोपरिभागम् एवंभूतत्वात् लङ्घनार्थं किंचिदुत्पतितमिव शरीरं निरुध्य रराजेत्यर्थ:। MY says *ṇirāa* दीर्घ। पीनतरतयालोक्यमान: अत एव प्रकट उपरिभागो यस्य तत् शरीरं तथा *rumbhiūṇa* रुद्ध्वा समुद्रदर्शनात् स्वयमेव उत्प्लवनोद्यतमिव देहं निरुध्येत्यर्थ:।

Kula says हर्षेण लङ्घनवशेन निरायतं यथा स्यात् तथा उन्नामितत्वात अधिकविततहृदयत्वेन पीनतरो विशाल:, आलोकेन स्फुरद्रूपतया प्रकट उपरिभगो यस्य तत् आत्मशरीरं समुद्रलङ्घनार्थम् अर्धोत्पतितमिव रुध्द्वा, प्लवगसैन्यसम्बन्धबलापेक्षया नियम्य इति भाव:, प्लवगाधिप: सुग्रीवोऽपि प्रेक्षते समुद्रमिति प्रकृतत्वात्।

41. गरुडेण व जलणणिहं समुद्दलङ्घणमणेण वाणरवइणा।
अवहोवासपसरिअं पक्खविआणं व पुलइअं कइसेण्णम्।।

[गरुडेनेव ज्वलननिभं समुद्रलङ्घनमनसा वानरपतिना।
उभयावकाशप्रसृतं पक्षवितानमिव प्रलोकितं कपिसैन्यम्।।]

Sugrīva, his heart set on traversing the sea, surveyed the army of apes, ranged on both sides, and bright as fire; like as Garuḍa, desiring to cross the sea, looks at his outspread wings (of gold).

Kula says गरुडेनेव समुद्रलङ्घनमनसा वानरपतिना सुग्रीवेण कनक पिङ्गलत्वात्, (पक्षे) कनकमयत्वात्, ज्वलननिभमुभयपार्श्वप्रसृतं कपिसैन्यं पक्षवितानमिव विततं पक्षद्वयमिव *pulaiaṁ* प्रलोकितं दृष्टम्। K says पक्षपटलमिव (वितानमिव *chāyā*). Muda says दृशे: पुल आदेश:, and refers to Hemacandra 4.181. *SC* text has *garuleṇa* for *–ḍena.*

42. साअरदंसणहित्था अक्खित्तोसरिअवेवमाणसरीरा।
सहसा लिहिअव्व ठिआ णिप्पन्दणिराअलोअणा कइणिवहा।।

---

[38] I.e. it seemed as if he was about to fly across the sea, but held himself back.

[39] Lit. stretched and raised in joy.

[सागरदर्शनत्रस्ता आक्षिप्तापसृतवेपमानशरीराः।
सहसा लिखिता इव स्थिता निःस्पन्दनिरायतलोचनाः कपिनिवहाः।।]

Terror-stricken, all of a sudden, at the sight of the sea and trembling and moving away, but held back (by shame), the apes stood like painted figures, with wide flickerless eyes.

Kula says सहसा तत्क्षणं सागरदर्शनेन त्रस्ताः। त्रस्ते हित्थशब्दो देशीयः। पूर्व भयादपसृतं लज्जया पश्चादाक्षिप्तं वेपमानं शरीरं यैस्ते तथा। लिखिता इव निर्व्यापारत्वात् चित्रन्यस्ता इव। K says पूर्वमपसृतं तत आक्षिप्तम् अपसरणात् निवर्तितं वेपमानं शरीरं येषां ते। MY says आक्षिप्तापसृतं भयेन हठात् गृहीत्वा पश्चादपनीयमानमिव वेपमानं शरीरं येषां ते। *ṇirāa* दीर्घ। Kula says अहो दुस्तरोऽयं समुद्र इति विस्मयात् निष्पन्दानि दरसंकुचितत्वात् (?) निरायतानि दीर्घाणि लोचनानि येषां ते कपिनिवहाः स्थिताः। R explains निरायत as विस्फारित।

43. पेच्छन्ताण समुद्दं चडुलो वि अउव्वविम्हअरसत्थिमिओ।
हणुमन्तम्मि णिवडिओ सगोरवं वाणराण लोअणणिवहो।।

[पश्यतां समुद्रं चटुलोऽप्यपूर्वविस्मयरसस्तिमितः।
हनूमति निपतितः सगौरवं वानराणां लोचननिवहः।।]

As they beheld the sea even their fickle eyes rested admiringly on Hanumat, fixed in a gaze of unwonted amazement.[40]

MY says सगौरवम् ईदृशोऽपि समुद्रोऽनेन लङ्घित इति सबहुमानमित्यर्थः। Kula says पूर्वमननुभूतत्वात् अपूर्वेण विस्मयरसेन स्तिमितो निश्चलो लोचननिवह . . . हनुमति निपतितः।

44. उअहिं अलङ्घणीज्जं दट्ठूण गआगअं च मारुअतणअम्।
मोहन्धआरिएसु वि गूढो भमइ हिअएसु सिं उच्छाहो।।४४।।

[उदधिमलङ्घनीयं दृष्ट्वा गतागतं च मारुततनयम्।
मोहान्धकारितेष्वपि गूढो भ्रमति हृदयेष्वेषामुत्साहः।।]

After they had seen the untraversable ocean and Hanumat, who had journeyed and returned, a vague ardour flickered even in their hearts, lost in bewilderment.

K, Muda and probably MY read शोक for मोह (R and Kula). K,

---

[40] Because he had leaped over to Laṅkā.

MY, Muda, Deva and probably Kula read मूढ for गूढ (R who gives the other reading as a variant).

Kula says उदधिमलङ्घनीयं दृष्ट्वा तमतिक्रम्य गतागतं मारुततनयं च दृष्ट्वा *siṁ* तेषां वानराणां मोहेन विषादकृतवेचित्त्येन अन्धकारितेषु प्रतिपत्तिशून्येष्वपि हृदयेषु मृतो (मूढो ?) निश्चयरहित: उत्साह: जलनिधिलङ्घनाध्यवसायो भ्रमति अस्मज्जातीयेन लङ्घितोऽयमिति बहुलान्धकारे खद्योत इव दृष्टनष्टो विचरित। MY says *siṁ* एषाम्। गतागतहनुमद्दर्शनात् उत्साह: सन्नपि समुद्रदर्शनजनितविषादान्धकारिततया हृदयेषु मूढ एवाभूदित्यर्थ:। Deva says समुद्रदर्शने त्वशक्यमिदमारब्धमिति प्रतिभाति। हनुमद्दर्शने: पुन: शक्यमिति च। अत: किंकर्तव्यतामूढ: एवं गमनोत्साह: तेषां हृदयेषु भ्रमति स्म।

45. तो ताण हअच्छाअं णिच्चललोअणसिहं पउत्थपआवम्।
आलेक्खपईवाण व णिअअं पइइचडुलत्तणं पि विअलिअम्।।

[ततस्तेषां हतच्छायं निश्चललोचनशिखं प्रोषितप्रतापम्।
आलेख्यप्रदीपानामिव निजकं प्रकृतिचटुलत्वमपि विगलितम्।।]

Thereafter even their natural agility vanished, like the flare of lamps depicted in pictures, while their lustre faded, the flame of their eyes ceased to stir, and their courage ebbed away.

K and MY read *taṁ* (तत्) for *to* तत: (R and Kula). Muda has *taṁ*, but his *chāyā* has तत:।

K says तेषां तत् निजमात्मीयं प्रकृतिचटुलत्वमपि विगलितम्। कथं विगलितम् – हतच्छायं हता छाया शोभा यथा भवति। शिखाशब्दो दीपापेक्षया प्रयुक्त:। निश्चललोचनमित्यर्थ:। अन्यत्र निश्चलज्वालम्। प्रोषितप्रतापं प्रोषितपौरुषं यथा। अन्यत्र प्रोषितोष्णम्। एवं तेषां कापेयमपि गलितम् किमिव – आलेख्यप्रदीपानामिव। चित्रप्रदीपानां यथा चटुलत्वमेवं न भवति तद्वदिति। Kula says निश्चलानि लोचनानि शिखा इव यत्र। प्रोषित: प्रताप: प्रभावो दाहशक्तिश्च यत्र तद् यथा स्यादिति सर्वं क्रियाविशेषणम् आलेख्यप्रदीपानामिव निजकमात्मीयं नित्यं च प्रकृतिचटुलत्वमपि विगलितम्।

46. कह वि ठवेन्ति पवङ्गा समुद्ददंसणविसाअविमुहिज्जन्तम्।
गलिअगमणाणुराअं पडिवन्थणिअत्तलोअणं अप्पाणम्।।

[कथमपि स्थापयन्ति प्लवङ्गा समुद्रदर्शनविषादविमुह्यमानम्।
गलितगमनानुरागं प्रतिपथनिवृत्तलोचनमात्मानम्।।]

Despondent on seeing the ocean, with the desire to proceed further gone, the apes somehow composed themselves as their eyes turned to the way back home.[41]

K says पूवङ्गाः समुद्रदर्शनविषादविमुह्यन्तम्, अत एव गलितगमनानुरागं, प्रतिपथे प्रतिनिवृत्तिमार्गे निवृत्तलोचनमात्मानं स्वामिभीत्या हनुमद्दर्शनेन च कथमपि स्थापयामासुरिति। Kula says कथमपि . . . कृच्छ्रादात्मानं समुद्रदर्शनात् विषादेन विमुखीक्रियमाणं यापयन्ति धारयन्ति। येन प्रतिनिवृत्त्य गृहं गम्यते स प्रतिपथः तेन निवृत्तं चलितं लोचनं यस्य तम्। MY says समुद्रदर्शनत्रस्तमनसां प्रतिपथं जिगमिषतां कपीनां तत्रावस्थानमपि अशक्यमासीत् किं पुनः तल्लङ्घनमित्याशयः।

It will be seen that Kula, like manuscript C of Goldschmidt, read *javenti* (cf. *SC* text) for *ṭhaventi* स्थापयन्ति। Deva mentions the former reading as a variant. He says *javenti* यापयन्ति वा, cf. Hemacandra 4.40.

इअ सिरिपवरसेणविरइए दसमुहवहे महाकव्वे
विइओ आसासओ समत्तो।।

[इति श्रीप्रवरसेनविरचिते दशमुखवधे महाकाव्ये
द्वितीय आश्वासकः समाप्तः।]

[41] Cf. 3.1, 51. According to Rāmadāsa: composed themselves, getting rid of the desire to go home, and withdrawing their eyes from the way back home (lit. the path of return).

तृतीय आश्वासकः
Third Āśvāsakaḥ

1–2. तो ते कइमाअङ्गे रूढविसाअमअभाविओमीलन्ते।
आलाणक्खम्भेसु वा बाहूसु सिलाअलट्ठिएसु णिसण्णे।।
आहासइ सुग्गीवो णिअअरवाहि फुडणिन्तजसणिग्घोसम्।
धीराहि सारगरुअं दन्तुज्जोआहि णिम्मलत्थं वअणम्।।
(जुग्गअम्)

[ततस्तान्कपिमातङ्गान्रूढविषादभावितानवमीलतः।
आलानस्तम्भेष्विव बाहुषु शिलातलस्थितेषु निषण्णान्।।
आभाषते सुग्रीवो निजकरवात्स्फुटनिर्यद्यशोनिर्घोषम्।
धैर्यात्सारगुरुकं दन्तोद्द्योतान्निर्मलार्थे वचनम्।।]
(युग्मकम्)

Sugrīva then addressed the apes, elephants, as it were, who were seated, supporting themselves on their arms resting on slabs of stone, like posts.[1] Their eyes were closed, and they were made restless by deep despondency, as elephants are by their periodic rut. His words were firmer than even his fortitude because of their depth, and proclaimed his fame[2] even more clearly than his voice, and conveyed a meaning clearer than even the brilliance of his teeth.

K, Kula and Muda read *bhāmia* for *bhāvia* (R).

K says ततः रूढेन अलंविजृम्भितेन विषादाख्यमदेन भ्रमितावमीलितान् निमीलल्लोचनान्, आलानस्तम्भेष्विव शिलातलस्थितेषु बाहुषु निषण्णान् कृतावलम्बान्[3] कपिमातङ्गान् कपिश्रेष्ठान् कपिरूपान् गजानिति च। आभाषते सुग्रीव इत्युत्तरत्र सम्बन्धः।

Kula says भ्रमितान् घूर्णितान् अतः अवमीलतः। Muda says अवमीलन्तो निचेष्टाः तान्। MY reads *āṇāla* for *ālāṇa* (R). Both Hemacandra and Vararuci commentary cite the word *āṇāla-kkhambho.* Muda cites the relevant rule. Cf. notes on 8.59.

---

[1] Lit. posts to which elephants are tied.

[2] I.e. his reputation as a powerful speaker.

[3] न्यस्तदेहभारान् Kula.

MY remarks विषादस्य मदतया रूपणं लज्जाविवेकादिशून्यतापादकतयेति ग्राह्यम्।

R says विषाद एव मदः तेन भावितान् सम्बद्धान।

K says सुग्रीवः निजकरवात् स्फुटर्नियद्यशोनिर्घोषं, यशो लोकप्रशंसा, घोषमयमेव हि यशो भवति, स्वधैर्यादपि सारेण गुरु, अर्थगौरवं सारः, दन्तोद्द्योतो दन्तप्रकाशः, ततोऽपि निर्मलार्थं वचनमाभाषते स्म। उच्चमानेषु वाक्येषु एते गुणाः क्रमात् द्रष्टव्याः।

MY says यशोनिर्घोषो यशःप्रकाशः।

3. धरणिधरणे भुअ च्चिअ महणम्मि सुरासुरा खअम्मि समुद्दा।
हन्तव्वम्मि दहमुहे एह्णिं तुम्हे त्थ महुमहस्स सहाआ।।

[धरणिधरणे भुजा एव मथने सुरासुराः क्षये समुद्राः।
हन्तव्ये दशमुखे इदानीं यूयं स्थ मधुमथनस्य सहायाः।।]

His own arms helped Viṣṇu to support the earth;[4] and the gods and demons to churn the ocean; and the oceans during the deluge. Yourselves be his[5] help now that Rāvaṇa has to be slain.

K says पूर्वं धरणिधरणे मधुमथनस्य भुजा एव सहाया आसन्। भुजबाहुल्यं च वेदेन प्रतिपादितम्। उद्धृतासि वराहेण कृष्णेन शतबाहुनेति, etc.

4. मा सासअसोडीरं कह वि णिअत्तन्तसँमुहसंठविअपअम्।
आअअवित्थक्कन्तं पणअन्तं व सुअणं परुम्हाह जसम्।।

[मा शाश्वतशौटीर्यं कथमपि निवर्तमानसंमुखसंस्थापितपदम्।
आगतवितिष्ठमानं प्रणयन्तमिव सुजनं प्रम्लापयत यशः।।]

Do not turn away fame, the source of constant pride, that hath come but falters and recedes and somehow steps forward (again); like a worthy suppliant that approaches and hesitates, and turns back and comes forward (again).[6]

K says यशसश्च सज्जनस्य च साधर्म्यमुच्यते। अभिमुखं यशः मा प्ररुन्द्ध मा निवारयत। अस्मासु निष्कारणोपकारिणो रामस्य प्रत्युपकारनिर्वर्तनात् आगमिष्यन्तीं कीर्तिं विषादविक्लवा यूयं मा निवारयतेत्यर्थः कथंभूतं यशः – शाश्वतशौण्डीर्यं, शौण्डीरः समर्थः तस्य भावः

[4] I.e. while raising it from the ocean during the Boar incarnation.

[5] Rāma is identified with Viṣṇu.

[6] The idea is, fame is approaching them slowly, but cannot be acquired without a spirit of enterprise which they are yet to show.

शौण्डीर्यम्, शाश्वतं कल्पान्तरावस्थायि शौण्डीर्यं यस्य तत् तथाभूतम्। सुजनोऽपि तथाविध एव कथमपि निवर्तमानसंमुखसंस्थापितपदम्। इयमस्य योजना – प्रथममभिमुखं भूत्वा युष्माकं समुद्रदर्शनसमये निवर्तमानं पराङ्मुखीभवत्, पुनर्युष्मत्सामर्थ्यावगमात् कथमपि संमुखमभिमुखं संस्थापितं पदं पदविन्यासो यस्य तत् तथाभूतम्। आगतमपि वितर्कयत् पुनः संशयानम्। किमिव – प्रणयन्तं याचमानं सुजनमिव। सज्जनस्तु दारिद्र्यात् किञ्चित् दातारं प्रार्थयितुमुद्यतः प्रथमं। कतिचित् पदानि गत्वा पुनरभिमानात् निवृत्तान्यपि पदानि गत्यन्तराभावात् अभिमुखस्थापितानि कृत्वा पुनः संशयानो भवति तद्वदित्यर्थः। प्रणयः स्यात् परिचये याञ्चायां सौहृदेऽपि च इति वैजयन्ती।

MY says *vitthakkantaṁ* व्याकुलीभवन्तम्। वितर्काक्रान्तमिति केचित्। *mā parumbhāha* मावमन्यध्वम्। मापरुन्ध इति वा। *sāsaa-soḍīraṁ* शाश्वतशौडीर्यं सुजनस्य स्वाभाविकं नैरपेक्ष्यरूपं शौडीर्यं, यशसस्तु स्वहेतुतया। . . . आगतव्याकुलीभवन्तं तदर्थोद्योगेनागतम्, अपारसमुद्रदर्शने शिथिलीभवत्। प्रणयार्थमागतस्यापि सुजनस्य तद्भङ्गभयात् व्याकुलीभावः स्फुटः।

Muda says यशो मा रुन्ध्वं मा निवारयतेत्यन्वयः।

Muda (*chāyā*) has आगतविलम्बमानं। He says *vitthakkantaṁ* फक्क नीचैर्गतौ। फक्कः थक्क इत्यादेशः (cf. Hemacandra 4.87, 259)। तिष्ठितेर्वा विलम्बमानमित्यर्थः (cf. ibid. 4.16).

Kula says प्रणयन्तं प्रार्थयमानं सुजनमिव यशः मा पराङ्मुखयत। सुजनयशसोस्तुल्यं विशेषणमाह। शाश्वतशौटीर्यं स्थिरगर्वं, सीतान्वेषणप्रेषितेषु (कपिषु) वृथानिवृत्तेषु निवर्तमानं, हनुमता ज्ञातायां सीतावार्तायां कथमपि संमुखसंस्थापितपदम्। सुजनोऽपि याञ्चालज्जया निर्वतमानः कुटुम्ब भरणादिनिर्वाहालोचनया कथमपि संमुखस्थापितपदो भवति। रामेण सह रिपुनिग्रहार्थमागतेषु (अस्मासु) आगतं भगवद्विषादोदयात् वितिष्ठमानम् (ref. to यशः)। सुजनोऽपि प्रार्थयमान आगतोऽपि कथं मया देहीति वक्तव्यमिति वितिष्ठमानः स्यात्।

5. रक्खसवहदुव्वोज्झो कज्जारम्भो समुद्दलङ्घणगरुओ।
पढुमं चिअ रहुवइणा उवरिं हिअअ तुलिओ भरो व्व विलइओ।।

[राक्षसवधदुर्घात्यः(पक्षे–रक्ष्यशपथदुर्वाह्यः) कार्यारम्भः समुद्रलङ्घनगुरुः।
प्रथममेव रघुपतिना उपरि हृदये तुलितो भर इव विगलितः।।]

This task hard, to fulfil because the demons have to be slain, and arduous because the ocean has to be traversed, was at the very outset assigned to us, like a burden, and pondered in our hearts, and accepted by us.[7]

---

[7] Translation follows the readings of Kṛṣna, Mādhava and Kulanātha. Kṛṣna has "you" for "us".

K (*chāyā*) read the second line as प्रथमेव रिचतो युष्मान् पश्चाद्हृदयेन तुलितो भर इवं विलग्नः। K seems to read *raio vo pacchā* for *rahuvaiṇā uvariṁ* रघुपतिना उपरि (R). MY and Kula agree with K, but MY has अस्मान् and Kula अस्माकम्। Muda has रघुपतिना like R.

K says राक्षसवधेन दुर्वाह्यो दुर्निर्वहः, समुद्रलङ्घनेन गुरुरयं कार्यारम्भः। एवंभूतोऽपि प्रथममेव रचितो भवद्भिः कल्पितः, पश्चात् हृदयेन तुलितः तोलितः शक्यो न शक्य इति परीक्षितः। ततः युष्मान् विलग्न आरूटः भर इव भार इव। भारोऽपि प्रथममेव रचितः पश्चात् तोलितः। ततः शिरसा धार्यत इति। तस्मादिदानीं विषादो न युक्त इत्यर्थः।

MY says रचितः बुद्ध्या पूर्वापरभावेनावस्थापितः। *ṇe* अस्मान्। हृदयेन तुलितः शक्यतया निरूपितः। अस्मान् वोढव्यतया प्राप्तः। प्रथममेव तोलयित्वातिमर इति बुद्ध्वैवारोपितः। किमत्र अपूर्ववत् विचार्यत इत्यर्थः।

Kula says राक्षसवधस्य दुष्करत्वात् तेन दुर्वहः, समुद्रलङ्घनेन गुरुकः कार्यारम्भो भार इव प्रथममेव क्रियाकरणपुरःसरं मैत्रीसमय एव नोऽस्माकम् अस्मभ्यं रचितो न चेदानीमिति भावः। स च पश्चात् वाह्यतया(?) हृदयेन तुलितः, इदानीञ्च अनुशिष्टत्वात् विगलितः (विलगितः?) गृहीतः। Kula reads *ṇe* like MY.

Muda (*chāyā*) has प्रथममेव रघुपतिना अनन्तरं हृदयतुलितो भर इव विगलितः (?)। He says पूर्वमेव श्रीरामहृदये तुलित्वा पश्चात् अस्मास्वारोपित इत्यर्थः।

6. तुम्ह च्चिअ एस भरो आणामेत्तप्फलो पहुत्तणसद्दो।
अरुणो छाआवहणो विसअं विअसन्ति अप्पणा कमलसरा।।

[युष्माकमेवैष भर आज्ञामात्रफलः प्रभुत्वशब्दः।
अरुणश्छायावहनो विशदं विकसन्त्यात्मना कमलसरांसि।।]

This responsibility is yours. The master's authority is restricted to command. The lotus beds in the pools burst into bloom by themselves. The sun only adds to their lustre.

K and Muda read अरुणच्छायाप्रधानानि (*aruṇa-cchāā-vahaṇā*) for *aruṇo chāā-vahaṇo* छायावहनः (R and Kula).

K says एष कार्यारम्भो युष्माकमेव भरः। मम प्रभुत्वशब्दः आज्ञामात्रफलः। तथाहि कमलसरांसि अरुणच्छायाप्रधानानि अरुणप्रभा प्रधानभूता येषां तानि आत्मनैव स्वयमेव हि विशदं स्पष्टं विकसन्ति। Muda says प्रधानशब्दे उत्खातादित्वात् ह्रस्वः (cf. Hemacandra 1.67).

Muda reads *appaṇo* for *appaṇā* (R), and quotes Hemacandra 2.209 calling it an अव्यय। H.C. quotes this line with *appaṇo*.

MY says कमलानां विकासवत् युष्माकमेव उल्लासरूपः स्वामिकार्यकरो युष्मास्वेवायत्त इत्यर्थः। अरुणेन स्वप्रभेव केवलमाज्ञैव मया प्रवर्तनीया इत्याशयः।

Kula says युष्माकमेवैष भरः, प्रभुत्वशब्दः प्रभुत्वेन व्यपदेशः आज्ञामात्रफलः, आज्ञापयति परं प्रभुः भृत्या एव कुर्वत इत्यर्थः। एतदेव प्रतिवस्तूपमया दर्शयति। अरुणो रविः छायां शोभामावहतीति छायावहनः परं, विशदं यथा स्यात् तथा कमलसरांसि स्वयमेव विकसन्ति। अथवा छायामातपरोधिनीमपहन्तीति व्याख्येयम्। *SC* text reads *appaṇā* like R.

7. तरिउं णहु णवर इमं वेलावणबउलकुसुमवासिअसुरहिम्।
हत्थउडेहि समत्था तुम्हे पाउं पि फलरसं व समुद्दम्।।

[तरितुं न खलु केवलमिमं वेलावनबकुलकुसुमवासितसुरभिम्।
हस्तपुटाभ्यां समर्था यूयं पातुमपि फलरसमिव समुद्रम्।।]

Verily ye are capable not only of traversing the sea, but even of drinking it up from your hands, like the juice of fruits, scented as it is by the *bakula* flowers of the woods on the shore!

8. चिरआलकङ्खिआणं धुआवमाणणिअलुण्णमन्तमुहाणम्।
एसो णवर अवसरो असरिससमसीसबन्धणविमोक्खाणम्।।

[चिरकालकाङ्क्षितानां धुतापमाननिगलोन्नमन्मुखानाम्।
एष केवलमवसरोऽसदृशसमशीर्षबन्धनविमोक्षाणाम्।।]

This is the sole opportunity for the long desired release from the bondage of rivalry with[8] the unworthy, as a result of which one could hold one's head high, by shaking off the fetters of humiliation[9]

K reads निगलावनमत्सुखानाम् for *ṇialuṇṇamanta-muhāṇaṁ* (R) निगलोन्नमन्मुखानाम्।[10]

K says असदृशैः अनुचितैः हीनपौरुषैः समं शीर्षबन्धनस्य केशबन्धस्य विमोक्षाणां विमोचनानामयं केवलमवसरः। उत्तमानां सेवकानां मध्यमैः सह वेतनकल्पनं शीर्षबन्धनशब्देनोच्यते। वक्ष्यति च –*Kai – samasīsa . . . raṇabhare* (12.53) इति। कथंभूतानाम् – चिरकालकांक्षितानामुत्तमैः चिराय कांक्षितानां, धुतावमाननिगलावनमत्-

---

[8] Or, "occupying the same rank with".

[9] Translation follows Rāmadāsa's reading. The idea is, the tasks ahead will give them a chance to prove their superiority to their unworthy rivals, and bring to an end the humiliation of competing with them for favours.

[10] R says धुतः त्यक्तोऽपमान एव निगलस्तेन उन्नमत् मुखं येभ्यस्तेषाम्।

सुखानाम् अवमान एव निगलं निरस्तावमाननिगलत्वात् आसीदत्सुखानाम्।[11] इदानीं युष्मासु यः समुद्रं लङ्घयति तस्य वेतनाधिक्यमवश्यं भविष्यतीत्यभिप्रायः।

MY reads *oṇamanta* rendered as उपनमत्, cf. H.C. 1.173. He says *ṇavara* केवलम्। समशीर्षबन्धनम् एकज्यारोपणम्। R says समशीर्षं स्पर्धा।

Muda (*chāyā*) has धुतावमाननिगलोपनमत्सुखानाम्। He says असदृशैः सह यत् समशीर्षबन्धनं तुल्यत्वेन माननादिकं तस्य विमोक्षाः तेभ्यः उत्कर्षोपलब्धेरित्यर्थः। The reading of K, MY and Muda appears to be the same except that the last two render *oṇamanta* as उपनमत्।

Kula seems to read *dhuāvamāṇaṇialo ṇamanta - muhāṇaṁ*. He says असमानजनसमीकरणलज्जया नमन्मुखानामित्यर्थात् न्यूनत्वात्, असदृशेन हीनजनेन या समीकरणं स्पर्धा बन्धनमिव तद्विमोक्षाणां चिरकालकांक्षितानामेष 'णवर' केवलोऽवसरः, शूरणां कातराणाञ्च व्यक्तिरिति भावः। किंभूतः समयः – धुतोऽपमाननिगडो येनावसरेण स तथा। धूत इत्याशंसायां भूतवत् क्तः। अथवा ध्रुवेण निश्चलेन अपमाननिगडेन अवनमन्मुखानामिति योज्यम्।

9. ते विरला सप्पुरिसा जे अभणन्ता घडेन्ति कज्जालावे।
थोअ च्चिअ ते वि दुमा जे अमुणिअकुसुमणिग्गमा देन्ति फलम्।।

[ते विरलाः सत्पुरुषा येऽभण्यमाना घटयन्ति कार्यालापान्।
स्तोका एव तेऽपि द्रुमा येऽज्ञातकुसुमनिर्गमा ददति फलम्।।]

Honest persons that achieve their tasks silently[12] are rare. Few also are the trees that yield fruit without their flowering being noticed.

K reads कार्यकलापे or कार्यकलापान् (*kajja-alāve*) for *kajjālāve* कार्यालापान् (R and Kula).

K says इह लोके ते सत्पुरुषाः विरलाः बहवो न सन्ति। ये अभणन्तः (Kula and Muda also) स्वामिने अकथयन्तः तस्य कार्यकलापे कार्यजाते घटन्ते प्रवर्तन्ते। घट चेष्टायामिति धातुः। अथवा कार्यकलापान् घटयन्ति साधयन्ति। ये अज्ञातकुसुमनिर्गमाः सन्तः फलं ददाति ते द्रुमा अपि स्तोका एव अल्पा एव। यूयं पुनः कार्याध्यवसायमध्ये विक्लबीभवथ इत्युपालम्भः।

Muda reads कार्यकलापान् like K, and says निदर्शनालङ्कारः।

Kula says कार्यालापान् कार्यमित्यालप्यन्ते इति कार्यशब्दवाच्या ये व्यापारास्तान्

---

11 Rāmadṛṣṭi says धुतेन निवृत्तेन अवमानेन असदृशसमशीर्षबन्धनाख्येनैव निगलेन अवनमन्ति प्रह्वीभूतानि सुखानि अङ्गनादिसंभावनोत्पन्नानि येषु तेषाम्।

12 Lit. without saying anything.

घटयन्ति कुर्वन्ति। अत्र प्रतिवस्तूपमामाह – स्तोका एव तेऽपि द्रुमा ये अज्ञातकुसुमनिर्गमाः कुसुमेनासूचितफलाः फलं ददति। R says कार्यालापान् आलपितकार्याणि।

10. खिण्णं चावम्मि करं चिरकालुक्कण्ठिअं अमरिसम्मि मणम्।
मा दा देउ रहुवई बाणाहिमुहिं च बाहगरुइं दिट्ठिम्।।

[खिन्नं चापे करं चिरकालोत्कण्ठितममर्षे मनः।
मा तावद्ददातु रघुपतिर्बाणाभिमुखीं च बाष्पगुर्वीं दृष्टिम्।।]

Let not Rāma apply his weary hand to his bow, surrender his long anxious mind to wrath, and direct his tearful eyes to his arrows.[13]

K remarks अस्मासु तिष्ठत्सु विरहपीडितो रामः चापव्यापारं करिष्यति चेत् तत् अत्यन्तमयुक्तमित्यर्थः। MY says विरहखिन्ने रामे तूष्णींभूय स्थिते युष्माभिरेवैतत् सर्वं निर्वहणीयमित्यर्थः।

MY has *mā ā* (for *dā*) मा तावत्। Muda says तावत् रामो मा ददातु इति त्रिष्वपि वाक्येषु सम्बध्यत इति मध्यमदीपकालङ्कारः।

11. ओवग्गउ तुम्ह जसो दहवअणपआवपत्थिवपरिग्गहिअम्।
विलुलिअसमुद्दरसणं णहभवणन्तेउरं दिसावहुणिवहम्।।

[अवक्रामतु युष्माकं यशो दशवदनप्रतापपार्थिवपरिगृहीतम्।
विलुलितसमुद्ररसनं नभोभवनान्तःपुरं दिग्वधूनिवहम्।।]

Let your fame dominate the ten regions of the sky, maidens as it were, by crumpling up their girdle, the ocean; (maidens) held captive by the king that is Rāvaṇa's might, and abiding in the recesses of their home, the sky.[14]

K says युष्मद्यशः लङ्घितसमुद्राणां युष्माकं यशो दशाननस्य प्रतापाख्येन पार्थिवेन परिगृहीतं, विलुलिता शिथिलिता समुद्रमयी रशना यस्य तम्, नभ एव अन्तःपुरभवनं यस्य तं दिग्वधूनिवहम् अभिभवतु। दशाननप्रताप पार्थिवसकाशात् आच्छिद्य स्ववशे करोतु इत्यर्थः।

MY : says *oaggau* अभिभवतु। युष्माभिः समुद्रे निस्तीर्णमात्रे रावणप्रतापोऽभिभूतो भवेदित्यर्थः।

---

[13] I.e. they should take the initiative and relieve Rāma from the necessity of fighting.

[14] Rāvaṇa's world-conquering might is fancied as a king, and the regions of the sky as women taken captive by the latter. The idea is, let them overcome the resistance of the sea, i.e. cross over to Laṅkā, and earn universal fame in a world dominated by Rāvaṇa's prowess. Cf. Kulanātha in Extracts.

Kula says दशाननस्य प्रतापः पार्थिव इव तेन परिगृहीतं स्वीकृतं, नभो भवनमिव तदेवान्तःपुरं निवासस्थानं यस्य तं, दिशो वध्व इव तासां निवहं युष्माकं यशः विलुलिता विद्रुता समुद्ररसना यथा स्यात् अववल्गतु[15] रसनामिव समुद्रं विधूय आक्रामतु। लङ्घ्यतां समुद्रो, रावणप्रतापमभिभूय युष्माकं यशः सर्वास्वपि दिक्षु प्रसरतु इत्यर्थः।

Muda says दिश एव वध्वस्तासां निवहं युष्मद्यशो व्याप्रोतु आक्रामत्वित्यर्थः। प्राकृते यशःशब्दस्य पुंस्त्वात् प्रतिनायकत्वध्वनिः।[16]

12. जं साहसं ण कीरइ तं दअमाणेण जीविअं किर दइअम्।
जो अपडिमुक्कसुकओ सो वि गणज्जइ जगम्मि जीअन्तमुओ।।

[यत्साहसं न क्रियते तद्दयमानेन जीवितं किल दयितम्।
योऽप्रतिमुक्तसुकृतः सोऽपि गण्यते जगति जीवन्मृतः।।]

When a person desists from daring deeds, it is surely because he wants to preserve his dear life. But, on the other hand, whoso fails to repay a kindness is counted in the world as dead even while alive.[17]

K says प्राणभयात् भवद्भिः साहसं न क्रियते चेत् अकरणेऽपि यूयं मृतकल्पा इत्याह – पुंसा साहसं न क्रियते यत् तत् दयितं जीवितं दयमानेन रक्षता किल। देङ् रक्षण इति धातुः। दयितं जीवं परिरक्षता पुंसा तत् क्रियत इत्यर्थः। किलशब्दोऽन्यथात्वं प्रकटयति। कुत इत्याह – यः पुमान् अप्रतिमुक्तसुकृतः पूर्वं सुकृतकारिणामकृतप्रत्युपकार इत्यर्थः, सोऽपि जगति जीवन्मृतः गण्यत इति। Rāmadṛṣṭi says साहसमशक्यकरणम्। Kula says यत् साहसं न क्रियते तत् किल दयितं प्रिय जीवितं दयमानेन रक्षता। तदपि वृथैव, यतो योऽप्रतिमुक्तसुकृतः प्रत्युपकारेण अपरिशोधितोपकारर्णः सोऽपि जगति जीवन्मृतो गण्यते जीवत्कार्याकरणात्। तस्मात् रामप्रत्युपकारार्थं साहसमेवाश्रयत इति भावः Muda says अधीगर्थ इत्यादिना कर्मणः शेषत्वेन विवक्षायां षष्ठी। अत्र तु शेषत्वाविवक्षया द्वितीयैव।

13. किं व ण आणह एअं कज्जं परिपेलवं पि जह परिणामे।
देह परं संमोहं कुसुमं विसपाअवस्स व मलिज्जन्तम्।।

[किं वा न जानीतैतत्कार्यं परिपेलवमपि यथा परिणामे।
ददाति परं संमोहं कुसुमं विषपादपस्येव मृद्यमानम्।।]

---

[15] This word is restored from *SC*.

[16] Rāmadṛṣṭi read वसनं for *rasaṇaṁ* – युष्माकं यशः दिग्वधूनिवहं विलुलितं मर्दितमाक्षिप्तमित्यर्थः समुद्र एव वसनं यस्मिन् तथा अभिभवतु बन्दीभावमानयतु इत्यर्थः। अत्र हेतुः, दशाननस्य प्रतापेनैव पार्थिवेन परिगृहीतम् प्रतिभटस्त्रीपरिभवो युक्त इति भावः।

[17] Sugrīva reminds his followers of their obligations to Rāma.

Are ye not aware of this — that even an easy task, pondered too much, leads to utter confusion in the end, like as the tender flower of a poisonous plant makes one unconscious while being crushed with the hand.[18]

K (*chāyā*) has किमिव न जानीथ। Kula has किं वा न जानीथ। K says परिणामे निर्वहणे। Kula says परं संमोहं कार्यानिश्चयं मूर्छां च ददाति। Deva says कार्यं मृद्यमानं चेदत्यन्तं विचार्यमाणं चेत्।

14. विहडन्तं पि समत्था ववसाअं पुरिसदुग्गमं णेन्ति वहम्।
भुवणन्तरविक्खम्भं दिअसअरो विहडिएक्कचक्कं व रहम्।।

[विघटमानमपि समर्था व्यवसायं पुरुषदुर्गमं नयन्ति पन्थानम्।
भुवनान्तरविष्कम्भं दिवसकरो विघटितैकचक्रमिव रथम्।।]

The valiant carry even their failing enterprise to the path (of success), inaccessible to others; just as the Sun drives his tottering one-wheeled chariot through the middle region of the universe.

K, Kula and Muda read समर्थः and नयति in the singular. They as well as MY read विगलित for *vihaḍia* विघटित (R).

K says समर्थो विघटमानमपि एवं समुद्रादिभिः प्रतिबन्धैः शिथिलीभवन्तमपि व्यवसायं कार्याध्यवसायमन्यैः पुरुषैः दुर्गमं पन्थानं पदं नयति। दिवसकरः विगलितैकचक्रत्वात् विघटमानं रथं यथा भुवनान्तरालविस्तारं नयति तद्वदिति। आदित्यरथस्य प्रसिद्धमेकचक्रत्वम्।

MY says व्यवसायं व्यवसितार्थम्। पन्थानमुपायभूमिम्। यथा रविर्विगलितैकचक्रमपि रथं भुवनस्य मध्यावकाशं सर्वगः सर्वतो नयतीत्यर्थः। Kula says व्यवसायं कार्यम्। R says भुवनान्तरं नभस्तदेव विष्कम्भं विवरम्। विष्कम्भो विवरे देश्याम्।

Muda says समर्थो विसामग्रीकमपि उद्योगमन्यपुरुषदुर्गमं मार्गं नयति। तत्रोपमा भुवनेत्यादि। विष्कम्भो विस्तारः। Kula syas एकस्मात् भुवनादन्यत् भुवनान्तरं तस्य विष्कम्भमन्तरालं विगलितं विशृङ्खलमेकं चक्रं यस्य तं रथं दिवसकर इव। Deva says यथा दिवसकरः विगलितैकचक्रं एकचक्रत्वादेव विकलं स्वं रथं भुवनान्तरविष्कम्भं भुवनान्तरसन्धिप्रदेशं यथा नयति तद्वदिति।

15. कअकज्जे तालसमे अइरा पेच्छह भुए अणुत्तालसमे।
णिहुओ राअसहाओ पडिवक्खस्स अ अवेउ राअसहाओ।।

[कृतकार्यास्तालसमानचिरात्पश्यत भुजाननुत्तालसमान्।
निभृतो राजस्वभावः प्रतिपक्षस्य चापैतु राजस्वभावः।।]

---

[18] This is a warning against weighing the pros and cons too much.

Behold before long your arms resembling palm trees, crowned with success without great toil. Let the sovereignty of the enemy,[19] characterized by lust, come to an end, assailed by you.[20]

K says अनुत्तालश्रमान् अनुत्ताल: अनुन्नत: श्रमो येषां तान्, तालसमान् दीर्घान् भुजान् अचिरात् कृतकार्यान् पश्यत। किञ्च निभृत: अप्रकाशमानो भवतां राजसभावो रासत्वमपैतु अपगच्छतु। रजोगुणविजृम्भणेनैव हि संरम्भ: स्यादिति भाव:। अपि च प्रतिपक्षस्य शत्रो: राजस्वभावश्चापैतु।

Kula explains *ṇihuo* as निधृत: (निधुत: ?), and says निधृतो नि:शेषेण धृत: (धुत: ?) प्रतिपक्षस्य च रावणस्य राजस्वभावो राजत्वमपैतु अपगच्छतु। रागसहाय:, राग: कामासक्ति: सहाय: सहचरो यस्य। अथवा राजस्वभावरूपेण व्यपदेशात् निभृत: छन्नो राजसो भाव इत्यर्थ:।

Muda has अनुत्तालश्रमान् like K and Kula. The latter says तालतरुसमान् भुजान् अनुत्तालश्रमान् अनुद्भटायासान् अचिरात् कृतकार्यान् प्रेक्षध्वम्। Muda says राजसभाव: राजसत्वं रावणस्यापैतु अपयातु। कीदृश: – राज्ञां स्वभाव: प्रकृतिभूत:। R says राजसो भावो रजोगुणविजृम्भितं मरणादिभयम्।

16. संखोहिअमअरहरो संभन्तुव्वत्तदिट्ठरक्खसलोओ।
वेलाअडमुज्झन्ते अह णे हसइ हिअएण मारुअतणओ।।

[संक्षोभितमकरगृह: संभ्रान्तोद्वृत्तदृष्टराक्षसलोक:।
वेलातट मुह्यतोऽथास्मान्हसति हृदयेन मारुततनय:।।]

Yonder Hanumat that perturbed the sea,[21] and saw the insolent demons panic-stricken (during the burning of Laṅkā), inwardly mocks at us as we stand bewildered on the seashore.

K reads युष्मान् for *ṇe* अस्मान्।

K says लङ्घनरभसेन संक्षोभितसमुद्र:, संभ्रान्त: अतिसंत्रस्त उद्वृत्तो वेपमानशरीर: दृष्टो राक्षसलोको येन स हनुमान् वेलातट एव मुह्यतो युष्मान् हृदयेन हसति अथ हसति नूनमित्यर्थ:।

---

[19] I.e. Rāvaṇa.

[20] Cf. Kulanātha in Extracts. The line is variously explained. According to Rāmadāsa, let your hidden fear as well as the sovereignty of the enemy come to an end.

[21] It is imagined that he disturbed the sea by trampling down the shore before leaping over to Laṅkā.

MY says उद्वृत्ततया दृप्ततया दृष्टो राक्षसनिवहः संभ्रान्तः कृतो येन स तथा। *aha* असौ। *ṇe* अस्मान्। Kula says संभ्रान्तः संविग्नः। *aha ṇe* अयमस्मान्।

Muda says अहेति अदसः प्रथमैकवचने रूपम्, and quotes Hemacandra 3.87 where Pravarasena's line is quoted.

SC says उद्वृत्तः परावृत्तः। R says उद्वृत्ता इतस्ततो गामिनः।

17. अव्वोच्छिण्णपसरिओ अहिअं उद्धाइ फुरिअसूरच्छाओ।
उच्छाहो सुभडाणं विसमक्खलिओ महाणईण व सोत्तो।।

[अव्यवच्छिन्नप्रसरितोऽधिकमुद्धावति स्फुरितशूर(सूर्य)च्छायः।
उत्साहः सुभटानां विषमस्खलितो महानदीनामिव स्रोतः।।]

The unremitting zeal of brave warriors that is aglow with heroism is heightened when thwarted by obstacles; just as the constantly flowing water of great rivers, glistening with the lustre of the sun, surges up, when obstructed in its course.

R and Kula read *mahā-ṇaīṇa*. The others have this in singular.

K says क्वचिदपि अव्युच्छिन्नप्रसृतः, स्फुरितशूरच्छायः स्फुरिताः प्रज्वलिता शूराणां छाया शोभा यस्य सः सुभटानामुत्साहः विषमेषु एवंविधेषु स्खलितः सन् अधिकमुद्धावति प्रवर्धते। किमिव – महरनद्याः स्रोत इव। नदीप्रवाहश्च अव्युच्छिन्नप्रसृतः, स्फुरितसूर्यच्छायः स्फुरितसूर्यप्रतिबिम्बो विषमेषु स्खलितः सन् अधिकमुद्धावति। तद्वदिति।

MY says *phuria sūra cchāo* स्फुरितशूरप्रशस्तिः, स्फुरितसूर्यप्रकाशश्च।

Muda has अव्युच्छिन्न like K, whose *pratīka* is *avvucchiṇṇa* for *avvo-* (R and Kula) अव्यवच्छिन्न। Muda and Kula render *uddhāi* as ऊर्ध्वायते। Kula says सुभटानामुत्साहः अव्यवच्छिन्नमविरतं प्रसृतः प्रवृत्तः, विषमे दुष्करे कृत्ये स्खलितः प्रतिहतः सन् महानदीनां स्रोत इव अधिकमूर्ध्वायते। महानदीनां स्रोतोऽपि विषमे प्रोन्नतभूभागादौ (?) स्खलितमधिकमूर्ध्वायते। उच्छलितत्वादेव स्फुरितसूरच्छायं प्रतिफलितादित्यप्रभं भवति।

Muda says स्फुरिता शूरस्य वीरस्य छाया कान्तिर्यत्र। स्रौतःपक्षे स्फुरिता सूरस्य सूर्यस्य छाया प्रतिबिम्बं यत्र।

Deva says प्रतिबद्धं चेत अधिकमुद्धावति बन्धमुल्लङ्घयति तदुपरिभागेनैव गन्तुमिच्छति तद्वदिति।

18. माणेण परिट्ठविआ कुलपरिवाडिघडिआ अणोणअपुव्वा।
चिन्तेउं पि ण तीरइ ओहुप्पन्ती परेण णिअअच्छाआ।।

[मानेन परिस्थापिता कुलपरिपाटिघटिता अनवनतपूर्वा।
चिन्तयितुमपि न तीर्यते आक्रम्यमाणा परेण निजकच्छाया।।]

It is unthinkable that one's prestige, never lowered before, should be humiliated by others, the prestige that hath been built up with a sense of pride, and maintained from one generation to another.

K and Muda read प्रतिष्ठापिता for परि- । (R and Kula).

K says पूर्वं कुलपरिपाटीघटिता कुलस्य वंशस्य परिपाट्या आनुपूर्व्या घटिता संपादिता, मानेन प्रतिष्ठापिता स्थैर्यं गमिता निजच्छाया वीराणां सहजा दीप्तिः परेणाभिभूयमाना सति पश्चात् अनेन छायावता पुंसा चिन्तयितुमपि न शक्यते। आत्मप्रतापस्य परपरिभवमुपैति चेत् ततः स्वीकर्तुं न शक्यत एव, परिभवः प्रागेव परिहरणीय इति यावत्। शकेस्तरचयतीरा इति कर्मणि तीरादेशः (Vararuci 8.70), says R निजकच्छाया निजप्रतिष्ठा।

Muda says तीरइ इति शकेश्चयतरतीरपारा इति (Hemacandra 4.86) तीरादेशः। छाया कीर्तिः प्रतिबिम्बञ्च। प्रतिबिम्बपक्षे मानं प्रमाणं, कुलं देहः। 'सजातीयजने गोष्ठे देहेऽपि कथितं कुलम्'। 'मानं प्रमाणे प्रस्थादौ मानं चित्तसमन्नतिः'। Deva says आत्माभिमानेन प्रतिष्ठापिता निजकच्छाया। MY says मानेन अभिमानेन राजसत्कारेण। कुलपरिपाट्या पुत्रपौत्रादिक्रमेण संबद्धा। निजच्छाया शौर्यादिना कृतं निजरूपम्।

SC text has *ahuvvantī* (अवघूयमाना) for *ppa*-Kula also has अवघूयमाना।

19. परिवड्ढन्तुच्छाहो विअलिअरणमच्छरेहिँ अप्पत्तगुणो।
अअसक्कन्तोसरिओ कड्ढिज्जइ दुक्करं भडत्तणसद्दो।।

[परिवर्धमानोत्साहो विगलितरणमात्सर्यैरप्राप्तगुणः।
अयशःक्रान्तापसृतः कृष्यते दुष्करं भटत्वशब्दः।।]

Martial reputation radiates enthusiasm, and its value cannot be appreciated by those who lack ardour for war. It is hard to regain it, once it departs, tarnished by disgrace

K and Muda read अल्पोऽपि पुनः for *oppatta-guṇo* अप्राप्तगुणः (R and Kula).

K says भटत्वस्य वाचकः शब्दो भटशब्दः इत्यर्थः। सोऽल्पोऽपि अयशःक्रान्तत्वात् अपसृतश्चेत् विगलितरणमत्सरैः रणं प्रति विगलितमत्सरैः वीरैः पुनर्दुष्करं कृष्यते अतिकृच्छ्रादाकृष्यते। तस्मात् पूर्वमेवायशःप्रवेशः परिहरणीय इत्यर्थः।

Kula seems to read परिमित for *vialia*. He says दुष्करेऽप्यर्थे परि समन्तात् वर्धमानः शृण्वतामपि उत्साहो येन स तथा परिमितो रणमत्सरः समरामर्षो येषां तैः अप्राप्तगुणः, नाममात्रोदाहरणेनापि शत्रुसंकोचहेतुः प्रतापविशेषः एवंभूतो यो भटत्वशब्दः

सुभटत्वख्यातिः अयशसा क्रान्तः समपसृतः पलायितः दुष्करं कृष्यते न शक्यते पुनरानेतुमित्यर्थः।.

20. आहिअसमराअमणा वसणम्मि अ उच्छवे अ समराअमणा।
अवसाअअविसमत्था धीरच्चिअ होन्ति संसए वि समत्था।।

[आहितसमरागमना व्यसने चोत्सवे च समरागमनसः।
अवशागतविषमार्था धीरा एव भवन्ति संशयेऽपि समर्थाः।।]

The valiant who welcome the advent of war, and preserve their equanimity in weal and woe, remain steadfast even in danger, faced with a calamity brought by fate.

K, Kula and Muda read *āḍhia* for *āhia* आहित (R). Muda says *āḍhia* इति आदृते ढिरिति ढिः (Hemacandra 1.143). The word is recorded in *Deśīnāmamālā* 1.74 with the meanings इष्ट, गणनीय, अप्रमत्त and गाढ।

K says आदृतसमरागमनाः, व्यसने उत्सवे च समरागं समाभिनिवेशं समप्रकारं मनो येषां ते समर्थाः अवशागतः यदृच्छागतः विषमो दुस्तरोऽर्थो वस्तुविशेषो येषां ते तथाभूताः संशयेऽपि आपद्यपि धीरा एव भवन्ति न विषीदन्ति। Kula says *āḍhiaṁ* गणनीयं समरागमनं येषाम्।

Muda says अवशोऽनायत्तः अतो दैवम्। MY says प्रतिपथदैवागत विषमार्था धीरा एव भवन्ति प्राणसंशयेऽपि समर्थाः। Kula reads अवसादित (*avasāia*, cf. *SC* text) for *avasāaa* (अवशागत) अवसादितः

अवसन्नीकृतो विषमः अर्थो यैः। He mentions the other reading and explains it: अवशोऽस्वतन्त्रः आगतो विषमो दुष्करोऽर्थो येषु। अथवा अवशं दैवम् अप्रतिक्रियत्वात्, तस्मादागतो विषमोऽर्थों येषाम्। अथवा अवशात् दैवात् आगते विषमे तिष्ठन्तीति तथोक्तास्ते समर्थाः सन्देहेऽपि धीरा एव भवन्ति।

R says आहितं समर्पितमर्थात् स्वस्मिन् समरस्य आगमनं यैः। संग्रामोऽपि कर्तव्य इति कृतनिश्चयाः।

21. ववसाअसप्पिवासा कह ते हत्थट्ठिअं ण पाहेन्ति जसम्।
जे जीविअसंदेहे विसं भुजंग व्व उव्वमन्ति अमरिसम्।।

[व्यवसायसपिपासाः कथं ते हस्तस्थितं न पास्यन्ति यशः।
ये जीवितसंदेहे विषं भुजंगा इवोद्वमन्त्यसमर्पम्।।]

Those who let loose their wrath when their life is in danger, even as serpents emit their venom when in peril of their life;

and show ardent zeal for manly endeavour — how can they fail to attain fame that is within their reach?

MY says व्यवसायेन सपिपासा व्यवसायरूपपिपासावन्तः। He reads *ṇa pāvanti* for *ṇa pāhenti* (पस्यन्ति), and says न पिबन्ति न प्राप्नुवन्तीति वा। Muda says *pāhenti* पास्यन्ति। पिबतेः पातेश्च रूपम्। Ms. C of Goldschmidt has-*he-* (*SC* text also). Kula says व्यवसाये सपिपासाः सतृष्णाः। *SC* text has *sappiāsā* for-*vā-*.

22. सीहा सहन्ति बन्धं उक्खअदाढा चिरं धरेन्ति विसहरा।
ण उण जिअन्ति पडिहआ अक्खण्डिअववसिआ खणं पि समत्था।।

[सिंहाः सहन्ते बन्धं उत्खातदंष्ट्राश्चिरं ध्रियन्ते विषधराः।
न पुनर्जीवन्ति प्रतिहता अखण्डितव्यवसिताः क्षणमपि समर्थाः।।]

Lions endure their captivity; and serpents live long, even when their fangs are taken out. But the valiant whose endeavour knows no check do not live even for a moment, when frustrated in their efforts.

K says उत्खातदंष्ट्रा विषधराः चिरं धरन्ति जीवन्ति। अखण्डितव्यवसिताः क्वचिदपि अखण्डितव्यवसितार्थाः समर्थाः प्रतिहताश्चेत् क्षणमपि न जीवन्ति। MY also says धरन्ति जीवन्ति। Kula says ध्रियन्ते अवतिष्ठन्ते। Muda has *dharanti* (ध्रियन्ते *chāyā*) for *dharenti* . He says धृङ् अवस्थाने। जीवन्तीत्यर्थः। Kula remarks अखण्डितव्यवसिता इति खण्डितव्यवसितास्तु पूर्वमपि सोढत्वात् सहन्तेऽपि।

23. अकअत्थपडिणिअत्ता कह सँमुहालोअमेत्तपडिसंक्कन्तम्।
दप्पणअलेसु व ठिअं णिअअ दच्छिह पिआमुहेसु विसाअम्।।

[अकृतार्थप्रतिनिवृत्ताः कथं संमुखालोकमात्रप्रतिसंक्रान्तम्।
दर्पणतलेष्विव स्थितं निजकं द्रक्ष्यथ प्रियामुखेषु विषादम्।।]

Returning without achieving your task, how will ye see your sorrow, mirrored in the countenances of your wives as soon as they see ye before them?

K and Kula read स्फुट (*phuḍa*) for *paḍi* found in R.

K says एवमकृतार्थाः प्रतिनिवृत्ताः यूयं प्रियामुखेषु संमुखालोकनमात्रेण स्फुटं संक्रान्तं दर्पणस्थलेष्विव स्थितं निजं विषादं कथं द्रक्ष्यथ। भवतां विषादो युष्माभिरदृश्यमानोऽपि प्रेयसीनां मुखेषु स्पष्टं द्रष्टव्यः। किं ततः कष्टमित्यर्थः। तस्मात कृतकार्यैरेव निवर्तितव्यमिति यावत्।

Kula says कृतकार्यागता: स्वामिन इति प्रथमं प्रसादयोगात् दर्पणतलेष्विव निर्मलेषु प्रियामुखेषु संमुखालोकमात्रस्फुटसंक्रान्तं निजमात्मीयं विषादं स्थितमकृतार्थप्रतिनिवृत्ता: कथं द्रक्ष्यथ। निजकलत्रैरपि गर्हणीया: किं पुनरन्यैरिति भाव:।

Muda seems to read मुख- or सुख-संक्रान्तम्। *SC* text and ms. C of Goldschmidt read *damcchiha* for *decchiha.*

24. णिज्जन्ति चिरपअत्ता समुद्दगहिरा व पडिपहं णइसोत्ता।
तीरेन्ति णिअत्तेउं असमाणिअपेसणा ण उण सप्पुरिसा।।

[नीयन्ते चिरप्रवृत्तानि समुद्रगम्भीराण्यपि प्रतिपथं नदीस्रोतांसि।
तीर्यन्ते निवर्तयितुमसंमानितप्रेषणा न पुन: सत्पुरुषा:।।]

The everflowing currents of rivers, even though deep as the sea, can be guided backwards. But honest persons cannot be induced to turn back without having achieved their task.

K says नदीस्रोतांसि चिरप्रयत्नात् प्रतिपथं नीयन्ते। Kula says चिरप्रवृत्तानि नदीस्रोतांसि like R. Muda renders *ṇijjanti* (नीयन्ते others) as निर्यान्ति।

MY read *tīranti* for *tīrenti* (शक्यन्ते)। He reads *asamāvia* (असमापित) for *asamāṇia* rendered as असंमानित by K and R who explains it as अनिष्पादित। Kula and Muda have असमापित, but the latter reads *asamāṇia,* as he says समापे: *samāṇa* इत्यादेश:। Cf. Hemacandra 4.142 who equates *samāṇai* with *samāvei.*

25. जो लङ्घिज्जइ रइणा जो वि खविज्जइ खआणलेण वि बहुसो।
कह सो उइअपरिहओ दुत्तारो त्ति पवआण भण्णउ उअही।।

[यो लङ्घ्यते रविणा योऽपि क्षप्यते क्षयानलेनापि बहुश:।
कथं स उदितपरिभवो दुस्तार इति प्लवगानां भण्यतामुदधि:।।]

How could it be said that it was beyond the power of the apes to traverse the ocean that is accustomed to humiliation, traversed as it is by the sun, and consumed by the fire of the epoch of universal ruin, time and again?

K and Muda read *volijjai* (अतिक्रम्यते) for *laṅghijjai* लङ्घ्यते (R, Kula and MY). K, Muda and Kula read भण्यते for *bhaṇṇau* भण्यताम् (R).

K and R explain *uia-parihao* as उदितपरिभव:। MY and Muda say उचितपरिभव: परिचितपरिभव: Kula says उदित: परिभवो यस्य। अथवा उचित: अभ्यस्त: परिभवो येन स उदधि:।

Muda says प्लवगानामिति साभिप्रायं सम्बन्धमात्रस्य विवक्षितत्वात् षष्ठी। यथा किमेषामस्ति दुष्करमिति।

K, MY and Muda put this verse after verse 26.

26. चिन्तिज्जउ दाव इमं कुलववएसक्खमं वहन्ताण जसम्।
लज्जाइ समुद्दस्स वि दोह्ण वि किं होइ दुक्करं बोलेउम्।।

[चिन्त्यतां तावदिदं कुलव्यपदेशक्षमं यशो वहताम्।
लज्जायाः समुद्रस्यापि द्वयोरपि किं भवति दुष्करं व्यतिक्रमितुम्।।]

Think of this: for those who possess a renown worthy of their family tradition, which of the two evil — the ocean and disgrace — is harder to overcome?[22]

K (*chāyā*), Muda and Kula read चिरं for *imaṁ* (R and K comm.). K, Kula and Muda read च (i.e. *a*) for *vi* अपि (R). K, MY and Muda read भवेत् for *hoi* (R and Kula ?).

K says इदं तावत् चिन्त्यताम्। किमिति चेत्, कुलव्यपदेशक्षमं वंशकथनयोग्यं वंशप्रवादानुरूपं यशो वहतां पुंसां लज्जायाः समुद्रस्य च द्वयोरपि अतिक्रमितुं किं दुष्करं भवेत्। समुद्रादपि लज्जा दुस्तरेत्यर्थः। MY says *hojja* भवेत्।

Kula says कुलव्यपदेशक्षमं वंशकीर्तनयोग्यम्। समुद्रलङ्घनमवोचितं न तु लज्जालङ्घनमिति भावः। Deva says कुलव्यपदेशक्षमं कुलप्रसिद्धियोग्यम्।

27. किरणासणिं रहुसुए सुहस्स किर णासणिं विमुंच मा दा।
सेलससारअमे हो तुम्हे जेऊण चन्दसारअमेहो।।

[किरणाशनिं रघुसुते सुखस्य किल नाशनीं विमुञ्चत मा तावत्।
शैलससारतमान्भो युष्माञ्जित्वा चन्द्रशारदमेघः।।]

Yea, let not the moon, an autumnal cloud as it were, after overcoming ye, strong as mountains, release on Rāma its thunder, the lunar rays, destructive of happiness.[23]

---

22 I.e. it will be easier for them to cross the sea than to bear the disgrace resulting from their failure to do so.

23 The rays of the moon supposed to be unbearable to *virahin*s are represented as thunder, while the moon is fancied as a white cloud of the autumn with its rumblings of thunder. The idea is, delay in the conquest of Laṅkā and the recovery of Sītā will add to the sufferings of Rāma as well as themselves, separated from their wives, and so *virahin*s like Rāma.

K says चन्द्राख्य: शारदमेघ: तावत् भो वानरा: शैलवत् ससारतमान् अत्यर्थं सारवतो युष्मान् जित्वा रावणवधोद्युक्तान् अध:कृत्य सुखस्य नाशनीं किल किरणाशनिं रघुसुते मा मुञ्चतु। MY remarks शक्यत्वे सति युष्माभि: देवीविरहदु:खं रामस्यावश्यं निरसनीयम्। . . . शैलगुहागतानामशनिभयाभावादिति भाव:।

Kula says *mā dā* इति मा तावत् *tubbhe* युष्मान् जित्वा, आरब्धकार्यविमुखान् कृत्वा इत्यर्थ:, चन्द्र: शारदमेघ इव धवलत्वात् किरणान् अशनिमिव दु:सहत्वात् सुखस्य किल नाशनीं विमुञ्चतु। अनतिक्रान्तायामेव शरदि शीघ्रं निष्पाद्यातां कार्यं, रामोऽपि निर्वृतिं लभतामिति भाव:। *SC* says युष्मान् जित्वा प्रारब्धकार्यासमर्थान् मत्वा। R says चन्द्र: किरणवज्रपातेन विरहिणो युष्मानभिभूय अतिवियोगिनं रामचन्द्रमभिभविष्यतीति सर्वतोऽनुचितमिति भाव:।

28. बन्धवणेहब्भहिओ होइ परो विणएण सेविज्जन्ता।
किं उण कओवआरो णिक्कारणणिद्धबन्धवो दासरही।।

[बान्धवस्नेहाभ्यधिको भवति परोऽपि विनयेन सेव्यमान।
किं पुन: कृतोपकारो निष्कारणस्निग्धवान्धवो दाशरथि:।।]

Even an enemy, served with humility, becomes kinder than a kinsman; let alone Rāma, a disinterested benign friend, who hath done good to us.[24]

K read प्रणयेन for *viṇaeṇa.*

Kula says ननु उपक्रियमाणोऽपि विजातीयत्वात् पर एवायं राम:। तत् किमेतदर्थं नियोजयसीत्याशङ्क्याह। परोऽपि शत्रुरपि विनयेन सेव्यमान: सन् बान्धवात् स्नेहेनाभ्यधिको भवति, किं पुन: निष्कारणस्निग्धबान्धव: कारणं विनैव अस्माकमुपकारक: कृतोपकार: उपकारेणोपगृहीत:। एतेन य एवं महात्मा शत्रुं निर्जित्य राज्यदानादस्माकमुपकर्ता स प्रत्युपकृत: किमिवाभीष्टं न करोतीत्यर्थ:।

K says परोऽपि य: कश्चित् प्रणयेन सेव्यमानश्चेत् बान्धवस्नेहाभ्यधिको भवेत्। पूर्वमेव कृतोपकारो निष्कारणस्निग्धबान्धवो दाशरथि: प्रणयेन सेव्यमान: किं पुन: अस्माकं किं न कुर्यादित्यर्थ:।

29. अइरपरूढ व्व लआ समरुच्छाहे उदुम्मि व विलम्बन्ते।
अज्ज वि दाव मह इमा मउलेइ च्चिअ फलं ण दावेइ सिरी।।

[अचिरप्ररूढेव लता समरोत्साहे ऋताविव विलम्बमाने।
अद्यापि तावन्ममेयं मुकुलायत एव फलं न दर्शयति श्री:।।]

---

[24] Translation takes the first *bāndhava* in the sense of "kinsman". Cf. 11.55.

Verily my royal fortune, like a new-grown creeper, is still in bud, and doth not bear fruit, because your martial ardour, like the right season, is slow to manifest itself.[25]

K says राघवेण दत्ता ममेयं श्रीः अचिरप्ररूढा लतेव भवन्ती युष्मत्समरोत्साहे ऋताविव फलप्रदायिनि ग्रीष्मादावृताविव विलम्बमाने सति अद्यापि मुकुलयत्येव (Muda also; मुकुलायते R and Kula)। फलं न दर्शयति। यथा लता फलं न दर्शयति तद्वदिति। राघवेण प्रतिपादिता राज्यश्रीः तस्य प्रत्युपकारे कृत एव मे भोग्या स्यादित्यर्थः।

Muda says यथा ऋतो विलम्बमाने लता मुकुलितैव तिष्ठति न फलति तथा श्रीरपि अस्मासु युद्धमानुत्सहमानेषु न फलति। वालिनमिवास्मान् उत्खाय अन्यस्मै रामो राज्यश्रियं दास्यतीति भावः।

30. केच्चिरमेत्तं व ठिई एअ विसंवाइआ ण मोच्छिहि रामम्।
कमलम्मि समुप्पण्णा तं चिअ रअणीसु किं ण मुञ्चइ लच्छी।।

[कियच्चिरमात्रं वा स्थितिरेवं विसंवादिता न मोक्ष्यति रामम्।
कमले समुत्पन्ना तदेव रजनीषु किं न मुञ्चति लक्ष्मीः।।]

How long will Rāma's patience, thus worn out, last without leaving him altogether? Doth not the beauty born of the day lotus leave it at night?[26]

K says एवं विसंवादिता एवं दैवेन प्रतिकूलिता स्थितिरवस्था कियच्चिरमात्रं वा रामं न मोक्ष्यति कियन्तं कालावयवं न मोक्ष्यति। अचिरात् मीक्ष्यतीत्यर्थः। अत्र दृष्टान्तं व्यतिरेकेण आह – कमले समुत्पन्नापि श्रीः रजनीषु तत् कमलमेव न मुञ्चति किम्। किमिति प्रश्ने। मुञ्चत्येव। पुनरुदिते सूर्ये तदेव कमलं प्राप्नोति। तद्वदेव सीता न चिरात् रामं प्राप्स्यतीति व्यतिरेकोक्तिः। अस्यां दुरवस्थायामेव रामस्य अस्माकं प्रतिकर्तुमवकाश इत्यभिप्रायः।

Muda says रामस्यैषा दुर्दशा . . . स्थितिर्दशा। He and MY seem to agree with K, Kula's interpretation of the verse is different. He says एवमिति प्रतिज्ञातार्थाकरणेन विसंवादिता विघटिता स्थितिर्मर्यादा कियच्चिरमात्रं वा कियन्तं कालं रामं न मोक्ष्यति। कमले समुत्पन्ना लक्ष्मीस्तदेव कमलं किं रजनीषु न मुञ्चति। एतेनैवं विसंवादनात् अस्मानेव तावदयं प्रथमं हनिष्यतीति भावः। R agrees with Kula — स्थितिः धैर्यमेवं भवतामव्यवसायेन विसंवादिता विचालिता सती, etc.। तथा सति आधीरो भवन् सर्वानपि नो निहनिष्यतीति भावः। (वि)संवादो विचलत्वम्।

31. सअलुज्जोइअवसुहे समत्थजिअलोअवित्थरन्तपआवे।
ठाइ ण चिरं रविम्मि व विहाणपडिआ वि मइलदा सप्पुरिसे।।

---

[25] Sugrīva, recently installed on the throne by Rāma, does not feel secure until he has required his obligations to the latter.

[26] The day lotus closes at night.

[सकलोद्द्योतितवसुधे समस्तजीवलोकविस्तीर्यमाणप्रतापे।
तिष्ठति न चिरं रवाविव विधान(विभात)पतितापि मलिनता सत्पुरुषे।।]

Indecision about an undertaking doth not abide long in an able person that hath illumined the entire earth (with his glory), and extended his power over all living beings; even as the faint light of early dawn doth not linger in the sun.[27]

K says विधानेन विधिना पतितापि मलिनता सदोषता सत्पुरुषे चिरं न तिष्ठति। कथंभूते – सकलमविकलंमुद्द्योतितवसुधे विरातिजभूतले, समस्त जीवलोकप्रसरत्प्रतापे। किमिव – एवंभूते रवौ विधानपतिता विधानेन प्रकारेण पतिता मलिनता मेघसंपर्कभवा यथा चिरं न तिष्ठति तद्वदिति।

MY reads *maulaṇā* for *mailadā*, and explains it as मलिनता सत्पुरुषे व्यसनं, रवावुपरागः। Muda also says यथा सूर्ये उपरागः Kula says समस्तजीवलोकविस्तीर्यमाणप्रतापे सत्पुरुषे रवाविव विधानं दैवं ततः पतिता मलिनता शोकादिकृतो विषादः, पक्षे प्रभातं, तत्र पतितः सन्ध्यारागो न चिरं तिष्ठति। Muda says विधानमितिकर्तव्यता तत्र पतिता (मलिनता)। रविपक्षे *vihāṇaṁ* प्रातः।

32. सप्पुरिसपाअडवहं पढमं जं राहवेण अम्हासु कअम्।
होज्ज व ण होज्ज व समं अम्हेहिँ कअं पि किं उण अकीरन्तम्।।

[सत्पुरुषप्रकटपथं प्रथमं यद्राघवेणास्मासु कृतम्।
भवेद्वा न भवेद्वा सममस्माभिः कृतमपि किं पुनरक्रियमाणम्।।

What we might do for Rāma might or might not be equal to what he first did for us, manifesting the way of a man of noble character; but should it remain undone?

K reads this verse after verse 27, and MY after 33.

K, MY and Muda read प्रकटसत्पुरुषपथं। K and Muda read भवेद्वा न वा तस्य समं for *hojja va ṇa hojja va samaṁ* भवेद्वा न भवेद्वा समं (R and Kula)।

K says राघवेण प्रकाशितसत्पुरुषस्वभावं प्रथममस्मासु यत् कृतम् अस्माभिः कृतमपि तस्य सुकृतस्य समं भवेत् वा न वा। अक्रियमाणं तु किं पुनः। Muda says अस्माभिः प्रत्युपकारलेशोऽपि न कृत एवेति भावः।

Kula says ननु अस्माभिः सीतान्वेषणेन प्रत्युपकृतमेवास्य इत्यत आह। सत्पुरुषस्य प्रकटः प्रकाशः पन्थाः विपदुद्धरणलक्षणों मार्गो यत्र तत् यत् प्रथममस्मासु राघवेण कृतम्

[27] Sugrīva asks his followers not to be discouraged by Rāma's indecision about what should be done to cross over to Laṅkā.

उपकृम्, तस्य रावणवधरूपं प्रधानं कार्यं कृतमपि समं भवेत् वा न भवेत् वा, किं पुनरक्रियमाणम्।

33. राहवपत्थिज्जन्तो उद्धो दीसिहइ केच्चिरं व दहमुहो।
दूरन्तपेच्छिअव्वो सिहरपडन्तविअडासणि व्व वणदुमो।।

[राघवप्रार्थ्यमान ऊर्ध्वो द्रक्ष्यते कियच्चिरं वा दशमुखः।
दूरान्तप्रेक्षितव्यः शिखरपतद्विकटाशनिरिव वनद्रुमः।।]

Assailed by Rāma, how long will Rāvaṇa be seen to hold his head high? He must be seen quickly (before he is destroyed), like a forest tree, with dreadful thunder crashing down on the top.

K, MY, Kula and Muda read त्वरमाण for *dūrānta* दूरान्त (R)।

K says राघवेण प्रार्थ्यमानः युद्धार्थमभियुज्यमानो दशमुखः कियन्तं चिरकालमूर्ध्वं तिष्ठन् दर्शिष्यते (द्रक्ष्यते others)। अभियोगानन्तरमेव विनङ्क्ष्यतीत्यर्थः। तस्मात् दशमुखं युद्धार्थं दिदृक्षुभिः त्वरमाणैरेव प्रेक्षितव्यः स शिखरे पतन्महाशनिः वनद्रुम इव।

Kula says यः सत्वरं पश्यति तेनैव परं यदि द्रक्ष्यते। MY says *tūranta-pecchiavvo* त्वरमाणप्रेक्षितव्यः आशुतरविनाशीत्यर्थः। Cf. Hemacandra 4.171.

Muda says प्रार्थ्यमानः अभियास्यमानः संरुध्यमानो वा। 'अभियाने च यच्ञायां प्रार्थना कथ्यते बुधैः'। 'प्रार्थितः शत्रुसंरुद्धे याचितेऽभिहितेऽपि च' इति वा। यथा – विशूलः प्रार्थ्यतामिति। Deva says प्रार्थ्यमानः युद्धार्थमाहूयमानः।

34. बालाअवं व एत्तं धुअअम्बालाअवंसुणिवहच्छाअम्।
कइसेण्णं रअणिअरा तमरअणिअर व्व पेच्छिउं पि अओग्गा।।

[बालातपमिवायद्धुतातास्रालातपांशुनिवहच्छायम्।
कपिसैन्यं रजनिचरास्तमोरजोनिकरा इव प्रेक्षितुमप्ययोग्याः।।]

The demons, like the massive darkness of the night, are not bold enough even to behold the army of apes, advancing like the rays of the morning sun, and glistening like the sparks thrown off by the glowing fire-brand when it is waved about.

K says धुतताम्रालातस्फुलिङ्गनिवहप्रभं धुतानां ताम्राणाम् उल्मुकानां स्फुलिङ्गनिवहसदृशम्। अत एव बालातपमिव यान्तं (?) कपिसैन्यं रजनिचराः प्रक्षितुमपि न समर्थाः। तमःशकलनिकरा यथा बालातपं द्रष्टुं न शक्नुवन्ति तद्वदिति। Kula says रजन्यां चरन्तीति तमोरेणवोऽपि रजनीचराः।

Muda says *entaṁ* आयत् आगच्छत् (MY and Kula also).

35. गुरुअम्मि वि पडिवक्खे होन्ति भडा अहिअवारिअप्पडिऊला।
पडिगअगन्धा इद्धा उद्धङ्कुसरुद्धमत्थअ व्व गइन्दा।।

[गुरावपि प्रतिपक्षे भवन्ति भटा अधिकवारितप्रतिकूलाः।
प्रतिगजगन्धाविद्धा ऊर्ध्वाङ्कुशरुद्धमस्तका इव गजेन्द्राः।।]

Even when the adversary is powerful, warriors become exceedingly restive, when restrained from fighting, even like spirited elephants, excited by the smell of their rivals, when their heads are held tight by the upright goad.[28]

K, My and Muda read गुरावेव (*garue ccia* MY) for *garuammi vi* (R and Kula,),

K says प्रतिपक्षे गुरावेव महत्येव भटाः वारिताः सन्तोऽधिकं प्रतिकूला भवन्ति निवारणमतिलङ्घयन्ति। प्रतिगजगन्धेन आविद्धा आहता गजेन्द्राः ऊर्ध्वाङ्कुशेन रुद्धमस्तका अपि यथा प्रतिकूला भवन्ति तद्वदिति। MY says वारितास्तु अधिकप्रतिकूला भवन्ति। सुभटा गजा इवेत्यर्थः।

36. विसमम्मि वि अविसण्णो धारेइ धुरं धुरंधरो च्चिअ णवरम्।
किं दिणअरोवराए दिणस्स होइ अवलम्बणं ससिबिम्बम्।।

[विषमेऽप्यविषण्णो धारयति धुरं धुरंधर एव केवलम्।
किं दिनकरोपरागे दिनस्य भवत्यवलम्बनं शशिबिम्बम्।।]

One that is capable of a task can alone achieve it, undaunted even in peril. Does the moon ever become the support of the day when there is an eclipse of the sun?

K says विषमेऽपि विपत्तावपि अविषण्णः धुरंधर एव समर्थ एव धुरं कार्यं धारयति। Kula says धुरंधर एव भारोद्वहनक्षम एव धुरं भारं केवलं धारयति।

37. मुक्कसलिला जलहरा अहिणवदिण्णफला अ पाअवणिवहा।
लहुआ वि होन्ति गरुआ समरमुहोहरिअमण्डलग्गा अ भुआ।।

[मुक्तसलिला जलधरा अभिनवदत्तफलाश्च पादपनिवहाः।।
लघवोऽपि भवन्ति गुरवः समरमुखावहृतमण्डलाग्राश्च भुजाः।।]

The clouds that have released the rains, and the trees that have given away their fresh fruit, and the arms that have

---

[28] I.e. to prevent them from charging.

wielded the sword in the forefront of the battle are worthy of esteem, even though they have diminished in weight.[29]

K and Muda read विटपाः for *ṇivohā* (R and Kula). They render *oharia* as अपहृत (अव – R)।

K says मुक्तवर्षा जलधराश्च, अभिनवदत्तफलाः पादपविटपाश्च, समरमुखे प्रयुक्तखडगा भुजाश्च लघवोऽपि कृतकार्यत्वात् गुरवो भवन्ति। अपहरणं प्रयोगः।

MY says *oharia* उत्कण्ठ (?)। भुजानां लाघवं संस्कारवैशद्योद्भूतप्रबोधः। गौरवं तु श्लाघ्यता। Muda says अवहृतमवपातितमित्यर्थः। एतेन कार्यवशात् लाघवेऽपि गौरवमित्यर्थः। Kula says समरमुखे रणोपक्रमे *oharia-maṇḍalaggā* व्यापारितखड्गा भुजाः। Deva says समरमुखव्यावृत्तमण्डलाग्रस्य भुजस्य लाघवं तु जाड्यप्रतियोगि वैशद्यमेवेति।

38. दप्पं ण सहन्ति भुआ पहरणकज्जसुलहा धरेन्ति महिहरा।
वित्थिण्णो गअणवहो णिज्जइ कीस गुरुअत्तणं पडिवक्खो।।

[दर्पे न सहन्ते भुजाः प्रहरणकार्यसुलभा ध्रियन्ते महीधराः।
विस्तीर्णो गगनपथो नीयते किमिति गुरुत्वं प्रतिपक्षः।।]

Your arms (still) retain their pride.[30] Mountains for use as weapons are readily found. Wide is the path of the sky.[31] Why do ye overrate the enemy's might?

K, Muda and Kula read मुञ्चन्ति (*muanti*) for *sahanti* (R)।

K says भवतां भुजाःदर्पं न मुञ्चन्ति दर्पवन्त एव । . . . महीधराः ध्रियन्ते अवतिष्ठन्ते। धृङ् अवस्थाने। MY says *kīsa* कस्मात् (Muda also). Kula says प्रतिपक्षः किं गौरवं नीयते दुर्जयत्वख्यातिं प्राप्यते। R says किमिति गुरुत्वं नीयते। K and Deva say प्रहरणकार्ये युद्धे सुलभा योग्याः।

39. धीरं परिरक्खन्ता गरुअं पि भरं धरेन्ति णवर सुउरिसा।
ठाणं चिअ अमुअन्ता णीसेसं तिहुअणं खवेन्ति रविअरा।।

[धैर्यं परिरक्षन्तो गुरुमपि भरं धारयन्ति केवलं सुपुरुषाः।
स्थानमेवामुञ्चन्तो निःशेषं त्रिभुवनं क्षपयन्ति रविकराः।।]

---

[29] The apparent literal meaning is: are heavy, even though they become light. The loss of weight in the case of the arms is the feeling of lightness after exertion.

[30] According to Rāmadāsa's reading: Your arms do not brook (the enemy's) pride.

[31] The apes described in the poem as capable of flying through the air.

The brave alone can achieve a task, even though arduous, by maintaining their fortitude. The rays of the sun scorch the entire universe by abiding in[32] their customary place.[33]

K reads गुर्वीमपि धुरं for *garuaṁ pi bharaṁ* (R and Kula). He and Kula read *taventi* (तपन्ति; तापयन्ति) for *khaventi* क्षपयन्ति (R and Muda)।

K says व्यसनेषु धैर्यं परिरक्षन्त एव सुपुरुषाः केवलं गुर्वीमपि धुरं धारयन्ति निर्वहन्ति। तथाहि रविकिरणाः स्थानं स्वावस्थानभूतं मण्डलममुञ्चन्त एव निःशेषं त्रिभुवनं तपन्ति। Kula says स्थानत्यागे रविं त्यजन्तो ज्वाला इव निर्वाणा अकिञ्चितकराः स्युरित्याशयः। Muda reads *dharanti* for-*re*-, and says धृञ् धारणे। Kula says स्थानं रविमण्डलं धैर्यस्थानीयम्। MY says धैर्यं नाम कृच्छ्रप्राप्तावव्यग्रतया पूर्वस्थानापरित्याग एव।

40. काअरपडिमुक्कधुरं जिणन्ति पत्थाणलङ्घिअग्गक्खन्धा।
पढमं ता णिअअबलं पच्छा पहरेहिँ सुउरिसा पडिवक्खम्॥

[कातरप्रतिमुक्तधुरं जयन्ति प्रस्थानलङ्घिताग्रस्कन्धाः।
प्रथमं तावन्निजकबलं पश्चात्प्रहरणैः सुपुरुषाः प्रतिपक्षम्॥]

The brave advance beyond the front ranks of the army as they push ahead, and first dominate their own troops, among whom the craven abandon the initative, and thereafter vanquish the enemy by striking hard.

K says सुपुरुषाः कातरैः भीरुभिः प्रतिमुक्तधुरं निजबलं निजसैन्यं प्रस्थानेन प्रयाणेन अवगाहनेन लङ्घिताग्रस्कन्धाः लङ्घितः आक्रान्तः अग्रस्कन्धः सैन्यस्याग्रव्यूहः येन ते तथाभूताः जयन्ति स्ववशे कुर्वन्ति। प्रथममात्मनः सेनां संस्थापयन्ति पश्चात् प्रहारैः (प्रहरणैः Kula) प्रतिपक्षं जयन्ति। Kula says कातरेण प्रतिमुक्ता धूरग्रेसरता यत्र तन्निजबलं स्वसैन्यम्।

41. अण्णेन्ति मङ्गलाइं अल्लिअइ सिरी जसो पवड्ढइ पुरओ।
पडिवण्णरणुच्छाहे पडिवक्खुद्धरणपत्थिअम्मि सुउरिसे॥

[अनुगच्छन्ति मङ्गलान्यालीयते श्रीर्यशः प्रवर्धते पुरतः।
प्रतिपन्नरणोत्साहे प्रतिपक्षोद्धरणप्रस्थिते सुपुरुषे॥]

When a man of noble character, inspired with martial ardour,

---

[32] Lit. without leaving. . . .

[33] I.e. the orb of the sun to which fortitude is likened.

sets out to destroy an enemy, fame precedes him, fortune draws near, and favourable signs follow in his wake.

K, Muda and Kula read प्रवर्तते for *pavaḍḍhai* (R).

K says सत्पुरुषे प्रतिपक्षोद्धरणाय प्रस्थिते सति मङ्गलानि कल्याणानि तमनुयन्ति। श्रीः विजयश्रीः आश्रयति। पुरतो यशः प्रवर्तते। शत्रुवधाय प्रस्थिता यूयमपि मङ्गलादीनि मा पराङ्मुखानि कुरुतेत्यर्थः।

MY says *aṇṇanti* (for *aṇṇe-*) अनुयान्ति। *alīai* प्राप्नोति प्रत्युद्गच्छतीत्यर्थः। Kula says आलीयते समालिङ्गति श्रीः। Muda says उपसर्पेरल्लिअ इत्यादेशः। Cf. Hemacandra 4.139 which gives *alliai* found in R who renders it as आलीयते – मिलति। Cf. H C 4.54.

42. वच्चन्ता अइभूमिं कड्ढिअसुहडासिवत्तवन्थावडिआ।
णवर ण चलन्ति वीअं लुअवक्खा महिहर व्व वेराबन्धा।।

[व्रजतोऽतिभूमिं कृष्टसुभटासिपत्रपथापतिताः।
केवलं न चलन्ति द्वितीयं लूनपक्षा महीधरा इव वैराबन्धाः।।]

Persistent animosities, reaching their climax, confront[34] the drawn swords of valiant warriors, and never retrace their steps; even as the mountains whose wings were clipped (by Indra) do not move to another place.[35]

Muda reads *verābaddhā* for *-bandhā* (R and Kula).

K says वैरमाबध्नन्तीति वैराबन्धा वीराः। कृष्टानां सुभटासिपत्राणाम्, असिपत्रमसिधेनुः खड्गविशेषः, कोशादाकृष्टानां शत्रुभटासिपत्राणां पथि प्रहारमार्गे आपतिताः, अतिभूमिं युद्धस्य काष्ठां व्रजन्तो वैराबन्धाः केवलं द्वितीयं न चलन्ति प्रथमावस्थानात् पुनर्द्वितीयं न चलन्ति पदान्तरं न प्राप्नुवन्ति। किमिव – लूनपक्षा महीधरा इव। शत्रुपक्षमवगाह्य प्रहरन्तः प्रहताश्च वीराः स्थानात् स्थानान्तरं न गच्छन्ति। तत्रैव शत्रूनुत्सादयन्तीत्यर्थः।

MY and Muda (*chāyā*) read अरिभूमिं for *aibhūmiṁ* (अतिभूमिम्)। My says अरिभूमिं शत्रूणाम् आसन्नतां भूमिम्। *viiaṁ* द्वितीयां भूमिमित्येव ततोऽनुकर्षः। *ṇavara* केवलम्। चलनस्य जयपराजयसाधारण्यं केवलशब्दार्थः। अथवा केवलशब्द एवकारार्थः। न चलत्येवेत्यर्थः।

34 Lit. fall in the way of . . . .

35 Cf. Devarāṭa in Extracts. According to Kulanātha, the animosities "never shift to another person, just as the mountains do not move to another place", that is, the enmity against Rāvaṇa shared by them with Rāma must be pursued to its bitter end by themselves, because the task cannot be delegated to others. Sugrīva reminds the apes that they had promised to help Rāma against Rāvaṇa, and must not back out.

Muda commentary has अतिभूमि, but the meaning is not clear. He says *vīaṁ* इति क्रियाविशेषणम्। वैरेणाबद्धाः। बद्धो हि पदमपि चलितुं न पारयति किमुत समन्तात् बद्धः। Muda (*chāyā*) renders *ṇavara* as अनन्तरम्।

Kula says सुभटाकृष्टासिपत्रपथापतिताः सन्तः, अतिभूमिं प्रकर्षं व्रजन्तो वैराबन्धा द्वितीयं पुरुषं केवलं न चरन्ति न यान्त्येव तैरेव(?) समाप्यमानत्वादित्यर्थः। लूनपक्षा महीधरा यथा द्वितीयं स्थानं न यान्ति। अतो युष्माभिरारब्धः कार्यभारो युष्माभिरेव निर्वर्तितः शोभत इति भावः। R says आबध्यमानवैराणि द्वितीयं पुरुषं न चलन्ति तत्र न संक्रामन्ति।[36]

Devarāta says अतिभूमिं परमकाष्ठां गच्छन्तः वैरबन्धाः कृष्टानां कोशाकृष्टानां सुभटासिपत्राणां क्षुरिकाणां पथि धारया न केवलं पतिता भवन्ति द्वितीयं च प्रयोगं न चलन्ति। Then he says वैरानुबन्धाः शत्रवः शात्रवं वा। वैरानुबनः प्रतिबलं दूरमवगाढाः समरे अतिभूमिं व्रजन्तो नासीरे स्थित्वा सर्वं साधयन्ति। . . . प्रतिभटेन उत्खातासिसञ्चरमार्गगताः तदानीं स्मृतेन वैरेण स्थिरीकृताः सुपुरुषाः ततो निवृत्य द्वितीयं पदं न चलन्ति। तत्रैव स्थिता भवन्ति। यस्मिन् देशे कृत्तपक्षा महीधरास्तत्रैव स्थिरा भवन्ति पुनर्नान्यत्र गच्छन्ति।

43. ता सोअइ रहुतणओ ताव अ सीआ वि हत्थपहत्थमुही।
ताव अ धरइ दहमुहो जाव विसाएण वो तुलिज्जइ धीरम्।।

[तावच्छोचते रघुतनयस्तावच्च सीतापि हस्तपर्यस्तमुखी।
तावच्च ध्रियते दशमुखो यावद्विषादेन वस्तुल्यते धैर्यम्।।]

Rāma will lament and Sītā lean her face on her elbows (in grief), and Rāvaṇa live so long as your courage is outweighed by dejection.

K says दशमुखश्च तावत् धरति जीवति यावत् वो धैर्यं विषादेन तुल्यते अधःक्रियते। MY says *tulijjai* तोल्यते चाल्यत इत्यर्थः। Kula says तावच्च ध्रियते स्वरूपेणावतिष्ठते दशमुखः यावद्वो युष्माकं धैर्यं विषादेन तुल्यते आकलय्यते। Muda says ध्रियते जीवति। धृङ् अवस्थाने। यथा – ध्रियते यावदेकोऽपि रिपुस्तावत् कुतः सुखमिति। *SC* says तुल्यते उत्क्षिप्यते। R says सदृशीक्रियते। उत्क्षिप्यते वा।

44. अण्णो अण्णस्स मणो तुम्ह ण आणे अणाहिओ मह अप्पा।
णिव्वण्णन्तस्स इमं दररूढवणप्पसाहणं हणुमन्तम्।।

[अन्यदन्यस्य मनो युष्माकं न जानेऽनाधिर्ममात्मा।
निर्वर्णयत इमं दररूढव्रणप्रसाधनं हनूमन्तम्।।]

Everyone's mind is different. I am not aware of yours. But I

---

[36] *SC* says यं प्रति येन यद्वैरमङ्गीकृतं तेनैव वैरेण स तेन व्यापादयितुमुचितः, न तु तस्मिन् भग्नोद्यमे तद्वैरमादाय अन्यैररिनिर्यातनं कर्तुमुचितमित्यर्थः।

do not value myself highly as I behold yonder Hanumat, adorned with his partly healed wounds.[37]

K, MY and Muda read अनादृतः for *aṇāhio (R)* rendered as अनाधिः। R says मम पुनरात्मा अनाधिर्भवद्भिर्विना कार्यं कथं सिध्येदिति अन्तर्व्यथाशून्यः।

K reads प्रगुण for दररूढ (R and Kula), and says अन्यस्य मनः अन्यदन्यप्रकारं भवति। युष्माकं मनो न जाने। ममात्मा अनादृतः[38] त्युक्तुमध्यवसितः। कथंभूतस्य – दरप्रगुणमीषद्रोपितं व्रणमेव प्रसाधनं यस्य तमिमं हनूमन्तं निर्वर्णयतः पश्यतः। समुद्रमुल्लङ्घ्य रावणं हनिष्यामि तेन हतो वा भविष्यामीत्यर्थः। Muda says हनूमन्तं पश्यतो मम मध्ये चानादरो जात इत्यर्थः। Their reading seems to be *aṇāḍhio*, found also in Kula and *SC* text. Kula says हनूमन्तं निर्वर्णयतः(मम) आत्मा *aṇāḍhio* अगणनीयः, अस्मिन्नेव बहुमानः न तु आत्मनि इति भावः। See notes on verse 20.

45. पडिवक्खस्स अ लच्छिअं आसाएन्तएणं
णिअअकुलस्स अ कित्तिअं आसाएन्तएणम्।
मरणं पि वरं लद्धअं णअणिम्माणएणं
पुरिसेण चिरं जीविअं ण अ णिम्माणएणम्।।

[प्रतिपक्षस्य च लक्ष्मीमास्वादयता
निजककुलस्य च कीर्तिमासादयता।
मरणमपि वरं लब्धकं नयनिर्मापकेण
पुरुषेण चिरं जीवितं न च निर्मानकेन।।]

Death, not long life, is preferable for one that hath lost his pride,[39] even if he takes possession of the enemy's wealth, maintains the renown of his family, and upholds the moral law.

R reads *āsāentaeṇaṁ* (आस्वादयता and आसादयता). K, MY and Muda seem to read *āsāsantaeṇaṁ* (from *āsāsai*) which they explain differently. Kula's reading is same as that of R, but he explains

---

[37] The references is to his recent fight with the demons during the raid on Laṅkā. Sugrīva speaks disparagingly of himself while admiring Hanumat. According to another interpretation, he does not value his life highly, i.e. will sacrifice it if necessary in trying to emulate Hanumat.

[38] Deva says अहमात्मानं शरीरमनादृतवामिति। He explains रदरूढ as ईषदुच्छून।

[39] I.e. self-respect.

it differently (प्रतिपक्षस्य लक्ष्मीम् आशातयता विनाशयता, निजककुलस्य च कीर्तिम् आसादयता स्वीकुर्वता)।

Muda has प्रतिपक्षस्य लक्ष्मीमाशासानेन शत्रोः श्रियमात्मन इच्छता। निजकुलस्य कीर्तिमाश्वासयता कुलस्य च कीर्तिमाश्वासयता अम्लानां कुर्वतः। K has आशासता ईषच्छासता निगृह्णता and आश्वासयता। MY has प्रतिपक्षस्य च लक्ष्मीमाशंसमानेन, निजकुलस्य (च)कीर्तिमाश्वासयता। K and Muda omit अ–(च) in the first and second lines.

K and MY read लब्धुं and जीवितुं। Kula has लब्धं and जीवितं like R. Muda has लब्धं and जीवितुं K says नयस्य निर्माणकेन संपादकेन नयप्रणेत्रापि (उचितकारिणा MY) निर्मानेन मरणमपि पुरुषेण लब्धुं वरं योग्यं, चिरं जीवितुं न वरम्। एवंभूतस्य पुरुषस्य जीवितादपि मरणमेव श्रेयस इत्यर्थः। Kula says नयनिर्माणको नीतिप्रयोक्ता, तेन मरणमपि वरं लब्धं, न च निर्मानकेन मानहीनेन चिरं जीवितं लब्धम्। पुरुषस्तावदेवासौ यावत् मानात् न हीयत इति भावः। R on verse 46 says मानोऽहंकारः।

Muda says नयस्य नीतेर्निर्मात्रा पुरुषेण मरणमपि लब्धं वरं मानरहितेन च चिरं जीवितुं न वरमित्यर्थः। *ṇimmāṇaeṇaṁ* इति निर्माणकेनेत्यर्थः। निर्मो णिम्माणणिम्मवाविति णिम्माणादेशः (Hemacandra 4.19, i.e. *ṇimmāṇai*) *āsāantaeṇaṁ* इति पाठे एकत्र आसादयता आशानां ददता वा। अन्यत्र आस्वादयता(?) इत्यर्थः।

46. एअ वि सिरीअ दिट्ठआ के सरलच्छिआए
करकमलस्स अ छिक्कआ केसरलच्छिआए।
मुज्झन्ति सविण्णाणआ समरसमाणअम्मि
एअ ममम्मि भणन्तए समरसमाणअम्मि।।

[एवमपि श्रिया दृष्टकाः के सरलाक्ष्याः
करकमलस्य च स्पृष्टया केसरलक्ष्म्या।
मुह्यन्ति सविज्ञानकाः समरसंमानदे
एवमपि भणति समरसमापके।।]

While I speak thus — I, who fight to a finish, and possess martial ardour and pride in equal measure — what discerning people will remain perplexed, even when they are thus[40] watched by the keen-eyed goddess of fortune, and touched by the beautiful filaments[41] of her lotus hands?

K and MY read इत्यापि for *ea* (एवं) in the last line. R, Kula and

[40] I.e. through his favour. He refers to his followers.

[41] The fingers are meant.

Muda have एवमपि। They *yamakas kesaralacchiāe* and *ke sara-* ; and *samarasamāṇaammi* (2) are explained differently in the commentaries.

K says सरलाक्ष्या सरसाक्ष्या श्रिया लक्ष्म्या एवं दृष्टा अपि, तस्याः करकमलस्य केसरलक्ष्म्या केसरशोभया स्पृष्टाश्च, एवं किष्किन्धाराज्यं प्राप्य साक्षात् लक्ष्म्या दृष्टाः, विहरन्त्याः तस्याः हस्तकमलकेसरश्रिया स्पृष्टाश्च के पुरुषाः सविज्ञानाः सन्तः समरसंमाने समरे संमानो यस्य तस्मिन्, समरसंमानके इति वा समरं बहु मन्यमाने, समरसमाने रसो वीररसः समौ रसमानौ यस्य तस्मिन् मयि इतीत्थं भणत्यपि मुह्यन्ति न केऽपि मुह्यन्ति। एवमतिश्रीमन्तो विज्ञानवन्तश्च पार्श्वस्थे स्वामिनि मयीत्थं वदत्यपि कथं मुह्यथेत्यर्थः।

Kula says एवमपि मत्प्रसादात् श्रिया सरलाक्ष्या प्रगुणदृष्ट्या दृष्टाः, श्रियैव करकमलस्य च केशरलक्ष्म्या किञ्जल्कनिकरेण *chikkaā* स्पृष्टाः। अनेन लक्ष्म्या दर्शनस्पर्शनकथनेन मध्यमोत्तमसम्पदः मया यूयं विभक्ताः, न तु केऽपि निकृष्टा इति सूचितम्। एवंभूते मयि सम यथा स्यात् तथा रसमानौ अनुरागसत्कारौ ददति। पुनः किंभूते – समरस्य संग्रामस्य समानके शत्रुवधात् कृतसत्कारे। एतेन विशेषणद्वयेनानुग्रहे क्षमता सूचिता।

MY says रणयोग्यं शरत्समयं सहकारिणं च लब्ध्वा कोऽत्र मुह्येत् प्रेक्षावानित्याह – एवमपि श्रिया दृष्टाः, केसरलक्ष्म्याः करकमलस्याक्षेप्तारः,[42] के शरल्लक्ष्म्या मुह्यन्ति सविज्ञानाः, समरसंमानदे[43] इत्यपि मयि भणति समरसमाने युद्धसमाने विक्रमेण तुल्य इत्यर्थः।

Muda says समौ रसो वीररसश्च मानो यस्य तस्मिन् (see K)। समरस्य समापके पारप्रापके मयि एवं भणति सति सचेतनाः के वा मुह्यन्तीति। न केऽपीत्यर्थः। कीदृशाः – पक्ष्मलक्ष्म्या श्रिया दृष्टाः श्रिया अनुगृहीताः श्रीमन्त इत्यर्थः। तथा शरलक्ष्म्या वाणसमृद्धेः करकमलेन स्पृष्टा युद्धेषु शरक्षताङ्गा इत्यर्थः। करकमलस्येति तृतीयार्थे षष्ठी। समापेः समाण इत्यादेशः (Hemacandra 4.142, see notes on verse 24) अग्रिमगलितकेन संदानितकम्। एवंशब्दस्य मांसादिषु चेति मलोपः। R says समरस्य समापके निर्वाहके।

47–48. मा सोइज्जउ दुहिआ सीआ लोअएणं
णलिणि व्व समोलुग्गआ सीआलोअएणम्।
दुहिए राहवहिअए कामइलन्तअम्मि
जीविअम्मि अहिलोहिआ का मइलन्तअम्मि।।

चन्दअ व्व मेहमइलिए रअणीसारअम्मि
कमलअम्मि व हिमडड्ढए रअणीसारअम्मि।

---

[42] I e. श्रियः करकमलस्य केसरलक्ष्मयाः आक्षेप्तारः।

[43] After this our copy has सदृशेच्छाभिमाने which seems to be an alternative explanation of the phrase construed as सम-रस-माने।

दुहिए राहवहिअअए भमरोअत्तअम्मि
    कुसुमम्मि व पव्वाअए भमरोअत्तअम्मि।।

[मा शोच्यतां दु:खिता सीता लोककेन
    नलिनीव समवरुग्णा शीतालोकेन।
दु:खिते राघवहृदये कामक्लाम्यमाने
    जीवितकेऽभिलोभिका का मलिनायमाने।।

चन्द्र इव मेघमलिनिते रजनीसारके
    कमल इव हिमदग्धे रजोनि:सारके।
दु:खिते राघवहृदये भ्रमरोदितिव्ये
    कुसुम इव प्रवाणे भ्रमरापवर्तितव्ये।।]

While Rāma's heart is full of sorrow, and afflicted with delusion, and is like the moon, the mainstay of the night, when obscured by clouds; like a lotus that is blasted by frost, and sheds its pollen; like a withered flower turned over by the bees — let the people not bewail the lot of Sītā, suffering like a day lotus plant wilted by the cold-rayed moon! While Rāma's heart, pining with love, is distraught with grief, what craving can one have for one's fading life?

The verses are interconnected. K, Muda and Kula put verse 48 first. My[44] has only one verse consisting of the first half of 48 and the second half of 47.

K, MY, Muda and Kula read राम for *rāhava* (R). Kula says दु:खितके रामहृदये, i.e. *duhiae rāma-hiae*. K and Kula read हिमावरुग्णा for *samoluggaā* समवरुग्णा (R). Muda has समारुग्णा।

K, MY and Muda have हिमावरुग्णे in verse 48. Kula has हिमदग्धे like R.

K says रजनीसारे रजन्या: सारभूते अवष्टम्भभूते चन्द्रे मेघमलिनित इव, रजोनि:सारके, रज: पराग: तत् नि:सारयति निर्गमयतीति रजोनि:सारकं ण्वुल्प्रत्ययान्तम्, अधिष्ठितै: भ्रमरैरपवृत्ते अविकासिते तस्मिन् कमले हिमावरुग्ण इव, भ्रमरोर्गाते भ्रम एव रोग: तेनार्ते रामहृदये दु:खिते सति। उत्तरत्र सम्बन्ध:।

दु:खिता सीता लोकेन जनेन मा शोच्यताम्। अस्मासु तिष्ठत्सु द;खितां सीतां प्रति लोको

---

[44] Only ms. A is available for this canto.

मा शोचतु इत्यर्थः। कथंभूता – शीतालोकेन चन्द्रेण हिमपीडिता नलिनी यथा शोच्यते जनेन तथा रावणेन दुःखिता सीतेति। किञ्च रामस्य हृदये[45] कामक्लान्ते दुःखिते सति मलिनान्ते मलिनस्वरूपे जीविते अभिलोभिता अभिलाषिता का। एवं रामे सीतायां च दुःखितयोः कश्मले जीवितो लोभो न कर्तव्य इत्यर्थः।

Deva says भ्रमरैः अपवृत्ते तद्भारातिशयेनाधोमुख एवंभूते कुसुमे प्रम्लान इव।

Kula says *pavvāae* शुष्के . . . भ्रमरेणापवृत्ते विमर्दवशादावर्तिते कुमुस इव। (verse 48). Most of this phrase is omitted in K (comm). K (*chāyā*) has however कुमुस इव प्रग्लाने भ्रमरापवृत्ते। Kula says धिक्कारमलिनायमाने जीविते का अभिलोभिता अतितृष्णा न युज्यत इति भावः। Muda has अतिलोभिता। Explaining 3.47 he says प्रथमार्धस्य पूर्वेण (i.e. 3.48) सम्बन्धः। उत्तरार्धं पृथग्भूतं वाक्यम्। काम्क्लान्ते रामहृदये दुःखिते सति मलिनीभवति जीविते का तृष्णा। एवं सति जीविते तृष्णा न करणीयेत्यर्थः। At the end of 3.48 he says सीता लोकेन मा शोच्यतामित्युत्तरेणान्वयः। Deva says मलिनान्ते अशोभनावसाने जीविते . . . अनवस्थिते जीविते प्रणयो न कर्तव्य इत्यर्थः।

49–50. कइआ णु विरहविरइअदोव्बल्लपसाहणुज्झिआहरणाइं।
णीसासवसपहोलिग्गलम्बालअमलिअपम्हलकओलाइं।।
पिहुलणिअम्बअलक्खलिअसिढिलवलअविवइण्णबाहुलआइं।
दच्छाम परिअणत्थुअकअपेसणलज्जिआ पिअकलत्ताइं।।
(जुग्गअम्)

[कदा नु विरहविरचितदौर्बल्यप्रसाधनोज्झिताभरणानि।
निःश्वासवशप्रघूर्णनशीललम्बालकमृदितपक्ष्मलकपोलानि।।
पृथुलनितम्बतलस्खलितशिथिलवलयविप्रकीर्णबाहुलतानि।
द्रक्ष्यामः परिजनस्तुतकृतप्रेषणलज्जिताः प्रियकलत्राणि।।]
(युग्मकम्)

Abashed to hear the achievement of our task being praised by our retainers,[46] when shall we see our dear wives that have discarded their ornaments, being only adorned with the langour caused by their separation from us; with their cheeks thrilling in contact with their long tresses waving in the wake of their sighs; and their creeper-like arms, stripped of the loose bangles, drooping on their ample hips?

---

[45] Kula's attempt to explain *duhiae rāma-hiae* as दुर्हृत्कृतवैरामथिते is a tour de force not in conformity with the style of the poem, see *SC*.

[46] I.e. when they return home after winning the war.

K says विरहेण विरचितं दौर्बल्यमेव प्रसाधनम्, तद्वत्तया उज्झिताभरणानि, निश्वासवशप्रघूर्णितैः लम्बैरकैर्मृदितः पक्ष्मलः पुलकितः कपोलो येषाम्। अलकस्य स्पर्शपारुष्यात् पुलकः। उत्तरत्र सम्बन्धः। Kula reads मिलित for *malia* (मृदित).

K and MY read विपुल (*viula*) for *puthula* पुथुल (R, Kula and Muda). K, Muda and Kula read तट (*aḍa*) for *ala* तल (R). K and Kula read विनिकीर्ण for *vivaiṇṇa* विप्रकीर्ण (R). *SC* text has *viṇiiṇṇa*.

K says विपुले नितम्बे स्खलिताः, प्रशिथिलैः करस्य कार्श्यादत्यर्थं शिथिलैर्वलयैः विनिकीर्णाः परित्यक्ताः बाहुलता येषां तानि। क्व नु मां त्वद-घीनजीवितां विनिकीर्य क्षणभिन्नसौहृद इति कुमारसंभवे (4.6)। एवंभूतानि प्रियाणि कलत्राणि वयं कदा नु द्रक्ष्यामः। कथंभूताः – परिजनस्तुतेन कृतेप्रेषणेन कृतेन प्रेषणेन राघवस्यादेशेन लज्जिताः। स्तोत्रश्रवणात् लज्जा।

K seems to read *ṇiamba-aḍa-khalia-pasiḍhila*. Kula and Muda have शिथिल। Cf. R (text). R com. has प्रशिथिल।

Kula says पृथुलनितम्बतटस्खलितेन विरहशिथिलेन वलयेन विनिकीर्णा विनिर्मुक्ता बाहुलता येषां तानि।

Muda reads रणप्रेषण। He says परिजनेन उच्चैः स्तुतं यत् रणप्रेषणम्, अनेन युद्धे एवमेवं कृतमिति तेन संजातलज्जाः कदा नु प्रियकलत्राणि द्रक्ष्याम इत्यन्वयः।

51–52. इअ जाहे भण्णन्तं ण चलइ चिन्ताभरोसिअन्तसरीरम्।
आअड्ढणणिच्चेट्ठं पङ्कक्खुत्तं व गअकुलं कइसेण्णम्।।
तो फुडसद्दुद्धाइअवणदवभरिअगिरिकंदराआरमुहो।
रिउविक्कमसहन्तो जम्पइ वाणरवई पुणो वि हसन्तो।।
(जुग्गअम्)

[इति यदा प्रभण्यमानं न चलति चिन्ताभरावसीदच्छरीरम्
आकर्षणनिश्चेष्टं पङ्कमग्नमिव गजकुलं कपिसैन्यम्।।
ततः स्फुटशब्दोद्धावितवनदवभृतगिरिकंदराकारमुखः।
रिपुविक्रममसहमानो जल्पति वानरपतिः पुनरपि हसन्।।]
(युग्मकम्)

When the host of apes, thus addressed by Sugrīva, did not stir, being weighed down with anxieties, and looked like a herd of elephants sinking in mire, and wearied with the efforts to pull them out; the lord of the apes, unable to tolerate the enemy's prowess, spoke again as he laughed;

his mouth resembling a mountain cave enveloped in the flames of a forest fire,[47] shooting up with a clear sound.

K and Muda read आकृष्टपरिश्रान्तं for *āaḍḍhaṇaṇiccet̤ṭhaṁ* आकर्षणनिश्चेष्टं (R). Kula has आक्षिप्तमाकृष्टं सत् परिश्रान्तम्।

K says एवं सुग्रीवेण भाष्यमाणं (भण्यमानं *chāyā*) चिन्ताभरेण हृदयदुःखगौरवेण अवसीदच्छरीरं कपिसैन्यं पङ्कमग्नं जनैराकृष्टत्वात् परिश्रान्तं गजकुलमिव दृश्यमानं यदा न चलति यदा न परिस्पन्दते तदा सुग्रीवः पुनरपि जल्पति इत्युत्तरगाथया सम्बन्धः। Kula has पङ्कक्षिप्तं गजकुलमिव।

आकृष्ट is *āaḍḍhai*, but MY says *āaṇṭhia* (*āaṭṭhia* ?) आकृष्ट। यूथपतिनेति शेषः। कपिसैन्यस्य तु आकर्षकः सुग्रीवः। Cf. Sañjīvanī 7.8 कथं कर्षतीत्यस्य कट्ठ इति। उच्यते – एवमन्येऽपीति बहुलग्रहणात् पक्षे ट्ठादेशस्य प्रवृत्तेः।

K says स्फुटशब्दं यथा उत्थापितेन उत्थितेन वनदवेन भरितगिरिकन्दरासदृशास्यः। Kula says ऊर्ध्वायितेन वनाग्निना भरितो यो गिरिकुहरस्तदाकारं मुखं यस्य। Muda has स्फुटशब्दोर्ध्वापित। R has उद्धावित।

53. इअ अत्थिरसामत्थे अण्णस्स वि परिअणम्मि को आसङ्घो।
तत्थ वि णाम दहमुहो तस्स ठिओ एस पडिहडो मज्झ भुओ।।

[इत्यस्थिरसामर्थ्येऽन्यस्यापि परिजने कोऽध्यवसायः(आसङ्गः)।
तत्रापि नाम दशमुखस्तस्य स्थित एष प्रतिभटो मम भुजः।।]

What confidence can others, too have in their followers, when their effciency is unreliable in this wise? Then there is Rāvaṇa to reckon with; and my arm stands as his adversary![48]

K says परिजने सेवकजने इति एवमस्थिरसामर्थ्ये अन्यस्यापि को विश्वासः। यथा मम युष्मासु विश्वासो नाभूत् एवमन्यस्यापि राज्ञः सेवकजने विश्वासः कीदृशः। तत्रापि शत्रुपक्षेऽपि दशमुखो नाम दशमुखः केवलमवशिष्यते। ममैष भुजस्तस्य प्रतिभटः स्थितः। किमिदानीं युष्माभिरित्यर्थः।

Muda renders *āsaṁgha* as संभावना। Kula is here corrupt, but *SC* has प्रत्याशा। Kula says नामशब्दः संभावनायाम्। तत्रापि रिपुसैन्येऽपि दशमुखः, etc.

54. अवहोआसम्मि महं हत्थअलाहअदलन्तपत्थिअसलिलो।
जा ण णिअत्तइ उअही बोलीणं ताव होउ वाणरसेण्णम्।।

[47] The red interior of the mouth is likened to fire.

[48] Sugrīva impilies that Rāvaṇa's followers might be as a unreliable as his own, and in that case they would have to engage in single combat.

[उभयावकाशे मम हस्ततलाहतदलत्प्रस्थितसलिलः।
यावन्न निवर्तते उदधिर्व्यतिक्रान्तं तावद्भवति वानरसैन्यम्।।]

Let the army of apes cross over to Laṅkā even before the sea, smitten with the palm of my hand, and parting asunder, with the waters rolling away on both sides, hath the time to return!

K, MY and Muda *pratīka* has *avahovāsa*. K and Muda read यावन्निवर्तते (*jāva ṇiattai*) for *jā ṇa* . . . यावन्न . . . (R and Kula)।

K says उभयोः पार्श्वयोः मम हस्ततलाहतत्वात् दलन् विदीर्यमाणः प्रस्थितसलिलः उदधिर्यावत् निवर्तते तावत् वानरसैन्यमतिक्रान्तं भवतु। समुद्रस्य आधारभूतेन स्थलेनातिक्रामत्वित्यर्थः।

55. अहिआणं तोसिहरे धरिअं मलअगिरिणो हसन्तो सिहरे।
गुरुभरविसअंसेणं णेज्जामि भुएण जोअणसअं सेणम्।।

[अहितानां तोषहरे धृतां मलयगिरेर्हसन्शिखरे।
गुरुभरविषमांसेन नयामि भुजेन योजनशतं सेनाम्।।]

I will carry the army as I laugh a hundred leagues[49] (across the ocean) on my arms, with the shoulders unbent[50] under the enormous weight; (the army) stationed on the summit of the Malaya that is destructive of the enemy's joy.[51]

K, My and Kula read *bhariaṁ* for *dhariaṁ* (R and Muda).

K says अथवा चन्दनवृक्षैः अहीनां तुष्टिकरे मलयगिरेः शिखरे भरितां पूरितां सेनामहं हसन् गुरुणा भरेण शक्तिगौरवेण विशदः प्रकटः अंसो येन तेन भुजेन योजनशतं नेष्यामि। अहितानां तुष्टिहरे इति वा छाया। शत्रूणां तोषहरे यशोहरे इत्यर्थः।

MY says *tosi-hare* तोषधरे तुष्टिकरेत्यर्थः। अहीनां तोषहरे भृतां, etc. MY also has विशदांसेन। Muda has अहीनां तोषिगृहे in *chāyā* and says *ahiāṇaṁ* इति स्वार्थे कः। तोषयत्यवश्यमिति तोषि तत्र चन्दनतरुबाहुल्यात्, तच्च तत् गृहं चेति कर्मधारयः। गृहस्य घरादेशे घस्य हत्वम्। तोषिधरे इति वा व्याख्येयम्। तोषिणश्चन्दनतरवः तान् धरतीति।

Kula says अहितानां शत्रूणां तुष्टिहरे, अथवा सुरभिशीतचन्दनालयत्वात् अभिकानां कामुकानां तुष्टिगृहे, किंवा अहीनां सर्पाणां तोषिणी धरा भूमिर्यत्र तस्मिन् मलयगिरेः शिखरे

[49] *Yojanas*.

[50] Lit. clearly visible.

[51] The summit of the mountain from which the expedition was to start is described as a source of misery to the inhabitants of Laṅkā.

भरितां सेनां गुरुणा भरेण विशदः उन्नमितत्वात् व्यक्तः अंसः स्कन्धो यस्य तेन भुजेन योजनशतं नेष्यामि। समुद्रस्य शतयोजनत्वात् उत्पारं प्रापयिष्यामीत्यर्थः।

56. समुहमिलिएक्कमेक्के को इर आसण्णसंसअम्मि सहाओ।
जाव ण दिज्जइ दिट्ठी काअव्वं दाव होइ चिरणिव्वूढम्।।

[संमुखमिलितैकैकस्मिन्कः किलासन्नसंशये सहायः।
यावन्न दीयते दृष्टिः कर्तव्यं तावद्भवति चिरनिर्व्यूढम्।।]

Who doth lend a hand in imminent peril, when each stands (helpess) before the other? The task must be accomplished long before others attend to it.[52]

K, MY, Muda and Kula read निर्वृत्तम् (*ṇivvuttaṁ*, cf. *SC* text) for *ṇivvūḍhaṁ* निर्व्यूढम् (R).

K says संमुखमिलितैकैके, एकश्च एकश्च एकैकः अन्योन्यमित्यर्थः, आभिमुख्येन मिलितपरस्परे मिश्रितद्वन्द्वे आसन्नसंशये आसन्नप्राणसंशये, युद्ध इत्यध्याहार्यम्, तत्र कः किल सहायः। न कोऽपि सहायो भवितुमर्हति। कुत इति चेत्, यावन्न दृष्टिर्दीयते साहाय्यं कर्तुकामेन दृष्टिः युद्धाय यावन्न दीयते तावत् अस्य कर्तव्यं चिरनिर्वृत्तं चिराय साधितं भवतीति।

MY says आसन्नसंशये आसन्ने प्राणसंशये यावन्न दीयते दृष्टिः सहकारिणेति वा, सहकारिष्विति वा शेषः, तावत् कर्तव्यं कार्यं चिरनिर्वृत्तं भवतीति योजना।

Muda and Kula have भवतु for *hoi*. Kula says यावन्न दीयते दृष्टिः प्रेक्षकैः इत्यर्थात्, तावत् कर्तव्यं शस्त्रग्रहणानुरूपं चिरं निर्वृत्तं भवतु। *SC* text has *tāva* for *dāva*. R says निर्व्यूढं निर्वृत्तं भवति।

57. अह व महण्णवहुत्तं पत्थन्तस्स गअणं महं ण वहुत्तम्।
रुहिरवसामिसवत्तं हन्तूण व णिव्वुओ वसामि सवत्तम्।।

[अथवा महार्णवाभिमुखं प्रतिष्ठमानस्य गगनं मम न प्रभूतम्।
रुधिरवसामिषपात्रं हत्वेव निर्वृतो वसामि सपत्नम्।।]

Or the sky will not be wide enough for me as I rush forth with the great sea before me![53] I will abide happy after slaying the enemy that lives on flesh, blood and marrow.[54]

---

[52] I.e. without waiting for help from others. Or, "before one looks about (for help)". Cf. Mādhava in Extracts. Sugrīva warns his followers that he will act on his own initiative without waiting for their help.

[53] I.e. as he files to the other shore.

[54] A reference to the *rākṣasas*.

K says हुतशब्दोऽभिमुखवाचकः। अहमेव शत्रुं हनिष्यामीत्युक्तम्। तत्र विप्रतिपत्तिमाह – अथवा शत्रुवधार्थं महार्णवाभिमुखं महार्णवमुल्लङ्घयितुं प्रतिष्ठमानस्य प्लवमानस्य मम गगनं न प्रभूतम्। मम शरीरविस्ताराय गगनं न पर्याप्तं भवेत्। अथवा यथाकथंचित् गत्वा सपत्नं शत्रुं हत्वा निर्वृतो वसामि वत्स्यामि। वर्तमानसामीप्ये वर्तमानवद्वेति लट्। कीदृशं सपत्नं – रुधिरवसामिषात् वृत्तं जीवनं यस्य तम्। राक्षसा हि पुरुषादाः। K (*chāyā*) हत्वा वा निर्वृतः, ete. (MY also) .

MY says रावणवधोद्युक्तस्य मम समुद्राभिमुखं गच्छतो मार्गभूतं गगनम प्रभूतमित्येतावत। प्रतिबन्धो वा स्यात्। रावणवधो निष्प्रतिबन्धः सिध्येदेव वा। न तु प्रतिबन्धान्तरशङ्केत्याशयः।

Muda renders *patthantassa* as प्रार्थ्यमानस्य। He says प्रार्थनमभियानमिति पूर्वमुक्तम्। Muda and MY render *vattoṁ* as पात्रम् like R. Muda says पत्रं वा। रुधिरवसामिषं पिबन्तीति कप्रत्ययः, तान् त्रायत इति पुनरातोऽनुपसर्गे क इति कप्रत्ययः।

Kula says अथवा महार्णवाभिमुखं गमनं (for गगनं) प्रार्थयमानस्य मम न प्रभुत्वं वाच्यमेव[55] च न स्यात्। R seems to refer to this interpretation – केचित्तु अथवा महार्णवाभिमुखं प्रार्थयतो गमनं मम न प्रभुत्वमिति संस्कृस्य अपि तु प्रभुत्वमेव इत्यर्थमाहुः। Kula th en says (सपत्नं शत्रु) किंवा सपत्रं सवाहनं, सपात्रं ससचिवं वा हत्वा निर्वृतो वसामीति योज्यम्।

58. णिसुढिज्जन्तभुअंगं मा मुज्झह मह सरोसचलणक्कन्तम्।
जत्तो णमइ महिअलं तत्तो णाम सअलो पअट्टउ उअही।।

[निपात्यमानभुजंगं मा मुह्यत मम सरोषचरणाक्रान्तम्।
यतो नमति महीतलं ततो नाम सकलः प्रवर्ततामुदधिः।।]

Be not perplexed. Let the entire sea roll into wherever the earth sinks, trampled down by me in a rage, with the serpents crushed under the weight.[56]

After verse 57 the order of verses in K is 62, 58, 59, 63. verse 60 is not found in K. For 61 see below.

In verse 58 K reads ततोऽभिमुखसलिलः (i.e. *tattohutta-salilo*) for *tatto ṇāma saalo* ततो नाम सकलः (R, Kula and Muda). MY's reading is same as K's except that he has सलिलं। K, MY, and Muda read *paloṭṭai* for *paaṭṭau* प्रवर्तताम् (R). Kula seems to read *paloṭṭau* (cf. *SC* text) explained as प्रसरतु। *SC chāyā* प्रलुठतु।

---

[55] Our copy has वाद्यमेव।

[56] I.e. the sea will empty into the sunken earth, enabling them to cross its dry bed.

K says अथवा मम सरोषचरणाक्रान्तं मम सरोषं यथा चरणाभ्यामाक्रान्तम् आहतमतएव अधः भज्यमानभुजङ्गं (निस्त्रुट्यद्भुजङ्गं *chāyā*) महीतलं यतो नमति यत्र नमति ततोऽभिमुखसलिलः भूत्वा उदधिः प्रलुठति। अवनते तस्मिन् महीतलप्रदेशे जलधिजलं सर्वं पतिष्यति। तो भवन्तः स्थलेनैव गच्छन्तु। यूयं च मा मुह्यत स्वस्था एव तिष्ठत।

MY says *ṇisuḍijjanta* (K *pratīka* also) अवपात्यमान। *paloṭṭai* (our copy has *paloṭṭhai*) प्रलुठति। महीतलं यतो नमति ततोऽभि मुखसलिलं प्रलुठत्युदधिः। तदा स्थलेनैव गन्तुं शक्यत इत्यर्थः।

Muda has *ṇisuḍhijjanta* (भराक्रान्तनमत्)। He says भाराक्रान्ते कर्तरि नमेः णिसुढादेशः, and quotes Hemacandra 4.158 which gives *ṇisuḍhai*. He has प्रत्यागच्छत्युदधिः, and quotes *H.C.* 4.166, which gives *paloṭṭai pacāgacchai*. Kula says आक्रमणभरपीड्यमानपातालस्थपन्नगं महीतलम्।

59. ओ जमलक्खम्भेहिँ व धरिएण भुएहिँ मह महोअहिमज्झे।
उम्मूलिआइएणं समइञ्छउ विञ्झसंकमेण कइबलम्।।

[उत यमलस्तम्भाभ्यामिव धृतेन भुजाभ्यां मम महोदधिमध्ये।
उन्मूलितानीतेन समतिक्रामतु विन्ध्यसंक्रमेण कपिबलम्।।]

Or, let the host of apes pass over to the other side by the Vindhya range serving as a causeway, after it is uprooted and brought here by me, and held over the surface of the ocean by my arms acting like twin pillars!

K, Muda and Kula read *vaṭṭhe* (पृष्ठे) for *majjhe* (R who mentions the other reading *asia* variant). They read उत्पाटित (*uppāḍia*) for *ummūlia* (R).

K says अथवा मया उत्पाटितानीतेन महोदधिपृष्ठे युगलस्तम्भाभ्यामिव मम भुजाभ्यां धारितेन विन्ध्यमयेन संक्रमेण सेतुना कपिबलं समत्येतु अतिलङ्घयतु।

MY says ओ उत। *samaiccau* समत्येतु। Muda says गमेरइच्छादेशः (*H.C.* 4.162 which gives *aicchai*)। *samaicchau* सम्यग्गच्छत्वित्यर्थः। Muda (*chāyā*) has संगच्छताम्। R has *samaiñchau* समतिक्रामतु। Kula also has the latter meaning, but his reading is not clear. *SC* text agrees with R. It has *āṇieṇaṁ* (आनीतेन) for *āieṇaṁ* (R) .

60. विवलाअन्तभुअंगं उव्वत्तिअजलअरं विहिण्णमहिहरम्।
मुहमारुअविहुअजलं पेच्छह रअणाअरं करेमि थलवहम्।।

[विपलायमानभुजंगमुद्वर्तितजलचरं विभिन्नमहीधरम्।
मुखमारुतविधुतजलं पश्यत रत्नाकरं करोमि स्थलपथम्।।]

Behold, I will turn the sea into a stretch of land, sweeping the waters away with my breath, with the serpents rushing away, and the water animals turned over, and the (submarine) mountains rent asunder!

The verse is not found in K and MY. Muda gives only the *chāyā*, and remarks केषुचित् पुस्तकेषु दृश्यते। The *chāyā* shows some variations, the *pratīka* being *ṇisuḍhijjanta* for *vivalāanta* (भराक्रान्तनमद्भुजङ्गमुद्वर्तितजलचरं चलन्महीधरम्, etc.)।

Kula has अथ मारुत – for *muha-mārua* (R). He says अथ मारुतेन विधूतजलम् उत्सारितपानीयं रत्नाकरं करोमि।

61. मज्झक्खुडिउम्मूलिअभुआभमाइअविमुक्कसेसद्धन्तम्।
एत्तोहुत्तसुवेलं तत्तोहुत्तमलअं करेमि समुद्दम्।।

[मध्यखण्डितोन्मूलितभुजाभ्रामितविमुक्तशेषार्धान्तम्।
इतोऽभिमुखसुवेलं ततोऽभिमुखमलयं करोमि समुद्रम्।।]

I will put the sea in a position in which the Suvela mountain will face this way,[57] and the Malaya thitherward,[58] after I have broken them in the middle, and uprooted and turned them round with my arms, and discarded the remaining parts![59]

K and MY have this verse after 8.23. K and probably MY read घटित for *sesa* (R, Kula and Muda).

K says मध्ये जलाधारतलस्य मध्ये करतलाग्रेण त्रुटित्वा छित्त्वा उन्मूलितौ, भुजाभ्यां भ्रमितौ निवर्तितौ, पुनर्विमुक्तौ घटितौ अर्धान्तौ यस्य तं समुद्रम्। अतएव इतोमुखसुवेलं ततोमुखमलयं च करोमि किम्। अयमर्थः – मलयसुवेलयोरन्तराले मलययुक्तमुत्तरं समुद्रं सुवेलयुक्तं दक्षिणं च समुद्रं द्विधा भुजाभ्यां मध्ये छित्त्वा द्वावपि समुद्रखण्डौ भुजयोः भ्रमणेन

---

[57] I.e. northwards. The Suvela is the mythical mountain of Ceylon.

[58] I.e. southwards, so as to face the Suvela.

[59] I.e. he will make the mountains face each other, after levelling them by breaking off the upper halves, and join them across the sea to serve as a bridge, throwing away the superfluous parts. This appears to be Rāmadāsa's interpretation. According to Kṛṣṇa and Mādhava, Sugrīva means that he will cleave asunder the bed of the sea, and reverse the positions of the northern and southern portions of the sea including the coastal mountains. The Suvela will thus take the place of the Malaya and vice versa, and it will be unnecessary for the army to cross over to Laṅkā which is situated on the Suvela!

विपर्यस्तौ[60] विमुच्य घटितच्छेदमार्गं समुद्रं करोमि किमिति। मलयस्य ततोमुखत्वे तु प्रयोजनमिदं पश्यामः। उद्‌धृतस्य मलयस्य स्थाने सुवेलस्य आनीतस्य स्थापनं[61] भवेदिति।

MY says दक्षिणोत्तरतटावस्थितसुवेलमलयसहितं प्राक् प्रत्यगर्वाक् चातिविस्तृततया संभविनि मध्यभागे प्रथममेकखण्डतया त्रुटितमथोन्मूलितम्, अथोत्तरतः सुवेलो दक्षिणतो मलयश्च यथा स्यात् तथा भुजाभ्यां भ्रामितम्, अथ त्रुटनावकाशे क्षिप्तमथ प्रतिसंहितपर्यन्तं (प्रतिसंहित) – त्रुटनामार्गम्, अतएव इतोभूतसुवेलं ततोभूतमलयं च करोमीत्यर्थः।... *pahuppantaṁ* प्रभूतमितिवत् *iahutta* इति इतोभूत इति, *tattohutta* इति ततोभूतेति च ग्राह्यम्। *hutta* इत्यस्य अभिमुखार्थत्वे वलितपदमुभयत्राध्याहार्यम्।

K (*chāyā*) has किमितोमुखसुवेलं for *etto-hutta-suvelaṁ* (R).

Muda has इतोऽभिमुखसुवेलं ततोऽभिमुखमलयं करोमि समुद्रम् like R. Muda says *bhamāḍiaṁ* (for *bhamāia*) भ्रमितम्। भ्रमयतेः भमाडेत्यादेशः (Hemacandra 3.151)। *addhanto perante* (i.e. पर्यन्ते) इति देशीमाला (1. 8)। *hutto* अभिमुख इति देशी (*Deśīnāmamālā* 8.70)। पूर्वार्धं क्रियाविशेषणम्।

Kula is somewhat corrupt, sut he reads *ukkhalia* explained as उत्खण्डित for–*kkhuḍia* खण्डित (R). He says *addhanta* एकदेशवाची (इति) देशीकोषे उक्तम्।

The sense of the verse according to K and MY is brought out by MY's introductory remark – अथवा अत्रैव शत्रुबलसहितसुवेलोपस्थापनात् कपिसैन्यस्य अनपेक्षितोत्तरणं समुद्रं करोमीत्याह। Kula says अथवा मलयमेव भवद्भिः सह समुद्रपारं नयामीत्याह। भुजाभ्रामितो बाहुना मथित, मथनोत्सारितजलत्वात् मध्ये उत्खण्डितश्चासौ उन्मूलित उत्क्षिप्ताधस्तनजलश्च, मध्यभाग एव आरम्भमाणजलत्वात् विमुक्तशेषार्धान्तः त्यक्तपूर्वपश्चिमपर्यन्तद्वयश्चेति तं तथा। अतो मूलजलोद्‌गमेन उन्मूलितत्वात् भ्रमज्जलरयेण भ्रमितत्वाच्च इतोऽभिमुखो मलयदेशाक्रमणाभिमुखः सुवेलो यत्र तं, ततोऽभिमुखः सुवेलाभिमुख मलयो यत्र तं समुद्रं करोमि।

After verse 57, the order of verses in MY is 58, 59, 62, 63; for 60 and 61 see above. Muda has them in the following order: 62, 58, 60, 59, 61, 63.

---

60 Corrected from MY who reproduces K's explanation. Ms. B of MY has भुजभ्रामणेन।

61 *SC* refers to an interpretation similar to K's, but with the reading *sesa* – केचित्तु उन्मूलित् उत्खातश्चासौ भुजाभ्रामितश्चेति स तथा, अनन्तरं मध्ये उत्खण्डित एकदेशभग्नत्वादेव विमुक्तशेषार्धान्तं यथा स्यात्तथा . . . ईदृशं समुद्रं करोमीति . . . क्रियाविशेषणतया उपपादयन्ति।

62. अह व सुवेलालग्गं पेच्छह अज्जेअ भग्गरक्खसविडवम्।
सीआकिसलअसेसं मज्झ भुआअट्टिअं लअं मिव लङ्कम्।।

[अथवा सुवेलालग्नां पश्यताद्यैव भग्नराक्षसविटपाम्।
सीताकिसलयशेषां मम भुजाकृष्टां लतामिव लङ्काम्।।]

Or, witness Laṅkā pulled down by my arms even today, like a creeper clinging to the Suvela, with the branches, the demons, smashed down, and only a tender shoot, Sītā,[62] left over.

Muda says लङ्कामद्यैव मद्भुजाकृष्टां पश्यतेति सम्बन्धः। लतापि कश्चित् गिरिमाश्रिता सुखेनाक्रष्टुं शक्यत इत्यभिप्रायेणोक्तं सुवेलालग्नामिति। Kula has this verse after 60. K has it after 57.

63. ओ भग्गरक्खसदुमं णिहअदसाणणमइन्दसुहसंचारम्।
रामाणुराअमत्तो मलेमि लङ्कं वणत्थलिं व वणगओ।।
[उत भग्न ('अवभग्न'वा) राक्षसद्रुमां निहतदशाननमृगेन्द्रसुखसंचाराम्।
रामानुरागमत्तो मृद्नामि लङ्कां वनस्थलीमिव वनगजः।।]

Frenzied by my devotion to Rāma, I will crush Laṅkā as does a wild elephant a forest: (Laṅkā) that will be safe owing to the lion, Rāvaṇa, being killed, with the trees, the demons, knocked down.

K says अथवा अहं रामानुरागेण मत्तः मदेनेव मत्तो भूत्वा लङ्कां भग्नराक्षसाख्यद्रुमां, निहतरावणाख्यमृगेन्द्रत्वात् सुखसंचारां च मृद्नामि। वनस्थलीं वनगज इव, पूर्वमेव निहतसिंहत्वात् सुखसंचारां वनस्थलीमिव यथा गजेन्द्रो मृद्नाति तद्वदिति। अथवा निहतदशाननगजेन्द्रसुखसंचारामिति पाठः। तदा गजेन्द्रः प्रतिगजः। अयमेव पाठः समीचीनः। Kula says भग्नाः पतिता राक्षसा द्रुमा इव यत्र। निहतोदशाननो मृगेन्द्र इव यत्र, etc.

Muda says अतिप्रबलो मत्तो गजः सिंहमपि हिनस्तीति भावः। Kula says गजस्याष्टौ मदावस्था भवन्ति। तत्र पष्ठ्यां मदावस्थायां गजः सिंहमपि हन्ति।

इअ सिरिपवरसेणविरइए कालिदासकए दहमुहवहे महाकव्वे
तइओ आसासओ समत्तो।।

[इति श्रीप्रवरसेनविरचिते कालिदासकृते दशमुखवधे महाकाव्ये
तृतीय आश्वासकः समाप्तः।]

---

62 Held captive in Laṅkā.

चतुर्थ आश्वासक:
Fourth Āśvāsakaḥ

1. अह पढमवअणणिहुअं पच्छा उम्हइअलज्जिअं कइसेण्णम्।
सससिदंसणपासुत्तं कमलवणं व दिअसागमेण विबुद्धम्।।

[अथ प्रथमवचननिभृतं पश्चादूष्मायितलज्जितं कपिसैन्यम्।
शशिदर्शनप्रसुप्तं कमलवनमिव दिवसागमेन विबुद्धम्।।]

Thereupon the army of apes that had kept still at the first words of Sugrīva, but were afterwards[1] provoked and ashamed, bestirred themselves; even as a day lotus bed that closes at the sight of the moon bursts into bloom at the advent of the day.

K, MY and Muda read प्रणय for *vaaṇa* वचन (R and Kula). K and Muda read अरुण for *diasa* (R and Kula).

K says प्रथमप्रणयनिभृतं प्रथमं प्रणयेन सुग्रीवस्य प्रार्थनया निभृतं तूष्णींभूतं, पश्चात् तस्योष्मायितेन पौरुषप्रकाशनेन लज्जितं कपिसैन्यं विबुद्धमालस्यमवधूय समुच्छ्वसितम्। शशिदर्शनेन प्रसुप्तं कमलवनमरुणागमेन यथा विबुध्यते तद्वदिति।

MY says *umhaviaṁ* (for *umhaia*) ऊष्मापितम्। विबोध: कमलिनीवने विकास:। कपिबले कार्यानुकूल उल्लास:।

Muda says प्रथमं प्रणयेन प्रार्थनया निभृतं पश्चादूषितमूष्मयुक्तं कृतमुत्साहितमित्यर्थ:। विबुद्धं प्रवृत्त्युन्मुखं बभूवेत्यर्थ:।

Kula says प्रथमवचनानि *dharaṇidharaṇe* (3.3) इत्यादीनि सामप्रधानानि तै: निभृतं निरुद्यमं, पश्चात् *ia atthira-sāmatthe* (3.53) इत्युतसाहवचनै: सहायमनादृत्य स्वयं विक्रमयितुमिच्छता सुग्रीवेण ऊष्मायितलज्जितमुद्वेजितव्रीडितं कपिसैन्यं कमलवनमिव शशिदर्शनेन सामवचनोपमेन प्रसुप्तं दिवसागमेन उत्साहवाक्येनेव विबुद्धं विगतमोहं विगतनिमीलितं चाभूत्।

2. णवरि अ कइहिअआइं धुअन्धआरविअडाइँ गमणुच्छाहो।
एक्को बहुआइ समं गिरिसिहराइँ अरुणाअवो व्व विलग्गो।।

[अनन्तरं च कपिहृदयानि धुतान्धकारविकटानि गमनोत्साह:।
एको बहूनि समं गिरिशिखराण्यरुणातप इव विलग्न:।।]

---

[1] Cf. 3.53 ff.

Ardour for advancing to Laṅkā dominated at the same moment the hearts of the numerous apes, elated and rid of gloom; just as the light of the morning sun spreads all at once over the numerous peaks of mountains coming into view, with the darkness swept away.

K and Muda read तरुण for अरुण (R and Kula).

K says अथ धुतान्धकारविकटानि निरस्तविषादान्धकारत्वात् विक्टानि प्रकाशानि कपिहृदयानि बहूनि सममेव एको गमनोत्साहः प्राप्तः, धुतान्धकारविक्टानि बहूनि गिरिशिखराणि तरुणातप इव। सर्वेषामपि लङ्कां प्रति गमनोद्योगेतसाहो जात इत्यर्थः।

My says कपिहृदयेषु अन्धकारः प्रकाशाभावः अप्रतिपत्तिरिति यावत्। Kula says एकत्रान्धकारो विषादः, अन्यत्र तिमिरम्। धुतान्धकारत्वात् विकटानि विशालानि हृदयानि गिरिशिखराणीव उन्नतत्वात्, गमनोत्साहः अरुणातप इव तेजःस्वभावत्वात् अनुरागयोगाच्च वहुषु एकः समं युगपत् आरूढः। R says विकटानि व्यक्तानि।

3. तो दप्पमुहपसाओ आढत्तो ताण हिअअहसिउज्जोओ।
रणविक्कमग्गहत्थो णिअअसहाओ व्व पहरिसो वित्थरिउम्॥

[ततो दर्पमुखप्रसाद आरब्धस्तेषां हृदयहसितोद्योतः।
रणविक्रमाग्रहस्तो निजकस्वभाव इव प्रहर्षो विस्तरितुम्॥]

Their joy, like their natural traits, began to be manifest more and more. It seemed to be the buoyant look of their pride;[2] the glow of the fervour of their heart; the prelude to their valour in war.

K reads अमर्षः (*amariso*) for *pahariso*.

K says ततो दर्पस्य मुखप्रसादः दर्पमयस्य पुरुषस्य मुखप्रसादो, हृदयहसितस्य हृदयविकासस्योद्द्योतः प्रकाशो, रणविक्रमस्य अग्रहस्तः विक्रमस्य प्रहारशीलत्वात् प्रहर्तुमुद्यतः अग्रहस्तः तेषाममर्षः निजस्वभाव इव कापेयमिव विस्तरितुमारब्धः। पूर्वं प्रकृतिचटुलत्वमपि गलितमित्युक्तम्। तदपि अमर्षेण सह पुनरागतमित्यर्थः। निजकसहाय इति वा।

MY says निजस्वभाव इवेति निजस्वभावोऽपीत्यर्थः। यथा हि पुंसां मुखप्रसादः अन्तर्गतस्य दर्पस्य व्यञ्जकस्तथा प्रहर्षोऽप्येव। हृदयस्य हसितं (?) विस्ताराख्या भूमिः। यथोक्तं रसविद्भिः –

स्वादः कार्यार्थसम्भेदादात्मानन्दसमुद्भवः।
विकारविस्तरक्षोभविक्षेपैः स चतुर्विधः ॥

[2] Pride is personified, the joy of the apes being figured as the cheerful aspect of their pride.

इति। एवं विक्रमस्य वीररसस्थायिभावयुद्धोत्साहस्य अग्रहस्तः प्रधानाङ्गं प्रहर्षः प्रहर्षजचेष्टाकारणेन कार्योपलक्षणात्। एवं च युद्धोत्साहो वीररसोत्पादे स्थायी भावः। गर्वहर्षावनुभावौ। यथोक्तम् –

वीरप्रतापविनयाध्यवसायसत्वामोहाविषादनयविक्रमविस्मयाद्यैः।
उत्साह . . . रणदानयोगास्त्रेधा किलात्र मतिगर्वधृतिप्रहर्षाः ।।

इति। एवं च दर्पहर्षकापेयचेष्टा युगपत् प्रावर्तन्तेति तात्पर्यम्।

Muda mentions अमर्ष as a variant. He says दर्पस्य मुखप्रसाद इव, . . . रणविक्रमस्याग्रहस्त इव, कपीनां निजस्वभाव इव अमर्षः प्रहर्षो वा विस्तरीतुं प्रारब्धः।

Kula is incomplete, but he seems to explain दर्पमुखप्रसाद as दर्पोल्लास। He says मुखप्रसादो हि यस्य भवति तस्योल्लासं सूचयति, and remarks दर्पहृदयोल्लासविक्रमाणां मूढत्वं तेषामुत्साहेन निरस्तमिति भावः। Deva says दर्पमुखप्रसादः दर्पसचिवः, हृदयहसितोद्द्योतः हृदयवैपुल्यप्रकाशकः, रणविक्रमाग्रहस्तः रणे क्रियमाणस्य विक्रमस्य पूर्वरङ्गभूतः अमर्षः। Kula says हृदयस्य हसितोद्द्योत् इव हृदयस्य सोत्साहत्वाविष्करणात्। रणविक्रमस्य अग्रः श्रेष्ठो हस्त इव रणव्यापारसाधकतमत्वात्।

4. बहलुद्धअधाउरअं रिसहेण धुओज्झराहअकओलअलम्।
भिण्णं वामभुअसिरे उम्मूलिअवलिअपण्णअं गिरिसिहरम्।।

[बहुलोद्धतधातुरज ऋषभेण धुतनिर्झराहतकपोलतलम्।
भिन्नं वामभुजशिरस्युन्मूलितवलितपन्नगं गिरिशिखरम्।।]

Ṛṣabha[3] rent asunder a mountain peak, and smashed it on his left shoulder, raising a cloud of dust from its red earth, with the uprooted serpents winding about; while his cheeks were hit by the splashing cascades.

K, MY, Muda and Kula read बहुल for बहल (R commmentary).

K says वृषभेण वानरेण वामभुजशिरसि गिरिशिखरं भिन्नं निपात्य विदारितम्। कथमिव – बहुलमुद्धूतं धातुरजो यथा भवति तथा, धुतेन निजनिर्झरेणाहतकपोलतलं यथा, उन्मूलिताः पन्नगास्तत्र निवासिनो वलिता यथा भवति तथा भिन्नम्।

5. पुलउब्भेआअम्बं णीलो परिपुसइ विसमकसणच्छाअम्।
हिअअणिहत्तपहरिसं ससिपडिभिण्णघणसंणिहं वच्छअडम्।।

---

[3] The names in this and the following verses are those of the leaders of the apes.

[पुलकोद्भेदाताम्रं नीलः परिप्रोञ्छति विषमकृष्णच्छायम्।
हृदयनिहतप्रहर्षे शशिप्रतिभिन्नघनसंनिभं वक्षस्तटम्॥]

Nīla rubbed his rugged and swarthy breast that appeared to be reddish as the hair stood on end. With joy hidden in the heart, it was like a cloud penetrated by the moon.[4]

K, MY and Kula read परिमृशति for *paripusai* परिप्रोञ्छति (R). Cf. 11.3.

K says नीलः पुलकोद्भेदाताम्रं यत एव नीलः कपिलेन पुलकोद्गमेन ईषत्ताम्रं, विषमकृष्णच्छायं व्रणकिणबहुलत्वात् विषमं कृष्णप्रभं च, हृदयनिहितप्रहर्षम् अत एव शशिप्रतिभिन्नघनसंनिभं वक्षस्तटं हर्षात् कराग्रेण परिमृशति स्म। तथा च माघकाव्ये – विचिन्तयन्नुपनतमाहवं रसादुरः स्फुरत्तनुरुहमग्रपाणिना। परामृशत् कठिनकठोरकामिनीकुचस्थलप्रमुषितचन्दनं पृथुः ॥ इति (17.11)।

MY says *parimusai* पर्यमृशत्। पुलकानुमेयान्तर्गतहर्षतया हृदयस्य शशिगर्भघनसादृश्यम्। Kula says हृदयनिहितप्रहर्षत्वात् द्योतितेन शशिना प्रतिभिन्नः संपृक्तो यो घनस्तत्सदृशं वक्षःस्थलं नीलः परिमृषति हस्तेन घट्टयति।

6. विहडन्तोट्ठउडदलं फुरन्तदन्तअरबहलकेसरवअरम्।
पहरिसचन्दालोए हसिअं कुमुएण सुरहिगन्धुग्गारम्॥

[विघटमानौष्ठपुटदलं स्फुरद्दन्तकरबहलकेसरप्रकरम्।
प्रहर्षचन्द्रालोके हसितं कुमुदेन सुरभिगन्धोद्गारम्॥]

In the moonlight of joy, *kumuda* burst into laughter, even as a night lotus bursts into bloom, breathing forth a sweet smell, with his lips opening like the petals, and the shimmer of his teeth plain to view like the dense filaments.[5]

K and Muda read cgqy for cgy (R)-

K says कुमदो नाम कश्चित् सेनापतिः तेन प्रहर्षाख्यचन्द्रालोके सति कुमुदेनेव हसितम्। कथम् – विघटमानं विकसदोष्ठपुटाख्यं दलं यथा भवति तथा, स्फुरद्दन्तकराख्यबहुलकेसरनिवहं च यथा तथा, सुरन्भिर्गन्धोद्गारो यथा भवति तथा हसितमिति। कुमुदपक्षे हासो विकासः। Kula says स्फुरन् प्रकटीभवन् दन्तकराणां केशराणांमिव प्रकरो यथा स्यात्, and विघटमानमोष्ठपुटं दलमिव यथा स्यात्।

---

[4] The breast is likened to a cloud, and the joy in the heart to the moon.

[5] There is a pun on the name K0umuda meaning a night lotus which blooms in the moonlight.

7. विहडन्तधरणिबन्धो उहअभुअक्खेवमुहलवेविरविडवो।
विसमपडन्तविसहरो वेलाचन्दणदुमो मइन्देण धुओ।।

[विघटमानधरणिबन्ध उभयभुजक्षेपमुखरवेपनशीलविटपः।
विषमपतद्विषधरो वेलाचन्दनद्रुमो मैन्देन धुतः।।]

Mainda shook a sandal tree on the seashore, loosening the earth, with the branches, pushed with both hands, quivering and rustling, and the serpents[6] dropping here and there.

K says मैन्दद्विविदावश्विनोः पुत्रौ वानरौ। तेन मैन्देन विघटमानभूमिबन्धः, उभयभुजप्रेरणमुखरवेपमानविटपः, इतस्ततः पतद्विषधरो वेलाचन्दनद्रुमो धुतः परिकम्पितः।

Muda has विघटमानधरणीबन्धम्। Kula reads वेष्ट, i.e. *veḍha* for बन्ध। He says विघटमानो धरणीवेष्टो महीवेष्टनं यस्य, . . . विषममस्तव्यसतं पतन्तो विषधरा यस्मात् स तथाभूतो वेलाचन्दनद्रुमः।

8. दिप्पन्तदुरालोआ दिविअस्स सधूमसिहिसिहावत्तणिहा।
सोम्मत्तणं ण पत्ता हरिसभरेन्ती वि विसहरस्स व दिट्ठी।।

[दीप्यमानदुरालोका द्विविदस्य सधूमशिखिशिखावर्तनिभा।
सौम्यत्वं न प्राप्ता हर्षभ्रियमाणापि विषधरस्येव दृष्टिः।।]

Fierce and glaring, and resembling the flicker of a smoky flame, Dvivida's eyes, like those of a serpent, did not regain their calm, even though full of joy.

K says द्विविदस्य दृष्टिः विषधरस्य दृष्टिरिव हर्षपूर्यमाणापि सौम्यत्वं प्रसन्नत्वं न प्राप्ता। हर्षस्य अमर्षसहितत्वात् दुर्दर्शाभूत्। सर्पस्य दृष्टिः हर्षावस्थायामपि क्रूरैव भवति।

K (*chāyā*) has हर्षह्रियमाणा। MY says *bharantī* ह्रियमाणा। तारकया सधूमवह्निसादृश्यम्। Others have भ्रियमाणा। Kula says अमर्षेण दीप्यमाना अतो दुरालोका, . . . सधूमो यः शिखिनः शिखावर्तः ज्वालाभ्रमणं तन्निभा।

9. सरहो वि दरिमुहग्गअपडिसद्दप्फुडिअमलअअडपब्भारम्।
मुञ्चइ विसअं णाअं मलेइ अङ्गं च रोमविसअण्णाअम्।।

[शरभोऽपि दरीमुखोद्गतप्रतिशब्दस्फुटितमलयतटप्राग्भारम्।
मुञ्चति विशदं नादं मृद्नात्यङ्गं च रोषविषार्द्रम्।।]

[6] I.e. the serpents that had coiled round the branches. Cf. 1.60.

Śarabha uttered a piercing yell that reverberated from the mouths of the caves, and seemed to rend the broad expanse of the Malaya slopes; while he pressed his limbs, dripping sweat in a fit of rage.

K and Muda and probably MY read *valei* for *malei* (R and Kula).

K says शरभोऽपि सेनापतिः दरीमुखोद्गतेन प्रतिशब्देन स्फुटतमलयतटविस्तरं यथा विशदमतिप्रकटं नादं मुञ्चति स्म। रोषविषेण रोषजलेन स्वेदेन आर्द्रमङ्गं वलयति च स्म च। मलेइ इति च पाठः। मृद्नातीत्यर्थः। विषशब्दो जलपर्यायः।

MY says अचलयदङ्गञ्च रोषविषार्द्रम्। रोष एव विषस्तेन जातस्वेदमित्यर्थः।

Muda says *taṇṇāaṁ* आर्द्रमिति देशी। समासमध्यवर्तित्वेन अनादित्वात् तलोपे यमकनिर्वाहः। एवमन्यत्रापि।

Kula says रोषविषेण रोषोद्गतेन स्वेदजलेन।

10. अरुणाअम्बच्छाए तक्खणमेत्तपडिबुद्धपङ्कअसोहे।
फुरइ णिसढस्स वि फुडं दिअसस्स मुहम्मि दिणअरो व्व अमरिसो।।

[अरुणाताम्रच्छाये तत्क्षणमात्रप्रतिबुद्धपङ्कजशोभे।
स्फुरति निषधस्यापि स्फुटं दिवसस्य मुखे दिनकर इवामर्षः।।]

Wrath clearly showed on Niṣādha's face, pink like Aruṇa, the charioteer of the sun, and beautiful like a lotus that had just opened; like as the sun gleams at dawn, rosy through the presence of Aruṇa, and beautiful with the lotus beds bursting into bloom at the moment.

K and Muda have मुखे दिवसस्य in *chāyā*.

K says निषधस्य सेनापतेः अरुणाताम्रच्छाये अरुणवत् आताम्रच्छाये, अन्यत्र अरुणेन आताम्रच्छाये, तत्क्षणमात्रप्रतिबुद्धपङ्कजकान्ते, अन्यत्र तत्क्षणप्रतिबुद्धैः पङ्कजैः शोभा यस्य तस्मिन् मुखे अमर्षः स्फुटमस्फुरत्, दिवसस्य मुखे दिनकर इव।

11. विअडाहरन्तरालं कअं सुसेणस्स रोसहसिएण फुडम्।
उप्पाअरुहिरअम्बं मज्झप्फुडिअरइमण्डलं मिव वअणम्।।

[विकटाधरान्तरालं कृतं सुषेणस्य रोषहसितेन स्फुटम्।
उत्पातरुधिराताम्रं मध्यस्फुटितरविमण्डलमिव वदनम्।।]

As Suṣeṇa burst out laughing in anger, his face, with the lips parted[7] for a long while, resembled the orb of the sun

[7] Lit. with the interval between the lips revealed. Cf. Kṛṣṇa in Extracts.

when it was rent in the middle and red as blood, portending evil.

K, Muda and Kula read चिरम् for *phuḍaṁ* स्फुटम् (R)।

K says सुषेणस्य वदनं रोषेण हसितेन चिरं विकटाधरान्तरालं विकटं प्रकाशितमधरयोः अन्तरालं यस्य तत् तथा कृतम्, उत्पातरुधिरेण आताम्रं मध्ये स्फुटितं रविमण्डलमिव अभूत्। MY says उत्पातरुधिरेण उत्पाते रुधिरवच्च ताम्रम्।

12. हरिसपरिअम्भिएण अ अद्धुल्लसिअरइबिम्बअम्बच्छविणा।
पुरओहुत्तारम्भो मुहेण दिअसो व्व पाअडो वालिसुओ।।

[हर्षपरिजृम्भितेन चार्धोल्लसितरविबिम्बाताम्रच्छविना।
पुरतोऽभिमुखारम्भो मुखेन दिवस इव प्रकटो वालिसुतः।।]

Aṅgada was shown to be ready for action by his face beaming with joy, and red like the partly emerging orb of the sun; like as the day as it starts in the east is revealed by the morning, aglow with the crimson lustre of the slowly rising sun.

K, MY, Muda and Kula read प्रविजृम्भितेन for परि (R). K and Kula read *darullasanta* (दरोल्लसत्) for *addhullasia* (R).

K says वालिसुतोऽङ्गदः हर्षात् प्रविजृम्भितेन विकसितेन, किञ्चिदुल्लसद्रविबिम्बताम्रच्छविना मुखेन पुरतोमुखारम्भः सर्वेभ्यः पूर्वमभिमुखारम्भः अभिमुखकार्यारम्भ इति प्रकटः प्रसिद्धोऽभूत्, दिवसः प्रातःकालेनेव। विशेषणं समानम्। Deva says सर्वेभ्यः पुरतः कार्येऽभिमुख इति प्रकट इत्यर्थः। . . . यथा दिवसः ईषत् रविबिम्बताम्रच्छविना मुखेन पुरतः पूर्वस्यां दिशि प्रकटो भवति। MY says पूर्वदिगुपक्रमत्वं सूर्यस्य, अग्रतःस्थितोद्योगत्वमङ्गदस्येति ग्राह्यम्।

Kula says हर्षप्रविजृम्भितेन प्रमोदविकसितेन, रोषेण(?)[8] असमग्रदर्शनत्वात् वानरमुखानामीषदुल्लसतो रविबिम्बस्येव, पक्षे ईषदुल्लसता रविबिम्बेन ताम्रा छाया द्युतिर्यस्य तेन मुखेन वदनेन, पक्षे प्रत्यूषेण, etc. R says दिवसश्च कीदृक् – पुरतोऽभिमुखः प्राच्यभिमख आरम्भ उपक्रमो यस्य तादृश इति।

13. णेच्छइ णिव्वूढभरो लहुअं दप्पुद्धअत्तणं पवणसुओ।
कअपेसणस्स सोहइ धीरं चिअ महइ रक्खिउं वअणिज्जम्।।

[नेच्छति निर्व्यूढभरो लघुकं दर्पोद्धतत्वं पवनसुतः।
कृतप्रेषणस्य शोभते धैर्यमेव महति रक्षितुं वचनीयम्।।]

---

[8] *SC* has रोमावृतत्वेन।

Hanumat, who had achieved the task assigned to him,[9] had no desire to make any trivial manifestation of pride. Self-restraint becomes one that hath fulfilled the master's command, and serves to avert calumny.[10]

K and Muda read दर्पोद्धुरत्वं for *dappuddhaattaṇaṁ* दर्पोद्धतत्वं (R and probaby Kula).

R says निर्व्यूढभर: निर्वर्तितकार्यो हनुमान् लघु तुच्छं दर्पोद्धुरत्वं दर्पेण उद्धुर: उद्धत: अहंकृत: दर्पोद्धुर: तस्य भावो दर्पोद्धुरत्वं तत् अन्यवानरवत् नेच्छति स्म। कथमित्याह – कृतप्रेषणस्य कृतस्वामिप्रेषणस्य सेवकस्य धैर्यमेव शोभते न चापलम्। कुत इत्याह – स वचनीयं वाच्यं रक्षितुं परिहर्तुमिच्छति। अनेकार्थत्वात् धातूनां रक्षतिरत्र परिहारे वर्तते।

MY says कृतप्रेषणस्य कृताज्ञापितकार्यस्य धैर्यमेव शोभावहम्। अतो दर्पमेव मारुति: नैच्छत्। प्रत्युत कृतकार्यस्य आत्मनो वचनीयरूपत्वं तदेव दर्पं परिहर्तुमैच्छदित्यर्थ:। Kula says धैर्यमेव वचनीयं परापवादं रक्षितुं *mahai* अर्हति नान्यदित्यर्थ:। R says तत् धैर्यं तस्य पुरुषस्य वचनीयं वाच्यतारूपं स्वगुणाविष्कारं करोतीति लोकापवादरूपां रक्षितुमेततपुरुषं प्रति अनागन्तुं महति वाञ्छति।

14. णिब्भच्छिओअहिरवं फुडिआहरणिव्वडन्तदाढाहीरम्।
इसइ कइदप्पपसमिअरोसविरज्जन्तलोअणो सुग्गीवो।।

[निर्भर्त्सितोदधिरवं स्फुरिताधरनिर्वलद्दंष्ट्राहीरम्।
हसति कपिदर्पप्रशमितरोषविरज्यमानलोचन: सुग्रीव:।।]

Sugrīva, whose eyes became serene, as his wrath was appeased at the sight of the high spirits of the apes, burst into laughter, drowning the noise of the sea, the sharp points of his teeth being revealed by the quivering lips.

K and Muda have लोचनं for *loaṇa* (R and Kula).

K says सुग्रीव: एवं हासशब्देन निर्भर्त्सितोदधिरवं अध:कृतोदधिरवं यथा, स्फुरिताधरत्वात् निर्व्यज्यमानदंष्ट्रामयवज्रं, वज्रो रत्नविशेष:, कपिदर्पेण प्रशमितरोषत्वात् विरज्यल्लोचनं प्रसीदल्लोचनं च यथा हसति स्म।

MY says *dāḍhā-hīraṁ* दंष्ट्राहीरं दंष्ट्रावज्रम्। Muda says त्रीण्यपि क्रियाविशेषणानि। He has स्फुरिताधरस्पष्टीभवद्दंष्ट्राहीरम्। Kula and R (text) have स्फुटित (*phuḍia*), explained as विकसित by Kula, who also

[9] See 1.36 ff.

[10] I.e. saves one from the charge of vanity.

says दंष्ट्राया हीरं तीक्ष्णाग्रम्। R says विरज्यमाने विशब्दस्य अभाववाचकत्वेन रागो लौहित्यं तच्छून्ये लोचने यस्य तथाभूतः।

15. णवरि सुमित्तातणओ आसङ्घन्तो गुरुस्स णिअअं च बलम्।
णअ चिन्तेइ ण जम्पइ उअहिं सदसाणणं तणं व गणेन्तो।।

[अनन्तरं सुमित्रातनयोऽध्यवस्यन्गुरोर्निजकं च बलम्।
न च चिन्तयति न जल्पत्युदधिं सदशाननं तृणमिव गणयन्।।]

Lakṣmaṇa, confident of his strength and that of his elder brother, neither talked nor worried, utterly despising the sea as well as Rāvaṇa.

āsaṁghanto is rendered as विश्वसन् in K (*chāyā*). K says लक्ष्मणः गुरोः ज्येष्ठस्य बलं निजं बलं च प्रमाणयन्। MY has आशंसमानः निश्चिन्वानः। Muda says गुरोः निजं च बलं संभावयन्। Kula has आशंसन्। He seems to read *ṇavara* (केवलम्) for *ṇavari* (अनन्तरम्)।

16. रहुणाहस्स वि दिट्ठी वाणरवइणो फुरन्तविद्दुमअम्बम्।
वअणं वअणाहि चला कमलं कमलाहि भमरपन्ति व्व गआ।।

[रघुनाथस्यापि दृष्टिर्वानरपतेः स्फुरद्विद्रुमाताम्रम्।
वदनं वदनाच्चला कमलं कमलाद्भ्रमरपङ्क्तिरिव गता।]

Rāma's gaze, emanating from his visage, rested on Sugrīva's face, red as shining coral, like as a flitting line of bees passes from a lotus to another lotus, red as coral.

K says रघुनाथस्यापि दृष्टिः वदनात् चला चलिता स्फुरद्विद्रुमवत् ताम्रं वानरपतेर्वदनं गता। कमलात् चला भ्रमरपङ्क्तिः कमलमिव। . . . . रघुपतिः अनन्तरं कर्तव्यमुद्दिश्य वानरराजस्य मुखमवलोकयामासेत्यभिप्रायः। Muda says श्रीरामस्यापि दृष्टिः तद्वदनाच्चला सुग्रीवस्य वदनं प्रापेत्यन्वयः। कपिषु विषादं परित्यज्य कार्यौन्मुख्यं गतेषु फुल्लवदनकमलो रामस्तादृशं सुग्रीवं सगौरवमालोकयामास इति भावः।

17–19. तो वअपरिणामोणअभुमआवलिरुब्भमाणदिट्ठिच्छेहो।
आसण्णधवलमिहिआपरिक्खलन्तोसहिप्पहो व्व महिहरो।।
करवारिअकइलोओ सुग्गीवविइण्णभासुरच्छिच्छेहो।
जालाहअदुमणिवहो फुलिङ्गपिङ्गलिअमहिहरो व्व वणदवो।।
जम्पइ रिच्छाहिवई उण्णामेऊण महिअलद्धन्तणिहम्।
खलिअवलिभङ्गदाविअवित्थअबहलवणकंदरं वच्छअडम्।।

(अन्त्यकुलअम्)

[ततो वयःपरिणामावनतभ्रूवल्लिरुध्यमानदृष्टिक्षेपः।
आसन्नधवलमेघिकापरिस्खलदोषिधिप्रभ इव महीधरः।।
करवारितकपिलोकः सुग्रीववितीर्णभाखराक्षिक्षेपः।
ज्वालाहतद्रुमनिवहः स्फुलिङ्गपिङ्गलितमहीधर इव वनदवः।।
जल्पति ऋक्षाधिपतिरुन्नमय्य महीतलार्धान्तनिभम्।
स्खलितवलिभङ्गदर्शितविस्तृतबहलव्रणकंदरं वक्षस्तटम्।।]

(अन्त्यकुलकम्)

Jāmavant then spoke, raising his chest, which was broad like a plot of ground, and revealed as the wrinkles disappeared numerous large cavities left by wounds (in wars).

With the lustre of his eyes hidden by the brows drooping with age, he looked as if he were a mountain, with the sheen of its plants obscured by an adjoining bank of white clouds.[11]

Holding the apes in check with a gesture of his hands, with his flashing eyes[12] fixed on Sugrīva, he seemed to be a forest fire touching the trees with the flames, and reddening the adjacent mountain with the sparks.[13]

K reads प्रतिफलत् for *parikkhalanta* परिस्खलत् (R)। Kula has प्रति।

K says ततो वयःपरिणामावनतयोः भ्रुवोः वलीभिरवलम्बनैः रुध्यमानदृष्टिप्रभः, तदानीमासन्ने धवलमेघे प्रतिफलदोषधिवृक्षज्वालो महीधर इव। पलितयोगात् धवलमेघस्थानीया भ्रूः, ओषधिप्रभास्थानीया दृष्टिः। जल्पतीति उत्तरत्र सम्बन्धः।

My says *ruṁbhamāṇa-diṭṭhicchoho* रुध्यमानदृष्टिशोभः। धवलमेघस्य स्वच्छतया तेजोगतेर्नातिप्रतिबन्धकत्वात् तत्प्रतिफलनेन नातिनिरोधं लक्षयति।

Muda (*chāyā*) has भ्रूपरिरुध्यमानदृष्टिच्छायः, and प्रतिस्खलत (Kula also) for परिस्खलत् (R). He says *mihiā* मेघपंक्तिः and quotes *Deśīnāmamālā* 6.132. R says महीधर इव। सोऽपि कीदृक् – आसन्नया मेघिकया स्वल्पमेघेन परिस्खलन्ती छन्नतया यथावदप्रकाशमाना ओषधिप्रभा यत्र सः।

---

[11] The white hair of Jāmavant's eyebrows is likened to the clouds, and the lustre of his eyes to that of the plants.

[12] Lit. the bright lustre of the eyes.

[13] The raised hands of Jāmavant as he enjoined discipline on the apes are likened to the flames, and the apes to the trees; while his eyes flashing fire and fixed on Sugrīva are likened to the sparks covering the mountain.

Kula says ततो वयःपरिणामेन शैथिल्यात् अवनतया भ्रूलेखया रुध्यमानदृष्टिविक्षेपः, अतश्च आसन्नायां धवलायां प्रतनुमेघिकायां प्रतिस्खलदोषधिप्रभो धरणीधर इव।

Goldschmidt reads *diṭṭhicchoho* (cf. *acchi-cchoho* in the next verse). In N.S. edition R has *-ccheho* (क्षेपः) which seems to be a mistake . *Choha* is a *deśī* word included in *Deśīnāmamālā* 3.39 in the sense of विक्षेप (cf. Kula above) and समूह. The word seems to be explained as प्रभा, शोभा, etc. by others (see K, MY and Muda above). *SC* says क्षिपधातोः छुहादेशः (cf Hemacandra 4.143). This explains the rendering क्षेप। Cf. Kula on the next verse.

K says करेण वारितचपलकपिलोकः, तदा सुग्रीवे दत्तभास्वरनेत्रप्रभः, ज्वालया आहतद्रुमनिवहः स्फुलिङ्गपिङ्गलितमहीधरो वनदव इव स्थितः।

Muda has सुग्रीववितीर्णभासुराक्षिच्छायः। Kula says सुग्रीवार्पितभास्वराक्षिक्षेपः, अत एव उत्क्षिप्तताम्राङ्गुलिनिकरनिभया ज्वालयाहतः कपिलोकनिभो द्रुमनिवहो येन, भास्वराक्षिक्षेपनिभैः स्फुलिङ्गैरग्निकणैः पिङ्गलितः सुग्रीवनिभो महीधरो येन तादृशो वनदव इव।

K and Muda read महीधर for *mahi-ala* (R and Kula); and बहुल for बहल (R). Kula also reads बहुल। K, MY and Muda read गलित for *khalia* (R and Kula).

K says ऋक्षाधिपतिः जाम्बवान् महीधरार्धान्तनिभं भूधरैकदेशनिभं गलितवलिभङ्गत्वात् दर्शितविस्तृतबहुलव्रणकन्दरं वक्षस्तटमुन्नमय्य जल्पति स्म।

20. सग्गं अपारिजाअं कोत्थुहलच्छिरहिअं महुमहस्स उरम्।
सुमिरामि महणपुरओ अमुद्धअन्दं च हरजडापब्भारम्।।

[स्वर्गमपारिजातं कौस्तुभलक्ष्मीरहितं मधुमथनस्योरः।
स्मरामि मथनपुरतोऽमुग्धचन्द्रं व हरजटाप्राग्भारम्।।]

I remember the heaven when it was without the *pārijāta* tree; Viṣṇu's bosom when it was without the *kaustubha* gem and the goddess of wealth; and the great mass of Śiva's matted hair when it was without the young moon, all before the churning of the ocean.[14]

Muda says हरजटासमूहमित्यर्थः, and refers to *Deśīnāmamālā* 6.66 which gives *pabbhāra* in the sense of संघात and गिरिगुहा। *SC* text has *sumarāmi* (स्मरामि) for *sumirāmi.*

[14] I.e. he existed even when the *pārijāta*, the moon and the rest were in the ocean, and had not yet been appropriated by the various gods as a result of the churning.

21. महुमहहत्थम्मि मए णक्खुक्खुडिअसरसं महासुरहिअअम्।
दिट्ठा अणुधावन्ती अक्खित्तं णिअअहत्थकमलं व सिरी।।
[मधुमथनहस्ते मया नखोत्खण्डितसरसं महासुरहृदयम्।
दृष्टा अनुधावती आक्षिप्तं निजकहस्तकमलमिव श्रीः।।]

I saw the Fortune (of Hiraṇyakaśipu) as she followed the bleeding heart of the mighty demon, torn out by Viṣṇu's nails, and held in his hands, as if it were her own lotus hand forcibly grasped by him.[15]

K reads नखत्रुटितं (*ṇaha-kkhuḍiaṁ*) for *ṇakkhu-kkhuḍia* नखोत्खण्डित (R and Kula).

K says मधुमथनहस्ते वर्तमानं नखत्रुटितं नखैरुद्धृतमत एव सरसं महासुरस्य हिरण्यकशिपोः हृदयं हृदयकमलमाक्षिप्तमपहृतं। निजहस्तकमलमिव अनुधावन्ती श्रार्मया दृष्टा। महासुरस्य हृदये समुत्पाटिते श्रीः साद्यो धावति स्म। तदेवमिवेत्युत्प्रेक्षितम्।

Kula says आक्षिप्तमाकृष्य गृहीतं निजकं स्वहस्तस्थितं कमलमिव अनुधावन्ती दैत्यानां श्रीर्मया दृष्टा। R says आक्षिप्तं परमेश्वरेण आक्रम्य गृहीतं निजकहस्तकमलमिव।

22. तं च हिरण्णक्खस्स वि सुमिरामि महावराहदाढाभिण्णम्।
महिमण्डलं व तुलिअं उक्खअहिअअगिरिबन्धणं वच्छअडम्।।
[तच्च हिरण्याक्षस्यापि स्मरामि महावराहदंष्ट्राभिन्नम्।
महीमण्डलमिव तुलितमुत्खातहृदयगिरिबन्धनं वक्षस्तटम्।।]

I remember how Hiraṇyākṣa's bosom pierced by the tusk of the Great Boar, was held aloft, with the heart, strong as a mountain rooted out; even like the earth that was raised from the ocean, with the mountains torn from their roots.[16]

K and Muda read विकटं for *tuliaṁ* (R and Kula). Kula seems to read च for *va* (इव) in the second line.

K says उत्खातहृदयगिरिबन्धनं महीमण्डलमिवेत्युक्तम्। R says महीमण्डलमपि दंष्ट्रयोत्थापनदशायां गिरिणामितस्ततो विशीर्य पतितत्वादुत्खातगिरिबन्धनमभूदिति साम्यम्। Kula says हिरण्याक्षस्यापि जलधिमग्नमहीमण्डलोद्धरणप्रवृत्तेन महावराहेण

[15] The bleeding heart of Hiraṇyakaśipu killed by Viṣṇu in his Man–Lion incarnation is fancied as the rosy hand of the demon king's Fortune seized by his victorious adversary.

[16] The demon Hiraṇyākṣa was killed by Viṣṇu in his Boar incarnation as he tried to prevent him from raising the earth submerged in the ocean.

दंष्ट्रया भिन्नं तुलितं (च) यद् वक्षःस्थलं तच्च स्मरामि महीमण्डलं च तथाभूतं स्मरामि। तस्यापि मे प्रत्यक्षं जातमित्यर्थः। हृदयं गिरिरिव दृढनिष्ठुरत्वात्, तस्य बन्धनं बन्धनस्थानं बध्यतेऽस्मिन् इति कृत्वा, उत्खातमुत्पाटितं हृदयगिरिबन्धनं यस्य तत्तथा। महीमण्डलं च उत्खातानि गिरय एव बन्धनानि यस्य। गिरिबन्धनैः सहैव इत्यर्थः।[17]

23. धीरं हरइ विसाओ विणअं जोव्वणमओ अणङ्गो लज्जम्।
एक्कन्तगहिअवक्खो किं सीसउ जं ठवेइ वअपरिणामो।।

[धैर्यं हरति विषादो विनयं यौवनमदोऽनङ्गो लज्जाम्।
एकान्तगृहीतपक्षः किं शिष्यतां यत्स्थापयति वयःपरिणामः।।]

Despondency destroys fortitude, the frenzy of youth discipline, and passion the sense of shame. Tell (me) if old age that maintains a definite attitude (towards such issues) lends support to any of these.[18]

K, Muda and probably MY read *khavei* (क्षपयति) for *ṭhavei* स्थापयति (R and Kula).

K says विषादो धैर्यं हरति। यौवनमदो विनयं हरति। अनङ्गो लज्जां हरति। कथंभूतः – एकान्तगृहीतपक्षः। पक्षः साध्यवस्तु । एकान्तेन नियमेन गृहीतसाध्यः। विषादादयो धैर्यादीनि साध्यत्वेन गृहीत्वा हरन्तीत्यर्थः। वयःपरिणामस्तु यत् क्षपयति नाशयति तत् किमस्ति शस्यताम्। अस्ति चेदुच्यतामित्यर्थः। पक्षः पार्श्वगरुत्साध्यसहायबलभित्तिषु। पार्श्वद्वारे विरोधेऽर्धमासे चुल्लिबिलेऽन्तिके ।। इति वैजयन्ती। तस्मात् परिणतवयसा मयोच्यमानं वचनं गृह्यतामित्यभिप्रायः।

MY says यथा युष्माकं विषादो धैर्यं हरति, यथा च लोके यौवनजो मदो विनयं, तत्त्वज्ञश्चानङ्गो लज्जां, नैवमियं वृद्धता तादृशं कमपि गुणं हरतीत्याह – धीर इत्यादि। एकान्तगृहीतपक्षः गृहीतधैर्यादिहरणनियमपक्ष इत्यर्थः। *sīsau* शिष्यताम्।

Muda says एकान्तेन नैयत्वेन गृहीतः पक्षो विरुद्धपक्षो येन स तथोक्तः। यथा विषादादयो धैर्यादीनां विरुद्धं पक्षं स्वीकृत्य तानि हरन्ति, तथा वयःपरिपाकोऽपि यत् क्षपयति तत् कथ्यताम्। न किंचित तादृगित्यर्थः। *sīsau* इति कथेः सीसादेशः। शिष्यतामिति वा।

---

17 Partly corrected from *SC*.

18 Cf. Kulanātha in Extracts. According to Rāmadāsa: Is there any need to aver what old age, coming to a definite conclusion, holds to be true, namely that despondency destroys fortitude, etc. The interpretation does not suit the context very well as Jāmavant's intention is to glorify old age to make his opinions more convincing.

Kula says प्रथमे वयसि विषयास्वादस्नेहेन विवेकलोपात् कार्यप्रतिपत्तिविच्छेदेन अप्रतिपत्तिः विषादो भवति। . . . एकान्तो निश्चयः तेन गृहीतः पक्षः साध्यः (?) येन स वयःपरिणामः तेषां विषादयौवनमदानज्ञानां मध्ये किं *sīsau* कथ्यतां यत् स्थापयति, न किमपि अपि तु सर्वमेतत् विनाशयतीत्यर्थः। अतः . . . तद्विरोधिवयःपरिणतिसाध्यानां धैर्यविनयलज्जानां योगो भवति। तेन च कार्यतत्त्वज्ञानं भवति। उच्चावचं त्यक्त्वा मम परिणतवयसः बुद्ध्या प्रवृत्तिः क्रियतामिति भावः। R says एकान्ततः तत्त्वतो गृहीतः पक्षः सिद्धान्त इदमित्थमेवेति निर्णयरूपो येन तादृशो वयःपरिणामो वार्धकं कर्तृ विषादो धैर्यं . . . हरतीत्येवमादिप्रकारेण यत् स्थापयति स्थिरीकरोति, निर्धारयतीति यावत्, तत् किं शिष्यतां कथ्यताम्।

24. अणुहूअमुणेअव्व विहडिअविसमक्खरे वि संघडिअत्थे।
जोव्वणमूढपहसिए मा अवमण्णह जरापरिणउल्लावे।।

[अनुभूतज्ञातव्यान्विघटितविषमाक्षरानपि संघटितार्थान्।
यौवनमूढप्रहसितान्मावमन्यध्वं जरापरिणतोल्लापान्।।]

Despise not the utterances of one that is bowed with age.[19] Their purport is based on experience,[20] and they are consistent in meaning, even though the words are incoherent and harsh. They are only ridiculed by those who are foolish because of their youth.

K and MY *pratīka* has *aṇuhūya* (अनुभूय)।

K says जरापरिणतस्य मादृशस्य उल्लापान् वाक्यानि यूयं मावमन्यध्वम्। कीदृशान् – अनुभूय ज्ञातव्यान्, विघटितानि विगलितानि विषमानि अक्षराणि येषां तान् तथाभूतानपि संघटितार्थान्, यौवनमूढैः प्रहसितान्।

MY says अनुभूतिः फलतः, ज्ञातव्यत्वं तु प्रामाण्यतः। फलाविसंवादात् प्रमाणतया ज्ञातव्यानित्यर्थः। स्वरूपे अक्षराणां विघटनमश्लिष्टत्वं, वैषम्यमुच्चावचता। एतच्च द्वयं स्थानकरणाद्यपाटवनिमित्तम्। विसंघटितार्थान् स्वरूपेण आपाततया प्रतीयमानान्। अथवा विघटिताक्षरानपि संघटितार्थान्।

Deva also says अनुभूय ज्ञातव्यान् केवलमनुभवेनैव ज्ञातव्यान् नोक्तिमात्रविश्वसनीयान्। विघटितविषमाक्षरान् विघटितानि अक्रमाणि विषमाण्यक्षराणि . . . येषां ते एवंभूतान्। वृद्धानां वचनानि . . . निषेधरूपत्वात् प्रथमं प्रथमं परुषाण्यपि सुखोदर्काणि भविष्यन्ति।

R, Muda and Kula have *aṇuhūa* (अनुभूत्)। R says अनुभूतो ज्ञातव्यभागो येषु तान्। मया सर्वमिदमनुभूय उच्यत इति भावः। अथ चानुभूते सति ज्ञातव्यान्।

---

[19] Or, "utterances matured by age".

[20] Or, "They should be comprehended by realizing their purport."

वृद्धवचनमनुभवानन्तरं ज्ञायत इति भवद्भिरप्यनुभूय ज्ञातव्यं यन्मयोक्तमिति तात्पर्यम्। Kula is corrupt, but *SC* seems to reproduce him – अनेकशास्त्राभ्यासेन ज्ञातमनुभूतमनुभवलिङ्गं येषु तान्, अथवा साक्षादनादृतानपि अनुभूतेनानुभवेन ज्ञातव्यान्। संघटितार्थान् सम्यक् प्रतिपादितार्थान्।

25. तुज्झ भुआसु णिसण्णो हरिसत्थो पब्बलो सुराण वि समरे।
मारुअलद्धत्थामो ओवग्गइ महिरओ वि ता दिअसअरम्।।

[तव भुजयोर्निषण्णो हरिसार्थः प्रबलः सुराणामपि समरे।
मारुतलब्धस्थामोऽवक्रामति महीरजोऽपि तावद्दिवसकरम्।।]

Leaning on thine[21] arms, the host of apes will prove valiant even in a war with the gods. Even the dust of the earth assails the sun, deriving its strength from the wind.

K says तव भुजयोः कृतावलम्बो हरिसार्थः सुराणां समरेऽपि वत्सलः समर्थः। नैनमवज्ञातुमर्हसीत्यर्थः। अत्र दृष्टान्तमाह – मारुतेन लब्धस्थाम लब्धबलं महीरजोऽपि तावत् दिवसकरमभिभवति हि। भटानां सामर्थ्यं स्वामिबलायत्तमित्यर्थः।

MY says वत्सलः श्रद्धालुः समर्थ इत्यर्थः। *oaggai* अभिभवति। Muda says *paccalo* इति समर्थः and quotes *Deśīnāmamālā* 6.69. This is probably also the reading of K and MY who seem to have Sanskritized it into वत्सल। Kula also has समर्थः, but he seems to read *pabbalo* (प्रबलः) like R. Cf. 6.33 and 9.3 below. MY on 6.33, however, says *vacchaiā* वत्सलाः समर्थाः। K also cites the word in his gloss on 9.3. *SC* text has *pabbalo*. It has *ovaggai*, like R, rendered as अववल्गति आस्कन्दति in *SC* commentary. Kula is here corrupt.

26. किं उण दुप्परिअल्ला मज्जाआइक्कमुप्पहवलिज्जन्ता।
उअहि व्व सारगरुआ घडिआ वि विसंघडन्ति कज्जालावा।।

[किं पुनर्दुष्परिकलनीया मर्यादातिक्रमोत्पथवल्यमानाः।
उदधय इव सारगुरवो घटिता अपि विसंघटन्ते कार्यालापाः।।]

But weighty projects whose course is hard to determine, fail, even though well planned, if conducted in the wrong way by violating established principles; like as the unfathomable oceans, prized for their riches, are reduced to a state of chaos, even though calm, when they go astray by overflowing their shores (during the deluge).

---

[21] Ref. to Sugrīva.

K and Muda read कार्यकलापा: for *kajjālāvā* कार्यालापा: (R and Kula)।

K says किं पुनः किंतु कार्यकलापाः कार्यजातानि घटिता अपि पुनः विघटन्ते (विसंघटन्ते *chāyā*) भिद्यन्ते। कथंभूताः – दुष्पारिकला दुष्परिच्छेदाः, मर्यादातिक्रमात् उत्पथे दुर्मार्गे वल्यमाना नीयमानाः। सारगुरवः सारः साध्यवस्तु तेन गुरवः। किमिव-उदधय इव। उदधयश्च दुष्परिच्छेदाः, मर्यादायाः कूलस्यातिक्रमात् उत्पथप्रवृत्ताः, सारगुरवश्च, घटिता अपि प्रकृतिस्था अपि प्रलये पुनः विघटन्ते विकारं भजन्त इति। मर्यादा कूलदेशोऽस्येति हलायुधः। तस्मात् भवतैव केवलेन संरम्भो न कार्य इत्यभिप्रायः।

R says दुष्परिकलनीयाः . . . इत्थंकर्तव्यतया दुरवधारणीया वा। (समुद्रपक्षे) दुखगाहनीयाः।

MY says दुष्परिकलनाः परिच्छेत्तुं परिमातुं चाशक्याः। मर्यादा शास्त्रदर्शितः क्रमो वेला च। शास्त्रं चात्र – सहायसाध्यं राजत्वं चक्रमेकं न वर्तत इत्यादि। सारः प्रयोजनममृतकौस्तुभादिश्च। उत्पथवल्यमाना अमार्गेण विक्रियां नीयमानाः। घटिता अपि घटितप्राया अपि। सत्यमधिष्ठातुरेव कार्यकरत्वं, किंतु सहायसहितस्यैव, न तु असहायस्य, अन्तरा प्रत्यूहबहुलतया विघ्न(?)-संभवादिति तात्पर्यम्।

Kula says किं पुनः कार्यालापाः कार्यशब्दवाच्याः कार्यविशेषा उदधय इव सारेणार्थेन रत्नादिना च गुरुकाः, *duppariallā* अशक्यावधारणाः अशक्यलङ्घनाः, दुरधिगमा हि गतिः कार्यस्येत्याशयः,[22] घटिता अपि विसंघटन्ते। अत्र हेतुः मर्यादातिक्रमो दर्पात् शास्त्रार्थलङ्घनं स एवोत्पथो विमार्गः तेन वल्यमाना नीयमानाः। पक्षे मर्यादा स्थितिः।

Muda says *duppariallā* अशक्याः and quotes *Deśīnāmamālā* 5.55. He says मर्यादा लोकस्थितिर्वेला च।

27. पच्चक्खा हि परोक्खं कह वि तुलग्गघडिआहि आगमसुद्धम्।
संचालिअणिक्कम्पं अणुहूआहि वि महं सुअं चिअ गरुअम्॥

[प्रत्यक्षात्परोक्षं कथमपि तुलाग्रघटितादागमशुद्धम्।
संचालितनिष्कम्पमनुभूतादपि मम श्रुतमेव गुरु॥]

My supersensual knowledge, derived from the scriptures, and conforming to trustworthy lore, and unshakable though assailed (by arguments), is weightier than even direct experience that is based on perception through the medium of the senses, and somehow tallies fortuitously with the truth.

[22] This is restored from *SC*. Our copy of Kula has त्वराधिगमा विपत्तिः(?) कार्यस्य which does not suit the context.

K says प्रत्यक्षादनुभवावस्थायामात्मनः प्रत्यक्षात्, कथमपि कथञ्चित यदृच्छया क्षणघटितात् काकतालीयसदृशात् अनुभूतादप्यर्थात् मम श्रुतमेव शास्त्रश्रवणमेव गुरु। कीदृशं – परोक्षं कालान्तरे फलप्रदम्। आगमेन उपदेशेन विशुद्धम्। अतएव संचालितनिष्कम्पं पूर्वपक्षयुक्तिभिः संचालितमपि सिद्धान्तयुक्तिभिः निष्कम्पम्। त्वरावद्भिः सहसा क्रियमाणं कार्यं यदृच्छया घटेत वा न वा। शास्त्रोक्तमार्गेण क्रियामाणं कार्यमेव सिध्यतीति मम पक्षः इत्यर्थः।

MY says प्रत्यक्षादपरोक्षज्ञानविषयात्, . . . कथमपि तुलाग्रघटितात् अवधानेन तुलासंमितात्। अनेन दृढनिर्णीतत्वं लक्ष्यते। तथा च लोकमनः-प्रणिधानादिसहकारिसम्पत्तिबलात् अव्यभिचारिप्रत्यक्षविषयीकृतादपीत्यर्थः। अथवा तुलाग्रघटितत्वेन अनुमाननिश्चितमुच्यते। तुलाग्रस्य मानसाधनस्य अवनमनोन्नमन-रूपलिङ्गनिश्चितादपीत्यर्थः। ततश्च प्रत्यक्षानुमानाभ्यां प्रमितादपि आगमसिद्धं श्रुतमेव गुरु इति। संचालितनिष्कम्पं संचलनानुगुणपूर्वपक्षयुक्तिरूपतद्व्यापारविषयीकृतत्वेऽपि निश्चलमित्यर्थः। अनेनानुकूलतर्कद्वारा अन्यथासिद्धिशङ्कानिरास उक्तः। अनुभूतादपि प्रत्यक्षगृहीतादपि श्रुतमेव आगमविषयीकृतमेव आभ्रान्ततया श्रद्धेयमित्यर्थः।

Muda says मम अनुभूतादपि श्रुतमेव गुरुकम्। अनुभूतमिन्द्रियजन्यज्ञानं, श्रुतं शास्त्रजन्यम्। कथं गुरु इत्यपेक्षायां विशेषणद्वारा हेतुमुपन्यस्यति। प्रत्यक्षात् – अनुभूत् हि अक्षाणीन्द्रियाणि प्रतिगतम्। एतेन इन्द्रियदेशकालस्वभावविप्रकृष्टव-स्त्वगाहित्वाभावात् अल्पविषत्वमुक्तम्। तथा कथमपि काकतालीयघटितात् – अनुभवस्य हि काकतालीयन्यायेन संवादात् प्रामाण्यम्। इन्द्रियाणां दोषबाहुल्यात्। श्रुतं कीदृशम् – प्रत्यक्षेभ्यः पराग्भूतम्, आगमेन आप्तवाक्येन विशुद्धम्। अतीन्द्रियवस्त्ववगाहि करणदोषविकलं चेत्यर्थः। श्रुतस्य प्रामाण्ये हेत्वन्तरमाह – युक्तिभिः संचालितं सत् निष्कम्पं शङ्ककुण्ठितं न भवतीत्यर्थः। *tulaggaṁ* काकतालीये इति देशीकोशे (*DN* 5.15).

Kula says प्रत्यक्षमिन्द्रियजज्ञानं तच्च भ्रान्तमपि भवति यथा शुक्त्यादौ रजतबुद्धिः। अथ कथमपि तुलाग्रवत् घटितात् स्थिरीकृतात् उपपन्नीकृतादिति यावत्। प्रत्यक्षादिन्द्रियसंनिकर्षजात् ज्ञानात् साक्षादनुभूतात् अपि परोक्षं साक्षादननुभूतमपि श्रुतमेव शास्त्राधिगतमेव मम गुरुकमादृतम्। अत्र हेतुः – आगमशुद्धमिति। आप्तानां . . . निश्चितवादिनां वचनमागमः। तेन शुद्धं निर्मलं शास्त्रस्य आगमाविरुद्धत्वात् अतएव संचालितनिष्कम्पं विचार्य सिद्धान्तीकृतत्वात् स्थिरम्। एतेन यदहमागमार्थगतं भणामि तत् तथेति गृह्यतामिति भावः।

R says परोमिन्द्रियप्रत्यासत्त्यजन्यम्।

28. जं साहेन्ति समत्था समसारपरक्कमा ण तं णिव्वडिआ।
एक्को पअवेज्ज दढं मिलिआ उण दिणअरा खवेन्ति तिहुअणम्।।

[यत्साधयन्ति समस्ताः समसारपराक्रमा न तं निर्वलिताः।
एकः प्रतपेद्दृढं मिलिता पुनर्दिनकराः क्षपयन्ति त्रिभुवनम्।।]

What those who are equal in strength and valour can achieve, when united, cannot be achieved, when they are divided. A single sun might intensely heat the universe, but the (twelve) united suns (of the epoch of ruin) destroy it altogether.

K says समसारपराक्रमाः समबलपराक्रमाः सेवकाः समस्ताः अपृथग्भूताः यत् साधयन्ति तत् कार्यं निर्व्यक्ताः पृथग्भूताः न साधयन्ति। एको दिनकरः दृढं प्रतपेत्। त्रिभुवनं पुनर्मिलिताः द्वादशापि दिनकराः सहिता एव क्षपयन्ति।

MY says *sāhanti* साधयन्ति। एकैकेन क्रियमाण उत्साहः सामुदायिकात् लघुफल् इत्युक्तम्। Muda renders *samartthā* as समर्थाः। The equivalent of समस्त is *samattha* according to Vararuci 3.12, and *samatta* according to Hemacandra 2.45. *SC* text has *samattā* explained as समस्ताः in the gloss. Kula on 6.53 objects to the explnation of *samatta* as समस्त।

29. ओवग्गइ अहिमाणं पडिवक्खस्स वि ण तारिसं देइ भअम्।
अमरिसगहिओ व्व सरो विद्दाइ अभाअसंधिओ उच्छाहो।।

[अवक्रामत्यभिमानं प्रतिपक्षस्यापि न तादृशं ददाति भयम्।
अमर्षगृहीत इव शरो विद्रात्यभागसंहित उत्साहः।।]

Misplaced zeal proves ineffectual, and humiliates one's pride, and causes no great fear to the enemy, like an arrow taken up in a fit of rage.

K says अभागसंहितः अस्थाने प्रवर्तित उत्साहः अभिमानमभिभवति। प्रतिपक्षस्य न तादृशं भयं ददाति स्थाने घटित उत्साहो यादृशं भयं ददाति। किं कुर्यादित्याह – विद्रात्येव विपद्यत एव। द्रा कुत्सिते गमने। किमिव – अमर्षेण गृहीतः शरः इव। स च अभिमानमभिभवति, शत्रोश्च न तादृशं भयं ददाति। अवसीदत्येव।

MY has विद्रवति। Muda says विद्राति विरुद्धं कुत्सितं भक्तीत्यर्थः। द्रा कुत्सायां गतौ। Muda (*chāyā*) has आक्रामत्यभिमानं।

Kula says अभागे अकाले अस्थाने च संहितो योजितः, अमर्षेण क्रोधेन गृहीत उत्साहः शरः इव[23] . . . निष्फल एव विद्राति विलीयते। तथा चौक्तम् – न पापाय पूर्वं लिम्पेत् कालं वीक्ष्य समुत्पतेत। पश्चात्तापाय निर्दिष्टा विक्रमैकरसज्ञता।[24]

30. णेअ तुमे मोत्तव्वं सुट्ठु वि तुरिएण धीर पत्थिवचरिअम्।
तुरवन्तस्स रविस्स वि मडइज्जइ दक्खिणाअणम्मि पआओ।।

---

[23] Kula is here corrupt. After इव *SC* has अभिमानमववल्गति आस्कन्दति।

[24] Partly restored from *SC*.

[नैव त्वया मोक्तव्यं सुष्ठ्वपि त्वरितेन धीर पार्थिवचरितम्।
त्वरमाणस्य रवेरपि मृदूयते दक्षिणायने प्रतापः॥]

Being in hurry, thou must not abandon the commendable way of the wise kings. Even the heat of the sun grows feeble as it hastens on its way in its winter course.[25]

K and MY read *ṇa vi a* (नापि च) for *ṇea* (R, Kula and Muda) नैव।

K says त्वरितेन त्वयापि च धीर पार्थिवचरितं सुष्ठु शोभनमपि न मोक्तव्यम्। राजानो हि विमृश्यकारिणः न त्वरावन्तः। त्वरायाः प्रतापविरोधिनीत्वात् दक्षिणायेन त्वरमाणस्य रवेरपि प्रतापो मृदूयते मन्दायते। दक्षिणस्यां दिशि रविः क्षिप्तेषुरिव सर्पतीति श्रीविष्णुपुराणे (Book 2; ch. 8)।

Muda (*chāyā*) has नैवं। He says *maulijjai* इति पाठे मुकुलीभवति संकुचतीत्यर्थः।

Kula says धीरा विमृष्यकारिणः ते च ते पार्थिवाश्चेति तेषां चरितं सुष्ठु त्वरितेनापि त्वया नैव मोक्तव्यम्। वैधर्म्येण दृष्टान्तयति। त्वरमाणस्य रवेरपि परमतेजस्विनो दक्षिणाशागमने प्रतापो मृदूयते। एतेन सहसा विदधीत न क्रियामिति भावः।

Deva says हिममिलितत्वात् प्रतापो मृदुर्भवतीत्यर्थः। दक्षिणायने रवेस्त्वरमाणत्वं ज्योतिःशास्त्रे प्रसिद्धम्।

31. किं अइराएण इमा अमग्गसमरसुहचिन्तिअकहाहि कआ।
पहरिसपणामिअमुही गोत्तक्खलणविमण व्व दे जअलच्छी॥

[किमतिरागेणेयममार्गसमरसुखचिन्तितकथाभिः कृता।
प्रहर्षप्रणामितमुखी गोष्टस्खलनविमना इव ते जयलक्ष्मीः।]

Because of thy inordinate zeal, why dost thou make yon goddess of victory that joyfully presents her visage to thee, look like a lady-love dejected at the mention of her rival's name, by thy utterances prompted by a desire to obtain the joy of war by wrong methods?[26]

K, MY and Muda read विस्तृत (*vitthaa*) for *cintia* (R and Kula). K and Muda have स्खलित for स्खलन।

K says त्वयि प्रहर्षादर्पितमुखी इयं जयलक्ष्मीरतिरागेण अत्यभिनिवेशेन हेतुना

---

[25] The lessening of the sun's power in the winter is fancied as being caused by its apparent haste on the shortening days.

[26] Victory and rashness are fancied as rivals. The former is in sight, but cannot be obtained by rash methods.

अमार्गसमरसुखविस्तृतकथाभिः अमार्गे अपथे समरसुखस्य विस्तृताभिः कथाभिरुक्तिभिः, गोत्रस्खलितेन सपत्नीनामग्रहणेन यथा विमनाः क्रियते तथा किमर्थं कृता। *samuha-miliekkamekke* (3.56) इत्यादिभिः कथाभिः गोत्रस्खलितविमना इव ते किं कृता। यथा प्रहर्षादर्पितमुखी दयिता सपत्नीनामग्रहणेन स्खलितेन विमनाः क्रियते तद्वदिति ते अतिरागेणेति सम्बन्धः। MY says ते त्वया अमार्गेण विस्तृत(समर)-सुखकथायामतिरागिणा। Muda says प्रहर्षार्पितमुखी इयं जयलक्ष्मीः अमार्गसमरसुखाय विस्तृतकथाभिः त्वया गोत्रस्खलितविमनस्का इव किमिति कृता इत्यन्वयः।

Kula reads अभिरागेण for *airāeṇa* (अतिरागेण)। He says दैवदोषादिकमनपेक्ष्य शौर्यवशेनैव केवलेन शास्त्रीयं मार्गं त्यक्त्वा अमार्गेण यच्चिन्तितं समरसुखं तस्य कथाभिरियं जयलक्ष्मीः . . . (विमनाः) किमिति त्वया कृता। ईप्सायां भूतवत् प्रयोगः। मा क्रियतामित्यर्थः। यथान्येषामभिरागेण नायकेन(?) नायिका प्रहर्षसंमुखीभूतापि अमार्गेण अनायकोचितेन(?) अधैर्येण यत् सुखचिन्तनं तेन याः कथास्ताभिः गोत्रस्खलितेन विमनाः क्रियत इति।

32. मा रज्जह रहस च्चिअ चन्दस्स वि दाव कुमुअवणणिप्फण्णो।
दूरं णिव्वलिअगुणो एक्करसस्स कमलेसु विद्दाइ जसो।।

[मा रज्यत रभस एव चन्द्रस्यापि तावत्कुमुदवननिष्पन्नम्।
दूरं निर्वलितगुणो एकरसस्य कमलेषु विद्राति यशः।।]

Persist not solely in obstinate zeal. Even the super-excellent renown earned by the moon by its action on the night lotus beds hath no effect on the day lotus, because the moon cleaves to a single mood.[27]

K, Muda and Kula read *ṇivvūḍhabharo* for *ṇivvalia-guṇo* (R).

K says रभस एव अभिनिवेश एव मा रज्यत मा स्नेहं कुरुत। को दोष इति चेत् एकरसस्य एकत्रैव अभिनिवेशिनः चन्द्रस्यापि तावत् कुमुदवने निष्पन्नं निर्वृत्तं दूरं चिरकालं निर्व्यूढभरं निर्व्यूढकुमुदकार्यं यशः कमलेषु विद्राति विपद्यते। तस्माद् युक्तं युक्तं विमृश्य कर्तव्यमिति। Muda says रसोऽनुरागः।

Kula says देशकालादिमनपेक्ष्य रभस एव उत्साह एव केवले मा रज्यत। यतः आस्तां तावदन्यः चन्द्रस्यापि एकरसस्य तावत् कुमुदमात्रानुरागिणो विकाशकत्वेन कुमुदवननिष्पन्नं यत् यशः ख्यातिः दूरमत्यर्थः निर्व्यूढभरं धृतोत्कर्षं तत् कमलेषु विद्राति तदविकाशनात् विलयं याति। एतेन रभसेन न संपतेदिति नयो दर्शितः।

---

[27] I.e. the moon cannot open the day lotus, because it is bent on opening the night lotus to the exclusion of any other flower. Jāmavant criticizes Sugrīva for sticking to a rigid policy as seen in his determination to go forward without the co-operation of his followers, as described in the previous canto.

33. किं अप्पणा परिअणो परस्स ओ परिअणेण दे पडिवक्खो।
सोहइ पत्थिज्जन्तो जिआहिमाणस्स किं जअम्मि वि गहणम्।।
[किमात्मना परिजनः परस्य उत परिजनेन ते प्रतिपक्षः।
शोभते प्रार्थ्यमानो जिताभिमानस्य किं जयेऽपि ग्रहणम्।।]

What would be proper — for thee to attack the enemy's troops thyself, or, for thy troops to attack the enemy? Is one whose pride hath been humiliated[28] held in esteem even if he wins the victory?[29]

K says आत्मना त्वयैव प्रार्थ्यमानः अभियुज्यमानः परस्य शत्रोः परिजनः शोभते किम्। उत ते परिजनेन प्रार्थ्यमानः प्रतिपक्षः किं शोभते उच्यताम्। तव सेवकजनैरभियुज्यमानः शत्रुरेव हि शोभते। तत् तव शोभाकारणमित्यर्थः। The remaining portion of K's gloss is missing, but his citation from canto 11, verse 98 containing the word *aggahaṇaṁ* shows that he takes *gahaṇaṁ* (ग्रहणम्) in the sense of आदर।[30]

MY says स्वयमेव परस्य परिजनं त्वरया प्रार्थयमानस्त्वं परस्यैव शोभामापादयिष्यसीत्याह – *kiṁ appaṇā* इत्यादिना।

अथवा स्वपरिजनप्रार्थित एव प्रतिपक्षः शोभते तव शोभायै नान्यथेति। अथवा उभयोरप्यनयोः पक्षयोरुचिततया कतरः शोभते युज्यत इत्यर्थः। *kiṁ jaammi vi gahaṇaṁ* जयेऽपि गहनं किम्। अस्थाने अभिमानमकुर्वतः तव सुप्राप एव जय इत्यर्थः।

Kula says क्षमत्वेऽपि सहानिरपेक्षा न युध्यन्ते इत्यभिप्रायेण . . . आह किमित्यादि। किमसहायगमनेन आत्मना स्वयमेव शत्रोः परिजनः प्रार्थ्यमानः अभियुज्यमानः शोभते युज्यते, उत सहायगमनेन तव परिजनेन हनूमदङ्गदादिना प्रतिपक्षो रावणः प्रार्थ्यमानः शोभते। निरूप्यतां तावत् उभयोर्मध्ये कः शोभाकरः पक्ष इति। सहायेनैव शत्रुः जीयत इति प्रभोः शोभेति भावः। तस्मादभिमानेन सहायनिरपेक्षता न युक्ता।

[28] I.e. a commander who has humiliated himself by fighting with the rank and file of the opposite army. Sugrīva had threatened to attack and destroy the demons himself. Cf. 3.57, 62, 63.

[29] Mādhava and others explain the line differently: What obstacle to victory is there for one that has conquered his pride? That is, it is easy for one who is not too proud to seek help from others to gain a victory over the enemy. The remark is directed against Sugrīva who had decried the idea of waiting for others to help in a danger. Cf 3.56 Jāmavant implies that Sugrīva could secure the willing co-operation of his followers if he only gave up his presumptuous self-confidence.

[30] Cf. R — जिताभिमानस्य असमेन समं साम्येनाधःकृताहंकारस्य पुरुषस्य जयेऽपि जाते किं ग्रहणं परेषां क आदरः। न्यूनकक्षजयेन प्रकर्षाभावात्।

प्रत्युताभिमान एव जेतुं युज्यत इत्याह – जिताभिमानस्य किं जगत्यपि गहनं कष्टम्। *SC* quotation has जगत्यपि किं गहनं दुर्लभमपि तु नेत्याह[31]। Kula renders *jaa* as जगत।

Deva says तव परिजनेन पर एव प्रार्थयितुं युक्तः। अभिमानेन किल वञ्च्यसे। अभिमानं वशीकुरु। वशीकृताभिमानस्य तव किं जये अप्राप्तव्यम्।

Muda also explains *gahaṇaṁ* as गहनम्। He says अभिमानेन खलु त्वया एवमुच्यते। एक एव ससैन्यं रावणं हनिष्यामीति। तत्र विचार्यतां किं त्वया शत्रोः सैन्यमभियुज्यमानं (?) शोभते उत त्वत्सैन्येन रावण इति। . . . (जितभिमानस्य) तदा जयविषये किं गहनं न किंचिदित्यर्थः। For this use of गहन cf. *Paumacariu* 12.6.9 — *kavaṇu gahaṇu kira rāvaṇu.*

34. हणुमन्ताइसएणं हणुमन्तमुहाण वाणराण अ वइणा।
धीर अणिव्वलिअजसं काअव्वं किं तुमे वि मारुइसरिसम्।।
[हनुमदतिशयितेन हनुमन्मुखानां वानराणां च पत्या।
धीर अनिर्वलितयशः कर्तव्यं किं त्वयापि मारुतिसदृशम्।।]

Wise one, superior to Hanumat, and the lord of Hanumat and the other apes as thou art, shouldst thou, too, do something similar to what he hath done, something that would not redound to thy fame?[32]

R text has *aṇivvalia* and *SC* text *-ḍi-*, both rendered as अनिर्वलित in the *chāyā.* K (*chāyā*) reads हनुमदतिशयिनां, and MY and Muda — दतिशयानां for *hanumantāisaeṇaṁ* हनुमदतिशयितेन (R and Kula)।

K says हे धीर हनुमन्तमपि अतिशयानानां हनुमत्प्रमुखानां च वानराणां पत्या अधिपतिना त्वयापि मारुतिसदृशं मारुतिचरितमात्रसदृशम् अनिर्व्यक्तयशस्कमप्रकाशयशस्कं कर्म कर्तव्यं किम्। स्वामिनो भवतः तस्य भटयोग्यकार्यकरणमयशस्करमेव। तस्मात् सपरिकर एव गत्वा शत्रून् जहीत्यर्थः।

MY says हनुमतः अतिशयो येषां ते हनूमदतिशयाः तेषां हनूमदतिशयानामित्यर्थः। (Muda also)।

Muda says अस्पष्टयश इति क्रियाविशेषणम्। अन्यसंदेशे क्रियमाणे यशः स्पष्टं न भवति किंतु तत्तुल्यं भवतीत्यर्थः। एतच्च दररूढव्रणप्रसाधनं हनूमन्तं पश्यतो ममात्मानादृत इत्येतत्कटाक्षं क्षिपित्वोक्तम् (see 3.44)।

---

[31] *SC* anonymously reproduces practically the whole of Kula's gloss, but gives the last two sentences as a quotation from अन्ये।

[32] I.e. if he flew across the ocean as he threatened to do (cf. 3.57), he would be only doing what had already been done by Hanumat.

Kula says हनूमदतिशयितेन (i.e. हनूमतः अधिकेन as explained by R) हनूमत्प्रभृतिवानराणां च पत्या त्वया किं मारुतिसदृशमिति यथा मारुतिना अकृतरावणवधत्वात् अनिष्पन्नं यशः कृतं तथा कर्तव्यम्। *SC* quotation has अनिष्पन्नयशो यथा स्यात् तथा। Hemacandra gives *nivvalai* निष्पद्यते (4.128) and *ṇivvaḍai* पृथक् स्पष्टो वा भवति (4.62)।

35. कह तम्मि वि लाइज्जइ जम्मि अइण्णप्फला अदूरपसरिआ।
पडिअम्मि दुमे व्व लआ स च्चिअ अण्णं पुणो वि लग्गइ आणा।।

[कथं तस्मिन्नपि लाग्यते यस्मिन्नदत्तफला अदूरप्रसृता।
पतिते द्रुम इव लता सैवान्यं पुनरपि लगत्याज्ञा ('पुनर्विलगति' वा)।।]

How can a task be trusted to one in whose hands it hath not progressed nor shown success? It must be reassigned to someone else; just as a creeper, when the supporting tree falls, is again trained against another, because it hath not flourished nor borne fruit.[33]

K says पूर्वं यस्मिन् सेवके त्वदीया आज्ञा अदूरप्रसृता अत्यन्तमप्रसृता अतएव अदत्तफलाभूत सैवाज्ञा पुनस्तस्मिन्नपि कथमारोप्यते[34]। अन्यं सेवकं विलगतु। आश्रयभूते द्रुमे पतिते लतेव। सैव लता यथापरं वक्षमारोहति तद्वदिति। तव सेवका हि बहवः सन्ति। तत्र हनूमानिव त्वदाज्ञां यो निर्वोढुं शक्नुयात् तमेव तत्र प्रेषय। त्वं पुनर्मा गम इत्यर्थः। MY says सन्ति हि बहवः शूराः सैनिकाः। तत्र यदि कतिपये अलसास्तान् विहाय समर्थेषु नियुज्यतां धूरित्याह।

K and Muda have विलग्यते (*vilāijjai*) and विलगति (*vilaggai*). Muda says विलग्यते आरोप्यते। कपीन् प्रत्युपालम्भोऽयम्।

Kula says निजोन्मार्गप्रवृत्तेन त्वया रामस्याज्ञा विफलीकृता यदि अन्यत्र लगति तदा तत्रैव कीर्तिः स्यादित्याशयमाह। *SC* has तदा तवैव अकीर्तिः स्यात्। R agrees with Kula — त्वयि अपि एवमविमृश्यकारितया रामाज्ञा तथैव स्यादिति भावः। Kula seems to read *lāijjau* (लाग्यताम्, cf. *SC* text) for *-i* (लाग्यते) found in R, who likewise takes *vi* separately. R reads *vi laggai* (अपि लगति) for विलगति (K and Muda). Kula is corrupt, but seems to agree with R (cf. *SC*).

---

[33] It is hinted that the command of the army might be transferred from Sugrīva to someone else owning to his wrong methods; but according to Kṛṣṇa and others, Sugrīva is here counselled to try more efficient persons if some of his followers have been found wanting.

[34] Deva alo says भवत आज्ञा यस्मिन् भटवर्गे अदूरप्रसृता तस्मिन् आरोपयितुं न शक्यते।

36. हन्तुं विमग्गमाणो हन्तुं तुरिअस्स अप्पणा दहवअणम्।
किं इच्छसि काउं जे पवअवइ पिअं ति विप्पिअं रहुवइणो।।

[हन्तुं विमृग्यन् हन्तुं त्वरितस्यात्मना दशवदनम्।
किमिच्छसि कर्तुं यत्प्लवगपते प्रियमिति विप्रियं रघुपतेः।।]

Lord of the apes, desiring to slay Rāvaṇa, dost thou wish to displease Rāma, thinking it would please him, eager as he is to slay him himself?[35]

K and Muda read अस्य (i.e. *se*) for *je* (R and Kula) in the second line. K, Muda and Kula read अप्रियं for *vippiaṁ* (R). Muda says हन्तुं विमार्गन् इच्छन् इति संबुद्ध्यन्तमेतत्। Kula says येशब्दः (*je* ?) पादपूरणे। Cf. Hemacandra 2.217.

37. इअ णिअमिअसुग्गीवो रामन्तेण वलिओ पिआमहतणओ।
परिमट्ठमेरुसिहरो सूराहिमुहो व्व पलअधूमुप्पीडो।।

[इति नियमितसुग्रीवो रामान्तेन वलितः पितामहतनयः।
परिमृष्टमेरुशिखरः सूर्याभिमुख इव प्रलयधूमोत्पीडः।।]

Having thus restrained Sugrīva, the son of Brahmā[36] turned towards Rāma; like as the dense smoke of the fire of universal destruction confronts the sun, after spreading over the summit of the Meru.[37]

K says इति नियोजितसुग्रीवः (*chāyā* has नियमित) जाम्बवान् रामान्तेन रामसमीपेन (Kula also; रामपार्श्वेन MY) वलितः रामाभिमुखं निवृत्त इत्यर्थः। यथा प्रलयकालधूमसमूहः प्रथमं मेरुशिखरं परामृश्य पश्चात् सूर्याभिमुखो भवति तद्वदिति। सुग्रीवस्य पिङ्गलत्वात् मेरुसादृश्यम्।

Muda has चलितः for वलितः। Kula says इत्युक्तप्रकारेण नियमितः असत्पक्षं त्याजितः सुग्रीवो येन स तथा। . . . परिमृष्टं स्पर्शादाच्छादिततेजो मेरुशिखरं येन स तथा, सूरस्याभिमुखः प्रलयधूमोत्पीड इव। सुग्रीवस्य कनकगौरत्वात्, श्रीरामस्य वैष्णवतेजसा दीप्तत्वात्, जाम्बवतः कृष्णत्वात् उपमेयत्वम्।

---

35 Cf. 15.60.

36 Jāmavant.

37 Sugrīva's tall reddish figure is likened to the golden Meru mountain round which the sun and the other planets are said to revolve; while the black figure of Jāmavant is likened to the smoke, and Rāma to the sun.

38. जम्पइ अ किरणपम्हलफुरन्तदन्तप्पहाणिहाओत्थइअम्।
विणअपणअं वहन्तो समुहागअधवलकेसरसडं व मुहम्।।

[जल्पति च किरणपक्ष्मलस्फुरद्दन्तप्रभानिघातावस्तृतम्।
विनयप्रणतं वहन्संमुखागतधवलकेसरसटमिव मुखम्।।]

He spoke with his face lowered in humility. Covered with the lustre of his bright sparkling teeth, it seemed to be hidden by his white hair streaming in front.

K says किरणैः पक्ष्मलानां पूर्णानां दन्तानां प्रभानिकायेन प्रभासमूहेन स्थगितम् (*chāyā* has अवच्छादितम्), तदानीं संमुखागतधवलकेसरसटमिव दृश्यमानं विनयेनावनतं मुखं वहन् जाम्बवान् जल्पति स्म च। जाम्बवान कृष्णवर्णः। तस्य तु दन्तप्रभा धवलकेसरत्वेनोत्प्रक्षिता।

My says *ṇihāa ṇinkāa otthaiaṁ* अवस्थगितम्[38]। *occhaiaṁ* (?) इति वा पाठः। तदा अवच्छादितमित्यर्थः। (cf. K above). Kula says स्फुरतां दन्तानां प्रभानिवहेन अवस्थगितम्। R *chāyā* has अवस्तृतम्।

39. रक्खिज्जइ तेल्लोक्कं पलअसमुद्दविहुरा धरिज्जइ वसुहा।
उअरद्धन्तपहुत्ते विमुहज्जइ साअरे त्ति विम्हअणिज्जम्।।

[रक्ष्यते त्रैलोक्यं प्रलयसमुद्रविधुरा ध्रियते वसुधा।
उदरार्धान्तप्रभूते विमुह्यते सागर इति विस्मयनीयम्।।]

Thou dost protect the universe, and support the earth, overwhelmed by the ocean during the deluge.[39] It is amazing that thou art perplexed in regard to the sea that fills only a part of thy belly.

K, MY and Muda read मह्यते for *vimuhijjai* विमुह्यते (R). Kula is here incomplete in our copy. MY says *mujjhijjai* मुह्यते।

K says उदरार्धान्तप्रभूते उदरैकदेशपर्याप्ते सागरे विषये मुह्यते मोहः प्राप्यते। MY says उदरैकदेशमात्रस्यापि कथंचित् पर्याप्ते। Kula says उदरैकदेशसंमिते। Muda says उदरपर्यन्तप्रभूते, as he explains *addhanta* as पर्यन्त, quoting *Deśīnamamālā* 1.8.

40. धणुवावारस्स रणे कुविअकअन्तणिमिसन्तरणिहस्स तुहम्।
फुडविज्जुविलसिअस्स व आरम्भो च्चिअ ण होइ किं अवसाणम्।।

---

[38] Our copy has अवस्थितं।

[39] The reference is to the Boar incarnation of Viṣṇu with whom Rāma is identified.

[धनुर्व्यापारस्य रणे कुपितकृतान्तनिमेषान्तरनिभस्य तव।
स्फुटविद्युद्विलसितस्येवारम्भ एव न भवति किमवसानम्।।]

Is not the very start of the action of thy bow in war also its end, like that of a brilliant flash of lightning, destructive as it is like a wink of the wrathful god of death?[40]

K says रणे तव कुपितकृतान्तनिमेषान्तरसदृशस्य धनुर्व्यापारस्य आरम्भ एव अवसानं (किं) न भवति। किमिव – स्फुटविद्युद्विलसितस्येव। विद्युतूस्फुरणस्य आरम्भ एव अवसानं यथा भवति तद्वदिति। यदा त्वद्धनुषि शरं संदधासि तदैव शत्रुः निहतः स्यादित्यर्थः।

MY says विद्युतः क्षणस्थितकालतया यथारम्भ एव अवसानं तथा धनुर्व्यापारस्यापि उत्पत्तिक्षण एव कृतसकलकार्यतया द्वितीयक्षणे नावस्थानमित्यर्थः। Muda says त्वदीयधनुर्व्यापारस्य आरम्भ एवावसानं न भवति किम्। अपि तु भवत्येव। उपक्रमसमन्तरमेव फलप्राप्तिर्भविष्यतीत्यर्थः। Kula says कुपितस्य कृतान्तस्य यत् निमेषान्तरं क्षयहेतुः सूक्ष्मकालविशेषः तन्निभस्य धनुर्व्यापारस्य। . . . धनुर्व्यापारारम्भ एव शत्रुविनाशक्षणः, तेन . . . धनुषा दुष्करमपि साध्यते किं पुनः समुद्र इति भावः। MY says अक्षिपक्ष्मस्पन्दक्षणनिभस्येति कृतान्तस्य कपोलोपलक्षितः निमेषक्षणो जातमात्र उव विनाशहेतुर्न द्वितीयक्षणं यावत् विलम्बित इति। स दृष्टान्तीकृतः। R says क्रुद्धस्य यमस्य निमेषान्तरं द्वितीयनिमेषः तत्तुल्यस्य। एकनिमेषा(न)न्तरं यावत् परो निमेषो भवति तावदभ्यन्तर एव सकलशत्रुनाशादिकार्यनिर्वाहकत्वात्।

41. णिव्वुब्भइ पलअभरो तीरइ वलवामुहाणलो वि विसहिउम्।
दिण्णं जेणेअ तुमे कह काहिइ साअरो तहिं चिअ धीरम्।।

[निरुह्यते प्रलयभरस्तीर्यते वडवामुखानलोऽपि विसोढुम्।
दत्तं येनैव त्वया कथं करिष्यति सागरस्तस्मिन्नेव धैर्यम्।।]

How will the ocean maintain even against thee the fortitude[41] bestowed on it by thyself, by dint of which it fulfils its task during the deluge,[42] and can endure even the submarine fire?

K says अनेन समुद्रेण प्रलयभरः प्रलये सति जगत्प्लावनभरो निर्वर्त्यते (निरुह्यते *chāyā*). Muda says निरुह्यते निर्वाहं नीयते इत्यर्थः। K says वडवामुखानलोऽपि

---

[40] Lit. like the second wink, i.e. the destruction is completed in the interval between two winks. The bow is fancied as destroying the enemy in the twinkling of an eye; its action thus ends as soon as it begins.

[41] I.e. its unyielding nature making it difficult to cross.

[42] I.e. submerges the earth.

सोढुं शक्यते। एतत् सर्व वैभवमस्मै येन त्वयैव दत्तं तस्मिन्नेव त्वयि स धैर्यं कथं करिष्यति। सर्वदा मार्गं दास्यत्येवेत्यर्थः।

42–43. तो पाअडदोव्वल्लं पम्हट्ठपिआपओहरप्फरिससुहम्।
वच्छं तमालणीलं पुणो पुणो वामकरअलेन मलेन्तो।।
उअहिस्स जसेण जसं धीरं धीरेण गरुअआइ गरुअअम्।
रामो वि थिईअ ठिइं भणइ रवेण अ रवं समुप्फुन्दन्तो।।
(जुग्गअम्)

[ततः प्रकटदौर्बल्यं प्रस्मृतप्रियापयोधरस्पर्शसुखम्।
वक्षस्तमालनीलं पुनः पुनर्वामकरतलेन मृद्रन्।।
उदधेर्यशसा यशो धैर्य धैर्येण गुरुतया गुरुताम्।
रामोऽपि स्थित्या स्थितिं भणति रवेण च रवं समाक्रामन्।।]
(युग्मकम्)

Rāma then spoke as he rubbed his breast, dark as the leaves of a *tamāla* tree, with his left hand time and again; it had manifestly weakened, and forgotten the joy of the touch of his beloved's bosom. He drowned the noise of the sea with his voice, and eclipsed its fame with his own fame; its fortitude with his own fortitude; its strength with his own strength; and its firmness with his own firmness.

K (*chāyā*) has प्रमुषितप्रियापयोधरसुखस्पर्शम्। K's gloss on this verse is incomplete. He says मृद्नन् परामृशन्। कार्यगौरवविमर्शात् वक्षःस्थलस्पर्शः। My says *pamhu*(*ṭṭha*) प्रस्मृतं। Muda has प्रमृष्टप्रियापयोधरस्पर्शसुखम्। Kula has प्रभ्रष्ट (*pabbhaṭṭha*, cf. *SC* text) for *pamhaṭṭha* (R who says प्रस्मृतं विस्मृतं प्रभ्रष्टं वा, etc.)।[43]

K (*chāyā*) has रामः स्थित्या च स्थिति in the second line. K says रामः उदधेर्यशःप्रभृतीन् गुणान् आत्मनो यशःप्रभृतिभिरधःकुर्वन् (समुन्मार्जन् *chāyā*) भणति स्म। स्थितिर्मर्यादा।

MY says *pundanto* (*phu-* ?) आक्रामन् (Muda adds न्यक्कुर्वन्)। यशःप्रभृतिभिर्गुणैः समुद्रमतिशयान इत्यर्थः। Kula's reading is illegible, but he renders it as आच्छादयन् – स्थित्या च त्रिभुवनव्यवस्थाकारिण्या

[43] Kula is here incomplete, but says . . . तमालनीलं वक्षः समाश्वासयन्निव वामाङ्गस्यात्यन्तप्रियापरिचितत्वात् वामकरतलेन पुनः पुनः मृद्नन् परिमृशन्।

स्थितिं, रवेण च सजलजलधरगम्भीरेण महापुरुषलक्षणेन रवं . . . आच्छादयन्। *SC* reproduces Kula, but it reads *samupphullanto* (?) for *samupphudanto*. R has समाक्रामन्। *SC chāyā* has समुद्भ्रंशयन्।

44. दुत्तारम्मि समुद्दे कइलोए विमुहिए ममम्मि विसण्णे।
हरिवइ तुमे च्चिअ इमा दुव्वोज्झा वि अवलम्बिआ कज्जधुरा।।

[दुस्तारे समुद्रे कपिलोके विमुग्धे मयि विषण्णे।
हरिपते त्वय्येवेयं दुर्वाह्याप्यवलम्बिता कार्यधुरा।।]

Lord of the apes,[44] while the ocean remains untraversable, and the apes are stupefied, and myself downhearted, thou alone hast assumed the burden of this enterprise, even though heavy.

K says इयं कार्यधुरा दुर्वहापि त्वयैव अवलम्बिता। अस्य कार्यस्य त्वमेव अवलम्बनमित्यर्थः। Muda and Kula slso have त्वयैव। R has त्वयि एव। Kula syas त्वयैव केवलमियं कार्यधुरां अध्यवसायादवलम्बिता गृहीता। MY says *vimuhie* विमूढे विमुखिते वा।

45. धीराहि सारगरुअं अलङ्घणिज्जाहि सासअसमुज्जोअम्।
रिच्छाहिवाहि वअणं रअणं रअणाअराहि व समुच्छलिअम्।।

[धीरात्सागरगुरुकमलङ्घनीयाच्छाश्वतिकयश उद्द्योतम्।
ऋक्षाधिपाद्वचनं रत्नं रत्नाकरादिव समुच्छलितम्।।]

Just as the precious, ever glorious gems emerge from the calm untraversable ocean; similarly, weighty words, the source of ever brilliant fame, emanated from Jāmavant who was sedate and unassailable.

K and Muda read समुच्चलितम् for समुच्छ – (R and Kula)। K says सारगुरु अर्थसारेण गुरु। Kula says एकत्र धीरात् विचक्षणात्, अन्यत्र धैर्यवतः। एकत्र साध्योपदर्शकत्वम्, अन्यत्र महार्घत्वं सारस्तेन गुरुकम्।

46. जत्थ परमत्थगरुआ ण होन्ति तुम्हारिसा थिरववट्ठम्भा।
महिहरमुक्क व्व मही अत्थाअइ तत्थ वित्थरा कज्जधुरा।।

[यत्र परमार्थगुरवो न भवन्ति युष्मादृशाः स्थिरव्यवष्टम्भाः।
महीधरमुक्तेव मही अस्तायते तत्र विस्तृता कार्यधुरा।।]

---

[44] Ref. to Sugrīva.

A vast enterprise collapses where there is no truly great stable support like yourselves; even as the earth sinks when deprived of the support of the mountains.[45]

K says परमार्थेन याथार्थ्येन गुरवो युष्मादृशाः पुरुषाः यत्र राष्ट्रे स्थिरव्यवष्टम्भाः स्थिरवलम्बा न भवन्ति कृच्छ्रेषु अवलम्बा न भवन्ति तत्र विस्तृता कार्यधुरा अस्तमेति नश्यति। स्थिरवष्टम्भभूतैः महीधरैः मुक्ता महीव। Muda says व्यवष्टम्भः सामर्थ्यम्। अस्तायते क्षिप्ता भवति। Kula says महीधरैः कुलशैलैः मुक्ता महीव विस्तृता महती कार्यधुरा अस्तायते नश्यति, जलधौ निमज्जति च।

47. पडिवत्तिमेत्तसारं कज्जं थोआवसेसिअं मारुइणा।
संपइ जो च्चेअ उरं देइ पवङ्गाण पिअइ सो च्चेअ जसम्।।

[प्रतिपत्तिमात्रसारं कार्यं स्तोकावशेषितं मारुतिना।
संप्रति य एव उरो ददाति प्लवगानां पिबति स एव यशः।।]

Hanumat hath almost achieved the task, the core of which was to know (the whereabouts of Sītā). Whosoever among the apes now applies himself to it can attain fame.

K and Muda read प्लवङ्गेषु for *pavaṁgāṇa* (R and Kula).

K says इदं कार्यं रावणवधकृत्यं मारुतिना स्तोकावशेषितं समुद्रमुल्लङ्घ्य लङ्कामवगाह्य दृष्ट्वा देवीं प्रमदवनमवचूर्ण्य बहूनक्षप्रभृतीन् राक्षसान् निहत्य रावणं च निर्भर्त्स्य पुनरागतेन हनुमता भूयिष्ठं निर्वर्तितमेव कार्यम्। अत एव प्रतिपत्तिमात्रसारं, बुद्ध्या ग्रहणं प्रतिपत्तिः, तावन्मात्रसारं कृतम्। संप्रति प्लवङ्गेषु य एव उरो ददाति अहमेतत् करिष्यामिति अभिमुखीभवतीत्यर्थः स एव यशः पिबति नान्य इति।

MY says हनूमता निर्वृत्तप्रायतया अल्पशेषमीषत्करं कार्यमिति हरीन् प्रोत्साहयति। प्रतिपत्तिः करिष्यामीत्यभ्युपगमः, तन्मात्रमेव साधनतया सारं यत्र तत्तथा। अथवा प्रतिपत्तिः देवीवृत्तान्तावगतिः। सा च हनूमता कृतेति स्वल्पमेवावशिष्यते रावणवधस्येषत्करत्वादिति। . . . उरो ददाति प्रतीच्छति प्रतिपद्यत इत्यर्थः। R says प्रतिपत्तिः सीतावार्ताज्ञानं तन्मात्रं सारं मुख्यं प्रयोजनं यत्र। . . . तथा च वार्ताज्ञानमेव दुःशकमासीत् तत् प्रकृते हनूमता निष्पादितमेव।

Muda says प्रतिपत्तिः ज्ञानम्। अत्र सीता तिष्ठतीति ज्ञानमेव कार्ये सारम्। उरोदानं प्रवृत्युन्मुखत्वम्। प्रतिपत्तिः पदप्राप्तौ प्रवृत्तौ (?) गौरवेऽपि च। प्रबुद्धे ज्ञानसंपत्तौ प्रतिपत्तिः प्रयुज्यत इति विश्वः। Printed edition of विश्वप्रकाश has प्रागल्भ्ये च प्रबोधे च प्रतिपत्तिः प्रयुज्यते। Kula says अस्ति सीतेति प्रतिपत्तिः बोधः (?) तन्मात्रमेव सारो यस्य तत् कार्यं मारुतिना स्तोकावशेषितम्। प्रतिपत्तिश्चेत् कृता कार्यं

[45] The mountains with their deep roots are fancied as supporting the earth.

सिद्धमेव . . . । संप्रति पूवङ्गानां मध्ये य एवोरः सत्त्वाधिष्ठानं (?) हृदयं ददाति स एव यशः पिबति।

48. ता सव्वे च्चिअ समअं दुत्तारं पि हणुमन्तसुहवोलीणम्।
अब्भत्थेम्ह सुरासुरणिव्वूढब्भत्थणाअरं मअरहरम्।।

[तावत्सर्व एव समं दुस्तारमपि हनूमत्सुखव्यतिक्रान्तम्।
अभ्यर्थयामः सुरासुरनिर्व्यूढाभ्यर्थनादरं मकरगृहम्।।]

So let us all together entreat the ocean,[46] which, though untraversable, hath easily been crossed by Hanumat, and hath treated with respect diverse requests of the gods and demons.

All except R read *taṁ* (तत्) for *tā* (तावत्)। K and MY *pratīka* has *taṁ savvaccia*. Kula says तत् तस्मात्।

K says वयं सर्वेऽपि मकरगृहं मार्गनिमित्तमभ्यर्थयामहे (Muda also). MY has अभ्यर्थयेमहि। K says सुरासुराणां निर्व्यूढो निर्वर्तितः अभ्यर्थनादरः अमृताद्यभ्यर्थनादरो येन तम्। अभ्यर्थनाभर इति च पाठः। Kula says सुरासुराणां निर्व्यूढ ईप्सितसंपादनात् निर्वाहितः अभ्यर्थनायामादरो गौरवं येन।

49. अह णिक्कारणगहिअं मए वि अब्भत्थिओ ण मोच्छिहि धीरम्।
ता पेच्छह बोलीणं विहुओ अहिजन्तणं थलेण कइबलम्।।

[अथ निष्कारणगृहीतं मयाप्यभ्यर्थितो न मोक्ष्यति धैर्यम्।
तत्पश्यत व्यतिक्रान्तं विधुतोदधियन्त्रणं स्थलेन कपिबलम्।।]

But if it doth not give up its obduracy maintained without reason, even when implored by me, ye will behold the host of apes gone to the other shore by land, having swept away the barrier of the sea!

K, Muda, Kula and probably MY read ततः (*to*) for *tā* (R text). R commentary has ततः। Kula says विधुतोदधियन्त्रणं निराकृतसमुद्रविरोधं कपिबलम्। MY says अपेक्षिताकरणलक्षणं धैर्यमस्मदवलेपाभावेऽपि यदि गृहीत्वा न मुञ्चेत् तदा चतुर्थोपायः प्रयोक्ष्यत इत्यर्थः। यन्त्रणा प्रतिबन्धः। Muda says स्थलेनातिक्रान्तं पश्यतेत्यन्वयः। अब्धिं स्थलीं करिष्यामीति भावः।

50. जत्थ महं पडिउत्थो वसिहिइ अण्णस्स कह तहिं चिअ रोसो।
दिट्ठिं पाडेइ जहिं दिट्ठिविसो तं पुणो ण पेच्छइ बिइओ।।

[46] I.e. for passage to Laṅkā.

[यत्र मम पर्युषितो वत्स्यत्यन्यस्य कथं तस्मिन्नेव रोषः।
दृष्टिं पातयति यत्र दृष्टिविषस्तं पुनर्न पश्यति द्वितीयः।।]

How will one who becomes the object of my wrath be the object of another's wrath?[47] He that is beheld by serpent with venom in its eyes is not seen again by another of its kind.[48]

K reads परिवृद्धः for *padiuttho* प्रत्युषितः (Muda); पर्युषितः (R and Kula)।

K says यत्र विषये मम रोषः परिवृद्धः तत्रैव अन्यस्य रोषः कथं वत्स्यति। अस्मद्रोषेणैव नाशितत्वादित्यर्थः। तथा हि दृष्टिविषः सर्पो यस्मिन् दृष्टिं पातयति तं पुनः द्वितीयः सर्पो न हि पश्यति। R says यत्र विषये मम रोषः परिसर्वतोभावेनोषितः अवस्थितः।

51. ताव अ सहसुप्पण्णा णवाअवालिद्धकसणमिहिआअम्बा।
मउलप्पहाणुविद्धा आढत्ता दीसिउं णिसिअरच्छाया।।

[तावच्च सहसोत्पन्ना नवातपाश्लिष्टकृष्णमेघिकाताम्रा।
मौलि मुकुटप्रभानुविद्धा आरब्धा द्रष्टुं निशिचरच्छाया।।]

Meanwhile, the suddenly emerging lustre of a multitude of demons began to be seen in the sky. Blending with the glitter of their crowns, it[49] appeared to be reddish like patches of dark clouds suffused with the glow of the morning sun.

K says तापच्च तस्मिन्नवसरे व सहसा उत्पन्ना, मकुटप्रभानुविद्धा मिश्रिता, अत एव नवातपस्पृष्टकृष्णमेघवत् आताम्रा निशिचराणां छाया प्रभा द्रष्टुमारब्धा। द्रष्टुमिति कर्मणि तुमुन्।

MY says *āliddhā* स्पृष्टा। *dīsiuṁ* आविर्भवितुम्। दर्शनस्य कर्म भवितुम्। Muda says द्रष्टुं दृग्गोचरीभवितुम्। He has नवातपश्लिष्ट। Kula says मेघिका तनुमेघावली। He seems to have नवातपालीढ (cf. *SC*). *SC* text has *mauḍa* for *maula* मुकुट।

52. तो गमणवेअमारुअमुहलपडद्धन्तणहणिराइअजलए।
पेच्छन्ति रविअरन्तरघोलाविअपिहुलविज्जुले रअणिअरे।।

[ततो गमनवेगमारुतमुखरपटार्धान्तनभोनिरायतजलदान्।
प्रेक्षन्ते रविकरान्तरघूर्णितपृथुलविद्युतो रजनीचरान्।।]

47 I.e. will not live to incur the wrath of another person.

48 Such a serpent is believed to kill its victim with its eyes.

49 I.e. the black colour of the demons.

They then beheld the demons, who scattered the clouds in the sky with the fringes of their robes, rustling in the gust of wind caused by their speed, with massive flashes of lightning playing in the sunlight.[50]

K, MY and Muda read विधुत (*vihua*) for *pihula* पृथुल (R and Kula)।

K says ततस्ते रजनिचरान् पश्यन्ति स्म। कथंभूतान् – गमनवेगमारुतमुखरैः पटार्धान्तैः पटप्रान्तैः नभसि दीर्घीकृतजलदान्, रविकरान्तरघूर्णितविधुतविद्युतः, अन्तरशब्दः सदृशपर्यायः, स्थानेऽन्तरतम इत्यादिवत्,[51] मेघेषु दीर्घीक्रियमाणेषु तद्गता विद्युतोऽपि दीर्घीभवन्ति, रविकरसदृशा घूर्णिताः भ्रमिता विधुताश्च मेघस्था विद्युतो यैरिति बहुव्रीहिः। तान् पश्यन्ति स्म रामादयः।

MY reads *ṇiha* for *ṇaha* — पटार्धान्तनिभ (cf. Kula). MY and Muda have *ṇirāvia* explained as दीर्घीकृत for *ṇirāia* (निरायत R) in the same sense. K (*chāyā*) has निरायतीकृत। R renders *ṇirāia* also as निराकृत। This is found in Kula whose reading seems however to be different. Kula says वेगगमने यो मारुतस्तेन मुखरैः पटार्धान्तैः नभसि निराकृता निर्भर्त्सिताः सशब्दत्वात् कृष्णत्वाच्च जलदा यैस्तान्। He seems to read *ṇirāaa*[52] as he mentions *ṇirāia* as a variant. He says (*ṇiha*) *ṇirāiajalae* इति पाठे तु ये पटार्धान्ताः तन्निभा निराजिताः शोभिता जलदा येषु तान्।[53]

Muda says पटपर्यन्तैः नभसि *ṇirāvia* दीर्घीकृता जलदा यैस्तान्। रविकरमध्ये भ्रमिता विधुता विद्युत् यैस्तान्। R says यद्वा तादृशैः पटार्धान्तैः नभसि निराकृता बहिःस्फोटिता जलदा येभ्यस्तान्। वस्त्रैरेव मेघानामपाकृतत्वादित्यर्थः।

MY reads *bolāvia* rendered as आक्रान्त for *gholāvia* (घूर्णित)। He says रविकराणामन्तरे करचणादिना लङ्घिताः पुनः विधुताश्च मेघमर्दजनिता विद्युते यैस्तान्। क्वचित् *gholāvia* इति पाठः। तदा दुर्दिनं विनैव कराणां मध्येऽपि घूर्णितविधुतविद्युतः उत्पातस्फरितविद्युत् इत्यर्थः। Kula says मेघसाम्य-पोषणार्थमेवाह – रविकरा एवान्तरे मध्ये घूर्णिता भ्रमिताः पृथुला विद्युतो येषु तान्। एतेन सशब्दस्फुरितविद्युन्नवमेघानिव व्यापकान् निशाचरान् प्रेक्षन्ते।

53. तो णहअलावडन्ते पलउप्पाअ व्व णिसिअरे अहिलेउम्।
उण्णामिअगिरिसिहरं चलिअं महिमण्डलं व वाणरसेण्णम्।।

---

[50] Regarded as phenomenon of bad omen. See Mādhava in Extracts.

[51] Pāṇini 1.1.50. *Kāśikā* says स्थाने प्राप्यमाणानामन्तरतम आदेशो भवति सदृशतमः।

[52] This reading is found in manuscript RH of Goldschmidt.

[53] *SC* which anonymously reproduces Kula has *ṇirājia*, which is hardly Prākṛta. Besides, राजित appears in our poem as *rāia* (1.56; 2.29; 7.43).

[ततो नभस्तलावपततः प्रलयोत्पातानिव निशिचरानभिलवितुम्।
उन्नामितगिरिशिखरं चलितं महीमण्डलमिव वानरसैन्यम्।।]

As the demons descended from the sky, like meteors at the epoch of universal ruin, the host of apes made a move to attack them, even as the earth moves at that epoch, raising the mountain peaks.[54]

K, MY, Muda and Kula read *ovaḍanta* for *āvaḍanta* (R).

K says ततः प्रलयोत्पातानिव नभस्तलादवपततः निशिचरान् अभिलेतुमभियोक्तुं वानरसैन्यं चलितम्। कथंभूतम् – प्रहरणार्थमुन्नमितगिरिशिखरं महीमण्डलमिव चलितम्।

MY says *ahileuṁ* प्राप्तुम्। प्रलयदशायामुत्पातेषु नभस्तलादवपतत्सु महीमण्डलमपि यथोर्ध्वं प्रत्युच्चलितं तथेत्यर्थः। Muda says अभिलेतुमभिगन्तुम्। लीङ्श्लेषणे।

54. ओसुम्मन्तजलहरं विसमट्ठिअकइबलवलन्तालोअम्।
दीसइ भमन्तविहडं थाणप्फिडिअसिढिलं पडन्तं व णहम्।।

[अवपात्यमानजलधरं विषमस्थितकपिबलवलदालोकम्।
दृश्यते भ्रमद्विह्वलं स्थानस्फेटितशिथिलं पतदिव नभः।।]

The sky, with the clouds scattered below,[55] and appearing to move as the host of apes took their stand on high and low ground,[56] seemed to be falling, displaced and loose, and helpless and reeling.

K and MY *pratīka* has *osubbhanta* for *osumbhanta*. K, Muda and probably MY read *calanta* for *valanta* (R and Kula). Kula reads *visamuṭṭhia* for *visama-* and *vialaṁ* (विकलं) for *vihaḍaṁ* (विह्वलं)। Cf. *SC* text.

K says विषमस्थितैरुत्तराधरभावेन स्थितैः प्लवगबलैः चलदालोकमनवस्थितदर्शनम्, अवपात्यमानजलदं नभः स्थानभ्रष्टशिथिलं भूत्वा पतदिवादृश्यत।

K says निपात्यमानमेघं, विषमोत्थितेन प्लवगबलेन देहवितानैरुत्क्षिप्तमिव वलमानालोकमावर्जितमिव दृश्यमानम्, अतएव स्थानभ्रष्टं सत् शिथिलं भ्रमद्विकलं नभः पतदिव दृश्यते। R says विषमस्थितमुपरिपतनभिया बहिर्बहिरवस्थितं यत् कपिबलं तस्य वलन् आलोको दर्शनं यत्र।

---

[54] The reference is to the convulsive movements of the earth at the epoch of destruction. Cf. Mādhava in Extracts.

[55] I.e. by the demons as they rushed down from the sky.

[56] Cf. Mādhava in Extracts.

MY says *vihalaṁ* विह्वलम्। आकाशसंयोगिनां मेघानां प्लवग(?)लोकस्य च पतनचलनाभ्यां नभस्तलमपि पतति चलतीति प्रतिभासादेवमुक्तम्। MY, Muda and Kula render *phiḍia* as भ्रष्ट like K. R renders it as स्फेटित अवक्षिप्त।

55. णवरि अ लङ्कादिट्ठो दिट्ठसहाओ विहीसणो मारुइणा।
णिअमेऊण कइबलं बीओदन्तो व्व राहवस्स उवणिओ।।

[अनन्तरं च लङ्कादृष्टो दृष्टस्वभावो विभीषणो मारुतिना।
नियम्य कपिबलं द्वितीयोदन्त इव राघवस्योपनीतः।।]

Thereupon Hanumat held the host of apes in check, and brought Vibhīṣaṇa to Rāma, as if he were a second message from Laṅkā;[57] (Vibhīṣaṇa) whom he had seen there, and whose nature he had observed.

Kula says सुचरितो धार्मिकः परमवैष्णवो विभीषणः परमाश्वासस्थानत्वात् द्वितीयोदन्त इव।

56. चलणोणअणिहुअस्स अ माणेण व करअलेण से रहुवइणा।
उण्णामिअं णणु सिरं जाअं रक्खसउलाहि दूरब्भहिअम्।।

[चरणावनतनिभृतस्य च मानेनेव करतलेनास्य रघुपतिना।
उन्नामितं ननु शिरो जातं राक्षसकुलाद्दूराभ्यधिकम्।।]

As he bowed down at Rāma's feet in humility, the latter raised his head from the ground with his hands, as a mark of honour; verily it was thereby exalted high above the race of demons.

K and Kula read रघुपतेः for *rahuvatṇā* (R and Muda).

K says चरणयोरवनतस्य निभृतस्य अतिप्रश्रितस्य चास्य शिरो रघुपतेः करतलेन मानेनेव पूजाविशेषेणेव उन्नमितं महीतलादुत्थापितं राक्षसकुलात् दूरमभ्यधिकं जातं ननु। MY says राक्षसवंशात् पृथग्भूय दूरमभ्यधिकं गुणातिशयवत् जातमित्यर्थः।

K says चरणोपनतश्चासौ निभृतः विनयसंयतश्चेति तस्य विभीषणस्य शिरः रघुपतेः करतलेनोत्साहजनकत्वात् मानेनेवोल्लासितं सत् ननु निश्चितं राक्षसकुलात् दूरभ्यधिकं दृष्टं जातम्। Kula seems to read *ullāsiaṁ* for *uṇṇāmiaṁ*.

57. ववसिअणिवेइअत्थो सो मारुइलद्धपच्चआगअहरिसम्।
सुग्गीवेण उरत्थलवणमालामलिअमहुअरं उवऊढो।।

---

[57] For the first message see 1.37 ff.

[व्यवसितनिवेदितार्थः स मारुतिलब्धप्रत्ययागतहर्षम्।
सुग्रीवेणोरःस्थलवनमालामृदितमधुकरमुपगूढः।।]

Vibhīṣaṇa, pleased with Hanumat's confidence in him, intimated his resolve (to side with Rāma). Sugrīva, thereupon, embraced him, crushing the bees hidden in the garland of sylvan flowers on his breast.

K, My, Muda and Kula red *hariso* for *harisaṁ* (R).

K takes व्यवसितनिवेदितार्थः। as निवेदितव्यवसितार्थः, and says अर्थश्च रावणं परित्यज्य रामस्य शेषीभावः। मारुतिसकाशात् लब्धविश्वासत्वात् आगतहर्षः। MY says *vavasia-ṇivediattho* व्यवसितोऽर्थो निवेदितो यस्य। अध्यवसितोऽर्थः स्वागमनकार्यं निवेदितो यस्य येन वा स तथोक्तः। मारुतिना लब्धेन स्वविश्वासेन आत्मनो विश्वासपात्रत्वेन हृष्टः। Muda says निवेदितोद्युक्तार्थ इत्यर्थः। Kula says व्यवसितो रामेण . . . प्रतिज्ञातः तदभिप्रायवेदिना हनूमता निवेदितः कथितः अर्थः राक्षसपतित्वं प्रयोजनं यस्मै स तथा। अथवा रामेण व्यवसितः अनुष्ठितः सोपायं कथितः अर्थो रावणवधलक्षणो येन स तथा। मारुतिसकाशात् लब्धो यः प्रत्ययो विश्वासः तेन करणभूतेन आगतोऽनुबद्धो हर्षो यस्मिन् स तथा। Jagaddhara in his commentary on *Sarasvatīkaṇṭhābharaṇa* 4.171, where this verse is quoted says यद्वा व्यवसितः चिकीर्षितो रामसाहाय्यरूपो निवेदितोऽर्थो येन सः।

58. तो जम्पइ रहुतणओ समअं दससु वि दिसामुहेसु किरन्तो।
पअइसुकअस्स धवलं णीसन्दं व हिअअस्स दन्तुज्जोअम्।।

[ततो जल्पति रघुतनयः समकं दशस्वपि दिङ्मुखेषु किरन्।
प्रकृतिसुकृतस्य धवलं निःस्यन्दमिव हृदयस्य दन्तोद्योतम्।।]

Rāma then spoke, radiating the lustre of his teeth in the ten directions together, as if it were a bright emanation from his heart, pure by nature.

K, MY and Muda read विमलस्य for *sukaassa* (R) सुकृतस्य। K and Muda read विमलं for धवलं (R). Kula's gloss on this verse is missing in our copy.

59. ठाणं दवग्गिभीआ वणम्मि वणहत्थिणि व्व परिमग्गन्ती।
पेच्छह लद्धासाआ मोत्तुं रक्खसउलं ण इच्छइ लच्छी।।

[स्थानं दवाग्निभीता वने वनहस्तिनीव परिमृग्यन्ती।
पश्यत लब्धास्वादा मोक्तुं राक्षसकुलं नेच्छति लक्ष्मीः।।]

Behold. Like as a wild female elephant, scared by a frost fire, seeks a safe place in the forest, unwilling to leave it, having lived there happily; similarly, the goddess of prosperity is unwilling to forsake the race of demons, being happy (in her sojourn with them).[58]

K has त्रस्ता (*hitthā*) for *bhīā* भीता (R and Kula).

K says चिरं राक्षसकुलेषु लब्धास्वादा लब्धसुखरसा लक्ष्मीः राक्षसकुलं भोक्तुं नेच्छति। पश्यत। किमिव–दवाग्नित्रस्ता वनकरिणीव। वन एव स्थानं मार्गन्ती यथा तद्वनं परित्युक्तुं नेच्छति तद्वत् रावणस्य दुर्नयैः उद्विग्नापि राक्षसश्रीः चिरं लब्धसुखानु-भवत्वात् तत्रैव स्थतुमाश्रयमासादितवतीत्यर्थः। अनया गाथया रामेण विभीषणाय लङ्काराज्यं दत्तमित्युक्तं भवति। Kula says सीताहरणादवधारितरावणमरणा विभीषणं राक्षसलक्ष्मीः राक्षसराज्यप्राप्तये मत्समीपागमनाय प्रेरितवतीति भावः (partly restored from *SC*)।

60. णज्जइ विहीसण तुहं सोम्मसहावपरिवड्ढिअं विण्णाणम्।
दिट्ठिविसेहि व अमअं उअहिस्स णिसाअरेहि वि अविद्दविअम्।।

[ज्ञायते विभीषण तव सौम्यस्वभावपरिवर्धितं विज्ञानम्।
दृष्टिविषैरिवामृतमुदधेर्निशाचरैरप्यविद्रावितम्।।]

Vibhīṣaṇa, thy wisdom, enriched by thy genial nature, is known to be unimpaired even by thy kinship with the demons, even as the nectar of the ocean[59] was unspoilt by the venomous serpents.

K and Muda read सहवर्धितं for परि (R and Kula), and न for *a* (*viddaviaṁ*). Kula says तव सौम्येन स्वाभावेन परिवृद्धं विज्ञानं विवेकः। K says तव सौम्येन कल्याणेन स्वाभावेनैव सह वर्धितं विज्ञानं ज्ञायते। He says न विद्रावितं न विनाशितम्। Kula says ज्ञायते सुशीलत्वात् प्रतीयते। तेन संसर्गजा दोषगुणा भवन्तीत्येतदपि त्वया (त्वय्येव *SC*) व्यभिचरितमित्यर्थः।

61. सुद्धसहावेण फुडं फुरन्तपज्जत्तगुणमऊहेण तुमे।
चन्देण व णिअअमओ कलुसो वि पसाहिओ णिसाअरवंसो।।

[शुद्धस्वभावेन स्फुटं स्फुरत्पर्याप्तगुणमयूखेन त्वया।
चन्द्रेणेव निजकमृगः कलुषोऽपि प्रसाधितो निशाचरवंशः।।]

[58] I.e. the prosperity of the demons, endangered by the misdeeds of Rāvaṇa, will yet be safe in the hands of Vibhīṣaṇa who will soon replace him as the ruler of Laṅkā.

[59] I.e. in the period before the churning.

Endowed with stainless character and the lustre of manifold brilliant virtues, thou hast clearly adorned even the impure race of demons; like as the moon, pure by nature, with excellent radiant rays, lends charm to its deer, though it is a stain.

Kula says शुद्धो र्निदोषो निर्मलः स्वभावो यस्य तेन। स्फुरन्तः पर्याप्ता ये प्रेष्ठा गुणा एव मयूखा यस्य। पक्षे स्फुरन्तः पर्याप्तगुणा मयूखा यस्य। तेन त्वया चन्द्रेणेव निजकमृगः कलङ्कः कलुषोऽपि निशाचरवंशः स्फुटं प्रसारितः (प्रसाधितः?)। K says only नात्र दुर्बोधमस्ति। R says पर्याप्ता बहवः।

62. कह इर सकज्जकुसला कज्जगइं मइगुणेहि अवलम्बन्ता।
कुलमाणववट्ठम्भा ण होन्ति राअसिरिभाअणं सप्पुरिसा।।

[कथं किल स्वकार्यकुशलाः कार्यगतिं मतिगुणैरवलम्बमानाः।
कुलमानव्यवष्टम्भा न भवन्ति राजश्रीभाजनं सत्पुरुषाः।।]

Persons of character, effcient in their task, who adopt a course of action by applying their intellectual powers, and take their stand upon family tradition and self-respect — how can they fail to attain royal fortune?

K says स्वकार्यसाधने कुशलाः। अष्टौ बुद्धिगुणाः। यथाहुः – शुश्रूषा श्रवणं चैव ग्रहणं धारणं तथा। ऊहापोहोऽर्थविज्ञानं तत्त्वज्ञानं च धीगुणाः।। इति। एभिः मतिगुणै कार्यस्य गतिमवस्थाविशेषमवलम्बमानाः। अनवसादयन्तः, कुलस्य मानस्य च अवष्टम्भा (व्यवष्टम्भाः *chāyā*) आधारभूताः पुरुषाः भवादृशाः कथं राजश्रियो भाजनं न भवन्ति, अवश्यं भवन्त्येव। MY says बुद्धिगुणैः कार्यगतिमङ्गीकुर्वाणा धारयन्तः।

The verse is missing in our copy of Kula.

R says कुलमभिजनो मानोऽहंकारस्तौ व्यवष्टम्भ आश्रयो येषां ते। तदनुसारेण व्यवहरन्त इत्यर्थः।

63. लद्धासाएण चिरं सुरबन्दिपरिग्गहे णिसाअरवइणा।
सीआ रक्खसवसहिं दिट्ठिविसहरं विसोसहि व्व उवणिआ।।

[लब्धास्वादेन चिरं सुरबन्दिपरिग्रहे निशाचरपतिना।
सीता राक्षसवसतिं दृष्टिविषगृहं विषौषधिरिवोपनीता।।]

Having long enjoyed the capture of celestial maidens, Rāvaṇa hath brought Sītā to the abode of the demons, like as a poison-destroying plant is brought into a lair of venomous serpents.[60]

K says चिराय सुरबन्दीनां परिग्रहे लब्धास्वादेन रावणेन सीतापि तादृशीति मत्वा राक्षसवसतिमुपनीता विनाशाय। किमिव – दृष्टिविषाणां गृहं विषहरौषधिरिव। Kula explains परिग्रह as कलत्रीकरण, and says रावणेन सीता राक्षसवसतिं दृष्टिविषैः सर्पैः विषौषधिरिवोपनीता समीपं प्रापिता। सीतैव[61] तस्य विनाशहेतुर्भविष्यतीत्यर्थः। Kula reads *diṭṭhi- visehiṁ* (cf. *SC* text) for *diṭṭhi-visa-haraṁ*. *SC* text has *vasaiṁ* for *vasahiṁ* वसतिम्।

64. फिडिआ सुरसंखोहा बन्दिअणक्कन्दिअं गअं परिणामम्।
जाआ दहमुहगहिआ तिहुवणडिम्बस्स जाणई अवसाणम्।।

[स्फेटिताः सुरसंक्षोभा बन्दीजनाक्रन्दितं गतं परिणामम्।
जाता दशमुखगृहीता त्रिभुवनडिम्बस्य जानकी अवसानम्।।]

The anxieties of the gods are dispelled and the wails of the captive maids have come to an end. Sītā, held captive by Rāvaṇa, marks the end of the oppression of the world.[62]

K says सुराणां संक्षोभाः भ्रष्टाः नष्टाः। वन्दिजनानामाक्रन्दितं परिणामं गतं परिणतं समाप्तम्। किं बहुना। दशमुखगृहीता सीता त्रिभुवनोपद्रवस्य अवसानं जाता।

MY says *phiḍiā* भ्रष्टाः, and explains *ḍimba* as उपप्लव। Muda and Kula have विप्लव। R explains it as भय।

Kula says भ्रष्टाः सुराणां संक्षोभा विद्रवाः। . . . दशमुखेन गृहीत नीता जानकी त्रैलोक्यविप्लवस्य अवसानहेतुत्वादवसानं जाता, यथा विषं मृत्युरिति। जातेत्याशंसायां भूतवत् प्रयोगः। R says संक्षोभाः स्फेटिता अपगताः।

65. अह णअणेसु पहरिसं कण्णेसु पवङ्गवड्ढिअं जअसद्दम्।
सीसम्मि अ अहिसेअं पल्हत्थइ अ हिअअम्मि से अणुराअम्।।

[अथ नयनयोः प्रहर्षं कर्णयोः प्लवंगवर्धितं जयशब्दम्।
शीर्षे चाभिषेकं पर्यस्यति च हृदयेऽस्यानुरागम्।।]

---

[60] I.e. to drive them away. Serpents are believed to be unable to endure the smell of certain plants. Cf. 7.68 and 9.45. This belief is referred to in *Nāyādhammakahāo* in one of the verses quoted at the end of Chapter17: *ghāṇiṁdiya-duddaṁtattaṇassa aha ettio havaï dosoAjam osahi-gaṁdheṇaṁ bilāo niddhāvaī urago* AA 6AA — ed. N.V. Vaidya, Poona, 1940.

[61] Our copy has शिवैव।

[62] I.e. his destruction in the impending war for her recovery will deliver the world from his acts of violence.

Rāma, thereupon, poured consecrated water on Vibhīṣaṇa's head and brought joy to his eyes and the cheers of the apes to his ears, and inspired loyalty in his heart.[63]

K renders *palhatthai* as पर्यासयति निपातयति। MY says पर्यासयति स्म आर्पयदित्यर्थ:। अनुरागमिति स्वविषयविशेष:। Muda says पर्यस्यति स्म निक्षिप्तवानित्यर्थ:। दीपकमलंकार:। Kula says पर्यासयति आरोपयति। R says रामोऽस्य विभीषणस्य नयनयो: प्रहर्षमानन्दं पर्यस्यति विस्तारयति, etc.

इअ सिरिपवरसेणविरइए कालिदासकए दहमुहवहे महाकव्वे
चउट्ठो आसासओ समत्तो।

[इति श्रीप्रवरसेनविरचिते कालिदासकृते दशमुखवधे महाकाव्ये
चतुर्थ आश्वासक: समाप्त:।]

---

63. The verse describes the coronation of Vibhīṣaṇa.

पञ्चम आश्वासकः
Fifth Āśvāsakaḥ

1. अह जलणिहिम्मि अहिअं मअणे अ मिअङ्कदंसणविअम्भन्ते।
विरहविहुरस्स णज्जइ णिसा वि रामस्स वड्ढिउं आढत्ता।।

[अथ जलनिधावधिकं मदने च मृगाङ्कदर्शनविजृम्भमाणे।
विरहविधुरस्य ज्ञायते निशापि रामस्य वर्धितुमारब्धा।।]

Thereupon as the ocean surged up ever more as did the emotion of love, at the sight of the moon, it seemed to Rāma that the night, too, began to lengthen, overcome as he was with the grief of separation from Sītā.

निशापि पूर्वस्मात् परिमाणात् वर्धितुमारब्धेत्यज्ञायत, रघुपतेर्मनसेत्यध्याहार्यम् K. विरहविधुरस्य निशापि वर्धितुं प्रवृत्ता अक्षया रात्रिर्जातेत्याशयः Kula. रामस्य सम्बन्धिनी निशापि वर्धितुमारब्धवती इत्युत्प्रेक्ष्यत इत्यर्थः। यद्वा रामस्येति तृतीयार्थे षष्ठी। रामेणाज्ञायीत्यर्थः Muda.

2. उइअमिअङ्कं च णहं णिअमट्ठिअराहवं च साअरपुलिणम्।
णेन्ति परं परिवड्ढिं आलिङ्गिअचन्दिअं महोअहिसलिलम्।।

[उदितमृगाङ्कं च नभो नियमस्थितराघवं च सागरपुलिनम्।
नयतः परां परिवृद्धिमालिङ्गितचन्द्रिकं महोदधिसलिलम्।।]

The sky, with the rising moon, swelled overmuch the waters of the ocean, wrapped in moonlight; while the beach, with Rāma observing his vow,[1] heightened their splendour.

K remarks अत्र क्रमः। उदितचन्द्रं नभः आश्लिष्टचन्द्रिकं समुद्रसलिलम् अधिकां वृद्धिं निनाय। नियमस्थितराघवं सागरपुलिनं समुद्रमधिकां शोभां निनायेति।

Kula says उदितमृगाङ्कं च नभः, नियमेन अनशनविधिना स्थितो राघवो यत्र तत् सागरपुलिनञ्च महोदधिसलिलं परिवृद्धिं नयतः। द्विधा हि वृद्धिः। द्रव्यतो गुणतः। उदितचन्द्रेण जलस्य वृद्धिः, नियमस्थितराघवेण पुलिनेन गौरवगुणवद्धिः कृतेत्यर्थः।

MY says सचन्द्रस्य नभसः सरामस्य च पुलिनस्य न केवलं स्वरूपतः साम्यम्, अपि तु समुद्रसलिलसंवर्धनार्थक्रियातोऽपि। सरामपुलिनोदधिवर्धनं च रामतेजश्चन्द्रिकायाः

---

[1] Undertaken to induce the ocean to yield a passage to Laṅkā.

श्यामलायाः प्रसरन्त्याः तज्जलसारूप्यात्। नभसस्तु मुख्ययैव चन्द्रिकया तज्जलक्षोभहेतुत्वादिति मन्तव्यम्।

3. तो से विओअसुलहा णिअमविइण्णहिअअक्खिवणसोटीरा।
खउरेन्ति धिइग्गहणं जाअं जाअं विसूरणाविक्खेवा।।

[ततस्तस्य वियोगसुलभा नियमवितीर्णहृदयक्षेपणशौटीर्याः।
कलुषयन्ति धृतिग्रहणं जातं जातं खेदविक्षेपाः।।

Outbursts of grief, constant in his forlorn state, and strong enough to disquiet his heart, bent on the vow, marred his recurring efforts to maintain his fortitude.

K, Kula and Muda read अवक्षेपाः for *vikkhevā* (R). MY also says *visūraṇāvakkhevā*[2] चित्तखेदावक्षेपाः।

K says ततोऽस्य रामस्य वियोगे सुलभा, नियमाय दत्तस्य हृदयस्य क्षेपणे क्षोभणे समर्थाः (शौण्डीराः *chāyā*) खेदावक्षेपाः खेदाभिघाताः जातं जातं धैर्यग्रहणं कर्बुरयन्ति कलुषयन्ति स्म। खिदेर्विसूर इति विसूरादेशः।

Kula says 'विसूरणा' उद्वेगास्त एव चित्तमवक्षिपन्तीत्यवक्षेपाः ते दृढं समाधाय नियमे वितीर्णस्य दत्तस्य हृदयस्य विघाते शौटीराः शूराः, अतएव जातं जातं धृतिग्रहणं चित्तनिवृत्तिस्वीकारार्थं *khaurenti* मिश्रीभूय कलुषयन्तीति।

My says हृदयस्याक्षेपणसमर्थाः। . . . पुनःपुनः कथंचित् धृत्याहरणं पुनःपुनरपि तद्विच्छेद इति वा पारम्पर्येण आवर्तन्त इत्यर्थः।

Muda says क्षपण for क्षेपण। He says कर्बुरयन्ति शवलयन्ति आत्मना सहितं कुर्वन्तीत्यर्थः। अभीष्टार्थस्य संप्राप्तौ स्पृहापर्याप्तता धृतिः। ग्रहणमाहरणम्।

4. काहिइ पिअं समुद्दो गलिहिइ चन्दाअवो समप्पिहिइ णिसा।
अवि णाम धरेज्ज पिआ ओ णे विरहेज्ज जीविअं ति विसण्णो।।

[करिष्यति प्रियं समुद्रो गलिष्यति चन्द्रातपः समाप्स्यति निशा।
अपि नाम ध्रियेत प्रिया उत नो विरहयेज्जीवितमिति विषण्णः।।]

He grieved as he thought, "Will the ocean do a favour? Will the moonlight decay?[3] Will the night cease? Is my beloved perchance alive, or would she deprive me of my life?"

K says प्रिया धरेत् जीवेदपि नाम। अपि नामेति वितर्के। ओ अथवा अस्मान्

[2] *vi* for *va* in our copy is obviously a mistake.

[3] As a *virahin* he is impatient of the moonlight.

जीवितं विरहयेत् परित्याजयेदिति मत्वा विषण्णोऽभूत्। Muda says अपि नामेति संभावनायाम्। प्रिया जीवेत् किंवा त्यक्तजीविता अस्मानपि जीवितेन वियोजयेदिति विषण्णोऽभूदित्यर्थः। त्याजितैः फलमितिवदणौ कर्तुः कर्मत्वम्।

5. णिन्दइ मिअङ्कंकिरणे खिज्जइ कुसुमाउहे जुउच्छइ रअणिम्।
झीणो वि णवर झिज्जइ जीवेज्ज पिएत्ति मारुइं पुच्छन्तो।।

[निन्दति मृगाङ्ककिरणान्खिद्यते कुसुमायुधे जुगुप्सते रजनीम्।
क्षीणोऽपि केवलं क्षीयते जीवेत् प्रियेति मारुतिं पृच्छन्।।]

He reproached the moonbeams; suffered because of the flower-sorrowed god, and hated the night. Even though languid, he languished still more even as he asked Hanumat, "Is my beloved haply alive?"

K reads *khippai kusumāuhaṁ* for *khijjai kusumāuhe* खिद्यतेः कुसुमायुधे। K explains his reading as कुसुमायुधं क्षिपति अधिक्षिपति। K and MY read क्षौणः केवलं याप्यते for *jhīṇo vi ṇavara jhijjai* (R) — क्षीणोऽपि केवलं क्षीयते।

K says क्षीणः सः प्रिया जीवेत् किमिति मारुतिं पृच्छन् तेन हनुमता यत्तदुक्त्वा याप्यते कालक्षेपं कार्यते स्म। MY says *javijjai* यापयति स्म कालमिति शेषः। अथवा प्रिया जीवेन्न वेति मारुतिं पृच्छन् मारुतिना याप्यते विनोद्यत इत्यर्थः।

Kula seems to read *jhīṇo ṇavara dharijjai* (cf. *SC* text), which is mentioned by R as a variant. He says केवलं क्षीणोऽपि संधार्यते मारुतिनेत्यर्थवशात्। But *SC* (commentary) which anonymously reproduces Kula's gloss on the verse has याप्यते संधार्यते so that Kula's reading might be same as that of K and MY (see above).

6. एत्तो वसइत्ति दिसा एणं सा णूण णिन्दइ त्ति मिअङ्को।
एत्त णिसण्णेत्ति मही एएण णिअ त्ति से णहं पि बहुमअम्।।

[इतो वसतीति दिक् एनं सा नूनं निन्दतीति मृगाङ्कः।
अत्र निषण्णेति मही एतेन नीतेत्यस्य नभोऽपि बहुमतम्।।]

He valued the southern region, because she lived thereabout;[4] the moon, because she verily reproached it;[5]

[4] I.e. in Laṅkā.

[5] I.e. tolerated the unpleasant moon, because it was censured by Sītā as she pined for him.

the earth, because she reposed thereon; and the sky, because she was carried off athwart it.[6]

7. धीरेण णिसाआमा हिअएण समं अणिट्ठिआ उवएसा।
उच्छाहेण सह भुआ बाहेण समं गलन्ति से उल्लावा।।

[धैर्येण निशायामा हृदयेन सममनिष्ठिता उपदेशाः।
उत्साहेन सह भुजौ बाष्पेण समं गलन्त्यस्योल्लापाः।।]

The watches of the night vanished with his patience. The fleeting counsel (of his friends) faded away along with his fortitude. His arms drooped as did his spirits, and incoherent utterances issued forth along with his tears.

K says अनिष्ठिता अलब्धास्पदाः (अस्थिराः R) उपदेशाः हनुमत्प्रभृतिभिरुच्यमानाः हृदयेन समं गलन्ति स्म। उत्साहेन सह भुजौ गलतः अधोगतौ।

MY says उल्लापानामपि साभिप्रायवाक्यात्मकानां प्रलापात्मकानां वा बाष्पसहभावविशिष्टानामेव गलनं निर्गमनं, साभिप्रायवाक्यपक्षे निवृत्तिः, उपदेशादीनां तु केवलानामपि। भुजयोस्तु गलनं प्रयत्नशैथिल्यलक्षणमित्यादि यथायोगमूह्यम्।

Muda remarks अत्र तृतीयान्तैः समं प्रथमान्ता गलन्तीति सम्बध्यन्ते। सहोक्तिदीपकसंकरः।

8. धीरेत्ति संठविज्जइ मुच्छिज्जइ मअणपेलवेत्ति गणेन्तो।
धरइ पिअ त्ति धरिज्जइ विओअतणुए त्ति आमुअइ अङ्गाइं।।

[धीरेति संस्थाप्यते मूर्छते मदनपेलवेति गणयन्।
ध्रियते प्रियेति ध्रियते वियोगतनुकेत्यामुञ्चत्यङ्गानि।।]

He consoled himself, because she was patient; fainted as he recalled that she was too feeble to endure the pangs of love; clung to life, because his beloved was alive; and languished, because she was pining away forlorn.

K, MY, Muda and Kula read *mujjhijjai* for *mucchijjai* मूर्च्छते। (R). K has मुह्यति, MY मोह्यते, Muda अमुह्यत्। Kula says मुह्यते मोहं याति। कर्मकर्तरि यका प्रायोगोऽयम्।

K says धीरा धैर्यवती दुरवस्थास्वपि पाणान् न परित्यक्ष्यतीति हनुमदाद्यैः संस्थाप्यते आश्वास्यते स्म (Kula also)। मदनपेलवेति कामपरवशा व्यसनं न सहेतेति गणयन् मुह्यति। सीता धरति तादृशेऽपि दुरिते जीवतीत्युक्त्वा तैर्धार्यते आलम्ब्यते। सा वियोगेन चिरविरहेण तन्वी अतिक्षीणेत्युक्त्वा अङ्गानि आमुञ्चति इतस्ततः क्षिपति स्म।

[6] I.e. by Rāvaṇa.

MY says अत्र गणयन्निति प्रतिवाक्यमावर्तनीयम्। गणनमालोचनं तेन संस्थाप्यते स्वयमपि धीरायते। मदनपेलवा मदनविह्वलहृदया। विरहविवशाङ्गीति विवशाङ्गश्च भवतीत्यर्थः।

Kula says ध्रियते जीवति प्रियते हनुमद्वचसा धार्यते जीव्यते। अङ्गानि आमुञ्चति दुर्बलो भवतीत्यर्थः।

Muda has समस्थापयत् and says आत्मानमिति शेषः। गणयन् विचारयन्। R explains *dharijjai* as ध्रियते, and says ध्रियते जीवति। स्वयं प्राणान् न त्यजति।

9. उब्भडहरिणकलङ्को मलअलआपल्लवुव्वमन्तमऊहो।
अरुणाहअविच्छाओ जाओ सुहदंसणो णवर तस्स ससी।।

[उद्भटहरिणकलङ्को मलयलतापल्लवोद्वमन्मयूखः।
अरुणाहतविच्छायो जातः सुखदर्शनः केवलं तस्य शशी।।]

The moon became pleasant in his eyes only when its lustre was eclipsed by the morning sun;[7] with its emblem, the deer, clearly visible; and its rays emptying into the foliage of the creepers of the Malaya mountain.[8]

K (*chāyā*) has जातस्तस्य सुखदर्शनः केवलं शशी। Muda's *chāyā* is same except that he has अनन्तरं for केवलं। K and Muda have निश्छायः for *vicchāo* (R and Kula). K says अरुणेनाहतत्वात् निश्छायः, अत एव उद्भटहरिणकलङ्कः अतिप्रकाशहरिणकलङ्कः, मलयलतापल्लवेषु पाश्चात्यस्य मलयपर्वतस्य लतापल्लवेषु दृश्यमयूखः शशी तस्य तदानीं केवलं सुखदर्शनः, अन्यत् सर्वं दुःसहमित्यर्थः।

MY is here somewhat corrupt, but he seems to say कोमले मलयलतापल्लवमात्रे . . . ईषन्निर्गलन्मयूखः। उद्वमदमलगङ्गाप्रवाहमिव जह्नुमित्यादि-दर्शनात्। एवंभूतः शशी केवलं विरहिणस्तस्यैव प्रियदर्शनः। अन्येषामतीवाप्रियदर्शन एवाभूदिति वाक्यार्थः।

Kula says मलयस्य लतापल्लवेषु चन्दनतरुशाखाविटपेषु उद्वमन्तो गलन्तो मयूखा यस्य स तथा, तदा तेषु शोभातिशयदर्शनात्। ततः किरणदर्शनात् (किरणादर्शनात ?) उद्भटहरिणकलङ्कः। इत्थं मदनोद्दीपनासमर्थ इति रामस्य सुखदर्शनः।

Muda says अनन्तरं तस्य श्रीरामस्य शशी सुखदर्शनो द्रष्टुं शक्यो जात इत्यर्थः।

---

[7] Rāma, being a *virahin*, could look at the moon with pleasure only when its lustre was gone.

[8] The reference is to the belief that at daybreak the moon deposits its rays in the plant world.

10. जह जह णिसा समप्पइ तह तह वेविरतरङ्गपडिमावडिअम्।
किंकाअव्वविमूढं घोडइ हिअअं व्व उअहिणो ससिबिम्बम्।।

[यथा यथा निशा समाप्यते तथा तथा वेपमानतरङ्गप्रतिमापतितम्।
किंकर्तव्यविमूढं घूर्णते हृदयमिवोदधेः शशिबिम्बम्।।]

As the night came to a close the orb of the moon, reflected in the tremulous waves, swayed as if it were the ocean's heart, perplexed as to what should be done.[9]

K says किंकर्तव्यविमूढं मार्गप्रतिपादनं प्रति किं कर्तव्यमिति बुद्ध्या मूढमुदधेर्हृदयमिव। Muda says आसन्नभयत्वात् किं कर्तव्यमिति विमूढं समुद्रस्य हृदयमिव।

11. णवरि अ मलअगुहामुहभरिउव्वरिअफुडणीहरन्तपडिरवम्।
पवणेण उअहिसलिलं पहाअतूरं व आहअं रहुवइणो।।

[अनन्तरं च मलयगुहामुखभृतोद्वृत्तस्फुटनिर्ह्लदत्प्रतिरवम्।
पवनेनोदधिसलिलं प्रभाततूर्यमिवाहतं रघुपतेः।।]

The wind then smote the surface of the sea, as if it were Rāma's war-drum at dawn, with the echoes reverberating as they filled and emerged from the caves of the Malaya.

K and Muda read विभात for *pahāa* प्रभात (R and Kula)।

K says अथ पवनेनोदधिसलिलं रघुपतेः विभाततूर्यमिव मलयगुहामुखेषु भरितोद्वृत्तत्वात् पूर्णपरिवृत्तत्वात् स्फुटनिर्ह्रादमानः प्रतिरवो यथा भवति तथा आहतम्।

MY says मलयगुहामुखं पूरयित्वोद्गीर्णो निर्ह्रदन् प्रतिशब्दो यथा स्यात् तथोदधिसलिलमाहतमित्यर्थः।

Muda says भृतोद्वृत्तं पूरितावशिष्टम्। Kula says मलयस्य गुहामुखेषु भृतः सन् उद्वृत्तः अधिकतां गतः स्फुटः प्रकटः निर्हरन् दूरं विसर्पन् प्रतिरवो यस्मात् तथा।

12. हंसउलसद्दमुहलं उग्घाडिज्जन्तदसदिसावित्थारम्।
ओसरिअतिमिरसलिलं जाअं पुलिणं व पाअडं दिअसमुहम्।।

[हंसकुलशब्दमुखरमुद्घाट्यमानदशदिग्विस्तारम्।
अपसृततिमिरसलिलं जातं पुलिनमिव प्रकटं दिवसमुखम्।।]

The morning became clear, like the sandy shore, ringing with the call of the swans, with the darkness receding like

---

[9] I.e. about Rāma's crossing over to Laṅkā.

the waters, and the expanse of the ten directions coming into view.

K (*chāyā*) has दृश्यते (*dīsai*) for *jāaṁ*. K says अपसृततिमिरं दिवसमुखम् अपसृतसलिलं पुलिनमिवेति योजना।

Muda says सहोक्तिरलंकारः।

13. अह गमिअणिसासमअं गम्भीरत्तणदढट्ठिअम्मि समुद्दे।
रोसो राहववअणं उप्पाओ चन्दमण्डलं व विलग्गो।।

[अथ गमितनिशासमयं गम्भीरत्वदृढस्थिते समुद्रे।
रोषो राघववदनमुत्पातश्चन्द्रमण्डलमिव विलग्नः।।]

As the ocean remained steadfast in its profundity,[10] the night having passed, wrath took possession of Rāma's countenance, even as an eclipse overtakes the orb of the moon.

K and Muda read समये for *samaaṁ* (समयं) found in R and Kula. K says गमितनिशायमये समुद्रे गम्भीरत्वेन दृढस्थिते किंचिदपि अप्रतिपद्यमाने सति। Kula says गमितो निशारूपः समयो यथा स्यात् तथा। गाम्भीर्याय (?) दृढस्थिते दृढं कृतप्रतिज्ञे समुद्र सति।

14. तो से तमालणीलं णिडालवट्टं पलोट्टसेअजललअम्।
भिउडी थिरवित्थिण्णं कडअं विज्झस्स विसलअ व्व विलग्गा।।

[ततोऽस्य तमालनीलं ललाटपट्टं प्रलुठितस्वेदजललवम्।
भ्रुकुटी स्थिरविस्तीर्णं कटकं विन्ध्यस्य विषलतेव विलग्ना।।]

A frown came over Rāma's firm and broad forehead, dark as a *tamāla* leaf and streaming with sweat; like as a poison creeper clings to the solid and extensive slope of the Vindhya, dark blue with *tamāla* trees and drenched with rain.

K (*chāyā*) renders *paloṭṭa* as प्रलुठित like R. K commentary has विगलत्, Kula प्रगलित, and Muda प्रत्यागत। MY says अन्यत्र (i.e. विन्ध्यपक्षे) प्रलुठितसेकजललवम्। Hemacandra 4.166 gives *paloṭṭai* प्रत्यागच्छति; also derives it from लुट् (4.230). Muda says विलग्ना आरूढा।

---

[10] I.e. seemed unwilling to yield a passage for Rāma.

15. अह जणिअभिउडिभङ्गं जाअं धणुहुत्तवलिअलोअणजुअलम्।
अमरिसविइण्णकम्पं सिढिलजडाभारबन्धणं तस्स मुहम्।।
[अथ जनितभ्रुकुटीभङ्गं जातं धनुरभिमुखवलितलोचनयुगलम्।
अमर्षवितीर्णकम्पं शिथिलजटाभारबन्धनं तस्य मुखम्।।]

As he knitted his brows the face quivered with wrath, the knot of his matted hair came loose, and his eyes turned to his bow.

K reads चलितं for *jāaṁ* (जातं)। He says अथ जातभ्रुकुटिरेखं, धनुरभिमुख-विवृत्तलोचनयुगलं . . . तस्य मुखं . . . चलितं विकृतिं गतमित्यर्थः।

Kula reads विभिन्नकर्णं for वितीर्णकम्पं, and says अमर्षेण विभिन्नकर्णमतः शिथिलजटाभारबन्धनं तस्य मुखं जातम्।

16. पणअपडिभङ्गविमणो थोअत्थोअपडिवड्ढिआमरिसरसो।
तह सोम्मो वि रहुसुओ जाओ पलअरइमण्डलदुरालोओ।।

[प्रणयप्रतिभङ्गविमनाः स्तोकस्तोकप्रतिवर्धितामर्षरसः।
तथा सौम्योऽपि रघुसुतो जातः प्रलयरविमण्डलदुरालोकः।।]

Vexed at the failure of his request,[11] his wrath increasing by degrees, Rāma, although so gentle, assumed a fierce aspect, like the sun of the epoch of destruction.

K, Muda and MY read *āaā-roso* (आयतरोषः K, आगतरोषः Muda and MY) for *amarisa-roso* (अमर्षरसः) found in R and Kula.

K says प्रणयपतिभङ्गेन प्रार्थनाभङ्गेन विमनाः विपरीतमनस्कः, स्तोकस्तोकेन शनैःशनैः परिवृद्धायतरोषः। Kula says प्रणयस्य प्रतिभङ्गेन अभ्यर्थनाया अकरणेन विमनाः।

17. तो साहसणिम्माणं अमित्तदीसन्तलच्छिसंकेअहरम्।
संठिअरोसालाणं गेह्णइ भुअदप्पबीअलक्खं चावम्।।

[ततः साहसनिर्माणममित्रदृश्यमानलक्ष्मीसंकेतगृहम्।
संस्थितरोषालानं गृह्णाति भुजदर्पद्वितीयलक्ष्यं चापम्।।]

He took up his bow, a tool for doughty deeds. It was the appointed goal of the goddess of prosperity abiding[12] with

[11] I.e. the request to the ocean to facilitate the crossing.

[12] Lit. seen.

his foes;[13] a post, buttressing his deep-rooted wrath. It was a subsidiary base[14] of the pride of his arms.

K, Muda and MY read रोषगजेन्द्रालानं for *saṁṭhia-rosālāṇaṁ* (R). Kula has संहित for संस्थित।

K says ततो रामः साहसस्य निर्माणं निर्मायकम्। कर्तरि ल्युट्। अमित्रेषु याश्च यावत्यश्च लक्ष्म्यो दृश्यन्ते तासां सर्वासां संकेतगृहं नायकसमागमाय संकेतस्थानं, रोषगजेन्द्रस्य आलानभूतं, भुजदर्पस्य द्वितीयं लक्ष्म्। लक्ष्यते अस्मिन्निति लक्ष्म् आस्पदमित्यर्थः। दर्पस्य भुजव्यतिरिक्तं लक्ष्मिति यावत्। दर्पो भुजे वा धनुषि वा लक्ष्यत इति। एवंभूतं चापमगृह्णात्।

Kula says साहसस्य निर्माणं निर्मितिसाधनम्, अमित्रेशु दृश्यमानायाः लक्ष्म्याः संकेतगृहमभिसारस्थानं, संहितरोषस्यालानं बन्धस्तम्भमिव, भुजदर्पस्य द्वितीय लक्ष्म्। तदीयभुजदर्पस्य एको लक्ष्यः शत्रुः द्वितीयश्चापः, तेनोभयोरशक्यभूतयोरपि नाम्यमानत्वात्, एवंभूतं चापं गृह्णाति।

18. अक्कन्तधणुभरोणअधरणिअलत्थलपलोट्टजलपब्भारो।
थोअं पि अणारूढे उअही चावम्मि संसअं आरूढो।।

[आक्रान्तधनुर्भरावनतधरणितलस्थलप्रवृत्तजलप्राग्भारः।
स्तोकमप्यनारूढे उदधिश्चापे संशयमारूढः।।]

The waters of the sea swept over the earth as it sank under the weight of the bow, planted thereon; and the ocean was in peril of its life, even though the bow was still unstrung.[15]

K and Muda read धरणितलोत्स्थल for *dharaṇi-alatthala* (धरणितलस्थल) found in R. For the renading उत्स्थल (*utthala*) cf. 8.9.

K says आक्रान्तस्य आरोपणार्थमाक्रान्तस्य भुवि प्रतिष्ठापितकोटेः धनुषो भरेण गौरवेण अवनते धरणितले उत्स्थलप्रलुठितः स्थलमुल्लङ्घ्य प्रचलितः जलप्राग्भारः जलसमूहः यस्य स तथाभूत उदधिः चापे स्तोकमपि अनारूढे अनारोपिते सति संशयमारूढः अस्ति नास्तीति संशयं प्राप्तः।

MY and Muda says अनारूढे अनाततज्ये।

Kula seems to read उत्स्थल (उच्छलत्), like K. He says

13 The bow is fancied as a trysting-place where the goddess of prosperity, forsaking the defeated enemies, met the victorious Rāma, like a *nāyikā* meeting her lover.

14 Lit. the second base, i.e. second in relation to Rāma's arms on which his valour was primarily based.

15 Rāma prepares to hit the ocean with his fiery arrows.

गुणारोपणार्थमाक्रान्तस्य धनुषो भरेण अवनतधरणितलत्वात् उच्छलन् उल्लङ्घिततलः जलप्राग्भारः जलोच्छ्रायः यस्य स उदधिः। Hemacandra 4.174 gives *utthallai* उच्छलति।

Muda explains *paloṭṭa* as प्रत्यागत।

19. धूमाइ धूमकलुसे जलइ जलन्तारुहन्तजीआबन्धे।
पडिरवपडिउण्णदिसं रसइ रसन्तसिहरे धणुम्मि णहअलम्।।

[धूमायते धूमकलुषे ज्वलति ज्वलन्नारोहज्जीवाबन्धे।
प्रतिरवप्रतिपूर्णदिग्रसति रसच्छिखरे धनुषि नभस्तलम्।।]

The sky smoked as the bow was darkened by smoke; blazed as the fiery string was joined to the bow; and roared as the crest of the bow roared, filling the regions with echoes.

20. भिज्जउ महि त्ति व फुडं णत्थि समुद्दो त्ति दारुणं व पइण्णम्।
णासउ जअं ति व मणे चिरं तुलेऊण विलइअं णेण धणुम्।।

[भिद्यतां मही इतीव स्फुटं नास्ति समुद्र इति दारुणामिव प्रतिज्ञाम्।
नश्यतु जगदितीव मनसि चिरं तुलयित्वा विगलितमनेन धनुः।।]

Rāma took up the bow, as if after long revolving a dire resolve in his mind: "Let the earth be riven asunder; verily the sea shall cease to exist; let the world perish."

K, Muda, MY and Kula (?) read भिद्यते for *bhijjau* भिद्यतां (R). Muda, Kula and MY read नश्यति for *ṇāsau* नश्यतु (R). K and Muda read स्फुटं (*phuḍaṁ*) for *maṇe* (R and Kula) मनसि or मन्ये।

K says आरोपितज्यं धनुरनेन रामेण चिरमिमां दारुणामिव प्रतिज्ञामेवं तुलयित्वा विचार्यैव विलगितं गृहीतम्। कथमिव – मही स्फुटं भिद्यते इति प्रतिज्ञां चिरं विचार्यैव, समुद्रो नास्तीति प्रतिज्ञां चिरं तुलयित्वेव, जगदेव स्फुटं नश्यतीति च दारुणां प्रतिज्ञां विचार्यैव धनुर्गृहीतमिति पार्श्वस्थैराशङ्कितमित्यर्थः।

Kula takes *paiṇṇaṁ* (प्रतिज्ञां) as प्रतीर्णं। He says अतः प्रतीर्णं[16] जगत् निःशेषं भुवनं नश्यति स्फुटमितीव चिरं तुलयित्वा *maṇe* मन्ये दारुणं भयानकं धनु . . . रामेण गृहीतम्।

Muda and MY take *paiṇṇa* as प्रतिपन्न। MY says अनेन चिरं तोलयित्वा धनुर्गृहीतम्। तत्र निमित्तं कविनोत्प्रेक्ष्यते। भिद्यते महीति वा स्फुटम्। नास्ति समुद्र

[16] This seems to be a mistake for प्रकीर्णम्। Cf. *SC*. The preceding sentence seems to be स्फुटं मही भिद्यते इतीव, स्फुटं नास्ति समुद्र इतीव।

इति दारुणं वा कर्म प्रतिपन्नम्। नश्यति जगदिति वा स्फुटम्। एवमेव भावीति पर्यालोच्यत्यर्थः। अथवा भिद्यते महीति वा स्फुटम्। नास्ति समुद्र इति दारुणां वा स्फुटां प्रतिज्ञां चिर तोलयित्वा अनेन विलगितं धनुः। चिरं विचार्य ईदृशीमीदृशं वा प्रतिज्ञामारोपितं धनुरिति वा वाक्यार्थः। अस्मिन् पक्षे *paiṇṇaṁ* इति प्रतिज्ञामित्यर्थः

MY mentions *pavaṇṇaṁ* as a variant for *paiṇṇaṁ*, and says तथा समुद्रोद्देशेन मुक्तः शरो महीमवश्यं भिन्द्यात्। एवञ्च महीभेदादिकं प्रपन्नमागतं दारुणं नृशंसं कर्म चिरं विचार्यापि कार्यवशात् धनुर्विलगितमारोपितमित्यर्थः।

21. तो चिरविओअतणुओ सइ बाहोमट्ठमउअजीआघाओ।
जाओ अण्णो च्चिअ से विलइअधणुमेत्तवावडो वामभुओ।।

[ततश्चिरवियोगतनुकः सदा बाष्पावमृष्टमृदुकजीवाघातः।
जातोऽन्य एवास्य विगलितधनुर्मात्रव्यापृतो वामभुजः।।]

His left arm, worn by the grief caused by prolonged separation from his beloved, with the scar left by the bowstring drenched and softened by his constant tears, assumed a different aspect as soon as it became active in contact with the bow.

K reads प्रकटः (*pāaḍo*) for *vāvaḍo* (व्यापृतः)। He says चिरवियोगेन तनुः कृशः, सदा बाष्पापमृष्टत्वात् मृदुभूतज्याघातकिणः तस्य वामभुजो विलग्नधनुर्मात्रेण प्रकटो धनुरारोपणस्य आत्मपौरुषस्मारकत्वात् पीनः अन्य एव जातः अन्याकारोऽभूत्। MY, who reads *vāvaḍo*,[17] like R. Kula and Muda say अन्यो जातः अतिपटुरेव जात इत्यर्थः।

K (*chāyā*) and Kula read अप or अववृष्ट (*ovaṭṭha*) for *omaṭṭha* (अपमृष्ट or अवमृष्ट)। Kula says बाष्पेण अववृष्टः सिक्तः मृदुको ज्याघातो गुणाघातस्थानं यत्र स वामभुजः विगलित (विलगित?) धनुर्मात्रव्यापृतः सन् अन्य एव जात इति भीषणोऽभूदित्यर्थः। दक्षिणे भुजे तु व्याप्रियमाणे किं भविष्यतीति भावः।

Muda has बाष्पावमृष्टमृदितज्याघातः, मृदितं मृदुकृतम्। His reading might be *malia* for *maua* (मृदु K, मृदुक R)।

22. अह वामभुअप्फालणपडिरवपडिउण्णदसदिसावित्थारम्।
संभरइ जाअसङ्कं पलअघणब्भहिअपेल्लणं तेल्लोक्कम्।।

[अथ वामभुजास्फालनप्रतिरवप्रतिपूर्णदशदिग्विस्तारम्।
संस्मरति जातशङ्कं प्रलयघनाभ्यधिकप्रेरणं त्रैलोक्यम्।।]

Thereupon the universe, with the expanse of the ten

[17] Our copy has *vāvuḍo*.

directions filled with echoes as Rāma brandished the bow, recalled as it trembled the crushing force of the rumble of the clouds at the epoch of destruction.[18]

K reads the verse thus — अथ रामकरास्फालितप्रतिरवपरिपूर्णदशदिग्विस्तारम्। उन्मार्ष्टि[19] जातकम्पं प्रलयघनस्तनितपीडितं त्रैलोक्यम्।।

K says रामकरेण आस्फालितस्य घोषितमौर्वीकस्य धनुषः प्रतिध्वनिपूरितदशदिग्विस्तारं त्रैलोक्यं जातकम्पं भूत्वा प्रलयमेघस्तनितपीडनमुन्मार्ष्टि। प्रलयमेघस्तनितसंभवां पीडामुन्ममार्ज[20] विजहौ। धनुर्ध्वनिप्रहारस्यातिदुःसहत्वात् प्रलयमेघध्वनिजन्यं भयं सह्यममन्यतेत्यर्थः।

Muda's reading is the same except that he has धनूरवप्रति पूर्ण; and जातशङ्कं (R). He says त्रैलोक्यं कर्ता। प्रलयक्षुभितपुष्करावर्तकादिमेघध्वनिकृतां पीडां व्यस्मार्षीदित्यर्थः। द्वयं तुल्यमिति भावः।

MY's reading seems also to be about the same. His *pratīka* is *aha rāma*, but he says प्रलयघनस्तनितपीडितम् *upphisai* उत्त्रस्यति। He seems to take प्रलयघन, etc. as an adjective qualifying त्रैलोक्यम्। With regard to *upphisai*, cf. *uppittha* (त्रस्त, उद्विग्न) used in 6.38, 49, etc. and R's remark in his gloss on 11.39; also *Deśīnāmamālā* 1.129. Cf. also *upphesa* त्रास, ibid. 1.94.

Kula reads *saṁbharai* (स्मरति) like R, but he reads राम for वाम (R). धनूरव for प्रतिरव, प्रतिभिन्न for प्रतिपूर्ण, and जातकम्पं for *jāa-saṁkaṁ* (R) जातशङ्कं। Kula says रामस्य करास्फालनेन यो धनूरवस्तेन प्रतिभिन्नः पाटित इव दशदिग्विस्तारो यत्र तत त्रैलोक्यं भयात् जातकम्पं प्रलयघनस्तनितस्य प्रेरणं पीडनं स्मरति।

It will be seen that Kula reads *pellaṇaṁ* like R, but, like K and others, has स्तनित (*thaṇia*) for *abbhahia* found in R, who says प्रलयघनानाम् . . . अभ्यधिकं यत् प्रेरणं संघट्टः तत् संस्मरति।

23. गेण्हइ अ सो अणाअरपरम्मुहपसारिअग्गहत्थावडिअम्।
खअसूरमऊहाण व एक्कं उअहिपरिवत्तणसहं बाणम्।।

[गृह्णाति च सोऽनादरपराङ्मुखप्रसारिताग्रहस्तापतितम्।
क्षयसूर्यमयूखानामिवैकमुदधिपरिवर्तनसहं बाणम्।।]

---

[18] See Extracts for the readings followed.

[19] *upphusai* ?

[20] Muda also.

He took an arrow that came to his hand as he heedlessly[21] stretched it backwards. It was like one of the rays of the sun of the epoch of universal ruin, capable of overturning the ocean.

K says क्षयकालसूर्यमयूखानां मध्ये एकमिव उदधेः परिवर्तनस्य अन्यतः प्रेरणस्य सहं समर्थं बाणमगृह्णाच्च।

Kula says अनादरेण पराङ्मुखप्रसारिते अग्रहस्ते आपतितं मिलितम्।

My remarks पराङ्मुखादीनि पदान्यनादरमेव द्योतयन्तीति मन्तव्यम्।

24. तो संधन्तेण सरं रसन्तरोलुग्गभिउडिभङ्गेण चिरम्।
णीससिऊण पुलइओ अणुअम्पादूमिआणणेण समुद्दो।।

[ततः संदधता शरं रसान्तरावरुग्णभ्रुकुटिभङ्गेन चिरम्।
निःश्वस्य प्रलोकितोऽनुकम्पादुःखिताननेन समुद्रः।।]

He heaved a deep sigh as he fixed the arrow in the bow, and looked at the ocean, his frown obliterated by another emotion,[22] and his countenance saddened by compassion.

K, Muda and MY read दयालुता for *rasantara* (R and Kula)।

Muda (*chāyā*) has दयालुतारुग्ण। He says दयालत्वेनावरुग्णः श्लथीभूतो भ्रकुटिभङ्गो यस्य तेन। मुक्ते बाणे असौ कष्टाश्रितो भविष्यतीति चिरं निःश्वस्य दृष्टः समुद्र इत्यर्थः।

K says दयालुतयावरुग्णभ्रकुटिरेखेण अनुकम्पया परितप्तमुखेन रामेण, etc. दया कृपा। अनुकम्पालक्षणमुक्तं भावविवेके – अनुकम्पा तु सा ज्ञेया दुःखितान् प्रति देहिनः। उपकारपरत्वं या कुरुते चित्तविक्रिया।। इति।

MY says *daāidā* (*daāludā* ?) — *lugga* दयालुतालून। The feminine ending in *dā* is used more than once in the poem (3.31; 8.87).

Kula says रौद्ररसनिवृत्या रसान्तरं करुणरसस्तेन अवरुग्णो भ्रकुटिभङ्गो यस्य तेन।

25. अह कड्ढिउं पउत्तो णिक्कम्पणिराअदिट्ठिसच्चविअसरम्।
वलिअभुअरुद्धमज्झं दढणिप्पीडिअगुणं धणुं रहुणाहो।।

[अथ क्रष्टुं प्रवृत्तो निष्कम्पनिरायतदृष्टिसत्यापितशरम्।
बलितभुजरुद्धमध्यं दृढनिष्पीडितगुणं धनू रघुनाथः।।]

---

[21] Indicates contempt for the ocean.

[22] I.e. pity.

Aiming the arrow with a long and steadfast gaze, Rāma began to draw the bow, grasped in the middle with his (left) hand slightly bent, with string firmly gripped.

R says सत्यापितो लक्ष्याभिमुख्येन स्थिरीकृतः शरो यत्र तत्। वलितेन किंचित् तिर्यक्कृतेन भुजेन रुद्धं मध्यं यस्य। K says अथ रघुनाथो निष्कम्पया निरायतया दृष्ट्या विलोकितशरं, वलितेन् तिर्यक् दीर्घीकृतेन वामभुजेन रुद्धमध्यं गृहीतमध्यं, दक्षिणकराग्रेण दृढनिष्पीडितमौर्वीकं धनुः आक्रष्टुं प्रवृत्तः। शरमोक्षसमये शरव्यं शरं च दीर्घया स्थिरया दृष्ट्या समं लक्षयित्वा मुञ्चति शरं वीरो जनः। तदुक्तं निष्कम्पेति।

Kula says वलितेन कृतकलुषमुष्टिना भुजेन रुद्धमध्यं दृढधृतमस्तकम्। MY says वलित पार्श्वप्रसृत। Muda says *saccaviaṁ* दृष्टम्। *SC* says वलितेन दृढमुष्टीकृतेन भुजेन अर्थात् वामेन।

26. सरमुहविसमप्फलिआ णमन्तधणुकोडिविप्फुरन्तच्छाआ।
णज्जइ कड्ढिज्जन्ता जीआसद्दगहिरं रसन्ति रविअरा।।

[शरमुखविषमफलिता नमद्धनुःकोटिविस्फुरच्छायाः।
ज्ञायते कृष्यमाणा जीवाशब्दगभीरं रसन्ति रविकराः।।]

(As he drew the bow) the rays of the sun, dazzlingly reflected on the tip of the arrow, and glistening on the bending ends of the bow, seemed to be rumbling while being drawn, deep with the sound of the bowstring.[23]

K says शरस्य कृष्यमाणस्य मुखे विषमं प्रभूतं फलिताः प्रतिफलिताः, नमन्त्योः धनुष्कोट्योः विस्फुरत्त्विषः, कृष्यमाणाः रविकराः ज्याशब्देन गभीरं रसन्तीति ज्ञायते स्म। शरस्य शल्ये प्रतिफलिताः नमद्धनुरग्रस्फुरच्छवयो रविकरा एव कृष्यमाणाः पीडया ज्याशब्दव्याजेन गभीरं रसन्तीति पार्श्वस्थैरज्ञायतेत्यर्थः।

MY says धनुषो मध्यगते शरमुखे स्वयोः कोट्योश्च प्रतिफलनवशात् धनुःसदृश-संस्थानतामनुभवन्तो धनुःसच्छायाः स्वयमेव प्रकाशमाना रविकराः मौर्व्याकर्षणमपि स्वयमेवानुभूय रसन्तीत्यज्ञायतेत्यर्थः।

Kula says शरस्य मुखे लोहभागे। *upphaliā* इति पाठे तु निपत्य उत्फलिताः उत्पतिताः। . . . रविकराः ज्याशब्दव्याजेन भृशाकर्षोप-(द्रुताः ?) क्रन्दन्तीवेत्युत्प्रेक्षा।

27. फुडजीआरवमुहलं तज्जेइ व बाणमुहजलन्तग्गिसिहम्।
जलणिहिवहपडिउद्धं आअण्णाअड्ढिअं विअम्भइ व धणुम्।।

---

[23] The bow twanged while being drawn, but it is the rays of the sun glistening thereon that are spoken of as being drawn with a heavy sound.

[स्फुटजीवारवमुखरं तर्जयतीव बाणमुखज्वलदग्निशिखम्।
जलनिधिवधप्रतिबुद्धमाकर्णाकृष्टं विजृम्भत इव धनुः।।]

The bow, drawn up to the ear, seemed to yawn, having woke up to destroy the ocean; and appeared to theaten it roaring with the clear sound of the bowstring, with flames blazing on the tip of the arrow.

K and Muda read प्रदीप्त (*palitta*) for *jalanta* (R). MY's reading seems to be same as he has ज्वलित।

K says बाणमुखप्रदीप्ताग्निज्वालं, स्फुटज्यारवेण मुखरं धनुः समुद्रं तर्जयतीव। तर्जनीस्थाने शरमुखाग्निज्वाला। आकर्णाकृष्टं तदानीं जलनिधिवधार्थं प्रतिबुद्धं सुप्तोत्थितं व्यजृम्भतेव जृम्भणमकरोदिव।

Muda says हस्तिवधार्थं प्रतिबुद्धस्य सिंहस्य सादृश्यं ध्वन्यते। Kula says (धनुः) आकर्णाकृष्टत्वात् स्फारीभवत् जृम्भत इव जृम्भिकां करोतीवेत्युत्प्रेक्षा।

28. खुहिअजलसिट्ठसारो मुहणिद्धाविअपसारिउक्काणिवहो।
आअड्ढिज्जन्तो च्चिअ णज्जइ पडिओ त्ति साअेर रामसरो।।

[क्षुभितजलशिष्टसारो मुखनिर्धावितप्रसारितोल्कानिवहः।
आकृष्यमाण एव ज्ञायते पतित इति सागरे रामशरः।।]

Rāma's arrow seemed to drop on the ocean even while it was being drawn, because the flames darted and spread from its tip, and its potency was seen[24] in the troubled waters.[25]

K, Muda and MY read दृष्ट for *siṭṭha* (शिष्ट) found in R and Kula.

K says क्षुभिते जले (दृष्टसारः) दृष्टशक्तिः, मुखनिर्गतप्रसारितज्वालानिवहो रामशरः आकृष्यमाण एव सागरे पतित इत्यज्ञायत।

Kula says अकस्मात् क्षुभितेन जलेन शिष्टः कथितः सारो यस्य . . . स रामशरः आकृष्यमाण एवापतितोऽपि सागरे पतित इति ज्ञायते उत्प्रेक्ष्यते।

Muda has दृष्टसारे। Besides, he reads निर्वापित (*ṇivvāvia*) for *ṇiddhāvia* (निर्धावित), and says आकृष्टिकाल एवाब्धिजलक्षोभात् आब्धिजलपर्यन्तं प्रसारितस्य ज्वालानिकरस्य उदकसंसर्गेण मुखनिर्वापणीयेत्यर्थः।

29. धुअविज्जुपिङ्गलाइं सरमुहणिग्गिण्णहुअवहपलित्ताइं।
उप्पाअलोअणाइँ व फुट्टन्ति दिसामुहाण घणविन्दाइं।।

---

[24] Lit. declared by. . . .

[25] I.e. the flames issuing from the arrow stirred up the ocean even before the arrow hit the waters.

[धुतविद्युत्पिङ्गलानि शरमुखनिगीर्णहुतवहप्रदीप्तानि।
उत्पातलोचनानीव स्फुटन्ति दिङ्‌मुखानां घनवृन्दानि।।]

In the regions of the sky, the clouds, ablaze with the flames bursting out from the tip of the arrow, and yellow with quivering flashes of lightning, seemed to break asunder as if they were the eyes of malignant planets.

K, Muda and Kula read भ्रियमाणानि (*bharantāiṁ*) for *palittāiṁ* प्रदीप्तानि (R). MY's reading seems to be same as that of K. cf. *SC* text.

K says धुताभिः विद्युद्भिः पिङ्गलानि, शरमुखनिर्गतहुतवहपूर्यमाणानि घनवृन्दानि स्फुटन्ति स्म। दिङ्मुखानाम् उत्पातलोचनानीव। उत्पातसमये दिङ्मुखेषु कानिचित् नयनानि संभूय स्फुटन्तीति वार्ता।

MY says दिग्वधूमुखेषु उत्पातलोचनानि यथा युगान्ते स्फुटन्ति तद्वदित्यर्थः। शरभिन्नानि हुतवहभृतानि चेति विग्रहः।

Muda and Kula explain *phuṭṭanti* in the sense of स्फुरण। Muda quotes Hemacandra 4.231 which gives *phuṭṭai phuḍai*.

K (*chāyā*) and MY have भिन्न for *ṇigginna* (निगीर्ण)। Possibly they read *ṇibbhiṇṇa* used several times in the poem.

30. तो भुअरहसाअड्ढिअधणुवट्ठप्फुलिअबअहलधूमुप्पीडम्।
मुअइ मुहणिग्गआणलसिहासमोलुग्गसूरकिरणं बाणम्।।

[ततो भुजरभसाकृष्टधनुःपृष्ठस्फुटितबहलधूमोत्पीडम्।
मुञ्चति मुखनिर्गतानलशिखासमवरुग्णसूरकिरणं बाणम्।।]

Thereafter he released the arrow, shrouded in dense smoke bursting out of the back of the bow, forcefully drawn by his arm. It eclipsed the rays of the sun with the flames issuing from the arrowhead.

K says ततो भुजस्य रभसाकर्षणेन धनुःपृष्ठात् स्खलितबहुलधूमसमूहं, मुखनिर्गतानलशिखाहतत्वात् अवरुग्णसूर्यकिरणं बाणममुञ्चत। Kula and Muda, like K, read आकर्षण (*āaḍḍhaṇa*) for *āaḍḍhia* आकृष्ट (R). K, Muda and Kula (?) read हतावरुग्ण (*haolugga*, cf. *SC* text) for *samolugga* समवरुग्ण (R). Kula and K read बहुल for बहल (R and Muda)।

Muda says अवरुग्णं म्लानं। शराग्नेरतितीक्ष्णतया सूर्यरश्मीनामपि म्लानिः। Muda has फलित, and K स्खलित for *phulia* स्फुटित (R). Kula has भ्रष्ट (*phiḍia*, cf. *SC* text).

Kula says अवरुग्णा विच्छायीकृताः सूरस्य किरण येन तं बाणम्, भुजरभसाकर्षणेन धनुःपृष्ठात् भ्रष्टो वह्निदेवतासान्निध्यजनितो बहुलधूमोत्पीडो यथा स्यात तथा मुञ्चति।

31. सो जलिऊण णहअले सलिलद्धत्थमिअहुअवहाअम्बमुहो।
पढमोइण्णदिणअरो दीहो दिहओ व्व साअरम्मि णिवडिओ।।

[स ज्वलित्वा नभस्तले सलिलार्धास्तमितहुतवहाताम्रमुखः।
प्रथमावतीर्णदिनकरो दीर्घो दिवस इव सागरे निपतितः।।]

Blazing up in the sky, the arrow dropped into the ocean, with its point, red with flames, half submerged in the water; even as the livelong day vanishes in the sea, preceded by the sun.[26]

K says दीर्घः स शरः प्रथमं नभस्थले ज्वलित्वा सलिले अर्धास्तमितहुतवहः आताम्रमुखश्च पश्चात् सागरे निपतितः। यथा दीर्घो दिवसः नभस्तले ज्वलित्वा प्रकाशं कृत्वा समुद्रावतीर्णदिनकरः पश्चात् सागरे पतितः अस्तमेति तद्वदिति। आदित्यस्थानीयो हुतवहः दिवसस्थानीयः शरः।

Kula says सलिले अर्धास्तमितं हुतवहाताम्रं मुखं यस्य स तथा शरस्य समस्तास्तमयेन नभसि तेजसोऽदर्शनं स्यादिति शङ्कानिरासार्थमर्धास्तमितमित्युक्तम्। प्रथमावतीर्णदिनकर इत्यत्रापि अर्धास्तमितमिति ज्ञेयं समस्तास्तमयेन नभसि दिवसादर्शनप्रसङ्गात्।

MY remarks दिवसस्य ज्वलनं प्रकाशनं निपातोऽनुपलम्भः।

Muda says जले अर्धास्तमितो योऽग्निः तेनाताम्रमुखः।

32. गअणे विज्जुणिहाओ खअन्तकालाणलो समुद्दुच्छङ्गे।
महिअम्पो पाआले होइ पडन्तपडिअ ट्ठिओ रामसरो।।

[गगने विद्युन्निघातः क्षयान्तकालानलः समुद्रोत्सङ्गे।
महीकम्पः पाताले भवति पतन्पतितः स्थितो रामशरः।।]

Flying into the sky, Rāma's arrow seemed to be a flash of lightning. Having dropped on the bosom of the ocean, it seemed to be the fire of the epoch of universal ruin. Settled in the nether regions, it had the effect of an earthquake.

MY says *vijju-ṇihāo* विद्युन्निकायः (K also)। पाताले भूकम्पः कम्पहेतुत्वात्।

K says क्षयान्तकालानलः, अन्तशब्दः स्वरूपवाची वनान्तवत्, क्षयकालाग्निः।

33. तस्स अ मग्गालग्गा अइन्ति णिद्धूमजलणअम्बच्छाआ।
उअहिं बाणणिहाआ अद्धत्थमिअस्स दिणअरस्स व किरणा।।

---

[26] The arrow is likened to the day, and the fiery arrowhead to the setting sun.

[तस्य च मार्गालग्ना आयान्ति निर्धूमज्वलनाताम्रच्छायाः।
उदधिं बाणनिघाता अर्धास्तमितस्य दिनकरस्येव किरणाः।।]

Masses of other arrows, red with smokeless flames, entered the ocean in the wake of that arrow, half submerged in the waters; even as the rays of the sun that hath half gone down follow it into the sea.

K and Muda read ज्वलित for *aādha* (R).

K says तस्य शरस्य मार्गालग्नाः, निर्धूमेन ज्वलनेन ताम्रच्छायाः बाणसमूहाः समुद्रं यन्ति स्म। ज्वलितास्तमितस्य दिनकरस्य किरणा यथा तन्मार्गानुगाः समुद्रं प्रविशन्ति तद्वदिति।

MY says मार्गालग्नाः पश्चादालग्नाः। *ainti* अतियन्ति[27] विशन्तीत्यर्थः। *ṇihāā* निकायाः। Muda says बाणसमूहा अब्धिं प्रविविशुरित्यन्वयः। *ainti* इति प्रविशन्तीत्यादेशः। Kula says बाणसमूहा उदधिमायान्ति like R.

Kula reads उदित (*uia*, cf. *SC* text) for *addha*. He says उदितास्तमितस्य दिनकरस्य मार्गालग्नाः किरणा इव। शराऽप्युदितास्तमितो यतो धनुष उदितो नभसि प्रसृत्य जलधौ मग्नः।

34. णवरि अ सरणिब्भिण्णो वलआमुहविहुअकेसरसडुग्घाओ।
उद्धाइओ रसन्तो वीसत्थपसुत्तकेसरि व्व समुद्दो।।

[अनन्तरं शरनिर्भिन्नो वडवामुखविद्युतकेसरसटोद्धातः।
उद्धावितो रसन् विश्वस्तप्रसुप्तकेसरीव समुद्रः।।]

Thereupon the ocean, pierced by the arrows, surged up, roaring like a lion that had been asleep without fear; and shook its flowing mane, the flames of the submarine fire.

K and Muda read विस्रब्ध (*vīsaddha*) for *vīsattha* विश्वस्त (R)।

K says विस्रब्धं निःशङ्कं प्रसुप्तः केसरीव। विधुतवडवामुखाख्यकेसरसटोद्घातः, विधुतवडवामुखः समुद्रो विधुतकेसरसटोद्घातः सिंह इति क्रमः। *uddhāio* is rendered as उद्धावितः by R. Kula says ऊर्ध्वायितः। Muda says ऊर्ध्वीभूत इत्यर्थः (ऊर्ध्वापितः *chāyā*)। K is here corrupt, but he seems to say ऊर्ध्वापितः उत्थितः।

Muda has स्फुरन् (*phuranto*) for *rasanto* (रसन्)।

35. दूराइद्धणिअत्ते समुहागअबहलसरणिहाअक्खुडिए।
दोहाइज्जइ व णहं टङ्कच्छेअरहसुट्ठिअम्मि समुद्दे।।

[27] Our copy has अउन्ति अतिअन्ति।

[दूराविद्धनिवृत्ते संमुखागतबहलशरनिघातोत्खण्डिते।
द्विधा क्रियत इव नभष्टङ्कच्छेदरभसोत्थिते समुद्रे।।]

The sky seemed to be divided in twain as the sea, rent by the vast oncoming mass of arrows, dashed high with the speed of a chip of rock torn off by a pick-axe,[28] and returned again, after being driven far into the air.

K, Muda and Kula read स्खलिते (*khalie*) for *khuḍie* (R) खण्डिते (cf. Hemacandra 1.53).

K says प्रथमशरप्रहारेण दूराविद्धे दूरं क्षिप्ते ततो निवृत्ते, तदानीं संमुखागतेन अभिमुखमापतता शरनिकायेन स्खलिते प्रतिहते। एवं टङ्कच्छेदेन, टङ्कशब्देन शराभिघात उच्यते, तेन रभसादुत्थिते उच्चैर्गते समुद्रे नभः द्विधाक्रियत इव। अयमर्थः प्रथमपतितशराभिघातेन दूरं प्रेरिते, ततः शनैः निर्वतमानावस्थायाम् अभिमुखमापतद्भिरन्यैः शरैः स्खलितत्वात् टङ्कच्छेदादिव समुद्रे रभसादूर्ध्वं गते सति मध्ये व्यवधानेन नभः द्विधाकृतमिवेति।

Kula says पूर्वप्रहितशरनिवहेन दूरमाविद्धे क्षिप्ते ततो निवृत्ते, संमुखागता बहुलशरसमूहाः[29] तैः प्रस्खलिते, ततः स्खलनात् टङ्कच्छेदे टङ्कच्छिन्नशिलाशकल इव विषमोत्थिते सति[30] समुद्रे नभो द्विधाक्रियत इव। Kula reads *visama* for *rahasa* (cf. *SC* text). *SC* says विषममत्यर्थम्।

Muda says टङ्को गिरिसानुभागः। यथा – हिमाद्रिटङ्कादिवेति भट्टिकाव्ये (1.8)। अत्र तूपचारादुपरिभागः। टङ्कच्छेदेन रभसोत्थिते समुद्रे। स्खलिते प्रतिबद्धे। कश्चित् टङ्कशब्देन शरो विवक्षित इत्याह। पूर्वप्रयुक्तरामशरच्छेदरभसेनोत्थितः समुद्रः दूरं नभोमध्ये गत्व। पश्चात्प्रयुक्तशरसमूहप्रतिबद्धो यदा निवृत्तः तदा नभ एव द्विधाक्रियत इति बुद्धिर्जातेत्यर्थः।

MY says अथवा निर्मलतया नभोनिर्विशेषं समुद्रसलिलं बाणैः छिन्नमुपरि अधश्च दृश्यमानं शरतैक्ष्ण्यात् आकाशं द्विधाकृतमिवालक्ष्यतेत्यर्थः।[31]

36. रअणाअरपरभाए मज्झच्छिण्णम्मि बाणघाउक्खित्ते।
णिवडइ वीअद्धन्तो फुडिओसरिओ व्व मलअअडपब्भारो।।

---

[28] See Extracts for other explanations. Translation follows Kulanātha.

[29] K and Kula read बहुल for बहल।

[30] Cf. *ṭaṅkaccheocchaliyā sarīrasayalāṇa saṁghāyā* (*Gauḍavaho* 701) टङ्कच्छेदेभ्य उच्छलिताः शरीरशकलानां संघाताः (commentary)।

[31] R says टङ्कच्छेदरभसेन टङ्कच्छिन्नस्य वेगेनोत्थिते यथा टङ्कादिच्छिन्नं काष्ठादि हठादूर्ध्वे गच्छति तथैवोच्छलिते। टङ्कः पाषाणदारणः। यद्वा टङ्कः कुठारः। तस्मिन्निव छेदाय खण्डनाय रभसेनोत्थिते। यथा छेदनाय कुठार ऊर्ध्वमुत्तिष्ठतीत्यर्थः।

[रत्नाकरपरभागे मध्यच्छिन्ने बाणघातोत्क्षिप्ते।
निपतति द्वितीयार्धान्तः स्फुटितापसृत इव मलयतटप्राग्भारः।।]

When the farther side of the ocean was rent in the middle, and flung skyward by the impact of the arrows, the hither side[32] dropped (into the gap), like a massive landslide down the Malaya mountain.[33]

K says रत्नाकरस्य परभागे, मध्ये शरैः छिन्ने, पुनः बाणघातेनोत्क्षिप्ते सति द्वितीयार्धान्तः शरैरपहृतः अर्वाचीनभागः निपतति गतस्य स्थाने निपपात। अशनिप्रभृतिभिः स्फुटितापसृतः मलयतटप्रदेश इव। मलयो हि समुद्रस्य आसन्नः।

Muda says उन्नतसमुद्रपरभागे छिन्ने शरैः क्षिप्ते सति अवारसम्बन्धी द्वितीयो भागो विशीर्णो मलयतटप्राग्भार इवापतदित्यर्थः। प्राग्भार उन्नतप्रदेशः। मध्यच्छिन्न इत्यत्र समुद्रस्य मध्यप्रदेशे छिन्न इति ज्ञेयम्।

37. भिण्णगिरिधाउअम्बा विसमच्छिण्णप्पवन्तमहिहरवक्खा।
खुब्भन्ति खुहिअमअरा आवाआलगहिरा समुद्दुद्देसा।।

[भिन्नगिरिधात्वाताम्रा विषमच्छिन्नप्लवमानमहीधरपक्षाः।
क्षुभ्यन्ति क्षुभितमकरा आपातालगभीराः समुद्रोद्देशाः।]

The regions of the ocean, deep down to the nether world, and reddened by the minerals of the submarine mountains riven by the arrows, were convulsed, with the sea monsters confounded, and the totally severed wings of the mountains floating on the surface.[34]

K, Muda and MY read मिलिताः for *gahirā* गभीराः (R and Kula). K, Kula, Muda and MY seem to read *uppaanta*, which they render differently, for *ppavanta* प्लवमान (R)।

K says आपातालं संस्पृष्टाः समुद्रोद्देशाः क्षुभ्यन्ति स्म। कथंभूताः भिन्नानां शरभिन्नानामन्तर्गतानां गिरीणां धातुभिः ताम्राः, विषमच्छिन्नोत्पतन्महीधरपक्षाः। Kula also says विषमं छिन्ना उत्पतन्तो महीधराणां पक्षा येषु।

MY says *uppaanta* उत्प्लवमान। आपातालमिलिताः पातालावधिमिश्रितजला यथा स्युः तथैवाक्षुभ्यन्नित्यर्थः।

32 I.e. the side not disturbed by the arrows.

33 More literally: like a massive side of the Malaya mountain that has cracked and slid down.

34 When Indra clipped the wings of the mountains with his thunderbolt, some of them escaped into the sea with their wings intact.

Muda has विषमोच्छिन्नोत्प्लवमान। He says पूर्वं हि पाकशासनप्रयुक्तपविप्रभीताः पर्वताः सपक्षा एव समुद्रं प्राविशन्। सांप्रतं रामशरनिकृत्ताः तेषामपि पक्षा उपरि प्लवन्ते स्मेत्यर्थः।

38. आअम्बरविअराहअदरविहडिअधवलकमलमउलच्छाअम्।
भमइ सरपूरिअमुहं उग्घाडिअपण्डुरोअरं सङ्खउलम्।।

[आताम्ररविकराहतदरविघडितधवलकमलमुकुलच्छायम्।
भ्रमति शरपूरितमुखमुद्घाटितपाण्डुरोदरं शङ्खकुलम्।।]

The conches, with their mouths filled with the fiery arrows, and their white interior laid bare, moved to and fro, looking like white lotus buds opening by degrees in contact with the crimson rays of the sun.

K says आग्नेयशरपूरितमुखं, तदानीमाताम्ररविकरस्पृष्टदरविकसितधवल-कमलमुकुलच्छायं, प्रकाशितपाण्डरोदरम् एवंभूतं शङ्खकुलं भ्रमति स्म।

Kula says आताम्रै रविकरैराहतानि दरविघटितानि स्तोकविकसितानि यानि धवलकमलमुकुलानि तेषामिव छाया द्युतिर्यस्य (तत्), . . . शरैः पूरितमुखं, प्रहारवेदनयोत्तानीकरणेन उद्घाटितं पाण्डरमुदरं येन तत् शङ्खकुलं भ्रमति। Muda says उद्घाटितानि प्रकटीकृतानि पाण्डुराणि उदराणि अभ्यन्तरभागा यस्य तत्।

39. वेवन्ति विहुअमच्छा सरघाउक्खुडिअमअरदाढाधवला।
मणिभरविसमोणामिअलुअविसहरघोलिरप्फणा जलणिवहा।।

[वेपन्ते विधुतमत्स्याः शरघातोत्खण्डितमकरदंष्ट्राधवलाः।
मणिभरविषमावनामितलूनविषधरघूर्णितफणा जलनिवहाः।।]

White with the fangs of the sea monsters, lopped off by the arrows, the waters swirled, with the fish scattered; while the severed hoods of the serpents whirled about, totally weighed down by their gems.[35]

K says जलनिवहाः विधुतमत्स्याः, शरघातत्रुटितमकरदंष्ट्राभिः धवलाः, मणिभरेण फणस्थानां मणीनां भरेण विषममवनमिता लूनाः विषधराणां घूर्णमानाः फणाः येषां ते तथाभूता वेपन्ते स्म। MY has *luva* for *lua* लून।

Kula has खण्डित, and Muda उत्खण्डित like R. Kula and K seem to read *sara-ghāa-kkhuḍia* for-*ghāu.*

---

35 I.e. the gems supposed to be embedded in a serpent's hood.

40. फुट्टन्तविद्दुमवणं संखोहुव्वत्तणिन्तरअणमऊहम्।
घोलइ वेलावडिअं फेणणिहुच्छलिअमोत्तिअं उवहिजलम्।।

[स्फुटविद्रुमवनं संक्षोभोद्वृतनिर्यद्रत्नमयूखम्।
घूर्णते वेलापतितं फेननिभोच्छलितमौक्तिकमुदधिजलम्।।]

The waters of the ocean rolled in to the beach, displaying the lustre of the emerging gems turned over by the commotion, with the coral-reefs rent asunder, and the pearls shooting up like foam.

K, Muda and Kula read *khuṭṭanta-vidduma-laaṁ* for *phuṭṭanta* (स्फुटत्) . . . *vaṇaṁ* (R). K (*chāyā*) has त्रुट्यद्विद्रुमलतं संक्षोभोद्वृत्तरत्न-निर्यन्मयूखं (Muda also). Kula says खण्ड्यमानविद्रुमलतम्।

Muda says तुड तोडन इत्यस्य खुट्टादेशः। *toḍaṇaṁ* छेदनम्।[36]

MY also has *khuṭṭanta*, and remarks मणिविद्धस्य त्रुट्यद्भूषणस्य प्रकीर्णकेशस्य फेनमुद्वमतो राज्ञः समाधिरनुसंधेयः। R explains his reading स्फुटत् as भिद्यमान।

K and Muda read उत्क्षिप्त (*ucchitta*) for *ucchalia* (R and Kula).

41. जलपव्वाडिअमुक्का खणमेत्तत्थइअपाअडिअवित्थारा।
होन्ति पसण्णक्खुहिआ मूअल्लइअमुहला समुद्दावत्ता।।

[जलप्लावितमुक्ताः क्षणमात्रस्थगितप्रकटितविस्ताराः।
भवन्ति प्रसन्नक्षुभिता मूकायितमुखराः समुद्रावर्ताः।।]

The whirlpools of the ocean, now engulfed, now released by the afflux of water, with their expanse now hidden for a moment, now laid bare, became calm and turbulent, silent and boisterous by turns.

K says समुद्रावर्ताः तदानीमेवमभवन्। कथम् – जलैः क्षुभ्यद्भिः प्लाविताः प्रथमं कबलिताः अनन्तर मुक्ताः, तस्मात् क्षणमात्रं स्थगितास्ततः प्रकटितो विस्तारो येषां ते, तथा प्रसन्नाः प्लावनावस्थायां प्रशान्ताः ततः क्षुभिताः, तथा प्रथमं मूकीकृताः ततो मुखराश्चाभवन्।

Muda says समुद्रावर्ता जलप्लावितमुक्ताः क्षणमात्रच्छन्नप्रकटितविस्ताराः प्रसन्नक्षुभिता मूकीभूतमुखरा अभवन्...। राम(शर)क्षुभितेन (जलेन) पूर्वं प्लाविताः क्षणमात्रस्थगिताः,

---

[36] Hemacandra 4.116.

प्रसन्नाः मूकी(भूताः), . . . पश्चात् जलेन मुच्यमानाः प्रकटितविस्ताराः क्षुभिता मुखराश्च अभूवन्नित्यर्थः।

MY says समुद्रावर्ता जलरूपेणान्तरा क्षणं प्लावाता अन्तः(?)-स्थगितविवराः, प्रसन्ना मूकीकृताश्च, पुनर्जलमुक्ताः प्रकटितविस्तारत्वादिना प्रकृतिं प्राप्ता इत्यर्थः।

Kula reads स्थापित (*ṭhavia*) for *thaia* (स्थगित)। He says क्षणमात्रं स्थापितः प्रकटितः विस्तारो येषां ते, तथा जलप्लावनात् प्रसन्नाः जलमुक्तत्वात् क्षुभिताः संचालिताः, मूकीभूताः मुखराः समुद्रावर्ता भवन्ति।

K, MY and Muda read *pavvālia* for *pabbāḍia* or *pavvāḍia* (R). Muda quotes Hemacandra 4.41 which gives *pavvālai* प्लावयति[37]।

R has *mūallaia* rendered as मूकायित। MY has *mūallea* (?) मूकीकृत। Muda has *mūallaulī* (?), but he quotes *Deśīnālāmālā* 6.137, which gives *mūalla* and *mūala* in the sense of मूक, while the illustrative verse has *mūallia* which does not suit the metre in our verse. K (*chāyā*) has, however, क्षणं मूकीकृतमुखाः (*kaṇamūalliamuhā* ?), but this does not agree with K's gloss (see above). *SC* text has *mūallia-pamuhalā* मूकायितप्रमुखराः (*chāyā*)।

42. वलमाणुव्वत्तन्तो एक्कं चिरआलपीडिअं सिढिलेन्तो।
बीएण व पाआले पासेण णिसम्मिउं पउत्तो उवही।।

[वलमानोद्वर्तमान एकं चिरकालपीडितं शिथिलयन्।
द्वितीयेनेव पाताले पार्श्वेन निषत्तुं प्रवृत्त उदधिः।।]

Rolling and heaving, the ocean seemed about to turn over[38] in its bed, seeking to give rest to its long pressed side.[39]

K says शरक्षोभणेन वलमानश्चलन् उद्वर्तमानो विवर्तमान उदधिः चिरकालपीडितं चिरकालमधोगतत्वात् पीडितमेकं पार्श्वं शिथिलयन् द्वितीयेन उपरिगतेन पार्श्वेन पाताले निषत्तुं शयितुं प्रवृत्त इव।

Muda says यथा कश्चित शय्यायामेकेन पार्श्वेन चिरं शयितश्चिरकालशयनपरिपीडितं तत् पार्श्वं शिथिलीकृत्य इतरेण शयितुं प्रवर्तते तथा समुद्रोऽपीत्युत्प्रेक्षा। क्षोभवशेन पातालस्थितस्य जलस्योपरिदर्शनात्। Kula says यदधोगत जलं तत् ज्वलनक्काथवशात् उपरिष्टाद्भूतं, यदुपरिवृत्ति तदधोगतमभूदित्यर्थः।

---

[37] In our copies K *pratīka* has *bavvolia;* and MY *pratīka* has *vavvāḍia*.

[38] Lit. about to lie down on the second side.

[39] I.e. the lower depths of the sea. The idea is, the surface waters seemed to go down, and those of the lower depths seemed to be driven upwards by the commotion.

43. सरवेअगलत्थल्लिअसुवेलरुब्भन्तसाअरद्धत्थइअम्।
ओसरिअदाहिणदिसं दीसइ उक्खण्डिएक्कपासं व णहम्।।

[शरवेगगलहस्तितसुवेलरुध्यमानसागरार्धस्थगितम्।
अपसृतदक्षिणदिग्दृश्यते उत्खण्डितैकपार्श्वमिव नभः।।]

The sky was half hidden by the sea, when it was driven (from the northern shore) by the impetus of the arrows, and obstructed by the Suvela mountain (in the south).[40] With the southern region vanishing from sight, it appeared to be curtailed on one side.[41]

K, MY and Kula read अवखण्डित (*okhaṇḍia*) for *ukkha-* (R and Muda) उत्खण्डित।

MY says *galatthallia* गलहस्तित (नुन्न K, क्षिप्रं प्रेरितमित्यर्थः Muda)। K says शरवेगनुन्नन पश्चात् सुवेलपर्वतनिरुध्यमानेन सागरेण अर्धस्थगितं छादितार्थम्। अतएवापसृतदक्षिणदिक् नभः अवखण्डितैकपार्श्वमिव अदृश्यत्।

44. आइवराहेण वि जे अद्दिट्ठा मन्दरेण वि अणालिद्धा।
खुहिआ ते वि भअअरा आवाआलगहिरा समुद्दुद्देसा।।

[आदिवराहेणापि येऽदृष्टा मन्दरेणाप्यनाश्लिष्टाः।
क्षुभितास्तेऽपि भयकरा आपातालगभीराः समुद्रोद्देशाः।।]

Even the terrible regions of the ocean, deep down to the nether world, and unseen even by the Primeval Boar,[42] and untouched even by the Mandara mountain,[43] were convulsed (by the arrows).

K reads मिलिताः for *gahirā* (गभीराः), and says आपातालं पातालं यावत् मिलिताः। Muda says मन्दरेणापि अनाश्लिष्टाः अस्पृष्टाः।

45. एक्केक्कम्मि वलन्तो बाणप्पहरविवरे णहणिरालम्बे।
खअकालाणलभीओ पडइ रसन्तो रसाअले व्व समुद्दो।।

---

[40] The legendary mountain of Laṅkā.

[41] Ie. the sea, obstructed by the Suvela mountain, rose sky-high, obscuring the southern region, and the sky seemed to be diminished in area owing to the virtual disappearance of the south.

[42] Viṣṇu in his Boar incarnation while lifting the earth from the ocean.

[43] During the churning of the ocean.

[एकैकस्मिन्वलन्बाणप्रहारविवरे नभोनिरालम्बे।
क्षयकालानलभीतः पतति रसन्रसातल इव समुद्रः।।]

The ocean, rolling into each of the chasms, deep as the sky, caused by the impact of the arrows, roared and tumbled into the nether regions, as if in dread of the fire of the epoch of destruction.

K, Muda and MY read निरायतप्रलम्बः (*ṇirāa-valamba*) for *ṇaha-ṇirālambe* (R). Kula reads निरायतप्रलम्बे।

K, Muda and MY read भृते (*bharie*) for *bhio* भीतः (R and Kula)।

The *pratīka* in Muda, Kula and MY is *ekkakkammi* for ekke- .

K says एकैकस्मिन् बाणप्रहारविवरे बलमान आवर्तमानो, निरायतप्रलम्बः नितरामायतः प्रलम्बमानो विवरपर्यन्तैरधोगच्छन्, रसन् समुद्रः क्षयकालाग्निपूरिते[44] रसातले निपपातेव। एकैकस्य बाणप्रहारविवरस्य रसातलद्वारसाम्यं विवक्षितम्।

Muda says सर्वाणि आग्नेय(शर)प्रहारविवराणि कल्पान्ताग्निपरिपूरितपातालसदृशानि। तेषु प्रत्येकं कल्पान्तकष्टां दशां सर्वोऽपि समुद्रः अन्वभूदित्यर्थः। MY says बाणप्रहारविवरे बलमानो दीर्घप्रलम्बो रसन् अपतत्। पतितमात्र एव अवाशुष्यदिति च फलतीति। Kula says निरायतप्रलम्बे अवक्रदीर्घे बाणप्रहारविवरे बलमानः समुद्रः क्षयकालानलभीत इव रसन् पाताले पतति। R says नभोवत् निरालम्बे शून्ये।

46. दीसन्ति दिट्ठमहणा पुट्ठिपडिट्ठिअपलोट्टमन्दरसिहरा।
आसाइआमअरसा बाणदढप्पहरमुच्छिआ तिमिमच्छा।।

[दृश्यन्ते दृष्टमथनाः पृष्ठपरिस्थितप्रलुठितमन्दरशिखराः।
आस्वादितामृतरसा बाणदृढप्रहारमूर्छितास्तिमिमत्स्याः।।]

The whales that had tasted nectar, being coeval with the churning of the ocean, with the fallen peaks of the Mandara mountain still on their backs, were now seen, stunned by the heavy impact of the arrows.[45]

K and Muda read मर्म for बाण (R and Kula)।

---

[44] Our copy has पूरितो which is against the *chāyā*, which has भरिते।

[45] I.e. having tasted nectar as it emerged during the churning of the ocean, these primeval animals were stunned, but not killed by Rāma's arrows. The Mandara mountain served as the churning rod.

K says तिमयो मत्स्याः दृष्टमथना मथनकाले विद्यमाना एवं पुरातनाः, पृष्ठप्रतिष्ठित-लुठन्मन्दरशिखराः . . . मर्मणि दृढप्रहारेण शरसंभवेन मूर्च्छिताः दृश्यन्ते स्म।

Muda says तिमिमत्स्याः शतयोजनविस्तारा मत्स्याः। दृष्टमथनाः चिरजीविन इत्यर्थः। अतएव मथनक्षोभात् निपतित आस्वादितोऽमृतरसो यस्ते तथा। अमृतपानादेव चिरजीविनो रामबाणप्रहारेऽपि न मम्रुः किंतु मुमूर्छुरित्यर्थः।

47. उक्खित्तमहावत्ता दरदड्ढविवण्णविद्दुमरअक्खउरा।
आवाआलवलन्ता दीसन्ति महाभुअंगणीसासवहा।।

[उत्क्षिप्तमहावर्ता दरदग्धविवर्णविद्रुमरजःकलुषाः।
आपातालवलमाना दृश्यन्ते महाभुजंगनिःश्वासपथाः।।]

Visible were the tracks left in the waters by the gaspings of the great serpents;[46] (tracks) meandering to the nether regions, and sending up large whirlpools, and grey with the ashes of the half-burnt and discoloured coral-reefs.

Muda remarks यथा द्रग्धस्थलीषु करीषादीनि (?) उत्क्षिपन्त्यो भस्मपुरुषा वात्या निःसरन्ति, एवं पातालस्थानां शराग्नितप्तानां (?) भुजङ्गानां निश्वासा उत्क्षिप्तावर्ताः दग्धविद्रुमरजःकर्बुराः पातालात् निःसरन्ति स्म। तेषां मार्गा अदृश्यन्तेति।

K says समुद्रक्षोभे सति संभ्रान्तानां महाभुजङ्गानां विश्वासपथा दृश्यन्ते स्म। कथंभूताः – उत्क्षिप्तमहावर्ताः ऊर्ध्वमुद्धूतमहावर्ताः, किंचिद्दग्धविवर्ण-विद्रुमरजःकर्णकर्बुराः, पातालं यावत् वलमानाः।

48. वेवइ पेम्मणिअलिअं सरसंदट्ठधणिओवऊहणसुहिअम्।
जीएण एक्कमेक्कं परिरक्खन्तवलिअं भुअंगममिहुणम्।।

[वेपते प्रेमनिगलितं शरसंदष्टधन्योपगूहनसुखितम्।
जीवेनैकैकं परिरक्षद्वलितं भुजंगममिथुनम्।।]

Transfixed by an arrow, a pair of serpents quivered, clasped in love, and happy in the fast embrace, coiling round and protecting each other with their lives.

K says भुजङ्गममिथुनं जीवेन आत्मनो जीवितेन अन्योन्यं परिरक्षत् आत्मजीवितनाशेनापि अन्योन्यं परिरक्षत् वलितं वेपते स्म। Muda says स्वीयस्वीयजीवेन अन्योन्यमग्ने रक्षत् बलितं विवृत्त(?)-रज्जुसदृशमित्यर्थः। MY says अन्योन्यरक्षणाय भोगावेष्टनादिव्यापृतमित्यर्थः।

[46] I.e. the serpents oppressed by the heated waters.

49. मोडिअविद्दुमविडवा धावन्ति जलम्मि मणिणिहंसणणिसिआ।
सिप्पिउडमज्झणिग्गअमुहलग्गत्थोरमुत्तिआ रामसरा।।
[मोटितविद्रुमविटपा धावन्ति जले मणिनिघर्षणनिशिताः।
शुक्तिपुटमध्यनिर्गतमुखलग्नस्थूलमौक्तिका रामशराः।।]

Rāma's arrows, sharpened by friction with the gems, darted through the waters, smashing the coral growths; with large pearls adhering to their points as they pierced their way through the oyster-shells.

K says मणिनिकषणेन मणिशिलासु निकषेण निशिताः, शुक्तिपुटमध्यनिर्गतानि मुखे लग्नानि स्थूलानि मौक्तिकानि येषां ते रामशराः जले धावन्ति स्म।

Kula says मणिनिघर्षणेन निशिताः, अतस्तीक्ष्णत्वात् शुक्तिसंपुटं भित्त्वा तन्मध्यात् निर्गताः मुखलग्नस्थूलमौक्तिकाः, अतः निशितमुखत्वात्[47] मोटितो भग्नो न तु विद्धो विद्रुमविटपो यैस्ते रामशराः जले धावन्ति।

Muda says 'मुट आक्षेपप्रमर्दनयोः'। मोटितो भग्नः।

50. विसवेओ व्व पसरिओ जं जं अहिलेइ वहलधूमुप्पीडो।
कज्जलइज्जइ तं तं रुहिरं व महोअहिस्स विद्दुमवेढम्।।

[विषवेग इव प्रसृतो यं यमभिलीयते बहलधूमोत्पीडः।
कज्जलयति तं तं रुधिरमिव महोदधेर्विद्रुमवेष्टम्।।]

Each coral-reef, which the dense volume of smoke covered up, permeating like the virulence of poison, was turned black, as if it were the ocean's blood.[48]

K and Muda read बहुल for बहल (R and Kula)।

K says प्रसृतो विषवेग इव बहुलधूमोत्पीडो धूमसमूहो यद् यद् विद्रुमवेष्टं विद्रुममण्डलमभिलीयते स्पृशति तत् तत् महोदधेः रुधिरमिव कज्जलीक्रियते स्म। महोदधेरन्तर्वर्तमानत्वात् वर्णसाम्याच्च विद्रुमो रुधिरत्वेन निर्दिष्टः। विषवेगस्पृष्टं रुधिरं सद्यः कृष्णं भवति।

My says *ahilei* अभिलीयते प्राप्नोति। *ahiledi*[49] इति वा। यथा विषवेगेन प्राप्तं देहस्य रुधिरं कज्जलीक्रियते तथा शराग्निधूमेन प्राप्तो विद्रुमवेष्ट इत्यर्थः।

---

[47] The phrase is doubtful. It ought to be मुखलग्नमौक्तिकत्वादेव। Cf. *SC*.

[48] The coral-reefs are fancied as the ocean's blood. The imagery is that of blood turned black by poison.

[49] Our copy has अभि।

Kula says धूमौघः प्रसृतो यं(यं) विद्रुमवेष्टं महोदधेरभिलीयते श्लिष्यति तं तं, विषवेग इव रुधिरं, कज्जलयति कृष्णं करोति। Muda also says अभिलीयते आभिमुख्येन श्लिष्यति। महोदधे रुधिरमिव तं तं कज्जलयति कज्जलीकरोति। धातोर्धात्वन्तरप्राप्तिर्विषवेग इति स्मृतः। सर्पादिदष्टस्य हि रुधिरं कृष्णं भवति। R says कज्जलयति कज्जलमिव करोति श्यामलयतीत्यर्थः।

51. खुहिअसमुद्दुप्पइआ बाणुक्कित्तपडिएक्कवित्थअवक्खा।
विसमभरोणअसिहरा णहद्धवन्थवलिआ पडन्ति महिहरा।।

[क्षुभितसमुद्रोत्पतिता बाणोत्कृत्तपतितैकविस्तृतपक्षाः।
विषमभरावनतशिखरा नभोर्धपथवलिताः पतन्ति महीधराः।।]

As they flew out of the raging sea, the mountains, with one of their broad wings lopped off by the arrows, slanted midway in the air and dropped, their peaks bowed down with the unequal weight.[50]

Muda says पूर्वमिन्द्रभयात् सपक्षा एव महीधरा अब्धौ निमग्नाः। ते इदानीं क्षुभितात् समुद्रादुत्पतिता उड्डीयमानाः, मध्ये बाणोत्कृत्तैकविस्तृतपक्षत्वात्। पार्श्वेन लम्बमानाः, तस्मिन्नेव भारे(ण) विषमावनमितशिखराः, नभोऽर्धपथे वलिताः पतन्ति स्म। यथा तरुकोटरकुलायनिलीनदवदहनक्षुभिता उड्डीय गच्छन्तः पक्षिणो मध्येमार्ग लुब्धकैर्विद्धाः पतन्ति तद्वत् पर्वताः पेतुरित्यर्थः।

K says विषमात् भरादवनतशिखराः, एकपक्षस्य पतनात् भारस्य वैषम्यम्। अत एव अवनतशिखराः, नभसोऽर्धपथे वलिताः परिवृत्ताः महीधराः समुद्रे पतन्ति स्म।

MY says अत्र पर्वतेषु पक्षिसमाधिरनुसंधेयः। भारवैषम्यं पार्श्वान्तराधारभूतपक्ष-विलोपादिति। Kula says एकेन पक्षेण स्थातुमशक्ताः पक्षपार्श्वेन विषमं तिर्यक् भरेणावनतशिखराः। R says विषमभरेण अधिकगौरवेण विषमं वक्रं सत् भरेण चावनतमेकं शिखरं येषां ते।

52. छिण्णविवइण्णभोआ कण्ठपडिट्ठविअजीविआगअरोसा।
दिट्ठीहि बाणणिवहे डहिऊण मुअन्ति जीविआइँ भुअंगा।।

[छिन्नविप्रकीर्णभोगाः कण्ठपरिस्थापितजीवितागतरोषाः।
दृष्टिभ्यां बाणनिवहान्दग्ध्वा मुञ्चन्ति जीवितानि भुजंगाः।।]

The serpents, their bodies severed and scattered, flew into

[50] The winged mountains (see verse 37), which had taken refuge in the ocean, now tried to escape; but, with one wing gone, lost their balance and dropped into the sea again.

a rage, with life lingering in the throat, and died after burning the arrows with the fire of their eyes.[51]

K and MY read *bhiṇṇa* for *chiṇṇa* (R, Kula and Muda). K and Muda have प्रतिष्ठापित for परि- (R *chāyā* and Kula).

Muda says अत्र भुजङ्गशब्दः सामर्थ्यात् दृष्टिविषभुजङ्गेषु वर्तते। K says भुजङ्गाः दृष्टिविषाख्याः स्वदृष्टिभिः बाणनिवहान् दग्ध्वा जीवितान्यमुञ्चन्। तीक्ष्णा हि तथा कुर्वन्ति।

53. आऊरेइ रसन्तो उक्खडिअभुअंगभोअपब्भाराइं।
सरमुहगलत्थणुक्खअसेलट्ठाणविवरोअराइ हुअवहो।।

[आपूरयति रसन्नुत्खण्डितभुजंगभोगप्राग्भाराणि।
शरमुखगलहस्तोत्खातशैलस्थानविवरोदराणि हुतवहः।।]

The roaring flames filled up the cavities, which were left by the submarine mountains uprooted by the thrusts of the arrows, and were replete with the massive severed bodies of the serpents.

K and MY have नुन्न, and so seem to read *galatthia* for *galatthaṇa* (R, Kula and Muda).

K says उत्त्रुटितभुजङ्गभोगसमूहानि, शरमुखैः नुन्नोत्खातानां शैलानां स्थानविवरोदराणि अवस्थानविवरोदराणि हुतवहो रसन् आपूरयामास जलात् पूर्वमग्निरेवापूरयत्।

MY says शरनुन्नोत्थितानां शैलानां स्थानविवराणि शराग्निः जलपूरवत् आपूरयति स्मेत्यर्थः।

Kula says उत्खण्डिता भुजङ्गानां भोगप्राग्भाराः शरीरोच्छ्राया येषु तानि। शरमुखप्रेरणेन टङ्कघातेनैवोत्खातं यत् शैलस्थानं तत्र यानि विवराणि तेषामुदराणि हुतवहः . . . सर्वथा पूरयति।

Muda says हुतवहः शरमुखोत्क्षेपोतखातानां शैलानां स्थानभूतानि यानि विवराणि (तेषाम्) उदराण्यभ्यन्तराणि रसन् शब्दायमान आपूरयति स्म। प्राग्भारः समूहः। *galatthaṇaṁ* क्षेपणम्।

54. भिण्णुव्वूढजलअरा दरदिण्णमहातरंगगिरिअडघाआ।
छिण्णपडिउद्धविद्धा फुडन्ति माअङ्गमअरदन्तप्फडिहा।।

[भिन्नोद्व्यूढजलचरा दरदत्तमहातरङ्गगिरितटघाताः।
छिन्नपतितोर्ध्वविद्धाः स्फुटन्ति मातङ्गमकरदन्तपरिघाः।।

[51] Reference to the belief that certain serpents kill their victim with the poison in their eyes. Cf. 4.50.

The mace-like tusks of the sea elephants, carrying aloft the animals pierced by them, flew in pieces, being severed (by the arrows) and flung up (by the waves), and lightly struck the billows resembling mountain slopes.

K reads भिन्न for *diṇṇa* दत्त (R, Kula and Muda ?). K and MY read पतन्ति, i.e. *paḍanti* for *phuḍanti* स्फुटन्ति (R and Kula). Muda has सरन्ति। R says स्फुटन्ति द्विधा भवन्ति।

K says शरैः छिन्नपतिताः जलक्षोभेण ऊर्ध्वं क्षिप्ताः, दरभिन्नमहातरङ्गाख्यगिरितटघाताः, भिन्नोदूढसत्त्वाः मातङ्गमकराणां दन्तपरिघाः पतन्ति।

MY says *danta-pphalihā* दन्तपरिघा उत्पतनदशायामेव जलचरभेदादिकं कृत्वा अनन्तरं न्यपतन्नित्यर्थः।

Kula says महातरङ्गा गिरितटा इव तेषु दरदत्तो घातो यैः (ते)।

Muda says भिन्नाः प्रोता उदूढा जलचरा यैस्ते तथा। . . . महातरङ्गा एव गिरितटाः . . . । तथा छिन्नपतितोर्ध्वविद्धाः रामशरैः छिन्नाः पतिताः पश्चाच्च ऊर्ध्वं क्षिप्ताः।

55. जालालोअविमुहिअं सलिलतरङ्गपरिसक्कणपरिक्खलिअम्।
परिहरइ विद्दुमवणं धूमाहअअम्बलोअणं मीणउलम्।।

[ज्वालालोकविमुग्धं सलिलतरङ्गपरिसर्पणपरिस्खलितम्।
परिहरति विद्रुमवनं धूमाहतताम्रलोचनं मीनकुलम्।।]

The fish, dazed by the glare of the flames, their eyes hurt and reddened by the smoke, shunned the coral-reefs[52] as they went astray, wandering through the waves.

K says मीनकुलम् अग्निशङ्कया विद्रुमवनं परिहरति स्म न प्रविवेश।

Vimukhiaṁ विमुखितं K and probably Kula; विमूढं Muda.

Parisakkaṇa परिसंक्रम K; परिसर्पण Kula; परिष्वक्कण Muda, who explains it further as चंक्रमण, and says ष्वक्कगत्यर्थः। MY has *parisaṅkaṇa* (?) परिचंक्रमण।

आलोको दर्शनमुद्द्योतो वा Muda. (परि)स्खलितं भ्रष्टम् Kula. परिस्खलितं स्थानान्तरं गतम् R.

56. उव्वत्तोअरधवला दरणिग्गअडङ्कजमलजीहाणिवहा।
संधेन्ति उप्पअन्ता थोरतरङ्गविअडन्तराइ भुअंगा।।

---

[52] Because they mistook them for fire.

[उद्वृत्तोदरधवला दरनिर्गतदग्धयमलजिह्वानिवहाः।
संदधत्युत्प्लवमानाः स्थूलतरङ्गविकटान्तराणि भुजंगाः।।]

The (dead) serpents, floating on the waters, their white bellies turned upwards, and the withered twin tongues slightly protruding, filled the wide gaps between the massive waves.

K says उतप्लवमानाः समुद्रवर्तिनो भुजङ्गाः स्थूलानां तरङ्गाणां विकटानि अन्तराणि संदधति स्म भोगाभोगेन तरङ्गमध्यानां संधानमकुर्वन्। Muda says मृता हि सर्पा उत्तानशया उत्प्लवन्ते।

Kula explains *uppaantā* as उत्पतन्तः, and says तरङ्गाणां विकटान्तरालानि महाप्रमाणत्वात् संदधते पूरयन्ति।

MY says *saṁdhanti* (for - *dhe* -) संदधिरे। *uvvaantā* उतप्लवमानाः। *SC* text has *uppavantā*.

57. दीसन्ति दरुत्तिण्णा हुआसणुत्तत्तवाअमअणीसन्दा।
पक्कग्गाहणहङ्कुसविसमसमक्कन्तमत्थआ करिमअरा।।

[दृश्यन्ते दरोत्तीर्णा हुताशनोत्तप्तवानमदनिःस्यन्दाः।
प्रग्राहनखाङ्कुशविषमसमाक्रान्तमस्तकाः कारिमकराः।।]

The sea elephants were partly emerging from the waters, with the flow of their ichor heated and dried up by the flames, and their heads cruelly torn by the claws of the sea lions.

K, Kula and Muda read समुत्कृत्त (*samukkatta*) for *samakkanta* समाक्रान्त (R). K reads *pikka* for *pakka*.

K says हुताशनेनोत्तप्तत्वात् शुष्कमदनिष्यन्दाः, पक्वानां परिणतानां ग्राहाणां नखाङ्कुशैः विषमं समुत्कृत्तमस्तकाः करिमकराः दरोत्तीर्णा दृश्यन्ते स्म। इदीषत्पक्वस्वप्ने-त्यादिनेकारः (Vararuci 1.3)।

Vāa वान शुष्क MY. cf. R वान इति 'ओ वै शोषणे' धातुः। Muda says 'वायं' म्लानं, and quotes Hemacandra 4.18 which gives *vāi* म्लायति। Kula has शुष्क।

Kula says समर्थानां ग्राहाणां नखाङ्कुशैः विषममस्तव्यस्तं समुत्कृत्तमस्तकाः करिमकराः। Muda renders *pakkaggāha* as दुष्टग्राह, and quotes *Deśīnāmamālā* 6.64 which gives *pakka* in the sense of दृप्त and समर्थ (cf. Kula above). R renders the word as प्रग्राह, and says that it is a *deśī* word meaning जलसिंह। MY says *dakkaggāha* पक्वग्राह सिंहमकरेत्यर्थः।

58. घोलइ गओणिअत्तं विसमट्ठिअमणिसिलाअलपलोट्टन्तम्।
झिज्जन्तसलिलविहलं वेलापुलिणगमणूसुअं सङ्खउलम्।।

[घूर्णते गतापनिवृत्तं विषमस्थितमणिशिलातलप्रलुठत्।
क्षीयमाणसलिलविह्वलं वेलापुलिनगमनोत्सुकं शङ्खकुलम्।।]

The conches, helpless in the dwindling waters, and anxious to go ashore, tumbled about on the rugged gem rocks as they moved back and forth.

K says शङ्खकुलं गतापनिवृत्तं प्रथमं गतं ततः अपनिवृत्तं गतागतं कुर्वाणं, विषमस्थितेषु मणिशिलातलेषु प्रलुठत् विवर्तमानं, क्षीयमाणसलिलत्वात् विह्वलं, जलस्य दुर्वसत्वात् वेलायां पुलिनेषु च गमनोतसुकं भ्रमति स्म।

59. मुक्कसमुद्दुच्छङ्गा पक्खक्खेवेहिँ संभमसमुप्पइआ।
अब्भुत्तेन्ति महिहरा एक्कक्कमसिहरसंठिअं सिहिणिवहम्।।

[मुक्तसमुद्रोत्सङ्गाः पक्षक्षेपैः संभ्रमसमुत्पतिताः।
अभ्युत्तेजयन्ति महीधरा एकैकशिखरसंस्थितं शिखिनिवहम्।।]

The mountains, abandoning the bosom of the sea, and flying aloft in confusion, stirred up the flames lingering on each other's peaks with the flutter of their wings.[53]

K, MY and Kula read *pakkhukkhevehi* for *-kkhā-* (R).

K says महीधराः मुक्तसमुद्रोत्सङ्गाः, संभ्रमेण भयेन समुत्पतिताः, एकैकशिखर-संस्थितमग्निनिवहं पक्षोत्क्षेपैः पक्षनिक्षेपैः अभ्युत्थापयन्ति उद्दीपयन्ति स्म। अन्तर्भूतणिजर्थस्तिष्ठतिः। तथा कालिदासः – भर्तापि तावत् क्रथकैशिकानाम् . . .। (प्रास्थापयद्राघवमन्वगाच्च।।) इति प्रायुङ्क्त (Raghu 7.32)।

MY says संभ्रमेण उत्पतिताः शैला अन्योन्यशृङ्गस्थमग्निं पक्षोत्क्षेपाभ्याम-भ्युदस्थापयन्नित्यर्थः।

K and MY seem to read *abbhuṭṭhenti*[54] for *abbhuttenti* (R and Kula) अभ्युत्तेजयन्ति उद्दीपयन्ति। Muda reads *abbhuttanti* प्रदीपयन्ति, and says प्रदीपरेब्भुत्तादेशः। He seems to refer to Hemacandra 4.152 which gives *abbhuttai*, *palīvai*, etc. as equivalents for प्रदीप्यते।

[53] See verses 37 and 51.

[54] Cf. *uṭṭhei* 12.11.

60. विहलुव्वत्तभुअंगा छिण्णमहासुरसिरुप्पअणगम्भीरा।
मूलुत्थङ्घिअरअणा णेन्ति रसन्ता रसाअलजलुप्पीडा।।

[विह्वलोद्वृत्तभुजंगाश्छिन्नमहासुरशिर उत्प्लवगम्भीराः।
मूलोत्तम्भितरत्ना निर्यन्ति रसन्तो रसातलजलोत्पीडाः।।]

The roaring waters of the nether regions issued forth, terrible with the severed heads of the demons emerging with them; with the helpless serpents turned upside-down, and the gems cast up from the bottom.

K says छिन्नानां महासुराणां शिरःसमुत्पतनेन गम्भीराः भयङ्कराः, मूलादधस्तलात् उन्मूलितरत्नाः (*chāyā* has मूलोत्तसम्भितरत्नाः) रसातलजलसमूहाः रसन्तो निर्यन्ति स्म। Kula also says छिन्नानां महासुरशिरसामुत्पतनैः गम्भीराः रसातजललोत्पीडाः। R says उत्प्लवनेन गम्भीरा भयानकाः।

Kula says मूलात् पातालात् उत्थितानि रत्नानि यैः।

MY seems to read *ṇinta* (निर्यत्) for *chiṇṇa*. He says *siruppaaṇa* शिरउत्पतन। *ṇinti* (for *ṇenti*) निरीयुः।

61. बाणणिहाउच्छित्ता हुअवहजालाहउप्पवन्तप्फेणा।
अट्टन्ति णहअले च्चिअ मारुअभिण्णलहुआ सलिलकल्लोला।।

[बाणनिघातोत्क्षिप्ता हुतवहज्वालाहतोल्प्लवमानफेनाः।
शुष्यन्ति नभस्तल ए मारुतभिन्नलघुकाः सलिलकल्लोलाः।।]

Raised aloft by the impact of the arrows, the waves, assailed by the flames, and breaking into foam, dried up in the sky, being scattered and thinned by the wind.

K, MY and probably Kula read उत्तरत् (*uttaranta*) for *uppavanta* (R) उत्प्लवमान्।

K says बाणनिकायेनोत्क्षिप्ताः . . . सलिलकल्लोलाः नभःस्थल एव शुष्यन्ति स्म, न पुनरपतन्। MY says हुतवहज्वालाहताश्च उत्तरत्फेनाश्चेति विग्रहः। R says बाणनिघातेनोत्क्षिप्ताः। Kula says सलिलकल्लोला नभःस्थल एव मुञ्चन्ति क्षीयन्ते। Unless it is a misake he seems to read मुञ्चन्ति for *aṭṭanti* (शुष्यन्ति)।[55] Besides, he puts this verse after verse 72.

62. णिव्वूढविसत्थवआ भोआअड्ढणगलन्तगमणुच्छाहा।
तुङ्गतरङ्गक्खलिआ विसमुव्वत्तोअरा वलन्ति भुअंगा।।

[55] In verse 73 Kula explains *aṭṭanta* as क्षीयमाण। see below.

[निर्व्यूढविषस्तबका भोगाकर्षणगलद्गमनोत्साहाः।
तुङ्गतरङ्गस्खलिता विषमोद्वृत्तोदरा वलन्ति भुजंगाः।।]

Washed up[56] by the lofty billows, the totally overturned serpents, loth to drag themselves along, crawled as they spurted jets of poison.

R says तरङ्गैः स्खलिताः समुद्रात् प्रच्याविताः। तीरभूमावानीता इति यावत्। K explains *ṇivvūḍha* (निर्व्यूढ) as निर्वान्त (निःशेषोद्गीर्ण MY)। K says निर्वान्तविषबिन्दवः . . . भुजङ्गा वलन्ते भ्रमन्ति स्म।

K reads *theva* (बिन्दु) for *thavaa* (स्तबक) found in R. See Notes on 1.40. Kula is corrupt, but quotation in *SC* shows that he also reads *theva*, i.e. *visa-ttheva* for-*tthavaā*.

63. वेवन्ति णिण्णआणं सरणिवहच्छिण्णसङ्खविहडिअबलआ।
हत्थ व्व उअहिणिमिआ मुक्करवक्कन्दणिवडिआण तरङ्गा।।

[वेपन्ते निम्नगानां शरनिवहच्छिन्नशङ्खविघटितवलयाः।
हस्ता इवोदधिनियोजिता मुक्तरवाक्रन्दनिपतितानां तरङ्गाः।।]

As the rivers fell into the sea, with loud wailing as it were, their waves quivered, as if they were their hands caressing the ocean;[57] while the conch shells split by the arrows seemed to be the bangles slipping off their hands.[58]

K, Kula and probably MY read विगलित for *vihaḍia* विघटित (R)।

K says भुर्तुरुदधेः शरदाहमुपलभ्य मुक्तरवमयाक्रन्दं यथा निपतितानां निम्नगानां पत्नीनां हस्ता इव तरङ्गा वेपन्ते स्म। कथंभूताः – शरनिवहच्छिन्नाः शङ्खा एव विगलितानि वलयानि येषां ते तथाभूता उदधौ निमिताः निहिताः।

MY says शरविद्धे भर्तरि व्याकुलगतानां क्रन्दन्तीनां गलच्छङ्खवलया (हस्ताः) तद्वपुषि सावेगं न्यस्ता इव अवेपन्त तरङ्गा इत्याशयः।

Kula says शरनिवहेन छिन्नाः शङ्खा विगलिता वलया इव येषां ते तरङ्गा मुक्तरवाक्रन्दं यथा स्यात् तथा निपतितानां निम्नगानां नदीनां हस्ता इव वेपन्ते।

64. हुअवहभरिअणिअम्बा जलअरसंदट्ट‌वक्खउडपब्भाराः।
चिरसंणिरोहमसिणा दुक्खेण णहं समुप्पअन्ति महिहरा।।

[56] Lit. slipping off. . . . .

[57] Lit. placed on the ocean.

[58] The rivers are figured as the wailing wives of the ocean, oppressed by Rāma's arrows; and the conch shells are fancied as the bangles slipping off their hands in the struggle to help their consort.

[हुतवहभृतनितम्बा जलचरसंदष्टपक्षपुटप्राग्भाराः।
चिरसंनिरोधमसृणा दुःखेन नभः समुत्पतन्ति महीधराः।।

The (submarine) mountains, with their slopes enveloped in flames, and their broad wings soaked in water, laboured skywards, being sluggish from long confinement in the sea.[59]

K and probably MY read जलभर for *jalaara* जलचर (R). K and Kula read विस्तारा: (*vitthārā*) for *pabbhārā* प्राग्भारा: (R)।

K says चिरं संनिरोधेन समुद्रे निरोधेन मसृणाः मन्दबलाः। अन्यत् सुबोधम्।

MY says हुतवहदाहेऽपि शैला जलसंदष्टपक्षतया चिरं निरोधमसृणतया चाशु उत्पतितुं नाशक्नुवन्नित्यर्थः।

Kula says जलस्य भावाभाव: (?) तेन संदष्टाः संलग्नाः पक्षपुटविस्तारा येषां ते।

65. जलइ जलन्तजलअरं भमइ भमन्तमणिविद्दुमलआजालम्।
रसइ रसन्तावत्तं भिज्जइ भिज्जन्तपव्वअं उअहिजलम्।।

[ज्वलति ज्वलज्जलचरं भ्रमति भ्रमन्मणिविद्रुमलताजालम्।
रसति रसदावर्ते भिद्यते भिद्यमानपर्वतमुदधिजलम्।।]

The waters of the ocean blazed with the animals aflame; whirled with the gems and coral-reefs whirling with them; roared with the whirlpools booming; and clove as the mountains clove asunder.

66. आवत्तविवरभमिरो मलअपणिसिलाअलक्खलिअसंचारो।
घोलिरतरङ्गविसमो जह दीसइ साअरो तहेअ हुअवहो।।

[आवर्तविवरभ्रमणशीलो मलयमणिशिलातलस्खलितसंचारः।
घूर्णमानतरङ्गविषमो यथा दृश्यते सागरस्तथैव हुतवहः।।]

The flames looked just like the ocean, now whirling in the abyss of the whirlpools, now impeded by the gem rocks of the Malaya mountain, now tossing on the rolling waves.

K and MY read *bhario* for *bhamiro* (R and Kula). K reads मृदित (*malia*) for *malaa* (R and Kula).

K remarks सागरहुतवहयोः तदानीं रूपभेदो नोपलब्ध इत्यर्थः।

---

[59] The winged mountains find it difficult to fly out of the blazing sea for lack of practice. See verses 37 and 51.

My says *bhario* भृतः। आवर्तोदराणि आपूर्य स्थितः क्षुभितः सागरो यथाभूतो दृष्टः तज्जलानुप्रविष्टः शराग्निरपि व्याप्ततया तथाभूत एवादृश्यतेत्यर्थः।

67. रहसपलित्तुच्छलिओ जे च्चिअ पडिवेइ मलअवणवित्थारे।
विज्झाअणिअत्तन्तो ते च्चेअ पुणो वि विज्झवेइ समुद्दो।।६७।।

[रभसप्रदीप्तोच्छलितो यानेव प्रदीपयति मलयवनविस्तारान्।
विध्मातनिवर्तमानस्तानेव पुनरपि विध्मापयति समुद्रः।।]

Violently blazing and overflowing, the ocean set the broad woods of the Malaya mountain on fire, and quenched them again as it flowed back with the flames quenched.

K reads उच्चलितः for *ucchalio* (R and Kula).

K says पूर्वं शरघातरभसात् प्रदीप्तोच्चलितः ज्वलन् उल्लङ्घिततीरः समुद्रो यान् मलयवनविस्तारान् प्रदीपयति प्रज्वलयति स्म, निर्वाणनिवर्तमानो दूरं गत्वा शान्ताग्निः निवर्तमानः समुद्रः तानेव प्रदेशान् पुनर्निर्वापयामास।

MY says *vijjhāya* निर्वाण (विध्मात R and Kula)। *vijjhavei* निरवापयत् (विध्मापयति R; निर्वापयति Kula)। MY remarks अनयापि गाथया समुद्रजलस्य अग्निना व्याप्तिरुक्ता।

Kula reads मलयतटप्राग्भारान्, i.e. *malaa - aḍa - pabbhāre* for मलयवनविस्तारान्।

68. उत्थम्भिअमअरहरो मअरवसामिसविसङ्खलसिहाणिवहो।
णिवहणिसुद्धमहिहरो महिहरकूडविअडो विअम्भइ जलणो।।

[उत्तम्भितमकरगृहो मकरवसामिषविशृङ्खलशिखानिवहः।
निवहनिपातितमहीधरो महीधरकूटविकटो विजृम्भते ज्वलनः।।]

Massive like mountain peaks, the fire raged, raising the sea, and burning the (submerged) mountains down in masses; the flesh and fat of the sea monsters adding to the fury of the flames.

SC text and My *pratīka* have *utthaṁghia* explained as उत्तम्भित। K *pratīka* is same according to Goldchmidt's manuscript. Our copy has *uttaṁvia* (?). R has *uttambhia* (उत्तम्भित)। Hemacandra 4.36, 144 gives *utthaṁghai* in the sense of उन्नमयति and उत्क्षिपति।

K says उत्क्षिप्तसमुद्रो, मकराणां दह्यमानानां वसामयेन आमिषेण भक्ष्येण निरर्गलज्वालानिवहो, निवहशो निपातितमहीधरो दग्धपातितपर्वतो, महीधरकूटवत विकटो व्यजृम्भत अग्निः।

MY says *ucchambhia* इति पाठः। तथा च समुद्रं क्रोडीकृत्य अग्निः स्थित इत्यर्थः। मकरगृहं समुद्रः। *maara-vaso* (?) इति क्वचित पाठः। . . . विजृम्भते[60] ज्वलन इति ज्वालाभिरुदधेरपि अधिकवृत्तिरासीदित्यर्थः।

Kula *pratīka* seems to have *utthaṁghia* like MY. Kula says उद्वर्तितमकरगृहः (?)[61] . . . महीधराणां कूटेषु शिखरेषु विकटो विशालो विजृम्भते ज्वलनः।

69. जलणुत्थङ्घिअमूला बाणुक्खित्तपडिअत्तणणिसुम्भन्ता।
णिवडन्ति जलुप्पीडा पडिलोमागअपडन्तविअडावत्ता।।

[ज्वलनोत्तम्भितमूला बाणोत्क्षिप्तपरिवर्तननिपात्यमानाः।
निपतन्ति जलोत्पीडाः प्रतिलोमागतपतद्विकटावर्ताः।।]

The masses of water, raised from the bottom by the flames, and flung up by the arrows, and forced down as they turned over, dropped, with the vast whirlpools rolling upside down.

K reads वलमान (*valanta*) for *paḍanta* पतत् (R) in the second line. Kula seems to agree with K.

K says ज्वलनवेगेन उत्तम्भितमूलाः जलोत्पीडा बाणोत्क्षिप्ताः परिवर्तनेन विपर्यासेन निपात्यमाना अधोमुखाः पतन्तः अतएव प्रतिलोमागतवलमानविकटावर्ता भूत्वा निपतन्ति स्म।

Kula says पातालात् उद्गच्छता ज्वलनेन उत्तम्भित(मूलाः), अनन्तरं पतद्भिः बाणैरुत्क्षिप्ताः सन्तः परिवृत्ताः परिवर्तनेन निपात्यमाना जलोत्पीडा जलसंघाताः उच्चात् पतनेन प्रतिलोमागतः अधोमुखवर्ती वलन् (?) विकट आवर्तो येषां ते तथाभूता निपतन्ति।

MY *pratīka* has *utthambhia*. He reads *ṇisubbhantā* अवपात्यमानाः for *ṇisumbhantā*. He says बाणोत्क्षिप्ताः परिवर्तनेनावपात्यमानाः, आग्नेयेन रामशरेणोत्क्षिप्ततया ज्वलनेनोत्सङ्गितमूलाः सन्तः . . . अपतन्।

70. धूमाइ जलइ विहडइ ठाणं सिढिलेइ मलइ मलउच्छङ्गम्।
धीरस्स पढमइण्हं तह वि हु रअणाअरो ण भञ्जइ पसरम्।।

[धूमायते ज्वलति विघटते स्थानं शिथिलयति मृद्गाति मलयोत्सङ्गम्।
धैर्यस्य प्रथमचिह्नं तथापि हि रत्नाकरो न भिनत्ति प्रसरम्।।]

---

[60] Our copy has विजृम्भित।

[61] Our copy has उद्वस्तित।

The sea smoked and burst into flames, parted asunder and loosened its grip on the bottom, and dashed over the slopes of the Malaya. Still it abated not its onward movement,[62] the first sign of fortitude.

K and MY read *mahai* (इच्छति) for *malai* मृद्राति (R and Kula). K reads पुलिन for *malaa* (R and Kula); च for *hu*; and मुञ्चति for *bhañjai* (R and Kula).

K says पुलिनोत्सङ्गमिच्छति स्म। क्षीयमाणत्वात् पुलिनानि विकटानि भवन्ति। तुङ्गेपुलिनोत्सङ्गे विश्रामितुमैच्छदित्यर्थः। तथापि व रत्नाकरः धैर्यस्यप्रथमचिह्नं प्रसरमात्मीयं विशालत्वं दुर्लङ्घत्वादिकं महत्त्वं न मुञ्चति स्म। रत्नाकर इति साभिप्रायं रत्नानामुत्तमद्रव्याणामाकर इति।

Kula renders *ṇa bhañjai* as न भनक्ति नान्यथा करोति।

K says विघटते द्विधा भिद्यते। स्थानं निजमवस्थानं शिथिलयति स्म। MY reads *indhaṁ* for *iṇhaṁ*. He renders *pasaraṁ* as विस्तारम, and says ज्वलनेन स्थानशैथिल्याद्यापन्नस्यापि उदघेरक्षय्यतारूपधैर्यसूचको विस्तारो नात्यन्तं गतइत्यर्थः।

71. भुवइन्दलोअणाणं फुट्टन्ताण अ तिमीण साअरमज्झे।
संवत्तजलहराण व रामसराणलहआण णीहरइ रओ।।

[भुजगेन्द्रलोचनानां स्फुटतां च तिमीनां सागरमध्ये।
संवर्तजलधराणामिव रामशरानलहतानां च निर्ह्रदति रवः।।]

As the whales and the eyes of the mighty serpents, struck by the fire of Rāma's arrows, burst in twain in the bosom of the sea, the sound echoed like the rumble of the clouds at the epoch of universal ruin.

The verse is not found in K and MY. Kula says संवर्तजलधराणां प्रलयमेघानामिव रवो निर्हरति[63] दूरं प्रसरति। R renders *ṇiharai* as निर्ह्रदति (प्रतिशब्दं जनयति)।

72. मुहपुञ्जिअग्गिणिवहा धूमसिहाणिहणिराअअड्ढिअसलिला।
णिवडन्ति णहुक्खित्ता पलउक्कादण्डसंणिहा णइसोत्ता।।

[62] I.e. its energy or spirit of resistance as seen in its refusal to yield to force and open a way for Rāma through its waters.

[63] Kula is corrupt, but seems to read निर्वहति। *SC* has निर्हरति with the same meaning.

[मुखपुञ्जिताग्निनिवहानि धूमशिखानिभनिरायतकृष्टसलिलानि।
निपतन्ति नभ उत्क्षिप्तानि प्रलयोल्कादण्डसंनिभानि नदीस्रोतांसि।।]

The rivers, flung up (by the fiery arrows) into the sky, dropped like meteors at the epoch of destruction, with the flames massed in their mouths, and the waters long drawn out like streaks of smoke.

K reads विस्तृत (*vitthaa*) for *aḍḍhia* कृष्ट (R and Kula)।

K says मुखपुञ्जिताग्निनिवहानि, शरैर्नभसि उत्क्षिप्तानि, धूमशिखानिभनिरायति-विस्तृतसलिलानि नदीस्रोतांसि प्रलयोल्कादण्डसंनिभानि भूत्वा निपतन्ति स्म। उल्काया धूमसंबन्धोऽस्ति।

MY says मुखे ज्वलन्त्यः पश्चात् धूमायमाना उल्का इव बाणोत्क्षिप्ता नद्योऽपि नभसो न्यपतन्नित्यर्थः।

73. अट्टन्तसलिलणिवहो थोअत्थोअपडिमुक्कपुलिणुच्छङ्गो।
दीसइ ओसक्कन्तो मग्गाहुत्तो पअं पअं व समुद्दो।।

[शुष्यत्सलिलनिवहः स्तोकस्तोकप्रतिमुक्तपुलिनोत्सङ्गः।
दृश्यतेऽपसरन्मार्गाभिमुखः पदं पदमिव समुद्रः।।]

Having by degrees left the expanse of the beach, the sea, with the waters subsiding, appeared to recede step by step.

K reads स्तोकस्तोकं विमुक्त – for *thoa - tthoa - paḍimukka* (R and Kula).

K says शुष्यज्जलनिवहः, शनैः शनैः विमुक्तपुलिनप्रदेशः, अपसंक्रान्त एवमपक्रामन् समुद्रः पदं पदं मार्गाभिमुख इवादृश्यत। तत्र वस्तुमशक्यत्वात् देशान्तरे वस्तुं क्षणे क्षणे गमनोन्मुख इवादृश्यत। पदं पदमिति कालाध्वनोरत्यन्तसंयोग इति द्वितीया।

My says *aṭṭanta* क्षीयमाण (Kula also)। *maggāhutto* मार्गाभिमुखः पश्चान्मार्गदेशाभिमुखा इत्यर्थः। क्षीयमाणतया पुलिनानि मुञ्चन् समुद्रो भीतः पृष्ठतोऽभिमुख एव प्रतिपदमपाक्रामिन्निव अदृश्यतेत्यर्थः।

R says मार्गशब्दः पश्चादर्थवाची। शुष्यन् सलिलनिवहो यस्य तादृक्। . . . समुद्रः पश्चादिभिमुखः पदं पदमपसरन्निव दृश्यते। *SC* says *magga* - शब्दः पश्चाद्भागे देशी। Kula renders *osakkanto* (अपसरन् R) as अपष्वक्कमाणः (?) अपसर्पन्। Cf. Muda on verse 55.

74. जलणणिवहम्मि सलिलं साणलणिवहुच्छलन्तसलिलम्मि णहम्।
सलिलणिवहोत्थअम्मि अ अत्थाअइ णहअले दसदिसाअक्कम्।।

[ज्वलननिवहे सलिलं सानलनिवहोच्छलत्सलिले नभः।
सलिलनिवहावस्तृते चास्तायते नभस्तले दशदिक्चक्रम्।।]

The waters disappeared in the flames, and the sky in the surging waters enveloped in flames, and the ten directions in the sky overrun by the waters.

K and probably MY read उच्चलत् for *ucchalanta* (R and Kula).

K says ज्वलननिवहे सलिलं स्थितं, सानलनिवहोच्चलिते सलिले (-च्चलतसलिले *chāyā*) नभः स्थितम्। सलिलनिवहावस्तृते च नभःस्थले (नभस्तले *chāyā*) दशदिक्चक्रमस्तमियाय। MY says सलिले शरोच्चलिते प्रसरति सति नभो दिशश्च नादृश्यन्तेति सारम्। Kula says ज्वलननिवहे सलिलम्, अनलनिवहसहिते उच्छलति सलिले नभः, सलिलनिवहेन अवस्तृते छन्ने नभस्तले (?) दशदिक्चक्रमस्तायते।

75. सिहिणा पअविज्जन्ते आअट्टन्तम्मि वित्थए जलणिवहे।
जाआ गिम्हविलम्बिअरविरहचक्कमसिणा समुद्दावत्ता।।

[शिखिना प्रताप्यमाने आवर्त्यमाने विस्तृते जलनिवहे।
जाता ग्रीष्मविलम्बितरविरथचक्रमसृणाः समुद्रावर्ताः।।]

As the waters spread out, heated and swirled by the flames, the whirlpools of the ocean lessened in speed, like the wheel of the sun's chariot slowed down by the summer.[64]

K and probably MY read विजृम्भित् (*viambhia*) for *vilambia* (R and Kula).

K says शिखिना प्रताप्यमाने विस्तृते जलनिवहे आवर्तमाने सति समुद्रावर्ताः ग्रीष्मविजृम्भितस्य रविरथस्य चक्रवत् मसृणाः श्लक्ष्णा जाताः। समुद्रजलस्य अग्निसवर्णत्वात् आवृत्तिशैघ्याच्च रविरथचक्रसाम्यम्। रविरथचक्रं च ग्रीष्मकाले तापातिशयात् अग्निवर्णं भवति।

My says *āaṭṭantammi* आवर्त्यमाने। निस्तरङ्गतया निर्यद्बुद्बुदफेनतया च मसृणत्वेनावर्तानां ग्रीष्मात्यन्तप्रज्वलत्तेजोमयरविरथचक्रसाधर्म्यमुक्तम्।

Kula says आवर्त्यमाने क्वाथ्यमाने विस्तृते जलनिवहे, ग्रीष्मे दीर्घत्वात् दिवसस्य विलम्बितो रविरथः तस्य चक्र(वत्) मसृणाः मन्दभ्रमणाः समुद्रावर्ता जाता। R says मसृणा मन्दगतयो जाताः। ग्रीष्मे रविरथो मन्दं चलतीति लोकप्रतिपत्तिः।

---

[64] The one-wheeled chariot of the sun is fancied as going slower on the long summer days.

76. णिव्वडिअधूमणिवहो उद्धाइअमरगअप्पहामिलिअसिहो।
वित्थिण्णम्मि समुद्दे सेआलोमइलिओ व्व घोलइ जलणो।।

[निर्वलितधूमनिवह उद्धावितमरकतप्रभामिलितशिखः।
विस्तीर्णे समुद्रे शेवालावमलिन इव घूर्णते ज्वलनः।।]

Emitting a dense volume of smoke, the fire rolled over the vast ocean, and seemed to be enveloped in moss as the flames blended with the emerging lustre of the emeralds.

K reads उत्तिष्ठतीव (*uṭṭhei va*, cf. 12.11) for *uddhāia* उद्धावित (R) He reads the second line as विस्तीर्णे समुद्रे शैवालित इव घूर्णित्वा हुतवहः।

K says पृथग्भूतधूमनिवहः, मरकतप्रभाभिः मिलितज्वालः हुतवहो विस्तीर्ण समुद्रे चिरं घूर्णित्वा शैवालितः शैवालवानिव उत्तिष्ठते स्मः

Kula agrees with R, but he explains *uddhāia* as ऊर्ध्वायित। Cf. K on 9.55. MY's reading of the verse seems to be same as that of K. He gives only the gist of the verse – निर्धूमो ज्वलनो मरतकप्रभाभिः मिलितशिखः क्वथितस्थालीसलिलवत् उद्धौ भ्राम्यमाणे विस्तृतजलभ्रमणात् चिरावस्थितदार्वादिवत् शैवालित इव ऊर्ध्वायत इत्यर्थः।

77. जलइ वलवाणलो विअ फुट्टइ सेलो व्व रामबाणाहिहओ।
रसइ जलओ व्व उअही खुहिओ लङ्घेइ मारुओ व्व णहअलम्।।

[ज्वलति वडवानल इव स्फुटति शैल इव रामबाणाभिहतः।
रसति जलद इवोदधिः क्षुभितो लङ्घयति मारुत इव नभस्तलम्।।]

Smitten by Rāma's arrows the raging sea blazed like the submarine fire, and clove like a mountain; rumbled like the clouds, and assailed the sky like a gale.

Kula reads प्रलयानलः for *valavāṇalo*.

78. होइ थिमिअम्मि थिमिओ वलइ वलन्तम्मि विहडइ विसंघडिए।
परिवड्ढिअम्मि वड्ढइ सलिले झीणम्मि णवर झिज्जइ जलणो।।

[भवति स्तिमिते स्तिमितो वलति वलमाने विघटते विसंघटिते।
परिवर्धिते वर्धते सलिले क्षीणे केवलं क्षीयते ज्वलनः।।]

The fire stood still when the waters became calm; rolled when they rolled; broke up when they parted asunder; swelled when they swelled; and subsided only when they subsided.

K and MY read ज्वलति (*jalai*) for *hoi* (R and Kula).

MY says इन्धनीभूतस्य अम्भसः क्षय एव परमग्निरक्षीयत। अन्यदा तुतदेकीभूततया तद्वत् स्वयमपि प्रावर्धतेत्यर्थः।

79. रामसराणलपअविअझिज्जन्तोअहिविहत्ततडविच्छेआ।
ते च्चिअ तहवित्थारा तुङ्गा दीसन्ति दीवमण्डलिबन्धा।।

[रामशरानलप्रतापितक्षीयमाणोदधिविभक्ततटविच्छेदाः।
त एव तथाविस्तारास्तुङ्गा दृश्यते द्वीपमण्डलीबन्धाः।।]

The groups of islands, with their coastline distinct on account of the sea subsiding, heated by the fire of Rāma's arrows, looked higher while remaining the same in extent.

K reads विस्तीर्णाः (*vitthiṇṇā*) for *vitthārā* (R and Kula). K and Kula read मण्डलनिवहाः for *maṇḍalibandhā* (R).

K says रामशरानलेन प्रतप्तत्वात् क्षीयमाणे उदधौ विभक्ततटविच्छेदाः परिस्फुटसन्धिबन्धाः त एव प्राक्तना इव द्वीपमण्डलनिवहाः तथाविस्तीर्णा यथापूर्वं विस्तीर्णा अपि जलक्षयात् तुङ्गा दृश्यन्ते स्म।

MY reads *taḍa-vocchea* (तटव्यवच्छेदाः) and explains it as तटसीमानः। He remarks उदधावतिक्षीणे तुङ्गत्वातिशयाविष्करणात् द्वीपानां सन्नपि पूर्ववत् विस्तारो नालक्ष्यतेत्यर्थः।

R says क्षीयमाणे उदधौ विभक्तः प्रव्यक्तः तटविच्छेदः तटविभागो येषां ते। Kula says क्षीयमाणेनोदधिना विभक्तः तटविच्छेदाः तटभागा येषां ते तथा।

80. इअ दाविअपाआलं जलणसिहावट्टमाणजलसंवाअम्।
रामो दलिअमहिहरं खविअभुअंगणिवहं खवेइ समुद्दम्।।

[इति दर्शितपातालं ज्वलनशिखावर्त्यमानजलसंघातम्।
रामो दलितमहीधरं क्षपितभुजंगनिवहं क्षपयति समुद्रम्।।]

Thus did Rāma overthrow the ocean, with its waters swirled by the flames, the mountains shattered, the serpents destroyed, and the bottom exposed.

K reads त्रुटित (*khuḍia?*) for *khavia* (क्षपित) found in R and Kula.

K says ज्वलनशिखाभिरावर्तमानजलसंघातं, त्रुटितभुजङ्गनिवहं यथा क्षपयति नाशयति

स्म समुद्रम्। MY has आवर्तमान like K[65]. R says ज्वलनशिखाभिरावर्त्यमानो दह्यमानो जलसंघातो यत्र। Kula says ज्वलनशिखया (क्व)थ्यमानजलसंघातम्। *SC* text has *āaṭṭamāṇa* for *āvaṭṭa-* = क्वाथ्यमान (*chāyā*)।

81. जलपब्भारपलोट्टिअभमन्तसङ्खउलविहलमुक्कक्कन्दम्।
फुडिअवडवामुहाणलपलित्तदरदड्ढसंचरन्तविसहरम्।।

[जलप्राग्भारप्रलुठितभ्रमच्छङ्खकुलविह्वलमुक्ताक्रन्दम्।
स्फुटितवडवामुखानलप्रदीप्तदरदग्धसंचरद्विषधरम्।।]

The conches piteously wailed, rolling and straying amidst the billows: and the half-burnt serpents wriggled, scorched by the blazing submarine fire.

K reads क्षुभित (*khuhia*) for *phuḍia* (स्फुटित) found in R and Kula. The order of verses in K after 81 is 84, 82, 83, 85.

K says जलप्राग्भारे प्रलुठितैः। (R also) शङ्खकुलैः। Kula says जलप्राग्भारात् भ्रष्टेन शङ्खकुलेन। He also says स्फुटितेन विकसितेन वडवामुखानलेन, etc.

82. झिज्जन्तजलालोइअकिरणमुणिज्जन्तरअणपव्वअसिहरम्।
थोरतरङ्गकराहअदिसालआभग्गपडिअजलहरविडवम्।।

[क्षीयमाणजलालोकितकिरणज्ञायमानरत्नपर्वतशिखरम्।
स्थूलतरङ्गकराहतदिग्लताभग्नपतितजलधरविटपम्।।]

The peaks of the (submerged) jewel mountains could be recognized by their lustre in the dwindling waters; and the clouds dropped, like broken branches, from the regions of the sky, creepers as it were, battered by the ocean's hands, its massive waves.

83. साणलसरणिद्दारिअसकेसरुज्जलिअसीहमअरक्खन्धम्।
आसण्णभीअविसहरवेढिअकरिमअरधवलदन्तप्फलिहम्।।

[सानलशरनिर्दारितसकेसरोज्ज्वलितसिंहमकरस्कन्धम्।
आसन्नभीतविषधरवेष्टितकरिमकरधवलदन्तपरिघम्।।]

Pierced by the fiery arrows, the hairy shoulders of the sea lions burst into flames; and the terrified serpents, near at

---

[65] B, however, has *āaṭṭamāṇa* आवर्त्यमान।

hand, twined round the stout white tusks of the sea elephants.

K reads सकेसर for सकेसरु (R and Kula). He says सानलैः शरनिर्दारितकेसरैः सह ज्वलितः सिंहमकरस्कन्धो यत्र। Kula says सकेसरा ऊर्ध्वं ज्वलिताः सिंहमकराणां स्कन्धा यत्र तम्।

84. धुअपव्वअसिहरपडन्तमणिसिलाभग्गविद्दुमलआवेढम्।
दरडड्ढविसहरुज्झिअविसपङ्कक्खुत्तविहलकरिमअरउलम्।।

[धुतपर्वतशिखरपतन्मणिशिलाभग्नविद्रुमलतावेष्टम्।
दरदग्धविषधरोज्झितविषपङ्कमग्नविह्वलकरिमकरकुलम्।।]

The gem rocks falling from the peaks of the mountain,[66] shaken by the arrows, shattered the spreading coral-reefs; and the sea elephants were helpless, being stuck in the clammy poison emitted by the half-burnt serpents.

K says शराभिघातेन धुतानां पर्वतानां शिखरेभ्यः पतन्तीभिः मणिशिलाभिः भग्नविद्रुमलतामण्डलम्। दरदग्धविषधरोत्सृष्टे विषपङ्के मग्नविह्वलकरिमकरकुलम्। Kula says विषपङ्केषु क्षिप्तं लग्नं विह्वलं करिमकरकुलं यत्र तम्। He seems to read *paṅkakkhitta*. Cf. *paṅkukkhitta* found in manuscript C of Goldschmidt. Others read *-kkhutta* (मग्न)। Cf. Hemacandra 4.101 - *khuppai*, *majjai*. Kula also reads दव for दर।

85. रुन्दावत्तपहोलिरवेलावडिएक्कमेक्कभिण्णमहिहरम्।
णहअरुविलग्गवेविरधूमलआविसमलङ्घिअदिसाआलम्।।

[स्थूलावर्तप्रघूर्णमानवेलापतितैकैकभिन्नमहीधरम्।
नभस्तरुविलग्नवेपनशीलधूमलताविषमलङ्घितदिग्जालम्।।]

The mountains, spinning in the vast whirlpools, were dashed against each other, and crumbled; and the regions were covered here and there by the quivering creeper-like smoke[67] ascending the tree that was the sky.

K reads उद्धावत् for *rundāvatta* (स्थूल or बृहदावर्त) found in R and Kula. He reads *veā-* for *velā* (R); and *disāhoaṁ* for *disāālaṁ* दिग्जालम् (R and Kula)।

[66] The mountains mentioned in this and the next two verses are the winged ones hidden in the ocean, for which see verses 37 and 51. Cf. also verse 82.

[67] I.e. the streaks of smoke visible towards the end of the conflagration.

K says शरभयादुद्धावद्भिः, अशक्त्या घूर्णमानैः, वेगेनापतितैः एकैकैः परस्परैरिव भिन्नमहीधरम्। नभस्तरुविलग्नाभिः वेपमानाभिः धूममयीभिः लताभिर्विषमव्याप्त-दिगाभोगम्।

My reads *uddhāanta* and explains it as उर्ध्वायमान। K's reading is same (see above). As in 9.69 he explains *uddhāanta* as उद्धावत्।

Kula says वेगेन (? cf. *SC*) अपहताः स्खलिता अन्योनभिन्ना महीधरा यत्र। He seems to read *avahaa* (cf. 14.28) for *āvaḍia*. R says वेलायामापतिता अत एव एकैकं परस्परं भिन्ना दलिता महीधरा यत्र तम्।

86. पक्खपरिरक्खणुट्ठिअसरणिवहाहअदिसापइण्णमहिहरम्।
फुडिअजलमज्झणिग्गअफुडरअणुज्जोअसंघिउब्भडविवरम्।।

[पक्षपरिरक्षणोत्थितशरनिवहाहतदिक्प्रकीर्णमहीधरम्।
स्फुटितजलमध्यनिर्गतस्फुटरत्नोद्दयोतसंहितोद्भटविवरम्।।]

The mountains were scattered on all sides, struck down by the arrows as they flew aloft to save their wings; and the yawning gaps[68] were filled with the radiant lustre of the gems emerging from the bosom of the waters rent in twain.

K says पक्षपरिरक्षणार्थमुत्थिताः तदानीं शरनिवहैः आतताः (*chāyā* has आहत), दिक्षु प्रकीर्णा महीधराः यथा भवन्ति। स्फुटितस्य जलस्य मध्यात् निर्गतैः स्फुटै रत्नोद्द्योतैः संहितं समाहितं छादितमुद्भटं गम्भीरं जलविवरं यत्र।

Kula says स्फुरितात् (स्फुटितात् ?) विघटितात् जलमध्यात्। K says स्फुटितात् शरप्रवेशपर्वताद्युत्थानेन सरन्ध्रीकृतात् जलमध्यात्।

87. हुअवहपडित्तगोविअणिअणअणुम्हाविसण्ठुलमहग्गाहम्।
परिवड्डिएक्कमेक्काणुराअसरपहरणिव्वलिअसङ्खउलम्।।८७।।

[हुतवहप्रदीप्तगोपितनिजनयनोष्मविसंष्ठुलमहाग्राहम्।
परिवर्धितैकैकानुरागशरप्रहारनिर्वलितशङ्खकुलम्।।]

Scorched by the fire, the sea monsters that hid their claws in their bodies were overpowered by the heat;[69] and the conches, clinging to one another with mutual affection,[70] were driven asunder by the impact of the arrows.

---

[68] I.e. those caused by the mountains escaping from the sea.

[69] Cf. Mādhava in Extracts.

[70] Lit. whose mutual affection was intensified.

K, MY and Kula read *ṇiaa-ṇahumhā* for *ṇia-ṇaaṇumhā* (R).

K says हुतवहप्रदीप्तत्वात् गोपितानामन्तःप्रवेशितानां नखानामूष्मणा दाहोष्मणा विह्वलमहाग्राहम्। ग्राहाणां नखाः त्वचा छन्न एव भवन्ति संरम्भसमये निर्गच्छन्तीति प्रसिद्धम्। परिवृद्धपरस्परानुरागं संश्लिष्टं, शरप्रहारेण निर्व्यक्तं पृथग्भूतं शङ्खकुलं यथा भवति तथा क्षपयामासेति।

MY reads *ṇūmia* rendered as गोपित for *govia* (R). This seems to be K's reading also. For Kula see below.

MY says हुतवहप्रदीप्ता, गोपितनिजनखा, ऊष्मविसंस्थुलाश्च महाग्राहा यथा भवन्ति तथेत्यर्थः। उदधिदाहरोषविनिर्गतानां प्रवृत्तदाहतया पुनर्निचुलितानां नखानामूष्मपातेन[71] विवशीभूतसिंहमकरमित्यर्थः।

Kula says हुतवहेन प्रदीप्ताः, स्वगात्रेष्वेव गोपिता ये निजकनखास्तेषामूष्मणा। परिवर्धितान्योन्यानुरागं कृतघनाश्लेषमित्यर्थः। Kula seems to read *ṇūmia* which is the manuscript reading of *SC* text. See editor's footnote. Hemacandra 4.21 gives *ṇūmai* as the equivalent of छादयति।

R says गोपितयोः मुद्रितयोः निजनयनयोरूष्मणा।

इअ सिरिपवरसेणविरइए कालिदासकए दसमुहवहे महाकव्वे
पञ्चमो आसासओ समत्तो।

[इति श्रीप्रवरसेनविरचिते कालिदासकृते दशमुखवधे महाकाव्ये
पञ्चम आश्वासकः समाप्तः।]

---

[71] तापेन B.

षष्ठ आश्वासकः
Sixth Āśvāsakaḥ

1. अह णिग्गओ जलन्तं दरडड्ढमहाभुअंगपाअवणिवहम्।
मोत्तूण धूमभरिअं पाआलवणं दिशागओ व्व समुद्दो।।

[अथ निर्गतो ज्वलद्दरदग्धमहाभुजंगपादपनिवहम्।
मुक्त्वा धूमभृतं पातालवनं दिग्गज इव समुद्रः।।]

Then did the Ocean emerge, like an elephant of the quarters, abandoning the blazing sea floor, which resembled a wilderness pervaded by smoke, and was full of huge half-burnt serpents like unto trees.

K says अथ समुद्रः ज्वलद्दरदग्धमहाभुजङ्गाख्यपादपनिवहं धूमपूरितं पातालवनं मुक्त्वा दिग्गज इव मूर्तिमान् निर्गतः। यथा दिग्गज आत्मनिवासस्थानं दवाग्निना प्रदीप्यमानं मुक्त्वा निर्गच्छति तद्वदिति।

2. मन्दरदढपरिमट्ठं पलअविअम्भिअवराहदाढुल्लिहिअम्।
विसमं समुव्वहन्तो रामसराघाअदूमिअं वच्छअडम्।।

[मन्दरदृढपरिमृष्टं प्रलयविजृम्भितवराहदंष्ट्रोल्लिखितम्।
विषमं समुद्वहन्रामशराघातदुःखितं वक्षस्तटम्।

His rugged bosom, once heavily crushed by the Mandara mountain,[1] and bruised by the tusk of the Primeval Boar that mightily arose at the epoch of destruction,[2] was afflicted by the impact of Rāma's arrows.

K and MY read तटपरिघृष्टं for *daḍha-parimaṭṭhaṁ* = दृढपरिमृष्टं (R). MY (B) has *parimaṭṭha* like R but this might be a mistake. K reads *dāḍhā-lihiaṁ* for *dāḍhuhihiaṁ* (R and Kula).

K says मथनावस्थायां मन्दरस्य तटैः परिघृष्टं निकषितं, प्रलयसमयविजृम्भितस्य महावराहस्य दंष्ट्रया लिखितं, इदानीं रामशराघातेन दूनं परितापितं, अतएव विषमं वक्षस्तटं वहन्।

---

[1] The mountain was used as a staff by the gods and demons to churn the ocean.

[2] See verses 12 and 13.

MY says *pariaḍḍha* (?) परिघृष्ट। भगवतस्तत्तदवतारोद्देश्यकार्यनिर्वर्तन-निमित्तव्रणाङ्कम्, अतएव निम्नोन्नतं वक्षः पुरो दर्शयितुमिवोद्वहन् इत्यर्थः। अथवा पूर्वं मन्दरतटवराहदंष्ट्राभ्यां घर्षणलेखनमात्राङ्कितमिदानीं तु रामशरक्षतविषमं वक्षो भारमिव दुर्वहमुद्वहन् इत्यर्थः।

Kula says विषममितस्ततो जातकिणत्वात्। He has परिघृष्ट like K and MY. SC Text has *parihaṭṭha* rendered in the *chāyā* as परिघृष्ट। The phrase is quoted in Hemacandra 2.174 as *mandarayaḍa-parighaṭṭhaṁ*. It will be seen that HC reads *aḍa* (तट) like K and MY for *aḍha* (R and Kula).

3. गम्भीरवणाहोए दीहे देहसरिसे भुए वहमाणो।
अहिणवचन्दणगन्धे अणहुक्खित्ते व्व मलअसरिआसोत्ते।।

[गम्भीरव्रणाभोगौ दीर्घौ देहसदृशौ भुजौ वहमानः।
अभिनवचन्दनगन्धावनघोत्क्षिप्ताविव मलयसरित्स्रोतसी।।]

His long arms, befitting his body, and covered with deep and large wounds, and fragrant with fresh sandal paste, resembled two freely overflowing streams of the Malaya mountain, lined with deep woods, and wafting the scent of the fresh sandal trees (on their banks).

K says गम्भीरशरव्रणविस्तारौ, दीर्घौ, देहानुरूपौ, अभिनवचन्दनगन्धौ शैत्यहेतोरर्पितस्याभिनवस्य चन्दनस्य गन्धयुक्तौ (भुजौ वहमानः)। अनघोत्क्षिप्ते अक्लेशेनानायासेन उद्धृते मलयसरित्स्रोतसीव दृश्यमानौ। तत्र गम्भीरवनाभोगे, अभिनवचन्दनगन्धे इति।

MY says *vaṇāhoa* व्रणाभोगो वनाभोगश्च। *aṇaha* अनघ अक्षत अविशीर्णेत्यर्थः। सलितात्मतया समुद्रस्य तदभुजयोः स्रोतःसाम्यौचित्यम्। Kula says अनघमपापं निःशेषं यथा स्यात् तथा उत्क्षिप्ते उद्वृत्ते मलयसरित्स्रोतसीव दीर्घौ भुजौ वहमानः, R says अनभसि अनाकाशेऽर्थात् भूमौ उत्क्षिप्ते पर्वतात् निपत्योच्छलिते। तथा च ते अपि मलयात् समुद्रे पतत इति। यथा ते वहमानस्तथा भुजावपीति सहोपमा।

4. लहुइअकोत्थुहविरहं मन्दरगिरिमहणसंभमे वि अमुक्कम्।
तारेक्कावलिरअणं ससिमइरामअसहोअरं वहमाणो।।

[लघूकृतकौस्तुभविरहं मन्दरगिरिमथनसंभ्रमेऽप्यमुक्तम्।
तारैकावलिरत्नं शशिमदिरामृतसहोदरं वहमानः।।]

He was wearing a radiant pearlstring, the best of its kind, which shared the qualities of the moon, wine and nectar, and lightened his sorrow at the loss of the *kaustubha* gem,[3] and which he had not surrendered even during the commotion caused by the churning with the Mandara mountain.

K reads रत्नं (*raaṇaṁ*) for *virahaṁ* (R and Kula)।

K says एकावलिरेव रत्नम्। तार: सुमौक्तिकम्। तारस्तु मुक्ताशुद्धौ सुमौक्तिके इति वैजयन्ती। तारै: कृतमेकावलारत्नं वहमान:। कीदृशं–लघूकृत–कौस्तुभरत्नं, मन्दरगिरिमथनसंभ्रमेऽपि अतिमहार्घत्वादमुक्तम्। Kula says सर्वस्वमपि दत्त्वा तथाविधनिग्रहेऽपि रक्षितमिति भाव:।

MY reads *viaṇaṁ* for virahaṁ. He says *viaṇā* वेदना।

Kula says शशिमदिरामृतसहोदरमिति शशिवदाह्लादकारि मदिरावत् मदहेतु: अमृतवत् सर्वदोषहरं तारा विशुद्धा या एकावली सैव रत्नं स्वजात्युत्कृष्टत्वात् तद वहमान:।

5. गरुअं उव्वहमाणो हत्थप्फरिसपडिसिद्धवणवेअल्लम्।
रुहिरारुणरोमञ्चं खलन्तगङ्गावलम्बिअं वामभुअम्।।
(आइकुलअम्)

[गुरुकमुद्वहमानो हस्तस्पर्शप्रतिषिद्धव्रणवैकल्यम्।
रुधिरारुणरोमाञ्चं स्खलद्गङ्गावलम्बितं वामभुजम्।।]
(आदिकुलकम्)

His weary left arm, with the bristling hair reddened by blood, was supported by his consort Gaṅgā as she came with faltering steps; while the suffering caused by the wounds was assuaged by the touch of her hand.

K says भयात् स्खलन्त्या गङ्गयावलम्बितं स्त्रीणां भर्तुर्वामपार्श्वाश्रयत्वात् भार्यया गङ्गयावलम्बितम्, अतएव तस्या हस्तस्पर्शेन प्रतिषिद्धशरव्रणवैकल्यम्। वैकल्यं विकलभाव: वेदनेत्यर्थ:। रुधिरेणारुणितरोमाञ्च, गुरुम् एवंभूतत्वात् दक्षिणहस्तादपि वरिष्ठं वामभुजमुद्वहमान:। MY also says हस्तस्पर्शेति गङ्गाया इति शेष: Kula says सवेदनत्वात् गुरुकं, गङ्गाया: प्रियाया: हस्तस्पर्शेन प्रतिषिद्धव्रणवैक्लव्यम्।

6. आलीणो अ रहुवइं णिअअच्छाआणुलित्तमलअमणिसिलम्।
संसिअसुहोअइव्वं दुमं लआए व्व जाणईअ विरहिअम्।।

---

[3] I.e. made him forget the loss of this gem, which was taken out of the ocean during the churning, like the moon and the rest.

[आलीनश्च रघुपतिं निजकच्छायानुलिप्तमलयमणिशिलम्।
संश्रितसुखोपजीव्यं द्रुमं लतयेव जानक्या विरहितम्।।]

He approached Rāma, who was easily accessible to those who sought refuge. Separated from Sītā, he was like a tree bereft of a creeper; while the gem rocks of the Malaya mountain were suffused with the lustre of his body.

K reads *mahiharaṁ* for *maṇi-silaṁ* (R and Kula). Kula *pratīka* has *allīṇo* for *ālīṇo* (R). MY agrees with Kula. K's *pratīka* seems to be same.

K says समुद्रः निजया छायया शोभया व्याप्तमलयमहीधरं, संश्रितैः सुखमुपजीव्यं, जानक्या विरहितं रघुपतिमाश्रितश्च। कमिव लतया विरहितं द्रुममिव। विशेषणमुभयत्र समानम्।

MY says allīṇo आलीनः प्राप्तः।

7. सरघाअरुहिरकुसुमो तिवहअवल्लीपिणद्धमणिरअणफलो।
रामचरणेसु उअही दढफ्वणाइद्धपाअओ व्व णिवडिओ।।

[शरघातरुधिरकुसुमस्त्रिपथगावल्लीपिनद्धमणिरत्नफलः।
रामचरणयोरुदधिर्दृढपवनाविद्धपादप इव निपतितः।।]

The Ocean fell at Rāma's feet, like a tree dashed down by a gale. The blood from the wounds caused by the arrows was the flowers, and the precious gems worn by Gaṅgā, slim as a creeper, were the fruit.

K and MY have an entirely different verse here, the general sense being the same. The *chāyā* in K is.

शीर्षरचिताञ्जलिपुटः शरवेदनादूनिताननः सलिलनिधिः। पादयोः दाशरथेः पवनवशक्षिप्तपादप इव निपतितः।। K only says स्पष्टोऽर्थः।

MY says *pāesu* पादयोः *osuddha* अवपातित। He seems to read *vasosuddha* for *vasa-kkhitta* (K) in the second line.

Kula agrees with R.

8. पच्छा अ हित्थहिअआ जत्तो च्चिअ णिग्गआ विवह्लत्थमुही।
हरिचरणम्मि तहिं चिअ कमलाअम्बम्मि तिवहआ वि णिवडिआ।।

[पश्चाच्च त्रस्तहृदया यत एव निर्गता विपर्यस्तमुखी।
हरिचरणे तत्रैव कमलाताम्रे त्रिपथगापि निपतिता।।]

Thereafter Gaṅgā, too, overcome with fear, and turning her face aside, fell at Hari's feet, rosy as the day lotus, the very feet from which she had emerged.[4]

K says त्रस्तहृदया, अतएव विपर्यस्तमुखी स्त्रीस्वाभावात् भयाच्च परावृत्तमुखी त्रिपथगा च पूर्वं यत एव निर्गता तस्मिन्नेव कमलाताम्रे हरिचरणे निपतिता।

Kula says पश्चाच्च यत एव हरिचरणात् निर्गता। अनेन दुहितृधर्मो दर्शितः। अतो भर्त्रा सह पितृसमीपागमनं लज्जाकरमित्याह। *hittha- hiaā* व्रीडितहृदया। हित्थं व्रीडितभीतयोरिति देशीयदर्शनात्। अतो विपर्यस्तमुखी तत्रैव हरिचरणे कमलाताम्रे त्रिपथगापि निपतिता . . . पितृपदप्रणाममकरोदिति भावः।

MY says *hittha* त्रस्त।

9. अह मउअं पि भरसहं जम्पइ थोअं पि अत्थसारब्भहिअम्।
पणअं पि धीरगरुअं थुइसंबद्धं पि अणलिअं सलिलणिही।।

[अथ मृदुमपि भरसहं जल्पति स्तोकमप्यर्थसाराभ्यधिकम्।
प्रणतमपि धैर्यगुरुकं स्तुतिसंबद्धमप्यनलीकं सलिलनिधिः।।]

The Ocean then uttered words that were cogent though soft in tone; deeply significant though brief; dignified though polite; and outspoken though accompanied with praise.

K says अथ सलिलनिधिः रामं प्रति एवं जल्पति स्म। मृद्वपि सुकुमारमपि प्रयोजनभरस्य सहम्। स्तोकं परिमितमपि अर्थस्य सारेण उत्कर्षेण अभ्यधिकमतिमहत्। प्रणतमपि प्रणतियुक्तमपि धैर्यात् गुरु उन्नतं, स्तुतिसंबद्धमपि अनलीकमवितथं वचनमित्यध्याहर्तव्यम्।

MY says मृद्वपि भरसहं कोमलसंदर्भमपि हेतुहेतुमद्भावावस्थितकर्कशार्थप्रतिपादकं, मिताक्षरमपि अमितसारार्थं प्रणयं प्रार्थनारूपम्।

Kula says भरसहं विमर्दक्षमं प्रकर्षेण नतमपि धैर्यगुरुकम् असुलङ्घ्यं अनलीकं यथार्थं सलिलनिधिर्जल्पति।

10. दुत्तारत्तणगरुइं थिरधीरपरिग्गहं तुमे च्चिअ ठविअम्।
अणुवालन्तेण ठिइं पिअं ति तुह विप्पिअं मए कह वि कअम्।।

[दुस्तारत्वगुर्वी स्थिरधैर्यपरिग्रहां त्वयैव स्थापिताम्।
अनुपालयता स्थितिं प्रियमिति तव विप्रियं मया कथमपि कृतम्।।]

Somehow have I incurred thy displeasure by maintaining my stability, fortified by my untraversable character, thinking

[4] Rāma is identified with Viṣṇu from whose feet the sacred river is said to have issued.

it would please thee, because it was obtained by thyself,[5] and sustained by me with unflinching fortitude.

K says दुस्तरत्वेन गुर्वी, स्थिरगाम्भीर्यपरिग्रहां, त्वयैव पूर्वं स्थापितां स्थितमवस्थानं तव प्रियमित्यनुपालयता मया कथमपि केनापि प्रकारेण तव विप्रियं कृतम्।

Kula says दुस्तरत्वेन गुरुं दर्वहां, स्थिरो धैर्यपरिग्रहो यस्यास्तां . . . त्वयैव स्थापितां स्थितिं त्रिभुवनव्यवस्थाकारिणीं मर्यादां कथं नाम देवस्याप्रीतिः स्यादिति प्रियबुद्ध्या अनुपालयता मया तव विप्रियं कथमपि कृतम्। अपिशब्दो नामार्थः। कथं नाम कृतं न कृतमेवेति भावः। अथवा कथमपीदं विप्रियकारणं, किं तदित्यहं तावन्न जानामीत्यर्थः। अतएव प्रभोरत्र न दोषो ममैवायं कर्मविपाक इति मधुरोपालम्भो दर्शितः।

11. विअसन्तरअक्खउरं मअरन्दरसुद्धुमाअमुहलमहुअरम्।
उदुणा दुमाण दिज्जइ हीरइ ण उणो तमप्यण च्चिअ कुसुमम्।।

[विकसद्रजःकलुषं मकरन्दरसाध्मातमुखरमधुकरम्।
ऋतुना द्रुमाणां दीयते ह्रियते न पुनस्तदात्मनैव कुसुमम्।।]

The seasons give the trees flowers in bloom, tinted by pollen, with the humming bees glutted with honey, but do not themselves take them away.[6]

K says विकसदवस्थायां रजोभिः शबलं, मकरन्दरसेन पूरितमुखरभ्रमरं कुसुमं ऋतुना द्रुमाणां दीयते, तत् पुनरात्मनैव कदापि ह्रियते खलु। तस्मात् भवता दत्तं पदं भवतैव न हर्तव्यमिति। K-(*chāyā*) has रजः कर्बुरं, रसाध्मात, and ह्रियते न पुनरपि आत्मनैव कुसुमम्।

Kula says विकसद्रजामिश्रकलुषं, मकरन्दरसाध्मातमुखरमधुकरम्, ऋतुना द्रुमाणां कुसुमं दीयते न पुनश्च आत्मनैव ह्रियते। एतेन देवेन इयं दुस्तरत्वगुर्वी स्थितिर्दत्ता नैनामपहर्तुं देवोऽर्हतीति भावः।

12. किं पम्हट्ठ म्हि अहं तुह चलणुप्पण्णतिवहआपडिउण्णम्।
खअकालाणलखविअं धरणिअलुद्धरणविलुलिअं अप्पाणम्।।

[किं प्रस्मृतवानस्म्यहं तव चरणोत्पन्नत्रिपथगाप्रतिपूर्णम्।
क्षयकालानलक्षपितं धरणितलोद्धरणविलुलितमात्मानम्।।]

---

[5] I.e. Rāma as Viṣṇu. The Ocean maintains that he resisted Rāma to preserve his preordained stability.

[6] I.e. the stability of the ocean is an irrevocable gift from Rāma himself, considered as Viṣṇu.

Have I forgotten that I was destroyed by the fire of the epoch of universal ruin; and was filled by the waters of the Gaṅgā emanating from thy feet;[7] and (again) crushed by thee at the time of uplifting the earth?[8]

K and MY read क्षयदुष्कालानुचरं for *khaa-kālāṇala-khaviaṁ* = क्षयकालानलक्षपितम् (R and Kula)।

K says तव चरणोत्पन्नया त्रिपथगया परिपूर्णं (प्रतिपूर्णं others), क्षयाख्यदुष्काले तवानुचरं सकलभुवनसंहारात् भवतः सहायभूतं, धरणितलोद्धरणे त्वया वराहरूपिणा विलुलितमात्मानमिदानीम् अहं किं विस्मृतोऽस्मि स्मराम्येव। तस्मात् भवतो नाहमवज्ञामाचरामि। Kula says विलुलितं विमर्दितम्।

Hemacandra 3.105 cites the initial phrase of the verse and reads *pamhuṭṭha* for *pamhaṭṭha* (प्रस्मृत)। K *pratīka* in our copy has *kiṁ pammuṭṭho*. My *pratīka* has *kiṁ pamhaṭṭha*, but manuscript B adds *pamhuṭṭho* प्रस्मृतः विस्मृतवानित्यर्थः। The *pratīka* in manuscript B is *kiṁ pamhaṭṭho mhi*.

13. चलणेहिँ महुविरोहे दाढाघाएहिँ धरणिवेढुद्धरणे।
सोअकिलिन्तेण तुमे इण्हिं दहमुहवहे सरेहिं विलुलिओ॥

[चरणाभ्यां(चलनैर्वा) मधुविरोधे दंष्ट्राघातैर्धरणिवेष्टोद्धरणे।
शोकक्लान्तेन त्वया इदानीं दशमुखवधे शरैर्विलुलितः॥]

I was crushed by thy feet during thy fight with the demon Madhu,[9] and by the thrusts of the tusk of the Primeval Boar at the time of raising the earth;[10] and overcome with grief, thou hast now whelmed me with thy arrows on the eve of slaying Rāvaṇa.[11]

K reads स चाहं नाथ त्वया (i.e. *so a ahaṁ ṇāha tume* for *soakilinteṇa tume* (R and Kula) = शोकक्लान्तेन त्वया। MY also says *so a* स च।

K says मधुकैटभविरोधे चराणाभ्यां विलुलितः अस्मि। धरणिमण्डलोद्धरणे दंष्ट्राघातैः

---

[7] Cf. verse 8.

[8] I.e. the earth submerged in the ocean during the deluge. A reference to the Boar incarnation of Viṣṇu. See 4.22, 39; 5.44.

[9] The fight took place in the ocean.

[10] See the preceding verse.

[11] The ocean recounts the exploits of Rāma as Viṣṇu, pointing out the cruelty with which he was treated in each of them.

क्षोभितोऽस्मि। एवंभूतः सोऽहमिदानीं दशमुखवधे शरैश्च विलुलितोऽस्मि। तव कार्यान्तरप्रसंगे सम पीडा सिद्धैवेत्युपालम्भः। R says विलुलितो विमर्दितः।

14. णिअआवत्थाहि वि मे एअं धीरेण विप्पिअं धीर कअम्।
जं णेण पअइसोम्मा कह वि विसंवाइआ तुह मुहच्छाआ।।

[निजकावस्थाया अपि मे एकं धैर्येण विप्रियं धीर कृतम्।
यदनेन प्रकृतिसौम्या कथमपि विसंवादिता तव मुखच्छाया।।]

Wise one, my fortitude[12] hath caused me a greater woe than even my physical suffering[13] in that I have thereby somehow ruffled thy countenance, serene by nature.

K reads निजावस्था हीयं for *ṇiaāvatthāhi vi me* = निजकावस्थाया अपि मे (R and Kula); and केवलं (*ṇavara*) for धीर (R and Kula)।

K says निजा मदीयावस्था हीयं त्वदीयेन रोषेण यादृशः कृतोऽस्मि सैषा खलु ममावस्था। एवं धीरेण एवं शक्तिमाता केवलं तव विप्रियं कृतमभूत। तव विप्रियं कर्तुं के वयम्। तथापि कृतमेव। कथमिति चेत्, अनेन कारणेन प्रकृतिसौम्या प्रकृत्या प्रसन्ना तव मुखशोभा कथमपि विसंवादिता विकृतेति यत् तस्मादिति।

MY says विप्रियमेतदेवेत्यर्थः। Kula says निजकावस्थातोऽपि अधिकमेवैतत् धैर्येण विप्रियं कृतम्। अतोऽप्यधिकं मम दुःखं वर्तत इत्यर्थः। किं तदिति यदनेन धैर्येण प्रकृतिसौम्या . . . तव मुखच्छाया कथमपि मदीयप्रमादेन समुदितरोषजननात् अन्या कृता (अन्यथा कृता R)। R explains *eaṁ* as एकम्।

15. एअं तुह एआरिससुरकज्जसहस्सखेअवीसामसहम्।
जअपव्वालणजोग्गं परिरक्खसु पलअरक्खिअं जलणिवहम्।।

[एवं (एतं वा) तवैतादृशसुरकार्यसहस्रखेदविश्रामसहम्।
जगप्प्लावनयोग्यं परिरक्षस्व प्रलयरक्षितं जलनिवहम्।।]

So save these waters, capable of inundating the world, and stored up for the deluge, that also allay thy fatigue caused by a thousand such tasks on behalf of the gods.[14]

K says एवं तवैतादृशानां सुरकार्यसहस्राणां निर्वर्तनजनिते खेदे सति विश्रामस्य सहायभूतम्, अतएव प्रलयार्थं रक्षितं रक्षणीयं, प्रलये जगतः प्लावनसमर्थं जलनिवहमिमं परिरक्ष मा विनाशय।

---

[12] As seen in his resistence to Rāma.

[13] Lit. condition.

[14] The ocean is the resting place of Viṣṇu with whom Rāma is identified.

Kula says जगत्प्लावनयोग्यं प्रलयरक्षितं प्रलयानलादपि रक्षितमेव जलनिवहं परिरक्षस्व। जलत्प्लावनार्थं च रक्षणमस्योचितमिति भाव:।

16. अपरिट्ठिअमूलतलं जत्तो गम्मइ तहिं दलन्तमहिअलम्।
ण हु सलिलणिब्भरं चिअ खविए वि ममम्मि दुग्गमं पाआलम्।।

[अपरिस्थितमूलअलं यतो गम्यते तत्र दलन्महीतलम्।
न खलु सलिलनिर्भरमेव क्षयितेऽपि मयि दुर्गमं पातालम्।।]

The sea floor is impassable not only when I am full of water,[15] but even when I am dried up, because its foundation is unstable, and the ground splits wherever it is trodden.

K and MY (ms. B) *pratīka* has *apaḍiṭṭhia* for *apari** (R). Kula *pratīka* has *avari**. K reads *ṇibbhara ccia* which is mentioned by R as a variant. Kula reads *ṇibbharaṁ cia* like R.

K says एवं क्षपितेऽपि मयि यतो येन प्रदेशेन युष्माभिर्गम्यते तत्रापि दलन्महीतलं पङ्कमयत्वात् दीर्यमाणस्थलं पातालं दुर्गमं स्यात्। मयि सलिलनिर्भर एव केवलं न खलु दुर्गमम्। तस्मात् जलशोषणमकिंचित्करमेव।

Kula says अक्षयिते मयि सलिलनिभरमेव जलभरितमेव पातालं दुर्गमं न खलु। क्षयितेऽपि मयि दुर्गमं पातालम्। कथमित्याह – अपरिस्थितम् अवधिशून्यं मूलस्य तलमधोभागो यस्य तत् तथा। यत्र गम्यते तत्र दलन्महीतलम्। एतेन तलस्य प्राप्ति: पङ्कदु:सरत्वं च दर्शितम्। R says अपरिस्थितं न परि सर्वतोभावेन स्थितम्। अदृढमित्यर्थ:।

17. तं कालस्स णिसम्मउ कह वि दरुक्कित्तदसमकण्ठक्खलिअम्।
घडिअगिरिसेउबन्धं चिरआलाउञ्चिअं दहमुहंम्मि पअम्।।

[तत्कालस्य निषीदतु कथमपि दरोत्कृत्तदशमकण्ठस्खलितम्।
घटितगिरिसेतुबन्धं चिरकालाकुञ्चितं दशमुखं पदम्।।]

So after a causeway composed of mountains hath been built, let the god of death anyhow plant his foot on Rāvaṇa;[16] it hath been held back for long, after it had slid off his partly severed tenth head.[17]

---

[15] The reading *salila-ṇibbhara ccia* is followed. See Extracts.

[16] Lit. let the foot of the god of death rest on Rāvaṇa.

[17] Rāvaṇa had cut-off nine of his heads to please Śiva, and was slashing the tenth when he was deterred by the god with a boon. Yama, balked of his prey, is waiting for another opportunity which will be provided when the suggested bridge to Laṅkā is built.

K reads दरत्रुटित (*darakkhuḍia*, cf. *SC* text) for *darukkitta* = दरोत्कृत्त (R). *SC chāyā* has दरखण्डित। Kula's reading seems to be same.

K says तस्मात् कालस्यान्तकस्य पदं दशमुखे निषीदतु। कथंभूतम् – दरच्छिन्नात् दशमकण्ठात् कथमपि स्खलितमीश्वरसांनिध्यात् प्रतिबद्धं, चिरकालमाकुञ्चितं निक्षेप्तुमुद्यतं, तथा निषीदतु वानरैः घटितसेतुबन्धं यथा। इत्येवमुक्त्वा समुद्रो विरराम।

MY says *taṁ* तस्मात्। जलक्षपणस्य अनुपायत्वादित्यर्थः। Kula says यत एवं तत् तस्मात् कालस्य यमस्य यत् पदं शङ्कराराधनाय नवसु कण्ठेषु छिन्नेषु सत्सु निधातुं प्रसारितम्, कथमपि अथार्धखण्डिते दशमे कण्ठे शङ्करस्य प्रसन्नत्वात् स्खलितं सत्, कदापि निधास्यत इति आरोपणाय चिरकालमाकुञ्चितम् उत्क्षिप्य वक्रयित्वा स्थापितं, तदिदानीं त्वया निःशेषलूनकण्ठे दशमुखे घटितो गिरिभिः सेतुबन्धो निषदनाय यस्मै तद् यथा स्यात् तथा निषीदतु। तत् बध्यतां गिरिसेतुरित्यर्थः।

18–19. अह जअदुप्परिअल्ले दहमुहकुविएण पवअवइपच्चक्खम्।
रहुणाहेण समुद्दे वालिम्मि व बाणणिअमिअम्मि पसन्ते।।

पवआहिवइविइण्णा रामाणन्ती पवंगमेसु विलग्गा।
सेसफणाविच्छूढा तिहुअणसारगरुई महि व्व भुअंगे।।
(जुग्गअम्)

[अथ जगद्दुष्परिकलनीये दशमुखकुपितेन प्लवगपतिप्रत्यक्षम्।
रघुनाथेन समुद्रे वालिनीव बाणनियमिते प्रशान्ते।।

प्लवगाधिपतिवितीर्णा रामाज्ञप्तिः प्लवंगमेषु विलग्ना।
शेषफणाविक्षिप्ता त्रिभुवनसारगुर्वी महीव भुजंगेषु।।]
(युग्मकम्)

When the ocean unfathomable in the world, became calm, subdued by Rāma with his arrows, because the latter was wroth against Rāvaṇa, even as the invincible Vāli was chastised in the presence of Sugrīva; then Rāma's command (to build a causeway), proclaimed by Sugrīva, lay heavy on the apes; even as the earth, heavy-laden with the riches of the universe, rests on the serpents when it is shifted from the hood of Ananta.[18]

---

[18] The great serpent that sustains the weight of the earth. Here, it is fancied as sharing the burden with other serpents.

K (*chāyā*) has जगद्दुष्परिकले। K says जगता परिकलयितुं परिच्छेतुमशक्ये समुद्रे। . . . वालिनीव बाणनियते (बाणनियमिते *chāyā*) प्रशान्ते सति। Kula says नियते दर्पशून्ये कृते। R says जगता दुष्परिकलनीये दुस्तरणीये, पक्षे दुर्जये।

K and MY read *pavaṁgame suvilaggā* for *pavaṁgamesu vilaggā* (R and Kula)।

K says रामस्याज्ञप्तिराज्ञा सेतुबन्धविषया प्लवगाधिपतिना वितीर्णा दत्ता प्लवङ्गमान् सुष्ठु विलग्ना, शेषस्य फणैर्विक्षिप्ता त्रिभुवनसारेण गर्वी मही किङ्करभूतान् भुजङ्गानिव।

MY says *pavaṁgame* प्लवङ्गमान्। *suvilaggā* दृढलग्ना। *bhuaṁge* भुजङ्गान्।

Kula says रामस्याज्ञाप्ति: प्लवगाधिपतिना स्वयं प्रतीष्य वितीर्णा दत्ता प्लवङ्गमेषु सेतुबन्धार्थं . . . आरूढा। शेषफणाविन्यस्ता भुवनसृजेत्यर्थात् त्रिभुवनसारेण गुर्वी महीव भुजङ्गमान्। He refers to the विभक्तिभेद of the उपमेय and the उपमान involved in the construction followed by him, and says अर्थाभेदात् न दोष:।

Kula seems to read *valaggā* (आरूढा) for *vilaggā* = विलग्ना। cf. Hemacandra 4.206. The manuscript reading of *SC* text also is *valaggā*. See editor's footnote. Besides, Kula has विन्यस्त (see above) for विक्षिप्त (*vicchūḍha*). *SC* text has *ṇivvūḍha* (निर्व्यूढ)।

Lokanātha, quoted by *SC*, says like K -रामस्याज्ञप्ति: प्लवङ्गमान् सुष्ठु विलग्ना। See editor's footnote.

20. तो हरिसपढमतुलिए चलिआ फुट्टन्तपम्हविसमूससिए।
वेउक्खअसीमन्ते पवआ धुणिऊण केसरसडुग्घाए।।

[ततो हर्षप्रथमतुलितांश्चलिता स्फुटत्पक्ष्मविषमोच्छ्वसितान्।
वेगोत्खातसीमन्तान्प्लवगा धूत्वा केसरसटोद्धातान्।।]

Thereupon the apes moved forward, shaking their massive hair, which first bristled with joy, and was parted by the speed of their march, spreading out with the hairs distinct.

K reads त्रुट्यत् for *phuṭṭanta* = स्फुटत् (R and Kula)। MY has *khuṭṭanta* त्रुट्यत्।

K says तत: प्लवगा हर्षेण प्रथममेव तुलितान् उच्छ्रितान्, चलनरभसेन त्रुट्यत्पक्ष्मत्वात् दलद्रोमत्वात् विषममुच्छ्वसितान् विकसितान्, वेगेन चलवेगेन उत्खातसीमन्तान् अतिस्फुटीकृतमध्यपद्धतीन् केसरसटोद्धातान् धूत्वा चलिता:।

MY says *ukkhaa* उत्खात अपनीतेत्यर्थ:।

Kula says हर्षेण प्रथमं तुलितानुल्लसितान्। एतेन कार्यारम्भे रोमाञ्चेन मन:प्रसाद:

कार्यसिद्धिहेतुर्दर्शितः। स्फुटत्पक्ष्म विकसत्सूक्ष्मरोम यथा स्यात् तथा विषममत्यन्तमुछ्वसितान् . . . केसरसटासमूहान्। He seems to explain उत्खात as उत्कीर्ण। R says उत्खात् प्रकटीकृतः। Kula remarks – तथाचोक्तम् – मनःप्रसादः सिद्धिलक्षणमिति।

21. पवअक्खोहिअमहिअलधुअमलअपडन्तसिहरमुक्ककलअलो।
उद्धाइओ अणागअघडन्तधरणिहरसंकमो व्व समुद्दो।।

[प्लवगक्षोभितमहीतलधूतमलयपतच्छिखरमुक्तकलकलः।
उद्धावितोऽनागतघटमानधरणिधरसंक्रम इव समुद्रः।।]

As the peaks of the Malaya, which were shaken when the earth was convulsed by the apes, tumbled into the waters the sea roared and surged up, as if the causeway was being built even before the mountains came on the scene.[19]

K says प्लवगक्षोभितेन महीतलेन धुतस्य मलयस्य पतद्भिः शिखरैर्मुक्तकोलाहलः समुद्रः अनागतैरेव धरणिधरैः घटमानसंक्रम इव उच्चलितः (उत्थापितः *chāyā*)। अनानीतेष्वपि पर्वतेषु बध्यमानसेतुरिवेत्यर्थः। Kula says अनागतं प्रागेव घटमानो बन्धं गच्छन् धरणीधरसंक्रमो यत्र तथाभूत इव समुद्र ऊर्ध्वायितः (?) (उद्धावितः उच्छलितः R)।

MY says सेतुबन्धे व्यवस्थिते (व्यवसिते B) समुद्रः स्वयमेव कृतहर्षरवः कपिबलेभ्यः प्रथमत एव सेतुकरणे प्रवृत्त इवलक्ष्यतेत्यर्थः। *aṇāara- ghaḍanta* इति पाठे तु अयत्नघटमानेत्यर्थः।

22. कम्पइ महेन्दसेलो हरिसंखोहेण दलइ मेइणिवेढम्।
सइदुद्दिण्णतणाओ णवर ण उद्धाइ मलअवणकुसुमरओ।।

[कम्पते महेन्द्रशैलो हरिसंक्षोभेण दलति मेदिनीवेष्टम् (पृष्ठं वा)।
सदादुर्दिनार्द्रं केवलं नोद्धावति मलयवनकुसुमरजः।।]

The Mahendra mountain trembled, and the surface of the earth cracked because of the commotion caused by the apes. Only the pollen of the flowers in the woods of the Malaya did not rise aloft, being moistened by the ever cloudy skies.

K reads उत्तिष्ठति (*uṭṭhei*, cf.12.11) for *uddhāī* = उद्धावति (R and Kula)।

K says महेन्द्रशैलः मलयस्य परिसरे महेन्द्रः।

---

[19] I.e. the scene described seemed to be a prelude to the building of the causeway by dropping mountains on the ocean, as described in canto VIII.

23. तो संचालिअसेलं कह वि तुलग्गेण समघडन्तक्कम्पम्।
दूरं पवंगमबलं णहमुहलग्गवसुहं णहं उप्पइअम्।।

[ततः संचालितशैलं कथमपि तुलाग्रेण समघटमानकम्पम्।
दूरं प्लवंगमबलं नखमुखलग्नवसुधं नभ उत्पतितम्।।]

The host of apes, with lumps of earth sticking to the tips of their nails,[20] flew high into the sky, stirring the mountains, and making somehow a simultaneous flight by chance.

K, MY and Kula read *ukkampaṁ* for *°kkampaṁ* (R). For *tulaggeṇa* (तुलाग्रेण) see also Notes on 7.39. It is variously explained as "in a moment", "by chance", "all of a sudden", etc.

K says ततः प्लवङ्गमबलं दूरं नभ उत्पतितम्। कथंभूतं – रभसेन संचालितशैलं, कथमपि केनापि प्रकारेण, तुलाग्रेण क्षणेन, समं युगपदेव घटमानभुवनोत्कम्पं, नखमुखलग्नवसुधम् अवगाढेषु नखमुखेषु लग्नमृत्तिकं भूत्वा उत्पातितम्।

My says *tulaggeṇa samaghaḍantukkampaṁ* एकक्षणोत्पन्नसर्वोत्पतनोद्योग-मित्यर्थः। अथवा मिथस्तुलासंमितोत्साहम्।

Kula says ततः क्षोभेण संचालितशैलं, शैलसंचालनादेव तुलाग्रेण समं सदृशं यथा स्यात् तथा घटमानोत्कम्पं तुलाग्रवदस्थिरमित्यर्थः। अस्थिरत्वादेव कथमपि प्लवङ्गमबलं दूरं नभ उत्पत्तितम्। उत्पतनाय भरदानात् नखमुखलग्नवसुधमिति। R says तुलाग्रंकाकतालीयसंवादः। (cf. *Deśīnāmamālā* 5.15), तेन सममेकदैव घटमानः कम्पः स्पन्दो यस्य।

24. उप्पअणोणअमहिअलणइमुहपडिसोत्तपत्थिओ सलिलणिही।
जलणिवहाहअसिढिले पवउच्छेवणसहे करेइ महिहरे।।

[उत्पतनावनतमहीतलनदीमुखप्रतिस्त्रोतःप्रस्थितः सलिलनिधिः।
जलनिवहाहतशिथिलान्प्लवगोत्क्षेपणसहान्करोति महीधरान्।।]

As the earth sank when the apes flew up,[21] the sea, flowing upstream through the mouths of the rivers, battered the mountains with its waves, loosening and making them capable of being uprooted by the apes.

K and MY read *mūle* for *siḍhile* = शिथिलान् (R and Kula); and *°suhe* for *°sahe* (R and Kula)।

---

[20] Because they had planted their feet firmly on the earth before leaning into the air.

[21] I.e. under the pressure of their feet planted on the earth.

K says कपीनामुत्पतनाडम्बरेण अवनते महीतले नदीमुखैः प्रतिस्रोतः प्रस्थितः समुद्रः जलनिवहाहतमूलान् पर्वतान् प्लवगानामुत्क्षेपणे सुखान् सुकरान् अकरोत्। वृक्षाणामुद्धरणे यथा मूलसेकं कुर्वन्ति तद्वदिति।

MY says *ucchippaṇa-suhe* उत्क्षेपणसुखान्। कपिबलोत्पतनवेगावनतायां भूमौ नदीमुखैः प्रतिस्रोतः प्रस्थितोऽब्धिः मूलतलार्द्रीकरणेन शैलानयत्नोत्पाट्यान् अकरोदित्यर्थः। अनेनापि समुद्रस्य सेतुकरणसाहायकमुक्तं[22] भवति।

Kula says उत्पतनेन अवनते महीतले सति नदीमुखेन प्रतिस्रोतः प्रस्थितः नदीस्रोतः प्रतीपं कृत्वा प्रसृतः सलिलनिधिः जलनिवहाहतत्वेन शिथिलान् . . . महीधरान् करोति।

R says सलिलनिधिर्महीधरान् प्लवगानामुत्क्षेपणसहानुत्थापनयोग्यान् करोति।

25. फुरमाणजलणपिङ्गलणिरन्तरुप्पइअपवअ(बल)पेल्लिज्जन्तो।
जत्तो दीसइ तत्तो णज्जइ धूमणिवहो त्ति गअणुद्देसो।।

[स्फुरज्ज्वलनपिङ्गलनिरन्तरोत्पतितप्लवग(बल)प्रेर्यमाणः।
यतो दृश्यते ततो ज्ञायते धूमनिवह इति गगनोद्देशः।।]

Covered up by the apes, reddish yellow like a blazing fire, and flying in serried ranks, the sky, wherever visible, seemed to be a mass of smoke.[23]

K says स्फुरज्ज्वलनवत् पिङ्गलैः निरन्तरमुत्पतितैः प्लवगैः पीड्यमानो गगनोद्देशः यत्र यत्रादृश्यत तत्र तत्र वानरमयस्य ज्वलनस्य धूमनिवह इव ज्ञायते स्म।

It will be seen that K reads *dhūma-ṇivaho vva* for . . . *tti* = इति (R and Kula). MY agress with K. He says *pellijjanto* पीड्यमानः प्रेर्यमाणो वा। अनलपिङ्गलकपिबलनिरन्तरमन्तरान्तरा दृश्यमानं नभो धूमवदलक्ष्यत।

26. दीसइ दूरुप्पइअं उअहिम्मि अहोमुहोसरन्तच्छाअम्।
पाआलं व अइन्तं धरणिहरुद्धरणकङ्खिअं कइसेणम्।।

[दृश्यते दूरोत्पतितमुदधावधोमुखापसरच्छायम्।
पातालमिवायमानं धरणिधरोद्धरणकाङ्क्षितं कपिसैन्यम्।।]

The host of apes, flying high into the air, and reflected in the sea, face downward, seemed to be entering the nether regions with the purpose of uprooting the (submarine) mountains.

---

22 . . . साहाय्य . . . B.

23 I.e. by contrast with the colour of the apes.

K says दूरमुत्पतितं, तदानीमुदधावधोमुखप्रसरत्प्रतिबिम्बं कपिसैन्यं धरणिधरोद्धरणे काङ्क्षितं काङ्क्षासहितं सपक्षपर्वतोद्धरणे साभिलाषं पातालं गच्छदिवादृश्यत्।

My says *aintaṁ* अतियत् प्रविशत्। बिम्बं यथा नभसि उपर्युपरि दूरदूरतरादौ वर्तते, यथा जलादेरन्तरधस्तात् दूरतरादौ प्रतिबिम्बं दृश्यते यतोमुखं च भवति तद्विपरीतं तत्र दृश्यत इति स्थिते दूरं नभसि समुत्पतदूर्ध्वमुखं कपिबलमुदधावधोमुखतया दूरावगाढप्रतिबिम्बं शैलोद्धरणाय पातालमप्यंशेन प्रविशदिवालक्ष्यतेत्यर्थः।

K (*chāyā*) has पातालमिव यत्। R says पातालमिव अयमानं गच्छत्। Kula says कपिसैन्यं पातालमिवागच्छत् दृश्यते। cf. *ainti* invariably explained as आयान्ति by R (5.33; 6.36; 7.55; 8.60)।

27. अद्दिट्ठदिसाणिवहं जाअं पवअबलसंणिरुद्धालोअम्।
विच्छिण्णाअवकसणं दिअसमुहे वि दिअसावसाणे व्व णहम्।।

[अदृष्टदिङ्निवहं जातं प्लवगबलसंनिरुद्धालोकम्।
विच्छिन्नातपकृष्णं दिवसमुखेऽपि दिवसावसान इव नभः।।

Obscured by the host of apes, the sky, with the regions invisible, was, even at daybreak, bereft of sunshine and gloomy as at the end of the day.

K says प्लवगबलैः निरुद्धप्रकाशम् अदृष्टदिङ्मण्डलं, विच्छिन्नातपत्वात् कृष्णं नभः दिवसमुखेऽपि पूर्वाह्णेऽपि दिवसावसान इव जातम्।

Kula says व्यवच्छिन्नातपत्वात् कृष्णं . . . नभः। He seems to read *vocchiṇṇa* for *vi*° cf. 8.98, 9.75. *SC* text also has *vo*°.

28. ओवइआ अ सरहसं तंसट्ठिअपुट्ठिणीसरन्तरविअरा।
सेलेसु मुक्ककलअलपडिरवभरिअकुहरोअरेसु पवंगा।।

[अवपतिताश्च सरभसं तिर्यक्स्थितपृष्ठनिःसरद्रविकराः।
शैलेषु मुक्तकलकलप्रतिरवभरितकुहरोदरेषु प्लवंगाः।।

With the sunlight passing through the gaps between their slanting backs, the apes swiftly descended on the mountains as the caves resounded with their cries.

K says प्लवगाः शैलेष्व(व)पतन्। कथंभूताः-अवपतनावस्थायां तिर्यक्स्थितपृष्ठावकाशेभ्यो निःसरद्रविकराः। MY says *taṁsa-ṭṭhia* त्र्यस्रस्थित तिर्यगूर्ध्वमुखतयावस्थितेत्यर्थः।

29. वेओवइआण अ सिं जाअं दलिअमहिसंधिबन्धणमुक्कम्।
उक्खलिअतुलेअव्वं कह वि भुअंगधरिअट्ठिअं गिरिआलम्।।

[वेगावपतितानां चैषां जातं दलितमहीसंधिबन्धनमुक्तम्।
उत्खण्डिततुलयितव्यं कथमपि भुजंगधृतस्थितं गिरिजालम्।।]

As they vehemently swooped down on the mountains they were detached from the earth with the link shattered, and somehow stood erect, held fast by the serpents;[24] and so could be lifted by the mere effort of uprooting.[25]

K and MY read अत्रुटित (*akkhuḍia* ?) for *ukkhalia* = उत्खण्डित (R). K reads *dhariaṁ dharāhara-jālaṁ* for *dhara-ṭṭhiaṁ giri- ālaṁ* (R and Kula).

K says वेगादवपतितानां च तेषां धराधरजालम् अत्रुटितमेव अच्छिन्नमेव साकल्येन समूलमेव उद्धर्तव्यं जातम्। कथमपि–अवपतनरभसात् दलितेन महीसन्धिबन्धेन मुक्तं, कथमपि भुजङ्गैः धारितमिति।

MY says दलितमहीसन्धिबन्धनमुक्तं दलितमहीसन्धिबन्धनावगलितम्। अतएव त्रुटनाभावेऽपि तोलयितुं शक्यमित्यासीत्। यत् महत्तरतया शेषेण प्रयत्नधृतं गिरिजालं तदपि शिथिलमूलतया मूलसहितमेव तोलयितुं शक्यं जातम्। न तु मूलतस्त्रुटितं चेति तात्पर्यम्।

Kula says कथमिव भुजङ्गैः धृतत्वात् स्थितम्, उत्खण्डितेन उन्मूलनमात्रेण तोलयितव्यं तोलनार्हं गिरिजालं जातम्। Kula has उत्खण्डित like R, but his reading might be *ukkhuḍia* found in *SC* text.

30. आढत्ता अ तुलेउं उरपडिअविसट्टगण्डसेलद्धन्ते।
कुविअमइन्दोवग्गिअसंखोहप्फिडिअवणगए धरणिहरे।।

[आरब्धाश्च तुलयितुमुरःपतितविशीर्णगण्डशैलार्धान्तान्।
कुपितमृगेन्द्रावगृहीतसंक्षोभस्फेटितवनगजान्धरणीधरान्।।]

They began to lift the mountains with the fragments of crumbling rocks falling on their bosom; while the elephants in the woods, attacked by the angry lions, escaped in the confusion.

K says वानराः धरणिधरानुद्धर्तुमारब्धाश्च। कथंभूतान्–उरसि पतितत्वात् विशीर्णगण्डशैलप्रदेशान्, कुपितैः सिंहैरभिभूताः गृहीताः संक्षोभात् भ्रष्टाः वनगजा येषु तान्।

MY says *oaggia* अभिभूत; *tuleuṁ* तोलयितुम। Kula says उरसि पतितानां

[24] Supposed to uphold the earth. Cf. verse 19.

[25] See Kulanātha in Extracts. According to Kṛṣṇa's reading, "could be lifted unbroken".

विशीर्णखण्डशैलानां च्युतस्थूलप्रस्तराणामर्द्धान्ता येषां . . . तान् धारणिधरान् तोलयितुमारब्धाः।

31. वच्छुत्थङ्घिअकडआ तो ते कडअपडिअट्टलिअवच्छअडा।
सेलेसु सेलगरुआ पवआ पवएसु महिहरा अ पहुत्ता।।

[वक्षउत्तम्भितकटकास्ततस्ते कटकप्रतिघृष्टवक्षस्तटाः।
शैलेषु शैलगुरवः प्लवगाः प्लवगेषु महीधराश्च प्रभूताः।।]

Massive like mountains, the apes matched them as they raised their flanks with their breast; and the mountains likewise matched the apes, bruising the latter's bosom with their flanks.[26]

K and MY (manuscript A) *pratīka* has *vacchuttaṁghia* (वक्षउत्तम्भित)। MY (manuscript. B) has °*ttha*°, like R.

K says कटकैः परिघृष्टवक्षस्तटाः, शैलवत् गुरवस्ते प्लवगाः शैलेषु पर्याप्ताः। तेषां वक्षोभिरुत्थापितकटकाः पर्वताश्च तेषु पर्याप्ता बभूवुः। उभयेषां भेदो नोपलब्ध इति।

R has *paḍiaṭṭalia* = प्रतिघृष्ट। MY has *pariaḍḍhia* परिघर्षित (परिकर्षित ?)। He says प्लवगाः शैलवहाः शैलेषु प्रभूताः कटकपरिघर्षितवक्षस्तटाः शैलाः प्लवगेषु च प्रभूताः नान्योन्यमहीयन्तेत्यर्थः। Kula's reading might be *pariaṭṭalia*, cf. *SC*. He says कटकैः परि . . .(?) परिकलितं परिच्छिन्नं वक्षःस्थलं येषाम्। अतः परस्परसाम्यात् शैलगुरुकाः प्लवगाः शैलेषु, महीधराः प्लगवेषु प्रभूताः संमिताः।

32. पवअभुअणोल्लिआणिअमहिहरपडिपेल्लणोणउण्णअविसमा।
जाआ पलोट्टिओअहिवारंवारभरिआ महिअलद्धन्ता।।

[प्लवगभुजनोदितानीतमहीधरप्रतिप्रेरणावनतोन्नतविषमाः।
जाता प्रलुठितोदधिवारंवारभृता महीतलार्धान्ताः।।]

The regions of the earth which became uneven, now sinking, now rising, under the pressure of the mountains while they were pushed and pulled by the arms of the apes, were intermittently filled by the rolling sea.[27]

K says वृक्षोन्मूलन इव प्लवगानां भुजैः नुन्नेन आनीतेन आकृष्टेन च महीधरेण या प्रतिपीडना तया पर्यायेण अवनतोन्नतत्वात् विषमा नैकरूपाः महीतलार्धान्ताः क्षोभात्

[26] I.e. in the process of uprooting.

[27] I.e. the waters of the sea flowed in and out as the earth alternately sank and rose while the mountains were uprooted.

प्रलोठितेनोदधिना वारं वारं पर्यायेण भरिता जाताः। अवनतावस्थायां पूरिता उन्नतावस्थायां विभुक्ता इत्यर्थः। एवं पर्वता उद्धरणाय क्षोभिताः।

MY says *ṇollia* नुन्न। प्लवगभुजैः नुन्नानीतत्वं नुन्नप्रतिनुन्नत्वमुत्पाटनार्थम्।

Kula says पर्यस्तेनोदधिना। He reads प्रेरित (*pellia*, cf. *SC* text) for *ṇollia* = नोदित R.

33. विसहिअवज्जप्पहरा उक्खम्भन्ति खअमारुअपडिक्खम्भा।
अगणिअवराहणिहसा पलअजलुत्थङ्घपब्बला धरणिहरा।।

[विषोढवज्रप्रहारा उत्खायन्ते क्षयमारुतप्रतिस्तम्भाः।
अगणितवराहनिघर्षाः प्रलयजलोत्तम्भप्रबला धरणीधराः।।]

Uprooted were the mountains that had endured the crash of the thunderbolt, and resisted the winds of the epoch of destruction, and disregarded the thrusts[28] of the Primeval Boar,[29] and were capable of withstanding the waters of the Deluge.

K and MY read प्रतिकूलाः for *paḍikkhambhā* (R and Kula); and वत्सलाः for *prabalā* = प्रबलाः (R and Kula)।

K says पर्वता वानरैरुत्खन्यन्ते स्म। कथंभूताः . . . क्षयकालमारुतस्य प्रतिकूलाः प्रत्यर्थिनः। . . . प्रलयजलस्यापि उत्तम्भने प्रतिबन्धे वत्सलाः समर्थाः।

MY says *paḍikkūlā* प्रतिकूलाः (cf. Hemacandra 2.97) वेगधारकाः। *vacchalā* वत्सलाः समर्थाः cf. 4.25 abave.

Kula says प्रतिस्कम्भाः प्रतिघातकाः। R says प्रतिस्तम्भाः प्रतिरोधार्गलाः।

34. जलओवट्ठविमुक्का अणन्तरोइण्णसरअवन्थावडिआ।
एक्कक्खेवुग्गाहिअदरवसुआअविसआ विसट्टन्ति गिरी।।

[जलदाववृष्टविमुक्ता अनन्तरावतीर्णशरत्पथावपतिताः।
एकक्षेपोद्ग्राहितदरशुष्कविशदा विशीर्यन्ति गिरयः।।]

Some mountains, drenched and abandoned by the rain clouds, and falling in the way of the succeding autumn,[30] crumbled when lifted with a single effort, because they were not perfectly dry and free from moisture.

---

[28] Lit. scrapings.

[29] See verse 13.

[30] Rāma's expedition took place in the autumn.

Lokanātha quoted is *SC*, says विशदा व्यक्ता विशीर्यन्ते सशब्दं खण्डशो भवन्ति। According to *SC*, others explain विशदा: as स्पष्टा विभिन्नावयवा:।

K and MY read *ekkukheva* for *ekka-kkheva* (R and Kula).

K says जलदैरपवृष्टविमुक्ता:, अनन्तरावतीर्णे शरत्पथे शरत्समये आपतिता: प्राप्ता गिरय प्लवगैरेकोत्क्षेपेण उद्गृहीता: अशुष्कभूमिबन्धत्वात् एकेनोत्क्षेपेणोद्गृहीता: ईषच्छुष्का विशदा जलसंरोधरहिता: विश्लिष्यन्ति छिन्नभिन्नं पतन्ति स्म। Kula says *visaṭṭanti* विक(स)न्ति विकटविस्तारा भवन्तीत्यर्थ:। R says गिरयो विशीर्यन्ति शतखण्डा भवन्तीत्यर्थ:।

K and My *pratīka* has *oaṭṭha* for *ovaṭṭha*. MY reads *vasuvāa* (शुष्क)। Kula says एकेन क्षेपेण एकयैवाकृष्ट्या। R says एकक्षेपेण एकप्रयत्नेन। Kula says अनन्तरम् अनु(अव ?)पतिताया अवतीर्णाया: शरद: पन्थानमापतिता:। He seems to read *ovaia* (cf. *SC* text) for *oiṇṇa* (अवतीर्ण)।

35. विहुणन्ति विहुव्वन्ता वलेन्ति सेला पवंगमवलिज्जन्ता।
णामेन्ति णमिज्जन्ता उक्खिप्पन्ता अ उक्खिवेन्ति महिअलम्।।

[विधूनयन्ति विधूयमाना वलयन्ति शैला: प्लवंगमवल्यमाना:।
नमयन्ति नाम्यमाना उत्क्षिप्यमाणाश्चोत्क्षेपयन्ति महीतलम्।।]

While they were shaken by the apes, the mountains shook the earth. While they were turned, they turned the earth. While they were bent, they bent the earth. While they were raised, they raised up the earth.[31]

K reads *ukkhivanti* for *ukkhiventi* = उत्क्षेपयन्ति (R)।

K says प्लवङ्गमैर्विधूयमाना: शैला महीतलं विधून्वन्ति। तैर्वल्यमाना भ्रम्यमाणा: भूतलं भ्रमयन्ति स्म। नाम्यमाना नामयन्ति। उत्क्षिप्यमाणास्ते भूतलमुत्क्षिपन्ति स्म। R says वल्यमाना वक्रीक्रियमाणा: सन्तो वलयन्ति वक्रयन्ति।

MY reads *valanti* for *valenti*, but he explains it as वलयन्ति (K *chāyā* also). He says धूननं स्थिरस्य प्रथमचलनम्। वलनं मूलत्रुटनायाभितो भ्रामणम्। नमनमध:प्रणोदनम्। उत्क्षेपणमूर्ध्वप्रेरणम्।

36. दलिअमहिवेढसिढिला मूलालग्गभुअइन्दकड्ढिज्जन्ता।
संचालिज्जन्त च्चिअ अइन्ति गरुआ रसाअलं धरणिहरा।।

[दलितमहीवेष्टशिथिला मूलालग्नभुजगेन्द्रकृष्यमाणा:।
संचाल्यमाना एवायान्ति गुरवो रसातलं धरणिधरा:।।]

---

[31] I.e. the earth seemed to rise along with the mountains.

Some of the heavy mountains, loose on account of the earth cracking, sank into the nether regions even while they were shaken by the apes, because they were dragged down by the mighty serpents at the base.[32]

K says धरणिधराः वानरैः संचाल्यमाना एव रसातलं यान्ति स्म (*chāyā* has यन्ति)।

MY says *ainti* अतियन्ति[33] प्रविशन्तीत्यर्थः। Kula says रसातलमायन्ति। R has आयान्ति।

37. णवपल्लवसच्छाआ जलओअरसिसिरमारुअविइज्जन्ता।
वाअन्ति तक्खणुक्खअहरिहत्थुक्खित्तभेम्मला मलअदुमा।।

[नवपल्लवसच्छाया जलदोदरशिशिरमारुतवीज्यमानाः।
वायन्ति तत्क्षणोत्खातहरिहस्तोत्क्षिप्तविह्वला मलयद्रुमाः।।]

Beautiful with fresh foliage, and fanned by the cold wind from the womb of the clouds, the sandal trees withered as they tossed about, being at the moment uprooted and flung up by the apes with their hands.[34]

K and MY read विधूयमानाः (*vihuvvantā*) for *viijjantā* = वीज्यमानाः (R and Kula)।

K says नवपल्लवैः सशोभाः, जलदोदरजैः शिशिरमारुतैः विधूयमाना एवं सुकुमारा मलयद्रुमाः चन्दनद्रुमाः तत्क्षणमुत्खाताः पर्वतेभ्य उद्धृताः कपिहस्तैर्नभसि दूरमुत्क्षिप्तत्वात् विह्वलाः व्याकुला म्लायन्ति स्म।

My says *vāanti* अशुष्यन्। अनेन शैलोत्पाटनाय तन्मूलरूढानां द्रमाणामुत्पाटनमुक्तं भवतीति वेदितव्यम्।

Kula has तिष्ठन्ति for *vāanti* (वायन्ति शुष्यन्ति R)। He says मलयद्रुमाश्चन्दन . . . तिष्ठन्ति। मलयादन्येष्वपि देवताधिवासपर्वतेषु तत्सुकृतवशात् चन्दनतरुयोगो न विरुध्यते। *Kaḍaa - dumā* इति पाठस्तु सुगम एव।

38. कम्पिज्जन्तधराहरसिहरसमाइद्धजलहररउप्पित्था।
गअसुहवत्तणिसण्णा वेवइ हंसी सहस्सवत्तणिसण्णा।।

[कम्प्यमानधराधरशिखरसमाविद्धजलधररवोद्विग्ना।
गतसुखपात्रनिःसंज्ञा वेपते हंसी सहस्रपत्रनिषण्णा।।]

---

32 The serpents supposed to bear the weight of the earth. See verse 19.

33 अतियान्ति A.

34 They were getting rid of the trees before uprooting the mountain.

Scared by the rumble of the clouds, pierced by the peak of a mountain shaken by the apes, a female swan, resting on a lotus, trembled as she fainted, with all trace of happiness gone.

K says प्लवगैः कम्प्यमानधराधरशिखरैः समाविद्धानां क्षिप्तानां जलधराणां रवैरुद्विग्ना पुनरपि घनसमयागमशङ्कया भीता, अतएव गतसुखवृत्ता गतसुखवृत्तिः निःसंज्ञा, सहस्रपत्रनिषण्णा गिरिशिखरःसंबन्धिनि पद्मे निषण्णा हंसी वेपते स्म। गतसुखवत्त्वा निःसंज्ञेति वा।

MY says *uppitthā* (*uvvitthā* B) उत्त्रस्ता। गतसुखपात्रनिःसंज्ञा (सुखवार्त B)। अथवा गतसुखवर्तन्या सन्ना खिन्नेति। अथवा गतसुखवत्त्वनिःसंज्ञा। The last explanation is missing in A.

Kula says *uppitthā* समाकुला। रोषपूर्णे समाकुले च *uppittha*- शब्दो देशीयः।[35] Then he seems to say सुखवर्त्म जलदात्ययः तस्य गतत्वात्, अथवा जलदागमबुद्ध्या सुखहेतुर्या वार्ता प्रवृत्तिः तस्या गतत्वात् निःसंज्ञा निश्चेतना।

39. पवओवऊढकड्ढिअसेलब्भन्तरभमन्तविसमक्खलिआ।
गहिरं रसन्ति वित्थअवच्छत्थलरुद्धणिग्गमा णइसोत्ता।।

[प्लवगोपगूढकृष्टशैलाभ्यन्तरभ्रमद्विषमस्खलितानि।
गम्भीरं रसन्ति विस्तृतवक्षःस्थलरुद्धनिर्गमानि नदीस्रोतांसि।।]

Rolling and swirling violently in the caverns of the mountains, clasped and pulled by the apes, the streams rumbled heavily, with their outflow obstructed by their wide bosoms.

K says प्लवगैरुपगूढकृष्टानां शैलानामभ्यन्तरेषु भ्रमन्ति विषमोन्नतेषु स्खलितानि, तेषां विस्तृतवक्षःस्थलरुद्धनिर्गमानि नदीस्रोतांसि गभीरं रसन्ति स्म।

40. अद्धुक्खित्तपसिढिले अद्धवहभुअंगकड्ढिअद्धत्थमिए।
उम्मूलेन्ति रसाअलपङ्कक्खुत्तसरिआमुहे धरणिहरे।।

[अर्धोत्क्षिप्तप्रशिथिलानर्धपथभुजंगकृष्टार्धास्तमितान्।
उन्मूलयन्ति रसातलपङ्कमग्नसरिन्मुखान्धरणीधरान्।।]

They uprooted the mountains, which, partly lifted and loose, had partly sunk, dragged down half the way by the serpents; with the outlets of the streams blocked by the mud of the nether regions.[36]

---

[35] Hemacandra says in *Deśīnāmamālā* 1.129 — उप्पित्थं त्रस्तं कुपितं विधुरं चेति त्र्यर्थम्।

[36] A variation of verse 36 q.v.

K and MY (A) read *ucchitta* for *ukkhitta* and *siḍhilie* (Kula also) for *pasidhile* प्रशिथिलान् (R)।

K says अर्धोत्क्षिप्तावस्थायां शिथिलितान्, अर्धपथे भुजङ्गैः कृष्टत्वादेव अर्धास्तमितान्, रसातलपङ्के मग्नसरिन्मुखान् परितो भूतलस्य विश्लिष्टत्वादधस्तात् पाताले लग्नसरित्प्रवाहान् पर्वतान् प्लवङ्गा उन्मूलयन्ति स्म।

MY says प्रथमं शिथिलतमूलान् अर्धोत्क्षिप्तानेव अन्तरा मूलावेष्टकभुजगावकृष्टतया पुनर्यावच्छिखरमत्यन्तान्तरितान् अतएव रसातलपङ्कखातसरिन्मुखान् उद्मूलयन् गिरीनित्यर्थः अथवा प्रथममर्धोत्क्षिप्तान् भारेण शिथिलानिति योजना।

Kula says रसातलपङ्कक्षिप्तसरिन्मुखान्। He seems to read °*kkhitta* for °*kkhutta* (मग्न) Ms C of Goldschmidt has *ukkhitta*.

41. उव्वेल्लइ व णिराअं पासल्लन्तेसु सिहरपडिमुच्चन्तम्।
उक्खिप्पन्तेसु पुणो संवेल्लिज्जइ व महिहरेसु णहअलम्॥

[उद्वेल्ल्यत इव निरायतं पार्श्वायितेषु शिखरप्रतिमुच्यमानम्।
उत्क्षिप्यमाणेसु पुनः संव्रियत इव महीधरेषु नभस्तलम्॥]

When the mountains leaned, the sky, rid of the peaks, seemed to be unrolled throughout its length; when they were raised, it seemed to be rolled up again.

K has परिमुच्यमानम् for प्रति।

K says प्लवगैः कम्प्यमानेषु महीधरेषु पार्वमाश्रयत्सु शिखरैः परिमुच्यमानं निरायतं नभस्तलमुद्वेष्ट्यते इव विस्तार्यते इव प्रतिभाति। उत्क्षिप्यमाणेषु पुनस्तेषां मूलविस्तारोत्क्षेपेण संवेष्ट्यते इव संकोच्यते इति प्रतिभाति।

R explains *uvvellai* as उद्वेल्ल्यते प्रकाश्यते, and *saṁvellijjai* as संव्रियते वर्तुलीक्रियते। K agrees with Hemacandra who derives them from वेष्ट् preceded by उत् and सम् respectively (4.222, 223)।

My says *uvvelai* उद्वेल्यते (A has *uvvellai* उद्वेष्यते which is a mistake for उद्वेष्ट्यते)। *ṇirāaṁ* दीर्घम्। *saṁvellijjai* सँवेल्ल्यते संवेष्ट्यत इत्यर्थः। *saṁpellijjai* इति पाठः। तदा संपीड्यत इत्यर्थः।

Kula is somewhat corrupt, but he seems to say . . . धरासन्धिबन्धादुन्मोच्य[37] स्वस्वस्थानगर्तात् उद्धृत्य स्थापितेषु, गर्तस्थानेषु निरायतं दीर्घं स्कन्धारोपणकाले पार्श्वायमानेषु (महीधरेषु), स्वशिखरेषु प्रतियुज्यमानं नमदिव,

[37] This is preceded by उद्वेल्लेषु उत्पाटितेषु महीधरेषु in *SC* which reads *uvvellesu* for *uvvellei va*.

स्कन्धारोपणानन्तरमुत्क्षिप्यमाणेषु (तेषु), नभस्तलं संवेष्ट्यते वर्तुलीकृत्य संकल्यत इव। He seems to read *paḍijujjantaṁ* for *paḍimuccantaṁ*.

42. उम्मूलेन्ति पवंगा भुअसिहरारुहणणिच्चलपरिग्गहिए।
कडआवडणत्थङ्घिअविसमविवत्तविवरम्मुहा धरणिहरे।।

[उन्मूलयन्ति प्लवगा भुजशिखरारोहणनिश्चलपरिगृहीतान्।
कटकापतनोत्तम्भितविषमविवृत्तविपराङ्मुखा धरणिधरान्।।]

The apes uprooted the mountains, which were held fast by supporting them with their shoulders, while they raised and turned their face aside and looked backwards for fear the flanks should crash down on them.

K reads आश्लिष्ट (*āliddha*, cf. HC 2.49) for *āruhaṇa* (R and Kula). MY reads आरूढ।

K says प्लवङ्गः भुजशिखरैराश्लिष्टत्वात् निश्चलगृहीतान् पर्वतान् कटकापतनोत्तम्भितेन पर्वतस्य भिन्नकटकपतनभयात् उन्नमितेन, विषमं विवृत्तेन् विपराग्भूतेन मुखेन युक्ताः सन्तः उन्मूलयन्ति स्म।

My says *ārūḍha* आरोपित नुन्नेति वा पाठः (i.e. *ṇollia*). *ārūḍhi* इति पाठे त्वारोपणमर्थः। कटकस्यावपतनात् उन्नमन्तो विषमविवृत्ता विपराङ्मुखाश्चेति विग्रहः। MY seems to read *ovaḍaṇa* for ā°.

Kula says भुजशिखरारोहणेन स्कन्धविनिवेशनेन . . . परिगृहीतान्। R says विपराक् पश्चाद्गतं मुखं येषां ते। गिरिणामंसवर्तिनां त्रुटितो नितम्बो मुख एव पतेदिति शङ्कया पश्चात्कृतमुखा इत्यर्थः। Kula says विषमं तिर्यक् विवर्तितं च विपराक्कृतं (?) मुखं येषां ते प्लवङ्गाः।

43. हरिभुअकड्ढिअमुक्का भुअङ्गदढवेढणावलम्बणधरिआ।
भिज्जन्ता वि महिअले ओअल्लन्ति ण पडन्ति चन्दणविडवा।।

[हरिभुजकृष्टमुक्ता भुजंगदृढवेष्टनावलम्बनधृताः।
भिद्यमाना अपि महीतलेऽवनमन्ति न पतन्ति चन्दनविटपाः।।]

Pulled and released by the arms of the apes, the branches of the sandal trees, though broken, did not drop to the ground, but hung loose, gripped by the tight coils of the serpents on the trees.

K and Kula read भज्यमानाः (*bhajjantā*) for *bhijjantā* = भिद्यमानाः (R). *Kchāyā* has भुज्यमानाः।

K says दृष्टिप्रसरनिरोधेन हरीणां भुजैराकृष्य मुक्ता, भुजङ्गदृढवेष्टनावलम्बनेन धृता, भज्यमाना अपि चन्दनानां विटपा महीतले न पतन्ति स्म अवलम्बन्त एव।

MY says *oallanti* अवलगन्ति अनवेल्लन्ति वा आलम्बन्त इत्यर्थः। Kula says *oannanti* (*oallanti* ?) अवलम्बन्ते। Kula has युज्यमानाः। Probably it is a mistake for भज्यमानाः, as it appears to be followed by भङ्गं गच्छन्तः। cf. *SC*.

44. पडिसमइ णहणिबद्धो चिरेण भरिअब्भणाअगम्भीरअरो।
हरिभुअविक्कमपिसुणो अअण्डभज्जन्तधरणिहरणिग्घोसो।।

[प्रतिशाम्यति नभोनिबद्धश्चिरेण भृताभ्रनादगम्भीरतरः।
हरिभुजविक्रमपिशुनोऽकाण्डभज्यमानधरणिधरनिर्घोषः।।]

The crash of a suddenly broken mountain,[38] revealing the prowess of the arms of an ape, and deep as the rumble of the heavy clouds, slowly died away, lingering in the sky.

K, MY and Kula *pratīka* has *paḍisāi* (प्रतिशाभ्यति K and MY; प्रतिसायति Kula) for *paḍisamai* (R). K reads प्रलय-घन for *bhariabbha* = भृताभ्र (R and Kula)।

K says नभोनिबद्धः नभसि प्रसृतः, प्रलयघननादवत् गम्भीरतरः अकाण्डे सहसा भज्यमानानां उद्ध्रियमाणानां धरणिधराणां निर्घोषश्चिरेण प्रशाम्यति स्म। Kula says गुरुघण्टाध्वनिरिव विलम्बेन क्षीयते।[39] क्षै जै सै क्षये इत्यस्य धातो रूपमिदम्। R and Kula say जलपूर्णस्य अभ्रस्य मेघस्य नादवत् गम्भीरतरः।

45. पासल्लन्ति महिहरा जत्तोहुत्ता पवंगमभुअक्खित्ता।
धुव्वन्तधाउअम्बा तत्तोहुत्ता वलन्ति सरिआसोत्ता।।

[पार्श्वायन्ते महीधरा यतोऽभिमुखाः प्लवंगमभुजक्षिप्ताः।
धाव्यमानधात्वाताम्राणि ततोऽभिमुखानि वलन्ति सरित्स्रोतांसि।।]

The mountain streams, reddened by the minerals washed by them, meandered in the direction in which the mountains leaned, pushed by the arms of the apes.

K *pratīka* has *pāsallanti* which he renders as पर्यस्यन्ते MY says पार्श्वमाश्रयन्ति Kula and R have पार्श्वायन्ते।

K (*chāyā*) has भुजाक्षिप्ताः। He says प्लवङ्गमभुजैराक्षिप्ता गिरयो यतोमुखाः

---

[38] While being uprooted.

[39] Our copy has क्षे डै सै।

पर्यस्यन्ते धाव्यमानधातुताम्राणि क्षाल्यमानधातुताम्राणि सरित्स्रोतांसि ततोमुखानि वलन्ते स्म।

MY says गाढप्रहृतरुधिरपतनसमाधिरत्रानुसंधेयः।

46. दीसन्ति पवअवलिआ आवत्तेसु व महोअहिस्स वलन्ता।
सरिआण घडिअपत्थिअवलन्तसलिलवलअन्तरेसु महिहरा।।

[दृश्यन्ते प्लवगवलिता आवर्तेष्विव महोदधेर्वलन्तः।
सरितां घटितप्रस्थितवलमानसलिलवलयान्तरेषु महीधराः।।]

The mountains, turned round by the apes,[40] seemed to turn round amidst the eddies of the waters of their streams swirling and rushing in a united flow, as if they were whirling in the whirlpools of the sea.[41]

K reads विस्तृत (*vitthaa*) and भ्रमत् (*bhamanta*) in the second line for *patthia* (प्रस्थित) and *vaḷanta* respectively found in R and Kula.

K says उत्क्षेपकाले प्लवगैः वलिता भ्रमिताः, तदानीमात्मीयसरितां अन्योन्यघटितस्य विस्तृतस्य (भ्रमतः) सलिलस्य वलयान्तरेषु वलमानाः भ्रमन्तः शैला महोदधेः आवर्तेषु वलमाना इवादृश्यन्त।

MY says *pavaa-valiā* उन्मूलनार्थं प्लवगैः भ्रामिताः। *ghaḍia* घटित। घटितत्वं निरन्तरावस्थितत्वम्।

Kula says वमन्ति (?) (वलन्ति *SC*) मण्डलाकारेण वहन्ति यानि सलिलवलयानि तेषामन्तरेषु।

47. मअरन्दगरुअवक्खं पासोअल्लन्तवणलआविच्छूढम्।
ण मुअइ कुसुमग्गोच्छं आसाइअमहुरसं पि महुअरमिहुणम्।।

[मकरन्दगुरुकपक्षं पार्श्वायमानवनलताविक्षिप्तम्।
न मुञ्चति कुसुमगुच्छमास्वादितमधुरसमपि मधुकरमिथुनम्।।]

A pair of bees, with the wings heavy-laden with the honey of flowers, could not leave a cluster of blossoms shed by a sylvan creeper leaning sideways,[42] even though they had partaken of the honey.

---

40 In the process of uprooting.

41 I.e. while the mountains were turned round, the streams ran into one another and became a whirling mass of water, in which the mountains seemed to whirl.

42 Because of the swaying of a mountain.

K says पर्वतेषु चलत्सु पार्श्वेषु आलीयमानवनलताभिः विक्षिप्तं कुसुमस्तबकं मधुकरमिथुनं नामुञ्चत्। कथंभूतं-मकरन्दसेकात् गुरुपक्षं, पीतमकरन्दमपि पक्षस्य गौरवभरात् मोक्तुं नाशक्नोदित्यर्थः। K (*chāyā*) has नो मुञ्चति कुसुमगुच्छम्।

My says *pāsoallanta* (*pāsa* + *oallanta*) पार्श्वावलम्बमान। वनलताविक्षिप्तमा-स्वादितमधुरसमिति च कुसुमगुच्छस्य विशेषणम्। मध्वार्द्रगुरुपक्षत्वमपरित्यागहेतुः।

Kula says पार्श्वे अवलम्बमानया वनलतया विक्षिप्तं प्रेरितमपि आस्वादितमधुरसमपि मधुकरमिथुनं मकरन्दगुरूकृतपक्षत्वात् कुसुमगुच्छं न मुञ्चति। अथवा पक्षपाते पक्षशब्दः। मकरन्दगुरुपक्षपातात् प्राप्तकृच्छ्रमपि न मुञ्चति। पक्षपातहेतुमाह-आस्वादितमधुरसमपीति अनुभूतमधुरसमपि भाविमकरन्दसंबन्धानुबन्धेन न मुञ्चतीत्यर्थः।

48. उप्पुअसुरहिगन्धमअरन्दरञ्जिआइं ठिअपरिलेन्तभमरभमरोअरञ्जिआइं।
कमलवणाइँ सूरपरिमासविअसिआइं उच्छलिए सराण सलिलम्मि
विअसिआइं।।

[उत्पुतसुरभिगन्धमकरन्दरञ्जितानि स्थितपरिलीयमानभ्रमद्भ्रमरोदराञ्जितानि।
कमलवनानि सूर्यपरिमर्षविकसितानि उच्छलिते सरसां सलिले
वियच्छ्रितानि।।]

When the waters of the mountain lakes surged up,[43] the lotus beds rose aloft, flowering in contact with the rays of the sun. Tinted by the fragrant honey of the flowers, they were darkened inside by the bees, some at rest, some hidden, and others flying about.

K reads *uddhaa* (cf. 1.51) for *uppua* = उत्प्लुत (R). K and MY read स्थिर and उच्चलिते for *ṭhia* स्थित and *ucchalie* (R and Kula)।

K says उद्धतसुरभिगन्धेन मकरन्देन रञ्जितानि, स्थिरपरिलीयमानमधुकरोदरैरञ्जितानि अक्तानि निर्व्यक्तानीत्यर्थः। व्यञ्जितानिति वा। अञ्जूव्यक्तिगमनम्रक्षणेषु। सूर्यकिरण-परिमर्शात् विकसितानि कमलवनानि सरसां सलिले उच्चलिते सति आकाशमाश्रितानि।

My *pratīka* has *upphusia* for *uppua*. He says उन्मृष्टसुरभिगन्धम-करन्दरञ्जितानि स्थिरपरिलीयमानभ्रमणशीलभ्रमरैरुदरे अञ्जितानि।

Kula *pratīka* seems to have *uppua* (उत्प्लुत) like R. He says उद्गतेन सुरभिगन्धिना मकरन्देन; and भ्रमरैः उदरे अञ्जितानि (?) कज्जलितानि कमलवनानि।

49. दढसंदाणिअमूला वलन्ति वाणरभुआवलम्बिअसिहरा।
रोसुप्पित्थभुअंगमविसमुद्धफणापणोल्लिआ धरणिहरा।।

[43] During the uprooting.

[दृढसंदानितमूला वलन्ति वानरभुजावलम्बितशिखराः।
रोषोद्विग्नभुजंगविषमोर्ध्वफणाप्रणोदिता धरणीधराः।।]

Deeply rooted in the earth, some mountains, when their peaks were clutched by the apes,[44] inclined only when they were pushed up by the huge erect hoods of the infuriated serpents at the base.[45]

K and MY read चलन्ति for *valanti* (R and probably Kula who says पार्श्वान्तरेण (?) भ्रमन्ति)। K, MY and Kula have फण for फणा। They seem to read °*pphaṇa.*

K says अधस्तात् दृढबद्धमूलाः केचित् शैलाः वानरभुजैः अवलम्बितशिखराः क्षोभ्यमाणाः, रोषेण क्षोभितानां मूलभाजां भुजङ्गमानां विषमोर्ध्वैः फणैः प्रणुन्नाः चलन्ति स्म, न पुनरुद्धर्तुमशक्यन्तेत्यर्थः।

MY says *uppittha* उत्त्रस्त। दृढमूलबन्धा अपि शैलाः कपिभुजैरुन्मूलनाय अवलम्बितशिखराः तत्क्षणोत्त्रस्तभुजगोर्ध्वफणविषमनुन्ना अचलन्नित्यर्थः। Kula has संक्षोभात् रोषपूर्णानां भुजङ्गानां विषमोर्ध्वफणैः तिर्यगूर्ध्वीकृतभोगैः cf. Kula on verse 38 above.

50. सरिआ सरन्तपवहा अण्णोण्णमहाणइप्पवह पल्लत्था।
खोहिअपङ्कक्खउरा वलन्तसेलवलिआ मुहुत्तं बूढा।।

[सरितः सरत्प्रवाहा अन्योन्यमहानदीप्रवाहपर्यस्ताः।
क्षोभितपङ्ककलुषा वलमानशैलवलिता मुहूर्त व्यूढाः।।

The ever-flowing brooks, swaying as the mountains swayed, and turbid with the mud that was stirred up, swelled for a moment as they ran into one another and became large streams.

K reads *sariā-salila-ppavahā* for *sariā saranta-pavahā* = सरितः सरत्प्रवाहाः (R)।

K says प्लवगैः महीधराणां भ्रमणे कृते तदीयानां बह्वीनां सरितां सलिलप्रवाहाः भ्रमणवेगेन अन्योन्यं मिश्रीभूय महानदीप्रवाहत्वेन पर्यस्ताः, खोभितपङ्ककलुषाः वलमानशैलवशेन वलिता मुहुर्तं वहन्ति स्म।

MY says उन्मूलनार्थं शैलेषु भ्राम्यमाणेषु भ्रामिताः तदीया बहवो निर्झराः सम्भूय महानदीप्रवाहो यथा स्यात् तथा परस्परमिलिताः शैलमभितः क्षणं प्रावहन्। अथवा *aṇṇaṇṇa* इति पाठे अन्यैरन्येः महानदीप्रवाहैः पर्यस्ता इत्यर्थः।

---

[44] For uprooting them.

[45] Cf. verse 36.

Kual says सरितां नदीनां सततप्रवाहा अविच्छिन्नप्रवाहाः। He seems to read *sariā-sada-ppavahā*, like manuscript C of Goldschmidt. cf. *SC* text.

The order of verse in K and MY is 48, 50, 49, 51 with and additional verse after 50.

51. कड्ढिज्जन्ति समन्ता विसमुव्वत्तन्तधवलकसणच्छाआ।
महिहरमूलालग्गा रसाअलद्धपडिघोलिरा भुअइन्दा।।

[कृष्यन्ते समन्ताद्विषमोद्वर्तमानधवलकृष्णच्छायाः।
महीधरमूलालग्ना रसातलार्धप्रतिघूर्णनशीलां भुजगेन्द्राः।।]

The mighty serpents adhering to the base of the mountains, were pulled out[46] as they gasped and twisted about, looking alternately black and white,[47] with half of their bodies writhing inside the earth.

K, MY and Kula read श्वसन्तः (*sasantā*) for *samantā* = समन्तात् (R). K has परि- for *paḍi-* in the second line.

K says उद्ध्रियमाणानां पर्वतानां मूलालग्ना भुजगेन्द्राः रसातले अर्धभागेन घूर्णमाना विषममुद्वर्तनवशेन दृश्यादृश्यपृष्ठोदरत्वात् धवलकृष्णवर्णाः श्वसन्तः कृष्यन्ते स्म।

Kula says अर्धकायेन परिभ्रमणशीला भुजगेन्द्राः क्रोधात् श्वसन्तः कृष्यन्ते।

52. गलइ सरसं पि कुसुमं वाइ अणालिद्धबन्धणं पि किसलअम्।
रहसुम्मूलिअमहिहरभअविवलाअवणदेवआण लआणम्।।

[गलति सरसमपि कुसुमं वात्यनालीढबन्धनमपि किसलयम्।
रभसोन्मूलितमहीधरभयविपलायितवनदेवतानां लतानाम्।।]

While the sylvan deities fled from the creepers in fear when a mountain was violently uprooted, even their fresh blossoms dropped, and the young shoots withered, even though the stems were unhurt.

K (commentary) reads ईषत् (*dara ?*) for *bhaa* in the second line, but the *chāyā* has भय।

K says रभसोन्मूलितस्य महीधरस्य सकाशात् ईषत्पलायितवनदेवतानां तदीयलतानां कुसुमं सरसमपि नवमपि कुसुमं गलति स्म। अस्पृष्टबन्धनमपि अस्पृष्टमूलमपि किसलयं म्लायति स्म। आधारस्य पर्वतस्योन्मूलनादेवमभूत्।

---

46 I.e. by the apes while uprooting the mountains.

47 Because the back was black and the belly white.

MY says *vāi* म्लायति। *aṇāliddha* अस्पृष्ट। Kula says अस्पृष्टबन्धनमपि अभग्नवृन्तभागमपि। R says वाति वृन्तादपगच्छति। *vāi* वायति शुष्यतीति केचित।

53. उक्खिप्पन्ति जं दिसासुं धरा समत्ता तेण खणेण णज्जइ वसुंधरा समत्ता।
कीरइ महिहरेहि गअणं दिसालआणं वड्डइ जलअसिहरपउणं दिसालआणम् ।।

[उत्क्षिप्यन्ते यद्दिशासु धरा समस्तास्तेन क्षणेन ज्ञायते वसुंधरा समाप्ता।
क्रियते महीधरैर्गगनं द्विशालमानं वर्धते जलदशिखरप्रगुणं दिशालतानाम्।।]

The earth seemed to disappear in a moment in the regions in which all the mountains were uprooted. Twin walls appeared to be built in the sky with the mountain;[48] and the clouds, the crest of the creepers that were the regions of the sky, dropped in increasing abundance.[49]

K, MY and Kula read *ukkhammanti* = उत्खन्यन्ते for *ukkhippanti* (R) = उत्क्षिप्यन्ते। They read *paḍaṇaṁ* (पतनं) for *paüṇaṁ* = प्रगुणं (R)।

K says दिक्षु धराः पर्वताः समस्ता उत्खन्यन्ते। यदुद्धृता इति यत् तेन हेतुना वसुन्धरा क्षणेन समाप्ता ज्ञायते। भूधराणामुद्धरणात् भूरपि नष्टेति ज्ञायते स्म। किंच उद्ध्रियमाणैः गिरिभिः गजनन्दिसालदानं क्रियते। गजनन्दी सल्लकी। सल्लकी स्यात् गजप्रियेति हलायुधः। सालो वृक्षः। गजनन्दिवृक्षाणां दानं खण्डनं क्रियते स्म। अपि च दिग्लतानां जलदमयस्य शिखरस्य पतनमवर्धत। पर्वतशृङ्गविघट्टितानां दिङ्मयलतानां तद्गतमेघमयस्य अग्रस्य पतनं बहुतरमभूदित्यर्थः।

MY says अकीर्यत महीधरैः गजनन्दिसालदानं सल्लकीखण्डः। दानं भङ्गः।

It will be seen that K and MY construe the third line as *kīrai mahiharehi gaaṇaṇḍi-sāla-āṇaṁ*. Kula construes it also as . . . *gaaṇaṁ di-sāla-āṇaṁ* cf. R.

Kula says यत् यस्मात् दिक्षु सर्वासु धराः पर्वताः समात्ताः[50] युगपत् गृहीता उत्खन्यन्ते तेन हेतुना ज्ञायते क्षणेन वसुन्धरा मही समाप्ता नष्टा। धराः समस्ता इति व्याख्यानमसङ्गतं समस्तशब्दस्य हि *samattha* इति रूपं भवति (Vararuci

[48] See Kulanātha in Extracts. The huge apes at the foot of the uprooted mountains constituted one wall, and the mountains the other. Mādhava offers a simpler explanation: the (uprooted) mountains scattered the broken fragments of the *sallakī* trees.

[49] I.e. the clouds, scattered by the peaks of the mountains while they were lifted up, seemed to drop in masses.

[50] Our copy has समन्ताः। *SC* (*chāyā*) has समात्ताः। *SC* which partly reproduces Kula has *samattā*.

3.12)। किंच गजनन्दिनश्च ते शाला वृक्षाश्चेति तेषां दानं दिशां लतानामिव महीधरैः क्रियते। अथवा दिक्षु आलयो येषां तेषां दिग्गजानामित्यर्थवशात् जलदाः शिखराणीव तेषां पतनं वर्धते। अथवा द्वयोः शालयोः प्राकारयो दानं (?) निर्माणं यत्र तथाभूतं गगनं . . . महीधरैः[51] क्रियते। अधः कपिमाला उपरि शैलमाला यस्मात् तस्मात् द्वौ प्राकाराविव नभसः कृतावित्युत्प्रेक्षागर्भोक्तिः। . . . अथवा द्विशालतानं द्वयोः प्राकारयोः तानो विस्तारो यत्र गगने तत्तथा। किंच दिशालतानामिव जलदाः शिखराणि अग्रविटपा इव तेषां पतनं शैलोन्मुखं . . . वर्धते (?)।

54. एक्कक्केण अ सेलं करअलजुअलधरिअं तुलन्तेण कअम्।
अद्धत्थमिअं च णहं अद्धुग्धाडिअरसाअलं च महिअलम्।।

[एकैकेन च शैलं करतलयुगलधृतं तुलयता कृतम्।
अर्धास्तमितं च नभोऽर्धोद्घाटितरसातलं च महीतलम्।।]

As each of the apes lifted up a mountain, held fast with his hands, the sky seemed to be half-hidden, and the depths of the earth seemed to be half-revealed.

K (*pratīka*) has *ekkekkeṇa,* with which MY (B) agrees. MY (A) has *ekkakkameṇa* omitting अ, and explain it as एकैकेन – एकैकेनापि कपिना एवं कृतं किं पुनः संभूयेति भावः। K and Kula read इव . . . इव (i.e. *va*) for च . . . च (R) in the second line. K reads *-tthaiam* (स्थगितं) for *-tthamiaṁ* (अ) स्तमितं R. Kula's reading seems to be the same.

K says करतलयुगलधृतं शैलं तुलयता उद्धरता एकैकेनैव कपिना नभः अर्धस्थगितमिव कृतं, महीतलं च अर्धप्रकाशितरसातलमिव कृतम्। एतेन पर्वतानामतिमहत्त्वमुक्तम्।

My says *tulateṇa* तोलयता उन्मूल्येति शेषः। रसातलस्योद्घाटनं विपुल-पर्वतोन्मूलनमार्गेण स्फुटदृश्यमानत्वम्। Kula says नभः अर्धावस्थगितमिव (कृतम्)। अर्धोद्घाटितरसातलमिव उत्पाटितपर्वतविवरैः पृथुभिः अर्धप्रकाशितपातालमिव महीतलं कृतम्।

55. सेलणिअम्बालग्गा पविरलणइमग्गपाअडतडच्छेआ।
भुअइन्दप्फणधरिआ णहं विलग्गन्ति मेइणिअलद्धन्ता।।

[शैलनितम्बालग्राः प्रविरलनदीमार्गप्रकटतटच्छेदाः।
भुअगेन्द्रफणधृता नभो विलगन्ति मेदिनीतटार्धान्ताः।।]

---

[51] *SC* has महीधरैः करणभूतैः क्रियते अर्थात् कपिभिः।

Portions of the earth, held together by the mighty serpents,[52] rose aloft, adhering to the slopes of the (uprooted) mountains, with sections of the river banks[53] revealed by the tenuous flow of the streams.[54]

K says उद्ध्रियमाणानां शैलानां नितम्बेषु आलग्ना: अधोनितम्बेषु दृढसंबद्धा:, प्रविरलेन नदीमार्गेण इतस्तो विशीर्णजलेन नदीप्रवाहेण प्रकाशतटच्छेदा: अधोगतेन जलप्रवाहेण प्रकाशनदीतटखण्डा: मेदिनीतलैकदेशा: अधो धारयतां भुजगेन्द्राणां फणैर्धारिता: सन्त: पर्वतै: सह नभो विलगन्ति स्म न निपतन्ति स्म। MY says यथाधस्तात् भूतलं तथा तादृशाकारापरित्यागेनैव नभो व्यलगन्नित्यर्थ:। Kula says वानरोत्क्षिप्तशैलै: सह मेदिनीखण्डैकदेशा नभो *va(lagganti)* (आ)-रोहन्ति।

56. धरणिहरेण अ चलिअं चलिअकंदरेण पुट्टइ गअउलं अणालिद्धकं दरेण।
गिरिसिहराइ सरसहरिआलवङ्किआइं समविसमं णमन्ति हरिआलवङ्किआइं।।

[धरणिधरेण च चलितं चलितकंदरेण स्फुटति गजकुलमनालीढकं दरेण।
गिरिशिखराणि सरसहरितालपङ्क्तिानि समविषमं नमन्ति हरिजालवक्रितानि।।]

An intrepid herd of elephants dispersed, being rocked by a mountain, with the caves rocking;[55] and the peaks of (other) mountains, moist with melting orpiment, inclined unsteadily when they were bent by the apes, thumping with the flat of the hand.

K, MY and Kula read *cāliaṁ* for *a caliaṁ* = च चलितं (R). K and MY read *visama-samaṁ* for *sama-visamaṁ* (R and Kula).

K (*chāyā*) अस्पृष्टकं दरेण in the second line. K says चलितकन्दरेण धरणिधरेण चालितं कन्दरासु वर्तमानत्वात् कन्दराचलनात् चलितं, दरेण भयेन अस्पृष्टम् (Kula also) इत: पूर्वं भयेनास्पृष्टं गजकुलं स्फुटति पृथग्भवति स्म। गिरिशिखराणि सरसहरितालपङ्क्तिानि, हरितालो धातुविशेष:, सरसैर्विलीनै: हरितालै: पङ्क्तिानि, हरिजालै: वानरसमूहै: वक्रितानि विषमं समं च बहुप्रकारं नमन्ति स्म।

MY says हरितालवक्रितानि हरीणां तालप्रहारेण वक्रितानीति वा हरिजालवक्रितानीति वा। Kula says हरीणां तालै: करतालै:।

---

[52] The serpents supposed to bear the weight of the earth. See verse 19.

[53] Or, "the indentations in the banks" caused by current and weather.

[54] I.e. large masses of earth came up with the uprooted mountains together with portions of the streams cut-off from their course.

[55] The elephants had taken shelter in the caves during the uprooting.

57. पाअवसिहरुत्तिण्णो मलअवणपवित्तपवणरअवित्थरिओ।
संझाराओ व्व णहं अप्फुन्दइ मलिअरविअरं कुसुमरओ।।

[पादपशिखरोत्तीर्णं मलयवनप्रवृपवनरयविस्तृतम्।
संध्याराग इव नभ आक्रामति मृदितरविकरं कुसुमरजः।।]

Rising from the top of the trees (on the mountains), and scattered by the force of the wind blowing from the Malaya woods, the pollen of the flowers pervaded the sky like the evening glow, obscuring the rays of the sun.

K (*chāyā*) and MY read परियत् (*parinta*)[56] for *pavitta* = प्रवृत्त (R). K and Kula read वश for *raa* = रय (R)।

K says उद्ध्रियमाणपर्वतानां पादपशिखरेभ्यः उत्तीर्णमुच्चलितं, मलयवनपरिवर्तमानपवनवशेन विस्तारितं कुसुमरजः। मृदितरविकरं नभः सन्ध्याराग इव व्याप्नोति स्म। K (*chāyā*) renders *apphundai* as अक्रामति like R.

MY says महत्यपि क्षोभे नित्यदुर्दिनतया मलये भूरजसोऽसंभवात् कुसुमरजः-समुत्थानमिति मन्तव्यम्।

Kula says मलयवनात् परिगच्छतः[57] प्रसरतः पवनस्य वशेन विस्तृतम्, and... सन्ध्याराग इव नभः स्थगयति। He seems to read *parinta* like K. See notes on 7.50 and 9.68, 88.

58. कड्ढिअमूलणिरन्तररसाअलुक्खित्तसलिलकद्दमघडिआ।
वड्ढन्ति त्ति मुणिज्जइ णज्जइ ण मुअन्ति महिअलं ति महिहरा।।

[कृष्टमूलनिरन्तररसातलोत्क्षिप्तसलिलकर्दमघटिताः।
वर्धन्त इति ज्ञायते ज्ञायते न मुञ्चन्ति महीतलमिति महीधराः।।]

As the mountains were hemmed in by the slush, rising from the nether regions, and thickly accumulating at their uprooted base, it seemed that they were growing in bulk, and had not been detached from the earth.

K says कृष्टैर्मूलैः सह निरन्तरं निरवकाशं यथा रसातलादुत्क्षिप्तेन सलिलमिश्रेण कर्दमेन घटिताः दीर्घीकृताः महीधराः वर्धन्त इति ज्ञायते स्म। महीतलं मुञ्चन्तीति न ज्ञायते स्म। पार्श्वस्थैः। Kula says न मुञ्चन्त्येव महीतलमिति ज्ञायते।

---

56 MY is here corrupt. Our copy has परीयत् and परितः (A), *paṭinta* (B). In the gloss on 14.57 MY explains *parinta* as परियत्। K here explains परियत् as परिवर्तमान। Cf. his gloss on 9.60. The word परियत् is often written by the scribes as परियत् and पर्यत्।

57 Restored from *SC*.

59. सिहराइ णिआइ णहं महिन्दलद्धाइं मलअस्स अ अइणिआइ महिं दलद्धाइं।
विज्झणिअम्बाण कई दप्पुण्णामाणं सज्झअडाण अ भरिआ धुअपुण्णामाणम् ।।

[शिखराणि नीतानि नभो महेन्द्रलब्धानि मलयस्य चातिनीतानि महीं दलार्धानि।
विन्ध्यनितम्बानां कपयो दर्पोन्नामानां सह्यतटानां च भृता धुतपुंनागानाम्।।]

The apes were loaded with the proudly soaring flanks of the Vindhya and the slopes of the Sahya with the swaying *punnāga* trees; so the peaks brought from the Mahendra were flung in the air, and portions of the Malaya cast on the earth.[58]

K (*chāyā*) reads the last two lines as follows.

विन्ध्यनितम्बानां कपयो दर्पोन्नतानां
सह्यतटानां भरिता भुजगापूर्णानाम्।

K thus reads *dappuṇṇaāṇaṁ* for *dappuṇṇāmāṇaṁ* दर्पोन्नामानां (R); and *bhuaappuṇṇaāṇaṁ* (?) for *dhuapuṇṇāmāṇaṁ* धुतपुंनागानाम् (R). K reads मलयगिरेः। for *malaassa a* (R) in the second line.

K says महेन्द्रात् पर्वतात् लब्धानि शिखराणि नभो नीतानि प्लवगैराकाशं गमितानि। मलयगिरेः दलार्धानि दलानां तटानामर्धानि खण्डानि भरस्य पर्याप्तत्वात् महीमतिनीतानि मह्यां परित्यक्तानि। कपीनां भुजदर्पेण दूरमुन्नतानामुद्धृतानां विन्ध्यनितम्बानां, भुजगापूर्णानां सह्यतटानां च कपयः पूर्णा नितम्बैः पूर्णा इत्यर्थः। पूरणगुणेत्यादिना ज्ञापिता षष्ठी। K reads *appuṇṇa* (आपूर्ण)। See Notes on verse 96.

MY's readings are same as those of K. Kula's readings are *dappuṇṇāāṇaṁ* and *dhua-puṇṇāāṇaṁ*. He says महेन्द्रात् पर्वतात् लब्धानि शिखराणि नभो नीतानि। चरणभरेण आक्रम्य गमनात् मलयस्य . . . दलार्धानि महीमानीतानि भूमिं प्रापितानि। किञ्च कपयः विन्ध्यनितम्बानां भरिताः पूर्णाः। पूरणार्थयोगे तृतीयार्थे षष्ठी, नितम्बैरित्यर्थः। दर्पेण दृप्ततया उन्नादानाम् उद्घुष्टानां न केवलं तेषां भरिताः, सह्यतटानां च, धुताः पुन्नागास्तरुभेदा येषां तेषाम्। *dappuṇṇāmāṇaṁ* इति पाठे तु दर्पेण . . . उन्नाम उन्नतिर्येषां, तथा धुताः पुन्नामानः[59] पुरुषाह्वयाः पुन्नागतरवो येषामिति च व्याख्या। तथाच पुन्नागः पुरुषस्तुङ्ग इत्यभिधानानि।

60. सिहराण भुअसिरेहिं कडआण अ माविअं उरेहि पमाणम्।
वणविवरेहि दरीणं तुलिआ पवआण अग्गहत्थेहि गिरी।।

[58] I.e. they discarded portions of the lesser mountains to lighten the burden.

[59] Our copy has पुन्नागान्। *SC* gives the word correctly.

[शिखराणां भुजशिरोभिः कटकानां च मापितमुरोभिः प्रमाणम्।
व्रणविवरैर्दरीणां तुलिताः प्लवगानामग्रहस्तैर्गिरयः।।]

While the mountains were lifted by the apes with their forearms, their shoulders resembled in extent the peaks, the breast the flanks, and the cavities left by wounds on their bodies the caves.[60]

K and MY read मुधा मितं for a *māviaṁ* = च मापितं (R and Kula)।

K says प्लवगानामग्रहस्तैः गिरयः तुलिताः उद्धृताः। तुलिता इत्युक्ते उपमिता इति च स्फुरति। तमर्थमालम्ब्य आह – शिखराणां प्रमाणं कपीनां भुजशिरोभिः मुधा व्यर्थं मितं समीकृतम्। तथा कटकानां प्रमाणमुरोभिः मुधा मितं, दरीणां प्रमाणं तेषां व्रणविवरैः मुधैव मितम्। कुतः अग्रहस्तैरेव गिरीणां तुलितत्वादिति।

MY says *muhā* मुधा। miaṁ मितम्। शिखरकटकादिपरिमाणसादृश्येऽपि कपिभ्यः सारतः शैला हीनतमाः संवृत्ताः तेषां तदग्रहस्तमात्रतुलितत्वादित्यर्थः। तुलिता इति सदृशीकृता इति च स्फुरति।

Kula says शिखराणां भुजशिखरैः (i.e. *bhua-siharehi* for °*sirehiṁ*) . . . कर्तृभिः प्रमाणं मापितम् इयत्तया परिच्छिन्नं, कटकानामुरोभिः, उरःस्थलस्थित-पृथुव्रणविवरैः दरीणाम्। *darīo* इति पाठे तुलिता इति योज्यम्। प्लवगानामग्रहस्तैः हस्ताग्रैः गिरयः कियन्नामैषां गौरवमिति हेलया तुलिता उत्क्षिप्ताः। R says प्रमाणं परिमाणं मापितं सदृशीकृतम्। अग्रहस्तैः हस्ताग्रैः गिरयस्तुलिताः सदृशीकृताः . . . वस्तुतस्तु तैस्तेषां प्रमाणं मापितमित्यध्यवसायानन्तरमग्रहस्तैः तुलिता उत्तोलिता इत्यर्थः।

61. पडिसन्तकण्णआलं ओवत्तमुहं पसारिओलुग्गकरम्।
झाइ णु सोआणिमिल्लं वीसमइ णु भमिअणीसहं हत्थिउलम्।।

[प्रतिशान्तकर्णतालमपवृत्तमुखं प्रसारितावरुग्णकरम्।
ध्यायति नु शोकनिमीलितं विश्राम्यति नु भ्रमितनिःसहं हस्तिकुलम्।।]

Were the elephants[61] in a trance, closing their eyes in grief? Tired out with wandering, were they reposing themselves? The flappings of their ears ceased, their faces were turned aside, and the languid trunks were stretched out on the ground.

---

[60] The literal sense is that the dimensions of the peaks were measured with the shoulders and so on, after which the mountains were lifted with the forearms. Cf. Kulanātha in Extracts.

[61] Those on the uprooted mountains.

K says पर्वतोद्धरणक्षोभेण भ्रान्तं निःसहमतिक्लिष्टं तद्गतं गजकुलमेवंभूतम्। Kula says अवरुग्णो भग्नः श्लथव्यापार इत्यर्थः करो यस्य तत् तथा।

62. पाअवा अ पासल्लसेलविसमाणिआ चुण्णिआ दलिज्जन्तदलुव्विसमाणिआ।
जलहरा अ विहडन्तमहिन्दरवाविआ वणलआ अ घोलन्ति महिं दरवाविआ।।

[पादपाश्च पार्श्वायितशैलविषमानीताश्चूर्णिता दल्यमानदलोर्वीसमापिताः।
जलधराश्च विघटमानमहेन्द्ररवावृता वनलताश्च घूर्णन्ते महीं दरवापिताः।।]

The trees, bent as a mountain leaned over,[62] were smashed and levelled with the ground with their shattered fragments; and the clouds resounded with the din of the Mahendra mountain as it parted asunder; while the creepers of its woods swayed, lightly touching the ground.

K reads पर्यस्त (*palhattha* ?) for *pāsalla* (पार्श्वायित R and Kula; पार्श्वाश्रित MY)। K and MY read *aluvvi* तलोर्वी for *daluvvi* दलोर्वी (R and Kula)।

K says पादपाश्च पर्यस्तेन शैलेन विषममानीताः विषममाकृष्टाः, उद्धरणरभसेन चूर्णिताः, दल्यमानतलया[63] उर्व्या समानीताः (समानिताः?) चूर्णितत्वात् पृथिव्या समीकृता अभवन्। जलधराश्च विघटमानेन विशीर्यमाणेन महेन्द्रेण राविताः। णे रावादेशः। शिखरगता मेघाः महेन्द्रेण विघटमानेन शब्दिता अभूवन्। तद्गता वनलताश्च महीमीषत् प्रापिताः सत्यो घूर्णन्ते स्म।

MY says समानीताः (समानिताः ?) समानीकृताः। Kula says दल्यमानैः विभिद्यमानैः दलैरवयवखण्डैरुर्व्याः समानिताः . . . भूमिसमाः कृता इत्यर्थः। He says राविताः शब्दं कारिताः। अथवा रवावृता आवृतरवा (?) इत्यर्थः। *vihaḍanti* इति पाठे तु जलधराश्च विघटन्ते। किंभूता – रवेणावृतो महेन्द्रपर्वतो यैस्ते। R says पार्श्वायिते वक्रीभूते शैले महेन्द्रनामनि विषमानीता वैषम्यमागताः। स्वयमपि वक्रीभूता इत्यर्थः।

63. टुट्टन्ता वि ससद्दं पवअभुअक्खेवमूलवलिअद्धन्ता।
भुअएहि भोअभारा सेलभरङ्कुसइअप्फणेहि ण णाआ।।

[त्रुट्यन्तोऽपि सशब्दं प्लवगभुजक्षेपमूलवलितार्धान्ताः।
भुजगैर्भोगभाराः शैलभराङ्कुशायितफणैर्न ज्ञाताः।।]

The serpents, with their hoods sunk in the heavy mass of

[62] While being uprooted.

[63] Our copy has . . . धरया। K (*chāyā*) has दल्यमानतलोर्वी।

the mountains, were not aware even when their massive bodies, with the lower half coiled up in the depths of the earth, snapped with a loud noise as the apes pulled up the mountains.[64]

K and MY *pratīka* has *khuṭṭantā* for *ṭuṭṭantā* (R) = त्रुट्यन्तः। K and Kula read प्लवगोत्क्षेपैः (*pavaükkhevehi*) for *pavaa-bhua-kkheva*° (R)।

K says शैलभराङ्कुशितफणैः शैलमूलेषु अतिदूरमग्नफणैः भुजगैः मूले अधस्तले वलितार्धान्ताः भोगभाराः प्लवगानामुत्क्षेपैः सशब्दं त्रुट्यन्तोऽपि न ज्ञाताः। भूधारणे पारवश्यातिशयात् भुजगैः स्वशरीरच्छेदोऽपि न गणित इत्यर्थः।

MY says पातालस्थितपश्चिमार्धा गिरिमूलवेष्टितपूर्वार्धाश्च भुजगाः शैलभराङ्कुशीकृतफणाः सशब्दत्रुट्यन्मध्यानपि भोगान् नाज्ञासिषुरित्यर्थः। R says मूलेऽर्थात् भूमेः वलितो वक्रीभूतोऽर्धान्तोऽन्तार्घं पुच्छभागो येषां ते।

Kula reads *phuṭṭantā*. He says प्लवगोत्क्षेपैः सशब्दं . . . स्फुटन्तोऽपि विदीर्यन्तोऽपि मूले वलितो भ्रमितोऽर्धान्तो यैः ते तथा भोगाः शरीराणि त एव गुरुत्वात् भाराः ; अज्ञाने हेतुमाह – शैलभरेण अङ्कुशीकृता आकुञ्चिताः फणा यैस्तैर्भुजङ्गैः न ज्ञाताः। भरापगमसुखादिति श्रीहर्षः।

64. दरदाविअपाआलं दरउक्खित्तविहलोसरन्तभुअंगम्।
दीसद हीरन्तं मिव कईहि दरतुलिअमहिहरं महिवेढम्।।

[दरदर्शितपातालं दरोत्क्षिप्तविह्वलापसरद्भुजंगम्।
दृश्यते ह्रियमाणमिव कपिभिर्दरतुलितमहीधरं महीवेष्टम्।।]

When a mountain was partly uprooted, the earth seemed to be lifted up by the apes, (as if) partly detached from the nether regions, with the partly extracted serpents sneaking away, crazed with fear.

K, MY and Kula read रेंचित (*reia*) for *dāvia* = दर्शित (R)।

K says कपिभिः किंचिदुद्धृतमहीधरं, तदानीं दरोत्क्षिप्तविह्वलापसरद्भुजङ्गं, दरशून्यीकृतपातालं महीवेष्टं कपिभिः ह्रियमाणमिव अदृश्यत। महीतलपर्वतयोः अपृथग्दर्शनात् महीमण्डलमपि ह्रियमाणमिव ददृशे।

MY says ईषदात्माना रिक्तीकृतपातालं किंचिदुन्मुक्तपातालं महीवेष्टमूर्ध्वं ह्रियमाणमिव अदृश्यत। अथवा लुण्ट्यमानमित्यर्थः तत्संबन्धिशैलादेरपहरणात् तदाश्रितानां च भुजगानामपसरणादिति।

---

[64] A reference to the underground serpents mentioned in verse 19.

65. मीणउलाइ अविअ सिढिलेन्ति जीविअं ण अ णदीहराइं
विअसन्ते मुअन्ति धरणिहरसंभमे णअणदीहराइं।
महिसउलाण (फलिह)मणिसिलावेल्लिआण वणचन्दणासिआणं
अवसेसो वि णत्थि तिमिरुग्गमाण जह चन्दणासिआणम्।।

[मीनकुलान्यपि च शिथिलयन्ति जीवितं न च नदीगृहाणि (नदीह्लदान्वा)
विकसति मुञ्चति धरणिधरसंभ्रमे नयनदीर्घाणि।
महिषकुलानां (स्फटिक)मणिशिलाप्रेरितानां वनचन्दनाश्रिताना-
मवशेषोऽपि नास्ति तिमिरोद्गमाणां यथा चन्द्रनाशितानाम्।।]

As the commotion of the mountains grew more violent, the long-eyed fish[65] disregarded their lives, and abandoned not their river homes; and not even a trace was left of the buffaloes that took shelter in the sandal groves, and were swept away by the (rolling) crystal rocks;[66] even as nothing remains of the emerging darkness destroyed by the moon.

K and MY read मत्स्यकुलानि शिथिलयन्ति जीवितं, and omit *avi* = अपि (R and Kula)।[67]

K says नयनवत् दीर्घतराणि मत्स्यकुलानि धरणिधरसंभ्रमे विकसति विजृम्भमाणे सति नदनदीगृहाणि, नदीविशेषाः नदाः, नदनदीमयानि गृहाणि मुञ्चन्ति स्म। अतएव जीवितं शिथिलयन्ति त्यजन्ति स्म। वनचन्दनाश्रितानां, मणिशिलाभिः पतन्तीभिः पीडितानां महिषकुलानां अवशेषमपि नास्ति निरवशेषं मृतानीत्यर्थः। चन्द्रनाशितानां तिमिरोद्गमानां यथावशेषो न स्यात् तद्वदिति।

MY says न च नदीह्रदान् नदीगृहाणि वा जीवितशैथिल्यं सोढ्वा ह्रदान् न त्यक्तवन्तो मत्स्या इत्यर्थः। MY reads महिषकुलानां घनशिलापीडितानां नवचन्दनाश्रितानाम्।

K and MY seem to read *pelliāṇa* for *ve*° (R Text). K usually renders *pellia* as पीडित। R (commentary) and Kula have प्रेरित which also gives *pellia*.

Kula says नयनवत् दीर्घाणि मीनकुलानि . . . जीवितमपि शिथिलयन्ति, न तु नदीगृहाणि मुञ्चन्ति। दुस्त्यजा खलु जन्मभूमिरिति भावः। किं च महिषकुलानां . . . वनचन्दनं चन्दनवनमाश्रितानां, मणिशिलाभिः[68] संक्षोभदलितस्फटिकशिलाभिः प्रेरितानाम्

[65] Those in the mountain streams.

[66] Lit. gem rocks, explained as above by Rāmadāsa and Kulanātha.

[67] R Text has *avi a* = अपि च।

[68] Our copy has सालशिलाभिः।

अभिहतानामवशेषोऽपि नास्ति न भवति, निःशेषं क्षीयन्त इत्यर्थः, etc. R says नयनवत् दीर्घाणि, नयनेन, दीर्घाणि, दीर्घनयनानीति वा।

66. अद्धेअद्धप्फुडिआ अद्धेअद्धकडउक्खअसिलावेढा।
पवअभुआहअविसढा अद्धेअद्धसिहरा पडन्ति महिहरा।।

[अर्धार्धस्फुटिता अर्धार्धकटकोत्खातशिलावेष्टाः।
प्लवगभुजाहतविशीर्णा अर्धार्धशिखराः पतन्ति महीधराः।।]

Some of the mountains tumbled down,[69] rent in the middle; some with the encircling rocks dislodged from half of the slopes; and others crumbling under the blows of the apes, with only half of the peaks left.

K says एकदेशवाचकः अर्धशब्दः सर्वनामसंज्ञः। अर्धे कतिचित् महीधराः अर्धे स्फुटिताः उन्मूलनरभसात् मध्यभागे स्फुटिताः। अर्धे केचित् उद्धरणसमये संभ्रमात् अर्धकटके कटकार्धे उत्खातशिलावेष्टाः पतन्ति। प्लवगभुजैराहतत्वात् शिथिलाः अर्धे केचित् अर्धशिखराः आनीयमानावस्थायां कपिभुजैराहतशिलाः अर्धशेषशिखरा भूत्वा पतन्ति स्म।

Kula says अर्धे अर्धप्रदेशे अर्धस्फुटिताः, अर्धे अर्धकटकेभ्यः कटकार्धेभ्यः उत्खातशिलावेष्टाः, प्लवगभुजाहता 'विसढा' विघटितप्रदेशा महीधरा अर्धे अर्धशिखराः खण्डशृङ्गाः पतन्ति। R renders *visaḍha* as विशीर्ण। K has शिथिल।

67. जस्स सिहरं विवज्जइ पडिअं फुडिओ अ जो धरिज्जइ सेलो।
सो च्चेअ विसज्जिज्जइ उक्खन्तूण वि अपूरमाणम्मि भरे।।

[यस्य शिखरं विपद्यते पतितं स्फुटितश्च यो ध्रियते शैलः।
स एव विसृज्यते उत्खायाप्यपूर्यमाणे भरे।।]

When the peak of a mountain was deemed inadequate,[70] or when a mountain had to be supported, because it cracked as it fell, it was discarded even after the effort of uprooting because it was deficient in weight.[71]

K, MY and Kula read तुल्यते (*tulijjai*) for *vivajjai* = विपद्यते (R). They read उत्क्षिप्य (*ukkhettūṇa*, cf. *samakkhettūṇa* = समाक्षिप्य 10.

[69] I.e. while being uprooted.

[70] According to Kulanātha (Mādhava also), "deemed inferior (to other)". Kṛṣṇa differs. See Extracts.

[71] I.e. not strong enough for the causeway.

74) for *ukkhantūṇa* = उत्खाय (R). They also read पतितस्फुटित: for *paḍiaṁ phuḍio* (R); i.e. *paḍiapphuḍio.*

K says उद्धियमाणस्य यस्य गिरे: शिखरं तुल्यते भिद्यते, उद्धृतोऽपि य: पतितस्फुटितश्च[72] अध:प्रदेशे पतित: पतितार्ध इत्यर्थ:, स्फुटितश्च यो धार्यते भुजाभ्यामवलम्ब्यते स एव शैलो विसृज्यते त्यज्यते स्म। कुत:-उत्क्षिप्यापि भरे भारे अपूर्यमाणे सति अपर्याप्तभारत्वात् कपिभि: परित्यक्त:।

MY says *tulijjai* तोल्यते। यस्य शिखरमतोल्यत तोलयित्वा अन्यैर्नीतं, यश्च नीयमानदशायाम् अन्तरा पतित: स्फुटितार्धान्तोऽधार्यत स गिरि: उत्क्षिप्य नीयमानोऽपि अपर्याप्तभरो व्यसृज्यतेत्यर्थ:। अथवा यस्य शिखरं तोल्यते लघुतया परिच्छिद्यते स व्यसृज्यत नोदमूल्यत। स्फुटितभाग: पतितो यस्य स: पतितस्फुटित:। यो धार्यमाणोऽपि पतिस्फुटितार्धान्त: सोऽपि व्यसृज्यत। यश्च उत्क्षिप्तोऽपि अपूर्यमाणभार: सोऽपि व्यसृज्यतेत्यर्थ:।

Kula says यस्य शैलस्य शिखरं तुल्यते अन्यापेक्षया हीनतया आकल्यते। यश्च उन्मूलनकाले पतित एकदेशे स्फुटितो हस्ताभ्यां धार्यते तदेव उत्क्षिप्य विसृज्यते। हेतुमाह-अपूर्यमाणे भरे। भारोऽनेन (न) पूर्यत इति। Lokanātha quoted in *SC* says स एवापूर्यमाणे भरे पर्वतान्तरवदिह महत्त्वं नास्तीति कृत्वा उत्क्षिप्यापि विसृज्यते लघुत्वादुपेक्षित् इत्यर्थ:।

68. लोअणवत्तन्तरिए कणे रुअन्तीओ धारेन्ति वाहमइए कणेरुअन्तीओ।
मण्णेन्ति अ आसाअं विसं णवअणस्स विरहम्मि जूहवइणो विसण्णवअणस्स।।

[लोचनपत्रान्तरितान्कणान्रुदत्यो धारयन्ति वाष्पमयान्करेणुपङ्क्तय:।
मन्यन्ते चास्वादं विषं नवतृणस्य विरहे यूथपतेर्विषण्णवदनस्य
(विसंज्ञवचनस्यवा)।।]

Because of separation from the dejected leader of the herd, the weeping cow elephants shed tears that were hidden by the eyelashes, and regarded the taste of the fresh grass as rank poison.

K seems to read *ruvantīo* (cf. *SC* text) for *rua°*, as he says रुदो व इति वकारादेश: (Vararuci 8.42). So in the second line his corresponding reading will be (*kaṇeru*)-*vantīo*, for *-antīo* (पङ्क्तय:)। He says विषण्णवदनस्य यूथपते: विरहे रुदत्य: करेणुपङ्क्तय: करिणीसङ्घा लोचनपत्रै: पक्ष्मभिरन्तरितान् बाष्पमयान् कणान् बिन्दून् धारयन्ति स्म। Kula says लोचनवर्त्मनो नेत्रावरणपुटादन्तरितान् पृथग्भूतान् बाष्पमयान् कणान् धारयन्ति।

---

[72] Our copy has पतति।

69. सेलुद्धरणारोसिअभुअइन्दणिराअअप्फणणिसम्मन्ती।
जह जह संखोहिज्जइ तह तह कइदेहभरसहा होइ मही।।

[शैलोद्धरणारोषितभुजगेन्द्रनिरायतफणनिषीदन्ती।
यथा यथा संक्षोभ्यते तथा तथा कपिदेहभरसहा भवति मही।।]

The earth was capable of sustaining the weight of the apes even while it was convulsed,[73] because it reposed on the outstretched hoods of the lord of serpents,[74] enraged by the uprooting of the mountains.

K and MY read निरुध्यमाना for *ṇisammantī* = निषीदन्ती (R and Kula). K reads सैन्य (*seṇṇa*) for देह (R and Kula).

K says मही शैलोद्धरणेनारोषितस्य भुजगेन्द्रस्यानन्तस्य निरायतैः फणैः निरुध्यमाना अधो धार्यमाणा कपिभिः यथा यथा संक्षोभ्यते तथा तथा कपिसैन्यभरस्य सहा सहिष्णुरभूत।

My says *ṇirumbhanta* निरुध्यमान He has *ṇirāia* (दीर्घीकृत) for *ṇirāaa*.

Kula says भुजगेन्द्रस्य शेषस्य निरायतेषु प्रसारितेषु फणेषु निषीदन्ती विश्राम्यन्ती।

70. संचालिअणिक्कम्पा भुआणिहाअविसमुक्खअसिलावेढा।
खुडिआ सिहरद्धेसु अ पवएहि णिअम्बबन्धणेसु अ सेला।।

[संचालितनिष्कम्पा भुजानिघातविषमोत्खातशिलावेष्टाः।
खण्डिताः शिखरार्धेषु च प्लवगैर्नितम्बबन्धनेषु च शैलाः।।]

The mountains that stood firm, even when pushed, were broken by the apes in the region of the peaks and along the base of the flanks; while the encircling rocks were dislodged here and there by thumping them with the hands.[75]

K says प्लवगैः संचालिता अतिमहत्त्वात् निष्कम्पाः केचित् शैलाः तेषां भुजानिघातेन भुजाघातेन विषममुत्खातशिलामण्डलाः शिखरार्धेषु च नितम्बबन्धनेषु च नितम्बसंधिषु च त्रुटिता बभूवुः।

Kula says ये शैलाः संचारिता अपि रसातले दूरप्रवेशात निष्कम्पा उन्मूलयितुमशक्यास्ते भुजानिर्घातेन (निघातेन ?) विषममितस्तत उत्खातशिलावेष्टाश्च

---

[73] I.e. by the uprooting of the mountains.

[74] Ananta is fancied as spreading out its thousand hoods to provide greater security.

[75] I.e. parts of the mountains were broken off to facilitate the uprooting.

सन्तः प्लवगैरूर्ध्वं शिखरार्धेषु अधो नितम्बेषु च खण्डिता मध्ये भञ्जयित्वा गृहीता इत्यर्थः।

71. उण्णामिअं मिव णहं दूरं ओसारिआ विव दिसाहोआ।
उम्मूलन्तेहि धरे पसारिअं मिव पवंगमेहि महिअलम्।।
[उन्नामितमिव नभो दूरमपसारिता इव दिगाभोगाः।
उन्मूलयद्भिर्धरान्प्रसारितमिव प्लवंगमैर्महीतलम्।।]

As the apes uprooted the mountains the sky seemed to be raised aloft;[76] the regions of the sky seemed to be driven wide apart, and the earth seemed to be expanded.[77]

K reads गिरीन् for *dhare* = धरान् (R and Kula)।

K says गिरीन् उन्मूलयद्भिः कपिभिः पर्वतानामत्यर्थमुन्नत्या नभः उन्नमितमिव उत्तम्भितमिवाभूत् तथा दिशामाभोगा विस्तारा दूरमपसारिता इव तिरोधायकानां गिरीणामुद्धरणादूरमुत्सारिता इवासन्। महीतलं च प्रसारितमधिकं विस्तारितमिवाभूत्।

72. दीसइ कइणिवहुक्खअधराहरट्ठाणगहिरविवरुत्तिण्णो।
उप्पाआअवअम्बो सेसाहिप्फणमणिप्पहाविच्छड्डो।।

[दृश्यते कपिनिवहोत्खातधराधरस्थानगभीरविवरोत्तीर्णः।
उत्पातातपाताम्रः शेषाहिफणमणिप्रभाविच्छर्दः।।]

Dark red as an ominous glow of the sky, the massive radiance of the gems, embeded in the hoods of the serpent Ananta,[78] was seen emerging through the deep cavities that marked the site of the mountains uprooted by the host of apes.

K says उत्पातभूत आतप उत्पातातपः। तस्य च ताम्रत्वं शास्त्रसिद्धम्। तद्वत् ताम्रः। अन्यत् सुबोधम्। SC says विच्छर्दः (i.e. *vicchaḍḍo*) समूहे देशी।

73. केलासदिट्ठसारं गरुअं पि भुजाबलं णिसाअरवइणो।
पवएहि पाडिएक्कं एक्ककरुक्खित्तमहिहरेहि लहुइअम्।।
[कैलासदृष्टसारं गुरुकमपि भुजाबलं निशाचरपतेः।
प्लवगैः प्रत्येकमेककरोत्क्षिप्तमहीधरैर्लघूकृतम्।।]

---

[76] I.e. by the raised peaks.

[77] I.e. the earth appeared to be wider after it was cleared of the mountains.

[78] Cf. verse 69.

The strength of Rāvaṇa's arms though it was great and seen at its best when applied to the Kailāsa mountain, was thrown into the shade by the apes, who each uprooted a mountain with a single hand.[79]

K says कैलासोद्धरणे दृष्टसारं दृष्टोत्कर्षम्। अयमुपालम्भः कैलासस्य केवलं चलनादिति। गुर्वपि निशाचरपतेः भुजानां बहूनां बलं प्रत्येकमेककरोत्क्षिप्तमहीधरैः कपिभिः लघूकृतम्।

MY says *pāḍiekkaṁ* प्रत्येकम्। एकैकेन अविशेषेण सर्वैरित्यर्थः।

Kula reads शिष्ट (*siṭṭha*) for *diṭṭha*. He says कैलासेन शिष्टसारं कथितोत्कर्षं गुरुकमपि निशाचरपतेः भुजानां (?) बलं प्लवगैः प्रत्येकमेकैकेन प्लवगेनापि लघूकृतमधरीकृतम्। अत्र हेतुः एककरोत्क्षिप्तमहीधरैरिति। रावणेन हि विंशत्या भुजैरुत्क्षिप्य[80] महारम्भवतापि कैलासो मनाक् चालितः। परं वानरैस्तु प्रत्येकमेककरेण हेलयोत्क्षिप्तमहीधरै रावणभुजबलमुपहसितमिति भावः।

74. उक्खअगिरिविवरोवइअदिणअराअवमिलन्ततमसंघातम्।
जाअं पविरलतिमिरं आवण्डुरधूमधूसरं पाआलम्।।

[उत्खातगिरिविवरावपतितदिनकरातपमिलत्तमःसंघातम्।
जातं प्रविरलतिमिरमापाण्डुरधूमधूसरं पातालम्।

The nether regions, with their dense gloom blending with the rays of the sun, entering through the chasms left by the uprooted mountains, became dusky like greyish smoke as the darkness grew sparse.

K and MY read जातमिव विरलविरलं in the second line for *jāaṁ pavirala-tumiraṁ* (R and Kula ?). K and MY read निर्भर for धूसरं (R and Kula). K and Kula have आपाण्डर for *āvaṇḍura* = आपाण्डुर (R)।

K says उत्खातगिरीणां विवरैः अवपतितदिनकरातपमिश्रिततमःसंघातं पातालं विरलविरलमतिविरलं यथा आपाण्डरैः धूमैः निर्भरं पूरितमिव जातम्।

MY says विरलविरलमिति क्वलित् क्वचिदित्यर्थः। आतपमिलत्तिमिरं पाताल-मीषत्पाण्डुरधूमनिर्भरमिव जातमित्यन्वयः।

75. पवएहि अ णिरवेक्खं कओ करन्तेहि गिरिसवासुद्धरणम्।
सामिअकज्जेक्करसो अअसमुहे वि जसभाअणं अप्पाणो।।

[79] Rāvaṇa had only moved the Kailāsa mountain with his twenty arms.

[80] Our copy has उत्क्षेप्यं।

[प्लवगैश्च निरपेक्षं कृतः कुर्वद्भिर्गिरिशवासोद्धरणम्।
स्वामिकार्यैकरसोऽयशोमुखेऽपि यशोभाजनमात्मा।।]

As the apes uprooted the mountains, their own abode, regardless of their own interest, they earned glory, in spite of being liable to blame, because they were solely devoted to their master's work.

K reads निरवशेषं for *a ṇiravekkhaṁ* = च निरपेक्षं (R and Kula). K, MY and Kula read गिरिववासोद्धरणम् for *girisa-vāsu*° = गिरिशवासो° (R)।

K says गिरिस्ववासोद्धरणं गिरय एव स्ववासाः स्वगृहाः तेषामुद्धरणं निःशेषमेव कुर्वद्भिः प्लवगैः स्वामिकार्यैकरसः स्वामिकार्ये एकोर सो रागः तात्पर्यं यस्य स तथाभूत आत्मा अयशोमुखेऽपि अयशःप्रसङ्गेऽपि स्वगृहोन्मूलनात् अपवादप्रसङ्गेऽपि यशोभाजनमेव (कृतः)। कुतः–स्वामिकार्यतत्परत्वादिति।

MY says *giri-savāsuddharaṇaṁ* गिरिस्ववासोद्धरणम्।

76. होन्ति गरुआ वि लहुआ पवंगभुअसिहरणिमिअवित्थअमूला।
रहसुद्धाइअमारुअदूरुक्खित्तोज्झरा धराधरणिवहा।।

[भवन्ति गुरुका अपि लघुकाः प्लवंगभुजशिखरनिवेशितविस्तृतमूलाः।
रभसोद्धावितमारुतदूरोत्क्षिप्तनिर्झरा धराधरनिवहाः।।]

The mountains, with their broad base held fast on the shoulders of the apes, became lighter, though heavy, because the streams were swept away by the wind rising from the speed of the apes.[81]

K's gloss on this verse is mutilated in our transcript. K (*chāyā*) has मारुतिक्षिप्यमाणनिर्झराः for *mārua-dūrukkhittojjharā* (R). Kula and MY read उत्क्षिप्यमाण (*ukkhippanta*) for *dūrukkhitta* (दूरोत्क्षिप्त), like manuscript C of Goldschmidt.

MY remarks असनियमितमूलतया मारुतोद्धूनितनिर्झरतया च गिरयो गुरवोऽपि लघवो जाता इत्यर्थः।

77. अह वेएण पवंगा सअलं आअड्ढिऊण महिहरणिवहम्।
ओवअणाहि वि लहुअं वीसज्जिअकलअलं णहं उप्पइआ।।

[अथ वेगेन प्लवंगाः सकलमाकृष्य महीधरनिवहम्।
अवपतनादपि लघुकं विसृष्टकलकलं नभ उत्पतिताः।।]

---

[81] See next verse.

Thereupon, having uprooted all the mountains, the apes quickly flew into the sky, raising cries, even more swiftly than when they alighted on them.[82]

K reads स्वाकृष्य for *āaḍḍhiūṇa* = आकृष्य (R and Kula). MY has *sāaḍḍhiūṇa* समाकृष्य। K takes *vīsajjia* separately विसृज्य (*chāyā*)।

K says अथ प्लवङ्गाः सकलं गिरिसमूहं स्वाकृष्य सुष्ठून्मूल्य गृहीत्वा कलकलं कृत्वा अवपतनादपि लघु आशु वेगेन नभ उत्पतिताः।

78. चडुलेहि णिप्पअम्पा उप्पइअव्वलहुएहि वित्थअगरुआ।
एक्कक्खेवेण णहं पक्खेहि व महिहरा कईहि विलइआ।।

[चटुलैर्निष्प्रकम्पा उत्पतितव्यलघुकैर्विस्तृतगुरुकाः।
एकक्षेपेण नभः पक्षैरिव महीधराः कपिभिर्विलगिताः।।]

The nimble and swift-flying apes carried the vast and heavy and unshakeable mountains to the sky with a single effort, as if with agile wings.

K and Kula (?) read एकोत्क्षेपेण for *ekka-kkheveṇa* = एकक्षेपेण (R)।

K says उत्पतनमेव उत्पतितव्यम्। कृत्यल्युटो बहुलमिति भावे तव्यप्रत्ययः। उत्पतने लघुभिः शीघ्रैः चटुलैः कपिभिः विस्तृतगुरवो निष्प्रकम्पाः पर्वताः पक्षैरिव नभ एकोत्क्षेपेण एकोद्योगेनैव विलग्नाः प्राप्ताः। यथा पर्वताः पूर्वं पक्षवत्त्वे पक्षैरुत्पतन्ति तद्वदिति।

Kula says चटुलैश्च पक्षैरिव कपिभिः . . . एकोत्क्षेपेण (?) एकोद्गमेन . . . महीधरा नभो विलगिताः प्रापिताः[83]। R says कपिभिः कर्तृभूतैः पर्वता नभो नीता उत्पतनकारणत्वात् पक्षैरिव इत्युक्तमिति केचित्।

79. पवअक्कन्तविमुक्कं विसमुद्धप्फुडिअपत्थिअणिअत्तन्तम्।
घडिअं घडन्तणइमुहसंदाणिअसेलणिग्गमं महिवेढम्।।

[प्लवगाक्रान्तविमुक्तं विषमोर्ध्वस्फुटितप्रस्थितनिवर्तमानम्।
घटितं घटमाननदीमुखसंदानितशैलनिर्गमं महीवेष्टम्।।]

The earth, trampled and abandoned by the apes, became level again when the cavities left by the mountains were filled by the united streams,[84] and the rugged masses of earth that had gone up (with the mountains) broke away and returned to the site.

---

[82] See verse 28.

[83] Our copy has प्लाविताः *SC* has प्रापिताः।

[84] I.e. the streams pouring down from the mountains when they were carried aloft.

K says उत्पतनसमये प्लवगैराक्रान्तं ततो विमुक्तं, विषमम् ऊर्ध्वभागेषु, ऊर्ध्वशब्देन पर्वतमूलपर्यन्तलग्नः प्रदेश उच्यते, तेषूर्ध्वभागेषु स्फुटितं छिन्नं भूत्वा प्रस्थितं गिरिमूलैः सह गतं पुनर्निवर्तमानम्। विषमार्धस्फुटितेति वा पाठः। विषमं यथा अर्धेषु एकदेशेषु स्फुटितं भूत्वा प्रस्थितं प्लवगानामुत्पतनरभसात् ऊर्ध्वं गतं, पुनर्निवृत्तं महीवेष्टं घटितं यथापूर्वं प्रकृतिस्थमभूत्[85]। कथमिति-घटमानैः नदीमुखैःस्फुटनावस्थायां विच्छिन्नैः पुनर्घटमानैः नदीप्रवाहैः संदानितशैलनिर्गमं संहितशैलनिर्गमस्थानमिति।

Kula is corrupt, but he says घटमानैरेकीभवद्भिः नदीमुखैः। घटितं समीभूतमण्डलमित्यर्थः। *SC* says अयं भावः। उत्पाटितगिरिविवराणां तत्रत्यनदीमुखजलैः प्रत्यागत्य पूरितानां स्फुटितोत्पतितैः भूपार्श्वभागैः पूरणात् भूतलसमतैव जातेत्यर्थः।

80. हीरन्तमहिहराहिं मईहि भअहित्थपत्थिअणिअत्ताहिं।
सोहन्ति खणविवत्तिअससंभमुम्मुहपलोइआइ वणाइं।।
[ह्रियमाणमहीधराभिर्मृगीभिर्भयोद्विग्नप्रस्थितनिवृत्ताभिः।
शोभन्ते क्षणविवर्तितससंभ्रमोन्मुखप्रलोकितानि वनानि।।]

While the mountains, their abode, were carried away, the hinds started to run, but turned back, distraught with fear; and the woods were beautiful as they turned round and looked up in bewilderment for a while.

K reads महीधराणां, मृगीणां, निवृत्तानां for *mahiharāhiṁ,* etc. (R and Kula),

K says ह्रियमाणानां महीधराणां वनानि शोभन्ते स्म। कथंभूतानि-भयत्रस्तप्रस्थितानां, भयशब्देनात्र भयहेतुरुच्यते, भयात् त्रस्तप्रस्थितानां पतनभयात् पुनर्निवृत्तानाम्, एवं गतागतं कुर्वन्तीनां मृगीणां क्षणविवर्तितानि ससंभ्रमत्वादुन्मुखानि उन्नमितमुखानि विलोकितानि विलोकनानि येष्विति बहुव्रीहिः।

Kula says क्षोभभयपलायिताभिः ह्रियमाणो महीधरो यासां ताभिः। भयेन आविग्ना व्याकुला अतः प्रस्थिताश्च निवृत्ताश्चेति तथा ताभिः। क्षणं विवर्तितं ससंभ्रममुद्गतं च मुखं यत्र तत् तथा चिरनिवासपरिचयात् मृगीभिः प्रलोकितानि वनानि शोभन्ते प्रीतिहेतवो भवन्तीत्यर्थः।

81. उम्मूलिआण खुडिआ उक्खिप्पन्ताण उज्जुअं ओसरिआ।
णिज्जन्ताण णिराआ गिरीण मग्गेण पत्थिआ णइसोत्ता।।

---

[85] R says महीवेष्टं घटितं प्रागिव मिलित्वा समीभूतम। . . . विषमं नतोन्नतं पूर्व(नि)पातानियमेन ऊर्ध्वप्रस्थितं सत् स्फुटितं त्रुटितं पश्चात् निवृत्तं तत्खाते पतितम्।

[उन्मूलितानां खण्डितान्युत्क्षिप्यमाणानामृजुकमपसृतानि।
नीयमानानां निरायतानि गिरीणां मार्गेण प्रस्थितानि नदीस्रोतांसि।।]

When the mountains were uprooted, their rivers were cut-off from their source. While they were lifted up, they poured straight down. While they were carried away, they rushed close behind them in a lengthening stream.[86]

K says गिरीणामुन्मूलितानां नदीस्रोतांसि उन्मूलनावस्थायां त्रुटितानि विच्छिन्नानि, उत्क्षिप्तानाम् (उत्क्षिप्यमाणानां *chāyā*) उद्धतानाम् अधः ऋजुकं यथापसृतानि प्रसृतानि, नीयमानानां तेषां गिरीणां निरायतानि पर्वतवेगवशात् नितरामायतानि भूत्वा मार्गेण प्रस्थितानि।

MY says गिरीणामुन्मूलने सति चिरप्रवृत्तमार्गविच्छेदात् त्रुटितानि, तदनन्तरमुत्क्षेपणेन अधस्तात् ऋजून्यवपतितानि, तिर्यक् नयनदशायां तिर्यञ्चि दीर्घीकृतानीत्यर्थः, तन्मार्गेणैव प्रस्थितानि स्रोतांसीति योजना। Kula says ऋजुकमपसृतानि प्रगुणं गर्तेषु अधः प्रसृतानि।

82. उम्मुहसारङ्गअणं अप्फुन्दइ मलिअमेहसारं गअणम्।
विवरब्भन्तरविहअं गिरिआलं सिहरपरिभमन्तरविहअम्।।

[उन्मुखसारङ्गगणमाक्रामति मृदितमेघसारं गगनम्।
विवराभ्यन्तरविहगं गिरिजालं शिखरपरिभ्रमद्रविहयम्।।]

Powerful as the clouds of the epoch of destruction, the mountains pervaded the sky, with the herds of deer looking skyward, the birds hidden in the caves, and the sun's steeds travelling across the peaks.

K, MY and Kula read प्रलय for *malia* मृदित (R); and परिभ्रान्त (*paribbhanta*) for *paribhamanta* (R). K and MY have *giri-ālaṁ* at the end of the *pāda*.

K says प्लवगैर्धार्यमाणं गिरिजालं गगनमाक्रामति स्म। कथंभूतमउन्मुखहरिणगणं भयादुन्मुखमृगसमूहं, प्रलयमेघसारं प्रलयकालमेघाः संवर्तादयः तत्सदृशबलं, विवराभ्यन्तरगतपक्षिसङ्घं, शिखरेषु परिभ्रान्तरवितुरङ्गम्।

Kula says *appūnnai* (*apphuṇṇai* ?[87]) आक्रामति स्थगयतीति यावत। cf. *apphuṇṇa* (आक्रान्त) 2.4; 9.84. R has *apphundai* (आक्रामति)। K and MY on vv. 59 and 96 have *appuṇṇa* for *apphu°*.

[86] I.e. the falling streams seemed to stretch behind the mountains as they sped through the air.

[87] This is the manuscript of *SC*. See editor's fn. *SC* reproduces Kula's gloss on the anonymously.

83. अंसट्ठविअमहिहरा उब्भिअदाहिणकरावलम्बिअसिहरा।
उत्ताणवामकरअलधरिअणिअम्बपसरा णिअत्तन्ति कई।।

[अंसस्थापितमहीधरा उच्छ्रितदक्षिणकरावलम्बितशिखराः।
उत्तानवामकरतलधृतनितम्बप्रसरा निवर्तन्ते कपयः।।]

The apes returned (to the sea), with the mountains fixed on their shoulders, the peaks supported with the upraised right hand, and the broad flanks held up with the upturned left hand.

K, MY and Kula read उच्छ्रित for *ubbhia* = उच्छ्रित (R). Hemacandra 2.59 derives *ubbha* from ऊर्ध्व।

K says अंसेषु वामांसेषु स्थापितमहीधराः, उच्छ्रितैरूर्ध्वीकृतैः दक्षिणकरैरवलम्बित-शिखराः, उत्तानितवामकरतलगृहीतनितम्बविस्ताराः कपयः समुद्रं प्रति निवृत्ताः।

MY says *ūsia* (*SC* text also) उच्छ्रित। Kula says उच्छ्रितेन उत्क्षिप्तेन दक्षिणकरेण।

84. पत्थाणच्चिअ पढमं भुअमेत्तपहाविआण जं ण पहुत्तम्।
कह तं चिअ ताणं चिअ पहुप्पइ कईण महिहराण अ गअणम्।।

[प्रस्थान एव प्रथमं भुजमात्रप्रभावितानां यन्न प्रभूतम्।
कथं तदेव तेषामेव प्रभवति कपीनां महीधराणां च गगनम्।।]

How was it that the sky that was not spacious enough for the apes, when at the outset of their journey[88] they rushed forth empty-handed, now had enough space for them as well as the mountains?

K *pratīka* has *patthāṇe* (*SC* Text also) for *-ṇa* (R). He says . . . न प्रभूतं न पर्याप्तमभूत . . . कथं प्रभवति कथं पर्याप्तं भवेत। Kula says न प्रभूतं न संमानक्षममभूत न संमिता एव ते तत्रेत्याशयः।

85. वहइ पवंगमलोओ समतुलिउक्खित्तमिलिअमूलद्धन्ते।
एक्कक्कमसिहरुग्गमणिहसुप्पुसिअसरिआमुहे धरणिहरे।।

[वहति प्लवंगमलोकः समतुलितोत्क्षिप्तमिलितमूलार्धान्तान्।
एकक्रमशिखरोद्गमनिघर्षोत्प्रोञ्छितसरिन्मुखान्धरणीधरान्।।]

The apes carried the mountains along, with their basic portions simultaneously uprooted and lifted, and coming

---

[88] I.e. the initial flight to uproot the mountains.

into contact with each other; and the outlets of the streams obliterated by the friction of each other's towering peaks.[89]

K says प्लवङ्गमलोकः सममेव तुलिता उद्धृता नभसि चोत्क्षिप्ताः मिलिता अन्योन्यं संघट्टिताः मूलार्धान्ता मूलप्रदेशाः येषां तान्, अन्योन्यशिखरोद्गमस्य शिखरोच्छ्रयस्य निकषेण उन्मृष्टसरिन्मुखान् धरणिधरान् वहति स्म।

Kula says एकैकशिखरोद्गमानां निघर्षेण उत्प्रोञ्छितं सरिन्मुखं येषु तान् महीधरान् कपिलोको वहति परस्परविजिगीषया युगपत् संघट्टनेन नयतीत्यर्थः।

86. णिव्वण्णेऊण चिरं पवआ बोलेन्ति महिहरभरक्कन्ता।
साअरपडिरूआइं पढमुक्खअविअडमहिहरट्ठाणाइं।।

[निर्वर्ण्य चिरं प्लवगा व्यतिक्रामन्ति महीधरभराक्रान्ताः।
सागरप्रतिरूपाणि प्रथमोत्खातविकटमहीधरस्थानानि।।]

Oppressed with the weight of the mountains, the apes passed on, having watched for a long while the ocean-like cavities left by the massive mountains, erewhile uprooted (by themselves).

K reads महीधराक्रान्तांसाः for *mahihara-bharakkantā* (R and Kula).

K says महीधराधिष्ठितभुजशिखराः कपयः सागरसदृशानि प्रथममुत्खातगिरीणां विकटानि स्थानानि चिरं निर्वर्ण्य निरीक्ष्य पश्चादतिक्रामन्ति स्म। अयमर्थः- असंस्थापितगिरयो गच्छतः केचिद्वानराः प्रथममन्यैः कपिभिः उन्मूलितमहीधराणामवस्थानप्रदेशान् सागरसदृशान् चिरं निरूप्य किमयमेव समुद्र इति चिरं विचार्य पश्चात् समुद्रं प्रति गता इति।

Kula says प्रथममुत्खाता ये विकटा विशाला महीधरास्तेषां स्थानानि . . . महीधरभराक्रान्ताः चिरं निर्वर्ण्य व्यवक्रामन्ति। *SC* has व्यप-।

87. खणसंधिअमेहअडा बेउक्खिप्पन्तगिरिणिराअट्ठविआ।
परिवड्ढन्ताआमा वहन्ति व णहङ्गणे महाणइसोत्ता।।

[क्षणसंहितमेघतटानि वेगोत्क्षिप्यमाणगिरिनिरायतस्थापितानि।
परिवर्धमानायामानि वहन्तीव नभोङ्गणे महानदीस्त्रोतांसि।।]

The large streams, stretching across the mountains[90] while they were speedily rushed through the air, seemed to flow

[89] The imagery is that of a compact procession of mountains rushing through the air with the outlets of the streams blocked up.

[90] I.e. the chain of mountains closely following each other, as described in verse 85. See Kṛṣṇa in Extracts.

in the sky, lengthening in their course, with the clouds that joined them for a moment serving as their banks.

K says महानदीस्रोतांसि क्षणसंहितमेघतटानि यदृच्छया मेघैः क्षणं घटितमेघमयतटानि, वेगेनोत्क्षिप्यमाणेषु गिरिषु अन्योन्यं निरन्तरघटितेषु निरायतस्थापितानि, परिवर्धमानायामानि भूत्वा नभोऽङ्कणे (नभोऽङ्गणे?) नभोमध्ये वहन्तीव।

My says क्षणमात्रसंहितमेघतटतया रभसनीयमानगिरिदीर्घीकृतत्वेन भूयोभूयाः तिर्यक् परिवर्धमानायामतया च नभसि महीतल इव नद्यः प्रावहन्नित्यर्थः।

R says क्षणं व्याप्य संहिता मिलिता मेघा एव तटानि येषां तानि। मेघा एव तटभूमयो भवन्तीत्यर्थः।

88. सेलेसु सेलतुङ्गा णहअलमिलिएसु मिलिअदन्तप्फलिहा।
पवअविहुएसु विहुआ णिव्वडिएसु वि ण णिव्वलन्ति वणगआ।

[शैलेषु शैलतुङ्गा नभस्तलमिलितेषु मिलितदन्तपरिघाः।
प्लवगविधुतेषु विधुता निर्वलितेष्वपि न निर्वलन्ति वनगजाः।।]

As the mountains came into contact with each other in the sky, the mountain-high wild elephants were locked in each other's tusks,[91] and rocked when the mountains were rocked by the apes, and did not part even when the mountains parted.

K says कपिभिर्नीयमानेषु शैलेषु नभस्तलमिलितेषु नभस्तले यदृच्छया घटितेषु तत्र वर्तमानाः शैलवत् तुङ्गा वनगजा अपि रोषात् परस्परं मिलितदन्तपरिघा बभूवुः। शैलेषु प्लवगैः विधुतेषु सत्सु वनगजाश्च विधुता आसन्। अतः शैलेषु निर्व्यक्तेषु पृथग्भूतेष्वपि गजा न निर्व्यज्यन्ते। युद्धाभिनिवेशात् मिलितदन्ताः सन्तः न पृथग्भूता इति।

Kula reads शैलगुरुकाः (*sela-guruā*) for *sela-tuṅgā*. He remarks वनगजाः पर्वतात् पर्वतान्तरं गत्वा लग्नाः पर्वतेषु पृथग्भूतेषु अपि परस्परं रोषवत्त्वात् (?) (न) पृथग्भवन्तीत्यर्थः।

89. वेविरपओहराणं दिसाण गिरिविवरदिट्ठतणुमज्झाणम्।
कुसुमरएण सुरहिणा अग्घाएण व णिमीलिआइं मुहाइं।।

[वेपनशालिपयोधराणां दिशां गिरिविवरदृष्टतनुमध्यानाम्।
कुसुमरजसा सुरभिणा आघ्रातेनेव निमीलितानि मुखानि।।]

The faces of the regions of the sky, with the quivering clouds

---

[91] I.e. in the course of the aerial journey the elephants of one mountain charged those of another, interlocking their tusks.

(maidens as it were with heaving bosoms), with tiny portions seen through the gaps between the mountains,[92] seemed to be covered[93] with the fragrant pollen of the flowers (of the mountain trees) inhaled by them.[94]

K says वेपमानपयोधराणां वेपमानमेघानां, वेपमानस्तनीनामिति च स्फुरति। गिरिविवरेषु गिरीणामन्तरालेषु दृष्टस्वल्पमध्यानां दृश्यमानकृशमध्यप्रदेशानां दिशां मुखानि सुरभिणा आघ्रातेन कुसुमरजसा पर्वतद्रुमसंभवेन पुष्पपरागेणेव निमीलितानि संकुचितानि। यथा कुसुमपरागाघ्राणेन स्त्रीणां मुखानि मिलिताक्षाणि भवन्ति तद्वदिति। Kula says अत्र तु पर्वतैः (?) निरन्तरपिहितत्वात् दिङ्मुखानि निमीलितानीवेत्युत्प्रेक्षा। *SC* says निमीलितानि छन्नानि।

90. पवआ करअलधरिए णहमुहणिब्भिण्णवेवमाणविसहरे।
गइवसविसट्टसिहरे बिइअकरेहि परिसंठवेन्ति महिहरे।।

[प्लवगाः करतलधृतान्नखमुखनिर्भिन्नवेपमानविषधरान्।
गतिवशविशीर्णशिखरान्द्वितीयकरैः परिसंस्थापयन्ति महीधरान्।।]

As the peaks crumbled owing to the speed of the flight, the mountains, held up by the apes with one hand, were steadied by them with the other hand; while the serpents quivered, pierced by their nails.

MY has *vīa* for *biia* (द्वितीय)। K says द्वितीयैरितरैः करैः यथापूर्वं स्थापयामासुः।

91. णहअलवेअपहाविअपवंगहीरन्तसेलसिहरक्खलिआ।
मग्गागअसेलाणं होन्ति मुहुत्तोज्झरा महाणइसोत्ता।।

[नभस्तलवेगप्रधावितप्लवंगह्रियमाणशैलशिखरस्खलितानि।
मार्गागतशैलानां भवन्ति मुहूर्तं निर्झरा महानदीस्रोतांसि।।]

Falling off the summit of the mountains carried by the apes as they rushed through the sky, the large streams became for a moment cascades on the succeeding mountains.[95]

K reads त्रुटित (*-kkhuḍuia* ?) for *-kkhalia* = स्खलित (R). Cf. Hemacandra 4.116.

---

[92] Means also: with the slender waist seen through the gaps. . . .

[93] Means also: seemed to have the eyes closed on account of. . . .

[94] The imagery is that of women closing their eyes as they inhale the sweet scent of flowers.

[95] I.e. poured down on the mountains that followed close behind.

K says नभस्तले वेगप्रधावितैः प्लवगैः ह्रियमाणानां शैलानां शिखरेभ्यः त्रुटितानि विच्छिन्नानि महानदीस्रोतांसि मार्गागतशैलानां पश्चादागतशैलानां मुहूर्तं निर्झरा अभवन्।

The gloss on this verse is missing in our copy of Kula.

92. वेउक्खअदुमणिवहे तडपब्भारणिहणिव्वलन्तजलहरे।
णेन्ति जरढाअवाहअदरिविवरणिसण्णगअउले धरणिहरे।।

[वेगोत्खातद्रुमनिवहांस्तटप्राग्भारनिभनिर्वलमानजलधरान्।
नयन्ति जरठातपाहतदरीविवरनिषण्णगजकुलान्धरणीधरान्।।]

They carried the mountains along with the trees uprooted by the speed; the clouds resembling the massive flanks parting asunder; and the elephants, oppressed with the intense heat of the sun, crouching within the caves.

K says वेगेनोत्खातद्रुमनिवहान्, तटप्राग्भारनिभाः पृथग्भवन्तः जलधराः येषां तान् विश्लिष्यत्तट [?] प्रदेशसदृशजलधरखण्डानित्यर्थः, तीव्रातपपीडितत्वात् दरीविवरेषु निलीनगजकुलान् पर्वतान् प्लवगा नयन्ति स्म। K (*chāyā*) has . . . निर्व्यज्यमानजलधरान्। R says निर्वलमानाः पृथग्भूता जलधरा येभ्यस्तान्। *SC* Text has *ṇivvaḍanta* for °*lanta*.

93. धावइ वेअपहाविअपवंगहीरन्तसेलसिहरन्तरिओ।
छाआणुमग्गलग्गो तुरिअं छिण्णाअओ व्व मलउच्छङ्गो।।

[धावति वेगप्रधावितप्लवंगह्रियमाणशैलशिखरान्तरितः।
छायानुमार्गलग्नस्त्वरितं छिन्नातप इव मलयोत्सङ्गः।।]

Covered by the peaks of the mountains carried by the vehemently rushing apes, the summit of the Malaya mountain, cut-off from the sunlight, seemed to run fast in the wake of the shadows.[96]

K and MY read *dhāi va* (धावतीव) for *dhāvai* (R and Kula); and प्लवगकरोत्क्षिप्त for *pavaṁga-hīranta* = प्लवङ्गह्रियमाण (R and Kula). K and MY read त्वरितच्छिन्नातपः for *turiaṁ chi*°.

K says वेगात् प्रधावितानां प्लवगानां करैः उत्क्षिप्तैः शैलशिखरैरन्तरितो मध्ये व्यवहितो मलयोत्सङ्गः मलयस्योपरिभागः धावतीव। प्लवगनीयमानानां गिरीणां

[96] Translation follows Rāmdāsa. According to others, the Malaya mountain seemed to run, "even as the sunlight seems to run when intersected (by passing clouds)". See Extracts.

मध्ये दृष्टो मलयोत्सङ्गः सर्वत्रैकरूप्येण दृश्यमानस्तेषां वेगगमने स्वयमपि धावन्निव प्रतिभाति स्म। सर्वत्रैकरूप्येण स्थित आतपः उभयत्र मेघच्छायागमने सति अविच्छन्नं तच्छायानुमार्गगतः स्वयमपि मध्ये त्वरितं त्वरितं छिन्नो धावतीव दृश्यते तद्वदिति।

MY says वेगप्रधाविप्लवङ्गकरोत्क्षिप्तशैलशिखरच्छन्नः छायानुमार्गलग्नः त्वरित-च्छिन्नातप इव मलयोत्सङ्गोऽपि स्वयं वेगादधावदिव[97] *turiaṁ chiṇṇāava vva* इति व्यस्तपाठे त्वरितमधावदिवेत्यन्वयः। प्रागपि तत्तद्देशे विद्यमानस्यैव वेगात् स्वावरणविगमानन्तरं तत्र तत्रोपलम्भात् धावनप्रतिभास इति हृदयम्।

Kula says वेगेन प्रधावितैः प्लवङ्गैः ह्रियमाणानां (शैलानां) शिखरैरन्तरित आच्छादितो (?) यो मलयोत्सङ्गः सोऽनन्तरं . . . तच्छायानुमार्गलग्नः सन् त्वरितं धावतीव इति प्रतीत्योत्प्रेक्षया (?) धावतीत्याह। छिन्नातप इव, यथा मेघानामन्तरालनिपतित आतपः पवनप्रेरितमेघप्रसरणे धावन्निव दृश्यते तथा मलयोत्सङ्गः अपीति भावः।

94. आलोइआ ण दिट्ठा सच्चविआ ण गहिआ समोवइएहिं।
उम्मूलिआ वि जेहिं तेहिं ण उअहिं णिआ कईहि महिहरा।।
[आलोकिता न दृष्टाः सत्यापिता न गृहीताः समवपतितैः।
उन्मूलिता अपि यैस्तैर्नोदधिं नीताः कपिभिर्महीधराः।।]

The apes who had seen the mountains (from afar) saw them no more;[98] those who had fixed their eyes on them seized them not;[99] nor did those who uprooted them, simultaneously alighting on the ground, bring them to the sea.[100]

K (*chāyā*) has उदधिं नैः न in the second line. K says सममवपतितैः कपिभिः ये पर्वता दूरादालोकिताः तैस्ते गिरयः पुनर्न दृष्टाः क्षिप्रमन्यैरुन्मूलितत्वात् पुनर्न दृष्टाः। यैर्ये सत्यापिता लक्षीकृताः पर्वताः तैस्ते न गृहीताः, अन्यैः गृहीतत्वात्। यैश्च ये उन्मूलिता गिरयः तेऽपि तैरुदधिं न नीताः, अन्यैर्नीतत्वात्। एवं प्लवगाः अहमहमिकया स्वामिकार्यमकुर्वन्नित्यर्थः।

Kula reads *saṁsṭhaviā* (संस्थापिताः) for *saccaviā* (सत्यापिताः) He says संस्थापिताः सज्जीकृताः (अपि न गृहीताः) ग्रहीतुं न प्राप्ताः, कृष्टाकृष्टिकया अन्यैः नीतत्वात्।

---

97 B says कपिबलनभोनीयमानशैलच्छायानुमार्गलग्नतया त्वरितविच्छिन्नातप इव मलयोत्सङ्गोऽपि स्वयं वेगादधावदिव।

R says छिन्न आतपो यस्मात्। शिखरैरेव छिन्नातपः।

98 Because they were quickly uprooted by others.

99 I.e. those who had purposed to uproot a mountain were forestalled by others.

100 Because others carried them off. The verse describes how the apes uprooted and brought the mountains to the sea in emulation of each other.

95. भग्गदुमभङ्गभरिओ उक्खित्तविसट्टपडिअमहिहरविसमो।
पवआण उअहिलग्गो लक्खिज्जइ बिइअसंकमो व्व गइवहो।।

[भग्नद्रुमभङ्गभृत उत्क्षिप्तविशीर्णपतितमहीधरविषमः।
प्लवगानामुदधिलग्नो लक्ष्यते द्वितीयसंक्रम इव गतिपथः।।]

The trail of the apes reaching to the sea looked like a second casuseway,[101] being strewn with fragments of broken trees, and uneven with the mountains that had crumbled to the ground when raised aloft.

K says भग्नद्रुमाणां भङ्गैः भग्नावयवैः भरितः उत्क्षिप्तत्वात् विशीर्णपतितैः पर्वतैर्विषमः पूरित उदधिलग्न उदधि यावत् प्रवृत्तः प्लवगानां गतिपथः, etc.

96. वेएण गहिअसेलं वेलाबोलेन्तपडिणिअत्तोवइअम्।
जाअं रामाहिमुहं अणुराउप्फुल्ललोअणं कइसेण्णम्।।

[वेगेन गृहीतशैलं वेलाव्यतिक्रान्तप्रतिनिवृत्तावपतितम्।
जातं रामाभिमुखमनुरागोत्फुल्ललोचनं कपिसैन्यम्।।]

The host of apes that had in their onward rush passed beyond the seashore, taking the mountains with them, returned and alighted on the ground, and stood in front of Rāma, their eyes beaming with affection for him.

K and MY read व्युत्कान्त for *bolenta* explained as व्यतिक्रान्त by R. Kula has व्यपक्रान्त MY says *vokkanta* व्युत्क्रान्त। K reads अनुरागपूर्णलोचनं, and mentions अनुरागफुल्ललोचनं as a variant.

K says एवं गृहीतशैलं वेगेनाधिकेन वेलाव्युत्क्रान्तं वेलामतिक्रम्य नभसा समुद्रं गतं ततः प्रतिनिवृत्त्यावपतितम्। अनुरागेण रामगतेन स्नेहेन पूर्णलोचनं कपिसैन्यं रामाभिमुखं जातम्। MY reads *appuṇṇa* अपूर्ण (आपूर्ण ?) आक्रान्तेति वा for *upphulla* = उत्फुल्ल (R and Kula). K's reading seems to be same as that of MY. Kula says कपिसैन्यं वेगेन रामादिभिरध्यासितां वेलां व्यपक्रान्तमतिक्रम्य गतं ततः प्रतिनिवृत्तं सत् अवपतितम्।

इअ सिरिपवरसेणविरइए कालिदासकए दहमुहवहे महाकव्वे
छठुओ आसासओ समत्तो।

[इति श्रीप्रवरसेनविरचिते कालिदासकृते दशमुखवधे महाकाव्ये
षष्ठ आश्वासकः समाप्तः।]

---

[101] With reference to the one that was to be built with mountains across the sea.

सप्तम आश्वासकः
Seventh Āśvāsakaḥ

1. अह ते विक्कमणिहसं दहवअणपआवलङ्घणग्गक्खन्धम्।
आढत्ता विरएउं सासअरामजसलञ्छणं सेउवहम्।।

[अथ ते विक्रमनिकषं दशवदनप्रतापलङ्घनाग्रस्कन्धम्।
आरब्धा विरचयितुं शाश्वतरामयशोलाञ्छनं सेतुपथम्।।]

Then did they begin to build the causeway that was to be the touchstone of their valour; the precursor of the otherthrow of Rāvaṇa's might; the abiding symbol of Rāma's fame.

K says विक्रमस्य निकषं वानराणां भुजबलस्य परिच्छेदकमित्यर्थः। दशवदनस्य प्रतापलङ्घनाय प्रतापाभिभवाय अग्रस्कन्धम्। स्कन्धः सेनाव्यूहः। अग्रिमस्कन्धः। रावणवधसाधनत्वात् सेतुः सेनाव्यूहत्वेनोक्तः।

MY says निकषः स्वविक्रमपरीक्षास्थानम्। आगामिनः समरविक्रमस्य व्यञ्जनम्। Kula says विक्रमस्य शक्तिसम्पदो निकषमुत्कर्षापकर्षपरीक्षाहेतुम्। R says निकषं कषपाषाणम्।

2. णवरि अ महिअलधरिआ मुक्का उअहिम्मि वाणरेहिँ महिहरा।
आइवराहभुएहिँ व पलउव्वहणदलिआ महिअलद्धन्ता।।

[अनन्तरं च महीतलधृता मुक्ता उदधौ वानरैर्महीधराः।
आदिवराहभुजैरिव प्रलयोद्वहनदलिता महीतलार्धान्ताः।।]

Thereupon the mountains, held up in the sky, were dropped by the apes on the sea, even as the portions of the earth that broke away while it was raised from the waters of the Deluge were dropped on the sea by the arms of the Primeval Boar.[1]

K, MY and Kula read *ṇaha* for *mahi* (R). K and probably MY read *bhariā* for *dhariā* (R and Kula)।

K says नभस्तले भरता घटिताः महीधरा वानरैरुदधौ सेतुरचनार्थं मुक्ताः। प्रलयोद्वहनदलिताः, बहुबाहुना वराहेण समुद्धृता मही चिरं जले स्थितत्वात् बहुधा खण्डिता हि भवति, एवमुद्वहनसमये दलिताः अधोगच्छन्तः महीतलविभागाः

[1] See 6.12, 13 for the allusion.

महावराहस्य भुजैर्यथा समुद्रे मुक्ताः क्लिन्नत्वादधःपतन्तो महीखण्डाः पुनर्गृहीत्वा समुद्रमध्यस्थायां भुवि यथा स्थापिता तद्वदित्यर्थः।

MY says प्रलयोद्धरणदलिता महीतलार्धान्ता महावराहभुजैः प्रथमं नभस्तले घटिताः पश्चादुदधौ यथा व्युमुच्यन्त तद्वदित्यर्थः।

Kula says अनन्तरं च आदिवराहभुजैः प्रलये यत् उद्वहनमुत्क्षेपणं तेन दलिता महीतलैकदेशा इव महीधरा वानरैः नभःस्थले धृताः सन्त उदधौ मुक्ताः।

3. णिवडन्तम्मि ण दिट्ठो दूरोवइअम्मि कम्पिओ गिरिणिवहे।
खणपडिअम्मि विलुलिओ अत्थमिअम्मि परिवड्ढिओ सलिलणिही।।
[निपतति न दृष्टो दूरादवपतिते कम्पितो गिरिनिवहे।
क्षणपतिते विलुलितोऽस्तमिते परिवर्धितः सलिलनिधिः।।]

As the mountains dropped the sea vanished from sight; it rocked as they plunged far down; it was convulsed as they slumped in a trice; and swelled as they disappeared in the waters.

K says गिरिनिवहे निपतति सति समुद्रः तद्विस्तारच्छादितत्वात् न दृष्टः। दूरमधः अवपतिते सति वेलानिलाघातात् कम्पितः। क्षणात् पतिते सति विलुलितः क्षुभितः। गिरिनिवहे जलेषु अस्तमिते सेतुविरचनाभावात् निमग्ने सति परिवृद्धोऽभूत्।

4. णिहउव्वत्तजलअरं कड्ढिअकाणणभमन्तभमिरुच्छङ्गम्।
जाअं कलुसच्छाअं पढमुच्छलिआगअं महोअहिसलिलम्।।

[निहतोद्वृत्तजलचरं कृष्टकाननभ्रमद्भ्रमणशीलोत्सङ्गम्।
जातं कलुषच्छायं प्रथमोच्छलितागतं महोदधिसलिलम्।।]

The waters of the ocean, first surging up, and then rolling into the beach, became turbid as they filled up with the whirling woods swept away from the mountains,[2] with the animals killed and overturned.

K, MY, Deva and Kula read *bharia* for *bhamira* भ्रमणशील (R). K reads *uccalia* (Deva also) for *ucchalia* (R and Kula).

K says अथ महोदधेः सलिलं निहतोद्वृत्तजलजन्तु, कृष्टभ्रमत्काननभरितोत्सङ्गं कृष्टैः भ्रमद्भिः काननैः पर्वतसंबन्धिभिः भरितोपरिभागं, पर्वतपतनात् प्रथममुच्चलितं नभसि उच्चलितं तत आगतं भूत्वा कलुषच्छायं जातम्।

MY says यथा कृष्टकाननं भवति तथा भ्रमत् तैरेव काननैः भृतोत्सङ्गमिति योज्यम्।

---

[2] Cf. Kṛṣṇa in Extracts.

Kula says निहता: सन्त उद्वृत्ता उत्तानीभूता जलचरा यत्र। पर्वतपतनात् प्रथमोच्छलितागतं, गमनागमनेन कृष्टैः काननैः भ्रमन् भरितश्च उत्सङ्गो यस्य तत् महोदधिसलिलं कलुषच्छायं जातम्। Deva says उद्वृत्ता: परिपूवमाना:।

5. सलिलत्थमिअमहिहरो पुणोविअद्दिट्ठमिलिअगिरिसंघाओ।
तह घडिअपव्वओ विअं दीसइ णहसाअरन्तरालुद्देसो।।

[सलिलास्तमितमहीधरः पुनरप्यदृष्टमिलितगिरिसंघातः।
तथा घटितपर्वत इव दृश्यते नभःसागरान्तरालोद्देशः।।]

Even with the mountains vanishing in the waters, the interval between the sky and the ocean appeared to be full of mountains as before, because masses of other mountains imperceptibly gathered again.[3]

K says सलिलास्तमितः पूर्वपतितो महीधरो यस्य स तथाभूतः, पुनरपि अदृष्टमिलितगिरिसंघातः उपर्युपरि अदृष्टघटितगिरिसंघातः नभःसागरान्तरालोद्देशः तथाघटितपर्वत इव दृश्यते, शैघ्र्यातिशयेन प्रतिक्षणं क्रियमाणस्य पर्वतघटनस्यादर्शनात् प्रथमघटितपर्वतवानिवादृश्यत्। MY says कदाचिदपि पर्वतरहितो नादृश्यतेत्यर्थः। Kula says सलिले अस्तमिता महीधरा यत्र स तथा। पुनरपि अदृष्टमिलितो गिरिसंघातो यत्र स नभःसागरयोरन्तरालोद्देशः तथा तेन प्रकारेण घटितपर्वत इव दृश्यते। एतेन निर्झरसंततिः यथा प्रतिक्षणं विच्छिद्यमानापि तथाव्यवस्थितैव लक्ष्यते, तथैवाविच्छिन्नमिलितप्रक्षिप्तपतितानां गिरीणां संतान इत्युक्तं भवति।

6. जणिअं पडिवक्खभअं तुलिआ सेला धुओ कईहिँ समुद्दो।
ण हु णवर हिअअसारा आरम्भा वि गरुआ महालक्खाणम्।।

[जनितं प्रतिपक्षभयं तुलिताः शैला धुतः कपिभिः समुद्रः।
न खलु केवलं हृदयसारा आरम्भा अपि गुरवो महालक्ष्याणाम्।।]

The mountains were uprooted, and the ocean rocked by the apes striking terror into the enemy. Not only the strength of will but also the enterprises of those who have lofty aims are great.

K says कपिभिः शैला उद्धृताः, समुद्रः कम्पितः। अतएव प्रतिपक्षस्य भयं जनितम्। तथाहि महालक्षाणां, लक्षशब्देन साध्यमुच्यते अक्षुद्रलक्षाणामतुच्छानुभवानां हृदयसारा हृदयशक्तय एव न केवलं गुरवः, आरम्भा अपि गुरवो भवन्ति हि। लक्षस्य महत्त्वात् आरम्भाश्च तदनरूपा भवन्तीत्यर्थः।

---

[3] The verse describes the unbroken succession of the mountains dropped by the apes.

MY says सारो बलम्। केवलं बुद्धिबलान्येव न गुरूणि किंतु प्रवृत्तयोऽपीत्यर्थः। Kula says महत् लक्ष्यं सिसाधयिषितं येषां ते महालक्ष्याः, तेषां न खलु केवलं हृदयस्य सारा व्यवसायविशेषाः गुरुकाः, किंतु आरम्भाः कार्य साधनोपाया अपि गुरुकाः . . .।

7. जो दीसइ धरणिहरो णज्जइ एएण वज्झइ त्ति समुद्दो।
उअहिम्मि उण वडन्ता कत्थ गअ त्ति सलिले ण णज्जन्ति धरा ॥

[यो दृश्यते धरणीधरो ज्ञायते एतेन बद्ध इति समुद्रः।
उदधौ पुनः पतन्तः कुत्र गता इति सलिले न ज्ञायन्ते धराः॥]

As the mountain came into view it seemed that it would span the sea; but none knew whither the mountains, plunging into the sea, were gone amidst the waters.

K reads the second line as उदधौ पुनः पतन् कुत्र गत इति सलिले न ज्ञायते शैलः। Kula agrees with R.

Veses 8 and 9 are not found in K and MY. Verse 8 is found in Kula, but after 10, the order of verses being 7, 10, 8, 11.

8. सअलमहिवेढविअडो सिहरसहस्सपडिरुद्धरइरहमग्गो।
इअ तुङ्गो वि महीहरो तिमिङ्गिलस्स वअणे तणं व पणट्ठो॥

[सकलमहीवेष्टविकटः शिखरसहस्रप्रतिरुद्धरविरथमार्गः।
इति तुङ्गोऽपि महीधरस्तिमिंगिलस्य वदने तृणमिव प्रनष्टः॥]

Broad as the earth, a mountain that blocked the path of the sun's chariot with its thousand peaks, vanished, even though so lofty, in the mouth of a whale-devouring monster, like a blade of grass.

9. पव्वअसिहरुच्छित्तं धावइ जं जं जलं णहङ्गणहुत्तम्।
तं तं रअणेहिँ समं दीसइ णक्खत्तमण्डलं व पडन्तम्॥

[पर्वतशिखरोत्क्षिप्तं धावति यद्यज्जलं नभोङ्गणाभिमुखम्।
तत्तद्रत्नैः समं दृश्यते नक्षत्रमण्डलमिव पतत्॥]

The volume of water that rushed skyward, thrown up by the mountain peaks (plunging into the sea), looked like a conglomeration of stars as it came down with the gems.[4]

---

[4] I.e. the gems that had gone up with the waters.

10. वाणरवेआइद्धा पिहुलवलन्तणिअओज्झरपरिक्खित्ता।
अप्पत्त च्चिअ उअहिं भमन्ति आवत्तमण्डलेसु व सेला।।

[वानरवेगाविद्धाः पृथुलवलमाननिजनिर्झरपरिक्षिप्ताः।
अप्राप्ता एवोदधिं भ्रमन्त्यावर्तमण्डलेष्विव शैलाः।।]

Swiftly flung by the apes, the mountains, encircled by their massive swirling cascades, seemed to move round in whirlpools even before reaching the sea.

K and Deva read विपुल for *pihula* = पृथुल (R). K says वानरैः वेगेनाविद्धाः भ्रमयित्वा विसृष्टाः, विपुलैः वलमानैः निजैः निर्झरैः परिक्षिप्ताः शैलाः उदधिमप्राप्ता एव आवर्तमण्डलेषु भ्रमन्तीव। Kula says आविद्धाः क्षिप्ताः। Besides he says निजाभिः वलन्तीभिः निर्झरावलीभिः परिक्षिप्ता वेष्टिताः। He reads *ṇiaa-valantojjharavali* cf. *SC* text.

11. खणमेलिआपविद्धो सिहरन्तरणित्तरित्तवाणरलोओ।
पच्छा पडइ समुद्दे अण्णो मिलइ पढमं णहे गिरिणिवहो।।

[क्षणमेलितापविद्धः शिखरान्तरनिर्यद्रिक्तवानरलोकः।
पश्चात्पतित समुद्रेऽन्यो मिलति प्रथमं नभसि गिरिनिवहः।।]

Even before a group of mountains, brought together in an instant and thrown down, dropped into the sea, with the apes flying out[5] empty-handed through the gaps between the peaks, another group of mountains gathered in the sky.

K says प्लवगैः क्षणात् मेलितो घटितः प्रविद्धः[6], शिखरान्तरेभ्यः निर्यन् निर्गच्छन् रिक्तः शून्यः गिरिभरवर्जितः वानरलोको यस्य स तथाभवन् गिरिनिवहः समुद्रे पश्चादेव पतितः। प्रथममेव नभसि अन्यो गिरिनिवहो मिलति घटते स्म। K (*chāyā*) has पश्चात् पतति।

It will be seen that K (Deva also) reads *melia-ppaviddho* for *meliāpaviddho* (R and Kula). R says मेलितो योजितः पश्चादपविद्धः प्रेरितो गिरिनिवहः। Kula is corrupt, but *SC* which reproduces him says क्षणादतर्कितं मेलितः समुपस्थापितः अपविद्धः क्षिप्तः।

MY says क्षणेन घटयित्वावपातितः पूर्वावपातितान्यगिरिनिवहतया रिक्तेन गिरिरहितेन . . . शिखरान्तरालैरूर्ध्वं निःसरता कपिलोकेनोपलक्षितः मध्यमो गिरिनिवहः समुद्रे

---

5 Lit. going out.

6 Deva says कपिभिः क्षणेन मेलितः प्रविद्धः घटयित्वा क्षिप्तः।

पश्चादपतत्, प्रथममेव त्वन्यस्तृतीयो नभस्यमिलत्। अत्र मिथ इति शेषः, अथवा समुद्रे पश्चात् पततः प्रथमं नभसि घटमानस्य च द्वयोर्गिरिनिवहयोः क्षणमेलितप्रतिविद्धत्वं शिखरान्तरनिर्यद्रिक्तवानरत्वं च क्रमादेकैकविशेषणमनुसंधेयम्। अतः पर्यायद्वयमेव सिद्धं भवति। अनेन गिरिघटनानैरन्तर्यं विवक्षितमिति।

12. दीहा वलन्तविअडा रसन्ति उवहिम्मि मारुअभरिज्जन्ता।
पाआलोअरगहिरा रहसोविद्धाण महिहराण गइवहा।।

[दीर्घा वलद्विकटा रसन्त्युदधौ मारुतभ्रियमाणाः।
पातालोदरगभीरा रभसापविद्धानां महीधराणां गतिपथाः।।]

When the mountains were speedily thrown into the sea, their long, winding and broad tracks, deep down to the bottom, rumbled as they filled with wind.

K says उदधौ वानरैः रभसक्षिप्तानां पर्वतानां गतिपथा दीर्घा वलमाना विकटाश्च, मारुतेन पूर्यमाणाः, पातालोदरवत् गभीरा भूत्वा रसन्ति स्म।

MY says *Osuddhāṇa* अवपातितानाम् (Deva *chāyā*). This is the reading of *SC* Text and Kula also, who has निपातितानाम्। R reads *oviddhāṇa* and says रभसेन वेगेनापविद्धानां प्रेरितानां महीधराणाम्।

13. उक्खित्तविमुक्काइं णहम्मि एक्केक्कमावडणभिण्णाइं।
वज्जभउव्विण्णाइँ व पडन्ति रअणाअरे गिरिसहस्साइं।।

[उत्क्षिप्तविमुक्तानि नभस्येकैकक्रमावपतनभिन्नानि।
वज्रभयोद्विग्नानीव पतन्ति रत्नाकरे गिरिसहस्राणि।।]

Lifted and released by the apes, thousands of mountains, crumbling as they dashed against one another in the sky, plunged into the sea, as if stupefied with terror of the thunderbolt.[7]

K, MY Deva and Kula read *aīnti raaṇāaraṁ* in the second line for *paḍanti raaṇāare* (R).

K says कपिभिः लीलयोत्क्षिप्य विमुक्तानि, नभसि अन्योन्यघट्टनेन भिन्नानि, वज्रभयात् उद्विग्नानीव गिरिसहस्राणि रत्नाकरं प्रविशन्ति स्म (यन्ति *chāyā*)। पूर्व गिरय इन्द्रवज्रभयादाविग्ना यथा समुद्रं प्रविष्टाः तथैव प्राविशन्।

MY says *ainti* (*SC* text also) अतियान्ति प्राप्नुवन्नित्यर्थः। Kula says

[7] I.e. like the mountains of old, which had plunged into the sea to save their wings from the thunderbolt of Indra. See 5.37.

रत्नाकरमायान्ति। Deva says अयन्ते गच्छन्ति। *SC* has अधिगच्छन्ति which is a mistake for अतिगच्छन्ति।

14. भिण्णसिलाअलसिहरा णिअअदुभोसरिअकुसुमरअधूसरिआ।
पढमं पडन्ति सेला पच्छा वाउद्धुआ महाणइसोत्ता।।

[भिन्नशिलातलशिखराणि निजकद्रुमापसरत्कुसुमरजोधूसरिताः।
प्रथमं पतन्ति शैलाः पश्चाद्वातोद्धतानि महानदीस्रोतांसि।।]

Grey with the pollen of the flowers swirling from the trees, the mountains, with the rocks and peaks torn asunder, dropped first, and thereafter their great streams stirred up by the wind.

K says शैलाः भिन्नशिलातलशिखराः भूत्वा प्रथमं प्रापतन्। निजतटात् (अपसृत) द्रुमकुसुमरजोधूसरितानि महानदीस्रोतांसि वायुनोद्धूतानि पश्चात् पतन्ति स्म। Kula says भिन्नानि शिलातलानि शिखराणि च येषां ते शैलाः R says शैलाः कीदृशाः – निजकद्रुमेभ्यः अपसरद्भिः कुसुमरजोभिः धूसरिताः।

15. णिम्मलसलिलब्भन्तरविहत्तदीसन्तविसमगइसंचारा।
णस्सन्ति णिच्चलट्ठिअपवंगमालोइआ चिरेण महिहरा।।

[निर्मलसलिलाभ्यन्तरविभक्तदृश्यमानविषमगतिसंचाराः।
नश्यन्ति निश्चलस्थितप्लवंगमालोकिताश्चिरेण महीधराः।।]

Watched by the apes as they stood still, the mountains slowly disappeared in the sea, with their winding course distinctly visible amidst the clear waters.

K says दूरादुत्खातनीतेषु पर्वतेषु समुद्रे लोष्टकपालादिवत् नश्यत्सु सत्सु तेषां सलिले विस्पष्टदृश्यमानान् गतिपथान् कपयः शोकविस्मयाभ्यां निश्चलाः सन्तो ददृशुरित्यर्थः।

MY explains *visama-gai* (विषमगति) as कुटिलप्रकार। He says गतिः प्रकारः। Kula says निर्मलसलिलाभ्यन्तरे विभक्तं[8] (स्फुटं) दृश्यमानो (विवर्तनवशात्) विषमगतिसञ्चारः अधःप्रवेशो येषां ते महीधरा, इयत्प्रमाणा अपि गिरयः अस्तायन्ते इत्यवधानात् निश्चलस्थितैः प्लवङ्गैरालोकिताः चिरेण नश्यन्ति अदर्शनं गच्छन्ति।

16. फेणकुसुमन्तरुत्तिण्णकेसराआरवेविरमऊहाइं।
सूएन्ति पवत्ताइं मूलुक्खुहिअं महोअहिं रअणाइं।।

---

[8] The words within brackets are restored from *SC*.

[फेनकुसुमान्तरोत्तीर्णकेसराकारवेपनशीलमयूखानि।
सूचयन्ति प्लवमानानि मूलोत्क्षुभितं महोदधिं रत्नानि।।]

The gems, rising to the surface, with their quivering filament-shaped rays emerging through the flower-like foam, showed that the ocean was stirred to its depths.

K reads मूलक्षुभितं for *mūlukkhuhiaṁ* = मूलोत्क्षुभितं (R). *SC* text has *mūla-kkhuhiaṁ* like K.

K says फेनमयानां कुसुमानामन्तरेभ्य उत्तीर्णाः तदीयकेसरसदृशाकारा (वेपमाना) मयूखाः येषां तानि, क्षोभातिरेकादुत्थितानि मूलतलस्थितानि रत्नानि महोदधिं मूलेऽपि क्षुभितं सूचयन्ति स्म।

MY says *paantāiṁ* प्लवमानानि। Kula has मूलखण्डितं। He seems to read *mūla-kkhuḍiaṁ*. cf. Hemacandra 1.53.

17. विहुणइ वेलं व महिं भिन्दइ समअं व धरणिधरसंघाअम्।
गेण्हइ भअं व गअणं मुअइ सहाअं व साअरो पाआलम्।।

[विधुनोति वेलामिव महीं भिनत्ति समयमिव धरणीधरसंघातम्।
गृह्णाति भयमिव गगनं मुञ्चति स्वभावमिव सागरः पातालम्।।]

The sea rocked the earth as it did the shore; shattered the mountains as it broke the customary law;[9] resorted to the sky[10] even as it resorted to fear; and forsook the nether regions[11] even as it abandoned its natural calm.

K says इवशब्दः प्रकारवचनः। पर्वताहतः समुद्रो वेलां तीरं यथा विधुनोति स्म तथा महीमपि व्यधुनोत्, etc. Kula says वेलामिवेत्यर्थात् सहोपमायां न केवलं वेला महीमपीत्यादि योज्यम्। K says समयं मर्यादाम्। Kula says समयं जगदवलम्बनमिव धरणीधरसंघातं भिनत्ति। R says समयं वेलालङ्घनं न कर्तव्यमिति व्यवस्थामिव।

18. पल्लत्थन्ति वलन्ता चलविडवन्तरणिअत्ततरुपारोहा।
मूलुण्णामिअजलआ अहोमुहन्दोलिओज्झरा धरणिहरा।।

[पर्यस्यन्ति वलमानाश्चलविटपान्तरनिवृत्ततरुप्ररोहाः।
मूलोन्नामितजलदा अधोमुखान्दोलितनिर्झरा धरणिधराः।।]

---

9 That of not overflowing its shore.

10 I.e. rose sky-high.

11 I.e. surged up from the bottom.

The mountains were thrown headlong into the waters as they slanted. The branch-roots of the trees issued through the moving branches.[12] The clouds were thrust upward by the (overturned) base of the mountains; and the cascades rolled upside down.

K says कपिभिः पर्वताः पर्यस्यन्ते भ्रामयित्वा अधोमुखं क्षिप्यन्ते स्म। कथंभूताः-वलमानाः। चलानां विटपानामन्तरेभ्यो निवृत्ताः ऊर्ध्वं निर्गताः तरूणां प्लक्षादीनां प्ररोहा येषां ते तथाभूताः। मूलैरुन्नमद्भिः उन्नमितजलदा, अधोमुखमान्दोलितनिर्झराः।

MY says हरिभिः गिरयो भ्राम्यमाणाः अधोमुखं क्षिप्यन्ते। अधोमुखावपतनदशायां कथंभूता इत्यत्राह चलेति। तत्र मूलाभिमुखत्वं विहायान्यथाभूतप्ररोहाः, मूलैरुन्नामितवैहायसमेघाः, शिखरप्रदेशेषु अधोमुखभ्राम्यन्निर्झरा इति। R says धरणिधरा वलमाना अधोमुखत्वेन वक्रीभवन्तः सन्तः पर्यस्यन्तीतस्ततः पतन्ति।

K, MY and Kula (see below) explain प्ररोह as "barnch-root" cf. 1.4; 2.19 above. R takes it as "ordinary root". He says निवृत्ता लम्बमानाः तरूणां प्ररोहाः शिफा यत्र ते। तरूणामप्यघोमुखत्वेन शिफा अप्यधोमुखा भवन्तीत्यर्थः।

Kula seems to read पतन्तः[13] (i. e. *paḍantā*, like manuscript C of Goldschmidt) for *valantā*. He says पर्यस्यन्ति परिवर्तन्ते। R says पर्यस्यन्ति इतस्ततः पतन्ति। Kula explains प्ररोह as शाखाशिफा। He says *valantā* इति पाठे आवर्तनत इत्यर्थः।

19. अट्ठिअपडन्तमहिहरदूरट्ठिअजलरअन्धआरत्थमिए।
साहइ णवर पडन्ते पक्खुहिअसमुद्दपडिरओ धरणिहरे।।

[अस्थितपतन्महीधरदूरोत्थितजलरयान्धकारास्तमितान्।
शास्ति केवलं पततः प्रक्षुभितसमुद्रपतिरवो धरणिधरान्।।]

As the mountains were hidden in the gloom caused by sea spray rising high into the air, as a result of more and more mountains incessantly falling, the roar of the raging sea alone proclaimed that they had dropped.

K and Kula read संक्षुभित for *pakkhuhia* (R).

---

[12] It is fancied that when the mountains were overturned the branch-roots of trees like the banyan instead of hanging down stood high among the branches. Cf. 2.19.

[13] Our copy has पदन्तः।

K says अस्थितमनवरतं पतद्भिः पर्वतैरुत्थापितैः सलिलरजोऽन्धकारैः अस्तमितान् सलिलबिन्दुसमूहमयैः अन्धकारैः छन्नान्, पततः पर्वतान् क्षुभितसमुद्रप्रतिरवः केवलं शंसति। MY says अवपततः शैलान् क्षुभितसमुद्रघोष एव केवलमशंसत्। न तु ते तथाभूता अदृश्यन्तेत्यर्थः। Kula says पतद्भिः महीधरैः दूरोत्थितस्य जलस्य रजोभिः कर्णैर्योऽन्धकारः तेन . . . अस्तमितान्, पततो धरणीधरान् केवलं संक्षुभितसमुद्रस्य प्रत्यग्रो रवः प्रतिरवः कथयति, अथवा दिक्कुहरव्यापी प्रतिरवः प्रतिध्वनिः।[14]

20. दरधोअकेसरसडा पाआलुम्हगिरिधाउकद्दमिअमुहा।
पडिसक्कन्ति पवंगा पल्हत्थिअमहिहरूससन्तक्खन्धा।।

[दरधौतकेसरसटाः पातालोष्मगिरिधातुकर्दमितमुखाः।
परिवर्तन्ते प्लवंगाः पर्यस्तमहीधरोच्छ्वसत्स्कन्धाः।।]

The apes moved about, with their hair wet with spray, and the face smeared with the minerals of the mountains melting from subterranean heat; while their shoulders were at ease, because the mountains were cast down.

K says प्रक्षिप्तपर्वतत्वात् उच्छ्वसद्भुजशिखरप्रदेशाः, पातालोष्णैः पर्वतमूलगतपातालसंयोगादुष्णैः गिरिधातुभिः कर्दमितमुखाः। पातालं तु नित्यसंवृतत्वात् ऊष्मलं भवतीति भावः। गिरिनिर्झरैः दरधौतकेसरसटाः प्लवङ्गाः परितः संक्रामन्ति (परिसंक्रामन्ति *chāyā*) चरन्ति स्म।

MY says *parisakkanti* परिसमचरन्। Kula says उष्णेन गिरिधातुना कदर्थितमुखाः। He seems to read *kavaṭṭia* (कदर्थित) for *kaddamia*. cf. Hemacandra 1.224. He renders *palhatthia* as पर्यासित।

21. विअलन्तोज्झरलहुआ पवणविहुव्वन्तपाअवुद्धपइण्णा।
पवएहिँ उद्धमुक्का सिहरेहिँ पडन्ति साअरम्हि महिहरा।।

[विगलन्निर्झरलघुकाः पवनविधूयमानपादपोर्ध्वप्रकीर्णाः।
प्लवगैरूर्ध्वमुक्ताः शिखरैः पतन्ति सागरे महीधराः।।]

Released by the apes with the peaks upward, the mountains learned over at the top, with the trees tossed by the wind, and dropped into the sea with the peaks down, growing lighter as the cascades poured out.

K, Deva and MY read विलग्नाः for *paiṇṇā* = प्रकीर्णाः (R) and

[14] Partly restored from *SC*.

उद्धूयमान (*uddhuvvanta*) for *vihuvvanta* (R).[15] Translation follows Goldschimdt's reading *paallā* (manuscript C) for *paiṇṇā* Hemacandra 4.70 has *payallai* शिथिलीभवति लम्बते वा।

K says प्लवगैरूर्ध्वं मुक्ता ऊर्ध्वशिखरं प्रक्षिप्ताः पर्वता विगलन्निर्झरत्वात् लघवः, पवनेन उद्धूयमानैः प्रेर्यमाणैः स्वपादपैरूर्ध्वं विलग्नाः ऊर्ध्वीकृतमूला इत्यर्थः, एवं भूत्वा शिखरैः गुरुभिः सागरे न्यपतन्। Deva explains ऊर्ध्वविलग्न as ऊर्ध्वनुन्न।

MY says निर्झरविगलनेन लघूकृततया पवनोद्धूयमाननितम्बतरुवनोर्ध्वलग्नतया च प्लवगैरूर्ध्वशिखरं मुक्ता अपि गिरयो गुरुभिः शिखरैः न्यपतिन्नित्यर्थः। Kula seems to read *mūlehi* for *siharehi*. *SC* says प्लवगैरूर्ध्वमुक्ता अधःशिखरीकृत्य क्षिप्ता महीधराः सागरे मूलैः पतन्ति।

22. अत्थमिअसेलमग्गा भिण्णणिअत्तन्तसलिलपुञ्जितअकुसुमा।
होन्ति हरिआलकविला दाणसुअन्धुप्पवन्तगअदुमभङ्गाः।।

[अस्तमितशैलमार्गा भिन्ननिवर्तमानसलिलपुञ्जितकुसुमाः।
भवन्ति हरितालकपिला दानसुगन्ध्युत्प्लवमाना गजद्रुमभङ्गाः।।]

Yellow with orpiment,[16] the tracks of the sinking mountains were covered with the flowers[17] piled up by the waters as they divided and returned, and with the broken fragments of the floating *sallakī* trees, fragrant with the ichor of elephants.[18]

K says अस्तमितानां शैलानां मार्गाः भिन्ननिवर्तमानसलिलपुञ्जितकुसुमाः, हरितालैः धातुविशेषैः कपिलवर्णाः, दानेन मदेन सुगन्धयः उत्प्लवमाना गजद्रुमाणां सल्लकीनां भङ्गा यत्र ते तथा बभूवुः। सल्लकी स्यात् गजप्रियेति हलायुधः।

My reads *uppaanta* (उत्प्लवमान) for *uppavanta*. Kula reads लाञ्छित for *puñjia*. He says अस्तमितानां निमग्नानां (शैलानां) मार्गाः . . . भिन्नेन अपसृतेन निवर्तमानेन (सलिलेन) लाञ्छितानि कुसुमानि येषां ते तथाभृताः हरितालकपिला भवन्ति।

---

15 Kula is corrupt, but to judge from *SC* which follows him closely, he reads प्रकीर्ण like R, and has उद्धूयमान like K with अवधूयमान as an alternative. *SC* text has *ohuvvanta* (अवधूयमान). *SC* says पादपैरुर्ध्वप्रकीर्णा उर्ध्वप्रचला वा। प्रकीर्णाः परिवर्तिता इति लोकनाथः। R says ऊर्ध्वेन मस्तकेन प्रकीर्णा विक्षिप्ताः (महीधराः)।

16 The yellow mineral embedded in the mountains.

17 Those of the mountain trees.

18 Elephants feed on the leaves of these trees.

23. अत्थाअन्ति सरोसा सलिलदरत्थमिअसेलसिहरावडिआ।
एक्कावत्तवलन्ता धुवआतम्बलोअणा वणमहिसो।।

[अस्तायन्ते सरोषाः सलिलदरास्तमितशैलशिखरापतिताः।
एकावर्तवलमाना धुताताम्रलोचना वनमहिषाः।।]

A herd of angry wild buffaloes, with rolling red eyes, that tumbled off the summit of a mountain, partly submerged in the waters, disappeared as they turned round in a whirlpool.

K, MY and Kula read अवपतिताः (*ovaiā*, cf. 6.28, 29) for *āvaḍiā* आपतिताः (R)।

K says जलेन धाव्यमानाताम्रलोचनाः (MY and Kula also). R says धूयमाने इतस्ततः प्रेर्यमाणे आताम्रे लोचन यैस्ते। Kula says विकटतटस्य असतमितस्य शैलस्य शिखरादवपतिताः। He reads *viaḍa-aḍatthamia* (cf. *SC* Text) for *salila-daratthamia* = सलिलदरास्तमित (R and K *chāyā*). K commentary says सलिलोदरास्तमितेभ्यः शैलशिखरेभ्यः अवपतिताः।

24. भिण्णमिलिअं पि भिज्जइ पुणो वि एक्कक्कमावलोअणसुहिअम्।
सेलत्थमणणउण्णअतरङ्गहीरन्तकाअरं हरिणउलम्।।

[भिन्नमिलितमपि भिद्यते पुनरप्येकैकक्रमावलोकनसुखितम्।
शैलास्तमननतोन्नततरङ्गह्रियमाणकातरं हरिणकुलम्।।]

Carried away by the heaving billows as the mountains sank, and in terror of their life, a herd of deer, although they parted and met, parted once more, content to have seen one another again.

K reads अस्तमय (*atthamaya*) for *atthamaṇa* अस्तमण (R, Deva and Kula ?)

25. दाढाविभिण्णकुम्भा करिमअराण थिरहत्थकड्ढिज्जन्ता।
मोत्तागब्भिणसोणिअभरेन्तमुहकंदरा रसन्ति मइन्दा।।

[दंष्ट्राविभिन्नकुम्भाः करिमकराणां स्थिरहस्तकृष्यमाणाः।
मुक्तागर्भितशोणितभ्रियमाणमुखकंदरा रसन्ति मृगेन्द्राः।।]

Dragged by the stiff trunks of the sea elephants, the lions[19] roared and pierced their temples with their fangs, the cavity

---

[19] Those on the sinking mountains.

of their mouths filling up with blood from the former's heads mixed with pearls.[20]

K says दंष्ट्राभिः करिमकराणां भिन्नकुम्भा दंष्ट्राभिन्नकरिमकरकुम्भा इत्यर्थः, तेषां स्थिरैः हस्तैः कृष्यमाणाः, मुक्तागर्भितैः तत्कुम्भशोणितैः पूर्यमाणमुखकन्दराः सिंहा रसन्ति स्म।

26. उव्वत्तिअकरिमअरा पडन्ति पडिअगिरिसंभमुब्भडरोसा।
ओवइअमअरणिद्दअलुअगत्तावरविसण्ठुला माअङ्गा।।

[उद्वर्तितकरिमकराः पतन्ति पतितगिरिसंभ्रमोद्भटरोषाः।
अवपतितमकरनिर्दयलूनगात्रावरविसंष्ठुला मातङ्गाः।।]

Infuriated by the commotion of the falling mountains, the elephants plunged into the waters, overturning the sea elephants, but were helpless with their hind legs savagely lacerated by the oncoming crocodiles.

K says मातङ्गा उद्वर्तितकरिमकराः विदारितकरिमकराः, उपरिपतितगिरिसंभ्रमेण उद्भटरोषा, अवपतितैः मकरमत्स्यैः निर्दयलूनगात्रापरत्वात् विसंस्थुला विह्वलाः पतन्ति स्म। गात्रापरशब्देन गजस्य पूर्वापरपादावुच्येते। 'गात्रं पूर्वोऽङ्घ्रिरस्य यः'; 'अपरः (?)[21] पश्चिमः पादः' इति वैजयन्ती।

MY says *lua-gattavara* लूनगात्रापर लूनापरगात्रेत्यर्थः। अपरगात्रशब्देनापरपादावुक्तौ। उद्वर्तितकरिमकराः स्वमदगन्धे- नोत्थापितकरिमकराः। मकराणामवपतनमहंपूर्विकया संभूयोपनिपातः (संभूयेवावनिपातः A)।

Vese 26 is missing in our transcript of Kula. R says उद्वर्तिता उत्तानीकृताः करिमकरा यैस्ते। . . . लूने गात्रावरे येषां ते। . . . छिन्नजङ्घापूर्वपश्चाद्देशाः। *SC*, quoting Amara, says गात्रं पूर्वजङ्घाभागः, अवरं पश्चिमजङ्घाभागः।

27. विहुलपवालकिसलअं सेलदरत्थमिअदरिमुहवलन्तीहिं।
आवेढपहुप्पन्तं वीईहिँ दुमेसु वणलआहिँ व भमिअम्।।

विधुतप्रवालकिसलयं शैलदरास्तमितदरीमुखवलमानाभिः।
आवेष्टप्रभवद्वीचिभिर्द्रुमेषु वनलताभिरिव भ्रमितम्।।]

Eddying at the mouth of the caves of the partly submerged mountains, the waves whirled round the trees, completely encircling them, and tossing the young coral growths, even

[20] I.e. the pearls supposed to be inside the head of an elephant.

[21] Printed text has अवरं।

as the sylvan creepers whirled, shaking their coral-like shoots.

K and Deva read सलिल for *sela* (R and Kula)।

K says सलिले दरास्तमितगिरिदरीमुखेषु वलमानाभिः वीचिभिः द्रुमेषु मज्जत्पर्वतदरीगतद्रुमेषु वनलताभिरिव भ्रान्तं भ्रमणं कृतम्। विधुतप्रवालकिसलयं विधुतविद्रुममयकिसलयं यथा, आवेष्टप्रभूतमावेष्टने पर्याप्तं यथा भवति तथा भ्रान्तम्। MY says वीचिभिः लताभिरिव . . . आवेष्टप्रभवच्च यथा भवेत् तथा द्रुमेषु भ्रान्तम्। लताभ्रमणे तत्किसलयानामिव वीचिभ्रमणेऽपि विद्रुमाणां विधुतत्वम्। R says वीचिपक्षे प्रवालानां किसलयं यत्र, लतापक्षे प्रवालवत् किसलयं यत्र। Kula says शैलस्य दरासतमितस्य दरीमुखे वलन्तीभिर्मण्डलायमानाभिः (वीचिभिः)। प्रमाणानुरूपदत्तावेष्टनमित्थर्थः।

28. गिरिणिवहेहि रसन्तं उक्खम्मन्तेहि णिवडिएहि अ समअम्।
धरणीअ साअरस्स अ उग्घाडिज्जइ णिरन्तरं पाआलम्॥

[गिरिनिवहै रसदुत्खायमानैर्निपतितैश्च समम्।
धरण्याः सागरस्य च उद्धाट्यते निरन्तरं पातालम्॥]

The rumbling nether regions of the earth as well as the ocean were likewise entirely laid bare; the former by the mountains while they were uprooted, and the latter by those plunging into the waters.[22]

K reads धरणिधरैः सरभसं for *giri-ṇivahehi rasantaṁ* = गिरिनिवहै रसत् (R and Kula ?)।

K says सरभसमुत्खन्यमानैः शैलेः धरण्याश्च, निपतितैः गिरिभिः समुद्रस्य च पातालं सममेव निरन्तरमुद्घाटितं निर्विशेषं प्रकाशितम्। Deva has गिरिनिवहैः सरभसं in the first line.

MY says धरणेरधोवर्ति पातालं शैलोत्पाटनमार्गैः प्रकाश्यते, सागरस्य तु शैलमज्जनमार्गैरित्यर्थः। *SC* says समं तुल्यं यथा स्यात् तथा। समं युगपदिति श्रीनिवासः।

29. वेआविद्धवलन्ता मुहलवलन्तोज्झरावलिपरिक्खित्ता।
संवेल्लिअघणणिवहा वलिअलआलिङ्गिआ पडन्ति महिहराः॥

[वेगाविद्धबलन्तो मुखस्खलन्निर्झरावलिपरिक्षिप्ताः।
संवेल्लितघननिवहा वलितलतालिङ्गिताः पतन्ति महीधराः॥]

---

[22] I.e. the depths of the earth were revealed by the cavities left by the uprooted mountains, and the bottom of the sea by the divided waters as the mountains plunged into them.

Turning round while they were swiftly pushed down, the mountains, which enveloped the clouds, and were surrounded by noisy swirling cascades, dropped into the sea, with the leaning creepers clinging to them.

K and Deva seem to read *valanta-ṇia-ojjhara* in the first line. K (*chāyā*) has वलमाननिजनिर्झर।

K says प्लवगैर्वेगेन आविद्धत्वात् क्षिप्तत्वात् वलमाना भ्रमन्तः, मुखरभ्रमन्निजनिर्झरपरिक्षिप्ताः[23], संपीडितघननिवहाः, चलिताभिः वृक्षलताभिरालिङ्गिताः पर्वता प्रापतन्। अयमस्याभिप्रायः यथा केचित् कुटुम्बिनो महापुरुषाः क्रूरेण विधिना स्थानात् भ्रंशिताः मुखरैः भ्रमद्भिरपत्यैः परिवृता दुःखपीडितसुहृज्जनाः चलिताभिः स्त्रीभिरवलम्बिताः पतन्ति तद्वदिति।

K and Deva read *calia* for *valia* (R and Kula) in the second line.

Kula reads *valantojjharāvali* like R — वलन्तीभिः निर्झरावलीभिः वेष्टिताः। He explains *saṁvellia* as संवेष्टित, and says संवेष्टिता घननिवहा यैस्ते। R says संवेल्लिताः चञ्चलीभूता घननिवहा येषु ते। वलिताभिः वक्रीभूताभिः लताभिरालिङ्गिताः।

30. एक्कक्कमावडन्ता णिअअभुअक्खेवभिण्णसेलद्धन्ता।
णिन्ति धुअकेसरसडा गअणुच्छलिअसलिलोत्थआ कइणिवहा।।

[एकैकक्रमापतन्तो निजकभुजक्षेपभिन्नशैलार्धान्ताः।
निर्यन्ति धुतकेसरसटा गगनोच्छलितसलिलावस्तृताः कपिनिवहाः।।]

The apes, who broke parts of the mountains as they hurled them down with their arms, and were bathed in the waters surging sky-high, came ashore one by one,[24] shaking their massive hair.

K *pratīka* has *ekkekka*. K, Deva and MY read शैलस्थगिताः (*sela-tthaiā*) for *seladdhantā* शैलार्धान्ताः (R and Kula); and *uccalia* for *ucchalia* (R and Kula)।

K says समुद्रे पर्वतं प्रक्षिप्य पुनः पर्वतग्रहणार्थं एकैकमागच्छन्तः, निजभुजक्षेपभिन्नैः शैलैरुपरि पतद्भिः स्थगिताः, धुतकेसरसटाः गगनोच्चलितसमुद्रजलच्छादिताः (सलिलावस्तृताः *chāyā*) भूत्वा कपयो निर्यान्ति स्म। R says निजकभुजाभ्यां यः क्षेपः त्यागः तेन भिन्नः त्रोटितः शैलार्धान्तो यैः।

---

[23] Deva says मुखरवलमानैः निजनिर्झरैः परिक्षिप्ताः।

[24] I.e. to bring in more mountains.

31. दीसइ वारंवारं गिरिघाउक्खित्तसलिलरेइअभरिअम्।
पाआलं व णहअलं णहविवरं व विअडोअरं पाआलम्।।

[दृश्यते वारंवारं गिरिघातोत्क्षिप्तसलिलरेचितभृतम्।
पातालमिव नभस्तलं नभोविवरमिव विकटोदरं पातालम्।।]

The nether regions looked like the vault of the sky with its empty expanse, and the sky looked like the nether regions, time and again, when they were respectively abandoned and filled by the waters of the sea, thrown up by the impact of the mountains.[25]

K says समुद्रे गिरिघातोत्क्षिप्तपानीये सति तत्सलिलै रेचितं विवजितं भरितं च नभस्तलं सलिलभरितावस्थायां पातालमिवाभूत्। सलिलरेचितावस्थायां नभोविवरमेवाभूत्। तथा पातालं च गिरिघातोत्क्षिप्तसलिलरेचितसमये नभोविवरमिव विकटोदरमभूत्। सलिलभरितावस्थायां पातालं पातालमेवाभूत्। एवं पातालं नभश्च पर्यायेण बहुशो विपर्यस्तमदृश्यतेत्यर्थः। R says विकटोदरं तुच्छोदरं, etc. He remarks केचित्तु पातालमिव नभो नभ इव पातालमित्युभयमपि तत्सलिलेन रेचितभृतं दृश्यते। नभ इव पातालं रेचितं तदिव नभो भृतमित्यर्थः।

32. संखोहभिण्णमहिअलगलिअजलोलुग्गपङ्कअवणुच्छङ्गा।
विहलगइन्दालम्बिअ फुडिअपडन्तसिहरा पडन्ति महिहरा।।

[संक्षोभभिन्नमहीतलगलितजलावरुग्णपङ्कजवनोत्सङ्गाः।
विह्वलगजेन्द्रालम्बितस्फुटितपतच्छिखराः पतन्ति महीधराः।।]

The mountains dropped into the sea, with the lotus beds at the summit withered, because the water of the lakes had run out through the bottom split by the commotion; while the peaks, with the panic-stricken elephants clinging to them, cracked and collapsed.

K says संक्षोभेण पतनक्षोभेण भिन्नात् विदारितात् महीतलात् सरसः अधस्तलात् गलितजलत्वात् अवरुग्णपङ्कजवनः म्लानपङ्कजवनः उत्सङ्ग उपरिप्रदेशो येषां ते तथा। विह्वलैः गजेन्द्रैः अवलम्बितत्वात् स्फुटितपतच्छिखरा महीधराः पतन्ति स्म। R says विह्वलैः व्याकुलैः गजेन्द्रैरालम्बितानि शुण्डादिना अवष्टब्धानि अत एव स्फुटितानि त्रुटितानि तत एव पतन्ति शिखराणि येषां ते।

---

[25] The waters of the sea, stirred up by the falling mountains, are fancied as alternately soaring to the sky and coming down, in the course of which the bed of the sea, when empty of the waters, looked like the sky; and the sky, when flooded with water, looked like the sea floor.

MY seems to read *jalahara* for *mahiala*. He says शैलोत्क्षेपणवेगभिन्नेभ्यो जलधरेभ्यो विगलिताभिः वर्षधाराभिः विलुलितपद्मवना इत्यर्थः। Kula says संक्षोभेण भिन्न द्विधाभूतं महीतलं [?] सरोजवनाधारभूमिः तेन गलितजलत्वात् अवरुग्णपङ्कजवना उत्सङ्गा येषाम्

33. रसइ गिरिघाअभिण्णो तीरं लङ्घेइ वलइ विसमक्खलिओ।
पावइ महणावत्थं णवर ण णिद्देइ साअरो अमअरसम्।।

[रसति गिरिघातभिन्नस्तीरं लङ्घयति वलति विषमस्खलितः।
प्राप्नोति मथनावस्थां केवलं न निर्ददाति सागरोऽमृतरसम्।।]

Rent by the impact of the mountains, the sea roared and overflowed its shore and swirled, dashing over the rugged ground. It was reduced to the condition of being churned; only did not bring forth nectar.[26]

K says रसतीत्यादिकस्य गाथाद्वयस्य पूर्वभागे (?) लिखितं व्याख्यानं द्रष्टव्यम्।

MY says निद्रावयति निश्च्यावयतीत्यर्थः। प्रागेवोद्धृतामृतत्वादिति भावः।

His reading might be *ṇiddavai* for *ṇiddei* = निर्ददाति (R). Kula is here mutilated. *SC* text has *ṇiddaai*.[27] *SC* says प्रागिवामृतरसं न मुञ्चति नाविष्करोति इत्यर्थः Some of these words appear in Kula.

34. उक्खअणिसुद्धसेलो संसइअसमुद्दघोरमुक्कक्कन्दो।
रक्खसपुरीअ कह आ गमणोवाओ वि दारुणसमारम्भो।।

[उत्खातनिपातितशैलो संशयितसमुद्रघोरमुक्ताक्रन्दः।
राक्षसपुर्याः कथं वा गमनोपायोऽपि दारुणसमारम्भः।।]

Lo, even the preparation to reach the city of the demons caused formidable efforts. Mountains were uprooted and cast into the sea, and the ocean uttered terrible groans in peril of its life.

Kula says आःशब्दो विस्मये। आः कथं कोऽयं प्रका(रः) . . . राक्षसपुर्या गमनोपायोऽपि भीषणसमारम्भः . . . He also says संशयितेन संशयकोटिं प्रापितेन समुद्रेण (मुक्ताः) घोरो भीषण आक्रन्दः परित्राणरवो यत्र स तथा। R renders *kaha ā* as कथं वा।

---

[26] As in days of old.

[27] *Chāyā* has निर्ददाति।

35. वेउक्खलिउद्धाइअणहभमिरफुरन्तकञ्चणसिलावेढम्।
कुसुमसुअन्धरआलं पह्लत्थइ पवअणोल्लिअं धरआलम्।।

[वेगोत्खण्डितोद्धावितनभोभ्रमणशीलस्फुरत्काञ्चनशिलावेष्टम्।
कुसुमसुगन्धरजोजालं पर्यस्यति प्लवगनोदितं धरजालम्।।]

Pushed by the apes, the mountains, covered with the fragrant pollen of the flowers, tumbled into the sea as their slabs of gold, shattered by the impact, rose aloft, flashing across the sky.

K *pratīka* has *Vea-kkhuḍia*. MY *pratīka* has *veükkhuḍia* (*SC* text also = वेगोत्खण्डित *chāyā*)।

K (*chāyā*) has वेगत्रुटितोत्थापित . . . K says क्षेपणवेगात् त्रुटितोद्गतं नभसि भ्रमत् सफुरत् शोभमानं काञ्चनशिलामण्डलं यस्य तत्, कुसुमानां सुगन्धिभिः रजोभिः युक्तं धरजालं प्लवगनुन्नं पर्यस्यते स्म (MY also)।

Kula has उत्खण्डित, like R whose reading is however *ukkhalia*. Kula says पर्यस्यति निपतति।

MY says *uddhāia* ऊर्ध्वायित ऊर्ध्वापितेति वा।

36. वड्ढइ पवअकलअलो वलइ वलन्तवलआमुहो सलिलणिही।
पवणणिराइअरुक्खा पडन्ति उद्धट्ठिओज्झरा धरणिहरा।।

[वर्धते प्लवगकलकलो वलति वलमानवडवामुखः सलिलनिधिः।
पवननिरायतवृक्षाः पतन्त्यूर्ध्वस्थितनिर्झरा धरणीधराः।।]

The cries of the apes swelled, and the sea rolled with the submarine fire rolling; while the mountains dropped, with the cascades shooting up, and the trees stretched out by the wind.

K says समुद्रश्च भ्रमद्वडवामुखः सन् भ्रमति स्म। Kula says सलिलनिधिः ध्वनति। He seems to read *rasai* for *valai*; and explains *ṇirāia* as निरावित – पवनेन निराविता अत्यर्थं शब्दिता वृक्षा येषाम्। Cf. K's explanation of *virāia* in his gloss on 2.29. The word is explained by R and MY as निरायत = दीर्घीकृत; निरायतीकृत दीर्घतरीकृत (K). According to *SC*, Śrīnivāsa explains *ṇirāia* as ऋजूकृत।

37. दूराइद्धणिअत्ता मोडिअमलिअहरिअन्दणमइज्जन्ता।
उअहिं रहसुक्खित्ता आसाएन्ति विरसं महाणइमच्छा।।

[दूराविद्धनिवृत्ता मोटितमृदितहरिचन्दनमुद्यमानाः।
उदधिं रभसोत्क्षिप्ता आस्वादयन्ति विरसं महानदीमत्स्याः।।]

Exhilarated by the sap of the broken and crushed sandal trees, the fish of the large streams,[28] returning after being thrown far into the sea, and briskly splashing about, tasted the brackish water of the sea.

K, Deva and probably MY read मिलन्तः (*milijjantā*) for (*maijjantā*) (R and Kula). Deva reads तुलित (= उद्गूढ) for *malia* (मृदित)।

K says पर्वतपतनक्षोभितेन समुद्रेण दूरमाविद्धाः पुनर्निवृत्ताः[29], त्रुटितमृदितैः हरिचन्दनैः मिलन्तः संसृज्यमानाः, रभसोत्क्षिप्ताः संभ्रमादुत्पतिताः महानदीनां पर्वतगतानां मत्स्याः उदधिं विरसमास्वादयन्ति स्म। MY says मोटितमृदितचन्दनेन अतिपरुषजलसंगताः उच्चलता जलेन रभसोत्क्षिप्ताः शैलनदीमत्स्याः। Kula says अभिमुखगिरिपतनेन दूरमाविद्धाः क्षिप्ताः ततो निवृत्ताः मोटितो भग्नो मृदितो यो हरिचन्दनः तेन माद्यमाना हर्षिता, अतो रभसोत्क्षिप्ता वेगेनोत्पतिता महानदीमत्स्याः क्षारजलत्वात् विरसमुदधिमास्वादयन्ति पिबन्ति। Kula renders *maijjantā* as माद्यमानाः। R has मुद्यमानाः। He says उत्क्षिप्ता उत्प्लुत्योत्प्लुत्य परितो गताः। Lokanātha quoted in *SC* says माद्यन्तो हर्षेण विस्मृतात्मानः।

38. आसीविसमणिअम्बा पल्हत्थन्ति विहडन्तविसमणिअम्बा।
दुमणिवहोवरि हरिआ दरीसु सेला रविप्पहावरिहरिआ।।

[आशीविषमण्याताम्राः पर्यस्यन्ति विघटमानविषमनितम्बा।
द्रुमनिवहोपरि हरिता दरीषु शैला रविप्रभापरिहृताः।।]

Green at the top because of the trees, and tinged with red by the gems embedded in the hoods of the serpents, and bereft of sunlight in the caves, the mountains tumbled into the sea, with their rugged slopes crumbling to pieces.

K says आशीविषाणां मणिभिस्ताम्राः, . . . विषमनितम्बा निम्नोन्नतनितम्बा, द्रुमनिवहैरुपरि हरिताः श्यामलाः, दरीषु रविप्रभाभिः परिहृताः (अन्धकारितदरीविवराः MY) शैलाः पर्यस्यन्ते स्म। Kula says विघटमानत्वात् विषमा नितम्बा येषां ते। He seems to have पर्यस्यन्ति। Cf. verse 35. R says शैलाः पर्यस्यन्ति समुद्रे निपत्य विशीर्यन्ति।

---

[28] I.e. the streams of the mountains thrown into the sea.

[29] Deva says दूराविद्धनिवृत्ताः पर्वतैः सह दूरमुदधौ क्षिप्ताः . . . गिरिक्षोभितोदधिप्रतिहतेन नदीपूरेण सह दूरापविद्धाः पुनर्निवृत्ताः।

39. धरिअं वेओवत्तं गिरिघाउच्छित्तपाणिअम्मि समुद्दे।
वलिऊण भुअअवइणा कह वि तुलग्गविसमाअअं महिवेढम्।।

[धृतं वेगापवृत्तं गिरिघातोत्क्षिप्तपानीये समुद्रे।
वलित्वा भुजगपतिना कथमपि तुलाग्रविषमागतं महीवेष्टम्।।]

As the earth slanted swiftly, and became unsteady all of a sudden, when the waters of the ocean were flung up by the impact of the mountains, it was somehow held up by the lord of the serpents by changing its posture.[30]

K says समुद्रे गिरिघातैरुत्क्षिप्तपानीये सति वेगादपवृत्तमधस्तात् अपसृतं, तुलाग्रेण[31] यदृच्छया विषममयथापूर्वमागतं महीवेष्टं भुजगपतिना वलित्वा शरीरं वक्रीकृत्य कथमपि धारितम्। R says वलित्वा तिर्यग्भूत्वा। MY says *tulagga* क्षण। विषमं कृच्छ्रम्। तुलाधृतमिव समोभयपार्श्वं भूगोलं मध्ये शिरः कुर्वन् खलु शेषो धारयति। इदानीं तु गिरिघातोत्क्षिप्तसमुद्रजलतया विषमभरभागं वेगेन भारगुरुणि पार्श्वान्तरे प्रवृत्तं भूवेष्टनं तत्रैव दूरं (दूरे B) संचार्य शिरः कथमपि धृतवानित्यर्थः।

Kula says समुद्रे गिरिघातोक्षिप्तपानीये सति वेगादपसृतं चलितं निर्जलसमुद्रप्रदेशे लघुत्वात्, अन्यत्र गुरुत्वात् अन्यत्र लघुत्वात् तुलाग्रवत् विषमागतं व्यर्थीभूतं सदापतितं (?) महीमण्डलं भुजगपतिना शेषेण बलित्वा . . . (धृतम् ?) *SC* says महीमण्डलमेकत्र सलिलशून्यतया लघुत्वादपरत्र सलिलभरेण गुरुत्वात् तुलाग्रवत् विषमागतं तिर्यग्भावापन्नं भुजगपतिनानन्तेन वलित्वा फणामण्डलं समाधाय धृतम्।

40. वज्जभअं धरणिहरा आइवराहखुरपेल्लणाइँ वसुमई।
समअं चिअ पम्हट्ठं संभरिओ महणसंभमं च समुद्दो।।

[वज्रभयं धरणिधरा आदिवराहखुरप्रेरणानि बसुमती।
समकमेव प्रस्मृतं संस्मृतवान्मथनसंभ्रमं च समुद्रः।।]

All at once, the mountains remembered their terror of the thunderbolt,[32] and the earth the thrusts of the hooves of the

---

[30] The serpent Ananta bears the earth poised on its numerous hoods. It is fancied that at the moment when the waters of the sea rushed upward, leaving the bed empty, the earth, becoming lighter on one side, lost its equilibrium, which was restored by Ananta by adjusting its hoods.

[31] R says तुलाग्रेण काकतालीयसंवादेन अकस्मात् विषमागतं तिर्यग्भूतं . . . वेगेन हठाद्पवृत्तमपवर्तितुमारब्ध म्। आदिकर्मणि क्तः।

[32] The wings of the mountains were once clipped by Indra with his thunderbolt. Cf. 5.37; 7.13.

Primeval Boar,[33] and the ocean the commotion of the churning — all that had been forgotten by them.[34]

K, Deva and MY read प्रति for खुर (R and Kula). K and Deva read चिर for *cia* = एव (R). K and Deva read *saṁbhariā* (cf. *SC* text) for *saṁbhario* (R) construed as संस्मृतवान्

K says पर्वतानामुद्धरणादिभिः क्षोभैः महीप्रभृतयः चिरविस्मृतानि वज्रभयादीनि सममेव संस्मृताः। संस्मृत इति कर्तरि क्तप्रत्ययः। Deva has संस्मारिताः।

K (*chāyā*) has सममेव चिरप्रमुषितं संस्मृतो मथनसंभ्रमं च समुद्रः। R says समकमेकदैवेत्यर्थः। प्रस्मृतं विस्मृतम्। MY says *paḍivellaṇāi* प्रतिपीडनानि। *pamhaṭṭhaṁ* प्रस्मृतम्। Kula says प्रभ्रष्टं (i.e. *pabbhaṭṭhaṁ)* प्रस्मृतम्, and quoted Pāṇini 1.2.69 (नपुंसकमनपुंसकेनैकवच्चास्यान्यतरस्याम्) to explain the neuter singular. The rest is corrupt.

41. मलअचन्दणलआहरे संभरमाणओ णिअअमहणदुक्खं मिव संभरमाणओ।
रसइ सेलसिहराहिहओ सरिआवई। दहमुहस्स दोसेण समोसरिआवई।।

[मलयचन्दनलतागृहान्संविभ्राणो निजकमथनदुःखमिव संस्मरन्।
रसति शैलशिखराभिहतः सरित्पति र्दशमुखस्य दोषेण समवस्तृतापत्।।]

Imerilled through Rāvaṇa's fault, the ocean that flooded[35] the sandal groves of the Malaya mountain, roared, battered by the mountain peaks, as if it remembered the pain caused when it was churned.

K, Kula and MY read °*haresu bhara*° for °*hare saṁbhara*° (R). K (*chāyā*) has मलयचन्दनलतागृहेषु भ्रियमाणः found in Kula also.

K says मलयस्य चन्दनलतागृहेषु पूर्यमाणो निजमथनदुःखं संस्मरन्निव सरित्पतिः रसति स्म। कथंभूतः – शैलशिखराभिहतो दशमुखस्य सीतापहरणदोषेण समुपसृतापत्। MY says समपसृतापत् गमितसकलमथनाद्यापदपि दशमुखदोषेण शैलाभिहतः सन् अरसत्। R says समवसृता समुपागता आपत् विपत्तिर्यस्य तथा। This agrees with Lokanātha quoted in *SC* (सम्यगवसृता उपस्थिता आपत् यस्मिन्)। Kula reads *samo sariāvaī* for *samosariāvaī* in the fourth line. He says सरित्पतिः समुद्रश्च (दशमुखस्य दोषेण) सीतापहारोपेक्षणेन समः तुल्यः

---

[33] During the Boar incarnation of Viṣṇu while lifting the earth submerged in the ocean.

[34] I.e. the uprooting and dropping of the mountains on the sea reawakened the memories of similar upheavals in days of old.

[35] Nourished, according to Rāmadāsa's reading.

'सृता प्रसृता आपद्' यस्य स तथा[36]। R says लतागृहाणि संबिभ्राणो धारयन्। पयःसेकादिना पुष्णन् इति वा। *SC* says लतागृहं पूरयन्। मलयचन्दनलतागृहेषु भ्रियमाण इति कुलनाथः।

42. जलवट्ठत्थमिएसु अ उद्धाइ गिरीसु मलिअविद्दुमअम्बो।
आवलिअचुण्णिएसुं धुअधाउरओ व्व सीहररउग्घाओ।।
[जलपृष्ठास्तमितेषु चोद्धावति गिरिषु मृदितविद्रुमाताम्रः।
आपतितचूर्णितेषु धुतधातुरज इव शीकररजउद्धातः।।]

As the mountains disappeared in the waters, crumbling as they crashed, a cloud of spray, tinged with red by the broken corals, rose aloft, even like the swirling dust from the minerals.

K, MY and Deva read *majjha* for *vaṭṭha* = पृष्ठ (R and Kula)।

K (*chāyā*) has जलमध्यास्तमितेषु उद्धावति and आपतितचूर्णेतेषु च धुतधातुरज इव शीकररजउद्घातः। My also has आपतित for *āvalia* (R), rendered as आपतित in R (commentary). *SC* text has *āvaḍia*.

K says गिरिषु जलमध्यास्तमितेषु सत्सु मृदितविद्रुमताम्रः चूर्णितैः विद्रुमैस्ताम्रः शीकररजःसंघात उद्धावति स्म। आपतितेषु अन्योन्यघट्टनात् चूर्णितेषु च गिरिषु धुतधातुरज इव च शीकररजउद्घातः उत्तस्थौ। अथवा गिरिषु जलमध्यास्तमितेषु तेषामुपरि आपतितचूर्णितेषु च गिरिषु मृदितैः विद्रुमैस्ताम्रः शीकरकणसंघातः धुतधातुधूलिरिव उत्तस्थाविति योजना।

MY says गिरिष्वापतितचूर्णितेषु च[37] जलमध्यास्तमितेषु च सत्सु चूर्णिततया धातुरजःसमुत्थानेऽपि प्राप्ते जलास्तमयेन तस्य प्रतिबद्धतया शीकरोद्घात् एवोदचलत्। स तु विद्रुमचूर्णसंपर्कात् धातुरजःसदृशो भूत्वा तत्प्रतीतिमस्याप्यजनयदित्यर्थः।

Kula says ऊर्ध्वायते उद्गच्छति।

43. सेलसिहरसंखोहिअकल्लोलन्तअं गलिअधाउरसराइअकल्लोलन्तअम्।
रसइ उअहिसलिलं धरेसु वलमाणअं भग्गचन्दणरसोसहिणिव्वलमाणअम्।।
[शैलशिखरसंक्षोभितकल्लोलान्तं गलितधातुरसराजितलोलकान्तम्।
रसत्युदधिसलिलं धरेषु वलमानं भग्नचन्दनरसौषधिनिर्वलमानकम्।।]

Heaving as they were stirred up by the mountain peaks, the broad waters of the sea, tinged with a different hue by the

---

[36] Restored from *SC*.

[37] B omits च।

sap of the broken sandal trees and by the broken plants, roared as they rolled amidst the mountains, with the waves coloured by the dissolving minerals.

K (*chāyā*) has

शैलशिखरसंक्षोभितालोलत्कं गलितधातुरजोरञ्जितकल्लोलान्तम्।
रसति उदधिसलिलं धरेषु पतत् भग्नचन्दनरसौषधिनिर्व्यज्यमानम्।।

MY agrees with K, but has . . . लोलत् in the first line. K and MY read रजोरञ्जित for *rasa-rāia* = रसराजित (R). Kula has रसरञ्जित। K, MY and Kula seem to read *rāvia* for *rāia*. Cf. HC 4.49.

K says धरेषु गिरिषु पतितेषु पतत्, अन्येषां पततां शैलानां शिखरैः संक्षोभितत्वात् (आ)लोलत्कं, स्वार्थे को वेति कः, लोलमित्यर्थः। गलितैः धातुरजोभिः रञ्जितकल्लोलान्तं, भग्नानां चन्दनानां रसैः भग्नाभिरोषधीमिश्च निर्व्यज्यमानं पृथग्विभाव्यमानम् आपादितवर्णान्तरमेवंभूतमुदधिसलिलं रसति स्म। K's पतत् in the third line, seems to stand for *valomāṇaaṁ* वलमानं (Kula, Deva and R who explain it as वक्रीभवत्)।

MY has भग्नचन्दनरसौषधिपृथग्भवत् in the fourth line and says पृथग्भावो भिन्नवर्णता। R says निर्वलमानं जलान्तरात् पृथग्भूतम्।

Kula says शैलशिखरैः संक्षोभितत्वात् कल्लोलायमानं, गलितेन गैरिकादिरसेन रञ्जितकल्लोलं, ततं विस्तृतं, तेषु गुहावियुक्तपर्वतेषु वलमानं तदुदधिसलिलं रसति ध्वनति। The rest of Kula's gloss is somewhat corrupt, but he says (भग्नचन्दनरसौषधिना) निर्वीर्यत्वात् सर्पवत् निर्बलमतएवानतम्।

44. गिरिणिव्वलिअपडन्ता उद्धअजलमूलमिलिअपत्तलविडवा।
लहुअत्तणुप्पवन्ता गअणमणाअड्ढिआ वि लग्गन्ति दुमा।।

[गिरिनिर्वलितपतन्त उद्धतजलमूलमिलितपत्रलविटपाः।
लघुत्वोत्प्लवमाना गगनमनाकृष्टा अपि लगन्ति द्रुमाः।।]

Severed from the mountains, and tumbling into the sea, the trees whose leafy branches reached the depths of the surging waters emerged, being light, and rose to the sky, even without being drawn above.[38]

K and MY read चल for जल; मृदित (*malia*) for *milia*; उत्पतन्तः (*uppaantā*) for *uppavantā* = उत्प्लवमानाः; and विलगन्ति for *vilagganti*

[38] I.e. rose sky-high on the crest of the waves.

= अपि लगन्ति (R)[39]. K (*chāyā*) has अकृष्टा अपि गगनं विलगन्ति द्रुमा :। *SC* Text Ms. has *valagganti,* i.e. आरोहन्ति।

K says गिरिभ्यो निर्व्यक्ताः पतन्तः पृथग्भूताः पतन्तः, उद्धतानि उद्धूतानि चलानि मूलानि शिफाश्च (मृदिताः) पत्रलाः पत्रबहुलाः विटपाश्च येषां ते तथा, लघुत्वेन उत्पतन्तो द्रुमा अनाकृष्टा अपि गगनमध्यारोहन्ति स्म। पततां पर्वतानां नितम्बेभ्यः परिभ्रश्य जले मग्ना अपि द्रुमाः गौरवाभावात् पुनरुत्पत्य गगनमारोहन्नित्यर्थः। MY says अनाकृष्टा अपि गगनं व्यलगन्। Kula says उद्धतस्य (?) ऊर्ध्वप्रसृतस्य (जलस्य) मूले मिलिताः पत्रलाः विटपा येषां ते तथा। अनाकृष्टा अपि जलोत्कर्षणेन तन्मूले लग्ना द्रुमा गगनं . . . आरोहन्ति। R has उद्धृत for उद्धत।

45. पवअबलेहिं राअसंजाअमच्छरेहिं गअणणिराअभिण्णघणभेसिअच्छरेहिं।
फुडधवलग्गदन्तपडिपेल्लिआहरेहिं भिज्जइ साअरस्स सलिलं धराहरेहिं।।

[प्लवगबलै रागसंजातमत्सरैर्गगननिरायतभिन्नघनभीषिताप्सरोभिः।
स्फुटधवलाग्रदन्तप्रतिप्रेरिताधरैर्भिद्यते सागरस्य सलिलं धराधरैः।]

Incensed by rivalry with one another, the hosts of apes cleft the waters of the sea asunder with the mountains, bitting the lower lip with their protruding white teeth, and striking terror into the nymphs as they scattered the clouds stretched out in the sky.

K, Deva and MY read तीव्र for *rāa* राग (R and Kula) and गमननिघात for *gaaṇa-ṇirāa* = गगननिरायत (R). Kula has गगननिपात, i.e. °*ṇivāa*. cf. *SC* text.

K says तीव्रः अतिदुःसहो यथा संजातो मत्सरः समुद्रविषयो येषां तैः, गमननिघातेन गमनाभिघातेन भिन्नैः घनैः मेघैः भीषिताप्सरोभिः, स्फुटधवलदन्ताग्रनिपीडिताधरैः प्लवगबलैः कर्तृभिः धराधरैः करणभूतैः सागरस्य सलिलं भिद्यते स्म। Kula says रागेण परस्परस्पर्धानिवेशेन संजातो मत्सरः क्रोधो येषां तैः। स्फुटेन व्यक्तेन धवलदन्ताग्रेण प्रतिपीडितः अधरो यैस्तैः प्लवगबलैः।

सागरस्य सलिलं भिद्यते। कैः करणभूतैरित्याह–धराधरैः। किंभूतैःगगननिपाते भिन्नो यो घनो मेघस्तेन भीषिता अप्सरसो यैः तैस्तथा। R says रागेण द्वेषेण रावणं प्रति संजातमात्सर्यैः।

46. पवणभरन्तदरिमुहं पवणसुअक्कन्तविहलिअसिलावेढम्।
पडइ सिहरोज्झरुग्गअमहिन्दधणुगब्भिणं महिन्दक्खण्डम्।।

[39] The other readings are common to R and Kula.

[पवनभ्रियमाणदरीमुखं पवनसुताक्रान्तविघटितशिलावेष्टम्।
पतति शिखरनिर्झरोद्गतमहेन्द्रधनुर्गर्भितं महेन्द्रखण्डम्।।]

Spanned with a rainbow rising across the cascades on the summit, a section of the Mahendra mountain, whose rocky frame had been damaged when trampled by Hanumat,[40] crashed into the sea, with the wind filling the caves.

K says पवनपूर्यमाणदरीमुखं, समुद्रलङ्घनार्थमुत्पतता पवनसुतेन आक्रान्तत्वात् विघटितशिलामण्डलं, शिखरनिर्झरात् उद्गतेन महेन्द्रधनुषा गर्भितं भरितम्। निर्झराणां निपातेषु प्रसृतैः शीकरैः आतपयोगादिन्द्रधनुर्मण्डलमाविर्भवति। तथा च कुमारसंभवे (81.31)–

शीकरव्यतिकरं मरीचिभिर्दूरयत्यवनते विवस्वति।
इन्द्रचापपरिवेषशून्यतां निर्झराः प्रसवितुर्व्रजन्ति ते।। इति।

एवभूतं महेन्द्रखण्डं महेन्द्रपर्वतस्यैकदेशः वानरसंरम्भक्षोभितं पतति स्म।

Kula says प्राक् लङ्कागमनार्थं समुद्रलङ्घनाय क्रमं कर्तुं पदभरं न्यस्यता पवनसुतेन, etc. He reads सलिल for *sihara*, and says सलिलोज्झरे निर्झरसलिले। उद्गतमुदितं यत् मदेन्द्रधनुः, etc. (quoted in *SC*).

47. गअणअलम्मि सेलसंघट्टवारिआणं ओत्थरिअं रवेण जलभरिअवारिआणम्।
वहमाणं लआहराइं सअन्दलाइं किं पडिअं ण होइ सिहरं सअं दलाइं।।

[गगनतले शैलसंघट्टवारितानामवस्तृतं रवेण जलभृतवारिदानाम्।
वहमानं लतागृहाणि सकन्दलानि किं पतितं न भवति शिखरं शतं दलानि।।]

The summit of a mountain, pervaded by the rumble of the water-filled clouds, obstructed by the clash of the mountains in the sky — was it not reduced to a hundred fragments as it dropped on the sea, carrying with it the leafy groves of creepers?

K and MY insert रुचिरं before *saandalāiṁ* (सकन्दलानि) in the third line.

K says गगनतले शैलानां पततां संघट्टेन वारितानां प्रतिबद्धगमनानां, जलभरितानां वारिदानां रवेण अवस्तृतं व्याप्तं, सकन्दलानि सपल्लवानि लतागृहाणि वहमानं रुचिरं शिखरं तेषामेव शिखरं शतं दलानि बहुधा शकलानि भूत्वा पतितं न भवतिः किं, पतितमेवाभवदित्यर्थः। R says कन्दलो नाम वृक्षविशेषस्तत्सहितानि लतागृहाणि।

[40] Hanumat had planted his feet on the Mahendra mountain to leap over to Laṅkā in quest of Sītā.

48. लक्खिज्जन्ति समुद्दे गिरिघाउव्वत्तमअरविसमुक्कित्ता।
छेअपसरन्तरुहिरा फेणमिलन्ता वि चमरिबालद्धन्ता।।

[लक्ष्यन्ते समुद्रे गिरिघातोद्वृत्तमकरविषमोत्कृत्ताः।
छेदप्रसरद्रुधिराः फेनमिलन्तोऽपि चमरीवालार्धान्ताः।।]

Parts of the white bushy tail of the *camarī* deer,[41] savagely torn off by the crocodiles, turned over by the impact of the mountains, could be recognized on the sea, even though covered with foam, because the blood welled out from the wounds.

K reads चमर for *camari*. He says समुद्रेप तितगिरिघातात् उद्वृत्तैः मकरैः विषमं समुत्कृत्ताः छेदप्रदेशात् प्रसरद्रुधिराश्चमराणां बालखण्डाः फेनैः मिलन्तोऽपि लक्ष्यन्ते स्म स्फुटमदृश्यन्त। R says चमरीणां बालार्धान्ताः पुच्छैकदेशाः। Kula says विषममस्तस्तव्यस्तम्।

49. सिद्धअणो भएण मुञ्चइ लआहराइं सुरअविसेसजाअसेओल्लआहराइं।
गिरिसरिआमुहाइं णासन्ति सासआइं भमइ महोअहिस्स सलिलं दिसासआइं।।

[सिद्धजनो भयेन मुञ्चति लतागृहाणि सुरतविशेषजातस्वेदार्द्राधराणि।
गिरिसरिन्मुखानि नश्यन्ति शाश्वतानि भ्रमति महोदधेः सलिलं दिक्शतानि।।]

The *siddhas*[42] abandoned in fear the groves of creepers, with the ground moist with perspiration caused by diverse modes of amorous dalliance practised by them. The agelong outlets of the mountain streams were wiped out, and the waters of the ocean rolled in a hundred directions.

K and MY read *harisalaā-harāiṁ* for *seollaāharāiṁ* स्वेदार्द्राधराणि (R)।

K says सिद्धजनः पर्वतवर्ती भयेन लतागृहाणि मुञ्चति स्म। कीदृशानि सुरतविशेषजातहर्षवत्ताभराणि पूर्वं सुरतविशेषजातो हर्षवत्ताया भरोऽतिशयो येषु। हर्षवत्ता हर्षवत्तं मत्वर्थीयो लप्रत्ययः (i.e., *harisala+ā*)[43]। शाश्वतानि गिरिसरिन्मुखानि नश्यन्ति स्म। महोदधेः सलिलं दिक्शतानि भ्रमति सर्वा दिशो व्याप्नोति स्म। Deva says सुरतविशेषजातोहर्षेण अधरा आर्द्रा भवन्तीति एवंभूतानि लतागृहाणि। This would give the reading found in Kula and *SC* (Text), but

41 Those on the sinking mountains.

42 A class of supernatural beings imagined as living on the mountains.

43 A marginal note in manuscript B of MY says *harisalayā* हर्षलता मत्वर्थीयो लच् प्रत्ययः।

with a different meaning for अधर। Kula says सुरतविशेषेण . . . जातहर्षत्वात् स्वेदेनार्द्राणि अधराणि[44] उत्सङ्गस्थानानि येषाम्। He seems to read *harisollaāharāiṁ* found in *SC* text. R says सुरतविशेषेण बन्धवैचित्र्यात् जातैः स्वेदैः आर्द्राणि अधराणि अधःस्थलानि येषां तानि।

50. भमइ समुक्खित्तकरं गअवइवारिअपवित्तपक्कग्गाहम्।
विहलुत्थङ्घिअकलहं विअडावत्तमुहमागअं गअजूहम्।।

[भ्रमति समुत्क्षिप्तकरं गजपतिवारितप्रवृत्तप्रग्राहम्।
विह्वलोत्थापितकलभं विकटावर्तमुखमागतं गजयूथम्।।]

A herd of elephants that entered a large whirlpool turned round and round, raising their trunks, and holding up a distressed cub, while the leader of the herd kept a prowling sea lion off.

K, Deva MY and Kula read परियत् (*parinta*)[45] for (*pavitta*) = प्रवृत्त (R). They read पक्कग्राह (*pakkaggāha*) for paggāha प्रग्राह (R). K and Deva read उत्सङ्गित (ucchaṁgia) for *utthaṁghia* उत्थापित (R). K and Deva read मुखमापितं for *mukhamāgaaṁ* मुखमागतं (R). The *chāyā* in our copy of Deva agrees with R, but the readings in his gloss agree with K.

K says विकटस्य विशालस्यावर्तस्य मुखेन मापितं परिमितं परितो रुद्धं (तिरोहितं Deva), नासिकया जलप्रवेशपरिहारार्थं समुत्क्षिप्तकरं, गजपतिना वारितः परियन् परितो रुन्धन् (परितो गच्छन् Deva) पक्कग्राहः प्रवृद्धो ग्राहो यस्य तत्, विह्वल उत्सङ्गितः अभ्यन्तरीकृतः कलभो यस्य तत् करियूथं भ्रमति स्म।

Deva and MY have पर्यत् which is a mistake for परियत्। MY says पक्कग्राहः सिंहमकरः। *māiaṁ* (?) मार्जितम्। अथवा मापितं प्रमापितम्। Deva explains पक्कग्राह as दुष्टग्राह।

Kula seems to read मुखमापितं like K, but construes it differently. He says गजपतिना वारिताः परिगच्छन्तः पक्वाः समर्थाः जलचराः ग्राहाः यत्र। गजपतिनैव विह्वला उत्तम्भिता उत्तोल्य धृताः कलभा यत्र। विकटावर्तमुखमापितं[46] प्रापितं गजयूथं भ्रमति। R says प्रग्राहो जलसिंहः।

51. समुहपडन्तविअडगिरिसिहरवेल्लिआणं वीइपरिक्खलन्तपवणवसवेल्लिआणम्।
दिट्ठिं देह राहवो कह वि जा णईणं ता विरहेइ णवर हिअअम्मि जाणई णम्।।

---

[44] Restored from *SC*.

[45] Kula has परिगच्छत्। See his gloss below and notes on 6.57, 9.68, 88.

[46] Our copy has माप्रियं।

[संमुखपतद्विकटगिरिशिखरप्रेरितानां वीचिपरिस्खलत्पवनशवेल्लितानाम्।
दृष्टिं ददाति राघवः कथमपि यावन्नदीनां तावद्विरहयति केवलं हृदये जानकीएनम्।।]

Sītā was somehow absent from Rāma's heart only so long as he watched the rivers (entering the sea), being driven back by the massive mountain peaks dropping in front of them, and rocked by the froce of the wind dashing against the waves.

K says संमुखं पतद्भिः विकटैः गिरिशिखरैः पीडितानां, वीचिषु परिस्खलपवनवेगवेल्लितानां वक्रीकृतानामेवमाकुलानां नदीनां[47] राघवः कथमपि दृष्टिं यावत् ददाति कौतुकात् यावन्तं कालं दृष्टिमर्पयति तावदेव जानकी एनं राघवं हृदये विरहयति त्यजति। अन्यदा सीता रामहृदयं न परित्यजतीत्यर्थः। MY says व्यरहयत् एनं राम स्वात्मना वियुक्तमकरोदित्यर्थः। देव्याः स्मृतिः सर्वदानुवर्तमानापि नदीनां दर्शनीयतातिशयेन तद्दर्शनक्षणे एव परमन्तरितेत्यर्थः।

Kula reads घात (*ghāa*, cf. *SC* text) for *sihara* in the first line. He says गिरीणां घातात् प्रेरितानामिति सप्तम्यर्थे षष्ठी, प्रेरितास्वित्यर्थः। It will be seen that the first — *vellia* stands for *pellia* (प्रेरित; पीडित)। The second *rellia* is वेल्लित explained as वक्रीकृत, or चञ्चलीकृत, (R). Lokanātha says प्रेरितानां प्रतिपथं नीतानाम्।

52. दरडङ्ढविद्दुमवणा उद्धावन्ति सिहिकज्जलिअसङ्खउला।
पाआललग्गकड्ढिअरामसरोलुग्गपत्तणा जलणिवहा।।

[दरदग्धविद्रुमवना उद्धावन्ति शिखिकज्जलितशङ्खकुलाः।
पातालग्नकृष्टरामशरावरुग्णपत्रणा जलनिवहाः।।]

The waters heaved, bringing up the partly burnt coral-reefs and the conch shells blackened by fire, and drawing out the broken feathers of Rāma's arrows stuck fast in the sea floor.[48]

The verse is not found in our copy of Kula. K and Deva read -लताः for *-vaṇā* (R); and उत्तिष्ठन्ति for *uddhāanti* उद्धावन्ति (R)।

K says समुद्रस्य पातालस्पृशो जलनिवहा उदतिष्ठन्। कथंभूताः – रामशराग्निना दरदग्धविद्रुमलताः तथैव शिखिना कज्जलितशङ्खकुलाः। पातालग्नानि कृष्टानि

[47] R says वीचिषु परिस्खलतो विषमसंचारस्य पवनस्य वशेन। *SC* says वीचिषु परिस्खलितस्य प्रतिहतगतेः।

[48] The relics of the conflagration of the sea caused by Rāma's arrows (see canto V) are fancied as emerging from the sea when the waters were troubled by the mountains.

रामशराणामवरुग्णानि भग्नानि पत्राणि यैस्ते तथाभूता उत्तिष्ठन्ति स्म। MY says अक्षोभ्यनिखातस्य रामशरस्य लघुतयोल्लूनं पत्रमात्रं येषां ते रामशरोल्लूनपत्रा इति। He seems to read *ullukka* for *olugga* (अवरुग्ण)। Hemacandra 4.116 gives *ullukkai* as an equivalent of तुडति।

SC says शराणां पत्ररचना पत्रणेत्यभिधीयते।

53. भीअणिसण्णजलअरं पलोट्टणिअअभरभिण्णवक्खमहिहरम्।
दीसइ विहिण्णसलिलं कुविउद्धाइअभुअंगमं पाआलम्।।

[भीतनिषण्णजलचरं प्रलुठितनिजकभरभिन्नपक्षमहीधरम्।
दृश्यते विभिन्नसलिलं कुपितोद्धावितभुजंगमं पातालम्।।]

The bottom of the sea, with the waters parted asunder (by the falling mountains), could be seen, with the terrified animals lying still, and the furious serpents darting upward, and the submarine mountains sent rolling,[49] with their wings broken under their own weight.[50]

K, MY, Deva and Kula read *bhagga* for *bhiṇṇa* (R)।

K says भीतनिषण्णजलचरं, प्रलुलिताः (?) (*chāyā* has प्रलुठित) इतस्ततः परिभ्रान्ताः निजभरेण भग्नपक्षाः भ्रमणपरिक्लेशजेन निजभरेण भग्नपक्षा महीधरा यत्र तत्, विभिन्नसलिलं विशीर्णसलिलं, कुपितोत्थितभुजगं पातालमदृश्यत। Kula says उपर्युपरि गिरिघातवशात् . . . पार्श्वेन पतिताः महीधरा यत्र। *SC* text has *paloṭṭha* for °*ṭṭa*.

54. खुहिअसमुद्दाहिमुहा तंसट्ठिअमहिहरोसरन्तक्खलिआ।
करिमअरबद्धलक्खा करिमअरपडिच्छिआ पडन्ति गइन्दा।।

[क्षुभितसमुद्राभिमुखास्तिर्यक्स्थितमहीधरापसरत्स्खलिताः।
करिमकरबद्धलक्ष्याः करिमकरप्रतीष्टाः पतन्ति गजेन्द्राः।।]

The mighty elephants, confronting the raging sea, tumbled into the waters, slipping off the slanting mountains, with their eyes fixed on the sea elephants, who in their turn accepted the challenge.[51]

K (*chāyā*) and MY render *taṁsa* as त्र्यस्र। K says तिर्यक्स्थितात् महीधरात् अपसरत्स्खलिता अपसरन्त एव स्खलिताः, करिमकरेषु बद्धलक्षाः, करिमकरैः

[49] I.e. by the incoming mountains.

[50] See 5.37, 51.

[51] Lit. (being) accepted by the sea elephants.

प्रतीष्ठाः अभियुक्ताश्च गजेन्द्राः पतन्ति स्मः। Kula says प्रतीष्ठा गृहीताः। R says प्रतीष्टा युद्धाय स्वीकृता इति संप्रदायः।

55. ण वि तह पवआविद्धा विअडणिअम्बगरुआ रसाअलमूलम्।
जह उच्छलिउद्धाइअसलिलभरोवाहिआ अइन्ति महिहरा॥

[नापि तथा प्लवगाविद्धा विकटनितम्बगुरुका रसातलमूलम्।
यथा उच्छलितोद्धाविअसलिलभरापवाहिता आयान्ति महीधराः॥]

Heavy with their massive flanks, the mountains plunged to the bottom, not so much because they were hurled down by the apes as because they were submerged under the weight of the splashing and surging waters of the sea.

K, Deva and MY read उच्चलित for *ucchalia* (R and Kula). K (*chāyā*) has उच्चलितोत्थापितसलिलभरावगाहिता यन्ति महीधराः।

K says महीधरा उच्चलितोत्थापितस्य पर्वतपतनक्षोभादुच्चलितस्य उत्थापितस्य दूरमुत्थापितस्य सलिलस्य उपरिपतितस्य भरेण अवगाहिता मज्जिता भूत्वा यथा रसातलं यन्ति प्रविशन्ति स्म, प्लवगैराविद्धाः क्षिप्ताः सन्तः पर्वतास्तथा न प्राविशन्। कथंभूताः – विकटैः नितम्बैः गुरवः।

MY says प्लवगाविद्धा विकटनितम्बगुरवोऽपि गिरयो न तथा रसातलमूलमत्यायन् प्राप्नुवन् यथा उच्चलितोर्ध्वापितसलिलभरावगाढा इति।

R says प्लवगैराविद्धाः प्रक्षिप्ता अपि महीधरास्तथा तेन प्रकारेण रसातलमूलं न आयान्ति न गच्छन्ति यथा . . . सलिलभरैः अपवाहिताः अधः प्रेरिता गच्छन्ति। Kula says महीधरा न तथा रसातलमायान्ति यथा उच्छलितोर्ध्वापितस्य सलिलस्य भरेणावगाढा (अ)त्यायान्ति।[52] Deva says उच्चलितेन ऊर्ध्वायितेन अतिदूरं गतेन सलिलभरेण अपवाहिता अधोनुन्नाः।

56. उत्थङ्घिअदुमणिवहा गिरिघाउव्वत्तमुच्छिअमहामच्छा।
वेलासेलक्खलिआ उद्धं भिज्जन्ति उअहिजलकल्लोला॥

[उत्तम्भितद्रुमनिवहा गिरिघातोद्वृत्तमूर्छितमहामत्स्याः।
वेलाशैलस्खलिता ऊर्ध्वे भिद्यन्ते उदधिजलकल्लोलाः॥]

The waves of the sea, carrying with them the huge fish overturned and stunned by the impact of the mountains, broke up high in the air as they dashed over the coastal mountains, hurling up the trees.

---

[52] The words रसातलमायान्ति are restored from SC.

Deva (*pratīka*) has *uttagghia*. Deva (*chāyā*) has उत्सङ्गित, cf. verse 50, but commentary has उत्तम्भित।

K *pratīka* has *uttaṁbhia* (उत्तम्भित *chāyā*) for *uttaṁghia* in the same sense (R). N.S. edn. has *uttaṁghia* MY(A) has *utthāghia*. K and Kula read *uddhā* for *uddhaṁ* (R). K says सुबोधोऽर्थः। Kula has this verse after 58.

Verses 57 and 58 are not found in K and MY. In verse 58 *SC* text reads *maventi* (मापयन्ति) for *miṇenti* in the same sense and rendered by R as मिन्वन्ति। Kula has मापयन्ति।[53]

57. अद्धत्थमिअविसण्ठुलगअजूहारूढसिहरविहलस्स णहम्।
जीअं व झत्ति णज्जइ गिरिस्स कुहराहि उग्गअं सुरमिहुणम्।।

[अर्धास्तमितविसंष्ठुलगजयूथारूढशिखरविह्वलस्य नभः।
जीव इव झटिति ज्ञायते गिरेः कुहरादुद्गतं सुरमिथुनम्।।]

As a mountain tottered, with its summit thronged by a bewildered herd of elephants, half immersed in the waters, a pair of deities suddenly flew into the sky from a cave, as if it were the mountain's soul.

58. धरिआ भुएहि सेला सेलेहि दुमा दुमेहि घणसंघाआ।
ण वि णज्जइ किं पवआ सेउं बन्धन्तिओ मिणेन्ति णहअलम्।।

[धृता भुजैः शैलाः शैलैर्द्रुमा द्रुमैर्घनसंघाताः।
नापि ज्ञायते किं प्लवगाः सेतुं बध्नन्ति उत मिन्वन्ति नभस्तलम्।।]

The mountains were held up by the apes with their arms, and the trees by the mountains, and the masses of clouds by the trees. It was not apparent whether the apes were building a causeway or measuring the sky.

59. रहसविसज्जिएक्कमेक्का वलन्तधुअपडिअमणिसिला साअरम्मि णिवडन्ति
धरणिहाआ मलिअमहाभुअंगभग्गप्फणोअरोसरिअसंपुडं रसाअलं दुम्मेन्ति
धरणिहाआ।

---

[53] Our copy has वाप°। Kula reads verse 57 differently from R. He says अर्धास्तमितमर्धमग्नं विसंष्ठुलं यत् गजयूथं तेनाक्रान्तशिथिलत्वात् विह्वलस्य व्याकुलस्य गिरेः शिखरात् निर्गतं सुरमिथुनं जीवितमिव नभः समुत्पतति (समुत्पतितम् *SC*)।

णासइ जं जलं साअरस्स चुण्णिअमणोसिलाअडपडन्तसेलसंदारुणं फलन्तं दरिअणिसाअरेन्दहीरन्तजाणईवाहणिब्भरपुलोइअस्स किर दारुणं फलं तम्।।

[रभसविसृष्टैकैके वलद्धुतपतितमणिशिलाः सागरे निपतन्ति धरनिघाता मृदितमहाभुजंगभग्नफणोदरापसृतसंपुटं रसातलं दुन्वन्ति धरणिघाताः। नश्यति यज्जलं सागरस्य चूर्णितमनःशिलातटपतच्छैलस्यन्दारुणं फलद्दृप्तनिशाचरेन्द्रह्रियमाणजानकीबाष्पनिर्भरप्रलोकितस्य किल दारुणं फलं तत्।।]

Heaps of mountains, dashing against one another as they were vehemently thrown down, dropped into the sea, with their gem rocks swaying and falling; and the convulsions of the earth overwhelmed the nether regions, flattening out the drooping hoods of the great serpent[54] crushed under the weight.

And, if splitting waters of the ocean, tinged with red by the mountains that fell, with the masses of realgar crushed, faced destruction, that was grievous result of Sītā's tearful looks while she was carried off by the insolent lord of the demons.[55]

K, Deva, MY (?) and Kula divide the verse into two halves:

(a) K, Deva and Kula read एकैकापतत् for *ekkamekkā valanta* (R). K (*chāyā*) has एकैकापतन, and MY एकैकापात।

K and Deva read the second line as मृदितमहाभुजङ्गफणापसृतसंपुटं रसातलपथं च दूनयन्ति धरणिखाताः। Deva, R and MY add भग्न (*bhagga*) before फणापसृत। MY reads रसातलपथं चाधून्वन् (अव्यथयन्) धरणिघाताः। R has °*pphaṇodara* (फणोदर)। Kula omits उदर like K and MY.

K says प्लवगै रभसविसर्जितत्वात् एकैकमापतन्तः अन्योन्यं श्लिष्यन्तः, आपतनवेगेन धुतपतितमणिशिलाः, धरणिखाताः धरण्याः खाता उद्धृताः धरनिकाया धराणां गिरीणां संघाताः सागरे निपतन्ति स्म। मृदितानां निजनितम्बनिपतनेन क्षुण्णानां महाभुजङ्गानां फणेभ्यः अपसृतसंपुटं, संपुटशब्देन अस्थिपटलमुच्यते, अपसृताः संपुटाः यथा भवन्ति तथा रसातलं च दूनयन्ति स्म।

Kula says रभसेन विसर्जिता एकैकमापतन्तः अन्योन्यमास्खलन्तः। He also

54 See footnote 21.

55 I.e. the sufferings of the sea were due to its indifference to Sītā's silent appeal for help.

says रसातलं धून्वन्ति[56] (cf. MY) पातालं पीडयन्ति। R has *dummenti* (*dūmenti SC* text) दुन्वन्ति (cf. K)।

(b) K and Kula read मणिशिला for *maṇosilā* मन:शिला (R, SC, Deva and MY). K, MY Deva and Kula read मन्दारुणं for *sandāruṇaṁ* स्यन्दारुणं (R). K, Deva and MY read समुद्रस्य for *sāarassa* (R)।

K says समुद्रस्य जलं चूर्णितमणिशिलातलं यथा पतद्भिः शैलेः मन्दारुणमीषदरुणं भूत्वा फलत् विशीर्यमाणं नश्यति यत्, ञि फला विशरण इति धातुः, दृप्तेन गर्वितेन निशाचरेन्द्रेण ह्रियमाणाया जानक्याः बाष्पनिर्भरस्य विलोकितस्य दारुणं फलं किल् तत्। रावणेन प्रसभं ह्रियमाणायाः सीतायाः दुरितस्य लोकपालो वरुणः साक्षीभूत इति समुद्रनाश इत्यभिप्रायः।

MY gives the gist of (a) and (b) together. He says शैलसंघाता यदेवं समुद्रे न्यपतन्, यच्च भूमिघाता रसातलपथमव्यथयन्, यत् चूर्णितमन:शिलातलैः पतद्भिः शैलैरीषदरुणं (जलं) फलत् क्वाथेन स्फुटच्चाभूत् तदेतत् सर्वं हरणदशायां जानक्याः समुद्रोऽयमस्मत्प्रत्यानयने रामस्य महान् प्रतिबन्धः कथं परिहरणीय इत्यभिप्रायेण सबाष्पावलोकितस्य घोरं फलमिति वाक्यार्थः। Kula says जानक्याः पतिव्रतायाः बाष्पनिर्भरं यथा स्यात् तथा सकरुणं प्रलोकितस्य, etc. He says 'फलन्त'मिति विसरत्।

60. सेलसिलाहआ समुद्दोअरे मणीणं चुण्णिज्जन्ति वित्थरा रअणगामणीणम्।
भरइ णहङ्गणं अणिव्विण्णमेहलाणं हंसउलावलीण वणराइमेहलाणम्।।

[शैलशिलाहताः समुद्रोदरे मणीनां चूर्ण्यन्ते विस्तारा रत्नग्रामणीनाम्।
भ्रियते नभोङ्गणमनिर्विण्णमेघलानं हंसकुलावलीनां वनराजिमेखलानाम्।।]

The spreading masses of gems, the best of the jewels, were reduced to dust, crushed by the rocks of the mountains in the depths of the sea; and the expanse of the sky, decked with unfaded clouds, was thronged with rows of swans, girdles, as it were, encircling the woods on the mountains.

K, Deva and MY read समुद्रोदरगाः for *samuddoare* (R and Kula)।

K says रत्नग्रामणीनां रत्नश्रेष्ठभूतानां मणीनां समुद्रोदरगाः समुद्रोदरगताः विस्ताराः शैलशिलाहताः चूर्ण्यन्ते स्म। अनिर्विण्णमेघलावण्यं अनिर्विण्णानां अक्लिष्टानां मेघानां लावण्यं कान्तिर्यस्य तत्[57] नभोऽङ्गणं वनराजिमेखलानां वनराज्या मेखला भूतानां हंसकुलावलीनां भ्रियते पूर्यते स्म। तृतीयार्थे षष्ठी। पूर्वं पर्वतनदीषु वर्तमानाभिः

---

[56] Our copy has धूवन्ति।

[57] Deva says अनिर्विण्णा जलपूरिता मेघाः तेषामिव लावण्यं यस्य।

हंसकुलावलीभिः नभोऽङ्गणं पूरितमिति। *meha-lāṇaṁ* इति वलालितादिशब्दवत् (?) लावण्ये वकारस्य लोपः। अधो मनयामिति यकारलोपः (Vararuci 3.2)। अथवा अनिर्विण्णमेघलानम्। ला आदान इति धातुः। अनिर्विण्णान् मेघान् लातीति अनिर्विण्णमेघलानम्। Kula says अनिर्विण्णान् अपरिखिन्नान् मेघान् लाति गृह्णाति इति अनिर्विण्णमेघलानं नभोऽङ्गणम्।

61. रसइ रसाअलं दलइ मेइणी णिसुब्भन्ति जलअणिवहा परीइ गअणङ्गणे
कविअणो ओसुब्भन्ति महिहरा महिहराहिहओ साअरो वि सुइरं थलम्मि
घोलइ अमुक्कविअणो।
कुसुमपसाहणं मिव समुद्धपल्लवं साअरम्मि पडिआण विडवलग्गं दुमावलीणं
जाअं भिण्णसिप्पिउडमज्झणिग्गअत्थोरधवल– मोत्ताविहूसणं विद्दुमावलीणम्।।

[रसति रसातलं दलति मेदिनी निपात्यन्ते जलदनिवहाः पर्येति गगनाङ्गने
कपिजनोऽवपात्यन्ते महीधरा महीधराभिहतः सागरोऽपि सुचिरं स्थलं
घूर्णतेऽमुक्तवेदनः।
कुसुमप्रसाधनमिव समुग्धपल्लवं सागरे पतितानां विटपलग्नं द्रुमावलीनां
जातं भिन्नशुक्तिपुटमध्यनिर्गतस्थूलधवलमुक्ताविभूषणं विद्रुमावलीनम्।।]

The nether regions rumbled; the earth cracked; and the clouds were forced down.[58] The apes moved about in the sky; the mountains were dropped; and the sea, pounded by the mountains, rolled on the beach for long, racked with pain.

The large and white ornamental pearls, issuing from inside the broken oyster-shells, and stuck in the coral-reefs, seemed to be flowery adornment furnished with tender shoots, when they came into contact with the branches of the trees that fell into the sea.[59]

K divides the verse into two halves.

(a) K, Deva and MY read शैल (*sela*) for *jalaa* जलद (R and Kula); and उत्खन्यन्ते (*ukkhammanti*) for *osubbhanti* अवपात्यन्ते (R and Kula).[60] R reads *mahiharāhihao* महीधराभिहतः MY and Kula have

[58] I.e. came down with the mountains as they dropped on the sea.

[59] I.e. in contact with the branches, the pearls looked like flowers, with the corals looking like rosy young shoots.

[60] Kula cites the word as *osumbhanti*, which shows that he also reads *nisumbhanti* for *ṇisubbhanti* in the first line. Cf. *SC* text.

महीधराहत:। This is the reading of K also according to manuscript B. A is here defective.

K says पूर्वं पर्वतोत्क्षेपणदशायां रसातलं रसातलगतो जन: क्रोशति स्म। मेदिनी च तदानीं दलति स्म। शैलनिवहा: समुद्रे निपात्यन्ते स्म। गगनाङ्गणे कपिजन: पर्येति परित: चरति स्म। उत्खन्यन्ते स्म पुन: महीधरा:। हत: सागरोऽपि अमुक्तवेदन: सन् सुचिरं स्थले घूर्णति स्म।

(b) K and MY have शुक्तिसंपुटमध्यनिर्गतं in the last line. Kula has शुक्तिमध्यविनिर्गतं। R has *sippi-uḍa* (शुक्तिपुट)।

K says भिन्नशुक्तिसंपुटमध्यनिर्गतं विद्रुमावलीनं विद्रुमेषु लग्नं स्थूलधवलमुक्ताविभूषणं सागरे पतितानां द्रुमावलीनां विटपलग्नं विटपेषु लग्नं भूत्वा समुग्धपल्लवं कुसुमप्रसाधनमिव जातं तेषां वृक्षाणां सपल्लवकुसुमबन्धनमिवाभूत्।

Deva and MY seem to treat the verse as a single unit. MY says पूर्वार्ध प्रतीतम् (i.e. स्फुटम्), and then . . . कुसुमप्रसाधनमिव जातमित्युत्तरा-र्धान्वय:। Kula appears to do the same as at the beginning of his gloss on 7.59 he says गलितकपञ्चकमाह, which seems to comprise 7.59 (a), 7.59 (b), 7.60, 7.61, and 7.62. But the *pratīka* कुसुमेत्यादि in his gloss on 61 shows that he possibly treats the second half as a separate verse. In that case, verse 62 would be outside the गलितकपञ्चक।

62. अत्थमिआण महिहराण समच्छरेहिं परिमलिआइ वणगएहि समच्छरेहिं।
साहइ कुसुमरेणुमइओ धओ व्वणाइं अविरअणिम्महन्तमहुगन्धओव्वणाइं।।

[अस्तमितानां महीधराणां समत्सरै: परिमृदितानि वनगजै: सममप्सरोभि:।
शास्ति कुसुमरेणुमयो ध्वजो वनानि अविरतनिर्यन्मधुगन्धयौवनानि।।]

The pollen of the flowers serving as a banner revealed the woods of the mountains sinking in the sea along with the nymphs; the woods that were crushed by the angry elephants, and unceasingly emitted the rich fragrance of the honey of flowers.

K, MY, Deva and Kula read अस्तमितानि for *atthamiāṇa* अस्तमितानां (R). K and Deva read समं स्थलै: and समन्थरै: for *samaccharehiṁ* समत्सरै: and सममप्सरोभि: (R and Kula). Kula says संशब्द: सममित्यर्थे।

K says स्थलै: अध:स्थलै: समं समुद्रे अस्तमितानि। अथवा महीधराणां स्थलै: सममस्तमितानि। समन्थरै:, मन्थरशब्देन सौन्दर्यमुच्यते, ससौन्दर्यै: वनगजै: परिलुलितानि, अविरतनिर्गच्छन्मधुगन्धयौवनानि। यौवनशब्देन गन्धस्यातिशय उच्यते। एवंभूतानि वनानि उपरिगत: कुसुमरेणुमयो ध्वज: शंसति व्यञ्जयति स्म।

It will be seen that k reads *samaṁ thalehiṁ* in the first line, and makes it rhyme with *samaṁtharehiṁ* on the basis of रलयोदभेद:। K, Deva and MY (A) read *pariluliāi* for *parimaliāi* परिमृदितानि (R and Kula). My (B) has the latter reading.

MY says अस्तमितानि महीधराणां समं स्तरै: (?)[61] प्रस्तरैरुपलैरित्यर्थ:। परिलुलितानि वनगजै: समात्सर्यै:, etc. He remarks महीधराणां प्रस्तरै: समं समुद्रेऽस्तमितान्यपि गजलोलितानि निर्यन्मधुगन्धानि वनानि कुसुमरेणुमयो ध्वजोऽशंसदित्यर्थ:।

MY seems to read *samaṁ tharehiṁ* (समं स्तरै:) in the first line and *samaṁtharehiṁ* in the second which he explains as समात्सर्यै:। The word *maṁthara* is recorded in *Deśīnāmamālā* 6.145, but neither मात्सर्य nor सौन्दर्य (see K above) appears among the meanings given there. The commentary says मंथरं बहु कुसुम्भं कुटिलं चेति त्र्यर्थम्। मन्दवाची तु संस्कृतसम:।

63. वहइ पवंगमलोओ पहुप्पइ णहङ्गणं पडिच्छइ उअही।
देइ मही वि महिहरे तह वि हु दूरविअडोअरं पाआलम्।।

[वहति प्लवंगमलोक: प्रभवति नभोङ्गणं प्रतीष्टे उदधि:।
ददाति मह्यपि महीधरांस्तथापि खलु दूरविकटोदरं पातालम्।।]

The apes brought over the mountains. The sky was spacious enough. The earth, too, surrendered the mountains, and the ocean received them. Yet verily the bottom of the sea was mostly empty.

K reads च (*a*) for *hu* खलु in the second line.

K says प्लवङ्गमलोक: पर्वतान् वहति स्म। प्रभवति नभोऽङ्गणमानीयमानानां पर्वतानां वानराणां च गगनं पर्याप्तावकाशमभूत (पर्वतसंमानाय प्रभवति Kula)। उदधिश्च प्रतीच्छति गिरीन् प्रत्यगृह्णात्। मह्यपि भूरपि गिरिं ददाति स्म। तथापि च पातालं समुद्रान्तरालम् अत्यन्तविकटोदरमेव (विशालकुक्षि Kula)। एवं सर्वसाधनसंपत्तावपि सत्यामुपायोपक्रमाभावत् तत् सर्वमकिञ्चित्करमभूदित्यर्थ:। R says तथापि खलु पातालं दूरादेव विकटोदरं तुच्छोदरम्।

64. इअ खोहेन्ति पवंगा थोअविराअगिरिपङ्कणिव्वुअमहिसम्।
दुममिलिअविद्दुमवणं थलसावअमिलिअजलअरं मअरहरम्।।

[61] समास्तरै: A; समस्तरै: B.

[इति क्षोभयन्ति प्लवङ्गाः स्तोकविशीर्णगिरिपङ्कनिर्वृतमहिषम्।
द्रुममिलितविद्रुमवनं स्थलश्वापदमिलितजलचरं मकरगृहम्।।]

Thus did the apes convulse the ocean. The buffaloes were happy to wallow in the mud of the mountains partly dissolving in the waters; the coral-reefs mingled with the trees; and the aquatic animals with those living on land.

K says प्लवङ्गा मकरगृहं स्तोकविलीनेषु किञ्चित् शिथिलीकृतेषु गिरिषु संजातेन पङ्केन निर्वृतवनमहिषं, द्रुमैः मिलितविद्रुमवनं, स्थलवर्तिभिः श्वापदैः सिंहव्याघ्रादिभिः मिलितजलचरसत्त्वं यथा भवति तथा इति क्षोभयन्ति स्म। न पुनः सेतो प्रसङ्गमप्यवापुरिति।

65. वणगअगन्धारोसिअजम्भाअन्तपडिउद्धकेसरिमअरम्।
समुहपडन्तधराहरभीअवलन्तभुअइन्दजणिआवत्तम्।।

[वनगजगन्धारोषितजृम्भायमाणप्रतिबुद्धकेसरिमकरम्।
संमुखपतद्धराधरभीतवलमानभुजगेन्द्रजनितावर्तम्।।]

The sea lions woke up and yawned, enraged by the smell of the elephants in the woods on the mountains; and the huge serpents caused whirlpools as they twisted about, scared by the mountains dropping in front of them.

K reas विजृम्भमाण (*viambhamāṇa*, cf. 1.43) for *jambhāanta* जृम्भायमाण (R); जृम्भमाण (Kula)।

K says अभिमुखपतद्धराधरभीतैः वलमानैः भुजगेन्द्रैः जनितावर्तं यथा क्षोभयन्ति स्म। Kula says वनगजगन्धेनारोषिता जृम्भमाणा विधूतमुखाः (विवृतमुखाः *SC*) प्रतिबुद्धाः केशरिमकरा यत्र।

66. अत्थाअन्तवणत्थलिपरिणामोलुग्गपण्डुवत्तत्थइअम्।
मअणदुमभङ्गणिग्गअकसाअरसमइअविहलघोलिरमच्छम्।।

[अस्तायमानवनस्थलीपरिणामावरुग्णपाण्डुपत्रस्थगितम्।
मदनद्रुमभङ्गनिर्गतकषायरसमत्तविह्वलघूर्णमानमत्स्यम्।।]

The sea was covered with pale withered leaves from the sinking woods; and the helpless fish tossed about, intoxicated by the astringent sap exuding from the broken *madana* trees.[62]

---

[62] Plants with toxic properties. See Introduction.

K says जलेषु अस्तं गच्छन्तीनां वनस्थलीनां संबन्धिभि: परिणामेनावरुग्णै: भग्नै: पाण्डुपत्रै: स्थगितम्। मदनद्रुमाणां भङ्गात् निर्गतेन कषायरसेन, कषायस्तुवर:, तेन रसेन निर्यासेन मत्तविह्वलघूर्णमानमत्स्यम्। मदनरसास्वादात् मत्स्या मूर्छन्तीति प्रसिद्धम्।

MY says *maia* मादित। Kula says मदयन्ति विह्वलयन्ति ये द्रुमा विषपादपादयस्तेषां . . . कषायरसेन मूदिता: (मृदिता: ?) विह्वला घूर्णनशीला मत्स्या यत्र तम्। Kula seems to read मृदित[63] (*malia*, cf. *SC*) for *maia*. *SC* says मदनद्रुमस्य करहाटस्य।

67. धरणिहरभारवेल्लिअपल्लवदलमुद्धवेल्लिअलआजालम्।
विसवण्णवाअवाहअपव्वाअन्तविसवण्णवाअवकुसुमम्।।

[धरणिधरभारप्रेरितपल्लवदलमुग्धवेल्लितलताजालम्।
विषवन्नवातपाहतप्रवायद्बिसवर्णपादपकुसुमम्।।]

The tender creepers were crumpled up with their leaves and shoots crushed under the weight of the mountains; and the flowers of the trees lost their colour, withering in contact with the trees with poisonous leaves.

K says धरणिधरभारपीडितपल्लवदलानां[64], मुग्धानां सुकुमाराणां, वेल्लितानां कुटिलीकृतानां लतानां जालं यत्र तम्[65]। विषपर्णपादपै: विषमयपत्रै: पादपैराहतत्वात् प्रम्लायत् विस्ववर्णं विगतस्वप्रभं पादपकुसुममितरेषां पादपानां कुसुमं यत्र तम्। MY also has विषपर्णपादपाहत . . . विगतस्ववर्ण, etc.

Kula reads शिखर for भार in the first line. Then he says विषवन्नवातपेन विषतुल्येन लभ्येन (नवेन ?) शरदातपेनाहतानि वायन्ति शुष्यन्ति विसवर्णानि मृणालधवलानि पादपकुसुमानि यत्र तम्। R says विषवन्त: सर्पा: त एव नवातपा: तापहेतुत्वात् तैराहतानि . . . अत एव प्रवायन्ति शुष्यन्ति, etc.

68. आवत्तभमिरमहिहरसिहरोज्झरसीहरन्धआरिअगअणम्।
पडिओसहिगन्धाहअपाआलसमुच्छलन्तविहलविसहरम्।।

[आवर्तभ्रमणशीलमहीधरशिखरनिर्झरशीकरान्धकारितगगनम्।
पतितौषधिगन्धाहतपातालसमुच्छलद्विह्वलविषधरम्।।]

The sky was obscured by the spray of the cascades on the

---

[63] Deva (*chāyā*) also reads मृदित, but his gloss on the verse is missing.

[64] The fiast *vellia* stands for *pellia* = पीडित (K) प्रेरित (R, *SC* and Kula who has प्रेषित)।

[65] R says वेल्लितानि चञ्चलानि लतानां जलानि यत्र। Cf. verse 51.

summit of the mountains spinning in the whirlpools; and the serpents, overpowered by the smell of the plants that fell into the water,[66] emerged helpless from the bottom of the sea.

The verse is not found in K. A corresponding verse with the same *pratīka* (*āvatta*) occurs in MY, but the only word explained by him (*uddhāanta*) is not found in the verse as read by R and Kula. The latter read पातालतलोच्छलत् for *pāāla-samucchalanta* in the second line. The verse occurs in Deva who reads पातालतल।

69. आवत्तमण्डलोअरवलन्तसेलकडअप्पहामिज्जन्तम्।
णिन्तरसाअलविसहरवित्थिण्णफणामणिप्पहामिज्जन्तम्।।

(कुलअम्)

[आवर्तमण्डलोदरवलमानशैलकटकप्रभ्राम्यमाणम्।
निर्यद्रसातलविषधरविस्तीर्णफणामणिप्रभामीयमानम्।।]

(कुलकम्)

The sea was churned up by the flanks of the mountains moving round in the depth of the whirlpools; and was marked by the lustre of the gems embedded in the spacious hoods of the serpents emerging from the nether regions.

K says आवर्तमण्डलोदरेषु वलमानैः शैलकटकैः प्रक्षोभ्यमाणं (प्रभ्राम्यमाणं *chāyā*) निर्यतां निर्गच्छतां रसातलविषधराणां विस्तीर्णाभिः फणामणिप्रभाभिः मीयमानं परिच्छिद्यमानमेवं ते क्षोभयन्ति स्म। Kula says मीयमानमियत्तया गृह्यमाणप्रमाणम्। R says मीयमानं ज्ञायमानम्।

70. अव्वोच्छिण्णविसज्जिअणिअन्तराआममिलिअपव्वअघडिओ।
दीसइ णहणिम्माओ णासइ उअहिम्मि णिवडिओ सेउवहो।।

[अव्यवच्छिन्नविसृष्टनिरन्तरायाममिलितपर्वतघटितः।
दृश्यते नभोनिर्मितो नश्यत्युदधौ निपतितः सेतुपथः।।]

Formed by the mountains, continuously released[67] and coming together in a long unbroken series, the causeway

---

[66] Serpents are believed to be unable to endure the smell of certain plants. See 4.63.

[67] I.e. by the apes from above.

appeared to be built in the sky, but vanished as it plunged into the sea.

auvocchiṇṇa is rendered by K (*chāyā*) as अव्युच्छिन्न (अव्यंवच्छिन्न R, Deva and Kula) K (commentary) says अविच्छिन्नं विसर्जितैः . . . मिलितैः परस्परं घटितैः पर्वतैः घटितो विरचितः सेतुपथः, etc.

71. तो घेप्पिउं पउत्ता थोअत्थोअं परिस्समेण पवंगा।
अणुराए व्व विराए लङ्काणत्थघडणक्खमे सेउवहे।।

[ततो ग्रहीतुं प्रवृत्ताः स्तोकस्तोकं परिश्रमेण प्लवंगाः।
अनुराग इव विशीर्णे लङ्कानर्थघटनक्षमे सेतुपथे।।]

Thereupon the apes began by degrees to be overcome by fatigue as the causeway that was to bring disaster to Laṅkā faded away, like their own zeal.

K says लङ्काया अनर्थसंपादनक्षमे सेतुपथे अनुराग इव सेतुनिर्माणाभिनिवेश इव विलीने सति ततः प्लवङ्गाः परिश्रमेण खेदेन कर्त्रा स्तोकस्तोकं ग्रहीतुं प्रवृत्ता ग्रहीतुमारब्धाः। प्रवृत्ता इति कर्मणि। परिश्रमेण गृहीता इति यावत्। प्रारम्भे निष्फले सति तेषां हृदयदुःखमभूदित्यर्थः। MY says सेतुचिकीर्षायां सेतौ च द्वयेऽपि विलीने परिश्रमः कपिषु पदं चक्रे इत्यर्थः।

इअ सिरिपवरसेणविरइए कालिदासकए दहमुहवहे महाकव्वे
सत्तमो आसासओ समत्तो।

[इति श्रीप्रवरसेनविरचिते कालिदासकृते दशमुखवधे महाकाव्ये
सप्तम आश्वासकः समाप्तः।]

अष्टम आश्वासकः
Eighth Āśvāsakaḥ

1–2. इअ जाहे णिवडन्ता सिहरोज्झरधोअसुरविमाणधअवडा।
अत्थाअन्ति समुद्दे वित्थारत्थमिअणहअला वि महिहरा।।

ताहे णिसुद्धसेसा वेवन्तुव्वत्तकरअलोसरिअअडा।
ठविआ वेलामूले खणलक्खिअगारवा कईहि महिहरा।।

(जुग्गअम्)

[इति यदा निपतन्तः शिखरनिर्झरधौतसुरविमानध्वजपटाः।
अस्तायन्ते समुद्रे विस्तारास्तमितनभस्तला अपि महीधराः।।

तदा निपातितशेषा वेपमानोद्वृत्तकरतलापसृततटाः।
स्थापिता वेलामूले क्षणलक्षितगौरवाः कपिभिर्महीधराः।।]

(युग्मकम्)

When thus the mountains vanished as they dropped into the sea, even though they had covered the sky with their expanse, and drenched the banners of the aerial cars of the gods with the cascades on their summit; the mountains left over were set down by the apes on the margin of the beach, their weight being felt by them for a moment as the flanks slipped off their tired quivering hands.

K reads *vitthārattaia* for *-tthamia* = विस्तारास्तमित (R and Kula); and धारणिधराः for *vi mahiharā* (R and Kula). K says विस्तारस्थगितनभस्तलाः R says विस्तारेणास्तमितं छन्नं नभस्तलं यैस्ते।

K and MY have म्लान for *uvvatta* उद्वृत्त[1] (R), i.e. they read *uvvāa* found in MY. Cf. Hemacandra 4.11, 18. This is the reading of Kula and Deva also, as they have परिश्रान्त। *Deśīnāmamālā* 1.102 (*uvvāa* खिन्न)। *SC* says *uvvāa* इति पाठे श्रान्तात् करतलादित्यर्थः।

3. गिरिसंखोहविमुक्का झीणा अप्पत्तपढमगमणोआसा।
मन्दन्दोलणमउआ गआगअ च्चिअ समुद्दसलिलुप्पीडा।।

---

[1] R says उद्वृत्तादूर्ध्वपृष्ठीकृतात् करतलात्।

[गिरिसंक्षोभविमुक्ताः क्षीणा अप्राप्तप्रथमगमनावकाशाः।
मन्दान्दोलनमृदुका गतागता एव समुद्रसलिलोत्पीडाः॥]

Rid of the upheaval caused by the mountains, the waters of the sea, placid with soft undulation, became calm even as they moved back and forth, without reaching the range of their former surge.

K, MY and Deva read उत्कम्पाः for *utpīḍā* = उत्पीडाः (R and Kula). K says समुद्रसलिलोत्कम्पाः अप्राप्तप्रथमगमनावकाशाः क्षोभावस्थायां गमनावकाशो यस्तमप्राप्ताः, मन्देनान्दोलनेन स्पन्दनेन मृद्वो भूत्वा गतागत एव गमनागमन एव क्षीणाः शान्ताः।

MY says सलिलोत्कम्पाः उत्कम्पमानानि सलिलानि यत एव मन्दान्दोलनमृदूनि, अतएव समुद्र एव गतागतमात्राणि, न तु पूर्ववदुत्स्थलानीत्यथः।

Kula says गिरिसंक्षोभेण विमुक्ताः, अतः क्षीणाः अनुच्छलिताः, अत एव अप्राप्तप्रथमगमनावकाशाः संक्षोभेण (प्रथमं) यावत् दूरं गताः तावत् दूरं न गता इत्यर्थः। सलिलोत्पीडाः जलसंघाताः।

4. भिण्णघडन्तावत्तो आवत्तन्तरभमन्तभिण्णमहिहरो।
महिहरसंभमविहुओ विहुअणिअत्तसलिलो णिअत्तइ उअही॥

[भिन्नघटमानावर्त आवर्तान्तरभ्रमद्भिन्नमहीधरः।
महीधरसंभ्रमविधुतो विधुतनिवृत्तसलिलो निवर्तत उदधिः॥]

Rocked by the commotion caused by the mountains, the sea returned to its former state. The whirlpools, broken up (by the mountains), formed again; the crumbling mountains moved round amidst the whirlpools; and the heaving waters receded from the shore.

उदधिर्निवर्तते पूर्वगतात् प्रदेशात् निववृते K. निवर्तते पूर्वावस्थां लभते R.

MY says क्षोभदशायां भिन्नो निवृत्तः पुनस्तत्प्रशमदशायां घटमान आवर्तो यत्र स तथा। अथवा भिन्नघटमानः द्विधाभूतः पुनर्घटमानः। अथवा पूर्वतो विपरीतघटमानावर्त इत्यर्थः। He reads *āattantara* and explains it as आवर्तोदर। Kula says आवर्तान्तरेषु भ्रमन्तो भिन्ना महीधरा यत्र। महीधरेभ्यः संभ्रमो भयं (*SC*) तेन कर्तृभूतेन विधुतो दिगन्तं गतः। विधुतं कम्पितं निवृत्तं सलिलं यस्य स उदधिः निवर्तते।

5. वोच्छिज्जन्तकलअलं जहोइअट्ठाणदरपअत्तावत्तम्।
दीसइ खणदुल्लक्खं तं चिअ थिमिअसलिलत्तणं जलणिहिणो॥

[व्यवच्छिद्यमानकलकलं यथोचितस्थानदरप्रवृत्तावर्तम्।
दृश्यते क्षणदुर्लक्ष्यं तदेव स्तिमितसलिलत्वं जलनिधेः।।]

The natural calm of the sea that was invisible for a while was seen again, with the din subsiding, and the whirlpools partly forming in the customary places.

vocchijjanta = व्युच्छिद्यमान K. MY has विच्छिद्यमान। K says पर्वतपतनाभावात् व्युच्छिद्यमानकलकलं, यथोचितेषु उचितानतिक्रामिषु स्थानेषु किंचित् प्रवृत्तावृत्तं, क्षणमात्रदुर्लक्षं क्षोभातिरेकात् क्षणमात्रं द्रष्टुमशक्यं तदेव प्राक्तनमेवोदधेः स्तिमितसलिलत्वं दृश्यते स्म पुनरपि अदृश्यत। Kula has व्यवच्छिद्यमान् like R. He says यथोचितप्रदेशेषु दरप्रवृत्त आवर्तो यत्र (R also)।

6. मोत्ताघडन्तकुसुमं सममरगअवत्तभङ्गभरिआवत्तम्।
विद्दुममिलिअकिसलअं ससङ्खधवलकमलं पसम्मइ सलिलम्।।

[मुक्ताघटमानकुसुमं सममरकतपत्रभङ्गभृतावर्तम्।
विद्रुममिलितकिसलयं सशङ्खधवलकमलं प्रशाम्यति सलिलम्।।]

The waters became calm, with flowers mingling with pearls, the whirlpools filled with broken leaves and emeralds, the young shoots combining with corals, and the white lotus blossoms mixed with conchshells.[2]

Pasammaī = प्रसीदति K and MY; प्रशाम्यति R and Kula. K says समशब्दः सहार्थः। समरतकैः सहमरतकैः पत्रभङ्गैः भग्नपत्रैः भरितावर्तं, विद्रुमैः मिलितकिसलयं, शङ्खैः सहितधवलकमलम् एवं समानवर्णैः समुद्रगतैः द्रव्यैः संगतकुसुमादिकं सलिलं समुद्रस्य प्रसीदति स्म। MY says अथवा क्षोभदशायां व्यथा उच्चलितमुक्तादिमत् उदधिसलिलं, तथा प्रसाददशायामपि तत्सदृशकुसुमादिमत्तया तुल्यरूपमलक्ष्यत इति तात्पर्यम्।

7. दीसइ समोसिअन्ती खणणिव्वलिउत्तरन्तविलुलिअकुसुमा।
झिज्जन्तारुणअम्बा समुद्दवट्ठम्मि धाउपङ्कच्छाआ।।

[दृश्यते समवसीदन्ती क्षणनिर्वलितोत्तरद्विलुलितकुसुमा।
क्षीयमाणारुणताम्रा समुद्रपृष्ठे धातुपङ्कच्छाया।।]

The lustre of the minerals of the mountains, soaked in water, was seen on the surface of the sea as it faded away, reddish like the decaying sunlight, and blending with the colour of

[2] The verse describes the mingling together of the products of the sea and those of the sinking mountains.

the crushed flowers as they emerged, being just detached from the trees.[3]

K and MY read *samosarantī* = समपसरन्ती for *samosiantī* = समवसीदन्ती (R and Kula), which they mention as a variant. K says पतितानां पर्वतानां संबन्धिनी धातुपङ्कच्छाया: गैरिकपङ्कच्छवि समुद्रपृष्ठ एवमदृश्यत। कथम् – समपसरन्ती अपगच्छन्ती। क्षणं निर्व्यक्तानि पृथग्भूतानि उत्तरन्ति प्लवमानानि कुसुमानि पतितगिरिवनसंबन्धीनि यस्यां सा। क्षीयमाणारुणवत् ताम्रा। अरुण: सूर्यसुत:। Kula says समवसीदन्ती मन्दतां गच्छन्ती उत्प्लवमानानि विलुलितानि म्लानानि कुसुमानि यत्र। R says अरुण: संध्यारागो वा। क्षणात् तदानीमेव।

8. वणगअगन्धुत्तिण्णा पुणो णिअत्तन्ति आअवाहअविहला।
णिअअकरसीहरोल्लिअणिव्वाअन्तमुहमण्डला करिमअरा।।

[वनगजगन्धोत्तीर्णा: पुनर्निवर्तन्त आतपाहतविह्वला:।
निजककरशीकरार्द्रितनिर्वाप्यमाणमुखमण्डला: करिमकरा:।।]

Overpowered by the heat of the sun, the sea elephants that had come ashore, scenting the elephants of the woods,[4] returned to the sea, their faces drenched and cooled by the spray from their trunks.

निर्वान्मुखमण्डला: सुखीभवन्मुखप्रदेशा: करिमकरा:। निर्वाति ह्लादते सौख्ये[5] निर्वृणोति सुखीभवेत् इत्याख्याते K. शीतलायमानानि मुखमण्डलानि येषां ते तथाभूता: Kula.

9. दुमभङ्गकलुसिआइं कसाअरसभिण्णपण्डुरप्फेणाइं।
जाआइँ णिण्णआणं उत्थलवलणरअधूसराइँ मुहाइं।।

[द्रुमभङ्गकलुषितानि कषायरसभिन्नपाण्डुरफेनानि।
जातानि निम्नगानामुत्स्थलवलनरजोधूसराणि मुखानि।।]

The mouths of the rivers (entering the sea), made turbid by the broken trees, with the white foam mingling with their astringent sap, became grey with dust as the waters surged over the banks.[6]

---

[3] Those on the sinking mountains.

[4] I.e. to fight with them.

[5] Our copy has सुख्ये, B has सुखै:।

[6] I.e. as a result of the sea dashing against the incoming streams during the disturbance.

K, Deva and Kula read पतन (*-vaḍaṇa*) for *valaṇa* (R). K says निम्नगानां मुखानि पर्वतद्रुमाणां भङ्गैः कलुषितानि, अतएव तेषां वृक्षाणां कषायेण तुवरेण निर्यासरसेन पाण्डरीभूतफेनानि, उत्स्थले पतनात् क्षोभसमये उत्तुङ्गस्थले पतनाद्रजसा धूसराणि जातानि। अयमत्र ध्वनिः – यथा भर्तरि व्यसनपीडिते पत्नीनां मुखानि कलुषितानि भूमौ पतनाद्रजोभिः धूसराणि भवन्ति तद्वत्।[7] My remarks अत्र भर्तृव्यसने स्त्रीणामार्त्तिचेष्टासमाधिः। Kula says उत्स्थलमुन्नतदेशः ततः पतनेन रजोधूसराणि जातानि। R says उत्स्थलेन तीरभूमावुन्मार्गेण यद्वलनमितस्ततो गमनं तेन।

10. खुहिओअहिविच्छूडा महिन्दकडएसु मलअभित्तिच्छेआ।
घडिआ मलिअगअउला मलअअडेसु अ महिन्दसेलद्धन्ता।।

[क्षुभितोदधिविक्षिप्ता महेन्द्रकटकेषु मलयभित्तिच्छेदाः।
घटिता मृदितगजकुला मलयतटेषु च महेन्द्रशैलार्धान्ताः।।]

Tossed about on the raging sea, portions of the flanks of the Malaya mountain joined the flanks of the Mahendra, and sections of the Mahendra joined the slopes of the Malaya, with the herds of elephants crushed (by the waves).

K and Deva read घटित (*ghaḍia*) for *malia* = मृदित (R); and कटक for *sela* (R). K says क्षुभितेन उदधिना विक्षिप्ता मलयपर्वतस्य भित्तिच्छेदाः, भित्तिशब्देन तटविशेष उच्चते, तटविभागा आसन्नस्य महेन्द्रपर्वतस्य कटकेषु घटिताः। कथंभूताः-घटितगजकुलाः घटितवनगजसमूहाः। तथा मलयस्य तटेषु महेन्द्रस्य कटकार्धान्ताश्च घटिता एवं विपर्यस्ताः। Deva says महेन्द्रकटकार्धान्ताः मलयकटकार्धान्ताश्च (?) व्यत्यस्तयोगं मिलिता इति। तदा मलयमहेन्द्रयोः स्थितानि गजकुलानि कटकानां भेदेन अर्धभिन्नानि तद्योगे तथैव युक्तानि स्वं स्वं यूथविरहं न जानन्ति। Kula reads शिखर (*sihara*) for *sela*; and *galia* for *malia*. He says महेन्द्रशिखरैकदेशाः गलितगजकुलाः।

11. दीसन्ति विअडधवला थिमिअणिअत्तन्तजलतरङ्गिअवट्टा।
वासुइणिम्मोअणिहा णिरन्तरालग्गमोत्तिआ पुलिणवहा।।

[दृश्यन्ते विकटधवलाः स्तिमितनिवर्तमानजलतरङ्गितपृष्ठाः।
वासुकिनिर्मोकनिभा निरन्तरालग्नमौक्तिकाः पुलिनपथाः।।]

The broad and white expanse of the beach, with the surface

---

[7] Deva says उत्स्थला भूत्वा पुनः पतिताः तेन रजःकलुषिता इति कारागृहादौ बध्यमाने कस्मिंश्चित् तस्य दारास्तत्रागत्य प्रवेष्टुमलभमाना महीतलभृशपतनपरिलुठनेन भग्नहस्ताद्यङ्गाः स्वेदविवर्णाङ्गरागा रजःकलुषितमुखा; चिरेण तत्र ताड़नावसाने प्रविशन्ति तद्वदिति।

rippled by the slowly receding waters, and thickly studded with pearls, looked like the (white and spotted) slough of Vāsuki.[8]

Kula says विकटधवला:, स्तिमितं यथा स्यात् शनैः शन निवर्तमानेन जलेन तरङ्गितपृष्ठाः, निरन्तरालग्नमौक्तिकाः पुलिनपथा वासुकिनिर्मोकनिभा दृश्यन्ते। तेऽपि विशालाः धवलाः तरङ्गिनः पुलकाचिता भवन्ति।

12. खोहेन्ति खुहिअणिहुअं उअहिं णहवन्धपडिणिअत्तोवइआ।
पव्वअघाउक्खित्ता चिरआलालोइआ सलितसंघाआ।।

[क्षोभयन्ति क्षुमितनिभृतमुदधिं नभःपथप्रतिनिवृत्तावपतिताः।
पर्वतघातोत्क्षिप्ताश्चिरकालालोकिताः सलिलसंघाताः।।]

The masses of water that had been flung up by the impact of the mountains (on the sea), and were visible for a long while as they descended back from the sky, again stirred up the sea that had been disturbed and calmed down.

K says पूर्वं पर्वतघातैरुत्क्षिप्ताः, नभसि अर्धपथात् प्रतिनिवृत्ताः पतिताः, चिरकालेन आलोकिताः सलिलसंघाताः क्षुभितनिभृतमुदधिं पुनः क्षोभयन्ति स्म।

13. अह णलविइण्णणअणो जम्पइ विहडन्तमणिसिलासणवट्ठो।
उव्वत्तिआअअट्ठिअवामअरारुहिअतिअभरो पवअवई।।

[अथ नलवितीर्णनयनो जल्पति निघटमानमणिशिलासनपृष्ठः।
उद्वर्तितायतस्थितवामकरारोपितत्रिकभरः पूवगपतिः।।

The lord of the apes (Sugrīva) then spoke, fixing his eyes on Nala;[9] while his bejewelled stone seat cracked as he rested his massive buttocks on his left hand, upturned and outstretched.

K and Deva read शिलातलपृष्ठे for *silāsaṇavaṭṭho* = °शिलासनपृष्ठः (R). He says विघटमाने गौरवातिशयेन भिद्यमाने मणिशिलातलपृष्ठे उद्वर्तितायतस्थितम् उद्वर्तितकरतलं यथायतस्थितं वामभुजमारूढः त्रिकभरः अंससंधिभरो यस्य सः पूवगपतिः। Kula reads शिलासनपट्टः (°*vaṭṭo*), and says उद्वर्तित आयतस्थितो यो वामकरः तत्रारूढत्रिकभरः परिवर्तनवशादेव विघटमानमणिशिला-सनपट्टः नले वितीर्णनयनः पूवगपतिः जल्पति।[10]

---

[8] The great serpent used as a rope by the gods and demons while churning the ocean with the Mandara mountain.

[9] One of the apes, a great architect.

[10] R says यद्वा उद्वर्तितस्तिर्यग्भूतः सन् आयतः स्थितो नलदर्शनाय मस्तकोन्नमनादथ च वामकरारोपितत्रिकभरश्चेति कर्मधारयः This is a slight amplification of Śrīnivāsa's gloss quoted in *SC*.

14. खविओ वाणरलोओ दूरट्ठिअविरलपव्वअं महिवेढम्।
ण अ दीसइ सेउवहो मा हु णमेज्ज गरुअं पुणो रामधणुम्।।

[क्षपितो वानरलोको दूरस्थितविरलपर्वतं महीवेष्टम्।
न च दृश्यते सेतुपथो मा खलु नमेद्गुरुकं पुना रामधनुः।।]

"The apes are worn out. The earth hath only a few remote mountains left. But the causeway is not visible. Let not Rāma's mighty bow be bent again.[11]

K and Deva read पर्वतनिवहः and पादपं for *vāṇara-loö* and *pavvaaṁ* (R and Kula who have प्लवङ्ग for *vāṇara*). K says पर्वतानिवहः क्षपतिः उद्धृत्यानीय नाशितः। महीमण्डलं दूरस्थितविरलवृक्षमभूत्। पर्वतानामुद्धृतत्वात् पादपाः शिष्टाः इत्यर्थः।

My remarks -*ṇamejja* नम्येत नमेदिति वा। गुरुकार्यसाधकतया गुरुभूतं रामधनुर्लघु सेतुमधिकृत्य मा पुनर्नम्येत। K says एवं कृतेऽपि सेतुपथो नोपलब्धः। तस्मात पुनरपि गुरु अतिमहत् रामधनुः मा खलु नमेत्। भूयोऽपि रामस्य धनुषो नमने सति भुवनमेव भस्मीभवेत्। तस्मात् अस्माभिरेवोपायान्तरमन्वेषणीयमिति वाक्यशेषः।

15. मइरा मुद्धमिअङ्को अमअं लच्छी सकोत्थुहं दुमरअणम्।
किं सेउबन्धलहुअं जं वोत्तूण रअणाअरेण ण दिण्णम्।।

[मदिरा मुग्धमृगाङ्कोऽमृतं लक्ष्मीः सकौस्तुभं द्रुमरत्नम्।
किं सेतुबन्धलघुकं यदुक्त्वा रत्नाकरेण न दत्तम्।।]

Wine, the young moon, nectar, the goddess of wealth, and *pārijāta*, the best of trees, together with the *kaustubha* gem, is all this of lesser value than the causeway[12] that the Ocean doth not grant it[13] despite his promise?[14]

K, Deva and MY read मुक्त्वा (*mottūṇa*) for *vottūṇa* = उक्त्वा (R and Kula). K says मदिरा सुरा, etc. एतत् सर्वं प्रशस्तवस्तु सेतुपथवत् किं लघू भवति यन्मदिरादिकं मुक्त्वा पूर्वं दत्त्वा स्थितेन रत्नाकरेण अस्माकमभिमतं न

---

[11] I.e. to chastise the ocean, as described in canto V.

[12] I.e. is the causeway more important than all these?

[13] I.e. does not allow it to be built.

[14] The idea is, during the churning by the gods and demons, the ocean had given up wine, nectar, etc. even without any promise; so it is unlikely that it will now break its promise by obstructing the building of the causeway. The idea of the causeway was suggested by the ocean as described in canto VI.

दत्तम्। अतिलघुः सेतुपथो न दत्तः। तत्र कारणमस्माकमविमृश्यकारित्वमेव। मदिरादयोऽपि देवैरुपायेनैव हि महता समुद्राल्लब्धाः। तस्मादुपाय एव चिन्त्यतामित्यर्थः। Deva also says: प्रशस्तमुपायान्तरमास्थेयमिति। But he mentions another interpretation अपरा व्याख्या। मदिरादिकं सर्वं किं सेतुबन्धाल्लघुकं भवति येनैतत् सर्वं मुक्त्वा (प्रदाय[15]) सेतुबन्धो न दत्तो भवति। तस्मात् तदपि दास्यत्येवेति। समुद्रस्य सेतुदानं सेतुबन्धनानुगुण्यम्।

MY says जं मोत्तं ण रअणाअरेण ण-इण्णमिति[16] पाठः। दिण्णं दत्तं अभ्युपगतमित्यर्थः। तथा च यन्मदिरादिकं पूर्वं मोक्तुं न नाभ्युपगतं तत् किं सेतुबन्धात् लघु अपि तु गुर्वेव इत्यर्थः। इयमेवोक्तिभङ्गिः कवेः प्रदेशान्तरेष्वपि तत्र तत्रानुगन्तव्या यथा — see 11.21.

Kula says मदिरा, etc. किं सेतुबन्धात् लघुकं किं लघुकान्येतानि सेतुबन्धो गुरुकः . . . यदेव प्रत्येकं त्रैलोक्यसारं मदिरादिकं तदेवानेव देवासुरेभ्यो दत्तम्। इदं तदपेक्षया कियन्मात्रं यत् प्रार्थितमभ्युमगम्यापि[17] न दत्तमिति अहो गरीयानस्माकं परिभव इति भावः।

16. धूमाअन्ति च्चिअ से अज्ज वि पाआलदेहदूरालग्गा।
आअट्टन्तजलाहअससद्दविज्झविअहुअवहा रामसरा।।

[धूमायन्त इवास्याद्यापि पातालदेहदूरालग्नाः।
आवर्त्यमानजलाहतसशब्दविध्यापितहुतवहा रामशराः।।]

Rāma's arrows, stuck deep in the bottom of the sea, are smouldering still,[18] with their flames beaten down and noisily quenched by the seething waters.

K says अस्य समुद्रस्य पातालमये देहे दूरमालग्नाः, आवर्तमानैर्जलैराहतत्वात् सशब्दं प्रशमितहुतवहा रामशराः अद्यापि धूमयन्त्येव न निःशेषं शान्ताः। MY says क्षीयमाणजलाहतसशब्दनिर्वापितहुतवहा रामशराः। MY explains *āaṭṭanta* as क्षीयमाण। Cf. his explanation of *aṭṭanti* in 13.32. Kula says रामशराः आवर्तमानेन . . . जलेनाहतः सशब्दं विध्मापितो निर्वापितो हुतवहो येषां तेऽद्यापि धूमायन्त एव नैतावता निर्वान्तीत्यर्थः। R say आवर्त्यमानेन क्वथ्यमानेन जलेन। *SC* says आवर्त्यमानेन क्वाथ्यमानेन क्षीयमाणेन वा।

---

15 मुक्त्वा is so explained in Deva's first interpretation.

16 Manuscript B has इति वा।

17 Refers to 6.17, Kula says अयं तु (सेतुबन्धः) घटितसेतुबन्धमित्यादिना रत्नाकरेणोदित्वापि अस्मभ्यं न दत्तः। एतदुक्तं भवति-यदेव प्रत्येकं, etc.

18 Sugrīva refers to the chastisement of the sea for failure to grant passage to Rāma's army, as described in canto V, and envisages the possibility of a similar catastrophe if there is further delay in building a causeway.

17. तं बन्धसु धीर तुमं सेउं अज्जेअ जाव दूरन्तरिआ।
एक्कं मलअसुवेला होन्तु दुहा अ विअडा समुद्दद्धन्ता।।
[ततो बधान धीर त्वं सेतुमद्यैव यावद्दूरान्तरितौ।
एकं मलयसुवेलौ भवतां द्विधा च विकटौ समुद्रार्धान्तौ।।]

Wise one, build therefore a causeway even today. Let the widely separated Malaya and Suvela[19] mountains unite, and the vast expanse of the sea divide in twain."

K read तावत् (Deva also) and समुद्रोद्देशा: for *jāva* (R and Kula) and *samuddaddhantā* (R, MY, Deva and Kula). Manuscript C of Goldschmidt has *samudduddesā*. MY remarks एकमिति सामान्यविवक्षया नपुंसकनिर्देशः।

18. तो पवअबलाहि फुडं विण्णाणासङ्घणिव्वलन्तच्छाओ।
पवअवइसंभमुम्मुहविइण्णभअहित्थलोअणो भणइ णलो।।

[ततः प्लवगबलात्स्फुटं विज्ञानाध्यवसायनिर्बलच्छायः।
प्लवगपतिसंभ्रमोन्मुखवितीर्णभयोद्विग्नलोचनो भणति नलः।।]

Distinct in lustre from the host of apes because of his confidence in his art, Nala thereupon clearly spoke, respectfully raising his timorous eyes before the lord of the apes.

K, Deva and MY read उत्साहः for *Cchāo* — च्छायः (R and Kula). K says प्लवगसैन्यादपि आत्मानि विज्ञानविश्वासेन व्यज्यमानोत्साहः। MY says *viṇṇāṇāsaṁgha* विज्ञानाशंसा। विज्ञानं शिल्पज्ञानं। तस्याशंसा निश्चयः। ततः पूर्वतः पृथग्भवदुत्साहः। K says प्लवगपतिं प्रति संभ्रमादुन्मुखं यथा वितीर्णभय-त्रस्तलोचनो भूत्वा भणति स्म। Kula says प्लवगपतेः संभ्रमेण आदरेण उन्मुखं यथा स्यात् तथा।

19. भण्णइ पवंगपुरओ रहुणाहस्स अ पवंगवइ वीसत्थम्।
तुह सेउबन्धजणिआ ममम्मि संभावणा ण होहिइ अलिआ।।

[भणति प्लवंगपुरतो रघुनाथस्य च प्लवंगपते विश्वस्तम्।
तव सेतुबन्धजनिता मयि संभावना न भविष्यत्यलीका।।]

"Lord of the apes, confidently do I speak before the apes as well as Rāma. The confidence thou hast reposed in me in respect of the causeway shall not be in vain.

[19] See verse 83.

प्लवंगपते प्लवंगानां पुरतः रघुनाथस्य च पुरतो विश्वस्तं विश्वासयुक्तं त्वया भण्यते K, MY says प्लवंगपुरत इति राज्ञः साक्षादनिर्देश्यतया तत्परिकरभूतप्लवंग-संनिधावित्युक्तम्। तेन तव पुरत इत्यर्थः। समासपदादप्यस्मात् निष्कृष्य पुरत इति रघुनाथस्येत्यत्रापि अनुषञ्जनीयम्। अथवा समानानां प्लवंगमानां (पुरतः) भण्यते रघुनाथस्य चेत्यत्र श्रूयत इति शेषः सामर्थ्यात्। अथवा तव रघुनाथस्य च मयि संभावना इत्यन्वयो द्रष्टव्यः। विस्रब्धं निःसंशयमित्यर्थः।

Kula says भोः प्लवगपते सजातीयानां प्लवगानां रघुनाथस्य च पुरतो विश्वस्तं यथाभूतं भण्यते, मयि सेतुबन्धजनिता तव संभावना योग्यत्वारोपणम् अलीका न भवति। नहि कर्तुमशक्यं प्रभुसमक्षं प्रकाश्यते। सेतुर्बद्ध एव इत्यवगच्छेत्याशयः।

20. खविओ पव्वअणिवहो दलिअँ व रसाअलं धुओ व्व समुद्दो।
जीअं व परिच्चत्तं अज्ज व संभावणा तुहं णिव्वूढा।।

[क्षपितः पर्वतनिवहो दलितं वा रसातलं धुतो वा समुद्रः।
जीवो वा परित्यक्तोऽद्य वा संभावना तव निर्व्यूढा।।]

Let the mountains be destroyed, the nether regions rent asunder,[20] the ocean convulsed, and my life sacrificed. But thy confidence in me shall be justified even today.

K (*pratīka*) has *khavio vva*. K, Deva and Kula read वा शैल for *pavvaa* — (R). K says शैलनिवहः सर्वः क्षपितो भवतु वा। पर्वतक्षेपणात् रसातलं वा दलितमस्तु। समुद्रो धुतो वा मम जीवितं परित्यक्तं वा भवतु। तव संभावना अद्यैव निर्व्यूढा स्यात्। शैलादीनां जीवितपर्यन्तानामेवं भावेऽपि तव संभावनामद्य निर्वक्ष्यामीत्यर्थः। Kula says क्षयितो वा शैलनिवहः, दलितं वा रसातलं, धुतो वा समुद्रः, जीवितं (वा) परित्यक्तम्। अथवा तव पदं (अद्य ?) संभावना निर्वूढा। (न) अपरः पक्ष इत्यर्थः।

R says अथ चाद्य तव संभावना प्रतिष्ठा निर्व्यूढैव। . . . मया सेतोरवश्यं बद्धव्यत्वादित्याशयः।

21. तं पेक्खसु महिविअलं महीवट्टम्मि व महं महोअहिवट्टे।
घडिअं घडन्तमहिहरघडिअसुवेलमलअन्तरं सेउवहम्।।

[तत्प्रेक्षस्व महीविकटं महीपृष्ठ इव मम महोदधिमध्ये(पृष्ठे)।
घटितं घटमानमहीधरघटितसुवेलमलयान्तरं सेतुपथम्।।]

So behold a causeway, wide as the earth, built by me across the great ocean as on the surface of the earth, with the gap

---

[20] I.e. by the mountains dropped into the sea.

between the Malaya and the Suvela filled up with mountains clinging together.

K and Deva *pratīka* has *pecchaha* rendered as पश्यत for *pekkhasu* = प्रेक्षस्व (R). MY and *SC* text have *pecchasu*. K and Deva read वेष्टे (*veḍhammi*) for *vaṭṭammi* = पृष्ठे (R and Kula); and मया (*mae*) for *mahaṁ* found in R. K says महीवेष्ट इव महोदधिपृष्ठे तिष्ठता मया घटितं, घटमानैरन्योन्यं शिलष्यद्भिः महीधरैरेकीकृतसुवेलमलयान्तरम्, अतएव महीवत् विकटं सेतुपथं पश्यत। *SC* text has *mae*.

22. किं उत्तरउ णिरन्तरघडन्तधरणिहरसंकमेण समुद्दम्।
ओ बोलेउ धुओअहिथोउत्तिण्णमहिमण्डलेण कइबलम्।।

[किमुत्तरतु निरन्तरघटमानधरणिधरसंक्रमेण समुद्रम्।
उत व्यतिक्रामतु धुतोदधिस्तोकोत्तीर्णमहीमण्डलेन कपिबलम्।।]

Shall the host of apes cross the sea by a bridge of mountains set firmly together; or shall it march across the slightly raised bed of the sea after its waters have been swept away?

K and Kula read उत्क्षिप्त (*ukkhitta*) for *uttiṇṇa* (R). K says अथवा धुतादुभयतो निरस्तादुदधेः स्तोकमुद्धृतेन महीमण्डलेन अधस्तलभूमिभागेन किमतिक्रामतु।

23. तं पेच्छह मलओ च्चिअ पत्थन्तो पडिगअं गओ व्व सुवेलम्।
मह भुअदढसंरुद्धो आइद्धं धुणउ मुहवडं व समुद्दम्।।

[तत्पश्यत मलय एव प्रार्थयमानः प्रतिगतं गज इव सुवेलम्।
मम भुजदृढसंरुद्ध आविद्धं धुनोतु मुखपटमिव समुद्रम्।।]

Or, behold. Let the Malaya, firmly held by my hands, and advancing upon the Suvela, sweep the intervening sea away, like as an elephant charging at its opponent shakes off the veil![21]

K, Deva, Kula and MY read ओ for तं (P). K and MY read *pecchasu* for *pecchaha* (R and Kula). अथवा पश्य K. ओशब्दः पक्षान्तरे अथवा Kula. K says मलय एव सुवेलं गजः प्रतिगजमिव प्रार्थयमानः अभियुञ्जानो नोदनवेगेनाविद्धं समुद्रं मुखपटमिव धुनोतु। MY reads सारुद्ध for संरुद्ध–दृढसारुद्धो

---

[21] Nala means that he will push the Malaya mountain through the sea to link it to the Suvela in Laṅkā, sweeping the waters away in the process! The Malaya advancing towards the Suvela is likened to a blindfolded elephant which charges at a rival elephant by shaking off its veil to which the sea is compared. See 2.22; 13.59.

दृढसंरूद्धः दृढनुन्न इति यावत्। ओ उत। एवं वा प्रकारो भविष्यति। प्रेक्षस्व इत्यन्वयः। R says आविद्धमन्तरा पातितम्। Kula says धुनोतु विधूय क्षिपतु।

24. ओ विरएमि णहअले तुरिअपहाविअपवंगसंचरणसहम्।
अणुपरिवाडिपरिट्ठिअघणकूडघडन्तमहिहरं सेउवहम्।।

[उत विरचयामि नभस्तले त्वरितप्रधावितप्लवंगसंचरणसहम्।
अनुपरिपाटीपरिस्थितघनकूटघटमानमहीधरं सेतुपथम्।।]

Or, I will build a bridge in the sky, composed of mountains, compact like clouds in massive array, and strong enough for the march of the swift-running apes!

K reads प्रतिष्ठित for *pariṭṭhia* (R and Kula). K says अथवा नभस्तले, अनुपरिपाटी अनुक्रमः, अनुक्रमेण प्रतिष्ठिता घनकूटाः दृढतरशिखराः घटमाना महीधरा यस्य तं, त्वरितप्रधावितानां प्लवङ्गानां संचरणसहिष्णुं सेतुपथं विरचयामि। MY says अनुपरिपाटी परम्परा। घन निरन्तर। Kula says अनुपरिपाट्या यथाक्रमेण परिस्थितो यो घनकूटो मेघसंघातः तद्वत् घटमानाः श्लिष्यन्तो महीधरा यत्र तं सेतुपथं विरचयामि।

25. ओ साअरोअरब्भन्तराणिओवरिपरिट्ठविअणिप्फन्दा।
जलहरलम्बिअवक्खा घडेन्तु लङ्कावहं रसाअलसेला।।

[उत सागरोदराभ्यन्तरानीतोपरिस्थापितनिःस्पन्दाः।
जलधरालम्बितपक्षा घटयन्तु लङ्कापथं रसातलशैलाः।।]

Or, let the mountains of the nether regions, brought out of the depths of the sea, and held motionless above the waters, form the road to Laṅkā, with their wings drooping under the load of water![22]

K reads प्रतिष्ठापित for परि° (R); and निष्कम्पाः for *ṇipphandā* (R and Kula). He also reads घटन्तां लङ्कापथे for *ghaḍentu laṅkāvahaṁ* = घटयन्तु . . . (R and Kula) रसातलगताः शैलाः लङ्कापथे सेतौ घटन्तां संबध्यन्ताम् K.

26. तं मह मग्गालग्गा विरएह जहाणिओअमुक्कमहिहरा।
अणुवाअदिट्ठदोसं अइराहोन्तसुहबन्धणं सेउवहम्।।

[तन्मम मार्गलग्ना विरचयत यथानियोगमुक्तमहीधराः।
अनुपायदृष्टदोषमचिराद्भवत्सुखबन्धनं सेतुपथम्।।]

[22] A reference to the winged mountain hidden in the sea for which see 5.37.

So build a causeway, following my lead, and methodically releasing the mountains. Vitiated heretofore by wrong methods, it will soon be built with ease."

K says मम मार्गालग्नाः पुरतोमार्गमनुगता, यथानियोगमेव मुक्तपर्वता यूयं पूर्वमनुपायात् उपायाभावात् दृष्टदोषमिदानीम् अचिरात् भवत्सुकरबन्धनं सेतुपथं विरचयत। Kula says यथा नियोजयामि तथा मुक्तमहीधराः। अनुपायेन दृष्टो दोषः अनिष्पत्तिलक्षणो यत्र तम्। R ays मम मार्गलग्नाः पश्चात् लग्नाः। यथा मयोच्यते तथा।

27. इअ णलवअणहरिसिअं गलिअपरिस्समणिराअमुक्ककलअलम्।
चलिअं तुलिअधराहरकअणिब्भरदसदिसं पवंगमसेण्णम्।।

[इति नलवचनहर्षितं गलितपरिश्रमनिरायतमुक्तकलकलम्।
चलितं तुलितधराधरकृतनिर्भरदशदिक्प्लवंगमसैन्यम्।।]

Cheered thus by Nala's words, the army of apes bestirred themselves as they uttered prolonged cries, with their fatigue gone, and filled the ten directions with the mountains lifted up by them.

K and MY read चलित for *tulia*. K reads भर for *kaa* = कृत (R and MY)।

K says प्लवङ्गमसैन्यं चलितानामुद्धतानां धराधराणां भरेण विस्तारेण पूरितदशाशं भूत्वा चलितं कार्ये प्रावर्तत। कृतनिर्भरदशदिगिति च पाठः। चलितैः पर्वतैः निर्भरीकृतदशदिक्कमित्यर्थः।

MY says चलितधराधरं च तत् कृतनिर्भरदशदिक् चेति विग्रहः। तत्रोद्योगरभसकम्पितमलयत्वं चलितधराधरत्वम्। कृताः स्थाननिर्भराः पूर्णा दश दिशो येन तत्तथा। सविशेषणे हि विधिनिषेधौ विशेषणमुपसंक्रामतः इति न्यायेन निर्भरतायामेव कारणं पर्यवस्यतीति निर्भरीकृतदशदिक्कमित्यर्थो लभ्यते। अथवा रअणिब्भरेति पाठः। चलितेन धराधररजसा निर्भरा दश दिशो यस्य तत्तथा।

R says तुलितैः उत्तोलितैः धराधरैः कृता निर्भराः पूर्णा दश दिशो येन। This and the next verse are missing in our copy of Kula.

28–29. अह णेण सुहप्फरिसे पिउणो सलिलम्मि मज्जिऊण सणिअमम्।
रामचरणाण पढमं पच्छा काऊण रविसुअस्स पणामम्।।

तो कअणधाउअम्बो सपल्लवासोअविडवभरिअदरिमुहो।
पढमं णलेण णिमिओ मङ्गलकलसो व्व जलणिहिम्मि महिहरो।।

(जुग्गअम्)

[अथानेन सुखस्पर्शे पितुः सलिले मङ्क्त्वा सनियमम्।
रामचरणयोः प्रथमं पश्चात्कृत्वा रविसुतस्य प्रणामम्।।

ततः कनकधात्वाताम्रः सपल्लवाशोकविटपभृतदरीमुखः।
प्रथमं नलेन नियोजितो मङ्गलकलश इव जलनिधौ महीधरः।।]
(युग्गकम्)

Thereupon, after a ceremonial bath in the pleasent waters of the sea, and paying obeisance first to his father,[23] and thereafter to Rāma's feet and to Sugrīva; Nala first planted in the ocean a mountain, red with gold and other minerals, with the mouths of the caves filled with leafy branches of *aśoka* trees, like an auspicious pitcher (of gold, decked with leafy *aśoka* twigs).

K and MY (*pratīka*) have *to ṇeha*. K reads the verse thus — ततः स्नेहसुखस्पर्शं पुनरपि सलिले मङ्क्त्वा सनियमं। रामचरणयोः प्रथमं पितुः कृत्वा सरित्पतेः प्रणामम्।। ततो नलेन सलिले समुद्रजले पुनरपि पुनः पुनः बहुशः स्नेहेन समुद्रगतेन सुखस्पर्शं यथा सनियमं च यथा निमज्य प्रथमं रामचरणयोः ततः पितुः विश्वकर्मणश्च अनन्तरं सरित्पतेश्च प्रणामं कृत्वा महीधरो निमित इत्युत्तरगाथया संबन्धः। MY says नियमो मनसः प्रणिधानम। K says नियमः प्राणायामादिः। *SC* says कुलनाथादिमते एतत् पद्यं नास्ति।

K and MY read *aha* for *to* (R and Kula).

30. तह पढमं विअ मुक्को वेलाअडसंठिओ णलेण महिहरो।
जह दीसिउं पउत्तं लङ्काणत्थस्स सेउबन्धस्स मुहम्।।

[तथा प्रथममेव मुक्तो बेलातटसंस्थितो नलेन महीधरः।
यथा द्रष्टुं प्रवृत्तं लङ्कानर्थस्य सेतुबन्धस्य मुखम्।।]

One of the mountains set down on the beach[24] was at the very outset dropped by Nala on the sea in such a way that the initial phase of the causeway that was to bring disaster to Laṅkā began to be seen.

K, Deva and MY read संश्रितः (*saṁsio*) for *saṁṭhio* (R and Kula)।

K says सेतुबन्धस्य मुखं यथा द्रष्टुमारब्धं लोकैरालोकितुमारब्धं तथा निक्षिप्तः।

[23] Viśvakarmā, the divine architect.

[24] See verse 2.

द्रष्टुमिति कर्मणि तुमुन्प्रत्ययः। MY says *dīsiuṁ* प्रकाशीभवितुम्। Deva says द्रष्टुमाविर्भवितुम्।

31. भमिओ अ तह धराहरपहरुच्छित्तसलिलो णहम्मि समुद्दो।
महिहररअमइलाइं जह धोआइ समअं दिसाण मुहाइं ।।

[भ्रमितश्च तथा धराधरप्रहारोत्क्षिप्तसलिलो नभसि समुद्रः।
महीधररजोमलिनानि यथा धौतानि समं दिशां मुखानि।

The sea, with the waters thrown up by the impact of the mountains (dropped by the apes), swirled in the sky in such a manner that the regions of the sky, grey with the dust of the mountains, were cleansed all at once.

K reads उच्चलित for *ucchitta* = उत्क्षिप्त।

32. जलतण्णाअघडन्ता अविभाविज्जन्तघडणमग्गोआसा।
ण मुअन्ति एक्कमेक्कं खुहिअसमुद्दविसमाहआ वि महिहरा।।

[जलार्द्रघटमाना अविभाव्यमानघटनमार्गावकाशाः।
न मुह्यन्त एकैकं क्षुभितसमुद्रविषमाहता अपि महीधराः।।]

Soaked in water, and clinging together, the mountains, with the join imperceptible, were not parted from each other, even though battered by the raging sea.

33. पडिवहपत्थिअसलिला वेलाअडपडिअमहिहरसमक्कन्ता।
जे च्चिअ अहिगममग्गा जाआ ते च्चेअ णिग्गमा वि णईणम्।।

[प्रतिपथप्रस्थितसलिला वेलातटपतितमहीधरसमाक्रान्ताः।
य एवाभिगममार्गा जातास्त एव निर्गमा अपि नदीनाम्।।]

Blocked by mountain dropped on the beach, the channels of the rivers by which they entered the sea became, in fact, outlets by which the waters flowed backwards.

The verse is not found in Kula.

MY says वेलापतितशैलाक्रान्ततया प्रतिस्रोतसः सन्तो य एव सरितां (समुद्र)प्रवेशमार्गाः त एव निर्गममार्गाः जाता इत्यर्थः।

34. णिवडन्ति तुङ्गसिहरा पवलविमुक्का अहोमुहा वि णलवहे।
भमिऊण मूलगरुआ जहेअ उम्मूलिआ तहेअ महिहरा।।

[निपतन्ति तुङ्गशिखराः प्लवगविमुक्ता अधोमुखा अपि नलपथे।
भ्रमित्वा मूलगुरुका यथैवोन्मूलिता तथैव महीधराः॥]

The mountains, even though released by the apes with the peaks downwards, turned over, being heavy at the base, and dropped on Nala's way,[25] with the peaks upwards, exactly in the position in which they were uprooted.

MY remarks हरिभिरधोमुखतया विमुक्ता अपि गिरयो भ्रमित्वा मूलगौरवादूर्ध्वशिखराः सन्तो मूलैरपतन्नित्यर्थः। K says नलपथे सेतावधोमुखाः प्लवगैः विमुक्ता अपि तुङ्गशिखरा मूले गुरवः पर्वताः नभसि भ्रान्त्वा विपयर्स्य मूलगुरुत्वात् ऊर्ध्वमुखा एवापतन् इत्यर्थः।

35. विहुणेन्ति विहुव्वन्ता करिमअरमुहाइ थिरणिहित्तणहमुहा।
मुहपज्जत्तदढुक्खअकुम्भअडभमन्तकेसरा केसरिणो॥

[विधूनयन्ति विधूयमानाः करिमकरमुखानि स्थिरनिहितनखमुखाः।
मुखपर्याप्तदृढोत्खातकुम्भतटभ्रमत्केसराः केसरिणः॥]

The lions,[26] tossed by the sea elephants, shook up the latter's faces, firmly thrusting their claws into them; while their mane moved about the temples (of the sea elephants), which were severely mangled and swallowed up in their mouths.

Kula says स्थिरनिहितानि दृढमारोपितानि नखमुखानि यैस्ते तथा। मुखेषु पर्याप्ताः (संमिताः *SC*) दृढोत्खाता ये कुम्भतटाः तेषु भ्रमन्तः केशरा येषां ते केशरिणः करिमकरमुखानि विधुन्वन्ति। विधूयमानाः करिमकरैरेव इत्यर्थात्। R says मुखे पर्याप्तं पूर्णं दृढं यथा स्यादेवमुत्खातं कवलीकृतं, etc.

36. पडिगअगन्धपसारिअकरिमअरच्छिण्णगलिअकरपब्भारे।
जाणन्ति णवर कुविआ लवणजलालिद्धवणमुहे वणहत्थी॥

[प्रतिगजगन्धप्रसारितकरिमकरच्छिन्नगलितकरप्राग्भारान्।
जानन्ति केवलं कुपिता लवणजलाश्लिष्टव्रणमुखान्वनहस्तिनः॥]

The infuriated wild elephants (on the mountains) became aware that their massive trunks, stretched out at the smell of their adversaries, the sea elephants, were torn away by the latter, only when the wounds came into contact with the briny water of the sea.

---

25 The causeway is thus designated in honour of Nala.

26 Those tumbling off the mountains into sea.

K reads व्रणमुखाः for °*muhe* = मुखान् (R, Deva and Kula). K *chāyā* translates *āliddha* as आलीढ।[27] R has अश्लिष्ट। Kula says करिमकरैः छिन्नाः सन्तो गलिता ये करप्राग्भाराः तान् लवणजलेनादिग्धं स्पृष्टं व्रणमुखं येषां तान् तथाभूतान् केवलं वनहस्तिनो जानन्ति क्रोधविद्रुतत्वादित्याशयः।

37. दरघडिअसेउबन्धा उप्पइऊण पवआ समुद्दुप्पइए।
कड्ढन्ति जमलकरअलसंदाणिअवक्खसंपुडे धरणिहरे।।

[दरघटितसेतुबन्धा उत्पत्य प्लवगाः समुद्रोत्पतितान्।
कर्षन्ति यमलकरतलसंदानितपक्षसंपुटान्धरणीधरान्।।]

Having built a position of the causeway, the apes flew aloft, and dragged down the submarine mountains as they flew out of the sea, grasping their wings with both their hands.[28]

38. बन्धर णलो वि तक्खणविसमुच्छलिअचलकेसरसडुग्घाओ।
तिअवलिअकरपसारिअहरिहत्थुक्खित्तमहिहरो सेउवहम्।।

[बध्नाति नलोऽपि तत्क्षणविषमोच्छलितचलकेसरसटोद्धातः।
त्रिकवलितकरप्रसारितहरिहस्तोत्क्षिप्तमहीधरः सेतुपथम्।।]

With the streaming mass of his hair ruffled up at the moment, Nala, too, put the causeway together as he lifted the mountains from the outstretched hands of the apes with his hands curved beside his hips.

K, Deva and MY read उच्चलित for *ucchalia* (R). K reads बहु for चल। He and Deva read प्रसारण for *pasāria* (R and Kula). K, MY and Kula read आक्षिप्त (*akkhitta*) for *ukkhitta* उक्षिप्त (R). K says नलोऽपि त्रिकप्रदेशे वलितयोः करयोः प्रसारणेन हरिहस्तेभ्य आक्षिप्तमहधरः सन् सेतुपथमबध्नात्। Kula says त्रिकप्रदेशेन प्रसारिताभ्यां कराभ्यां प्रसारितेभ्यो हरिहस्तेभ्य आक्षिप्ता महीधरा येन स तथा। Deva says क्षिप्तमहीधरः कपिहस्तैर्दत्तमहीधरः।

39. जं बहुपव्वअजणिअं विच्छूढसमुद्दपाअडं महिविवरम्।
तं एक्को पडिरुम्भइ वित्थारब्भहिअसंठिओ धरणिहरो।।

---

[27] K says वनहस्तिनः प्रतिगजमदगन्धाघ्राणात् प्रसारितान् तदानीं करिमकरैः छिन्नत्वात् गलितान् करप्राग्भारान् करविस्तारान् केवलं लवणजलस्पृष्टव्रणमुखाः जानन्ति। पूर्वे कोपपारवश्यात् छिन्नगलितानपि हस्तान् अजानन्तः सद्यो लवणजलस्पृष्टव्रणमुखाः सन्तः केवलमजानन् इत्यर्थः।

[28] See 5.51 for a similar picture. Here, the winged mountains try to escape from the sea to avoid being crushed by the causeway.

[यद्बहुपर्वतजनितं विक्षिप्तसमुद्रप्रकटं महीविवरम्।
तदेकः प्रतिरुणद्धि विस्तराभ्यधिकसंस्थितो धरणीधरः।।]

When a cavity at the bottom, caused by the numerous mountains (dropped by the apes), was discovered in the heaving sea, it was covered up by a single mountain, larger in extent, and fixed firm (by Nala).

K says पूर्वं वानरक्षिप्तैः बहुभिः पर्वतैः जनितं, विक्षिप्ते विधूते समुद्रे प्रकटं यन्महीविवरम् अधस्तान्महीतलस्पर्शि विवरं तत् नलेन विस्ताराभ्यधिकसंस्थितः मूलविस्तारेण (?) अभ्यधिकं स्थापित एक एव पर्वतः प्रतिरुणद्धि छादयति स्म। R says (विक्षिप्ते ?) पतत्पर्वतैः द्विधाभूते समुद्रे प्रकटं व्यक्तम्।

40. साअरलद्धत्थाहं णिमेन्ति जं जं धराहरं कइणिवहा।
बज्जइ पुरओ हुत्तो काऊण पअं तहिं तहिं सेतुवहो।।

[सागरलब्धस्थाघं नियोजयन्ति यं यं धराधरं कपिनिवहाः।
बध्यते पुरतोऽभिमुखः कृत्वा पदं तत्र तत्र सेतुपथः।।]

As the apes fixed each mountain that reached to the bottom of the sea, Nala, planting his foot thereon, built the causeway further and further.

K, Deva and MY read *thāma* for *thāha* (R and Kula). See 15.19 below, लब्धस्थामानं (K *chāyā*); लब्धस्थैर्यम् (K Comm.). लब्धस्थेमानम् MY (B has लब्धस्थानम्)। Deva says लब्धस्थेम लब्धस्थैर्यं यथा तथा निपिन्वन्ति निक्षिपन्ति (K also) आरोपयन्ति Kula. MY says सागरगाढमूल-निष्प्रकम्पान् महत्तरान् महीधरान पुरतोऽवस्थितानालम्ब्यालम्ब्य पदं तेषु कृत्वैव सेतुः शीघ्रमगच्छदिवेत्यर्थः। He seems to read *vajjai* or *vaccai* (व्रजति) for *bajjhai* (बध्यते). K says कपिनिवहाः सागरे लब्धस्थैर्यं यं यं पर्वतं निक्षिपन्ति सेतुपथः तस्मिन् पदं कृत्वा पुरतोमुखो बध्यते स्म।

R says पुरतोऽभिमुखः अग्निमाग्रिमः सेतुपथो नलेन बध्यते।

41. समअं पवअविमुक्के सेउवहम्मि समअं अभाअपडन्ते।
परिपेल्लेइ रएइ अ समअं च णलो पडिच्छिऊण महिहरे।।

[समकं प्लवगविमुक्तान्सेतुपथे समकमभागपततः।
प्रतिप्रेरयति रचयति च समकं च नलो प्रतीक्ष्य महीधरान्।।]

Receiving the mountains (accurately) released by the apes as well as those dropping at the wrong place in the causeway,

Nala put them in position and joined them together, all at once.

पर्वतान् नलश्च सममेव प्रतीष्य प्रतिगृह्य प्रतिपीडति यथास्थानं निवेशयति स्म K. समकालमेवापीडयत् स्थानस्थितानकरोदिति MY.

42. अवलम्बइ णलघडिए अभाअवलिआणिए घडेइ महिहरे।
सेउवहस्स समुद्दो उव्वेलन्तसलिलो पवड्ढइ पुरओ।।

[अवलम्बते नलघटितानभागवलितान्घटयति महीधरान्।
सेतुपथस्य समुद्र उद्वेलसलिलः प्रवर्धते पुरतः।।]

The sea supported the mountains set firmly together by Nala, and brought into position those dropping at the wrong place; while it surged in front of the causeway with a heavy swell.

K and Deva read प्रवर्तते (*pavaṭṭai*) for *pavaḍḍhai* (R and Kula). K and Kula read पतित for *valia* (R). K says समुद्रः नलेन घाटितान् पर्वतान् अवलम्बते स्म न पुनरधः पातयति स्म। अस्थाने पतितान् पुनरानीतान् गिरीन् स्थाने घटयति स्म। सेतुपथस्य पुरतो मार्गं प्रदर्शयन् उद्वेल्लत्सलिलः प्रचलत्सलिलो भूत्वा पुरतः प्रावर्तत। . . . समुद्रः सेतुपथस्य आनुकूल्यमकरोदित्यर्थः।

43. जं जं आणेइ गिरिं रहिरहचक्कपरिमट्टसिहरं हणुमा।
तं तं लीलाइ णलो वामकरुत्थम्बिअं रएइ समुद्दे।।

[यं यमानयति गिरिं रविरथचक्रपरिमृष्टशिखरं हनूमान्।
तं तं लीलया नलो वामकरोत्तम्भितं रचयति समुद्रे।।]

As Hanumat brought each mountain, with its summit worn by the wheel of the sun's chariot,[29] Nala fixed it in position in the sea as he lifted it with his left hand with ease.

K (both *chāyā* and comm.) says वामकरेण गृहीहतम्। R (*chāyā*) has उत्तम्भितम् renderd as उत्थापितम्। This corresponds to the reading *utthambhiaṁ* mentioned by Goldschmidt who reads *utthaṁghiaṁ*. Kula says वामकरेण उत्स्थलितम्[30] उत्तोलितम्। He seems to read *utthalliaṁ*.[31] Besides he reads प्लवगाः for *Haṇumā* and says यं यं गिरिं प्लवगा आनयन्ति (*āṇenti*)।

---

[29] Indicates the height of the mountain.

[30] Our copy has उत्थलितं।

[31] This reading is found in *SC* text.

44. वित्थअसरकमलसिरे सेले दरघडिअसेउसंकमलसिरे।
जलणिहिसेआलग्गा पाआलधरा धरेन्ति सेआलग्गा।।

[विस्तृतसर:कमलशिरस: शैला दरघटितसेतुसंक्रमलसनशीलान्।
जलनिधिसेवालग्ना: पातालधरा धारयन्ति शैवालाग्र्या:।।]

The mountains of the nether regions, devoted to the service of the ocean, and crowned with moss, sustained the mountains tottering in the partly built causeway, with extensive lotus beds in the pools on their summit.

लसनान् प्रचलत: शैलान् K. लसनशीलान् Kula. स्खलनोद्यतान् *SC.*

45. बेलाअडसंबद्धा गओणिअत्तन्तजलरअविहुव्वन्ती।
हल्लन्तकिरणविडवा अन्दोलइ मरगअप्पहावणराई।।

[बेलातटसंबद्धा गतापनिवर्तमानजलरयविधूयमाना।
लसत्किरविटपा आन्दोल्यते मरकतप्रभावनराजी।।]

Starting from the margin of the beach, the emerald-green stretch of woods (on the mountains of the causeway), with the glistening branches, swayed as it was rocked by the rush of waters moving back and forth.

K says निपततां शैलान् क्षोभेण गतानां प्रणुन्नानां पुनरपनिवर्तमानानां च जलानां रयेण विधूयमाना, वेलातटे संबद्धा, वेपमानकिरणमयविटपा मरतकप्रभाख्या वनराजिरान्दोलति प्रेङ्खोलति स्म। MY says सेतुपथस्य उभयपार्श्वयो: प्ररूढवनराजिरिवान्तर्गतमरकतगिरिप्रभा समुच्चलन्ती जलरयेणाघूर्णतेत्यर्थ:। वेलातट: पर्यन्तसलिलप्रदेश:।

R says यद्वा मरकतवत् प्रभाशस्या इति हरिद्वर्णा वनराजी सेतुपर्वतोपरिस्था आन्दोल्यते।

Kula says वेला जलविकृति: वेला समुद्रतट:, अथवा वेलैव तट: (तत्र संबद्धा) . . . मरकतप्रभा: वनानि च, अथवा मरकतप्रभा एव वनानि तेषां राजि: पंक्ति:, हल्लन्त: प्रेङ्खन्त: विरला: विटपा: यद्वा किरणा एव विटपा यस्या: सा तथा आन्दोलायते सततं गतिं करोति। प्रभा: किरणद्युतय:।

R says 'हल्लन्त' इति लसदर्थे देशी।

46. दन्तेसु बलिअलग्गा खोहुप्पित्थगअसंपहारुक्खित्ता।
करिमअराण भुअंगा पडन्ति कालासमण्डलपडिच्छन्दा।।

[दन्तेषु वलितलग्ना क्षोभोद्विग्नगजसंप्रहारोत्क्षिप्ताः।
करिमकराणां भुजंगा पतन्ति कालायसमण्डलप्रतिच्छन्दाः॥]

The serpents coiled about the tusks of the sea elephants, and looking like iron rings, fell to the ground when they were tossed up during the latter's fight with the elephants (on the mountains), scared by the commotion of the sea.

K says करिमकराणा दन्तेषु भयेन वलितलग्नाः, क्षोभत्रस्तैः पर्वतगजैः सह संप्रहारे सति दूरमुत्क्षिप्ता भुजंगाः तथैव वलितरूपा दन्तेषु मण्डनार्थं प्रत्युप्तकालायसवलयनिभा भूत्वा पतन्ति स्म।

47. पव्वअवडनाइद्धो जो चिअ उअहिस्सा डिणिअत्तइ पडमम्।
सो चिअ सलिलद्धन्तो अण्णोहुतविसमं वलेइ णलवहम्॥

[पर्वतपतनाविद्धो य एवोदधेः प्रतिनिवर्तते प्रथमम्।
स एव सलिधार्धान्तोऽन्यतोऽभिमुखविषमं वलयति नलपथम्॥]

The volume of sea water that returned after being driven far afield by the falling mountains was the first to adjust Nala's way when it inclined in another direction.[32]

K says पर्वतपतनैराविद्धः उदधेः यः सलिलार्धान्तो दूरं प्रेरितः स एव प्रतिनिवर्तमानो नलपथम् अभिघातात् अन्यतोमुखं चलयति स्म। K *chāyā* has वलयति।

Kula says पर्वतपतनेन आविद्धः क्षिप्तः य एवोदधेः सलिलैकदेशः प्रतिनिवर्तते स एव अन्याभिमुखविषमं नलपथं सेतु प्रथमं वलयति प्रगुणयति, पश्चान्नल इत्यर्थः।

48. खुहिअसमुद्दस्थमिआ खुडेन्ति अक्खुडिअमअजलोज्झरपसरा।
चलणालग्गभुअंगे पासे व्व णिराअकड्डिए माअङ्गा॥

[क्षुभितसमुद्रास्तमिताः खण्डयन्त्यखण्डितमदजलनिर्झरप्रसराः।
चरणालग्नभुजंगान्पाशानिव निरायतकृष्टान्मातङ्गाः॥]

The elephants half submerged in the heaving waters, with their ichor streaming freely, tore the serpents clingnig to their feet, like ropes, stretching and pulling them (with their trunks).[33]

K, Deva and Kula read जलार्ध (*jaladdha*) for *samudda* (R). K says क्षुभिते जले अर्धमस्तमिताः, अखण्डितमदजलनिर्झरप्रसरा मातङ्गाः। MY reads *khuḍanti* for °*ḍe*° = त्रोटयन्ति छिन्दन्ति K; खण्डयन्ति R and Kula.

---

[32] Illustrates the co-operation of the sea. Cf. verse 42.

[33] Literally stretched and pulled.

49. रअणच्छविविमलअरा फलरसभरिअदरभिण्णमरगअणिवहा।
ओधुव्वन्ति तरङ्गा चुणिअसङ्खउलपण्डुरअरफेणा।।
[रत्नच्छविविमलतराः फलरसहरितदरभिन्नमरकतनिवहाः।
अवधूयन्ते तरङ्गाश्चूर्णितशङ्खकुलपाण्डुरतरफेनाः।।]

The waves rolled, made brighter by the lustre of the gems, with the broken emeralds greener in contact with the juice of the fruits (dropping from the trees on the mountains), and the foam made whiter by the shattered conchshells.

Deva reads भरिततर (*bharia-ara*) for *bharia-dara* (R Text). He says फलरसो मरकतनिवहश्च तरङ्गेशु वर्तन्ते . . . फलरसात् भरिततरो मरकतनिवहः प्रतिभाति।

K and probably Kula read हरिततर for *bharia-dara*.

K reads अवक्षुभ्यन्ति for *odhuvvanti* = अवधूयन्ते (R and kula) R says तरङ्गा अवधूयन्ते गिरिपतनेन दिशि दिशि नीयन्ते। K says क्षुण्णानां पर्वतवृक्षफलानां रसैः भ(ह ?)रिततराःश्यामलतराः भिन्ना मिश्रिताः मरकतनिवहा येषु ते (तरङ्गाः). R has हरितदर and says फलरसैः हरिंताः किंचित् किंचित् खण्डिता मरकतनिवहा येषु। Kula also has हरित। MY reads *ohuppanti* for *odhuvvanti*, and first renders it as अभ्यभवन्। He says रत्नच्छायादिना पूर्वतोऽतिशयितवैमल्यादियोगिनो भूत्वा तरङ्गाः सेतुमाक्रामन्नित्यर्थः। Then he says अथवा उपर्युच्चलितरत्नप्रभाभिः शोभातिशयमुपजनयन्तीभिरभ्यमृयन्त। तरङ्गाः तिरस्कृतनिजरूपशोभा अक्रियन्तेत्यर्थः। *SC* text has *ohuvvanti* = अवधूयन्ते।

Kula is somewhat corrupt, but seems to says रत्नानां माणिक्यादीनां या छविः द्यूतिः तया विमलतराः, गलितानां फलानां रसैः हरिततरा (?) भिन्नाः चूर्णिता मरकतनिवहा येषु, चूर्णितैः शङ्खकुलैः पाण्डरतरा अतिधवलाः फेना येषु ते तरङ्गाः शैलसंप्रहारवशात्(?) अवधूयन्ते।

50. घडमाणेहि अ समअं झिज्जइ सेलेहि जेत्तिअं चिअ उअही।
उच्छलइ तेत्तिअं चिअ उत्थङ्घिअमूलसलिलपरिपूरन्ती।।
[घटमानैश्च समं क्षीयते शैलैर्यावन्मात्रमेवोदधिः।
उच्छलति तावन्मात्रमेवोत्तम्भितमूलसलिलपरिपूर्यमाणः।।]

Replenished by the waters surging from the bottom, the sea swelled as much as it sank under the weight of the mountains set firmly together.

Kula reads जीयते (*jivvai*, *SC* text) for *jaijjai* = क्षीयते। He says समं घटमाने . . . अन्योन्यं मिलिद्भिः शैलैरुदधिः यावदेव जीयते (सेतुवर्त्मनाक्रम्यते *SC*)।

K reads अपि (*vi*) for a = च (R). K and MY read उत्स्थलति (*utthalai* according to MY) for *ucchalai* उच्छलति (R and Kula). MY says सरभसक्षिप्तैः शैलैः समन्ततो वेगविधुतसलिलतया तत्प्रवृत्तेः प्राक् यावत् क्षीयते तावत् मूलसलिलप्रतिपूर्यमाणः पूर्वतोऽप्यधिकमुत्स्थलीबभूव। K says समं घटमानैरपि पर्वतैः उदधिः यावदेव क्षीयते स्म तेषां कन्दरादिभिः ग्रस्यमानजलः समुद्रो यावत्प्रमाणं क्षीयते, उत्तम्भितैः मूलसलिलैः पूर्यमाणः तावदेव उत्स्थलति अवर्धत।[34] Deva has उच्चलति उद्गच्छति।

51. उद्धप्फुडिअणइमुहा णिअअट्ठाणसिढिलोसरन्तमहिहरा।
अन्दोलन्तसमुद्दा अन्दोलन्ति व णहं धरणिसंखोहा।।

[ऊर्ध्वस्फुटितनदीमुखा निजकस्थानशिथिलापसरन्महीधराः।
आन्दोलत्समुद्रा आन्दोलयन्तीव नभो धरणिसंक्षोभाः।।]

Earthquakes seemed to rock the heavens, making the ocean rock; while the waters of the rivers entering the sea were scattered high in the air, and the mountains tottered in their foundations.[35]

K, MY and Deva read अर्ध for *uddha* (R and Kula)। अर्धे स्फुटितनदीप्रवाहाः K. स्फुटितैकदेशसरिन्मुखाः MY.

52. अद्धुट्ठिअसेउवहं होइ खणं अद्धदिण्णहरिहिअअसुहम्।
अद्धोवइअमहिहरं अद्धोसारिअरसाअलं उअहिजलम्।।

[अर्धोत्थितसेतुपथं भवति क्षणमर्धदत्तहरिहृदयसुखम्।
अर्धावपातितमहीधरमर्धापसारितरसातलमुदधिजलम्।।]

With half of the causeway emerging, and half of the mountains dropped on the sea, and half of the sea floor[36] covered up[37] the waters of the ocean gave for a moment partial[38] joy to the hearts of the apes.

---

[34] K remarks अयमत्र समाधिः – सममेव घटमानैः चेष्टमानैः बहुभिरपि यः पूर्यमाणः प्रथमं क्षीयते स पुनर्मूलपुरुषैः आपूर्यमाणः सन् प्रवृद्धो भवतीति। *SC* says बहुपर्वतपूरितोदरत्वात् उत्थापितमूलसलिलेन प्रतिपूर्यमाणः तावदेव उच्छलति वर्धते।

[35] The verse describes the convulsions of nature that took place when the mountains were cast into the sea.

[36] Literally the nether regions.

[37] I.e. by the mountains. Literally removed, or ecliped.

[38] Because the causeway was not yet complete.

समुद्रस्य जलं क्षणमात्रमर्धविरचितसेतुपथम्, अर्धप्रतिपादितवानरहृदयसुखम्, अर्धपतितपर्वतमर्धतिरोहितपातालं च बभूव K.

53. णिम्माओ त्ति मुणिज्जइ दूराइद्धम्मि साअरे सेतुवहो।
सो चिअ सलिलभरन्तो थोआरद्धो व्व दीसइ णिअत्तन्ते।।

[निर्मित इति ज्ञायते दूराविद्धे सागरे सेतुपथः।
स एव सलिलभ्रियमाणः स्तोकारब्ध इव दृश्यते निवर्तमाने।।]

When the sea was driven afar off,[39] the causeway appeared to be built;[40] but when it was flooded as the sea returned, it looked as if it had been just[41] begun.

समुद्रे पर्वतपतनरभसेन दूराविद्धे सति K. दूरं व्याप्यविद्धे प्ररिते R. अपवारिते Kula.

54. अवि पूरइ पाआलं ण अ कुविअदिसागइन्दगमणविहाआ।
उअहिविइण्णोआसा पूरेन्ति महावराहपअणिक्खेवा।।

[अपि पूर्यते पातालं न च कुपितदिग्गजेन्द्रगमनविघाताः।
उदधिवितीर्णावकाशाः पूर्यन्ते महावराहपदनिक्षेपाः।।]

Even the nether regions were filled by the mountains, but not the footprints of the Great Boar,[42] which pervaded the ocean, and impeded the movements of the irate elephants of the quarters.[43]

पर्वतैः पातालमपि पूर्यते। कुपितानां मिथोयुद्धाय कुपितानां दिग्गजेन्द्राणां गमनस्य विघ्नकारिणः, उदधौ विततावकाशाः महावराहस्य पदनिक्षेपाः न पूर्यन्ते स्म K. उदधिवितीर्णावकाशा उदधेरपि गाम्भीर्यदायिन इत्यर्थः MY. उदधये वितीर्णो दत्तः अवकाशः स्थानं यैः ते महावराहपदनिक्षेपाः। एतेन समुद्रादपि अतिगाम्भीर्यमुक्तम Kula.

55. जाअं महिहरमहिअं धातुअडक्खलणसरसपल्लवराअम्।
दुमभङ्गतुवरसुरहिं उप्पज्जन्तमइरं व साअरसलिलम्।।

[जातं महीधरमथितं धातुतटस्खलनसरसपल्लवरागम्।
द्रुमभङ्गतुवरसुरभि उत्पद्य[मान]मदिरमिव सागरसलिलम्।।]

---

39 I.e. by the falling mountains.

40 I.e. the portion built was clearly visible.

41 Literally slightly.

42 The Boar incarnation of Viṣṇu. See 5.44.

43 Supposed to hold up the earth.

Churned up by the mountains, the waters of the sea, which assumed the colour of the young shoots of plants[44] by dashing against the slopes of the mountains rich in minerals, and were astringent to the taste and fragrant in contact with the broken trees, seemed to be producing wine (as in days of old).[45]

K says निपतद्भिः महीधरैः मथितं क्षोभितम्, अन्यत्र मन्दरेण मथितम्। धातुतटेषु स्खलनेन सरसोऽभिनवः पल्लवरागः किसलयवर्णो यस्य तत्। द्रुमाणां चन्दनादीनां भङ्गेन तुवरं कषायरसं सुरभि सुगन्धि च सागरसलिलं तदानीमुत्पद्यमानमदिरमिव जातम्। मथने सति अमृतात् पूर्वं मदिरा समुत्पन्ना। सा तु रक्तवर्णा सुरभिगन्धिश्च भवति।

56. संचालेइ समुद्दो जह जह विरलट्ठिअं धराहरणिवहम्।
तह तह विराअसिहरो पूरिअविवरत्थिरो घडइ सेउवहो।।

[संचालयति समुद्रो यथा यथा विरलस्थितं धराधरनिवहम्।
तथा तथा विशीर्णशिखरः पूरितविवरस्थिरो घटते सेतुपथः।।]

Whilst the sea rocked the mountains standing apart in the causeway, it became compact as the peaks crumbled and filled up the gaps.

K says सेतौ विरलस्थितं पर्वतनिवहं समुद्रो यथा यथा चालयति, तथा विलीनशिखरः सन् सेतुपथो घटते श्लिष्टोऽभूत। Kula says विशीर्णैः शिखरैरवपूरितविवरः स्थिरः सेतुपथः। He reads *siharopūria* for *siharo pūria*. K *chāyā* has पूरितविवरस्थितः for *–tthiro*

57. पडइ णु णहअलघडिओ कड्ढिज्जइ णु मलआहि चिरणिम्माओ।
घडइ णु समुद्दसलिले घडिओ णीह णु रसाअलाहि णलवहो।।

[पतति नु नभस्तलघटितः कृष्यते नु मलयाच्चिरनिर्मितः।
घटते नु समुद्रसलिले घटितो निरेति नु रसातलान्नलपथः।।]

Did Nala's Way[46] drop on the sea, fashioned in the sky? Built long ago, was it hauled from the Malaya mountain? Did it come into being in the waters of the sea? Did it emerge from the nether regions, complete in structure?

ṇīi = निर्यात K; निर्गच्छति Kula; निरेति R.

---

[44] I.e. were coloured red.

[45] Wine was one of the objects produced by the churning of the ocean. See verse 15.

[46] Cf. verse 34.

58. गअणम्मि उअहिसलिलं सलिलविमुक्के रसाअलम्मि णहअलम्।
दीसइ तीसु वि समअं णहसलिलरसाअलेसु पव्वअजालम्।।

[गगने उदधिसलिलं सलिलविमुक्ते रसातले नभस्तलम्।
दृश्यते त्रिष्वपि समं नभःसलिलरसातलेषु पर्वतजालम्।।]

The waters of the sea were seen in the sky, and the sky on the sea floor emptied of the waters,[47] but the mountains[48] in the sky and the waters and on the sea floor, in all three alike.

59. वेलालाणणिअलिओ रसिऊण रसाअलट्ठिअं पि समुद्दो।
चालेइ सेउबन्धं खम्भं आरण्णकुञ्जरो व्व वलन्तो।।

[वेलालाननिगलि(डि)तो रसित्वा रसातलस्थितमपि समुद्रः।
चालयति सेतुबन्धं स्तम्भमारण्यकुञ्जर इव वलन्।।]

The rolling sea, restrained by the shore as by a chain, roared and rocked the causeway, even though it reached into the nether regions, like as a wild elephant, moving to and fro, bellows and shakes the post to which it is tied.

K reads सलिलनिधिः for *pi samuddo* (R and Kula). K (*pratīka*) has वेलानाल (MY also, but with ण as recorded by Vararuci 4.29 and Hemacandra 2 .117. R has वेलालाण। K says वेलानालेन वेलामयेन शृङ्खलेन[49] निगलितो वलमानः समुद्रः। MY says अत्रालानत्वं वेलाया पादनिगलस्थानीयप्रतिबन्धहेतुतयेति सेतुबन्धात्मना स्तम्भेन न पौनरुक्त्याशङ्केति रहस्यम्। आलानो गजबन्धस्तम्भः। निगलितः संजातनिगलः। निगलः पादबन्धः। आरण्यकुञ्जर इति नवग्रह इति विशेषः।

60. पेल्लिज्जन्ति दढअरं जह जह पवएहि खुहिअजलतण्णाआ।
ओहट्टन्ताआमा तह तह एक्कक्कमं अइन्ति महिहरा।।

[प्रेर्यन्ते दृढतरं यत्र यत्र प्लवगैः क्षुभितजलार्द्राः।
अपसरदायामास्तत्र तत्रैकैकमायान्ति महीधराः।।

---

47 I.e. the empty seafloor looked like the sky when the waters were hurled up by the falling mountains. Cf. 7.31.

48 I.e. the mountains dropped by the apes on sea from above, and reaching to the bottom.

49 Kula says वेला कूलं सैवालानं शृङ्खलादिरूपम्। *SC* says आलानपदेन रज्जुरप्युच्यते . . .। आलानं बन्धस्तम्भ इत्यत्रामरटीकायां समाहारं कृत्वा बन्धनरज्जौ स्तम्भे चेति व्याख्यातम्।

As the mountains, soaked in the heaving waters, were firmly pressed together by the apes, they adhered to each other, shrinking in dimensions.

तथा तथा एकैकं यन्ति K (*chāyā*). K says सेतौ पतिता: पर्वता: प्लवगैर्यथा यथा दृढतरं पीड्यन्ते नुद्यन्ते, क्षुभितैर्जलै: आर्द्राभ्यन्तरा: वर्धमानायामा भूत्वा तथा तथा परस्परं श्लिष्यन्ति स्म। MY says परिवर्धमानायामा:। *ainti* अत्यायन् प्राविशन्नित्यर्थ:। K and MY seem to read *āvaḍḍhanta* for *ohaṭṭanta* = अपसरत् (R). *āḍhanta* in MY seems to be a scribal error. Kula is corrupt, but *SC* renders *ohaṭṭanta* as अवघट्टमान-अवघट्टमानायामा निष्पीडनात् विगलद्विस्तारा एकैकमायान्ति (R and Kula also) अन्योन्यं श्लिष्यन्ति।

61. पवअभुअगलत्थल्लिआ विप्पइण्णरअणा धरणिहरा पडन्ति भअचुण्णइंणरअणा।
खुहिओ साअरो रसई उण्णअं ण ईणं मोअन्तो व्व तिव्वभअउण्णअं णईणम्।।

[प्लवगभुजगलहसिता विप्रकीर्णरत्ना धरणिधरा: पतन्ति भयचूर्णकिंनरगणा:।
क्षुभित: सागरो रसति उन्नतं न दीनं मोचयन्निव तीव्रभयपूर्णतां नदीनाम्।।]

Pushed by the arms of the apes, the mountains dropped into the sea, scattering its gems, with the *kinnaras* living on them crazed with fear. Boldly, not meekly, did the boisterous ocean roar, as if it were dispelling the panic fear of the rivers.[50]

K seems to read *puṇṇa* or *uṇṇa* for *cuṇṇa* = चूर्ण (R). K says भयपूर्ण। MY has भयाक्रान्त। Kula and SC read *hittha* = आविग्न Kula; व्याकुल *SC*.[51]

K says प्लवगभुजै: प्रणुन्ना: (नुन्ना MY), विप्रकीर्ण (रत्ना:), भयपूर्णशिखरस्थकिंनरगणा: पर्वता: पतन्ति स्म। क्षुभित: सागरो नदीनां भार्याणां भयपूर्णतां मोचयन्निव उन्नतं रसति स्म। न तु दीनं रसति स्म।

62. भरइ व दूराइद्धो धुव्वइ व पडन्तधरणिहरकद्दमिओ।
रुम्भइ व पडिणिअत्तो भिण्णो घडइ व मणिप्पहाहि समुद्दो।।

[भ्रियत इव दूराविद्धो धाव्यत इव पतद्धरणिधरकर्दमित:।
रुध्यत इव प्रतिनिवृत्तो भिन्नो घटत इव मणिप्रभाभि: समुद्र:।।]

When the sea was driven afar off,[52] it seemed to be filled with the rays of its gems; while it seemed to be impeded by them

[50] Supposed to be the ocean's wives.

[51] In our copy Kula has only हि।

[52] I.e. by the falling mountains. Cf. verse 53.

when it returned.[53] Bespattered with mud by the mountains as they dropped, it seemed to be cleansed by the rays; and when it parted asunder, it seemed to be closed up by them.

Kula says पर्वतघातेन दूरमाविद्धोऽपसारितजलः समुद्रः मणिप्रभाभिः भ्रियत इव। . . . भिन्नो भिदां लम्भितो घटत इव निर्विबाधो भवतीव। भ्रियत इव पूर्यत इव R. घटत इव एकीभवतीव R; संहित इवासित् K.

63. करिमअराण खुहिअसाअरविसासिआणं
सेउवहम्मि पडिअगिरिणिवहविसासिआणम्।
समअं वणगआण णिवहा धरोसिआणं
समुहं आवडन्ति मअगन्धरोसिआणम्।।

[करिमकराणां क्षुभितसागरविषाश्रितानां
सेतुपथे पतितगिरिनिवहविशासितानाम्।
समकं वनगजानां निवहा धरोषितानां
संमुखमापतन्ति मदगन्धरोषितानाम्।।]

The herds of elephants on the mountains of the causeway, maimed by the mountains that dropped on the bridge, confronted in a body the sea elephants abiding in the heaving waters, because they were enraged at the smell of their ichor.

K reads विषे श्रितानां and विष्लेषितानां (i.e. *visesiāṇaṁ*) for *visāsiāṇaṁ* (R and Kula). MY's reading is same as K's, but his explanation is somewhat different. K and My read रव for *ṇivaha* (R) in the second line, while Kula and *SC* text read वर। K says सेतुपथे पतितगिरिरवेण विश्लेषितानां, धरेषु पर्वतेषु नित्युमुषितानां, करिगकराणां मदगन्धेन रोषितानां वनगजानां निवहाः क्षुभितस्य सागरस्य विषे जले श्रितानां करिमकराणां संमुखमापतन्ति स्म। MY has करिमकराणां क्षुभितसागरस्य विषेऽनले (जले B) श्रितानां, सेतुपथे पतितगिरिरवेण विशेषितानां जनितविकाराणां, etc. Kula says करिमकराणं क्षुभितस्य सागरस्य विषं जलमाश्रितानां, सेतुपथे पतितैर्गिरिवरैर्विशेषण प(पा ?)तितानां[54] मदगन्धवासितानां संमुखं धरेषु पर्वतेषु (वा)सितानां (?) वनगजानां (च) समूहाः समं तुल्यमापतन्ति[55]। Kula seems to read वासित for *rosia* in the last two lines.

---

[53] I.e. the waters seemed to pass slowly through a compact mass of rays.

[54] *SC* has विशेषेण शासितानां धर्षितानाम्।

[55] Cf. R — करिमकराणां वनगजानां च निवहाः सममेकदैव संमुखमापतन्ति। युद्धाय परस्परमभिमुखीभवन्तीत्यर्थः।

64. उत्थङ्घिअदुमणिवहा सुइरं परिमलिअसेउवहपासल्ला।
धाउकलङ्कक्खउरा दूरं गन्तूण उद्वमन्ति तरङ्गा:।।

[उत्थापितद्रुमनिवहा: सुचिरं परमृदितसेतुपथपार्श्वा:।
धातुकलङ्ककलुषा दूरं गत्वा उद्वमन्ति तरङ्गा:।।]

Having long battered the sides of the causeway, and thrown up the trees, the waves, tinged with the colour of the minerals,[56] died away after rolling far into the sea.

MY reads *utthaṁghia* (explained उत्तम्भित) for *uttaṁghia* (see Goldschmidt) = उत्थापित (R and *SC*). K (*pratīka*) has *uttaṁvia* (*uttaṁbhia* ?), rendered as उत्तंभित found in Kula also.[57] K says (उद्वमन्ति) तरङ्गा दूरं गत्वा शाम्यन्ति। MY says उदवमन् प्रकृतत्वात् द्रुमनिवहानिति। Kula is corrupt, but *SC* says उद्वमन्ति आविलत्वं त्यजन्ति प्रसन्ना भवन्तीत्यर्थ इति कुलनाथ:। लीयन्त इति श्रीनिवास: R says उद्वमन्ति विलीयन्ते। समाप्ता भवन्तीत्यर्थ:।

65. दीसइ मअउलेहि उअही णलो अणेहिं समअं सेल(उ)पडणभअउण्णलोअणेहिं।
जं खलिअं अईइ सलिलं णईण ऊरं तं उद्धाइ पवअकलकलविइण्णऊरम्।।

[दृश्यते मृगकुलैरुदधिर्नलो जनै:
समं शैल(सेतु)पतनभयपूर्णलोचनै:।
यत्स्खलितमत्येति सलिलं नदीनां पूरं
तदुद्धावति प्लवगकलकलवितीर्णतूर्यम्।।]

The deer (on the mountains of the causeway) looked at the ocean, and the people at Nala, all together, with eyes full of fear lest the mountains should topple down; and the waters of the streams[58] that cascaded far into the sea rose aloft as they dashed (against the waves) to the music provided by the jubilation of the apes.[59]

K and Deva read गज for *maa* = मृग (R, Kula and MY). K and MY read वलितं for *khaliaṁ* (R and Kula). K says शैलपतनभयपूर्णलोचनै:

[56] Those embedded in the mountains of the causeway.

[57] *SC* gives उत्तम्भित as a variant.

[58] Those on the mountains of the causeway.

[59] Rāmadāsa refers to a belief that water rises to the sound of musical instruments.

गजकुलैरुदधिरदृश्यत। उपरि किमस्य शैल: पततीति भयपूर्णलोचनैः जनैर्नलश्च दृश्यते स्म। K and MY explain *ūraṁ* (third line) as दूरम्[60] K says पतत्पर्वतनदीनां वलितं यत् सलिलं दूरमत्येति निपतति तत् सलिलं पू(वगकलकलैः वितीर्णवाद्यं भूत्वा उद्धावति अत्तिष्ठति स्म अभिघातात् पुनरूर्ध्वमुत्पपात। MY and Deva read सेतु for *sela*. Deva says सेतुना सहासौ सागरै पतिष्यतीति एवं भीतैर्जनैः नलः सादरं दृश्यते। MY reads *a ṇehiṁ* (च एभिः, cf. Hemacandra 3.77) for *aṇehiṁ* (जनैः) MY renders the first line as अदृश्यत मृगकुलैरुदधिर्नलश्चैभिः। Kula is here corrupt. *SC* has एभिः like MY. possibly it is Kula's reading also, as he does not say जनैः।

MY translates the thrid line as यद्बलवदत्येति सलिलं नदीनां दूरं and remarks — वलिअं फलिअं वेति पाठः। *phaliaṁ* फलितं विभिन्नम्। समाप्तप्राये सेतुबन्धे निपात्यमानैर्गिरिभिः प्रतिबन्ध(द्ध ?)-प्रवेशमार्गेशु तीरनदीमुखेषु विशीर्णतयोर्ध्वमुत्पतत्सु विस्मयात् कपयः कलकलं कृतवन्त इत्यर्थः – Deva says नदीनां यत् सलिलं दूरमत्येति प्रविशति तदिदानी फलितं विशीर्णं भूत्वा प्लवगकलकलदत्ततूर्यं च भूत्वा उद्धावति उत्तिष्ठति।

Kula says शैलपतनभयोद्विग्नलोचनैर्मृगकुलैः उदधिर्दृश्यते। He seems to read *bhaa-vuṇṇa* for *uṛṇa* (पूर्ण)। This is also the reading of Manuscript C of Goldschmidt, cf. *Deśīnāmamālā* 7.94 which gives *vuṇṇa* in the sense of भीत and उद्विग्न।[61] Kula explains *aīi* as आयाति – यन्नदीनां सलिलमायाति समुद्रं प्रविशति तूरं(?)त्वरमाणं(?)तत् प्लवगकलकलैः वितीर्णतूर्ये यथा स्यात् तथा स्खलितं सत् (ऊर्ध्वायते ऊर्ध्व धावतीत्यर्थः *SC*)। R says यद्वा नदीनामेव सेतुस्थानामित्यर्थात् सलिलमिति कर्तृ। समुद्रतरङ्गाभिघातात् स्खलितं सत् यद्दूरमतिक्रामति समुद्रजलमित्यर्थात्।

66. इअ सअलमहिअलुक्खअमहिहरसंघाअणिम्मिअमहारम्भम्।
णिअअच्छाआवइअरसामलइअसाअरोअरजलद्धन्तम्।।

[इति सकलमहीतलोत्खातमहीधरसंघातनिर्मितमहारम्भम्।
निजकच्छायाव्यतिकरश्यामलितसागरोदरजलार्धान्तम्।।]

Thus did they build Nala's Way. Its mighty structure was built with heaps of mountains uprooted from the entire

---

[60] *SC* text and *chāyā* have तूरं। *SC* commentary says यन्नदीनां सलिलं त्वरमाणं सत् अतिगच्छति समुद्रं प्रविशति। This might be Kula's reading also, but our copy is corrupt and has दूरन्तं त्वरमार्दे।

[61] *SC* commentary also has उद्विग्न like Kula, but *SC* text and *chāyā* have respectively -*uṇṇa* and पूर्णे।

earth; and, in contact with its reflection was darkened a part of the waters even in the depths of the sea.

K merely paraphrases the verse. R says आरम्भ उच्छ्राय:।

67. विसमोसरिअसिलाअलदढघाउक्खित्तमच्छपच्छिमभाअम्।
मज्झच्छिण्णभुअंगमवेड्ढप्पीडणविआरिअसिलावेढम्।।

[विषमापसृतशिलातलदृढघातोत्कृत्तमत्स्यपश्चिमभागम्।
मध्यच्छिन्नभुजंगमवेष्टोत्पीडनविदारितशिलावेष्टम्।।]

The tail fins of the fish were lopped off, violently hit by the rocks falling sideways from the causeway; while the serpents, rent in twain by a rock, split it with the pressure of their coils.

K reads उत्त्रुटित for *ukkitta* (R). R (com.) has उत्कृत्त (*ukhitta*). Kula has उत्खण्डित। The reading of K and Kula seems to be *ukkhuḍia* (cf. Hemacandra 4.116 and *SC* text). Manuscript C of Goldschmidt has *ukkhalia*. K has विलीन for *viāria* = विदारित (R), but this is invariably given by him as an equivalent of *virāa* which here does not suit the metre, probably he reads *virāia*; see 9.45 below. Kula says चूर्णितशिलापीठम्। His reading might be *vicuṇṇia* used elsewhere in the poem without the *upasarga*. *SC* says विदारितो विदीर्णो वा शिलावेष्टो यत्रेति लोकनाथ:। *virāvia* इति पाठो लोकनाथसंमत:; अतएवेदृशी व्याख्या।

K says पर्वतात् विषममपसृतस्य शिलातलस्य दृढेन घातेन उत्त्रुटितमत्स्यपृष्ठभागम्। देहमध्ये छिन्नस्य भुजङ्गमस्य वेष्टनोत्पीडनेन विलीनशिलामण्डलम्। Kula says मध्यच्छिन्नभुजङ्गमेन अमर्षात् गात्रावेष्टोत्पीडनेन चूर्णितशिलापीठम्। He reads *visamāvaḍia* for *visamosaria* (cf. *SC* text), and says विषमं तिर्यक् आपतितस्य शिलातलस्य।

68. सेलुम्मूलणसंभमगहिअप्फिलिअगअमग्गधाइअसीहम्।
गिरिसिहरणिसण्णाणिअगिरिपेल्लिअणिन्तमुहलजलहरसलिलम्।।

[शैलोन्मूलनसंभ्रमगृहीतभ्रष्टगजमार्गधावितसिंहम्।
गिरिशिखरनिषण्णानीतगिरिप्रेरितनिर्यन्मुखरजलधरसलिलम्।।]

The lions chased the elephants who, when seized, ran away in the confusion caused by the uprooting of the mountains;[62] while torrents of water poured down from the rumbling

[62] I.e. while the mountains were uprooted and brought to the causeway.

clouds, settling on the peaks of the mountains, and wafted to the causeway, because they were pressed by other mountains that followed.[63]

K says गिरिशिखरनिषण्णत्वादानीतेभ्यः पुनर्गिरिणा पीडितेभ्यः जलधरेभ्यो निर्यन्मुखरसलिलम्। *SC* text has *phiḍia* fo *philia* (भ्रष्ट)।

69. पासल्लपडिअवणगअरुद्धमहोज्झरदुहापहाविअसलिलम्।
धरणिहरन्तरिअट्ठिअचन्दणवणमुणिअमलअसिहरक्खण्डम्।।

[पार्श्वपतितवनगजरुद्धमहानिर्झरद्विधाप्रधावितसलिलम्।
धरणिधरान्तरितस्थितचन्दनवनज्ञातमलयशिखरखण्डम्।।]

The cascades[64] gushed forth in twin streams, because their outlets were blocked by the elephants that fell beside them; while the sections of the Malaya peaks could be distinguished by sandal groves standing in between the mountains.[65]

K and Kula read *muho* for *maho* . . . (R). K says पार्श्वात् पतितेन वनगजेन रुद्धमुखनिर्झरात् द्विधाप्रसृतसलिलं। R says पार्श्वे पार्श्वायमानेन वा पतितेन। Kula says वनगजेन बद्धमुखस्य निर्झरस्य द्विधाप्रधावितं सलिलं यत्र। R says अन्तरितमन्तर्गतम्।

70. वीईपडिऊलाहअथोउव्वेल्लिअदुमाबलम्बन्तलअम्।
विसमसिहरन्तरागअसंवेल्लिअसाअरं घडेन्ति णलवहम्।।
(कुलअम्)

[वीचिप्रतिकूलाहतस्तोकोद्वेल्लितद्रुमावलम्बमानलतम्।
विषमशिखरान्तरागतसंवेल्लितसागरं घटयति नलपथम्।।]
(कुलकम्)

The creepers hung loose from the trees, partly uncoiled, being lashed by the waves; and the sea swirled, entering through the gaps between the thinly scattered peaks.

K and Kula read विरल for *viisama* (R). K says वीचिभिः प्रतिकूलाहतत्वात् स्तोकमुद्वेष्टिता गलितवेष्टनाः अतएव द्रुमेभ्योऽवलम्बमाना लता यत्र तम्। गिरीणां

[63] The clouds are fancied as accompanying the mountains carried to the causeway through the air, closely followed by other mountains, as described in canto VI.

[64] Those on the mountains of the causeway.

[65] I.e. sandal trees were visible on the peaks of the Malaya mountain interspersed in the causeway.

शिखरान्तरैः शिखरान्तरालैरागतः संवेल्लित इतस्ततश्चलितः सागरो यत्र तं तथाभूतं नलपथं वानरा घटयन्ति स्म। Kula says उद्वेल्लिता विश्लेषिताः। विरलानां शिखराणामन्तरेणागतः अपरेण शैलेन संपातितः सागरो यत्र तम्। *SC* says विरलेन शिखराणामन्तरेण आगतः संवेल्लितो निबिडद्रुमपाषाणादिभिः सम्यक् वेष्टितः सागरो यत्र। संवेल्लितः शैलान्तरेण पीडित इति कुलनाथः। R says संवेल्लितः चञ्चलीभूतः।

71. वित्थरइ सेउबन्धो विहुव्वइ धराहराहओ सलिलणिही।
दिट्ठसुवेलुच्छङ्गं रसइ दिसाइण्णपडिरवं कइसेण्णम्॥

[विस्तीर्यते सेतुबन्धो विधूयते धराधराहतः सलिलनिधिः।
दृष्टसुवेलोत्सङ्गं रसति दिक्कीर्णप्रतिरवं कपिसैन्यम्॥]

The causeway stretched ahead; the sea rocked, battered by the mountains; and as they saw the Suvela range[66] the host of apes set up a yell, filling the regions with echoes.

कीर्णप्रतिरवम् R. दत्तप्रतिरवम् K, Kula and MY who has *diṇṇa* for *iṇṇa*. Kula says विस्तीर्यते वर्धते। विधूयते कम्पते। कर्मकर्तरि प्रयोगोऽयम्।

72. दीसन्ति भिण्णसलिले समुद्दमज्झम्मि सेउबन्धक्कन्ता।
संभमकड्ढणलुग्गा भअचुण्णपलाअसेलपक्खद्धन्ता॥

[दृश्यते भिन्नसलिले समुद्रमध्ये सेतुबन्धाक्रान्ताः।
संभ्रमकर्षणावरुग्णा भयचूर्णपलायितशैलपक्षार्धान्ताः॥]

In the midst of the sea, with the waters parting asunder, were seen portions of the wings of the submarine mountains, crushed by the causeway, and torn as they hurriedly tugged at them when they fled from the ocean, crazed with fear.[67]

K and MY read *puṇṇa* (पूर्ण) for *cuṇṇa* = चूर्ण (R). K has छिन्नाः[68] for *luggā* (R and Kula). Kula says रुग्णा भग्नाः। MY says *lukkā* लूनाः। K and MY seem to read *lukkā* for *luggā*. Hemacandra 4.116 mentions *lukkai* in the sense of तुडति "tear". R mentions the reading *bhaa-puṇṇa* for *-cuṇṇa*. *SC* explains *cuṇṇa* as उद्विग्न, and says it is a *deśī* word.[69]

---

[66] In Laṅkā.

[67] A variation of the picture given in verse 37.

[68] लूनाः according to Goldschmidt.

[69] *SC'S cuṇṇa* seems to be a scribal error for *vuṇṇa*. The reading of *SC* and that of Kula (missing in our copy) appears to be *bhaa-vuṇṇa* as in 8.65. See above.

73. महिहरपहरक्खोहिअसलिलपरिक्खअविराअमूलमहिहरम्।
थोअत्थोओसरिअं बन्धेन्ति पवंगमा पुणो वि णलवहम्।।

[महीधरप्रहारक्षोभितसलिलपरिक्षतविशीर्णमूलमहीधरम्।
स्तोकस्तोकमपसृतं बध्नन्ति प्लवंगमाः पुनरपि नलपथम्।।]

The apes restored Nala's Way when it by degrees tended to break up, the mountains at the base being eroded and worn away by the waters, stirred up by the impact of the mountains (dropped on the sea).

K reads पतन for *pahara* (K and Kula). R and Kula read वर्धयन्ति for *bandhenti* (R). K says महीधरपतनैः क्षोभितेन सलिलेन परिक्षतत्वात् विलीन्मूलपर्वतम्, अतएव किंचित् किंचिदपसृतं नलपथं प्लवंगमाः पुनरपि पर्वतान्तरैः वर्धयन्ति स्म (i.e. *vaḍḍhenti*). MY says परिक्षतविलीनसेतुमूलनिहितशैलम्। Kula says विलीना मूलमहीधरा मुखपतितपर्वता यस्येति। अतः स्तोकस्तोकेनापसृतं भ्रष्टायामं नलपथम्।

74. जह जह अच्चासण्णो उअहिं जेऊण होई सेउवहवरो।
उच्छलइ धराहिहअं दूरं थोअत्तणेण तह तह सलिलम्।।

[यथा यथात्यासन्न उदधिं जित्वा भवति सेतुपथवरः।
उच्छलति धराभिहतं दूरस्तोकत्वेन तथा तथा सलिलम्।।]

As the great causeway reached very near the farther shore, conquering the sea, the intervening water, because of its smaller extent, dashed high when hit by the mountains.

K and Deva read तटः for *varo* (R and Kula). K reads विस्तीर्यते (*vittharai*) for *uccalai* (Deva) and *ucchalai* (R and Kula) K and probably Deva read स्तोकत्वेऽपि for *thoattaṇeṇa* = स्तोकत्वेन् (R and Kula probably). K says सेतुपथस्य तटः मुखभागः उदधिं जित्वा अतिक्रम्य यथा यथा परतीरस्य अत्यासन्नोऽभूत्, सलिलं स्तोकत्वे सत्यपि धरैः पतद्भिरभिहतत्वात् तथा तथा विस्तृतमभूत्। MY says अभिमुखः पार (पार ?) तीरप्रदेशः . . . सलिलं स्वल्पीभवदपि सुदूरमुत्स्थलीबभूवेत्यर्थः। He seems to read *utthalai* for *ucchalai*. Cf. 50 above.

75. महिहरपहरुच्छित्ता उअरिं सेउस्स जे पडन्ति खलन्ता।
ते चिअ सलिलुप्पीडा होन्ति वलन्तविसमा महाणइसोत्ता।।

[महीधरप्रहारोत्क्षिप्ता उपरि सेतोर्ये पतन्ति स्खलन्तः।
त एव सलिलोत्पीडा भवन्ति वलद्विषमा महानदीस्रोतांसि।।]

The masses of water, thrown up by the impact of the mountains on the sea, spattered down on the causeway, and turned into large swirling streams.

Only the *chāyā* of the verse is found in our copy of K. Kula says स्खलन्तः संभ्रमानाः।

76. देइ समत्तच्छाअं दरमिलिअसुवेलमहिहरतडद्धन्तो।
बीओआसपहाविअतिमिपूरिअसाअरन्तरो सेउवहो।।

[ददाति समाप्तच्छायां दरमिलितसुवेलमहीधरतटार्धान्ताः
द्वितीयावकाशप्रधावितितिमिपूरितसागरान्तरः सेतुपथः।।]

The causeway, with part of the slope of the Suvela almost touching it, appeared to be complete, the intervening stretch of sea being filled up by the whales rushing in from either side.

K, Kula, Deva and MY read द्वितीयार्धान्त *bīddhanta* for *bīoāsa* = द्वितीयावकाश (R). Kula reads नव for दर। K says द्वितीयार्धान्तं प्रति सेतोरपरसमुद्रार्धान्तं प्रति प्रधावितेन तिमिना। R says द्वितीयावकाशात् प्रधावितेन . . .। अयं भावः – एकपार्श्वादपरपार्श्वं प्रति . . . सत्वरं गच्छता तिमिना।

77. जाहे सेउणिबद्धं धुणइ णलो विसमसंठिअमहासेलम्।
ताहे चिरेण सअलो सअलक्कन्तवसुहो णिअत्तइ उअही।।

[यदा सेतुनिबद्धं धुनोति नलो विषमसंस्थितमहाशैलम्।
तदा चिरेण सकलो सकलाक्रान्तवसुधो निवर्तते उदधिः।।]

As Nala shook up the causeway, because the big mountains stood uneven, the ocean flooded the entire earth, and slowly receded.

K, Kula Deva and probably MY also read सेतुनिबन्धं for *seu-ṇibaddhaṁ* (R). K, Deva and MY read सलिलं for *saala* (R and Kula). K says वानराणां प्रक्षेपरभसात् विषमस्थितमहापर्वतं सेतुं नलो वीक्ष्य सम्यगवस्थानार्थं यदा धुनोति स्म, तदा समुद्रः सकलः सेतुना प्रणुन्नः सन् सलिलाप्लावितवसुधो भूत्वा निवृत्तः। MY says विषमस्थितमहाशैलं सेतुं प्रतिचिकीर्षुः नलो यदा व्यधुनोत् तदा सलिलाक्रान्तवसुधो भूत्वा समुद्रः चिरेण न्यवर्तत। R says सेतौ निबद्धं विषमसंस्थितं समीभूय न लग्नं महाशैलं सुसज्जीकरणाय नलो यदा धुनोति।

78. लहुइअपेसणहरिसिअकइणिवहणिसुद्धसेलपहरवलन्तो।
णइसोत्तो व्व समुद्दो सेउसवेलन्तरे मुहुत्तं वूढो।।

[लघुकृतप्रेषणहर्षितकपिनिवहनिपातितशैलप्रहारवलमानः।
नदीस्रोत इव समुद्रः सेतुसुवेलान्तरे मुहूर्त्तं व्यूढः।।]

The sea flowed for a moment, like a stream, in the gap between the causeway and the Suvela, heaving as it was hit by the mountains dropped by the apes, who rejoiced at their task being almost finished.

K reads चलन् for *valanto* (R and Kula). K says वलन् अल्पीभवन्। K says प्रेषणेन स्वामिकार्येण। व्यूढः वहति स्म। MY says लघूकृतः समापितप्रायः। प्रेषणं सेतुविषयराजाज्ञा। व्यूढः कर्तरि क्तः। R says वलमानो दोलायमानः।

79. जह जह णिम्माविज्जइ वाणरवसहेहि सेउसंकमसिहरम्।
तह तह दहमुहहिअअं फाडिज्जइ साअरस्स सलिलेण समम्।।

[यथा यथा निर्मीयते वानरश्रेष्ठैः सेतुसंक्रमशिखरम्।
तथा तथा दशमुखहृदयं पाट्यते सागरस्य सलिलेन समम्।।]

As the powerful apes built the forepart of the causeway Rāvaṇa's heart was rent asunder along with the waters of the sea.

Not found in K and MY.

80. पाआलमिलिअमूलो अव्वोच्छिण्णपसरन्तसरिआसोत्तो।
ठाणट्ठिओ वि पडिओ मुहम्मि धरणिहरसंकमस्स सुवेलो।।

[पातालमिलितमूलोऽव्यवच्छिन्नप्रसरत्सरित्स्रोताः।
स्थानस्थितोऽपि पतितो मुखे धरणीधरसंक्रमस्य सुवेलः।।]

The Suvela, with its foundations reaching into the nether regions, and its streams incessantly flowing, fitted in with the forepart of the bridge of mountains, even standing where it stood.[70]

avvocchiṇṇa = अव्यवच्छिन्न (R and Kula); अव्युच्छिन्न K (*chāyā*). K says पाताले सक्तमूलः, अविच्छिन्नप्रवहन्नदीप्रवाहः सुवेलः स्वस्थाने स्थितोऽपि धरणिधरसंक्रमस्य सेतोः मुखे पतितः। वानरैः क्षिप्रं क्षिप्यमाणेन पर्वतनिवहेन

[70] I.e. the Suvela became the last mountain of the causeway on the southern shore.

समाप्यमानस्य सेतुमुखस्य दुर्लक्षं शैघ्र्यमनया गाथया प्रतिपादितम्। MY says शैलसंक्रमस्य मुखे (= पुरोभागे Kula) भवितुं महान् शैलोऽपेक्षितः स्थानस्थित एव तथाभूतः सुवेलः तथा जात इत्यर्थः Manuscript A has महाशैलापेक्षित-स्थानस्थितएव।

81. मलउच्छङ्गगएण वि रहुवइपासट्ठिएण वाणरवइणा।
कइकलअलेण णाओ णिप्पच्छिमसेलपूरिओ सेउवहो।।

[मलयोत्सङ्गगतेनापि रघुपतिपार्श्वस्थितेन वानरपतिना।
कपिकलकलेन ज्ञातो निष्पश्चिमशैलपूरितः सेतुपथः।।]

The lord of the apes (Sugrīva), even though he was on the summit of the Malaya, standing beside Rāma, knew from the jubilation of the apes that the causeway was completed with the last of the mountains.

पश्चात् पर्वतविनाशनिरपेक्षः शैलो निष्पश्चिमशैलः K. पश्चिमः शेषः तद्रहितेन सर्वशेषेण शैलेन पूरितो निष्पादितः सेतुपथः R.

82. आरम्भन्ते सअलो तिहाअविसमो दरुट्ठिअम्मि णलवहे।
होइ दुहा अ समत्ते सो चिअ अण्णो पुणो पुणो वि समुद्दो।।

[आरभ्यमाणे सकलस्त्रिभागविषमो दरोत्थिते नलपथे।
भवति द्विधा च समाप्ते स एवान्यः पुनः पुनरपि समुद्रः।।]

The self-same sea appeared to be different now and again. When Nala's Way was begun, it looked entire; when it was partly erected, the sea was divided unequally into three parts;[71] and when it was complete, it was divided in twain.

K reads *vva* for *vi* (R). K says सेतौ आरभ्यमाणे सति समुद्रः सकलः अविकलो दृष्टः। तस्मिन् किञ्चित् बद्धे सति त्रिभागविषमः पुरस्तात् उभयतश्च विमुक्तैः त्रिभिः भागैः विषमोऽभूत। समाप्ते सति द्विधा बभूव। स एव समुद्रः एवंभूतत्वात् पुनः पुनः क्षणे क्षणे अन्य इवाभूत्।

83. मलउच्छङ्गपउत्तो चलन्तवाणरभरोणओ सेउवहो।
गरुओ तिऊडगिरिणा पल्हत्थन्तो दुमो दुमेण व धरिओ।।

[मलयोत्सङ्गप्रवृत्तश्चलद्वानरभरावनतः सेतुपथः।
गुरुकस्त्रिकूटगिरिणा पर्यस्यमानो द्रुमो द्रुमेणेव धृतः।।]

[71] I.e. the two sides of the causeway and the open front.

The massive causeway, starting from the summit of the Malaya, and weighed down by the passing apes, was supported as it rocked by the Suvela, like as a falling tree is supported by another tree.[72]

K, Kula and MY read *malaa-niambosario* for *malaucchaṅgapaüìtto* = मलयोत्सङ्गप्रवृत्तः (R)।

K says मलयनितम्बादपसृतः प्रवृत्त इत्यर्थः। पर्यस्यमानः प्रसार्यमाणः। R says पर्यस्यमानः समुद्रवीचिभिरितस्ततः प्रेर्यमाणः। *SC* says दृष्टान्तमाहपर्यस्यन् पतन् द्रुमो द्रुमेणेव।

84. दीसइ सेउमहावहदोहाइअपुव्वपच्छिमदिसाभाअम्।
ओव्वत्तोहअपासं मज्झुक्खित्तविसमं णमन्तं व णहम्।।

[दृश्यते सेतुमहापथद्विधायितपूर्वपश्चिमदिग्भागम्।
अपवृत्तोभयपार्श्वे मध्योत्क्षिप्तविषमं नमदिव नभः।।]

With the eastern and western regions divided by the great causeway, the sky seemed to be raised up in the middle and uneven, inclining with both sides sloping downwards.[73]

Kula says अववृत्तावनतावुभयपार्श्वौ यस्य तत् तथाभूतं नभः मध्योत्क्षिप्तविषमत्वात् पतदिवोत्प्रेक्ष्यते। He reads *paḍaniaṁ* for *ṇamantaṁ* (नमत्)। Besides, he reads जलधिपूर्वपश्चिमभागम् for *puvva-pacchima-disā-bhāaṁ*. He says सेतुमहापथेन द्विधाकृतौ जलधेः पूर्वपश्चिमभागौ यत्र तत् तथा। K says शतयोजनमायतेन सेतुपथेन द्विधाकृतपूर्वपश्चिमदिग्भागम्, अत्युन्नतेन सेतुना मध्ये उत्क्षिप्तत्वात् विषमम्, अपवृत्तोभयपाश्र्वं निम्नोभयपाश्र्वं नभो नमदिव मध्योत्क्षेपवेगात् . . . अदृश्यत्।

85. मलअसुवेलालग्गो पडिट्ठिओ णहणिहम्मि सागरसलिले।
उअअत्थमणणिराओ रविरहमग्गो व्व पाअडो सेउवहो।।

[मलयसुवेलालग्नः परिस्थितो नभोनिभे सागरसलिले।
उदयास्तमननिरायतो रविरथमार्ग इव प्रकटः सेतुपथः।।]

Stretching across the waters of the sea resembling the sky,

---

[72] The causeway extended from the Malaya mountain on the northern shore to the Suvela in Laṅkā.

[73] The sky is likened to a pavilion with the eastern and western regions looking like sloping roofs, with the bridge of mountains standing in the middle like a row of pillars.

the causeway, joined to the Malaya and the Suvela, was clearly visible, like the track of the sun's chariot extending from the mount of sunrise to that of sunset.

K (*chāyā*) has प्रतिष्ठितः। R and Kula have परिस्थितः। K says सेतुपथः उदयास्तमयपर्वतयोः मध्ये निरायतो रविरथमार्ग इव प्रकटोऽभूत्।

86. दीसइ पवणविहुव्वन्तसाअरोअरपरिट्ठिअमहासिहरो।
विअडपसारिअवक्खो उप्पवमाणो व्व महिहरो सेउवहो।।

[दृश्यते पवनविधूयमानसागरोदरपरिस्थितमहाशिखरः।
विकटप्रसारितपक्ष उत्प्लवमान इव महीधरः सेतुपथः।।]

With the great mountain peaks resting on the bosom of the sea,[74] rocked by the wind, the causeway looked like a floating mountain with its widespread wings.[75]

K reads सागरोपरिप्रतिष्ठित for *sāaroara-pariṭṭhia* = सागरोदरपरिस्थित (R). MY says *uppaamāṇa* उत्प्लवमान। उत्पतन् वा। The verse is not found in Kula.

87. अरई थोरूसासा णिद्दाणासो विवण्णदा दौव्वल्लम्।
सेउम्मि रइज्जन्ते रामादो रावणम्मि संकन्ताइं।।

[अरतिः स्थूलोच्छ्वासा निद्रानाशो विवर्णता दौर्बल्यम्।
सेतौ रच्यमाने रामाद्रावणे संक्रान्तानि।।]

Discontent, deep sighs, loss of sleep, pallor and weakness passed from Rāma to Rāvaṇa while the causeway was being built.

Not found in K and MY.

88. अह थोरतुङ्गविअडो णेउं णिहणं सबन्धवं दहवअणम्।
दोहाइअसलिलणिही कअन्तहत्थो व्व पसरिओ सेउवहो।।

[अथ स्थूलतुङ्गविकटो नेतुं निधनं सबान्धवं दशवदनम्।
द्विवायितसलिलनिधिः कृतान्तहस्त इव प्रसृतः सेतुपथः।।]

Massive and lofty and formidable, the causeway stretched

---

74 I.e. reflected in the sea.

75 The reflections of the mountain peaks on both sides of the causeway are likened to the legendary wings of the mountains that took refuge in the sea. See 5.37.

away, parting the sea in twain, like the hand of death, to destroy Rāvaṇa with his kinsmen.

Not found in our copy of K. Found in MY and Kula.

89. विसमेण पअइविसमं महिहरगरुएण समरसाहसगरुअम्।
दूरत्थेण वि भिण्णं सूलेण व सेउणा दसाणणहिअअम्।।

[विषमेण प्रकृतिविषमं महिधरगुरुकेण समरसाहसगुरुकम्।
दूरस्थेनापि भिन्नं शूलेनेव सेतुना दशाननहृदयम्।।]

Rāvaṇa's heart, unrelenting by nature, and steadfast in martial zeal, was pierced by the rugged causeway, heavy with the mountains, as by a spear, even though it was far away.

शैलशिखरसंकटत्वात् विषमेण, महीधरैः घटितत्वात् गुरुणा सेतुना शूलेनेव सता प्रकृत्या विषममतिक्रूरं, समरसाहसेन गुरु महीयो दशाननस्य हृदयम् K. विषमेण निम्नोन्नतेन। प्रकृतिविषमं स्वभावतो दुष्प्रधर्षम् MY.

90. दीसन्ति खुहिअसाअरसलिलोल्लिअकुसुमणिवहलग्गमहुअरा।
सेतुस्स पासमहिहरपअडन्तोव्वत्तकिसलआ कडअदुमा।।

[दृश्यन्ते क्षुभितसागरसलिलार्द्रितकुसुमनिवहलग्नमधुकराः।
सेतोः पार्श्वमहीधरप्रकट्यमानोद्वृत्तकिसलयाः कटकद्रुमाः।।]

The trees on the slopes of the causeway were plain to view, with the bees clinging to the flowers drenched with the water of the heaving sea, and the dropping young shoots flickering on the mountains on the flanks.

K and Deva read प्रचलत् (*paalanta*) for *paaḍanta* = प्रकट्यमान (R). They have प्रचलदपवृत्तकिसलयाः, and seem to read *ovvatta* = अपवृत्त as in 8.84. R has *uvvatta* उद्वृत्त, cf. 5.56, 60, etc. He says उद्वृत्तानि भ्रमरभरात् विपरीत्य स्थितानि किसलयानि येषाम्। Kula is corrupt; *SC* reads *paalanta* like K, but explains it as प्रगलत्। *SC* says अपवृत्ताः सलिलभरेणानताः किसलया येषां ते सेतोः कटकद्रुमाः। Deva explains अपवृत्त as उद्वृत्त।

91. थिमिओअहिसच्छाया कत्थ वि दीसन्ति महिहरन्तरवडिआ।
फलिहसिलाअलघडिआ मज्झच्छिण्ण व्व सेउबन्धोआसा।।

[स्तिमितोदधिसच्छायाः कुत्रापि दृश्यन्ते महीधरान्तरपतिताः।
स्फटिकशिलातलघटिता मध्यच्छिन्ना इव सेतुबन्धावकाशाः।।]

Portions of the causeway, built of crystal rocks, and interspersed between the mountains, seemed at places to be rent in the middle, being similar in colour to the tranquil sea.[76]

K says कुत्रापि क्वचित् प्रदेशे स्फटिकशिलातलघटिता:, स्तिमितेनोदधिना समानवर्णा: अन्त:प्रतिबिम्बितसमुद्रत्वात् समुद्रसमानवर्णा:, महीधरान्तरेषु पतिता: सेतुबन्धप्रदेशा मध्ये-मध्ये छिन्ना इवादृश्यन्त।

92. हिमपडनौत्थइआइं घडिआइं वि णलवहम्मि णज्जन्ति फुडम्।
सिहराइं सिहरिवइणो मलअस्स अ मलिअचन्दणसुअन्धाइं।।

[हिमपतनावस्थगितानि घटितान्यपि नलपथे ज्ञायन्ते स्फुटम्।
शिखराणि शिखरिपतेर्मलयस्य च मृदितचन्दनसुगन्धानि।।]

Peaks of the Himalaya covered with snow, and those of the Malaya, fragrant with the crushed sandal trees, could be clearly recognized, even though built into Nala's Way.

K, MY, Deva and Kula read पटल (*paḍala*) for *paḍaṇa* (R). K reads दृश्यन्ते (*dīsanti*) for *ṇajjanti* = ज्ञायन्ते (R and Kula; and अवच्छादितानि) for *otthaiāiṁ* (अवस्थगितानि) found in R and Kula. K seems to read *occhaiāiṁ*. Cf. Hemacandra 2.17 — क्वचित् स्थगित शब्देऽपि। छइअं।

93. जाआ फुडवित्थारा गओणिअत्तन्तजलरअविहुव्वन्ता।
पक्कग्गाहसमग्गा सेउम्मि वि साअरस्य वेलामग्गा।।

[जाता: स्फुटविस्तारा गतापनिवर्तमानजलरयविधूयमाना:।
प्रग्राहसमग्रा: सेतावपि सागरस्य वेलामार्गा:।।]

The causeway looked like the extensive shoreline of the sea[77] being rocked by the rush of the waters advancing and receding, and filled with the monsters of the deep.

K, MY, Deva and Kula read सगर्भा: (*sagarbbhā*) for *samaggā* (R). MY says पक्वग्राहो दुष्टग्राह:। पक्वग्राहै: सगर्भा: गर्भसहिता: तद्गर्भा इत्यर्थ:। K says परिणतग्राहगर्भिता: वेलामार्गा: तीरपथा: सेतावपि जाता: सेतुपार्श्वयोरपि

---

[76] I.e. the waters of the sea, visible through the transparent rocks, seemed to flow through gaps in the causeway.

[77] Literally the extensive paths of the seashore appeared also on the causeway. Some take *velā* in the sense of waves, which are explained as sweeping over the causeway.

बभूवुः। R says सागरस्य वेला कल्लोलरूपं जलं तन्मार्गाः . . . प्रग्राहो जलसिंहः तेन समग्राः संपूर्णाः। Deva says सागरस्य वेलाया मार्गाः समुद्रजलवृद्धिप्रतिरयाः सेतावपि जाताः।

94. सेलाइञ्छणपडिआ सलिलोल्लिअगरुअकेसरभरक्कन्ता।
दीसन्ति दरुत्तिण्णा संकमपासल्लसंठिआ केसरिणो।।

[शैलातिक्रमपतिताः सलिलार्द्रितगुरुककेसरभराक्रान्ताः।
दृश्यन्ते दरोत्तीर्णाः संक्रमपार्श्वसंस्थिताः केसरिणः।।]

The lions that fell into the sea when the mountains were thrown in, were seen slowly emerging from the waters, and resting on the flanks of the causeway, cumbered with their heavy mane drenched with water.

K (*pratīka*) has *selālaṁghaṇa* (rendered in the *chāyā* as शैलक्षेपण) for *selāiñchaṇa* (R and Kula ?). MY (manuscript B) has *selāiṁghaṇa*, and says *aiṁghaṇaṁ* रभसक्षेपणं प्रेरणमिति यावत्। MY (manuscript A) has *aṁ*(*ā*?)*laṁghanaṁ*, cf. K's reading. Kula says गिरिप्रेषणेन पतिताः। *SC* says *selāiñchaṇeṇa* गिरिप्रेरणेन पतिताः। शैलाकर्षणात् पतिता इति केचित्। R says शैलस्यातिक्रमेण आकर्षणेन पतिताः। K says शैलक्षेपावस्थायां पतिताः, सलिलार्द्रितानां केसराणां भारेण आक्रान्ताः, समुद्रात् किंचिदुत्तीर्णाः संक्रमस्य सेतोः पार्श्वस्थिताः केसरिणः अदृश्यन्त। Deva has शैलक्षेपणपतिताः। His *pratīka* is missing in our copy.

95. पुव्वावरोअहिगआ दट्ठुं पुव्वावरोअहिसमुप्पणा।
सेउपडिसिद्धपसरा पुणो ण पेच्छन्ति कुलहराइं जलअरा।।

[पूर्वापरोदधिगता द्रष्टुं पूर्वापरोदधिसमुत्पन्नाः।
सेतुप्रतिषिद्धप्रसरा पुनर्न पश्यन्ति कुलगृहाणि जलचराः।।]

The animals of the eastern and western parts of the sea that had gone to see the western and eastern parts respectively,[78] saw their homes no more,[79] their way being barred by the bridge.

K and Kula read पूर्वापरावतिगताः (i.e., *puvvāvare aigaā*, cf. *SC* text) for *puvvāvaroahi-gaā* = पूर्वापरोदधिगताः (R). K says मध्यस्थस्य सेतोः पूर्वापरयोः समुद्रयोः संजाता जलचरा महामत्स्या पूर्वापरौ, अपरपूर्वाविति योज्यम्,

---

[78] I.e. before the building of the causeway.

[79] I.e. could not return.

नात्र कविना क्रमो विवक्षितः, पूर्वसमुद्रसंभवा अपरभागं कुतूहलात् द्रष्टुम् अतिगता अतिदूरं गताः। तथापरसमुद्रसंभवाः पूर्वभागं द्रष्टुं गताः सन्तः सहसा निर्मितेन सेतुना प्रतिषिद्धगतयो भूत्वा पुनः कुलगृहाणि नैवापश्यन्नित्यर्थः। Kula says ये जलचराः . . . पूर्वापरावुदधी द्रष्टुमागताः सेतुबन्धात् पूर्वं स्वस्थानमतिक्रम्य गताः, तेऽधुना बद्धेन सेतुना प्रतिषिद्धप्रसराः सन्तः पुनः कुलगृहाणि जन्मस्थानानि न प्रेक्षन्ते। Deva's reading is same as that of K and Kula, but he says पूर्वापरौ द्रष्टुमभिगताः। The word अतिगताः also appears in his gloss.

96. दीसन्ति धाउअम्बा मारुअविहुअधवलोज्झरपडद्धन्ता।
सेउस्स तुङ्गसिहरा उहअतलपरिट्ठिआ धअ व्व महिहरा।।

[दृश्येते धातुताम्रौ मारुतविधुतधवलनिर्झरपटार्धान्तौ।
सेतोस्तुङ्गशिखरावुभयतटपरिस्थितौ ध्वजाविव महीधरौ।।]

The high-peaked mountains, red with minerals, standing on either shore, looked like flagstaffs marking the causeway, with the white, wind-swept cascades serving as banners.

K reads परिक्षिप्ताः for *paḍaddhantā* = पटार्धान्तौ (R and Kula). He says धवलेन निर्झरेण परिक्षिप्ता महीधराः। K reads प्रतिष्ठिताः for *pariṭṭhiā* (R and Kula). Kula says सेतोरुभयतटपरिस्थितौ महीधरौ मलयसुवेलौ।

97. अह णिम्मिअसेउवहं सेउवहब्भहिअथलपइण्णमहिहरम्।
चलिअं चलन्तराहवहिअअणिहिप्पन्तरणसुहं कइसेणम्।।

[अथ निर्मितसेतुपथं सेतुपथाभ्यधिकस्थलप्रकीर्णमहीधरम्।
चलितं चलद्राघवहृदयनिधीयमानरणसुखं कपिसैन्यम्।।]

Having built the causeway, and scattered on the ground the mountains left over, the host of apes set out on their march, inspired by Rāma with martial ardour as he marched with them.

K says कपिसैन्यं प्रचलता राघवेण हृदये निधीयमानयुद्धसुखं भूत्वा चलितुं प्रवृत्तम्। MY says सेतुरचनापेक्षितेभ्योऽतिरिक्ता आनीताः शैलाः वैफल्यात् पुनः स्थले प्रकीर्णा येन तत्तथा।

98. पेच्छन्ति अ वोलन्ता संकमदोहाइअक्खविअवित्थारम्।
वलआमुहणिट्ठविएक्कपासवोच्छिण्णपाणिअं मअरहरम्।।

[प्रेक्षन्ते च व्यतिक्रामन्तः संक्रमद्विधायितक्षपितविस्तारम्।
वडवामुखनिष्ठापितैकपार्श्वव्यवच्छिन्नपानीयं मकरगृहम्।।]

As they passed they beheld the sea, divided in twain by the causeway, and reduced in extent, with the waters diminished on one side, being consumed by the submarine fire.[80]

K and MY read क्षीयमाण (*jhijjanta* for *vocchiṇṇa* = व्यवच्छिन्न) (R and Kula). MY says सेतुना द्विधाकृतस्योदधेः निरुद्धपरस्परपार्श्वसलिलप्रसरतया एकस्मिन् साग्निके पार्श्वे अग्निना पीयमानसलिले सति पार्श्वान्तरसलिलस्य तत्र संचारणजन्यपूरणाभावात् क्षीणसलिलत्वं जातमित्यर्थः। K says अतिक्रामन्तः ते वानराः संक्रमेण सेतुना द्विधाकृतत्वात् क्षपितविस्तारं, वडवामुखेन वह्निना निष्ठापिते नाशिते दह्यमाने एकत्र पार्श्वे क्षीयमाणजलं समुद्रं पश्यन्ति स्म। Deva has व्युच्छिन्नमल्पीभवत् पानीयं यस्य।

99–100.सङ्खउलधवलकमले फुडमरगअहरिअवत्तभङ्गणिहाए।
विद्दुममिलिअकिसलए उहअतडाबद्धसंकमम्मि णलवहे।।

संचरइ वाणरबलं णमइ विसट्टन्तमहिहरो सेउवहो।
ओआहिअपाआलं सव्वत्थामगरुअं धरेइ समुद्दो।।
(जुग्गअम्)

[शङ्खकुलधवलकमले स्फुटमरकतहरितपत्रभङ्गनिघाते।
विद्रुममिलितकिसलये उभयतटाबद्धसंक्रमे नलपथे।।

संचरति वानरबलं नमति विशीर्यमाणमहीधराः सेतुपथः।
अवगाहितपातालं सर्वत्थामगुरुकं धारयति समुद्रः।।]
(यग्मकम्)

The host of apes marched over Nala's Way, the bridge linked to both shores, that was full of white lotus blossoms as well as conch shells, heaps of broken green leaves as well as bright emeralds, and young shoots mingling with corals.[81]

The causeway bent under the weight, with the mountains coming loose; but the ocean supported it firmly with all its strength, pressing hard upon the nether regions.

K reads *jua* (युत) for *-ula* = कुल (R, Deva, Kula and MY)।

---

[80] I.e. the waters consumed by the submarine fire could not be replenished by the waters from the other side of the causeway which reached to the bottom of the sea, like a wall.

[81] The flowers and leaves belonged to the mountains of the causeway, and the corals, emeralds, etc. were those washed up by the waves.

समुद्रसंभवैः शङ्खैः युक्तपर्वतसरोवर्तिधवलकमले, तथा मरतकसंपृक्तपत्रभङ्गसमूहे K. MY remarks शङ्खादीनां पुण्डरीकादिकतया रूपणमार्गात् मङ्गलाभिप्रायेणात्र समचरद्वानरबलमित्युत्तरेण संबन्धः।

K, Deva and MY read द्विधाकृत (*dohāia*) for *oāhia* = अवगाहित; अवगाढ (R and Kula). K says अथ समुद्रः अधःप्रवेशेन द्विधाकृतपातालं तं सेतुं सर्वस्थाम्ना सह बलेन गुरु दृढं धारयति स्म। MY remarks अधारयत् सेतुमिति लभ्यते प्रकृतत्वात्। द्विधाकृतपातालमित्यध्याहृतसेतुपदविशेषणमिच्छन्ति केचित्। अन्ये क्रियाविशेषणमिति। अन्यथा तु . . . द्विधाकृतपातालं भरवशदलिताधस्तनभूतलं यथा स्यात्तथा समुद्रः कपिबलं सर्वप्राणमधारयदिति योज्यम्। K says तस्मिन् वानरबलं चरति गच्छति स्म। तेषां गौरवात् विशिलष्यन्महीधरः सेतुपथः नमति स्म। Kula says आक्रमभरेण विसंघटमाना महीधरा यत्र स सेतुपथो नमति। अवगाढपातालं पातालमूले दत्तभरं यथा स्यात्, सर्वस्थाम्ना गुरुकं च यथा स्यात् तथा धारयति समुद्रः।

101. संचालेइ णिअम्बं धारेइ उअरि तरङ्गकरपब्भारम्।
खम्भम्मि वणगओ विअ आबद्धो सेतुसंकमम्मि समुद्दो।।

[संचालयति नितम्बं धारयत्युपरि तरङ्गकरप्राग्भारम्।
स्तम्भे वनगज इवाबद्धः सेतुसंक्रमे समुद्रः।।]

Obstructed by the causeway, the sea, like a wild elephant tied to a post, rocked the flanks of the bridge, and spread over it its massive waves, even as an elephant stretches out its trunk and shakes the post (to uproot it).

The verse is not found in K, Deva and MY. R says नितम्बं सेतोरेव मूलभागं संचालयति। *SC* says नितम्बं मध्यभागं सेतोरित्यर्थादिति कुलनाथः।

102. उत्तिण्णा अ पवङ्गा सेलभरुव्वहणजणिअसेअतुसारा।
धाउमइले करअले पासट्ठिअमहिहरोज्झरेसु धुवन्ता।।

[उत्तीर्णाश्च प्लवङ्गाः शैलभरोद्वहनजनितस्वेदतुषाराः।
धातुमलिनानि करतलानि पार्श्वस्थितमहीधरझरेषु धावयन्तः।।]

Bathed in sweat after they had carried loads of mountains, the apes crossed the sea, and laved their hands, soiled by the minerals, in the cascades of the mountains on the flanks of the causeway.

K says शैलभरोद्वहनेन जनितस्वेदशीकराः। तुषारः शीकरेऽपि चेत्त्यमरशेषे। My reads *sea-jala-lavā* for *sea-tusārā*.

103. पत्ता अ दहमुहाणिअणन्दणवणपाअवोइअवणुद्देसम्।
जलभरणिसण्णजलहरभरमोडिअवणलअं सुवेलुच्छङ्गम्।।

[प्राप्ताश्च दशमुखानीतनन्दनवनपादपोचितवनोद्देशम्।
जलभरनिषण्णजलधरभरमोटितवनलतं सुवेलोत्सङ्गम्।।]

They reached the summit of the Suvela that had groves befitting the trees brought from the Nandana garden by Rāvaṇa; where the sylvan creepers were crushed under the weight of the clouds settling on them with their load of water.

पादपाचितवनाद्देशमिति वा पाठः K.

104. सोऊण समुत्तिण्णं उअहिमविद्दविअविक्कमं कइसेण्णम्।
जाओ रक्खसलोओ रक्खसणाहस्स पेलवाणत्तिअरो।।

[श्रुत्वा समुत्तीर्णमुदधिमविद्रावितविक्रमं कपिसैन्यम्।
जातो राक्षसलोको राक्षसनाथस्य पेलवाज्ञप्तिकरः।।]

Hearing that the host of apes had crossed the sea, with their valour unresisted, the demons became remiss in carrying out the orders of their master.

K, Deva and MY read *uahiṁ acchera-vikkamaṁ* (आश्चर्यविक्रमं) for *uahimaviddavia-vikkamaṁ* (R and Kula); and गलितप्रतापक्षुभितः for *pelavāṇattiaro* (R and Kula). K says वानराणां समुद्रलङ्घनादेव राक्षसनाथस्य गलितेन प्रतापेन राक्षसजनः क्षुभितोऽभूदिति। MY says *accheraṁ* आश्चर्यम् *paāva* प्रताप। Kula says अविक्रातः (अविद्राणः ?) अनुपहतो विक्रमो यस्य तत् कपिसैन्यमुदधिमुत्तीर्णं श्रुत्वा राक्षसलोको राक्षसनाथस्य पेलवं मृदु यथा स्यात् तथा आज्ञप्तिमाज्ञां करोतीति तथाविधो जातः। R has अविद्रावितविक्रमम्।

105. जाव अ महोअहिअडे आवासग्गहणवावडं कइसेण्णम्।
ताव कअन्तेण कओ रावणसीसम्मि वामहत्थप्फंसो।।

[यावच्च महोदधितटे आवासग्रहणव्यापृतं कपिसैन्यम्।
तावत्कृतान्तेन कृतो रावणशीर्षे वामहस्तस्पर्शः।।]

While the host of apes was busy stationing themselves on the seashore, death touched Rāvaṇa's head with his left hand.[82]

[82] Indicates the ease with which Rāvaṇa would be destroyed.

Not found in K, Deva and MY. Kula's readings differ somewhat from those of R. He reads *suvela-kaḍae* for *mahoahi-aḍe* (महोदधितटे); Dahamuha for रावण; and *-ppaṇao* for *-pphaṁso* (स्पर्शः)। Kula says यावच्च विश्रामार्थं सुवेलकटके आवासग्रहणव्यापृतं कपिसैन्यं तावत् दशमुखस्य शीर्षे कृतान्तेन वामहस्तप्रणयः कृतः। अनन्तरमेव (वानर)सैन्यं ममाभिलषितं पूरयिष्यति इति अविध्यनार्थं वामहस्तस्य (असिद्धि)हेतुत्वात् तेनासिद्धिकरीमिव रक्षामकरोदित्यभिप्रायः। *SC* adds प्रणयः स्वीकारः। R says वामहस्तेन स्पर्शः कृतः . . . इति रावणस्य हठादेव मृत्युः व्यञ्जितः।

106–07. रामस्स रावणस्स अ लोआलोअन्तरालसरिसामण्णे।
वड्ढन्तणिव्वअन्ते पाआरन्तरदहाइअम्मि पआवे।।

जाआ लच्छीअ समं सोहा महिअस्स सागरस्स पसण्णा।
तिअसजणिआणुराए उत्तिण्णम्मि मअलञ्छणम्मि व रामे।।

[रामस्य रावणस्य च लोकालोकान्तरालनिस्सामान्ये।
वर्धमाननिवर्तमाने प्राकारान्तरद्विधायिते प्रतापे।।

जाता लक्ष्म्या समं शोभा मथितस्य सागरस्य प्रसन्ना।
त्रिदशजनितानुरागे उत्तीर्णे मृगलाञ्छन इव रामे।।]

While Rāma's power and that of Rāvaṇa, unparalleled in the region encompassed by the Lokāloka mountain,[83] expanded and receded respectively, divided by the intervening wall of Laṅkā,[84] and when Rāma, beloved of the gods, crossed the ocean, like the moon that rose from it,[85] the disturbed sea assumed a serene beauty accompanied with splendour (as it once did when lovely wine emerged with

---

[83] I.e. in the entire world. The mountain belt, called Lokāloka, is the circular boundary between *loka* (the region illumined by the sun and other luminaries) and *aloka* (the region of perpetual darkness). As the *Bhāgavata* says, "it was placed by *Īśvara* on the limit of the three worlds; and its height and breadth are such that the rays of the heavenly luminaries, from the sun to the polar star, which spread over the regions within the mountain, cannot penetrate beyond it". See *Viṣṇu Purāṇa*, Bk. II, chapter 4 and Wilson's translation and *Bhāgavata* 5.20.34ff. and the commentary of Śrīdharasvāmin. Kālidāsa refers to the mountain in a simile in *Raghu* 1.68.

[84] I.e. Rāma's power extended as far as the wall of Laṅkā, while that of Rāvaṇa was confined within the limits of the city.

[85] I.e. during the churning of the ocean by the gods and demons.

the goddess of wealth from its waters while it was churned).[86]

K says रामस्य रावणस्य च लोकालोकान्तरालनि:सामान्ये निरुपमाने, इदानीं वर्धमाने रामस्य प्रतापे, रावणस्य तु निर्वतमाने प्रसरान्निवर्तमाने, प्राकारान्तरेण प्राकारव्यवधानेन द्विधाकृते सति रामप्रतापो लङ्कां न प्रविष्ट:। रावणप्रताप: प्राकारात् भग्न इति। एवं द्विधाकृते सति उत्तरत्र संबन्ध:।

MY says रामस्य प्रताते लोकालोकावृतस्य भूगोलस्यान्तरालं सर्वं यथाभिव्याप्नुयात् तथा लङ्काप्राकारं यावत् बहि: सर्वत्र प्रसरणेन वर्धमाने, दशमुखस्य तु प्रतापे प्राक् ब्रह्माण्डोदरमभिव्याप्य स्थितेऽपि इदानीं प्राकारात् बहिर्देशं सर्व विहायान्तरेव यथावस्थितं स्यात् तथा निर्वतमाने सतीत्यर्थगति:। प्राकार एवान्तरं व्यवधानं तेन द्विधाकृते एकस्मिन् प्रतापे प्रतापान्तरात् भिन्नदेशतयावस्थिते सति। प्रताप इति जात्यपेक्षया द्वित्वेऽपि एकवचनमिति शब्दगति: Kula says लोकालोकान्तराले रवि(?)-तेजोविधेयीभूतचक्रवालगिरिपरिच्छन्नभुवनोदरे। . . . लङ्काप्रकारमध्ये परं रावणप्रताप:, अन्यत्र सर्वत्र रामस्येत्यर्थ:।

K says त्रिदशानां जनितानुरागे रामे चन्द्र इव, मथितात् समुद्रात् चन्द्र इव, उत्तीर्णे सति मथितस्य पर्वतपतनक्षोभितस्य सागरस्य लक्ष्म्या समृद्ध्या सह प्रसन्ना शोभा जाता। यथा पूर्वं मथितस्य (सागरस्य) लक्ष्म्या सह प्रसन्ना मदिरा जाता तद्वदिति।

MY says मथने लक्ष्मीर्धनाधिदेवता, शोभातीता काचिद्देवतैव, प्रसन्ना मदिरेति स्फुटम्। सम्प्रति तु सागरे भवत्प्रसादस्थायां शोभायामुपचर्यते, प्रसन्ना शोभा भवति। तेन प्रसादजनिता शेभेत्यर्थ:। लक्ष्मीस्तु सेतो रामसंचरणजनिता शोभेति भेदो द्रष्टव्य:। उत्तीर्णे समुद्रमतिक्रान्ते रामे, चन्द्रे तु समुद्रादुदिते सतीति। त्रिदशानुरागजननं तु द्वयो: साधारणम्।

Kula says लक्ष्म्या समं जयलक्ष्म्या सह रामे जगदाह्लादकत्वात् मृगलाञ्छन इव रावणादिजगत्कण्टकक्षयहेतुत्वात् त्रिदशजनितानुरागे उत्तीर्णे सति मथितस्य क्षोभितस्य सागरस्य शोभा प्रसन्ना अनाविला जाता। यथा पूर्वं देवदानवै: मथितस्य सागरस्य लक्ष्म्या सह चन्द्रे सुधानिधानत्वात् त्रिदशजनितानुरागे (?) उत्थिते सति शोभा प्रसन्नाभूत्। R says शोभायतीति शोभारूपा प्रसन्ना मदिरा। अथवा शोभानाम्नी काचिदप्सर:श्रेष्ठा।

इअ सिरिपवरसेणविरइए कालिदासकए दहमुहवहे महाकव्वे
अट्ठमो आसासओ समत्तो।

[इति श्रीप्रवरसेनविरचिते कालिदासकृते दशमुखवधे
महाकाव्येऽष्टम आश्वासक: समाप्त:।]

---

[86] According to Kulanātha: When Rāma, beloved of the gods, like the moon, crossed the ocean, accompanied by the goddess of victory, the disturbed sea assumed a serene beauty (as it did when the moon emerged with the goddess of wealth while it was churned).

नवम आश्वासकः
Ninth Āśvāsakaḥ

1. अहं पेच्छन्ति पवङ्गा सअलजअक्कमणवड्ढिअमहासिहरम्।
णिट्ठविअदाहिणदिसं सेसदिसामुहवहाविअं व सुवेलम्।।

[अथ प्रेक्षन्ते प्लवङ्गाः सकलजगदाक्रमणवर्धितमहाशिखरम्।
निष्ठापितदक्षिणदिशं शेषदिङ्मुखप्रधावितमिव सुवेलम्।।]

The apes beheld the Suvela mountain that seemed to engulf the southern region, and stretch away to cover the remaining regions, extending its great peaks to pervade the entire world.

सकलजगतामाक्रमणाय वर्धितमहाशिखरं, निष्ठापितदक्षिणदिशं तिरोहितदक्षिणदिङ्मुखं, शेषदिङ्मुखाच्छादनाय प्रधावितमिव K, Kula reads *ghaṭṭavia* explained as आक्रान्त fo *ṇiṭṭhavia* = निष्ठापित, नाशित (R and MY)।

2. भुवणस्स व महुमहणं भुवणभरज्झीणमहुमहस्स व सेसम्।
सेसस्स व सलिलणिहिं सरिआवइणो विसम्मिअव्वभरसहम्।।

[भुवनस्येव मधुमथनं भुवनभरक्षीणमधुमथनस्येव शेषम्।
शेषस्येव सलिलनिधिं सरित्पतेर्विश्रमितव्यभरसहम्।।]

It was capable of sustaining the weight of the ocean, just as Viṣṇu is capable of sustaining the weight of the universe, and the serpent Ananta that of Viṣṇu, worn out with the burden of the universe, and the ocean likewise that of Ananta.[1]

K and MY read *āsīṇa* for *-jjhīṇa* = क्षीण (R and Kula ?). K, MY and Kula read = निषत्तव्य, i.e. *ṇisammiavva* for *vi*° = विश्रमितव्य (R). K says भुवनस्य निषत्तव्यभरसहं, निषत्तव्यमिति भावे तव्यप्रत्ययः निषदनमित्यर्थः। त्रिभुवननिषदनभरस्य सहं समर्थ मधुमथनमिव। उदरगतेन भुवनभरेण सहासीनस्य तस्य मधुमथनस्योपरि शयानस्य भरसहं शेषमिव, तस्य शेषस्य भरसहं समुद्रमिव, तस्य समुद्रस्यापि निषत्तव्यभरसहं सुवेलं ददृशुः। अयं मालोपमाप्रकारः। MY says भुवनभरासीनः भुवनभरेण निषण्ण इत्यर्थः। R says समुद्रस्य विश्रमितव्यं विश्रामः।भावे तव्यः। तत्र भरसहं भारक्षमम्। समुद्रस्याप्यवलम्बनमित्यर्थः।

---

[1] Viṣṇu reposes on the coils of Ananta in the ocean.

3. धरणिहरेअव्वसहं उअहिभरेअव्वपव्वलणइप्पवहम्।
णहमाअव्वसमत्थं खअमारुअरुम्भिअव्वजोग्गणिअम्बम्॥

[धरणीधर्तव्यसहमुदधिभर्तव्यप्रबलनदीप्रवाहम्।
नभोमातव्यसमर्थं क्षयमारुतरोद्धव्ययोग्यनितम्बम्॥]

It was capable of bearing the weight of the earth. Its streams were capable of filling the ocean. It was able to measure the sky. Its flanks were strong enough to withstand the winds of the epoch of destruction.

K and MY read वत्सल for *pabbala* = प्रबल (R and Kula). See Notes on 4.25. K says उदधेः पूरणे समर्थनदीप्रवाहम्। वत्सलशब्दः समर्थपर्यायः। प्रागप्युक्तम् – *vacchalo surāṇa vi samare* (4.25). MY says *dhareavva* धारयितव्य। धारणेत्यर्थः। धारयितव्येत्यादिः तव्यप्रत्ययो धारणादिभावपरतयानुसंधेयः। *bhareavva* धारण(भरण?) पूरणेति यावत्। वत्सलः समर्थः। *meavva* (for *mā*-) मातव्य मानेत्यर्थः।

4. दूरपरिपेल्लिअदिसं दूरोणामिअसमत्थपाआलअलम्।
दूरअरुक्खित्तणहं णवर करासण्णपाअवप्फलकुसुमम्॥

[दूरपरिप्रेरितदिशं दूरावनामितसमस्तपातालतलम्।
दूरतरोत्क्षिप्तनभः केवलं करासन्नपादपफलकुसुमम्॥]

It seemed to have driven the regions of the sky afar off, and weighed down the entire nether world deep below, and raised the sky to a greater altitude. Only the fruits and flowers of its trees were within easy reach.

K (*pratīka*) has *dūra-paḍi*°. He has प्रतिपीडित for *paripellia* = परिप्रेरित (R). MY also has *paḍipellia*. Several verses after this are missing in both the manuscripts of MY. Kula says दूरं प्रतिप्रेरिताः पीडयित्वापसारिता दिशो येन तम्। He reads *ovāhia* = अवगाढ़ (cf. HC 4.205) for *oṇāmia* (अवनामित); and *samatta* for *samattha*. He says दूरावगाढमतः समाप्तं पातालं येन। *samattha* इति पाठे समस्त इत्यर्थः। *SC* text has *ovāhia*.

5. पासल्लागअसरिअं अमुक्कपाआलसाअरजलुच्छङ्गम्।
आइवराहुव्वत्तणखणपडिउद्धट्ठिअं व मेइणिवेढम्॥

[पार्श्वागतसरितममुक्तपातालसागरजलोत्सङ्गम्।
आदिवराहोद्वर्तनक्षणपतितोर्ध्वस्थितमिव मेदिनीवेष्टम्॥]

Rivers flowed down its flanks. It was firmly planted in the nether regions and the depths of the sea. It seemed as if it were the earth, slanting for a moment, while being lifted from the ocean by the Primeval Boar.[2]

K reads *valia* for *paḍia* (R) in the second line. He says पार्श्वप्रसृतसरितम्, अमुक्तपातालममुक्तसागरजलोत्सङ्गं च। तदानीमादिवराहस्योद्वर्तनेनोद्धरणार्थं क्षणमात्रं वलितम् ऊर्ध्वस्थितं मेदिनीमण्डलमिव स्थितम्। Kula says विनीतोर्ध्वस्थितमिव मेदिनीवेष्टम्। Kula's विनीत seems to be a mistake for वलित। *SC* text has *valia*. *SC* says आदिवराहस्य उद्वर्तनेन उत्क्षेपणेन क्षणात् वलितोर्ध्वस्थितं तिर्यगूर्ध्वीभूतं मेदिनीवेष्टमिव। अन्ये तु . . . वलितं मण्डलाकारं समुत्थितं मेदिनीवेष्टमिव। पासल्लशब्दः पार्श्वे देशी।

6. पाआलभरिअमूलं वज्जमुहाओडणट्ठविअणिक्कम्पम्।
आलाणक्खम्भं मिव सुरहत्थिक्खन्धणिहसमसिणिअपासम्।।

[पातालभृतमूलं वज्रमुखाकोलनस्थापितनिष्कम्पम्।
आलानस्तम्भमिव सुरहस्तिस्कन्धनिघर्षमसृणितपार्श्वम्।।]

Its foundations filled the nether regions. It was fixed firm by ramming it down with the tip of the thunderbolt. It seemed to be a post to which the elephants of the god were tied, with its sides smoothed down by the rubbing of their shoulders.

āoḍaṇa is translated in K (*chāyā*) as त्रोटन्। K (commentary) says पाताले भरितमूलं पूर्णमूलम्, इन्द्रस्य वज्रमुखाभिघातेन निष्कम्पं स्थापितं, सुरहस्तिनामैरावतादीनां स्कन्धनिकाषेण मसृणित पार्श्वंश्लक्ष्णीकृतपार्श्वमेवंभूतत्वात् आलानस्तम्भमिव स्थितम्। आलानस्तम्भश्च दूरमधस्तात् प्रतिष्ठितः मूलदेशमभितः काष्ठदण्डाभिघातैः निष्कम्पस्थापितश्च भवतीति। Kula says वज्रमुखाकोटनेन पक्षच्छेदाघातेन . . . स्थिरीकृत्य स्थापितमित्यर्थः। R says वज्रस्य मुखेन यदाकोलनं मृत्तिकामभिहत्य दृढीकरणं तेन स्थापितम् अत एव निष्कम्पम्।

7. विमलिअरसाअलेण वि विसहरवइणा अदिट्ठमूलच्छेअम्।
अप्पत्ततुङ्गसिहरं तिहुअणहरणपरिवड्ढिएण वि हरिणा।।

[विमर्दितरसातलेनापि विषधरपतिनादृष्टमूलच्छेदम्।
अप्राप्ततुङ्गशिखरं त्रिभुवनभरणपरिवर्धितेनापि हरिणा।।]

[2] I.e. the Boar incarnation of Viṣṇu. Cf. 7.2.

The extremity of its base was not seen even by the lord of serpents[3] that crushed the nether regions (with its weight). Its lofty peaks were not reached even by Viṣṇu when he extended his frame to wrest the universe (from the demon Bali).[4]

K reads *vilulia* for *vimalia* = विमर्दित (R and Kula). K says सर्वतोऽपि गाढरसातलेनापि शेषेणादृष्टमूलावसानं, त्रिभुवनहरणाय बलिना महासुरेण गृहीतस्य त्रिभुवनस्य हरणार्थं परिवृद्धेन त्रिविक्रमेणापि अप्राप्ततुङ्गशिखरम्। Kula says विषधरपतिनापि न दृष्टो मूलस्य छेदः पर्यन्तो यस्य तम्।

8. विच्छूढोअहिसलिलं कडअभमन्तभुअइन्ददिण्णावेढम्।
पासट्ठिएण रइणा करेहिं हरिणा व्व मन्दरं उवऊढम्।।

[विक्षिप्तोदधिसलिलं कटकभ्रमद्भुजगेन्द्रदत्तावेष्टम्।
पार्श्वस्थितेन रविणा करैर्हरिणेव मन्दरमुपगूढम्।।]

It drove back the waters of the sea, and was encircled by the great serpents moving about its slopes, and encompassed by the sun with its rays as it stood beside it;[5] just as the Mandara mountain, encircled by the great serpent (Vāsuki), and held fast by Viṣṇu with his arms, convulsed the waters of the ocean (during the churning).[6]

विस्तारेण विक्षप्तोदधिसलिलं, कटकेषु भ्रमद्भिः महाभुजङ्गैः दत्तावेष्टनम्। अन्यत्र कटके भ्रमता मन्थनरज्जुभूतेन वासुकिना दत्तावेष्टनम्। उत्तुङ्गतरत्वात् पार्श्ववर्तिना रविणा करैः किरणैरुपगूढम्। हरिणा करैः मन्दरमिव K.

9. सेससिररअणघट्टिअमणिमूलुज्ज्ञोअहअरसाअलतिमिरम्।
विसमुद्धसिहरसंकडपणट्ठरविमण्डलन्धआरिअगअणम्।।

[शेषशिरोरत्नघट्टितमणिमूलोद्द्योतहतरसातलतिमिरम्
विषमोर्ध्वशिखरसंकटप्रनष्टरविमण्डलान्धकारितगगनम्।।]

It dispelled the gloom of the nether regions with the radiance of its bejewelled base, scraped by the gems on the head of the serpent Ananta;[7] while it plunged the sky into darkness,

---

[3] A reference to Ananta sustaining the earth on its numerous hoods.

[4] Cf. verse 51.

[5] See verse 38.

[6] The ocean was churned by the gods and demons, using the Mandara mountain as a churn-staff, with Vāsuki serving as a rope.

[7] See verse 7.

because the orb of the sun disappeared in the recesses of its rugged and lofty peaks.

शेषस्य शिरोरत्नैर्घट्टितस्य मणिमयमूलस्योद्द्योतेन प्रभया हतरसातलतिमिरम्। K संकटेषु मिथोऽन्तरालेषु R संकटे गहनदेशे Kula. K says विषमाणामूर्ध्वशिखराणां संकटे संकटमार्गे प्रणष्टरविमण्डलत्वात् अन्धकारितगमनम्। एवं रसातले गगनधर्मं गगने रसातलधर्मं च कुर्वाणम्।

10. ससिबिम्बपासणिहसणकसणसिलाभित्तिपसरिआमअलेहम्।
जोण्हाजलपव्वालिअविसमुम्हाअन्तमुणिअरविरहमग्गम्।।

[शशिबिम्बपार्श्वनिघर्षणकृष्णशिलाभित्तिप्रसृतामृतलेखम्।
ज्योत्स्नाजलप्रप्लावितविषमोष्मायमाणज्ञातरविरथमार्गम्।।]

Streaks of nectar ran down its dark rocky wall, scraped by the side of the (passing) moon;[8] and the track of the sun's chariot could be recognized, because it profusely emitted vapours, when flooded with moonbeams.[9]

K and Kula read निकषित for *ṇihasaṇa* = निघर्षण (R). K reads शिखर for *kasaṇa* = कृष्ण (R and Kula). K (*chāyā*) has प्रक्षालित for *pabbālia* = प्रप्लावित (R); and ज्वलित for *muṇia* = ज्ञात (R and probably Kula). K says अन्तिके गच्छतः शशिनो बिम्बस्य पार्श्वेन निकषितायां शिखरशिलाभित्तौ प्रसृततदीयामृतधारम्। ज्योत्स्नाजलसिक्तत्वाद्विषममूष्मायमाणरविरथ-पथम्। Kula says शशिबिम्बेन पार्श्वे निकषिता निघृष्टा या कृष्णशिलाभित्तिः तत्र प्रसृता अमृतलेखा यत्र। ज्योत्स्नाजलेन प्रेरितत्वात् (?) विषममत्यर्थमूष्मायमाणः अतएव ज्ञातः (?) स्मष्टमुपलक्षितो रविरथमार्गो यत्र तम। R says विषमं यथा स्यात् तथोष्मायमाणो बाष्पायमाणः।

11. सिहरालीणमिअङ्कं विरलट्ठिअगहिअसलिलजलअक्खण्डम्।
खुडिउव्वूढमुणालं णिसासु विसमहिअकद्दमं व सुरगअम्।।

[शिखरालीनमृगाङ्कं विरलस्थितगृहीतसलिलजलदखण्डम्।
खण्डितोद्व्यूढमृणालं निशासु विषमहितकर्दममिव सुरगजम्।।]

With the moon clinging to the summit, and patches of water-filled clouds thinly scattered on the flanks, the mountain at

---

[8] The moon is supposed to be composed of nectar.

[9] The misty exhalation on the mountain at night is fancied as being caused by the flaming track of the sun being quenched by the rays of the moon, cool as a shower.

night looked like an elephant of the gods, holding aloft a torn lotus-stalk (with its trunk), with its body spattered here and there with mud.[10]

निशि शिखरालीनमृगाङ्कं, विरलमवस्थिता गृहीतासलिला जलदखण्डा यत्र तम्। एवंरूपत्वात् जलक्रीडया त्रुटितोदूढमृणालमण्डलं हृतकर्दम[11] सुरगजमिव स्थितम् K. विषमं यथा स्यात् तथा हृतः क्वचित् क्वचित् तनावारोपितः कर्दमो येन गजास्वाभाव्यात् R. विषमहृतकर्दमं कचित् कचित् लग्नपङ्कम् *SC*.

12. हरिअवणराइपिसुणिअदूरअरालोअसिहरसरिआमग्गम्।
पवणुक्खुडिअकिलामिअमिअङ्कपुट्ठिपडिउस्ससन्तकिसलअम्।।

[हरितवनराजिपिशुनितदूरतरालोकशिखरसरिन्मार्गम्।
पवनोत्खण्डितक्लाम्यन्मृगाङ्कपृष्ठप्रत्युच्छ्वसत्किसलयम्।।]

The courses of the streams flowing from the summit were seen from afar, revealed by lines of verdant woods; and the young shoots, torn and withered by the wind, were refreshed in contact with the back of the moon.

K and Kula seem to read *ukkhuḍaṇa* for °*ḍia* = उत्खण्डित (R). K says दूरतरालोकः अत्युच्छ्रायेणातिदूरे दृश्यमानः शिखरसरिन्मार्गः शिखरात् प्रसृतायाः सरितो मार्गो गमनपथः हरितया श्यामलया वनराज्या केवलं पिशुनितः सूच्यते यत्र तम्। पवनाभिघातजनितात् त्रुटनात् क्लान्तानि . . . किसलयानि यत्र तम। Kula says पवनोत्खण्डनेन क्षयितानि मृगाङ्केन प्रत्युच्छ्वसन्ति किसलयानि यत्र तम्। K says मृगाङ्कपृष्ठे पतितत्वात् उच्छ्वसन्ति किसलयानि। K's construction is *paḍia+ūsasanta*, while Kula and R take *paḍi* as an *upasarga* (प्रति)। R says प्रत्युच्छ्वसन्ति प्रत्युज्जीवन्ति।

13. दूरुद्धाइअसिहरं जलणिहिजलदिट्ठविअडपाअडपडिमम्।
उप्पाआसणिपहअं उद्धप्फुडितपडिएक्कपासं व ठिअम्।।

[दूरोद्धावितशिखरं जलनिधिजलदृष्टविकटप्रकटप्रतिमम्।
उत्पाताशनिप्रहतमूर्ध्वस्फुटितपतितैकपार्श्वमिव स्थितम्।।]

The peaks soared, and the vast and clear reflection of the mountain was seen in the waters of the sea. It seemed as if it

[10] The moon is likened to a torn lotus stalk, and the patches of clouds to spattered mud.

[11] K is here corrupt. But see quotation from *SC* and K on 10.10 हृतातपरजसि . . . सुरगजे, i.e. हृत for his.

were struck by portentous lightning, and being riven asunder at the top, one side of it had fallen into the sea.

dūruddhāia is rendered by Kula as दूरोद्धापित। K (*chāyā*) has दूरोत्थापित। K says दूरमुच्छ्वसितशिखरम् जलनिधिजले दृश्यमानविशाल- परिस्फुटप्रतिबिम्बम्। एवंरूपत्वात् प्रलयकाले उत्पातरूपेण अशनिना प्रहतं ताडितम्, ऊर्ध्वादारभ्य स्फुटितपतितैकपार्श्वमिव तिष्ठन्तम्।

14. गुरुभरसेसाहिप्फणवारंवारपडिरुद्धमूलुच्छङ्गम्।
खअमारुउक्खआणिअतुङ्गअडावडिअभिण्णसेसमहिहरम्।।

[गुरुभरशेषाहिफणवारंवारप्रतिरुद्धमूलोत्सङ्गम्।
क्षयमारुतोत्खातानीततुङ्गतटापतितभिन्नशेषमहीधरम्।।]

The broad expanse of its base was sustained by Ananta's heavy hoods by turns;[12] while the other mountains were dashed to pieces, when uprooted and blown on to its lofty slopes by the winds of the epoch of destruction.

गुरुभारैः शेषहिफणैः पर्यायेण प्रतिरुद्धमूलप्रदेशं भरातिरेकात् फणैः क्रमेण धारितमूलस्थलम्। क्षयमारुतेनोत्खातानीताः तुङ्गेषु तटेष्वापतिताः अत एव भिन्नाः शेषमहीधरा यस्य तम् K.

15. गहिअजलमेहपेल्लिअणिव्वाअन्तणिहुअट्ठिअमहामहिसम्।
णिहअगअकुम्भलोहिअसिलाअलोसुक्खबद्धमुत्तावडलम्।।

[गृहीतजलमेघप्रेरितनिर्वाप्यमाणनिभृतस्थितमहामहिषम्।
निहतगजकुम्भलोहितशिलातलावशुष्कबद्धमुक्तापटलम्।।]

The huge buffaloes on the mountain lay still and refreshed as the water-filled clouds pressed against them; and the pearls that were inside the temples of the elephants, killed (by lions), stuck fast as they dried on the blood-stained slabs of stone.[13]

गृहीतजलैर्मेघैः पीडितत्वादाक्रान्तत्वात निर्वान्तः सुखीभवन्तो निभृतं स्थिताः महामहिषा यत्र तम् K. गृहीतजलैर्मेघैः प्रेरिताः सन्तः Kula. सिंहनिहतानां गजानां कुम्भलोहितेन कुम्भरुधिरेण शिलातले बद्धावशुष्कमुक्तापटलम् K.

16. लवणजलसीहराहअदरुव्वमन्तदुममुद्धपल्लवराअम्।
सींहरवभीपअत्थिअणिउज्झिएक्कचलणट्ठिउक्कण्णमअम्।।

---

[12] I.e. Ananta used its thousand hoods in turn to bear the weight of the mountain.

[13] See verse 24.

[लवणजलशीकराहतदरोद्वमद्द्रुममुग्धपल्लवरागम्।
सिंहरवभीतप्रस्थितनिकुञ्चितैकचरणस्थितोत्कर्णमृगम्।।]

The colour of the young leaves of the trees faded slightly in contact with the briny sea spray; and the deer ran away, scared by the roar of lions, but stopped short, bending a leg, and pricking up their ears.

लवणजलशीकरैराहतत्वात् दरोद्वमन् किञ्चित् प्रणश्यन् द्रुमाणां मुग्धस्य पल्लवस्य रागो यत्र तम्। K. MY says *uvvamanta* उद्वमत् निःसरत् विनश्यदिति यावत् Kula says विच्छायीभवन्।

17. कडअपरिपेल्लिआणं रइअरपाअडिअकन्दराभरिआणम्।
अब्भन्तरट्ठिआणं परिल्लपासपरिसंठिअं व दिसाणम्।।

[कटकप्रतिप्रेरितानां रविकरप्रकटितकन्दराभृतानाम्।
अभ्यन्तरस्थितानामपरपार्श्वपरिसंस्थितमिव दिशाम्।।]

The mountain seemed to encompass the regions of the sky,[14] which stood within its limits, enveloped by its slopes, and enclosed within its sunlit caves.

K and MY read दृष्टानां for °*ṭṭhiāṇaṁ* (R and Kula). K (*chāyā*) has कटकपरिपीडितानां . . . परिपार्श्वतः परिसंस्थितमिव दिशाम्। K says कटकैः पीडितानां तिरोहितानां, रविकिरणैः प्रकटितासु विशालतरासु कन्दरासु भरितानाम्, एवमभ्यन्तरे दृष्टानां दिशां परितः पार्श्वे परिसंस्थितमिव। तदीयैः कटकैः व्याप्तत्वाद्दिशां बहिः अप्रकाशतया तदभ्यन्तरे दृष्टत्वाच्च दिशां परिपार्श्वे स्थितमिवेत्यर्थः। MY says *parilla-pāsa* परिपार्श्व (B has पर°)। बहिः कटकपीडितानां रविकर-प्रकाशितदर्युदरप्रविष्टपरिसमाप्तदृष्टानां दिशां परतोऽवस्थितमिवेत्यर्थः। Kula says दशानामपि दिशां परपार्श्वे बहिःपार्श्वे।[15] *Parilla-pāsa* seems to be same as *parilla-vāsa* mentioned in *Deśīnāmamālā* 6.33 in the sense of अज्ञातगति। The meaning is applicable here, i.e. the extent of the Suvela was unknown to the regions of the sky enveloped by the mountain.

18. रअणिआसु दूरुग्गअसिहरअणंतअं
सुहणिसण्णमअखण्डिअसिहरअणन्तअम्।

[14] Literally seemed to stand all around the regions of the sky.

[15] R says वयं तु दिशामपरपार्श्वे परितो बहिःस्थितमिव।

कुविअरामभिण्णोअहिदढसरणोल्लिअं
सिहरलग्गससिमण्डलणीसरणोल्लिअम्।।

[रजनिकासु दूरोद्गतशिखररत्नैस्ततं
सुखनिषण्णमृगखण्डितशिखरतृणान्तम्।
कुपितरामभिन्नोदधिदृढशरनोदितं
शिखरलग्नशशिमण्डलनिःसरणार्द्रितम्।।]

It was vast in extent, and at night the flaming lustre of its gems spread far into the sky. The antelopes, lying at ease, nibbled the tips of grass on its peaks. It was rocked heavily by the arrows, with which Rāma in his wrath had cloven the sea asunder.[16] It was drenched with oozings of nectar from the orb of the moon[17] resting upon its summit.

K and MY read *rāaa-sudūra* for *raaṇiāsu dūra* (R). K says राजतानि रजतमयानि सुदूरमुद्गतानि अनन्तानि शिखराणि यस्य तम्। सुखनिषण्णैर्मृगैः खण्डितशिखराणि[18] शष्पशङ्कया लीढकिरणानि (रत्नानि) मरकतादीनि यत्र तम्। तत विस्तृतम्। कुपितस्य रामस्य भिन्नोदधिभिः शरैः दृढं प्रणुन्नम्। शिखरै लग्नस्य शशिनः निःसरणेन अमृतनिष्यन्देन आर्द्रितम्।

MY says *rāaa* (i.e. रागद) रञ्जक। सुदूरोद्गतशिखाररत्नं ततं सुखनिषण्णमृगखण्डितशिखरतृणान्तम्। Kula says रात्रिषु दूरोद्गतशिखानि रत्नानि यत्र तम्। (ततं) विस्तृतम्। . . . मृगैः खण्डितशिखरतृणोऽन्तः पर्यन्तः यस्य तम्। Kula seems to read *rāiāsu* found in *SC* text.

19. दूरोवाहिअमूलं रविअरवोलीणसिहरणट्ठालोअम्।
अद्धत्थमिआआमं जहेअ उअहिसलिले तहेअ णहअले।।

[दूरापवाहितमूलं रविकरव्यतिक्रान्तशिखरनष्टालोकम्।
अर्धास्तमितायामं यथैवोदधिसलिले तथैव नभस्तले।।]

Its foundations reached into the depths of the sea, and it was invisible[19] at the top which was beyond the range of the

---

[16] See canto V.

[17] Cf. verse 10.

[18] खण्डितशिखानि ? cf. Kula's explanation below. R says शिखा तेजोधारा। He also says मृगैः खण्डितः शिखरतृणानामन्तोऽग्रं यत्र तम्।

[19] Or, bereft of light.

rays of the sun. So its dimensions were half hidden in the sky as they were in the waters of the sea.

K (*pratīka*) has *dūroāhia*. He reads *raha* for *-ara* = कर (R and Kula). He says अधस्तात् दूरमवगाढमूलम् उपरि रविरथमतिक्रान्तैः शिखरैर्नष्टालोकम्। MY says उदधेरधस्तात् मूलेनेव नभस्यपि उपरिष्टाच्छिखरैरर्धास्त-मितायाममदृश्यार्धायामं स्थितमित्यर्थः। *ovāhia* अवगाढ। *bolīṇa* अतिक्रान्त। उभयत्र कर्तरि क्तः। Kula says नष्टालोकमदृश्यतां गतम्।

K says एवंभूतत्वात् उदधिसलिले यथा अर्धास्तमितं तथैव नभस्तले अर्ध-स्थगितायामम्। R renders *ovāhia* as अपवाहित explained as अधःप्रापित।

20. पवणन्दोलिअचन्दणसंघट्टुट्ठिअसुगन्धिधूमुप्पीडम्।
दरपीओअहिगरुइअसेसद्धन्तजलआवलम्बिअसिहरम्।।

[पवनान्दोलितचन्दनसंघट्टोत्थितसुगन्धिधूमोत्पीडम्।
दरपीतोदधिगुरुकितशेषार्धान्तजलदावलम्बितशिखरम्।।]

It was enveloped in a dense mass of fragrant vapour rising from the friction of the sandal trees swayed by the wind. The clouds that had partly absorbed the waters of the sea held on to its peaks, being heavy-laden at the other end.[20]

K says दरपीतोदधित्वात् गुरूकृतस्य जलदस्य शेषार्धान्तेन पश्चिमार्धेन अवलम्बित-शिखरम्। R says शेषार्धान्तः पश्चाद्भागः।

21. तलपडिहअसाअरअं उद्धोज्झरविहुअसीहरोसाअरअम्।
गहमालामेलिअअं सिहरट्ठिअचन्दमण्डलामेलिअअम्।।

[तलप्रतिहतसागरकमूर्ध्वनिर्झरविधुतसिंहरोषाकरम्।
ग्रहमालामेलितकं शिखरस्थितचन्द्रमण्डलापीडम्।।]

It withstood the waters of the sea with its base, and caused the anger of the lions, knocked down by the cascades at the top. It was crowned with a garland of planets, and wore a wreath, the orb of the moon resting upon its peaks.

K and MY read तट for तल; नित्य for *uddha*; शब्द for *vihua*; and गण for माला। K reads प्रमेलितं for *meliaaṁ*. K and MY read यक्ष for *canda*.

---

[20] The clouds are fancied as clinging to the peaks because they were dragged down by the load at the lower end.

K says तटेषु प्रतिहतसमुद्रं, नित्यनिर्झरशब्देन सिंहानां रोषे आदरप्रदं रोषातिशयप्रदमित्यर्थः। ग्रहगणैश्चन्द्रादित्यादिभिः प्रमेलितं संपृक्तं, शिखरस्थितैर्यक्षमण्डलैः आम्रेडितं चिरमभ्यस्तम्। MY says ग्रहगणेन वामेतरितं प्रदक्षिणीकृतं, वामेतरितमिति च वर्णस्थितिपरिवृत्त्या लभ्यते। अथवा ग्रहणव्यामेलितम्, i.e. *gaha-gaṇa-vāmeliaaṁ* for *gaha-gaṇa-ppameliaaṁ* (K), and *gaha-mālā-me°* (R). The verse is not found in Kula.

22. ससिपुरओ पसरिअअं कुहरेसु णिवाअणिप्पअम्पसरिअअम्।
मणिमअपासुत्तमअं कणअसिलासीणसुहिअपासुत्तमअम्।।

[शशिपुरतः प्रसृतकं कुहरेषु निवातनिष्प्रकम्पसरित्कम्।
मणिमयपार्श्वोत्तमं कनकशिलासीनसुखितप्रसुप्तमृगम्।।]

Its summit toward over the moon. The streams in its caverns were windless and calm. It dispelled darkness with its flanks rich in gems; and the deer lay sound asleep on the slabs of gold.

K and MY read परतः (*paraa*) for *purao* (R and Kula ?); and *ṇirāa* = निरायतं for *ṇivāa* निवात (R and Kula). K says सूर्यस्योपरि वर्तमानस्य शशिनोऽपि परतः उपरि प्रसृतं प्रवृद्धम्। कुहरेषु निरायतप्रसृतनिष्कम्पसरितम्। MY says दीर्घनिष्प्रकम्पसरित्कम्। Kula says मणिमयैः पार्श्वैः उत्तमस्कम् उत्क्षिप्ततिमिरम् उत्तमं वा।

23. भिण्णुक्खित्तपरम्मुहवलन्तसद्दूलगहिअगअकुम्भअडम्।
बिलपासुत्तभुअंगमजलधाराआरणिग्गअमणिच्छाअम्।।

[भिन्नोत्क्षिप्तपराङ्मुखवलमानशार्दूलगृहीतगजकुम्भतटम्।
बिलप्रसुप्तभुजंगमजलधाराकारनिर्गतमणिच्छायम्।।]

Pierced and tossed by the elephant (with its tusks), the tiger turned back and pounced on the former's temples; while the lustre of the gems on the hoods of the serpents, asleep in the cavities, issued forth like a jet of water.

24. अट्ठिअसमुद्दसीहरदुप्परिमासणिहकण्टअन्तमणिअडम्।
णहलग्गमोत्तिआफलगअसीसारूढणीहरन्तमइन्दम्।।

[अस्थितसमुद्रशीकरदुष्परिमर्षनिभकण्टकायमानमणितटम्।
नखलग्नमौक्तिकफलगजशीर्षारूढनिर्ह्रादमृगेन्द्रम्।।]

The slopes, rich in gems, seemed to bristle with thorns, like nettles, on account of the incessant sea spray;[21] and the lion roared, riding on the elephant's head, with the pearls[22] stuck in its claws.

K (*pratīka*) has *aḍḍia* (*aṭṭia* ?) rendered as शुष्क। MY has *atthia* (*ṭṭhia* in B) अस्थित अविरत अविच्छिन्न (Kula also). K says उपरिप्रसृतशुष्कसमुद्रजलशीकरत्वात् दुष्परिमर्शनिभं, दुष्परिमर्शो दुष्पर्श ओषधिविशेषः स्पर्शादिव देहे कण्डूं जनयति, तत्सदृशं भूत्वा कण्टकीभवन्मणितटम्। समुद्रजलशीकराः शोषाद्घनीभवन्ति। नखलग्नमौक्तिकफलाः गजशीर्षारूढा एव निःसरन्तो मृगेन्द्राः यत्र तम्। R says निर्ह्लादशालिनो मृगेन्द्राः। Cf. Hemacandra – *ṇīharai nīsarai* 4.79; *ṇīharai akkandai* 4.131. Kula has निर्ह्रदन्तः cf. *SC*.

25. ओवट्ठकोमलाइं वहमाणं मेहविमलिअविमुक्काइं।
कप्पलआवसुआइअपवणुद्धुअधवलअंसुआइ वणाइं।।

[अववर्षकोमलानि वहमानं मेघविमार्दितविमुक्तानि।
कल्पलताशोषितपवनोद्धूतधवलांशुकानि वनानि।।]

The woods on the mountain, heavily pressed by the clouds and then released were sodden with rain, with the white scarves hanging from the celestial creepers[23] drying and fluttering in the breeze.

SC text has *ovaṭṭa* for *ovaṭṭha*. According to Śrīnivāsa quoted by *SC*, it is a *deśī* word meaning मेघजलसेक। K and MY have *oaṭṭha* = अपवृष्ट MY.[24] MY says अथवा *oatta* इति पाठः। तत्रापवृत्तेति छाया। K reads विलुलित for *vimalia* (R, MY and Kula), cf. verse 7.[25] K and MYreadविमल for धवल (R and Kula). K says कल्पलतानां तत्रत्यानां

[21] The reference is to sea-water that has dried. In verse 41 the poet refers to "the salt taste of hardened sea spray". Here the salt crust formed by sea spray on the slopes of the mountain is likened to small thorns. The Greek verb *epantheō*, to bloom, be in flower, was likewise used of a salt crust forming on a surface, as in *Herodotus* II.12.

[22] I.e. the pearls inside the head of the elephant mangled by the lion. The reference is to the belief that an elephant's head contains pearls.

[23] Explained by Kṛṣṇa as the branches of the all-giving *kalpa* trees, See 14.74.

[24] अववृष्टेन अववर्षणेन कोमलानि Kula. His *pratīka* is *ovaṭṭha*. K (*chāyā*) has अव° and commentary अभि°।

[25] MY says *vimalia* (ā° manuscript A) विमृदित। विमृदितमुक्तानि विमृद्य विमुक्तानीत्यर्थः।

कल्पवृक्षशाखानां संबन्धीनि पवनेन शोषितत्वात् उत्थापितानि विमलान्यंशुकानि येषु तानि वनानि वहमानम्। MY also has उत्थापित।

26. आरूढोअहिसलिले अद्धुक्खअसरसविसमपासल्लदुमे।
कुसुमभरिए वहन्तं फलिहअडुत्ताणपत्थिए णइसोत्ते।।
[आरूढोदधिसलिलान्यर्धोत्खातसरसविषमपा श्र्वद्रुमाणि।
कुसुमभृतानि वहन्तं स्फटिकतटोत्तानप्रस्थितानि नदीस्त्रोतांसि।।]

Overrun by the waters of the sea, the streams, partly uprooting the moist leaning trees on the banks, and laden with flowers, ran shallow over the crystal slopes.

K reads मूल for सरस (R and Kula). K says समुद्रजलवृद्धौ नदीमुखैः आरूढोदधिसलिलानि, जलरयेणार्धोत्खातमूलत्वात् विषमाः पार्श्वद्रुमा येषां तानि . . . नदीस्त्रोतांसि वहन्तम्। MY says *pāsalla* पार्श्व। Kula says विषमं पार्श्वायिता द्रुमाः येषु तानि। R says स्फटिकतटे उत्तानानि अगभीराणि सन्ति प्रस्थितानि[26] तत्र खातं कर्तुमशक्तत्वादिति भावः।

27. रविरहतुरंगमाणं वाआइद्धसिहरोज्झरेहि धुवन्तम्।
थोओल्लपग्गहाइं लालाफेणलवगब्भिणाइ मुहाइं।।
[रविरथतुरंगमाणां वातोद्धूतशिखरनिर्झरैर्धावयन्तम्।
स्तोकार्द्रप्रग्रहाणि लालाफेनलवगर्भितानि मुखानि।।]

With the wind-swept cascades on the summit, the mountain cleansed the mouths of the horses of the sun's chariot, which were full of froth, and partly moistened the reins.

वाताविद्ध K (*chāyā*), वातप्ररितैः शिखरनिर्झरैः क्षालयन्तम्। K. वाताहतैः Kula, *dhuantaṁ* धावन्तं क्षालयन्तमिति यावत् MY.

28. दीहरसिहरालग्गं पज्जिलओसहिसिहाहअं वहमाणम्।
पाअडिअमअकलङ्कं णिसासु कज्जलइओअरं व मिअङ्कम्।।
[दीर्घशिखरालग्नं प्रज्वलितौषधिशिखराहतं वहमानम्।
प्रकटितमृगकलङ्कं निशासु कज्जलितोदरमिव मृगाङ्कम्।।]

The moon, resting upon its extensive summit, and touched by the flames of the plants blazing at night, clearly showed its stain, the deer, as if its inner surface was covered with soot.

---

[26] K says कुसुमभरितानि। स्फटिकमये तटे कटके उत्तानप्रस्थितानि स्फटिकतटवर्ण- निर्विशेषं प्रस्थितानि नदीस्त्रोतांसि।

प्रज्वलितौषधिशिखाहतम् K (*chāyā*). K says दीर्घतरे शिखरे लग्नं, निशासु प्रज्वलितौषधिज्वालाभिराहतं, प्रकटितमृगकलङ्कं, ज्वालाहतत्वात् कज्जलितोदरमिव मृगाङ्कं दधतम्।

29. उद्धरिअधरणिविअडं आइवराहहिअवङ्कदूरोआढम्।
णइसोत्तिहिब्भरन्तं खअरइसंतावसोसिअं मअरहरम्।।

[उद्धृतधरणीविकटमादिवराहहृतपङ्कदूरांवगाढम्।
नदीस्रोतोभिर्भरमाणं क्षयरविसंतापशोषितं मकरगृहम्।।]

With its streams it was filling the ocean that had been dried up by the heat of the sun of the epoch of destruction; the wide ocean, with the earth lifted out of its waters, and extremely deep, because the ooze was carried away by the Primeval Boar.[27]

उद्धृतया धरण्या हेतुना विशालम्, आदिवराहस्य महता शरीरेण हृतपङ्कत्वाद्दूरमवगाढम् अगाधं . . . समुद्रं नदीस्रोतोभिः पूरयन्तम् K.

30. अण्णाआगमणदिसे पुरओ पडिसद्दभेसिअणिअत्तमए।
विवरभरिए वहन्तं उक्कणिअवणगए मइन्दणिणाए।।

[अज्ञातागमनदिशः पुरतः प्रतिशब्दभीषितनिवृत्तमृगान्।
विवरभृतान्वहन्तमुत्कर्णितवनगजान्मृगेन्द्रनिनादान्।।]

The roar of lions filled the caves, making the elephants in the woods prick up their ears; while the direction from which the sound came being unknown, the deer fled straight on, but turned back, scared by the echoes.

K reads आकर्णितवनचरान् for *ukkaṇṇia-vaṇa-gae* = उत्कर्णितवनगजान् (R and Kula). He says कुतः संभवतीति अविज्ञातागमनमार्गान्, वनचराकर्णितान् मृगेन्द्रनिनादान् वहन्तम्। MY says *āaṇṇia* आकर्णित। कर्तरि क्तः। शब्दानामागमनदिशोऽपरिज्ञानं तारतया प्रतिशब्दसन्निधानाद्वा अशेषदिग्व्यापितत्वात्।

31. तामरसरआअम्बं सरेसु सुव्वन्तमुहुरसरआअम्बम्।
गहिआमिसहरिअइअं वेलाणिलसीहरोल्लवणहरिअइअम्।।

[तामरसरजआताम्रं सरस्सु श्रूयमाणमधुरस्वरकादम्बम्।
गृहीतामिषहरिदयितं वेलानिलशीकरार्द्रवनहरितायितम्।।]

[27] I.e. the Boar incarnation of Viṣṇu while lifting the earth submerged in the ocean.

The mountain was tinged with red by the pollen of the lotus blossoms; and on its lakes were heard the geese with their melodious notes. It was the favourite resort of lions pouncing on their prey. It was verdant with woods drenched with spray wafted by the sea breeze.

गृहीतामिषाणां गृहीतभक्ष्याणां हरीणां सिंहानां दयितं, वेलानिलशीकरार्द्रेण वनेन हरितीकृतं श्यामलितम्। K. MY says गृहीतामिषहर्यतिगतं[28] प्राप्तं हरिदयितमिति वा। वेलानिलशीकरार्द्रवनहरितीकृतमिति, भरितमिति वा। Kula says वेलानिलेन शीकरैर्यदार्द्रीकरणं तेन हरिताचितं तृणव्याप्तम्। He seems to take *ollavaṇa* as one word in the sense of आर्द्रीकरण।

32. मिलिअसमुद्दद्धन्ते पाअडणहमण्डले पहुत्तदसदिसे।
उइअत्थमिअदिणअरे भुवणविहाए व्व कंदरे वहमाणम्।।

[मिलितसमुद्रार्धान्तान्प्रकटनभोमण्डलान्प्रभूतदशदिशः।
उदितास्तमितदिनकरान्भुवनविभागानिव कंदरान्वहमानम्।।]

It had caves that seemed to be divisions of the world, with portions of the sea entering them, the firmament visible inside, the ten regions of the sky included in them, and the sun rising and setting within their confines.

Kula says प्रभूताः। संमिता दशं दिशो येषु तान्। K says मिलितसमुद्रैकदेशान्, अन्तःप्रकटनभोमण्डलान्, पर्याप्तदशदिशः, निजाभ्यन्तर एव उदितास्तमितदिनकरान्, एवंभूतत्वात् भुवनविभागानिव दृश्यमानान् कन्दरान् वहन्तम्।

33. उच्छलिओअहिभरिए थोअत्थोओसरन्तणिव्वूढजले।
आइमुहरे वहन्तं पुरओहुत्तलखणे सिहरणीसन्दे।।

[उच्छलिखोदधिभृतान्स्तोकस्तोकापसरन्निर्व्यूढजलान्।
आदिमधुरान्वहन्तं पुरतोऽभिमुखलक्षणाञ्शिखरनिःस्यन्दान्।।]

The brooks on the summit, issuing by degrees and growing in volume, were sweet at the source, and briny in their onward course, being overrun by the surging sea.

K and MY read उच्चलित for *ucchalia* (R and Kula). K reads °सलिलान् for *bharie* = भृतान् (R and Kula ?). K says उच्चलितसमुद्र-सलिलान्, स्तोकस्रबदविच्छिन्नजलान् आदौ मूले मधुरान्, पुरतः प्रदेशे लवणान् शिखरजलप्रवाहान् वहन्तम्। MY says *ṇivvūḍha* निर्व्यूढ निःशेषनिर्गत। आदिमधुरान्

[28] i.e. *aia* = अतिगत। Cf. *ainta* 6.26 = अयमान, गच्छत् R.

प्रभवप्रदेशभूतगिरितटोपरि मधुरान् . . . जलधिजलारूढप्रदेशे लवणरसानित्यर्थः। Kula says उच्छलितोदधिना हृतान् (भृतान् ?)। R says निर्व्यूढानि संभूयोपचितानि जलानि येषु तान्।

34. रअणच्छविहुव्वन्तं वलन्तसेसपिहुलप्फणविहुव्वन्तम्।
सरपरिवड्ढिअकमलं कडअलआलग्गसूररहअक्कमलम्।।

[रत्नच्छविधाव्यमानं वलच्छेषपृथुलफणविधूयमानम्।
सरःपरिवर्धितकमलं कटकलतालग्नसूररथचक्रमलम्।।]

It was brightened by the lustre of its jewels, and shaken by the massive hoods of the serpent Ananta as it turned about (under the weight).[29] Lotus beds expanded on its lakes, and the rust from the wheels of the sun's chariot adhered to the creepers on the slopes.

K and MY read विपुल for *pihula* = पृथुल (R and Kula). K says भारातिशयाद्वलमानस्य वक्रीकृतशरीरस्य शेषस्य विपुलैः फणैः धूयमानम्। Kula says परिवर्तमानस्य।

35. णहणीले वहमाणं उम्हाहअमहिसमग्गिओवरणवहे।
पासपसरन्तकिरणे मअतण्हावेढिए सरे व्व मणिअडे।।

[नभोनीलान्वहमानमुष्माहतमहिषमार्गितावतरणपथान्।
पार्श्वप्रसरत्किरणान्मृगतृष्णावेष्टितान्सरांसीव मणितटान्।।]

The sky-blue sapphire slopes, gleaming all around, and enveloped in a mirage, looked like lakes, with the buffaloes, oppressed with the heat, seeking a path for descending into them.[30]

K says नभस्तलवत् नीलान्, जलभ्रान्त्या उष्णाहतमहिषमार्गितावतरणपथान्, पार्श्वतः प्रसरत्किरणान् मणितटान् इन्द्रनीलवैडूर्यमणितटान् संरासीव वहमानम्। Kula seems to says मृगैः तृष्णया पिपासया वेष्टितान्। *SC* says मृगतृष्णा मरीचिका इति केचित्। R says मृगतृष्णया आवेष्टितान् व्याप्तान् and explains the word as मरीचिका। MY says सरःसाम्यादेव पार्श्वप्रसरत्किरणानि मृगतृष्णावेष्टितानि स्थितानि चटुलोर्मिसंकुलानि सलिलभृतानि सरांसीव। अथवा पार्श्वप्रसरत्किरणानि तदानीं मृगतृष्णावेष्टितानि स्थितानि सरांसीव किरणावरुद्धतया मृगतृष्णावेष्टिततया च

---

[29] I.e. while sustaining the earth made heavier by the mountain.

[30] I.e. the animals mistook the blue rocks for a sheet of water.

वृतिवेष्टितानीति मत्वा महिषैः अवतरणमार्ग- मार्गणमित्यवसेयम्। R has उष्माहत, and Kula उष्णायित।

36. गअमलिअतमालवणं सीहमुहोरुद्धरअअसिहरक्खण्डम्।
महिसाहअकसणसिलं अणुरूअट्ठाणमुक्कवणअररोसम्।।

[गजमृदिततमालवनं सिंहमुखावरुद्धरजतशिखरखण्डम्।
महिषाहतकृष्णशिलमनुरूपस्थानमुक्तवनचररोषम्।।]

There, the wild animal unleashed their fury on objects similar to themselves. The elephants crushed the *tamāla* woods; the lions seized with their mouths fragments of the silver peaks; and the buffaloes hit the black rocks (with their horns).

K (*chāyā*) has नखक्षिप्त for *muhoruddha* = मुखावरुद्ध (R). K (commentary) says सिंहैः प्रतिसिंहबुद्ध्या नखैरुत्क्षिप्तरजतशिखरखण्डम्। Kual has मुख like R, but seems to read अवरुग्ण, i.e. *olugga* for *oruddha*, cf. *SC*.

37. केसरिचलणतलाहअभिण्णपइण्णगअकुम्भमोत्तारअणम्।
वणदवभीअपहाविअगअउलमलिअणइसंगमोत्तारअणम्।।

[केसरिचरणतलाहतभिन्नप्रकीर्णगजकुम्भमुक्तारत्नम्।
वनदवभीतप्रधावितगजकुलमृदितनदीसंगमोत्तारतृणम्।।]

There, precious pearls were scattered from inside the temples of the elephant mangled by the lion's paws;[31] and the luxuriant grass on the approaches to the streams was crushed by the herds of elephants that ran thither, scared by the forest fires.

K, like R, explains उत्तार as उत्ताल, and says नदीसंगमेषु नदीनां संगमपदेषु उत्तालंप्रभूतं तृणं यत्र तम्। रलयोरदभेदः। MY says गजकुलमृदितनदीसंगमोत्तारवनम्। उत्तीर्यते तेनेत्युत्तारस्तीर्थम्। नदीसंगमावतारवनं वा। R seems to say नदीनां संगमे प्रवेशे। Kula seems to say नदीसंगमोत्तारस्य नदीसंगमतीरस्य तृणानि। Cf. *SC* which gives Lokanātha's explanation नदीसंगमसंबन्धिनः अवतरस्य घट्टस्य तृणानि।

38. कडअवलन्तरविरहं तलवणराइपडिघोलिरुब्भडतारम्।
पासल्लणिसण्णस्स वि उअरि वीअभुअणस्स व णिस्संमन्तम्।।

[31] Cf. verse 24.

[कटकवलद्रविरथं तालवनराजिप्रतिघूर्णमानोद्भटतारम्।
पार्श्वनिषण्णस्याप्युपरि द्वितीयभुवनस्येव निषीदन्तम्।।]

The chariot of the sun wound its way along the slopes of the mountain. The radiant stars wandered through the woods on its flanks. It seemed to tower over the firmament lying by its side.

K and Kula read तट for तल। K says उपरितटस्य वनराजिषु परिघूर्णमाना: भ्रमन्त: उद्भटा: अतिप्रकाशा: तारा नक्षत्राणि यस्य तम्। K reads भुवनत्रयस्य[32] for *bīa-bhuaṇassa* = द्वितीयभुवनस्य (R and Kula). K (*chāyā*) has एव त्रिभुवनस्य। K says एवमतितुङ्गत्वात् पार्श्वे निषण्णस्य परित: प्रदेशेषु स्थितस्यापि भुवनत्रयस्योपरि तिष्ठन्तमिव। चन्द्रादित्यनक्षत्राणां शिखरात् अधस्तादेव संचारादेव-मुत्प्रेक्षितम्। Kula says द्वितीयभुवनस्य गगनस्योपरीव निषीदन्तं तद्गतचन्द्रादित्यग्रहन-क्षत्राणामधोलक्ष्यमाणत्वादिति भाव:। MY says त्रिभुवनस्योपरि परितश्च व्याप्यावस्थितत्वाच्चेत्यर्थ:।

39. अद्धच्छिण्णरविअरे असमत्तपहुत्तसअलचन्दमऊहे।
छिण्णकडए वहन्तं उद्धाअणिअत्तगरुडमग्गिअसिहरे।।

[अर्धच्छिन्नरविकरानसमाप्तप्रभूतसकलचन्द्रमयूखान्।
छिन्नकटकान्वहन्तमुद्धावितनिवृत्तगरुडमार्गितशिखरान्।।]

The rays of the sun were half cut-off from its jagged cliffs,[33] and the rays of the full moon covered only a portion of them. The bird king Garuḍa who set out in quest of their summit, returned, worn out with fatigue.

K and MY read भिन्न for छिन्न (R and Kula). K reads म्लान (परिश्रान्त Kula) for *uddhāa* = उद्धावित (R). The reading of K and Kula appears to be *uvvāa* (cf. *SC* and notes on 8.2). K says अर्धावकाशे पर्यवसितरविकिरणान्, समस्तप्रदेशेषु अप्रभूतसकलचन्द्रकिरणान् अपर्याप्तचन्द्रभास:, अतिदूरगमनात् म्लानेन गरुडेन विश्रामितुं मार्गितशिखरान् भिन्नकटकानतिपुराणतया विशीर्णान् कटकान् वहन्तम्। भिन्नकटका अप्येवमतिविस्तीर्णावकाशा: किं पुन: अभिन्नकटका इत्यभिप्राय:। MY says *asamatta* असमस्त। भिन्नकटकानां कटकान्तरारोहपरिणाहयोस्तुल्यत्वेऽपि भेदमार्गेषु तयो: स्फुटोपलभ्यतया विशेषप्रतीति-

[32] i.e. *bhuaṇa-ttaassa*, an expression like *rayaṇa-ttaya* (Yogīndu's *Paramātma-prakaśa* 2.95).

[33] I.e. did not reach the upper part of the cliffs.

दर्शनाभिप्रायेण भिन्नेत्युक्तम्। भ्रान्त्या पश्चादुपनतरूपणात् मार्गणात् निवृत्तेन गरुडेन मार्गितशिखरान् दिदृक्षितशिखरान्, न तु मार्गितदृष्टशिखरानित्यर्थः। भिन्नकटका अप्येवंभूताः किं पुनरविकलावस्थिता इति चावगम्यते। Kula says असमाप्ते असमग्रप्रदेश एकदेश इत्यर्थः। प्रभूताः संमिताः सकलचन्द्रस्य पूर्णशशिनो मयूखा यत्र। . . . तान् वज्रादिघातादिना छिन्नकटकान् वहन्तम्। . . . छिन्नानामपि कटकानामियान् परिणाहातिशय इति भावः (partly corrected from *SC*). R says 'दुरालोकं दुरारोहं कटकान्तरसंगतम्। भृगुप्रायं गिरेः शृङ्गं तच्छिन्नकटकं विदुः'।।

40. सुरवहूण हिअअट्ठिअरअणवसारअं साअरस्स रइअं मिव रअणवसारअम्।
णलिणिवत्तउडजाअमहुरसामोअअं वउलवणणिम्महन्तमुहुरसामोअअम्।।

[सुरवधूनां हृदयस्थितरत्नप्रसाधकं सागरस्य रचितमिव रत्नप्रसारकम्।
नलिनीपत्रपुटजातमधुरश्यामोदकं बकुलवननिर्यन्मधुरसामोदकम्।।]

It fulfilled with marvellous perfection the desire for pleasure in the hearts of the celestial nymphs.[34] It seemed to be a mart set up for the gems of the ocean.[35] The water in its pools was sweet and dark in contact with the leaves of the lilies; and a fragrance like that of wind issued from the groves of *bakula* trees.[36]

K says सुरवधूनां हृदये स्थितः नवरतस्य अभिनवस्य रतस्य सार उत्कर्षो यत्र तम्। सागरस्य कृते रचितं रत्नप्रसारकमिव। रत्नानि प्रसारयतीति रत्नप्रसारको रत्नापणः। सागरोऽपि तदीयैरेव रत्नैः रत्नाकरो भवतीति भावः। नलिनीपत्रान्तरेषु श्यामं जातं मधुरमुदकं यस्य, नलिनीपत्रमध्यगतत्वात् तत्प्रभया श्यामलितमुदकमिति। अथवा नलिनीपत्रपुटजातेन नलिनीपत्रपुटसमूहेन मधुरश्याममुदकं यत्र। बकुलवनेभ्यो निःसरन् मधुरसस्य आमोदो यत्र। बकुलकुसुमगन्धो मदिरामोदसदृश इति प्रसिद्धम।

MY says सागरस्य रचितमिव रत्नकोशम्। प्रसारकं कोशः। Kula says सुरवधूनां हृदयेप्सितस्य रतस्य नवमपूर्वं सारकं संपादकम्। *SC* text has *hiaacchia* = हृदयेप्सित *chāyā*. Kula says नलिनीपत्रपुटैः यातमनुगतम्।

41. तिव्वजरढाअवाहअहरिआलामोअविम्हराइअहरिणम्।
संखोओअहिसीअरलवणरसासाअमहिसलिब्भन्तसिलम्।।

---

[34] Cf. the last verse of the canto.

[35] The gems washed up by the waves are fancied as being set out as on a market stall.

[36] The smell of *bakula* flowers is often likened to that of wine. Cf. 1.56; 12.14.

[तीव्रजरठातपाहतहरितालामोदविमूर्च्छितहरिणम्।
संस्त्यानोदधिशीकरलवणरसास्वादमहिषलिह्यमानशिलम्।।]

The deer fainted on account of the smell of the yellow orpiment heated by the fierce midday sun; and the buffaloes licked the rocks for the taste of the salt crust formed by sea spray.[37]

K says तीव्रेण जरठातपेन परिणतातपेनाहतस्य विलीनस्य हरितालस्य आमोदेन विह्वलीकृतहरिणम्[38]। हरिणानां हरितालगन्धो मोहकर इति वार्ता। शोषात् संघातभूतानामुदधिशीकराणां संबन्धिनो लवणरसस्यास्वादनार्थं महिषैर्लिह्यमानशिलम्। MY says *vimharāvia* (for °*rāia*) विह्वलीकृत। *saṁkhāa* संस्त्यान्। Kula says आतपेनाहतं तप्तं यत् हरितालं तस्यामोदेन विस्मारिता अपस्माररोगेण हृता:[39]। *Deśīnāmamālā* 6.3 mentions *pamhāra* (= अपस्मार ?) in the sense of अपमृत्यु।

42. तुङ्गरअअसिहरुग्गमेहि तारं गअं
सीहणिहअगअलोहिअमोत्तारङ्गअम्।
गरुअधीरणिव्वाहिअबहुजुअसंखअं
उअहिसलिलसंकन्तसरुज्जुअसङ्खअम्।।

[तुङ्गरजतशिखरोद्गमैस्तारां गतं
सिंहनिहतगजलोहितमुक्तारङ्गदम्।
गुरुकधैर्यनिर्वाहितबहुयुगसंक्षय-
मुदधिसलिलसंक्रान्तसरऋजुकशङ्खगम्।।]

The surface of the mountain was bright with its lofty silver peaks. With the blood of the elephants killed by lions it coloured the (scattered) pearls.[40] With steadfast fortitude it had passed through many an epoch of destruction. To its

---

37 See verse 24.

38 *SC* says मूर्च्छितहरिणम्। विस्मापितेति कश्चित् (cf. R)। तन्न, 'विम्हरावेइ' इति मुच्छिते देशी इति देशीसारदर्शनात्।

39 *SC* has अपस्माररोगिण: कृता:। Kula goes on to say अथवा नष्टचेतनीकृता विकला (विह्वला ?) इति यावत् हरिणा यत्र तम् (partly restored form *SC*) उपर्युपरि पातात् लवणरूपेण घनीभूतो य उदधिशीकर:, etc.

40 I.e. the pearls supposed to be inside the head of elephants were stained with blood when they were killed by the attacking lions.

lakes came conches in straight rows from the waters of the sea.

K and MY read रत्न for *raaa* = रजत (R and Kula). K reads ताराग्रं and लग्नं for *tāraṁ gaaṁ* and *(mo)ttā-raṅgaaṁ* (R, Kula and MY); and सरिद्युत for *sarujjua* (R and others). K says तुङ्गरत्नशिखराणामुद्गमैः ताराग्रमुज्ज्वलाग्रम्। सिंहनिहतानां गजानां लोहितेन मुक्ताभिश्च लग्नं व्याप्तम्। He seems to read *tāraggaaṁ* and make it agree with his reading *(mo)ttā-laggaaṁ* in the second line by the रलयोरभेदः rule (cf. verses 37 and 44). He explains the last two lines as follows — गुरुणा धैर्येण निर्वाहितो यापितो बहूनां युगानां संक्षयो येन। उदधिसलिले संक्रान्ताभिः सरिद्भिः युताः शङ्खा यत्र तम्। Kula says तुङ्गैः रजतशिखरैस्तारं विशुद्धमङ्गं यस्य तम्, and explains निर्वाहित in the third line as अतिक्रान्त। MY construes *sarujjua* as सरउद्यत or सरऋजु। R says उदधिसलिलात् संक्रान्ताः सरसि ऋजुकाः संमुखा शङ्खका यत्र। *SC* says यस्य सरसि समुद्रादागत्य शङ्खा विहरन्तीत्यर्थः। सरसि ऋजुकाः प्रगुणपङ्क्तय इति लोकनाथः।

43. मणिपहम्मसामोअअं मणिपहम्मसामोअअम्।
सरसरण्णणिद्दावअं सरसरण्णणिद्दावअम्।।

[मणिप्रहर्मश्यामोदकं मणिपहर्म्यसामोदकम्।
सरःशरण्यनिर्दावकं स्मरशरज्ञनिद्रापदम्।।]

It was gay with the mansions of the *yakṣas*. The waters were dark in the pools containing gems. It was free from fires because of the ever fresh woods. It brought sleep to those who resorted to its lakes.

MY says *pahamma* देवखात (B adds अकृत्रिमसरः)। Kula says स्मरशरण्या मन्मथविधेयास्तेषां निद्रापदं निधुवनक्रीडाश्रान्तानां निद्रासुखदमित्यर्थः। अथवा सरःशरण्याः करिमहिषशूकरादयः तेषां निद्राकरं निद्राजनकम्। K says मणीन् पातीति मणिपः सर्पः। मणिपानां हर्म्यवत् सुष्ठु आमोदम् (मणिपाः सर्पाः मणिपानां हर्म्यैः सामोदम् MY)। मणिभिः मरकतादिभिः प्रहतत्वात् श्यामोदकम्। अथवा 'पहम्म'शब्दो भाजनवाचकः। मरकतादिमणिश्वभ्रेषु श्यामोदकम्। सरसेषु जलपस्रवणसहितेषु अरण्येषु निर्दावं दावाग्निरहितम्। सरःपरिसरमाश्रिताः सरःशरण्याः। सरः शरण्यं येषामिति बहुव्रीहिः। तेषां सौख्यातिशयात् निद्रापदम्। लोपोऽरण्य इति अकारलोपः (Vararuci 1.4). R says मणीन् पान्तीति मणिपाः यक्षाः सर्पा वा।

44. दरिअरक्खसामोअअं दरिअरक्खसामोअअम्।
विसअरुप्पहाअन्तअं विसअरुप्पहाअन्तअम्।।

[दृप्तराक्षसामोदकं दरीवराख्यश्यामोदकम्।
विशदरूप्यप्रभातान्तं विषतरुप्रभान्तकम्।।]

It gave pleasure to the proud demons.[41] The water was darknened by the *bibhītaka* trees growing in its caves; while the summit was beautiful with the clear effulgence of its silver. It was destructive with the potency of its poison trees.

Unlike R and Kula, K and MY read here two verses. The first is a Mahāyamaka formed with the phrase *daria-rakkhasā-moaaṁ*.

(i) K says एकरूपपादचतुष्टयं महायमकमेतत्। यथोक्तमाचार्येण। एकाकारचतुष्पादं यन्महायमकाह्वयम् इति।

तत्र दृप्तराक्षसामोदकमिति प्रथमः पादः। दृप्तानां राक्षसानामामोदकं प्रीतिकरमतिगहनत्वात् राक्षसानामावासभूतमित्यर्थः। दरीग – ऋक्षश्यामोदयमिति द्वितीयः पादः[42]। दरीगतैः दरीवर्तिभिः ऋक्षैः भल्लूकैर्हेतुभूतैः श्यामाया रात्रेरुदयो यत्र। ऋक्षाणामतिकृष्णवर्णत्वाद्दरीषु सदा रात्रिर्वर्तत इति प्रतिभातीत्यर्थः। दलितलक्षसामोदयमिति तृतीयः पादः। रलयोरभेदः। सामोदयो गजः। सामोद्भवः सिन्धुर इति हलायुधः। दलितानि विदारितानि लक्षाणि प्रतिगजा यैस्ते सामोदया यत्र तम्। दरीचरखश्यामोदकमिति चतुर्थः पादः। दरीषु स्पन्दमानं खमिव श्याममुदकं यत्र तम्। दरीषु प्रस्रवणादयः संभवन्तीति। Kula says दरीचरैरक्षैः बिभीतकैः श्याममुदकं यत्र तम्।

(ii) The second vese introduced by K and MY is rendered by K as follows:

रम्यसलिलपार्श्वलतं[43] रामासलीलवासालयम्।
विषतरुप्रभावार्तं विशदरूप्यप्रभापात्रम्।।

The second line is the same as the corresponding line of the verse as recorded by R and Kula except that MY and K seem to read *attaaṁ* for *antaaṁ*. K says रम्याः सलिलपार्श्वेषु लताः यत्र तम्। रामाणां सलीलवासायालयं सलीलनिवासार्थमालयभूतम्। विषतरूणां विषवृक्षाणां प्रभावेण आर्तम् आर्तमृगविहङ्गममित्यर्थः। विशदस्य रूप्यस्य रजतस्य प्रभायाः पात्रभूतम्। R says विशदरूप्यप्रभाभिः कान्तं कमनीयमित्यर्थः।

---

[41] I.e. the *rākṣasa*s of Laṅkā.

[42] MY says दरीचराक्षश्यामोदयमिति द्वितीयः पादः। दरीवर्तिजननयनानां श्यामाया रात्रेरुदयः प्रदोषः तं दरीणां नित्यनिरातपतया अन्धकारास्पदत्वान्। *akkha* इत्यत्र 'स्क ष्क-क्षां खः' इति (Vararuci 3.29) खत्वमेव। न 'अक्ष्यादिषु छः' इति (ibid. 3.30) छत्वम्। Dhummakkha इत्यादिवत्।

[43] This might be *ramma-salila-pāsa-laaṁ* (or even *vāsa-laaṁ*, but the derivation) of रामासलील, etc. from it is a *tour de force* not usual in the poem.

45. जरढविसोसहिवेढिअभुअंगपरिहरिअचन्दणदुमक्खन्धम्।
वोलन्तविसहरप्फणमणिप्पहाहअविराइअदुमच्छाअम्।।

[जरठविषौषधिवेष्टितभुजंगपरिहृतचन्दनद्रुमस्कन्धम्।
व्यतिक्रामद्विषधरफणमणिप्रभाहतविराजितद्रुमच्छायम्।।]

The trunks of the sandal trees, surrounded with full-grown poison-destroying plants, were shunned by serpents;[44] while the lustre of the gems on the hoods of the serpents that passed by dispelled the shadows of the trees.

K says जरठाभिः परिणताभिः विषौषधिभिः विषहराभिरोषधिभिः वेष्टितत्वात् भुजङ्गैः परित्यक्तचन्दनद्रुमस्कन्धम्. *virāia* (विराजित R) is explained as विलीन by K — अतिक्रामतां गच्छतां विषधराणां फणामणिप्रभाभिराहतत्वात् विलीना नष्टा द्रुमच्छाया यत्र तम्। Kula explains the word as विलीनीकृत। K seems to derive *virāia* from *virāa* = विशीर्ण, which he invariably translates as विलीन्। Cf. Hemacandra 4.56 — विलीङेर्विरा – *virāi vilijjai*.

46. फडिहकिरणणिवहेहिं धरणिधवलाअअं सुव्वमाणसुरसुन्दरिमुद्धवलाअअम्।
पलअसमअसलिलेण वि असअलधोअअं विवरणिन्तणवचन्दसरिसअलधोअअम्

[स्फटिककिरणनिवहैर्धरणीधवलायकं श्रूयमाणसुरसुन्दरीमुग्धप्रलापकम्।
प्रलयसमयसलिलेनाप्यसकलधौतं विवरनिर्यन्नवचन्द्रसदृशतटधौतम्।।]

The mountain whitened the earth with the radiance of its crystal rocks. On it was heard the sweet speech of the celestial nymphs. It could not entirely be washed even by the waters of the epoch of destruction. Silver resembling the new moon emerged from its caves.

प्रलयसमयजलेनापि असंपूर्णं क्षालितम् K.

47. रम्मअन्दराअच्छअं रम्मअन्दराअच्छअम्।
सग्गग्गहणिसामग्गअं सग्गग्गहणिसामग्गअम्।।

[रम्यचन्द्रागच्छदं रम्यकंदरावृक्षकम्।
साग्रग्रहनिःश्यामाग्रकं स्वर्गग्रहणीसामग्र्यम्।।]

---

[44] Sandal trees are usually described as being haunted by serpents. Here they avoid the trees owing to the presence of the poison-destroying plants. See 4.63 and 7.68.

It had beautiful caves and riverbanks. It was covered with the delightful hue of gold, and at night showed the way to the planets on its summit. It sheltered all the celestial nymphs held captive (by Rāvaṇa).[45]

K says रम्याः कन्दराः कच्छा नदीतीरप्रदेशाश्च यत्र तम्। रमिः रतिः प्रीतिः तद्योग्यं रम्यं चन्द्रं हिरण्यं तस्य रागो वर्णो स छदः छादनं यस्य तथाभूतम्। प्रियङ्गुरस्वर्णप्रभाच्छादितमित्यर्थः। स्वर्गस्य ग्रहे ग्रहणे प्राप्तौ नितरां सामग्र साधनसंपत्तिः यत्र तम्[46]। निशब्दो भृशार्थः। नि न्यग्भावनिकामयोरिति वैजयन्ती। स्वाग्रे स्वस्य शिखरे ग्रहाणां निशासु मार्गप्रदम्। गाङ्गेयं स्यात् गैरिकं भूरि चन्द्रं राः कल्याणं निष्कमष्टापदं चेति हलायुधः R says स्वर्गग्रहणीनां स्वर्गबन्दीनां सामग्र्यं साकल्यं यत्र। Kula's explanation is same except that he says सुरबन्दीनां सामग्र्यं समुदयं दयते रक्षतीति तम्।

48. पङ्कुत्तरन्तलङ्घिअपरिवत्तवराहवञ्चिआहअसीहम्।
सरसलिलोअरणिबडिअणिअअभरत्थमिअकणअपल्लवगोच्छम्।।

[पङ्कोत्तीर्णलङ्घितपरिवृत्तवराहवञ्चिताहतसिंहम्।
सरःसलिलोदरनिपतितनिजभरास्तमितकनकपल्लवगुच्छम्।।]

There, the boar as it came out of the mire was attacked by the lion, but turned back, eluding and baffling the latter; and the clusters of leaves, dropping from the golden trees into the waters of the lakes, disappeared because of their weight.

पङ्कोत्तरणदशायामभिभूतेन पुनः प्रतिनिवृत्तेन (प्रवृत्तेन A) वराहेण वञ्चिताहतः सिंहो यत्र तम् MY. पङ्कादुत्तरता तदानीमेव सिंहलङ्घितेन पुनः परिवृत्तेन अभिमुखीभूतेन वराहेण, etc. K.[47]

49. णहसिरिं सअलणीलमेहलावण्णिअं बद्धजोइसाउव्वमेहलावण्णिअम्।
सिहरेहिं बाहूहि व पच्छाअन्तअं मण्णुअं दिसाणं मिव पच्छा अन्तअम्।।

[नभःश्रियं सजलनीलमेघलावण्यां बद्धज्योतिषापूर्वमेखलावर्णितम्।
शिखरैर्बाहुभिरिव प्रच्छादयन्तं मन्युं दिशामिव पश्चादायान्तम्।।]

---

[45] Translation follows Kṛṣṇa except in the last line for which see Kulanātha in Extracts.

[46] MY says स्वर्गग्रहणसामग्र्यगं स्वर्गग्रहणं स्वर्गस्पर्शनम्।

[47] Kula is incomplete. *SC* says पङ्कादुत्तरन्तः सिंहैः लङ्घिता आक्रान्ताः पश्चात् परिवृत्ता से वराहाः तैः वञ्चिता आहताश्च सिंहा यत्र तम्। तैः वञ्चिताः त्यक्तप्रहारा इति कुलनाथः R says आहतः ताडित इव।

With its peaks, like arms, the mountain embraced the beautiful sky, lovely with the blue clouds full of water, and bedecked with the marvellous girdle of stars worn by her, and seemed thereby to give offence to the regions of the sky.[48]

K and MY read सेक for *ṇīla* (R). Kula has स्निग्ध। K says सजलसेकानां जलसेकसहितानां मेघानां लावण्यं यत्र। अथवा सजलसेका मेघा ऐव लावण्यं यस्यास्ताम्। अथवा सजलसेकस्य मेघस्येव लावण्यं यस्यास्ताम्। ज्योतीषि नक्षत्राणि ज्योतिर्मय्या अपूर्वमेखलया वर्णितां शोभिताम्। वर्णो नीलादिविप्राद्योः कीर्तौ गीतिक्रमे स्तुतौ। . . . लेपशोभयोः।। इति वैजयन्ती। एवंभूतां नभःश्रियं बाहुभिरिव शिखरैः प्रच्छादयन्तम् आलिङ्गन्तं, तस्मात् कारणात् पश्चाद्दिशां मन्युं कोपं ददतमिव नभःश्रीविषयात् सापत्न्यात् दिगङ्गनानां कोपं कुर्वाणमिव। MY says नभःश्रियं सजलसेकमेघलावण्यितां संजातलावण्यां, बद्धज्योतिरपूर्वमेखलावर्णिताम्। अत्र ज्योतिर्नक्षत्रम्। . . . मन्युं दिशामिव पश्चाद्ददतं तासां मुखदीप्तिसंकोचात् मन्युं ददतमिवेत्याशयः। Kula says प्रच्छादयन्तमुपगूहयन्तमिव, अत एव पश्चादनन्तरं दिशामपरनायिकानामिव मन्युमपराधं यान्तं प्राप्नुवन्तं ददतं वा (corrected from *SC*).

50. असुरबन्दिसाहारणं असुरवं दिसाहारणम्।
सूरअं तमणिवालअं सूरअन्तमणिवालअम्।।

[असुरबन्दिसाधारणमसुरवं दिगाधारकम्।
सूरगं तमोनृपालयं सूरकान्तमणिपालकम्।।]

It was the common abode of the maidens held captive by the demons,[49] and full of dismal cries. It concealed the regions of the sky from view. Its flanks were composed of sunstones; and it touched the sun, and harboured darkness (in its caves).

K, Kula and MY read *vāsaaṁ* (पार्श्व and वासं) for *vālaaṁ* (R). K and MY read the second line first. K says सूर्यकान्तमणिमयपार्श्वम् (Kula also)। सूरगं बहुभुजङ्गमित्यर्थः। तमसो निवासप्रदं गुहास्विति शेषः। असुरबन्दीनामसुरैः गृहीतानां बन्दीनां बन्दीभूतानां दिव्याङ्गनानां साधारणं सामान्यमावासम्, अत एव असुरवम् अशोभनशब्दयुक्तं तासां स्त्रीणामाक्रन्दनशब्दयुक्तमित्यर्थः। दिशां हारणमात्मविस्तारेण दिशामपहारकं, दिशां धारणमिति वा।

MY says सूर्यकान्तमणिपार्श्वं, सूरगं सुष्ठूरगं सूर्यस्पृशं वा। तमोनिवासम्। . . . असुरवं व्याकुलरवं, दिशाहारणं दिक्कवलनं दिग्व्यापिनमित्यर्थः। Kula says

[48] The sky is personified as the mountain's mistress; while the regions of the sky, overshadowed by the mountain, are figured as disgruntled rivals.

[49] Cf. verse 47.

तमसो निवासदम्। अथवा शूराः कान्ताश्च ये मणिपा यक्षास्तेषामाश्रयम् (i.e. *maṇiva + ā saaṁ*).

51. हरिणा बलिमहिहरणे समए जलएहि जलणिहोहि जुअन्ते।
जं ण चइअं भरेउं तं देहेण भुअणं भरेऊण ठिअम्।।

[हरिणा बलिमहीहरणे समये जलदैर्जलनिधिभिर्युगान्ते।
यन्न शकितं भर्तुं तद्देहेन भुवनं भृत्वा स्थितम्।।]

It stood filling the world with its expanse, the world that could not be filled by Viṣṇu[50] while wresting the earth from the demon Bali; by the clouds in the seasons of rains; and by the oceans at the epoch of destruction.

bhareuṁ पूरयितुम् MY (K and Kula also); भर्तुम् R. *bhareūṇa* = पूरयित्वा K and Kula; भृत्वा R.

52. अत्थाअं व वहन्तं जालन्तरणिग्गउद्धअम्बमऊहम्।
आसण्णसिहरवणदववोलीण पणठ्ठमण्डलं दिअसअरम्।।

[अस्तायमानमिव वहन्तं जालान्तरनिर्गतोर्ध्वताम्रमयूखम्।
आसन्नशिखरवनदवव्यतिक्रान्तं प्रणष्टमण्डलं दिवसकरम्।।]

The sun, with its orb vanishing from sight, being enveloped in the forest fires on the adjoining peaks of the mountain, seemed to be setting, with its reddish rays shooting up through the flames.

K says आसन्नशिखरवनदवेन अतिक्रान्तत्वात् कवलितत्वात् प्रणष्टमण्डलमदृष्टमण्डलम्, अग्निज्वालान्तरेभ्यो निर्गतोर्ध्वताम्रमयूखम्, अत एव अस्तमितमिव दिवसकरं वहन्तम्।

My says *atthāaṁ* अस्तमितम्। अधः शिखरप्रज्वलद्वनदवज्वालान्तरालेषु ऊर्ध्वस्फुरद्द्विवर्णकिरणमात्रव्यक्तमण्डलम् उपरि अतिक्रामन्तं रविमकालेऽस्तमितमिव वहन्तमित्यर्थः।

53. वडवामुहसंतावे भिण्णअडेअ गरुए तरङ्गप्पहरे।
अविरहिअकुलहराण व सरिआण कए ण साअरस्स सहन्तम्।।

[वडवामुखसंतापाद्भिन्नतटान्गुरुकांस्तरङ्गप्रहारान्।
अविरहितकुलगृहाणामिव सरितां कृते न सागरस्य सहमानम्।।]

It endured the heat of the submarine fire, and the heavy blows

---

[50] Viṣṇu as Trivikrama.

of the waves of the sea, eroding its slopes, as if for the sake of its streams that were loth to quit their paternal home.[51]

K and Kula read संतापं for *saṁtāve* (R). K reads कटकान् for *aḍe a* = तटान् च (R and Kula). As K omits व in the second line, he seems to read –*Kulaharāṇaṁ sariāṇa* (cf. *SC* text) for *Kulaharāṇa va sariāṇa*. K says वडवामुखेन कृतमात्मनः संतापं, समुद्रजलेषु अतिदूरमवगाढत्वात् वडवामुखाग्निसंतापः सुवेलस्य संभवतीति भावः, तथा भिन्नकटकान् गुरुन् तरङ्गप्रहारांश्च समुद्रस्य संबन्धिनः एतान् सरितामात्मसंभवानां कृतेन कृते सहमानम्। कथंभूतानाम्–अविरहितपितृगृहाणां समुद्रं प्रविष्टानामपि अपरित्यक्तपितृगृहाणाम्। यथा श्वसुरो जामातुरविनयं स्वसुतामुद्दिश्य सहते तद्वदिति।

MY says अत्राविरहितकुलगृहत्वं सरितां लालनप्रकाशनपरं स्रोतोविच्छेदविरहपरं च। *sariāṇa kaaṁ va* इति पाठः। *kaeṇa* इति पाठे इवेत्यध्याहार्यम्।

54. रअणीसु उव्वहन्तं एक्कक्का अम्बमणिसिलासंकन्तम्।
मुद्धमिअङ्कच्छाअं खुरमुहमग्गं व रइतुरंगाण ठिअम्।।

[रजनीषूद्वहन्तमेकैका ताम्रमणिशिलासंक्रान्ताम्।
मुग्धमृगाङ्कच्छायां खुरमुखमार्गमिव रवितुरङ्गाणां स्थितम्।।]

At night it carried the reflections of the young moon on each block of ruby, as if they were a series of hoof-marks left by the horses of the sun.

K says रजनीषु आताम्रमणिमयीषु पद्मरागमयीषु शिलासु एकैकं प्रत्येकं संक्रान्तां रवितुरङ्गमाणां गच्छतां खुरमुखमार्गमिव खुरस्य मुखविन्यासपरम्परामिव स्थितां मुग्धमृगाङ्कच्छायां बालेन्दुप्रतिबिम्बमुद्वहन्तम्। MY remarks अत्र स्फटिकादेः परभागाभावादिन्द्रनीलादेस्तमःसहकारित्वाच्च रजन्यां प्रतिबिम्बग्रहणासामर्थ्येन तत्समर्थस्य पद्मरागादेराताम्रपदेनोपादनमिति रहस्यम्। Kula reads अर्ध for *muddha* — अर्धमृगाङ्कस्य अर्धचन्द्रस्य।

55. विसमपरिसंठिएहिं विसमुद्धाइअलआहरोत्थइएहिं।
कंचणसिलाअलेहिं छिण्णाअवमण्डलेहिं व परिक्खित्तम्।।

[विषमपरिसंस्थितैर्विषमोद्धावितलतागृहस्थगितैः।
काञ्चनशिलातलैश्छिन्नातपमण्डलैरिव परिक्षिप्तम्।।]

It was surrounded with slabs of gold, lying uneven, and

[51] The streams are figured as the daughters of the mountain married to the ocean. The delay in settling in their new home makes the angry son-in-law chastise the father with the waves and the submarine fire.

covered with groves of high-grown creepers here and there, as if they were circles of light intersected by shadows.

K (*chāyā*) has विषमोर्ध्वायित। K says विषमपरिसंस्थितैः, विषममूर्ध्वीभूतलता-गृहस्थगितैः, एवंरूपत्वात् छिन्नातपमण्डलैरिव अन्तरान्तरामेघच्छायान्तरितातपमण्डलैरिव काञ्चनशिलातलैः परिक्षिप्तम्। MY says *paricchittaṁ* परिक्षिप्तम्। अत्र शिलातलेषु विषमत्वं निम्नोन्नतत्वम्। Kula says काञ्चनशिलानां दलैः खण्डैः। परिक्षिप्तं वेष्टितम्। *SC* says विषमोर्ध्वायितेन क्वचित् क्वचिदुद्गतेन लतागृहेणावस्थगितैः काञ्चनशिलातलैः।

56. अप्पत्तदिणअराइं आअवभअसिहरसंठिअभुअंगाइं।
कडएहि उव्वहन्तं वणाइ उद्धपरिवड्ढिअच्छाआइं।।

[अप्राप्तदिनकराण्यातपभयशिखरसंस्थितभुजंगानि।
कटकैरुद्वहन्तं वनान्यूर्ध्वपरिवर्धितच्छायानि।।]

It bore on its slopes woods that were beyond the range of the sun, with the shadows deepening above, and the serpents abiding at the top for fear of the heat of the sun.[52]

MY says अप्राप्तो दिनकरो येषु तानि। अप्राप्त इति कर्तरि क्तः। सूर्यपथमुल्लङ्घ्य वर्तमानानि। K says अप्राप्तदिनकराणि दिनकरपथमतीत्यं स्थितानि, अतएवोर्ध्वप्र-वृत्तच्छायानि, आतपभयात् शिखरेषु स्वाग्रेषु स्थितभुजङ्गानि वनानि वहन्तम्। Kula says अधःस्थित दिनकरत्वादेवोर्ध्वपरिवृद्धच्छायानि वनानि कटकैरुद्वहन्तम्।

57. तुङ्गत्तणपज्जन्ते वित्थअविक्खम्भसिट्ठमुहवित्थारे।
तिअसगआण वहन्तं दन्तप्फलिहजुअलंकिए कडअअडे।।

[तुङ्गत्वपर्याप्तान्विस्तृतविष्कम्भशिष्टमुखविस्तारान्।
त्रिदशगजानां वहन्तं दन्तपरिघयुगलाङ्कितान्कटकतटान्।।]

The lofty flanks of the mountain, dented by the mace-like tusks of the elephants of the gods, declared the size of their mouths through the wide space between the marks left by the tusks.

K and MY read क्षतान् for *aṅkie* (R and probably Kula). MY has *juala-kkhae*. K reads कनक for *kaḍaa* = कटक (R). K says त्रिदशगजानां दन्तपरिघयुगलक्षतान् दन्तपरिघयुगलैः प्रहतान्, विस्तृतेन विष्कम्भेण दन्तयोरन्तरालेन शिष्टः कथितो व्यञ्जितः मुखविस्तारो येषु तान् कनकतटान् वहन्तम्। MY says विष्कम्भः अवकाशः। Kula says तुङ्गत्वेन पर्याप्तान् संपन्नान् तुङ्गानित्यर्थः।

52 See verse 19.

विस्तृतेन . . . अन्तरालेन मध्यभागेन।[53] Kula reads स्फटिक (*phaliha*) for *kaḍaa*.

58. तिअसगआण वहन्तं हत्थुम्हाहअकिलन्तपल्लवराए।
कडपरिघोलणकविले चिरवूढविमुक्कपारिआअअविडवे।।

[त्रिदशगजानां वहन्तं हस्तोष्माहतक्लाम्यत्पल्लवरागान्।
कटकपरिघूर्णनकपिलांश्चिरव्यूढविमुक्तपारिजातकविटपान्।।]

Here the branches of the *pārijāta* tree, borne by the celestial elephants for a long while, were discarded after they had turned yellowish brown by being whirled round their cheeks, with the leaves discoloured by the hot breath from the trunk.[54]

K reads हस्तोष्ठ for *hatthumhā*° = हस्तोष्मा° (R and Kula). K says त्रिदशगजानां हस्तोष्ठेन आहतत्वात् क्लान्तपल्लवरागान्, कटेषु गण्डेषु परिघूर्णनेन कण्डूयनार्थं भ्रमणेन कपिलान् मदेन कपिलवर्णान्, तैश्चिरमूढविमुक्तान् क्रीडयोढ्वा विमुक्तान् पारिजातविटपान् वहन्तम्। Kula seems to say चिरमूढविमुक्तान् उद्गालितपारिजातकविटपान्।

59. पासाअअं वहन्तं मणिकडअमऊहधवलिअमअच्छाअम्।
पुट्ठोवइअमहोज्झरजलघाउव्वत्तमण्डलं व मिअङ्कम्।।

[पार्श्वगतं वहन्तं मणिकटकमयूखधवलितमृगच्छायम्।
पृष्ठावपतितमहानिर्झरजलघातोद्वृत्तमण्डलमिव मृगाङ्कम्।।]

It bore the moon clinging to its flank, with its dark emblem, the deer, whitened by the rays of the crystal slopes. It seemed as if the lunar orb had been turned over by the impact of the waters of the great cascades falling on its back.[55]

K says स्फटिकमणितटमयूखधवलितमृगच्छविं, तदानीं पृष्ठे निपतितस्य महानिर्झरस्य जलाभिघातात् विपर्यस्तमण्डलमिव मृगाङ्कं वहन्तम्। चन्द्रस्योपरिभागे कलङ्को न संभवतीति भावः। MY says उद्वृत्तमण्डलतया निष्कलङ्कपश्चिमपार्श्वप्रकाशनं

[53] Cf. *Deśīnāmamālā* 7.88. *vikkjaṁbho* स्थानमन्तरालं च। विस्तारवाचकस्तु विष्कम्भशब्दभवः।

[54] The verse describes the elephants of the gods disporting themselves on the mountain, whirling with their trunk the branches of the *pārijāta* tree which they had brought from heaven. Cf. verse 61.

[55] As the lunar spot was no longer visible, it is fancied that the cascades pouring down the mountain-side had turned over the moon, exposing the all-white back.

विवक्षितम्। Kula says चन्द्रस्य क्रोडभाग एव कलङ्को न पृष्ठे . . . *SC* says माघेऽपि चन्द्रस्योपरिभागे कलङ्कशून्यत्वं वर्णितम्। उत्सङ्गसङ्गिहरिणस्य मृगाङ्कमूर्तेरित्यपि माघे दृष्टत्वात्।[56]

60. सलिलदरधोअकुसुमं दीसन्तोवरिपरिल्लजरढालोअम्।
मअरहरस्स वहन्तं अब्भासब्भहिअसामलं वणराइं।।

[सलिलदरधौतकुसुमां दृश्यमानोपर्युपरिजरठालोकाम्।
मकरगृहस्य वहन्तमभ्याशाभ्यधिकश्यामलां वनराजिम्।।]

The woods were deep blue because of the proximity of the sea, with the flowers washed by the spray, and brilliant sunshine coming into view as it spread above and around them.

K, MY and Kula read *raa* for *dara* (R). K (*chāyā*) has परियत् for *parilla* (R). K (commentary) has परिवर्तमान्, and his reading appears to be *parinta* (see verses 68 and 88). Manuscript B of K has परिवृत्त which is less correct.

My says *salila-raa* सलिलरजः। *rao* जवो वा। Kula says सलिलरजोभिः जलशीकरैः। K says सदा समुद्रजलसिक्तमूलत्वात् अभ्याशगता वनराजिः सलिलकणिकाधौतकुसुमा हरितबहुपत्रविटपबहुला च भवति। तस्मादुपरिदृश्यमान-परिवर्तमानजरठातपाम्। मध्यन्दिनेऽपि तीव्रातपः पत्रबहुलतया तदधस्तात् प्रवेष्टुं न शुक्नुयादिति मकरगृहस्याभ्याशत्वात् अभ्यधिकश्यामलां वनराजि वहन्तम्। Kula is corrupt. *SC* has परिल्ल (?); परिगत (*chāyā*). It says दृश्यमान उपरि परिगतो जरठः कर्कशः आलोकः सूर्यद्युतिः यत्र ताम्। R explains *uvari-parilla* as उपर्युपरि।

61. तिअसगआण वहन्तं दूरुण्णिअमग्गणहणिअत्तमुहुअरे।
ओवअणपअत्तन्ते उप्पअणपणट्ठणिग्गमे गइमग्गे।।

[त्रिदशगजानां वहन्तं दूरोन्नीतमार्गनभोनिवृत्तमधुकरान्।
अवपतनप्रवर्तमानानुत्पतनप्रणष्टनिर्गमान्गतिमार्गान्।।]

It bore the tracks left by the elephants of the gods as they descended the slopes, with no visible sign of departure,

---

[56] Kula is corrupt, but the quotation from Māgha 4.22 appears in his gloss.

because they flew off (after their sports); while the bees that followed far in their wake returned from the sky.[57]

K and MY read *aṇṇia* (अन्वित, अनुगत) for *uṇṇia* = उन्नीत (R), cf. Goldschmidt's footnotes on 13.77. Kula seems to read *aṇṇia*. K says त्रिदशगजानां गतिमार्गान् वहन्तम्। कथंभूतान् – अवपतने प्रवर्तमानान् गगनात् शिखराग्रे निपत्य क्रीडितुमधस्तादवतरणसमये प्रवर्तमानान् प्रवृत्तपदविन्यासान्। चिरं विहृत्य पुनरुत्पतने प्रणष्टनिर्गमान् गगनचारित्वात् सहसा गगनोत्पतनसमये अदृष्टनिर्गमान्। वनमध्यादेव गगनमुत्पतन्तीति। णश अदर्शने। (मदजलपानार्थं *SC*) दूरान्वितमार्गा दूरमनुगतमार्गाः नभसि गन्तुमशक्यत्वात् निवृत्ताः तत्रत्या मधुकरा येषु तान्।

MY says दूरानुगतमार्गा गजोत्पतनदशायां नभसो निवृत्ता गिरिवनभृङ्गा येषु ते तथा (भूतान्)। गगनावपतनादारभ्य प्रवृत्तान्, वनविहारानन्तरं गगनोत्पतने सति प्रणष्टनिर्गमान् मार्गान् गमनमार्गानित्यर्थः। Kula is somewhat corrupt. He seems to say अवपतने समुद्रावगाहनार्थमवतरणे वृक्षतृणादेः तिर्यग्भावात् अधोमुखीभावात् प्रवर्तमानान्। उत्पतने च वृक्षतृणादेः प्रगुणीकरणात् प्रणष्टः अलक्ष्यतां गतः निर्गमः स्वर्गगमनं यत्र।

62. थोआअहतिमिराइं वहमाणं थोअणिग्गअमऊहाइं।
णिंतग्गिगब्भिणाइ व थोउत्तिण्णरअणङ्कुरट्ठाणाइं।।

[स्तोकाहततिमिराणि वहमानं स्तोकनिर्गतमयूखानि।
निर्यदग्निगर्भितानीव स्तोकोत्तीर्णरत्नाङ्कुरस्थानानि।।]

Places with partly exposed sprout-like gems gleamed faintly, dispelling the darkness a little, and seemed to be covered with sparks.

K reads उब्भिन्न (*ubbhiṇṇa*) for *uttiṇṇa* (R). Kula is uncertain, but *SC* has उब्भिन्न। K says निर्यदग्निना गर्भितानीव दृश्यमानानि स्तोकमुत्पन्न-रत्नाङ्कुरस्थानानि किञ्चिदुत्पन्नानां रत्नाङ्कुराणां स्थानानि आकरस्थानि वहन्तम्।

63. मोडिअपव्वाअदुमे उव्वेल्लावेढभग्गपुञ्जइअलए।
वणगअजुज्झ परिमले वहमाणं पहरपडिअदन्तप्फडिहे।।

[मोटितप्रवानद्रुमानुद्वेलावेष्टभग्नपुञ्जितलतान्।
वनगजयुद्धे परिमलान्वहमानं प्रहारपतितदन्तपरिघान्।।]

---

[57] The elephants walked down the slopes of the mountain, but flew back after their sports; and the bees pursued them for some distance to partake of their ichor. Cf. verse 85 and 10.45.

The mountain bore traces of the elephants fighting in the woods, with the massive tusks knocked down, the trees smashed and withered, and the creepers, uncoiled and broken, lying about in heaps.

त्रुटितप्रम्लानद्रुमान, उद्वेल्लितावेष्टाः उद्ग्रथितावेष्टना भग्राः पुञ्जिताश्च लता येषु तान्। वनगजानां युद्धपरिमर्दान् वहन्तम्। परिमर्देऽपि परिमल इति वैजयन्ती K.

MY says *pavvāa* म्लान् शुष्केत्यर्थः। युद्धपरिमलान् युद्धोन्नायकान् मोटितद्रुम-त्वादिप्रकारान् युद्धोन्नायकान् वहन्तमित्यर्थः। R says युद्धपरिमलान् युद्धविमर्दान्।

64. मन्दरपहरुच्छलिए अज्जवि वित्थिण्णमणिपहम्मणिहत्ते।
जलणिहिजलवोच्छेए अणिग्गआमअरसे समुव्वहमाणम्।।

[मन्दरप्रहारोच्छलितानद्यापि विस्तीर्णमणिप्रहर्म्यनिहितान्।
जलनिधिजलव्यवच्छेदाननिर्गतामृतरसान्समुद्वहमानम्।।]

Stored in its vast caverns, studded with gems, were isolated masses of sea water, thrown up by the impact of the Mandara mountain (during the churning), that still retained the taste of nectar.[58]

K and MY read *uccalie* for *uccha°* (R and Kula). K reads विच्छेदान् for *vocchee* (R, Kula and MY), MY says *pahamma* प्रखात। *vocchea* व्युच्छेद। R and Kula have व्यवच्छेद। Kula explains प्रहर्म्य as देवखात। K says पुरा मन्दरस्य प्रहारैः उच्चलितान्, अद्यापि विस्तीर्णेषु मणिमयेषु श्वभ्रेषु निहितान्, अनिर्गतामृतरसान् जलनिधिजलस्य एकदेशान् वहन्तम्।

65. जलसंखोहालग्गं वहमाणं विसमलग्गपत्तणणिवहम्।
राहवसरसंघाअं वज्जमुहक्खुडिअपक्खसेसं व ठिअम्।।

[जलसंक्षोभालग्नं वहमानं विषमलग्नपत्रणानिवहम्।
राघवशरसंघातं वज्रमुखोत्खण्डितपक्षशेषमिव स्थितम्।।]

It carried a mass of Rāma's arrows that had, during the upheaval of the sea,[59] stuck in its slopes, with the feathers broken here and there, as if they were the remnants of its wings clipped by Indra's thunderbolt.[60]

---

[58] Because the water had entered the caverns before nectar was taken out of the ocean by the gods and demons who churned it with the Mandara mountain.

[59] I.e. during the chastisement of the sea by Rāma with the fiery arrows.

[60] It is fancied that the Suvela, like all other mountains, had wings until they were clipped by Indra.

K, MY and Kula read शर for जल (R). K and Kula read बाणसमूहं for *sara-saṁghāaṁ* (R). K says शरक्षोभकाले समुद्रमतीत्य लग्नमात्मनि लग्नं विषमभग्नपत्रसमूहं वज्रमुखत्रुटितस्य पक्षस्य शेषमिव दृश्यमानं राघवबाणसमूहं वहन्तम्।

66. कुम्भोवग्गणणिवडिअकरिहत्थुक्खुडिअसीहकेसरभारम्।
सहअरिविरुआअण्णणवलन्तभमरपरिवत्तिअलआकुसुमम्।।

[कुम्भावक्रमणनिपतितकरिहस्तखण्डितसिंहकेसरभारम्।
सहचरीविरुताकर्णनवलद्भ्रमरपरिवर्तितलताकुसुमम्।।]

There, the elephant fell as the lion sprang upon its temples, but tore up the latter's heavy mane with its trunk; and the bee turned about on hearing the hum of its mate, upsetting the flower of the creeper on which it lay.

कुम्भाभिभवेन निपतितस्य करिणो हस्तेन त्रुटितसिंहकेसरसमूहम्। अन्यत्र विहृत्यागच्छन्त्याः सहचर्या विरुताकर्णनात् वलमानेन भ्रमता भ्रमरेण परिवर्तित व्यावर्तितमधिष्ठितं लताकुसुमं यत्र तम् K. My says *oaggoṇa-ṇivaḍia* अभिभावनेन निपतितः। R says कुम्भयोरवक्रमणादतिक्रमणात् निपतितेन करिणा हस्तेन खण्डितः सिंहस्य केसरभारो यत्र तम्। Kula says कुम्भाववल्गनेन (?) निपतितः अभितोऽभिमुखमागत्य मिलितः करिहस्तेन चोत्खण्डितः (सिंहकेसरभारः यत्र)।

67. हिमसीअले वहन्तं पवणोमासविसमोससिअसेआले।
दिअसासारक्खुडिए दरवसुआअसलिले ससिमणिप्पवहे।।

[हिमशीतलान्वहन्तं पवनावमर्षविषमोच्छ्वसितशैवालान्।
दिवसासारखण्डितान्दरशुष्कसलिलाञ्शशिमणिप्रवाहान्।।]

Snow-cold streams of water, oozing from the moon-stones (at night), ceased to flow during the day, with the waters partly drying up, and the moss stirred here and there by the gusts of wind.

K reads आघात for *omāsa* (R and Kula) = अवमर्ष। K says दिवसासारत्रुटितान्, दिवसं कालाध्वनोरत्यन्तसंयोगे इति द्वितीया, सर्वस्मिन् दिवसे त्रुटितासारान् विच्छिन्ननिष्यन्दान्, अत एव दरशुष्कसलिलान्, पवनाघातेन विषममुद्गतशैवालान् शशिमणिप्रवाहान् वहन्तम्। MY says *ūsasia* उच्छ्वसित उन्नमित। यत एव दिवसेषु आसारेण क्षरणेन त्रुटिता रहिता अत एव ईषच्छुष्कसलिलाः तान् प्रवाहानित्यर्थः। Kula says दिवसे अवतारेण खण्डितान्। This is amplified by *SC* — आसरणमासार आगमनमिति यावत्। दिवसे अवतारेण प्रसारेण खण्डितान् दिवसे प्रस्यन्दशून्यतया खण्डितप्रसरानित्यर्थः।

68. विसमुल्ललिअपरिमले कमलिणिवत्तपरिघोलिरजलच्छाए।
मरगअसिलाअलोवरि पवित्तपारअरसे समुद्दहमाणम्।।

[विषमोल्लुलितपरिमलान्कमलिनीपत्रपरिघूर्णनजलच्छायान्।
मरकतशिलातलोपरि प्रवृत्तपारदरसान्समुद्वहमानम्।।]

Quicksilver moved about on slabs of emerald, with its traces flickering here and there, and looked like water rolling on lotus leaves.

K and MY read परियत् for *pavitta* = प्रवृत्त (R). Their reading seems to be *parinta* found in manuscript C of Goldschmidt.

K says विषममुल्ललितः उत्प्लुतः परिमलः परिभ्रमो येषां तान्। कमलिनीपत्रघूर्णमान-जलच्छवीन्[61]। मरतकशिलातलोपरि परियतः परिस्फुरतः पारदरसान् पारदो नाम् रसायनसाधनभूतः क्वचिदप्यनश्वरो द्रवद्रव्यविशेषः MY says विषमोल्ललित विषमोन्मीलित। परिमल लिङ्गम् (cf. verse 63)। क्वचित् क्वचिदभिव्यक्त-तत्तद्देशसंसर्गविशेषान् इतस्ततः परीयत् (परीयतः ?) पारदरसानित्यर्थः।

Kula reads *ullasia* (*SC* text also) for *ullalia*. Kula says विषमं स्पष्टं यथा स्यात्तथा उल्लसितः परिमलो गतागतविशेषो येषां तान्। मरकतशिलातलोपरि परीतान् पारदरसान् समुद्वहमानम्। Here परीतान् stands for परिगतान् (cf. *SC*), which shows that Kula's reading might be same as that of K and MY. See verse 88 below.

69. आरुहइ व दिवसमुहे उद्धाअन्तुद्धमण्डलाउरतुरओ।
सममण्डलबोलीणो ओअरइ व जं दिणावसाणम्मि रई।।

[आरोहतीव दिवसमुखे उद्धावमानोर्ध्वमण्डलातुरतुरगः।
सममण्डलव्यतिक्रान्तोऽवतरतीव यं दिनावसाने रविः।।]

The sun seemed to ascend the mountain at dawn, with the upright orb rising aloft, and his horses worn out with fatigue; and having journeyed with the orb evenly balanced, seemed to descend it at the end of the day.

My says *uddhāanta* ऊर्ध्वायमान। अथवा उद्धावत् उच्चलदित्यर्थः। Kula also says ऊर्ध्वायमानम् ऊर्ध्वं गच्छत्। K says रविः दिवसमुखे उद्धावदूर्ध्वमण्डलः

---

[61] K (*chāyā*) has जलच्छायान्।

आरोहणक्लेशात् आतुराश्वश्च भूत्वा यमारोहतीव। आरुह्य सममण्डलः सन् अतिक्रान्तः ततो दिनावसाने अधोमुखरथः सन् यम् अवतरतीव अवरोहतीव। Kula says ऊर्ध्वमतिर्यक् मण्डलं यस्य सः, ऊर्ध्वोयमानोर्ध्व- मण्डलश्चासौ . . . तथोक्तः सन् रविरारोहति। आरुह्य च सममण्डलः दिवसमध्ये व्यवक्रान्तः प्रसृतः दिनावसाने चावतरतीव यस्मात् (partly corrected from quotation in *SC*).

70. छुन्दन्ति जत्थ वन्थे णिसासु विसमपरिहारपरिअत्तन्ता।
कडएसु कउज्जोआ पुरओ बोलन्ततारआहि वणअरा।।

[क्षुदन्ति यत्र पथो निशासु विषमपरिहारपरिवर्तमानाः।
कटकेषु कृतोद्योताः पुरतो व्यतिक्रान्ततारकाभिर्वनचराः।।]

There, at night, the inhabitants of the woods, going round to avoid the rugged places on the slopes, trod the paths, lighted on their way by the stars journeying ahead of them.

In our copies K and MY (*pratīka*) have *puddanti*, *pudanti*, and *phudīti*. Their reading seems to be *phundanti* for *chundanti* = क्षुन्दन्ति (R). K renders it as क्रामन्ति (आक्रामन्ति MY)। Kula seems to agree with R, cf. *SC*. K and MY read प्रचार (*-ppacāra*) for परिहार (R and Kula). K says यत्र निशासु तिमिरे विषमैः प्रचारैः परिवर्तमानाः, कटकेषु पुरतोऽतिक्रामन्तीभिः तारकाभिः कृतोद्द्योताः कृतप्रकाशाः वनचराः पथः मार्गान् क्रामन्ति गच्छन्ति। MY says *panthe* पथि। विषमे दुर्गमार्गे प्रचारो विषमप्रचारः। कृतोद्द्योताः तारकप्रभाभिः प्रकाश्यमानाः तत्परिहाराय गूढमृगवधार्थिनो व्याधास्तारकाणि पादाक्रमणेन छादयन्तीत्यर्थः। MY seems to read *tāraāi* for *tāraāhi*, taking it as the object of *phundanti*.

71. पिअअमविओइआणं जत्थ अ सिहरमिलिअं चिलाअहूवणम्।
बोलेइ वाहमइलिअकुसुमञ्जलिसमुअताडिअं ससिबिम्बम्।।

[प्रियतमवियोजितानां यत्र च शिखरमिलितं किरातवधूनाम्।
व्यतिक्रामति वाष्पमलिनितकुसुमाञ्जलिसंमुखताडितं शशिबिम्बम्।।]

The orb of the moon, lingering on the summit, moved along, being directly hit by the Kirāta maidens, separated from their lovers, with handfuls of tear-stained flowers.[62]

MY remarks अत्र विरहिणीभिः स्वप्रतिकूलं शशिबिम्बम् अत्यासन्नतया

[62] I.e. the maidens chastized the moon, the traditional enemy of forlorn lovers, finding it near at hand on the summit of the mountain.

कुसुमाञ्जलिव्याजेन प्रद्वेषात् संमुखं ताड्यत इत्यर्थः। K says शशिबिम्बम् अपक्रामति प्रहारभयात् धावतीति भावः।

72. णहअलं व गहसोहिअं सविआणअं सिहररुद्धखअमारुअरहसविमाणअम्।
रअणसिहरकिरणुग्गमेहि घणराअअं। दरिमुहेसु गुप्पन्तसीहघणराअअम्।।

[नभस्तलमिव ग्रहशोभितं सविमानकं शिखररुद्धक्षयमारुतरभसविमानदम्।
रत्नशिखरकिरणोद्गमैर्घनरागदं दरीमुखेषु व्याकुलायमानसिंहघनसवकम्।।]

Adorned with the heavenly bodies, like the sky, the mountain had on it the aerial cars of the gods. It scorned the vehemence of the winds of the epoch of destruction, resisted by its peaks. It coloured the clouds with the soaring rays of its bejewelled peaks, and resounded with the deep roar of the restless lions in the caves.

. . . नभश्चराणां विमानैः सहितम्। शिखररुद्धस्य क्षयमारुतस्य रभसस्य वेगस्य विमानकम्। विमाननमवज्ञा। अवज्ञाकरम्। रत्नशिखरस्य किरणोद्गमैः घनानां रागदं वर्णविशेषप्रदम्। दरीषु व्याकुलीभवतां सिंहानां घनेन गम्भीरेण रावेण युक्तमित्यर्थः। K, MY mentions *suvvanta* (श्रूयमाण) as a variant for *guppanta*.

73. जम्मि समत्त व्व दिसा झीण व्व मही कआवसाणं व णहम्।
अत्थमिओ व्व समुद्दो णट्ठं व्व रसाअलं णिसण्णं व जअम्।।

[यस्मिन्समाप्ता इव दिशः क्षीणेव मही गतावसानमिव नभः।
अस्तमित इव समुद्रो नष्टमिव रसातलं निषण्णमिव जगत्।।]

On it the diverse regions of the sky seemed to terminate. The earth seemed small beside it. The sky seemed to end with it. The ocean seemed to disappear thereabout. The nether regions seemed to have vanished underneath. The world seemed to repose thereon.

K remarks पर्वतस्यातिमहत्त्वेन मह्यादेः पृथग्दर्शनाभावात् तत् सर्वमस्मिन्नेव निषण्णमिवेति प्रतर्कः। Kula says यस्मिन् समाप्ता इव दिशः; तस्मिन्नेव (सर्वासां) दिशामुपलम्भात्। क्षीणेव मही, दिग्व्यापकत्वेन तस्यैव सर्वत्र प्रतीयमानत्वात्। कृतावसानमिव नभः, सकलनभोमण्डलाच्छादकत्वे तस्यैव दृश्यमानत्वात्। अस्तमित इव समुद्रः, यत्रस्थैस्तद्व्यतिरिक्तसमुद्रस्थानस्यासम्भाव्यमानत्वात्। नष्टमिव रसातलम् उन्मूलिताशेषपातालकुक्षित्वात्। निषण्णमिव जगत्, क्षितिनभःसुरलोकनिवासिनां (तत्रैवावस्थानात् *SC*)।

74. जस्स सिहरेसु बहुसो वलन्ति वलमाणजुअवलन्तक्खन्धा।
भीआरुणपरिवत्तिअघोणाघोलन्तचामरा रइतुरआ।।

[यस्य शिखरेषु बहुशो वलन्ति वलमानयुगवलत्स्कन्धाः।
भीतारुणपरिवर्तितघोणाघूर्णमानचामरा रवितुरगाः।।]

Amidst its peaks the horses of the sun's chariot leaned frequently, curving their shoulders as the yoke slanted; while the charioteer Aruṇa turned them round in alarm, making the flywhisks flap against their snouts.

MY says यस्य तुङ्गेषु शिखरेषु गतिपथं निरुध्यावस्थितेषु प्रतिदिनं गतिभङ्गभीरुणारुणेन परिवर्तिता अश्वा अतएव घोणाघूर्णमानचामराः पार्श्वैः परिवृत्त्य गच्छन्तीत्यर्थः। Kula says आदित्यपथमतीत्य स्थितेषु यस्य शिखरेषु गतिराधस्खलनात् भीतेनारुणेन च परिवतर्तितघोणा व्यावर्तितनासिकाः, अतएव घूर्णमानचामराः, वलमाने व्यावर्त्यमाने युगे वलमानस्कन्धा रवितुरगा बहुशो वलन्ते गच्छन्ति। R says रवितुरगा यस्य शिखरे बहुशो वलन्ति वक्रीभवन्ति।

75. दीसन्ति जोइसवहे णिसासु वोढूण कुसुमणिवहं व जहिं।
गहिअपढमुच्चआइ व पहाअवोच्छिण्णतारआइ वणाइं।।

[दृश्यन्ते ज्योतिःपथे निशासूढ्वा कुसुमनिवहमिव यत्र।
गृहीतप्रथमोच्चयानीव प्रभातव्यवच्छिन्नतारकानि वनानि।।]

There, the woods were seen high in the sky, carrying the stars[63] like clusters of flowers at night; and when the stars vanished at dawn it seemed as if the flowers were culled in the first plucking of the day.

Kula reads निवहान् (*ṇivahe*, cf. *SC* text) for *ṇivahaṁ*. K and MY read अपचय for *uccaa* (R and Kula). K reads विभातविच्छिन्न। K says ज्योतिष्पथवर्तमानानि यस्मिन् वनानि निशासु कुसुमनिवहमिव नक्षत्रसमूहमूढ्वा विभाते विच्छिन्नतारकाणि अस्तमितनक्षत्राणि तानि गृहीतप्रथमापचयानीव दृश्यन्ते। गृहीतः कृतः प्रथमं कुसुमारामेभ्यः पूर्वमेव कुसुमापचयो येषामिति।

MY says *joisavahe* ज्योतिष्पथे नक्षत्रमार्गे। *voḍhūṇa* ऊढ्वा। यस्मिन् निशासु नक्षत्रमार्गे वनानि निरन्तरतारकानिचिततया कुसुमनिवहमूढ्वेव स्थितानि, पश्चात् प्रभातव्युच्छिन्नतारकाणि सन्ति गृहीतप्रथमापचयानीव दृश्यन्ते। अपचीयत इत्यपचयः कुसुमनिवहः। *Joisavahaṁ* इति वा पाठः। तदा स्पष्टोऽर्थः। Kula says यत्र

---

[63] Cf. verse 38.

निसासु ज्योतिषां तारकाणां वहान् निवहान् कुसुमनिवहानिव (ऊद्वा) प्रभातव्यच्छिन्नतारकाणि वनानि गृहीतप्रथमोच्चयानीव दृश्यन्ते इति व्याख्या।[64]

76. जत्थ अ गमेन्ति णिद्दं णिसासु णीसासविहुअपेलवजलआ।
चन्दपरिमासपअडिअससिमणिसलिलोज्झराहआ वणमहिसा।।

[यत्र च गमयन्ति निद्रां निशासु निःश्वासविधुतपेलवजलदाः।
चन्द्रप्रतिमर्षप्रकटितशशिमणिसलिलनिर्झराहता वनमहिषाः।।]

There, at night, the wild buffaloes slumbered, scattering the soft clouds by their breath, with streams of water, issuing from the moon-stones by contact with the lunar rays, lapping against them.

K reads वेल्लित for पेलव (R and Kula); and विगलित for *paaḍia* = प्रकटित (R). K says यत्र वनमहिषाश्च निशासु निश्वासवायुना विधुतपरिवृत्तजलदाः, चन्द्रकिरणपरिमर्शात् विगलितैः शशिमणिसलिलनिर्झरैराहता भूत्वा निद्रां गमयन्ति। Kula reads प्रगलित (*paalia*, cf. *SC*) for विगलित।

77. जत्थ अ सिहरावडिअं वलइ सिलाभित्तिविसमपासल्लइअम्।
भुअइन्दमणिणिहंसणपणट्ठउज्जोअसंचअं ससिबिम्बम्।।

[यत्र च शिखरापतितं वलति शिलाभित्तिविषमपार्श्वायितम्।
भुजगेन्द्रमणिनिघर्षणप्रणष्टोद्योतसंचयं शशिबिम्बम्।।]

The lunar orb, on reaching the summit of the mountain, passed by, slanting along the rocky wall, with its massive radiance worn away as it rubbed against the gems embedded in the hoods of the mighty serpents (at the top).[65]

K reads बन्ध for *visama* (R and Kula). K (*chāyā*) has घनबद्ध for *paṇaṭṭha* (R and Kula). MY seems to agree with K. K says यत्र च शिखरेषु आपतितं शिलाभित्तिबन्धस्य शिलामयस्य भित्तिनिवेशस्य पार्श्वगतं शशिबिम्बं तत्रत्यानां भुजगेन्द्राणां मणिषु निकषणेन बहुलबद्धप्रभासञ्चयं भूत्वा वलति। शिलाभित्तिविषमपार्श्वगतमिति च पाठः।

MY says यत्र तुङ्गशिखरनिरुद्धपदं शशिबिम्बं शिलाभित्तीनां संकटपार्श्वगतं,

[64] Kula seems to have an alternative explanation. *SC* which reproduces Kula says अथवा ज्योतिःपथो गगनं तस्मिन् वर्तमानानि वनानि यत्र निशासु कुसुमनिवहानिव इत्यर्थात् तारकानिवहानूद्वा प्रभातव्यवच्छिन्नतारकाणि सन्ति गृहीतप्रथमोच्चयानीव दृश्यन्त इति व्याख्या।

[65] The pallor of the moon is fancied as being caused by the friction of the lunar orb and the gems. Cf. verse 56.

तत्रत्यभुजगफणामणिनिकषणसंबद्धोद्द्योतसञ्चयं भूत्वा वलति पार्श्वगतः परावृत्त्य गच्छतीत्यर्थः। Kula has शिलाविषमभित्तिपार्श्वीकृतम्। R says शिलाभित्तौ विषमं यथा स्यात् तथा पार्श्वायितं तिर्यक् विवृत्तं पुरतः प्रतिरोधादित्यर्थः। *SC* says वलति तिर्यक् गच्छति। भुजगेन्द्रमणीनां पाषाणकर्कशत्वात्। तन्निघर्षेण दर्पणादीनामिव प्रणष्ट उद्द्योतसंचयो यस्येदृशं शशिबिम्बिं वलति वर्णान्तरेण गच्छतीति लोकनाथः।

Kula reads प्रद्योत (*pajjoa*, cf. *SC* text) for *ujjoa.*

78. आमोइअपाआलो जस्स खउप्पाअकम्प णिद्दअविहुओ।
पव्वालेइ महिअलं अवलिच्छिअसेससाअरो मअरहरो।।

[आमोचितपातालो यस्य क्षयोत्पातकम्पो निर्दयविधुतः।
प्लावयति महीतलमप्रतिष्ठशेषसागरो मकरगृहः।।]

Violently convulsed by the mountain as it rocked during the disaster of the epoch of destruction, the ocean by its side, abandoning the nether regions, flooded the earth without the aid of the remaining oceans.

K, MY and Kula read *ummoia* (उन्मोचित) for *āmoia* (R).

K says यस्य क्षयकालोत्पातजनितेन कम्पेन निर्दयविधुतः समुद्रः उन्मुक्तपातालः सन् अप्रतीक्षितशेषसागरो भूत्वा भूतलं प्लावयति सागरान्तरनिरपेक्षः स्वयमेव प्लावयतीति।[66] Kula also says अप्रतीक्षितशेषसागरः। MY says *apaḍicchia* अप्रतीष्ट (cf.7.54,10.41). *SC* text has *avaḍikkhia* (अप्रतीक्षित)। R has *avalicchia* (अप्रतीष्ट)। He says अप्रतीष्टाः अनासादिताः शेषसागराः येन।

79. जत्थ भमन्ति णहंकुससिहरसमासण्णमुहलकड्ढिअजलआ।
मुहपडिअविज्जुमण्डलदरपज्जलिअधुअकेसरा केसरिणो।।

[यत्र भ्रमन्ति नखाङ्कुशशिखरसमासन्नमुखरकृष्टजलदाः।
मुखपतितविद्युन्मण्डलदरप्रज्वलितधुतकेसराः केसरिणः।।]

The lions roamed about, pulling at the rumbling clouds resting upon the peaks with their sharp claws; while their ruffled mane was singed by the streaks of lightning flashing across their face.

नखाङ्कुशैः प्रतिगजशङ्कया कृष्टा मुखराः शिखरसमासन्ना जलदाः यैस्ते केसरिणः K.

[66] MY says यस्य प्रलयोत्पातरूपेण कम्पेन गाढविधुतः पार्श्ववर्ती समुद्र एव पातालमपि उन्मुच्य उच्चलितः शेषसागरानपेक्षो भुवं प्लावयतीत्यर्थः।

80. ओज्झरमज्जणसुहिआ जत्थ पुणो वि दिवसाअवकिलिम्मन्ता।
णिव्वाअन्ति णिसण्णा खन्धुग्घुट्टहरिचन्दणदुमेसु गआ।।
[निर्झरमज्जनसुखिता यत्र पुनरपि दिवसातपक्लाम्यमानाः।
निर्वान्ति निषण्णाः स्कन्धोद्घृष्टहरिचन्दनद्रुमेषु गजाः।।]

There, the elephants, soothed by bathing in the cascades, but again worn out with the heat of the day, were refreshed as they lay beside the sandal trees, rubbed by their shoulders.

K says यत्र गजाः निर्झरमज्जनेन सुखिताः पुनरपि दिवसातपेन क्लाम्यन्तः स्कन्धैरुद्घृष्टेषु निकषितेषु हरिचन्दनद्रुमेषु निषण्णा अपाश्रिताः सन्तः निर्वान्ति सुखीभवन्ति। MY reads *khandhugghaṭṭha* for *°gghu°*. Kula says हरिचन्दनद्रुमेषु गोशीर्षचन्दनतरुषु सुशीतलेषु निषण्णा निर्वाणा भवन्ति गजाः प्रशान्ततापा भवन्तीत्यर्थः।

81. जत्थ अ भमिरमहुअरं कडअलआलग्गधवलचामरपम्हम्।
ससिउद्धुअकुसुमरअं णज्जइ तुरिआण रइतुरंगाण गअम्।।
[यत्र च भ्रमणशीलमधुकरं कटकलतालग्रधवलचामरपक्ष्मम्।
श्वसितोद्धुतकुसुमरजो ज्ञायते त्वरितानां रवितुरङ्गाणां गतम्।।]

The course of the swift horses of the sun on the mountain could be recognized, being marked by the pollen of flowers scattered by their breath, with the bees flying about, and hairs from their white *cāmara* whisks settling on the creepers on the slopes.

K says रवितुरगाणां गमनरभसात् भ्रमन्मधुकरं . . . रवितुरगाणां गतं गमनं ज्ञायते। MY reads *bhamia* for *bhamira*, and explains it as भ्रामित, भृङ्गभ्रमणादिगमनवेगादिति ग्राह्यम्। R and Kula says भ्रमणशीला मधुकरा यत्र।

82. अञ्जणराएण सइ धूसरन्तआइं
गण्डअलेसु खलिअविसमोसरन्तआइं।
सुरबन्दीण णअणगलिआइं अंसुआइं
कप्पलआण जत्थ मइलेन्ति अंसुआइं।।

[अञ्जनरागेण सदा धूसरायमाणानि
गण्डतलेषु स्खलितविषमापसरन्ति।
सुरबन्दीनां नयनगलितान्यश्रूणि
कल्पलतानां यत्र मलिनयन्त्यंशुकानि।।]

There, the tears of the captive nymphs,[67] rolling down their cheeks, and always coloured dark by the collyrium paint of their eyes, soiled the scarves hanging from the celestial creepers.[68]

K says अञ्जनवर्णेन सदा धूसरस्वरूपाणि गण्डतलेषु स्खलितत्वात् विषममपसरन्ति सुरबन्दीनां नयनगलितानि अश्रूणि यत्र कल्पलतानामंशुकानि किसलयमयानि मलिनयन्ति।

83. एक्कसिहरे समप्पइ जस्स अ सोसविअमलिअदुमसंघाओ।
सइदक्खिणुत्तराअणणहगमणागमणविलुलिओ रइवन्थो।।

[एकशिखरे समाप्यते यस्य च शोषितमृदितद्रुमसंघातः।
सदा दक्षिणोत्तरायणनभोगमनागमनविलुलितो रविपथः।।]

The track of the sun, marked by clumps of trees withered and crushed, and worn out by its constant journeys through the sky in its northern and southern courses, seemed to terminate on a single peak of the mountain.

विलुलितः प्रहृतः K. दक्षिणायनोत्तरायणाभ्यां नभोगमनागमनक्षुण्णो रविमार्गः यस्य एकस्मिन् शिखर एव समाप्यते पर्यवस्यति। यस्मिन् शृङ्गे रवेर्दक्षिणायनं रवेः तत्रैव उत्तरायणपीत्यर्थः MY.

84. जेण भरभिण्णवसुहं अप्फुण्णसाअलं समोत्थइअणहम्।
सव्वदिसाविच्छूढं परिवड्ढन्तेण वड्ढिअं व तिहुअणम्।।

[येन भरभिन्नवसुधमाक्रान्तरसातलं समवस्थगितनभः।
सर्वदिग्विक्षिप्तं परिवर्धमानेन वर्धितमिव त्रिभुवनम्।।]

Spreading in all directions, it seemed to extend the three worlds as it grew in extent, cleaving the earth with its weight and enveloping the nether regions, and covering up the sky.

K says भरेण गौरवेण भिन्नवसुधम्, अवपूर्णरसातलम्, अवच्छादितगगनं, विक्षिप्तसर्वदिक्कं यथा वर्धमानेन येन त्रिभुवनं वर्धितमिव। K seems to read *samocchaia*[69] for *samotthaia* = समवस्थगित (R and probably Kula). MY has *ācchuṇṇa* (*occhuṇṇa* ?) अवक्षुण्ण for *apphuṇṇa* (R, K and Kula). It is a *deśī* word explained as आक्रान्त by R and Kula, cf.

---

[67] Cf. verses 47 and 50.

[68] I.e. they wiped their eyes with the scarves for which see verse 25.

[69] Hemacandra 2.17 derives छइअ from स्थगित।

Hemacandra 4.258. K takes it in the sense of अवपूर्ण, cf. *Deśīnāmamālā* 1.20. K and R explain *vicchūḍha* as विक्षिप्त (= प्रेरित R)। Kula says सर्वासु दिक्षु विच्युतं विक्षिप्तं प्रेरितम्। *SC* text reads *vivvūḍha* (see editor's fn.), though *SC* commentary has निर्व्यूढ.

85. गन्धावद्धमहुअरा वसन्ति जत्थ समअं सुरअणाणुगआ।
अण्णोण्णं पडिऊला एक्कक्खम्भल्लिआसुरगअ व्व उदू।।

[गन्धाबद्धमधुकरा वसन्ति यत्र समकं सुरवनानुगताः।
अन्योन्यं प्रतिकूला एकस्तम्भनिगलितसुरगजा इवर्तवः।।]

There, the mutually hostile seasons abode all together, attached to the groves of celestial beauty, with the bees attracted by the fragrance of the flowers; even as the elephants of the gods, resorting to the celestial garden, are tied to a single post, with the bees following the scent (of their ichor).[70]

K and MY read *gandhāiddha* (गन्धाविद्ध) for *gandhāvaddha* (R and Kula ?). K reads अनुचराः for *aṇugaā* (R); *aṇuraā* = अनुरताः (Kula). K says गन्धैः पुष्पगन्धैः आकृष्टमधुकराः, अन्यत्र मदगन्धाकृष्टभ्रमराः, सुरवनं कल्पवृक्षवनं तत्र चारिणो वर्तमानाः। भिन्नलिङ्गत्वादन्योन्यं प्रतिकूला ऋतवो यत्र सममेव वसन्ति। एकस्तम्भे नियमिताः सुरगजा इव। MY reads *ekkakkhambhāliā* and explains it as एकस्तम्भानीताः (स्तम्भालानिताः B)। He says *udū* ऋतवः। एकस्तम्भबद्धाः सुरगजा इव मिथोविरुद्धा अप्यृतव उक्तसाधर्म्यवन्तो यत्र समं वसन्तीत्यर्थः। K (*chāyā*) has एकस्तम्भालीनाः, and his reading seems to be same as that of MY. The reading as recorded by MY is *ālia* and K seems to derive it from आलीन (cf. *lua* = लून)। *Ālia* however appears to be a *deśī* word used at least twice in Svayambhū's *Paümacariu* in the sense of "tied" : *ālāṇakhambhe jaṁ āliyau* (also *āliu*) 19.14.3; 79.12.6. *SC* text has *ekkakhambha-ṇialiā suragaa va udū*. *SC* says एकस्मिन् स्तम्भे *ṇialiā* निगडिताः। Kula is corrupt in our copy, but *SC* here reproduces Kula *in toto*. R agrees with Kula.[71]

86. दीसइ वि वलाअन्तो जत्थ समासण्णदहमुहभआविग्गो।
सिहरन्तरालपडिलग्गमोइआणिक्कमण्डलो दिवसअरो।।

---

[70] See verse 61.

[71] R says एकस्तम्भनिगलिताः सुरगजा इव। Goldschmidt's tentative reading *ekkakkhambhallia* (see his footnote) has been taken over in the N.S. edition.

[दृश्यतेऽपि पलायमानो यत्र समासन्नदशमुखभयाविग्नः।
शिखरान्तरालप्रतिलग्नमोचिततिर्यङ्मण्डलो दिवसकरः।।]

The sun, overcome by fear of Rāvaṇa abiding nearby, was seen to slink away, extricating its slanting orb when it got stuck between the peaks of the mountain.

K reads अपि पलायमानः like R for *vivalāanto* = विपलायमानः (Kula). K says आदित्य आत्मनोऽपर्याप्ते शिखरयोरन्तराले ससंभ्रमं प्रतिलग्नं कथंचिन्मोचितं तिर्यग्भूतं मण्डलं यस्य स तथाभूत्वा पलायमानो दृश्यते। MY says भयात् सप्रकाशं गन्तुमशक्नुवन् यस्मिन् शृङ्गान्तरालमार्गेण गूढं पलायत इत्यर्थः।

87. जत्थ अ मआण मणहरकिंणरगीअसुहिओणिमिल्लच्छाणम्।
विसमिअरोमन्थाणं एइ विउद्धं चिरेण रोमं त्थाणम्।।

[यत्र च मृगाणां मनोहरकिंनरगीतसुखितावमीलदक्षाणाम्।
विश्रमितरोमन्थानामेति विबुद्धं चिरेण रोम स्थानम्।।]

There, as the deer, delighted to hear the charming songs of the *kinnaras*, closed their eyes, and stopped chewing the cud, their hair, standing on end, slowly become smooth again.

K (*chāyā*) has सुखितावनिमीलिताक्षाणाम्। K and MY read *visaria* (विस्मृत) for *visamia* (R). Kula reads विघटित (*vihaḍia*). K says विस्मृतरोमन्थानां मृगाणां विबुद्धं रोम आनन्दादुच्छ्वसितं रोम चिरेण पुनः स्थानमेति प्रकृतिं भजते। R explains *visamia* as विश्रमित्, or विस्मृत, or विषमित (अन्तरान्तरा विच्छेदित)।

88. तीरपवित्तमुहलकलहंसरोअएसुं
कुविअगइन्दबद्धकलहं सरोअएसुं।
कुमुअवणाण जत्थ णहअन्दलग्गआणं
रविअरदंसणे वि ण हअं दलग्गआणम्।।

[तीरप्रवृत्तमुखरकलहंसरोचकेषु
कुपितगजेन्द्रबद्धकलहं सरोवरेषु (सर उदकेषु, उदरेषु, वा)।
कुमुदवनानां यत्र नभश्चन्द्रलग्नानां
रविकरदर्शनेऽपि न हतं दलाग्रतानम्।।]

The angry elephants quarrelled in the waters of the lakes, resounding with the call of the noisy swans moving about on the banks; and the tips of the petals of the night lotus beds suffered no harm even at sunrise, because they touched the moon in the sky.[72]

K and MY read परियत्[73] for *pavitta* = प्रवृत्त (R). Their reading seems to be *parinta*. See verse 68 above. K says तीरे परियतां परिचरतां मुखराणां कलहंसानां रोदः शब्दः तद्वत्सु सरउदरेषु कुपितैर्गजेन्द्रः बद्धकलहं सुवेलं ददृशुः। यत्र नभश्चरे चन्द्रे लग्नानाम् आसन्नं चन्द्रमाश्रितानां कुमुदवनानां दलाग्राणां रविकरदर्शनेऽपि भयं नास्ति तम्। K (*chāyā*) has तीरपरियन्मुखरकलहंसरोदवत्सु . . . सरउदरेषु।

MY says तीरपर्यन्मुखरकलहंसरोदरेषु[74] रोदरश्चक्रवाकः[75] कुपितगजेन्द्रबद्धकलहं सरउदरेषु। बद्धकलहमिति शैलविशेषणम्। हंसानां चक्रवाकानां च सरोऽन्तर्गजक्षोभात् तीराभिगमनम्। यत्र कुमुदवानानां नभश्चन्द्रलग्नानां दलाग्राणां रविकरदर्शनेऽपि न भयं, हतं हानिर्वा। Kula is here corrupt, but *SC* reproduces him correctly यत्र सरउदकेषु कुपितैः गजेन्द्रैः बद्धकलहं यथा स्यात् तथा तीरं परीताः परिगताः (परिगाः Kula) मुखरा विरुवन्तो ये कलहंसाः तेषां रोचकेषु रुचिकारकेषु। Kula seems to read *parinta* like K and MY. Cf. notes on 6.57 and 7.50.

89. वलमाणम्मि महुमहे जत्थ अ पाउच्छलन्तरअणुज्जोअम्।
विअडं फणपब्भारं गाढभरुत्ताणिअं णिमेइ अणन्तो।।

[वलमाने मधुमथने यत्र च पादोच्छलद्रत्नोद्द्योतम्।
विकटं फणप्राग्भारं गाढभरोत्तानितं नियोजयत्यनन्तः।।]

As Viṣṇu turned over while asleep on the serpent Ananta, the latter propped its large massive hoods, flattened by the heavy weight, against the mountain, with the lustre of their gems[76] spreading over the foothills.

---

[72] The night lotus shrinks at sunrise and blooms by moonlight. Here the plants on the lakes at the top of the mountain were in constant bloom owing to the proximity of the moon.

[73] Our copy has परीयत्।

[74] रोदारेषु of the manuscript is a mistake as it goes against the Yamaka. पर्यत् is a mistake for परियत्।

[75] B has रोदारः; A says रोदाश्चक्रवाकाः। Monier-Williams records रोदर in this sense.

[76] I.e. the gems supposed to be embedded in the hoods of serpents. Ananta sustains the weight of the earth, and is sometimes represented as the couch of Viṣṇu.

K and MY read पाश्र्वोच्चलत् (*pāsuccalanta*) for *pāucchalanta* (R). K says मधुमथने कदाचित् प्रतिबुध्य वलमाने विवर्तमाने सति तस्य गाढेन अतिमात्रेण भेरण उत्तानितं विकटं पार्श्वोच्चलद्रत्नोद्द्योतं फणविस्तारम्। अनन्तश्च यत्र निक्षिपति विश्रमार्थं निदधाति। MY says *ṇimei* निक्षिपति (अर्पयति Kula)। वलमाने पार्श्वपरिवृत्त्या शयाने सर्वदिग्विसृमरो रत्नालोको भारार्त्या शैलनितम्बनिहिते फणे ऊर्ध्वपार्श्वमात्र एवोच्चलन् ज्ञायत इति पार्श्वोच्चलदित्युक्तम्। Kula reads विषदोच्छलत्, which seems to be a mistake for विषमो⁰, cf. *SC*. R explains his reading (see above) as पादेषु प्रत्यन्तपर्वतेषु उच्छलद्रत्नानाम् उद्द्योतो यस्मात् तम्।

90. दीसइ कडअल्लीणो जस्स अ विवरसरिसुब्भडमअच्छाओ।
अवहोवासमऊहो सिहरुज्झरभिण्णमण्डलो व्व मिअङ्को।।

[दृश्यते कटकालीनो यस्य च विवरसदृशोद्भटमृगच्छायः।
उभयावकाशमयूखः शिखरनिर्झरभिन्नमण्डल इव मृगाङ्कः।।]

The moon, clinging to the mountain side, was seen with the conspicuous shadow of its deer looking like a cavity, with the rays manifest on either side, as if the lunar orb had been hollowed out by the cascades rushing down from the summit.[77]

K says यस्य कटकमाश्रितो (कटकालीनो *chāyā*) गच्छन् विवरसदृश-प्रकाशमृगच्छायः, अतएव कलङ्कप्रदेशस्योभयपार्श्वप्रसरन्मयूखो मृगाङ्कस्तदानीं शिखर-निर्झरपातेन छिद्रितमण्डल इव दृश्यते। MY says *avahovāsa* उभयपार्श्वं। ऊर्ध्वाधोभागप्रसृतमयूखत्वं निर्झरपतनप्रतीत्यापादकम्।

91. मज्झकरालाइ जहिं तिण्णि वि समअं णिरन्तरपहुत्ताइं।
थोरुण्णए हरिभुए वलआइ व भुअणमण्डलाइ ठिआइं।।

[मध्यकरालानि यत्र त्रीण्यपि समकं निरन्तरप्रभूतानि।
स्थूलोन्नते हरिभुजे वलयानीव भुवनमण्डलानि स्थितानि।।]

All the three worlds lay round the mountain, like the three bangles round the massive and lofty arm of Viṣṇu,[78] close-fitting alike and hollowed in the middle.[79]

---

[77] The lunar spot is fancied as a hole torn by the cascades pouring down the mountain-side.

[78] Viṣṇu as Trivikrama in the Dwarf incarnation.

[79] I.e. the mountain seemed to have emerged, piercing its way through the nether regions, the earth and the sky.

SC says यथा हरिभुजं वेष्टयित्वा वलयानि तथैनमपि वेष्टयित्वा भुवनानि स्थितानीत्यर्थः।

K says मध्ये करालानि सान्तरालानि बहिरण्डकटाहावृतत्वात् सान्तरालमध्यानि, निरन्तरप्रभूतानि अन्योन्यनिर्विवरपर्याप्तानि (निरन्तरमशिथिलं प्रभूतानि सम्मितानि Kula त्रीण्यपि भुवनमण्डलानि यत्र समं स्थितानि। यत्र परितः स्थितानि। स्थूलोन्नते हरिभुजे त्रीणि वलयानीव, MY says स्थूलोन्नते हरेः त्रिविक्रमस्य भुजे वलयानीति। Kula says सममेककालं वलयानीव स्थितानि। R says समकं तुल्यम्।

92. सोसिअदुमा रइवहा णववणराइसुहसीअरा ससिवन्था।
जत्थ वणन्तरतणुआ णवर ण णज्जन्ति तारआगइमग्गा।।

[शोषितद्रुमा रविपथा नववनराजिसुखशीतलाः शशिपथाः।
यत्र वनान्तरतनुकाः केवलं न ज्ञायन्ते तारकागतिमार्गाः।।]

The tracks of the sun, marked by the withered trees, could be recognized as well as those of the moon, pleasant and cool with the lush woods. The faint trail of the stars through the woods only remained untraced.

रवेः पन्थानः ऋतावृतौ भिन्नाः पन्थानः K. *SC* text has *sīalā* for *sīarā*.

93. अलअपडिलग्गगन्धं तिअसवहूणं सिलाअलोत्थअमलिअम्।
अक्खिवइ जत्थ पवणो ओसुक्खन्तसुरहिं तमालकिसलअम्।।

[अलकप्रतिलग्नगन्धं त्रिदशवधूनां शिलातलावस्तृतमृदि(मलि)तम्।
आक्षिपति यत्र पवनोऽवशुष्यत्सुरभिं तमालकिसलयम्।।]

There, the wind scattered the *tamāla* leaves that were spread by the nymphs on slabs of stone and crumpled (during their amorous sports), and were redolent of their perfumed locks, and gave out a sweet smell as they withered away.

K and MY read त्रिदशवधूशिलातलान्तर[80] for *tiasa-vahūṇaṁ silā-ala* (R and Kula). K says यत्र त्रिदशवधूभिः शिलातलान्तरेषु अवस्तृतं मृदितं, तासामलकेषु प्रतिलग्नगन्धमलकेभ्यः प्रतिलग्नगन्धं वा, अवशुष्यदवस्थायां सुरभि तमालकिसलयं पवनः आक्षिपति (आकर्षति Kula) MY says त्रिदशवधूभिः शयनीयतया शिलातलान्तरावस्तृतमृदितम्।

---

[80] Metre requires °*vahu*° for *vahū,* cf. Hemacandra 1.4.

94. पवणाहअपल्हत्था दरीसु जस्स अ पुणो वि लग्गन्ति णहम्।
पडिसोत्तपत्थिउम्मुहमुहुत्तपीअसलिलोज्झरा सलिलहरा।।

[पवनाहतपर्यस्ता दरीषु यस्य च पुनरपि लगन्ति नभः।
प्रतिस्रोतःप्रस्थितोन्मुखमुहूर्तपीतसलिलनिर्झराः सलिलधराः।।]

The clouds, swept into the caves by the wind, drove in the opposite direction; and as they rose aloft quaffed for a moment the waters of the cascades, and ascended the sky again.

K and MY read *siharo°* for *salilo°* (R). Kula is corrupt; *SC* agrees with K. K and Kula read *vilagganti* विलग्गन्ति for *vi la°* (R). K says यस्य च दरीषु पवनाहतपर्यस्ताः मेघाः निर्झराणां प्रतिस्रोतः प्रस्थितत्वादुन्मुखाः सन्तः मुहूर्तं पीतशिखरनिर्झरा भूत्वा पुनर्नभ आरोहन्ति। R says प्रतिस्रोतसा विपरीतमार्गेण प्रस्थिताः, अत एव उन्मुखा ऊर्ध्वमुखाः। MY says यत्र शिखरनिर्झरेषु पातुमारब्धाः जलधराः मध्ये पवनेनाधस्तात् पर्यस्ता दरीषु पातिताः पुनरपि प्रतिस्रोतस्कमुन्मुखं मुहूर्तपीतसलिला भूत्वा नभो विलगन्तीत्यर्थः[81]। Kula says पवनाहतत्वेन दरीषु पर्यस्ताः पतिताः ततः प्रतिस्रोतः, etc.

95–96. अद्दिट्ठगअपणोल्लिअपडन्ततडघाअमुच्छिउट्ठिअसीहे।
सद्दूलरवविसंठुलणिवडिअअण्णोण्णलग्गकिंणरमिहुणे।।

तुङ्गअडोज्झरमुहले जस्स अ कसणमणिगण्डसेलद्धन्ते।
सेवन्तीण ण पत्तो तिअसवहूण सिढिलत्तणं अणुराओ।।
(जुग्गअम्)

[अदृष्टगजप्रणोदितपतत्तटघातमूर्च्छितोत्थितसिंहान्।
शार्दूलरवविसंष्ठुलनिपतितान्योन्यलग्नकिंनरमिथुनान्।।

तुङ्गतटनिर्झरमुखरान्यस्य च कृष्णमणिगण्डशैलार्धान्तान्।
सेवमानानां न प्राप्तस्त्रिदशवधूनां शिथिलत्वमनुरागः।।]
(युग्मकम्)

The ardour of the nymphs did not flag as they frequented the sapphire rocks, resonant with the cascades pouring down the lofty slopes. Here, the lion sprang up after being stunned by the impact of a falling rock, pushed down by an unseen

[81] वल्गन्ति A, वलगन्ति B.

elephant; and the *kinnara* couples sank to the ground and clung to each other, appalled at a tiger's growl.

The verse is not found in K, MY and Kula. Found in R and *SC* which says स्कन्धकमिदं कुलनाथे न धृतम्।

अनुरागः संभोगाभिलाषः K, MY says तुङ्गतटेभ्यः सशब्दं पतद्भिः निर्झरैः मुखरानिन्द्रनीलमयान् गण्डशैलप्रदेशान् सेवमानानां त्रिदशवधूनां तद्विषयोऽनुरागः अभिलाषः शैथिल्यं (न) प्राप्तः।

इअ सिरिपवरसेणविरइए कालिदासकए दहमुहवहे महाकव्वे
सुवेलवण्णणो णवमो आसासओ समत्तो।

इति श्रीप्रवरसेनविरचिते कालिदासकृते दशमुखवधे महाकाव्ये
सुवेलवर्णनो नवम आश्वासकः समाप्तः।

दशम आश्वासकः
Tenth Āśvāsakaḥ

1. अह णिअअमहिहरेसु व सुवेलसिहरेसु णिव्वडिअवीसत्थम्।
परिसंट्ठिअं हअम्मि व अहअम्मि विदहमुहे पवंगमसेण्णम्।।

[अथ निजकमहीधरेष्विव सुवेलशिखरेषु निर्वलितविश्वस्तम्।
परिसंस्थितं हत इवाहतेऽपि दशमुखे प्लवंगमसैन्यम्।।]

Thereafter the host of apes stayed on the peaks of the Suvela as on their native mountains, confidently in separate groups, as if Rāvaṇa, even though undestroyed, had been slain.

K reads विस्रब्ध[1] for *vīsattha*, and says निर्व्यक्तविस्रम्भं (निर्व्यक्त)स्थैर्यम्। विस्रब्धः स्थिर उच्यते इति हलायुधः। विस्रब्धमिति भावे निष्ठा, i.e. *vīsaddhaṁ*. MY says *ṇivvaḍia-vīsatthaṁ* निर्भयतया पृथग्भूत्वा विश्वस्तमवस्थितमित्यर्थः।

2. रइणा वि अणुच्छुण्णा वीसत्थं मारुएण वि अणालिद्धा।
तिअसेंहि वि परिहरिआ पवंगमेहि मलिआ सुवेलुच्छङ्गा।।

[रविणाप्यनुत्क्षुण्णा विश्वस्तं मारुतेनाप्यनालीढाः।
त्रिदशैरपि परिहृताः प्लवंगमैर्मृदिताः सुवेलोत्सङ्गाः।।]

The apes trampled the summit of the Suvela that was unassailed even by the sun, and untouched even by the wind with confidence, and was shunned even by the gods[2]

My says *aṇocchuṇṇā*[3] अनवक्षुण्णाः (K and Kula also) अनाक्रान्ता इति वा। *aṇāiddhā* अस्पृष्टाः (K also). अनाश्लिष्टाः Kula. त्रिदशैरपि परित्यक्ताः सुवेलप्रदेशाः K. विस्रब्धं निःशङ्कम् K. Kula reads *addhanta* (अर्धान्त) = एकदेश for *ucchaṁga.*

3. रिउणअरि त्ति सरोसं जणअसुआ एत्थ णिवसइ त्ति सहरिसम्।
पहुणा लङ्काहिमुही उहअरसन्दोलिआ विइण्णा दिट्ठिः।।

---

[1] Also in verses 2, 55 and 80.

[2] I.e. for fear of Rāvaṇa.

[3] Cf. *occhundaï* in verse 55. R has *aṇu*⁰ (अनुत्क्षुण्णाः)।

[रिपुनगरीति सरोषं जनकसुतात्र निवसतीति सहर्षम्।
प्रभुणा लङ्काभिमुखी उभयरसान्दोलिता विकीर्णा(वितीर्णा,वा) दृष्टिः।।]

The mighty Rāma cast a look at Laṅkā that was rooted in two different emotions: with wrath, because it was the foeman's city; and with joy as he thought "Here lives my beloved".

K and MY read this verse after 12.29. K and Kula read अत्र मम वसति प्रियतमेति (*ettha mahaṁ vasai piaamatti*, cf. *SC* text for *jaṇaa . . . tti* (R). K reads आबद्धोभयरसा for *uhaa-rasandoliā* (R). Kula seems to read प्रतिबद्धोभयरसा, and प्रभोः (*pahuṇo*) for *pahuṇā* and निपतिता (*ṇivaḍiā*) for *viiṇṇā* = वितीर्णा।

4. तो सुअरामागमणो पवअक्कन्तसिहरेण जाआमरिसो।
रोसेण गलितधीरो समं सुवेलेण कम्पिओ दहवअणो।।

[ततः श्रुतरामागमनः प्लवगाक्रान्तशिखरेण जातामर्षः।
रोषेण गलितधैर्यः समं सुवेलेन कम्पितो दशवदनः।।]

Having heard of the advent of Rāma, Rāvaṇa, disconcerted and full of spite, trembled with rage, even as the Suvela trembled with its peaks trampled by the apes.

5. ताव अ आसण्णट्ठिअकइबलणिग्घोसकलुसिअस्स भअअरम्।
दसवअणस्स समोसरिअपरिअणं मुअइ दिट्ठिवाअं दिवसो।।

[तावच्चासन्नस्थितकपिबलनिर्घोषकलुषितस्य भयकरम्।
दशवदनस्य समपसृतपरिजनं मुञ्चति दृष्टिपातं दिवसः।।]

Meanwhile, the day shunned the terrible looks of Rāvaṇa,[4] who was enraged by the yells of the neighbouring host of apes, while his attendants slunk away in fear.

K says तावच्च तत्रान्तरे च आसन्नस्थितकपिबलनिर्घोषेण कलुषितस्य क्षुभितहृदयस्य दशवदनस्य भयङ्करं दृष्टिपातं दिवसो मुमोच। समापसृतपरिजनं दृष्टिपातस्य भयङ्करत्वात् सममेवापसृताः परिजनाः यथा भवन्ति तथा मुमोच। परिजनवत् भीतो दिवसो जगामेत्यर्थः। R says समपसृताः पलायिताः परिजना यस्मात् तम्।

6. सुरगअणिहस्स रइणो कड्ढन्तस्स णलिणिं व दिअसच्छाअम्।
वलइ हरिआलकविलो कमलरअक्खउरिओ व्व करपब्भारो।।

[4] The departing day is fancied as leaving the fearful presence of Rāvaṇa.

[सुरगजनिभस्य रवेः कर्षतो नलिनीमिव दिवसच्छायाम्।
वलति हरितालकपिलः कमलरजःकलुषित इव करप्राग्भारः।।]

As the sun drew behind it the lustre of the day, like an elephant of the gods trailing a lotus plant, the mass of its rays, reddish yellow like orpiment, verged (towards the west); even as the elephant's massive trunk curls up, coloured with the pollen of the lotus blossoms.

यथा सुरगजस्य कमलरजोभिः शबलितः करविस्तारो वलते तद्वदिति K. रवेः करसमूहो वलति परावर्तते। सर्वतो वर्तुलीभवतीत्यर्थः R. वलति प्रतीच्यामावर्जितो भवति Kula.

7. ओलुग्गप्फरिसाणं झिज्जन्तसारिआअवणिराआणम्।
आआमिज्जन्तीण व जाअं तलिणत्तणं दुमच्छाआणम्।।

[अवरुग्णस्पर्शानां क्षीयमाणप्रसारितातपनिरायतानाम्।
आयम्यमानानामिव जातं तलिनत्वं द्रुमच्छायानाम्।।]

The shadows of the trees, lengthening as the pervasive daylight faded, with their coolness[5] impaired,[6] thinned as if they were being stretched.

K says अस्तमयसमये सति प्रसारितस्य सर्वतः प्रसृतस्य आतपस्य क्षीयमाणत्वात् निरायतानाम्, अवरुग्णस्पर्शानां स्पर्शगुणविहीनां द्रुमच्छायानामायम्यमानानामिव अतिदीर्घीक्रियमाणानामिव तलिनत्वम् अतितनुत्वं जातं, यथा तप्तस्य लोहस्य लोहान्तराघातात् अत्यायतीक्रियमाणस्य अतिलघुत्वं जायते तद्वदिति। Kula says आतपस्य क्षीयमाणत्वात् अवरुग्णो यथावत् त्वगिन्द्रियग्राह्यः स्पर्शो यासाम्। *SC* says अवरुग्णस्पर्शानां पूर्वमातपप्राचण्ड्यात् छायासुशीतलस्पर्शो गृहीत आसीत्, इदानीमातपमान्द्येन स्पर्शानुपलब्धेरिति भावः।

8. दीसइ विद्दुमअम्बं सिन्दूराहअगइन्दकुम्भच्छाअम्।
मन्दरधाउकलङ्किअवासुइमण्डलनिअक्कलं रइबिम्बम्।।

[दृश्यते विद्रुमाताम्रं सिन्दूराहतगजेन्द्रकुम्भच्छायम्।
मन्दरधातुकलङ्कितवासुकिमण्डलनिश्चक्रलं रविबिम्बम्।।]

Red as coral, the orb of the sun resembled the head of a mighty elephant painted with vermilion and was round like

[5] Literally touch.

[6] I.e. the coolness was not felt in the evening as during the day.

the coils of the serpent Vāsuki, coloured by minerals of the Mandara mountain.[7]

K does not explain the verse fully. K (*chāyā*) has वासुकिमण्डलसदृशम्। MY says *ṇiakkalaṁ* सदृशम्[8]। K remarks भोगस्य मण्डलावृत्तिकरणत्वं मण्डलम्। Kula says मन्दरस्य धातुना गैरिकेण कलङ्कितस्य लिप्तस्य वासुकेः कुण्डलीभूतशरीरमण्डलमिव निश्चक्रलं वर्तुलं रविबिम्बं दृश्यते।

9. मउलेन्ति दिसाहोआ छाआसामलइओअरं महिवेढम्।
दिअसो कलावसेसो सिहरालग्गतणुआअवा धरणिहरा।।

[मुकुलायन्ते दिगाभोगाश्छायाश्यामलितोदरं महीवेष्ट(पृष्ट)म्।
दिवसः कलावशेषः शिखरालग्रतनुकातपा धरणिधराः।।]

The expanses of the regions of the sky appeared to shrink, and the circle of the earth was darkened by the shades of evening. A tiny part of the day still remained, and a faint light lingered on the peaks of the mountains.

छाया भूच्छाया तम इति यावत्। कलावशेषः अल्पावशेषः MY.

10. अत्थणिअम्बपरिणए हिआअवरअम्मि सुरगअम्मि व दिअसे।
दीसहिं पल्हत्थन्तं विहडिअधाउसिहरं व दिणअरबिम्बम्।।

[अस्तनितम्बपरिणते हृतातपरजसि सुरगज इव दिवसे।
दृश्यते पर्यस्यद्विघटितधातुशिखरमिव दिनकरबिम्बम्।।]

As the day, like an elephant of the gods, hit the slope of the mountain of sunset, raising a cloud of dust, the evening glow, the orb of the sun appeared to be tumbling like a dislodged peak of the mountain composed of red earth.

K says हृतातपरजसि संहृतातपशेषे। अन्यत्र हृतरजसि आहृतमहीपांसौ। दिवसे सुरगज इव अस्तपर्वतनितम्बे परिणते समाप्ते सति। अन्यत्र दन्तप्रहारं कृतवति सति। पर्यस्यमानम् अधोमुखीभवत् दिनकरबिम्बं दन्तप्रहारेण विपर्यस्यमानं विघटितं धातुशिखरमिवादृश्यत। MY says परिणतवति तिर्यग्दन्तप्रहारवति। (तथा) च मुक्तगगनतया अस्तनितम्बमात्रपर्यवसिते इत्यर्थद्वयम्। हृतातपरजसीति रजसो हरण-मुपादानम्। आतपस्य त्वपनयनम्। Kula says परिणते निषण्णे कृतदन्ताघाते (च)। *SC* and R say पर्यस्यत् पतत्। R says परि सर्वतोभावेन नते उपनते प्राप्ते।

[7] Vāsuki served as a rope coiled round the Mandara mountain with which the ocean was churned by the gods and demons.

[8] *Deśīnāmamālā* 4.39 gives the word in the sense of वर्तुल, like R and Kula.

11. कमलाण दिअसविगमे संबज्झन्ति गलिआअवकिलिन्ताइं।
मअरन्दमत्तमहुअरचलपक्खुप्पुसिअमहुरसाइ दलाइं।।

[कमलानां दिवसविगमे संबध्यन्ते गलितातपक्राम्यति(क्लान्तानि)।
मकरन्दमत्तमधुकरचलपक्षोत्प्रोञ्छितमधुरसानि दलानि।।]

The petals of the day lotus blossoms, drooping on account of the fading daylight, closed at the end of the day, with the dripping honey wiped away by the agile wings of the bees, enlivened by the honey of the flowers.

K reads विरामे (*virame*) for विगमे (R). He renders *uppusia* as उन्मृष्ट। Kula is incomplete. but *SC* has *virame* like K. Kula reads *milanta* (मिलत्) for *kilinta* (क्लान्त), and says कमलानां दलानि गलितातपत्वात् मिलन्ति संकुचन्ति, . . . संबध्यन्ते मुकुलीभवन्तीत्यर्थः।

12. दीवन्ति दो वि सरिसा कइचलणाइद्धमहिरअसमक्कन्ता।
अव्थाअन्तो अ रई आसण्णविणासणिप्पहो दहवअणो।।

[दृश्येते द्वावपि सदृशौ कपिचरणाविद्धमहीरजःसमाक्रान्तौ।
अस्तायमानश्च रविरासन्नविनाशनिष्प्रभो दशवदनः।।]

The setting sun as well as Rāvaṇa, bereft of lustre because of impending ruin, both looked alike, hemmed in by the dust of the earth struck by the feet of the apes.

कपिचरणैराहताया मह्या रजोभिः समाक्रान्तौ K.

13. अद्धत्थमिअदिणअरो तुङ्गोवासपरिसंठिआअवसेसो।
गअणे मुक्कमहिअलो परिप्पवन्ततलिणो किलिम्मइ दिअसो।।

[अर्धास्तमितदिनकरस्तुङ्गावकाशपरिसंस्थितातपशेषः।
गगने मुक्तमहीतलः परिप्लवमानतलिनः क्लाम्यति दिवसः।।]

Abandoning the earth, the day, faint as it hovered in the sky, faded away, with the sun half gone down, and the remaining light lingering on the mountain heights.[9]

परिप्लवमान चञ्चलीभवदीत्यर्थः। *kilammai* (for *kili*⁰) अक्लाम्यत् MY. K (*chāyā*) has परिवर्तमानतलिनः K (commentary) says परिवर्तमानत्वात् परिप्लवमानत्वात् तनुः।

---

[9] Literally on the high places.

14. दिअसेण वणगएण व परंमुहाइद्धपाअवस्स व रविणो।
दीसइ थोरकरालो उद्धो मूलणिवहो व्व करपब्भारो।।

[दिवसेन वनगजेनेव पराङ्मुखाविद्धपादपस्येव रवेः।
दृश्यते स्थूलकराल ऊर्ध्वो मूलनिवह इव करप्राग्भारः।।]

As the sun was flung (to the west) by the day, even as a tree is thrown backwards by a wild elephant, its extensive, thinly scattered mass of rays, shooting upward, looked like the roots (of an uprooted tree).

MY reads *osuddha* (अवपातित) for *āiddha* (आविद्ध)। Kula's reading might be the same as he says दिवसेन वनगजेनेव पराङ्मुखपा(ा)-तितपादपस्येव रवेः। K seems to explain आविद्ध as क्षिप्त, and says वनगजेनेव दिवसेन आहत्य पराङ्मुखक्षिप्तस्य वृक्षस्येव रवेः स्थूलः करालः सान्तराल ऊर्ध्वः करप्राग्भारः मूलनिवह इव वृक्षस्य शिफासमूह इवादृश्यत। Kula says स्थूलकरालो विरलस्थितत्वात्। R says वनगजेनेव दिवसेन पराङ्मुखमन्यतोमुखं प्रेरितस्य सतः पादपस्य इव। *SC* says प्राग्भारः समूहः, and explains पराङ्मुखाविद्ध as अधःशिखरीकृतनिपातित।

15. णवरि अ दिणअरबिम्बं संझामइअम्मि णिअअरुहिरप्पङ्के।
दहवअणस्स भअअरं पढमसिरच्छेअमण्डलं व णिउड्डम्।।

[अनन्तरं च दिनकरबिम्बं संध्यामये निजकरुधिरपङ्के।
दशवदनस्य भयंकरं प्रथमशिरश्छेदमण्डलमिव निमग्नम्।।]

Thereupon the orb of the sun sank in its own blood, the evening glow, as if it were the terrible first head of Rāvaṇa, severed and immersed in its gore.

K says अथ दिनकरबिम्बं सन्ध्यामये, तेजसीत्यध्याहार्यम्, निमग्नमभूत्। किमिव – रामबाणच्छिन्नस्य दशवदनस्य प्रथमशिरसो भयङ्करं छेदमण्डलं छेदप्रदेशमण्डलं भूतलगते निजरुधिरपङ्के यथा निमग्नं भविष्यति तद्वदित्यर्थः।

Kula says दिनकरबिम्बं सन्ध्यामये स्वकीयरुधिरसंघाते आसन्नविनाशस्य दशवदनस्य प्रथमशिरश्छेदमण्डलमिव निमग्नम्। MY says सन्ध्यारुणमस्तमयमानं रविबिम्बं तत्क्षणोच्चलद्रुधिरनिमग्नदशमुखप्रथमकण्ठच्छेदबुद्धिमजनयत् लोकस्येत्याशयः।

16. भमरभरोवत्ताइं परिणअकेसरपलोट्टरअगरुआइं।
रविविरहमिलन्ताइं वि होन्ति करालाइ पङ्कआण दलाइं।।

[भ्रमरभरापवृत्तानि परिणतकेसरप्रलुठितरजोगुरुकाणि।
रविविरहमिलन्त्यपि भवन्ति करालानि पङ्कजानां दलानि।।]

The petals of the day lotus blossoms, even though closed in the absence of the sun, parted, because they were bowed down with the weight of the bees, and made heavy by the pollen issuing from the mature filaments.

K says अन्तर्गतेन भ्रमरभरेण अपवृत्तानि आक्रान्तानि, परिणतेभ्यो विकसितेभ्यः केसरेभ्यः प्रलुठितेन रजसा गुरूकृतानि, रविविरहात् म्लायन्ति पङ्कजानां दलानि करालानि संकोचक्रमेण मिथः सान्तरालानि अभवन्। K omits वि in the second line, so he seems to read *milantāiṁ metric*. Others take *milanta* as मिलत् instead of म्लायत् (K). R says अपवृत्तानि अवनतानि।

MY reads *oagga* (अभिभूत) for *ovatta* (अपवृत्त)। Kula says भ्रमरभरावभग्नानि। He seems to read *obhagga*. MY says रविविरहात् मिलन्त्यपि घटमानान्यपि करालानि मध्यच्छिद्राणि (दलानि)। Kula says रविविरहे मिलन्ति पङ्कजानां दलानि करालानि दन्तुराणि भवन्ति। He also omits *vi* like K. R says रविविरहे सति परस्परं मिलन्त्यपि।

17. अवरदिसावित्थिण्णो दीहमऊहविसमप्पहासंघाओ।
रअणिब्भरो व्व दीसइ कालमुहक्खित्तदिअसकड्ढणमग्गो।।

[अपरदिशाविस्तीर्णो दीर्घमयूखविषमप्रभासंघातः।
रजोनिर्भर इव दृश्यते कालमुखक्षिप्तदिवसकर्षणमार्गः।।]

The massive lustre (of the setting sun), uneven with lengthening rays, and spreading in the west, seemed to be the dusty trail of the day while it was snatched away by the jaws of death.

Kula and K read विषमः (*visamo*). K says अपरदिशि विस्तीर्णो दीर्घैः किरणैः विषमः प्रभासंघातः अस्तमितस्य रवेः प्रकाशसमूहः कालमुखेन आक्षिप्तस्य आकृष्टस्य दिवसस्य रजोनिर्भरो निकर्षणमार्ग इवादृश्यत्। अवयवभूतस्य अहोरात्रस्य प्रधानभूतसंवत्सरः कालशब्देनोच्यते। Kula says दीर्घा ये मयूखाः तैः विषमो नतोन्नतः प्रभासंघातः कालस्य मुहूर्तादेः मुखे पतितस्य दुःखेन आकृष्टस्य दिवसस्य, etc.[10]

18. उद्धोवअत्तबिम्बे वेएण महिं व दिणअरम्मि अइगए।
उच्छलिआअवअम्बा संझाराअमिहिआ णहम्मि णिहित्ता।।

[10] *SC* says अपरस्यां पश्चिमायां दिशि विस्तीर्णः। . . . दीर्घेण मयूखेन विषमः अतिशयितः प्रभासंघातः . . . कालस्य अस्तसमयस्य मुखे क्षिप्तस्य दिवसस्य कर्षणमार्ग इव दृश्यत इति लोकनाथः।

[ऊर्ध्वापवृत्तबिम्बे वेगेन महीमिव दिनकरेऽतिगते।
उच्छलितातपाताम्रा संध्यारागमेघिका नभसि निहिता।।]

A bank of light clouds, suffused with the evening glow, clung to the sky, as if reddened by the rays that shot up when the orb of the sun, falling from above, appeared to dash against the earth.

K, MY and Kula read अवपतत् (*ovaanta*) for *avaatta* (अपवृत्त) found in R.[11] They also read उच्चलित for उच्छ॰ (R).

K says ऊर्ध्वान्नभःप्रदेशात् अवपतद्बिम्बे दिनकरे वेगेन महीमतिगत इव प्रविष्ट इव सति तस्योच्चलितातपवत् ताम्राः सन्ध्यारागयुक्ता मेघा नभसि प्रसृताः। R says मेघिका स्वल्पमेघः (Kula also). MY says *ovaanta* अवपतत्। ऊर्ध्व-दिशोऽवपतद्बिम्बे। *saṁjhā-rāa-mihiā* सन्ध्यारागवान् मेघः इति छायाद्रुमादिवत् द्रष्टव्यम्। लाक्षारसादिपूरिते घटादौ नभसो वेगेन प्रतियाति पृथिव्यादिमूर्तद्रव्योपरि निपतिते तत्क्षणोच्चलदन्तर्गतलाक्षादिनोपरि नभःस्थितानां पटादीनां यथोपरञ्जनं स्यात् तेन न्यायेनेत्याशयः।

19. अत्थसिहरम्मि दीसइ मेरुअडुग्घुट्ठकणअकद्दमअम्बो।
वलमाणतुरिअरविरहपडिउट्ठिअधअवडो व्व संझाराओ।।

[अस्तशिखरे दृश्यते मेरुतटोद्घृष्टकनककर्दमाताम्रः।
वलमानत्वरितरविरथपतितोत्थितध्वजपट इव संध्यारागः।।]

The evening glow appeared on the summit of the sunset mountain, as if it were the banner, rising after it had gone down, of the sun's swift chariot as it wound its way round the Meru mountain; (the banner) reddened by the molten gold of the mountain rubbed off its slopes.[12]

K reads (i) उन्मृष्ट for *ugghuṭṭha* (उद्घृष्ट) found in R and Kula; and (ii) वलितस्थित for *paḍiuṭṭhia* = पतितोत्थित (R and Kula). With regard to (i), K's reading might be *uppusia* which he often renders as उन्मृष्ट (cf. verse 11). MY, however, reads *upphaṭṭha*

---

[11] R says ऊर्ध्वादपवृत्तं स्खलितं बिम्बं यस्य तादृशि दिनकरे।

[12] Meru is the golden mountain at the centre of Jambudvīpa round which the planets were supposed to revolve. Here, the gold of the mountain is fancied as being melted by the sun; and the glow of the sky at sunset is figured as the banner of the sun's chariot that had brushed against the molten gold.

(*upphuṭṭha* ?) and renders it as उन्मृष्ट। See his gloss on verse 35 below and 11.102.

K says अस्तगिरिशिखरे सन्ध्यारागोऽदृश्यत। किमिव–मेरुमभितो वलमानस्य त्वरितस्य रविरथस्य वलितस्थितो ध्वजपट इव। कथंभूत: ध्वजपट:–मेरुतटस्यात्यासन्नतया दीप्ततरेण आतपेन विलीनस्य मेरुतटस्य उन्मृष्टेनोज्ज्वलेन कनककर्दमेन ताम्र: कर्दमस्पर्शात् ताम्र:। अथवा मेरुतटात् स्फुटितविलीनस्य कनकस्य कर्दमेन ताम्र:।

20. विअसइ धवलाअम्बं गअरुहिरालिद्धकेसरिसडच्छाअम्।
पवणन्दोलणचडुलं संझारज्जन्तकेसरं कुमुअवणम्।।

[विकसति धवलाताम्रं गजरुधिरालीढकेसरिसटाच्छायम्।
पवनान्दोलनचटुलं संध्यारज्यमानकेसरं कुमुदवनम्।।]

The night lotus bed burst into bloom while being swayed by the breeze. With the filaments coloured by the gleam of the evening, it assumed a white a reddish hue, resembling a lion's mane smeared with the blood of the elephant (killed by it).

K and MY read दृश्यते (*dīsai*) for *viasai* = विकसति (R and Kula). K says गजरुधिरस्पृष्टसिंहसटासदृशवर्णं कुमुदवनमदृश्यत।

21. होइ अपाअडदीहा दरवोच्छिज्जन्तविसमसंझाराआ।
ओधूसरिअदसदिसा अबद्धतिमिरा दिणावसाणच्छाआ।।

[भवत्यप्रकटदीर्घा दरव्यवच्छिद्यमानविषमसंध्यारागा।
अवधूसरितदशदिक् अबद्धतिमिरा दिनावसानच्छाया।।]

The shadows at the end of the day that made the ten directions grey were faint and long, and still free from the onset of darkness, with the partly dissolving gleam of the evening scattered here and there.

K and My read °दीपा for *dīhā* (R and Kula). My says अनुपजाततिमिरा प्रदोषशोभा नि:शेषाव्युच्छिन्नविरलावस्थितसन्ध्यारागा, अत एव तदभिभवेन नातिभास्वरदीपा।

K says दिनावसानस्य छाया छविरेवमभूत्। कथम्–अविच्छिद्यमानविषमसन्ध्यारागा, अबद्धतिमिरा असंजाततिमिरा, अत एव अप्रकटदीपा, etc. Kula takes the अ in *apāaḍa* (अप्रकट) separately as he says भवति च प्रकटदीर्घा ईषद्व्यवच्छिद्यमानविषमसन्ध्यारागा, etc.

22. संझाअवमुच्चन्तं जलिअपसम्मन्तहुअवहट्ठाणणिहम्।
दूरत्थमिअदिणअरं जाअं संवत्तसरिसरूअं गअणम्।।

[संध्यातपमुच्यमानं ज्वलितप्रशाम्यद्धुतवहस्थाननिभम्।
दूरास्तमितदिनकरं जातं संवर्तसदृशरूपं गगनम्।।]

Bereft of the evening glow, with the sun far down, the sky looked everywhere alike, resembling a hearth where a blazing fire was dying down.

K, MY and Kula read सर्वत्र for *saṁvatta* found in R who mentions the other reading (*savvattha*) as a variant. K says सर्वत्र प्रदेशे सदृशरूपं जातम्। R says संवर्तेन प्रलयेन सदृशं रूपं यस्य तादृक् जातम्। My remarks पूर्वं रवावस्तमितमात्रे सन्ध्यारागानुवृत्त्या प्रदेशभेदेन उज्ज्वलानुज्ज्वल-रूपमासीन्नभः। इदानीं तु दूरास्तमिते तस्मिन् संध्यायाश्चोपरमे सर्वदिक्षु अनुज्ज्वलमेव जातमित्यर्थः।

23. संझाराअत्थइआ दरसंरूढन्धआरकअपरभाआ।
दिअसच्छविपरिसेसे झिज्जन्ते णिव्वलन्ति दीवुज्जोआ।।

[संध्यारागस्थगिता दरसंरूढान्धकारकृतपरभागाः।
दिवसच्छविपरिशेषे क्षीयमाणे निर्बलन्ति दीपोद्द्योताः।।]

As the remaining splendour of the day faded away the light of the lamps, dimmed by the evening glow, became distinct, being set off by the partly accumulating darkness.

K, MY and Kula read अस्तमित for *tthaia* = स्थगित (R). K and probably MY read दूरारूढ for दरसंरूढ (R). Kula has नवसंरूढ। K says पूर्वं सन्ध्यारागादस्तमिताः अप्रकाशाः, दूरमारूढेन भृशं प्ररूढेन तमसा कृतवर्णोत्कर्षो दीपप्रभाः दिवसच्छवेः परिशेषे क्षीयमाणे सति स्फुटं व्यज्यन्ते स्म। MY has विवृद्धतमः . . . Kula says कृतः परभागः शोभा येषां ते। *nivvalanti* स्वरूपेण निष्पाद्यन्ते[13] दीपोद्द्योताः। MY says अभिव्यज्यन्ते। R says परभागः अभ्यतः शोभा and explains दर as ईषत्। With regard to *ṇivvalanti*, Hemacandra says *ṇivvaḍai* पृथक् स्पष्टो वा भवति (4.62), but derives *nivvalai from* निष्पद्यते (4.128). *SC* says *ṇivvaḍanti* पृथगुपलभ्यन्ते निष्पन्ना भवन्तीति वा[14]

[13] निष्पद्यन्ते ?।

[14] The commentary on *Gaüḍavaho* (431) renders *ṇivvaḍaï* as निर्वर्तते प्रकटीभवति, and explains *ṇivvaḍia* (ibid 383) as निवृत्तं संपन्नमभिव्यक्तम्। Also *ṇivvaḍaï* = निर्वर्तते संपद्यते (ibid. 502)।

24. विहडन्तराअणिअलं उहअतडट्ठिअमिलन्तदिट्ठिरइसुहम्।
अवसं चक्काअजुअं हुंकाराअत्तजीविअं वोच्छिण्णम्।।

विघट्टमानरागनिगडमुभयतटस्थितमिलद्दृष्टिरतिसुखम्।
अवशं चक्रवाकयुगं हुंकारायत्तजीवितं व्यवच्छिन्नम्।।]

A helpless pair of red geese parted from each other,[15] with the bond of passion rent asunder, and their life reduced to moans, their only joy of love being the meeting of their eyes as they lingered on the opposite banks of a stream.

K reads विच्छिन्न for *vo°* = व्यव° (R and Kula). K says उभयतटयोः सरसः तटद्वये पृथक्स्थितत्वात् मिलद्दृष्टिमात्ररतिसुखम्। अवशं दैवात परवशम्। शोकातिरेकजनितो दीर्घनिश्वासपवनाक्रन्दो हुङ्कारः। हुङ्कार आयत्तमधीनं जीवितं यस्य तत्तथा। संस्तभ्यमानः स हुङ्कारो यदि निर्गच्छेत् तदा तेनैव सह जीवितमपि निर्गच्छतीति हुङ्कारायत्तजीवितं तत् चक्रवाकमिथुनं विच्छिन्नं विश्लिष्टमभूत्। MY says अथवा अन्योन्यजीवितधारणसूचकशोकविरुतरूपहुङ्कारश्रवणमात्रेण स्वजीवितं धारयदित्यर्थः। Kula says अवशं दैवगतिपरतन्त्रम्। He reads *pemma* for *rāa* (राग), i.e. विघटमानप्रेमनिगडं, and explains प्रेम as प्रेमभावारब्धालिङ्गनादिव्यापार, and remarks that it is not स्नेह, तस्याविघटितस्यैव स्थितत्वात्।

25. ताव अ तमालकसणो कञ्चणकडअं व बहलसंझाराअम्।
परिपेल्लिऊण अ तमो हिअकद्दमसुरगइन्दणिहसो व्व ठिओ।।

[तावदेव तमालकृष्णं काञ्चनकटकमिव बहलसंध्यारागम्।
प्रतिप्रेर्य च तमो हृतकर्दमसुरगजेन्द्रनिघर्ष इव स्थितम्।।]

Black as a grove of *tamāla* trees, darkness, meanwhile, pressed heavily on the extensive evening glow, even as the mud-covered body of a mighty elephant of the gods, rubbed against a mountain's golden slope, presses it hard.

K reads बहुल for बहल। He says तावच्च तमालकृष्णं तमः काञ्चनतटमिव दृश्यमानं बहुलं सन्ध्यारागं च प्रतिषिध्य स्थितम्। हृतकर्दमस्य गृहीततटाकपङ्कस्य सुरगजेन्द्रस्य निकष इव शरीरनिकष इव। हृतपङ्कस्य गजेन्द्रस्य देहनिकाषो हेमकटकं निर्भिद्य यथा प्रकाशते तद्वदन्धकारः सन्ध्यारागमपनुद्य स्थित इत्यर्थः। निकर्ष इति निकषणक्रिया न विवक्षिता। किं तर्हि निकषणतत्परगजस्य देह एवाभिप्रेतः। . . . इदानीं दिवसच्छविप्रणाशात् अन्धकारः सन्ध्यारागमपनुद्य स्वैरमवस्थित इति न पुनरुक्तदोषः (with reference to verse 23).

[15] The reference is to a pair of *cakravāka* birds supposed to separate at nightfall.

Kula says तमालवत् कृष्णं तमः हृतः गात्रेणोढः कर्दमो येन सुरगजेन्द्रेण तस्य निकष इव कर्दमालेपो गात्रनिघर्ष इव[16] सन्ध्यारागं काञ्चनटकमिव गात्रघर्षणयोग्यं प्रतिप्रेर्येव स्थितम्। प्रेरणं द्युतिप्रच्छादनमेव। K (*chāyā*) has प्रतिपीड्य = प्रतिषिध्य (commentary).

26. आसण्णम्मि पविरलं बहलं थोअन्तरम्मि दूरम्मि घणम्।
ओभग्गदिट्ठिपसरं सव्वत्थ समट्ठिअं पि दीसइ तिमिरम्।।

[आसन्ने प्रविरलं बहलं स्तोकान्तरे दूरे धनम्।
अवभग्नदृष्टिप्रसरं सर्वत्र समस्थितमपि दृश्यते तिमिरम्।।]

The darkness, even though present everywhere alike, appeared to be sparse at close quarters, diffuse a little farther, and dense at a distance, obstructing the power of vision.

K reads बहुल for बहल (R and Kula). He also reads अथ भग्न (*o bhagga* ?) for *obhagga* (अवभग्न)।

आसन्ने समीपदेशे प्रविरलं, स्तोकान्तरे किञ्चित् परतः। प्रदेशे बहुलमदृश्यत। ततो दूरे घनमतिबहुलम्, अथ भग्नदृष्टिप्रसरमभूत् K.

27. घणविडवट्ठिअतिमिरा तिमिरालिद्धमइलन्तमुद्धकिसलआ।
किसलअणिसण्णकुसुमा कुसुमामोएण णवर णज्जन्ति दुमा।।

[घनविटपस्थिततिमिरास्तिमिरालीढमलिनायमानमुग्धकिसलयाः।
किसलयनिषण्णकुसुमाः कुसुमामोदेन केवलं ज्ञायन्ते द्रुमाः।।]

Thick darkness settled on the branches of the trees; the tender foliage, enveloped in darkness, assumed a dull colour; and the flowers were hidden in the foliage. The fragrance of the flowers alone revealed the presence of the trees.

K does not explain the verse. The *chāyā* has तिमिरस्पृष्टमुकुलमुग्धकिसलयाः। K seems to read *maülanta* for *mailanta* (R and Kula). Kula says तिमिरेणादिग्धानि विलिप्तानि मलिनायमानानि मुग्धकिसलयानि येषां (ते द्रुमाः) Kula quotaion in *SC* has आलिद्धानि। R says आलीढानि स्पृष्टानि।

28. मेलाविअसव्वदिसं आसण्णम्मि वि पणट्ठणअणालोअम्।
सूएअव्वमहिअलं जाअं सूरवडणाणुरूअं तिमिरम्।।

---

[16] *SC* says निकषः कर्दमालेपनं गात्रघर्षणमिति कुलनाथः। गात्रनिघर्षस्थानमिति श्रीनिवासः। The correct reading of Kula seems to be कर्दमालेपेन गात्रनिघर्षः।

[मेलितसर्वदिगासन्नेऽपि प्रनष्टनयनालोकम्।
सूचयितव्यमहीतलं जातं सूरपतनानुरूपं तिमिरम्॥]

The darkness fitted in with the hour of the sun's downfall. It mixed up all the directions, and destroyed vision even at close quarters; and even the presence of the earth had to be surmised.

K and MY read अनुसदृशं (*aṇusarisaṁ*) for *aṇurūaṁ* (R and Kula).

K says मिश्रीकृतसर्वदिक्कं, सूचयितव्यभूतलं स्पर्शानुमेयभूतलं तिमिरं सूर्यपतनानुसदृशं सूर्यस्य पतनस्य नाशस्य अनुसदृशमनुरूपं बभूव। अयमत्र ध्वनिः। अतिप्रतापे महति राजनि मृते सति सद्यः प्रतिपक्षपरिभवात् क्षुभिते तद्विषये सर्वमर्यादा भिन्ना भवन्ति। तत्रत्यानां नराणामासन्नदेशेऽपि सञ्चारो नश्यतीति। Kula says तिमिरं सूरस्यादित्यस्य पतनानुरूपं जातम्। शूरप्रधानपुरुषपतनेऽपि भग्नसैन्यस्य भयान्ध्यादीदृशं तिमिरं भवतीति भावः। He also says सूचयितव्यं गतिस्खलितविभाव्यमाननतोन्नतं महीतलं यत्र तत् तथाभूतम्।

29. ओक्खण्डेअव्वदढो पसरइ उक्खम्मिअव्ववहलुग्घाओ।
अवलम्बिअव्वजोगो ससिणा भेअव्वसंघओ तमणिवहो॥

[अवखण्डयितव्यदृढः प्रसरत्युत्खनितव्यबहलोद्घातः।
अवलम्बितव्ययोग्यः शशिना भेत्तव्यसंहतस्तमोनिवहः॥]

The darkness spread. It seemed firm enough to be hewn, and dense enough to be lifted; seemed capable of being grasped, and solid enough to be penetrated by the moon.

K and MY read उत्तम्भयितव्य (*utthambhiavva*, cf. 5.68); and बहुल for *ukkhammiavva* = उत्खनितव्य[17]; and *bahala* respectively (R). K reads सान्द्रः for *joggo* = योग्यः (R and Kula) K says अन्धकार एवं प्रसरति स्म। कुठारादिना अवखण्डयितव्यः छेत्तव्यो यथा भवति तथा दृढः। भार इव शिरसोत्तम्भयितव्यः धारयितव्यो बहुल उद्घातो घनीभावो यस्य स तथाभूतः। नीलपटादिवत् अवलम्बितव्यसान्द्रः। शशिना मेत्तव्यसंहतः पर्वत इव भेदनयोग्यः संहतोऽतिनिबिडः। MY says द्रव्यवदुत्तम्भयितुं कराभ्यामुत्क्षेप्तुं यथा शक्येत तथा बहुलोद्घातः बहुलोच्चयः। Kula seems to explain *avalambiavva* as अवलम्बन।

---

[17] Kula is corrupt, but quotation in *SC* shows that he reads उत्क्षेप्तव्य (*ukkhippiavva* cf. *SC* text).

30. वहइ व महिअलभरिओ णोल्लेइ व पच्छओ धरेइ व पुरओ।
पेल्लेइ व पासगओ गरुआइ व उवरिसंठिओ तमणिवहो।।

[वहतीव महीतलभृतो नोदयतीव पश्चाद्धारयतीव पुरतः।
प्रेरयतीव पार्श्वगतो गुरुकायत इवोपरिसंस्थितस्तमोनिवहः।।]

Pervading the earth, the expanse of darkness seemed to carry all things. It seemed to push from behind, and hold up in front, and press from either side; and appeared to grow heavy as it spread overhead.

K and probably Kula read मार्गतः (*maggao*, cf *SC* text) for *pacchao* = पश्चात् (R). K says अतिसान्द्रः तमोनिवहो मूर्तद्रव्यवत् एवमकरोदिव। कथम्–महीतले भरितः बहुलः तमोनिवहो भुवि तिष्ठन्तं पुरुषमधस्तादाधारत्वेन वहतीव। मार्गतः पृष्ठभागतः तिमिरनिवहः तमेव नुदतीव। पुरतो गतः तिमिरनिवहः पृष्ठनोदात् पतन्तं पुरुषं धारयतीव अवलम्बत इव। पार्श्वगतस्तु तं पीडयतीव (MY also)। उपरि मूर्ध्नि स्थितोऽन्धकारः तस्य भारवत् गुरुर्भवतीवेति। Kula says भृतमहीतलो जलौघः तृणादिकमिव वहतीव लोकमित्यर्थात्। मार्गतः पश्चात् प्रेरयतीव।

31. दीसइ अ तिमिरमिलिओ कसणसिलाभिण्णसलिलसीभरधवलो।
थोउम्मिल्लन्तदिसो उअअन्तरिअतणुओ ससिअरुज्जोओ।।

[दृश्यते च तिमिरमिलितः कृष्णशिलाभिन्नसलिलशीकरधवलः।
स्तोकोन्मीलद्दिगुदयान्तरिततनुकः शशिकरोद्द्योतः।।]

The lustre of the moonbeams blending with darkness appeared to be white as a cloud of spray suffused with the hue of sapphire. It was faint, being hidden by the mountain of the east, with the regions of the sky partly revealed.

K says तिमिरेण मिलितः, तदानीं कृष्णशिलया इन्द्रनीलशिलया मिश्रितसलिलशीकरवत् धवलः, स्तोकमुन्मीलद्दिक् किञ्चित्प्रकाशमानदिग्भाग, उदयपर्वतान्तरितत्वात् तनुः शशिकिरणप्रकाशश्च दृश्यते स्म।

32. दीसइ जुअक्खअम्मि व महिअलपरभाअससिअराहअतिमिरा।
णिव्वडिअधूमहुअवहडज्झन्तसमुद्दसंणिहा पुव्वदिसा।।

[दृश्यते युगक्षय इव महीतलपरभागशशिकराहततिमिरा।
निर्वलितधूमहुतवहदह्यमानसमुद्रसंनिभा पूर्वदिक्।।]

The eastern region of the sky, with the darkness assailed by the rays of the moon over a section of the earth, appeared to resemble the ocean consumed by a smokeless fire as at the epoch of destruction.

K reads महीधर for *mahi-ala* (R and Kula). He says उदयगिरेः परभागेऽपरभागे स्थितस्य उदयरागवतः शशिनः करैराहततिमिरा, तदानीं पृथग्भूतधूमेन कालाग्निना वडवामुखेन वा दह्यमानसमुद्रसन्निभा पूर्वदिक् युगक्षय इवादृश्यत्। MY says *ṇivvaḍia-dhūma* पृथग्भूतधूम निर्धूमेत्यर्थः। R says परभाग एकदेशः।

33. णवरि अ अच्छालोआ उअअगिरिक्खलिअबहलजोह्णाणिवहा।
जाआ पणट्ठतिमिरा मुद्धमिअङ्कपरिपण्डुला पुव्वदिसा।।

[अनन्तरं चाच्छालोका उदयगिरिस्खलितबहलज्योत्स्नानिवहा।
जाता प्रनष्टतिमिरा मुग्धमृगाङ्कपरिपाण्डुरा पूर्वदिशा।।]

Thereafter the east, white with the young moon, assumed a clear aspect, with the darkness vanishing from sight, and a vast mass of moonbeams surging out of the mountain of the east.

K reads बहुल for बहल (R); and प्रोषित (i.e. *pauttha*) for *paṇaṭṭha* (R). K and MY have मूढ for *muddha*.

K says मूढेन अनुदितेन मृगाङ्केन परिपाण्डरा, उदयपर्वतात् स्खलितबहुलज्योत्स्नानिवहा, अत एव प्रोषिततिमिरा व्यपगततिमिरा पूर्वाशा अच्छालोका जाता प्रसन्नप्रकाशा अभूत्। MY reads *paatta-timirā*[18] explained as प्रसरणोद्यततिमिरा। He remarks मृगाङ्कस्य मूढत्वमालोकप्रवृत्तावपि उदयगिरिगर्भवर्तितया स्वरूपतो नाभिव्यक्तिः। अत एव मूढमृगाङ्का। अत एव अच्छालोका विरलालोका। अथवा मूढत्वं नातिविशदप्रभत्वम्। MY explains उदयगिरिस्खलित as उदयाद्रेर्निर्गतः।

34. णवकमलोअरअम्बं केसरसउमारसंगलन्तमऊहम्।
विरलेइ समासण्णं णीसेसेइ तिमिरं ण ता ससिबिम्बम्।।

[नवकमलोदराताम्रं केसरसुकुमारसंगलन्मयूखम्।
विरलयति समासन्नं निःशेषयति तिमिरं न तावच्छशिबिम्बम्]

The lunar orb, reddish like the inside of a fresh lotus blossom, with streaming rays soft as the filaments, thinned the oncoming darkness, but did not yet destroy it.

---

[18] *paatta* = प्रवृत्त।

MY has *ṇa ā* for *ṇa tā* (तावत्)। K says तावत् तस्मिन् क्षणे। K and Kula have ताम्र for आताम्र (R). My remarks उदितमात्रं शशिबिम्बमसमग्रप्रभतया मुग्धताम्रं कमलेनोपमितमिति मन्तव्यम्।

35. तो उअअसिहरमिलिअं जाअं उप्पुसिअतिमिरधवलच्छाअम्।
इअहुत्तच्छिअसुरगअदन्तच्छेअपरिमण्डलं ससिबिम्बम्।।

[तत उदय(गिरि)शिखरमिलितं जातमुत्प्रोच्छिततिमिरधवलच्छायम्।
इतोऽभिमुखस्थितसुरगजदन्तच्छेदपरिमण्डलं शशिबिम्बम्।।]

Reaching the summit of the mountain of the east, the moon, resplendently white, with the darkness wiped away, became round like the stump of the severed tusk of an elephant of the gods turned towards the earth.

K (*chāyā*) reads निहितं for *miliaṁ* (R). He says ततः क्रमात् उदयगिरिशिखरस्थितम्, उन्मृष्टतिमिरत्वात् धवलशोभं शशिबिम्बम् इतोऽभिमुखस्थितस्य सुरगजस्यैरावतस्य दन्तच्छेदवत् छिन्नस्य दन्तस्य छेदमण्डलवत् परिमण्डलं जातम्।

MY says *upphaṭṭha* (*upphu*° B) उन्मृष्ट। छेदः छेदमार्गः।

Kula's gloss on 35 and 36 is mutilated.

36. णवरि अ ससिअरणिसुड्डिअविवलाइअतिमिरकलुसताराणिवहम्।
जाअं बहुकुसुमोत्थअसिलाआरसंणिहं गअणअलम्।।

[अनन्तरं च शशिकरनिपातितविपलायिततिमिरकलुषतारानिवहम्।
जातं बहुकुसुमावस्तृतशिलातलाकारसंनिभं गगनतलम्।।]

Thereupon the sky, covered with clusters of dim stars, with the darkness routed by the rays of the moon, looked like a rock strewn with numerous flowers.

Not found in K and MY.

37. दरमिलिअचन्दकिरणा दरधुव्वन्ततिमिरपरिपण्डुरालोआ।
दरपाअडतनुविडवा दरबद्धच्छाहिमण्डला होन्ति दुमा।।

[दरमिलितचन्द्रकिरणा दरधाव्यमानतिमिरपरिपाण्डुरालोकाः।
दरप्रकटतनुविटपा दरबद्धच्छायामण्डला भवन्ति द्रुमाः।।]

The trees, partly touched by the moonbeams, and variegated by the partly dissolving darkness, with the smaller branches partly visible, cast partly formed patches of shadows.

K reads *ṇimia* (निमित *chāyā*) for *milia* (R, Kula and MY). K, MY and Kula read *khaüria* for *paripaṇḍura* (R). See N.S. edn. Goldschmidt adopts the former reading.

K says दरनिहितचन्द्रकिरणा दरविधूयमानेन तिमिरेण मिश्रितच्छवयः (द्रुमाः) K (*chāyā*) has दरधूयमानतिमिरकर्बुरितालीकाः।

MY says *dhuvvanta* धाव्यमान। तमसः पङ्कादिन्यायेन धाव्यमानत्वमभिप्रेतम्। *khauria* कर्बुरित। आलोक्यत् इत्यालोको रूपम्। कल्माषितरूपा इत्यर्थः। प्रकाशे सत्येव छायासंभवात् चन्द्रोदये बद्धच्छायता द्रुमाणामुक्ता। Kula says दरधाव्यमान-तिमिरत्वात् मिश्रकलुषः प्रकाशो येषाम्।

38. होइ णहलङ्घणसहं जाअत्थामकिरणाहउक्खअतिमिरम्।
विअलिअमुद्धसहाअं जरठाअन्तधवलं णिसाअरविम्बम्।।

[भवति नभोलङ्घनसहं जातस्थामकिरणाहतोत्खाततिमिरम्।
विगलितमुग्धस्वभावं जरठायमानधवलं निशाकरबिम्बम्।।]

The orb of the moon, growing white as it matured, and discarding its tender aspect, became capable of traversing the sky, having assailed and extirpated the darkness with its strengthened rays.

K says जरठायमानत्वात् परिणतत्वात् धवलं निशाकरबिम्बं जातस्थामभिः जातबलैः किरणैः आहतोन्मूलिततिमिरं, विगलितो मुग्धस्वभावः। अभिनवत्वस्वाभावो यस्य तत्, नभोलङ्घनसहं गगनारोहणसमर्थभूत्। MY remarks अत्र समुपजातोत्प्लवनपाटवस्य गजावस्कन्दनक्षमस्य केसरिकिशोरकस्य समाधिरनुसंधेयः।

39. तहपरिसंठिअसेलं वित्थिण्णदिसं तहुज्जुअणइप्पवहम्।
खन्तूण व उक्किण्णं ससिणा तमसंचअं पुणो वि महिअलम्।।

[तथापरिसंस्थितशैलं विस्तीर्णदिक्तथर्जुकनदीप्रवाहम्।
खनित्वैवोत्कीर्णं शशिना तमःसंचयं पुनरपि महीतलम्।।]

With the mountains standing as before, and the rivers flowing straight as ever, the earth, with its vast regions, seemed to be carved anew by the moon, by digging up the accumulated mass of darkness.

K and MY read *ukkhittaṁ* for *ukkiṇṇaṁ* (R and probably Kula). K says यथापूर्वमवस्थितशैलसंनिवेशं, विस्तीर्णदिङ्मण्डलं, तथैव ऋजवोऽवक्रा नदीप्रवाहा यत्र तन्महीमण्डलं शशिना तमःसञ्चयं खात्वा विदार्य पुनरपि उत्क्षिप्तमिव। तमसि निमग्नं भूतलं जलधिनिमग्नम् आदिवराहेणेव जलधिमिव तमःसमूहं विधूय पुनरुद्धृतमिवाभूत।

MY says *ujjua* ऋजु उद्यतमिति वा प्रवृत्तमिति यावत्। उपरिस्थितं पङ्कादिकमपनीय पाषाणादिवत् तमो निरस्य भूतलमुत्क्षिप्तमिवेत्यर्थः।

Kula reads विच्छिन्न for *vitthiṇṇa* (विस्तीर्ण)। *SC* says *jaha ujjua* इति पाठे यथा ऋजवो नदीप्रवाहा यत्र इत्यर्थः। This might be Kula's reading, but our copy seems to have यथोज्ज्वला नदीप्रवाहा यत्र।

40. बहलम्मि वि तमणिवहे णिव्वालेऊण सच्चविअरूवाओ।
अणुबन्धन्ति ससिअरा घेत्तुं ण चअन्ति पाअवच्छाआओ।।

[बहलेऽपि तमोनिवहे निर्वाल्य सत्यापितरूपाः।
अनुबध्नन्ति शशिकरा ग्रहीतुं न शक्नुवन्ति पादपच्छायाः।।]

The shadows of the trees, with their outlines distinctly perceived even in the dense darkness, were hemmed in but could not be seized by the rays of the moon.

K, MY and Kula read बहुल for बहल (R). K (*chāyā*) has बहुलेऽपि तमोनिवहे निर्व्यज्य (i.e. पृथग्भूय) सत्यापितरूपाः।

K says तमोनिवहे बहुले सत्यपि पृथक्त्वेन (i.e. पृथग्भूय) लक्षितरूपाः पादपच्छायाः शशिकरा अनुबध्नन्ति परितो रुन्धन्ति। ग्रहीतुं न शक्नुवन्ति स्म। तमःप्रसरावसरेऽपि वृक्षाणां बहुलपत्रशाखाबहुलत्वात् पिण्डितान्धकारा इव पृथगुपलब्धस्वरूपाः पादपच्छायाः चन्द्राशवः तमःशङ्कया परितो वेष्टयन्त्येव। न पुनः प्रणाशयितुम- शक्नुवन्नित्यर्थः।

My says *ṇivvāḍeūṇa* पृथक्कृत्य, न तु पृथग्भूयेति। *ṇivvāḍeūna ṇahe* (13.58) इत्यादिषु तस्यार्थस्य दुर्घटत्वात्। *saccavia* लक्षित्। प्रतिबन्ध इव बहुलतमेऽपि तमसि तन्निरस्य ततः पृथक्कृत्य लक्षितरूपा अपि तरुच्छाया रिपुबन्दीरिव केवलं निरुध्यावतस्थिरे। द्रुमदुर्गावस्थिततया ग्रहीतुं नाशक्नुबान्नत्यर्थः। केचितु अन्यथा व्याचक्षते। यदा चन्द्रोदयात् पूर्वं बहुलतमं तमस्तदा केवलाकाशस्थिततमसः पृथग्भूय अभिव्यक्तरूपाः छायाः शशिकरा अन्वबध्नन्, न तु ग्रहीतुमशक्नुवन्निति। तदसत् पृथग्भवनार्थे *ṇivvāḍeūṇa* इत्यस्याप्रयोगात् . . . R has *ṇivvāleūṇa* (निर्वाल्य पृथक्कृत्य)। *SC* says *ṇivvāheūṇa* (?) पृथक् कृत्वेति कुलनाथः। The reading in our copy is corrupt, and followed by पृथक्कृत्य।

41. णवर करालेइ ससी मुहपरिहट्टणसमूससन्तदलउडम्।
अवडिच्छिएक्कमेक्का विसअं फालेन्ति महुअर च्चिअ कुमुअम्।।

[केवलं करालयति शशी मुखपरिघट्टनसमुच्छ्वसद्दलपुटम्।
अप्रतीष्टैकैके विषदं पाटयन्ति मधुकरा एव कुमुदम्।।]

The moon only parted the petals of the night lotus; it was

the bees that clearly ripped it open, without waiting for one another, opening out the petals by striking on the top.

K and MY read परिमर्शन for *parihaṭṭaṇa* = परिघट्टन (R and Kula). They read अप्रतीष्टैकैकं for *avaḍicchiekkamekkā* = अप्रतीष्टैकैके (R). Kula's readsing is same as R's, but he has अप्रतीक्षित। See below. K says शशी कुमुदं केवलं करालयति दलानामन्तरालं करोति छिद्रयत्येव। मधुपानोत्सुका भ्रमरास्तु मुखपरिमर्शनेन संमुखस्पर्शनेन समुच्छ्वसद्दलपुटं कुमुदम-प्रतीष्टैकैकं परस्परमप्रतीष्टमन्योन्यस्य अवसरमप्रदाय एकैकमेव ते विशदं पाटयन्ति विकासयन्ति स्म।

MY has *apaḍicchia* for *ava⁰*; *muha parimāsaṇa* (explained as अग्रपरिमर्शन); and *pāḍenti* for *phālenti*. *SC* has अप्रतीक्षित for अप्रतीष्ट, i.e. *avaḍikkhaia*. Kula says *ekkamekka* शब्दः अन्योन्यार्थे देशीयः।

42. पुसिओ णु णिरवसेसं समअं थोरकरपेल्लिओ णु विराओ।
ओत्थइओ णु समत्तो ससिणा पीओ णु णिद्दअं तमणिवहो।।

[प्रोञ्छितो नु निरवशेषं समं स्थूलकरप्रेरितो नु विशीर्णः।
अवस्तृतो नु समस्तः शशिना पीतो नु निर्दयं तमोनिवहः।।]

The darkness seemed to be wiped away without leaving a trace; seemed to melt away, driven all at once by the massive rays; seemed to be totally covered up, and ruthlessly engulfed by the moon.

SC says नुशब्द इवार्थ इति श्रीनिवासः (Kula also). MY has *phusio* for *pusio* (उन्मृष्ट K.)। K, Kula and MY render *otthaio* as अवस्थगितः। K and MY render *virāo* as विलीनः। K renders *pellio* as पीडितः (प्रेरितः R and Kula)। Kula renders *samatto* as समाप्तः (समस्तः R and K)। Kula says अवस्थगित इव, निर्दयं पीत इव समाप्तोऽवसितः। K says समस्तः तमोनिवहः शशिना निरवशेषमुन्मृष्टो नु। सममेव स्थूलैः करैः पीडितो नु। निष्पिष्टो विलीनो नु। स्थगितो नु। निर्दयं पीतो नु। कथं नष्ट इति नाज्ञायत।

43. मंसलचिक्खिल्लणिहं हत्थग्गेज्झं व मइलिअदिसाअक्कम्।
खन्तूण व तमणिवहं चन्दूज्जोएण खउरिअं व णहअलम्।।

[मांसलकर्दमनिभं हस्तग्राह्यमिव मलिनितदिक्क्रम्।
उत्खायेव तमोनिवहं चन्द्रोद्द्योतेन मुण्डित(धवलित)मिव नभस्तलम्]

Having dug up, as it were, the mass of darkness, resembling thick mud, that obscured the regions of the sky, and seemed capable of being grasped with the hand, the radiance of the moon seemed to give a dappled look to the firmament.

Not found in K and MY.

With regard to *khaüriaṁ*, Kula who reads this verse after verse 36 says चन्द्रोद्द्योतेन नभःस्थलं मिश्रकलुषीकृतमिव। R says मुण्डितमिव धवलितमिवेति वा। Cf. verse 37 above. Kula's gloss on this verse is incomplete. *SC* has *maülia* (मुकुलित) for *mailia* = मलिनित (R). *SC* says मुकुलितं संकुचितं दिक्चक्रं यस्मात्।

44. भिण्णतमदुद्दिणाइं विडवन्तरविरलपडिअचन्दकराइं।
थोअसुहालोआइं पअडन्ति व मुद्धपल्लवाइं वणाइं।।

[भिन्नतमोदुर्दिनानि विटपान्तरविरलपतितचन्द्रकराणि।
स्तोकसुखालोकानि प्रकट्यन्त इव मुग्धपल्लवानि वनानि।।]

With the darkness vanishing like a rainy day, the partly distinct woods, with lovely foliage, seemed to be dripping as the moonbeams came scattered through the branches.

K and MY read प्रचलन्ति (*paalanti*) for *paaḍanti* = प्रकट्यन्ते। (R). Kula is corrupt, but *SC* also has *paalanti* rendered as प्रगलन्ति। K says वनानि प्रचलन्तीव। चन्द्रकिरणैर्विरलसंस्पृष्टत्वाद चलन्निव, प्रज्वलन्तीवेति वा। Kula reads धौत *dhoa* for *thoa* (स्तोक)—धौतानीव सुखालोकानि।

45. परिमलिअद्दुमकुसुमा उअहुत्तदिसागइन्दमअणीसन्दा।
निव्विट्ठपङ्कअवणा ओवग्गन्ति कुमुओअराइ महुअरा।।

[परिमृदितद्रुमकुसुमा उपभुक्तदिग्गजेन्द्रमदनिस्यन्दाः।
निर्घृष्टपङ्कजवना आक्रामन्ति कुमुदोदराणि मधुकराः।।]

The bees that had heavily pressed the flowers of the trees, and partaken of the streaming ichor of the great elephants of the quarters, and enjoyed the day lotus beds, forced their way into the night lotus blossoms.

MY says *ṇivviṭṭha* निर्विष्ट (K *chāyā* and Kula also) उपमुक्तेत्यर्थः। *oagganti* अध्यतिष्ठन्। अनेकरसंज्ञा एव भृङ्गाः कुमुदासवं संभावितवन्त इत्यर्थः।

K (*chāyā*) has परिमृदितद्रुमकुसुमा उपयुक्तदिग्गजेन्द्रमदनिष्यन्दाः, not explained in the commentary which has only उपभुक्तपङ्कजवना मधुकराः विकसितकुमुदोदराणि मधुपानरभसादभिभवन्ति स्म। K seems to read *uautta* or *uvautta* (उपयुक्त) for *uahutta* (उपभुक्त) in the first line. The word *uautta* occurs in Gauḍavaho (350), but the commentary renders it as उपभुक्त।

46. होइ णिराअअलम्बो गवक्खपडिओ दिसागअस्स व ससिणो।
कसणमणिकुट्टिमअले गेह्णन्ती सरजलं व्व करपब्भारो।।

[भवति निरायतलम्बो गवाक्षपतितो दिग्गजस्येव शशिनः।
कृष्णमणिकुट्टिमतले गृह्णन्सरोजलमिव करप्राग्भारः।।]

The mass of moonbeams, entering through the windows, and stretching lengthwise on the sapphire floors, seemed to be the long and pendent trunk of an elephant of the quarters, taking in water from a lake.

K and Kula read *ṇirāa-valambo* (निरायतप्रलम्बः) found in *SC* text and manuscript C of Goldschmidt, for *nirāaa-lambo* (R).

47. दीसन्ति गअउलणिहे ससिधवलमइन्दविद्दुए तमणिवहे।
भवणच्छाहिसमूहा दीहा णीसरिअकद्दमपअच्छाआ।।

[दृश्यते गजकुलनिभे शशिधवलमृगेन्द्रविद्रुते तमोनिवहे।
भवनच्छायासमूहा दीर्घा निःसृतकर्दमपदच्छायाः।।]

When the massive darkness resembling a herd of elephants was routed by the moon, a white lion as it were, the long shadows of the mansions looked like the muddy tracks of their feet.

K says गजकुलमलिने तमोनिवहे मृगेन्द्रधवलेन शशिना विद्राविते सति दीर्घाः भवनच्छायासमूहा विद्रुतानां गजानां निसृतकर्दमपदन्याससदृशा दृश्यन्ते स्म। निसृतं नितरां सृतं दीर्घीभूय गतम्। MY says निसृते कर्दमो येषां तानि पदानि तथा भवनच्छायाः तत्सदृशशोभा इत्यर्थः। Kula says निःसृते पलायने कर्दमलिप्त-पादच्छायाकृतयो दृश्यन्ते।

48. तंसुण्णमन्तबिम्बो जालन्तरणिग्गओसरन्तमऊहो।
भिण्णविवरन्धआरो भग्गच्छाहिपसरो विलग्गइ चन्दो।।

[तिर्यगुन्नमद्बिम्बो जालान्तरनिर्गतापसरन्मयूखः।
भिन्नविवरान्धकारो भग्नच्छायाप्रसरो विलगति चन्द्रः।।]

Destroying the darkness in the hallows, and diminishing the length of the shadows, the moon ascended the sky, with its orb mounting sideways, and its receding rays sweeping out of the windows.

K and MY read जालमुखाकृष्ट[19] for *jālantara-ṇiggaa* (R and Kula). K says तिर्यगुन्नमद्बिम्बः, जालं गवाक्षः तदीयरन्ध्रेभ्यः आकृष्टप्रसरन्मयूखो, नाशितश्वभ्रान्धकारो, भग्नवृक्षादिच्छायादैर्ध्यः चन्द्रो विलगति गगनमिति शेषः। MY says पूर्वं गवाक्षमुखप्रविष्टानां मयूखानां चन्द्रस्योन्नमनक्रमेण अनुपलम्भात् जालमुखाकृष्टेत्युक्तम्। भग्नच्छायाप्रसरं निरस्तवृक्षादिच्छायादैर्ध्यं विलगतीत्यत्र नभ इति शेषः। MY seems to read *pasaraṁ* for *pasaro*. Kula says पूर्वं जालान्तरेण निर्गता इदानीमपसरन्तो मयूखा यस्य स तथा।

49. विच्छड्डिअचुण्णनिहा आवीअंसुअविसेसिअब्भच्छाआ।
विअडगवक्खोवइआ दीवुज्जोअमिलिआ किलिम्मइ जोह्णा।।

[विच्छर्दितचूर्णनिभा आपीतांशुकविशेषिताभ्रच्छाया।
विकटगवाक्षावपतिता दीपोद्द्योतमिलिता क्लाम्यति ज्योत्स्ना।।]

Entering through the wide windows, and resembling scattered powder, the moonlight, with its clear lustre set off by the yellowish curtains, faded as it blended with the flare of the lamps.

K (*pratīka*) has *vicchaḍḍia* like others. K says विकटेन गवाक्षेण प्रविष्टा, दीपप्रभाभिः मिलिता, तदानीं प्रसारितकुङ्कुमादिचूर्णनिभा, ईषत्पीतांशुकेन विशेषिता अतिशयिता अच्छा छाया छविः यस्या सा तथाभूता ज्योत्स्ना क्लाम्यति स्म। K explains *vicchaḍḍia* as प्रसारित। R (*chāyā*) has विच्छर्दित explained in commentary as पञ्जीकृत। *SC* says विच्छर्दितं त्यक्तं विकीर्णमिति यावत्। MY says *āpīaṁsua* ईषत्पीतांशुक। ईषत्पीतेभ्योशुकेभ्यो व्यावर्तितस्वकीय-धवलशोभेत्यर्थः। It will be seen that K and MY (*SC* text also) read अच्छ for *abbha* (अभ्र) found in R, who mentions अच्छ as a variant. Kula here is corrupt, but his अच्छाया seems to stand for अच्छच्छाया.[20] R says यद्वा–आपीतांशुकेन पीतवस्त्रेण विशेषितं विशिष्टं यदभ्रकं तद्वत् छाया यस्याः। वस्त्रपीतिमप्रतिबिम्बादभ्रकस्यापि किर्मीरितत्वादिति भावः।

50. परिणामदरुम्मिल्लं ओवत्तेअव्वबहलजोह्णाभरिअम्।
थोअत्थोअमउलिअं भरवित्थारिअदलं व वेवइ कुमुअम्।।

---

[19] I.e. *jāla-muhāaḍḍhia*.

[20] Kula seems to say . . . विकीर्णपटवासरजस्तुल्य। ईषीत्पीतेन अंशुकेन विशेषिता सदृशीकृता अच्छा छाया यस्याः सा तथा। विकटगवाक्षेण अवपतिता दीपोद्द्योतेन मिलिता ज्योत्स्ना दुर्गवर्त्मावतरणश्रान्ता परपुरुषसंपर्कात् कोमलप्रकृतिर्युवतिरिव ग्लायतीत्यर्थः। Cf. quotations in *SC*.

[परिणामदरोन्मीलमपवर्तयितव्यबहलज्योत्स्नाभृतम्।
स्तोकस्तोकमुकुलितं भरविस्तारितदलमिव वेपते कुमुदम्।।]

Closing by degrees (during the day), and partly opening (at nightfall) on account of maturity, the night lotus, filled with dense[21] moonlight, seemed to quiver, with the petals expanded by the weight of the rays.

K and MY read बहुल for बहल (R). K reads मृदूकृतं (*mauiaṁ* cf. *SC* text) for *mauliaṁ* = मुकुलितं (R); and प्रवेपते for *va vevai* (R). K says परिणामात् परिपाकाद्दरमुन्मीलितं चन्द्रोदयात् पूर्वमेव किञ्चिद्विकसितम्, अपवर्तयितव्यं करेणोत्क्षेपयितव्यं यथा तथा बहुलया ज्योत्स्नया पूरितम्। अत एव स्तोकस्तोकं मृदूकृतं, ज्योत्स्नाभरेण विस्तारितदलं कुमुदं प्रवेपते स्पन्दते स्म। अयमत्र ध्वनिः – अपक्वं घटादिपात्रं सलिलेन परिपूरितमत्यन्तं मृदु भूत्वा भेदेन विस्तारितं कम्पते तद्वदिति। MY says अपवर्तयितव्येत्यादि[22] क्षीरादिवत् बहिरपवाहयितुं यथा शक्येत तथा बहुलज्योत्स्नाभृतमिति। *bhara-vitthāria* ज्योत्स्नाभरविस्तारित। दलानां परस्परविभागरूपविस्तारजनकक्रियासंक्षोभात् कुमुदस्य वेपनमिवेत्यवसेयम्[23]। Kula is corrupt. *SC* has मृदूकृतं like K.

51. पवणाअम्पिअसिहरा गओणिअत्तन्तविडवविहुअच्छाआ।
ससिकिरणपरिक्खित्ता जोह्णावेअवडिआ पवन्ति व रुक्खा।।

[पवनाकम्पितशिखरा गतापनिवर्तमानविटपविधूतच्छायाः।
शशिकिरणपरिक्षिप्ता ज्योत्स्नावेगपतिताः प्लवन्त इव वृक्षाः।।]

The trees, hemmed in by the lunar rays, and rocked at the top by the wind, with the shadows wavering on account of the branches moving to and fro, seemed to swim as they swayed in the current of moonlight.

K, Kula and probably MY read किरणपरिक्षिप्यमाणाः (*kiraṇa-parikkhippantā*) for *sasi-kiraṇa-parikkhittā* (R). K and MY read वलिता भ्रमन्ति for *vaḍiā pavanti* = पतिताः प्लवन्ते (R). Kula has वलिताः सन्त प्लवन्त इव (वृक्षाः)। MY says शशिकिरणपरिक्षिप्यमाणा वृक्षा ज्योत्स्नावेगवलिता भूत्वा अभ्रमन्निव।

---

[21] Literally dense enough to be turned over.

[22] A has it in Pkt : *avavattaïdavva*, इत्यादि।

[23] वेपनमित्यवसेयम् A.

52. घरमणिमऊहभिण्णो सलिलाहअबहलचन्दणरसच्छाओ।
उद्देसुल्ललिअतमो दीसइ विवरविसमो व्व जोह्लाणिवहो।।

[गृहमणिमयूखभिन्नो सलिलाहतबहलचन्दनरसच्छायः।
उद्देशोलुलिततमो दृश्यते विवरविषम इव ज्योत्स्नानिवहः।।]

Resembling a vast mass of sandal paste sprinkled with water, the moonlight, blending with the flare of the lamps, and eclipsed at places, seemed to be dotted with holes.[24]

K and probably MY and Kula read निभः (*niho*) for *tamo* (R). K and MY read बहुल for बहल। K says गृहाणां प्रासादानां मणिमयूखैः बहुवर्णैः भिन्नः, अत एव क्वचित सलिलबिन्दुमिश्रबहुलचन्दनरसच्छायः, क्वचिदुद्देशेषु उल्ललितनिभः अन्तरेऽन्तरे क्षुभिताकार इत्यर्थः, विवरैः छिद्रैर्विषम इव चादृश्यत।

My says अन्तरान्तरा गृहमणिमयूखसंभिन्नः, तदानीं सलिलाहतबहुलचन्दन-रसच्छायः, क्वचित् क्वचित् प्रदेशे अविद्यमानवत् लक्ष्यमाणो ज्योत्स्नानिवहो विवरैः छिद्रैः विषमरूप इवादृश्यतेत्यर्थः।

Kula says उद्देशेषु मिलितस्थानेषु उल्ललित इव उत्पाटित इव।

R says उद्देशेषु क्वचित् क्वचिदुल्लुलितं विपर्यस्य स्थितं तमो यत्र, शाखापत्रादिच्छायारूपत्वात्। He explains *ghara-maṇi* as दीप, and quotes *Hārāvalī* which gives this meaning for गृहमणि। Cf. *SC*.

53. विअलिअणिअअच्छाअं जाअं जोह्लापरिप्पवन्तमिअङ्कम्।
विच्छूढव्वमऊहं अविभाविअसह्लतारअं गगणअलम्।।

[विगलितनिजकच्छायं जातं ज्योत्स्नापरिप्लवमानमृगाङ्कम्।
विक्षेप्तव्यमयूखमविभामवितश्लक्ष्णतारकं गगनतलम्।।]

Pervaded by the dense rays, the sky lost its own colour, with the tiny stars invisible, and the moon floating on the flood of its light.

K reads शशिकरं for *maūhaṁ* (R and Kula). MY has *parivvaanta* (परिप्लवमान) for *parippavanta*. K says गगनतलं . . . करेण क्षेप्तव्यचन्द्रकिरणं . . . जातम्। Kula says विक्षेपयोग्या मयूखा यत्र।

54. णिव्वडिअतुङ्गसिहरा धवला दीसन्ति दिट्ठमहिअलबन्धा।
णहमज्झट्ठिअससहरवोच्छिण्णच्छाहिमण्डला धरणिहरा।।५४।।

[24] The areas lighted by the lamps are fancied as gaps in the expanse of moonlight.

[निर्वलिततुङ्गशिखरा धवला दृश्यन्ते दृष्टमहीतलबन्धाः।
नभोमध्यस्थितशशधरव्यवच्छिन्नच्छायामण्डला धरणीधराः।।]

The mountains looked white, with the lofty peaks distinctly visible, and the base coming into view, with the expanse of their shadows obliterated by the rays of the moon at the zenith.

K and Kula read शशिकर for *sasahara* (R). K reads विच्छिन्न for *vo*° (R and Kula) = अवच्छिन्न Kula व्यव° R.

K says नभोमध्यस्थस्य शशिनः करैः विच्छिन्नच्छायामण्डलाः (धरणीधराः) MY says *ṇivvaḍia* अभिव्यक्त (निर्व्यक्त K)। Kula says दृष्टो-महीतले बन्धो मूलभागो येषाम्। R says बन्धः संधि। Kula says निर्वलितानि पृथक् दृश्यमानानि।

55. विवरं ति परिहरिज्जइ बहलद्दुमच्छाहिमण्डलागअतिमिरम्।
ओच्छुन्दइ वीसत्थं जोह्णाणिवहभरिअं थलं मिव विवरम्।।

[विवरमिति परिह्रियते बहलद्रुमच्छायामण्डलागततिमिरम्।
आक्रम्यते विश्वस्तं ज्योत्स्नानिवहभृतं स्थलमिव विवरम्।।]

A place dark amidst the deep shadows of the trees was shunned (by people) thinking it was a hollow; while a hollow, flooded with moonlight, was confidently traversed like level ground.

K reeads इव (*va*) for *ti* = इति (R and Kula). He rads बहुल for बहल (R and Kula). K and probably Kula read विस्रब्धं (*vīsaddhaṁ*) for *vīsatthaṁ* = विश्वस्तं (R). MY and R render *occhundai* as आक्रम्यते। K says अवक्षुद्यते आक्रम्यते।

56–57. इअ वम्महजग्गाविअतीरविसूरन्तणिव्वलिअचक्काए।
जाअम्मि मउलिउप्पलदुक्खपहुप्पन्तमहुअरम्मि पओसे।।
वम्महपरव्वसाइं रामागमणपरिवड्ढिआवेआइं।
अहिलक्खन्ति मुअन्ति अ रइवावारं विलासिणीहिअआइं।।
(जुग्गअम्)

[इति मन्मथजागरिततीरखिद्यमाननिर्वलितचक्रवाके।
जाते मुकुलितोत्पलदुःखप्रभवन्मधुकरे प्रदोषे।।
मन्मथपरवशानि रामागमनपरिवर्धितावेगानि।
अभिलषन्ति मुञ्चन्ति च रतिव्यापारं विलासिनीहृदयानि।।]
(युग्मकम्)

When thus the even tide came, while the red geese,[25] separated from their mates, and kept awake by love, pined on the banks of streams; and the bees had hardly enough of space inside the closing day lotus blossoms; the hearts of the young women (of Laṅkā), overcome by passion, and beset with anxieties at the advent of Rāma, both desired and shrank from the acts of love.

K says इति मन्मथेन जागरिता निद्रामप्रापिता:, तीर स्थित्वा खिद्यमाना विरलवेदनया तप्यमाना:, निर्व्यक्ता: पृथग्भूताश्चक्रवाका यत्र तस्मिन्। मुकुलितेषूत्पलेषु दु:खेन कृच्छ्रात् प्रभवन्त: पर्याप्नुवन्तो मधुकरा यत्र तस्मिन् प्रदोषे जाते। MY says कृच्छ्रेण सावकाशीभवदिति यावत्। Kula says प्रभवन्त: संमान्त:।

K and MY read अभिलङ्घयन्ति, and Kula अभिलङ्घन्ति for *ahilakkhanti* (अभिलषन्ति) found in R. Their reading seems to be *ahilaṁghanti*[26].

K says मन्मथेन परवशानि, रामस्यागमनेन परिवर्धितोद्वेगानि विलासिनोहृदयानि रतिव्यापारमभिलंघयन्ति कामपारवश्यात् स्पृशन्ति रामागमनावेगात् मुञ्चन्ति च। MY says अभिलंघयन्ति अभिनिविशन्ते। मदनवशतया रतिव्यापारमभिन्यविशन्त रामागमनोद्वेगादमुचंश्चेत्यर्थ:।

Kula says ग्रहणे मोक्षे च यथाक्रमं हेतुद्वयमाह। मन्मथपरवशानि, रामागमनेन परिवर्धित: आतापो येषां तानि।

58. लद्धगलन्तासाअं आवेअविहिण्णवम्महुल्ललिअसुहम्।
छिण्णघटिज्जन्तरसं णावज्जइ दइअचुम्बणं जुवईणम्।।

[लब्धगलदास्वादमावेगविभिन्नमन्मथोल्ललितसुखम्।
छिन्नघट्यमानरसं नाबध्यते दयितचुम्बनं युवतीनाम्।।]

The kisses of the lovers were lost upon the young women, as the sweetness felt melted away, and the joy was marred by passion slackened by anxieties, and the emotion subsided as it rose.

K, MY and Kula read भिन्न for *chiṇṇa* (R). R explains *ullalia* as उत्तरलीकृत। Cf. verse 52. K says दयितेन चुम्बनं युवतीनां नाबध्यते हृदि न संबद्धम्। कथंभूतम्। लब्धगलदास्वादमावेगेन विभिन्नमन्मथत्वात् उल्ललितसुखम्।

[25] Cf. verse 24.

[26] Hemacandra 4.192 gives *ahilaṁghaï* and *ahilaṁkhaï* in the sense of काङ्क्षति। *SC* text has *ahilaṁghenti* — काङ्क्षन्ति अभिनाटयन्ति गृह्णन्तीति कुलनाथ: (*SC* commentary)।

एवं भिन्नघटमानरसं घटमानभिन्नरसम्। आस्वादो माधुर्यं, सुखं हृदयनिर्वृतिः, रसः सुरतरागः इत्येषां भावनामयं विशेषः।

My says प्रथमं लब्धः पुनर्गलन्नास्वादः सुखविषयानुभवोऽस्येति तत् तथा। कुत एतदित्याह। *āvea* इत्यादि। भयशिथिलेन मन्मथेन ज्ञातमात्रविच्छिन्नसुखं, तत् किमत्यन्ततो विच्छिन्नरसमेव। नेत्याह भिन्नेति। एवं विच्छिन्नोऽपि पुनः प्रतिसंधीयमानो रसोऽस्येति तत् तथोक्तम्। एवं दयितैः कृतं चुम्बनं युवतीनां नाबध्यत नाविच्छेदेन हृदि व्यलगदित्यर्थः। Kula says पूर्वं लब्धः पश्चात् गलन् आस्वादो माधुर्यं यस्य। आवेगेन विभिन्नमन्मथत्वात् पतितं सुखं यत्र। आवेगेनैव भिन्नो यत्नेन घटमानो रसोयत्र। तत् दयितचुम्बनं युवतीनां नाबध्यते हृहये न लगतीत्यर्थः। SC says आवेगेन विभिन्नेन मन्मथेन उल्ललितमस्थिरीकृतं सुखं यत्र।

59. वेवइ ससइ किलिम्मइ सअणे आमुअइ णीसहो अङ्गाइं।
ण विणज्जइ किं भाओ ओ मअणपरव्वसो विलासिणिसत्थो।।

[वेपते श्वसिति क्लाम्यति शयने आमुञ्चति निःसहोऽङ्गानि।
न विज्ञायते किं भीत उत मदनपरवशो विलासिनीसार्थः।।]

The young women trembled and sighed and languished. Faint- hearted, they tossed about on the bed. None knew whether they were scared or overcome by passion.

शयने अङ्गानि आमुञ्चति क्षिपति स्म K. निःसहः अवसन्न K.

60. पिअअमवच्छेसु वणे ओवइअदिसागइन्ददन्तुल्लिहिए।
वेवइ दट्ठूण चिरं संभाविअसमरकाअरो जुवइजणो।।

[प्रियतमवक्षःसु व्रणानवपतितदिग्गजेन्द्रदन्तोल्लिखितान्।
वेपते दृष्ट्वा चिरं संभावितसमरकातरो युवतिजनः।।]

Having seen on the breast of their beloved the scars left by the thrusts of the tusks of the attacking elephants of the quarters,[27] they trembled for a long while, affrighted as they remembered the impending battle.

K reads स्तनान् (*thaṇe*) for *vaṇe* (व्रणान्) found in R and Kula.

K reads गजेन्द्रदन्तमार्गस्खलितान् for *disā-gainda-dantullihie* (R and Kula). K, MY and Kula read *sambhāria* for *sambāvia* (R).

K says स्तनानात्मीयस्तनान् प्रियतमवक्षःसु पूर्वमवपतितानां गजेन्द्रदन्तानां मार्गेषु प्रहारव्रणेषु स्खलितान् दृष्ट्वा संस्मृतसमरत्वात् कातरो युवतिजनो वेपते स्म।

---

[27] In previous battles with the gods.

MY says *saṁbhāria* संस्मारित (Kula also). Kula says इदानीमपि दृश्यन्ते पुनरपि व्रणा भविष्यन्तीति भीति इत्यर्थ:। R says संभावित उपस्थितो य: समरस्तेन कातर:। *SC* explains संभावित as उत्प्रेक्षित।

61. सुरअसुहद्धमउलिअं भमरदरक्कन्तमालईमउलणिहम्।
साहइ समरुप्पेसं उप्पित्थुम्मिल्लतारअं णअणजुअम्।।

[सुरतसुखार्धमुकुलितं भ्रमरदराक्रान्तमालतीमुकुलनिभम्।
शास्ति समरोत्पेषमुत्पित्सोन्मीलत्तारकं नयनयुगम्।।]

Their eyes, half closed in the joy of dalliance, and resembling *mālatī* buds, lightly pressed by bees, opened with a panicky stare and betrayed their dread of war.

K reads कुसुम for *maüla* = मुकुल (R and Kula). K says समरत्रासं प्रियेभ्य: शंसति स्म। Kula says नयनयुगं समरोत्पेषं साधयति कथयति। My says *sāhai* अशंसत्। *upphesa* उत्त्रास। *uppittha* उत्त्रस्त। *ummilla* उन्मीलित नयनयुगं समरत्रासमशंसदित्यर्थ:।

Deśināmamālā (1.94, 129) mentions *upphesa* = त्रास and *uppittha* = त्रस्त (also कुपित and विधुर)। R and *SC* text read *uppesa*. Kula remarks समरोत्पिष्टसुभटानामपि ईदृगेव नयनयुगं भवतीति भाव:।

62–63. अह ससिजणिआमोए मअपरिवड्ढिअपिआहिसारणसोक्खे।
मअणुम्मूलिअमाणे राअपराहीणरइसुहम्मि पओसे।।
वलइ अ दूमिअकुविओ अवसाइअहरिसिओ अईइ सरीरम्।
ससइ अ चुम्बिअसुहिओ मअपाअडिअहिअओ विलासिणिसत्थो।
(जुग्गअम्)

[अथ शशिजनितामोदे मदपरिवर्धितप्रियाभिसारणसौख्ये।
मदनोन्मूलितमाने रागपराधीनरतिसुखे प्रदोषे।।
वलति च दूनकुपितोऽप्रसादितहर्षितोऽत्येति शरीरम्।
श्वसिति च चुम्बितसुखितो मदप्रकटितहृदयो विलासिनीसार्थ:।।]
(युग्मकम्)

Thereupon at nightfall when the moon brought joy, and the exhilaration caused by wine heightened the pleasure of meeting the beloved, and passion rooted out pride, and the joy of love was dominated by mutual affection; the young women, with their hearts revealed by the effect of wine, appeared to turn away from their lovers, angry even though unoffended; yielded to them, cheerful even though unappeased; and sighed, happy even though unkissed.

K and MY read verse 66 between 62 and 63. Both the manuscripts of K (*chāyā* and commentary) have मदनोन्मीलितमाने (प्रदोषे) for मदनोन्मूलितमाने।

K and MY read प्रियतमान् (*piaame*) for *sarīraṁ* (R and Kula).

K says विलासिनीसार्थः प्रियतमैः (अ)परितापितोऽपि कुपितो भूत्वा वलतै परावर्तते पश्चात् प्रियतमैरप्रसादितोऽपि स्वयमेव हृष्टः प्रियतमानत्येति आश्लिष्यति। अचुम्बितोऽपि सुखितः श्वसिति। मदप्रकटितहृदयो मधुमदेन प्रकाशितहृदयः। अदूनितकुपितत्वादयः सर्वे मदविकारा इति द्रष्टव्यम्।

My says *adūmia* अनुपतापित। *aīi* अत्यगच्छत्प्राप। उपतापनिमित्ता- पराघाभावेऽपि कुपितः सन् अवलत् पराङ्मुखोऽभूत्। प्रसादनं मानस्य भङ्गोपायाः सामादयः। तदभावेऽपि प्रीतियुक्तः प्रियानभ्यगच्छत्। मदनवशात् कोपादिकमपि नाकरोत्। हृदयं च प्रकाशयदिति सारम्।

K and *SC chāyā* has अदूनितकुपितः। R says अदूनकुपितः कुपितोऽपि अदूनः अनुपतप्तः। प्रियैः अप्रसादितोऽपि हर्षितः सन् शरीरमत्येति तदुपरि पातयतीत्यर्थः। Kula says शरीरम् अङ्गमेति।

64. रोसपुसिआहराणं दइअबलामोलिचुम्बणपरुण्णाणम्।
णिव्वलिअमण्णुगरुअं हरइ पराहुत्तजम्पिअं जुअईणम्।।

[रोषप्रोञ्छिताधराणां दयितबलामोटितकचुम्बनप्ररुदिता(दती)नाम्।
निर्वलितमन्युगुरुकं हरति पराङ्मुखजल्पितं युवतीनाम्।।]

The words, stern with manifest wrath, uttered by the maidens, with the face turned away, as they angrily wiped their lips and wept, when forcibly kissed by their beloved, delighted the latter.

K reads स्फुरित? (*phuria*) for *pusia* = प्रोञ्छित (R and Kula). K and Kula read चुम्बित for *cuṁbaṇa* (R and MY). K says रोषेण प्रणयकोपेन स्फुरिताधराणां, तदानीमेव दयितैः बलात्कारेण चुम्बितत्वात् प्ररुदितानां युवतीनां निर्व्यक्तमन्युना कोपेन गुरु पराङ्मुखं जल्पितमुपालम्भवचनं हरति दयितानां हृदयमिति शेषः R says निर्वलितेन स्पष्टेन मन्युना। *SC* text has *ṇivvaḍia* for *ṇivvalia*.

MY says बलात्कारचुम्बनं तु पादपतनहठाश्लेषचुम्बनकचग्रहाः सखीश्लाघा प्रणयोपालम्भोक्तिः स्नेहपरीक्षा च बहुमानः शृङ्गारवृद्धिरभिभवो विपक्षस्य लाभभेदाश्च अनुभवसौख्यान्येवं मानस्याश्रयगतान्याहुरिति मानानुभवसौख्येषु अन्यतममुक्तं भोजेन।

प्ररोदनं च चक्षुर्निमीलनमुखप्रसादपुलकाश्रूणि उपालब्धिः प्रत्युपालब्धिश्च प्रक्रमनिन्दा गमनजुगुप्सा मानानुशययोग्ये अनुद्यमः दोषोद्भेदश्च मानोपशमौ द्वादशलक्षणाविति मानोपशमचिह्नेषु अन्यतमम्। जल्पितं चात्रोपालम्भदोषोद्भेदादिरूपं द्रष्टव्यम्। हरतीत्यस्य मनोहारित्वकथनेन ललितरूपो भ्रम एव रोष उक्तः। स्त्रीणां ललितकोपो भ्रम इति लक्षितत्वात्।

65. अहिसारणं ण गेह्णइ ण संठवेइ अलअं ण पुच्छइ दूइम्।
चन्दालोअपडिहओ वेवइ मूढहिअओ विलासिणिसत्थो।।

[अभिसारणं न गृह्णाति न संस्थापयत्यलकं न पृच्छति दूतीम्।
चन्द्रालोकप्रतिहतौ वेपते मूढहृदयो विलासिनीसार्थः।।]

The young women did not set out to meet their lovers nor did they dress their hair nor question the messenger girls (about the mission to the beloved). Bewildered by the moonlight, they trembled as they stood perplexed.

K says चन्द्रालोकेन प्रतिहतो ध्वंसितधैर्य इत्यर्थः, अतएव मूढहृदयो विलासिनीसार्थः अभिसारणं न गृह्णाति प्रियतमान् नाभिसारयति स्म। परिशिथिलमलकं न संस्थापयति सम्यक् स्थापयति। दूतीं किमत्र कर्तव्यमिति न पप्रच्छ, केवलं वेपते स्म।

MY says नाग्रहोदिति नाकरोदित्यर्थः। मूढहृदयः अप्रतिपत्त्या किञ्चिदपि अकुर्वन्नित्यर्थः। He reads *muñcai* for *pucchai*, as he says अमुञ्चत् प्राहिणोत्।

66. अवमाणिअरामकहं जहापुरपअट्ट जुअइजणवावारम्।
सोहइ रअणिअराणं आसङ्घिअदहमुहं पओसागमणम्।।

[अवमानितरामकथं यथापुरःप्रच्छन्नयुवतीजनव्यापारम्।
शोभते रजनीचराणामध्यवसितदशमुखं प्रदोषागमनम्।।]

Delightful was the advent of the evening to the demons. The talk about Rāma was ignored, and confidence reposed in Rāvaṇa; while the activities of the young women proceeded as before.

K and My read *avamaṇṇia* (अवमत, अवज्ञात) for *avamāṇia* (R and Kula). K (*chāyā*) has विश्वासितदशमुखं। K (commentary) says प्रमाणीकृतदशमुखम्। रावणे तिष्ठति रामःकिं करिष्यतीति प्रमाणीकृतरावणबलमित्यर्थः। My says *āsasaṁghia* आशंसित। प्रदोषो नाम महोत्सवो दशमुखबलप्रत्ययेन रामभयापगमात् रजनीचरमिथुनानां यथापूर्वं शोभावानेव प्रवृत्त इत्यर्थः। Kula explains *āsaṁghia* as आशाविषयीकृत। SC (*chāyā*) has संभावित agreeing with Hemacandra 4.35.

67. पिअपासाहि णिअत्तो समुहं अलिअं पि जं भणइ दूइजणा।
तं चिअ कामिणिसत्थो दूमेन्तिं पि बहुसो णिअत्तेइ कहम्।।
[प्रियपार्श्वान्निवृत्तः संमुखमलीकमपि यद्भणति दूतीजनः।
तामेव कामिनीसार्थो दुन्वन्ती(ती)मपि बहुशो निवर्तयति कथाम्।।]

What the messenger girls reported openly, returning after meeting the lovers, the young women caused to be repeated many a time, although it was false and brought them sorrow.[28]

K says प्रियस्य पार्श्वं गत्वा ततो निवृत्तः दूतीजनः अलीकामपि यां कथां प्रियस्य आगमनुयुक्तां कथां संमुखं कथयति स्म तां कथां परितापयन्तीमपि कामिनीसार्थो बहुशो निवर्तयति आवर्तसति स्म। . . . प्रियतमेनोपेक्षितया निवृत्तया दूत्या कथ्यमानां तदागमनसंबन्धामलीकामपि कथां बहुश आवर्तयामास। कीदृशीम्- दूनयन्तीमपि। प्रदोषे व्यतिक्रामति दूत्या सार्धं तस्यानागमनात् आश्वासनमात्रहेतुत्वात् मानवासनाहृदयं परितापयन्तीमपि रागपारवश्यात् पुनः पुनराम्रेडयति स्मेति।

MY says *ṇivattei* न्यवर्तयत् आवर्तयदिति यावत्।

68. सअणेसु पणअकलहे समुहणिसण्णपिअवेलविज्जन्तीहिं।
परिवत्तिउं ण चइअं णवरं णअणेसु विअलिअं बाहजलम्।।

[शयनेषु प्रणयकलहे संमुखनिषण्णप्रियव्यावर्त्यमानाभिः।
परिवर्तितुं न शकितं केवलं नयनयोर्विगलितं वाष्पजलम्।।]

During quarrels of love, the maidens, harassed by their beloved, sitting in front of them on the bed, could not turn the back upon them. Tears only welled up in their eyes.

K and MY read घूर्णितं (*gholiaṁ*) for *vialiaṁ* = विगलितं (R and Kula). K says प्रणयकलहे सति संमुखनिषण्णैः प्रियैः यत् किञ्चिदुक्त्वा व्याकुलीक्रियमाणाभिः प्रलोभ्यमानाभिः[29] प्रणयिनीभिः परिवर्तितुं पराङ्मुखीभवितुं न शक्तम्। केवलमासां नयनेषु बाष्पजलं घूर्णितम्। प्रणयकोप कलुषा प्रणयिन्यः प्रियैरनुनीयमानाः परिवतितुमभिमुखीभवितुं च नाशक्नुवन्। गाम्भीर्यात् केवलं रुदितवत्य इत्यर्थः।

Laṭakana says पराङ्मुखीभिरेव रुदितमिति भावः। अनुनयार्थं संमुखनिषण्णैः

[28] The messengers had brought assurances from the lovers, which proved to be false. According to another explanation, they made a false report obviously to tease the *nāyikā*s that the attitude of the *nāyaka*s was unfavourable. Cf. verse 79.

[29] Hemacandra (4.93 an 156) gives *velavaï* in the sense of वञ्चन and उपालम्भ। Cf. MY and Kula.

प्रियैः प्रतिकामिनीसंगचिह्नप्रकटनादिना व्याकुलीक्रियमाणाभिरुद्दीपितक्रोधाभिः। अतएव परिवर्तितुं न शक्नुवन्ति ताः।

MY says *velavijjantīhiṁ* प्रज्ञार्यमाणाभिः। प्रतारणं च संमुखनिषण्णेन (प्रियेण) निःशङ्कगाढालिङ्गनचुम्बनकचग्रहणादि। अत्रापि बाष्पजलघूर्णनं मानोपशम-लिङ्गमित्यवसेयम्। Kula says *velavijjantīhiṁ* खिद्यमानाभिः *velavia* खेदिते प्रतापिते (प्रतारिते ?) च देशोयम्। *SC* says *velaviaṁ* व्याकुले खेदिते च देशी।

69. अणुणअखणलद्धसुहे पुणो वि संभरिअमण्णुदूमिअविहले।
हिअए माणवईणं चिरेण पणअगरुओ पसम्मइ रोसो।।

[अनुनयक्षणलब्धसुखे पुनरपि संभृतमन्युदुःखितविह्वले।
हृदये मानवतीनां चिरेण प्रणयगुरुकः प्रशाम्यति रोषः।।]

The anger of the proud women, heightened by love, died away slowly in their hearts, gratified for a moment by the entreaties of the lovers, but saddened and perturbed again by the remembered offence.

K and MY read अनुनयसोढोऽपि पुनः सुचिरं for *aṇuṇaa-khaṇa-laddha-suhe puṇo vi* (R and Kula).

K says मानवतीनां रोषश्चिरेण प्रशाम्यति स्म। कथमिति–अनुनयात् सोढोऽपि प्रियकृतादनुनयात् सोढोऽपि सुचिरं प्रियापराधं स्मृत्वा मन्युना शोकेन दूनिते विह्वले च सति हृदये प्रणयगुरुत्वात् चिरेण प्रशशामेति। It will be seen that K takes *saṁbharia* separately as a gerund. Cf. 11.92.

MY says *sahio* सोढः शान्त इति यावत्। प्रियानुनयनप्रशान्तोऽपि मानिनीनां रीषो व्यलीकस्मरणादिनोद्दीपनेन मानः कथं कथमपि चिरेणाशाम्यदित्यर्थः।

Kula says अनुनयेन क्षणलब्धसुखे, पुनरपि संस्मृतेन मन्युना अपराधेन दुःखितविह्वले हृदये।

70. अलअं छिवइ विलक्खो पडिसारेइ वलअं जमेइ णिअत्थम्।
मोहं आलवइ सहिं दइआलोअणडिओ विलासिणिसत्थो।।

[अलकं स्पृशति विलक्षः प्रतिसारयति वलयं यमयति निवसनम्।
मोघमालपति सखीं दयितालोकनर्तितो विलासिनीसार्थः।।]

Flurried at the sight of the beloved and abashed, the young women touched their hair and adjusted their bangles, and tightened their attire and talked aimlessly to their maiden friends.

K and MY read पतितः (*paḍio*) for *ṇaḍio* (R and Kula). R says नर्तितः चञ्चलीकृतः, but see below. K says दयितस्यालोके पतित आलोकेन

परवशीकृतः विलासिनीसमूहः यत् किञ्चित् चेष्टते स्म। हस्तगतं वलयं प्रतिसारयति गलितमिव दृढयति स्म। सखीं मोघमप्रस्तुतं किमप्यालपति स्मेति। R says प्रतिसारयति स्थानान्तरं प्रापयति। MY says आलोकपतिता आलोक्यमानाः। दयितैरालोक्यमानाः स्त्रियो लज्जावशादेवमाचरन्तीत्यर्थः। R says विलक्षः प्रतिभाशून्यः। सलज्ज इति वा। K says विलक्षः रागाभिभूतत्वात् लक्षितः (विलक्षितः ?) Kula says संकेतितं समयमतिक्रम्य आगतस्य दयितस्यालोकेन दर्शनेन नटितः खेदितः। अतएव समीहिताकरणात् विलक्षः अलकं स्पृशति अतिसारयति[30] वलयं संस्थितमपि चालयित्वा स्थानस्थं करोति। संयम्य नियतमपि वस्त्रं *jamei* संयमयति, etc. *SC* says *ṇaḍio* व्याकुले देशी। *Deśīnāmamālā* 4.18 gives the word in the sense of वञ्चित and खेदित।

71. अब्भुट्ठणतुरिआणं सोहइ दइओवऊहणविराआणम्।
असमत्तमण्डणाणं तहेअ सअणगमणं विलासवईणम्।।

[अभ्युत्थानत्वरितानां शोभते दयितोपगूहनविशीर्णानाम्।
असमाप्तमण्डनानां तथैव शयनगमनं विलासवतीनाम्।।]

It was a pretty sight as the gay women, hastening to receive their lovers, and enraptured by the beloved's embrace, went to bed without having finished their adornment, just as they were.

virāa is rendered as विलीन by K, MY and Kula. K says आगतानां दयितानामम्युत्थानाय त्वरितानां, दयितोपगूहनेन विलीनानां विद्रुतहृदयानाम्। *SC* says विलीनानां द्रवतामापन्नानामिति लोकनाथः, विरागाणां विशिष्टरागाणामिति श्रीनिवासः।

72. अवसाइअदिण्णसुहो सहीहिं थिरदिट्ठिणिहुअवारिअविडिओ।
हित्थहिअओ सुणिज्जइ पिएहिं अलिअकुविओ विलासिणिसत्थो।।

[अप्रसादितदत्तसुखः सुखीभिः स्थिरदृष्टिनिभृतवारितव्रीडितः।
त्रस्तहृदयो ज्ञायते प्रियैरलीककुपितो विलासिनीसार्थः।।]

The young women, who greeted their lovers even without being appeased by them, were abashed when covertly admonished by their maiden friends with severe looks. As they stood scared their beloved knew that they only pretended to be angry.[31]

---

[30] प्रति°?।

[31] They pretended anger to please their girl friends, who had advised them to practise *māna*, and silently reproved them for being cordial to the lovers without waiting to be appeased by them for past offences.

K, MY and Kula read दत्तमुखः for *diṇṇa-suho* (R). R has *hittha-hiao muṇijjai* = त्रस्तहृदयो ज्ञायते। K has त्रस्तहृदयैर्ज्ञायते in which case metre would require *ṇajjai* for *muṇijjai*, as pointed out by Goldschmidt.

K says प्रियैरप्रसादितोऽपि तेषां दत्तमुखः तद्द्रष्टवा सखीभिः स्थिरया दृष्ट्या निभृतं निगूढं निवारितोऽतएव व्रीडितो विलासिनीसार्थः त्रस्तहृदयैः कोपमुद्रां द्रष्टवा त्रस्तहृदयैः प्रियैरलीकमेव कुपित इति ज्ञायते स्म। त्रस्तहृदयश्चेति च पाठः। सखीभिर्वारितत्वात् त्रस्तहृदयश्चेति, i.e. *hittha-hiao a ṇajjai*. MY says *apasāia* अप्रसादित। अप्रसादितोऽपि प्रियाणां संमुखीभूतः, सपदि सखीभिः निभृतसंज्ञानिवारितो व्रीडितश्च त्रस्तहृदयश्च पुनर्भावितरोषो युवतिजनः प्रियैरलीककुपित इति ज्ञायते इत्यर्थः। माने क्रियमाणे मुखप्रदानादिवारणं[32] सखीदूत्योः कर्म। प्रतिबोधनमुपदेशः प्रतिषेधश्च उपजाप(?)परिहासौ (परिहासाः A) स्खलितस्य गोपनमथो कर्माण्याहुः सखोदूत्योरित्युक्तत्वात्। Kula says अप्रसादित एव दत्तमुखः सखीभिः वरितो व्रीडितः सखीनिन्दितत्वात्। He also reads त्रस्तहृदयः like R.

73. सह वड्ढिअं सहिं मिव वड्ढन्तिं पिअअमाहिसारणविग्घे।
वारेइ चिरेण मओ लज्जं विच्छुहइ वम्महो च्चिअ पढमम्।।

[सह वर्धितां सखीमिव वर्धमानां प्रियतमाभिसारणविघ्ने।
वारयति चिरेण मदो लज्जां विक्षिपति मन्मथ एव प्रथमम्।।]

It was the god of love that first dissipated the bashfulness of the damsels that had grown up with them, like a maiden friend, standing in the way of their meeting the beloved. Frenzy brought by wine held it off but slowly.

K and Kula read वर्तमानां (*vaṭṭantiṁ*) for *vaḍḍhantiṁ* found in R who mentions the former reading as a variant.

K says सखीमिव सहप्रवृद्धां, प्रियभिसारणस्य विध्ने वर्तमानां स्त्रीणां लज्जां मधुमदश्चिरेण वारयति स्म। प्रथमं मन्मथ एव क्षोभयति स्म लज्जाम्। K (*chāyā*) has विक्षोभयति। MY says *vicchuhai* व्यक्षिपत् व्यपोहयदिति यावत्। Kula has विक्षिपति (R also).

74. सहिअणहत्थाहि मुहं दररइअविसेसअं समक्खेतूण।
जुवईहि वलिअविसमं अप्पाहिज्जइ ससंभमं दूइजणो।।

[सखीजनहस्तान्मुखं दररचितविशेषकं समाक्षिप्य।
युवतीभिर्वलितविषममध्याप्यते ससंभ्रमं दूतीजनः।।]

---

[32] मुखप्रसादनादिवारणं-B।

The young women, withdrawing the face from the hand of the maiden friend who was adorning it, and turning aside, with the ornamental dot still unfinished, hurriedly instructed the messenger girls about the mission to the beloved.

K reads समुद्गृह्य (*samugghettūṇa*) for *samakkhettūṇa* (समाक्षिप्य) found in R and Kula. MY's reading is different. K says दररचिततिलकं मुखं सखीजनहस्तात् समुद्गृह्य उत्क्षिप्य युवतिभिर्दूतीजनः . . . आभाष्यते स्म। MY says *samukkhantūṇa* समुत्खाय बलादाक्षिप्येत्यर्थः। *appāhijjai* व्याह्रियत (संदिश्यते Kula) Hemacandra 4.180 has *appāhai* = संदिशति। R says अध्याप्यते शिक्ष्यते। *SC* says वलितविषमं तिर्यग्वलितं यथा स्यात्।

75. अण्णं सहिअणपुरओ अप्पाहेन्तो अ अण्णहा दूइजणम्।
जम्पइ विमुक्कधीरं अण्णं चिअ दइअदंसणे जुवइजणो।।

[अन्यत्सखीजनपुरतोऽध्यापयंश्चान्यथा दूतीजनम्।
जल्पति विमुक्तधीरमन्यदेव दयितदर्शने युवतिजनः।।]

They spoke in one way before their maiden friends, and in another way while instructing the messenger girls, and something quite different, excitedly, at the sight of the beloved.

K (*chāyā*) has अन्यत् सखीजनपुरतः आभाषमाणः। He says युवतिजनः सखीजनस्य पुरतः अन्यत् मानधैर्ययोरुचितमाभाषमाणः, दूतीजनमन्यथा साभ्यर्थनमाभाषमाणश्च सन् तदानीमागतस्य दर्शने पुनरन्यदेव विमुक्तधैर्यं प्रणयानुरूपं जल्पति स्म। MY says *appāhento* a व्याहरंश्च। प्रदोषचन्द्रोदयमदैर्मानिनीनां धैर्यभङ्गो जात इत्यर्थः। उक्तं च –

त्रासो भयं मद ऋतूपगमः प्रदोषः,
चन्द्रोदयः पिकरुतं रजनीविरामः।
हृद्यो मरुद्विकसितोपवनं विविक्तमाद्यः
प्रवास इति माननिबर्हणानि।।इति।

Kula says अन्यदिति किं तेन शठेनेत्यादि सखीजनपुरतः। दूतीजनं संदिशन् चान्यथेति यथाशक्ति दयितमानयेति विमुक्तधैर्यं युवतिजनो जल्पति। अन्यदेव दयितदर्शने। सबहुमानमिति भावः। R says युवतिजनः सखीजनस्य पुरतः अन्यत्, अन्यथा च दूतीजनमध्यापयन् अग्रिमकृत्यमुपदिशन्, अन्यदेव विमुक्तधैर्यं यथा स्यात् तथा दयितदर्शने जल्पतीति . . . संप्रदायः।

76. कह वि समुहाणिअङ्कं कह कह वि वलन्तचुम्बिओवत्तमुहो।
देइ खलन्तुल्लावे णववहुसत्थे विसूरिअरअं पि धिइम्।।

[कथमपि संमुखानीताङ्के कथं कथमपि वलच्चुम्बितापवृत्तमुखे।
ददाति स्खलदुल्लापे नववधूसार्थे खिन्नरतमपि धृतिम्।।]

Even the uneasy gaiety of love with the newly-wedded brides brought joy to their consorts while they were somehow taken into their arms, face to face, muttering to themselves, with the face drooping and turned away, while being somehow kissed.

K reads आलाप for *ullāva* (R and Kula).

K says भर्त्रा कथमपि संमुखमानीताङ्के अङ्कमानीते, कथं कथमपि अतिकृच्छ्रात् चुम्बितावस्थायामपवृत्तमुखे, स्खलदालापे नववधूसमूहे संभूतं क्लिष्टसुरतमपि दयितस्य धृतिं प्रीति ददौ।

Kula reads अङ्ग for अङ्क, and says कथमपि संमुखमानोतानि अङ्गानि यस्य। कथं कथमपि वलमानं तिर्यक् भवत् चुम्बितमपवृत्तम् अवनतं मुखं यस्य R says अपवृत्तं तिर्यग्भूतम्, but on 8.84 and 10.16 he explains the word as अवनत।

77. सासइ विमुक्कमाणो वहलुब्भिण्णपुलउग्गमेण पिआणम्।
पुरओहुत्तणिसण्णो गओणिअत्तहिअओ अवलासिणिसत्थो।।

[शास्यते विमुक्तमानो बहलोद्भिन्नपुलकोद्गमेन प्रियाणाम्।
पुरतोऽभिमुखनिषण्णो गतापनिवृत्तहृदयो विलासिनीसार्थः।

The constant thrills of the young women assured their beloved that their anger was appeased, and their hearts favourably inclined[33] as they sat looking straight ahead.

K, MY and Kula read *sīsai* (शस्यते)[34] for *sāsaī* (शास्यते) found in R. K and Kula read बहुल for बहल (R). K and MY read *paraohutta* for *purao°* = पुरतोऽभिमुख (R and Kula). K has इतोनिवृत्त for *gaoṇiatta* = गतापनिवृत्त (R). Kula has इतोमुख। K, Kula and probably MY seem to read *ettohutta*, cf. *SC* text. R says पुरतो नायकस्याग्रे तदभिमुखनिषण्णोऽपि प्राचीमुखस्य प्रियस्य पुरः प्राचीमुख एव स्थित इति मानसमये पराङ्मुखीभूत इत्यर्थः। K says मानमुद्रया परतोमुखनिषण्णः पराङ्मुखं निषण्णो विलासिनीजनः रागाद्बहुलोद्भिन्नेन अविरलमुद्गतेन पुलकान्द्रमेन कर्त्रा विमुक्तमान इतोनिवृत्तहृदयश्चेति प्रियाणां कथ्यते स्म। MY says *sīsai* अशिष्यत अकथ्यत प्राकाश्यतेत्यर्थः।

[33] The reading *ettohutta* (literally facing hitherward) is followed.

[34] K (*chāyā*).

paraohutta-ṇisaṇṇo परतोऽभिमुखनिषण्णमपि विमुक्तमानं स्वाभिमुखहृदयं च मानिनीसार्थं पृष्ठपुलकोद्गम एव कामिनामशंसदित्यर्थः।

Kula says पुलकोद्गमेन विमुक्तमान इतोमुखहृदयः प्रियेभ्यः *sīsai* कथ्यते।

78. ण पिअइ दिण्णं पि मुहं ण पणामेइ अहरं ण मोएइ बला।
कह वि पडिवज्जइ रअं पढमसमागमपरम्मुहो जुवइजणो।।

[न पिबति दत्तमपि मुखं न प्रणामयत्यधरं न मोचयति बलात्।
कथमपि प्रतिपद्यते रतं प्रथमसमागमपराङ्मुखो युवतिजनः।।]

The maidens did not suck the beloved's proffered lips[35] nor did they offer their own[36] nor forcibly withdraw them. Inhibited by their first union with their lovers, they somehow yielded to the joys of love.

K and Kula read गृहीतम् (*grahiaṁ*) for *aharaṁ* = अधरम् (R). K and Kula read परवशः (*paravvaso*) for *paraṁmuho* (R) = पराङ्मुखः My has *ṇa paṇāvei*[37] (नार्पयत्)। K says पत्या प्रथमसमागमेन परवशः स्त्रीजनः भर्त्रा दत्तमपि मुखं न पिबति स्म। स्वमुखं च नार्पयति स्म। भर्त्रा बलाद्गृहीतं स्वमुख बलान्न मोचयति स्म।

79. अवलम्बिज्जउ धीरं ण अ सो एहिइ इहुग्गए वि पओसे।
इअ दूईहि तुलिज्जइ पढमाणिअपिअअमो विलासिणिसत्थो।।

[अवलम्ब्यतां धैर्यं न च स एष्यति इहोद्गतेऽपि प्रदोषे।
इति दूतीभिस्तुल्यते(?) प्रथमानीतप्रियतमो विलासिनीसार्थः।।]

"Have patience. He will not come here even when the night is far spent." Thus saying, the messenger girls tested the feelings of the young women whose lovers had already been brought by them (and were in hiding).

K and MY read इह गते (*ihaṁ gae*) for *ihuggae* = इहोद्गते (R). Kula reads अतिगते (*aiggae, SC* text) K says दूतीभिः प्रथममेवानीतप्रियतमः विलासिनीजनः प्रियतमं बहिः स्थापयित्वा दूतीभिरेवं तुल्यते परिच्छिद्यते स्म परिहासात् परीक्ष्यते स्म। कथं देवि त्वया धैर्यमवलम्ब्यतां न विषादः कार्यः। अस्मिन् प्रदोषे गतेऽपि स दयितो नैष्यति नागमिष्यति। तस्मात् धैर्यमवलम्बस्वेति। MY says *olambijjaü* अवलम्ब्यताम्। *ihaṁ* इह।

35 Literally mouth.

36 Literally the lower lip.

37 *ṇa vaṇāmei* A.

Kula has न हि *ṇa a* = न च। *SC* has *ṇa hu* = न खलु। Kula says तुल्यते किमेवमुक्तः अभिदधातीति ज्ञाप्यते (ज्ञातुमिष्यते *SC*)।

80. देइ विलासवईणं सुहे अ दुक्खे अ पाअडिअसब्भावा।
अणवेक्खिअलज्जाइं सहि व्व वीसत्थजम्पिआइ पसण्णा।।

[ददाति विलासवतीनां सुखे च दुःखे च प्रकटितसद्भावा।
अनपेक्षितलज्जानि सखीव विश्वस्तजल्पितानि प्रसन्ना।।]

Wine that reveals one's true sentiments in weal and woe, like a maiden friend that shows her amity in joy and sorrow, made the young women talk freely, irrespective of shame.

K reads अनालक्षित for *aṇavekkhia* = अनपेक्षित (R); and विस्रब्ध for *vīsattha* (विश्वस्त)। K says स्त्रीणां सुखे च दुःखे च प्रकटितसद्भावा। पीतं मद्यं पीतवतः सुखं वा दुःखं वा यथावत् प्रकाशयतीत्यत एवमुक्तम्[38] सखीव। सखी तु नायिकायाः सुखे च दुःखे च प्रकटितशोभनस्वभावा भवति। एवंभूता प्रसन्ना सुरा स्त्रीणाम् अनालक्षितलज्जानि विस्रब्धजल्पितानि निःशङ्कभाषितानि ददौ। सखी च भर्तुः पुरो नायिकाया निःशङ्कवाक्यानि शिक्षयति।

MY says *aṇalakkhia* अलक्षित। This is the reading of both K and MY. cf. Hemacandra 2.190. Kula says सुखे दुःखे च प्रकटितः। सद्भावः परमार्थो यया सा प्रसन्ना मदिरा सखीव अनवेक्षिता (?) अधरीकृता लज्जा यत्र तानि . . . ददातीति उत्पादयतीत्यर्थः। R says अनपेक्षिता लज्जा यत्र तानि। यथा सखी लज्जानपेक्षाणि विश्रम्भजल्पितानि ददातीत्यर्थः। Kula's reading seems to be same as R's. *SC* says अनपेक्षिता अवधीरिता।

81. चन्दुज्जोएण मओ मएण चन्दाअवो णु वड्ढिअपसरो।
दोहिं वि तेहिं णु मअणो मअणेण णु दो वि ते णिआ अइभूमिम्।।

[चन्द्रोद्द्योतेन मदो मदेन चन्द्रातपो नु वर्धितप्रसरः।
द्वाभ्यामपि ताभ्यां नु मदनो मदनेन नु द्वावपि तौ नीतावतिभूमिम्।।]

Did the effulgence of the moon heighten the frenzy brought by wine; or, did the frenzy heighten the effect of the moonlight? Did both of them heighten the power of passion; or, did passion bring both to the acme of perfection?

---

[38] K here aptly quotes Māgha 10.18:

या कथंचन सुखीवचनेन प्रागभिप्रियतमं प्रजगल्भे।
व्रीडजाड्यमभजन्मधुपा सा स्वां मदात् प्रकृतिमेति हि सर्वः।।

K says चन्द्रातपेन यूनां मदो वर्धितप्रसरोऽभूत नु। अथवा मदेन चन्द्रातप एव वर्धितप्रसरो नु। मधुमदस्य भूयस्तया चन्द्रातपः प्रवृद्ध इव प्रत्यभादित्यर्थः। ताभ्यां द्वाभ्यामपि मदनो वर्धितप्रसरो नु। अथवा मदनेन तौ द्वौ मदचन्द्रातपावतिभूमिम् अतिरेकं नीतौ नु। एवमन्योन्यहेतुकं भूत्वा तत् त्रयं प्रवृद्धमित्यर्थः। Kula says अतिभूमिं परमोत्कर्षं नीतौ। MY remarks एतेन मदचन्द्रातपहेतुको मदनो व्याख्यातः।

82. चन्दअरेण पओसे णिज्जइ मअणेण महुमएण अ समअम्।
दूरं दूरारूढो जुवईण पिएसु बहुरसो अणुराओ।।

[चन्दकरेण प्रदोषे नीयते मदनेन मधुमदेन च समम्।
दूरं दूरारूढो युवतीनां प्रियषु बहुरसोऽनुरागः।।]

The deep-rooted affection of the young women for their beloved, fervid with emotion, was intensified at nightfall by the moonbeams, passion and frenzy brought by wine, acting all together.

K, MY and Kula read *canda-arehi* for *areṇa* (R).

MY says प्रदोषे चन्द्रकरैर्मदनेन मधुमदेन च युगपत् युवतीनां प्रियेषु दूरारूढो बहुरसोऽनुरागो दूरमनीयतेत्यर्थः। K says युवतीनां प्रियेषु दूरारूढोऽतिप्रवृद्धो बहुरसो, रसो माधुर्यं, तस्य बहुत्वं चन्द्रातपमधुमदमदनैः, अनुरागः स्नेहः प्रदोषे चन्द्रकरैः मदनेन मधुमदेन च समम् अवैषम्येण दूरं नीयते अतिभूमिं नीयते स्म।

इअ सिरिपवरसेणविरइए कालिदासकए दहमुहवहे महाकव्वे
दसमो आसासओ समत्तो।

[इति श्रीप्रवरसेनविरचिते कालिदासकृते दशमुखवधे महाकाव्ये
दशम आश्वासकः समाप्तः।]

एकादश आश्वासकः
Eleventh Āśvāsakaḥ

1–2. इअ पडिसारिअचन्दे दूरुक्खण्डिअणिसापअत्तविरामे।
चित्तविअकामिणिअणे जामच्छेअविसमं गअम्मि पओसे।।
दीहं रक्खसवइणा चिन्तारेअविअधीरदाविअहिअअम्।
दसहि वि मुहेहि समअं आलोइअसुण्णदसदिसं णीससिअम्।।
(जुग्गअम्)

[इति प्रतिसारितचन्द्रे दूरोत्खण्डितनिशाप्रवृत्तविरामे।
चेतितकामिनीजने यामच्छेदविषमं गते प्रदोषे।।
दीर्घं राक्षसपतिना चिन्तारेचितधैर्यदर्शितहृदयम्।
दशभिरपि मुखैः समकमालोकितशून्यदशदिग्निःश्वसितम्।।]
(युग्मकम्)

When thus the evening advanced beyond the (second) watch of the night, with the moon ascending high in the sky, and all activity ceased as the night was far spent, and the young women worried (at the prospect of war); the lord of the demons heaved a deep sigh, revealing his heart, impatient with anxiety, and saw the ten directions empty as he turned his ten faces all at once.

K reads दूरावखण्डित for *dūrukkhaṇḍia* दूरोत्खण्डित (R and Kula). K and Kula read *cintavia* for *cittavia* (R).

K says इति एवमुक्तप्रकारेण प्रतिसारितचन्द्रे दूरं गगनारूढचन्द्रे। प्रागप्युक्तम् – *paḍisārei valaam* . . . इति। (10.70)। दूरमवखण्डितायां न्यूनायां निशायां प्रवृत्तावसाने। चिन्तितकामिनीजने। चिन्तित इति कर्तरि निष्ठा। चिन्तिता रामेण सह व्यतिकरे रावणस्य किं भविष्यतीति चिन्तापराः कामिनीजना यत्र। *cittavia* . . . इति च पाठः। निर्वृतकामिनीजन इत्यर्थः[1]। तस्मिन् प्रदोषे यामच्छेदविषमं गते द्वितीययामस्य छेदेन विषमं किञ्चिदधिकं गते सति। Deva says यामच्छेदेन यामार्धेन विषममधिकं गते सति। अध्यर्धयामात्मकः प्रदोषः। यामद्वयेऽतीतेऽयं विषमं गतो भवति।

---

[1] निभृत° in our copy is incorrect. Goldschmidt mentions the correct reading, which is also found in the Trivandrum manuscript.

Kula reads *visame* for *visamam* and takes *paatta* as प्रयत्न also. He says प्रसारितचन्द्रे, दूरोत्खण्डितायां निशायां प्रवृत्तविरामे, अथवा दूरोत्खण्डितया निशया लोकानामभीष्टार्थं प्रति प्रयत्नस्य विरामः पर्यवसानं यत्र चिन्तां गमितः खण्डितः कामिनीजनो यत्र, यामच्छेदोऽवर्धियस्य स चासौ विषमश्चेति तथाभूते प्रदोषे गते। My says गगनोद्गाढचन्द्रे, गतप्रायेण प्रदोषेण दूरच्छिन्नया निशया प्रवृत्तो लोकस्य विरामो व्यापारविरहो यत्र तस्मिन्, सुखितकामिनीजने, याममात्रस्य छेदेन गमनेन विषमं सावशेषं गते निशायाः त्रिभागरूपे प्रदोषे इति। अथवा यामस्य छेदो द्विधाकरणं यामार्धखण्डनं तदेव विषमं कृच्छ्रम्; अस्यावसानापादकत्वात् तत् (?) गते प्राप्ते सति। अतएव खण्डितया गतयामार्धया निशया दूरप्रवृत्तविरामे प्राप्तभूयिष्ठावसाने सतीति योज्यम्। पादोनघटिकाचतुष्टयमात्ररूपत्वात् प्रदोषस्येति।

SC says प्रदोषे यामिनीयामस्य द्वितीयप्रहरस्य छेदेन खण्डनेन विषमं प्राप्तवैषम्यं यथा स्यात् तथा गते सतीति लोकनाथः।

Deva reads दूरोत्कण्ठित for *dūrukkhaṇḍia*. He says दूरोत्कण्ठितनिशाप्रवृत्त-विरामे निशायाः प्रवृत्तो विरामः . . . दूरत्वादुत्कण्ठितः प्रार्थितो यस्मिन् तस्मिन् (प्रदोषे) प्रवृत्तविरामापि निशा अलब्धसुरतस्य रावणस्य दीर्घत्वात् अप्रवृत्तविरामेव प्रतिभाति। He gives another interpretation: दूरमुत्कण्ठितायाः अर्धरात्राधिकं गतायाः (निशायाः) प्रवृत्तः प्रारब्धो विरामो यस्मिन्।

MY seems to read *cittavia* as he says सुखितकामिनीजने (see K above). R says चेतितः प्राप्तचैतन्यः कामिनीजनो यत्र पूर्णकामतया मदापगमात्। Śrīnivāsa explains *cittavia* as परिपोषित according to *SC*.

K says चिन्तया रेचितधैर्यत्वात् परित्याजितधैर्यत्वात् दर्शितहृदयं प्रकाशितहृदयम्।

3. चिन्तेइ ससइ जूरइ वाहुं परिपुसइ धुणइ मुहसंघाअम्।
हसइ परिओससुण्णं सीआणिप्पसरवम्महो दहवअणो।।

[चिन्तयति श्वसिति खिद्यते बाहुं परिप्रोञ्छति धुनोति मुखसंघातम्।
हसति परितोषशून्यं सीतानिष्प्रसरमन्मथो दशवदनः।।]

Rāvaṇa, frustrated in his passion for Sītā, was lost in thought, sighed and grieved, rubbed his arms and shook his faces, and laughed without joy.

K, MY and Kula read *purimusai* for *paripusai* (R), rendered as परिप्रोञ्छति परिमार्ष्टि। MY says *purimusai* परिममार्ज। K says बाहुबलेन किमत्र क्रियत इति बाहुं परिमृशति स्म।

K says ज्वरति तप्यते। MY says *jūrai* अखिद्यत। Kula says क्रुध्यति क्रोधादेव बाहुं परिमृशति स्पृशति। Hemacandra 4.132, 135 gives *jūrai* in the sense of खिद्यते and क्रुध्यति।

K says सीतायां निष्प्रसरः रावणहेतोः प्रसरः प्रवेशो यस्य नास्ति स मन्मथो यस्येति बहुव्रीहिः। Kula says सीतायां निष्प्रसरो निरवकाशो मन्मथो यस्य स तथाभूतो दशवदनः।

4. बहु मण्णइ वच्छअडं हीरन्तुव्वत्तजणअतणआलिद्धम्।
णिन्दइ अ वअणणिवहं अप्पत्तपिआमुहामअरसासाअम्।।

[बहु मन्यते वक्षस्तटं ह्रियमाणेद्वृत्तजनकतनयाश्लिष्टम्।
निन्दति च वदननिवहमप्राप्तप्रियामुखामृतरसास्वादम्।।]

He valued his bosom, touched by Sītā as she quivered, while being carried off, but abhorred his mouths, deprived of the nectar-sweet taste of his beloved's lips.

K, MY and Kula read this verse after verse 8. K says रावणः पूर्वं ह्रियमाणतया तदानीमुद्वृत्तया परिवृत्तया जनकतनयया स्पृष्टं निजवक्षस्तटं बहु मेने। Kula also has स्पृष्ट। MY says ह्रियमाणोद्वृत्तया आवेगात् स्फुरन्त्या।

5. पडिरुद्धन्तस्स वि से भग्गणिअत्तपरिसंठविअभिज्जन्ते।
विसमुद्धाइअकम्पे हिअए उल्ललइ अलहुअम्मि वि धीरम्।।

[प्रतिरुन्धतोऽप्यस्य भग्ननिवृत्तपरिसंस्थापितभिद्यमाने।
विषमोद्धावितकम्पे हृदये उल्ललत्यलघुन्यपि धैर्यम्।।]

Despite his efforts to the contrary, his patience wore out in his intermittently throbbing heart, which, though firm, despaired and cheered up, and became steady and despondent by turns.

K reads भज्यमानं for *bhijjante* = भिद्यमाने (R and probably Kula).

K says प्रतिरुन्धतोऽपि यथाशक्ति निवारयतोऽपि अस्य धैर्यमुल्ललति गलति स्म। कथंभूतम्–प्रथममुत्कण्ठया भग्नं पुनः स्वेन बलेन प्रतिनिवृत्तं, परिस्थापितं यत्नात् स्थापितं च तत्क्षणमेव पुनरुत्कण्ठया भज्यमानं भूत्वा गलति स्म। धैर्यस्याधारे अलघुन्यपि अतिगुरुण्यपि हृदये विषमं भृशमुत्थितकम्पे[2] सति गलति स्म। प्रतिरुन्धत इत्यानादरे षष्ठी। K (*chāyā*) has विषमोत्थापित।

MY reads *bhijjantaṁ* for *bhijjante.* He says प्रथममुत्कण्ठया भग्नं पुनः स्वाभाविकतया प्रतिनिवृत्तं, यत्नात् स्थापितं च पुनरुत्कण्ठाबलात् भिद्यमानम्। अतएव उल्ललति स्म। *visamuddhāia* इति कादाचित्ककम्पे भ्रमति हृदय इत्यर्थः।

---

[2] Our copy has भृशमर्थित . . .।

Kula says हृदये धैर्यं . . . स्थितिं न लभते। किंभूते हृदये – उपायशून्यतया भग्ने तदनभिमुखे (?) तत्प्रीत्या पुनर्निवृत्ते तदभिमुखीभूते, ततश्च मनोरथैः परिसंस्थापिते स्थिरीकृते, दुर्घटतया तच्चिन्तावर्जनस्य पुनरपि भिद्यमाने (?), विषमोद्गतकम्पे कामावेगादुद्भूतवेपथावित्यर्थः।

6. तो से विसमुव्वत्तिअविरलपसारिअकरङ्गुलिदरत्थइअम्।
खलिअं अंसम्मि मुहं विअम्भिआआसगलिअवाहुप्पीडम्।।

[ततोऽस्य विषमोद्वर्तितविरलप्रसारितकराङ्गुलिदरस्थगितम्।
स्खलितमंसे मुखं विजृम्भितायासगलितबाष्पोत्पीडम्।।]

His faces, streaming with tears on account of overmastering anguish, and partly covered with the sparse fingers of his outstretched and upturned hands, drooped on his shoulders.

K says विजृम्भिका विजृम्भणम्। विजृम्भणकर्णविवरघट्टनादयो रताख्यस्य स्थायिभावस्य अनुभावा बोधका इत्यर्थः। ततोऽस्य विजृम्भिकायासेन गलितबाष्पपूरं, तदानीं विषममुद्वर्तितस्य विपर्यासितस्य प्रसारितस्य करतलस्य विरलाभिरङ्गुलिभिः दरस्थगितं मुखमंसे स्खलितम्।

Kula says विषमोद्वर्तिताभिः तिर्यगुत्तानिताभिः विरलप्रसारिताभिः कराङ्गुलीभिः। R says अंसे मुखं स्खलितं संबद्धम्। . . . एवं विजृम्भितेन वर्धितेनायासेनोद्वेगेन गलितो बाष्पोत्पीडो यस्मादिति रोदनमुक्तम्।

7. विसमुग्गाहिअमहुरं दूमिअदन्तव्वणाहरपरिक्खलिअम्।
आअण्णेइ पिआणं वलन्तहिअआवहीरिअं जअसद्दम्।।

[विषमादुग्राहितमधुरं दूनदन्तव्रणाधरपरिस्खलितम्।
आकर्णयति प्रियाणां वलमानहृदयावधीरितं जयशब्दम्।।]

He heard the greetings of his mistresses, lispingly uttered and sweet, and indistinct because of the lips hurt by amorous bites; but now ignored by his inconstant heart.

K says पार्श्वगतानां प्रेयसीनां जयशब्दमाकर्णयति स्म। कथंभूतम्उद्ग्राहणमुपन्यासः। उद्गृहीतमुपन्यस्ते बद्धग्राहितयोरपीति वैजयन्ती। लीलया विषममुपन्यस्तत्वात् मधुरम्, अक्षरस्पर्शेन दूनितदन्तव्रणेऽधरे परिस्खलितमव्योक्तोच्चारणं, वलमानेन जयशब्दाकर्णनस्यानिष्टत्वात् परावर्तमानेन हृदयेनावधीरितमवज्ञातम्।

R says पूर्वनिपातानियमात् दन्तव्रणेन दूनादधरात् परिस्खलितम् ओष्ठ्यवर्णस्यासम्यगुच्चारणादपरिस्फुटमित्यर्थः। उद्ग्राहितमुच्चारितम्।

MY says वलमानेन सीताभिमुखं परावर्तमानेन।

8. आमुअइ महइ सअणं मग्गइ रअणिविरमं जुउच्छइ दिअसम्।
णीइ णिअत्तेइ पुणो रइलम्भोवाअमग्गणाउरहिअओ।।

[आमुञ्चति महति शयनं मार्गति रजनीविरामं जुगुप्सते दिवसम्।
निरैति निवर्तते पुना रतिलम्भोपायमार्गणातुरहृदयः।।]

Weary of seeking a means of gratifying his passion, he left his bed and yearned for it again; sought the end of the night, but hated the day; sallied out, turned back again.

K has श्रयति for *mahai* (R, Kula and MY). He says शयनं श्रयति। पुनर्मुञ्चति। MY has *jugucchai* for *juü°*. Kula says महति अभिलषति।

9. पच्छाअन्तस्स वि से बहुसो हिअअट्ठिओ पिआण वि पुरओ।
समअं मुहणिवहेम्मि वि सीआमइओ पअट्टइ समुल्लावो।।

[प्रच्छादयतोऽप्यस्य बहुशो हृदयस्थितः प्रियाणामपि पुरतः।
समकं मुखनिवहेऽपि सीतामयः प्रवर्तते समुल्लापः।।]

Even in the presence of his mistresses, Sītā's name, abiding in heart, even though he tried to suppress it, emerged simultaneously from all his mouths time and again.

K says सीताप्रसङ्गं प्रच्छादयतोऽपि अस्य हृदयस्थितः सीतामय आलापः प्रियाणामपि पुरो मुखनिवहेऽपि सममेव बहुशः प्रावर्तत।

10. तं पुलइअम्मि पेच्छइ उल्लावन्तो अ तीअ गेह्णइ गोत्तम्।
ठाइ अ तस्स समअणे अण्णम्मि वि चिन्तिअम्मि स च्चिअ हिअए।।

[तां प्रलोकिते पश्यत्युल्लपंश्च तस्या गृह्णाति गोत्रम्।
तिष्ठति च तस्य समदनेऽन्यस्मिन्नापि चिन्तिते सैव हृदये।।]

He saw her wherever he glanced, and uttered her name whenever he talked. In his heart, inflamed with passion, she alone stayed even when he thought of aught else.

MY says *pulaiammi* प्रलोकिते प्रलोकनक्रियायाम्। K says विलोकिते प्रदेशे तमेव पश्यति स्म।

11. साहइ से संतावं वासहरद्धन्तविसमपुञ्जिअकुसुमो।
आअअणीसासहओ किलिन्तसग्गतरुपल्लवो उवआरो।।

[शास्त्यस्य संतापं वासगृहार्धान्तविषमपुञ्जितकुसुमः।
आयतनिःश्वासहतः क्लाम्यत्स्वर्गतरुपल्लव उपचारः।।]

The cooling remedies in the shape of the flowers heaped here and there in his chamber, and the fading leaves of the celestial trees, all marred by his sighs, betokened his grief.

sāhai = शंसति K and MY; शास्ति कथयति R.

12. देहपरिणाहविअडे वलइ भरोव्वत्तदलिअपासद्धन्ते।
दूरोणामिअमज्झे विसमं भूमिसअणे पहोलिरहत्थो।।

[देहपरिणाहविकटे वलति भरोद्वृत्तदलितपार्श्वार्धान्ते।
दूरावनामितमध्ये विषमं भूमिशयने प्रघूर्णनशीलहस्तः।।]

Swaying his hands, he tossed about on a bed on the floor, enough for his bulky frame, and sunk in the middle, with the sides turned down and crushed by his weight.

K, MY and Kula take *bharovvatta* as *bhara* + *ovvatta* (अपवृत्त). See below. R takes it as *uvvatta* (उद्वत्त)।

K says देहस्य परिणाहो विस्तारः तदनुरूपं विकटे विशाले, भरेण देहभरेण अपवृत्तं प्रेरितं दलितं च पार्श्वयोरर्धान्तं यत्र तत्र, दूरमवनतमध्ये भूमिशयने भूमावेव आस्तीर्णे शयने प्रघूर्णमानहस्तो भूत्वा विषमं वलते परिवर्तते स्म। Kula says भरापवृत्ते(न) अपवर्तनभरेण दलितपार्श्वैकदेशे। MY says स्वदेहभरावनमितपार्श्वे भूमिनिहितास्तरणे। Cf. *veovattia* = वेगापवर्तित 14.74. *SC* text has *bharovatta*.

13. दक्खिण्णमेत्तदिण्णो जणअसुआहुत्तहिअअदिण्णुक्कण्ठो।
उल्ललइ खणविलक्खो णिअअन्तेउरमुहेसु से मुहणिवहो।।

[दाक्षिण्यमात्रदत्तो जनकसुताभिमुखहृदयदत्तोत्कण्ठः।
उल्ललति क्षणविलक्षो निजकान्तःपुरमुखेष्वस्य मुखनिवहः।।]

His lips, touching those of his mistresses out of mere courtesy, slipped aside, compelled by momentary shame, and unsteady because his heart was bent on Sītā.

Kula reads *jaṇiükkaṇtho* (cf. *SC* text) for *diṇṇukkaṇṭho*. K says अस्य मुखनिवहः . . . कृतोत्कण्ठः (दत्तोत्कण्ठः *chāyā*), अतएव च क्षणं विलक्षः लज्जित उल्ललति तासां मुखेभ्यः स्खलति स्म। Kula says दाक्षिण्यमात्रेण दत्तः संमुखीकृतः, जनकसुताभिमुखेन हृदयेन जनितोत्कण्ठः विहितवैवश्यः तस्य मुखनिवहो निजान्तःपुरमुखेषु उल्ललेति नावतिष्ठते।

14. जा अण्णेण हसन्तो गमेइ उम्मच्छरं विलासिणिसत्थम्।
ता दूसहसंतावं अण्णं से सोअदुम्मणं होइ मुहम्।।

[यावदन्येन हसन्गमयत्युन्मात्सर्यं विलासिनीसार्थम्।
तावद्दुःसहसंतापमन्यदस्य शोकदुर्मनस्कं भवति मुखम्।।]

While he deceived his jealous mistresses by laughing with one face, another face of his was clouded with grief, bearing traces of unbearable suffering.

K and Kula read *ṇīsāsaṁ* for *saṁtāvaṁ* (R).

R says गमयति प्रतारयति। My says अगमयत् कथंचिदनयदित्यर्थः। Kula is mostly corrupt, but *SC* reproduces him in the initial portion of its gloss on the verse — यावदन्येन मुखेन *ummacchiaṁ* ईर्षोद्विग्नं विलासिनीसार्थं हसन् गमयत्यभिव्यथं करोति। यद्वा सानुरागं पश्यत्यर्थात् रावणः। Others read *ummaccharaṁ*, i.e. उन्मत्सरम्। *SC* says *ummachia*- शब्दः क्रोधे तज्जन्योद्विग्नतायामेव देशी।

K says उन्मत्सरम् उद्भूतमत्सरं विलासिनीजनमन्येन केनचिन्मुखेन हसन् रावणो यावत् गमयति यत् किञ्चिदुक्त्वा यापयति, तावत् तस्यान्यत् मुखं शोकेन दुर्मनो दुःखितं, दुःसहनिश्वासमभूत। दाक्षिण्येन प्रणयिनीः विनोदयितुकामो हसन् अन्यतमेन मुखेन यावत् आभाषते तावदन्यत् मुखं उत्कण्ठया विषण्णं दीर्घनिश्वासं च बभूवेत्यर्थः।

15. णिउणहसिआणुविद्धं सीआलम्भावहारणविसंवाअम्।
सुणइ ण लक्खेइ फुडं अण्णविइण्णहिअओ पिआण दहमुहो।।

[निपुणहसितानुविद्धं सीतालम्भावधारणविसंवादम्।
शृणोति न लक्षयति स्फुटमन्यवितीर्णहृदयः प्रियाणां दशमुखः।।]

With his heart fixed elsewhere, Rāvaṇa heard, but did not clearly comprehend the talk of his mistresses, accompanied by ironic smiles, as they ruled out the certainty of his winning Sītā.

K and MY read अवधीरण for *avahāraṇa* = अवधारण (R and Kula). K reads शून्य for *aṇṇa* (R and Kula).

K says प्रियाणामुपालम्भनिपुणेन हसितेनानुविद्धं युक्तं, सीतालाभस्यावधीरणमवज्ञारूपं सीता तव वशं न यास्यतीति विसंवादम्, आनुकूल्यं संवादः, विसंवादं प्रतिकूलवचनं शून्यदत्तहृदयो रावणः शृणोति स्म। केवलमशृणोदेव, स्फुटं न लक्षयति स्म शून्यहृदयत्वात्।

MY says अवाप्तसकलत्रैलोक्यवर्तियुवतिरत्नस्यापि ते मानुषीलाभोऽपूर्वः प्रार्थनीय एवेत्येवं परिहासानुगतं, सीतालाभस्याप्रार्थनीयत्वेन अवज्ञानात् यो विसंवादः

स्वाभिप्रायविरुद्धवचनं तदित्यर्थः। Kula explains विसंवाद as अन्यथाभाव। R says सीताया लम्भस्य प्राप्तेरवधारणम् अनेनोपायेन सीतालाभ इति निश्चयस्तस्य विसंवादमन्यथाकरणं साध्वी सीता कथमनेन लब्धव्येत्यादिवचनरूपम्।

16. ईसामच्छरगरुए साहिक्खेवपरिवड्ढितोवालम्भे।
कह कह वि गमेइ खणं विलक्खहसिएहिं कामिणिसमुल्लावे।।

[ईर्ष्यामत्सरगुरुकान्साधिक्षेपपरिवर्धितोपालम्भान्।
कथं कथमपि गमयति क्षणं विलक्षहसितैः कामिनीसमुल्लापान्।।]

Laughing in his confusion, he somehow endured for a moment the utterances of his mistresses, full of jealousy and wrath, and conveying opprobrious and stern rebukes.

K says अमक्षा ईर्ष्या, परविभूतेरसहिष्णुत्वं मत्सरः, ताभ्यां गुरुन्। अधिक्षेपो जुगुप्सा, उपालम्भो दोषारोपणम्, अधिक्षेपेण सह प्रवृत्तोपालम्भवाक्य कामनीनां वल्लभानामालापान् विलक्षहसितैः कथं कथमपि गमयति यापयति स्म। MY says परगुणसंभावनासहिष्णुता मात्सर्यमिति भोजः। स्वान्यप्रवृत्तिगर्हा स्यादुपालम्भः प्रियं प्रतीति कथनात् अधिक्षेपः प्रियस्यैव प्रवृत्तेर्गर्हेति विवेकः। कामिनीसमुल्लापान् विलक्षहसितैरगमयदिति कामिनीसमुल्लापेषु विलक्षहसितमेव परमकरोदित्यर्थः।

Kula says गमयति प्रेरयति। R says वैलक्ष्यमप्रतिभा। अधिक्षेपः तर्जनासंवलिता निन्दा। उपालम्भोऽपकारोक्तिः।

17. तस्स पडिरुद्धसेसं वाहोत्थअकण्ठविसमपअणिक्खेवम्।
सङ्किज्जइ विमणाहिं फुडं ण णज्जइ पिआहि गोत्तक्खलिअम्।।

[तस्य प्रतिरुद्धशेषं बाष्पावस्तृतकण्ठविषमपदनिक्षेपम्।
शङ्क्यते विमनोभिः स्फुटं न ज्ञायते प्रियाभिर्गोत्रस्खलितम्।।]

Dejected, his mistresses suspected, but failed to comprehend clearly his fortuitous mention of their rival's name, because the last letter was suppressed, and the utterance indistinct, his throat being choked with tears.

K and Kula (?) read प्रतिबद्ध for *paḍiruddha* (R).

K says भयेन प्रतिबद्धस्य वचसः शेषं शेषभूतमुत्कण्ठया बाष्पपूर्णे कण्ठे विषमपदविन्यासं तस्य गोत्रस्खलिततं नामधेयस्खलितं विषण्णाभिः प्रियाभिः शङ्क्यते स्म। विकलाक्षरत्वात् स्फुटं न ज्ञायते स्म।

MY says सीतागतमनसा बाष्पावस्थगितकण्ठतया विषमोपक्रान्तं, पुनः प्रतिसंधानेन अपह्नोतुमनसानुच्चारितवर्णशेषं गोत्रस्खलितमस्फुटतया शङ्क्यते, परं स्फुट न तु

निरचीयतेत्यर्थः। R says बाष्पावस्तृतेन कण्ठेन विषमः स्फुटास्फुटः पदनिक्षेपः पदोच्चारणं यत्र।

18. कह वि ठवेइ दहमुहो किं ति अणालविअमोहदिण्णालावम्।
दइआहि गलिअवाहं रोसणिरुत्तरपुलोइअं अप्पाणम्।।

[कथमपि स्थापयति दशमुखः किमित्यनालपितमोघदत्तालापम्।
दयिताभिर्गलितबाष्पं रोषनिरुत्तरप्रलोकितमात्मानम्।।]

Having responded[3] in vain when no one had spoken to him,[4] Rāvaṇa somehow composed himself as his mistresses looked at him in speechless rage, with tears welling up in their eyes.

K, Kula and probably MY have यापयति for *ṭhavei* = स्थापयति (R). Their reading is *javei*, cf. *SC* text. K (*chāyā*) has दत्तमोघोल्लापम्। Kula and MY also have उल्लापम्। K and probably MY read दयितानां for *daiāhi* (R and Kula). *SC* text has *aṇālatta* for *aṇāla via*; and *paloiaṁ* for *pu°*. K says केनचित् अनालपिते सति चित्तविभ्रमात् किमिति दत्तमोघालापं, तदानीं रोषेण निरुत्तराभिः प्रियाभिः विलोकितं गलितबाष्पमात्मानं रावणः कथंचित् यापयामास। दयितानामिति तृतीयार्थे षष्ठी। MY says स्त्रीणामनालसत्वेऽपि आलापाभावेऽपि वृथा दत्तः किमिति प्रश्नरूपः उल्लापो येन तत् यथा। गुरुबाष्पं भवति (यथा) तथा। रोषेणोत्तरमनुक्त्वा ताभिः केवलं प्रलोकितमात्मानं कथमपि व्यवास्थापयदित्यर्थः। MY seems to read *garua-bāhaṁ* for *galia°*. Kula says सीताप्रसक्तिवैमनस्यात् अनालपिते अपृष्टे किमिति निरर्थकदत्तोल्लापम्, दयिताभिः गलितबाष्पं यथा स्यात् तथा . . . प्रलोकितमात्मानं दशमुखः कथमपि यापयति व्यवस्थापयति।

19. अणहिअओ वि पिआणं उन्मच्छपसारिअग्घविअहुंकारम्।
अहिणन्दइ दहवअणो समत्तणिव्वेलिआहरोट्ठपुलइअम्।।

[अन्यहृदयोऽपि प्रियाणामुन्मत्सरप्रसारितार्थितहुंकारम्।
अभिनन्दति दशवदनः समस्तनिर्वेल्लिताधरोष्ठप्रलोकितम्।।]

Even though his heart was elsewhere, he welcomed the (angry) looked of his mistresses, with their lips all aquiver, because their mutterings occasioned by jealousy were suppressed (by decorum).[5]

---

[3] Literally having said "What?"

[4] I.e. in his absent-mindedness he imagined that someone was speaking to him.

[5] Cf. Kṛṣṇa in Extracts.

K reads क्षपित (क्षयित Kula), i.e. *°kkhavia* for *agghavia* = अर्घित (R). MY reads स्खलित (*°kkhalia*). See below. K says रावण: प्रियाणामुन्मत्सरत्वात् प्रसारित: प्रारब्ध: आभिजात्येन क्षपितो हुङ्कारो यत्र तत्, रुषा समस्तनिष्पीडिताधरोष्ठं यथा विलोकितं विलोकनम् अहृदयोऽप्यन्यत्रगतहृदयोऽपि अभिनन्दति तासां वाल्लभ्यादभिनन्दति स्म। अथवा अन्यहृदय: सन्नपि। प्राकृतलक्षणस्वातन्त्र्यमेतत्।

MY reads *ṇivvolia,*[6] like manuscript C of Goldschmidt, for *ṇivvellia*, and explains it as निष्क्रामित। K seems to explain *ṇivvellia* as निष्पीडित (see above). R says दशवदन: प्रियाणां समस्तं संपूर्ण निर्वेल्लितं प्रस्फुरितमधरोष्ठं यत्र तादृशं प्रलोकितं दर्शनमभिनन्दति। किंभूतम–उद्गतेन मत्सरेण प्रसारित: समुत्थापित:, अथ च अन्यचित्तत्वात् रावणेन विलासबुद्ध्या अर्घित: अर्चित: सत्कृतो हुंकारो यत्र तत्। MY says मत्सरेण प्रवर्तितो रोषातिशयेन मध्ये स्खलितश्च हुङ्कारो यस्य तत् समस्तनिष्क्रामिताधरोष्ठं प्रलोकितमहृदयोऽपि अनन्ददित्यर्थ:। अत्र कोपस्य ललितत्वेन भावाख्यत्वं ग्राह्यम्। Kula says ईर्षोद्वेगेन प्रसारित: रावणशङ्कया क्षयित: संहृतो हुङ्कारो यत्र। समस्तो निर्मल: (?) . . . अधरोष्ठो यत्र तत् प्रियाणां प्रलोकितम् अहृदयोऽपि हृदयशून्योऽपि दशवदनोऽभिनन्दति सौभाग्यसूचकत्वात् बहु मन्यत इत्यर्थ:। *SC* which reproduces Kula's gloss anonymously has समस्त – *ṇivvellia* समग्रदष्टोऽधरोष्ठ उत्तराधरो यत्र। *SC chāyā* has निर्वेल्लित।

20. दुच्चिन्तिआवसेसं पिआहि उन्मच्छसंभमकआलोअम्।
हसइ खणं अप्पाणं अणहिअअविसज्जिआसणणिअत्तन्तम्।।

[दुश्चिन्तितापदेशं प्रियाभिरुन्मत्सरसंभ्रमकृतालोकम्।
हसति क्षणमात्मानमन्यहृदयविसृष्टासननिवर्तमानम्।।]

As he absent-mindedly left his seat and returned to it, offering an ill-conceived excuse, he laughed at himself for a moment; while his mistresses looked at him in perplexity with jealous eyes.

K says दुश्चिन्तितापदेशम् सीताविषयं दुश्चिन्तितमुद्दिश्य अहृदयत्वात् विसर्जितासनम् आसनादुत्थाय गच्छन्तं पुनर्निवर्तमानं तदानीं प्रियाभिरुन्मत्सरंससंभ्रमं यथा कृतालोकमात्मानं क्षणं हसति किं कृतवानस्मीति स्वयमेव जहास।

Kula says दुश्चिन्तितापदेशम् उन्मादकृतं किमप्यनिष्टं। यत् तस्यापदेशो यथा स्यात् तथा प्रियाभिरुद्वेगसंभ्रमाभ्यां कृतालोकं प्रयुक्तसंवरणवादमात्मानं हसति

---

[6] Hemacandra 4.69 gives *ṇivvolaï* in the sense of मन्युना ओष्ठं मलिनं करोति।

असंबद्धक्रियाया हासहेतुत्वात् उपहसतीत्यर्थः। Kula explains *ummaccha* as ईर्षोद्वेग in verse 19, and here as उद्वेग।

R explains अपदेश as व्याज, MY also says अनुचितचिन्तितापदेशम् असंगत(?)निरूपितोक्तस्वगमनव्याजं प्रियाभिरुन्मत्सरं संभ्रमेण कृतालोकम्। *SC* says दुःखेन चिन्तितोऽपदेशः संवरणं यत्र ईदृशम्। R mentions *uvaesa* (उपदेश) as a variant for *ava°* (अपदेश) – रम्भानलकूबरयोः शापतः स्वनाशहेतुत्वेन दुश्चिन्तितो बलादेव सीतामानयामीत्येवंरूप उपदेशः सीताप्राप्त्युपायो येनेत्यर्थः।

21. तह स गओ अइभूमिं जह ण विणिज्जन्तणं पिआहि ण णाओ।
णा अ णाऊण ण हसिओ ण अ हसिऊण अणुसोइउं ण अ तिण्णो।।

[तथा स गतोऽतिभूमिं यथा न विनियन्त्रणं प्रियाभिर्न ज्ञातः।
न च ज्ञात्वा न हसितो न च हसित्वानुशोचितुं न च तीर्णः।।]

He went to such extremes (in his distraction) that his mistresses did know his condition for certain; and having known it, did laugh at him; but having laughed, could not help pitying him.

K and MY read च for स (R), and अनुकम्पितुमपि न दत्तः for *aṅusoiuṁ ṅa a tiṇṇo* = अनुशोचितुं न च तीर्णः (R).[7] K says रावणस्तदा तथा चातिभूमिं गतः उन्मादकाष्ठां गतः यथा प्रियाभिः विनिर्यन्त्रणं विशेषेण निर्यन्त्रणमनर्गलं यथा न न ज्ञातो, निःसंशयम् असावुन्मादमोहित इति यथा ज्ञात एवाभूत् तथा अतिभूमिमगात्। . . . ज्ञात्वा च ताभिर्यथा न न हसितः हसित एव तथोन्मत्तः। किञ्च हसित्वा च ताभिरनुकम्पितुमपि यथा न न दत्तः दत्त एव, अनुकम्पाया विषयीकृत इत्यर्थः। अभीष्टार्थदानादयं जीवतु इत्येवमनुकम्पितुमपि उचितो यथाभूत् तथातिभूमिं गत इत्यर्थः। अनुकम्पालक्षणमुक्तं भावविवेके –

अनुकम्पा तु सा ज्ञेया दुःखितान् प्रति देहिनः।
उपकारपरत्वं या कुरुते चित्तविक्रया।। इति।
R says न च न तीर्णः शकितः, अपि तु शकितः।

22. चिन्तेउं च पउत्तो अवहोवासपसरन्तणीसासहअम्।
दोसु णिमेऊण समं एक्कं आसण्णमुहकवोलेसु करम्।।

[चिन्तयितुं च प्रवृत्त उभयावकाशप्रसरन्निःश्वासहतम्।
द्वयोर्नियोज्य सममेकमासन्नमुखकपोलयोः करम्।।]

---

[7] Kula's reading seems to be same as that of R, but he reads च and अनुकम्पितुम् like K and MY.

Placing one of his hands evenly between two of his contiguous faces, he began to think as he covered it with his sighs coming on both sides.[8]

ṅimeūṇa निधाय MY (K also). K says अनन्तरं स आसन्नमुखकपोलयोः बहूनां निरन्तराणां मुखानामासन्नयोः द्वयोः मुखकपोलयोरन्तराले एकं करं समं निधाय चिन्तयितुं च प्रवृत्तः। कथंभूतम–उभयपार्श्वप्रसरदुष्णनिश्वासहतम्।

23. अङ्कागअं सहिज्जइ पओसरइविग्घसंकिएण कइबलम्।
तं कस्स वि सोअत्थं वलइ अलद्धसुरअं महं चिअ हिअअम्।।

[अङ्कागतं सह्यते प्रदोषरतिविघ्नशङ्कितेन कपिबलम्।
तत्कस्यापि शोकार्थं वलत्यलब्धसुरतं ममैव हृदयम्।।]

"I have put up with the host of apes that is close at hand, because I am afraid to disturb the pleasures of the night. That is to the advantage of someone else; while deprived of the joys of love, it is my heart that grows restless.[9]

K has स्वास्थ्यं for *soatthaṁ* rendered as शोकार्थम् by R and MY.

K says अङ्कमागतमासन्नं कपिबलं प्रदोषरतिविघ्नशङ्कितेन प्रदोषे राक्षसानां संभोगविघ्नः स्यादिति, मम च यदि कथंचित् सीता मदभिमुखीभवेत् तदा ममापि सुरतविघ्नः स्यादिति शङ्कमानेन मया सह्यते स्म। न विनाशितमिति यत् तत् कस्यापि पुरुषस्य स्वास्थ्यमभूत्। कस्यापीत्यनेन राम उक्तः। प्रदोषश्च व्यतीतः। तस्मादलब्धसुरतं मम हृदयमेव वलते भ्रमति व्यथत इत्यर्थः। K seems to take *soatthaṁ* in the same sense as *sovatthaṁ* mentioned in *Deśīnāmamālā* 8.45 in the sense of उपकार।

MY says कस्यापि यादृशतादृशस्य शोकार्थमेतत् कपिबलम् आसन्नस्थितमपि पूर्वं रतिलाभशङ्कया तद्विघ्नबुद्ध्या उपेक्षितम्। इदानीं तु तदलाभे निश्चिते क्षुद्राणां शोकजननं तत् कपिबलं प्रति ममैव रावणस्यापि हृदयं वलते अभिगच्छति।

Kula takes *soatthaṁ* as शोकास्तम्। He says ममैव हृदयं शोकास्तं सीतासंभोगाप्राप्तेः शोके मग्नम् अतएवालब्धसुरतम्। तत् कस्यापि वलति, न ज्ञायते किं शुभायाशुभाय वा प्रवर्तत इत्यर्थः।

R says ममैव हृदयं यद्वलति सुरताभावाकुलतया यत् चञ्चलीभवति तत् कस्यापि

---

[8] Literally (the hand) struck by his sighs, etc.

[9] The second line of the verse is variously explained. Translation follows Kṛṣṇa. The idea is, he has refrained from attacking the apes at night to allow the demons to enjoy their amorous sports undisturbed. This has benefited Rāma; while he suffers frustrated in his passion for Sītā.

रामस्य वा सीताया वा ममैव वा शोकार्थम्। Laṭakana says अलब्धसुरतं ममैव हृदयं कस्यापि शोकार्थं वलते प्रवर्तते . . . रामस्यैव शोकमुत्पादयामिति भावः। कस्यापीति सामान्येन रामस्यैवाभिधानमिति।

24. किं भुअविवरपहोलिरसंखोहप्फिडिअगहिअकड्ढिअणिहअम्।
अत्थाक्कासण्णठिअं णिप्फलचटुलमुहलं मलेमि कइबलम्।।

[किं भुजविवरप्रघूर्णनशीलसंक्षोभस्फेटितगृहीतकृष्टनिहतम्।
अकस्मादासन्नस्थितं निष्फलचटुलमुखरं मृद्गामि कपिबलम्।।]

Shall I crush the horde of apes as they draw near unawares, and move about and chatter in vain, and wriggle out of my arms and flee in confusion, and lie still when seized and dragged by me?

K reads त्रस्त and MY उत्त्रस्त (*uppittha*) for °*pphiḍia* = स्फेटित (R and Kula). K, MY and Kula read निभृतं (*ṇihuaṁ*) for *ṇihaaṁ* (R). K reads स्थित (°*ṭṭhia*) for *ṭhiaṁ* (R and Kula). K says अतर्कितमेव आसननस्थितेन मदासन्नस्थित्या निष्फलं कापेयात् चटुलं मुखरं च यथा भवति तथा मृद्नामि किम्। MY says अभिमुखप्रसारितभुजश्रेणीमध्यभ्रमित-संक्षोभोत्त्रस्तनिरस्ताकृष्टनिश्चेष्टं (कपिबलम्)। K says गृहीताकृष्टं कपिबलम्। R says संक्षोभेण भयेन (संचलनेन Kula) स्फेटितं भ्रष्टं पलायितमिति यावत्। Kula says निरुद्धचेष्टत्वात् निभृतं निष्पन्दम्।

25. ओ ससिकराहनुम्मिल्ललोअणन्दोलमाणवाहतरङ्गम्।
आसाएमि कअग्गहणिरुत्तरुत्ताणिआणणं जणअसुअम्।।

[उत शशिकराहतोन्मीलल्लोचनान्दोलमानबाष्पतरङ्गाम्।
आस्वादयामि कचग्रहनिरुत्तरोत्तानिताननां जनकसुताम्।।]

Or, shall I enjoy Sītā, her silent face turned upwards as I seize her by the hair, while ripples of tears well up in her eyes opening in contact with the moonbeams?

K reads *andola-galia* for *andolamāṇa* (R and Kula). K reads अभिभूत (*ovaggia*) for *uttāṇia* (R and Kula). MY's reading is same as K's. K says अथवा शशिकिरणाहतत्वात् उन्मीलितयोराघातादुन्मीलितयोः नयनयोरान्दोलन-गलद्बाष्पतरङ्गं[10], कचग्रहेण अभिभूतमुखीं जनकसुतामास्वादयामि। *SC* says कचग्रहेत्यादेः क्रियाविशेषणत्वमेव साधीयः। MY reads *āsāsemi* (आश्वासयामि)

---

[10] K (*chāyā*) has आन्दोलनगलितबाष्पतरङ्गम्।

for *āsāemi* (आस्वादयामि)। He says *oaggia* लङ्घित। Laṭakana says आसादयामि गृह्णामि।

26. कह विरहप्पडिऊला होहिइ समुहहिअआ पइम्मि उवगए।
णेच्छइ इअरा वि ससिं किं उण दिट्ठम्मि दिणअरम्मि कमलिणी।।

[कथं विरहप्रतिकूला भविष्यति संमुखहृदया पत्यावुपगते।
नेच्छतीतरथापि शशिनं किं पुनर्दृष्टे दिनकरे कमलिनी।।]

Hostile to me even in her husband's absence, how will she be friendly now that her lord hath come? Does the day lily that is averse to the moon,[11] even in the absence of the sun, ever desire it, when the sun comes into view?

K says इतरापि (Kula also) दिनकरविरहितापि। MY says इतरथापीति रवेरदर्शनेऽपीत्यर्थः। R agrees with MY.

27. अब्भत्थणं ण गेह्णइ तिरई तिहुअणसिरीअ वि ण लोहेउम्।
ण गणेइ सरीरवहं कह मण्णे होज्ज जाणई साणुणआ।।

[अभ्यर्थनां न गृह्णाति शक्यते त्रिभुवनश्रियापि न लोभयितुम्।
न गणयति शरीरवधं कथं मन्ये भवेज्जानकी सानुनया।।]

Sītā doth not accept entreaties, nor can she be tempted even with the riches of the three worlds, nor is she afraid of any danger to her life. How could she, I wonder, be favourable to me?

K and Kula read शरीरभयं for °*vahaṁ* (R). Manuscript. C of Goldschmidt reads °*bhaaṁ*.

28. पइमाहप्पणिसण्णा अवमाणिअसेससप्पुरिससौडीरा।
जइ णवर होज्ज व वसा लुअराहवसीसदंसणा जणअसुआ।।

[पतिमाहात्म्यनिषण्णावमानितशेषसत्पुरुषशौटीर्या।
यदि केवलं भवेद्वा वश्या लूनराघवशीर्षदर्शना जनकसुता।।]

Relying on the greatness of her consort, she depises the valour of all other brave men. She might perhaps yield only if she saw the severed head of Rāma.

K, Kula and MY read केवलमियाद्वशं (यायात् MY) for *ṇavara hojja*

[11] The day lily closes at nightfall.

va vasā (R). Their reading is *ṇavaraṁ ejja vasaṁ* (cf. *SC* text). Manuscript. C of Goldschmidt has *ṇavaraṁ*. Father, K, MY and Kula read दर्शने for *°daṁsaṇā* (R) = दर्शना।

K says पत्युर्माहात्म्ये निषण्णा कृतास्पदा, अतएवावधीरितशेषसत्पुरुषसामर्थ्या सीता लूनस्य मायामयस्य राघवशिरसो दर्शने सति केवलं वशमियात् उपेयात् यदि तदा वश्या भवेत् यदि इति वाक्यशेषः।

MY says भर्तृवैभवे व्यवस्थिते। अवज्ञातशेषपुरुषशौर्यातिशया। Kula says शौटीर्यं वीर्याभिमानः।

29. अद्दिट्ठलज्जणिज्जो भग्गपरित्ताणविअलिआसाबन्धो।
अवसो अबन्धुलहुओ भएण ठिइभङ्गसाहसं कुणइ जणो।।

[अदृष्टलज्जनीयो भग्नपरित्राणविगलिताशाबन्धः।
अवशोऽबन्धुलघुको भयेन स्थितिभङ्गसाहसं करोति जनः ।।]

People dare violate their cherished principle, out of fear, when they are helpless and humble for lack of friends, and see no cause for shame, with all hope gone owing to loss of protection."

K and MY read वित्रुटित (*vikhuḍia* ?) for *vialia* (R and Kula). K says वित्रुटितः छिन्नः। लज्जाविषयो लज्जनीयो लज्जानिमित्तभूतः। स्थितिर्मर्यादा प्रातिव्रत्यादिः। MY says भयेन धृतिभङ्गसाहसं करोति। He seems to read *dhii* for *ṭhii*. Kula says अदृष्टो लज्जनीयो लज्जाहेतुर्येन।

30. णवरि अ णं खेआलसजिम्भाअत्तवलिउद्धमुहसंघाअम्।
भुमआभङ्गाणत्तो समअं पासेसु परिअणो अल्लीणः।।

[अनन्तरं चैनं खेदालसजृम्भायमाणवलितोर्ध्वमुखसंघातम्।
भ्रूभङ्गाज्ञप्तः समकं पार्श्वयोः परिजन आलीनः।।]

Thereupon his attendants, summoned by a movement of his eyebrows, fearfully approached him on either side as his faces, held high with a weary yawn, turned towards them.

K and Kula read सभयं for *samaaṁ* (R). MY has *pāsehi* (पार्श्वाभ्याम्) for *pāsesu*. He says *jambhāanta* जृम्भमाण (K also). *allīṇo* प्राप्तः (आश्रितः K, आलीनः K *chāyā*)। K says खेदात् उत्कण्ठाखेदात् अलसजृम्भमाणो वलित उर्ध्वीकृतः मुखसंघातो यस्य तं रावणम्।

31. तो एक्कहिअअगुणिअं दसहि वि समअं मुखेहि अप्पाहेउम्।
ण पहुप्पइ दहवअणो चिरकङ्खिअलम्भगब्भिणक्खरगुरुअम्।।

[तत एकहृदयगुणितं दशभिरपि समकं मुखैरध्यापयितुम्।
न प्रभवति दशवदनश्चिरकाङ्क्षितलम्भगर्भिताक्षरगुरुकम्।।]

Even with his ten mouths he could not utter at once what was thought out in his mind, because it was cumbered with words, choked with joy, at the prospect of fulfilling his long cherished resolve.

K and MY read वचनं दशभिरपि मुखैः for *dasahi vi samaaṁ muhehi* (R and Kula).

K says एकत्र हृदये गुणितं प्रगल्भाभ्यस्तम्। MY says गुणितं कृताभ्यासम्। R says हृदयेन मनसा गुणितं चिन्तितं प्रमेयम्। Kula says एकेन हृदयेन गुणितमावर्तितम्। चिरकाङ्क्षितस्य रामवधप्रदर्शनेन सीतायत्तीकरणस्य लाभेन गर्भितैरक्षरैः हास्याङ्गत्वात्[12] गुरुकं दुःखोच्चार्यम्। K says एवंभूतं वचनं मायामयरामशिरोनिर्माणवचनं रावणः संभ्रमवशात् दशभिरपि मुखैर्युगपत् व्याहतु (आभाषितुं *chāyā*) न प्रभवति न शशाक।

MY says चिरप्रार्थितस्यार्थस्य लाभेन गर्भितैः तत्तदुपायप्रतिपादकैरक्षरैः गुरु वचनं दशभिरपि मुखैर्वक्तुं न प्राभवदित्यर्थः। R says गर्भितानि तत्कालोत्पन्नहर्षेण गद्गदकण्ठतयास्फुटीभूतानि यानि वक्तव्याक्षराणि तैः गुरुकमतिशयितम्।

32. अण्णेण समारद्धं वअणं अण्णेण हरिसगहिअप्फिडिअम्।
अण्णेण अद्धभणिअं मुहेण अण्णेण से कह वि णिम्मविअम्।।

[अन्येन समारब्धं वचनमन्येन हर्षगृहीतस्फेटितम्।
अन्येनार्धभणितं मुखेनान्येनास्य कथमपि निर्मि(र्मापि)तम्।।]

One of his mouths began the words; another took them over in joy, but let them slip; another uttered them half; while yet another somehow finished them.

K says पूर्वप्रस्तुतं वचनं तस्य एकेन मुखे समारब्धमन्येन हर्षात् गृहीतभ्रष्टं, पुनरन्येनार्धभणितं भूत्वा पुनरपरेण कथमपि समापितमिति।

33. तो उग्गाहिअसोअं तेण भणन्तेन मुहपहोलिरधूमम्।
संताविएक्कहिअअं दसकण्ठक्खलिअपलहुअं णीससिअम्।।

---

[12] Quotation in *SC* has हासगर्भत्वात्।

[तत उद्ग्राहितशोकं तेन भणता मुखप्रघूर्णनशीलधूमम्।
संतापितैकहृदयं दशकण्ठस्खलितप्रलघुकं निश्वसितम्।।]

As he spoke sadly, his mouths shrouded in fumes, and his heart aggrieved, he heaved a sigh that became faint as it passed through his ten throats.

K and MY read फलित for *°kkhalia* = स्खलित (R and Kula). K says मायारामशिरोदर्शनमूलस्य सीताधिगमोपायस्य अतीव दैन्यस्वरूपत्वात् अनन्यगतिकत्वाच्च . . . तस्य वचनकथने सहसा शोकः समभूत्। एवमुद्गृहीतशोकं भणता तेन संतापितैकहृदयं शोकोष्मणा संतापितहृदयं यथा, दशसु कण्ठनालेषु फलितत्वात् प्रशीर्णत्वात् प्रलघुकं च यथा भवति तथा निश्वसितम्। ञि फला विशरण इति धातुः।

MY says उपात्तचित्तवैधुर्यं भणता तेन मुखनिःसृतधूमं, संतापितैक . . . हृदयं, दशकण्ठी विभक्तलघु निश्वसितम्। R explains उद्ग्राहित as प्रकाशित।

34. आहासइ अ णिसिअरे आण्णासमकालदिण्णपडिसंलावे।
महिणिमिओहअकरअलतंसट्ठिअतिअभरुण्णमिअदेहद्धे।।

[आभाषते च निशिचरानाज्ञासमकालदत्तप्रतिसंलापान्।
महीनिवेशितोभयकरतलतिर्यक्स्थितत्रिकभरोन्नमितदेहार्धान्।।]

He addressed the demons, who responded simultaneously as he gave the orders, and (knelt before him) with both hands placed on the ground, and the raised half of the body resting on the curved hips.

K and MY read अवनमित for *uṇṇamia* (R and Kula).

K says मह्यां निहितोभयकरतलत्वात् तिर्यग्भूतेन त्रिकभरेण अवनमितपश्चिमदेहभागान्।

MY says *ṇimia* निक्षिप्त। महीनिहितोभयकरतलाश्च ते त्र्यस्रावस्थितैः त्रिकभरैरवन-मितदेहपश्चाद्भागाश्च इति विग्रहः।

K says प्रभोराज्ञायाः समकालमेव दत्तप्रतिसंलापानुक्तप्रतिवचनान् आदरेण भयेन च रावणस्य वाक्यविभागानां विरामे विरामे तथा क्रियत इति कृतप्रतिवचनानित्यर्थः।

R says तिर्यक् स्थितं यत् त्रिकं तत्र भरेणोन्नमितो देहार्धो देहपश्चाद्भागो यैस्तान्।

35. तं माआणिम्मविअं रिउदंसणविसमवलिअणिच्चलणअणम्।
दावेह कण्ठरहिअं सीआइ विओअपण्डुरं रामसिरम्।।

[तन्मायानिर्मि(र्मापि)तं रिपुदर्शनविषमवलितनिश्चलनयनम्।
दर्शयत कण्ठरहितं सीताया वियोगपाण्डुरं रामशिरः।।]

Show to Sītā Rāma's neckless head created by magic, with the face pale on account of separation from her, and the fierce staring eyes turned sideways to look at the foe.

K says तदिति वाक्योपक्रमे लोकोक्तिः। माययानिर्मितं रामशिरः सीतायै दर्शयत। कीदृशं – युद्धसमये रिपुदर्शनेन वलितम् ईषत्तिरश्चीनं विषमं क्रूरं निश्चलं च नयनं यस्य तत्, etc. MY says *ṇimmavia* निर्मापित। Kula says मायया निर्मितं (K also), रिपुदर्शनाय वलिते व्यापारिते विषमे निश्चले नयने यत्र तत्।

36. तो अमरिसमेलाविअभुमउग्गाहिअतरङ्गिअणिलाडअडम्।
छिण्णाणिअं व्व तं चिअ ताहे च्चिअ तेहि णिम्मिअं रामसिरम्।।

[ततोऽमर्षमेलितभ्रूद्ग्राहिततरङ्गितललाटतटम्।
छिन्नानीतमिव तदैव तदेव तनिर्मित रामशिरः।।]

Thereupon, at that very moment, they produced the very head of Rāma, as if it had just been severed and brought thither, with the forehead furrowed by an angry frown.

K says अमर्षमिलिताभ्यां भ्रूभ्यामुद्गृहीतत्वात् तरङ्गितललाटतटम्। MY says अमर्षमेलितभ्रूकं च तत् उद्गृहीततरङ्गितललाटं चेति समासः। ललाटोद्ग्रहणं च करग्रहणादिति बोद्धव्यम्। Kula says अमर्षमेलितयोः भ्रुवोः उद्ग्राहितेन उत्क्षेपेण भ्रुकुटिरचनयेत्यर्थः तरङ्गितं ललाटतलं यत्र तत् (रामशिरः)। R says अमर्षेण मेलिताभ्यामेकीभूताभ्यां भ्रूभ्यामुद्ग्राहितमुत्क्षिप्तम् अतएव तरङ्गितं सभ्रुकुटीकं ललाटतटं यत्र।

K says छिन्नानीतं साक्षात्तदेव रामशिर इव तदानीमेव मायामयं रामशिरो विरचितम्।

37. संपत्थिआ अ संभमचलणोवडणविसमुट्ठिआ षमअवणम्।
कह वि समत्तप्पाहिदशवअणाणत्तिवावडा रणणिअरा।।

[संप्रस्थिताश्च संभ्रमचरणावपतनविषमोत्थिताः प्रमदवनम्।
कथमपि समस्ताध्यापितदशवदनाज्ञप्तिव्यापृता रजनीचराः।।]

Hurriedly getting up with eager footsteps, the demons started for the pleasure garden, occupied with Rāvaṇa's command that had somehow been fully explained by him.

K and MY (?) read चरणावनतनिपतितोत्थिताः for *calaṇ-ovaḍaṇa-visamuṭṭhiā* (R).

K says संभ्रमेण रावणचरणयोरवनतनिपतिताः पुनरुत्थिता, उत्कण्ठादुःखेन कथंचित् समस्तं व्याहतायां दशवदनाज्ञप्तौ आज्ञापने व्यापृता राक्षसा रामशिरो गृहीत्वा प्रमदवनं क्रीडावनमशोकवनिकां प्रस्थिताश्च।

MY says कार्यत्वरिततया जानुभ्यां महीस्पर्शनमात्रेण प्रणतोत्थिता वक्तुमुपक्रान्तायां कथमपि मुखपरस्परया समापितायां दशमुखाज्ञायां व्यापृता रजनिचराः संप्रस्थिता इत्यर्थः। Kula's reading is uncertain, but विषमोत्थिताः appears in his gloss. He renders *samatta* as समाप्त instead of समस्त। *SC* says कथमपि समाप्तं *appāhiaṁ* संदेशो येन हर्षजाड्यात् एवंभूतस्य दशवदनस्य आज्ञप्तिव्यापृताः इति श्रीनिवासः।

38. पत्ता अ फुडिअमणिअडविवरुट्ठिअसलिलबद्धपङ्कअमउलम्।
पवणसुअभग्गपाअवभङ्गुग्गअबालकिसलअं पमअवणम्।।
[प्राप्ताश्च स्फुटितमणितटविवरोत्थितसलिलबद्धपङ्कजमुकुलम्।
पवनसुतभग्नपादपभङ्गोद्गतबालकिसलयं प्रमदवनम्।।]

They reached the pleasance where lotus-buds were springing up in the water stored in cavities in the crystal embankments; and young shoots had issued from the broken stems of the trees smashed by Hanumat.[13]

K and Kula read स्फटिक (*phaliha*) for *phuḍia* = स्फुटित (R). K and MY read विवरस्थित for *vivaruṭṭhia* (R). K says स्फटिकमणितटस्य विवरस्थेषु सलिलेषु बद्धानि कमलमुकुलानि यत्र तत् (प्रमदवनम्)। Kula is corrupt, but *SC* has विवरस्यित like K and MY. Laṭakanamisra reads *paḍia* for *phuḍia*, *maṇiala* for *maṇiaḍa*, and *raaṇa* for *salila*. He says पतितानां मणितलानां हरिन्मणीनां विवरस्थितैरवकाशावस्थितै रत्नैः बद्धानि पंकजमुकुलानि यत्र। हरिन्मणिस्थले जलाकारे रत्नद्युतयः पङ्कजमुकुलानीव दृश्यन्ते।

39. पेच्छन्ति अ सइसंठिअवअणविसंवइअथणणिसण्णकरअलम्।
दहवअणागमसङ्किअपअसदुप्पित्थलोअणं जणअसुअम्।।
[प्रेक्षन्ते च सदासंस्थितवदनविसंवादितस्तननिषण्णकरतलाम्।
दशवदनागमशङ्कितपदशब्दोत्पित्सलोचनां जनकसुताम्।।]

There they saw Sītā, with her eyes terror-stricken at the sound of their footsteps making her fear that Rāvaṇa might have come; while her hands lay on her bosom, having slipped from the face that had always rested on them.

K and MY read वितीर्ण (*viiṇṇa*) for *ṇisaṇṇa* (R and Kula). K reads वदनसंस्थित। He says सीतामपश्यंश्च। कथंभूताम – सदा शोकात् वदने

[13] Reference to the damage caused by Hanumat during his mission to Sītā.

स्थितं ततो विसंवादितं शिथिलितमित्यर्थः, स्तने वितीर्णमर्पितं करतलं यस्यास्ताम्। दशवदनागमशङ्कितत्वात् अन्यपदशब्देऽपि स एव पाप इति बुद्ध्या त्रस्तलोचनाम्।

MY and Kula read संस्थितवदन like R. MY says सवर्दा शोकेन स्वोपरि अवस्थितात् वदनात् विसंवादितमपनीतं स्तने दत्तं च करतलं यस्यास्ताम्। Kula says सदासंस्थितात् वदनात् विसंवादितम् आकृष्टम्। *SC* says सदासंस्थितादर्थात् करतलनिलीनात् वदनात्। R says विसंवादितं स्खलितम्।

40. पिअअमसहत्थपेसिअमणिसुण्णइअसिढिलद्धवेणीबन्धम्।
धोअकलधोअपाण्डुरपडन्तबाहपहउण्णअत्थणअलसम्।।

[प्रियतमस्वहस्तप्रेषितमणिशून्यीकृतशिथिलार्धवेणीबन्धाम्।
धौतकलधौतपाण्डुरपतद्बाष्पप्रहतोन्नतस्तनकलशाम्।।]

Her half-tied braid was loose, being stripped of the jewel, which she had sent to her beloved as a sign of recognition;[14] and her high bosom, white as refined silver, was drenched with streaming tears.

K and MY read एक for *addha* (R). K says स्वहस्तशब्देन अभिज्ञानद्रव्यमुच्यते। तथा विक्रमोर्वशीये राजा –

वासार्थं हर संभृतं सुरभिणा पौष्पं रजो वीरुधां
किं मिथ्या भवतो हृतेन दयितास्नेहस्वहस्तेन मे।
जानीते हि मनोविनोदनफलैरवंविधैर्धारितं
कामांर्तं जनमञ्जनां प्रति भवानालक्षितप्रार्थनः।।

इति। प्रियतमाय स्वहस्तत्वेन प्रेषितेन चूडामणिना शून्यीकृतशिथिलैकवेणीबन्धां, धौतकलधौतं विशुद्धरजतं तद्वत् पाण्डरैः पतद्भिः बाष्पैः आहतोन्नतस्तनकलशाम्। *SC* text has *paṇḍara* for *paṇḍura* (R). MY says प्रियतमं प्रति स्वहस्ततया प्रेषितेन मणिना शून्यीकृतः शिथिलश्चैकीभूतो वेणीबन्धो यस्यास्ताम्। Kula reads मणिवर for मणि, and वेणी for *addha-veṇī* (R). Cf. *SC* text.

41. अजमिअपम्हलवेणिं वाहजलपहाविआलओत्थइअमुहिम्।
रसणासुण्णणिअम्बं विच्छड्डिअमण्डणग्घविअलावण्णम्।।

[अयमितपक्ष्मलवेणीं बाष्पजलप्रधावितालकावस्तृतमुखीम्।
रसनाशून्यनितम्बां विच्छर्दितमण्डनार्घितलावण्याम्।।]

Her locks were unkempt and ruffled, and her face was covered with her tresses drenched with tears, and the hips

[14] See 1.39-42.

were without the girdle; but her beauty was heightened because she had discarded the ornaments.

K, MY and Kula *pratīka* has *aamia* for *ajamia* (R). K (*chāyā*) has धूसरदीर्घतरालकावस्तृतमुखीं . . . परित्यक्तमण्डनार्पितलावण्याम् K says अयमितत्वात् असंस्कृतत्वात् पक्ष्मलवेणीं, पक्ष्मशब्देन केशाग्राण्युच्यन्ते, केशाग्रैर्बहुलवेणीम्। धूसरै रजोबहुलैः दीर्घतरैरलकैः छादितमुखीम्। रशनाशून्यनितम्बां, परित्यक्तमण्डनत्वेऽपि पुञ्जितलावण्यां प्रकाशितकान्तिविशेषाम्।

MY says अयमितत्वादेव पक्ष्मला उच्छ्वासितकेशान्ता वेणीयस्यास्ताम्। धूसरितदीर्घ-तरालकावस्थगितमखीं[15], विच्छर्दितेन विगलितेन मण्डनेन स्थितसहजलावण्यां छादकाभावादित्याशयः। K and MY seem to read *dhūsaria dīha-arālaotthaia-muhiṁ* for *bāha-jala-pahāviā*⁰ (R). Kula's reading is same as R's, but he says बाष्पजलावमलिनितेन अलकेनावस्थगितं मुखं यस्याः (ताम्)। He reads अवमलिनित (*omailia*, cf. *SC* text) for *pahāvia* (प्रधावित)। He renders *agghavia* as अर्घित बहुमत।

42. थोअमउआअअट्ठिअपिअअमगअहिअअसुण्णणिच्चलणअणम्।
कइवलसद्दाअण्णणवाहतरङ्गपरिघोलमाणपहरिसम्।।

[स्तोकमुकुलायतस्थितप्रियतमगतहृदयशून्यनिश्चलनयनाम्।
कपिबलशब्दाकर्णनबाष्पतरङ्गपरिघूर्णमानप्रहर्षाम्।।]

Her partly closed, dilated eyes were motionless and vacant, her heart being absorbed in her beloved; while joy flickered in the ripples of her tears as she heard the noise of the host of apes.

K and MY read मुकुलीकृत for *maüāaa* (मुकुलायत) found in R and Kula. *SC* text has *maülā*°. K says स्तोकं मुकुलीकृतस्थितं प्रियतमगतेन हृदयेन शून्यत्वात् निश्चलं नयनं यस्यास्ताम्। कपिसैन्यशब्दस्याकर्णनेन बाष्पतरङ्गेषु परिघूर्णमानप्रहर्षां प्रकाशमानहर्षामित्यर्थः। MY says *maülāvia* मुकुलीकृत। . . . बाष्पतरङ्गेषु परिस्फुरन् प्रहर्षो यस्यास्ताम्। जातानन्दबाष्पामित्यर्थः। Kula says स्तोकमुकुलत्वात् आयतस्थिते . . . नयने यस्याः ताम्। . . . बाष्पतरङ्गेषु परिघूर्णमानो गतागतं कुर्वन् प्रहर्षा यस्यास्ताम्। R says स्तोकमीषन्मुकुलिते अत एवायतस्थिते दीर्घीभूते।

43. ईसरअभिण्णपाडलवसुआअप्फरुसवाहबिन्दुट्ठाणम्।
विच्छड्डिअपरिधूसरणिअअसहावपरिसंठिआहरराअम्।।

[ईषद्रजोभिन्नपाटलशुष्कपरुषबाष्पबिन्दुस्थानम्।
विच्छर्दितपरिधूसरनिजकस्वभावपरिसंस्थिताधररागम्।।]

[15] Our copy has अवस्थितमुखीं।

The traces of her tear-drops, partly mingling with the dust on her body, were pale red, dry and coarse; while her unadorned and pallid lips revealed their natural hue.

K reads क्षालितव्य (*khāliavva* ?) for *vicchaḍḍia* = त्यक्त (R and Kula). The word occurs in verse 41 also. K says ईषत् रजसा भिन्नं मिश्रम् अतएव पाटलं शुष्कं परुषं च बाष्पबिन्दुस्थानं बाष्पबिन्दूनां पतनस्थानं यस्यास्ताम्। क्षालितव्यधूसर: क्षालनयोग्यमिलन: निजस्वभावेन परित: स्थित: अधररागो यस्यास्ताम्।

44. वअणं समुव्वहन्ति ओलुग्गकओलणिव्वलन्ताआमम्।
असमत्तकलादीहं कइदिअहासण्णपूरिअव्वं व ससिम्।।

[वदनं समुद्वहन्तीमवरुग्णकपोलनिर्वलदायामम्।
असमस्तकलादीर्घं कतिदिवसासन्नपूरयितव्यमिव शशिनम्।।]

Her face appeared to be drawn out because of her worn cheeks, and resembled a crescent moon that fills out in the course of a few days.

K and MY read कतिपयाहासन्न for *kai-diahāsaṇṇa* = कतिदिवसा° (R and Kula).

K says अवरुग्णकपोलत्वात् शुष्ककपोलत्वात् व्यज्यमानायामं, कला: चन्द्रभागा:, असमाप्तकलत्वात् दीर्घं, कतिपयैरहोभिरासन्नम् अचिरात् पूरयितव्यं शशिनमिव वदनं वहन्तीम्। K (*chāyā*) has निर्व्यज्यमान् for *ṇivvalanta*. MY takes *pūriavva* as a noun — कतिपयैरहोभिरतिप्रत्यासन्नपूरणं शशिनमिवेत्यर्थ:। Kula also says कतिभिरपि दिवसै: संनिहितपूरणम्। He rendrs *ṇivvalanta* as निष्पद्यमान and says अवरुग्णकपोलत्वात् निष्पद्यमान आयामो दैर्घ्यं यस्य तत् वदनम्। R says निर्वलन् स्पष्टीभवन् आयाम:।[16]

45. देहच्छविणिव्वलिए भिण्णदरुव्वत्तरोअणासच्छाए।
भूसणबन्धणमग्गे लक्खिज्जन्ततलिणत्तणे वहमाणम्।।

[देहच्छविनिर्वलितान्भिन्नदरोद्वृत्तरोचनासच्छायान्।
भूषणबन्धनमार्गांल्लक्ष्यमाणतलिनत्वान्वहमानाम्।।]

She had on her the faint traces of her (discarded) ornaments, made distinct by the lustre of her body, and resembling yellow pigment applied to the body, but slightly rubbed off.

---

[16] Hemacandra gives *nivvalaï* for निष्पद्यते (4.128), and *ṇivvaḍaï* in the sense of पृथक् स्पष्टो वा भवति (4.62)।

K, MY and Kula read दत्त for *bhiṇṇa* (R). K and MY read म्लान (*uvvāa*) for *uvvatta* = उद्वृत्त = (R). Cf. Notes on 8.2. K and Kula read तलिनस्थितान् for *taliṇattaṇe* = तलिनत्वात् (R).

R says देहस्य स्वभावसिद्धा या छविर्गौरता तया निर्वलितान् पृथग्भूय प्रकाशमानान्।

K says देहवर्णात् पृथग्भूतान् (देहच्छविनिर्व्यक्तान् *chāyā*), दत्तया निहितया दरम्लानया रोचनया समानच्छायान्, लक्ष्यमाणावस्थायां तलिनस्थितान् तनुतरस्थितान् भूषणविन्यासप्रदेशान् वहन्तीम्। MY says दत्तया न्यस्तया ईषत् (म्ला)नया रोचनया सच्छायान् Kula says लक्ष्यमाणं तलिनं तनुकं स्थितं स्थानं येषां तान् वहमानाम्। The rest of Kula is corrupt. *SC* says दरमीषत् उद्वृत्ता दूरीकृता या रोचना।

46. दट्ठव्वचडुलणअणं उवऊहणलालसप्फुरिअवाहुलअम्।
आसण्णट्ठिअदइअं रसेण एक्कसअणम्मि व विसूरन्तिम्।।

[द्रष्टव्यचटुलनयनामुपगूहनलालसस्फुरितबाहुलताम्।
आसन्नस्थितदयितां रसेनैकशयन इव खिद्यमानाम्।।]

With her beloved close at hand,[17] she was pining, with her eyes longing to see him, and her quivering arms eager to embrace him; even like an offended lady suffering on account of love, with her beloved close to her in the bed.[18]

K reads लोलप्रस्फुरित for *lālasa-pphuria* (R and Kula).

K says द्रष्टव्ये राघवे चटुलनयनाम्, उपगूहनाय लोला लम्पटा स्फुरिता च बाहुलता यस्यास्ताम्। आसन्नस्थितप्रियतमाम् एकत्र शयन इव रसेन खिद्यमानाम्। भर्त्रा सहैकशयनगता वनिता केनचित् कारणेन पराङ्मुखीभूतत्वात् ततो रसेन प्रियोपभोगलोलुपा यथा खिद्यते तथा खिद्यमानामित्यर्थः।

Kula reads अवगूहन (*oūhaṇa*, cf. *SC* text) for *uva°* (उपगूहन)। MY says दर्शनमेव द्रष्टव्यं तदुत्सुकनयनाम्। आसन्नदयितामित्युक्तत्वात् दर्शनोपगूहने दयितस्यैवेति लभ्यते। *SC* says रसेनानुरागेण।

47. दूसहमिअङ्कदंसणदुउणअरुक्कण्ठणीसहणिसण्णङ्गिम्।
गअजीविअपरिसङ्किअणिसिअरिहत्थपरिमट्ठणिच्चलहिअअम्।।

[दुःसहमृगाङ्कदर्शनद्विगुणतरोत्कण्ठानिःसहनिषण्णाङ्गीम्।
गतजीवितपरिशङ्कितनिशिचरीहस्तपरिमृष्टनिश्चलहृदयाम्।।]

---

[17] I.e. outside the walls of Laṅkā.

[18] The imagery is that of a *māninī* who keeps aloof from her offending husband, but secretly yearns for him. Literally as if suffering on account of love, etc.

Her limbs were languid and drooping because of redoubled anguish at the sight of the unbearable moon;[19] and her inert bosom was felt by the female demons, fearing she was dead.

SC text read *viuṇa* for *duuṇa* (द्विगुण)।

48. हत्थेण वाहगरुइअदूरपलम्बालओत्थएण वहन्तिम्।
पिअपेसिणङ्गुलीअअमणिप्पहापाअडेक्कपासं व मुहम्।।

[हस्तेन बाष्पगुरूकृतदूरप्रलम्बालकावस्तृतेन वहन्तीम्।
प्रियप्रेषिताङ्गुलीयकमणिप्रभाप्रकटैकपार्श्वमिव मुखम्।।]

Her face seemed to be covered, on one side, with the lustre of the (blue) gems of the ring, sent by her beloved,[20] because she rested it on her hand covered with her flowing tresses, drenched with tears.

K, MY and Kula read प्रावृत (*pāvia*) for *pāaḍa* (प्रकट) found in R who mentions the former reading as a variant.

Kula says प्रियप्रेषितस्याङ्गुलीयकस्य मणेर्नीलवर्णस्येत्यर्थात् प्रभया प्रावृतैकपार्श्वमिव मुखं वहन्तीम्।

My reads *alaotthaaṁ vahamāṇiṁ*, and says अलकैरवस्तृतं, रामेण स्वहस्ततया[21] प्रेषितस्याङ्गुलीयकस्येन्द्रनीलप्रभाभि: प्रावृतैकपार्श्वमिव मुखं वहन्तीम्। अत्रेवशब्द: चार्थे। अलकैश्च मणिप्रभाभिश्च अवच्छादितमित्यर्थ:। *alaotthaeṇa vahaṇtiṁ* इति पाठे तु अवस्तृतेनावस्तरणेनैवंभूतमिव लक्ष्यमाणमिति व्याख्येयम्। अत्र तु अङ्गुलीयकमणिप्रभाणामपि परमार्थत: सत्त्वादुपमानवैयर्थ्यदोष इति विभावनीयम्।

K says बाष्पेण गुरुकत्वात् दूरप्रलम्बैरलकैरवस्तृतेन छन्नेन हस्तेन धृतत्वात् प्रियेण प्रेषितस्य हनुमता दत्तस्य अङ्गुलीयस्य हस्तगतस्य सम्बन्धिनो मणेरिन्द्रनीलमयस्य प्रभया प्रावृतैकपार्श्वमिव दृश्यमानं मुखं दधानाम्।

49. आसण्णजुज्जविमणं रामभुआसङ्गणिट्ठविअसंतावम्।
हिअआवलिअदहमुहं किं मण्णे होहिइ त्ति विमुहिज्जन्तिम्।।

[आसन्नयुद्धविमनसं रामभुजाध्यवसायनिष्ठापितसंतापाम्।
हृदयापतितदशमुखां किं मन्ये भविष्यतीति विमुह्यन्तीम्।।]

She was disquieted by the impending battle, but her anxiety

[19] Unbearable because she was *virahiṇī*.

[20] Brought by Hanumat on his mission to Sītā.

[21] See verse 40 above.

was stifled by her confidence in Rāma's arms. But when Rāvaṇa came to her mind, she was in a puzzle about what would come to pass.

K, MY and Kula read कथं (*kaha*) for किं (R). K says आसन्नात् युद्धात् विमनसं, रामभुजबलविश्वासेन पृथग्भूतसंतापाम् (निर्व्यक्तसंतापाम् *chāyā*), सहसा हृदयापतितरावणां हृदयगतरावणप्रतापाम्, रावणेन सह युद्धे कथं भविष्यति नूनमिति मुह्यन्तीम् (विमुह्यन्तीम् *chāyā*)।

K reads *ṇivaḍia* for *ṇiṭṭhavia* = निष्ठापित (R). My reads *ṇivvavia* (निर्वापित)। R says रामभुजयोरध्यवसायेन निष्ठापितो नाशितो युद्धे किं स्यादित्यादिसंतापो यस्यास्ताम्। MY says *āsaṁgha* आशंस निश्चय इत्यर्थः। कथं भविष्यतीति मन्य इति भङ्गोऽपि संभाव्यत इति पश्यामीति विमुखीभवन्तीम्। Kula says कथं मन्ये भविष्यतीति किं रामो जेष्यति रावणो वति विमुह्यमानाम्। The rest of Kula is corrupt, but *SC* reproduces him. He reads *ṇivvavia* like MY and says रामभुजाशाबन्धेन निर्वापितसंतापाम्।

50. समुहालोअणविडिअं विडिअणिमिल्लपिअदंसणुसुअहिअअम्।
ऊसुअहिअउम्मिल्लं उम्मिल्लोसरि अपइमुहकिलिम्मन्तिम्।।
(आइकुलकम्)

[संमुखालोकनव्रीडितां व्रीडितनिमीलितप्रियदर्शनोत्सुकहृदयाम्।
उत्सुकहृदयोन्मीलितामुन्मीलितापसृतपतिमुखक्लाम्यन्तीम्।।]
(आदिकुलकम्)

She was abashed to see Rāma before her (in her imagination); but when she closed her eyes in abashment, her heart became eager to see her beloved again. She opened her eyes in the eagerness of her heart, but became sad as the face of her consort vanished with the opening of the eyes.

Kula says रामस्य विरहेऽपीयच्चिरं जीवामिति संमुखालोकने व्रीडितां, व्रीडितनिमीलितं च लज्जासंकुचितं च प्रियदर्शनोत्सुकं च हृदयं यस्याः ताम्, उत्सुकेन हृदयेनोन्मीलितां विकासितामुल्लासितामित्यर्थः, रामरावणयोः वीर्यपर्यालोचने उन्मीलितं चापसृतं च पतिमुखं यस्याः सा चासौ क्लाम्यन्ती चेति तथा ताम्। R says उन्मीलितेन नयनोन्मीलनेन भावनापरित्यागादपसृतेऽदृष्टे सति पतिमुखे क्लाम्यन्तीम्। K reads रतिसुख for *pai-muha* (R and Kula). K says संकल्पमयस्य परितः स्थितस्य प्रियस्य सहसा संमुखालोकनेन व्रीडितां, व्रीडया निमीलितनयनत्वान् प्रियस्य संकल्पमयस्य दर्शनोत्सुकहृदयाम्, उत्सुकहृदयत्वात् पुनरुन्मीलितनयनाम्, उन्मीलितनयनावस्थायां संकल्पभ्रंशादपसृतेन नष्टेन रतिसुखेन क्लाम्यन्तीं सीतां ददृशुः।

MY's reading seems to be same as K's. He says उन्मीलिते सति अपगतसमागमतया खिद्यन्तीमित्यर्थः।

51. दट्ठूण अ णं दूमिअहिअअपहोलन्तसंभरिअकाअव्वा।
अल्लीणा माआमअरामसिरुल्लअणकाअरा रअणिअरा।।

[दृष्ट्वा चैनां दूनहृदयप्रघूर्णमानसंस्मृतकर्तव्याः।
आलीना मायामयरामशिरउल्लयनकातरा रजनीचराः।।]

The demons recalled their task that was slipping from their minds, saddened on seeing her, and drew near, loth to present to her the magic head of Rāma.

K says सीतां च दृष्ट्वा तस्यास्तथाविधक्लेशातिशयदर्शनात् परितप्ते हृदये प्रघूर्णमानं प्रभ्रश्यमानं पुनः संस्मृतं कर्तव्यं येषां ते रजनिचराः मायामयरामशिरआनयनेन कातरा विक्लवा भूत्वा आलीनाः सीतासमीपमाश्रिताः।

MY (probably K also) reads *alliaṇa* explained as प्रापण for *ullaaṇa* found in R who says उल्लयनेऽर्पणे कातराः। Kula says रामशिरसः अर्पणे कातरा व्यथितहृदयाः He seems to read *alliaṇa* which is the manuscript reading of *SC* text. See editor's fn. MY says *paholanta* प्रघूर्णमान विस्मृतेति यावत्।

52. अह तेहि तीअ पुरओ छेअसमुव्वत्तमासदिण्णावेढम्।
ठविअं राहववअणं लुअमज्झविलग्गवामहत्थं च धणुम्।।

[अथ तैस्तस्याः पुरतश्छेदसमुद्वृत्तमांसदत्तावेष्टम्।
स्थापितं राघववदनं लूनमध्यविलग्नवामहस्तं च धनुः।।]

They then placed before her Rāma's head, with the flesh swollen all round on account of the cut; also a bow with the severed left hand attached to the middle.

K says (छेद)प्रदेशे समुद्वृत्तेन मांसेन समुद्गतेन दत्तावैष्टम् आवेष्टितं राघववदनम्। My says लूनश्च धनुर्मध्ये विलग्नश्च वामहस्तो यस्य तत्तथा। Kula says छेदसंभृतेन अथोद्गतेन मांसेन। R says छेदेन कर्तनेन समुदवृत्तमुच्छ्वसितं यत् मांसं तेन। Kula seems to read *ālagga* for *vilagga*.

53. आलोइए विसण्णा उवणिज्जन्तम्मि वेविउं आढत्ता।
सीआ रअणिअरेहि रामसिर त्ति भणिए गअ च्चिअ मोहम्।।

[आलोकिते विषण्णोपनीयमाने वेपितुमारब्धा।
सीता रजनीचरै रामशिर इति भणिते गतैव मोहम्।।]

Sītā was seized with grief when she espied it, and began to tremble as the demons brought it near, and fainted when they said it was Rāma's head.

54. पडिआ अ हत्थसिढिलिअणिरोहपण्डरसमूलसन्तकवोला।
पेल्लिअवामपओहरविसमुण्णअदाहिणत्थणी जणअसुआ।।

[पतिता च हस्तशिथिलितनिरोधपाण्डुरसमुच्छ्वसत्कपोला।
प्रेरितवामपयोधरविषमोन्नतदक्षिणस्तनी जनकसुता।।]

She fell with her left breast pressed on the ground, and the right raised and slanting, and the pale cheeks filling out, being released from the grip of her hands.

K reads विरहापाण्डर for *ṇiroha-paṇḍara* (R and Kula). K says शोकात् शश्वन्निहितेन हस्तेन करतलेन तदानीं शिथिलितत्वात् विमुक्तत्वात् उच्छ्वसन् उन्नमन् विरहापाण्डरः कपोलो यस्याः सा। वामपार्श्वेन पतनात् भुवि पीडितवामपयोधरा अतएव विषमोन्नतदक्षिणस्तनी भूत्वा सीता पतिता च। *SC* says समुच्छ्वसन् यन्त्रणापायादुच्छूनतां गच्छन् कपोलो यस्याः। MY says पूर्वमाधारतया स्थापितेन हस्तेन पीडितावस्थितमिदानीं तदपगमात् प्रकृतिस्थं सत् कपोलं यस्याः सा तथा Kula says वामपयोधरेण भूमिनिषण्णेन प्रेरिता धृता च सा विषमोन्नत(दक्षिण)स्तनी चेति तथाभूता जनकसुता पतिता च। It will be seen that Kula puts *pellia* after *paöhara*, cf. *SC* text.

55. मरणम्मि बन्धवाणं जणस्स किं होइ बन्धवो च्चिअ सरणम्।
तह गुरुसोअकवलिआ धरम्मि पडिआ विमुच्छिआ धरणिसुआ।।

[मरणे बान्धवानां जनस्य किं भवति बान्धव एव शरणम्।
तथा गुरुशोककवलिता धरायां पतिता विमूर्छिता धरणिसुता।।]

At the death of one's kinsfolk, the kindred alone become one's refuge. Hence, the daughter of the Earth[22] swooned, and fell on the earth, overwhelmed with so great a grief.

The verse is not found in K, MY and Kula, nor in Deva, *SC* and Laṭakana.

56. ण कओ वाहविमुक्खो णिव्वण्णेउं पि ण चइअं रामसिरम्।
णवर पडिवण्णमोहा गअजीविअणीसहा महिम्मि णिसण्णा।।

---

[22] I.e. Sītā.

[न कृतो बाष्पविमोक्षो निर्वर्णयितुमपि न शकितं रामशिरः।
केवलं प्रतिपन्नमोहा गतजीवितनिःसहा मह्यां निषण्णा।।]

She shed no tears nor could even look at Rāma's head. Having fainted, she only sank to the ground, helpless like one dead.

K says गतजीवितेन निःसहा विह्वला। MY says जीवनं हि मनःशरीरधारणं,[23] तस्य गमनं नाम सुषुप्तवदिन्द्रियात्मप्रदेशेऽवस्थानं संज्ञाविरह इति यावत्।

57. खणणिच्चलणीसासं जाअं मोहन्धआरसामच्छाअम्।
विरलमिलिअच्छिवत्तं मुच्छाहीरन्ततारअं तीअ मुहम्।।

[क्षणनिश्चलनिश्वासं जातं मोहान्धकारश्यामच्छायम्।
विरलमिलिताक्षिपत्रं मूर्छाह्रियमाणतारकं तस्या मुखम्।।]

Her face was clouded by the gloom of unconsciousness, with the breath still for a moment, the eyelashes partly joined, and the pupils rolling in her swoon.

K reads पक्ष्म (*pamha*) for *vatta* = पत्र (R and Kula). K says तदानीं तस्या मुखं क्षणनिश्चलनिश्वासं, मोहान्धकारेण श्यामीकृतवर्णं, विरलघटिताक्षिपक्ष्म, मूर्च्छया व्यपनीयमानतारकं जातम्। R says विरलमल्पं मिलिते किंचित् मुद्रिते अक्षिपत्रे पक्ष्मणी यत्र।

58. विसरिअविओअदुक्खं तक्खणपब्भट्ठरामरणाआसम्।
जणअतणआइ णवरं लद्धं मुच्छाणिमीलिअच्छीअ सुहम्।।

[विस्मृतवियोगदुःखं तत्क्षणप्रभ्रष्टराममरणायासम्।
जनकतनया केवलं लब्धं मूर्छानिमीलिताक्ष्या सुखम्।।]

With eyes closed as she swooned, she felt only bliss free from the pangs of separation, with the sorrow caused by Rāma's death forgotten for the moment.

K, MY and Kula read *vialia* (विलगित) for *visaria* (विस्मृत) found in R; and वेदना (*viaṇā*) for *dukkhaṁ* (R), i.e. विगलितवियोगवेदनं as found in K (*chāyā*) and Kula.

K (*chāyā*) has प्रमुषित (विस्मृत commentary) for *pabbhaṭṭha* (प्रभ्रष्ट) found in R and Kukla. K's reading is same as that of MY who says *pamhuṭṭha* प्रस्मृत। Manuscript C of Goldschmidt reads

[23] Our copy has शरीरे।

pamhaṭṭha. R explains प्रभ्रष्ट as प्रस्मृत। K explains *ṇavaraṁ* as अनन्तरम्। R and Kula have केवलम्। Hemacandra 2.187, 188 gives *ṇavara* (*v. r. ṇavaraṁ*) in the sense of केवल and *ṇavari* in that of आनन्तर्य, but says that acording to some उभावप्युभयार्थौं।

K says मूर्च्छानिमीलिताक्ष्या सीतया अनन्तरं निद्रायमाणयेव सुखं लब्धम्। कीदृशं – विगलितभर्तृविरहव्यथं, तत्क्षणमेव विस्मृतराममरणदुःखम्।

59. थणपरिणाहोत्थइए तीए हिअअम्मि पअणुअं पि ण दिट्ठम्।
दीहं पि समूससिअं सूइज्जइ णवर वेविरे अहरोट्ठे।।

[स्तनपरिणाहावस्थगिते तस्या हृदये प्रतनुकमपि न दृष्टम्।
दीर्घमपि समुच्छ्वसितं सूच्यते केवलं वेपनशीलेऽधरोष्ठे।।]

On her bosom covered with the breasts, even her deep breathing was not observed in the least; it was only on her quivering lower lip that it was discerned.

K and Kula read परिणाहस्थगिते (*pariṇāha-tthaie* for °*ho*° (अवस्थगिते) found in R. K reads विषमोच्छ्वसितं for *pi samūsasiaṁ* (R and Kula).

60. अपरिप्फुडणीसासा तो सा मोहविरमे वि णीसहपडिआ।
अणुवज्झबाहगरुइअदुक्खसमुव्वूढतारअं उम्मिल्ला।।

[अपरिस्फुटनिश्वासा ततः सा मोहविरामेऽपि निःसहपतिता।
अनुबद्धबाष्पगुरूकृतदुःखसमुद्व्यूढतारकमुन्मीलिता।।]

She lay weary on the ground even at the end of her swoon, breathing faintly; and opened her eyes, with the pupils slowly rolling, and bedewed with streaming tears.

K, MY and Kula read बध्यमान (*bajjhanta*) for *aṇuvajjha* (अनुबद्ध) found in R. K reads समुद्वृत्त (*samuvvatta*) for *samuvūḍha* (R). Kula reads समुद्गूढ।

K says ततः अपरिस्फुटनिश्वासा सा मोहविरामेऽपि निःसहत्वात् अतिविह्वलत्वात् पतिता सती बध्यमानेन समुत्पतता बाष्पेण गुरूकृता दुःखेन कृच्छ्रेण समुद्वृत्ता पुनरावृत्ता तारका यथा भवति। तथोन्मीलिता।

MY says निःसह विवशः। बध्यमानः उत्पाद्यमानः। जायमानबाष्पगुरुतया कृच्छ्रेण उन्मीलिता तारका यथा स्यात् तथा।

R says दुःखेन समुद्व्यूढे उत्तानिते तारके गोलके यत्र तद् यथा स्यात्।

61. पेच्छइ अ सरहसोहरिअमण्डलग्गाहिघाअविसमच्छिण्णम्।
दूरधणुसंधिअञ्चिअसरपुङ्खालिद्धसामलिअआवङ्गम्।।

[पश्यति च सरभसावहृतमण्डलाग्राभिघातविषमच्छिन्नम्।
दूरधनुःसंहिताञ्चितशरपुङ्खालीढश्यामलितापाङ्गम्।।]

She beheld Rāma's head roughly lopped off by the impact of a forceful sword, the corners of the eyes being blackened by friction with the feathers of the arrows, drawn full length as they were fixed in the bow.

K and MY read संघान-ऋजूकृत (probably *saṁdhaṇujjua*)[24] for *saṁdhiañcia* (R). See below.

K says दूरं भृशं धनुषि संधानार्थमृजूक्रियमाणस्य शरस्य पुङ्खेन स्पृष्टत्वात् श्यामलितापाङ्गम्। अथवा धनुःसंधानोद्यतशरपुङ्खेति पाठः। दूरं धनुषि संधानवेलायाम् उद्यतस्योत्कृष्टस्य शरस्य पुङ्खेन स्पृष्टश्यामलितापाङ्गं रामशिरः पश्यति स्मेति संबन्धः। MY says क्रियमाणस्य धनुःसंधानस्य ऋजुः अतएव शरपुङ्खेन स्पृष्टः श्यामलितश्च आपाङ्गो यस्य तत्तथा।

R says दूरं व्याप्य धनुःसंहिताञ्चितस्य धनुरारोपिताकृष्टस्य शरस्य, etc. Kula also says धनुःसंहिताकृष्टस्य शरस्य। *SC* text has *aḍḍhia*[25] (आकृष्ट) for *añcia* in the same sense. Cf Hemacandra 4.187.

K says सरभसमपहृतस्य निपातितस्य मण्डलाग्रस्य खड्गस्याभिघातेन प्रहारेण विषमच्छिन्नं विषमच्छिन्नकण्ठम्।

MY says *oharia* अवगूरित व्यापारितेति यावत्। Kula also says व्यापारितस्य मण्डलाग्रस्य।

62. णिव्वूढरुहिरपण्डुरमउलन्तच्छेअमासपेल्लिअविवरम्।
भज्जन्तपडिअपहरणकण्ठच्छेअदरलग्गधाराचुण्णम्।।

[निर्व्यूढरुधिरपाण्डुरमुकुलायमानच्छेदमांसप्रेरितविवरम्।
भज्यमानपतितप्रहरणकण्ठच्छेददरलग्नधाराचूर्णम्।।]

The passage of the throat was blocked by the flesh, shrinking around the cut, and grown pale from bleeding; while the saffron powder on the blade of the sword had partly

[24] For *saṁdhaṇa* see *Païa-sadda-mahaṇṇavo* sub voce. Cf. विधनं for विधानं in Aśoka's Rock Edict XIII.

[25] The manuscript reading of *SC* text according to the editor's fn. is *aṭṭhia*. This form is provided in *Sañjīvanī* on Vararuci, p. 336.

adhered to the slit in the neck, when the weapon menacingly descended upon it.

K, MY and Kula read *tajjanta* for *bhajjana* = भज्यमान (R). K and MY read प्रति for दर (R).

K says निर्व्यूढरुधिरत्वात् निर्गतरुधिरत्वात् पाण्डरेण ईषत्पाण्डुना मुकुलीभवता छेदमांसेन छेदप्रदेशमांसेन पीडितविवरं रुद्धकण्ठनालं, तर्जयत्पतितस्य पतनरभसात् तर्जनं कुर्वतः पतितस्य प्रहरणस्य खड्गस्य कण्ठच्छेदे प्रतिलग्नं धाराचूर्णं खड्गस्य धारागतं चूर्णं कुङ्कमादिरजी यस्य तत्। MY says तर्जयतः अभिभवतः पतितात् खड्गात् कण्ठच्छेदमार्गे प्रतिलग्नं धारानिहितं चूर्णं यस्य तत्तथा।

My (*pratīka*) has *ṇivvūḍha* like R and K, but he says निर्वान्तः निर्गतः।

Kula reads तट for दर। He says गलितरुधिरत्वात्(?) पाण्डरं च तत्, संकुचता छेदमांसेन प्रेरितविवरं चेति। तथा तर्ज्यमानं सत्, पतितप्रहरणस्य कण्ठच्छेदतटे लग्नं धाराचूर्णं यत्र तत् तथा।

K and Kula seem to read *paṇḍara* for *paṇḍura* (R).

63. णिद्दअसंदट्ठाहरमूलुक्खित्तदरदिट्ठदाढाहीरम्।
संखाअसोणिअप्पङ्कपडलपूरेन्तकसणकण्ठच्छेअम्।।

[निर्दयसंदष्टाधरमूलोत्क्षिप्तदरदृष्टदंष्ट्राहीरम्।
संस्त्यानशोणितपङ्कपटलपूर्यमाणकृष्णकण्ठच्छेदम्।।]

The tips of the teeth were slightly visible, clenched at the root of the severely bitten lower lip; while the gash in the throat was black, being filled with a lump of gore.

K reads मग्न[26] for *ukkhitta* = उत्क्षिप्त (R). K and MY read *saṁghāa* for *saṁkhāa* (R) = संस्त्यान। K (*chāyā*) has संघात। K (commentary) says संहतेन शोणितपङ्कपटलेन पूर्यमाणकृष्णकण्ठच्छेदम्।

K says निर्दयं संदष्टस्याधरस्य मूले मग्नदरदृष्टदन्तवज्रम्। MY reads *ukkhāa* for *ukkhitta*. He says रोषेण संदाष्टाधरमूलादुत्खातं शिथिलमीषदृष्टं च दंष्ट्रावज्रं यस्य। अथवा मूलखातेति पाठः। तदा मूललग्नेत्यर्थः। *saṁghāa* संस्त्यान K remarks हीरशब्दो वज्रपर्यायः। वज्रं रत्नभेदः। R says दंष्ट्राहीरकं दंष्ट्राग्रम्।

Kula reads *mūla-kkhitta* as he says अधरमूले क्षिप्तं लग्नम्। He reads the second line differently. He says संस्त्यानेन शोणितोत्पीडेन बहलः पूर्यमाणः कृष्णकण्ठच्छेदो यस्य तत्, i.e. *soṇiuppīla-bahala* for *soṇiappaṅka-paḍala*.

[26] *I.e.* °*kkhutta*, cf *paṁka-kkhuttaṁ* 3.51.

64. णिसिअरकअग्गहाणिअणिलाडअडणट्ठभिउडिभुमआभङ्गम्।
गलिअरुहिरद्धलहुअं अणहिअउम्मिल्लतारअं रामशिरम्।।
(कुलअम्)

[निशाचरकचग्रहानीतललाटतटनष्टभ्रुकुटिभ्रूभङ्गम्।
गलितरुधिरार्धलघुकमहृदयोन्मीलत्तारकं रामशिरः।।]
(कुलकम्)

The frown and the movement of the eyebrows seemed to have disappeared from the forehead, while it was brought by the demons, seizing it by the hair; and it had become lighter from loss of blood, with the pupils fixed in a lifeless stare.

K reads रुधिरप्रलघुकं (i.e.°*ppalahuaṁ*) for *ruhiraddhalahuaṁ* (R and Kula). K says निशिचरैः कचग्रहेण अनीतत्वात् क्वचेषु प्रगूह्यनीतत्वात् ललाटतटे नष्टा भ्रुकुटिः रेखात्रयं भ्रूभङ्गश्च यस्य तत्। गलितरुधिरत्वात् प्रलघुकम्, अहृदयत्वात् ऊर्ध्वगततारकं रामशिरः पश्यति स्म। अथवा अनधिगतोन्मीलिततारकमिमि पाठः। Kula says अहृदयं हृदयानधिष्ठितमुन्मीलितं तारकं यत्र तत्। R says अहृदयमचैतन्यादनभिप्रायम्।

MY says कचग्रहानीततया ललाटतटे नष्टो रोषोद्धतया भ्रकुटीरूपयोः भ्रुवोर्भङ्गो यत्रेति।

65. तह णिमिअ च्चिअ दिट्ठी मुक्ककवोलविहुरो उर च्चिअ हत्थो।
गअजीविअणिच्चेट्ठा णवरं सा महिअलं थणभरेण गआ।।

[तथा नियोजितैव दृष्टिर्मुक्तकपोलविधुर उरस्येव हस्तः।
गतजीवितनिश्चेष्टा केवलं सा महीतलं स्तनभरेण गता।।]

Her eyes remained fixed on the head as before, and her weary hand, leaving the cheeks, rested on her bosom. Inert like a corpse, she only sank to the ground[27] under the weight of her breasts.

K and Kula read एव करः (i.e. *ccea karo*) for *ccia hattho* (R).

K says तस्या दृष्टिर्दर्शनात् प्रभृति तस्मिन् तथैव निहिता। प्रागेव मुक्तकपोलो विधुरो वेपमानः करः उरस्येव निहितः। MY says निमिता निश्चलेत्यर्थः। विधुरः विवश। स्तनभरो यत्र वलति तत्रैव पतिता न तु स्वबुद्ध्येत्यर्थः।

---

[27] The poet overlooks the fact that she was already prostrate in state of exhaustion, as described in verse 60.

Kula says तथा मिलितैव रामशिरसि . . . दृष्टिः। He says अनन्तरं च सा महीतलं, etc. He reads *navari a* (cf. *SC* text) for *navaraṁ* (केवलम्)।

66. सो मुच्छिउट्ठिआए किं एअं ति गअणे दिसासु अ समअम्।
सुण्णपरिघोलिअच्छं जाअं मूढपरिदेविअं तीअ मुहम्।।

[ततो मूर्छितोत्थितायाः किमेतदिति गगने दिक्षु च समकम्।
शून्यपरिघूर्णिताक्षं जातं मूढपरिदेवितं तस्या मुखम्।।]

When she rose up after having swooned, her visage bore the imprint of silent mourning, with the listless eyes rolling simultaneously in different directions, and towards the sky; wondering what it all could be.

K says ततो मूर्च्छितायाः पश्चादुत्थितायाः किमिदमिति भ्रान्त्या गगने दिक्षु च समं शून्यं लक्षहीनं घूर्णितं भ्रमितमक्षि यस्य तत् तस्या मुखं मूढपरिदेवितम् अव्यक्तपरिदेवितं जातम्। न तु मुक्तकण्ठं रोदितं शक्ताभूदित्यर्थः। MY says वचःस्तम्भेन सतोऽपि परिदेवितस्य अनभिव्यक्तेः उन्नेयपरिदेवितं जातमित्यर्थः।

67. णिव्वण्णेऊण अणं तत्तोहुत्तट्ठिओसिअन्तणिसण्णो।
काङ्क्षन्तीअ ण पत्तो वअणं मरणं च से कह वि अप्पाणो।।

[निर्वर्ण्य चैतत्ततोऽभिमुखस्थितावसीदन्निःसंज्ञः।
काङ्क्षन्त्या अपि न प्राप्तो वचनं मरणं चास्या कथमप्यात्मा।।]

Languid and drooping as she confronted the head, she found no words nor death, even though, on seeing it, she had longed for both.

K reads ततोमुखोत्थितावसीदन्त्याः करः (i.e. *tatto-huttuṭṭhi-osiantīa karo*), and explains *vaanaṁ* as वदनम्। My's reading is the same.

K says तत् रामशिरो निर्वर्ण्य वीक्ष्य च तदभिमुखम् उत्थितायाः, अवसीदन्त्याः, कांक्षन्त्याः प्रेम्णा तथाभूतं तद्वदनं स्प्रष्टुं कांक्षन्त्या अपि अवसादात् करो वदनं न प्राप्तः। उद्यतः करः पुनः पतितः। तथा मर्तुं कांक्षन्त्याः तस्याः आत्मा कथमपि मरणं च न प्राप्तः। MY says कथमपि सर्वैरपि प्रकारैः।

Kula agrees with R whose reading is altogether different (अस्या आत्मा वचनं मरणं च न प्राप्तः, etc.)। Kula seems to read इव (*va*) for च (cf. *SC* text). *SC* says यद्वा वचनं मरणं वा द्वयमपि न प्राप्तमित्यर्थः। R explains *ṇisaṇṇa* as निःसंज्ञ and निषण्ण।

68. णवरि अ पसारिअङ्गी रअभरिउप्पहपइण्णवेणीबन्धा।
पडिआ उरसंदाणिअमहीअलचक्कलिअत्थणी जणअसुता।।

[अनन्तरं च प्रसारिताङ्गी रजोभृतोत्पथप्रकीर्णवेणीबन्धा।
पतितोरःसंदानितमहीतलचक्रीकृतस्तनी जनकसुता।।]

Sītā then fell prostrate, her hair dishevelled and filled with dust, and her breasts pressed close[28] against the ground, covered with her bosom.

K read प्रविद्ध for *paiṇṇa* = प्रकीर्ण (R and Kula).

K says ततः अधोमुखं प्रसारिताङ्गी रजोभरितो धूलिधूसर उत्पथे इतस्ततः प्रविद्धो विक्षिप्तः वेणीबन्धः यस्याः सा। उरसा संदानिते संस्पृष्टे महीतले चक्रीकृतस्तनी भूत्वा पतिता। MY says उरसा सह संगतेन महीतलेन चक्रितौ स्तनौ यस्याः सा तथा। Kula says उरसा संदानितेन बद्धेन महीतलेन।

69. सव्वङ्गणिसण्णाअ वि णीसेसक्खविअवलिविभङ्गणिराओ।
तीए मज्झपएसो थणजहणकरालिओ ण पावइ वसुहम्।।

[सर्वाङ्गनिषण्णाया अपि निःशेषक्षपितवलिविभङ्गनिरायतः।
तस्या मध्यप्रदेशः स्तनजघनकरालितो न प्राप्नोति वसुधाम्।।]

Even though she outstretched, her waist, slim[29] with the fleshy folds entirely smoothed out, did not touch the ground, being held between the breasts and the hips.

K says भुवि सर्वाङ्गैः निषण्णाया अपि तस्याः निःशेषं क्षपितास्तिरस्कृताः त्रयो वलिविभङ्गा यथा भवति तथा निरायतः स्तनयोः जघनस्य (च) मध्ये करालितः सान्तरालः उन्नताभ्यां स्तनाभ्यां बृहता जघनेन च करालितो मध्यप्रदेशो वसुधां न प्राप्नोति न स्पृशति स्म। Kula says निरायतो दीर्घः स्तनजघनाभ्यां करालितो मध्ये सावकाशीकृतो मध्यप्रदेशः।

70. सहसालोअविराअं दइअमुहे तम्मि साणुसअदट्ठव्वे।
मोहं गन्तूण चिरं समअं वाहेण आगअं से हिअअम्।।

[सहसालोकविशीर्णं दयितमुखे तस्मिन्सानुशयद्रष्टव्ये।
मोहं गत्वा चिरं समं बाष्पेणागतमस्या हृदयम्।।]

---

[28] Literally rounded.

[29] Literally elongated.

Her consciousness, disrupted at the sudden appearance (of the severed head), while she had hoped to see her beloved's face with soothing words,[30] returned along with her tears, after being long eclipsed by the swoon.

K, MY and Kula read सानुनय for *sāṇusaa* = सानुशय (R). K says दयितस्य मुखे सानुनयम् अनुनयवचनैः सह द्रष्टव्ये। MY says स्वप्रसादपरे द्रष्टव्ये। Kula seems to say अनुनयवादान्विते।

K and MY translate *virāa* as विलीन् (विशीर्ण R)। R says अनुशयः पश्चात्तापः, तथा च सानुशयं द्रष्टव्ये वियोगेन रावणवधाविलम्बेन च सक्रोधं द्रष्टव्यमित्यवधारिते तस्मिन् दयितस्य रामस्य मुखे। Laṭakana says इदं मुखं पुरा मया न प्रकाममवलोकितं न चुम्बितमित्यनुशयः पश्चात्तापः।

71. तो कह वि लद्धसण्णा वाहोवग्गिअकवोलअलसंदट्ठम्।
मग्गइ संगोवेउं अलअं तीअ विहलो ण पावइ हत्थो।।

[ततः कथमपि लब्धसंज्ञा बाष्पाक्रान्तकपोलतलसंदष्टम्।
मार्गति संगोपयितुमलकं तस्या विह्वलो न प्राप्नोति हस्तः।।]

Having somehow recovered consciousness, she tried to arrange her tresses adhering to her cheeks, bedewed with tears, but her weary hand failed to move.

K reads संस्थापयितुं for *saṁgoveuṁ* = संगोपयितुं (R and Kula).

K says मार्गति कांक्षति स्म। MY says *oaggia* अभिभूत (K also). R says संगोपयितुं संगमयितुम्। *SC* says यथास्थानं नेतुमित्यर्थः इति केचित्।

72. आवेअसमुक्खित्तं तो से खेआगमोसिअन्तावत्तम्।
पडिअं णिअउच्छङ्गे अप्पत्तं चिअ पओहरे करजुअलम्।।

[आवेगसमुत्क्षिप्तं ततोऽस्याः खेदागमावसीददपवृत्तम्।
पतितं निजोत्सङ्गेऽप्राप्तमेव पयोधरौ करयुगलम्।।]

Her eagerly lifted hands,[31] worn out with fatigue and unsteady, dropped on her lap without having reached the breasts.

MY says आवेगेन स्तनाघातायोत्क्षिप्तं खेदागमावसीददपवृत्तम्। Only the *chāyā*

---

[30] According to Rāmadāsa's reading (see Extracts): remorsefully, i.e. with a sense of guilt for having caused him so great hardship and suffering.

[31] I.e. to beat the heat.

of this verse appears in our copy of K. R says अपवृत्तं स्खलितम्। (Kula also).

73. मूढहिअआइ दट्ठुं अचअन्तीअ समुहं कह वि रामसिरम्।
तंसोणमन्तणीसहवअणच्छन्दवलिआणणाइ पुलइअम्।।

[मूढहृदयया द्रष्टुमशक्नुवत्या संमुखं कथमपि रामशिरः।
तिर्यगवनमन्निःसहवदनच्छन्दवलिताननया प्रलोकितम्।।]

Bewildered and unable in any wise to look straight at Rāma's head she beheld it as her weary face leaned sideways, with her tresses moving in its wake.

K reads उन्नमत् for *oṇamanta* (अवनमत्) found in R, MY and Kula. K reads चन्द्र for छन्द (R and MY). K says मूढहृदयया रामशिरः संमुखं द्रष्टुं कथमपि अशक्नुवत्या तया पश्चात् तिर्यगुन्नमति ततो निःसहे परवशे वदनचन्द्रे वलितालकया भूत्वा तद्विलोकितम्। R says निःसहं . . . यद्वदनं तस्य छन्देन वशेन वलिता वक्रीभूता अलका यस्यास्तया। यथा यथा शिरोदर्शनाय मुखं तिर्यक्कृत्यावनतं क्रियते तथा तथा विकीर्णा अलका अपि तिर्यगवनमन्तीत्यर्थः। Kula is partly corrupt, but according to quotation in *SC* he reads छद्म (*chamma*) for छन्द–एवंभूतस्य वदनस्य छद्मना व्याजेन वलितालकया।

MY says त्र्यश्रमवनमतः निःसहस्य वदनस्य छन्देन आनुकूल्येन।

MY reads *ṇa pārantīe* for *acaantīa* (अशक्नुवत्या)। This would require elimination of *kaha* metric.

74. परिदेविउं पउत्ता णिअअसरीरपडिमुक्कराहवदुक्खम्।
करमग्गुट्ठिअसोणिअविवण्णउण्णअपओहरा जणअसुआ।।

[परिदेवितुं प्रवृत्ता निजकशरीरप्रतिमुक्तराघवदुःखम्।
करमार्गोत्थितशोणितविवर्णोन्नतपयोधरा जनकसुता।।]

Sītā began to wail, venting her grief for Rāma upon her own body, with her plump bosom blood-stained on account of blows with her hands.

K and MY read शरीरे विमुक्त° for *sarīrapaḍimukka* (R). K and probably MY read °दुःखा for *dukkhaṁ* (R and Kula).

K reads विस्तीर्ण[32] for *vivaṇṇa* (R and Kula).

K says करमार्गः करतलप्रहारः तेनोत्थितैः शोणितैः विशेषेण छादितोन्नतपयोधरा।

[32] I.e. *vitthaa*.

MY says रामं प्रत्यात्मनो हृदयं यद्दुःखं तत् स्वदेहे करप्रहारादिना मुञ्चन्तीति निजशरीरे विमुक्तेत्यादेरर्थः। K says निजकशरीरे विमुक्तराघवदुःखा। पूर्वं निजदुःखं राघवदुःखं चोभयं राघवे निहितमभूत्। अद्य तन्नाशभ्रान्त्या राघवगतं दुःखं स्वशरीरे करप्रहारादिना निहितवतीत्यर्थः। (cf. K's gloss on verse 76)। अथवा राघवं प्रत्यात्मनो हृदये यत् दुःखं वर्तते तस्य नाशात् तद्दुःखं स्वशरीरे कृतवतीत्यर्थः। Kula reads to *ṇiaa- sarīra-mukka°.*

He says ततो निजकशरीरे स्तनधातादिना मुक्तं राघवदुःखं यस्यास्तत् तथा।

75. आवाअभअअरं चिअ ण होइ दुक्खस्स दारुणं णिव्वहणम्।
जं महिलावीहत्थं दिट्ठं सहिअं च तुह मए अवसाणम्।।

[आपातभयंकरमेव न भवति दुःखस्य दारुणं निर्वहणम्।
यन्महिलाबीभत्सं दृष्टं सोढं च तव मयावसानम्।।]

"Suffering is terrible only at the outset; its sequel is not severe since I have seen and endured thy end, something abhorrent to a woman.

K and MY read दुःखानां for *dukkhassa* (R and Kula).

K says दुःखमापाते आगमसमय एव भयङ्करं भवति। दुःखानां निर्वहणं चिरमनुभवः न दारुणं शनैर्यापनीयमित्यर्थः। कुत महिलाबीभत्सं महिलानां स्त्रीणां जुगुप्सनीयं यथा भवति तथा तवावसानं मया दृष्टं सोढं च यत् तस्मादिति।

MY says दुःखानां निर्वहणं निष्ठा आपातभयङ्करमात्रमेव, न पुनः स्वरूपतो दारुणम्। अथवा दुःखानां दारुणं निर्वहणमापातभयङ्करमेव न भवति प्रमुखेऽपि असह्यं न भवति। महिलाबीभत्सं महिलानां लोकगर्हितम्। अथवा महिलानां बीभत्सं यथा भवति तथा दृष्टं सीदं चेत्यर्थः। Kula says दुःखस्य निर्वहणं समापनं न दारुणं भवति प्राणान्तं न करोतीत्यर्थः। *SC* says आपाततो यथा भयं तथा परिणामे न भवतीत्यर्थः।

76. वाहुल्लं तुज्झ उरे जं मोच्छिहिमि त्ति संठिअं मह हिअए।
घरणिग्गमणपअत्तं साहसु तं कम्मि णिव्वविज्जउ दुक्खम्।।

[बाष्पोष्णं तवोरसि यन्मोक्ष्यामीति संस्थितं मम हृदये।
गृहनिर्गमनप्रवृत्तं शाधि तत्कस्मिन्निर्वाप्यतां दुःखम्।।]

Tell me how I am to assuage my grief, which began since my departure from home, and which I had purposed to allay by shedding ardent tears on thy bosom.

K reads मूर्च्छिष्यति (*mucchihii*) for *mochihimi* (मोक्ष्यामि) found in

R. K and MY read अर्पितं (*appiaṁ*) for *saṁṭhiaṁ* = संस्थितं (R and Kula). K reads निर्याप्यतां[33] for *ṇivvavijjaü* = निर्वाप्यतां (R). The first line of the verse is quoted in Prākṛta in K's gloss on verse 74. K says गृहनिर्गमनात् प्रवृत्तं बाष्पोष्णम् अनवरतं गलता शोकतीवेण बाष्पेणोष्णं मम हृदये वर्तमानं यत् दु:खं मयि मूर्च्छिष्यतीति मत्वा तवोरसि त्वयार्पितं तदिदानीमेवंभूते त्वयि कस्मिन् निर्याप्यतां स्थाप्यतां शंस।

MY reads *mocchihii* (मोक्ष्यते) and *ṇijjaijjaü* (निर्यात्यता)। He says गृहनिर्गमनादारभ्य उष्णबाष्पवत् तवीरसि माक्ष्यत् इति यत् मम हृदये अर्पितं तत् दु:खं कस्मिन् निर्यात्यतां शंसेत्यन्वय:।

Kula seems to read *ṇiveijjaü*, and, like MY, *mocchihii.*

He says यत् दु:खं गृहनिर्गमात् प्रभृति प्रवृत्तं तवोरसि क्रीडे बाष्पोष्णं मोक्ष्यत इति मम हृदये संस्थितं तत् कथय कस्मिन् निवेद्यताम् (?)।

R says दु:खं बाष्पणोष्णं सत् तवोरसि मोक्ष्यामि तवोरसि रुदित्वा त्यक्ष्यामि इति यन्मम हृदये संस्थितमवधारितम्, etc.

77. विरहम्मि तुज्झ धरिअं दच्छामि तुमं त्ति जीविअं कह वि मए।
तं एस मए दिट्ठो फलिआ वि मणोरहा ण पूरेन्ति महम्।।

[विरहे तव धृतं द्रक्ष्यामि त्वामिति जीवितं कथमपि मया।
तदेष मया दृष्ट: फलिता अपि मनोरथा न पूर्यन्ते मम।।]

During separation from thee, I kept somehow alive in the hope of seeing thee, and thus have I seen thee. My hopes, although they were coming to fruition, were not fulfilled.

K and MY read त्वमेवमसि मे दृष्ट: (*taṁ ea si me diṭṭho*) for *taṁ esa mae,* etc. (R). MY has . . . मया दृष्ट:। Kula reads तदेवमसि मया दृष्ट:।

78. पुहवीअ होहिइ पई वहुपुरिसविसेसचञ्चला राअसिरी।
कह ता महं चिअ इमं णीसामण्णं उअत्थिअं वेहव्वम्।।

[पृथिव्या भविष्यति पतिर्बहुपुरुषविशेषचञ्चला राजश्री:।
कथं तावन्ममैवेदं नि:सामान्यमुपस्थितं वैधव्यम्।।]

The Earth will have another lord, and Royal Fortune pass to many an eminent man. How is it that this uncommon widowhood hath befallen me alone?

K says त्वयि अतीतेऽपि पृथिव्या: पति: अन्यो भविष्यति। राजश्रीश्च बहुपुरुषविशेषेषु

[33] I.e. *ṇijjavijjaü*. Hemacandra 4.40 gives *javaï* and *jāveï* for यापयति।

राजपुरुषेषु चञ्चला भविष्यति। कथमिदं ममैव तावत् निःसामान्यमनन्यसाधारणं वैधव्यमुपस्थितम्। तव पृथिवी श्रीरहं च परिग्रहाः। ते तु द्वे यथाकथंचित् भर्तृमत्यौ भविष्यतः। ममैव कथभिदमसाधारणं वैधव्यं जातमिति।

MY says *kaha ā* (for *tā*) कस्मात् तावत्। Kula's reading is same, but he says आ संतापे। ममैव एवं (इदं ?) कथं निःसामान्यं वैधव्यमुपस्थितम्।

79. किं एअ त्ति पलत्तं विसउम्मिल्लेहि लोअणेहि अ दिट्ठम्।
विअलिअलज्जाइ मए होइ फुडं णाह तुह मुहं ति परुण्णम्।।

[किमेतदिति प्रलपितं विषमोन्मीलिताभ्यां लोचनाभ्यां च दृष्टम्।
विगलितलज्जया मया भवति स्फुटं नाथ तव मुखमिति प्ररुदितम्।।]

I exclaimed 'what is this?' and stared at the head with wide eyes. When, my lord, it clearly turned out to be thine, I merely wept,[34] bereft of shame.

K says हे नाथ प्राप्तवैधव्या मया तव मुखमेवंभूतं दृष्ट्वा प्रथमं किमेतदिति भ्रान्त्या प्रलपितं, ततो मोहापगमे सति विषममुन्मीलिताभ्यां लोचनाभ्यां च दृष्टम्। ततो विगलितलज्जया मया तव मुखमिति निश्चित्य स्फुटं प्ररुदितं भवति। न पुनः स्नेहानुरूपो मरणाध्यवसायः कृतः। MY says प्रलापाद्येव कृतं न तु मरणमित्यर्थः। Kula says विषादोन्मीलिताभ्यां लोचनाभ्याम्। *SC* says विशदं विस्पष्टम्। R has both विषम and विशद for *visaa*.

80. सहिओ तुज्झ विओओ रअणिअरिहि समअं सहीहि व वुत्थम्।
दट्ठुं तुमं ति होत्तं जइ एत्ताहे वि जीविअं विअलन्तम्।।

[सोढस्तव वियोगो रजनीचरीभिः समकं सखीभिरिव व्युषितम्।
द्रष्टुं त्वामिति भवद्यदीदानीमपि जीवितं विगलत्।।]

It would have been true to say that I endured separation from thee, and sojourned with the *rākṣasa* women as with friends, only to see thee, had my life departed even now.[35]

K reads वृत्तम् for *vuttham* (R) rendered as व्युषितम्। MY says *uttham* उषितम्। इदं सर्वं द्रष्टुं त्वामित्यभविष्यत् यदीदानीमपि जीवितं व्यगलिष्यत्। Kula has उषितम्। Manuscript C of Goldschmidt also has *uttham*. K says एतत् सर्वं व्यसनं त्वां द्रष्टुमनुभूतमित्यभविष्यत् इदानीमपि मम जीवितं यदि व्यगलिष्यत्। तच्च न गलितम्। अतो लोको मामन्यथा ज्ञास्यतीति शेषः।

---

[34] Instead of dying.

[35] I.e. as she did not die on seeing Rāma's severed head, she could not claim that she had preserved her life only in the hope of seeing him again.

81. जाए परलोअगए तुमम्मि ववसाअमत्तसुहदट्ठव्वे।
हरिसच्छाणे वि महं डज्झइ अदिट्ठदहमुहवहं हिअअम्।।

[जाते परलोकगते त्वयि व्यवसायमात्रसुखद्रष्टव्ये।
हर्षस्थानेऽपि मम दह्यतेऽदृष्टदशमुखवधं हृदयम्।।]

Although there is ground for joy, because I could see thee with ease by a mere effort,[36] now that thou hast gone to the other world, my heart is on fire, because I did not see Rāvaṇa killed.

K says प्रसह्य मरणव्यसायमात्रेण त्वयि परलोकगतेऽपि द्रष्टव्ये जाते सति मम हृदयं हर्षस्थानेऽपि हर्षावसरेऽपि दह्यते। कुतःअदृष्टरावणवधत्वादिति।

82. वाहं ण धरेइ मुहं आसाबन्धो वि मे ण रुम्भइ हिअअम्।
णवरि अ चिन्तिज्जन्ते ण विणज्जइ केण जीविअं संरुद्धम्।।

[बाष्पं न धारयति मुखमाशाबन्धोऽपि मे न रुणद्धि हृदयम्।
अनन्तरं च चिन्त्यमाने न विज्ञायते केन जीवितं संरुद्धम्।।]

My face is not stained with tears,[37] nor does any bond of hope restrain my heart. Then on reflection, I know not what holds my life back.

K reads कथं तावत्चिन्त्यमानं[38] for *ṇavari a cintijjante* = अनन्तरं च चिन्त्यमाने (R). Kula is partly corrupt, but he has विचार्यमाणे, i.e. चिन्त्यमाने। *SC* text has *ṇavaraṁ* (केवलं)। K says एंव मरणव्यवसायात् बाष्पप्रसरं मुखं न धारयति। बाष्पो न निर्गच्छतीत्यर्थः। यः कश्चित् आशाबन्धोऽपि म हृदयं न रुणद्धि विनाशोन्मुखं हृदयं न निवारयति। जीवितं तावत् केन संरुद्धमिति चिन्त्यमानमपि न विज्ञायते।

MY says मुखं बाष्पं न रुणद्धि। आशाबन्धोऽपि न हृदयम्। जीवितं तु केन रुध्यते इति न ज्ञायते। बाष्पजीवितयोः निर्गमने पूर्वं प्रतिबन्धकद्वयं जातम्। अमङ्गलाशङ्का चाशाबन्धरचेति। तयोः प्रथमाभावादिदानीं बाष्पस्तावत् निर्याति। न तु द्वितीयाभावेऽपि जीवितमित्यत्र किं निमित्तमिति न ज्ञायत इति भावः। त्वद्दर्शनप्रत्याशायामसत्यामपि केवलं रोदिमि न म्रिय इत्यर्थः।

SC says मुखं कर्तृ बाष्पं न धारयति सदा बाष्पो वहत्येवेत्यर्थः। आशाबन्धोऽपि

---

36 I.e. by suicide

37 I.e. her grief is too deep for tears. This indicates also desperation. Cf. verse 117. According to some commentators: my face does not check the tears.

38 I.e. *kaha tā cintijjantaṁ*. cf. verse 105.

मे हृदयंन रुणद्धि आशाबन्धं परित्यज्य हृदयं मरणमेव धावतीत्यर्थः। R says न धारयति न प्रतिबध्नाति।

83. वोलीणो मअरहरो मज्झ कएण मरणं पि दे पडिवण्णम्।
णिव्वूढं णाह तुमे अज्ज वि धरइ अकअण्णुअं मह हिअअम्।।

[व्यतिक्रान्तो मकरगृहो मम कृतेन मरणमपि ते प्रतिपन्नम्।
निर्व्यूढं नाथ त्वयाद्यापि ध्रियतेऽकृतज्ञं मम हृदयम्।।]

Thou didst cross the ocean, and accept even death for my sake. Thy task, my lord, was fulfilled, but my ungrateful heartbeats[39] even now.

K says एवं त्वया निर्व्यूढं मयि वात्सल्यानुरूपं सर्वं कृतमित्यर्थः। अकृतज्ञं मम हृदयमद्यापि ध्रियते अवतिष्ठते। धृङ् अवस्थान् इति धातुः। MY has *maraṇaṁ pi tae* (for *de*), i.e. मरणमपि त्वया। He seems to read *kae* for *kaeṇa* (कृतेन), K and MY *pratīka* has *bolīṇo* for *volīṇo* (R). See N.S. edn. and *SC* text.

84. उग्गाहिइ राम तुमं गुणे गणेऊण पुरिसमइओ त्ति जणो।
गलिअमहिलासहावं संभरिऊण अ ममं णिअत्तिहिइ कहम्।।

[उद्गास्यति राम त्वां गुणान्गणयित्वा पौरुषमय इति जनः।
गलितमहिलास्वभावां संस्मृत्य च मां निवर्तयिष्यति कथाम्।।]

Recounting by virtues, O Rāma, people will praise thee as valiant, but will cease to talk about me, remembering me as one that lacked womanly character.[40]

K says जनस्तावकान् गुणान् गणयित्वा बहुश आवर्त्य त्वां पुरुषमयः पौरुषमय इति उद्ग्रहीष्यति प्रशंसिष्यति। गलितस्त्रीस्वभावां मा च संस्मृत्य मत्संबद्धां कथां निवर्तयिष्यति मद्गतं किञ्चिदपि गुणान्तरं न वक्ष्यति ग्रहीष्यतीत्यर्थः।

K *pratīka* has *uggāhii* like R.

My *pratīka* has *uggāhai* like manuscript C of Goldschmidt. He says उद्गृह्णाति उत्कीर्तय। पुरुषमय इति पुरुषैकस्वभावः क्लैब्यादिरहित इत्यर्थः। Kula says त्वां जनः पुरुषमतिक इति पुरुषाभिमानवानिति[41] गीतेन वर्णयिष्यति। (i.e. उद्गास्यति as construed by R)। पतिमरणेऽपि अमरणात् गलितम्

[39] Literally abides.

[40] I.e. the courage to die.

[41] Our copy has पुरुषातिमान°।

हिलास्वभावां मम कथां संस्मृत्य निवर्तिष्यते कथां संत्यक्ष्यतीति भावः। *SC* says पुरुषमयः पुरुषप्रकृतिक इति श्रीनिवासः।

85. तुह वाणुक्खअणिहअं दच्छिम्मि दहकण्ठमुहणिहाअं ति कआ।
मह भाअधेअवलिआ विवराहुत्ता मणोरहा पल्हत्था।।

[तव बाणोत्खातनिहतं द्रक्ष्यामि दशकण्ठमुखनिघातमिति कृताः।
मम भागधेयवलिता विपराङ्मुखा मनोरथाः पर्यस्ताः।।]

My hopes that I shall see Rāvaṇa's heads, severed by thy arrows, and flung to the ground, are reversed, being thwarted by fate.

K and Kula read पतितं (*paḍiaṁ*) for *ṇihaaṁ* (R).

K (*chāyā*) has मुखनिकायं। K says दशकण्ठस्य मुखसमूहं तव बाणीत्खातपतितं द्रक्ष्यामीति कृता मनोरथा मम भागधेयेन विधिना वलिताः स्खलिता, विशेषेण पराङ्मुखा भूत्वा पर्यस्ता विपर्यस्ताः तस्यैव आयुधेन तवेदृशी दशा जातेत्यर्थः। MY has *dacchaṁ* (द्रक्ष्यामि) for *dacchimi*. He says मम भागधेयैः पूर्वकृतकर्मभिः विपराङ्मुखा वलिताः विपर्यस्ता इति। विपर्यासः द्विषदस्त्रेण तवैव वधो जात इति।

86. जं तणुअम्मि वि विरहे पेमाबन्धेण सङ्कइ जनस्य जनो।
तं जाअं णवर इमं पेच्छन्तीए अ तारिसं मज्झ फलम्।।

[यत्तनुकेऽपि विरहे प्रेमाबन्धेन शङ्कते जनस्य जनः।
तज्जातं केवलमिदं पश्यन्त्याश्च तादृशं मम फलम्।।]

A sequel of this sort to what one fears in respect of another, out of affection for him, even in a brief separation, hath become manifest in my case alone."

K reads मनः for *jaṇo* (R and Kula). K, MY and Kula read प्रत्यक्षं तस्य for *pecchantīe a* = पश्यन्त्याश्च (R). K says अल्पेऽपि विरहे जनस्य मनः स्निग्धं जनमुद्दिश्य प्रेमाबन्धेन यद्दुरितं शङ्कते तस्य शङ्कितस्य दुरितस्य तस्य तादृशं शङ्कानुरूपं फलं ममैव केवलं प्रत्यक्षं जातम्। शङ्क्यमानेन दुरितेन येत् फलति तन्ममैव प्रत्यक्षमभूदित्यर्थः।

MY says तस्य विरहस्य तादृशं शङ्कितरूपं फलं ममैव केवलं प्रत्यक्षं जातम्। Kula says यत् . . . जनस्य जन आशङ्कते . . . तस्यानिष्टाशङ्कितस्य तत्तादृशमिदं प्रत्यक्षं फलं मम केवलं जातम्।

87. तो विलविआणप्फन्दं गलन्तहिअअपरिसुण्णलोअणजुअलम्।
मधुरं आसासन्ती हत्थुण्णामिअमुही भणइ णं तिअडा।।
[ततो विलपितनिस्पन्दां गलद्धृदयपरिशून्यलोचनयुगलाम्।
मधुरमाश्वासयन्ती हस्तोन्नामितमुखीं भणत्येनां त्रिजटा।।

Thereupon Trijaṭā[42] raised Sītā's face with her hands, and consoled her with sweet words as she lay worn out with mourning, with a vacant stare void of all feeling.

K and Kula read निस्थामान (*ṇitthāmaṁ*, cf. *SC* text) for *ṇipphandaṁ* (R). MY has निस्थेमानम् = विवशाम्। K says निस्थामानं निःशक्तिम्। Kula says निःस्थामानं निःसहाम्।

K remarks त्रिजटानामा विन्ध्यनाम्नो राक्षसाध्यक्षस्य धर्मशीला दुहिता।

88. अवरिगलिओ विसाओ अखण्डिआ मुद्धआ ण पेच्छइ पेम्मम्।
मूढो जुवइसहाओ तिमिराहि वि दिणअरस्स चिन्तेइ भअम्।।
[अपरिगलितो विषादोऽखण्डिता मुग्धता न प्रेक्षते प्रेम।
मूढो युवतिस्वभावस्तिमिरादपि दिनकरस्य चिन्तयति भयम्।।]

"Unthinking sorrow, undiscerning simplicity, and love do not see the truth; and the foolish mind of a young woman apprehends danger to the sun even from darkness.

K reads अपरिगणकः for *avarigalio* = अपरिगलितः (R). K and Kula read अपण्डिता for *akhaṇḍia* (R). K reads जानाति for *pecchai* (R and Kula).

K says विषादस्तावत् अपरिगणकः। इदमेवं संभवति न वेति न परिगणयिता परिगणयितुमक्षम् इत्यर्थः। परिगणयतीति परिगणकः। मुग्धता नाम स्त्रीणामाभिजात्यनिबन्धनो विवेकशून्यो भावविशेषः। मुग्धता अपण्डिता मौग्ध्यादेव स्वभावात् विवेक्तुमनिपुणा भवति। प्रेम स्नेहः। तत् किञ्चिदपि न जानाति। प्रकृत्या मूढः एतैर्युक्तो युवतिस्वभावः तिमिरादपि दिनकरस्य भयं निरूपयतीति सामान्योक्तिः।

Kala says अपरिगलितः (अपरिगणितः ?) परिचारशून्य (विचारशून्यः ?) विषादः। अपण्डिता विवेकशून्या मुग्धता मोहाक्रान्ता चित्तवृत्तिः। प्रेम कर्तृ युक्तं न पश्यति युक्तं न चिन्तयतीत्यर्थः। युवतिस्वभावो मूढो निश्चयशून्यो यतः तिमिरादपि दिनकरस्य भयं चिन्तयति। रावणादपि राममरणमाशङ्कत इति भावः। MY reads *apariganio* (cf. Kula) mentioned by R as a variant. *SC* says परिगणना विचार इति यावत्। विषादे विचारो न स्यादित्यर्थः।

---

[42] A *rākṣasa* woman friendly to Sītā.

R explains the first line differently — अपरिगलित: पूर्णो विषाद:, अक्षुण्णा मुग्धता, प्रम च त्र्यमपि न प्रेक्षते। वस्तुविचारक्षमं न भवतीत्यर्थ:।

89. तिहुअणमूलाहारं विसढमहिन्दपडिमुक्कवूढरणधुरम्।
जाणन्ती कीस तुमं तुलेसि सेसपुरिसाणुमाणेण पइम्।।

[त्रिभुवनमूलाधारं विह्वलमहेन्द्रप्रतिमुक्तव्यूढरणधुरम्।
जानती किमिति त्वं तुलयसि शेषपुरुषानुमानेन पतिम्।।]

Knowing thy consort to be the primal foundation of the universe, one that assumed the respsonsibility (of protecting the world), when it was abandoned by the helpless Indra,[43] why dost thou judge him to be on a par with other men?

K and MY *pratīka* has *tihuraṇa.*

K reads परिमुक्त for *paḍi°* (R and Kula). K and read निर्व्यूढधुरं for *vūḍha-raṇa-dhurṁ* (R). Kula reads विधुर, i.e. *vihura*, cf. *SC* text for *visaḍha* (विश्लथ K; विह्वल R) K says त्रिभुवनस्याधारभूतानि पञ्च महाभूतानि। तेषामप्याधारभूतत्वात् मूलाधार इत्युक्तम्। विश्लथेन श्रान्तेन महेन्द्रेण परिमुक्ता आत्मना निर्व्यूढा धूस्त्रिभुवनस्य रक्षाभरो येन तं पतिमेवंभूतं . . . जानानापि त्वं शेषपुरुषानुमानेन, अयमपि अन्य-पुरुषसाधारण इति बुद्धिरनुमानं, तेनानुमानेन कि तुलयसि किमध:करोषि। तन्न युक्तमित्यर्थ:।

MY says शेषपुरुषानुमानेन पुरुषत्वादिना तस्यापि तादृशत्वनुमायेत्यर्थ:। Kula says . . . निर्जितेन विधुरेण महेन्द्रेण प्रतिमुक्ता, निर्व्यूढा दैत्यान् निर्जित्य धारिता धूर्येन तं नारायणं पतिं जानतीं किं त्वं शेषपुरुषानुमानेन तुलयसि इतर पुरुषमिव शत्रुच्छिन्नशिरसं संभावयसीति भाव:।

90. अमिलिअसाअरसलिला अणहट्ठिअमहिहरा अणुव्वत्तअला।
रामस्स छिण्णपडिअं कह पत्तिअसि धरणी धरेइ त्ति सिरम्।।

[अमिलितसागरसलिला अनघस्थितमहीधरानुद्वृत्ततला।
रामस्य छिन्नपतितं कथं प्रत्येषि धरणी धारयतीति शिर:।।]

How canst thou believe that the earth could hold Rāma's severed and fallen head, without being overturned, and without the waters of the different oceans mingling together, or, with the mountains standing unharmed?[44]

---

[43] I.e. on account of his defeat by the demons.

[44] I.e. had Rāma died, unprecedented convulsions of nature would have heralded his death.

K reads °पर्वता for *mahiharā* (R and Kula), and भिन्न for *chiṇṇa* (R and Kula).

K says रामस्य भिन्नपतितं शिरः धरणी परस्परमसंकीर्णसागरजला, उत्पातवातैरुत्क्षिप्ता नभसि स्थिताः पर्वताः यस्या भवन्ति सा तथा, तैरेव वायुभिः अनुद्धततला भूत्वा धारयेदिति कथं त्वं प्रत्येषि प्रमाणयसि। तस्य शिरःपतने सति भूमिरेवमाकुला भवेत। तदभावात् न सत्यमित्यर्थः।

MY says अनघः निरुपद्रवः। *aṇuvvattaalā* अनुद्वृत्ततला (K *chāyā* also). R says अनघा अविशीर्णाः स्थिता महीधरा यत्र। *SC* says अनुद्वृत्तमविपर्यस्तं तलं यस्या एवंभूता धरणी।

91. मारुअमोडिअविडवं मिअङ्ककिरणपडिमासमाउलिअकमलम्।
कह होइ रामवडने इअ णिच्छाअं दसाणणघरुज्जाणम्।।

[मारुतमोटितविटपं मृगाङ्ककिरणप्रतिमर्षमुकुलितकमलम्।
कथं भवति रामपतने इति निच्छायं दशाननगृहोद्यानम्।।]

In the event of Rāma's death, how could Rāvaṇa's palace garden be thus shorn of its beauty, with the branches of the trees broken by the wind, and the day lotus blossoms closing in contact with the rays of the moon?[45]

K's gloss on this verse is incomplete in our copy. K (*chāyā*) has परिमर्श for *paḍimāsa* (प्रतिमर्ष = स्पर्श), and त्रुटित for *moḍia* = मोटित (R and Kula). K (commentary) only says रामेणाभिभूतत्वात् रावणस्य गृहोद्यानं मारुतोदयपरिभवं निच्छायम् इति। Kula remarks वातचन्द्रयोरपि रावणानभीष्टाचरणात् मृषैव राममरणमिति भावः।

92. मा रुअसु पुससु वाहं उअऊहेऊण अंसपरिअत्तमुहम्।
संभरिअ विरहदुक्खं रोत्तव्वं दे पुणो पइस्स वि अङ्के।।

[मा रोदीः प्रोञ्छ बाष्पमुपगूह्यांसपरिवृत्तमुखम्।
संस्मृत्य विरहदुःखं रुदितव्यं ते पुनः पत्युरप्यङ्के।।]

Weep not. Wipe thy tears away. On thy consort's lap wilt thou weep again, remembering the pangs of separation, and embracing him with thy face leaning on his shoulders.

The verse is not found in Kula.

---

[45] I.e. the wind and the moon dare interfere with the beauty of Rāvaṇa's garden, because Rāma is alive, and allows the forces of nature to function undisturbed.

K says बाष्पं च उन्मृश मार्जय। He takes *saṁbharia* as संस्मृत। R has संस्मृत्य। MY reads *phusasu* (मार्जय)। He reads *apaāseūṇa* (अप्रकाश्य) for *uaūheūṇa* (उपगूह्य), and says आलिङ्ग्येति केचित्। K has the latter reading.

93. अइरा अ दच्छिहि तुमं तुह विरहोलुग्गपण्डुरं मुहछाअम्।
गअरोससुहालोअं ओआरिअवावणिव्वुअं दासरहिम्।।

[अचिराच्च द्रक्ष्यसि त्वं तव विरहावरुग्णपाण्डुरं मुखच्छायम्।
गतरोषसुखालोकमवतारितचापनिर्वृतं दाशरथिम्।।]

Soon wilt thou see Rāma happy with his bow unstrung, and serene and free from wrath, with his face worn and pallid on account of separation from thee.

K, MY and Kula omit अ in *airā a dacchihi* (R). K and Kula have अचिरात् द्रक्ष्यसि। They seem to read *dacchihisi* like *SC* text and manuscript C of Goldschmidt. MY however reads *daṁsihisi* = द्रक्ष्यसि। K and Kula have *paṇḍara* for *paṇdura* (R).

K says अवतारितचापत्वात् न्यस्तचापत्वात् निर्वृतम्। MY says अवरोपितज्येति यावत्।

94. पत्तिहि अमरिसभरिअं हरेण वि अपत्थणिज्जकण्ठच्छेअम्।
फुट्टन्तं जइ होन्तं छिण्णं वि कअग्गहुग्गअं रामसिरम्।।

[प्रतीह्यमर्षभरितं हरेणाप्यप्रार्थनीयकण्ठच्छेदम्।
स्फुटद्यदि भवच्छिन्नमपि कचग्रहोद्गतं रामशिरः।।]

Believe me. Had it been Rāma's head, the cutting of which could not be imagined even by Śiva, it would have burst in a rage, even though severed, when affronted (by the demons) by seizing it by the hair.

K, MY and Kula *pratīka* has *pattia* for *pattihi* (R). K says प्रतीहि विश्वसिहि प्रमाणीकुरु।

MY and Kula read कचग्रहावधुतं (*kaa-ggahodhuaṁ*) for *kaaggahu-ggaaṁ* = कचग्रहोद्गतं (R). K (*chāyā*) has वधूतं। K (commentary) says राक्षसकृतेन कचग्रहेण विधूतम्। R says हरेणाप्यप्रार्थनीयो वक्तुमप्यशक्यः कण्ठच्छेदो यस्य तत्, and quotes 'प्रार्थितः शत्रुसंरुद्धे याचितेऽभिहितेऽपि च।' *SC* says अप्रार्थनीयोऽसंभावनीयः।

95. किं ति समाससिअव्वे मुज्झसि दहवअणदप्पभङ्गुप्फालम्।
पेच्छन्ती पमअवणं रामाणत्तिअरपवअआविद्धदुमम्।।

[किमिति समाश्वसितव्ये मुह्यसि दशवदनदर्पभङ्गोत्फालम्।
पश्यन्ती प्रमदवनं रामाज्ञप्तिकरप्लवगाविद्धद्रुमम्।।]

Why art thou stupefied when there is cause for joy, seeing as thou dost the pleasance that is a witness to the humiliation of Rāvaṇa's pride, with its trees prostrated by an ape that was but a servant of Rāma?[46]

K and MY read च for *ti* (R and Kula). They read भङ्गोत्पातं for *bhaṁgupphālaṁ* (R and Kula), and प्रविद्ध (*pavviddha* as stated by MY) for आविद्ध (R), explained as पातित। Kula reads प्रविद्ध। K says दशवदनस्य दर्पभङ्गार्थमुत्पातभूतम्। MY says भङ्गोत्पातं भङ्गसूचकमुत्पातम्।

MY reads *samūsasiavve* for *samā°* as he says समुच्छ्वसितव्ये समुच्छ्वासे हर्षे कर्तव्ये। R says समाश्वसितव्ये हर्षस्थाने। Kula is corrput, but *SC* which reproduces him says रामाज्ञप्तिकरेण प्लवगेन हनुमता प्रविद्धा भग्ना: पर्यासिता द्रुमा यत्र तत् प्रमदवनं दशवदनस्य दर्पभङ्गोत्फालं भज्यमानेन दर्पेण कृतमङ्गविक्षेपमिव पश्यन्ति किं मुह्यसि। यस्यैकस्य किंकरस्य एवंविधो विक्रमस्तस्य सुग्रीवविभीषणादिपुर:सरस्य कथं मोहादेवंविधं मरणं प्रत्येषीति भाव:। R says दशवदनस्य यो दर्पभङ्गस्तदुत्फालं तत्सूचकं प्रमदवनम्।

96. णिहउक्खअसुरलोअं दरिअणिसाअरणिहाअपल्हत्थन्तम्।
कह तेण खणं वि विना धरेइ जस्स भुअणं भुअववट्ठम्भम्।।

[निहतोत्खातसुरलोकं दृप्तनिशाचरनिघातपर्यस्यमानम्।
कथं तेन क्षणमपि विना ध्रियते यस्य भुवनं भुजव्यवष्टम्भम्।।]

How will the world, supported by his arms, subsist without him even for a moment, overwhelmed by the proud hordes of demons, with the abode of the gods ravaged and destroyed?

K says भुवनमिदं यस्य भुजव्यवष्टम्भं भुजाधारं विष्ठति तेन रामेण विनाभूतं, निहतोत्खातस्वर्गं, दृप्तै राक्षससमूहै: पर्यस्यमानं परितो ध्वस्यमानं भूत्वा क्षणमपि कथमवतिष्ठते। K (*chāyā*) and MY take *ṇihāa* (निघात R) as निकाय

[46] She refers to the devastation of Rāvaṇa's pleasure garden by Hanumat during his mission to Sītā.

(समूहेति यावत् MY) Kula says भुवनं यस्य भुजविधृतम् MY syas यस्य भुजापाश्रयमिदम्। *SC* says निघातेन समूहेन।

97. तह तं सि गआ मोहं मुच्छागअपडिअणीसहविसण्णङ्गी।
रक्खसमाएति फुडं जाणन्ती जइ इमं अहं पि विसण्णा।।

[तथा त्वमसि गता मोहं मूर्छागतपतितनिःसहविषण्णाङ्गी।
राक्षसमायेति स्फुटं जानती यथेदमहमपि विषण्णा।।]

Fainting and sinking to the ground, languid and drooping, thou art under such a delusion that even knowing it clearly to be a deception of the demons, I am likewise stricken with grief.

K and Kula read आगम for *gaa* (R), and निषण्ण (K *chāyā*) for *visaṇṇa* (R).

K says मूर्च्छागमेन पतितविह्वलनिलीनाङ्गी त्वं तथा मोहं गतासि। कथमिति चेत्, इदं सर्वं राक्षसमायेति स्फुटमेव जानती अहमपि यथा विषण्णा तथेति। Kula says मूर्च्छागमेन पतितानि निःसह–निषण्णानि अङ्गानि यस्याः सा। *SC* says निःसहानि करणव्यापारशून्यान्यङ्गानि यस्या इति लोकनाथः।

98. मिलितणिसारअरपुरओ सुवेलमलअन्तरालणिम्मविअवहे।
पेल्लिअतिऊडसिहरे अज्ज वि किं तुज्झ राहवे अग्गहणम्।।

[मिलितनिशाचरपुरतः सुवेलमलयान्तरालनिर्मापितपथे।
प्रेरितत्रिकूटशिखरेऽद्यापि किं तव राघवेऽग्रहणम्।।]

Why hast thou no confidence in Rāma even now? He hath built a causeway between the Suvela and the Malaya before the eyes of the united demons, and stormed the peaks of the Suvela."[47]

K reads पुरे (i.e. *purae*) for *purao* (R and Kula) = पुरतः।

MY also says मिलितानां निशाचराणां पुरतः, but he remarks *ṇisāara-purae* इति वा पाठः। तदा प्राप्तनिशाचरनगरे निशाचरनगरं प्राप्ते इत्यर्थः।

K says इतः पूर्वमादित्यादिभिरपि अनवगाढं निशाचरपुरं लङ्का येन मिलिता अवगाढा तस्मिन्, सुवेलमलययोरन्तराले समुद्रे निर्मितसेतुपथे, पीडितानि लङ्काधिष्ठानभूतानि त्रिकूटशिखराणि येन तस्मिन् राघवेऽद्यापि तव किमग्रहणं किमविश्वासौ भवति। MY says *aggahaṇaṁ* अप्रत्ययः अनिश्चयः। Kula says

[47] The mountain on which Laṅkā stood.

प्रेरितमाक्रान्तं . . . शिखरं येन तस्मिन्। He takes अग्रहण as अनादर like R. राघवे किं तवाद्यापि अग्रहणमनादरो येनेदं सत्यमेव मन्यस इति भावः।

99. मलिआ मलअणिअम्बा थले व्व चङ्कम्मिअं महोअहिसलिले।
वुत्थं सुवेलसिहरे अज्ज वि किं तुज्ज राहवे अग्गहणम्।।

[मर्दिता मलयनितम्बा स्थल इव चङ्कमितं महोदधिसलिले।
व्युषितं सुवेलशिखरेऽद्यापि किं तव राघवेऽग्रहणम्।।]

[48].

The verse is not found in K, MY and Kula.

100. तो अगहिओवएसा गओणिअत्तन्तजीविअमुहिज्जन्ती।
तिअडाअ जणअतणआ सहिसब्भावसरिसं उरम्मि णिसण्णा।।

[ततोऽगृहीतोपदेशा गतापनिवर्तमानजीवितमुह्यन्ती।
त्रिजटाया जनकतनया सखीसद्भावसदृशमुरसि निषण्णा।।]

Stupefied as she hovered between life and death, and paying no heed to the admonition, Sītā sank down upon Trijaṭā's bosom with confidence worthy of the latter's affection for her.

K and MY read *jīva-vimuhijjantī* for *jīvia-mu°* (R). Kula says गतापनिवर्तमानेन जीवितेन विमुह्यमाना हृतचैतन्या। His reading might be same as that of K and MY. His gloss on the verse is mutilated, and that on the next three verses is missing in our copy.

K says ततो गतापनिवर्तमानेन मुहुर्गच्छता मुहुर्निवर्तमानेन जीवेन विमुह्यन्ती, अत एव अगृहीतत्रिजटावाक्योपदेशा जनकसुता त्रिजटायाः सखीसद्भावस्य सख्यास्तस्याः सद्भावस्य सदृशमुरसि निषण्णाभूत्।

MY says सखीसद्भावः सखीस्वभावः।

101. लोअणवइअरलग्गं तंसणिसण्णाअ तीअ तिअडावच्छे।
गलिअं कपोलपेल्लणपीडिज्जन्तालउग्गअं वाहजलम्।।

[लोचनव्यतिकरलग्नं तिर्यङ्निषण्णायास्तस्यास्त्रिजटावक्षसि।
गलितं कपोलप्रेरणपीड्यमानालकोद्गतं बाष्पजलम्।।]

As she reclined sideways on Trijaṭā's bosom, the mingled

[48] A variation of the preceding verse. Found only in Rāmadāsa.

tears of their eyes[49] issued in a stream from her tresses hard pressed by her cheek.

K reads वेल्लन for *pellaṇa* (R). K (*chāyā*) has उद्गमं for *uggaaṁ* (R), but K commentary has अग्रं i.e. *aggaaṁ*.

K says त्रिजटाया वक्षसि त्रिर्यक् निषण्णाया: तस्या: पूर्वं लोचनान्तराललग्नं बाष्पजलं कपोलवेल्लनेन कपोले परिवर्तनेन[50] पीड्यमानं तत्र पतितमलकाग्रं यथा भवति तथा गलितम्। R says कपोलेन यत् प्रेरणं तेन पीड्यमानालकेभ्य उद्गतं नि:सृतं (बाष्पजलम्)। MY says लोचनव्यतिकरवशं सखीदृष्टिसंमिश्रणजनित-मित्यर्थ:। *SC* says लोचनयोर्व्यतिकरेण संपर्केण लग्नमिति कुलनाथ:।

102. तो जम्पिउं पउत्ता पुणो वि अत्थैक्कउट्ठिअसमूससिआ।
उरघोलिरवेणीमुहथणलग्गुग्घुट्टमहिरआ जनअसुआ।।

[ततरे जल्पितुं प्रवृत्ता पुनरप्यकस्मादुत्थितसमुच्छ्वसिता।
उरोघूर्णनशीलवेणीमुखस्तनलग्नोद्घृष्टमहीरजा जनकसुता।।]

Sītā, then, suddenly recovered herself, and began to speak again wiping away the dust on her breasts with her hair waving on her bosom.

K reads वेणीमुखा (i.e. *veṇi-muhā*) for *veṇī-muha* (R), and स्फुट for *ugghuṭṭha* (R), i.e. probably *pphuḍa-mahī*⁰.

K says पुनरपि अतर्कितोदितसंज्ञा, उरसि घूर्णमानवेणीमुखा, स्तनलग्नबहुभूमिरजस्का सीता विलपितुं प्रवृत्ता।

MY says सखीवक्षस: अतर्कितोत्थिता समुच्छ्रवसिता च। He reads *upphuṭṭha* = उन्मृष्ट ro *ugghuṭṭha*, and remarks उन्मार्जनमपि रजसो वेणीमुखेनेत्यवसेयम्। cf. R who says उरसि घूर्णमानेन वेणीमुखेनोद्धृष्टमुत्प्रोञ्छितं स्तनलग्नं महीरजो यस्या:।

103. साहसु ज च्चिअ पढमं दट्ठूण अहं इमं महिम्मि णिसण्णा।
स च्चिअ मोहुम्मिल्ला पेच्छामि अ णं पुणो धरेमि अ जीअम्।।

[शाधि यैव प्रथमं दृष्ट्वाहमिदं मह्यां निषण्णा।
सैव मोहोन्मीलिता पश्यामि चैतत्पुनर्धारयामि च जीवम्।।]

---

[49] Cf. Mādhava in Extracts. Literally tears accumulated owing to the contact of their eyes. Might mean also: tears accumulated on Trijaṭā's bosom owing to the contact of her eyes with it.

[50] Our copy has परिवर्तमानेन। The Trivandrum manuscript has also this reading.

"Tell me if I am the same that first saw this head and sank to the ground, and, then, recovering from the swoon, see it again, and cling to life.

K reads वदनं यदेव . . . तदेव for *sāhasu ja ccia . . . sa ccia* (R). MY's reading is the same as his *pratīka* is *vaaṇaṁ* like K's.

K says प्रथमं यदेवेदं वदनं दृष्ट्वाहं मह्यां पतिता, मोहादुन्मीलिता मोहापगमादुन्मीलित-नयना पुनः तदेवेदं पश्यामि स्वस्था भूत्वा पश्यामि, इदानीं (च) जीवितं धारयामि। अहो कष्टम्।

MY says मोहादुन्मीलिता मोहं विहाय लब्धसंज्ञेत्यर्थः। प्रथमं मूर्छापि तावदासीत् इदानीं सापि गतेति सा हृदयमुपालभते स्म।

R says शाधि कथमं। इदं रामशिरो दृष्ट्वा प्रथमं यैवाहं मह्य निषण्णा मूर्च्छितास्मीत्यर्थः, सैवाहं मोहे सति उन्मीलिता पुनः प्राप्तचैतन्या सती एतत् शिरः पश्यामि, etc.

104. सहिआ रक्खसवसही दिट्ठं तुह णाह एरिसं अवसाणम्।
अज्ज वि वअणिज्जहअं धूमाइ च्चिअ ण पज्जलइ मे हिअअम्।।

[सोढा राक्षसवसतिर्दृष्टं तव नाथ ईदृशमवसानम्।
अद्यापि वचनीयहतं धूमायत एव न प्रज्वलति मे हृदयम्।।]

I have endured life among the demons, and seen, my lord, such an end of thee; but my heart, overwhelmed with disgrace, still smoulders, and doth not burst into flame.

MY says वचनीयहतं रामात्ययेऽपि जानकी जीवति इत्यनेन परिवादेन हतमपीत्यर्थः।

105. पुरिससरिसं तुह इमं रक्खससरिसं कअं णिसाअरवइणा।
कह ता चिन्तिअसुलहं महिलासरिसं ण संपडइ मे मरणम्।।

[पुरुषसदृशं तवेदं राक्षससदृशं कृतं निशाचरपतिना।
कथं तावच्चिन्तितसुलभं महिलासदृशं न संपद्यते मे मरणम्।।]

This thy end is worthy of a man,[51] and the lord of the demons hath done what befits a demon. Why is it that death, worthy of a woman, and available at will,[52] doth not befall me?

K reads चिन्त्यमानं (*cintijjantaṁ*) for *cintia-sulahaṁ* (R, MY and Kula), which is mentioned by him as a variant.

MY says *kaha ā* (for *tā*) कस्मात् तावत्। चिन्तितसुलभमित्यत्र अपिशब्दो

[51] Because, as she thinks, he died fighting.

[52] I.e. by suicide.

व्याहर्तव्यः। K says मम तावत् चिन्त्यमानं मरणं महिलानां स्त्रीणां समुचितं कथं न संपतति।

106. पवणसुअसिट्ठतुरिअं इह एन्तस्स अवलम्बिउं मह जीअम्।
विरहलहुअं पि राहव मए जिअन्तीअ जीविअं तुज्झ हिअम्।।

[पवनसुतशिष्टत्वरितमिहागच्छतोऽवलम्बितुं मम जीवम्।
विरहलघुकमपि राघव मया जीवन्त्या जीवितं तव हृतम्।।]

Thou hadst sped hither, O scion of Raghu, as soon as Hanumat delivered his message, to save my life, worn by the sorrows of sepration; but I destroyed thy life, myself remaining alive."

K and MY read दृष्ट for *siṭṭha* (शिष्ट) found in R who says शिष्टे कथिते सति। Kula also has कथित।

K says हे राघव इतः प्रतिनिवृत्तेन पवनसुतेन दृष्टत्वात् त्वरितम् इह मम जीवितमवलम्बितुम् आगच्छतः तव जीवितं विरहव्यथया लघुभूतमपि जीवन्त्या मया हृतमभूत।

MY says पवनसुतेन मरणाय त्वरिततया दृष्टं मम जीवितमवलम्बितुमागच्छतस्तव मद्विरहदुःखक्लिष्टमपि जीवितं प्रत्युत जीवन्त्या मया हृतमित्यर्थः। R says विरहेण लघुकमपि गत्वरमपि मम जीवमवलम्बितुं रक्षितुमिहागच्छतस्तव जीवितं जीवन्त्या मया हृतम्।

107. अलअन्धआरिअमुही समुहागअकण्ठभमिअवेणीबन्धा।
मोहपडिवण्णहिअआ दरजम्पिअणीसहं पुणो वि णिसण्णा।।

[अलकान्धकारितमुखी संमुखागतकण्ठभ्रमितवेणीबन्धा।
मोहप्रतिपन्नहृदया दरजल्पितनिःसहं पुनरपि निषण्णा।।]

Stupefied in her heart, she sank to the ground again as she wearily moaned in a faint voice, with the face hidden[53] by her tresses, and the hair spreading about the neck in front.

MY reads जीवितं for *jampia* (R and K).

He says मोहप्राप्तहृदया ईषज्जीवितनिःसहं गतप्रायजीविततया परवशा यथा स्यात् तथा पुनरपि विसंज्ञा जातेत्यर्थः। K (*chāyā*) has दरजल्पितनिःसहं। K says लम्बैरलकैरन्धकारितमुखी, संमुखं पुरोभागमागतेन पुनः कण्ठे परिवृत्तेन वेणीबन्धेन युक्ता सा मोहगृहीतहृदया भूत्वा दरविलपितविह्वलं यथा पुनरपि निषण्णा। The verse is not found in our copy of Kula.

[53] Literally darkened.

108. तो फुडिअवेणिबन्धणभङ्गुग्गअविसमकेसपल्हत्थरणे।
पडिआ रामोरत्थलसअणणिरासहिअआ महिअलुच्छङ्गे।।

[ततः स्फुटितवेणीबन्धनभङ्गोद्गतविषमकेशपर्यास्तरणे।
पतिता रामोरःस्थलशयननिराशहृदया महितलोत्सङ्गे।।

Bereft of all hope of reposing on Rāma's bosom, she lay on the ground covered with the wavy, dishevelled hair of her loosened braid.

K and MY read शिथिल for *phuḍia* = स्फुटित (R and Kula). They read उन्नत for *uggaa* (R and Kula ?). They and Kula read प्रत्यास्तरणे for *palhatharaṇe* (प्रर्यास्तरणे) found in R.

K says ततो मूर्च्छिता सा शिथिलस्य विश्लिष्टस्य वेणीबन्धन(स्य) सम्बन्धिनः भङ्गवदुन्नताः तरङ्गवदुन्नताः विषमाः केशा एव प्रत्यास्तरणं शयनं यत्र तस्मिन महीतलोत्संङ्गे रामोरःस्थलशयने निराशहृदया पपात। MY says *paccattharaṇe*[54] प्रत्यास्तरणे। शिथिलस्य वेणीबन्धस्य भङ्गेन कुटिलतया क्वचित्। क्वचिदुन्नतः अतएव विषमः केश एव प्रत्यास्तरणं यत्र तद्भूतलं तथा तस्मिन् निपतितेत्यर्थः।

Kula says स्फुटितं विश्लिष्टं यत् वेणीबन्धनम्। R says वेण्या बन्धनस्य बन्धनपाशस्य भङ्गेनापगमेन उद्गताः प्रसृताः अत एव विषमा व्यस्ता ये केशाः, etc. *SC* says भङ्गेन कौटिल्येनोद्गताः।

109. तीअ णवपल्लवेण व पहराअम्बविहलेण हत्थेण मुहम्।
परिमज्जिउं ण चइअं एक्ककवोलमिलिआलअं कह वि कअम्।।

[तया नवपल्लवेनेव प्रहाराताम्रविह्वलेन हस्तेन मुखम्।
परिमार्ष्टुं न शकितमेककपोलमिलितालकं कथमपि कृतम्।।]

She could not wipe her face with her feeble hand, turned red, like a new leaf, by beating the breast, but somehow put aside her tresses on one cheek.[55]

K and Kula read केवले for *kaha vi* = कथमपि (R). K says स्तनप्रहारैः ताम्रविह्वलेन नवपल्लवेनेन तस्या हस्तेन बाष्पविह्वलायाः तस्या हस्तेन बाष्परजोदूषितं मुखं परिमार्ष्टुं न पारितं, केवलमेकत्र कपोले मिलितालकं कृतम्।

110. समुहमिलिअं पि जाहे रूअं वाहविहला ण गेह्णइ दिट्ठी।
ताहे कह कह वि कअं उहअकरुप्पुसिअलोअणं तीअ मुहम्।।

[54] Manuscript C of Goldschmidt has this reading.

[55] I.e. to be able to look at the head.

[संमुखमिलितमपि यदा रूपं बाष्पविह्वला न गृह्णाति दृष्टिः।
तदा कथं कथमाप कृतमुभयकरोत्प्रोच्छितलोचनं तस्या मुखम्।।]

When her vision, bedimmed with tears, failed to apprehend even the things lying in front of her, she somehow rubbed her eyes with both hands.

K reads मिलिता for *miliaṁ* (R and Kula).

K says राघवमुखस्याभिमुखं प्रसृतापि बाष्पविह्वला तस्या दृष्टिः यदा रूपं न गृह्णाति स्म, तदा कथं कथमपि मुखम् उभयकरोन्मृष्टलोचनबाष्पं कृतम्। MY says तया तद्दिदृक्षारभसेन लोचनयुगलं करयुगलेन प्रमृष्टमित्यर्थः।

R says संमुखमिलितमपि रूपं घटादिस्वरूपं यदा न गृह्णाति।

111. तो सा भमन्तमारुअविसमपइण्णालउप्पुसिअवाहजला।
पेच्छइ राहववअणं णिसाअरोच्छुण्णमहिअलपहोलन्तम्।।

[ततः सा भ्रमन्मारुतविषमप्रकीर्णालकोत्प्रोच्छितबाष्पजला।
प्रेक्षते राघववदनं निशाचरावक्षुण्णमहीतलप्रघूर्णमानम्।।]

With the tears wiped away by her tresses, scattered by a gust of wind, she looked at Rāma's head, vibrating on the ground, as if it had just been severed by the demons.[56]

K and Kula read प्रविद्ध for *paiṇṇa* = प्रकीर्ण (R). K and MY read रजोनिकरच्छन्न for *ṇisāarocchuṇṇa* = निशाचरावक्षुण्ण (R). K reads प्रलुठत् (*paloṭṭantaṁ*) for (*paholantaṁ*) = प्रघूर्णमानम्। (R and Kula). MY's reading is same as K's.

K says ततो भ्रमता मारुतेन विषमविक्षिप्तैरलकैः। उन्मृष्टबाष्पजला सा रजोनिकरच्छन्ने पांसुनिवहेन छन्ने महीतले . . . प्रलुठत् राघवमुखं पश्यति स्म। My says *raa-ṇiara-cchaṇṇa-mahi-ala-paloṭṭantaṁ* रजोनिकरच्छन्ने महीतले प्रस्फुरत् रामशिरः।

K says राघववदनं (निशाचरैः ?) छिन्नं महीतले प्रघूर्णमानम्। He reads *°cchiṇṇa* for *occhuṇṇa* (अवक्षुण्ण)। *SC* says तत्कालच्छिन्नमिव विचेष्टमानम्।

112. लक्खिज्जन्तबिसाआ अब्भहिउम्मिल्लणिच्चलट्ठिअणअणा।
रामसिरबद्धलक्खा धुव्वइ वाहेण से ण रुम्भइ दिट्ठी।।

[लक्ष्यमाणविषादाभ्यधिकोन्मीलन्निश्चलस्थितनयना।
रामशिरोबद्धलक्ष्या धाव्यते बाष्पेणास्या न रुध्यते दृष्टिः।।]

[56] See Kulanātha in Extracts.

Her mournful eyes, fixed on the head, with the pupils much dilated and motionless, were washed, not hindered by her tears.[57]

K says तस्या दृष्टिर्दर्शनक्रिया बाष्पेण धाव्यते क्षाल्यते स्म विशदीकृता (MY also)। न पुनर्बाष्पप्रसरेण रुध्यते स्म। बाष्पश्च प्रबहत्येव। दृष्टिश्च रामवदनमेव पश्यति स्म।

MY says दृष्टिः दर्शनक्रिया तारका वा। *SC* says अत्र नयनं तारका, दृष्टिः नेत्रमिति श्रीनिवासः। K says अभ्यधिकोन्मीलितनिश्चलस्थितनयनसन्निवेशा, रामशिरसि बद्धलक्षा तस्या दृष्टिः।

113. तो तं दट्ठूण पुणो मरणेक्करसाइ वाहणीसारच्छम्।
आउच्छसु मं ति कअं तिअडागअलोअणाइ दीणविहसिअम्।।

[ततस्तद्दृष्ट्वा पुनर्मरणैकरसया बाष्पनिःसाराक्षम्।
आपृच्छस्व मामिति कृतं त्रिजटागतलोचनया दीनविहसितम्।।]

She beheld it once more; and intent on death, glanced at Trijaṭā with tearless eyes, and piteously smiled as she said "Suffer me (to die)".

K reads निर्भरनयनं for *ṇīsāracchaṁ* = निःसाराक्षम् (R and Kula), and विलोकितं (*pulaiaṁ*) for *vihasiaṁ* (R and Kula). K says तत् रामवदनं चिरं दृष्ट्वा ततः पुनः मरणैकरसया मरणैकरागया मरणैकनिश्चयया, त्रिजटागतनयनया तया मरिष्यन्तीं माम् आपृच्छस्व आभाषस्व इत्यक्त्वा बाष्पनिर्भरनयनं दीनं विलोकितं दर्शनं कृतम्। MY says *āvuchasu* आपृच्छस्व। आप्रश्नश्च प्रस्थातुकामस्य जनस्य संभाषणादिरिति। Kula reads आपृच्छ इति, i.e. *āücchāmi tti* (cf. *SC* text) for *āüchasu maṁ ti* (आपृच्छस्व मामिति)। Kula's gloss is corrupt, but *SC* says आपृच्छे मरणोद्यमेऽनुज्ञां गृह्णामीति कृत्वा। R says मामापृच्छस्व संवद मरणकृतोद्यमां मामनुजानीहि।

114. सहिअम्मि रामविरहे दारुणहिअअप्पडिच्छिए वेहव्वे।
सहसु गअणेहलहुअं मह णिल्लज्जमरणं इमं ति परुण्णा।।

[सोढे रामविरहे दारुणहृदयप्रतीष्टे वैधव्ये।
सहस्व गतस्नेहलघुकं मम निर्लज्जमरणमिदमिति प्ररुदिता।।]

"Forgive my shameless death, despicable because of lack of love, since I endured separation from Rāma, and accepted

[57] I.e. in spite of her tears she could see the head clearly.

widowhood with a cruel heart."[58] Thus saying, she burst into tears.

K and MY read हस for *sahasu* = सहस्व (R and Kula). My says दारुणे क्रूरे हृदये मया प्रतीष्टे वैधव्ये, *hasasu* हस, ममेदं निर्लज्जं मरणं हसेति प्ररुदितेत्यन्वयः। K says प्रतीष्टे गृहीते। Kula says हे दारुण हृदय मम निर्लज्जं मरणमिदं सहस्व अनुभवेति प्ररुदिता।

115. सव्वस्स अ एस गई ण उणो माणुण्णआण इममवसाणम्।
अणुसरिसं ति भणन्ती आहन्तूण पडिआ थिरं थणअलसम्।।

[सर्वस्य चैषा गतिर्न पुनर्मानोन्नतानामिदमवसानम्।
अनुसदृशमिति भणन्ती आहत्य पतिता स्थिरं स्तनकलशम्।।]

"This is the fate of all, but such an end is unbecoming to those who have an exalted sense of the their dignity."[59] As she uttered these words she threw herself on the ground, beating her breast.

K and Kula read अपि (*vi*) for *a* = च (R). K reads मानोन्नतजातेरयमवमानः for *ṇa uṇo*, etc. (R). MY's reading seems to be same as that of K except for a difference in construction (see below).

K and MY read अपमृष्ट इति (*opusio tti*) for *aṇusarisaṁ ti* = अनुसदृशमिति (R). K and Kula read युगलं for *°alasaṁ* = कलसम् (R).

K says सर्वस्यापि स्त्रीजनस्य एषैव गतिः। युदत वैधव्यम्। किंतु मानोन्नताया जाते क्षत्रियस्त्रीजातेरयमवमानः[60] अपमृष्टः[61]। पतिमरणं सोढ्वा पश्चात् स्वबुद्धया मरणं वैधव्यावलम्बनं वा अवमानः। स क्षत्रियस्त्रीभिः अपमृष्ट एव परिहृत एवेति भणन्ती हा हतास्म्यहमिति स्थिरं स्तनयुगलमाहत्य पतिता। *opusia tti* टाबन्तपाठे तु मानोन्नतजातेः परिमरणात् पश्चात् मरणं वैधव्यं वा अवमान एव। अहमित्यध्याहार्यम्। अहमपमृष्टास्मि सर्वैः परिभूतास्मीति व्याख्येयम्। R says स्थिरं पतिता भूमावित्यर्थात्।

MY says सर्वोऽप्यविशेषादन्ततो म्रियत एव। तथा मानोन्नतया जात्या अयमस्मासु आपतितः पतिव्यसनेऽपि हृदयास्फुटनात्मकोऽवमानः अपमृष्टः परिहृत एव इतः पूर्वम्। तथा च स्त्रीषु मयि एवायमपूर्वः अवमानो जात इति भणन्तीत्यर्थः। . . . टाबन्तपाठे तु मानोन्नतजात्याः (?) मानोन्नतानां स्त्रीणां पतिमरणं सोढ्वापि पश्चात् स्वबुद्ध्या मरणमवमान एव तथा च अवमृष्ठास्मि दैवादहं तथाविधतयापि नष्टास्मीति

[58] Instead of dying on seeing the severed head.

[59] Translation follows Rāmadāsa's reading.

[60] K seems to read *māṇuṇṇaa-jāle aamavamāṇo*.

[61] *Chāyā* has अव°।

भणन्तीति व्याख्येयम्। MY mentions the Prākṛt reading, but our copy is here corrupt.

R reads *ṇa uṇo māṇuṇṇaāṇa imamavasāṇaṁ*. He says सर्वस्य एषा गतिः। . . . मानोन्नतानां पुनरिदमवसानम् एवंरूपेण मरणं नानुसदृशं न योग्यम्। Kula is mostly corrupt, but *SC* seems to follow him. He reads *māṇuṇṇa ṇāha tuha imaṁ avasāṇaṁ, aṇusarisaṁ ti*, i.e. (हे) मानोन्नत नाथ तव इदमवसानम् असदृशमिति।

116. तह जीवलज्जिआए विलवन्तीअ वि विसाअणीसहमउअम्।
दासरहि त्ति पलन्तं पिओ त्ति सीआइ ण चइअं वाहत्तुम॥

[तथा जीवलज्जितया विपलन्त्यापि विषादनिःसहमृदुकम्।
दाशरथिरिति प्रलपितं प्रिय इति सीतया न शकितं व्याहर्तुम्॥]

Even as she wailed in this wise, ashamed of her life, wearily in a voice faint from grief, Sītā addressed Rāma as the son of Daśaratha, but could not say "Beloved".

K and Kula omit *vi* (अपि) after *vilavantīa* (R). They seem to read *vilavantīe*. K puts सीतया before प्रियेति।

117. अणुसोइउं ण इच्छइ ण देइ अङ्गम्मि सा परम्मि पहारम्।
वाहं मुअइ ण रुम्भइ मरिअव्वे लद्धपच्चअं से हिअअम्॥

[अनुशोचितुं नेच्छति न ददात्यङ्गे सा परस्मिन्निव प्रहारम्।
बाष्पं मुञ्चति न रुणद्धि मर्तव्ये लब्धप्रत्ययमस्या हृदयम्॥]

No more did she wish to lament, nor smote her breast,[62] like an enemy. She shed no tears, but checked their flow. Her heart was bent on death.

K reads शीर्षे सा उरसि च (*sīsammi sā urammi a*) for *aṁgammi sā parammi va* (R and Kula).

K says शिरसि उरसि व प्रहारं न ददौ। . . . बाष्पं नं मुञ्चति स्म। रुणद्धि पिर्गच्छन्तं बाष्पं रुरोध।

MY says *mariavve* मर्तव्ये मरणे लब्धप्रत्ययं लब्धनिश्चयम्।

118. तो तं मरणणिमित्ते अणिअत्तन्तहिअअं पअत्ता वत्तुम।
तिअडा धुअग्गकरअलदरपडिअपडिच्छिअङ्गविसमो अण्णम्॥

[62] Literally body.

[ततस्तां मरणनिमित्ते अनिवर्तमानहृदयां प्रवृत्ता वक्तुम्।
त्रिजटा धुताग्रकरतलदरपतितप्रतीष्टाङ्गविषमावनताम्।।]

Trijaṭā then began to speak to her. Yearning for death, she was drooping heavily with her body held up (by her friend) as she, with quivering hands, almost fell to the ground.

K reads परिवर्तमान for *aṇiattanta* = अनिवर्तमान (R and Kula). He reads विषमालीनां (*visamallīṇaṁ* ?) for *visamoaṇṇaṁ* = विषमावनताम् (R). *SC* text has *visamoallaṁ* rendered as विषमोत्कम्पात् in the *chāyā*. This is also the reading of manuscript C of Goldschmidt and of Kula who has दारुणकम्पा। See below. *Deśīnāmamālā* 1.165 gives कम्प and पर्यस्त among the meanings of *oalla*. See also Notes on 13.43 where *oalla* is explained as अवनत by Kula. This agrees with R's explanation of *oaṇṇa*.

R says धुताग्राभ्यां करतलाभ्यां किंचित् पतितं सत् प्रतीष्टमवलम्बितं यदङ्गं तेन विषमं व्यस्तं यथा स्यात् तथावनतां, etc.

K says ततो मरणस्य निमित्ते उद्बन्धनादौ परिवर्तमानहृदयां परिभ्रमन्मानसां त्रिजटा धुताभ्याम् अग्रकरतलाभ्यां दरपतितावस्थायां प्रतीष्टैः गृहीतैरङ्गैः विषममालीनामङ्के निलीनां तां वक्तुं प्रवृत्ता। MY says धुताग्रकरतलाम् ईषत्पतितां त्रिजटया प्रतीष्टाङ्गविषमावलम्बनां त्रिजटया पतनदशायामेव प्रतीष्टदेहामीत्यर्थः। Kula says धुताग्रकरतला चासौ दरपतितप्रतीष्टेषु अङ्गेषु विषमावचला दारुणकम्पा चेति ताम्।[63]

119. जाणइ सिणेहभणिअं मा रअणिअरि त्ति मे जुउच्छसु वअणम्।
उज्जाणम्मि वणम्मि अ जं सुरहिं तं लआण गेह्णइ कुसुमम्।।

[जानकि स्नेहभणितं मा रजनीचरीति मे जुगुप्सस्व वचनम्।
उद्याने वने च यत्सुरभि तल्लतानां गृह्यते कुसुमम्।।]

"Sītā, despise not affectionate words, because I am a *rākṣasa* woman. Whether in a garden or in a wood, it is the fragrant flowers of the creepers that are culled.

K and MY *pratīka* has *jāṇasu* (जानीहि) for *jāṇai* = जानकि (R and Kula).

K, MY and Kula put this verse after 121.

120. किमु जीअन्तीअ तुमे जइ अलिअं सहि ण होज्ज राहवमरणम्।
अणहे उण रहुणाहे तुह मे मरणविहुरं किलिम्मइ हिअअम्।।

[63] This explanation is anonymously reproduced in *SC* which has विषमावगला।

[किमु जीवन्त्या त्वया यद्यलीकं सखि न भवेद्राघवमरणम्।
अनघे पुना रघुनाथे तव मे मरणविधुरं क्लाम्यति हृदयम्।।]

Friend, if Rāghava were really dead, what would indeed be the use of thy living? But my heart is weighed down with sorrow, because thou art dying even when Rāma is safe.

K and Kula *pratīka* has *kim va* for *kimu* (R). K says किमिव, Kula किं वा। My *pratīka* has *kīva*. The readings of K, Kula and MY require *jiantīa metri c.* for *jī°* (R).

K says राघवस्य मरणं यद्यलीकं न भवेत् सत्यं यदि भवेत् तदा जीवन्त्या त्वयां किं प्रयोजनं तदा मरणमेव श्रेय इत्यर्थः। रघुनाथे पुनरनघे क्लेशरहिते सति तव मरणेन विधुरं पीडितं मे मनः क्लाम्यति।

121. चिन्तेउं पि ण लम्भइ जह संभावेसि तह इमं जइ होन्तम्।
तो दाणि किं जणम्मि व तुमम्मि संठावणा महं अणुरूवा।।

[चिन्तयितुमपि न लभ्यते यथा संभावयसि तथेदं यदि भवत्।
तदेदानीं किं जन इव त्वयि संस्थापना ममानुरूपा।।]

It is impossible even to imagine what thou hast surmised. If it were so, would my consolation be now in place in regard to thee, as in the case of the common people?[64]

K and MY have शक्यते, and Kula पार्यते fro *labbhai* = लभ्यते (R). Their reading is *tīrai* found in *SC* text and manuscript C of Goldschmidt. *kīrai* mentioned by MY seems to be a mistake for *tī°*. Kula reads *saṁbhāvaṇā* for *saṁṭhā°* (संस्थापना)।

K says तथा संभावयसि यथा त्वं मन्यसे तथा तत् चिन्तयितुमपि न शक्यते। तथेदं यदि भवेत् तत इदानीं जन इव प्राकृतजने यथा तथा त्वयि मम संस्थापना समाश्वासना किमनुरूपा।

Kula says किं जन इव त्वयि संभावना ममानुरूपा। मृतपतिकायास्तवानुमरणं किं वारयामीति भावः। He says चिन्तयितुमपि न पार्यते किं पुनरवधारयितुमिति भावः। यथा संभावयसि तथेदं यद्यभविष्यत्। R says न लभ्यते न युज्यते।

122. सअला निसाअरपुरी घरपरिवाडिसमणीहरिअरुण्णरवा।
एक्केण कआ कइणा कह होइहि अणहरक्खरं रहुवडणम्।।

---

[64] I.e. if Rāma were really dead, it would be unnecessary to comfort Sītā like an ordinary woman, because she would commit suicide as a matter of course.

[सकला निशाचरपुरी गृहपरिपाटिसमनिर्ह्लदितरुदितरवा।
एकेन कृता कपिना कथं भविष्यत्यनघराक्षसं रघुपतनम्।।]

A single ape[65] reduced the entire city of the demons to such a plight that the loud wail rang through the rows of houses. How could Rāma's death come about with the demons unscathed?

K reads स्फुट for सम (R, MY and Kula ?).

K reads अनघराक्षसो रामवधः for *aṇaha-rakkhasaṁ rahu-vaḍaṇaṁ* = अनघराक्षसं रघुपतनम् found in R.

K says निशाचरपुरी सर्वा गृहपरिपाटिषु गृहपंक्तिषु स्फुटनिर्ह्रादिरोदनशब्दा परिस्फुटगम्भीररुदितशब्दा एकेनैव कपिना कृता। R says निर्ह्रदितः शब्दान्तरोत्पादी रुदितरवः। MY says निर्गतेति केचित्।

Kula says कथं भविष्यति अनघराक्षसं 'रामवधं' i.e. he reads *aṇaha-rakkhasaṁ rāma-vahaṁ* found in *SC* text. He remarks वधशब्दश्च प्राकृते नपुंसकलिङ्गोऽपि दृश्यते। K says एवंविधबहुसहस्रवानरपरिवारस्य रामस्य वधः कथमनघराक्षसो भविष्यति। तस्य वधे प्रस्तुते राक्षसानां कथं बाधा न भवेत्।

123. णत्थि णिहम्मइ रामो अइरा लोहिइ अरक्खसं तेल्लोक्कम्।
दिट्ठं ति भणामि फुडं पत्तिअ कस्स वि पिओ कुलस्स विणासो।।

[नास्ति निहन्यते रामोऽचिराद्भविष्यत्यराक्षसं त्रैलोक्यम्।
दृष्टमिति भणामि स्फुटं प्रतीहि कस्यापि प्रियः कुलस्य विनाशः।।]

It is impossible. Rāma cannot be killed. The world will soon be without any demons. I say so because I have foreseen it clearly. Believe me. To whom is the destruction of his race dear?

K and Kula read *ṇa hammai* for *ṇihammai* (निहन्यते) found in R who mentions the other reading as a variant.

K says त्वया शङ्कितमं नास्ति, रामो न हन्यते। . . . प्रतीहि विश्वसिहि। MY says नास्तीति एतदिति शेषः। Kula says न भवत्येव तदित्यर्थः। तदेव द्रढयति, न हन्यते राम इति।

124. उट्ठसु मुएसु सोअं पुस एअं वाहमइलिअं थणवट्ठम्।
सुणसु सउणेण वट्ठइ समराहिमुहे पइम्मि अंसुणिवाओ।।

---

[65] Hanumat.

[उत्तिष्ठ मुञ्च शोकं प्रोच्छ बाष्पमलिनितं स्तनपृष्ठम्।
शृणु शकुनेन वर्तते समराभिमुखे पत्यावश्रुनिपातः।।]

Rise. Give up thy sorrow. Wipe thy bosom soiled with tears. Hearken. The shedding of tears is inauspicious when one's consort confronts a battle.

K and Kula read युगलं for *vaṭṭhaṁ* = पृष्ठम् (R). K and MY read स्वप्नेऽपि for *saüṇe* = शकुने (R and Kula). They read *suṇa* for *suṇasu*. MY says *suṇa* शृणु मयोच्यमानमिति शेषः। *siviṇe vi* स्वप्नेऽपि। Lokanātha quoted by *SC* explains न वर्तते (*ṇa vaṭṭai*) as अनुचित। Kula says शकुने मङ्गले।

125. मोत्तूण अ रहुणाहं लज्जागअसेअबिन्दुइज्जन्तमुहो।
केण व अण्णेण कअ पाआरन्तरिअणिप्पहो दहवअणो।।

[मुक्त्वा च रघुनाथं लज्जागतस्वेदबिन्दूयमानमुखः।
केन वान्येन कृतः प्राकारान्तरितनिष्प्रभो दशवदनः।।]

Excluding Rāma, who else hath confined Rāvaṇa within the walls (of Laṅkā), bereft of lustre, with sweat dripping from his face on account of shame?

K reads अन्येनापि केन कृतः for *keṇa va aṇṇeṇa kao* = केन वान्येन कृतः (R and Kula). K says रघुनाथं मुक्त्वा अपहाय दशवदनः केनान्येन लज्जया आगतैः स्वेदबिन्दुभिः चीयमानमुखः पूर्यमाणमुखः, प्राकारेणान्तरितो व्यवहितः प्राकारान्तरालवर्ती निष्प्रभश्च कृतः। इतः पूर्वमन्येनापि केनैवं कृतो रावणः।

MY has *lajjāaa* (लज्जागत)। He says *lajjāama* इति पाठे लज्जागमात्, etc. This reading is found in Kula who also says स्वेदबिन्दुकीर्यमाणमुखः (cf. K and *SC*), i.e. °*bindu-ijjanta*° for *binduijanta* = बिन्दूयमान (R). Kula says प्राकारान्तरिते प्राकारबहिर्देशे निष्प्रभः। *SC* says प्राकाराद् बहिः प्रतापशून्य इत्यर्थः।

126. अइरा अ दे रहुसुओ तण्णाअन्तग्गहत्थमउइअपम्हम्।
मोच्छिहि वेवन्तङ्गुलिगुप्पन्तुक्खित्तविसमभाअं वेणिम्।।

[अचिराच्च ते रघुसुतो आर्द्रायमाणाग्रहस्तमुकुलितपक्ष्माम्।
मोक्ष्यति वेपमानाङ्गुलिगुप्यन्नुत्क्षिप्तविषमभागां वेणीम्।।]

Soon will Rāma loosen thy braid, with the tresses softened

by his perspiring[66] hands, and the curls[67] ruffled and raised by his trembling fingers.

K and Kula read रघुपतिः for *-suo* (R). K reads मोचित (*moia*) for *maüia* = मुकुलित (?) R, मृदुकृत Kula. K and MY read आक्षिप्त for *ukkhitta* = उत्क्षिप्त (R and Kula).

MY reads *moihii* = मोचयिष्यति for *mocchihi* (R) = मोक्ष्यति।

The reading of K and Kula is not clear, but they also say मोक्ष्यति। *SC* text has *mocchihi*.

MY says केशाग्रस्पर्शरसजनितवेपथुभिरङ्गुलिभिः आक्षिप्ताः समाकृष्टाः व्याकुलीभवन्तश्च विषमभागा यथा स्युस्तथा। मोचनदशायां वेण्या विशेषणमेतत्। MY seems to read *vevia* for *vevanta* = वेपमान (R, K and Kula).

K says अचिरात् रावणे हते रघुपतिस्ते वेणीं मोक्ष्यति चोद्वेष्टयति च। कथंभूताम् – स्पर्शसंभवेन स्वेदेन आर्द्रीभवता हस्ताग्रेण मोचितकेशां, स्पर्शरसात् वेपमानाभिरङ्गुलिभिः आक्षिप्ता आकृष्टा गुप्यन्तो व्याकुलीभवन्तः विषमभागा यथा भवन्ति तथा भूतां मोक्ष्यति। R says वेपमानाभिरङ्गुलोभिरुत्क्षिप्ताः समीकृता विषमभागा यस्याः। प्रोषितो भर्ता समागत्य प्राक्कृतं विरहिण्या वेणीबन्धं मोचयतीति भावः।

127. विअलिअलज्जालहुअं एअ करन्तस्स रहुवइम्मि धरन्ते।
ण अ तह दुक्खामि तुमे जह पविवत्तम्मि दहमुहस्स सहावे।।

[विगलितलज्जालघुकमेतत्कुर्वतो रघुपतौ ध्रियमाणे।
न च तथा दूये त्वया यथा परिवृत्ते दशमुखस्य स्वभावे।।]

I am aggrieved not so much on thy account as at the changed character of Rāvaṇa, thus acting meanly, without shame, while Rāma is alive.

K, MY and Kula read अपि (*vi*) for अ (R) in the second line. K and MY read प्रतापे for *sahāve* = स्वभावे (R and Kula).

MY says *ea karantassa* एवं कुर्वतः (K and Kula also)। *Tume* त्वयि त्वया वा। जीवत्यपि रामे लज्जां विहाय छलमेवं कुर्वतो रावणस्य प्रभावे परिवृत्ते तथा दूये न तथा त्वयि एवमवस्थायामपीत्यर्थः। Kula says न तथा त्वयापि[68] दुःस्थितया। K says विगलितलज्जत्वात् लघु अतिक्षुद्रमेवं कुर्वतः।

---

[66] Literally moist.

[67] Literally the uneven parts.

[68] Our copy has तथापि।

128. वालिवहदिट्ठसारं बाणगलत्थिअसमुद्ददिण्णथलवहम्।
रोहिअलङ्कावलअं मा लहुअं प्रेच्छ राहवस्स भुअबलम्।।

[वालिवधदृष्टसारं बाणगलहस्तितसमुद्रदत्तस्थलपथम्।
रोधितलङ्कावलयं मा लघुकं पश्य राघवस्य भुजबलम्।।]

Think not that the power of Rāma's arms counts for little. Its efficacy was seen in the slaying of Vāli. On account of it, the ocean, driven by his arrows, hath granted a land-track across its waters.[69] On account of it, Laṅkā is besieged.

K, MY and Kula read मलय for *valaa* = वलय (R).

K says कक्षान्तरे रावणं प्रक्षिप्य चतुःसमुद्रेषु सान्ध्योपास्तिं कृतवतो वालिनो वधे दृष्टसारम्। रोधिती वानरैरुपरोधिती लङ्कामलयाख्यः शैलो येन तत्तथाभूतं राघवस्य भुजबलं त्वं मा लघु पश्य। MY says आरूढलङ्कामलयाख्यशैलम्।

MY has *galatthalia*[70] = नुन्न for *galatthia* (R). K says बाणविलोलितेन समुद्रेण दत्तसेतुपथम्। Kula says बाणपीडितसमुद्रदत्तस्थलपथम्। . . . रोधितौ व्याप्तौ वा लङ्कामलयौ येन तत्। *SC* has रोधितौ गतागतैराक्रमितो वा व्याप्तौ वा।

129. दिट्ठासि मए सिविणे ससिसूरालिहणसोहिउम्मुहपडिमा।
खन्धुट्ठिअसुरगअकण्णआलविहुअधवलंसुअदसद्धन्ता।।

[दृष्टासि मया स्वप्ने शशिसूर्यालिहनशोभितोन्मुखप्रतिमा।
स्कन्धोत्थितसुरगजकर्णतालविधुतधवलांशुकदशार्धान्ता।।]

I have seen thee in a dream, riding on an elephant of the gods, with the fringes of thy white scarf shaken by the flappings of its ears; while thy joyful figure shone in contact with the sun and the moon.

K *pratīka* has *diṭṭhā tuvaṁ*. K reads स्कन्धस्थित for *khandhuṭṭhia* = स्कन्धोत्थित (R). K says स्वप्ने त्वं मयैवं दृष्टा। कथम्–शशि सूर्यालेहनेन शोभितोन्मुखप्रतिमा। अयमर्थः – सुरगजस्कन्धस्थिता त्वम् आसन्नगतं शशिमण्डलं सूर्यमण्डलं च कौतुकात् विलोकितवती। तदा तयोर्मण्डलयोरालेहनेन अवगाहनेन शोभितमुन्मुखभिमुखं प्रतिबिम्बं यस्याः सा तथा। सुरगजस्कन्धस्थितत्वात् तदीयकर्णतालेन कर्णचलनेन विधुतोत्तरीयपटार्धान्ता। It will be seen that K reads पट for *dasā* (R and Kula).

---

[69] Reference to the causeway.

[70] MY's reading is against metre. Perhaps he reads *sara* for बाण।

MY says दृष्टासि च मे मया, i.e. *a me* for *mae* = मया (R and Kula). K seems to read *diṭṭhaā tuvaṁ a*.

MY is somewhat corrupt here. He seems to say *sasi- sūrā-lihaṇa* . . . तयोरुपजातप्रतिबिम्बेत्यर्थः। आलेहन[71] स्पर्शनम्।[72]

MY reads *khandha-ṭṭhia* like K, but he construes it as *khandha+aṭṭhia* (cf. 1.35). He says स्कन्धे आस्थितस्य अधिष्ठितस्य सुरगजस्येत्यर्थः। Kula also says स्कन्धास्थितस्य आरूढस्कन्धस्य सुरगजस्य कर्णतालेन विधूतः कम्पितो धवलाशुकस्य दशैकदेशो यस्या सा तथा।

R says शशिसूर्ययोरालिहनेन मिलनेन शोभिता उन्मुखी प्रतिभा आकृतिर्यस्याः सा। Kula explains प्रतिमा as प्रतिकृति. *SC* says शशिसूर्ययोः आलेहनेन संपर्केण शोभितोन्मुखी हर्षादुन्नतमुखी प्रतिमा प्रतिकृतिः यस्याः सा तथा चन्द्रसूर्यप्रतिबिम्बितेत्यर्थः।

130. दिट्ठो अ मे दहमुहो दहमुहपरिवाडिविअडकड्ढणमग्गो।
कालदढ पासकड्ढिअदरघडिउग्घडिअखलिअमुहसंघाओ।।

[दृष्टश्च मे दशमुखो दशमुखपरिपाटि विकटकर्षणमार्गः।
कालदृढपाशकृष्टदरघटितोद्घाटितस्खलितमुखसंघातः।।]

I have also seen Rāvaṇa, with his heads, partly adhering to the body, but disjoined and fallen, while being dragged by the god of death with a stout halter, with the trail of the ten heads clearly visible one after the other.

K reads मुखर for *khalia* = स्खलित (R *chāyā*). K (*chāyā*) has दरघटितोद्घटितमुखरमुखसंघातः।

K says दशमुखश्च मया स्वप्ने (दृष्टः)। कालेन दृढेन पाशेन कृष्टत्वात् दरघटितविघटितमुखरमुखसमूहः। दशानां मुखानां परिपाट्यां पङ्क्त्यां विकटकर्षणमार्गो दशधा प्रकटितकर्षणपथः।

MY says me मया। . . . घटितोद्घटित। उद्घटितमुत्क्षेपात् विघटनम् He reads *vihala* (विह्वल) for *khalia*.

Kula reads उत्खण्डित, i.e. *ukkhuḍia* (cf. *SC* text and Hemacandra 1.53) for *ugghaḍia* = उद्घटित। He says कालस्य यमस्य पाशेन कृष्टो दरघटितः किंचित् भग्नश्च उत्खण्डितश्च मुखसंघातो यस्य स तथा।

---

[71] Our copy has आहेनं।

[72] *ālihaṇa* comes from *ālihaï* = स्पृशति। See Hemacandra 4.182, Cf . *sasi-kiraṇā-lihaṇa-kabburo . . . viṁjha-selo vva* (*Līlāvaï*, 456) where, however, the *chāyā* takes *ālihaṇa* as आलिखन।

SC text has *paḍia* for *khalia* like manuscript C of Goldschmidt. R (commentary) follows this reading — पतितो भूमावित्यर्थात् मुखसंघातो यस्य।

131. तं अवलम्बसु धीरं णासउ संपइ अमङ्गलं जाव इमम्।
मुणिअपरमत्थलहुई अवहीरिअणिप्फला णिअत्तउ माआ।।

[तदवलम्बस्व धैर्यं नश्यतु संप्रत्यमङ्गलं यावदिदम्।
ज्ञातपरमार्थलघुकावधीरितनिष्फला निवर्ततां माया।।]

So take heart. Let all this inauspicious behaviour[73] now cease. Let the illusion vanish, ignored and futile, and empty because the truth is known.

K reads तावत् for *jāva* = यावत् (R, MY and Kula). MY says यावत् साकल्येनेत्यर्थः। *ohīria-ṇipphalā* (for *ava°*) त्वयानादृतत्वे विनिष्फला वैमनस्याख्यफलरहिता निवर्ततां माया।

Kula says यावदिदं सर्वमेतत् अमङ्गलं संप्रति नश्यतु।

132. होत्तं जइ रामसिरं एआवत्थं पि तो समूससमाणम्।
अमअं मिव णाअरसं आसाएउण तुह क्करप्फरिससुहम्।।

[भवद्यदि रामशिर एतावदवस्थमपि ततः समुच्छ्वसत्।
अमृतमिव ज्ञातरसमासाद्य तव करस्पर्शसुखम्।।]

Had it been Rāma's head, it would have returned to life even in such a plight, having obtained the familar touch of thy hands, sweet as nectar."

The verse is not found in our copy of Kula. K and MY read करतलस्पर्शम् for *kara-ppharisa-suhaṁ* (R).

K says एतदवस्थमपि छिन्नमपि। करतलस्पर्शमास्वाद्य। MY has आसाद्य।

133. इअ रामपेम्मकित्तणदूसहवज्जाहिघाअदूमिअहिअआ।
संभरिअ मुक्ककण्ठमण्णमअं मरणणिच्चआ वि परुण्णा।।

[इति रामप्रेमकीर्तनदुःसहवज्राभिघातदुःखितहृदया।
संस्मृय मुक्तकण्ठमन्यमयं मरणनिश्चयापि प्ररुदिता।।]

Agonized by the mention in this wise of Rāma's love for her, an unbearable crash of thunder, she wept aloud in a different manner, remembering the past, even though she was intent on death.

[73] I.e. weeping.

K says अन्यमयम् अन्यप्रकारम् अधिकतरम्। MY reads *saṁbharia- mukka-kaṇṭhā*. He says *saṁbharia* संस्मारित। संकीर्तनेन प्रेम स्मारिता मुक्तकण्ठा प्रलपन्तीत्यर्थः। संस्मृत्येति ल्यबन्धमिति केचित्। K, Kula and R take *saṁbharia* (संस्मृत्य) separately and read °*kaṇṭhaṁ*.

134. तो तिअडावअणेहि वि ण संठिआ जाव तीअ पवअकलअलो।
रणसंणाहगभीरो ण सुओ राहवपहाअमङ्गलपडहो।।

[ततस्त्रिजटावचनैरपि न संस्थिता यावत्तया प्लवगकलकलः।
रणसंनाहगभीरो न श्रुतो राघवप्रभातमङ्गलपटहः।।]

She was not consoled even by Trijaṭā's words until she heard the yelling of the apes and the auspicious beat of Rāma's drum at morn, deep as it heralded the preparation for the battle.

K and MY read निश्रुतः for *ṇa suo* = न श्रुतः (R and Kula). K reads विभात for *pahāa* = प्रभात (R and Kula).

K says ततस्त्रिजटावचनैरपि यावत् न संस्थिता न समाश्वस्ता (निश्चिता MY) तावत् तया प्लवगानां कलकलः निरतां श्रुतः।

MY says *nisuo*[74] निश्रुतः cf. निपाति (*Ṛgveda* 1.73.2) = नितरां पालयति Sāyaṇa.

Kula *pratīka* has *tā* (तावत्) for *to* (ततः)। He says तावत् त्रिजटावचनैरपि (न) संस्थिता यावत् तया प्लवगकलकलः रणसंनाहगभीरो न श्रुतो राघवस्य प्रभातमङ्गलपटह इव।

135. अह बहुविहसंठावणपच्चाणिज्जन्तजीविआसाबन्धम्।
तीअ गअसोअविसअं दूरुण्णामिअपओहरं णीससिअम्।।

[अथ बहुविधसंस्थापनप्रत्यानीयमानजीविताशाबन्धम्
तया गतशोकविषदं दूरोन्नामितपयोधरं निश्वसितम्।।]

Thereupon, with a heaving bosom, she breathed freely, without any sorrow, with the hope of life brought back by the manifold consolations (of Trijaṭā).

K *pratīka* has *ti* (इति) for *aha* (R). MY has *ia*. K reads उच्छ्वसितं (*ūsasiaṁ*) for *ṇī*° (R).

---

[74] The word is frequently used along with cognate forms in Koūhala's *Līlāvaī* (ed. Upadhye, 1949).

K says एवं बहुविधैः संस्थापनैराश्वासनैः प्रत्यानीयमानः पुनरानीयमानः जीविते आशाबन्धः यथा भवति तथा तया गतशोकत्वात् विषममधिकं च दूरोन्नमितस्तनभरं च उच्छ्वसितम् उच्छ्वासो विमुक्तः। MY says विषमं पूर्वाभ्यधिकम्। The verse is not found in our copy of Kula. R says गतेन शोकेन विषदमानन्दजत्वादनुष्णम्। *SC* says विशदं स्पष्टम्। K and MY seem to read *visama* for *visaa*.

136. तो आसासिअसुहिए तीए पुणरुत्तसच्चविअवीसत्थे।
विहडिअवेहव्वभए पुणो वि संघडइ विरहदुक्खं हिअए।।

[तत आश्वासितसुखिते तस्याः पुनरुक्तसत्यापितविश्वस्ते।
विघटितवैधव्यभये पुनरपि संघटते विरहदुःखं हृदये।।]

The pangs of separation then re-entered her heart, consoled and relieved, and doubly reassured, with the fear of widowhood gone.

K and Kula read विगलित for *vihaḍia* = विघटित (R text and *chāyā*). R commentary has विगलित। K and MY read संगलति for *saṁghaḍaī* = संघटते (R). According to Hemacandra 4.113 *asṁgalai* is an alternative form of *saṁghaḍai*.

K (*chāyā*) has पुनरुक्तसत्यापितविश्वस्ते। He says तत आश्वासितत्वात् सुखिते, पुनरुक्तदृष्टविश्वासे, विगलितवैधव्यभये तस्या हृदये पुनरपि विरहदुःखं संगलति स्म। वैधव्यसंभ्रमादपक्रान्तं विरहदुःखं प्रकृतिस्थे हृदये पुनरपि प्रविष्टम्।

MY says कपिकलकलेन पुनरुक्तसत्यापिते विश्वस्ते तस्या हृदये पुनरपि विरहदुःखं समगलत् समापतदित्यर्थः। *SC* says पुनरुक्तमतिशयितं दृष्टविश्रम्भे निश्चितविश्वस्त इति केचित्। *SC* text reads *saṁgalai* like K and MY. Kula is corrupt, but quotation in *SC* has तस्या हृदये पुनरपि संमिलति विरहदुःखम्। As *SC* text often preserves Kula's readings his reading might be *saṁgalai* rendered as संमिलति।

137. माआमोहम्मि गए सुए अ पवआण समरसंणाहरवे।
जणअतणआइ दिट्ठं तिअडाणेहाणुराअभणिअस्स फलम्।।

[मायामोहे गते श्रुते च प्लवगानां समरसंनाहरवे।
जनकतनयया दृष्टं त्रिजटास्नेहानुरागभणितस्य फलम्।।]

When the delusion created by magic vanished, and the sound of the apes preparing for the battle was heard, Sītā realized the meaning of Trijaṭā's words, prompted by affection and loyalty to her.

MY says सहजस्नेहात् संस्तवजाताच्च अनुरागात् त्रिजटया यदुक्तं तस्या मरणव्यवसायनिवृत्तिरूपफलं देव्या दृष्टमनुभूतमित्यर्थः। R says फलं तात्पर्यं पर्यवसानं वा।

इअ सिरिपवरसेणविरइए कालिदासकए दहमुहवहे महाकव्वे
एआरहो आसासओ समत्तो।

[इति श्रीप्रवरसेनविरचिते कालिदासकृते दशमुखवधे महाकाव्ये
एकादश आश्वासकः समाप्तः।]

द्वादश आश्वासकः

Twelfth Āśvāsakaḥ

1. ताव अ दरदलिउप्पलपलोट्ट्धूलिमइलन्तकलहंसउलो।
जाओ दरसंमीलिअहरिआअन्तकुमुआअरो पच्चूसो।।

[तावच्च दरदलितोत्पलप्रलुठितधूलिमलिनायमानकलहंसकुलः।
जातो दरसंमीलितहरितायमानकुमुदाकरः प्रत्यूषः।।]

Meanwhile came the morning, with the swans darkened by the swirling pollen of the partly open blue lotus blossoms, and the night lotus pools turning green as the flowers partly closed their petals.[1]

K says नीलोत्पलानां प्रलुठिताभिः प्रसृताभिः धूलीभिः परागैः मलिनीभवत्-कलहंसकुलः . . . प्रत्यूषो जातः।

2. अरुणाअम्बच्छाओ णवसलिलाकलुसचन्दिमाहअमूलो।
धाउकलङ्कक्खउरो ओसरइ तडो व्व रअणिपच्छिमभाओ।।

[अरुणाताम्रच्छायो नवसलिलाकलुषचन्द्रिकाहतमूलः।
धातुकलङ्ककलुषोऽपसरति तट इव रजनीपश्चिमभागः।।]

The last watch of the night, suffused with crimson by the rising sun, and knocked at the base by the moonlight, grey like a flood, vanished like a stretch of riverbank, tinged with the colour of red earth.[2]

K and probably MY read अर्धानतः for °*cchāo* = °च्छायः (R and Kula). K and Kula read यामः for *bhāo* = भागः (R).

K says अरुणेन उदयता किञ्चिदाताम्रैकदेशः, तदानीं नवसलिलवत् ईषत्कलुषया चन्द्रिकयाहतमूलो रजन्याः पश्चिमयामः अपसरति अपजगाम। किमिव–कस्याश्चित् गिरिनद्याः तटः प्रवृद्धकलुषनवसलिलाहृतमूलः पर्वतस्नुतैः धातुकलङ्कैः कर्बुरः शबलश्च भूत्वा यथापसरति शनैः पतति तद्वदिति।

---

[1] The day lotus opens and the night lotus closes in the morning.

[2] The fading twilight with the first gleams of the morning sun is likened to a riverbank with layers of red earth, eroded by a flood to which the pale moonlight is compared.

MY says अरुणेन आताम्रापरभागो, धातुकलङ्ककर्बुरो, नवसलिलवत् अकलुषया चन्द्रिकया आहतपूर्वभागः[3] सन् तटवत् अवासरदित्यर्थः। अत्र रजनी नदीत्वेन विवक्षिता।

Kula says अरुणेन रविसारथिना आताम्रच्छायः, तत्सम्पर्कात् नवसलिलवदाकलुषा चन्द्रिका तया हतमूलः क्षयितपूर्वभागः पतिताधोभागः (च) रजनीपश्चिमयामः गैरिककलङ्केन मिश्रकलुषः तट इव अपसरति अपगच्छति। पक्षे पतति।

3. णिव्वण्णिज्जइ रूअं अरुणसिहोलुग्गचन्दिअम्मि महिअले।
ओव्वत्तधूसराणं णवर चलन्तीण पाअवच्छाआणम्।।

[निर्वर्ण्यते रूपमरुणशिखावरुग्णचन्द्रिके महीतले।
अपवृत्तधूसराणां केवलं चलन्तीनां पादपच्छायानाम्।।]

On the surface of the earth, with the moonlight eclipsed by the gleams of the morning sun, only the outline of the receding grey shadows of the trees could be seen as they moved.[4]

K, Kula and probably MY read उद्वृत्त (*uvvatta*) for *ovvatta* = अपवृत्त (R).

K says अरुणस्य शिखया प्रभया रुग्णचन्द्रिके महीतले तमःसमुदयात् उद्वृत्तधूसराणाम् उद्वृत्तत्वात् धूसराणां मसृणानां केवलं वायुना चलन्तीनां पादपच्छायानां रूपं निर्वर्ण्यते आलक्ष्यते स्म।

MY says (महीतले) अरुणस्य प्रथमोद्गतप्रभया परिम्लानज्योत्स्ने सति प्राग्भागं विहाय प्रत्यग्भागे प्रसृतानां छायानां रूपं चलनदशायामेव परमदृश्यत न त्वन्यदा धूसरतयेत्यर्थः।

Kula says उद्वृत्तधूसराणाम् उत्पृष्ठीकृतकदल्यादिपत्रवत्. ईषत् पाण्डूनां चलन्तीनां पादपच्छायानां[5] रूपं केवलं निर्वर्ण्यते, चक्षुर्ग्राह्यो गुणः परं प्रतीयते, न त्वशेषविशेषावगमो भवतीति भावः।

R says अपवृत्तानामपगतानाम्।

4. संमीलइ कुमुअवणं अद्धत्थमिअगलिअप्पहं ससिबिम्बम्।
विअलइ रअणिच्छाआ अरुणाहअमुद्धतारआ पुव्वदिसा।।

[संमीलति कुमुदवनमर्धास्तमितगलितप्रभं शशिबिम्बम्।
विगलति रजनीछायारुणाहतमुग्धतारका पूर्वदिक्।।]

---

[3] Our copy has अहत . . .।

[4] Cf. Mādhava in Extracts.

[5] *SC* says उद्वृत्तत्वात् परिवृत्तपार्श्वत्वात् इव धूसराणां महीरजोभिरीषत्पाण्डूनां पादपच्छायानाम्।

The night lotus bed closed its petals, and the orb of the moon that had half gone down was bereft of lustre. The splendour of the night faded away, and the feeble stars of the eastern sky were overpowered by the rising sun.

K and MY *pratīka* has *saṁmillai* for *saṁmīlai* (R and Kula). K and *SC* text read मन्द for *muddha* (R).

K (*chāyā*) has संमीलति commentary says कुमुदवनं निमीलति स्म। K says रजनेः छाया स्वरूपशोभा गलति स्म। पूर्वा दिक् अरुणप्रभयोपहतत्वात् मन्दा मसृणास्तारका यस्याः सा तथाभूत्।

MY says प्रतिबलाक्रान्तस्य समित्रान्तःपुरस्य न्यग्भूतस्य राज्ञः समाधिरत्रानुसंधेयः।

Kula says अरुणाहतचन्द्रिका पूर्वदिक्। His reading seems to be different unless it is a mistake. Besides he reads विगलितरजनीछाया (पूर्वदिक्) for *vialai* (विगलति), etc.

5. दीसइ अ तिमिररेइअपल्लवअम्बतरुणारुणाहअमिहिअम्।
विसमविहिण्णमणसिलाभङ्गप्फरुसमणिपव्वअद्धं व णहम्।।

[दृश्यते च तिमिररेचितपल्लवाताम्रतरुणारुणाहतमेघिकम्।
विषमविभन्नमनःशिलाभङ्गपरुषमणिपर्वतार्धमिव नभः।।]

Free from darkness, the sky, with patches of clouds, permeated by the rays of the rising sun, red as the young foliage of trees, resembled a part of a jewel mountain, bristling with slabs of realgar crumbling to dust.

K and MY read शिलातल for *maṇasilā* (R); and पर्वतमिव नभस्तलं for *pavvaaddhaṁ va ṇahaṁ* (R and Kula). K and MY read तलिन for तरुण (R and Kula). Kula reads *cuṇṇa* for भङ्ग।

K says तिमिरेण रेचितं परित्यक्तं, पल्लववत् ताम्रेण तरलितेन[6] तनुना अरुणेन आहतमेघं स्पृष्टमेधकलयुक्तं नभस्तलं विषमभिन्नैः शिलातलभङ्गैः मणिशिलातलभङ्गै पुरुषेण निम्नोन्नतेन मणिपर्वतेन युक्तमिवादृश्यत। एतदुक्तं भवति तिमिरेण रहितमरुणप्रभापाटलितमेघखण्डपूरितं नभस्तलं विषमभिन्नमणिशिलासङ्कटमणिपर्वत-सदृशमदृश्यतेति।

MY reads भङ्ग for ताम्र। He says तिमिरेण रेचितं च तत्, पल्लवभङ्गतलिना-रुणाहतमेघं चेति विग्रहः। तदानीं विषमभिन्नैः शिलातलभङ्गैः परुषमणिपर्वतयुक्तमिव वियदलक्ष्यतेत्यर्थः।

[6] Seems to be a mistake for तलिनेन। Goldschmidt's manuscript has तलिन।

Kula seems to read *maṇasilā* like R. He says नभो विषमविभिन्नैः सम्यक् दलितैः मनः शिलाचूर्णैः परुषं रूक्षं मणिपर्वतार्धमिव दृश्यते। He explains *mihiā* differently — तरुणारुणेन बालार्केण आहतमिहिकमुत्सारित-निशातुषारं नभः।

6. ताव अ अत्थणिअम्बं णवसलिलाउण्णगअपअच्छविकलुसो।
पत्तो अरुणुण्णामिअपासल्लन्तगअणोसरन्तो व्व ससी।।

[तावच्चास्तनितम्बं नवसलिलापूर्णगजपदच्छविकलुषः।
प्राप्तोऽरुणोन्नामितपार्श्वायमानगगनापसरन्निव शशी।।]

Meanwhile the moon, greyish like an elephant's footprint, filled with rain-water, reached the slope of the western mountain, as if it had slid down the sky when it slanted on being raised by the morning sun.

K and probably Kula read पर्यस्यमान (i.e. *palhatthanta*, cf. 8.83, 11.96) for *pāsallanta* (R and MY) = पार्श्वायमान।

K says तावत् शशी च अस्तमयरागयोगात् नवजलपूर्णगजपदस्य भूमिगतस्य नवसलिलपूर्णस्य गजपदविन्यासस्य छविवत् कलुष ईषदरुणो भूत्वा अरुणेनोन्नमितत्वात् पर्यस्यमानात् गगनात् अपसरन्निव भ्रश्यमान इव अस्तगिरिनितम्बं प्राप्तः। अथमभिप्रायः–पूर्वं तिमिरपूरितत्वात् नष्टस्वरूपं गगनमरुणेन उद्गच्छता समुन्नतमिव प्रकाशीभवत् पश्चिमाशायां पर्यस्यमानमिव आभाति। चन्द्रः तद्गतत्वात् आधारे पर्यस्यमाने तस्मात् भ्रश्यमान इव अस्तनितम्बं गत इति।

MY says गजपदच्छविकलुषः गजपदच्छायश्च यत् कलुषश्चेति विग्रहः। *pāsallanta* पार्श्वमाश्रयत्। R says पार्श्वायमानं पूर्वपार्श्वेनोत्थितम्।

Kula says शशी नवसलिलापूर्णं यत् गजस्य पदस्थानं तद्वत् कलुषछविश्च। प्राकृतत्वात् पूर्वनिपातानियमः अरुणोल्लासितपूर्वभागात् पर्यस्य(मानात्) गगनात् अपरसन्निव . . . अस्तनितम्बं प्राप्तः।

7. होन्ति पवणाहआइँ फुडमहुरविहंगणीहरन्तरुआइँ।
गुञ्जन्तमहुअराइँ धुससिल्हालहुअकिसलआइ वणाइँ।।

[भवन्ति पवनाहतानि स्फुटमधुरविहंगनिह्रदद्रुतानि।
गुञ्जन्मधुकराणि धुतशीतलघुककिसलयानि वनानि।।]

The wind-swept woods were resonant with the clear and sweet notes of the birds, with the bees humming, and the foliage lighter, being rid of frost.

K and Kula read श्रुत (*sua*) for *phuḍa* (R). K and MY read भ्रमत and ज्योत्स्ना for *guñjanta* and *silhā* (R and probably Kula).[7]

K says वनानि . . . भ्रमन्मधुकराणि, धुतया अपगतया उपरिस्थया ज्योत्स्नया हेतुना लघुभूतकिसलयानि अभवन्। He also says श्रुतानि मधुराणि विहङ्गानां निर्ह्रादमानानि उच्चतराणि रुतानि येषां तानि।

MY says रुधन्त (?) भ्रमत्। धुतानि ज्योत्स्नया रिक्तानि च किसलयानि येषां तानि धुतज्योत्स्नालघुकिसलयानि। सुप्तप्रबुद्धसमाधिरत्रानुसंधेयः। K remarks अयमत्र ध्वनिः। यथा केचित् महत्तरा रात्रौ सुखं प्रसुप्ताः प्रत्यूषे संवाहकैः स्पृष्टचरणाः श्रुतमधुरबन्दिमङ्गलवादाः भ्रमत्परिजना विधुतनिद्रानुबन्धतया लघुपाणिपदा भूत्वा प्रबुध्यन्ते तद्वदिति ध्वनिः।

R says *silhā* शीते देशी। Kula says धूतशिशिरत्वात् लघुककिशलयानि वनानि।

8. अरुणक्कन्तविअलिअं णिअअङ्काणुगअबहलजोह्लाभरिअम्।
अत्थसिहराहि पडिअं उक्खडिअकरावलम्बणं ससिबिम्बम्।।

[अरुणाक्रान्तविगलितं निजाङ्कानुगतबहलज्योत्स्नाभृतम्।
अस्तशिखरात्पतितमुत्खण्डितकरावलम्बनं शशिबिम्बम्।।]

Overpowered and displaced by the morning sun, the lunar orb, heavy with the dense moonbeams nestling on its bosom, dropped on[8] the summit of the western mountain, having lost the support of its rays.[9]

This verse is missing in our copy of K. According to Goldschmidt's manuscript, K reads कलुषितं for *vialiam;* बहुल for बहल; शिखरे (Kula also), i.e. *siharaṁmi* for *siharāhi* (R); and *garuaṁ* for *bhariaṁ.*

MY remarks रिपुतिरस्कृतस्य बहिरप्रसृतेन अभिमानमात्रावशेषेण तेजसा गुरुकृतस्य सहायरहितस्य पततो राज्ञः समाधिर्द्रष्टव्यः।

Kula reads *vialiam* and बहल like R, but, like K and MY, he has गुरुकम् for *bhariaṁ* (R). He also says अरुणाक्रान्तत्वात्। विगलितं भ्रष्टशोभम् (स्थानभ्रष्टम् R)।

9. पिअअमवियोअदुक्खं कह वि गमेऊण जामिणीअ पहाए।
अणुधाइ पडिरुअन्ती अब्भुट्ठाउं व सहजरी चक्काअम्।।

---

[7] Our copy of Kula has कुञ्जत्। *SC* text has *kūjanta.*

[8] "from", according to Rāmadāsa's reading.

[9] *Kara* means also "hand" which brings into relief the idea of helplessness.

[प्रियतमवियोगदु:खं कथमपि गमयित्वा यामिन्यां प्रभाते।
अनुधावति प्रतिरुवत्यभ्युत्थातुमिव सहचरी चक्रवाकम्।।]

Having somehow endured the grief of separation from her beloved at night, the female *cakravāka* bird ran to her mate, responding to his call, as if to welcome him at dawn.[10]

The verse is not found in K, MY and Kula.

10. जाअं समल्लिअन्ते अब्भहिओसहिसिहाकरालिअपासम्।
अत्थसिहरं मिअङ्के अण्णमअपअट्टचन्दमणिणीसन्दम्।।

[जातं समालीयमानेऽभ्यधिकौषधिशिखाकरालितपार्श्वम्।
अस्तशिखरं मृगाङ्केऽन्यमयप्रवृत्तचन्द्रमणिनिस्पन्दम्।।]

As the moon clung to the summit of the western mountain its flanks were lit up by the enhanced lustre of the plants; and the oozing of water from the moonstones increased more than ever.[11]

K says मृगाङ्के समाश्रयति सति (प्राप्तवति सति MY) अस्तशिखरम् अभ्यधिकारभिरोषधिवृक्षाणां शिखाभि: ज्वालाभि: प्रकाशितपार्श्वमुज्ज्वलीकृतपार्श्वम्, अधिकतरप्रवृत्तचन्द्रकान्तमणिनिष्यन्दं जातम्। Kula says पुन:-प्रवृत्त, etc. MY says पूर्वाधिकप्रभवच्चन्द्रकान्तस्त्रोतस्कम्। R says अन्यममयन्यादृशं यथा स्यात्। *SC* says करालितं विच्छुरितमिति कुलनाथ:।

11. दूरोणअणक्खत्तं अरुणसिहाहअगलत्थिओणअजोह्णम्।
अत्थमइ व ससिसहिअं उट्ठेइ व उअअपव्वआहि णहअलम्।।

[दूरावनतनक्षत्रमरुणशिखाहतगलहस्तितावनज्योत्स्नम्।
अस्तायत इव शशिसहितमुत्तिष्ठतीवोदयपर्वतान्नभस्तलम्।।]

The sky, with the stars sliding far down, and the moonbeams verging (towards the west), being driven by the rays of the morning sun, seemed to sink along with the moon, and rise (at the other end) from the sunrise mountain.

K and MY read उन्नतज्योत्स्नं for *oṇaa*° (R and Kula) = अवनतं°।

K says पश्चिमाशां प्रति दूरमवनतनक्षत्रं, शशिना सहितं नभ: अस्तं गच्छदिवादृश्यत।

---

[10] The birds (red geese) are believed to separate at nightfall.

[11] I.e. owing to the contiguity of the moon whose influence on plants and moonstones is often mentioned in *kāvya* poetry.

अरुणप्रभया समाहतत्वात् प्रेरितोन्नतज्योत्स्नं पूर्वस्यां दिशि नभ उदयपर्वतात् उद्गच्छदिवाभूत्। चक्रभ्रान्तिसमाधिरत्र विवक्षितः।

MY says उन्नतज्योत्स्नमिति विमुक्तप्रसरोर्ध्वमिात्रावस्थितज्योत्स्नम्। आधेय-पतनोत्थानाभ्याम् आधारपतनोत्थानप्रतिभास इति तात्पर्यम्।

My reads *atthāi va* (*SC* text also) for *atthamai va* = अस्तायत इव (R).

12. पइलम्भेण पओसो जाओ दिण्णप्फलो रइसुहेण णिसा।
आणिअविरहुक्कण्ठो गलइ अणिव्विण्णवम्महो पच्चूसो।।

[पतिलम्भेन प्रदोषो जातो दत्तफलो रतिसुखेन निशा।
आनीतविरहोत्कण्ठो गलत्यनिर्विण्णमन्मथः प्रत्यूषः।।]

The even-tide gave joy to the damsels by bringing their consorts, and the night by affording the pleasures of love. But the morning wore on, causing the anguish of separation, with passion unquenched.

K, MY and Kula read *pia* (प्रिय) for *pai* (R).

K says प्रदोषः प्रियलाभेन स्त्रीणां दत्तफलोऽभूत्। निशा रतिसुखेन दत्तफला। प्रत्यूषस्तु तासाम् आनीतप्रियविरहात्कण्ठः, अतएव अनिर्विण्णमन्मथः। नक्तं यूनां सुरतसंविधानैः खिन्नः निर्विण्णः कामः, दिवा तद्भावात् अनिर्विण्णमदनः तथाभूतो गलति स्म। निर्वेदः खेद उच्यते इति हलायुधः।

Kula is corrupt. R explains अनिर्विण्ण as अनिर्वाण or उद्दीप्त। *SC* has अक्षान्त।

13. वीसम्भवड्ढिअरसं अइराअक्खलिअसेससंठिअरसणम्।
विअलिअमएण णिउणं पच्चूसरअं पओसदूरब्भहिअम्।।

[विश्रम्भवर्धितरसमतिरागस्खलितशेषसंस्थितरसनम्।
विगलितमदेन निपुणं प्रत्यूपरतं प्रदोषदूराभ्यधिकम्।।]

The morning dalliance was much more delightful than that of the evening, perfect because the frenzy brought by wine had worn off, and the joy was enhanced by confidence, with the girdle torn to shreds[12] in the ardour of love.

K, MY and Kula read रतिराग for *ai* — अति (R). K and MY read त्रुटित, and Kula उत्खण्डित for °*kkhalia* स्खलित found in R. Their readings seem to be °*kkhuḍia* and *ukkhuḍia* respectively (*HC*

[12] Literally with only a remnant left of the girdle torn. . . .

1.53, 4.116). K reads मदवक्तव्यं and MY मदवचनीयं, i.e. *maa-vaaṇi-jjaṁ* (cf. 11.104) for *maeṇa ṇiuṇam* मदेन निपुणं (R). Kula reads मदप्रवीणं। *SC* text has *maa-ppatuṭṭaṁ*. *SC* commentary says *patuṭṭaṁ* प्रवीणे देशी। It also says *patuṭṭaṁ* निर्व्याजमालिङ्गनादिप्रवीणमिति कुलनाथः। The reading recorded in *SC* is doubtful. Our copy of Kula has *patta* which no doubt stands for *pattaṭṭha*. This reading is also found in the verse as quoted in Bhoja's *Śṛṅgāraprakāśa* 22.25. Kula thus seems to read *maa-pattaṭṭhaṁ* like Bhoja.[13]

K says विस्रम्भेण प्रणयकोपमानग्रहप्रसङ्गाभावात् रात्रौ च संभोगसुखेन विस्रम्भः अन्योन्यं विश्वासस्तेन वर्धितरसं, रतिरागेण सुरताभिनिवेशेन त्रुटितावशेषत्वेन अवस्थिता रशना यत्र तत्, तत् अपगतमधुमददोषं यूनां प्रत्यूषसमये रतं प्रदोषसुरतात् दूरमत्यन्तम् अभ्यधिकमभूत्।

MY says मानलज्जाविरहात् विस्रम्भः तेन वर्धितरसम्। प्रदोषे छिन्नशेषा स्थिता रशना इदानीं रतिरागेण त्रुटिता यत्र तत्तथा। मद एव वचनीयं दोषो गलितो यत्रेति तथोक्तम्। प्रदोषः प्रदोषरतम् उपचारात् मञ्चाः क्रोशन्तीति वत्।

R says विगलितमदत्वेन हेतुना निपुणं चतुरं (प्रत्यूषरतम्)।

Kula says सुरतविमर्दनोत्खण्डिता शेषसंस्थिता स्तोकावशिष्टा रसना यत्र तत्। . . . अतः प्रत्यूषरतं प्रदोषरतात् अत्यधिकमुत्कृष्टम्।

14. संकन्ताहरराअं थोअसुरासंठिउप्पलद्धत्थइअम्।
चसअं कामिणिमुक्कं किलिन्तबउलतणुओ ण मुञ्चइ गन्धो।।

[संक्रान्ताधररागं स्तोकसुरासंस्थितोत्पलार्धस्थगितम्।
चषकं कामिनीमुक्तं क्लाम्यद्बकुलतनुको न मुञ्चति गन्धः।।]

The wine-bowl, abandoned by the young women, and smeared with the paint of their lips, and half covered with the lotus left in the remnant of wine,[14] still emitted a mild fragrance like that of fading *bakula* flowers.

Kula says प्रदोषे कामिनीभिः पीतमुक्तं, संक्रान्ताधरालक्तकरसं, स्तोकसुरायां पीतशेषस्वल्पमद्ये स्थितेनोत्पलेन अर्धस्थगितं चषकं क्लान्तबकुलपुष्पगन्धवत् तनुः मृदुर्गन्धो मधुगन्धो न मुञ्चति स्म। मद्यगन्धस्य बकुलपुष्पगन्धसादृश्यं प्रसिद्धम्। यथा रघुवंशे-सुवदनावदनासवसंभृतः, etc. (9.30). MY says कामिनीभिरिदानीम् उपेक्षितं चषकं बकुलगन्धो नामुञ्चत्। अतिमन्दः अन्ववर्ततेति तात्पर्यम्।

---

[13] For the meaning of *pattaṭṭha* see notes on verse 34.

[14] The lotus was placed in the bowl to perfume the wine during the revels of the night.

15. पसिढिलकेसकलाओ उव्वत्तिअमेहलावरुद्धणिअम्बो।
छाआलग्गपरिमलो पिअअममुक्कतणुओ विलासिणिसत्थो।।

[प्रशिथिलकेशकलापो उद्वर्तितमेखलावरुद्धनितम्बः।
छायालग्नपरिमलः प्रियतममुक्ततनुको विलासिनीसार्थः।।]

The young women, allowed to leave by their beloved, were worn out with fatigue, their hair loose, and the hips encompassed by the girdle worn inside out;[15] while faint traces of perfumed paint still adhered to their bodies.

K and MY read निवसन for *ṇiamba* = नितम्ब (R and Kula). K reads भुक्त for *mukka* (R and Kula ?).

K says प्रियतमैः परिभुक्तमुक्तत्वात्[16] तनुर्मृदितशरीर इत्यर्थः। विलासिनीजनः . . . उद्वर्तितया बहिःप्रकाशितया मेखलया निरुद्धवसनः, छायालग्नपरिमलः शोभारूपेण लग्नपरिमर्दचिह्नः। परिमर्देऽपि परिमल इति वैजयन्ती। तथा किरातार्जुनीये – अथ परिमलजामवाप्य लक्ष्मीं, etc. (10.1).

MY says उद्वर्तितः बहिर्भावितान्तःपार्श्वः। *ṇiattha* निवसन। शोभारूपेणालग्नोपभोगचिह्नः। *taṇuo* तनुः कृशः खिन्न इति यावत्।

Kula says छायालग्नपरिमल आभासमात्रस्थितानुलेपनः। R says छायया आभामात्रेण यत्किंचिदित्यर्थः।

16. दुण्णिमिअवामचलणं वलन्तपीणोरुबिसमपाउद्धारम्।
दुक्खेण संठविज्जइ पिअहुत्तणिअत्तपत्थिअं जुवईहिं।।

[दुर्नियोजितवामचरणं वलत्पीनोरुविषमपादोद्धारम्।
दुःखेन संस्थाप्यते प्रियाभिमुखनिवृत्तप्रस्थितं युवतीभिः।।]

Wearily the young women set about returning home, turning to their beloved as they parted;[17] listlessly setting their left foot down, and stepping forth unsteadily because of the plump faltering thighs.

K reads स्खलत् for *valanta* (R and Kula). K (*chāyā*) has युवतीनाम् in the scond line.

K says (युवतीनां) प्रियैर्भुक्तसमनन्तरं प्रत्यासन्ननिजावासं प्रति निवृत्तप्रस्थितं

[15] Indicates the listlessness of the damsels at the time of departure.

[16] K (*chāyā*) has प्रियतमभुक्ततनुः।

[17] Or, retiring from the presence of their beloved.

निवृत्त्य प्रस्थानं गमनं दुःखेन कृच्छ्रात् संस्थाप्यते निर्वाह्यते स्म। कथंभूतम्– दुर्निहितवामचरणं, स्त्रीणां वामपार्श्वे सविशेषमदनस्याधिष्ठानमिति वार्ता[18]। तेन मदनपारवश्येन दुःखनिक्षिप्तवामपादं स्खलद्भ्यां पीनाभ्यामूरुभ्यां विषमः पादोद्धारो निक्षिप्तस्य पादस्योद्धरणं यत्र तत्तथा।

It will be seen that K takes *hutta* as भुक्त। Others take it in the sense of अभिमुख।

MY says प्रथमतो वामपादक्षेपः स्त्रीणां माङ्गलिकं कथयति। आप्रश्ने सति भर्त्रभिमुखं पुनर्निवृत्तं प्रस्थितं प्रस्थानं विरहोत्कण्ठया संभोगक्लान्त्या च कृच्छ्रेणापद्यतेत्यर्थः। अथवा *pia-hutta* (प्रियभुक्त)। प्रियभुक्तमुक्तानां प्रगे स्वगृहप्रस्थितं कथमपि कृतमित्यर्थः। तत्र स्त्रीणां वामैरङ्गैः प्रथमप्रवृत्तिरिति वामेत्युक्तम्।

Kula says स्त्रीणां वामाङ्ग एवं नखक्षतादिकं विहितम्। अतो दुर्निमित ऊरुसन्धिगतनखक्षतपीडया दुःखेन निहितो वामचरणो यत्र। वलमानाभ्यां सुरतायासात् तिर्यगुन्नमद्भ्यां (?)[19] पीनाभ्यामूरुभ्यां विषमो वक्रः पादस्योद्धारः उत्क्षेपो यत्र तत्, प्रियाभिमुखात् निवृत्तं सत् प्रस्थितं गमनं कथमपि युवतिभिः संस्थाप्यते प्रगुणीक्रियते कष्टेन साध्यत इत्यर्थः।

17. संखोहिअकमलसरो संझाअवअम्बधाउकद्दमिअमुहो।
ठाणप्फिडिओ व्व गओ रत्तिं भमिऊण पडिणिअत्तो दिअसो।।

[संक्षोभितकमलसराः संध्यातपाताम्रधातुकर्दमितमुखः।
स्थानस्फिटित इव गजो रात्रिं भ्रमित्वा प्रतिनिवृत्तो दिवसः।।]

Stirring the lotus pools into bloom, the day returned, having travelled all night, with the visage decked with the gleam of the morning; even as an elephant, gone astray, returns after roaming through the night, with its face smeared with red earth, having troubled the water of the lotus pools.

K says दिवसस्य गजस्य च श्लेषः। संक्षोभितकमलाकरः सायं संमीलितकमलाकरः, अन्यत्र विगाहनेन क्षोभितकमलिनीकः, संन्ध्यातपमयेन धातुना कर्दमितमुखः दिवसः स्थानभ्रष्टो गज इव रात्रिं सकलां[20] भ्रान्त्वा, अन्यत्र चरित्वा, प्रतिनिवृत्तः।

MY says संक्षोभो विकासात्मा। *phiḍio* भ्रष्टः। रात्रिमिति कालाध्वनोरत्यन्तसंयोग इति द्वितीया।

Kula says ताम्रधातुः गैरिकम्।

[18] R says स्त्रियो हि प्रथमं वामपादमग्रे विन्यस्य पश्चात् दक्षिणपादमुत्थाप्य चलन्तीति स्वभावः।

[19] *SC* has तिर्यग्भूय चलद्भ्यां, etc.

[20] Our copy has सकमलां।

18. अरुणपडिबोहिआए अब्भुत्थन्तीअ आअअं व दिणअरम्।
साहेन्ति विहडिआइँ णिमिअं कमलाइं दिअसलच्छीअ पअम्।।

[अरुणप्रतिबोधिताया अभ्युत्तिष्ठन्त्यागतमिव दिनकरम्।
शासति विघटितानि नियोजितं कमलानि दिवसलक्ष्म्याः पदम्।।]

The opening lotus blossoms seemed to declare that the beauty adorning the day had planted her foot on them as she awakened by the morning glow, rose to greet the sun that had come.

K reads दिवसकरं for *va* (इव) *diṇaaraṁ* (R and Kula); and विकसितानि for *vihaḍiāiṁ* = विघटितानि (R and Kula).

K says अरुणेन बोधितया प्रकाशितया, आगतं दिवसकरं भगवन्तमभ्युत्तिष्ठन्त्या दिवसलक्ष्म्या भवि निहितं पदं विकसितानि कमलानि शंसन्ति स्म। प्रातरेव विकसितानि कमलानि दिवसागममावेदयामासुरित्यर्थः। अयमत्र ध्वनिः – यथा काचित् नायिका प्रवासादागतं नायकं सखीजनप्रतिबोधिता प्रत्युद्गच्छन्ती ससंभ्रमं पदानि करोति तद्वदिति।

Kula reads दिवसलक्ष्म्या निहितं पदं . . . कमलानि कथयन्तीव।

19. एक्केक्कमवोच्छिण्णं पओसवीसत्थविहडिअं उअहिजले।
जणणिं व चन्दपडिमं अल्लिअइ विहाअकाअरं सङ्खउलम्।।

[एकैकक्रमव्यच्छिन्नं प्रदोषविश्वस्तविघटितमुदधिजले।
जननीमिव चन्द्रप्रतिमामालीयते विभातकातरं शङ्खकुलम्।।]

Separating without fear at nightfall in the waters of the sea, the conches, isolated from one another, and helpless in the morning closed in on the reflection of the moon, as if it were their mother.

K reads विच्छिन्नं and विस्रब्ध for *vo°* and *vīsattha* (R0. K and probably MY read विचलितं for *vihaḍiaṁ* (R).

K says प्रदोषे विस्रब्धं यथासुखमुदधिजले विचलितं, परस्परं विश्लिष्टं शङ्खकुलं विभाते कातरं भीतं भूत्वा चन्द्रस्य प्रतिमां जलगतां जननीमिव दृश्यमानामाश्रयति जननीति बुद्ध्या समाश्रयति स्म।

MY says निशि मिथो वियुक्तं, जलधौ स्वैरदूरगतं शङ्खकुलं शैत्यप्रियं धर्मारम्भकातरं सत् चन्द्रप्रतिमां जननीमिव प्रापेत्यर्थः। बाधकसंभावनया जननीमपि प्रापेत्यर्थः। R says यद्वा–जननीमिव चन्द्रप्रतिमामालीयते इत्युत्प्रेक्षा।

The order of verses in K and MY is 17, 19 18. Verse 19 in not found in Kula.

20. होइ कमलाअराणं समूससन्ताण चिरणिरोहेक्कमुहो।
संचालिअमहुमहुरो मारुअभिण्णो वि मंसलो च्चिअ गन्धो।।

[भवति कमलाकराणां समुच्छ्वसतां चिरनिरोधैकमुखः।
संचालितमधुमधुरो मारुतभिन्नोऽपि मांसल एव गन्धः।।]

The scent of the day lotus beds as they burst into bloom was rich, even though scattered by the wind, because it issued all at once after long confinement (within the petals);[21] and was sweetened by the honey of the flowers stirred (by the breeze).

Kula says समुच्छ्वसतां विकसतां कमलाकाराणां, चिरनिरोधेन (चिरनिरोधात् नक्तं निरोधात् K) एकमुखः पिण्डीभूय निर्गच्छन्, संचालितेन पवनोत्क्षिप्तेन मधुना मधुकृत्यः (? for मधुरः), मारुतेन भिन्नोऽपि विकीर्णोऽपि मांसल एव गन्धो भवतीत्यर्थः। K says संचालितेन मधुरसेन मधुरो गन्धः। *SC* text has *māsalo* for *maṁsalo*.

21. अं चिअ कामिणिसत्थं आउच्छन्ताण मुक्कवाहत्थबअम्।
रक्खसभडाण तं चिअ जाअं णिप्पच्छिमोवऊहणसौक्खम्।।

[य एव कामिनीसार्थः आपृच्छमानानां मुक्तबाष्पस्तबकः।
राक्षसभटानां स एव जातो निष्पश्चिमोपगूहनसौख्यः।।]

As the *rākṣasa* warriors took leave of their mistresses, who were shedding tears, the pleasure of embracing them was the last they ever had.[22]

K reads बाष्पबिन्दुं for *bāha-tthavaaṁ* = बाष्पस्तबकं (R). See 15.43 below. Kula has बाष्पबिम्बं,[23] which seems to be a mistake for ⁰बिन्दुं। Cf. 5.62, 14.75, 15.43.

K says शोकात् मुक्तबाष्पबिन्दुं कामिनीसार्थं गमनार्थमापृच्छमानानां राक्षसभटानां यदेवोपगूहनसौख्यमभूत् तदेव तेषां निष्पश्चिमं पश्चिमरहितमुपगूहनसौख्यं जातम्।

K says विरहखेदात् मुक्तबाष्पबिम्बं कामिनीसार्थमापृच्छमानानां प्रभाते गमनानुज्ञां

---

21 The petals of the day lotus remain closed during the night.

22 Because they never returned from the war with Rāma.

23 *SC* has स्तबकं, but the manuscript reading of *SC* text is *-tthevaṁ* which points to बिन्दु। See notes on 1.40.

प्रार्थयमानानां राक्षसभटानां यदेवोपगूहनसौख्यं जातं तदेव निष्पश्चिमं पश्चाद्भाविशून्यम्[24] उपगूहनसौख्यं जातम्।

22. अह समरन्तरिअसुहो दहमुहवेरपडिमुञ्चणाअअदिअहो।
लद्धामरिसावसरो अलद्धणिद्दो वि राहओ पडिउद्धो।।

[अथ समरान्तरितसुखो दशमुखवैरप्रतिमोचनागतदिवसः।
लब्धामर्षावसरोऽलब्धनिद्रोऽपि राघवः प्रतिबुद्धः।।]

Rāma woke, even though he had not really slept. The day had arrived for him to requite the wrong done by Rāvaṇa, and the time was ripe for letting loose his wrath; while the joy (of meeting Sītā) was delayed only by the impending war.

K and Kula read प्राप्त for *laddha* (R).

K says समरमात्रेण अन्तरितसीतासङ्गमसुखः, दशमुखवैरस्य दशमुखेन कृतस्यापकारस्य प्रतिमोचनाय (R also) प्रत्यपकारार्थमागतदिवसः, प्राप्तामर्षावसरः प्राप्तः अमर्षमोक्षस्य अवसरो यस्य स राघवः अलब्धनिद्रोऽपि प्रतिबुद्धः युद्धाय उद्युक्तः।

MY says समरमात्रव्यवहितदेवीसमागमसुखो, दशमुखवैरनिर्यातानार्थागतदिवसो, विरहादनिद्राणो विप्रतिबुद्धः शयनोत्थानादि कर्म कृतवानित्यर्थः।

Kula says दशमुखवैरस्य प्रतिमोचनायां[25] गतं हृदयं यस्य . . . विबुद्धः शयनादुत्थितः। It will be seen that Kula reads *gaa-hlao* for (*ā*)*aa-diaho* (आगतदिवसः)। R says दशमुखे यद्वैरं तत्प्रतिमोचनाय आगातो दिवसो यस्य। Manuscript C of Goldschmidt seems to have *paḍimoaṇā* for ^{0}*muñcanā* found in *SC* text. R takes it as ^{0}*muñcaṇa*.

23. सीआविओअदुक्खं विसहन्तस्स चउजाममेत्तन्तरिअम्।
दीहो अ गओ कालो ण समा एक्का अ सा णिसा रहुवइणो।।

[सीतावियोगदुःखं विषहमाणस्य चतुर्याममात्रान्तरितम्।
दीर्घश्च गतः कालो न समैका च सा निशा रघुपतेः।।]

Unequal in suffering was that night and the long time that had elapsed as Rāma endured the grief of separation from Sītā, which was to persist only for the four watches of that night.[26]

---

[24] Our copy has अपरगूह . . .।

[25] Our copy has प्रतिलोचनायां।

[26] I.e. the night preceding the battle that was to end in the recovery of Sītā seemed to Rāma to be longer than the years of separation from her.

MY says अन्तरं स्वरूपं चतुर्याममात्रस्वरूपवत् इत्यर्थः। सैकापि निशा दीर्घो गतश्च कालो न समौ, किंतु निशैव असह्यतरविरहदुःखा आसीत्। अरिवधाय प्रभातस्य आकांक्षिततमत्वादिति हृदयम्।

K says सीतावियोगदुःखं विषहमाणस्य निशा च गतो दीर्घः कालश्च, उभौ (न) समौ भवतः। निशैव दीर्घतराभूदित्यर्थः। पञ्चवर्षयुक्तोऽप्यस्य सीतावियोगकालो विरहदुःखेन युगसहस्रायमाणोऽभवत्। सा निशा तु प्रभाते विरहदुःखशान्तिसंभावनया सदाकांक्षितप्रभाता। ततोऽस्य जाग्रतो रामस्य तस्मादपि द्राघीयसी बभूवेत्यर्थः।

Kula says चतुर्याममात्रान्तरितं सीतावियोगदुःखं विषहमाणस्य रघुपतेः पूर्वं दीर्घश्च कालो गतः। तेन कालेन एका (च) निशा न समा। . . . सा रात्रिरक्षयेव भूता इति भावः।

24. उम्मिल्लन्ती चिअ से णिद्दासेसोणअच्छिवत्तक्खलिआ।
गुरुओलइअरणभरे दिट्ठी दिट्ठसमरे धणुम्मि णिसण्णा।।

[उन्मीलन्त्येवास्य निद्राशेषावनताक्षिपत्रस्खलिता।
गुरुकावलगितरणभरे दृष्टिर्दृष्टसमरे धनुषि निषण्णा।।]

His eyes, sparkling from within the lids drooping at the end of sleep, rested as they opened on his bow that had seen many a battle, and on which lay the heavy burden of war.

K says उषसि उन्मीलन्त्येव निद्राशेषादवनतेभ्यः अक्षिपत्रेभ्यः लोचनपक्ष्मभ्यः स्खलिता प्रसृता तस्य दृष्टिः गुर्वारोपितरणभरे दृष्टसमरे बहुशो दृष्टसमरव्यापारे धनुषि निषण्णा। कार्यगौरवात् उन्मीलनावसर एव रामो धनुरालोकयामासेत्यर्थः। K (*chāyā*) has गुरुकावलग्नरणेभर, etc.

R and Kula have गुरुकावलगित। R says अक्षिपत्राभ्यां स्खलिता पृथग्भूता।

25. मुअइ अ किलिन्तकुसुमं अवहोवासमलिओवहाणद्धन्तम्।
सइपरिअत्तणविसमं हिअआवेअपिसुणं सिलासअणीअम्।।

[मुञ्चति च क्लाम्यत्कुसुममुभयावकाशमृदितोपधानार्धान्तम्।
सदापरिवर्तनविषमं हृदयावेगपिशुनं शिलशयनीयम्।।]

He left his bed of stone that betokened the agony of his heart, being made rugged by his constant tossing about, with the pillows crushed on both sides, and the flowers withered.

K says रामः अवमर्दात् क्लान्तकुसुमम्, उभयोः पार्श्वयोरामर्देन मृदितोपधानप्रान्तं, सदादेहपरिवर्तनेन विषमं, हृदयावेगस्य हृदयदुःखस्य पिशुनं शिलागतं शयनीयं मुमोच च।

26–27. तो सेलसारगरुअं अइराहोन्तदइआसमागमपिसुणम्।
अहिणन्दिऊण सुइरं फुरमाणब्भहिअपीवरं वामभुअम्।।

खणसंमाणिअधम्मो धणुकङ्कणमग्गमोइअपरिट्ठविअम्।
बन्धइ मलिअविसज्जिअतमालसअणसुरहिं जडापब्भारम्।।
(जुग्गअम्)

[ततः शैलसारगुरुकमचिराद्भविष्यद्दयितासमागमपिशुनम्।
अभिनन्द्य सुचिरं स्फुरदभ्यधिकपीवरं वामभुजम्।।

क्षणसंमानितधर्मो धनुःकर्षणमार्गमोचितपरिस्थापितम्।
बध्नाति मृदितविसृष्टतमालशयनसुरभिं जटाप्राग्भारम्।।]
(युग्मकम्)

For a long while he watched with joy his (right) arm, which, strong as a mountain, grew sturdier as it twitched, pre-saging his union with his beloved, about to take place.[27] Instantly he performed the ceremonial rites, and bound his mass of matted hair, which was drawn aside and fixed away from the track of the bow,[28] and was made fragrant by the crumpled bed of *tamāla* leaves just left by him.

K and Kula read निज and निजक respectively, i.e. *ṇiaa* for वाम (R). K says ततो रामः शैलवत् सारेण बलेन गरुं, स्फुरन्तं स्पदमानं रणरागादभ्यधिकं पीनं, स्पन्दमानत्वात् भविष्यत्सीतामसमागमपिशुनं निजं दक्षिणं भुजं सुचिरमभिनन्द्य। उत्तरगाथया सम्बन्धः। Kula also says स्फुरत्त्वात् स्फुरणशीलत्वात् अत्यधिकपीवरं निजकभुजं दक्षिणमित्यर्थात्। MY has only भुजं, and his reading is probably same as that of K and Kula.

K and MY read निर्मित for *saṁmāṇia* (R and Kula). MY says *ṇimmāṇia* निर्मित। K and Kula read नियमः for *dhammo* (R). K reads प्रतिष्ठापितं for परि° (R and Kula).

K says युद्धत्वरया क्षणे निर्मितसन्ध्यावन्दनादिनियमः रामः पूर्वत्रिकभागे समवृत्तबन्धं जटामण्डलं धनुषः कर्षणमार्गात् मोचयित्वा किञ्चिदुन्नतं बबन्ध। कथंभूतम्– मृदितविसर्जितेन तमालपल्लवशयनेन सुरभिम्।

Kula says क्षणं संमानितनियमः कृतसन्ध्यावन्दनादिनित्यकृत्यः धनुःकर्षणमार्गात्

[27] The twitching of the right arm or eye is believed to be of good omen for a man. See 15.76, 77.

[28] I.e. in a manner to facilitate the drawing of the bow.

मोचितम्[29] अपसारितं परिष्ठापितं निवेशितं . . . जटाप्राग्भारं बध्नाति।

28–29. दाऊण गलिअवाहं चिरधरिआऊरमाणरोसाअम्बम्।
दिट्ठिं लङ्काहिमुहिं समत्थणिव्वडिअतारआदुप्पेच्छम्।।

गेह्णइ गहिअत्थामं सीआसुण्णइअसअणमग्गट्ठविअम्।
बहुसो विरहुक्कण्ठिअणिमिअमुहोरुण्णमइअकोडिं चावम्।।
(जुग्गअम्)

[दत्त्वा गलितबाष्पां चिरधृतापूर्यमाणरोषाताम्राम्।
दृष्टिं लङ्काभिमुखीं समस्तनिर्वलिततारकादुष्प्रेक्ष्याम्।।

गृह्णाति गृहीतस्थामं(म) सीताशून्यीकृतशयनमार्गस्थापितम्।
बहुशो विरहोत्कण्ठितनियोजितमुखावरुदितमृदितकोटि चापम्।।]
(युग्मकम्)

He directed his eyes, bedewed with tears, towards Laṅkā; they were red with long-standing anger reaching its culmination, and fierce with their glare.[30] He then took up his bow, known for its prowess; it lay on the side of the bed, vacant in the absence of Sītā, with its end soiled by his tears as he rested his face thereon in anguish caused by separation from her.

K says अथ रामो विरहवेदनया रोषेण च गलितबाष्पां, चिरं धारितेन तदानीमापूर्यमाणेन रोषेण ताम्रां, समस्तव्यक्तया तारकया कनीनिकया दुष्प्रेक्षां लोकैः दुरालोकां दृष्टिं लङ्काभिमुखीं कृत्वा। उत्तरगाथया सम्बन्धः। R says समस्तं निर्वलितया विस्फारणात् पृथग्भूतया तारकया।

K (*chāyā*) has मार्ग like R and Kula, but K (commentary) has भाग। K and MY read मलिन (*maila*) for *maia* = मृदित (R). They read मुख first in *ṇimia-muha* (R and Kula).

K says गृहीतस्थाम परिज्ञातस्थैर्यं, सीतया शून्यीकृते शयनभागे स्थापितं, बहुशो विरहोत्कण्ठितेन, उत्कण्ठैव उत्कण्ठितम्, उत्कण्ठया शयनकाले मुखे निहिता अतएव रुदितेन मलिना कोटिः यस्य तच्चापं जग्राह रामः।

Kula says गृहीतस्थाम युद्धेषु विज्ञातसामर्थ्यं . . . बहुशो विरहोत्-(कण्ठितेन) निमितं निहितं यत् मुखं तस्यावरुदितेन . . . कोटिं चापं गृह्णाति। *SC* has

[29] Our copy has सेवितम्।

[30] Literally hard to look at on account of the all too conspicuous eyeballs.

मलिनकोटिं like K and MY. *SC* text has *maliṇa*. R rendres *ṇimia* as नियोजित; निवेशित।

MY says उत्कण्ठैव उत्कण्ठितं, शयनदशायामेव उत्कण्ठितेन मुखेन संश्लेषिता अवरुदितेन च मलिनीकृता च कोटिर्यस्य तत्।

K and MY read 10.3 after this verse.

30. तो तं महिअलणिविअं वामकरावेढणिट्ठुरपरिग्गहिअम्।
दाहिणहत्थेण कअं वलन्तदेहभरणामिअं सज्जीअम्।।

[ततस्तन्महीतलनिवेशितं वामकरावेष्टनिष्ठुरपरिगृहीतम्।
दक्षिणहस्तेन कृतं वलद्देहभरनामितं सजीवम्।।]

The bow, planted on the ground, and held fast by gripping it with his left hand, was strung with the right hand as it bent under the weight of his stooping frame.

K omits *to* (R) and reads तन्महीतलार्धनिमितं (*chāyā*). Kula's reading is about the same.

K says अथ तेन तत् धनुः महीतलैकदेशे निहितमूलं, ततो वामकरावेष्टनेन निष्ठुरमतिदृढं गृहीतं, वलमानस्य ईषन्नमतो देहस्य भरेण नामितं, सज्यं कृतम्[31]।

Kula has *to*, but omits तं। He says ततो महीतले अर्धनिमितं निहितैकदेशं . . . दक्षिणहस्तेन दृष्टेन मह्यामारोपितं (स)गुणं कृतम्।

31. काऊण ससिअमन्थरगरुअसिरोअम्पतज्जिअं पडिवक्खम्।
चलिओ चलन्तपव्वअविलइअधणुमेत्तसाहणो रहुणाहो।।

[कृत्वा श्वसितमन्थरगुरुकशिरःकम्पतर्जितं प्रतिपक्षम्।
चलितश्चलत्पर्वतविलगितधनुर्मात्रसाधनो रघुनाथः।।]

Rāma set out, armed only with his bow, the mountain[32] rocking (under his feet). He struck fear into the enemy with the slow and heavy swaying of his head as he gasped (with rage).

K says स रामः प्रतिपक्षं श्वसितमन्थरेण श्वसितभरितेन गुरुणा शिरःकम्पेन तर्जितं कृत्वा[33] चलत्पर्वतविलग्नधनुर्मात्रसाधनः चलत्पर्वतसदृशं गृहीतधनुर्मात्रं साधनं यस्य स तथा, अथवा भरन्यासरभसेन चलत्पर्वतश्च विलग्नधनुर्मात्रसाधनश्चेति योज्यम्। एवंभूतश्चलितः योद्धुमिति शेषः।

---

[31] Our copy has नामितं भूत्वा सज्जं कृतम्।

[32] I.e. the Suvela.

[33] MY says रोषजनितेन श्वसितेन मन्थरगुरुणा च शिरःकम्पेन प्रतिपक्षं तर्जयन्निव।

R says चलति पर्वते विलगितं निवेशितं यत् धनुः तन्मात्रं साधनं सिद्धिसामग्री यस्य। Kula says चलत्–पर्वतश्चासौ, विलगितं गृहीतं धनुर्मात्रं[34] साधनं येन स चासाविति तथाभूतः। MY says चलितपर्वतश्च विलगितधनुर्मात्रसाधनश्च चलित इत्यर्थः।

32. चलिअं च तुलिअपव्वअमिलन्तसिहरणहणिम्मिएक्कमहिहरम्।
अणुरूअभुअपरिट्ठिअविडवमुणिज्जन्तपाअवं कइसेणम्॥

[चलितं च तुलितपर्वतमिलच्छिखरनभोनिर्मितैकमहीधरम्।
अनुरूपभुजपरिस्थितविटपज्ञायमानपादपं कपिसैन्यम्॥]

The host of apes also advanced, appearing to make up a range of mountains in the sky with the united peaks of the mountains held aloft by them; while the trees, carried in their arms of similar proportions, were distinguished by their branches.[35]

K says वानरसैन्यं चोद्धृतानां पर्वतानां मिलद्भिः शिखरैः नभसि निर्मितैकमहीधरं घटितैकमहापर्वतम्, अनुरूपेषु केषांचित् भुजेषु वृक्षसदृशाकारेषु स्थिता गृहीतस्थिताः विटपैश्छिन्नैः ज्ञायमानाः पादपा यस्य तत्तथाभूतं चलितम्।

MY says अनुरूप समानरूप तुल्याकार।

33. संणज्झन्ति कुउरिसा संणाहभरेण किं करेन्ति समत्था।
णिअअवलं चिअ कवअं कइणाप्पडिहआ भुआ अपहरणम्॥

[संनह्यन्ति कुपुरुषाः संनाहभरेण किं कुर्वन्ति समर्थाः।
निजकवलमेव कवचं कपीनामप्रतिहतौ भुजौ च प्रहरणम्॥]

The craven arm themselves. Of what use is the load of armour to the strong? Their own strength was the armour of the apes, and their unvanquished arms the weapons.

संनह्यन्ति कवचं बध्नन्ति K. कवचायुधाद्युपकरणग्रहणं संनाहः MY.

34. णाअणिसाअरसारं माआणिक्कलुसजुज्झगइप्पवुद्धम्।
अग्गक्खन्धम्मि कअं लङ्कामग्गणिउणं विहीसणसेणम्॥

[ज्ञातनिशाचरसारं मायानिष्कलुषयुद्धगतिप्रबुद्धम्।
अग्रस्कन्धे कृतं लङ्कामार्गनिपुणं विभीषणसैन्यम्॥]

---

[34] Our copy has धर्ममात्रं।

[35] The apes fought with mountains and trees as their weapons, as described in the next canto.

The troops of Vibhīṣaṇa were placed in the forefront of the army; they were conversant with the path to Laṅkā, and familiar with the resources of the demons and skilled in deceitful as well as straightforward methods of war.

K says मायायुद्धे निष्कलुषयुद्धे च समर्थं, लङ्कायाः मार्गे प्रवेशमार्गे निपुणं विभीषणसैन्यम्। MY says मायानिष्कलुषः रिपुमायाजन्यापायारहितः।

R reads *pabbuddhaṁ* (see Goldschmidt) = प्रबुद्धम् explained as प्रवीणम्। K (*chāyā*) has निपुणम् and K (commentary) समर्थम्। MY's reading is corrupt, but he also says समर्थम्। Kula says *puttacchaṁ* (?) प्रवीणम्, but this seems to be a mistake for *pattaṭṭhaṁ*. See notes on verse 13. The reading of K and MY might also be the same as that of Kula. The word *pattaṭṭha* is explained in *Deśīnāmamālā* 6.68 as बहुशिक्षित; as प्राप्तार्थः प्रतिष्ठां प्राप्तो निपुण इत्यर्थः in commentary on *Līlāvaī* 110; also as कुशल (ibid. 657).

Kula's gloss on this verse is reproduced almost verbatim in *SC* : मायासु निष्कलुषा अनाविला संमोहरहिता इति यावत्, ईदृशी या युद्धगतिः तत्र प्रवीणम्। *SC* text, however, has *patuṭṭhaṁ*, प्रतुष्टम् (*chāyā*), which does not give the rquired meaning.

35. समरतुरिअस्स सुकअं कह मोत्तव्वं ति दूमिओ सुग्गीवो।
महिआउहम्मि रामे सोअइ अ विहीसणो निसाअरवंसम्।।

[समरत्वरितस्य सुकृतं कथं मोक्तव्यमिति दुःखितः सुग्रीवः।
गृहीतायुधे रामे शोचति च विभीषणो निशाचरवंशम्।।]

When Rāma took up arms, Sugrīva became sad, being at a loss to requite his kindness, now that he was hasting to the battle;[36] while Vibhīṣaṇa grieved over the fate of the *rākṣasa* race.

K reads कथमस्य प्रतिमोक्तव्यम् (*kaha se paḍimottavvaṁ*) for *sukaaṁ* (सुकृतं) *kaha mottavvaṁ* (R).

K says गृहीतायुधे रामे सुग्रीवः समराय त्वरितस्य अस्य कथं मया प्रतिमोक्तव्यं प्रत्युपकर्तव्यमिति दूनः परितप्यते स्म।

MY and Kula agree with K.

---

36 The idea is, Rāma's eagerness to fight deprived Sugrīva of the opportunity to show his gratitude by taking the initiative in the fighting.

36. अप्फालिए धनुम्मि अ खोहिअगिरिविहुअसाअरे रहुवइणा।
कम्पिअघरपाआरा अङ्गक्खिवणविसमं व वेवइ लङ्का।।
[आस्फालिते धनुषि च क्षोभितगिरिविधुतसागरे रघुपतिना।
कम्पितगृहप्राकाराङ्गक्षेपणविषममिव वेपते लङ्का।।]

As Rāma brandished his bow, convulsing the Suvela and rocking the sea, Laṅkā, with its wall and mansions quivering, seemed to tremble, flinging its limbs about.

K and MY read विवर for *vihua* = विधुत (R and Kula). K reads प्रवेपते for *va* (इव) *vevai* (R and Kula).

K says रघुपतिना धनुषि क्षोभितगिरिविवरसागरे घोषेण संक्षोभितगिरिगुहासमुद्रे, आस्फालिते निर्घोषिते सति।

MY says क्षोभितगिरिविवरसागरं यथा निर्ह्लादेन तथा धनुष्यास्फालित इत्यर्थः। *aṁga-cchivaṇa-visamaṁ* अङ्गाक्षेपणक्विमम्। K says कम्पितगृहप्राकारा लङ्का अङ्गाक्षेपणविषमं प्रवेपते स्म केनाप्यङ्गक्षेपणे क्रियमाण इव प्राकम्पत, R says अङ्गानामवयवानां यत् क्षेपणमितस्ततः प्रापणं तेन विषमं यथा स्यादेवं वेपत इव। R has *aṁga-kkhivaṇa*. Kula says क्षोभितो गिरिः सुवेलो विधुतः सागरः येन तस्मिन् धनुषि च रघुपतिना आस्फालिते सति गिरिसमुद्रयोः संक्षोमेणैव कम्पितगृहप्राकारा लङ्का, etc.

37. झीणपुलआइअङ्गी अउव्वहरिसमिलिआणणा जणअसुआ।
सोऊण समासत्था पढमुल्लावं व राहवस्स धणुरवम्।।

[क्षीणपुलकाचिताङ्ग्यपूर्वहर्षमिलितानना जनकसुता।
श्रुत्वा समाश्वस्ता प्रथमोल्लापमिव राघवस्य धनूरवम्।।]

Sītā was solaced to hear the sound of Rāma's bow that came like his initial greeting to her, her frail body thrilling with rapture, and her face beaming with unwonted joy.

K reads प्रथमालापम् for *paḍhamullāvaṁ* (R and Kula).

38. मुच्छाविअजुवइजणो रक्खसवइहिअअमहिहरासणिघाओ।
वामोहेइ पुरिअणं सीआकण्णसुहओ पवङ्गकलअलो।।

[मूर्छितयुवतीजनो राक्षसपतिहृदयमहीधराशनिघातः।
व्यामोहयति पुरीजनं सीताकर्णसुखदः प्लवङ्गकलकलः।।]

The yelling of the apes pleasing to Sītā's ears, confounded the people of Laṅkā, making the young women faint, and acting like a crash of thunder on the mountain that was Rāvaṇa's heart.

K reads पात:[37] for *ghāo* = घात: (R and Kula). K (*chāyā*) has परिजनं but commentary has पुरजनं।

Kula says व्यामोहयति किंकर्तव्यताविमूढं करोति।

MY remarks पुरीजनशब्दस्य गोबलीवर्दन्यायेन युवतिजनव्यतिरेकविषयतया न पौनरुक्त्यम्।

39. कइवररहसुद्धाइअधुअसमअपहाविओअहिसमंक्कन्तो।
सलिलभरेन्तदरिमुहो रसइ पसम्मन्तपडिरवं धरणिहरो।।

[कपिवररभसोद्धावितधुतसमयप्रधावितोदधिसमाक्रान्तः।
सलिलभ्रियमाणदरीमुखो रसति प्रशाम्यत्प्रतिरवं धरणीधरः।।]

Assailed by the sea, overflowing its shore on account of the violent onrush of the host of apes,[38] the Suvela whose caves were filled with water roared with the echoes dying away.[39]

K and MY read बल for वर (R); and *pahammanta* (प्रहन्यमान) for *pasammanta* = प्रशाम्यत् (R and Kula). K reads धुतसमाव- पातित for *dhua-samaa-pahāvia* = धुतसमयप्रधावित (R and Kula). K's reading seems to be *dhua-sama-ovāia*. Cf. *ṇivāia* 13.2, 77 and *ovaia* (अवपतित) used frequently in the poem.

K says कपिबलानां रभसादुत्थापितेन उत्क्षिसेन, धुतेन, समं युगपत् अवपातितेन अधःपातितेन उदधिना समाक्रान्तः, अतएव सलिलपूर्यमाणदरीमुखः धरणिधरः सुवेलः प्रहन्यमानप्रतिरवं दिङ्मुखेषु आहन्यमानप्रतिरवं यथा रसति स्म।

MY seems to read *samuha* for *samaa*. He says संमुखमृजु। कपिबलस्य रभसादूर्ध्वायितैः[40] उत्प्लवनैः धूतेन पुनः प्रतिनिवृत्त्य प्रतीपमृजु अपसृतेन उदधिना समाक्रान्तः (?)। *pahammanta-paḍiravaṁ* उत्थाप्यमानप्रतिशब्दम्। अभिभूयमानान्यरवमिति वा। MY has *bharanta* for *bharenta* (भ्रियमाण)।

---

[37] Manuscript C of Goldschmidt has *vāo*.

[38] The seashore is fancied as sinking under the weight of the apes, causing the sea to overflow.

[39] I.e. the roar of the waters did not reverberate from the flooded caves of the mountain.

[40] Our copy has ऊर्ध्वान्वितैः।

Kula says कपिबलस्य (?) रभसोद्धावितेन . . . नामितत्वात् धूतसमयो लङ्घितमर्यादो य उदधिः प्रधावितस्तेन समाक्रान्तः। *SC* has बल।

40. णिज्जिअसेसकलअलो पढमप्फालिअरसन्तधणुणिग्घोसो।
सामरिसविअम्भिआणणदहवअणाअण्णिओ चिरेण पसन्तो।।

[निर्जिताशेषकलकलः प्रथमास्फालितरसद्धनुनिर्घोषः।
सामर्षविजृम्भिताननदशवदनाकर्णितश्चिरेण प्रशान्तः।।]

The sound of the bow as it rumbled, when first swung by Rāma, drowning all other noise, fainted away slowly as Rāvaṇa heard it with amazement and wrath.

K and Kula read विस्मितानन for *viambhiāṇaṇa* (विजृम्भितानन) found in R (see N.S. edn.). R's reading is against metre as pointed out by Goldschmidt who reads *vimbhiāṇaṇa*.

K says रामधनुषो निर्घोषः सामर्षेण विस्मितेन दशवदनेन चाकर्णितः चिरेण प्रशान्तः। Our copy of Kula has विमित which no doubt stands for विस्मित, i.e. *vimhia* of which *vimbhia* is a *variant*. Cf. *Līlāvaī*. ed. Upadhye, verse 134, footnote, *SC* text has *vimhia*.

41. ताव अ रक्खसणाहो पाआरन्तरिअकडइअं कइसेणम्।
रणमहिअं अगणेन्तो णिअए णिद्दापरिक्खअम्मि विउद्धो।।

[तावच्च राक्षसनाथः प्राकारान्तरितकटकितं कपिसैन्यम्।
रणमहितमगणयन्निजके निद्रापरिक्षये विबुद्धः।।]

Meanwhile, Rāvaṇa woke at the end of his slumbers, taking no heed of the host of apes, glorious in war, who stood encircling Laṅkā's wall.

प्राकारान्तरितं व्यवहितं, कटकितं कटको निवेशः कटकयुक्तं निविष्टमित्यर्थः। रणमहितं रणे पूजितं कपिसैन्यम् K. प्राकारेण अन्तरितं व्यवहितं, कटकीकृतं कटकवदावेष्ट्य अवस्थितमित्यर्थः MY. प्राकारान्तरितकटकितं वलयाकारेण बहिः कृताप्रकारवेष्टनम्। निजके निद्राक्षये विबुद्धः, न तु संभ्रमादकाले प्रबुद्ध इत्यर्थः। Kula कटकं वलयः, तद्वत् लङ्कामावेष्ट्य स्थितम् R.

42. वहइ विवलाअणिद्दं विइओवासपरिअत्तणावद्धसुहम्।
विसमसुअमङ्गलरवं ओहीअन्तपअलाइअं दहवअणो।।

[वहति विपलायमाननिद्रं द्वितीयावकाशपरिवर्तनाबद्धसुखम्।
विषमश्रुतमङ्गलरवमवहीयमानप्रचलायितं दशवदनः।।]

His sleep wore off as he ceased to roll, and took his ease by turning over in bed, hearing confusedly the auspicious music of the morning.

K, MY and Kula read *ohīranta* which they explain differently for *ohīanta* = अवहीयमान (R). Cf. next verse.

R says दशवदनोऽवहीयमानं क्रमेण ह्रसमानं प्रचलायितं तल्पे आलस्यात घूर्णनं वहति।

K says विपलायितनिद्रां विपलायितामपगच्छन्तीं निद्रां वहति स्म। कथंभूता–शयने द्वितीयस्य शरीरपार्श्वस्य परिवर्तनैराबद्धसुखां, विषमश्रुतमङ्गलध्वनिम् असकलश्रुत-बन्दिमङ्गलध्वनिम्, 'अपह्रियमाण'–प्रचलायितां, निद्राशेषेण शरीरस्य घूर्णनं प्रचलायितं, बोधेन शनैरपह्रियमाणप्रचलायिताम्।

MY says *ohīranta* मूर्छत्। अपक्षीयमाणेति वा। *paalāia* ईषत्स्वापानुवृत्त्या देहस्य प्रचलनम्।

Kula says विपलायिता निद्रा यत्र, द्वितीयपार्श्वपरिवर्तनेन आबद्धं सुखं यत्र, विषममसम्यक् श्रुतो मङ्गलरवः प्रभाततूर्यादिध्वनिः यत्र तत् तथाभूतम्, 'अवधीरयत्' विषयान्तरावज्ञां विदधत् प्रचलायितं (निद्राशेषघूर्णितं[41] वहति)। *SC* says विषममस्फुटमिति श्रीनिवासः। क्षणं श्रुतं क्षणमश्रुतमिति केचित्। अवहीयमान इति श्रीनिवासः। तन्मने *ohijjanta* इति पाठः। Śrinivāsa has this reading for *ohīranta* in 13.33 also, and says अवहीयमाना अवसीदन्तः। See *SC*.

43. तो महुमअमुच्चन्तामसिणोहीरन्तलोहिअच्छिणिहाअम्।
धणुसद्दामरिसहअं णिद्दासेसं दसाणणस्स विअलिअम्।।

[ततो मधुमदमुच्यमानामसृणापह्रियमाणलोहिताक्षिनिघातम्।
धनुःशब्दामर्षहतं निद्राशेषं दशाननस्य विगलितम्।।]

Disturbed by wrath at the sound of Rāma's bow, the remnant of Rāvaṇa's sleep, free from the effect of wine, came to an end as it slowly departed from the multitude of his eyes, red with drink.

K and Kula read *muccantaṁ* for *muccantā°* found in R who mentions the other reading as a variant. R mentions also *ohīanta* (अवहीयमान = अपचीयमान) as a variant for *ohīranta* = अपह्रियमाण।

K says ततः मधुमदेन मुच्यमानं, मसृणं मन्दमपह्रियमाणः शनैस्त्यज्यमानो लोहितः अक्षिसमूहो येन तत् रावणस्य निद्राशेषं रामधनुःशब्दश्रवणामर्षेण विगलितम्। R says

[41] Supplied from *SC*.

mucantaṁ इति पाठे निद्राशेषस्यैव विशेषणम्। मधुमदस्यापि तदानीमपगमादित्यर्थः। He explains his own reading thus — मधुमदेन मुच्यमानः अत एव आ ईषत् मसृणमपह्रियमाणो मन्दं मन्दमुन्मील्यमानो लोहिताक्षिसमूहो यत्र।

MY says *ohīranta* मूर्छत् विवशेत्यर्थः। *ṇihāa* निकाय (K *chāyā* also). Kula is mutilated, but *SC* says कुलनाथस्तु ततः प्रदोषपीतस्य मधुनो मदेन मुच्यमानं निद्रागौरवात् मसृणो मन्दः स्वव्यापारमवधीरयन् च निद्राच्छेदात् लोहितः अक्षिसमूहो यत्र इत्याह।

44. तुङ्गमणितोरणाइ व एक्कक्कमलङ्घिअङ्गुलिंकरालाइं।
उद्धं भुअजुअलाइं मुअइ वलेऊण णिअअसअणुच्छङ्गे।

[तुङ्गमणितोरणानीव एकैकक्रमलङ्घिताङ्गुलिकरालानि।
ऊर्ध्वं भुजयुगलानि मुञ्चति वलयित्वा निजकशयनोत्सङ्गेः।।]

As he lay in bed he moved and lifted up his (ten) pairs of arms, which, standing apart, with the fingers interlaced resembled lofty bejewelled gates.[42]

K says ततो रावणः प्रबुध्यमानः अन्योन्यं लङ्घितैरङ्गुलिभिः करालानि सान्तरालानि, तदानीं तुङ्गानि मणितोरणानीव दृश्यमानानि भुजयुगलानि बलयित्वा निजे शयनोत्सङ्गे ऊर्ध्वं मुञ्चति जृम्भमाणत्वात् ऊर्ध्वं मुमोच।

वलयित्वा उत्क्षिप्य Kula. अन्योन्याधिष्ठिताङ्गुलितया मध्यच्छिद्राणि भुजयुगलानि MY. Kula is somewhat corrupt, but *SC* says कुलनाथस्तु अङ्गुलीनां सन्धिषु अङ्गुलीनां न्यासेन प्रत्येकलंघिताङ्गुलीनि च तानि करालानि चेति तथा भूतानि भुजयुगलानि कृष्णदेहत्वात् तुङ्गेन्द्रनीलमणितोरणानीव इत्याह।

45. अह भअचलिएरावणभज्जन्तक्खम्भदिण्णसुरसंखोहम्।
आहम्मिउं पअत्तं रणसंणाहपिसुणं दशाणणतूरम्।।

[अथ भयचलितैरावणभज्यमानस्तम्भदत्तसुरसंक्षोभम्।
आहन्तुं प्रवृत्तं रणसंनाहपिशुनं दशाननतूर्यम्।।]

Thereafter Rāvaṇa's war-drum began to be beaten, heralding the preparations for the battle; while the gods were perturbed as the Airāvata elephant broke its post, crazed with fear.[43]

---

[42] The raised arms are compared to the pillars of a gate, and the interlaced fingers to the carved decorations at the top.

[43] I.e. they were reminded of Rāvaṇa's war with Indra, to whom the elephant belonged. Cf. verse 76.

MY says *āhammiuṁ* आहन्तुम् आहतं भवितुम्। रणसंनाहो रणोद्योगः। K remarks रावणस्य रणोद्योगः शक्र प्रत्येव भवति। (अतः) भयमैरावतस्य।

46. रणसण्णापडिउद्धा गहिअजहासण्णपहरणा रअणिअरा।
मीलन्तकण्ठलग्गं थोअं घेत्तूण णिग्गआ जुवइजणम्।।

[रणसंज्ञाप्रतिबुद्धा गृहीतयथासन्नप्रहरणा रजनीचराः।
मीलत्कण्ठलग्नं स्तोकं गृहीत्वा निर्गता युवतिजनम्।।]

Awakened by the warning of the battle, the demons, seizing hold of whatever weapons came to hand, sallied out after caressing a little their young mistresses who hugged them with their eyes closed.

Kula reads वेपमान (*vevanta*) for *mīlanta* (मीलत्)। K and MY read संनाहविबुद्धाः for *saṇṇā-paḍiuddhā* = संज्ञाप्रतिबुद्धाः (R and Kula).

K says रणसंनाहतूर्येण विबुद्धाः . . . राक्षसा मीलन्नयनमेव कण्ठे लग्नं युवतिजनं किञ्चिदादाय निर्गताः। R says मीलन्नेव मुद्रितनेत्र एव, etc.

MY says रणसंनाहः रणार्थं तूर्याघातः। *mīlanta* मीलत् मुह्यत्। एवंभूतं युक्तिजनं गृहीत्वा स्तोकं निर्गता इति योज्यम्।

R says रणाय संज्ञा संकेतो वाद्यरवः तेन प्रतिबुद्धाः जागरिताः।

47. आउच्छमाणगहिआ सुअम्मि अत्थेक्कसमरसण्णावडहे।
जुअइमुहाहि पियाणं णेन्ति अमुक्कसिढिलट्ठिआ अहरोट्ठा।।

[आपृच्छ्यमानगृहीताः श्रुते आकस्मिकस्मरसंज्ञापटहे।
युवतिमुखात्प्रियाणां निर्यान्त्यमुक्तशिथिलस्थिता अधरौष्ठाः।।]

When the sudden beat of the drum, a call to arms, was heard, the lips of the lovers, held fast by the young women as they took leave of them, parted from their mouth, slackening even though unreleased.

K says गन्तुमापृच्छमानानां प्रियाणां युवतिभिः गृहीता अधरोष्ठाः[44] अतर्कितमेव समरसंज्ञापटहे समरसूचनापटहे श्रुते भीतानां युवतीनां मुखात् अमुक्ता अपि शिथिलस्थिताः सन्तः निर्यान्ति स्म स्वयमेव गलन्ति स्म। *SC* text has *ṇinti* for *ṇenti* (निर्यान्ति)।

MY says *āucchamāṇa-gahiā* आपृच्छ्यमानाभिः गृहीताः। *attha-kkaṁ*

[44] Kula says प्रभाते स्वगृहगमनाय आपृच्छमानाः सन्तो गृहीताः युवतिभिः प्रियाणाम धरौष्ठाः।

अतर्कितम्। अमुक्ता अपि विरहकातरतया भिया च स्वयमेव। शिथिलाः स्थिता निरीयुरित्यर्थः।

48. पिअअमकण्ठोलइअं जुअईण सुअम्मि समरसण्णाहरवे।
ईसिणिहं णवर भअं सुरअक्खेएण गलइ बाहाजुअलम्।।

[प्रियतमकण्ठावलगितं युवतीनां श्रुते समरसंनाहरवे।
ईषन्निभं केवलं भयं सुरतक्षेपेण गलति बाहायुगलम्।।]

When the sound of arming for the battle was heard, the arms of the young women, clinging to their beloved's neck, slackened because of the pause in dalliance; fear was only a minor pretext.[45]

K and probably MY read ईषद्वितीर्णरणभयं for *īsi-ṇihaṁ ṇavara bhaaṁ* = ईषत् निभं केवलं भयं found in R who says तत्र भयं केवलं किंचित् निभं व्याजः।

K says प्रियतमानां कण्ठलग्नं युवतीनां बाहायुगलं बाहुयुगलं समरसंनाहरवे श्रुते ईषद्दत्तरणभयं यथा सुरतक्षेपेण चिकीर्षितस्य सुरतस्य क्षेपेण निरासेन गलति स्म।

K (*chāyā*) has कण्ठावलग्नं। MY has कण्ठावलगितं। He says सुरतखेदेन शिथिलीबभूव।

Kula reads *īsi-ṇaaṁ ṇavara kaaṁ*, and says प्रियतमकण्ठे अवलगितमासक्तं बाहुयुगलं सुरतखेदेन ईषन्नतं केवलं कृतं श्रुते समरसंनाहरवे गलति भयात् भ्रश्यतीत्यर्थः।

49. सुअसण्णारवतुरिआ पडिवण्णाउहविहत्थवलिअकरअला।
उव्वेल्लन्ति णिसिअरा वच्छवलन्तत्थणं पिआवेढसुहम्।।

[श्रुतसंज्ञारवत्वरिताः प्रतिपन्नायुधविहस्तवलितकरतलाः।
उद्वेल्लयन्ति निशाचरा वक्षोबलत्स्तनं प्रियावेष्टसुखम्।।]

Hastening on hearing the alarm, the demons, impatient as they took up arms, their hands unsteady, allowed the delightful embrace of their beloved to slacken as the breasts slipped from their bosom.

K reads गलित करतलं (cf. MY) for *valia-kara-alā* (R).

K says श्रुतसंज्ञारवत्वात् त्वरिता राक्षसा वक्षसि वलमानस्तनं प्रियाश्लेषसुखं प्रतिपन्नायुधत्वेन आसन्ने गृहीतायुधत्वेन विहस्ततया व्याकुलतया गलितकरतलं यथा उद्वेल्लयन्ति परिश्लथयन्ति स्म।

---

[45] I.e. the real cause was the coolness of the lovers due to anxiety.

MY say गृहीतायुधं रणदोहलव्याकुलं स्वकामिन्याश्लेषात् शिथिलं च करतलं यथा स्यात् तथेत्यर्थः। *uvvellanti* उदवेल्लयन्[46] उदमोचयन्नित्यर्थः। प्रियावेष्टसुखं सुखरूपं प्रियावेष्टम्।

Kula reads *gahia-kara-alā*. He says श्रुतेन संज्ञारवेण त्वरिताः, प्रतिपन्नं यत् आयुधं तेन विहस्ता व्यग्राश्चेति, उन्मोचनाय गृहीतप्रियाकरतलाश्चेति तथाभूता निशाचराः वक्षसि वलन्तो लुठन्तो स्तनो यत्र तत् प्रियावेष्टसुखं प्रियाभुजपाशाश्लेषसुखम् उद्वेष्टयन्ति (?) उन्मोचयन्ति (?). Hemacandra 4.223 derives *uvvellai* from उद्वेष्टयति। R says उद्वेल्लयन्ति चञ्चलयन्ति।

50. रुम्भन्तीण पिअअमे अक्कअउव्वे वि पणअभङ्गम्मि कए।
जुअईण चिरपरूढो भअहित्थम्मि हिअए ण लग्गइ माणो।।

[रुन्धतीनां प्रियतमानकृतपूर्वेऽपि प्रणयभङ्गे कृते।
युवतीनां चिरप्ररूढो भयोद्विग्ने हृदये न लगति मानः।।]

As the young women held their beloved back their long-standing anger born of jealousy no longer found place in their hearts, smitten with fear, even though the lovers refused their entreaty,[47] something that they had not done before.

K *pratīka* has *rumbhantīṇa* (MY also) and not *rubbha°* as in Goldschmidt's manuscript.

K says प्रियतमान् रुन्धतीनां गमनात् वारयन्तीनां युवतीनां चिराय प्रवृद्धो मानः . . . तासां हृदये न लगति न तिष्ठति स्म। मानमप्यपास्य प्रियतमान् निवारयामासुरित्यर्थः। इदं च दुर्निमित्तमिति द्रष्टव्यम्। R says नायकैरकृतपूर्वेऽपि प्रणयस्य भङ्गे नायिकान्तरासङ्गादिना कृते सति चिरप्ररूढो युवतीनां मानः। K says मानः अकृतपूर्वे प्रणयभङ्गे अभ्यर्थनाभङ्गे कृतेऽपि भयत्रस्ते तासां हृदये न लगति, etc.

MY says स्वोत्पत्तिरकारणैश्चिरोत्पन्नो मानोऽपक्षीयमाण उपेक्षारूपेण प्रणयभङ्गेनोद्दीपितोऽपि भयत्रस्तहृदये न व्यलगदित्यर्थः। . . . अथवा चिरप्ररूढ इति चिराभ्यस्त इति तेन शेषमपि तदनुगुणं व्याख्येयम्। MY has *akaaa-puvve pi* (अकृतपूर्वेऽपि) and explains प्रणय as प्रार्थना। Cf. verse 52.

51. जह जह पिआइ रुब्भइ संभाविअसामिआवमाणब्भहिअम्।
तह तह भडस्स वड्ढइ संमाणिअमच्छरेण समरुच्छाहो।।

[यथा यथा प्रियया रुध्यते संभावितस्वाम्यपमानाभ्यधिकम्।
तथा तथा भटस्य वर्धते संमानितमत्सरेण समरोत्साहः।।]

[46] Our copy has उव्वेलन्ती उद्वेलयत्।

[47] I.e. the request of the mistresses to delay their departure. Cf. verse 52.

Even as their mistresses restrained the martial zeal of the warriors it grew more ardent because of the rancour harboured (against the enemy), all the more because they were reminded of the possible humiliation of their master.[48]

K, MY and Kula read प्रियाभि: for *piāi* = प्रियमा (R); and संस्मृत (संस्मारित Kula) for *saṁbhāvia* (R). K reads संमानितमत्सराणां for ^{0}*maccharena* (R, MY and Kula). K reads भटानां for *bhaḍassa* (R and Kula).

K says प्रियाभि: यथा यथा रुध्यते गमनमिति शेष: तथा तथा संस्मृतेन स्वाम्यवमानेन स्वामिनो रावणस्यावमानो यो रामेण करिष्यमाणस्तेन अभ्यधिकं यथा (स्यात् तथा भटानाम्) उत्साहो वर्धते न हीयते स्म। कीदृशानाम्–संमानितमत्साराणां संमानित: समारोपित: मत्सरो राघ(वे यै: तेषाम्)।

MY says प्रियाभि: समरोत्साहो यथा यथारुध्यत तथा तथा स्वामिपूर्वकृता-वमानस्मरणेन स्वामिसंमानितै: सह मात्सर्येण च अवर्धतेत्यर्थ:।

Kula says यथा यथा प्रियाभि: संस्मारितेन स्वामिकापमानेनाभ्यधिकं यथा स्यात् तथा रुध्यते वार्यते, तथा तथा भटस्य संमानितेन सह मात्सर्येण समरोत्साहो वर्धते। R says संमानितेनादृतेन शत्रुं प्रति मात्सर्येण सह वर्धते।

It will be seen that K and others read *saṁbhāria* for *saṁbhāvia*. See above and cf. 10.60. R says संभावितेन तर्कितेन।

52. दइआकरेहि धरिआ खलिआ पणएण पेम्मराएण हिआ।
माणेण ववट्ठविआ रणपरिओसेण णिग्गआ रअणिअरा।।

[दयिताकराभ्यां धृता स्खलिता: प्रणयेन प्रेमरागेण हृता:।
मानेन व्यवस्थापिता रणपरितोषेण निर्गता रजनीचरा:।।]

Held by their beloved's hands, and delayed by their entreaties, and swayed by love and passion, but made resolute by their sense of honour, the demons departed, because of their delight in war.

K's gloss on this verse is somewhat incomplete, and the *chāyā* is missing. He has वलिता: for *khaliā* (R, Kula and MY). K says रणपरितोषेण भोगादभ्यधिकेन समरप्रहर्षेण निर्णीता निर्गता इत्यर्थ:।

MY says प्रणयेन प्रार्थनया स्खलिता विलम्बिता:[49] प्रेमरागाभ्यां (राग: संभोगाभिनिवेश:

---

[48] I.e. the possible defeat of Rāvaṇa by Rāma.

[49] Kula says प्रणयेन स्खलिता: कृतविघाता:।

K) हृता अप्यभिमानेन योद्धुं व्यवस्थापिता रणदोहलेन *ṇimiā* (?) निष्क्रामिता इत्यर्थः।

It will be seen that K reads निर्णीताः and MY *ṇimiā* for *ṇiggaā* = निर्गताः (R and Kula). MY's reading is against metre and obviously a scribal error. The reading of K and My seems to be *ṇiṇṇiā* from *nir+ṇī* "to go" (Hemacandra 1.93; 4.162), rendered as निर्णीताः and explained as निर्गताः by K. The verb *ṇīi* rendered as निरेति, निर्याति, etc. including the present participle *ṇinta* is frequently used in the poem. The past participle *ṇia* occurs in Svayambhū's *Paümacariu* 3.12.6 (*ṇiya . . . vāhaṇahi caḍeppiṇu*). Here the gloss explains *ṇiya* as निर्गतः। Hemacandra (ibid.) mentions another verb *ṇīṇai* in the same sense, of which the past participle is used in Puṣpadanta's *Jasaharacariu* 3.12.14 (*ṇīṇiy a-jīhahu* in the sense of निर्गतजिह्वस्य)। But this is probably not the reading intended here.

53. सुरसमरुच्चच्छन्दा कइसमसीसलहुआइअम्मि रणभरे।
लज्जन्ति अ संणहिउं ण अ विसहन्ति पसरं परस्स णिसिअरा।।

[सुरसमरोच्चच्छन्दाः कपिसमशीर्षलघुकायिते रणभरे।
लज्जन्ते व संनद्धुं न च विषहन्ते प्रसरं परस्य निशिचराः।।]

Ambitious to fight with the gods, they were ashamed to put on armour in a martial enterprise, trivial on account of rivalry with the apes. None the less they could not tolerate the aggression of the foe.

K (*chāyā*) and Kula read लघुकागते for *lahuāiammi* (R) = लघुकायिते।

K says देवैः सह युद्धेषु उन्नताभिप्रायाः राक्षसाः कपिभिः समशीर्षत्वात् तिर्यग्भिः कपिभिः समं शीर्षबन्धात् कपिभिः साम्यसंबन्धात् लघुत्वेनागते सति रणभरे संनद्धुं संनाहं कर्तुमपि लज्जन्ते च। परस्य शत्रोः प्रसरं परितः प्रसर्पणं च न सहन्ते स्म। ततः संनाहमकुर्वन्। Kula says कपिसमानस्पर्धया लघुके आगते रणभरे। *SC* says सादृश्ये *samasīsa*- शब्दो देशीयः। . . . अन्ये तु देवेन सह समरे उच्चाभिलाषत्वात् कपिभिः समरे समशीर्षेण तुल्यतया लघुनि आगते लघूकृते वा इति वदन्ति। R says कपिभिः समं समशीर्षेण स्पर्धया लघुके।

54. वणविवरेसु करालं वणवेढेसु मुहलं खलन्तद्धन्तम्।
होइ उरत्थलविसमं पुट्ठिणिराअट्ठिअं महोअरकवअम्।।

[व्रणविवरेषु करालं व्रणवेष्टेषु मुखरं स्खलदर्धान्तम्।
भवत्युरःस्थलविषमं पृष्ठनिरायतस्थितं महोदरकवचम्।।]

Mahodara's armour was hollow over the cavities left by old wounds, but clattered when parts of it rubbed against the swollen flesh round the scars. It was uneven on the chest, but flat on the back.[50]

K says महोदरस्य राक्षसस्य कवचं वक्षःस्थलेषु व्रणविवरेषु करालं सच्छिद्रं, व्रणवेष्टेषु महत्सु व्रणकिणेषु मुखरम् आयसत्वात् शब्दायमानं, स्खलदर्धान्तम्, अतएवोरःस्थले विषमं पुञ्जितं, पृष्ठे पुनः आयुधव्रणरहितत्वात् निरायतमेव स्थितम्।

MY says उरोगतगम्भीरव्रणविवरेषु तत्स्पर्शनरहितं, व्रणवेष्टेषु कर्कशतया मुखरं, स्खलदेकदेशं चेत्येवमुरःस्थले विषमं सत् महोदरकवचं पृष्ठे निम्नोन्नताभावात् ऋजु अवस्थितमित्यर्थः। स्वयं महोदरतया वक्षःस्थलस्य व्रणसंकटतया च वक्षसो नापासरदिति तात्पर्यम्। Our copy of Kula has only the *pratīka* of this verse but quotaion in *SC* shows that he reads *muhala-kkhalanta* for *muhalṁ kha°* — मुखरस्खलदेकदेशमिति कुलनाथः।

55. सुरसमरदिट्ठसारो रक्खसणाहस्स जङ्गमो पाआरो।
सरमोक्खेसु सुहत्थो संणज्झइ हरिसिओ कमेण पहत्थो।।

[सुरसमरदृष्टसारो राक्षसनाथस्य जङ्गमः प्राकारः।
शरमोक्षेषु सुहस्तः संनह्यते हर्षितः क्रमेण प्रहस्तः।।

Skilled in archery, Prahasta, a mobile rampart to the lord of the demons, whose might was seen in the wars with the gods, was delighted that he was methodically equipped with armour.

The verse is not found in K, MY and our transcript or Kula.

56. तिसिरस्स समुक्खित्तो बहुकण्ठन्तरकरालिओ संणाहो।
सिढिलं चिअ ओसरिओ एक्कमुहुक्खित्तहत्थतणुअम्मि उरे।।

[त्रिशिरसः समुत्क्षिप्तो बहुकण्ठान्तरकरालितः संनाहः।
शिथिलमेवापसृत एकमुखोत्क्षिप्तहस्ततनुके उरसि।।]

The upraised armour of Triśiras (three-headed) that had openings for his several necks slipped down loose over his chest, which contracted when the (six) hands were simultaneously raised (to let them into the arms of the coat of mail).

---

[50] I.e. the armour fitted the back, but not the chest because of the swollen flesh.

The verse is missing in our transcript of Kula. K says त्रिशिरसो राक्षसस्य बहुकण्ठान्तरकरालित:[51] बहूनां त्रयाणां कण्ठानाम् अनुरूपं छिद्रयुक्त:, उत्क्षिप्तनिहित: संनाह: एकमुखमुत्क्षिप्तहस्तत्वात् तनावुरसि शिथिलमेवापसृत: अधोगत:।

MY says त्रिशिरसो यथार्थनाम्नोऽन्त:प्रवेशितै: ऊर्ध्वमुखोत्क्षिप्तै: षड्भिर्हस्तैरुरसि तनूकृते संनह्यमानेनोत्क्षिप्तं कवचमयत्नेन शरीरं व्यासक्तं प्रावुणोदित्यर्थ:। *SC* says समुत्क्षिप्त: करयोरुत्क्षेपणादूर्ध्वीकृत:। R says एकमुखेन एकोपक्रमेण उत्क्षिप्तै: संनाहबाहुमध्यप्रवेशनाय उत्तोलितै: हस्तै: तनुके।

57. दिण्णमहिअम्पगरुअं संचालेन्ते महोअरे अप्पाणम्।
वच्छत्थलपुञ्जइओ ओसरइ भरेण अप्पणो संणाहो।।

[दत्तमहीकम्पगुरुकं संचालयति महोदर आत्मानम्।
वक्ष:स्थलपुञ्जितोऽपसरति भरेणात्मन: संनाह:।।]

As Mahodara[52] flung himself about violently, the ground trembling under him, his armour, which had stuck on his chest, slid down under its own weight.

K and MY have अकम्पन for महोदर (R and Kula) already mentioned in verse 54.

K says स संनाह: भरेण आत्मना स्वयमेव (भरवशात् स्वयमेव MY) अपसरति स्म। Cf. Hemacandra 2.209 — स्वयमित्यस्यार्थे *appaṇo* वा प्रयोक्तव्यम्। R says संनाह आत्मन: संनाहस्यैव भरेण अपसरति। Kula says आत्मानो भरेणावसरति अवतरति।

58. णीसरिएरावणदन्तमुसलदीसन्तमसिणणिहसच्छाअम्।
कवअं मज्झकरालं उत्तम्भिज्जइ उरत्थले इन्द्रहणो।।

[नि:सृतैरावणदन्तमुसलदृश्यमानमसृणनिघर्षच्छायम्।
कवचं मध्यकरालमुत्तभ्यते उर:स्थले इन्द्रजित:।।]

Indrajit's armour, hollow in the middle,[53] bulged on his (high) bosom; it glistened with the clearly visible smooth scrape left by the stout tusk of the Airāvata elephant that had glanced off the coat of mail[54] (in the fight with Indra).

---

51 *SC* says बहूनां कण्ठानामन्तरेषु करालित: कण्ठानुरूपनिर्माणेन दन्तुरित इत्यर्थ:। बहूनां कण्ठानामन्तरालेषु करालितो विरलासक्त इति कुलनाथ:।

52 See Extracts.

53 I.e. in the region of the waist.

54 The elephant had hit the armour with its tusks, but failed to pierce it. See Kulanātha in Extracts.

K and MY read लोह for *ṇihasa* = निकष (R and Kula).

K says इन्द्रजितो वक्षसि कृतप्रहारस्य ऐरावतस्य दन्तमुसला वक्षःकाठिन्येन तत्र प्रवेष्टुमशक्नुवन्तः कवचमेव भित्त्वा निःसरन्ति। निःसृतैरावतदन्तमुसलत्वात् दृश्यमानमसृणितलोहच्छायम्, अत एव मध्ये सान्तरालं कवचमिन्द्रजित उरःस्थले उत्तभ्यते विषमोन्नतमतिष्ठत्।

MY says वक्षस्तटपरिणतैरावणदन्तनिःसरणमार्गेषु दृश्यमाना मसृणच्छेदस्य लोहस्य दीप्तिर्यस्य तत्तथा। अत एव मध्यकरालिततया तत्र तत्र व्रणवेष्टेषु लग्नं कवचमुरःस्थलादिन्द्रजितो नापासरदित्यर्थः।

Kula says निःसृतः सुखप्रवेशाप्राप्त्या स्खलितो य ऐरावणदन्तमुसलः तस्य दृश्माना कषणच्छाया धर्षणद्युतिः यत्र तत् कवचं कृशत्वादुदरस्य मध्ये करालं सावकाशम् इन्द्रजित उरःस्थले उत्तभ्यते उरःस्थलस्य विशालत्वात् कवचस्य च ऐरावतनिकाषसंकोचितत्वात् उन्नम्यते। R says निःसृतानां भित्त्वा बहिर्गतानामैरावण-दन्तमुसलानां . . . निघर्षस्य निघर्षणस्थानस्य छाया कान्तिरुज्ज्वलता यत्र तत्।

59. अइकाअस्स वि कवए चिरेण ऊरूसु ठिअपलम्बोसारे।
देहप्पहाविमुक्कं जाअं वोच्छिण्णकसणमिहिअं व णहम्।।

[अतिकायस्यापि कवचे चिरेणौर्वोः स्थितप्रलम्बावसारे।
देहप्रभाविमुक्तं जातं व्यवच्छिन्नकृष्णमेघिकमिव नभः।।]

As the armour of Atikāya slowly reached down to the thighs, the sky, no longer suffused with the lustre of his body,[55] looked as if it were rid of a patch of black cloud.[56]

K and MY seem to read *uddha-ṭṭhie* for *ūrūsu ṭhia°* (R). K reads देहं separately, and विच्छिन्न for *vocchiṇṇa* (R).

R says ऊर्वेः स्थितः प्रलम्बोऽवसारः प्रस्तारो यस्येत्यूरुपर्यन्तलम्बितेऽतिकायस्यापि रावणपुत्रस्य कवचे।

K says अतिकायस्यापि कवचे ऊर्ध्वं स्थितं (स्थिते ?) चिरेण प्रलम्बावसारे सति प्रभाविमुक्तं निजया प्रभया विमुक्तं तस्य देहं विच्छिन्नकृष्णमेघच्छादितं नभ इव जातम्।

MY says अतिकायस्य कवचे कायमहत्त्वेन उर्ध्वावस्थिते सुचिरेण प्रलम्बापसारे सति प्रलम्बो यथा स्यात् तथापसारो यस्य तस्मिन् तथा देहप्रभाविमुक्तं गमनं सहसा व्युपाच्छिन्नकृष्णमेघमिव जातमित्यर्थः।

Kula's readings are different. He says अतिकायस्यापि कवचं प्रलम्बापसारं

[55] Literally bereft of the lustre of his body.

[56] I.e. the sky was no longer darkned by the huge swarthy figure of the demon, because it was hidden in the armour. Cf. Mādhava in Extracts.

बृहत्परिणाहमपि कायस्य महत्त्वात् चिरेण उरसि संस्थितं, देहप्रभाया वियुक्तं, जातं व्यवच्छिन्नकृष्णमिहिकमिव नभः . . . लोहकवचं नभ इव कृष्णं विशालं चेत्यर्थः।

The reading कवचं found in Kula is metioned by R as a variant. Kula explains अपसार as परिणाह (प्रस्तार according to R who has अवसार)। It will be seen that Kula reads उरसि संस्थितं, i.e. *urasaṁṭhiaṁ* for *ūrūsu ṭhia°*. Cf. *SC* text, which however reads *dehappahāṇuviddhaṁ*.

60. समरतुरिओ विसूरइ उरत्थलुव्वत्तदाविअंसोवासम्।
आवन्धिऊण कवअं वज्जमुहच्छिण्णवन्धणं धुम्मक्खो।।

[समरत्वरितः खिद्यते उरःस्थलोद्धृतदर्शितांसावकाशम्।
आबद्ध्य कवचं वज्रमुखाच्छिन्नबन्धनं धूम्राक्षः।।]

Eager for battle, Dhūmrākṣa was annoyed to have worn a coat of mail, which, because the clasp had been torn away by the thunderbolt,[57] turned over on his bosom, laying bare his shoulders.

K says समराय त्वरितो धूम्राक्षः वज्रमुखच्छिन्नबन्धनम्, अतएवोरःस्थले उद्वृत्तं विवृत्तं दर्शितांसप्रदेशं कवचमाबध्य, खिद्यते शत्रुवधाय खिद्यते स्म। MY reads वज्रधर for वज्रमुख, and takes *sovāsaṁ* separately. He says वज्रधरायोधने वज्रधरात् त्रुटितबन्धनमतएव उरःस्थलादुद्वृत्तं दर्शितं सावकाशं (i.e. *sovāsaṁ*) च कवचमाबध्य समरत्वरितः कवचान्तरग्रहणविलम्बादखिद्यतेत्यर्थः। Kula is corrupt, but seems to say दर्शितां सावकाशमनावृतांसम्।

61. रोसेण चिरपरूढे फुडिए असणिप्पहस्स वर्णसंघाए।
कवअविवरेहि गलिअं सुइरं उप्पाअजलहरस्स व रुहिरम्।।

[रोषेण चिरप्ररूढे स्फुटितेऽशनिप्रभस्य व्रणसंघाते।
कवचविवरैर्गलितं सुचिरमुत्पातजलधरस्येव रुधिरम्।।]

The long healed wounds of Aśaniprabha burst in a rage, and blood trickled for a long while through the apertures of his coat of mail, like a stream of blood from a portentous cloud.

K says चिरप्ररूढे चिरं रोपिते बद्धकिणे व्रणसंघाते रोषेण शरीरपोषात् स्फुटिते सति। R says रोषजन्यस्पन्दनेनोत्फुल्लतया कवचघर्षणात्।

---

[57] In Rāvaṇa's war with Indra.

62. उक्खिप्पन्तणिराआ अमरिसवेअवलिए णिउम्भस्स उरे।
फुडदाविअसीमन्ता विअलिअलोहवलआ विसट्टइ माढी।।

[उत्क्षिप्यमाणनिरायतामर्षवेगवलिते निकुम्भस्योरसि।
स्फुटदर्शितसीमन्ता विगलितलौहवलया विशीर्यते माढी।।]

As Nikumbha's bosom heaved with wrath, his ring-mail, being strained[58] and stretched cracked, with the chinks clearly visible, and the iron rings torn asunder.

K and Kula read *akkhippanta* (आक्षिप्यमाण) for *u*° (R and MY). K, Kula and probably MY read विघटित (*vihaḍia*) for *vialia* (R) = विगलित।

K says निकुम्भस्य उरसि अमर्षवेगेन वलिते विस्तारिते सति आक्षिप्यमाणत्वात् नितरामायता[59] माढी कवचं स्फुटदर्शितसीमन्ता स्पुटदर्शितभेदरेखा भूत्वा विश्लिष्यति विघटिताभूत्[60]। जगरः कंकटो माढी दंसनं जालिका स्मृतेति हलायुधः।

MY says माढी माथी बन्धनसिरा। निकुम्भस्योरसि अमर्षवेगेन उत्तम्भिते सति तत एवोत्क्षिप्यमाणा दीर्घा च कवचसंधानसिरा स्फुटदर्शितबन्धनमार्गा बन्धनार्थानां लोहवलयानां वित्रुटनात् व्यशीर्यतेत्यर्थः। R says वलिते उच्छ्वसिते।

Kula says वलिते तिर्यगाक्षिप्ते। विघटिता लौहवलया यत्र, छेदात् विश्लिष्टलौहकटिका। *visaṭṭai* विकसति उल्लसति। विकासादेव स्फुटदर्शितसीमान्ता व्यक्तीकृत-सीमन्ताकारपार्श्वसन्धिरित्यर्थः। With regard to माढी, he says यत्र निबिडस्यूते कवचाञ्चलपर्यन्ते सन्धिबन्धदाढ्यार्थं लौहादिघटितकटिका आबध्यते सा माढी। R says माढी देश्यां लौहाङ्गुलीयघटितो 'जिरह' इति प्रसिद्धः संनाहः। *SC* explains it as कवचबन्धनखिल्लिका।

63. सुरपहरणघाअसहं सुओ बि सुपरिच्छअं णिवन्धइ कवअम्।
समुहट्ठिअं ण आणइ पुरओ दुव्वाररामसरदुज्जाअम्।।

[सुरप्रहरणघातसहं शुकोऽपि सुपरिच्छदं निबध्नाति कवचम्।
संमुखस्थितं न जानाति पुरतो दुर्वाररामशरदुर्जातम्।।]

Śuka[61] put on a well-protected armour, capable of resisting

---

[58] Forced upward, according to Rāmadāsa's reading.

[59] Kula says आक्षिप्यमाणत्वात् निरायता प्रसारिता।

[60] K (*chāyā*) has विघटितलोहवलया विश्लिष्यति माढी।

[61] Rāvaṇa's minister.

the weapons of the gods, but was unaware of the imminent danger from Rāma's irresistible arrows.

K and MY read सुपरीक्षितं for *suparicchaaṁ* (R and Kula). K, Kula and MY read समुपस्थितं for *samuha-ṭṭihiaṁ* (R).

MY says *suparicchiaṁ*. सुपरीक्षितम्। He mentions the other reading and says सुपरिच्छदं सम्यक् सिराबन्धनवलयादिनिर्मितमित्यर्थः। रामशरा एव दुर्जातं व्यसनम्। सुरावहे सुपरीक्षितमभेद्यं कवचं शुको न्यबध्नात्। पुरतः समुपस्थितं दुर्वारं रामशरदुर्जातं नाज्ञासीदित्यर्थः। R says दुर्जातमुपद्रवम्।

Kula says सुपरिच्छेदं विचित्रसुवर्णादिरचनम् पुरतः समुपस्थितं दुवरैः रामशरैर्दुर्जातमनर्थोपनिपातं न जानाति।

64. तुरिआउच्छिअकामिणिवलन्तधणिओवऊहणाहिण्णाणम्।
थणपरिमलं दअन्तो णीइ च्चिअ सारणो ण बन्धइ कवअम्।।

[त्वरितापृष्टकामिनीवलद्धन्योपगूहनाभिज्ञानम्।
स्तनपरिमलं दयमानो निरैत्येव सारणो न बध्नाति कवचम्।।]

Sāraṇa[62] went forth without wearing any armour preserving thereby the imprint of the ornamental paint of the bosom of his mistress on his body, as a token of her eager and close embrace as he hastily took leave of her.

K says त्वरितमापृष्टायाः कामिन्या वलमानधन्योपगूहनस्याभिज्ञानभूतं स्तनपरिमलं स्तनविमर्दं दयमानः केवलमेव निर्याति स्म। R says निरैति युद्धाय गच्छत्येव। Kula says रणगमनाय आपृष्टायाः त्वरिताया जातत्वरायाः (?) वलन्त्याः संमुखीभवन्त्याः कामिन्याः गाढोपगूहनस्याभिज्ञानं स्तनपरिमलं स्तनसंपर्कलग्नमङ्गरागं दयमानो रक्षन् सारणो निर्यात्येव, न बध्नाति कवचम्। प्राकृतत्वात् पूर्वनिपातानियमः। MY says त्वरितमापृष्टायाः कामिन्या वलमानेनानेन कृतस्य गाढोपगूहनस्य चिह्नं स्तनपरिमलं स्तनचन्दनादि संक्रान्तं दयमानः। R says तदैव वलतो धन्योपगूहनस्य गाढालिङ्गनस्य।

65. जुत्ता कुम्भस्स रहे माआबद्धमुहलन्धआरधअवडे।
सुररुहिरदट्ठकेसरगुप्पन्तभुअङ्गपग्गहा केसरिणो।।

[युक्ताः कुम्भस्य रथे मायाबद्धमुखरान्धकारध्वजपटे।
सुररुधिरदृष्टकेसरव्याकुलभुजङ्गप्रग्रहाः केसरिणः।।]

Kumbha's chariot, which had for its banner a roaring shadow created by magic, was yoked with lions; while the

---

[62] Another minister of Rāvaṇa.

serpents, twisting about on their mane, stuck in the gore of the gods,[63] served as the reins.

K reads बहुल and MY बहल for *muhala* = मुखर (R and Kula). K and MY reads दिग्ध for *daṭṭha* = दष्ट (R and Kula ?). Kula says सुराणां रुधिरेण दष्टैः[64] लिप्तसंयुक्तैः केसरैः। K says कुम्भस्य रथे सुराणां रुधिरेण दिग्धेपु लिप्तेषु केसरेषु गुप्यन्तो व्याकुलीभवन्तो भुजङ्गमयाः प्रग्रहाः रज्जवो येषां ते केसरिणो युक्ताः योजिताः।

66. णिम्माएइ अमरिसं पडिहत्थेइ गरुअं पि सामिअसुकअम्।
विहुणइ पराहिमाणं णिमिओ मुट्ठिम्मि मण्डलग्गस्स करो।।

[निर्मापयत्यमर्षं प्रतिहस्तयति गुरुकमपि स्वामिसुकृतम्।
विधुनोति पराभिमानं नियोजितो मुष्टौ मण्डलाग्रस्य करः।।]

The hand, gripping the hilt of the sword, excited wrath; repaid the master's kindness, however great; and destroyed the foeman's pride.

K, MY and Kula *pratīka* has *ṇimmāṇei* (निर्मिमीते K and MY, निर्मापयति = उत्पादयति Kula) for *ṇimmāei* (R). K (*chāyā*), MY and Kula have निमितः (निहितः K commentary)। R has नियोजितः।

MY says खड्गमुष्टिनिमितो भटानां करः शत्रुषु अमर्षमजनयत्। गुर्वपि स्वामिसुकृतमत्यशेत। परेषां शौर्याभिमानं च व्यधुनोदित्यर्थः।

K says गुरुतरमपि स्वामिनः सुकृतं प्रतिहस्तयति अमित्रवत् प्रतिबन्धनं करोति। अमित्रोऽपि कृतापकारः प्रतिकर्तव्य एव। स्वामिना कृतमपि प्रतिमोक्तव्यमिति तथोक्तम्। तथा परस्याभिमानं दर्शनादेव धुनोति स्म।

Kula says गुरुकमपि स्वामिनः सुकृतमुपकारं प्रतिहस्तयति स्वामिहस्तं गमयति। पराभिमानं स्वामिशत्रुगर्वं धुनोति निरस्यति। R says प्रतिहस्तयति प्रतिस्वीकरोति प्रत्युपकरोतीत्यर्थः।

67. संणज्झन्ति समत्था ण सहिज्जइ कलअलो विसूरइ हिअअम्।
विरएइ सुरवहुजणो विमाणतोरणगआगओ णेवच्छम्।।

[संनह्यन्ति समर्था न सह्यते कलकलः खिद्यते हृदयम्।
विरचयति सुरवधूजनो विमानतोरणगतागतो नेपथ्यम्।।]

---

[63] I.e. the dry blood of the gods wounded in previous battles with the demons.

[64] Our copy has दन्तै।

The strong armed themselves, and could not endure the yelling (of the apes), and were aggrieved (at the delay); while the celestial maidens kept on coming to the door of their aerial cars and going back to adorn themselves.[65]

एवं समर्था: समनह्यन्। द्विषतां कलकलो न समर्थैः सेहे। तेषां हृदयं च शत्रुवधाय खिद्यते स्म K. रिपुकलकलश्रवणेन संनाहविलम्बादखिद्यत। भटस्वयंग्रहकौतुकात् विमानतोरणं प्रति गतश्च आगतश्च सुरवधूजनो नेपथ्यं व्यरचयदित्यर्थः MY. खिद्यते हृदयं समरकालाक्षेपादिति भावः। औत्सुक्यादसमाप्तनेपथ्य एव विमानद्वारं गच्छति, पुनः नेपथ्यविधानाय आगच्छतीत्यर्थः, Kula.

68. इअ जा समरसअह्णो संणज्झइ हरिसिओ णिसाअरलोओ।
ता रहुवइदीसन्तं अल्लीणं चिअ समन्तओ कइसेणम्।।

[इति यावत्समरसतृष्णः संनह्यति हर्षितो निशाचरलोकः।
तावद्रघुपतिदृश्यमानमालीनमेव समन्ततः कपिसैन्यम्।।

While the demons were thus arming themselves, delighted and eager for the battle, the host of apes, watched by Rāma, closed in upon Laṅkā.

MY says *allīṇaṁ* प्राप्तम्। Kula says रघुपतिना दृश्यमानं रामस्याग्रत इत्यर्थः कपिसैन्यं समन्तत आलीनमेव उपगमेव। K says इति राक्षसजनो हृष्टो भूत्वा समरे सतृष्णः सन् यावत् समनह्यत् तावत् रामेण दृश्यमानं युद्धगमनाय दृशा चोद्यमानं कपिसैन्यं समन्ततः राक्षसपुरीं प्राप्तमेव।

69. भग्गारामविओलं दलिउज्जाणभवणोवणिग्गमलहुइम्।
ओवग्गन्ति पवङ्गा सोहाविणिअंसणं णिसाअरणअरिम्।।

[भग्नारामविलोलां दलितोद्यानभवनोपनिर्गमलघुकाम्।
अवक्रामन्ति प्लवङ्गाः शोभाविनिदर्शनं निशाचरनगरीम्।।]

The apes attacked the city of the demons, which was panic-stricken, with the parks laid waste, and was denuded of splendour, being desolate with the pleasure gardens and the gateways to the (suburban) mansions destroyed.[66]

---

[65] They wished to ascertain if the battle had begun, as they were getting ready to accept as their lovers the heroes coming to heaven after their death on the battlefield.

[66] The verse describes the attack on the outskirts of Laṅkā. See Kṛṣṇa in Extracts.

K and MY read मृदित (*malia*) for *dalia* (R and Kula).

K says प्लवङ्गमा लङ्कामभिभवन्ति स्म। भग्नारामत्वात् विलोलां सभयाम्। मृदितैरुद्यानैः भवनोपनिर्गमैः भवनानामुपनिर्गमैः, शाखानगरगतानां भवनानां समीपनिर्गममण्डपैरित्यर्थः, एवंभूतत्वात् लघ्वीं, शोभाविनिदर्शनां शोभायां विगतनिदर्शनां विरहितदृष्टान्तां लङ्कामेवं परिभवन्ति स्म। आरामो नगरस्य बहिः परितो वृक्षवनम्। उद्यानं गृहारामः। शाखानगरमाख्यातं तथोपनगरं बुधैः इति हलायुधः।

MY says भग्नारामत्वेन विलोलां[67] व्याकुलपौराम्। . . . मृदितैरुद्यानैः भवनैरुपनिर्गमैश्च लघूकृताम्। यत्र राजा स्वभवनोपकण्ठे शुद्धान्तैः जनैर्वा सह रमते तदुद्यानं, तदेव मण्डपिकादिसहितमुपनिर्गमः, नगरनिष्क्रमणा रथ्या वा। तेषां भङ्गात् लघूकृतां शोभाविनिवसनां शोभारूपनिवसनरहिताम्। अत्र प्रतिराजमहिष्याक्रमणसमाधिः द्रष्टव्यः। R says भवनैः गृहैरुपनिर्गमैः द्वारैः।

Kula says भग्नैरारामैः कृत्रिमैर्वनैः विकलां, दलितैरुद्यानैः क्रीडावनैः गृहैरुपनिर्गमैः प्रधानमार्गैः लघ्वीं परिगलितच्छायां शोभाविनिवसनामिव वसनभूतया शोभया त्यक्तां नग्नामिव अववल्गन्ति[68] आक्रामन्ति। R says शोभाया विशेषतो निदर्शनं दृष्टान्तभूताम्। शोभैव विशिष्टं निवसनं वस्त्रं यस्या इत्यर्थो वा। *SC* adds सहजशोभैव स्थितेति भावः। *SC* quotes Amara — आरामः स्यादुपवनं कृतिमं वनमेव यत्।

70. अङ्काअअरअणिअरं धीराअन्तपवआहिवधरिज्जन्तम्।
रसइ विसमाअअपअं रोसुद्धाइअपरिट्ठिअं पवअबलम्।।

[अङ्कागतरजनिचरं धीरायमाणप्लवगाधिपध्रियमाणम्।
रसति विषमागतपदं रोषोद्धावितपरिस्थितं प्लवगबलम्।।]

Hemmed in by the demons, and hard put to it, the host of apes, held together by Sugrīva, who kept calm, roared as they sprang up in a rage and rushed (at the enemy).

K and Kula (probably MY also) read प्रधावितं for *pariṭṭhiaṁ* (R) = परिस्थितं।

K says अङ्कागतरजनिचरम्[69] आसन्नागतराक्षसबलम्, अतएव विषमागतपदम्। अत्र पदशब्देन अवस्थाविशेषो लक्ष्यते। विषममागतदशं, तदानीं धीरायमाणेन सुग्रीवेण धार्यमाणम्। अथ रोषादूर्ध्वायितं भूत्वा प्रधावितं वानरबलं रसति स्म। सहसा राक्षसैरवष्टब्धत्वात् दुःसहागतदशं भ्रान्तं तदानीं धीरेण स्वामिना समाश्वास्य धार्यमाणं कपिबलं पुनः प्रतिपक्षं प्रति रोषादूर्ध्वं प्रधावितं भूत्वा नादमकरोदित्यर्थः।

---

[67] *Viola* rendered as विलोल is a *deśī* word meaning आविग्न। See *Deśīnāmamālā* 7.63. *SC* says विलोलामङ्गवस्त्रशून्यामिति श्रीनिवासः।

[68] Our copy has अवगलन्ति।

[69] Cf. अङ्कमभ्यागतस्य *Bhāravi* 17.64. Mallinātha says अङ्कमन्तिकम्।

MY says युयुत्सावेगेन स्वमध्यप्रविष्टरजनिचरमतएव विषमागतपदं कृच्छ्रप्राप्तस्थानं प्रथमस्थाने अवस्थातुमशक्तमिति यावत्। धीरायमाणेन हरिराजेन धार्यमाणं कृतोत्तम्भनं कपिबलं रोषेण नभस्युद्धावितम् उत्प्लुतम्। प्रतिबलाभिमुखं च कपिबलमरसदित्यर्थः।

Kula says अतिसंनिहितत्वात् अङ्कागता रजनिचरा यस्य तत् तथा। तद्दर्शनात् रोषस्य उद्धावितेन (?) उद्गमेन धावितं, परस्परोल्लंघनरभसात् विषमागतपदं विषमपदसंचारं, etc.

71. रहसल्लिअन्तगव्विअकइसेण्णच्छन्दणहअलल्लीणसुरम्।
वन्दित्तणदट्ठव्वं पेच्छइ सुरवहुजणो णिसाअरणअरिम्।।

[रभसाल्लीयमानगर्वितकपिसैन्यछन्दनभस्तलालीनसुराम्।
वन्दीत्वद्रष्टव्यां प्रेक्षते सुरवधूजनो निशाचरनगरीम्।।]

While the gods gathered in the sky, hidden by the proud host of apes[70] as they rushed forward, the celestial maidens looked down at the city of the demons, which they could hitherto see on as captives.

K, MY and Kula read छन्न for छन्द (R). K says रभसादालीयमानैः गर्वितैः कपिसैन्यैः छन्ने नभस्तले आलीनसुरां कौतुकात् द्रष्टुमागतसुरां, बन्दित्वे द्रष्टव्यां बन्दित्वावस्थायां द्रष्टव्यां लङ्कामप्सरसां गणो निःशङ्कं यथेष्टं पश्यति स्म।

MY says *allianta* प्राप्नुवत्। *allīṇa* प्राप्त। सुरस्त्रियोऽपि स्वभर्तृभिः सार्धं रणदिदृक्षवो बन्दित्वेन विना द्रष्टुमशक्यां लङ्कामपश्यन्नित्यर्थः।

Kula says कपिसैन्येन छन्ने तिरोहिते गगनतले आलीनाः समरदर्शनकौतुकादुपगताः सुराः[71] यस्यां तां निशाचरनगरीम्।

R says यत् कपिसैन्यं तच्छन्देन तद्वशेन नभस्तले आलीना अवतीर्णाः सुरा यत्र तथाभूताम्। राक्षसभिया कापिसंनिधिमाश्रित्य नभसि देवता अपि स्थिताः।

72. रणरहसपत्थिआणं उरुवेअविसट्टसेलसिहरक्खलिआ।
पवआण पढमभग्गा पडन्ति समइच्छिआण मग्गेण दुमा।।

[रणरभसप्रस्थितानामूरुवेगविशीर्णशैलशिखरस्खलिताः।
प्लवगानां प्रथमभग्नाः पतन्ति समतिक्रामतां मार्गेण द्रुमाः।।]

---

[70] I.e. hidden by the gigantic figures of the apes. According to Rāmadāsa's reading (see Extracts), the gods gathered at a point in the sky corresponding to the position of the apes below, as they wished to be near the latter for fear of the *rākṣasa*s.

[71] Our copy has रमा।

As the apes rushed forth, hasting to the battle, the trees, broken and severed from the peaks of the mountains[72] crumbling on account of their vehement speed, dropped on the ground only after they had passed.

K and Kula read प्रस्थितानां च, i.e. *patthiāṇa a* for *patthiāṇaṁ* (R). K and MY read उरोवेग, i.e. *ura°* for उरु (K). K and MY read त्रुटिता:, and Kula खण्डिता: for *°kkhaliā* = स्खलिता: (R). Their reading seems to be *°kkhuḍia* (cf. Hemacandra 1.53).

K says रणरभसात् प्रस्थितानां समतीतानामतिदूरमतिक्रान्तानां च प्लवङ्गानां मार्गेण पृष्ठतो द्रुमाः पतन्ति स्म। कीदृशाः–तेषामुरोवेगेन विश्लिष्टेभ्यः शैलशिखरेभ्यः त्रुटिताः, प्रथमं भग्ना अपि शनैरपतन्। अनेन वानराणां वेगातिशय उक्तः।

MY says *samaiṁchiāṇa* समतीतानाम्। मार्गेण पश्चाद्भागेन। प्रथमभग्ना अपि तरवः अतिक्रान्तानामेषामनुमार्गमपतन्। अनेनैषां वेगातिशयोऽभिहितः।

R takes उरु as ऊरु Kula's reading is same, but he says उरुणा महता वेगेन विशीर्णात् शैलशिखरात् खण्डिता द्रुमाः। Cf. *SC*.

73. णहअलसमुट्ठिएहिं पाआरन्तरिअधअवडेहिं पवङ्गाः।
सूएन्ति गुडिअवारणरइअघडाबन्धसंठिए रअणिअरे।।

[नभस्तलसमुत्थितैः प्राकारान्तरितध्वजपटैः प्लवङ्गाः।
सूचयन्ति गुटितवारणरचितघण्टाबन्धसंस्थितान्रजनीचरान्।।]

The apes surmised from the banners rising high in the sky from within the city wall that the demons were mounted on the armoured elephants arrayed in battle formation.[73]

K, MY and Kula read समुच्छ्रितैः for *samuṭṭheihiṁ* = समुत्थितैः (R).

K says आकाशगताः प्लवङ्गा कवचितानां वारणानां रचिते विरचिते घटाबन्धे समूहसंनिवेशे स्थितान् रजनिचरान् नभस्तलसमुच्छ्रितैः प्राकारेणान्तरितैः ध्वजपटैः सूचयन्ति सम ध्वजपटचिह्नैरेव राक्षसान् गजारूढस्थितान् परस्परं सूचयन्ति स्म। Kula says सूचयन्ति अनुमिन्वन्तीत्यर्थः।

MY says *samūsiehiṁ* समुच्छ्रितैः। *guḍia* कवचित कवचितैर्वारणैः विरचितघटा-बन्धानन्तरावस्थितान् राक्षसान् प्राकारव्यवहितैरपि नभःस्थलोच्छ्रितैः ध्वजपटैर-लक्षयन्नित्यर्थः।

---

[72] Those carried by the apes for use as weapons. See verse 32.

[73] The banners were held up on the back of the elephants.

74. भमइ पवणाणुसारी पवअबलस्स खलिउट्ठिअपउच्छलिओ।
दुमभङ्गसद्दविसमो महिणीहरिअगरुओ समुल्लवणरओ।।

[भ्रमति पवनानुसारी प्लवगबलस्य स्खलितोत्थितपदोच्छलितः।
द्रुमभङ्गशब्दविषमो महीनिर्ह्लदितगुरुकः समुल्लपनरवः।।]

The sound of the approach of the host of apes, spreading as their feet rose and fell, followed the course of the wind; harsh with the crash of trees,[74] and growing louder as it reverberated from the earth.

K seems to read *ṇīharaṇa* for *ṇīharia* = निर्ह्लदित (R). K and Kula read समालयन (*samalliaṇa*, cf. *SC* text) for *samullavaṇa* (R). समुल्लपन।

K says तस्य प्लवगबलस्य लङ्कां प्रति गमनध्वनिः (MY also) गमनसमयशब्दः पवनानुसारी भूत्वा भ्रमति स्म। कथंभूतः – स्खलितोत्थितेभ्यः पदेभ्य उत्थितो, द्रुमभङ्गशब्दैः विषमः अभ्यधिको, मह्या निभरणेन नितरां भरणेन पूरणेन गुरूः। अथवा मह्या निर्ह्लादनगुरुः निर्ह्लादनेन गुरूः। Cf. R - मह्या निर्ह्लदितेन गुरुको मांसलः।

MY says रणकौतुकातिशयेन स्खलितोत्थितानामेषां पदैरुत्थापितो, जववशभज्यमानानां द्रुमाणां भङ्गजैः शब्दैः विषमस्तारकारादिरूपः, तदाक्रमणकम्पितमहीनिर्ह्लादेन गुरुकृतः कपीनां गमनरवो वेगपवनसहितः अभ्राम्यदित्यर्थः।

Kula says समालयनस्य सम्यगर्पणस्य रवो निर्घोषः द्रुमाणां भङ्गशब्दैः विषमो दुःसहः पवनानुसारी . . . भ्रमति विश्वमाक्रामतीत्यर्थः।

The equivalent of *mahi-ṇīharia-garuo* is missing in Kula. *SC* has *asaṇi-gghosa-garuo*.

75. णिद्दलिअमणिअडाणं देन्ति जहासण्णविवरपल्हत्थाणम्।
विहडिअसुवेललम्बिअदिसावलन्तोज्झरत्तणं फडिहाणम्।।

[निर्दलितमणितटानां ददति यथासन्नविवरपर्यस्तानाम्।
विघटितसुवेललम्बितदिग्वलन्निर्झरत्वं परिखाणाम्।।]

The moats of Laṅkā looked like the brooks streaming down the damaged Suvela mountain[75] and meandering on all sides, because their bejewelled embankments were smashed down by the apes, and the water poured into the neighbouring hollows.[76]

---

[74] I.e. the trees carried as weapons and broken during the march. Cr. verse 72.

[75] I.e. trampled by the apes.

[76] Literally the apes made the moats look like, etc.

K reads यथादृष्ट for *jahāsaṇṇa* (R). K and MY read पतत् for *valanta* (R).

K says लङ्कामाक्रामन्तो वानराः निर्दलितमणिमयतटानमितएव यथादृष्टेषु यथासंभवेषु विवरेषु पर्यस्तजलानां परिखानां विघटितात् शिथिलीकृतात् सुवेलत् लङ्काया अधिष्ठानभूतात् लम्बिताः लम्बमाना दिक्षु पतन्तो निर्झरा यासां ताः तथाभूताः तद्भावो विघटितसुवेललम्बितदिक्पतन्निर्झरत्वं तद् ददति स्म अकुर्वन्। भिन्नतटास्ततः ततः स्रवन्त्यः पतन्त्यः परिखाः सुवेलस्य परितो निर्झरत्वमगमन्नित्यर्थः। MY says तटनिर्मलेन परिखानां सुवेलशिखरात् विश्लिष्टनभोमार्गपतदपूर्वनिर्झरत्वं कृतवन्त इत्यर्थः। निर्झराणां विघटनं च सुवेलात् विच्छिद्य (नभो)मार्गेण पतनमित्यवसेयम्।

Kula reads निर्गलित (*ṇiggalia*) for *ṇiddalia*, यथालब्ध (*jahāladdha*) for *jahāsaṇṇa*, and probably पतत् for *valanta*. He says निर्गलितमणितटानां[77] तटभङ्गादेव यथालब्धैर्विवरैः . . . पर्यस्तानां निर्गच्छज्जलानां परिखानां प्राकारखातानां पूर्वं प्लवगाक्रमणेन विघटितात् सुवेलात् लम्बिताः दिक्षु पतन्तो[78] ये निर्झराः तत्सादृश्यं ददति प्लवगा इत्यर्थः।

76. जे चिरआलपरूढा समराइञ्छिअमहिन्दपअणिक्खैवा।
ते णवर गोनुरन्तरविहडणचडुलेहि वाणरेहि विडहिआ।।

[ये चिरकालप्ररूढाः समरातिक्रान्तमहेन्द्रपदनिक्षेपाः।
ते केवलं गोपुरान्तरविघटनचटुलैर्वानरैर्विघटिताः।।]

The long-preserved footprints of Indra, who had fled from battle (with Rāvaṇa) could only be effaced by the apes, who swiftly demolished the interior of the fortified gate of the city.[79]

K reads समरोत्खण्डित in the first line. K and MY read वित्रुटिताः for *vihaḍiā* = विघटिताः (R and Kula). Their reading might be *vikhuḍiā* or *vituḍiā* (cf. Hemacandra 4.116).

K says चिरकालप्ररूढाः चिरकालं प्रसिद्धाः अत्यन्तचिरन्तनाः समरे खण्डितस्य पराजितस्य महेन्द्रस्य ये पदनिक्षेपाः। पदशब्दश्चिह्नवाचकः। पदं स्थाने शरे त्राणे पादाङ्के पादचिह्नयोः इति वैजयन्ति। महेन्द्रस्य पदानां राजचिह्नानां किरीटसितातपत्रादीनां ये निक्षेपाः[80]। निक्षिप्यते इति निक्षेपः। सर्वेषां दर्शनार्थं गोपुरप्रदेशेषु स्थापिता

[77] निर्गलित might be a scribal error for निर्दलित।

[78] Our copy has पान्ता।

[79] The footprints were preserved at the place from where Indra had fled. Kṛṣṇa interprets the phrase as the captured royal insignia of Indra preserved inside the structure as a trophy. See Extracts.

[80] Cf. *SC* — द्वारलिखिताः पराजितशत्रुव्यवसाया इति केचित्।

महेन्द्रस्य मुकुटादयो ये ते केवलं गोपुरान्तरविघटनाय गोपुरान्तरभेदनार्थं चटुलैः वानरैः वित्रुटिताः त एव केवलं भग्नाः। न तु गोपुराणि भेत्तुमारूढा वानराः। तत्र रावणेन निजयशःप्रख्यापनाय स्थापितानि देवराजस्य राजलिङ्गानि दृष्ट्वा कोपात् तान्येव प्रथमं बभञ्जुरित्यर्थः।

MY reads पदविक्षेपाः in the first line, and says रणदत्तपृष्ठस्य धावतो महेन्द्रस्य ये पदविक्षेपाः चिरावस्थिताः गोपुरे निर्मिताः ते केवलं कपिभिरेव त्रुटिता न तु महेन्द्रेणान्येन वेति भावः। MY seems to read *samarāiñchia* like R who says समरादतिक्रान्तस्य पलायितस्य महेन्द्रस्य।

Kula reads *ṇavari* (अनन्तरं) for *ṇavara* (केवलं); and समरापवर्तित, i.e. *samarovattia*.[81] Cf. *veovattia* = वेगापवर्तित 14.74. He says ये चिरकालप्ररूढाः प्रविख्याताः समरापवर्तितस्य समरगृहीतानीतस्य महेन्द्रस्य पदनिक्षेपाः पादन्यासाः (ते) अनन्तरं . . . वानरैः विघटिता विलुप्ताः। *SC* says *ṇavari* अनन्तरमिति कुलनाथः।

77. जाआ णिसाअरपुरी पाआरब्भन्तरावसेसधअवडा।
खणवाणरसंवेल्लिअफलिहाविज्झविअरक्खसेन्दपआवा।।

[जाता निशाचरपुरी प्राकाराभ्यन्तरावशेषध्वजपटा।
क्षणवानरसंवेल्लितपरिखाविध्मापितराक्षसेन्द्रप्रतापा।।]

The city of the demons, with the remaining banners flying inside the wall, was reduced to a state in which the flame of Rāvaṇa's might seemed to be quenched by the waters of the moat, which was encircled in a moment by the apes.

K reads संपीडित for *saṁvellia* (R, MY and Kula). K says सा लङ्का प्राकाराभ्यन्तर एव अवशिष्टध्वजपटा, क्षणेन वानरैः पीडितया भग्नया परिखया स्रवन्त्या प्रशमितरावणप्रतापा जाता (*chāyā* has निर्वापितः . . . प्रतापा)।

MY explains *saṁvellia* as संवेष्टित।[82] Kula says वानरैः संवेल्लितया विधुतया परिखया। MY remarks जलासत्तेरग्निनिर्वापणसमाधिरित्यनुसंधेयः। R explains संवेल्लित as चञ्चलीकृत।

78. विअडगिरिऊडसंणिहणिरन्तरासण्णवाणरपरिक्खित्ता।
जाआ पाआरोहअमज्झव्वूढफडिह व्व रक्खसणअरी।।

[विकटगिरिकूटसंनिभनिरन्तरासन्नवानरपरिक्षिप्ता।
जाता प्राकारोभयमध्यव्यूढपरिखेव राक्षसनगरी।।]

[81] *SC* text has *samaroattia*.

[82] Hemacandra 4.222.

Beleaguered by the serried ranks of the apes, resembling massive mountain peaks, the city of the demons seemed to have the moat lying between twin walls.[83]

K and Kula read निषण्ण for *āsaṇṇa* (R). Kula says निरन्तरं निषण्णै: निविष्टैर्वानरै: परिक्षिप्ता वेष्टिता। K and Kula read दृश्यते (*dīsai*) for *jāā* (R). MY's reading seems to be the same. He says परिखाया बहि:पार्श्वमावेष्ट्य स्थितै: कपिभि: प्राकारद्वयमध्यगतपरिखेव लङ्का समलक्ष्यतेत्यर्थ:। Kula says उभयप्राकारमध्यक्षिप्तपरिखेव राक्षसनगरी दृश्यते परिखातटस्थित-कपिसैन्यस्यापि प्राकारसादृश्यात्। It will be seen that Kula reads क्षिप्त, i.e. °*kkhitta* for *vvūḍha* = व्यूढ explained as उपचित (R), प्रवृत्त (K).

79. तो तं वलन्तविअडं वाणरसेण्णं विहत्तदाराहोअम्।
जाअं णिवहणिरन्तरलङ्कापाआरघडिअमण्डलिबन्धम्।।

[ततस्तद्वलद्विकटं वानरसैन्यं विभक्तद्वाराभोगम्।
जातं निवहनिरन्तरलङ्काप्राकारघटितमण्डलीबन्धम्।।]

The host of apes, vast as it spread out, formed a circle round Laṅkā's wall, massing close together, and allotting the wide gates (to the leaders).

K reads विवर्जित for *vihatta* = विभक्त (R). He reads मण्डल for *maṇḍali* (R, Kula and MY).

K says ततस्तत् वलमानविकटं[84] परित:स्थितविशालं, विवर्जितद्वारविस्तारं वानरसैन्यं निरन्तरनिवहत्वात् लङ्काया: प्राकारत्वेन घटितमण्डलबन्धं जातम्। लङ्कां परितो निरन्तरनिषण्णं तद्वानरसैन्यं गोपुररहितप्राकारमण्डलमिव जातमित्यर्थ:।

MY says *virikka* विरिक्त (for *vihatta*), विमुक्तद्वारावकाशमिति यावत्। This seems to be the reading of K also, who has विवर्जित। See above. K (*chāyā*) has, विविक्त, which might be a scribal error for विरिक्त। MY goes on to says *ṇivaha* इति संघशो निरन्तरावस्थिततया लङ्काप्राकारस्य घटितो मण्डलीबन्धो वेष्टनं येन तत्तथा।

Kula reads *vivikka-dāḍhāhoaṁ* (cf. *SC* text) for *vihatta-dāṛāhoaṁ* विभक्तद्वाराभोगम् found in R. He says विविक्तदंष्ट्राभोगं प्रकटिताशेषदंष्ट्रम्। He explains *valanta-viaḍaṁ* as वेष्टमानोच्छ्रितं (वानरसैन्यम्)।

---

[83] I.e. the existing wall and the surrounding apes on the other side of the moat, looking like another wall.

[84] R says वलत् प्रवेशाय दिशि दिशि गच्छत् सत् विकटं विस्तीर्णम्।

R's reading *vihatta* is also found in Śrīnivāsa quoted in *SC*: ममेदं द्वारं तवेदमिति कृत्वा विभक्तद्वाराभोगम्। R says विभक्तः कपिमुख्येभ्यो विभज्य दत्तो द्वाराणामाभोगो येन। It may be noted that the reading *virikka* may also mean the same thing, as one of the meanings of विरिक्क (from वि+रिंच) is विभक्त see *Pāiasadda°* *sub voce*. Cf. रज्जं च . . . जणवयं च एक्कारसभाए विरिञ्चइ *Nirayāvaliyāo* I.

80. बिइओअहिगम्भीरे फलिहावत्तम्मि बिइअबद्धगिरिवहा।
आढत्ता लङ्घेउं बिइअसुवेलं व वाणरा पाआरम्।।

[द्वितीयोदधिगम्भीरे परिखापृष्ठे द्वितीयबद्धगिरिपथाः।
आरब्धा लङ्घयितुं द्वितीयसुवेलामिव वानराः प्राकारम्।।]

Having built a second causeway composed of mountains across the deep moat, as if it were another sea, the apes began to scale the wall, as if it were another Suvela.

K and Kula read *phalihā-bandhammi* for *vattammi* (R). K says द्वितीयसमुद्रवत् गभ्भीरे परिखाबन्धे बद्धगिरिपथाः पुनरपि घटितगिरिपथाः। R has परिखापृष्ठे। Manuscript C of Goldschmidt has *vaṭṭammi*.

81. णवरि अ मुक्ककलअलं वाणरतुलिअम्मि दहमुहाहिट्ठाणे।
चलिअं रअणिअरबलं खअग्गिविहुए व्व महिअले उअहिजलम्।।

[अनन्तरं च मुक्तकलकलं वानरतुलिते दशमुखाधिष्ठाने।
चलितं रजनीचरबलं क्षयाग्निविधुत इव महीतल उदधिजलम्।।]

Thereafter when Rāvaṇa's city was stormed by the apes, the army of the demons began to move, setting up a yell, even as the waters of the ocean flow over the earth, ravaged by the fire of the epoch of destruction.

वानरैः दशमुखाधिष्टाने लङ्कापुरे तुलिते परिभूते सति K. वानरैः तुलितै आक्रान्तत्वात् परिकलिते Kula तुलिते आक्रान्ते R. *SC* quotes विश्वअधिष्ठानं पुरे, etc.

82. आरूढो णीह रहं आसण्णगइन्दलङ्घणवलन्तेहिँ।
सरहेहिँ समरतुलिओ जुत्तं जुअभग्गकेसरेहिँ णिउम्भो।।

[आरूढो निरैति रथमासन्नगजेन्द्रलङ्घनबलमानैः।
शरभैः समरत्वरितो युक्तं युगभग्नकेसरैर्निकुम्भः।।]

Hasting to the battle, Nikumbha went forth, mounted on a chariot drawn by Śarabhas,[85] whose mane was heavily pressed by the yoke as they turned aside to attack the elephants close at hand.

K reads महितः for *tulio* = त्वरितः (R). Kula also has त्वरितः। K reads भुग्न for *bhagga* (R). Kuḷa seems to read लग्न, i.e. *lagga*.

K says समरपूजितः निकुम्भः सेनापतिः आसन्नानां गजेन्द्राणां लङ्घनाय प्रहाराय वलमानैः, युगभुग्नकेसरैः ग्रीवागतेन युगेन कुटिलीकृतकेसरैः शरभैर्युक्तं स्थमारूढो नगरात् निर्ययौ। शरभः सिंह इव गजशत्रुः। तथा वैजयन्ती–शरभस्तु गजारातिरुत्पादश्चाष्टपादपि।

83. कह वि पडिबद्धकवओ समरासङ्घिअसमत्थवाणरलोओ।
णीइ धणुकोडिताडणतूरविअतुरङ्गमो रहेण पअङ्घो।।

[कथमपि प्रतिबद्धकवचः समराध्यवसितसमस्तवानरलोकः।
निरैति धनुष्कोटिताडनत्वरिततुरङ्गमो रथेन प्रजङ्घः।।]

Prajaṅgha, who wore his armour in the nick of time, rode on a chariot, spurring on the horses with the end of his bow, and determined to fight with the entire host of apes.

K and MY *pratīka* has *kiha vi* (कथमपि) for *kaha vi* (R and Kula). K and MY read आसादित for *āsaṁghia* (R and Kula).

K says अतित्वरया कथमपि बद्धकवच समराय स्वबुद्ध्या प्रार्थितसकलवानरलोकः प्रजङ्घः . . . निर्ययौ।

My says *kiha vi* कथमपि विलम्बासहतयेति भावः। समरासादित समरप्रतीष्ट। Cf. Pāli *āsādeti*, to lay hand on, strike, assail, etc.

R says समरेऽध्यवसितः सर्वैः सह मयैव योद्धव्यमिति स्थिरीकृतः समस्तवानरलोको येन। Kula says समरे आसङ्कितः शक्यो जेतुमिति अवधारितः समस्तो वानरलोको येन सः। K explains *tūravia* as त्वरित (R *chāyā* also). *SC chāyā* has त्वरायित। R commentary says त्वरां कारिताः तुरङ्गमा येन।

84. चडुलवडाआणिवहो कञ्चणघरभित्तिविअडकूवरबन्धो।
इन्दइणो वि पसरिओ एक्कुद्देसो व्व रक्खसउरीअ रहो।।

[चटुलपताकानिवहः काञ्चनगृहभित्तिविकटकूवरबन्धः।
इन्द्रजितोऽपि प्रसृत एकोद्देश इव राक्षसपुर्या रथः।।]

[85] A legendary animal with eight feet.

The chariot of Indrajit, with the pole-frame broad as the golden wall of a palace, advanced, with flags flying, as if it were a segment of the city of the demons.

85. खणपरिअत्तमइन्दा खणलक्खिअकुञ्जरा खणन्तरमहिमा।
तस्स खणमेत्तमेहा रहं वहन्ति खणपव्वआ अ तुरङ्गा।।

[क्षणपरिवृत्तमृगेन्द्राः क्षणलक्षितकुञ्जराः क्षणान्तरमहिषाः।
तस्य क्षणमात्रमेघा रथं वहन्ति क्षणपर्वताश्च तुरङ्गाः।।]

His chariot was drawn by horses that were transformed every moment into lions, or elephants, or buffaloes, or clouds, or mountains.

86. अविसज्जिअणिक्कन्ते अत्थाणक्खोहहलहलुट्ठिअमुहले।
दहवअणस्स सुहावइ आण्णाभङ्गो वि तक्खणं णिअअबले।।

[अविसर्जितनिष्क्रान्ते अस्थानक्षोभहलहलोत्थितमुखरे।
दशवदनस्य सुखायत आज्ञाभङ्गोऽपि तत्क्षणं निजकबले।।]

When the *rākṣasa* troops sallied out without waiting for orders, starting off with loud shouts as fury and excitement prevailed at the royal court, even their breach of discipline at the time delighted Rāvaṇa.

K (*chāyā*) has आस्थानी K says आस्थानमण्डपमास्थानी तस्याः क्षोभेण तद्गतजनक्षोभेण यो हलहलः कोलाहलः तेन कारणेनोत्थितमुखरे उत्थाय शब्दायमाने निजबले, etc.

Kula says आस्थानीक्षोभेणास्थानश्रितानां रोषावेशेन (?) यत् हलहलं रणौत्सुक्यतरलत्वं तेनोत्थितमुखरे कृतकोलाहले। R says अस्थानक्षोभात् आकस्मिकक्षोभात् उत्थितेन हलहलेन कलकलेन मुखरे शब्दायमाने पूर्वनिपातानियमात्। यद्वा हलहलशब्दो युद्धोत्कण्ठायां देशी। युद्धोत्कण्ठायां मुखर इत्यर्थः। Kula says अविसर्जितनिष्क्रान्ते आदेशं विना निर्गते निजकबले।

87. गुडिअगुडिज्जन्तभडं सोहइ रणतुरिअजुत्तजुज्जन्तरहम्।
घडिअघडेन्तगअघडं चलिअचलन्ततुरअं णिसाअरसेणम्।।

[गुटितगुट्यमानभटं शोभते रणत्वरितयुक्तयुज्यमानरथम्।
घटितघट्यमानगजघटं चलितचलत्तुरङ्गं निशाचरसैन्यम्।।]

The army of the demons was splendid; warriors were armed and being armed; chariots were harnessed and being harnessed by warriors eager for the battle; rows of elephants were arrayed and being arrayed; and horses had moved and were moving.

K says रणाय त्वरितं युक्ता अश्वैर्युक्ता युज्यमानश्च रथा यत्र तत्। MY says रणत्वरितै रथिभिर्युक्त–युज्यमानरथमिति। K (*chāyā*) has संनद्धसंनह्यमानभटं . . . घटितघटमानगजघटं। R has घट्यमान। Kula has घटमान।

88. हत्थिगअवरिअराअं रहगअसच्चविअपवअवइसोमेत्ति।
आसगअवरिअहणुमं भूमीगअवरिअकइबलं णीइ बलम्।।

[हस्तिगतवृतरामं रथगतसत्यापितप्लवगपतिसौमित्रि।
अश्वगतवृतहनूमद्भूमीगतवृतकपिबलं निरैति बलम्।।]

The army advanced, the troops mounted on elephants chose Rāma as their antagonist; those on chariots purposed to engage Sugrīva and Lakṣmaṇa; the horsemen chose Hanumat, and the foot-soldiers the host of apes.

K (*chāyā*) has सत्यापित for *saccavia*. K (commentary) says रथगतैर्लक्षीकृतसुग्रीवलक्ष्मणम्। K (*chāyā*) has भूमिगतपरीयमाणवानरं निरेति बलम्। K (commentary) says पदातिभिः परीयमाणशेषवानरसैन्यं भूत्वा निर्ययौ। K seems to read *bhūmi-gaa-parinta-vāṇaraṁ* for *bhūmī-gaa-varia-kai-balaṁ* (R). For *parinta* see notes on 9.88. Here it is passive. Cf. forms like *bharanta* (भ्रियमाण) 8.53, *pūrenta* (पूर्यमाण) 11.63, etc.

R says रथगतैः सत्यापितावेताभ्यां सहास्माभिः योद्धव्यमिति स्थिरीकृतौ सौमित्रिप्लवगपती यत्र। *SC* says सत्यापितौ स्वीकृतौ।

MY says *varia* वृत पार्थितेति यावत्। *saccavia* लक्षित अन्विष्टेति यावत्। *virikka* शून्यीकृत। MY seems to read *bhūmi-gaa-virikka-vāṇaraṁ*. He says भूमिगतैः पत्तिमात्रैः विरिक्ता अपक्रान्ताः शेषवानरा यस्य तत्तथा।

Kula says भूमिगतैः वियुक्ता (विविक्ताः *SC*) पृथक्कृता एकैकशो वृता (*SC* also) वानरा यत्र तत् बलं (i.e. राक्षसबलं) निर्याति। His reading might be *bhūmi-gaa-vivikka-vāṇaraṁ*.

89. रहसंघट्टक्खलिअं गोउरमुहपुञ्जइज्जमाणगअघडम्।
भवणन्तरगुप्पन्तं अघडेन्तेक्कमुहणिग्गमं वलइ वलम्।।

[रथसंघट्टस्खलितं गोपुरमुखपञ्ज्यमानगजघटम्।
भवनान्तरव्याकुलमघटमानैकमुखनिर्गमं वलति बलम्।।]

The army took a devious route, unable to make its exit all at once; it was impeded by the congestion of the chariots, and crammed into the space between the mansions, with the elephant corps crowded into the gateways of the city.

K and Kula read भ्रमति for *valai* (R). Kula says भ्रमति इतस्ततो याति। K (*chāyā*) has, अघटमानैकमुखनिर्गमं, but commentary says भवनान्तरेषु व्याकुलीभवत् एवमयमानैकमुखनिर्गमं बलं भ्रमति स्म एकेनैव गोपुरमुखेन युगपन्निर्गमेन भ्राम्यति स्म। His reading seems to be *aamāṇa* for *aghaḍenta* = अघटमान (R and Kula). R on 6.26 translates *ainta* as अयमान (गच्छत्), but that does not suit the metre here. Unless it is a scribal error, K's reading may be construed as एकमुखेनिर्गमेन अयमानम् by the पूर्वनिपातानियम् rule. R says तत् बलम् अघटमानोऽसंपद्यमान एकमुखेनैकोपक्रमेण, एकदेति यावत् निर्गमो यस्य तथा सत् वलति निर्गमव्यग्रतया दिशि दिशि मण्डलीमाचरतीत्यर्थः। Kula says स्खलितं विघ्नितम्।

90. दुक्खेण गोउराइं वलन्तजुअकोडिविहडिअकवाडाइं।
वोलन्ति रक्खसरहा तंसोणामिअधआहओवरितडिमा।।

[दुःखेन गोपुराणि बलद्युगकोटिविघटितकपाटानि।
व्यतिक्रामन्ति राक्षसरथास्तिर्यगवनामितध्वजाहतोपरितडिमाः।।]

The chariots of the demons laboured through the gateways, striking the lintels above with their banners, lowered sideways; while the doors were scratched[86] by the ends of the slanting yokes.

K reads धनुः for *jua* = युग (R) and विलिखित (*vilihia*, cf. *SC* text) for *vihaḍia* = विघटित (R) K (*chāyā*), *SC* and MY have तलिम for तडिम (R). Kula's readings are uncertain.

K says राक्षसरथा वलमानाभिरवनमन्तीभिः धनुष्कोटिभिः विलिखितकपाटानि गोपुराणि तिर्यगवनमितैः ध्वजैराहतोपलाः सन्तो दुःखेन अतिक्रामन्ति स्म।

MY says महतामति पुरद्वाराणां निष्क्रामणापर्याप्तावकाशतया तदुपरिभागप्रतिबन्धतया त्र्यस्त्रीभूतैरेव नमितैः ध्वजैः स्पृश्यमानोपरितलिमा रथा गोपुराण्यत्यक्रामन्।

Kula says उपरित(लि)मं द्वारकूटपटलतलभागः। R says उपरितडिमं

[86] Translation follows the reading *vilihia*.

द्वारस्योपरिभागः। *SC* says तलिमं कवाटोपरिकाष्ठविशेष इति केचित्। उपरिवितानमिति केचित्, and quotes विश्व which gives वितानक as one of the meanings of तलिम।

91. णिसुढिअदिसागइन्दं भग्गभुअङ्गप्फणं दलिअपाआलम्।
गरुअं पि रक्खसाणं अइराहोन्तलहुअं भरं सहइ मही।।

[निपातितदिग्गजेन्द्रं भग्नभुजङ्गफणं दलितपातालम्।
गुरुकमपि राक्षसानामचिराद्भविष्यल्लघुकं भरं सहते मही।।]

The elephants of the quarters sank to the ground, and the hoods of the serpent Ananta[87] were crushed, and the nether regions split under the weight of the army of the demons. The earth endured it, even though heavy, because it was to lighten ere long.[88]

K has निस्त्रुटित for *ṇisuḍhia* = निपातित (R). K *pratīka* is *ṇisuḍia* K and MY read फणान्तरित for °*pphaṇaṁ dalia*° (R). R says भग्ना भुजङ्गस्य शेषस्य फणा यस्मात्। तथा दलितं पातालं येन। भूपतनादित्यर्थः।

K says असहिष्णुतया विरुग्णदिग्गजेन्द्रं, भग्नैर्भुजङ्गफणैरन्तरितपातालं राक्षसानां प्रसरतां भरं गौरवातिशयं गुरुमपि अचिरात् लघुर्भविष्यतीति भूमिः सहते स्म।

MY reads *ṇisuḍhia* explained as अवपातित। He says अन्तरित व्यवहित। Kula reads निलुटित[89] निलुटिता आक्रान्ता; पृथिवीं (धारयन्तः) दिग्गजेन्द्रा येन। He says भग्नाभिः भुजङ्गस्य शेषस्य फणाभिः अपसृतं संकुचितं पातालं यत्र तम्। Kula's reading is °*pphaṇosaria*.

92. अग्गक्खन्धावडिअं मज्झे दारमुहरुद्धपुञ्जिअपिहुलम्।
ऊसासिअसाहिमुहं कूलाभरिअभवणङ्गणं णीइ बलम्।।

[अग्रस्कन्धापतितं मध्ये द्वारमुखरुद्धपुञ्जितपृथुलम।
उच्छ्वासितरथ्यामुखं कूलभृतभवनाङ्गणं निरैति बलम्।।]

The army moved on, reaching the forward ranks (of the enemy forces). It swelled at the centre, being held up and

---

[87] The elephants of the quarters and Ananta are believed to uphold the earth. The latter has many hoods.

[88] As a result of the destruction of the *rākṣasa*s in the impending battle.

[89] *ṇiluḍhia* ? The *pratīka* in our copy is *niluṭia* which is a mistake.

massed at the gates; relieving the congestion on the highway, but filling the courtyards with the rear.

K reads विह्वलं (*vihalaṁ*) for *pihulaṁ* = पृथुलं (R and Kula). He reads रसति for *ṇīi* = निरैति, निर्याति (R and Kula).

K says अग्रस्कन्धो युद्धभूमिः तां प्राप्तां, मध्यप्रदेशे द्वारमुखरुद्धत्वात् पुञ्जितविह्वलं, पूरितरथ्यामुखं, कुलेन पृष्ठभागेन आपूरितभवनाङ्गणं भूत्वा रसति स्म। कूलं तीरे चभूकटाविति वैजयन्ती। R says यद्वा अग्रस्कन्धे कपिसैन्याग्रे आपतितं स्वाग्रभागेनैवेत्यर्थात्। MY says अग्रस्कन्धवपतितं यत्र योद्धव्यं तत्रैव प्राप्तम्। *ūsasia* उच्छ्वसित (K *chāyā* also)। शाखी तिर्यग्रथ्या पूरिततिर्यग्रथ्यामुखमिति यावत्। K and MY seems to read *ūsasia-sāhī* for *ūsāsia-sāhi* (R and Kula ?). Kula says अग्रस्कन्धे प्लवगबलेनापतितं शत्रु सैन्ये लग्नम्। He seems to say उच्छ्वासितशाखामुखम्, 'साही' रथ्या, सावकाशीकृतरथ्यामुखम् (?)। R says उच्छ्वासितं कियतां निर्गमनादसंबाधीकृतं रथ्यामुखं येन। साहिशब्दो राजमार्गे देशी।

93. इअ दारकअत्थम्भं णीइ विहिण्णविअडं णिसाअरसेणम्।
एक्कमुहदरिविणिग्गअसमत्थलुत्ताणपत्थिअणइच्छाअम्।।

[इति द्वारकृतस्तम्भं निरैति विभिन्नविकटं निशाचरसैन्यम्।
एकमुखदरीविनिर्गतसमस्थलोत्तानप्रस्थितनदीच्छायम्।।]

Thus impeded at the gates, the army of the demons moved out of the city, dispersed along a wide front, like unto a river issuing from a cave with a single entrance, and flowing wide over the plains.

K and MY read उत्तम्भं for °*tthambhaṁ* (R). K reads दर for *dari* (R and Kula).

K says तन्निशाचरसैन्यं द्वारे गोपुरमुखे कृतोत्तम्भं कृतसंमर्दं सङ्कटं, ततो विभिन्नविकटं पृथग्भूय प्रसृतं, तदानीमेकेन मुखेन दरं विनिर्गम्य समस्थले उत्तानप्रस्थितनदीप्रवहनिभं भूत्वा निर्ययौ। Cf. R on 9.26.

MY says *kaütthambhaṁ* (*SC* text also) कृतोत्तम्भं कृतप्रतिबन्धम्। Kula says इत्युक्तप्रकारेण द्वारे . . . कृतान्योन्यघर्षं निर्याति विभिन्नं पृथग्भूतं ततो विकटं विततं निशाचरसैन्यम्। एकमुखदरिविनिर्गतायाः समस्थाने उत्तानमगम्भीरं प्रस्थिताया विततजलायां नद्या इव छाया यस्य तत्तथा।[90] *SC* says द्वारेण कृत उत्तम्भो रोधो यस्येति केचित्।

[90] Partly restored from *SC* which preproduces Kula anonymously. After द्वारे *SC* omits a word which is partly corrupt in our copy, but seems to stand for कृतोत्तम्भं।

94. जाआइ तं मुहुत्तं पुण्णज्झीणसरिआपुलिणसोहाइँ।
रक्खसघरङ्गणाइं गअसमराहिमुहजोहपइरिक्काइँ।।

[जातानि तन्मुहूर्तं पूर्णक्षीणसरित्पुलिनशोभानि।
राक्षसगृहाङ्गणानि गतसमराभिमुखयोधप्रतिरिक्तानि।।]

At that moment, the courtyards of the mansions of the demons, vacant, with the troops gone to the front, looked like the sandy banks of a river that had subsided after a flood.

K (*chāyā*) has व्यतिरिक्तानि (विशेषेण रिक्तानि commentary), i.e. *vairikkāiṁ* for *pai°* (प्रतिरिक्तानि शून्यानि R)।

My seems to read *puṇṇojjhāa* which he renders as पूर्णावक्षीण for *puṇṇa-jjhīṇa* (पूर्णक्षीण)। He says समरार्थं गतैर्योधैः शून्यीकृतानि भवनाङ्गणानि पूर्णतत्क्षणावक्षीणानां सरितां पुलिनसदृशानि आसन्नित्यर्थः।

95. लङ्कावेढणतुरिओ आलोइअदारणिन्तरक्खसलोओ।
रसिऊण पवअणिवहो खरपवणाइद्धवणदओ व्व पचलिओ।।

[लङ्कावेष्टनत्वरित आलोकितद्वारनिर्यद्राक्षसलोकः।
रसित्वा प्लवगनिवहः खरपवनाविद्धवनदव इव प्रचलितः।।]

The apes, who were quick to encircle Laṅkā, yelled and rushed forth, like a forest fire driven by a violent gale, when they saw the demons come out through the gates.

K explains only a phrase of this verse, K (*chāyā*) has वात (Kula and MY also) for *pavaṇa* (R), and विचलितः for *paca°* (R). In our transcript K (*chāyā*) has दवः, like R and Kula, but Goldschmidt's manuscript has तरुः। MY has द्रुम, and विवलितः for विचलितः। MY says लङ्कावेष्टनार्थं व्यग्रः कपिनिवहो निर्यद्राक्षसबलावलोकनेन प्रवलवाताहतद्रुमवत् विवलितः परावृत्त इत्यर्थः।

Kula says खरवातप्रेषितवनदव इव चलितः तदभिमुखं प्रस्थितः। He seems to reads *vaṇa-davo via calio* as in manuscript C of Goldschmidt. Cf. *SC* text.

96. पहरुज्जअपाइक्कं परिवड्ढइ पक्खपसरिआसारोहम्।
मुक्कङ्कुसमाअङ्गं सिढिलिअरहपग्गहं णिसाअरसेणम्।।

[प्रहारऋजुकपदाति परिवर्धते पक्षप्रसृताश्वारोहम्।
मुक्ताङ्कुशमातङ्गं शिथिलितरथप्रग्रहं निशाचरसैन्यम्।।]

The army of the demons swelled, the infantry ready to strike, and the cavalry advancing on the flanks; the elephants urged on by the goad, and the chariots driven at full speed.[91]

MY says *paharujjua-pāikkaṁ* प्रहारोद्यतपादातं (K also). *SC* text has *paharujjaa*. K explains मुक्ताङ्कुशमातङ्ग as प्रयुक्ताङ्कुशमातङ्गः। MY remarks उद्योजितमातङ्गम् उद्योजितरथं च राक्षससैन्यं जातमिति यावत्।

Kula reads परिवर्तते for *parivaḍḍhai* — निशाचरसैन्यं परिवर्तते कपिसैन्यस्याभिमुखनित्यत्वात्। *SC* says परिवर्तते वानराभिमुखीभूय धावति।

R says प्रहारे ऋजुका वेध्यसंमुखीकृतकुन्ताः पदातयो यत्र।

SC says त्वरार्थं मुक्ता अङ्कुशा यत्र एवंभूता मातङ्ग यत्र।

97. तो एक्काअअवेअं एक्कक्कमदिण्णमहिअलब्भहिअपअम्।
ठाइ अणोहीणभडं तह परिमण्डलपहाविअं कइसेणम्।।

[तत एकागतवेगमेकैकक्रमदत्तमहीतलाभ्यधिकपदम्।
तिष्ठत्यनवहीनभटं तथा परिमण्डलप्रधावितं कपिसैन्यम्।।]

Thereupon, coming at a uniform speed, and striving to outdo one another in their onward rush,[92] the host of apes, composed of warriors of unflagging zeal, stood (before the enemy) as they swept forward in an encircling movement as before.[93]

This is the last verse of the canto in K, MY and Muda, adapted to introduce the usual concluding word अनुराग। Sea below.

K, MY and Kula read नसोढ (*ṇasahia*, cf. *SC* text for *mahiala* (R). K and Muda read धावति (*dhāi*) for *ṭhāi* = तिष्ठति (R and Kula). K, Muda and MY read गृहीतानुरागम्, i.e. *gahiāṇurāaṁ* for *aṇohīṇa-bhaḍaṁ* अनवहीनभटं (R).

K says ततः कपिसन्यमेकत्वेन आगतवेगम् एकरूपागतवेगम् अग्रतो दत्तमभ्यधिकं पदं परस्परं न सोढं येन तत्तथाभूतं, गृहीतयुद्धानुरागं, तथैव परितो मण्डलाकारेण प्रधावितं भूत्वा राक्षसबलमभितो धावति स्मेति[94]।

---

[91] Literally (the army) with the chariot reins slackened.

[92] A more literal rendering would be: intolerant of one another's forward step. For the reading followed see Extracts.

[93] I.e. as at the beginning of the attack. Cf. Mudamalla in Extracts.

[94] Muda says गृहीतानुरागं गृहीतयुद्धाभिनिवेशं कपिसैन्यं तथा परिमण्डलप्रधावितमेव भूत्वा धावतीति। तथा परिमण्डलं प्रधावितं, यथा आरम्भदशायां परिमण्डलं भवति उत्तरदशायामपि तथैव परिमण्डलं सत् प्रधावितमिति।

MY says *ekkakkama* अन्योन्य। तुल्यागतवेगम्, अन्योन्येन पराभिमुखदत्तमभ्यधिकपवमसहमानं, स्वीकृतरणानुरागं, तथा परिमण्डलीभूय प्रधावितम्। यथा राक्षससैन्यं निरगात् तथा परिमण्डलीभूय तत्प्रतीच्छामकरोत् कपिबलमपीत्यर्थः।

R says अनवहीना अनपगतधैर्या भटा यत्र। Kula reads भर for भट। He says एकैकेन दत्तं न सोढमभ्यधिकं पदं येन तत् तथा cf. K *chāyā* — एकैकदत्तनसोढ़ाभ्यधिकपदं)। अनवहीनभरम् अपरित्यक्तरणभारं यथा पूर्वं तथा परिमण्डलप्रधावितं कपिसैन्यं तिष्ठति। अभिमुखागतानपि राक्षसान् दृष्ट्वा तथैव सोत्साहं स्थितमित्यर्थः। The beginning of Kula's gloss is missing, but *SC* says एकरूपतया आगतो वेगो यस्य, समकृतवेगमिति कुलनाथः।

98. पत्थन्ति आअरोसा पत्थिज्जन्ति अ महग्घरणसोडीरा।
णिहणन्ति णिहण्णन्ति अ अणुराएण णवरं ण भज्जन्ति भडा।।

[प्रार्थयन्ते जातरोषाः प्रार्थ्यन्ते च महार्घरणशौटीर्याः।
निघ्नन्ति निहन्यन्ते चानुरागेण केवलं न भज्यन्ते भटाः।।]

The wrathful warriors assailed the enemy, and were assailed in turn. Full of exalted martial pride, they slew and were slain. Only they yielded not on account of their zeal.

K and MY put this as the concluding verse of *their* canto 13 as explained in the Introduction.

MY says केवलं रणानुरागेण न भज्यन्ते कदाचिदपि भग्नरणानुरागा न भवन्तीत्यर्थः। R says प्रार्थयन्ते परानुपरुन्धन्ति युद्धायाकारयन्ति वा। Kula says प्रार्थयन्ते वरयन्ति परानित्यर्थात्। *SC* says अभियुञ्जन्ति।

The phrase *ṇa bhajjanti bhaḍā* recurs in 13.4 (न भज्यन्ते नापसरन्ति R)।

इअ सिरिपवरसेणविरइए कालिदासकए दहमुवहे महाकव्वे
वारहो आसासओ समत्तो।

[इति श्रीप्रवरसेनविरचिते कालिदासकृते दशमुखवधे महाकाव्ये
द्वादश आश्वासकःसमाप्तः।]

त्रयोदश आश्वासकः
Thirteenth Āśvāsakaḥ

1. अह णिग्गअमिलिएहिं अल्लीणसमागएहि अ विमुक्करवम्।
रअणिअरवाणरेहिं दिण्णं सहिअं च गरुअरणपत्थाणम्।।

[अथ निर्गममिलिताभ्यामालीनसमागताभ्यां च विमुक्तरवम्।
रजनिचरवानराभ्यां दत्तं सोढं च गुरुकरणप्रस्थानम्।।]

Thereupon the demons, who joined battle as soon as they sallied out, and the apes, who closed in upon them, initiated and bore the brunt of heavy fighting, uttering loud cries.

K says अनन्तरं लङ्कायाः निर्गतमिलितैः निर्गस्य समूढैः, पूर्वमालीनैः लङ्कासमीपाश्रितैः ततः समागतैः रजनिचरैः वानरैश्च विमुक्तरवं यथा गुरु अतिमहत् रणप्रस्थानं रणार्थं प्रयाणं दत्तं कृतम। परस्परेण सोढं च Kula says निर्गतमिलितैः निष्क्रम्य लग्नै रजनिचरैः आलीनसमागतैः ढौकित्वा मिश्रीभूतैश्च वानरैः।

Muda says निर्गतमिलितैः पुर्या निर्गतमात्रं गत्वा युद्धार्थं श्लिष्टैः, आलीनसमागतैः द्वीपान्तरादागत्य समालीनैः यथाक्रमं रजनीचरवानरैः गुरुकं रणप्रस्थानं रणप्रक्रिया दत्तं सोढ़ं च। निर्गतमिलिताः रजनीचराः यथा प्रहरन्ति सहन्ते च समागतालीनवानरा अपि तथैव प्रहरन्ति सहन्ते चेत्यर्थः।

Kula says गुरुकरणप्रस्थानं महासमराघटनम्।

2. तह अ पुरिल्लणिवाइअदेहोवरिणिमिअचलणपत्थणतुरिआ।
एक्कक्कमं अहिगआ थोअं जह पहरलालसा ओसरिआ।।

[तथा च पुरोगनिपातितदेहोपरिनिवेशितचरणप्रस्थानत्वरिताः।
एकैकमभिगता स्तोकं यथा प्रहारलालसा असृताः।।]

As the warriors rushed forward, trampling on the fallen bodies of those in front of them, they came so close to one another that they drew back a little in their eagerness to strike.

K reads *taha vi* (तथापि) for *taha a* (तथा च)। K, MY. Kula and Muda read *patthia* for *patthaṇa* = प्रस्थान (R); and *aigaā* (अतिगताः) for *ahigaā* = अभिगताः (R).

K says पुरोभवतां प्रतिभटानां निपातितेषु देहेषु उपरिनिहितचरणाः सन्तः प्रस्थिताश्च

सैनिका अन्योन्यं तथातिगता अतिक्रम्य गताः (Kula also) कथमिति चेत्। प्रहारलालसाः ते यथा स्तोकमपसृताः। एतदुक्तं भवतियुद्धार्थमतिसंरब्धाः ते राक्षसवानराः प्रस्थानवेगातिशयात् पुरःस्थान् प्रत्यर्थिनो निपात्य तेषामुपरि कृतपदन्यासाः परस्परयोः अभ्यन्तरमवगाह्य पुनः प्रहारार्थं किंचिदपसृता इति।

MY says *purilla* पुरोगत। पुरोगतानां योधानां वेगवशात् निपातितदेहोपरि कृतपदाः त्वरया प्रस्थिताः सैनिकाः तथात्यन्तं मिलिता यथा प्रहारावकाशार्थं पुनरपासरन् इत्यर्थः। अतिगता अतिसंश्लिष्टाः। Muda says त्वरितं प्रस्थिताः प्रतिपुरुषाः तथा एकैकमतिगताः अत्यन्तमासन्नाः, प्रहारलालसाः प्रहारेच्छवः यथा स्तोकमपसृताः। Kula says एकैकं प्रत्येकम्।

3. जह हिअएहिं ववसिअं रअकलुसेहिं णअणेहिं जह सच्चविअम्।
रअणिअरेहिं रणमुहे तह पडिवक्खम्मि पहरणं ओहरिअम्।।

[यथा हृदयैर्व्यवसितं रजःकलुषाभ्यां नयनाभ्यां यथा सत्यापितम्।
रजनीचरै रणमुखे तथा प्रतिपक्षे प्रहरणमवपातितम्।।]

The demons wielded their weapons against the enemy in the forefront of the battle just as they had purposed in their hearts, and determined with their dust-covered eyes.

K says पूर्वं हृदये यथा युद्धे व्यवसितम् एवमेवं करिष्यामीति यथा अध्यवसितं, ततः समरभूमौ रजसा कलुषितैः नयनैः यथा लक्षितं (सत्यापितं *chāyā*), राक्षसैः प्रतिपक्षे तथा प्रहारणमवहृतं प्रयुक्तम् (विसृष्टम् Muda; व्यापारितम् Kula)।

MY says *saccavia* लक्षित (दृष्ट Kula; लक्षीकृत Muda)। Kula reads रजनीचरवानरैः (i.e. *raaṇiara-vāṇarehiṁ*, like manuscript C of Goldschmidt) for *raaṇiarehi raṇamuhe*. Kula says यथा हृदयैर्व्यवसितं चिन्तितम्।

4. पअलम्भव्भहिअजवा मुट्ठिपरिट्ठविअणिप्पअम्पक्खग्गा।
सच्चविअलद्धलक्खा पढमपहारविसआ ण भज्जन्ति भडा।।

[पदलम्भाभ्यधिकजवा मुष्टिपरिस्थापितनिष्प्रकम्पखड्गाः।
सत्यापितलब्धलक्ष्याः प्रथमप्रहारविषया न भज्यन्ते भटाः।।]

Quick to secure vantage ground, and adroit in striking the first blow,[1] the warriors, who wielded firmly gripped unwavering swords, and hit the mark, never yielded ground to the enemy.

---

[1] Cf. Kulanātha in Extracts.

K and Muda read प्रतिष्ठापित (Kula also) for परि°; भुजाः for *bhaḍā* (भटाः) and *sajjanti* for *bhajjanti* = भज्यन्ते (R and Kula ?).

K says पदशब्देन स्वामिना तत्काल एव प्रतिपादितः अधिकारविशेष उच्यते। तस्य लाभात् अभ्यधिकजवाः अतिप्रकृष्टप्रहाररभसा, मुष्टिषु प्रतिष्ठापितनिश्चलखड्गा, लक्षितलब्धलक्षा (सत्यापितलब्धलक्षाः *chāyā*) भटानां भुजाः प्रहारविशदाः प्रथम एव विदारितलक्षा न सज्यन्ति (सज्यन्ते?) न कुत्रचित् प्रतिहन्यन्ते स्म।

MY says पदं प्रहारस्थानं प्रहारविषयः तस्य लाभः। लक्षितलब्धलक्षाः यथा लक्षितं तथा लक्षं लब्धं यस्ते तथा। प्रथमप्रहारात् नाश्राम्यन् किंतु संस्कारोद्बोघात् लघवः शक्त्यतिशययोगिनोऽभवन् इत्यर्थः।

Kula says सत्यीकृतो दृष्टो लब्धो लक्ष्यः प्रहर्तव्यदेशो यैस्ते तथा। प्रथमप्रहारे अजातखेदत्वात् विशदाः पटवः . . .अतएव जितश्रमत्वात् . . . नावसीदन्ति। He seems to read *bhajjanti* like R who says न भज्यन्ते न पराजयन्ते। Kula says also पदलाभाय, प्रहारस्थानप्राप्तये, अथवा पदलाभेन . . . पदन्यासप्राप्त्या अत्यधिकजवाः वेगेन परिसृताः। It is not clear whether he read *bhuā* or *bhaḍā* (R). See above.

R takes *visaa* (विशद) as विषय (प्रथमप्रहारस्य विषया अपि), but mentions the other explanation.

Muda *pratīka* has अव, and he reads अवलम्बित for *paalambha*. He also reads प्रसार for प्रहार। He says अवलम्बिताभ्यधिकजवाः स्वीकृतात्यर्थवेगाः, मुष्टिप्रतिष्ठापितत्वात् दृढगृहीतत्वात् निष्प्रकम्पखड्गाः, लक्षीकृतबद्धलक्षाः भुजाः प्रथमप्रसार एव विशदाः प्रथमप्रसार एव प्रहारकत्वेन प्रसिद्धाः भुजाः पुनर्न सज्यन्ते प्रथमप्रयोग एव कर्तव्यस्य परिसमापितत्वात् पुनर्न सज्यन्ते नोद्युक्ता भवन्ति। Muda seems to read बद्ध for लब्ध in the second line.

5. विहुणन्ति चलिअविडवे मुहमण्डलघोलणुप्पुसिअसिन्दूरे।
पवअसहत्थाइद्धे कुम्भअडुक्खुत्तपाअवे माअङ्गा।।

[विधुन्वन्ति चलितविटपान्मुखमण्डलघूर्णनोत्प्रोञ्छितसिन्दूरान्।
प्लवगस्वहस्ताविद्धान्कुम्भतटभग्नपादपान्मातङ्गाः।।]

The elephants of the demons tried to shake off the trees with the swaying branches, hurled by apes, which had penetrated their temples, wiping off the vermilion paint as they whirled round the face.

K says मातङ्गाः प्लवगैः स्वहस्तेन आविद्धान् क्षिप्तान्, चलितशाखान्, मुखमण्डले घूर्णनेन अपमृष्टसिन्दूरविन्यासान्, कुम्भतटे मग्नान् वृक्षान् धून्वन्ति स्म। MY says *khutta* खात् (for *ukkhutta*).

6. रोसस्स दासरहिणो मअणस्स अ दूसहस्स रक्खसवइणो।
समअं चिअ अङ्ढत्तो दोएह वि अणुरूअदारुणो परिणामो।।

[रोषस्य दासरथेर्मदनस्य च दुःसहस्य राक्षसपतेः।
सममेवारब्धो द्वयोरप्यनुरूपदारुणः परिणामः।।]

The justly grievous consequences of both Rāma's terrible wrath and Rāvaṇa's irresistible passion began to be manifest all at once.

Kula says रामस्य रोषस्य राक्षसपतेः . . . दुःसहस्य मदनस्य (च) सममेव द्वयोरपि राक्षसप्रक्षयहेतुत्वात् अनुरूपदारुणः परिणामः आरब्धः वृत्तः।

7. णिहणन्ति गएहिं गए तुरएहिं तुरङ्गमे रहेहिं अ रहिणो।
जाअं पवङ्गमाणं पडिवक्खो पहरणं च रक्खससेण्णम्।।

[निघ्नन्ति गजैर्गजांस्तुरगैस्तुरङ्गमान्रथैश्च रथिनः।
जातं प्लवङ्गमानां प्रतिपक्ष्यः प्रहरणं च राक्षससैन्यम्।।]

The *rākṣasa* army provided both the targets and the means of attack[2] for the apes, since they killed the elephants with the elephants, the horses with the horses, and the chariot-fighters with the chariots.

वानरा इत्यध्याहार्यम् K. प्रतिपक्षः प्रहारविषयः *SC.*

8. सरविक्किणण्महिहरा सरविहडिअसेसमुग्गराहअसेला।
पहरणमग्गाइञ्चिअभुअचुण्णिअपव्वआ भमन्ति णिसिअरा।।

[शरविकीर्णमहीधरा शरविघटितशेषमुद्गराहतशैलाः।
प्रहरणमार्गाञ्चितभुजचूर्णितपर्वता भ्रमन्ति निशाचराः।।]

The demons moved about piercing the mountains (hurled by the apes) with their arrows, and breaking up with their clubs what remained of pierced by the arrows; while they smashed with their arms those that were out of reach of their weapons.

K and Kula read निर्भिन्न (*ṇibbhiṇṇa* used many times in the poem) for *vikkiṇṇa* = विकीर्ण (R).

K says तत्र राक्षसाः शरैः निर्भिन्नमहीधराः शरैः भिन्ना वानरमुक्ता महीधरा यस्ते।

[2] Literally, The . . . army became both the adversary and the weapon. . . .

तथा शरविघटितशेषा शरैः विदारितशेषाः मुद्गरैः आहताः शैला यस्तै। तथा प्रहारमार्गमतीता आसन्नत्वात् आयुधगोचरमतीताः भुजैरेव चूर्णिताः पर्वता यैस्ते। तथा भूत्वा भ्रमन्ति स्म।

MY says शरमुद्गराद्यशेषायुधैरपि अक्षता आसन्नतमा ये ते भुजैरेव राक्षसैः चूर्ण्यन्त इत्यर्थः। He says *aiñcia* अतिगत। Cf. 13.28 below. In 13.86 also he explains the word as अतिगत, and says जम्बुमालिनं हत्वा हनुमानतिगत इत्यर्थः।

K (*chāyā*) has प्रहरणमार्ग। Kula says प्रहरणमार्गादतिक्रान्ता भुजैः चूर्णिताः पर्वताः यैस्ते निशाचराः।

9. भाअपडिओ वि वित्थअगिरिपरिणाहविअडे पवङ्गक्खन्धे।
अपहुप्पन्तावेढो उल्ललइ गअस्स थोरकरपब्भारो।।

[भागपतितोऽपि विस्तृतगिरिपरिणाहविकटे प्लवङ्गस्कन्धे।
अप्रभवदावेष्ट उल्ललति गजस्य स्थूलकरप्राग्भारः।।]

The massive trunk of an elephant, even though it accurately hit the shoulder of an ape, broad as the expanse of a mountain, slipped aside, failing to hem it round.

K says विस्तृतस्य गिरेः परिणाहवत् विस्तारवत् विकटे विशाले प्लवङ्गस्य स्कन्धे ग्रीवामूले भागपतितोऽपि यथास्थानपतितोऽपि गजस्य स्थूलः करविस्तारः अप्रभवदावेष्टः अपर्याप्नुवदावेष्टनो भूत्वा उल्ललति विगलति स्म। MY says अपर्याप्तदावेष्टनानुगुणदैर्घ्यः उल्ललति विषमं स्खलितीत्यर्थ। Kula says भ्रमति। R says चञ्चलीभवति।

10. रअणिअरोरत्थलचुण्णिअस्स कइरोसपेसिअस्स सिहरिणो।
उद्धं उद्धाइं रओ ओसरइ अहोमुहो सिलासंघातो।।

[रजनिचरोरःस्थलचूर्णितस्य कपिरोषप्रेषितस्य शिखरिणः।
ऊर्ध्वमुद्धावति रजोऽपसरत्यधोमुखः शिलासंघातः।।]

As a mountain, furiously hurled by an ape, crumbled on the chest of a demon, the dust rose aloft, while the mass of rocks slumped down to the ground.

K says कपिना रोषात् प्रेषितस्य क्षिप्तस्य, रजनिचरोरःस्थले चूर्णितस्य शिखरिणो गिरेः रजो धूलिः ऊर्ध्वामुद्धावति स्म। तस्य शिलासंघातः अधोमुखोऽपसरति स्म।

11. रिउवलमज्झणिराआ णिहअणिरन्तरणिसुद्धणज्जन्तभडा।
विक्कमणीसामण्णा दट्ठुंपि भडाण दुक्करा गइमग्गा।।

[रिपुबलमध्यनिरायता निहतनिरन्तरनिपातितज्ञायमानभटाः।
विक्रमनिःसामान्या द्रष्टुमपि भटानां दुष्करा गतिमार्गाः।।]

The tracks of the warriors, stretching right through the enemy troops, and exhibiting uncommon valour, were a formidable sight,[3] with distinguished warriors slain and falling in succession.

K says रिपुबलस्य मध्ये निरायताः, निहताः निरन्तरं निपातिताः ज्ञायमानाः प्रख्याताः भटाः येषु, तेषां विक्रमणे कृते निःसामान्या निरुपमा, एवंभूताः भटानां गतिमार्गा द्रष्टुमपि दुष्कराः किं पुनः कर्तुमिति।

MY says भटानां ज्ञायमानत्वं प्रसिद्धता। विक्रमनिःसामान्या विक्रमेण निरुपमाः, A has विक्रमणे। Kula says निरायता दीर्घाः। निहिता निचूर्णनिपतिताः ज्ञायमानाः सुप्रसिद्धा भटा येषु ते तथा। (विक्रमेण) निःसामान्या असाधारणाः। अन्यैः भयहेतुत्वात् द्रष्टुमपि न शक्यन्त इत्यर्थः। Kula seems to read *ṇicuṇṇia* for *ṇirantara*.

12. णिव्वुब्भइ सोडीरं अप्पडिहत्थलहुओ हसिज्जइ पहरो।
वड्डइ वेरावन्धो अइसंधिज्जन्ति साहसेसु समत्था।।

[निवार्ह्यते शौण्डीर्यमप्रतिहस्तलघुको हस्यते प्रहारः।
वर्ध्यते वैरावन्धोऽतिसंदधति साहसेषु समर्थाः।।]

Martial ardour was brought into play. One's own blow was derided as trivial because of the lack of a worthy counter-blow. The urge of enmity prevailed. The strong persisted in daring exploits.

K says युद्धे योधैः शौण्डीर्यं स्वं सामर्थ्यं निरुह्यते निर्वर्त्यते स्म। अप्रतिहस्तलघुः – प्रतिहस्तः प्रतिद्वन्द्वी, अयोग्यप्रतिद्वन्द्वत्वात् लघुः प्रहारः आत्मीयः शस्त्रप्रहारः तैः हस्यते स्म। अथवा असदृशप्रतिभटत्वात् लघुः प्रहारः शत्रुणा कृतः शस्त्रप्रहारो वीरैरपहस्यते स्म। वीराणां वैर(ा)बन्धो ववृधे। समर्थाः साहसेषु अतिसन्धीयन्ते अतीव अभिनिविष्टा आसन् इत्यर्थः। कर्मकर्तरि पदम्। For प्रतिहस्त see also verse 92.

MY says निरुह्यते प्राणव्ययेनापीति भावः। अप्रतिहस्तलघुः प्रतिप्रहाराभावलघुः। प्रहर्त्रैव स्वयमपहस्यते। समर्था एव साहसकरणेषु परैः अतिसन्धीयन्ते हन्यन्त इत्यर्थः। अथवा साहसेषु समर्थाः साहसानुष्ठातारः तदति शायिसाहसकरणात् स्पर्धमानैः अतिसंधीयन्त इत्यर्थः। *SC* says जीयन्त इति श्रीनिवासः। Kula says शौटीर्यं

[3] Literally, hard even to look at.

शौर्याभिमानः। अप्रतिहस्तेन प्रतिहाराप्रदानेन लघुकः परिभवनीयः प्रहारः प्रहारवान् पुरुषो हस्यते। Kula reads अभिसन्धीयन्ते, i.e. *ahi°* for *ai saṁdhijjanti* (अतिसंधीयन्ते)। He says समर्थाः . . . प्राणनिरपेक्षकर्मसु अभिसन्धीयन्ते वञ्चयन्ते[4]।

13. ण पडइ पडिए वि सिरे सूलविहिण्णं पि णेअ भिज्जइ हिअअम्।
दुप्परिइअं ण लग्गइ लाविज्जन्तं पि पडिभडाण रणभअम्।।

[न पतति पतितेऽपि शिरसि शूलविभिन्नमपि नैव भिद्यते हृदयम्।
दुष्परिचितं न लगति लाग्यमानमपि प्रतिभटानां रणभयम्।।]

The heart did not sink, even though the head sank to the ground; nor did it lose courage, even though pierced by the spear. The fear of war, even though brought nearby the warriors, found no place in the hearts of their antagonists, because it was unfamiliar to them.

K says शिरसि पतितेऽपि धैर्येण देहो न पतति स्म। शूलेन विभिन्नमपि हृदयं नैव भिद्यते अन्तर्न बिभिदे। अहङ्कारेण भटैः लभ्यमानमपि (*chāyā* also) आवेश्यमानमपि रणभयं दुष्परिचितत्वात् प्रतिभटानां हृदये न लगति स्म। K's लभ्यमानम् might be a mistake for लाग्यमानम् = (*lāvijjantaṁ* (R). R says लाग्यमानमपि शत्रुभिराधीयमानमपि। Cf. MY below.

R says शिरसि पतितेऽपि हृदयं न पतति . . . न कातरतामवलम्बत इत्यर्थः। Kula says शूलेन समन्तात् भिन्नमपि न भिद्यते उन्नतमपराङ्मुखं च[5] तिष्ठतीत्यर्थः। दुःपरिचितमननुभूतपूर्वम्।

MY says हृदयं न भिद्यते इति न भिद्यते नान्यथा भवति हृदयस्य व्यवसाय-भूयस्कत्वादित्यर्थः। He has *lāijjantaṁ* लिह्यमानम् (?), and says भटैः प्रतिभटानां प्रहारादिभिः आपाद्यमानमपि रणभयमपरिचिततया नालगदित्यर्थः। MY's लिह्यमानम् is a mistake for लाग्यमानम्। Kula is corrupt, but *SC* text has *lāijjantaṁ*, translated as लाग्यमानम् in the *chāyā*.

14. सहइ पहरेसु दप्पो दप्पट्ठाणेसु सहइ पुरिसासङ्गो।
णिद्दोसेसु भडाणं ओसारेसु वि ण ओसरइ रोसरसो।।

[सहते प्रहारेषु दर्पो दर्पस्थानेषु सहते पुरुषाध्यवसायः।
निर्दोषेषु भटानामपसारेष्वपि नापसरति रोषरसः।।]

---

[4] The word is restore d from Kula quotation in *SC* which, however, has अर्धाकृष्टा वञ्चयन्ते।

[5] Partiallly restored from *SC*.

The pride of a warrior ignored the enemy's blow. Manly self-confidence achieved success in the thick of the fight.[6] The wrath of the warriors did not abate even during strategic[7] withdrawals.

K, MY and Kula read *hasai* for the first *sahai* = सहते (R). K and MY read प्रहार (*pahara*) for *dappa°* (R). K (*chāyā*) has अपसारेषु भटानां निर्दोषेष्वपि (*SC* text also).

K says प्रहारेषु सत्सु प्रहतानां भटानां दर्पः हसति विकसति स्म। पुरुषविश्वासः पुरुषः खलु अहमिति विश्वासः प्रहारस्य स्थानेषु विषयेषु प्राप्तेषु बलवत्तरेषु प्रतिभेदेषु (प्रतिभटेषु ?) प्रहर्तव्येषु सत्सु पुरुषाभिमानः सहते शक्नोति स्म। अतिभारेषु अभिमानिनामभिमानः साध्यं साधयतीति भावः। निर्दोषेषु अपसारेषु करस्य वशादागतेषु (?) अपगतेषु भटानां रोषरसो नापसरति स्म। *SC* says *pahara-ṭṭhāṇesu* इति पाठे प्रहारस्थानेषु प्रतिपक्षप्रहारसंकटेषु इत्यर्थः।

MY says प्रहारेषु दर्पो हसति। प्रहतः सन् भटः प्रहारमवजानातीति वा, प्रहतस्य भटस्य दर्पो वर्धत इति वार्थः। स्थानेषु अवसरेषु प्रहारं पुरुषाशंसा सहते। प्रहर्तव्यस्य शूरतया प्रसिद्धिः। अभ्युद्यतं प्रहारमनुजानातीत्यर्थः। MY seems to read *paharaṁ ṭhāṇesu* for *pahara-ṭṭhāṇesu*, which is K's reading.

MY mentions another explanation सहते शोभत इत्यर्थः (cf. Hemacandra 4.100) इति केचित्। हृदयस्थानेषु (प्रहारस्थानेषु ?) अपराङ्मुखस्य यः परकृतः प्रहारः तत्र तस्य पुरुषाशंसा शूरतराभिमान शोभत इत्यर्थः। He explains the second line thus: आश्रयभूतेषु भटेषु अजनितभग्नदोषमपसरत्सु अमित्रदर्शनादिना तदाश्रितो रोषो नापसरतीत्यर्थः। R says निर्दोषेषु अपसारेषु न भयेन, किंतु प्रहारसौकर्याय पश्चादागमनेष्वपि।

Kula says प्रहारेषु दर्पो हसति अवज्ञां करोति। पुरुषासङ्गः[8] पुरुषस्य शत्रुवधं प्रत्यासङ्ग(?)करत्वात् व्यवसायः[9] परप्रस्थानेषु पराभिमुखगमनेषु शोभते। भटानामिति सर्वत्र योज्यम्। Kula seems to read *para-paṭṭhāṇesu* (cf. *SC* text) and explains *sahai* as शोभते (cf. MY above).

15. रिउगअभिण्णुक्खित्ता रोसविहुव्वन्तचडुलकेसरणिवहा।
दढदट्ठदन्तमूला रसिऊण समच्छरं णिमिल्लन्ति कई।।

---

[6] Kṛṣṇa's reading (*pahara*) is followed.

[7] Literally, innocent. See Rāmadāsa in Extracts.

[8] Kula seems to say here *āsaṁgha* — शब्द आशायां देशीयः। पुरुषाकांक्षा पुरुषस्य, etc.

[9] *SC* says पुरुषस्य आशंसा शत्रुवधं प्रत्युत्साहः।

[रिपुगजभिन्नोत्क्षिप्ता रोषविधूयमानचटुलकेसरनिवहाः।
दृढदष्टदन्तमूला रसित्वा समत्सरं निमीलन्ति कपयः।।]

The apes yelled furiously when pierced and thrown up by the elephants of the enemy. Clenching their teeth, and shaking their flowing hair in anger, they closed their eyes in death.

K reads दर for *daḍha* = दृढ (R and Kula); and मुसल for मूल (R and Kula).

K says निमीलन्ति मृता इत्यर्थः। अन्यत् सुबोधम्। Kula says दृढं दष्टं दन्तमूलं दन्तनिर्गमस्थानं यैस्ते। समत्सरं सक्रोधम्।

16. अवहीरणा ण किज्जइ सुमरिज्जइ संसए वि सामिअसुकअम्।
णगणिज्जइ विणिवाओ दट्ठे वि भअम्मि संभरिज्जइ लज्जा।।

[अवधीरणा न क्रियते स्मर्यते संशयेऽपि स्वामिसुकृतम्।
न गण्यते विनिपातो दृष्टेऽपि भये स्मर्यते लज्जा।।]

The resolve of a warrior was not broken, and he thought of the master's kindness even in peril. Death was set at nought, and honour prevailed even in face of danger.[10]

K, MY and Kula read *avahāraṇā* (अवधारणा) for *avahīraṇā* अवधीरणा (R). K reads *bhajjai* and Kula *bhijjai* for *kijjai* = क्रियते (R). They read *cintijjai* for *sumarijjai* = स्मर्यते (R). K reads संशये, i.e. *saṁsaammi* for *saṁsae vi* (R and Kula).

K says योधानामवधारणा अवश्यमेतं हनिष्यामित्यध्यवसायः कदाचित् न भज्यते। संशये प्राणसंदेहे सति स्वामिना कृतं सुकृतं चिन्त्यते स्म। न तु स्वमरणम्। विनिपातो विपत्तिः वाहनविनाशादिः न गण्यते स्म। भये दृष्टेऽपि लज्जा स्मर्यते पलायनप्रसङ्गे लज्जा स्मर्यते स्म।

MY says अवधारणा व्यवसायः। विनिपातो वधः। दृष्टे भये भयहेतो, his *pratīka* is *ohāraṇā*.

Kula says अवधारणा प्रतिज्ञा न भिद्यते। संशयेऽपि जीवितसंदेहेऽपि स्वामिसुकृतं चिन्त्यते। R says विनिपातो मरणम्।

17. पढमाणिआहि सुइरं जे जीविअसंसअम्मि वि परिच्छूढा।
ते च्चिअ अहिमुहणिहआ सुरबन्दीहि अहिसारिआ रअणिअरा।।

[10] Literally, shame was remembered even when the cause of fear was seen. Cf. verse 78.

[प्रथमानीताभिः सुचिरं ये जीवितसंशयेऽपि परिक्षिप्ताः।
त एवाभिमुखनिहताः सुरबन्दीभिरभिसारिता रजनीचराः॥]

The captive nymphs, who had when first brought to Laṅkā rejected the demons for long, even at the risk of their life, accepted as their lovers those very demons when they were slain in the forefront of the battle.[11]

K says राक्षसैः प्रथमानीताभिः सुरबन्दीभिः बन्दीभूताभिः सुरस्त्रीभिः ये राक्षसाः जीवितसंशयेऽपि सुचिरं त्यक्ता अपरिगृहीताः, युद्धेऽभिमुखं निहिताः त एव ताभिरभिसारिता देवत्वं गताः त एव ताभिः गृहीता इति। My has *paḍicchūḍhā* (for परि⁰) प्रतिक्षिप्ताः प्रत्याख्याता इति यावत्।

18. रअणिअरबद्धलक्खो अबद्धरुहिरपरिपण्डुरङ्गच्छेओ।
अगणिअवणसंतावो उण्हपहारसरसो समल्लिअइ कई॥

[रजनीचरबद्धलक्ष्योऽबद्धरुधिरपरिपाण्डुराङ्गच्छेदः।
अगणितव्रणसंताप उष्णप्रहारसरसः समालीयते कपिः॥]

A wounded ape, profusely bleeding and pale, but eager to fight despite the severe blow inflicted upon him, drew near regardless of the agony of his wounds, fixing his eyes on a demon.

K reads भुजप्रहार[12] for अङ्गच्छेद (R). He says अबद्धरुधिरत्वात् छेदलाघवेन अनुत्पन्नरुधिरत्वात् परिपाण्डरभुजप्रहारः, अगणितब्रणवेदनः, उष्णेन तीव्रेण प्रहारेण सरसः साभिनिवेशः कपि रजनिचरेषु बद्धलक्षो भूत्वा प्रविवेशेत्यर्थः।

MY says उष्णप्रहारसरसः प्रत्यग्रप्रहारेण सोल्लासः। *samalliai* प्राप्नोति (समाश्रयति K *chāyā*). Kula says समालीयते ढौकते।

Kula says अगृहीतः रणकृतः संतापो येन। He reads *agahia-raṇa*⁰[13] for *agaṇia-vaṇa*⁰. He says उष्णो दाहकारी प्रहारो यस्य स, तथापि सरसः सानुरागः।

R says अबद्धेन प्रवहता रुधिरेण परिपाण्डरः अङ्गच्छेदः क्षतं यस्य तथा। Kula says अबद्धेन गलता रुधिरेण परिपाण्डरव्रणच्छेदः। He thus reads *paripaṇḍaravaṇa-ccheo* (cf. *SC* text).

---

[11] A reference to the belief that warriors who die on the battlefield become gods. Cf. 12.67.

[12] I.e. *paripaṇḍara-bhua-ppaharo.*

[13] This is the reading of manuscript C of Goldschmidt.

19. ण पडिक्खन्ति अवसरं ओच्छुन्दन्ति जणिअं परेण पआवम्।
बोलेन्ति जहाभणिअं साहुक्कारपुरओ अइन्ति समत्था।।

[न प्रतीक्ष्य(क्ष)न्तेऽवसरमाक्रामति जनितं परेण प्रतापम्।
व्यतिक्रामन्ति यथाभणितं साधुकारपुरत आयान्ति समर्थाः।।]

The valiant did not wait for a chance to come, but crushed the valour displayed by the enemy. They performed more than they promised and came forward (to fight), followed by applause.[14]

K says समर्थाः पराक्रमस्य अवसरं न प्रतीक्षन्ते न प्रतिपालयामासुः। परेण जनितं प्रतापं पौरुषमवक्षुन्दन्ति बभञ्जुः। यथाभणितं प्राक् पतिज्ञातमर्थम् अतिक्रामन्ति स्म तस्मादधिकं चक्रुः। साधुकारपुरतः अन्यैः क्रियमाणं साधुवादं पुरः कृत्वा प्रविशन्ति स्म (यन्ति *chāyā*)। अथवा साधुकारं साधुक्रियां पुरस्कृत्य प्राविशन्निति।

My says *occhundanti* अवक्षुन्दन्ति। *opphundanti* इति पाठे आक्रामन्तीत्यर्थः (cf. *apphundai* 6.57, 82) *bolanti* अतिक्रामन्ति। ततोऽपि अतिशयेन कुर्वन्तीत्यर्थः। अतियान्ति साधुकारस्य पुरतोऽतियान्ति। यत्र यत्र रिपून् घ्नन्तः शूराः प्रविशन्ति तत्र पश्चात् (तत्र तत्र A) भटैः कृतः साधुकारोऽपि प्रवर्तत इत्यर्थः। अत्र लट्प्रयोगेऽपि भूतविहितो लकारः तत्र तत्र निक्षेप्तव्यः।

Kula says अवसरं न प्रतीक्षन्ते कालक्षेपं न कुर्वन्ति। He also says साधुकारपुरतः इति यत्र साधुकारं शृण्वन्ति तदभिमुखं समर्था आयान्ति[15] इत्यर्थः। R says साधुकारपुरतः प्रतिपक्षप्रहारादिकं द्रष्ट्वा साधु साध्वित कृत्वा आयान्ति। तमेव (प्रति)प्रहर्तुमित्यर्थात् विपक्षकृतसाधुकारस्य पुरतः संमुखे आयान्ति इति वा।

20. इअ ताण तं विअम्भइ सुरङ्गणासुरअलम्भसंकेअहरम्।
भग्गजमलोअवन्थं महेन्दभवणुज्जुआइअवहं जुज्झम्।।

[इति तेषां (तयोर्वा) तद्विजृम्भते सुराङ्गनासुरतलम्भसंकेतगृहम्।
भग्नयमलोकपथं महेन्द्रभवनऋजुकापितपथं युद्धम्।।]

Thus did their battle rage. It destroyed the path to the world of Yama, and straightened the way to Indra's palace[16]: it was, as it were, the appointed bower where the celestial maidens met to secure the joys of love.[17]

---

[14] Cf. Mādhava in Extracts. Or, "meeting with applause".

[15] Kula quotation in *SC* has अतिगच्छन्ति।

[16] I.e. heaven.

[17] I.e. by choosing as their lovers the warriors killed in the battle. See verse 17.

K says इति तेषां तत् युद्धं व्यजृम्भत। कीदृशम्—सुराङ्गनानाम् अभिनवदयितप्राप्त्या सुरतलाभस्य संकेतगृहं धर्मयुद्धत्वात् भग्नयमलोकपथं खिलीभूतयमलोकमार्गं, महेन्द्रभवनममरावतीं तां प्रति ऋजूकृतमार्गम्। MY also has ऋजूकृत। R says ऋजुकायितः संमुखीकृतः।

21. कइवच्छत्थलपरिणअणिअअमुहत्थमिअदन्तिदन्तप्फलिहम्।
णिहअभडमहिअणिवडिअसुरवहुचलवलअमुहलपवअगइवहम्।।

[कपिवक्षःस्थलपरिणतनिजकमुखास्तमितदन्तिदन्तपरिघम्।
निहतभटमहितनिपतितसुरवधूचलवलयमुखरप्लवगगतिपथम्।।]

The stout tusks of an elephant that hit an ape on the bosom sank deep into its own mouth;[18] while the tracks of the apes on the battlefield were resonant with the moving bangles of the celestial maidens, who came down in quest of the warriors that were killed.[19]

K and Kula read हस्ति° for दन्ति°। The beginning of K's gloss is not well preserved in our manuscript. He says कपीनां वक्षस्तलपरिणतस्य (?) . . . निजे (?) मुखे गजस्य मुख एवास्तमिता वक्षस्तलस्य काठिन्यातिशयात् प्रतिहता भूत्वा मूलभाग एवातिदूरं मग्ना हस्तिनां दन्ताख्याः परिघा यत्र तत्। निहतानां भटमहितानां भटप्रवराणां ग्रहणाय निपतितानां सुरवधूनां चलैः गमनरभसात् चलैः वलयैः मुखराः प्लवगानां गतिपथा यत्र। वानरैः हतानां राक्षसभटानां ग्रहणाय वानराणां गतिपथाननुगच्छन्ति सुरस्त्रिय इत्यर्थः।

MY says कपिवक्षःसु तिर्यङ्निखाताः, तद्दाढर्यात् निजमुखेषु अस्तमिताश्च गजानां दन्तपरिघा यत्र तत्तथा।

R says निहतभटानां महितेन समीहया (Kula also) निपतितानां स्वर्गादागतानां सुरवधूनां, etc.

Kula says कपिवक्षःस्थले परिणताः कृताघाता, निजकमुखेषु अस्तमिताः . . . हस्तिदन्तपरिघा दन्तार्गला यत्र। R says कपीनां वक्षःस्थलेषु परिणतानां पश्चादागत्य दत्तदन्तप्रहाराणां पूर्वनिपातानियमादत्राकर्षणात् दन्तिनां निजकमुख एवास्तमिता . . . दन्तपरिघा यत्र।

22. ओवअणोसुद्धरहं उप्पअणोच्छित्तविहडमाणगइन्दम्।
गहिअप्फिडिअतुरङ्गं अणुधाविअपवअणिहअरक्खसजोहम्।।

---

[18] I.e. the tusks were driven into the mouth of the animal without being able to penetrate the chest of the ape.

[19] See the preceding verse.

[अवपतनावपातितरथमुत्पतनोत्क्षिप्तविघटमानगजेन्द्रम्।
गृहितस्फेटिततुरङ्गमनुधावितप्लवगनिहतराक्षसयोधम्।।]

The chariots were dashed on the ground as the apes swooped down on them. The elephants, thrown up by the apes as they sprang into the air, had their limbs broken.[20] The captured horses ran away, and the *rākṣasa* warriors were slain by the pursuing apes.

K reads रुद्ध for *pavaa* = प्लवग (R and Kula) in the second line. He says प्लवगैः कृतेन अवपतनेन उपरि पतनेन निपातितरथम्। तेषामुत्पतनेन उत्क्षिप्तत्वात् विदार्यमाणगजेन्द्रम् (विघटमान . . . *chāyā*)। तैः गृहीतभ्रष्टतुरङ्गम्। अनुधावितरुद्धाः ततो निहतराक्षसयोधा यत्र तत्।

MY says *phiḍia* भ्रष्ट। प्रथमं भ्रष्टाः पुनर्गृहीताः तुरङ्गः यत्र तत्तथा। R says गृहीताः सन्तः स्फेटिताः चञ्चलत्वात् बहिर्गताः तुरङ्गा यत्र। Kula says गृहीताः प्रेषिता तुरङ्गा यत्र। He reads मथित (*mahia*, cf. *SC* text) for *ṇihaa*. He also says तेषामेवोत्पतनेन उत्क्षिप्य विघटमाना गजेन्द्रा यत्र[21]।

23. रसणिव्वाओरत्थलसुहविसहिज्जन्तचन्दणदुमप्पहरम्।
कलअललोहुग्घाडिअमुहबोलीणसरमग्गणिन्तणिणाअम्।।

[रसनिर्वृतोरःस्थलसुखविषह्यमानचन्दनद्रुमप्रहारम्।
कलकललोभोद्घाटितमुखव्यतिक्रान्तशरमार्गनिर्यन्निनादम्।।]

The impact of the sandal trees (hurled by the apes) was endured with ease by the demons, because the chest was cooled by the sap (of the broken trees); while the apes screamed when the arrows pierced through their mouths as they opened them in their eagerness to chatter.

K reads निनद for *lohv* = लोभ (R and Kula). He says उरसि चूर्णितस्य चन्दनविटपस्य रसेन शीतलेन निर्वृतेन (निर्वाण *chāyā*) उरःस्थलेन सुखं विषह्यमानचन्दनद्रुमप्रहारम्। कलकलनिनदार्थम् उद्घाटिते विवृत्ते मुखे सहसा पतित्वा निष्क्रान्तस्य भित्त्वा निर्गतस्य शरस्य मार्गेण निर्गमद्वारेण निर्यन्निनादम्।

---

[20] According to the Bengal school of commentators: the elephants (that had fallen when seized by the apes) rose up and away as the apes leaped into the air. See Extracts. This interpretation goes well with what is said about the horses, but strains the meaning of *ucchitta* (*utkṣipta*).

[21] This is amplified by *SC* — पूर्वमारूढेषु कपिषु तद्भरात् पतिता ये गजेन्द्रास्त एव तेषामुत्पतनेन गात्रमुत्क्षिप्य यत्र पलायिता इत्यर्थः।

Kula says कलकललोमेन विवृतेषु मुखेषु व्यतिक्रान्तानां निर्भिद्य गतानां शराणां मार्गैः निर्यान्तो निनादा यत्र तत् तथा।

24. भिण्णघडिज्जन्तघडं पडिरुद्धोसरिअचक्कलिअपाइक्कम्।
सहिरोहिण्णरहवहं मुहसुक्खप्फेणणिहुअहेसिअतुरअम्।।

[भिन्नघट्यमानघटं प्रतिरुद्धापसृतचक्रितपदाति।
रुधिरापभिन्नरथपथं मुखशुष्कफेननिभृतह्रेषिततुरगम्।।]

The ranks of the elephants broke up, and were formed again. The foot-soldiers, checked in their advance, retreated and formed a circle. The path of the chariots was covered with blood, and the horses neighed faintly because of the dry foam in the mouth.

K reads °विद्ध for °रुद्ध (R and Kula ?). K and Kula read आपूर्ण for *ohiṇṇa* = अपभिन्न = प्रतिहत (R). Their reading is *āuṇṇa* used in 12.6 (cf. *SC* text).

K says भिन्नपुनर्घटमानगजसमूहं, प्रतिविद्धत्वात् अपसृत्य पुनः चक्रीकृतपदातिकं, पतितानामुपरि गमनात् रुधिरपूर्णरथपथं, हर्षाभावात् मुखेषु शुष्केषु फेनेषु लालाफेनेषु मन्दहेषिततुरगम्। (निभृत° *chāyā*)।

Kula says मुखमुक्तैः फेनैः निभृतह्रेषिताः अव्यक्तध्वनयः तुरङ्गा यत्र तत् तथा। He reads *mukka* for *sukkha* (शुष्क)।

25. रिउपहरणपरिओसिअसाहुक्काररवगब्भिणपडन्तसिरम्।
णिब्भिण्णपहरमुच्छिअवअणब्भन्तरविदाअभडचुक्कारम्।।

[रिपुप्रहरणपरितोषितसाधुकाररवगर्भितपतच्छिरम्।
निर्भिन्नप्रहारमूर्च्छितवदनाभ्यन्तरविशीर्णभट्टचुक्कारम्।।]

The heads of the warriors, pleased with the foeman's striking power, rang with applause as they fell;[22] and the battle-cry died away in the mouth of those mangled and stunned by the enemy's assault.

MY says *virāa* विलीन। K says रिपोः प्रहरणेन प्रहारेण परितोषितत्वात् साधुवादगर्भितं भूत्वा पतच्छिरस्कम्। प्रहारनिर्भिन्नमूर्च्छितत्वात्[23] वदनाभ्यन्तरे विलीनो

[22] Literally, were full of the sound of praise, i.e. the warriors fell praising the bravery of the enemy.

[23] Our copy of Kula has निर्गत for निर्भिन्न–निर्गतानां प्रहारमूर्छितानां वदनाभ्यन्तरे, etc. This is a mistake, *SC* has निर्भीक (*ṇibbhīa*) for *ṇibbhiṇṇa*.

भटानां घूत्कारो निनदो यत्र तत्। K (*chāyā*) has भटहुङ्कारम्। R says चुक्कारशब्दो देश्यां शब्दवाची। Kula is partly corrupt, but according to quotations in *SC* he reads बुक्कार for चु° and explains it as सिंहनाद।[24]

26. सेलपहरुव्विआइअदुक्खववट्ठविअहत्थिपत्थिअजोहम्।
भग्गधअचिह्नविमुहिअपणट्ठणिअअभडदुक्खणज्जन्तरम्।।

[शैलप्रहारोद्वेदितदुःखव्यवस्थापितहस्तिप्रार्थितयोधम्।
भग्नध्वजचिह्नविमुषितप्रनष्टनिजकभटदुःखज्ञायमानरथम्।।]

The *rākṣasa* troops were hemmed in[25] by their elephants, controlled with toil and trouble, because they took fright at the impact of the mountains (hurled by the apes); while the chariots, with their flags and emblems broken, could hardly be recognized by their puzzled fighters who had withdrawn from the fray.[26]

K says शैलप्रहारेण उद्वेजितत्वात् दुःखं कृच्छ्रात् व्यवस्थापितैः हस्तिभिः प्रस्थितयोधम्। भग्नध्वजचिह्नाः विमुखिताः प्रणष्टा अन्यत्र गताः निजैः भटैः दुःखेन कथंचित् ज्ञायमाना रथा यत्र तत्।

K seems to read *uvveia* (उद्वेजित)। Cf. *pahāruvveia* which is the reading of manuscript C of Goldschmidt. R reads *uvviāia* rendered as उद्वेदित। *SC* text has *uvviāvia* rendered as उद्वेजित (शैलप्रहारेण उद्वेजितेषु त्रासात् विमुखीभवत्सु *SC* commentary). This seems to be Kula's reading. Kula is here partly corrupt, but he has विमुखीभवत्। See below.

MY says दुःखव्यवस्थापितहस्तिप्रार्थितयोधं दुःखेनाभिमुखीकृतैः गजैः जिघृक्षितयोधम्। *indhaṁ* (for *ciṇha*) चिह्नम्। *vimuhia* विमूढ। प्रथमं प्रनष्टैः, ध्वजचिह्नभङ्गात् सहसा ज्ञातुमसमर्थैः . . . भटैः कृच्छ्रेण उन्नीयमानरथमित्यर्थः।

R says शैलप्रहारोद्वेदितैः, अत एव दुःखेन व्यवस्थापितैः स्थिरीकृतैः हस्तिभिः प्रार्थिता रुध्यमाना योधा यत्र। Kula says शैलप्रहारेण[27] . . . विमुखीभवन्तो

---

24 Manuscript C of Goldschmidt reads वोक्काररवं for भड-चुक्कारं। *SC* remarks वस्तुतस्तु चुक्कारः सिंहनादे स्यादिति हारावली। Kula's reading बुक्कार is however found in *Goüḍavaho* (10) where it is explained as गर्जित in the commentary.

25 Or, attacked.

26 I.e. they had abandoned the chariots damaged by the apes.

27 Our copy has सैन्य।

दु:खेन . . . स्थिरीकृता ये हस्तिनः तैः पराभिमुखं प्रस्थिता योधा यत्र। भग्नध्वजचिह्नत्वात् विमोहितैरजातनिश्चयैः प्रनष्टनिजकभटैः निहतस्वयोधैः दु:खेन ज्ञायमाना रथा यत्र तत् तथा। *SC* says प्रनष्टैरपसृतैः निजभटैः।

27. गिरिपेल्लिअरहकड्ढणविहलविसारिअमुहत्थणन्ततुरङ्गम्।
महिअलपलोट्टमहिहररअअरसोमलिअभिण्णपण्डुररुहिरम्।।

[गिरिप्रेरितरथकर्षणविह्वलप्रसारितमुखस्तनत्तुरङ्गम्।
महीतलप्रलुठितमहीधररजतरसावमृदितभिन्नपाण्डुररुधिरम्।।]

The horses groaned with wide open mouths, worn out with fatigue, as they pulled out the chariots squeezed by the mountains; while the pools of blood became palish white, commingling with the silver of the fallen mountain crushed to dust.[28]

K (*chāyā*) has रजआवलिविभिन्न (*raāvali-vihiṇṇa*) for *rasomalia-bhiṇṇa* = रसावमृदितभिन्न (R). Kula seems to read *rasovalia* (रसाववलित)[29]।

K says पर्वतेन आक्रान्तस्य रथस्य कर्षणेन विह्वलत्वात् प्रसारितमुख- निनदत्तुरङ्गम्। महीतले प्रलुठितानां चूर्णितानां (पतितानां R) महीधराणां रजतरजसां रजतशकलानाम् आवलीभिः भिन्नत्वात् पाण्डररुधिरम्। K (*chāyā*) renders *pellia* as पीडित। MY says विभिन्न मिश्र। प्रसारितमुखत्वं गुरुभाराकर्षणादिति ग्राह्यम्।

SC says कुलनाथस्तु महीतले प्रलुठितेन महीधरस्य रजतरसेन रूप्यद्रवेण अववलितं प्रेरितं भिन्नं मिश्रीभूतं पाण्डरं रुधिरं यत्र तदित्याह। रथसंघट्टोष्मणा द्रवत्वम्। R says रजतरसेन रूप्यक्षोदेन।

28. कइमुक्कचुण्णिअट्ठिअसेलमुणिज्जन्तसरससरिआमग्गम्।
ओहरिअविञ्छिआसिमग्गोवडन्तवाणरजोहम्।।

[कपिमुक्तचूर्णितस्थितशैलज्ञायमानसरससरिन्मार्गम्।
अवपातितवञ्छितासिमार्गावपतद्वानरयोधम्।।]

The moist traces of the streams could be discerned on the mountains hurled by the apes and reduced to dust; and, while the fighting apes came within range of the swords

---

[28] Kṛṣṇa's reading (silver dust) is followed. See Extracts. The mountains are those hurled by the apes.

[29] Kula's gloss on this verse is missing in our copy, but it is quoted in *SC*.

wielded by the demons, they were evaded by others going out of range.[30]

K and MY read *sotta* for *magga* (R and Kula ?) in the first line. The word *aiñcia* is missing in the N.S. edition. K reads अपसृत (*osaria*) for *oharia* (अवहृत) in the second line.[31] K (*chāyā*) renders the second line as अपसृतवञ्चितातीतासिमार्गावपतद्वानरयोधम्।

Kula reads आपतत् (*āvaḍanta*) for *ovaḍanta* (अवपतत्)।

K says कपिमुक्तेषु राक्षसैः चूर्णितेषु शैलेषु ज्ञायमानानि सरसानि जलार्द्राणि सरित्स्रोतांसि यत्र तत्। उद्यतं खड्गमालोक्य अपसृताः, राक्षसैः वञ्चितत्वात् अतिगता अतिलङ्घिता, असिमार्गेषु अवपतन्तो वानरयोधाः यत्र तत्।

MY says विमुक्तैः चूर्णितस्थितैः शैलैः पूरिततया दुर्लक्षाणि केवलं सरसतया आर्द्रतया उन्नीयमानानि सरित्स्रोतांसि यत्र तत्तथा। *oharia* अवगूरित। *aiñcia* अतिक्रान्त (see verse 8)। असिगोचरीभूतः, अवगूरितो, वञ्चनया गलितश्च वानरयोधो यत्र तत्तथा।

MY on 13.55 says *oharia* अवगूरित। कर्तरि क्तः। कृतप्रहार इति यावत्। Kula explains *oharia* (अवहृत) as व्यापारित as elsewhere. His gloss is somewhat corrupt, but anonymously reproduced in *SC*. He says अवहृतानां व्यापारितानां वञ्चितानां परिहृताघातानाम् आकृष्टानामसीनां खड्गानां मार्गेण आपतन्तः अभिमुखं धावन्तो वानरयोधा यत्र तत् तथा। Kula seems to read *āiñchia* (आकृष्ट) found in *SC* text for *aiñcia*. Cf. Kula on 14.59.

29. अहिधावन्तपवङ्गममुक्कंसणिराजकेसरसडुग्घाअम्।
मज्झन्तभाअणिवडिअदण्डाउहभिण्णमहिअलोविद्धभडम्।।

[अभिधावत्प्लवङ्गममुक्तांसनिरायतकेसरसटोद्घातम्।
मध्यान्तभागनिपतितदण्डायुधभिन्नमहीतलापविद्धभटम्।।]

The long hair of the apes spread over their shoulders as they rushed forward; while the warriors wounded by clubs hitting them on the waist slumped down to the ground.

---

30 Translation follows Rāmadāsa. According to Mādhava (see Extracts): the apes, who came within range of the swords (of the demons), struck a blow and got away, eluding the foe.

31 R explains *oharia* as अवपातित, and says रक्षोभिरवपातितानामथ च कपिभिः निःसृत्य वञ्चितानामसीनां मार्गे पतनपथेऽवपतन्तो वानरयोधा यत्र तथाभूतम्। तथा च यत्र ये स्थितास्ते बहिर्गताः, अन्ये पुनस्तत्र पतन्तः खण्डिताः, etc.

K reads पर्यास्तभाल for *majjhanta-bhāa* = मध्यान्तभाग (R and Kula).

K says अभिधावतां प्लवङ्गमानामंसेषु मुक्ता: वितता: निरायता: केसरसटोद्धाता यत्र तत्। फालेषु (भालेषु ?) ललाटेषु पर्यास्तं निपतितेन दण्डायुधेन भिन्ना महीतले पतिता: (निपातित *chāyā*) वानरभटा यत्र तत्।

My reads पर्यास्त (*pajjatta*) like K, but has भाग like R and Kula. He says मुक्ता अनाकुलिता: (अनाकुञ्चिता: A) अंसे दीर्घाश्चेति विग्रह:। *pajjata-bhāa-ṇivaḍia* भागे प्रहारस्थाने पर्यास्तनिपतित। R says मुक्तो विकीर्ण:।

Kula says मध्यान्तभागे शरीरमध्यदेशे निपतितै: दण्डायुधै: तोमरादिभि: भिन्ना महीतले अवविद्धा: कीलिता: भटा यत्र तत् तथा। R says मध्यस्यान्तभागेन निपतितं यत् दण्डरूपमायुधं तेन भिन्ना: सन्तो महीतलेऽपविद्धा: पातिता भटा यत्र तत्। *SC* says मध्यान्तभागे शरीरमध्यभागे अन्तभागे च निपतितेन, etc.

The commentary of Kṛṣṇa on canto 13 (after verse 29) and canto 14 is missing in our manuscripts. On this portion of the poem fuller extracts are given here from the commentaries of Mādhavayajvan and Kulanātha. The readings of Kṛṣṇa mentioned in this section are from those recorded by Goldschmidt in his edition.

30. गहिअसिरदट्ठवाणरणिसाअरोरत्थलद्धरोविअदाढम्।
णहधरिअपव्वओज्झरसीअरतण्णाअगरुइओसण्णरअम्।।

[गृहीतशिरोदष्टवानरनिशाचरोर:स्थलार्धरोपितदंष्ट्रम्।
नभोधृतपर्वतनिर्झरशीकरार्द्रगुरुकितावसन्नरज:।।]

The apes, seized and bitten on the head by the demons, thrust their teeth half into their chest; while the dust settled on the battlefield, being moistened and made heavy by the spray of the cascades on the mountains held aloft by the apes.

MY reads रुष्ट for *daṭṭha* = दष्ट (R and Kula) in the first line. He reads *bharia* for *dharia* (R and Kula) in the second line.

MY says प्रहर्तुं निशाचरकरावरुद्धशिरसा रुष्टेन कपिना तदुर:स्थ–लार्धारोपितदंष्ट्रमिति। प्रहरणतया वानरोन्नीतानां नभसि भरितानां पूरितानां (पर्वतानां निर्झर)–शीकरै: अवसन्नरजस्कमित्यर्थ:। Kula says गृहीतै: शिरसि दष्टै: वानरै: निशाचराणामुर:-स्थानार्धेषु रोपिता दंष्ट्रा यत्र। He explains अवसन्न as निरुद्गम। R says नभसि धृतानां पर्वतानां निर्झरशीकारै: आर्द्रत्वात् गुरूणि सन्ति अवसन्नानि पतितानि रजांसि यत्र।

31. सारहिहत्थअलाहअमुहपडिउट्ठिअतुरङ्गणिव्वूढरहम्।
सरघाअचुण्णिओवडिअपव्वआवीअरुहिरसरिआसोत्तम्।।
(आइकुलअम्)

[सारथिहस्ततलाहतमुखपतितोत्थिततुरङ्गनिर्व्यूढरथम्।
शरघातचूर्णितावपतितपर्वतापीतरुधिरसरित्स्रोत:।।]
(आदिकुलकम्)

The horses drew the chariots as they fell headlong and rose up, struck by the drivers with the hands; while the streams of blood were absorbed by the mountains crumbling to dust under the impact of the arrows of the demons.[32]

Kula says सारथिना हस्ततलेनाहतै: मुखेन पतितै: उत्थितैश्च तुरङ्गै: निर्व्यूढा रथा यत्र। MY says मुखेन पतितै: सारथिहस्ततलाघातात् (उत्थितै:), etc. R says प्रथमं संभ्रमेण पतिता: तदनु सारथिना हस्ततलेन आहतमुखत्वादुत्थिता ये तुरङ्गा: तैर्निर्व्यूढा: संचारिता रथा यत्र।

32. अट्टन्ति असहणाइं खण्डिज्जन्तपडिसारिअद्धन्ताइं।
वोच्छिज्जन्तमुहाइं भिज्जन्तोसरिअपडिभडाइं बलाइं।।

[आवर्तन्तेऽसहनानि खण्ड्यमानप्रतिसारितार्धान्तानि।
व्यवच्छिद्यमानमुखानि भिद्यमानापसृतप्रतिभटानि बलानि।।]

The armies,[33] intolerant (of each other's advance), suffered losses, with the foremost ranks annihilated, sections of the troops worsted and repulsed, and the opposing forces dwindling and taking to flight.

MY (B) *pratīka* has *agganti*. A has *aḍḍanti*[34] (*aṭṭanti* ? like R). MY explains it as नश्यन्ति क्षीयन्ते (K also). MY says प्रतिसारितेति खण्डेन सति अपसृतैकदेशानि (बलानि)। मुखं नासीरं, मुखशब्देन मुखस्थिता भटा विवक्षिता:। व्युच्छिद्यमानत्वं हन्यमानत्वम्। R explains प्रतिसारित as पराङ्मुखीकृत।

K, MY and Kula read क्षीयमाण (*jhijjanta*) for *bhijjanta* (भिद्यमान) found in R.

Kula says असहमानानि असोढपराह्वनानि। The rest is missing in our copy, but the following quotation from Kula is found in *SC*–

---

[32] Verses 29-31 form a *kulaka*.

[33] Those of the demons and the apes.

[34] Kula *pratīka* also looks like *aḍḍanti*.

व्यवच्छिद्यमानं विरलीभवत् मुखमग्रस्कन्धो येषाम्। क्षीयमाणा हीनबलाः सन्तः अपसृताः प्रतिभटा येषु तानि बलानि अट्यन्ते हिंस्यन्ते। R says (*aṭṭanti*) आवर्तन्ते परस्परमुपर्युपरि पतन्तीत्यर्थः।

MY says क्षीयमाणावस्थितप्रतिभटानीति पर्यायेणेति शेषः।

33. वाणरपहरुक्खडिआ अणिरूविअलक्खपेसिआसिपहरणा।
मुच्छाणिमीलिअच्छा ओहीरन्ता वि अल्लिअन्ति णिसिअरा।।

[वानरप्रहारोत्खण्डिता अनिरूपितलक्ष्यप्रेषितासिप्रहरणाः।
मूर्च्छानिमीलिताक्षा अपह्रियमाणा अप्यालीयन्ते निशिचराः।।]

Reeling under the blows of the apes, and striking at undetermined targets with their swords, with the eyes closed as in a swoon, the demons drew near, even though they were in a daze.

K and Kula read स्खलिताः (*°kkhaliā*) for *ukkhuḍiā* (उत्खण्डिताः) found in R. Kula says वानराणां प्रहारैः स्खलिता विह्वलगतयः।

MY says *ohīrantā vi* विह्वलीभवन्तोऽपि[35]। Kula says अनिरूपितलक्ष्यं प्रेषितासिप्रहरणाः क्षिप्तखड्गप्रहाराः, मूर्च्छानिमीलिताक्षाः अवह्रियमाणा अपि मृत्युना आकृष्यमाणा अपि निशाचरा आलीयन्ते ढौकन्ते। R says अपह्रियमाणाः स्वीयैः पश्चान्नीयमाना अपि निशिचराः . . . शत्रुणा आलीयन्ते मिलन्ति।

34. चुण्णिअगरुअपडिभडो फुरइ अणल्लीणरक्खसाहअविहलो।
खण्डिज्जन्तपअट्टो ओलिच्छिण्णपडिओ पवङ्गमजोहो।।

[चूर्णितगुरुकप्रतिभटः स्फुरत्यनालीनराक्षसाहतविह्वलः।
खण्ड्यमानप्रवृत्तः पङ्क्तिच्छिन्नपतितः प्लवङ्गमयोधः।।]

A warrior ape, who crushed a powerful adversary, but was staggered by a blow dealt by a demon standing at a distance, quivered as he dropped out of the ranks, with his efforts brought to nought.

MY reads *bahua* for *garua* = गुरुक (R and Kula). He has *paatta* (प्रयत्न) for *paaṭṭa* = प्रवृत्त (R). Kula is here corrupt, but *SC* has प्रयत्न like MY.

Kula explains *oli-cchiṇṇa* as आवलिछिन्नः पङ्क्तिभ्रष्टः। R says *oli* is a

---

[35] See also Extracts on 12.42, 43.

deśī word, but he says पङ्क्तिक्रमेण छिन्नः। MY reads *ūlu-cchiṇṇa* (ऊरुच्छिन्न)। Cf. *laa* for *raa* (रजस्) in 13.57.

MY says स्फुरति व्याचेष्टत इत्यर्थः। Kula says स्फुरति तेजसा न हीयत इत्यर्थः। R says स्फुरति कम्पते।

35. सोडीरेण पआवो छाआ पहरेहिं विक्कमेहिं परिअणो।
जीएण अ अहिमाणो रक्खिज्जइ अ गरुओ सरीरेण जसो।।

[शौण्डीर्येण प्रतापश्छाया प्रहारैर्विक्रमैः परिजनः।
जीवेन चाभिमानो रक्ष्यते च गुरुकं शरीरेण यशः।।]

Power was maintained with manly effort, and prestige by striking hard; while one's followers were protected with valour. Honour was preserved at the cost of life, and the valued fame at the expense of the body.

K and MY read *pahareṇa* for °*hi* (R and Kula). K, MY and Kula read *vikkameṇa* for °*hi* (R). MY seems to read *pahariso* for *pariaṇo* (R and Kula).

Kula says शौटीर्येण पुरुषकारेण प्रतापः, प्रहारैः छाया संभावना, विक्रमेण परिजनः . . . रक्ष्यत इति सर्वत्र योज्यम्। MY says शौर्येण सत्त्वगुणेन दुष्प्रधर्षता, छाया रूपं शूरतमप्रहारेण, आयोधनप्रहर्षणं (प्रहर्षं = प्रहर्षो A) धारामार्गसंचरणेन, जीवत्यागेनापि वीर्याभिमानः, शरीरक्षत्यापि यशो रक्ष्यत इत्यर्थः।

SC says छाया गोत्रपरम्परागतख्यातिः कान्तिर्वा। Cf. 3.18. R says शौण्डीर्येणाहंकारेण युद्धचातुर्येण वा।

36. भिज्जइ उरो ण हिअअं गिरिणा भज्जइ रहो ण उण उच्छाहो।
छिज्जन्ति सिरणिहाआ तुङ्गा ण उण रणदोहला सुहडाणम्।।

[भिद्यते उरो न हृदयं गिरिणा भज्यते रथो न पुनरुत्साहः।
छिद्यन्ते शिरोनिघातास्तुङ्गा न पुना रणदोहदाः सुभटानाम्।।]

The bosom of the warriors was pierced, but not their resolute heart. The chariots were broken by the mountain,[36] but not the will. Heads were cut-off, but not the high resolve to fight.

Kula reads भिद्यते (*bhijjai*) for *bhajjai* (भज्यते)।

MY says वक्षःस्थले भिन्नेऽपि व्यवसायो न भिद्यते। एकरूप एवेति यावत्। उत्साहः प्रयत्नः। शिरोनिकायच्छेदेऽपि रणश्रद्धा न छिद्यते इत्यर्थः।

[36] Those used by the apes as missiles.

37. सेलोज्झरेहिं गअणे धुअलोहिअसीअरेहिं धारामग्गे।
मअसलिलेहिं घडासु अ वोच्छिज्जइ पसरिअं महिरउट्ठाणम्।।

[शैलनिर्झरैर्गगने धुतलोहितशीकरैर्धारामार्गे।
मदसलिलैर्घटासु च व्यवच्छिद्यते प्रसृतं महीरजउत्थानम्।।]

The dust as it rose and spread was laid in the sky by the cascades of the mountains (held aloft by the apes), on the battlefield by the scattered spray of blood, and amidst the elephants in battle array by the flow of their ichor.

K and MY seem to read *sībhara-lohieṇa* (शीकरलोहितेन K) for *lohia-sībharehi* (R and Kula). K, MY and Kula read *salileṇa* for *salilehi* (R). K and MY read *vocchijjanta-viralaṁ* for *vocchijjai pasariaṁ* (R and Kula). K seems to have *vi°* for *vo°*.

MY says कपिभिः प्रहरणतया क्षिप्तानां गिरीणां निर्झरैः गगने, हन्यमानानां प्रतिभटानां समुच्चलितशीकरेण रुधिरेण सुभटधारामार्गे, मदसलिलेन गजघटासु च महीरजउत्थानं व्युच्छिद्यमानतया विरलं जातमित्यर्थः।

Kula says शैलानां निर्झरैः . . ., धुतैः लोहितशीकरैः रुधिरकणैः धारामार्गे रथगतिपथे,[37] मदसलिलेन (गज)घटासु च व्यवच्छिद्यते प्रसृतं महीरजउत्थानम्।

SC quotes विश्व–'धारा सैन्याग्रिमस्कन्धसंतत्यां'; and Śrīnivāsa who says धारामार्गे खड्गादिसंचरणपथे। R says धारामार्गे रणस्थाने।

38. विसहिअखग्गप्पहरा गइन्ददन्तलिहिअग्गलापडिरूआ।
सेलाइञ्छणवलिआ विसमं भज्जन्ति पवअबाहुप्फडिहा।।

[विसोढखड्गप्रहारा गजेन्द्रदन्तलिखितार्गलाप्रतिरूपाः।
शैलातिक्रमवलिता विषमं भज्यन्ते प्लवङ्गबाहुपरिघाः।।]

The stout arms of an ape, which had endured sword-cuts, and resembled a bar dented by the tusks of a mighty elephant, were fractured as they bent under the pressure of the mountain held by him.

K and MY read विशदं (*visaaṁ*) for *visamaṁ* (R). Kula's gloss is incomplete, but his reading might be same as that of K, as *SC* text has *visaaṁ*.

MY says *selāiñchaṇa-valiā* शैलविक्षेपणवलिता निष्कम्पतया सौकर्यवशात् विशदमभज्यन्तेत्यर्थः।

[37] Restored from quotation in *SC*.

Kula says गजेन्द्रदन्तनिर्गताश्चाकुलाः प्रतिरूपाश्च (बाहुपरिघाः)। He seems to read *gainda-danta-ṇiggaāula-paḍirūa* for . . . *lihiaggalā* . . . R says गजेन्द्रदन्ताभ्यां लिखिता यार्गला तत्प्रतिरूपाः तत्तुल्याः। शैलानामतिक्रमेण क्षतोत्पत्त्या धारणासामर्थ्यादधःपततनेन वलिता यन्त्रणमासाद्य वक्रीभूताः *SC* (*chāyā*) has शैलातिक्रमण।

39. तेण्हाइओ वि सुइरं संणाहच्छेअगब्भिणम्मि वणमुहे।
णिव्वलिअलोहविरसं ण पिअइ आमुअइ चक्खिऊण विहङ्गो।।

[तृषितोऽपि सुचिरं संनाहछेदगर्भिते व्रणमुखे।
निर्वलितलोहविरसं न पिबत्यामुञ्चत्यास्वाद्य विहङ्गः।।]

Having tasted the blood in a warrior's wound containing fragments of his armour, a bird, though thirsty, did not drink but shunned it, because it was flavourless on account of the presence of iron splinters.

MY says *taṇhāvio* तृषितः। R has *teṇhāio*. Kula reads *taṇhāio*. He says तृष्णाजितोऽपि तृष्णाभिभूतोऽपि विहङ्गः काकादिः।

MY, Kula and K (?) read *ruhiraṁ* (*SC* text also) for *suiraṁ* = सुचिरम् (R). MY says *ṇivvaḍia-loha-virasaṁ* पूर्वतः पृथग्भूतं यथा स्यात् तथा लोहेन विरसम्। विहङ्गः गृध्रः रुधिरं न पिबति किंतु किञ्चिदास्वाद्य त्यजतीत्यर्थः।

Kula's gloss is incomplete, but *SC* says कुलनाथस्तु लौहस्य संनाहस्य छेदैः गर्भिते व्याप्तमध्ये व्रणमुखे निर्वलितेन गृहीतसारेण लौहेन विरसमुद्वेजकं रुधिरं न पिबतीत्याह। *SC*'s own explanation is निःशेषेण वलितैः चिरं संभक्तैः लोहैः . . . विरसम्। R says निर्वलितेन पृथग्भूतेन संनाहस्य लोहेन तत्कणेन विरसम्।

40. वेवइ पडिओ वि भुओ ओसुद्धम्मि वअणम्मि धरइ अमरिसो।
लुअसीसं पि कबन्धं धावइ उक्खित्तकण्ठलोहिअधारम्।।

[वेपते पतितोऽपि भुजोऽवपातिते वदने ध्रियतेऽमर्षः।
लूनशीर्षोऽपि कबन्धो धावत्युत्क्षिप्तकण्ठलोहितधारः।।]

The severed arm of a warrior quivered even after it had dropped. Wrath was manifest even on the prostrate face. The trunk ran along, even though the head was lopped off, with streams of blood spurting out of the throat.

The verse is missing in our copy of Kula, but *SC* says छिन्नपतितेऽपि

वदनेऽमर्षः क्रोधो भ्रकुट्यादिरूपेण ध्रियते अवतिष्ठत इति कुलनाथः। Kula seems to read *osuddhe vi*, which occurs, also in MY, and is explained as अवपातितेऽपि। R reads *osuddhammi*. MY says *dharai* अनुवर्तते।

R reads *dhāvai ukkhitta*, etc. and says छिन्नमौलिरपि कबन्ध उत्क्षिप्ता कण्ठस्य लोहितधारा यत्र तथाभूतः सन् धावति। K reads *ṭhāi raükkhitta* (रयोत्क्षिप्त)। MY has the latter reading and explains it as रणवेगोत्क्षिप्त। It is found also in *SC*, which says कबन्धं . . . रयेण वेगेनोत्क्षिप्तकण्ठलोहितधारं धावति (i.e. *,dhāi* as required by the metre). पाठान्तरे तिष्ठति (i.e., *ṭhāi* as read by K) न पततीत्यर्थः।

41. देइ रसं रिउपहरो वहइ धुरं विक्कमस्स वेरावन्धो।
आअडिअरणरहसो दप्पं वडेइ आअओ अइभारो।।

[ददाति रसं रिपुप्रहारो वहति धुरं विक्रमस्य वैराबन्धः।
आकृष्टरणरभसो दर्पं वर्धयत्यागतोऽतिभारः।।]

The enemy's onslaught stimulated the ardour of the warriors. Inveterate hatred sustained their valour. The heavy task that confronted them enhanced their pride, bringing on the urge to fight.

Kula reads पर for रण in the second line. He says रिपुकृतः प्रहारो रसं ददाति उत्साहयति। बन्धुवधकृतो वैराबन्धो विक्रमस्य धुरं वहति शक्त्यनुरूपं चेष्टतं। आकृष्टपररभसः अपनीतपरोत्साहः अतिभारो बलवता सह संग्राम आगतो दर्पं वर्धयतिसहर्षेण शक्स्यतिशयं जनयति। MY says अतिभारः अतिमात्र प्रतिबलोपनिपातः।

42. साहेइ रिउं व जसं ण सहइ आआरिअं व कालक्खेवम्।
लहइ सुहं मिव णासं जीअं मुअइ समुहं पहरणं व भडो।।

[साधयति रिपुमिव यशो न सहते आकारितमिव कालक्षेपम्।
लभते सुखमिव नाशं जीवं मुञ्चति संमुखं प्रहरणमिव भटः।।

The warriors acquired fame, just as they subdued the enemy. They were impatient of delay, just as they were intolerant of the enemy's challenge. They accepted death like joy, and gave up their life, just as they flung a missile.

K reads सुकृतमिव मानम् for *suhaṁ miva ṇāsaṁ* (R). MY says सुकृतं स्वामिनां प्रतिसुकृतम्। K and MY seem to read *sukaaṁ va*, but it is not clear whether MY also reads मानम्। Kula reads *ṇāmaṁ* for *ṇāsaṁ*.

MY says *sāhei* साधयति। साधनमर्जनं निरसनं च। *āāriaṁ* आकारितम् आह्वानमित्यर्थः।

Kula says साधयति मारयति पक्षे उपार्जयति, रिपुमिव यशः। लभते सुखमिव नाम ख्यातिम्। R says यथा परप्रहारादिनां सुखं लभते तथा तेनैव नाशमपि।

43. विसहिअखग्गप्पहरा विअलिअलोहिअकिलिन्तणीसारभुआ।
मुच्छिज्जन्तो अल्ला अक्कन्ता णिअअमहिहरेहि पवङ्गा।।

[विसोढखड्गप्रहारा विगलितलोहितक्लाम्यन्निःसारभुजाः।
मूर्छायमाना अवमीलन्त आक्रान्ता निजकमहीधरैः प्लवङ्गाः।।]

Those of the apes who endured sword-cuts were crushed by their own mountains as they fainted, bowed down with the weight, their arms weary and feeble from loss of blood.

mucchijjantoallā is explained by R as मूर्च्छायमानाः सन्तः अवमीलन्तो निमीलन्नयनाः। Kula says मूर्च्छ्यमानावनताः। *SC* says ओअल्लशब्दोऽवनते देशी। This occurs in Kula in a corrupt form.

44. दअइ कुसुअं व माणं वड्ढन्तं पि अणहं ण पत्तिअइ जसम्।
ण करेइ लोअगरुए जीअ च्चिअ णवर आअरं भडसत्थो।।

[दयते कुसुममिव मानं वर्धमानमप्यनघं न प्रत्येति यशः।
न करोति लोकगुरुके जीव एव केवलमादरं भटसार्थः।।]

The warriors preserved their honour like a flower, and did not believe their fame to be perfect, however much it increased. Only they had no craving for life, held in high esteem in the world.

MY says न प्रत्येति न विश्वसिति भङ्गशङ्कया बिभेतीति यावत्। जीवितव्येनापि मानयशसोरेव रक्षामकरोदित्यर्थः।

Kula says कुसुममिव मानं दयते रक्षति न म्लापयति। वर्धमानमपि अहतमक्षतम् अम्लानं (?) यशो न प्रत्येति न श्रद्दधाति। लोकगुरुके लोकबहुमते जीवित एव केवलं भटसार्थः आदरं न करोति। Kula seems to read *ahaaṁ* (अहतम्) for *aṇahaṁ* (अनघम्) explained as निष्कलुषम् by R.

45. णिहआलक्खिअजोहे जाए लहुअम्मि णिअअधारमग्गे।
परिवड्ढन्ताइभरं गरुअं परसंकुलं अइन्ति समत्था।।

[निहतालक्षितयोधे जाते लघौ निजकधारामार्गे।
परिवर्ध्यमानाजिभरं गुरुकं परसंकुलमायान्ति समर्थाः।।]

When their own sector became quiet, with the distinguished warriors slain, the valiant went over to an area of heavy combat with the enemy where the press of battle was at its height.

MY says आलक्षिताः प्रसिद्धाः। प्रसिद्धयोधवधात् स्वधारामार्गे लधूकृतेऽतिभार-वदन्यस्यायोधनं व्यतिगच्छन्तीत्यर्थः।

Kula says निहता आलक्षिताः हन्तुं लक्ष्यीकृता योधा यत्र, तत्र निजकधारामार्गे खड्गव्यापारपथे लघुके जाते परिवर्धमानातिभरं गुरुकं परसंकुलं शत्रुसंमर्दमायान्ति समर्थाः। R says निजकधारामार्गे स्वारब्धसंग्रामे लघौ जाते सति निर्वाहिते सति समर्थाः परसंकुलं परचक्रमायान्ति। कीदृशम्—परिवर्धमान आजिभरो येन।

संकुल in the sense of संमर्द is used in *Arthaśāstra* 14.1: . . . धूमः . . . संग्रामावतरणावस्कन्दनसंकुलेषु प्रणीतः सर्वप्राणिनां नेत्रघ्नः।

46. धारेन्ति जसस्स धुरं एन्तं ण सहन्ति विक्कमस्स परिहवम्।
रोसस्स करेन्ति धिइं माणं वड्ढेन्ति साहसस्स समत्था।।

[धारयन्ति यशसो धुरामायान्तं न सहन्ते विक्रमस्य परिभवम्।
रोषस्य कुर्वन्ति धृतिं मानं वर्धयन्ति साहसस्य समर्थाः।।]

The strong strove to achieve fame, and could not brook any humiliation of their valour. They appeased their wrath (by slaying the enemy), and increased the tempo of daring exploits.

Kula says धारयन्ति यशसो धुरं यशोहेतु कर्म न त्यजन्तीत्यर्थः। विक्रमस्य परिभवमागच्छन्तं शत्रुणा क्रियमाणं न सहन्ते। शत्रुवधेन रोषस्य कुर्वन्ति धृतिम्। *SC* says रोषस्य धृतिं धारणं कुर्बन्ति। यद्वा शत्रुवधेन सरसीकरणात् तस्य प्रीतिमुत्पादयन्तीत्यर्थः।

MY says *entaṁ* आयान्तम्। साहसस्य मानं कुर्वन्ति साहसं बहु मन्यन्त इत्यर्थः। R says साहसस्य प्राणानपेक्षकर्मणो मानं परिमाणं वर्धयन्ति।

47. पयरासाइअहरिसं खणमुच्छागलिअरणमणोरहसोक्खम्।
जीअविढन्तच्छरसं सिरपरिवत्तिअजसं विअम्भइ समरम्।।

[प्रहारासादितहर्षः क्षणमूर्छागलितरणमनोरथसौख्यम्।
जीवार्जिताप्सराः शिरःपरिवर्तितयशा विजृम्भते समरः।।]

The battle raged, the blows bringing pleasure,[38] and the joy of fighting interrupted by momentary swoon; while nymphs were won at the cost of one's life,[39] and heads bartered for fame.

K and MY read क्षपित (*khavia*) for *galia* (R). Kula reads *ghaḍia*. K and MY read विभक्त (*vihatta*) for *viḍhatta* = अर्जित (R and Kula).

Kula says प्रहरणेन परप्रयुक्तेन आसादित: प्राप्तो हर्ष: प्रीतिर्यत्र। क्षणमूर्च्छया घटितं रणमनोरथसौख्यं रणकीर्तितं[40] निर्वाणसुखं यत्र। जीवेन जीवदानेन अर्जिता: अप्सरसो यत्र . . . (तत्) समरं युद्धं विजृम्भते विकसति।

MY says जीवविभक्ताप्सरस्कं जीवद्दशायामेव भटानां भर्तृतया विभागं कृतवत्योऽप्सरसो यत्र तत्तथा।

48. संदेहेसु हसिज्जइ रज्जिज्जइ साहसे रमिज्जइ वसणे।
मुच्छासु वीसमिज्जइ णिव्वूढं ति णवरं गणिज्जइ मरणे।।

[संदेहेषु हस्यते रज्यते साहसेषु रम्यते व्यसने।
मूर्छासु विश्रम्यते निर्व्यूढमिति केवलं गण्यते मरणे।।]

They laughed in the face of mortal danger, took delight in daring deeds, and rejoiced in peril; paused only during swoon, and deemed their task fulfilled only when they died.

MY says प्राणसंदेहेषु हस्यते, ततो न भयमिति यावत्। मरणे सत्येव केवलं शौर्यधुरा निर्व्यूढेति गण्यत इत्यर्थ:। Kula says हस्यते उत्साह: क्रियते। विश्रम्यते निर्व्यापारै: स्थीयते। R says मरणे सति निर्व्यूढं स्वकृत्यं निर्वाहितमिति गण्यते।

49. चलिओ अ चरणपहओ अनुव्वदिण्णरइमण्डलगहासङ्को।
अत्थेक्ककड्ढिअणिसो अभाअभग्गदिअसो महिरउग्घाओ।।

[चलितश्च चरणप्रहतोऽपूर्वदत्तरविमण्डलग्रहाशङ्क:।
अकस्मादाकृष्टनिशोऽभागभग्नदिवसो महीरजउद्घात:।।]

A cloud of dust that rose from the movements of the troops gave rise to the strange notion of a solar eclipse, and evoked the night all of a sudden, having brought the day to a premature end.

MY says *gaha* ग्रह। उपरागेति यावत्। अभागे असमये (अनवसरे Kula)।

---

[38] Literally with pleasure obtained through blows.

[39] I.e. by going to heaven after death on the battlefield.

[40] *SC* quotation has रणकांक्षितं।

50\. मूले वहलुग्घाओ मज्झोआसे पसारिअत्तणतडिणो।
णहपुञ्जिअवित्थरिओ पडइ दिसासु गरुअत्तणेण महिरओ।।

[मूले बहलोद्धातं मध्यावकाशे प्रसारितत्वतडिनम्।
नभःपुञ्जितविस्तृतं पतति दिक्षु गुरुत्वेन महीरजः।।]

The dust, thickly accumulated on the ground, and sparse as it spread out in mid air, became dense and pervasive in the sky, and being heavy, descended on all sides.

Kula says मूले . . . बहलोद्धातं प्रचुरनिचयं, मध्यावकाशे प्रसारितत्वेन तलिनं तनुकं . . . महीरजो दिक्षु गुरुत्वेन पतति। R says तडिनं विरलम्। तदुक्तं तडिनं विरले तुच्छे। Kula seems to read *taliṇo* (*SC* also) for *taḍiṇo*.

51\. मुअइ भरेइ णु वसुहं णीइ दिसाहिं थएइ णु दिसाअक्कम्।
अद्दिट्ठणिग्गमवहो पडइ णहाहिं गअणं विलग्गइ णु रओ।।

[मुञ्चति बिभर्ति नु वसुधां निरैति दिग्भ्यः स्थगयति नु दिक्चक्रम्।
अदृष्टनिर्गमपथं पतति नभसो गगनं विलगति नु रजः।।]

Did the dust, with the starting-point unseen, leave or fill the earth? Did it issue from the regions of the sky, or envelop the horizon? Did it fall from the sky, or rise to the firmament?

Kula says मुञ्चति बिभर्ति नु वसुधाम्, दिशो निर्याति न स्थगयति दिक्चक्रम्, नभसो गगनात् पतति नु गगनमारोहति नु। Our copy of Kula has न throughout for नु, but it might be a mistake.

52\. दीसइ रअणिअरबलं पवङ्गजोहेहिं मंसलरअन्तरिअम्।
ओसाअहअस्स ठिअं पुरओ मणिपव्वअस्स व हअच्छाअम्।।

[दृश्यते रजनीचरबलं प्लवङ्गयोधैर्मांसलरजोन्तरितम्।
अवश्यायहतस्य स्थितं पुरतो मणिपर्वतस्येव हतच्छायम्।।]

The army of the demons along with the fighting apes confronting it was covered with thick dust. Bereft of lustre, it seemed to stand in front of a jewel mountain enshrouded in mist.[41]

Kula says सान्द्ररजसा अन्तरितं, हतच्छायं विगलितप्रभं रजनीचरबलं प्लवङ्गमयोधैः

---

[41] The red-haired apes are compared to a jewel mountain, and the dust covering them to mist.

स्फुरद्रूपैः करणभूतैः अवश्यायेन नीहारेण हतस्य तिरोहितस्य मणिपर्वतस्येव पुरतः स्थितं दृश्यते। एतेन रजसां नीहारसाम्यं मणिपर्वतसाम्यं च वानराणामुक्तम्।

MY says *gahia-cchāaṁ* इति पाठः (for *va haa-cchāaṁ* found in R and Kula) सान्द्ररजोऽन्तरितं (रजनीचर)बलं हिमच्छन्नेन्द्रनीलशैलस्य गृहीतशोभं शोभां गृहीत्वा पुरतः स्थितं प्लवङ्गैरदृश्यतेति योजना।

53. ओधूसरिअधअवडो पसरइ मइलिअतुरङ्गममुहप्फेणो।
कसणमिहिअ व्व तणुओ णहम्मि सामलइआअवो रअणिवहो।।

[अवधूसरितध्वजपटः प्रसरति मलिनिततुरङ्गममुखफेनः।
कृष्णमेघिकेव तनुको नभसि श्यामलितातपो रजोनिवहः।।]

A mass of fine dust spread in the sky like a somber cloud, it turned the banners grey, discoloured the foam in the horses' mouth, and obscured the sunlight.

Kula says श्यामलितः आतपः सूर्यकिरणो येन स रजोनिवहः कृष्णमेघिकेव तनुको नभसि प्रसरति।

54. वाणररहसविसज्जिअणहङ्गणोवइअसेलमग्गणिराओ।
रइणो कलुसच्छाओ पडइ पणालोज्झरो व्व किरणुज्जोओ।।

[वानररभसविसर्जितनभोङ्गणावपतितशैलमार्गनिरायतः।
रवेः कलुषच्छायः पतित प्रणालनिर्झर इव किरणोद्द्योतः।।]

The dim rays of the sun, lengthening in the wake of the mountains swiftly hurled by the apes, and dropping from the sky, descended like a torrent of water from a conduit.

Kula says वानरै रभसेन (विसर्जितस्य) निवर्तितस्य (?) नभोऽङ्गनादवपतितस्य शैलस्य मार्गैः निरायतो दीर्घः रजसः सम्पर्कात् कलुषच्छायो रविकिरणानुघातः (किरणानामुद्धातः ?) प्रकाशः प्रणालनिर्झर इव पतति। Kula seems to read *kiraṇugghāo* for *kiraṇujjoö* (किरणोद्द्योतः)। R on 13.49 says उद्धातः घनीभूतः समूहः।

55. कुविओहरिअणिसाअरपवअदढक्खन्धपूरिअद्धन्तासु।
मंसलमहुकोसणिहो बज्झइ बज्झरुहिरासिधारासु रओ।।

[कुपितावहृतनिशाचरप्लवगदृढस्कन्धपूरितार्धान्तासु।
मांसलमधुकोषनिभं बध्यते बद्धरुधिरासिधारासु रजः।।]

Resembling a dense beehive, the dust settled on the gory blades of the swords that were partly broken[42] as the infuriated demons brought them down on the tough shoulders of the apes.

Kula says प्राकृते पूर्वनिपातानियमात् कुपितैः निशाचरैः अवहृता व्यापारिताः, प्लवगानां दृढस्कन्धेषु विशीर्णा[43] अर्धान्ता एकदेशा यासां तासु, बद्धरुधिरासु असिधारासु मांसलमधुकोषनिभं घनमधुवाससदृशं रजो बध्यते युक्तं भवति।

MY says *oharia* अवगूरित। कर्तरि क्तः। कृतप्रहार इति यावत्। कुपितावगूरितैः निशाचरैः प्लवङ्गानां दृढस्कृन्धे चूर्णीकृतार्धान्तासु तत्क्षतजसिक्तासिधारासु रजः संबध्यत् इत्यर्थः।

Kula seems to read *virāa* (विशीर्ण), and MY *cuṇṇia* (चूर्णित), for *pūria* (पूरित) found in R in the first line. R says कुपितैः निशाचरैरवहृतः अवपातितः अत एव प्लवगमानां दृढेऽपि स्कन्धे पूरितो व्यस्तः मग्न इति यावत्, अर्धान्तः अग्रभागो यासां तासु (असिधारासु)। The words *virāa* and *cuṇṇia* are frequently used in the poem.

56. रणपरिसक्कणविहला रइकिरणाहअकिलिन्तमणुलिअणअणा।
णिव्वाअन्ति गइन्दा सीअरसंवलिअरेणुकद्दमिअमुहा।।

[रणपरिसर्पणविह्वला रविकिरणाहतक्लाम्यन्मुकुलितनयनाः।
निर्वान्ति गजेन्द्राः शीकरसंवलितरेणुकर्दमितमुखाः।।]

The elephants, worn out with their movements in the battle, with the eyes closed being overpowered by the sun's rays, were refreshed when the face was coated with dust moistened by the spray of their trunks.

MY says *parisakkaṇa* परिसंचरण। Kula has परिभ्रम। He then says शीकरैः मदजलकणैः[44] संवलिता मिश्रिता ये रेणवः तैः कर्दमितानि मुखानि येषां ते तथाभूता गजेन्द्रा निर्वान्ति निर्वाणं निर्वृतिं (गच्छन्ति)।

57. मूलाहोअकराला सोणिअसोत्तणिवहन्तरालपसरिआ।
एक्कक्कमेण समअं संबज्झन्ति उअरिं महिलउप्पीडा।।

[मूलाभोगकरालाः शोणितस्रोतोनिवहान्तरालप्रसृताः।
एकैकक्रमेण समं संबध्यन्ते उपरि महीरजउत्पीडाः।।]

---

42 Cf. Kulanātha in Extracts.

43 Our copy has शीर्णा।

44 Restored from quotation in *SC*.

The masses of dust, with gaps at the bottom, because they rose only in the intervening spaces between the streams of blood, combined with one another in the upper air all at once.

MY says *ekkakkameṇa* अन्योन्येन एकैकेन वा। शोणितस्रोतोभिः मूले सान्तरालानि रजांसि उपरि मिथः संबध्यन्त इत्यर्थः। Kula says मूलाभोगे (उत्पत्तिदेशे *SC*) कराला मध्ये सावकाशा महीरजःसमूहाः प्रत्येकमन्योन्यमुपरि संसक्ता भवन्ति।

58. णिव्वालेऊण णहे गअसुक्कारिअवलन्तधअवडतणुइम्।
पवणो कड्ढइ विसमं छाआवहपट्ठधूसरं रअलेहम्।।

[निर्वाल्य नभसि गजसूत्कृतवलद्ध्वजपटतनुकाम्।
पवनः कर्षति विषमं छायापथपृष्ठधूसरां रजोलेखाम्।।]

The wind trailed a streak of dust here and there in the sky, making it distinct. Grey like the Milky Way, it was thinned by the banners fluttering on account of the snorting of the elephants.

My *pratīka* has *ṇivvāḍeūṇa* explained as पृथक् कृत्य for *ṇivvāleūṇa*. Kula's gloss is corrupt and mutilated, but he seem to say *ṇivvāheūṇa*[45] पृथक् कृत्वा। This reading is found in the manuscript of *SC* text. See editor's footnote.

SC says गजानां सूत्कारितेन सशब्दनासापवनेन चलद्भिः ध्वजपटैः तन्वीं . . . छायापथस्य दक्षिणोत्तरगमनप्रसृतस्य देवमार्गस्य पृष्ठमिव धूसरां रजोलेखां विषममितस्ततो नभसि पृथक् कृत्वा पवनः कर्षति।

59. संरुम्भइ दिट्ठिवहं गआण अहिमुहपहाविआण रणमुहे।
मारुअकम्पिज्जन्तो वअणब्भासम्मि मुडवडो व्व महिरओ।।

[संरुणद्धि दृष्टिपथं गजानामभिमुखप्रधावितानां रणमुखे।
मारुतकम्प्यमानो वदनाभ्यासे मुखपट इव महीरजः।।]

Swirled by the wind, the dust obstructed the vision of the elephants as they rushed forth in the forefront of the battle, as if it were a veil drawn over the face.[46]

Kula merely paraphrases this verse.

---

[45] Our copy has निर्वाहेतुन।

[46] A reference to the veil covering the eyes of a war elephant to prevent it charging at the wrong moment. Cf. 2.22; 8.23.

60. णवरि अ भडवच्छत्थलवणमग्गणिराअपत्थिउच्छलिआए।
रुहिरणईअ महिरओ उम्मूलिअकूलपाअवो व्व णिसुद्धो।।

[अनन्तरं भटवक्षःस्थलव्रणमार्गनिरायतप्रस्थितोच्छ्लितया।
रुधिरनद्या महीरज उन्मूलितकूलपादप इव निपातितम्।।]

The dust was thereafter settled by the river of blood, spouting from the chest wounds of the warriors, as if it were a tree on the eroded bank of a river.

Kula reads विवर for *magga* = मार्ग (R). He says अनन्तरं च भटवक्षःस्थलव्रणविवरेभ्यः निरायतप्रस्थितोच्छलितया रुधिरनद्या महीरजः उन्मूलितकूलपादप इव पातितं प्रशमितमित्यर्थः। R says व्रणमार्गेभ्यो निरायतं दीर्घं यथा स्यादेवं प्रस्थितोच्छलितया, etc. K reads मुखपर्यस्त for *magga-ṇirāa*. See Goldschmidt's footnote.

61. पलहुअणीहारणिहं संघाइअकमलणालतन्तुच्छाअम्।
घोलइ दरवोच्छिण्णं मारुअभिण्णतलिणट्ठिअं रअसेसम्।।

[प्रलघुकनीहारनिभं संघटितकमलनालतन्तुच्छायम्।
घूर्णते दरव्यवच्छिन्नं मारुतभिन्नतडिनस्थितं रजःशेषम्।।]

Dispersed by the wind and thinly scattered, and partly swept away, the remnant of the dust floated in the air, like thin mist, and resembling a pile of lotus stalk fibres.

MY says *saṁghāia* संघातित (K also) समूहीकृत। R's rendering संघटित seems to be incorrect.

Kula says संहारितानां भग्नानां कमलनालानां तन्तुच्छायं सूत्रसदृशं, दरव्यवच्छिन्न-मीषद्विघटितं, मारुतेन छिन्नमुत्सारितं (*SC*) सत् तलिनस्थितं रजःशेषं घूर्णते भ्रमति। R says मारुतेन भिन्नं खण्डखण्डीकृतम्, अतः तडिनस्थितं विरलस्थितं सत् घूर्णते।

Kula's reading संहारित for *saṁghāia* might be *saṁhāria* or perhaps *saṁghāria*. Cf. *saṁghaa* (संहत) used in 10.29.

62. रुम्भन्तुज्जुअमग्गं धराहरन्तरबलन्तणइसोत्तणिहम्।
बलइ वलन्तधअवडं पडिअगइन्दणिवहन्तरालेसु बलम्।।

[रुध्यमानर्जुकमार्गं धराधरान्तरवलन्नदीस्रोतोनिभम्।
बलति वलद्ध्वजपटं पतितगजेन्द्रनिवहान्तरालेसु बलम्।।]

Unable to move straight ahead,[47] the troops, with banners swaying, wound their way through the gaps between the heaps of fallen elephants, like unto a stream meandering through the hills.

MY says शैलनिवहान्तरालेन सरिदिव निहतगजकुलरुद्धमार्गा चमूः कुटिलमगच्छ-दित्यर्थः। R says वलति घूर्णते (भ्रमित्वा प्रसरति Kula)।

63. दूसहसहिअप्पहरा दुव्वोज्झविलग्गसमरणिव्वूढभरा।
ओच्छुण्णदुग्गमपहा कअदुक्करपेसणा पडन्ति पवङ्गा॥

[दुःसहसोढप्रहारा दुर्वहविलग्नसमरनिर्व्यूढभराः।
अवक्षुण्णदुर्गमपथाः कृतदुष्करप्रेषणाः पतन्ति प्लवङ्गा॥]

The apes fell in battle, they had endured unbearable blows, and achieved the heavy task of fighting imposed upon them; had trodden and impassable path, and carried out their master's command that was hard to fulfil.

MY says दुर्वहश्च आरोपितश्च समरस्य निर्व्यूढो भरो यैस्तै तथा। *valagga* (for *vilagga*) अवलग्न। *occhuṇṇa* आक्रान्ता (अवक्षुण्ण R)।

Kula says दुर्वहः, विलग्नः प्रतीष्टः, समरस्य निर्व्यूढो भरो यैः। अवक्षुण्णः (?) . . . दुर्दशः (for *duggama*) पन्था यैः। R says दुर्वहस्य . . . विलग्नस्य उपगतस्य समरस्य निर्व्यूढो निर्वाहितो भरो यैः।

64. बन्धुवहबद्धवेरं सहस्सपूरणकबन्धजणिआमोअम्।
वड्ढइ भडदिण्णरसं भुजपव्वलपहुअवीरपडणं जुज्झम्॥

[बन्धुवधबद्धवैरं सहस्रपूरणकबन्धजनितामोदम्।
वर्धते भटदत्तरसं भुजप्रबलप्रभूतवरिपतनं युद्धम्॥]

The battle raged, bringing joy to the warriors. Hatred was intensified by the killing of one's kinsmen. The headless trunk of the thousandth soldier caused delight (with its dance).[48] No heed was paid to the death of brave warriors because of confidence in one's arms.[49]

---

[47] Literally with the straight path barred.

[48] This was supposed to take place when a thousand soldiers were killed.

[49] The readings of Kṛṣṇa and Mādhava are followed.

K and MY read *paccaa* (प्रत्यय) for *pabbala* = प्रबल (R). Kula reads *pavva* (पर्वत)। K, MY and Kula read लघुक (*lahua*) for *pahua* found in R and explained as प्रभूत (?)।

MY says स्वभुजविश्वासात् ईषत्करतया कलितप्रतिवीरपतनमित्यर्थः। Kula says सहस्रपूरणस्य कबन्धस्य जनित आमोदो यत्र। सहस्रे पतिते एकः कबन्धो नृत्यतीति वार्ता। भटस्य दत्तः . . . (रसः) अनुरागो येन। रिपोः भुजपर्वतात् गृहीतोत्क्षिप्तस्य लघुकवीरस्य पतनं यत्र तत् तथाभूतं युद्धं (प्र)वर्तते।

R says भुजाभ्यां प्रबलानां प्रभूतानामसंख्यानां वीराणां पतनं यत्र।

65. मणिबन्धागअपुञ्जिअसंणाहच्छेअवलअदिण्णावेढम्।
णेउं ण चएइ सिआ मूलुच्छिण्णगरुअं णिसिअरस्स भुअम्।।

[मणिबन्धागतपुञ्जितसंनाहच्छेदवलयदत्तावेष्टम्।
नेतुं न शक्नोति शिवा मूलोच्छिन्नगुरुकं निशिचरस्य भुजम्।।]

A jackal could not carry off the arm of a demon, torn off at the root (by an ape), because it was heavy, being encased in the severed piece of armour that had stuck fast on the wrist.

K and Kula read हर्तुम् (*hariuṁ*) for *ṇeuṁ* = नेतुम् (R). K and MY read *mūla-cchea* for *mūlucchiṇṇa* (R). Kula has *mūla-cchiṇṇa*.

MY says मणिबन्धप्राप्ताः तत्रैव पुञ्जिताः संनाहच्छेदा एव वलयानि तैः दत्तावेष्टम्। अत्र निशिचरभुजस्य मूलच्छेदः कपिभिः हठाकर्षणात् शिलापातनाद्वा।

Kula says मणिबन्धागतेन हस्तपुच्छलग्नेन पुञ्जितेन संनाहच्छेदेन वलयेनेव दत्तावेष्टं मूलच्छिन्नं . . . गुरुकं निशाचरस्य भुजं शृगाली हर्तुं न शक्नोति।

66. आवत्तन्तरवलिआ रुहिरणिहाएसु पासबद्धप्फेणा।
ओल्लन्तपम्हगरुआ अत्थाअन्ति पडिऊण चमरुप्पीडा।।

[आवर्तान्तरवलिता रुधिरनिघातेषु पार्श्वबद्धफेनाः।
आर्द्रायमाणपक्ष्मगुरुका अस्तायन्ते पतित्वा चामरोत्पीडाः।।]

Heaps of *cāmara* whisks[50] fell into the pools of blood. Fringed with foam, and heavy with the hair soaked in blood, they sank as they moved round and round in the eddies.

Kula reads भ्रान्ताः (*bhamiā*) for *valiā* in the first line, and भ्रान्त्वा (*bhamiūṇa*) for *paḍiūṇa* (पतित्वा) in the second line. Cf. *SC* text.

[50] Used to decorate chariots, horses and elephants. Cf. 1.33; 9.74, 81; 15.49.

67. उद्धमुहमुक्कणाआ पुव्वद्धभरोसिअन्तपच्छिमभाआ।
कुम्भे पवअसिलाहअखुप्पन्तुद्धङ्कुसे धुणन्ति गइन्दा।।

[ऊर्ध्वमुखमुक्तनादाः पूर्वार्धभरावसीदत्पश्चिमभागाः।
कुम्भान्प्लवगशिलाहतनिखायमानोर्ध्वाङ्कुशान्धुन्वन्ति गजेन्द्राः।।]

The elephants shook their head, with the erect goad thrust into them by the stones hurled by the apes, and bellowed, face upwards, the hind quarters sinking under the weight of the forepart of the body.[51]

MY says *khuppanta* खन्यमान। निमज्जदिति यावत्। *osianta* अवसीदत्। निमज्जदङ्कुशान् कुम्भान् धून्वन्तीत्यर्थः।

Kula says क्षेप्यमाणार्धा मग्नार्धा अङ्कुशा येषु तान् कुम्भान् गजेन्द्रा धुन्वन्ति. He seems to read *khuppantaddha* for o *ntu* o. Cf. *SC* text. *SC* commentary says क्षेत्यमाणार्धा निमज्जदर्धा अङ्कुशा, etc. Hemacandra 4.101 has *khuppai = majjai*

68. अह पवअभरुब्भन्ता पहरुज्जुअतिअसभङ्गदाणसमुइआ।
जाआ रक्खसजोहा पढमुग्गअदुक्करं पडिवहाहिमुहा।।

[अथ प्लवगभरोद्भ्रान्ताः प्रहारऋजुकत्रिदशभङ्गदानसमुचिताः।
जाता राक्षसयोधाः प्रथमोद्गतदुष्करं प्रतिपथाभिमुखाः।।]

Thrown into confusion by the heavy onslaught of the apes, the *rākṣasa* warriors, strong enough to vanquish the gods, ever ready for war, took to flight, a thing hard for them to do, because it was the first time that they had ever fled.

K, MY and Kula read प्रहारोद्यत for *paharujjua* = प्रहारऋजुक (R). MY reads *paḍhamullaa* for *paḍhamuggaa* = प्रथमोद्गत(R).

MY says *paharujjaa* प्रहारोद्यत। प्रहारो युद्धम्। *paḍhamullaa*[52] प्राथमिकभङ्गस्येदम्। प्रथमतयाभियानात् दुष्करमित्यर्थः। K has प्रथमाश्रय।

The beginning of Kula's gloss is corrupt, but *SC* says अथानन्तरं वानरदरेण प्लवगेभ्यो भयेनोद्भ्रान्ताः संत्रस्ता व्याकुला इति कुलनाथः। Kula thus reads दर for भर।

---

[51] I.e. the animals reared themselves up and cried with pain when they were hit by the stones.

[52] *Paḍhamullaa = paḍhama+ulla+a*. See Hemacandra 2.163; 4.430. Cf. *piullaa* ibid. 2.164.

Kula then says प्रहारोद्यतानां त्रिदशानां भङ्गदानाय समुचिता योग्या राक्षसयोधाः प्रथमत्वात् पूर्वमह(त)त्वात् (?) दुष्करं यथा स्यात् तथा प्रतिपथाभिमुखाः पलायनोद्यता जाताः Kula seems to read *paḍhamullaa* like K and MY (see above). The manuscript of *SC* text also has this reading. See editor's footnote.

R says प्रथममुद्गतमुपस्थिमत एव दुष्करं यथा स्यात्। राक्षसानां युधि पलायनमिदं प्रथममेवोपस्थितमिति लज्जावशादिति भावः।

R's reading *paḍhamuggaa* (प्रथमोद्गत) is an idiomatic expression found also in Hāla, verse 15 — *paḍhamuggaa-dohaliṇīa* (Weber).

69. भग्गोणिअत्तिअगअं भमिअं ठाणपरिवत्तिओभग्गरहम्।
एक्कपअवलिअजोहं मण्डलिदिण्णतुरअं णिसाअरसेण्णम्।।

[भग्नापनिवर्तितगजं भ्रमितं स्थानपरिवर्तितावभग्नरथम्।
एकपदवलितयोधं मण्डलीदत्ततुरगं निशाचरसैन्यम्।।]

The army of the demons turned round; the elephants, dispersed in flight, were turned back; the broken chariots were moved out of position; the troops broke ranks all at once; and the horses moved in a circle.

MY says युद्धात् प्रतिनिवर्तमानदशायां निशाचरसैन्यमेवंभूतगजरथादिकं जातमित्यर्थः। Kula says भग्नापनिवर्तिता विमुखीकृता गजा यत्र। निजकस्थानात् परिवर्तिता अवभग्ना रथा यत्र। एकस्मिन् पदे वलिताः पुनर्निवृत्ताः योधा यत्र[53]। परिवर्तनेन दत्तमण्डलीकाः तुरगा यत्र तत् तथा निशाचरसैन्यं जातमित्यर्थात्।

It will be seen that Kula reads *ṇiaa-ṭṭhāṇa* (cf. *SC* text) for *bhamiaṁ ṭhāṇa°* found in R who says निशाचरसैन्यं भ्रमितं युद्धाय पुनः परावृत्तमित्यर्थः। स्थाने परिवर्तिता युद्धाय भ्रामिता अवभग्ना विमुखा रथा यत्र। He refers to the earlier interpretation of the verse — केचित्तु भ्रमितं पश्चादुगतमिति व्याख्याय पलायनपरतयैव स्कन्धकमिदं व्याचक्षते। The reading *bhamiaṁ* is found also in Lokanātha according to *SC*.

70. अमरिसवित्थक्कन्ता वि वलाअन्ति भमिऊण गलिआमरिसा।
ईसिविअत्तच्छूडा णिब्भीअल्लीणवाणरा रअणिअरा।।

[अमर्षवितिष्ठमाना वि(अपि)पलायन्ते भ्रमित्वा गलितामर्षाः।
ईषद्विवृत्तक्षिप्ता निर्भीतालीनवानरा रजनीचराः।।]

[53] R says एकपदेन एकोपक्रमेण वलिता वक्रीभूता योधाः पत्तयो यत्र।

The demons who stood their ground in anger, but were repulsed when they returned to flight for a while, turned and fled, with all wrath gone, pursued by the intrepid apes.

MY says *vitthakkantā* व्याकुलीभवन्तः वितर्कयन्तो वा। अमर्षपरावृत्ताः प्रहारार्थं भ्रमित्वा प्लवगेष्वलब्धच्छिद्राः पश्चादनुधावतो निर्भयान् प्रतिभटान् भयेन वलितकन्धरा एव पश्यन्त एव पलायन्तेत्यर्थः।

MY's gist of the verse seems to agree with K's reading निवृत्ताक्षमुखाः (*ṇiattacchamuhā* ?) for *viatta-cchūḍhā* (विवृत्तक्षिप्ताः) found in R.
Kula says अमर्षेण क्रोधेन वितिष्ठमानाः, प्रतिपक्षपीडितत्वात् गलितामर्षाः, ईषन्निवृत्य (?) क्षिप्ता असयः तैः वञ्चिताः . . . मन्दीकृता आलीनाः समीपोपगता वानरा यैः ते निशाचरा भ्रान्त्वा विपलायन्ते। Kula seems to read *ṇiatta-cchūḍhāsi-vañciallīṇā*° for *viatta-cchūḍhā ṇibbhīallīṇa*° found in R who says निर्भीता अत एवालीनाः संगता वानरा येषां ते रजनीचरा युद्धाय ईषद्विवृत्ताः परावृत्ताः, अथ क्षिप्ताः प्रेरिताः सन्तः, कपिभिरित्यर्थात्, पुनरपि भ्रमित्वा परावृत्त्य पलायन्ते। He explains वितिष्ठमानाः as विलम्बिताः।

SC text has *vivatta-vvūḍhāsi-vañciallīṇa-*. *SC* commentary says ईषद्विवृत्तैः वलितकन्धरैः सद्भिः व्यापारिता व्यूढा येऽसयः तै वञ्चिता आलीनाः पृष्ठगता वानरा यैस्तै रजनीचराः।

71. रहसंदाणिअतुरअं तुरङ्गमोरत्थलक्खलिअपाइक्कम्।
पाइक्कावलिअगअं गअभज्जन्तरहसंकुलं वलइ बलम्।।

[रथसंदानिततुरगं तुरङ्गमोरःस्थलस्खलितपदातिकम्।
पदात्यावलितगजं गजभज्यमानरथसंकुलं वलति बलम्।।]

The troops scattered, with the tangled mass of chariots broken by the elephants, and the horses trapped in the chariots, and the foot-soldiers stumbling over the horses, and the elephants tumbling over the former.

Kula says रथैः संदानिता बद्धाः (?) तुरगा यत्र। तुरगोपरि प्रस्थिताः (स्खलिताश्च) पायिक्याः पदातयो यत्र। पायिक्येषु आपतिता गजा यत्र। गजैः भज्यमानं रथसंकुलं रथसमूहो[54] यत्र तत् तथाभूतं बलं . . . पलायते। It will be seen that Kula reads तुरगोपरिप्रस्थित (*turaovari-patthia*) for *turaṁgamora-ṭṭhala* found in R who says तुरङ्गमाणामुरःस्थलात् स्खलिता घटिताः (पतिताः ?)

---

[54] Cf. *Silā-saṁkula* 1.57. See Extracts. *SC* says रथैः संकुलं व्याप्तं दुःखगभ्यम्।

पदातयो यत्र। K reads तुरगोपरिसंस्थित which is about the same as Kula's reading.

R says पदातिभिरावलिताः पृष्ठे तुरङ्गमातिक्रमादुपरुद्धा गजा यत्र तत्। Kula (see above) construes *āvalia* as आपतित। R also on 7.42 and 11.49 explains *āvalia* as आपतित, i.e. taking it as *āvaḍia* which occurs as a variant. See Goldschmidt ad *loc.*

72. ससइ विसमुद्धकम्पं गरुआअन्तभुअलम्बिओभग्गदुमम्।
विहलोसरिअपडिभडं सण्णोवाहिअणिसाअरं पवअबलम्।।

[श्वसिति विषमोर्ध्वकम्पं गुरुकायमानभुजलम्बितावभग्नद्रुमम्।
विह्वलापसृतप्रतिभटं सन्नापवाहितनिशाचरं प्लवगबलम्।।]

Having routed the dispirited demons, the host of apes whose adversaries fled in confusion gasped for breath, swaying the upper part of the body, with the broken trees[55] dangling from their weary hands.

MY says गुरूभवन्तो भुजलम्बिताश्च अवभग्ना द्रुमा यस्य तत्तथा।

R says सन्ना अवसन्ना अपवाहिताः पातिता निशाचरा येन तत्तथा। *SC* says सन्नमवसन्नं सत् अपवाहितं निष्क्रामितं निशाचरबलं येन तत् प्लवगबलं श्वसिति। Kula seems to says अनुपथमागता[56] अनुगता निशाचरा येन तत् प्लवगबलम्। His reading might be *aṇuvanthāgaa* for *saṇṇovāhia* (R). The form ⁰*vantha* occurs frequently in the poem.

K reads अन्योन्यविभिन्ननिशिचरम्।

Kula has अवभुग्न for *obhagga* (अवभग्न) in the first line. He reads *obhugga* like manuscript C of Goldschmidt.

73. अक्खण्डिअसोडीरा पवआणिअपढममाणभङ्गावसरा।
भग्गा वि भमन्ति पुणो णीसेसं रक्खसा ण गेह्णन्ति भअम्।।

[अखण्डितशौण्डीर्याः प्लवगानीतप्रथममानभङ्गावसराः।
भग्ना अपि भ्रमन्ति पुनर्निःशेषं राक्षसा न गृह्णन्ति भयम्।।]

But the demons, with their martial ardour unimpaired, and humiliation first brought to them by the apes, returned again, even though they had fled, and did not wholly give way to fear.

---

[55] Those used as weapons.

[56] As in similar cases, our copy has मार्थता।

MY says *soḍīra* शौर्य। अभ्रमन् कपिबलाभिमुखं युद्धाय परावर्तन्तेत्यर्थः। Kula says अखण्डितं शौटीर्यं शौर्याभिमानो[57] येषाम्। पूर्वगैः प्रथममानीतः मानभङ्गावसरः पराजयो येषां ते राक्षसाः भग्ना अपि पुनर्भ्रमन्ति निवर्तन्ते, निःशेषमेकान्तं भयं न गृह्णन्ति।

74. तह वि अ दरपरिवत्तिअचक्कलइज्जन्तगरुअचक्करहवहम्।
वित्थक्कन्तपहाविअसमत्थसंठावणाविढत्तरणजसम्।।

[तथापि च दरपरिवर्तितचक्रायमाणगुरुकचक्ररथपथम्।
वितिष्ठमानप्रधावितसमर्थसंस्थापनार्जितरणयशः।।]

Nevertheless the army of demons fled again. The track of the heavy-wheeled chariots formed a circle as they slowly turned round (in their flight); and the brave, who stood their ground and moved swiftly, earned martial fame by infusing fresh courage into the troops.

MY says तथापि च अत्यन्तभयाग्रहणेऽपि पलायमाना एवेत्यर्थः। *viḍhatta* आर्जित व्यवस्थितेति वा (°तेति यावत् A)।

Kula says यद्यपि नाभिहितं तथापि निबद्धोत्साहत्वात् दरपरिवर्तितानामीषत् भ्रमितानां, चकलीक्रियमाणानां(मण्डलीक्रियमाणानां[58]), गुरुकाणां मन्दगतीनां (रथचक्राणां[59]) पन्था यस्य तत् तथा। वितिष्ठमानैः, प्रधावितैः समर्थैः संस्थापनया भग्नसैन्याश्वासनेन अर्जितं (रणे यशो) यत्र तत् तथा। The reference is to निशाचरसैन्यम् mentioned in verse 77.

R says दरपरिवर्तितः किंचित् भ्रामितः अतएव चक्रायमाणः चक्राकृतिः गुरुकचक्रस्य रथस्य पन्था यत्र।

75. वाणरपरंमुहोणामिअद्धमोडिअलिलाडवट्टणिसिअरम्।
परसेण्णकलअलाहित्थपडिणिअत्तन्तगअविओलारोहम्।।

[वानरपराङ्मुखावनामितार्धमोटितललाटपट्टनिशिचरम्।
परसैन्यकलकलोद्विग्नप्रतिनिवर्तमानगजविलोलारोहम्।।]

The demons were held down, face backwards, and their foreheads half broken by the apes; while the mahouts were struck with dismay as the elephants fled, scared by the yelling of the enemy troops.

---

[57] शौर्य is restored from *SC*.

[58] Added from *SC*.

[59] Restored from *SC*.

MY says *āhittha* त्रस्त। कपिकलकलत्रस्तपलायमानानां करिणां प्रतिबलाभिमुखी-करणाय प्रयतमाननिषादिकमित्यर्थः।

Kula says वानरैः पराङ्मुखावनमिताः, केशेषु अपकृष्य अर्धमोटितललाटपट्टाः निशाचरा यत्र। परसैन्यस्य कलकलेन आविग्नानां प्रतिनिवर्तमानानां हस्तिनां विकला आरोहा यत्र तत् तथा। Kula reads *hatthi-vihalārohaṁ* (*SC* text also) for *gaa-violārohaṁ* (R). MY has *kari* for *gaa*. R says पलायमानेभ्यो गजेभ्यो विलोलाः चञ्चलाः, पतिता इति यावत् आरोहा हस्तिपका यत्र। *viola* rendered as विलोल by R is however a *deśī* word. D.N. 7.63 gives it in the sense of आविग्न। MY seems to explain it as प्रयतमान (see above).

76. चलवाणराणुधाविअवालधरिज्जन्तणिच्चलट्ठिअतुरअम्।
णिहअभडपडिअसारहिपवङ्गभेसिअतुरङ्गहीरन्तरहम्।।

[चलवानरानुधावितवालध्रियमाणनिश्चलस्थिततुरगम्।
निहतभटपतितसारथिप्लवङ्गभीषिततुरङ्गह्रियमाणरथम्।।]

The horses stood motionless, pursued and seized by the tail by the impetuous apes; and the chariots, with the fighters killed and the drivers fallen, were whirled away by the horses, frightened by the apes.

Kula says चलैः चपलैः वानरैरनुधावितैः वालेषु ध्रियमाणा निश्चलस्थिताः तुरगा यत्र। निहतभटाः पतितसारथयः प्लवङ्गनिर्भरा वानराक्रान्ताः तुरङ्गैः ह्रियमाणा रथा यत्र।

Kula reads निर्भर (*ṇibbhara*) for *bhesia* = भीषित (R and MY).

77. धारामग्गणिवाइअबलपडिहअविरलबाणरुण्णिअमग्गम्।
भग्गं गलन्तपहरणसुण्णइओहअभुअं णिसाअरसेण्णम्।।
(अन्त्यकुलअम्)

[धारामार्गनिपातितबलप्रतिहतविरलवानरोन्नीतमार्गम्।
भग्नं गलत्प्रहरणशून्यीकृतोभयभुजं निशाचरसैन्यम्।।]
(अन्त्यकुलकम्)

The apes in small groups went in pursuit, impeded by the troops fallen in battle; and the hands of the demons were empty with the weapons gone.[60]

[60] Verses 74-77 form a *kulaka*.

Kula is here mutilated, and has only the words तत् निशाचरसैन्यं भग्नम्।

K, MY and *SC* read आन्वित for *uṇṇia* = उन्नीत (R). MY says *aṇṇia* अन्वित अनुगतेति यावत्। प्रथमं धारामार्गसंचारेषु निपातितेन राक्षसबलेन गतिप्रतिबन्धात् कतिपयैरेव वानरैरनुगतमार्गम्।

K and MY read *bhagga* for *bhaggaṁ* (R and Kula), and therefore *galanta-ppaharaṇa* for °*paharaṇa*. MY says भग्नैः गलद्भिश्च आयुधैः शून्यीकृतोभयभुजं जातमित्यर्थः।

R explains उन्नीत as ऊहित–वानरैरुन्नीता ऊहिता मार्गा यस्य . . . अत्र संचारचिह्नमनेन गता इत्यादि कपितर्कप्रसक्तिरित्यर्थः।

SC says धारामार्ग इति खड्गधारा अश्वगतिर्वा। R says धारामार्गे संग्रामे।

78. अह हिअमच्छरलहुआ एक्कक्कमचक्खुरक्खणाहिअहिअआ।
हिअआवडिअदहमुहा वलिजा पडिमुक्करणभआ रअणिअरा।।

[अथ हृतमत्सरलघुका एकैकक्रमचक्षूरक्षणाहितहृदयाः।
हृदयापतितदशमुखा वलिताः प्रतिमुक्तरणभया रजनीचराः।।]

Thereafter the demons, reduced to impotence, with all wrath gone, remembered Rāvaṇa and returned once more, discarding the fear of battle, and bent on preserving their honour[61] before each other.

---

[61] Literally eye, i.e. "shame of the eye", phrase used in some Indian languages (e.g. Assamese and Bengali), and meaning *sense of shame, feeling of honour.* Cf. verse 16. According to another interpretation, the demons bethought themselves of the shame they would feel before each other if they took to flight. In this case the expression *cakkhu-rakkhaṇa* "preserving the eye" is taken in the sense of shame on the strength of *deśī* lexicon. See Extracts. Homer speaks of shame on the battlefield.

ō philoi, aneres este kai alkimon ētor helesthe allēlous t'aideisthe kata krateras husminas. — Iliad V.529-30.

Murray (Loeb) translates the lines literally: My friends, be men, and take to you hearts of valour, and have shame each of the other in the fierce conflict. The Penguin translation gives the sense: . . . and in the field fear nothing but dishonour in each other's eyes. This is better than the alternative explanation, *have respect unto one another,* based on another meaning of *aideomai*. Cf. Pierron's edn., vol. I, p. 187, Paris, 1883. The above lines recur in Iliad XV.561ff. with a notable change in the first line: *aidō thesth' eni thumō — take ye shame in your hearts* (Loeb); *think of your honour* (Penguin)

MY says भङ्गातिशयेन हृतान्योन्यमत्सरा अपि अन्योन्यभङ्गावलोकनपरिहारा-भिनिविष्टमनसो दशमुखस्मरणेन रणभयं त्यक्त्वा पुनर्योद्धुं प्रतिनिवृत्ता इत्यर्थः।

K and Kula read *bhamiā* for *valiā* = वलिताः explained as घूर्णिताः (R). Kula reads पक्ष for *cakkhu*. He says अथानन्तरं हृतेन मत्सरेण अमर्षेण लघुकाः, प्रत्येकपक्षस्य रक्षणे पार्श्वरक्षाविधौ आहितहृदयाः कृतनिश्चयाः, हृदये आपतितः स्मृतिपथं गतो . . . दशमुखो येषाम्,

"रामादपि मर्तव्यं, मर्तव्यं रावणादपि,
उभयादपि मर्तव्ये वरं रामान्न रावणात्।।"

इति मत्वा प्रतिमुक्तरणभयाः रजनीचरा भ्रान्ताः परिवृत्त्य स्थिताः[62]।

R says एकैकक्रमेण परस्परं चक्षुषां रक्षणे आहितानि अर्पितानि हृदयानि यैस्ते। चक्षुःसंमुखे लज्जया परस्परं त्यक्तुमपारयन्त इति सहैव परावृत्ता इति भावः। *SC* says केचित्तु हृतमात्सर्यत्वेन लघुका अपि लज्जायामाहितं हृदयं यैरेवंभूताः सन्तो भ्रमिता निवृत्त्यागता इत्यर्थः। '*cakkhu-rakkhaṇaā* लज्जा', इति देशीसार इति प्राहुः। *SC* mentions another reading, *cakka* (चक्र) for *cakkhu*.

79. वोच्छिण्णसंधिअजसा होन्ति णिअत्तसँमुहट्ठविअसोडीरा।
कइबलदुप्परिअल्ला सिढिलिअपडिवण्णरणधुरा रअणिअरा।।

[व्यवच्छिन्नसंहितयशसो भवन्ति निवृत्तसंमुखस्थापितशौण्डीर्याः।
कपिबलदुष्परिकलनीयाः शिथिलितप्रतिपन्नरणधुरा रजनीचराः।।]

The demons resumed the burden of war abandoned by them, and summoned their fading courage, and retrieved their lost renown, and became unconquerable by the martial hosts of apes.

MY says निवृत्तं कथमपि संमुखस्थापितं च शौर्यमेषामिति ते तथोक्ताः। *duppariallā* दुष्परिकलनाः दुष्प्रधर्षा इति यावत्।

Kula says व्यवच्छिन्नमपसूत्रं संहितं पुनः समारोपितं यशो यैः। निवर्तमानं संस्थापितं शौटीर्यं यैः। शिथिलिता[63] . . . प्रतिपन्ना गृहीता रणधूः यैः। रजनीचराः कपिसैन्यस्य दुष्परिकलनीयाः जेतुमशक्या भवन्ति। *dupparialla* शब्दो देश्यामशक्यः (cf. *Deśīnāmamālā*, 5.55). *SC* says अशक्यलङ्घने देशीति कुलनाथः। DN, however, has only अशक्य like Kula.

It will be seen that Kula reads *ṇiattanta-saṁṭhavia* for *ṇiatta-samuha-ṭṭhavia* found in R and MY.

---

[62] These two words are restored from *SC*.

[63] R says शिथिलिता त्यक्ता।

80. तो भङ्गलज्जिआणं परिवड्ढिअपसरहरिसिआण अ गरुअम्।
रअणिअरवाणराणं वरिआआरिअभडं पवट्टइ जुज्झम्।।

[ततो भङ्गलज्जितानां परिवर्धितप्रसरहर्षितानां च गुरुकम्।
रजनीचरवानराणां वृताकारितभटं प्रवर्तते युद्धम्।।]

A momentous combat then ensued between the demons, ashamed of their defeat, and the apes, elated by their enhanced success, the leading warriors (on each side) being chosen and challenged.

MY says *pasara* प्रसर। प्रतिबलप्रघर्षणेति यावत्। *variāāria* वृताकारित स्वयंगृहीताहूत।

Kula reads *bhagga* for भङ्ग (R and MY), and प्रवृत्तम् (*paattaṁ*) for *pavaṭṭai* = प्रवर्तते (R). K has प्रवृद्धम्।

Kula says भग्नलज्जितानां राक्षसानां परिवर्धितप्रसरत्वेन हृष्टानां च वानराणा वृता योद्धुमङ्गीकृता आकारिता (आहूता: *SC*) भटा यत्र तत् युद्धं प्रवत्तम्।

81. सुग्गीवेण पअङ्घो सत्तच्छअपाअवेण दिण्णरणसुहो।
वणगअदाणसुरहिणा वच्छुच्छलिअकुसुमट्टहासेण हओ।।

[सुग्रीवेण प्रजङ्घः सप्तच्छदपादपेन दत्तरणसुखः।
वनगजदानसुरभिणा वक्षउच्छलितकुसुमाट्टहासेन हतः।।]

Prajaṅgha,[64] who gave the joy of battle (to his adversary), was hit by Sugrīva with a *saptaparṇa* tree, which, fragrant with the ichor of wild elephants,[65] seemed to burst into laughter as the former's bosom was strewn with its flowers.[66]

MY reads *paccuccalia* (प्रत्युच्चलित) for *vacchucchalia*=वक्षउच्छलित (R and probably Kula). MY says हन्यमानाभिमुखोच्चलित।

MY remarks दत्तरणसुख इति रणस्य सुखतया वर्णनं सुग्रीवस्य शौर्यातिशयक-थनपरम्। कुसुमितस्य सुरभेश्च सप्तच्छदस्य वधसाधनत्वकथनं च तद्वधानायास-

[64] One of the leaders of the demons.

[65] The animals had rubbed themselves against the tree. Haribhadra, for instance, refers to groves of *saptaparṇa* trees smashed by elephants in the autumn. *Samarāiccakahā*, p. 194.

[66] The followers are fancied as the laugh of the tree, pleased with Sugrīva's skill in hitting his adversary.

प्रतिपादनार्थम्। कुसुमस्य अट्टहासतया रूपणं तु रिपुशौर्योपालम्भकरणोत्प्रेक्षासूचनाभिप्रायेणेति मन्तव्यम्।

82. दिविआहअस्स समरे सुरहिं उरपडिअसरसचन्दणगन्धम्।
असणिप्पहस्स जीअं अग्घाअन्तसुहिओणिमिल्लस्स गअम्।।

[द्विविदाहतस्य समरे सुरभिमुर:पतितसरसचन्दनगन्धम्।
अशनिप्रभस्य जीवमाजिघ्रत्सुखितावनिमीलतो गत:।।]

The life of the demon Aśaniprabha, who was struck by Dvivida with a sandal tree in the combat, ebbed away as he, with eyes closed, inhaled with delight the fragrance of the sappy tree crashing on his bosom.

MY *pratīka* (B) has *viviāhaassa* for *divi°* (द्विविदाहतस्य)। The first word is missing in A. MY says *oṇimillassa* अवनिमीलितस्य (अप° A) अत्रापि पूर्ववदेव वधानायासे तात्पर्यम्।

Kula says द्विविदनाम्ना यूथपतिनाहतस्य समरे मधुरं मनोहरम् उरसि पतितस्य सरसचन्दनद्रुमस्य गन्धमाजिघ्रत: सुखितावनिमीलितस्य अशनिप्रभनाम्नो राक्षसस्य जीवितं गतम्। Kula reads मधुरम् (*mahuraṁ*) for *surahiṁ*.

83. हन्तूण वज्जमुट्ठिं हसइ मइन्दो वि मुट्ठिघाअणिसुद्धम्।
आहित्थदिट्ठिणिग्गअजलणसिहाअम्बफुडिअलोअणजुगलम्।।

[हत्वा वज्रमुष्टिं हसति मैन्दोऽपि मुष्टिघातनिपातितम्।
उद्विग्नदृष्टिनिर्गतज्वलनशिखाताम्रस्फुटितलोचनयुगलम्।।]

Having slain the demon Vajramuṣṭi, laid low with a punch (on the head), Mainda laughed as the former's eyeballs shot out in the wake of the flame of wrath issuing from his bewildered eyes.

K, MY and Kula read शिखामार्गपतित। (*sihā-magga-paḍia*) for *sihāamba-phuḍia* = शिखाताम्रस्फुटित (R).

MY says *āhittha* आत्रस्त। त्रस्तदृष्टिनिर्गताया रोषज्वलनशिखाया अनुमार्गनिपतितलोचनयुगलो यथा स्यात् तत्तथा हत्वा मैन्दो जहासेति योज्यम्।

Kula reads आयस्त (*āattha*, *SC* text) for *āhittha*.

Kula says मैन्दनामापि यूथपति: शिरसि मुष्टिघातेन पातितम्, आयस्ताया: क्रोधादीप्ताया दृष्टे: निर्गतानां क्रोधज्वलनशिखानां मार्गेण पतितं लोचनयुगलं यस्य तं वज्रमुष्टिनामानं राक्षसं हत्वा हसति।

SC says मुष्टिघातेन पातितम्, आविद्धाया 'मइन्दं' प्रति क्षिप्तायाः दृष्टेः सकाशात् निर्गताया ज्वलदनलशिखाया मार्गे पश्चात् पतितं लोचनयुगलं यस्य तमिति लोकनाथः। The latter seems to read *āiddha* for *āhittha*.

84. कुविएण विज्जुमाली चिरजुज्झिअहरिसिओ सुसेणेण कओ।
चलणजुअलावलम्बिअणक्खुक्खित्तखुडिओहअभुअप्फडिहो।।

[कुपितेन विद्युन्माली चिरयुद्धहर्षितः सुषेणेन कृतः।
चरणयुगलावलम्बितनखोत्क्षिप्तखण्डितोभयभुजपरिघः।।]

Vidyunmālin, who was elated by the prolonged fight, was held down by the angry Suṣeṇa with his feet, and both the massive arms of the demon were torn asunder by the ape with his nails and hurled aloft.

K and MY read कक्ष (*kakkha*) for *ṇakkha* = नख (R).

MY says *cira-jujjhia* चिरयोधित (Kula also). R and *SC* have चिरयुद्ध।

MY says चरणयुगलाक्रान्ताभ्यां कक्षाभ्याम् उत्पाटितौ भुजौ यस्य स तथा। *SC* says चरणयुगलेनावलम्बित आक्रान्तः, कक्षायाः सकाशादुत्क्षिप्य खण्डयित्वा ऊर्ध्वक्षिप्तौ भुजपरिघौ यस्येति लोकनाथः। Kula's reading is uncertain. He says धन्धक्षिप्तखण्डितोभयभुजपरिघः। If धन्ध stands for स्कन्ध, his reading might be *khandha* for *kakkha*.

85. सहिअपहरं णलेण वि तवणस्स तलाहिघाअमोडिअकण्ठम्।
णिहिअं देहम्मि सिरं देहो अद्धणिमिओ महिअलम्मि कओ।।

[सोढप्रहारं नलेनापि तपनस्य तलाभिघातमोटितकण्ठम्।
निहितं देहे शिरो देहोऽर्धनिवेशितो महीतले कृतः।।]

Having endured a blow dealt by Tapana, Nala[67] broke the demon's neck with a slap, and thrust the head into the body, and made the body sink half into the earth.

K, MY and Kula read *ṭhio* for *kao* = कृतः (R). K and probably MY read ऊर्ध्वं for *addha* (R and Kula).

Kula says सोढप्रहारं यथा स्यात् तथा नलेनापि यूथपतिना तपननाम्नो राक्षसस्य तलाभिघातेन चपेटप्रहारेण (R also) मोटितकण्ठं शिरो देहे निहितं, देहः अर्धनिहितः अर्धमग्नो महीतले स्थितः। MY says तपनस्य शिरो देहे लग्नं, देहस्तु भूतले अर्धनिमग्नोर्ध्वावस्थित इत्यर्थः।

[67] The architect among the apes who built the causeway.

86. हन्तूण जम्बुमालिं झत्ति विहिण्णो अइश्चिओ पवण्णसुओ।
सअलतलगाढताडणभिण्णुच्छलिअसिरमेअसित्तदसदिसम्।।

[हत्वा जम्बुमालिनं झटिति विभिन्नोऽतिक्रान्तः पवनसुतः।
सकलतलगाढताडनभिन्नोच्छलितशिरोमेदःसिक्तदशदिक्।।]

Pierced by Jambumālin with a lance, Hanumat slew him, and moved away as the brain bursting out of the demon's head, broken with a heavy blow with the palm, was scattered about on all sides.

K, MY and Kula read शक्ति (*satti*) for *jhatti* = झटिति (R). They read मन्द for गाढ (R). MY has स्वकरतल for *saala-tala*.

Kula says पवनसुतो हनूमान् जम्बुमालिना शक्त्या विभिन्नः जम्बुमालिनं सकलतलस्य समग्रचपेटस्य मन्दताडनेन भिन्नात् शिरस उच्छलितेन मेदसा सिक्तदशदिशं हत्वा *aiñcio*[68] अतिक्रान्ताः।

MY says *aiñcio* अतिगतः। तच्छक्त्या प्रथमं भिन्नः पश्चात् स्वकरतलमन्दताडन-भिन्नशीर्षोच्चलितमेदःसिक्तदशदिशं जम्बुमालिनं हत्वा हनूमानतिगत इत्यर्थः। MY reads *uccalia* for *ucchalia* as he and K often do.

87. अह गेण्हइ अइभूमिं इन्दइवालितणआण रणसोडीरम्।
णिहएक्कमेक्कपरिअणसहत्थपडिवण्णसंसअतुलारोहम्।।

[अथ गृह्णात्यतिभूमिमिन्द्रजिद्वालितनययो रणशौण्डीर्यम्।।
निहतैकैकपरिजनस्वहस्तप्रतिपन्नसंशयतुलारोहम्।।]

The martial ardour of Indrajit and Aṅgada then reached its culmination, making them risk their lives in single combat, the followers of each having been killed in battle.[69]

Kula says इन्द्रजिद्वालितनययोः मेघनादाङ्गदयो रणशौटीर्यमतिभूमिं गृह्णाति प्रसरमासादयति। निहतान्योन्यपरिजनत्वात् स्वहस्तेन प्रतिपन्नः संशयतुलारोहो यत्र तत् तथा। R says स्वहस्तेन स्वकृत्या प्रतिपन्नः स्वीकृतः संशयरूपतुलायामारोह आरोहणं यस्मात्। ताभ्यामेवेत्यर्थात्। MY says मिथो निहतपरिजनतया स्वहस्ताभ्यामेव प्राप्तं प्राणसंशयेन साम्यं यत्र तत्तथा।

88. बाणन्धआरिअदिसं धणुमण्डलपरिगअं विसेसेइ परम्।
आलोइउक्खआणिअमुक्कपडन्तेहि गिरिसहस्सेहि कई।।

---

[68] Our copy has भूत्वा *sahañjio*. *SC* says मन्दताडनेन लीलयाभिधातेन।

[69] The remaining verses describe the encounter between Indrajit or Meghanāda and Aṅgada, the son of Vāli.

[बाणान्धकारितदिशं धनुर्मण्डलपरिगतं विशेषयति परम्।
आलोकितोत्खातानीतमुक्तपतद्गिरिसहस्रैः कपिः।।]

With thousands of mountains dropping from the sky while they were observed, uprooted, brought over and released by the ape, the latter[70] gained an advantage over his adversary who stood within the circle of his bow,[71] darkening the regions of the sky with his arrows.

MY says विशेषयति स्म स्वस्मात् निकर्षयति स्मेत्यर्थः। Kula says आकर्षाकृष्टस्य धनुषो मण्डलेन परिगतं परं शत्रुं मेघनादं कपिरङ्गदः . . . गिरिसहस्रैः विशेषयति तस्मादतिशयितो भवति। R says विशेषयति अतिक्रामति।

89. णिवडन्ति कुसुमणिब्भरमिलिअवलन्तविडवोवऊढमहुअरा।
विवइण्णप्फललहुआ धुतमज्झक्खुडिअपल्लवा दुमणिवहा।।

[निपतन्ति कुसुमनिर्भरमिलितवलद्विटपोपगूढमधुकराः।
विकीर्णफललघवो धुतमध्योत्खण्डितपल्लवा द्रुमनिवहाः।।]

The trees (hurled by Aṅgada) fell (over Indrajit), with the bees crowding round the flowers, and hidden by the swaying branches. They were lighter, because the fruits were scattered about; while the quivering leaves were rent in the middle.

Kula says कुसुमेषु निर्भरं मिलिता, वलद्भिः विटपैरुपगूढा मधुकरा येषु, विप्रकीर्णफलत्वेन लघुकाः, धुतमध्याः खण्डिताः पल्लवा येषां ते द्रुमनिवहा निपतन्ति। R says धुताः सन्तो मध्ये अन्तरादेशे उत्खण्डिताः पल्लवा येषां ते।

90. वालितणअं ण पावइ गअणे गुप्पइ दुमेहि सरसंघाओ।
छिज्जन्ति अद्धवत्थे एन्ता दहमुहसुअं ण लङ्घन्ति दुमा।।

[वालितनयं न प्राप्नोति गगने गोप्यते द्रुमैः शरसंघातः।
छिद्यन्तेऽर्धपथे आयान्तो दशमुखसुतं न लङ्घन्ते द्रुमाः।।]

The arrows of Indrajit did not reach Aṅgada; they were smothered in the sky by the trees hurled by the latter; nor did the trees reach Indrajit; they were cut down by his arrows midway as they came.

MY reads *entaṁ* (आयान्तम्) for *entā* = आयान्तः (R and Kula). Kula

---

[70] I.e. Aṅgada

[71] Indrajit is fancied as being encircled by the bow stretched to its full compass.

reads *dumesu* for *dumehi,* and प्राप्नुवन्ति (*pāventi*, cf. *SC* text) for *laṁghanti* (R).

Kula says मेघनादमुक्तः शरसंघातः गगने द्रुमेषु गुप्यते तिरोधीयते। अतएव वालितनयं न प्राप्नोति। अङ्गदक्षिप्ता द्रुमा आगच्छन्तः अर्धपथे छिद्यन्ते, दशमुखसुतमिन्द्रजितं न प्राप्नुवन्ति। R says मेघनादस्य शरसंघात अङ्गदक्षिप्तैः द्रुमैः गोप्यते तिरोधीयते व्याकुलीभवति वा।

91. विक्खित्तलोद्धकुसुमं सरदलिउद्धाअमाणचन्दणगन्धम्।
उद्धुतमन्दाररअं सरसलवङ्गदलगब्भिणं होइ णहम्।।

[विक्षिप्तलोध्रकुसुमं शरदलितोर्ध्वायमानचन्दनगन्धम्।
उद्धूतमन्दाररजः सरसलवङ्गदलगर्भितं भवति नभः।।]

Flowers of *lodhra* trees were strewn about; and the fragrance of the sandal trees, cleft asunder by the arrows, was wafted through the air; the pollen of the flowers of *mandāra* trees flew aloft; and the sky filled with the sappy fragments of clove trees.[72]

My *pratīka* has *vitthiṇṇa* for *vikkhitta* = विक्षिप्त (R). Kula reads *vicchiṇṇa*. K and MY read उत्थितत्तमाल for *uddhāamāṇa* (R and Kula). K and Kula read लव for दल (R).

MY says शरदलितोत्थितेत्यत्र तमालचन्दनयोः शरदलितत्वं तद्गन्धे तु उत्थितत्वमिति योज्यम्।

Kula says विच्छिन्नानि लोध्रकुसुमानि यत्र। शरदलितानां चन्दनानामूर्ध्वायमानो गन्धो यत्र। R says ऊर्ध्वायमान ऊर्ध्वप्रसारी उद्धावमानो वा गन्धो यत्र।

92. इअ तं समपडिहत्थं वारंवारवलदिण्णसाहुक्कारम्।
इन्दइवालिसुआणं परं पमाणं गअं पि वड्ढइ जुज्झम्।।

[इति तत्समप्रतिहस्तं बारंबारबलदत्तसाधुकारम्।
इन्द्रजिद्वालिसुतयोः परं प्रमाणं गतमपि वर्धते युद्धम्।।]

Thus did the combat between Indrajit and Aṅgada, repeatedly cheered by the troops, and marked by equal resistance, rage ever more, even though it had reached a climax.

MY says समप्रतिहस्तं समप्रतिद्वन्द्वम्। Kula explains the expression as तुल्यप्रतिकृतम्। R says समः प्रतिहस्तः परप्रहारनिवारणादिरूपा प्रतिक्रिया प्रतिपक्षो वा यत्र। *SC* says तुल्यप्रतीकारमिति लोकनाथः।

[72] The trees were those hurled by Aṅgada and intercepted by Indrajit's arrows.

K reads विजृम्भते (*viambhai*) for *pi vaḍḍhai* = अपि वर्धते (R and Kula).

93. दुमकुसुममज्झणिग्गअसरपुङ्खालग्गणिज्जमाणमहुअरम्।
णिव्वावारोवसिअट्ठिओहआविग्गसेण्णविम्हअदिट्ठम्।।

[द्रुमकुसुममध्यनिर्गतशरपुङ्खालग्ननीयमानमधुकरम्।
निर्व्यापारापसृतस्थितोभयाविग्नसैन्यविस्मयदृष्टम्।।]

The bees were carried away as they clung to the feathered shaft of Indrajit's arrows, which pierced their way through the flowers of the trees hurled by Aṅgada;[73] while the fight was watched in amazement by both armies,[74] standing aloof, motionless and anxious.

Kula says द्रुमकुसुममध्यनिर्गतानां शराणां प्राङ्मुखालग्ना नीयमाना मधुकरा यत्र तत् तथा। R says किंभूतं युद्धम्-अस्त्रीकृतवृक्षस्य कुसुमानां मध्येन निर्गतैः इन्द्रजितः शरैः पुङ्खेष्वालग्नाः सन्तो नीयमाना मधुकरा यत्र *ṇajjamāṇa* इति पाठे शरणां पुङ्खालग्नाः सन्तो ज्ञायमाना मधुकरा यत्रेत्यर्थः। This reading is found in *SC* (commentary) which mentions *ṇijjamāṇa* and *sajjamāṇa* as variants.

94. दहमुहतणअविसज्जिअसरभरिअणहङ्गणुप्पइअवालिसुअम्।
वालिसुअरोसपेसिअसालसिलासेलरुद्धदहमुहतणअम्।।

[दशमुखतनयविसृष्टशरभृतनभोङ्गणोत्पतितवालिसुतम्।
वालिसुतरोषप्रेषितशालशिलाशैलरुद्धदशमुखतनयम्।।]

Aṅgada sprang out of the sky, filled with the arrows discharged by Indrajit; while the latter was hemmed in by the trees, stones and mountains wrathfully hurled by the former.

Kula says अवस्थगित (*otthaia*) for *uppaia* = उत्पतित (R). K reads अवपतित (*ovaia*) Kula seems to read *visama* for *silā* in the second line.

Kula says दशमुखतनयेन विसर्जितैः मुक्तैः शरैः भृतं नभोऽङ्गनम्, अवस्थगितः (च) वालिसुतो यत्र। वालिसुतेन रोषेण प्रेषितैः (शाल)विषमशैलै रुद्धो दशमुखतनयो यत्र तत् तथा।

---

[73] I.e. the arrows sped through the flowers with the displaced bees clinging to them.

[74] I.e. the apes and the demons.

R says शरैः भृतात् पूरितात् नभोऽङ्गणात् उत्पतितः प्रहारवारणाय ऊर्ध्वगतो वालिसुतो यत्र। एवम्-वालिसुतेन रोषतः प्रेषितैः शालो वृक्षः शिलाः शैलाश्च तै रुद्धो न तु प्रतिहतः . . . दशमुखतनयो यत्र तत्।

95. णिसिअरसरणिद्दारिअवाणरदेहरुहिरारुणदिसाहोअम्।
वाणरपहरपअत्तिअरक्खसरुहिरोहकद्दमिअभूमिअलम्।।

[निशिचरशरनिर्दारितवानरदेहरुधिरारुणदिशाभोगम्।
वानरप्रहारप्रवर्तितराक्षसरुधिरौघकर्दभितभूमितलम्।।]

The sky was reddened by the blood spurting out from the body of the ape, pierced by the demon's arrow; while the ground was turned into mire by the flow of the demon's blood caused by the blows dealt by the ape.

K and Kula read *ṇahābhoaṁ* (cf. *SC* text and Goldschmidt's footnote) for *disāhoaṁ* (R).

Kula says निशाचरस्येन्द्रजितः शरैः निर्दारितस्य वानरस्याङ्गदस्य देहरुधिरेण अरुणो नभआभोगो गगनविस्तारो यत्र।

K reads *ruhira-dara* for *ruhiroha* = रुधिरौघ (R) Kula has only रुधिर। His reading might be same as R's.

96. रिउसूलदूमिओहीरमाणवालिसुअदिण्णवाणरसोअम्।
सेलाहिघाअमुच्छिअदहमुहतणअभअभिण्णरअणिअरबलम्।।

[रिपुशूलदुःखितावह्नियमाणवालिसुतदत्तवानरशोकम्।
शैलाभिघातमूर्छितदशमुखतनयभयभिन्नरजनीचरबलम्।।]

The host of apes lost heart when Aṅgada fainted, wounded by the adversary's spear; while the *rākṣasa* troops fled affrighted when Indrajit was stunned by the impact of a mountain hurled by Aṅgada.

K and Kula read दीनवानरसैन्यम् for *diṇṇa-vāṇara-soaṁ* = दत्तवानरशोकम् (R).

Kula says रिपोः इन्द्रजितः शूलेन व्यथितः अवह्रियमाणो मूर्च्छा(य)मानो यो वालिसुतः तेन दीनं निरुत्साहं वानरसैन्यं यत्र। R says अवह्रियमाणः अवपात्यमानः यो वालिसुतः तेन दत्तो वानरेभ्यः शोको यत्र। MY says *ohīramāṇa* मूर्च्छत्।

97. तारातणअविसेसिअरअणिअरपअत्तपवअसेण्णकलअलम्।
मन्दोदरिसुअदूमिअवाणरपरिओसमुहलरक्खसलोअम्।।

[तारातनयविशेषितरजनीचरप्रवृत्तप्लवगसैन्यकलकलम्।
मन्दोदरीसुतदु:खितवानरपरितोषमुखरराक्षसलोकम्।।]

The host of apes broke into loud cheers when the demon was overpowered by the son of Tārā;[75] while the demons shouted for joy when the ape was wounded by the son of Mandodarī.[76]

MY says तारातनयातिशायितात् इन्द्रजितो हेतो: प्लवङ्गै: कृतहर्षरवम्। मन्दोदरीसुताभितापितात् अङ्गदात् हेतो: हर्षमुखरराक्षसबलमित्यर्थ:। Kula says अङ्गदेन विशेषिते न्यक्कृते रजनीचरे मेघनादे प्रवृत्त: प्लवगसैन्यस्य कलकलो यत्र।

K reads योधम् (*johaṁ*) for *loaṁ* (R and Kula) in the second line.

98. भुअपडिअणिप्फलप्फलिहभङ्गहेलाहसन्तवाणरजोहम्।
उरभिण्णसिलाअलमेहणाअमुक्कट्टहासपण्डुरिअणहम्।।
(आइकुलअम्)

[भुजपतितनिष्फलपरिघभङ्गहेलाहसद्वानरयोधम्।
उरोभिन्नशिलातलमेघनादमुक्ताट्टहासपाण्डुरितनभ:।।]
(आदिकुलकम्)

The warrior apes laughed merrily when Indrajit's club broke as it fell ineffectively on Aṅgada's arm; and the sky was brightened by the loud laugh of Meghanāda when a boulder hurled by Aṅgada broke to pieces on his chest.[77]

Kula reads पाण्डरित (*paṇḍaria*, cf. *SC* text) for *paṇḍuria* in the second line.

99. अह इन्दइम्मि वालितणएण समराणुराअभग्गुच्छाहे।
णिहओ त्ति हसन्ति कई माआइ ठिअ त्ति हरिसिआ रअणिअरा।।

[अथेन्द्रजिति वालितनयेन समरानुरागभग्नोत्साहे।
निहत इति हसन्ति कपयो मायया स्थित इति हर्षिता रजनीचरा:।।]

Thereafter when Indrajit's spirit was broken by Aṅgada by dint of martial zeal, the apes made merry, thinking that he

---

[75] Aṅgada.

[76] Indrajit.

[77] Verses 92-98 form a *kulaka*.

was killed; but the demons rejoiced, because they knew that he had disappeared by magic.

Kula says इन्द्रजिति वालितनयेन समरानुरागेण भग्नोत्साहे निरुद्यमे[78] कृतान्तर्धाने सति निहत इति हसन्ति कपयः, etc. R says समरानुरागे भग्न उत्साहो यस्य तथाभूते सति।

इअ सिरिपवरसेणविरइए कालिदासकए दहमुहवहे महाकव्वे
तेरहो आसासओ समत्तो।

[इति श्रीप्रवरसेनविरचिते कालिदासकृते दशमुखवधे महाकाव्ये
त्रयोदश आश्वासकः समाप्तः।]

[78] Restored from *SC*. Our copy has only द्य।

चतुर्दश आश्वासकः
Fourteenth Āśvāsakaḥ

1. अह णिप्फलगअदिअसो जहिच्छिआ संपडन्तदहमुहलम्भो।
जूरइ लङ्काहिमुहो अलसाअन्तहतरक्खसो रहुणाहो।।

[अथ निष्फलगतदिवसो यदृच्छाया संपद्यमानदशमुखलम्भः।
खिद्यते लङ्काभिमुखोऽलसायमानहतराक्षसो रघुनाथः।।]

Rāma, with the day wasted, not having encountered Rāvaṇa as desired by him, because sad as he, looking towards Laṅkā, tardily slew the demons.

MY, says *jūrai* अखिद्यत। गतदिवसानां निष्फलत्वम्। दशमुखेन सह समरालाभात् एतदेवाह। प्रतीष्टासंघटमानेति अलसायमानो भूत्वा हतराक्षसः। रावणनिष्क्रमणप्रत्याशया लङ्काभिमुख इति ग्राह्यम्।

Kula says प्रतीक्षितः असंघटमानो दशमुखलाभो यस्य स तथा। अतएव गतो निष्फलो दिवसो यस्य। अलसायमानेन मन्दयुद्धेन[1] हता राक्षसा येन स रघुनाथो रामः रावणं दिदृक्षुः लङ्काभिमुखः क्रुध्यति।

MY seems to read *paḍicchiāsaṁghaḍanta*. Kula reads *paḍikkhiāsaṁghaḍanta* found also in *SC* text. K reads प्रतीक्षितासंपतत् according to Goldschmidt. R reads *jahicchiāsaṁpaḍanta*, translated as यदृच्छासंपद्यमान, but *saṁpaḍanta* is not = संपद्यमान, though it may serve as the meaning. R says यदृच्छया स्वेच्छया संपद्यमानः (असंपद्यमानः ?) दशमुखस्य लम्भः प्राप्तिर्यस्य। R explains *jahicchiā* as यदृच्छा, but his reading may also be construed as *jahicchia* (यथेत्सित)+ *asaṁpaḍanta*, which practically gives the same meaning as the readings of K, MY and Kula.

2. एएसु सुहणिसण्णो ण णीइ समरं दसाणणो त्ति गणेन्तो।
इच्छइ दिण्णाआसे रअणिअरेसु पडिमुञ्चिउं सरणिवहे।।

[एतेषु सुखनिषण्णो न निरैति समरं दशानन इति गणयन्।
इच्छति दत्तायासान्नजनिचरेषु प्रतिमोक्तुं शरनिवहान्।।]

[1] Restored from *SC*.

He resolved to discharge his arrows that had proved burdensome[2] at the demons as he thought: "Care-free because of his confidence in them, Rāvaṇa doth not come out to fight."

K and MY read निश्वासान् (ṇīsāse) for *sara-ṇivahe* = शरनिवहान् (R). Kula is corrupt, but his reading might be same as R's, to judge from *SC* (text and commentary). The reading of K and MY is given as a variant in *SC*.

MY says एतेषु एतानधरीकृत्य स्वयं सुखेन स्थितः। रावणोद्देशेन प्रवृत्तान् समरालाभात् आत्मन एव दत्तायासान् कोपनिश्वासान् राक्षसेष्वेव प्रतिमोक्तुमैच्छत्। निश्वासमोक्षमात्रमेव चास्य व्यापारः प्रतिबलवधाय पर्याप्तः तद्वधाव्यभिचारी चेति तात्पर्यम्। *SC* says स्वरनिवहान् निश्वाससमूहान मुञ्चतीति श्रीनिवासः अर्थान्तरं वदति। तथा च विश्वः "स्वरो . . . ध्वनौ। उदात्तादिष्वति प्रोक्तः स्वरो नासासमीरण।।" इति।

3. दिट्ठम्मि पत्थिअम्मि अ आवडिअम्मि अ परे सरणिसुम्भन्ते।
समरम्मि विसूरन्ता मोहुक्करिसिअदुमा भमन्ति पवङ्गा।।

[दृष्टे प्रस्थिते चापतिते च परे शरनिपात्यमाने।
समरे खिद्यमाना मोघोत्कृष्टद्रुमा भ्रमन्ति प्लवङ्गाः।।]

As Rāma's arrows killed the enemy at sight, or as he retreated or drew near, the apes moved about the battlefield downhearted, holding up their trees in vain.[3]

MY says *patthiammi* प्रार्थिते। प्रस्थिते इति केचित्। आपतिते प्राप्ते। Kula says परे शत्रौ शरैः पात्यमाने हन्तव्याभावात् मोघोत्कर्षितद्रुमा निष्फलोल्लासितवृक्षाः प्लवङ्गमाः खिद्यमानाः समरे भ्राम्यन्ति। R says रणाभिमुखं प्रस्थिते च पलायिते वा परे, आपतिते निकटमागते च परे।

4. भेत्तूण तुरिअमुक्के अणुलोमपहाविए सिलासंघाए।
पढमं साहेन्ति परं विहडिअवाणरमणोरहा रामसरा।।

[भित्त्वा त्वरितमुक्ताननुलोमप्रधाविताञ्शिलासंघातान्।
प्रथमं साधयन्ति परं विघटितवानरमनोरथा रामशराः।।]

Rāma's arrows pierced their way through the swifty hurled boulders of the apes, flying in the same direction, and killed the enemy first, disappointing the apes in their hopes.

---

[2] Because the desired target could not be found. See the preceding verse.

[3] I.e. without any opportunity to kill the enemy.

K, MY and Kula read *tulia* for *turia* = त्वरित (R). MY seems to read *sela* for *silā*. Kula reads *dharāhara-ṇivahe* for *silā-saṁghāe.*

MY says नासोरगतकपिभिः तुलितमुक्तानपि शैलसंघातान् भित्त्वा मध्ये सुषिरं कृत्वा निर्गता रामशराः शिलाभ्यः पूर्वमेव परानसाधयन्नित्यर्थः।

Kula says प्लवगैः तुलितमुक्तान्, स्वात्मनोपप्रधावितान् धराधरनिवहान् भित्वा। R says त्वरितं यथा स्यात् तथा मुक्तान्, अथानुलोमं शरगन्तव्यदिगभिमुखं प्रधावितान् शिलासंघातान् भित्वा। *SC* says तुलितमुक्तान् . . . तोलयित्वा परिकलय्य मुक्तान्। But the reading *tulia* may also be taken as *turia* as in *samara-tulia* = समरत्वरित 12.82.

5. छिज्जइ करेण समअं पवए णल्लिअइ रक्खसाण पहरणम्।
पावइ तुरिअविमुक्कं अणहं ण अ रक्खसं पवङ्गपहरणम्।।

[छिद्यते करेण समं प्लवगे नालीयते राक्षसानां प्रहरणम्।
प्राप्नोति त्वरितविमुक्तमनघं न च राक्षसं प्लवङ्गप्रहरणम्।।]

The weapons of the demons were rent asunder by his arrows all at once, and did not reach the apes; nor did the swiftly flung missiles of the apes find any demon unhurt.[4]

K and MY read *bhijjai* for *chijjai* (R and Kula). K and Kula read शरैः (*sarehi*) for करेण (R). K reads प्लवङ्गमप्रहारः (*pavaṁgam-apaharo*) for *pavaṁga-paharaṇaṁ* (R). Kula and MY also read प्रहारः like K.

Kula says राक्षसानां प्रहरणं रामस्य शरैः समं छिद्यते। R says राक्षसानां प्रहरणं शरादि करेण समं छिद्यते। रामशरैरित्यर्थात्।

MY says *ṇa alliai* (*ṇalliai*) न प्राप। प्रहारः प्रहरणमायुधमित्यर्थः। Kula says प्लवगानां प्रहारः अनघमक्षतशरीरं राक्षसं न प्राप्नोति।

6. भिण्णे वच्छम्मि सिला गिरिसिहरं छिण्णपाडिअसिरट्ठाणे।
णिवडइ सराहिसंधिअपरक्कमेहि पवएहि रोसविमुक्कम्।।

[भिन्ने वक्षसि शिला गिरिशिखरं छिन्नपातितशिरःस्थाने।
निपतति शराभिसंहितपराक्रमैः प्लवगै रोषविमुक्तम्।।]

The mountain peaks, wrathfully hurled by the apes, whose valour was frustrated[5] by Rāma's arrows, dropped on the heads of the demons, already severed and dashed on the

---

[4] Because they were already wounded by Rāma's arrows.

[5] I.e. rendered superfluous.

ground; while the boulders hurled by them likewise dropped on their chest already pierced by the arrows.

Kula says शरैः अभिसंहितः[6] विफलीकृतः पराक्रमो येषां तैः। प्लवगैः रोषविमुक्तं गिरिशिखरं छिन्नपातितशिरःस्थाने निपतति। भिन्ने वक्षसि शिला निपतति। एतेन रामशराणां शीघ्रत्वं दर्शितम्।

R says रामस्य शरेणाभिसंहितो वञ्चितः पराक्रमों येषां तैः। शत्रुमारणस्य तत एव सिद्धत्वात्। K reads अतिसंहित for *ahisaṁdhia* (अभिसंहित), according to Goldschmidt, cf Extracts on 13.12.

7. सइ संधिओ च्चिअ सरो रहुणाहस्स सइ चक्कलइअं च धणुम्।
अच्छिज्जइ अ सराहअसइपल्हत्थन्त रक्खससिरेहि मही।।

[सदा संहित एव शरो रघुनाथस्य सदा चक्रीकृतं च धनुः।
आच्छाद्यते च शराहतपर्यस्यद्राक्षसशिरोभिर्मही।।]

Rāma's arrows appeared to be all the time fixed to the bow, and the bow all the time curved; while the ground was strewn with the ever rolling heads of the demons struck off by the arrows.

R has *acchijjai* = आच्छाद्यते ? MY reads *avathakkai* translated as अवस्तीर्यते। B has *atthakkai*. Kula and K have आस्तीर्यते = *atthijjai* ?. *SC* text has *otthijjai* = अवस्तीर्यते *SC* commentary.

8. विसमालग्गहुअवहा विसहररेअविअबिलमुहपडिच्छन्दा।
दीसन्ति बाणमग्गा रक्खसदेहेसु से ण दीसन्ति सरा।।

[विषमालग्नहुतवहा विषधररेचितबिलमुखप्रतिच्छन्दा।
दृश्यते बाणमार्गा राक्षसदेहेष्वस्य न दृश्यन्ते शराः।।]

The tracks of the arrows, fiery at places, but not the arrows, were seen in the bodies of the demons, and resembled the mouth of holes abandoned by serpents.

Kula reads *dari* for बिल in the first line. He says विषधरैः सर्पैः रेचितानां दरीमुखानां बिलद्वाराणां प्रतिच्छन्दाः प्रतिरूपा बाणमार्गाः राक्षसदेहेषु (दृश्यन्ते)। तस्य रामस्य शरा अग्निबाणा निर्भिद्य गतत्वात् न दृश्यन्ते।

9. उक्करिसन्तस्स करे पत्थन्तस्स हिअए रसन्तस्स मुहे।
दीसन्ति णवर पडिआ णिबद्धसिरपडणसूइआ रामशरा।।

---

[6] Restored from *SC*.

[उत्कर्षतः करे प्रार्थयमानस्य हृदये रसतो मुखे।
दृश्यन्ते केवलं पतिता निबद्धशिरःपतनसूचिता रामशराः॥]

Rāma's arrows, their course revealed by the fall of heads in unbroken succession, were visible only when they dropped on the foeman's hand as he drew his sword, or on his bosom as he resolved to attack, or on his face as he yelled.

MY says उत्कर्षतः कोशात् खड्गमिति शेषः। Kula says खड्गम् (?) उत्कर्षतः उन्नामयतः करे, प्रार्थयमानस्य अभियोद्धुमिच्छोः हृदये, रसतो निनदतो मुखे पतिताः केवलं दृश्यन्ते निबद्धानां पतञ्जिकानिखातानां भटानां[7] शिरःपतनैः सूचिता निर्णीताः रामशराः।

My explains निबद्ध as अविच्छिन्न। He says वेगवशादविच्छिन्न शिरःपतनोन्नेशः शरा यदा वेगक्षयस्तदापि यैरङ्गैरुद्युञ्जते परे तेष्वेव परं न्यपतन् न पुनर्वृथेत्याशयः।

SC says निबद्धानां शिक्षणकौशलेन छिन्नलग्नानां शिरसां पतनेन सूचिताः। निबद्धानां मिलितानां शिरसां पतनेन सूचिता युगपत् पतितानां बहूनामित्यर्थ इति केचित्। R says निबद्धानां व्यूहे संयोजितानां वीराणां शिरःपतनेन सूचिताः प्रकाशिताः। यद्वा निबद्धं शिरस्त्राणादिसंबद्धं यच्छिरः तत्पतने, etc.। संप्रदायस्तु निबद्धं कबन्धसंगतं यच्छिरः तत्पतनेन सूचिता इति व्याचष्टे।

10. जो जत्थ च्चिअ दिट्ठो सुओ जहिं जस्स विअलिओ वि णिणाओ।
चलिओ अ जो जहिं चिअ तस्स तहिं चेअ णिवडिआ रामसरा॥

[यो यत्रैव दृष्टः श्रुतो यस्य विगलितोऽपि निनादः।
चलितश्च यो यत्रैव तस्य तत्रैव निपतिता रामशराः॥]

His arrows dropped wherever the enemy was seen, wherever his firm voice was heard, and wherever he betook himself.

K and MY read *avihalo vva* (अविह्वलो वा) for *vialio vi* = विगलितोऽपि (R). Kula seems to read चाविकलः, i.e. *avihalo a*. Lokanātha quoted in *SC* says यत्र यस्याविकलः सावष्टम्भश्च निनादः श्रुतः। MY reads *calio vva* (K also) = चलितो वा for *calio a* (च) found in R and Kula. MY reads *jatto ccia* and says यत एव यत्रैव इति यावत्। R has *jattha ccia* = यत्रैव (Kula also).

---

[7] This word is added from quotation in *SC*, which however has पञ्जिकालिखितानां भटानां।

11. हअहत्थिभडतुरङ्गा दीहा दीसन्ति तम्मि रक्खससेण्णे।
अग्गक्खन्धपअत्ता कूलं भेत्तूण णिग्गआ रामसरा।।

[हतहस्तिभटतुरङ्गा दीर्घा दृश्यन्ते तस्मिन्राक्षससैन्ये।
अग्रस्कन्धप्रवृत्ताः कूलं भित्त्वा निर्गता रामशराः।।]

The long chain of Rāma's arrows that killed elephants, horses and troops was seen amidst the army of the demons as they entered through the front ranks and went out, piercing through the rear.

MY says दीर्घा दीर्घाध्वगा इत्यर्थः। कूलं कूलानीकस्कन्धं सेनापश्चाद्भागः। R says अग्रस्कन्धेन सेनामुखेन प्रवृत्ताः प्रविष्टाः . . . रामशराः . . . Kula says पुरोभागे पतिताः।

12. जं चिअ उअलद्धभअं काहिइ समअं पडाइअव्वारम्भम्।
तं रामसराहिहअं दिट्ठं णवर पडिअं णिसाअरसेण्णम्।।

[यदेवोपलब्धभयं करिष्यति समं पलायितव्यारम्भम्।
तद्रामशराभिहतं दृष्टं केवलं पतितं निशाचरसैन्यम्।।]

The troops of the demons were seen to fall, hit by Rāma's arrows, even as they were on the point of fleeing affrighted all at once.

MY says *jaccia* यावदेव for *jaṁ cia* यदेव (R and Kula). He says *tā* तावत् for *taṁ* = तत् (R and Kula). MY and K read समरे for *samaaṁ* = समम् (R and Kula). *SC* text has *palāiavva* for *paḍā*°.

MY says समरभूमिसंगतस्य निशाचरसैन्यस्य सहसैव रामशरनिकरव्याप्तावकाशतया पलायनावसरोऽपि न लब्ध इत्यतो निरवशेषं निहतमेवासीदिति तात्पर्यार्थः।

13. इअ तं बाणुक्कित्तं पडन्तसमकालदिट्ठसिरसंघाअम्।
सुअसारणावसेसं खणेण रक्खसबलं कअं रहुबइणा।।

[इति तद्बाणोत्कृत्तं पतत्समकालदृष्टशिरःसंघातम्।
शुकसारणावशेषं क्षणेन राक्षसबलं कृतं रघुपतिना।।]

In this wise Rāma destroyed in an instant the army of demons with his arrows, the falling heads seen all at once, with Śuka and Sāraṇa[8] as the sole survivors.

[8] Ministers of Rāvaṇa.

14. ताव अ सलोहिआरुणरक्खसबलणिव्विसेससंझातिमिरो।
परमत्थओ चिरस्स व णिव्वाओ गलिअरक्खसभओ दिअहो।।

[तावच्च सलोहितारुणराक्षसबलनिर्विशेषसंध्यातिमिरः।
परमार्थश्चिरस्येव निर्वाणो गलितराक्षसभयो दिवसः।।]

Meanwhile the day, with the evening twilight resembling the host of demons red with blood,[9] came to an end, as if for ever in reality, with all danger from the demons gone.[10]

Kula says यावदेवं तावच्च सरुधिरत्वादवशं यत् राक्षसबलं तेन निर्विशेषं समानरूपं सन्ध्यातिमिरं यत्र स दिवसो गलितराक्षसभयः चिरस्य चिरेण परमार्थत इव[11] निर्वाणः, न केवलमस्तंगतत्वात् परमनिवृत्तिप्राप्त्या च निर्वाण इत्यर्थः। Kula seems to read अवश for अरुण in the first line. His explanation of the verse is better than R's.

K reads राग for तिमिर and अपि *(vi)* for *va* (इव)। MY says *ṇivvāo* निर्वाणः अस्तमित (अन्तरित A) इत्यर्थः। परमार्थतः यथाकालम्।

15. अह उग्गाहिअचाओ एक्को वालिसुअमोडितरहुप्पइओ।
संचरइ मेहणाओ णिअअच्छविमेलिअन्धआरम्मि णहे।।

[अथोद्ग्राहितचाप एको वालिसुतमोटितरथोत्पतितः।
संचरति मेघनादो निजकच्छविमेलितान्धकारे नभसि।।]

Thereupon Meghanāda, flying aloft from his chariot broken by Aṅgada,[12] and holding up his bow, moved about alone in the sky, the darkness blending with the lustre of his body.

MY says *uggāhia* उद्गृहीत (उद्ग्राहित R)।

16. तो णिट्ठविअणिसिअरा इन्दइणा गरुअवेरमूलाहारा।
समअं चिअ सच्चविआ अद्दिट्ठेण विहिणेव्व दहरहतणआ।।

[ततो निष्ठापितनिशिचराविन्द्रजिता गुरुकवैरमूलाधारौ।
सममेव सत्यापितावदृष्टेन विधिनेव दशरथतनयौ।]

---

[9] The dark colour of the demons streaming with blood is likened to the approaching darkness blending with the glow of the sky at sunset.

[10] I.e. the day along with the danger from the demons seemed to pass for ever without any chance of returning.

[11] Kula is here corrupt, but परमार्थत इव occurs more than once in *SC*.

[12] See the last verse of the previous canto.

The invisible Indrajit, like Fate unseen, fixed his eyes at the same moment on both the sons of Daśaratha,[13] who had destroyed the demons, and were at the root of the deep animosity against them.

saccaviā लक्षीकृतौ। MY; दृष्टो Kula; सत्यापितौ नागपाशलक्ष्यत्वेन व्यवस्थापितौ R.

17. मुअइ अ सअम्भुदिण्णे ताण भुअङ्गमुहणिग्गआणलजीहे।
णीसेसणिहअरक्खसवीसत्थपलम्बिओहअभुआण सरे।।

[मुञ्चति च स्वयंभूदत्तांस्तयोर्भुजङ्गमुखनिर्गतानलजिह्वान्।
निःशेषनिहतराक्षसविश्वस्तप्रलम्बितोभयभुजयोः शरान्।।]

As they stood, with both arms hanging down, free from care, because all the demons had been slain, Indrajit let fly at them the arrows, granted by Brahmā, which had serpents for tips, with the fiery tongues shooting out.

MY says *tāṇa* ताभ्याम्। चतुर्थ्यन्तमेतत्। भुजङ्गमुख भुजङ्गाकारमुख।

18. तो भिण्णङ्गअदेसा णिद्दारिअबीअबाहुपाअडिअमुहा।
राहवदेहम्मि ठिआ तिअसंदाणिअभुआ भुअङ्गमबाणा।।

[ततो भिन्नाङ्गददेशा निर्दारितद्वितीयबाहुप्रकटितमुखाः।
राघवदेहे स्थितास्त्रिकसंदानितभुजा भुजङ्गमबाणाः।।]

The serpent arrows, piercing through the upper part of one arm, penetrated the other arm, revealing their mouths, and remained embedded in the bodies of the scions of Raghu, fastening their arms to their hips.

MY says (भुजङ्गमबाणाः) त्रिकसंदानितभुजाः, एकस्य भुजस्य अङ्गददेशं भित्त्वा भुजान्तरस्यापि तत्प्रदेशविदारणेन दर्शितमुखा, उभावपि भुजौ पृष्ठतो नीत्वा यावत्त्रिकमाकृष्य बद्ध्वा संश्लिष्टौ कृतवन्त इत्यर्थः।

Kula reads पार्श्व (*pāsa*) for बाहु, and says भिन्नाङ्गददेशाः, निर्दारिते द्वितीयपार्श्वे प्रकटितमुखाः . . . भुजङ्गमबाणाः। He seems to read *viia-vāsa* as found in *SC* text. K reads देहयोः (*dehesu*) for *dehammi* (देहे)। Kula has राघवयोः देहे सुस्थिताः for *rāhava-dehammi ṭhiā* (R). *SC* text has *rāhava-dehe a ṭhiā* (राघवदेहे च स्थिताः)।

[13] I.e. Rāma and Lakṣmaṇa.

19. णिद्धोआअसणीला णिन्ति विसाणलफुलिङ्गपज्जलिअमुहा।
धणुसंधाणविमुक्का अउव्वणाराअविब्भमा भुअइन्दा।।

[निर्धौतायसनीला निर्यान्ति विषानलस्फुलिङ्गप्रज्वलितमुखाः।
धनुःसंधानविमुक्ता अपूर्वनाराचविभ्रमा भुजगेन्द्राः।।]

Dark blue like tempered[14] iron, the serpents, released after fixing them to the bow, and looking like miraculous arrows, issued forth with their mouths aflame with the sparks of their fiery venom.

MY says *pajjalia-muhā* प्रज्वलितमुखाः। K and Kula read दशाननसुतस्य for *visāṇala-phuliṅga* (R). K reads संस्थाननिबन्धाः for *saṁdhāṇa-vimukkā* (R and Kula).

R says निर्धौतं दाहोत्तरं जले क्षिप्तं यदायसं लौहं तद्वन्नीलाः।

20. णिवडन्ति विज्जुमुहला तारसमब्भहिअलोहलट्ठि च्छाआ।
कसणजलओअराहि व रक्खसमाअन्धआरिअणहाहि सरा।।

[निपतन्ति विद्युन्मुखरास्तालसमभ्यधिकलौहयष्टिच्छायाः।
कृष्णजलदोदरादिव राक्षसमायान्धकारितनभसः शराः।।]

Resembling iron rods brightened by heating, and rumbling like thunder, the arrows dropped from the sky enveloped in darkness by the magic of the demon, and seemed to issue from the murky clouds.

K and Kula read ताप (*tāva*) for तार (R). R says शराः किंभूताः–तालवृक्षात् समभ्यधिका महत्यो या लौहयष्टयः तच्छाया कान्तिः येषां ते। *SC* says तारेण मार्जनशुद्ध्या, पाठान्तरे तापेन समभ्यधिकाया अधिकोज्ज्वलाया लौहयष्टेरिव छाया येषां ते।

21. पढमं रविबिम्बणिहा पलउक्कासंणिहा णहद्धपडन्ता।
भिन्दन्ता होन्ति सरा दरणिब्भिण्णभमिआ भुआसु भुअङ्गा।।

[प्रथमं रविबिम्बनिभाः प्रलयोल्कासंनिभा नभोर्धपतन्तः।
भिन्दन्तो भवन्ति शरा दरनिर्भिन्नभ्रमणशीला भुजासु भुजङ्गाः।।]

[14] *ṇiddhoā*, washed, i.e. dipped into water after heating, as explained by Rāmadāsa, a reference to "the process of tempering iron by dipping it red-hot into cold water, when the sudden contraction hardens the metal". It is mentioned in *Odyssey* IX.391ff. (see Stanford's commentary, 1959) and the *Ajax* of Sophocles (651) where it is called *baphē* (dipping).

Looking at first like the solar orb, and resembling meteors as they passed half-way through the sky, they appeared to be arrows as they pierced their limbs, and became serpents on their arms, coiling round the lightly bitten parts of the body.

MY says प्रथमं धनुषो निर्गमने तेजःपुञ्जरूपतया रविबिम्बच्छायाः, ततो नभोऽर्धपथापतिताः, गमनाविच्छेदेन उल्कावत् दीर्घाः, ततः अङ्गेषु भिन्दन्तो बाणीभवन्तः, ईषन्निर्भिन्ने अङ्गे आवेष्टनाय भ्रमिता (भुजेषु) भुजङ्गा बभूवुरित्यर्थः।

Kula says प्रथमं रविबिम्बनिभाः, उल्कावर्णा नभोऽर्धपथापतिताः। Kula's reading is *ukkā-vaṇṇā ṇahaddha-vanthāvaḍia* (cf. *SC*, text) for *palaükkā-saṁṇihā ṇahaddha-paḍantā* = प्रलयोल्कासंनिभा नभोऽर्धपतन्तः found in R. MY's reading is same as Kula's except that he reads *ukkā-dīhā*. K's reading is given by Goldschmidt is imperfect, but closely resembles that of Kula and MY.

Kula has भ्रमणशीलाः (*bhamirā*, cf. *SC* text) for *bhamiā* (MY and R Text). R (*chāyā* and commentary) has भ्रमणशीलाः।

The expression °*vanthāvaḍia* (see above) in Kula and MY's readng occurs elsewhere in the poem. Cf. 6.34. See also Extracts on 15.45.

R says तयोर्भुजासु दर ईषन्निर्भिन्नं दष्टं यैस्ततथाभूताः कृतकिंचिद्दंशाः, अथ च भ्रमणशीला भोगेन वलयाकाराः सन्तो भुजङ्गा भवन्तीति सर्वत्र संबध्यते।

22. बज्झन्ति दहरहसुआ दरभग्गमणोरहा किलिम्मन्ति सुरा।
अद्दिट्ठमेहणाआ उण्णामिअपव्वआ भमन्ति पवङ्गा।।

[बध्येते दशरथसुतौ दशभग्नमनोरथाः क्लाम्यन्ति सुराः।
अदृष्टमेघनादा उन्नामितपर्वता भ्रमन्ति प्लवङ्गाः।।]

The sons of Daśaratha remained fast bound. The gods were dispirited, being somewhat frustrated in their hopes; while the apes who did not see Meghanāda moved about aimlessly, holding up their mountains.

K and MY read *vijjhanti* (विध्येते) for *bajjhanti* = बध्येते (R and probably Kula).

23. रसइ णहम्मि णिसिअरो भिण्णमभिण्णहिअअं दिसासु कइबलम्।
भिज्जन्तो वि ण भिज्जइ रिउदंसणदिण्णलोअणो दासरही।।

[रसति नभसि निशिचरो भिन्नमभिन्नहृदयं दिक्षु कपिबलम्।
भिद्यमानोऽपि न भिद्यते रिपुदर्शनदत्तलोचनो दाशरथिः।।]

The demon yelled in the sky. Disconsolate, the host of apes went in differnt directions (in quest of the foe). Rāma, though pierced by the arrows, was not downhearted, and looked about to have a glimpse of the enemy.

R reads *bhiṇṇamabhiṇṇa-hiaaṁ* and says अभिन्नहृदयमपराङ्मुखचित्तं कपिबलं दिक्षु भिन्नं . . . घूर्णितम्। Kula says भिन्नहृदयं व्यथितचित्तं कपिबलं दिक्षु भिन्नमितस्ततो गतम्। K and MY also have भिन्नहृदयं like kula except that K has भिद्यते (*bhijjai*) for भिन्नम् (Kula). MY says भिन्नं विशीर्णं हृदयं यस्य तत्तथा। गलितधैर्यमिति यावत्।

24. रोसाणलपज्जलिअं जलन्तवडवामुहाणलपडिच्छन्दम्।
अङ्गेसु लद्धपसरा हिअअं से णवर परिहरन्ति भुअङ्गा।।

[रोषानलप्रज्वलितं ज्वलद्वडवामुखानलप्रतिच्छन्दम्।
अङ्गेषु लब्धप्रसरा हृदयमस्य केवलं परिहरन्ति भुजङ्गाः।।]

The serpents permeated through his limbs; only they avoided his heart, aglow with the fire of wrath, and like unto the blazing submarine fire.

MY says अनेन रोषानलप्रज्वलिततया वाडववत् दुरासदस्य हृदयस्य नागास्त्रैः परिहृतत्वेन जीवितस्थितिनिमित्तं सूचितम्।

25. ताण भुअङ्गपरिगआ दुक्खपहुव्वन्तविअडभोगावेढा।
जाआ थिरणिक्कम्पा मलअअडुप्पण्णचन्दणदुम व्व भुआ।।

[तयोर्भुजङ्गपरिगता दुःखप्रभवद्विकटभोगावेष्टाः।
जाताः स्थिरनिष्कम्पा मलयतटोत्पन्नचन्दनद्रुमा इव भुजाः।।]

The arms of Rāma and Lakṣmaṇa, ringed about with serpents, but not easily encompassed by their massive coils, became stiff and motionless, like the sandal trees[15] growing on the Malaya slopes.

MY says यथा मलयजा भुजङ्गैः वेष्टिताः सुनिश्चला भवन्ति तथानयोः भुजा अपि नागास्त्रबद्धतया निष्कम्पा जाता इत्यर्थः। Kula says तयोः भुजङ्गैः परिगता वेष्टिताः, दुःखेन प्रभवन्तः समाप्तिं यान्तो विकटभोगावेष्ठा येषु ते, मलयतटोत्पन्नचन्दनद्रुमा इव भुजाः। R says महत्त्वात् झटिति वेष्टयितुं न पारयन्तीत्यर्थः।

26. तह पडिवण्णधणुसरा सरणिब्भिज्जन्तणिच्चलभुअप्फलिहा।
दट्ठोट्ठमेत्तलक्खिअणिप्फलरोसलहुआ कआ रहुतणआ।।

[15] Frequently associated with serpents in *kāvya* poetry. Cf. 1.60; 6.43.

[तथा प्रतिपन्नधनुःशरैः शरनिर्भिद्यमाननिश्चलभुजपरिघौ।
दष्टौष्ठमात्रलक्षितनिष्फलरोषलघुकौ कृतौ रघुतनयौ।।]

The scions of Raghu, who held their bows and arrows as before, with their arms pierced and paralysed by the serpent arrows, were rendered helpless, with their futile wrath perceptible as they merely bit their lips.

MY says तहेत्यादि–धनुषि शरेषु च गृहीतेष्वपि निर्व्यापारौ इत्यर्थः।

K and Kula read सीव्यमान (*sivijjanta*) for *ṇibbhijjanta* = निर्भिद्यमान (R). They read निश्चलस्थापितभुजौ (*ṇiccala-ṭṭhavia-bhuā*) for *ṇiccala-bhua-pphalihā* = निश्चलभुजपरिघौ (R).

27. सरणिब्भिण्णसरीरा जाआ आलोअमग्गिअव्वावअवा।
दरदिट्ठपत्तणन्तरणिहित्तसंखाअलोहिआ रहुतणआ।।

[शरनिर्भिन्नशरीरौ जातावालोकमार्गितव्यावयवौ।
दरदृष्टपत्रणान्तरनिहितसंस्त्यानलौहितौ रघुतनयौ।।]

Their bodies being pierced through and through by the arrows, the limbs had to be searched out to be seen; while the clotted blood accumulating on the feathers of the arrows could partly be seen.

MY says *pattaṇa* पत्र। शरैः निरन्तरभिन्नतया प्रदीपादिना मार्गणीयावयवौ। यावत्पुङ्खमावेष्टनात् ईषद्दृष्टेषु पत्रान्तरेषु निहितं संस्त्यानं रुधिरं ययोः तौ तथा। एवंभूतौ कृताविति वाक्यार्थः। Kula says पत्रणान्तरेषु पक्षसन्धिषु। R says पत्रणा पुङ्खः तदन्तरे तन्मध्ये। *SC* says शराणां दूरनिखाततया ईषद्दृष्टानां पत्रणानामन्तरेषु निहितानि संस्त्यानानि लोहितानि ययोरीदृशौ।

28. सरसीविओरुजुअलं संकीलिअविहलणिच्चलट्ठिअचलणम्।
णिअलिअदेहावअवं संचरिअव्वं पि रहुसुआण अवहअम्।।

[शरस्यूतोरुयुगलं संकीलितविह्वलनिश्चलस्थितचरणम्।
निगलितदेहावयवं संचारितव्यमपि रघुसुतयोरपहतम्।।]

Even their power to move was lost, with the thighs transfixed by the arrows, and the feet held fast, feeble and motionless, and all the limbs bound tight.

K, and MY seems to read *avagaaṁ* (अपगतम्) for *avahaaṁ* = अपहतम् (R). Kula has व्यपरतम् (व्यु° ?) अवसितम्। *SC* text has *uvaraam̐.* SC commentary says उपरतमवसितमिति केचित्।

MY says अत्र शरस्यूतोरुयुगलत्वादिकं संचरणापगमनक्रियाविशेषणत्वेन योज्यम्। Manuscript A has संवीत for स्यूत, and अवगमन for अपगमन।

29. तो सुरहिअएहि समं पडिअं विहलन्तपढमसंठिअबाणम्।
अद्दिट्ठरिउविसज्जिअसरपहरङ्कुसिअवामहत्थाहि धणुम्।।

[ततः सुरहृदयैः समं पतितं विघटमानप्रथमसंस्थितबाणम्।
अदृष्टरिपुविसृष्टशरप्रहाराङ्कुशितवामहस्ताद्धनुः।।]

Thereupon as the spirits of the gods drooped the bow fell from Rāma's hand, crippled by the arrows discharged by the unseen foe; while the arrow fixed aforetime slipped from the bow.

K and Kula read विगलत् (*vialanta*) for *vihalanta* = विघटमान (R). They read *sam̐dhia* (संहित) for *sam̐ṭhia* = संस्थित् (R). K, Kula and MY read राम for वाम (R) in the second line.

MY says रामेण धनुर्न त्यक्तम्। अपि तु विवशात् तस्य करात् स्वयमेवापतदित्याशयः। रिपोरदृश्यत्वकथनमस्य शौर्यक्षतिशङ्कानिरासार्थम्।

30. उद्धाइओ अ सहसा विवलाअविमाणतडिमपच्छिमदेसे।
सुरवहुविसमक्कन्दो एक्कमुहाहअरसन्ततन्तिच्छाओ।।

[उद्धावितश्च सहसा विपलायितविमानतडिमपश्चिमदेशे।
सुरवधूविषमाक्रन्द एकमुखाहतसत्तन्त्रीछायः।।]

All of a sudden the piercing cry of the celestial maidens, like unto the notes of the strings of a lyre sounding in unison, rose in the rear of their fleeing aerial cars.[16]

MY says राघवयोः निर्व्यापारतया पतनात् प्रभृति पलायमानेषु विमानेषूपरितन-प्रवृत्तिजिज्ञासया तज्जघनप्रदेशावस्थितानां विलोकयन्तीनां सुरवधूनां धनुःपतनदर्शनात् युगपदनेकवीणाशब्दोत्थानवत् भयशोकाभ्यामाक्रन्दः समुद्भूत इत्यर्थः।

Kula reads मुक्त (*mukka*) for *visama* in the second line. He says सहसा तत्क्षणं विपलायितानां विमानानां तलिमस्य (?) कुट्टिमस्य पश्चिमदेशे रामावलोकनार्थं विमानपश्चिमभागोत्थिताभिः सुरवधूभिः मुक्त आक्रन्दो रवः एकमुखाहतानां युगपत् ताडितानां रसन्तीनां तन्त्रीणां छाया ध्वनिसादृश्यं यस्य स ऊर्ध्वापितश्च उत्थितः। R says सुरवधूनां विषम आक्रन्द उद्धावित् उत्थितश्च।

[16] They had come to the rear of their cars to watch the happenings below.

31. तो पडिओ रहुणाहो भञ्जन्तो तिहुवणस्स आसाबन्धम्।
सीहणहङ्कुसपहओ तुङ्गं आसण्णपाअवं व वणगओ ।।

[ततः पतितो रघुनाथो भञ्जस्त्रिभुवनस्याशाबन्धम्।
सिंहनखाङ्कुशप्रहतस्तुङ्गमासन्नपादपमिव वनगजः।।]

Thereafter Rāma sank to the ground, shattering the hope of the universe, even as a wild elephant, mauled by the claws of a lion, falls, breaking a tall neighbouring tree.

K, MY and Kula *pratīka* has *aha* for *to* (R). Kula reads रघुतनयः for *rahuṇāho*.

32. पडिअस्स अ रहुवइणो पडिओ अणुमग्गअं सुमित्तातणओ।
उद्धट्ठिअस्स पणओ पल्हत्थस्स व दुमस्स छाआणिवहो।।

[पतितस्य च रघुपतेः पतितोऽनुमार्गं सुमित्रातनयः।
ऊर्ध्वस्थितस्य प्रणतः पर्यस्तस्येव द्रुमस्य छायानिवहः।।]

When Rāma fell, Lakṣmaṇa fell after him, like the reclining shadow in the wake of a lofty tree crashing to the ground.

MY says *paṇao* प्रणतः। तदाश्रित इत्यर्थः। K and Kula read अनुमार्गतः (i.e. *aṇumaggaö* for °*aṁ*). R says पतितस्य रघुपतेरनुमार्गं पश्चात्।

33. धरणिपडिएसु तेसु अ णिव्वण्णन्तसमुहोणअभरुव्वत्ता।
उत्ताणिएक्कचक्का सुराण तंसतडिमा चिरं आसि रहा।।

[धरणिपतितयोस्तयोश्च निर्वर्ण्यमानसंमुखावनतभरोद्वृत्ताः।
उत्तानितैकचक्राः सुराणां तिर्यक्तडिमाश्चिरमासन्रथाः।।]

And when they sank to the ground, the chariots of the gods tarried long (in the sky), lurching under the weight of the occupants as they bent forward and looked on, with one wheel turned upwards, and the side walls turning aslant.[17]

MY says *taṁsa* त्र्यस्र। *āsi* आसन्। निर्वर्णयन्तो भूत्वा संमुखागताः तत्पतनदर्शनेन भयाविग्नाश्चेति विग्रहः। अत्र भयाविग्नत्वं स्थाननिमित्तोपचारात् मञ्चाः क्रोशन्तीतिवत्। उत्तानितैकचक्राः उत्पतनोपक्रमात् ऊर्ध्वमुखैकचक्राः।

MY seems to read *samuhāgaa-bhaāhitthā* for *samuhoṇaa-*

[17] The occupants of the chariots, apparently two-wheeled, had gathered on one side to look down at the battlefield.

bharuvvattā found in R, who says सुराणां रथा निर्वर्ण्यमाने रामलक्ष्मणौ जीवतो न वेति निरूप्यमाणे सति संमुखीभूय अवनतानामधोमुखानाम्, अर्थात् सुराणाम्, भरेण उद्वृत्ता नतोन्नता: चिरमासन्। K's reading is same as MY's.

Kula's reading is same as R's, but he reads *bharakkantā* for *bharuvvattā*. Kula says सुराणां रथा निर्वर्णयतां निरूपयतां संमुखावनतानां भरेण आक्रान्ता:। Kula reads *taṁsa-valiā* (त्र्यस्रवलिता:) for *taṁsa-taḍimā*. R says तिर्यक्तडिमा: तिर्यग्गतपार्श्वभित्तय इत्यर्थ:।

34. हिअअपडणे व्व मूढं रइपडणे व्व सहसा तमम्मि णिवडिअम्।
रामपडणम्मि जाअं सिरपडणे व्व गअजीविअं तेल्लोक्कम्।।

[हृदयपतन इव मूढं रविपतन इव सहसा तमसि निपतितम्।
रामपतने जातं शिर:पतन इव गतजीवितं त्रैलोक्यम्।।]

When Rāma fell, the world was stupefied as when the mental faculties fail. It was suddenly plunged into gloom as at the setting of the sun. It appeared to be bereft of life as when the (severed) head falls to the ground.

K, MY and Kula read निमग्नम् for *ṇivaḍiaṁ* = निपतितम् (R). MY reads *vihalaṁ* (विह्वलम्) for मूढं।

MY says *ṇiūḍḍaṁ* निमग्नम्। हृदयपतनं संज्ञाप्रतिरोध:। तम: तिमिरं शोकश्च। MY (both manuscripts) has *ṇiūḍḍha*, but °*ḍḍa* occurs elsewhere in the poem (10.15; 15.74). Cf. Hemacandra 4.101.

35. अह रामपरित्ताणं सुण्णदिसामुहपलोअणणिरुच्छाहम्।
भअणिच्चलपुञ्जइअं ण मुअइ पडिअं पि राहवं कइसेण्णम्।।

[अथ रामपरित्राणं शून्यादिङ्मुखप्रलोकननिरुत्साहम्।
भयनिश्चलपुञ्जितं न मुञ्चति पतितमपि राघवं कपिसैन्यम्।।]

The host of apes whose security depended on Rāma lost heart as they looked at the directions that seemed to be empty. Paralysed with fear, and huddling together, they did not forsake Rāma, even though he had fallen.

Kula says राम: परित्राणं रक्षा बलं यस्य तत् कपिसैन्यं भयेन . . . भुञ्जीकृतं, etc.

36. दीणं भग्गुच्छाहं उव्विग्गमणं विसाअपेल्लिअहिअअम्।
राहवविइण्णणअणं आलेक्खगअं व संठिअं कइसेण्णम्।।

[दीनं भग्नोत्साहमुद्विग्नमनो विषादप्रेरितहृदयम्।
राघववितीर्णनयनमालेख्यगतमिव संस्थितं कपिसैन्यम्।।]

Dejected, disheartened and anxious, the host of apes kept still as in a picture, their eyes fixed on Rāma, and hearts smitten with grief.

The verse is not found in K, MY and Kula.

37. पडिअस्स वि रहुवइणो दीसन्तो देइ पवअवइसंलावम्।
अविसाअमहग्घविओ सासअधीरधरिओ मुहस्स पसाओ।।

[पतितस्यापि रघुपतेर्दृश्यमानो ददाति प्लवगपतिसंलापम्।
अविषादमहार्धितः शाश्वतधैर्यधृतो मुखस्य प्रसादः।।]

Even though Rāma had fallen, the visible serenity of his face, maintained with abiding fortitude, and highly prized because there was no trace of anguish, assured the host of apes that there was no cause for fear.

MY says रामस्य मुखप्रसादो जीवनाव्यभिचारी प्लवगेभ्यो ददावभयमित्यर्थः। *pavaa-bala-mābhāiṁ* प्लवगबलस्य मा भैरिति वार्ताम्, अभयमिति यावत्। *mahagghavio* महार्घितः। Manuscript A has मा भैषीरिति।

K has बल and अभयम्, and his reading seems to be same as MY's. Kula's reading is also same as that of MY. He says पतितस्यापि रघुपतेरविषादेन महार्घीकृतो बहुमानपात्रीकृतः मुखस्य प्रसादो दृश्यमानः प्लवगबलस्य माभीतिं[18] ददाति। *SC* text has *mābhīiṁ*, but *Deśīnāmamālā* 6.129 says *mābhāī* अभयप्रदानम्, which is also MY's reading.

R's reading is *pavaa-vai saṁlāvaṁ*. He says रघुपतेः मुखस्य प्रसादो दृश्यमानः सन्, अर्थात् सुग्रीवेण, प्लवगपतये सुग्रीवायैव संलापमाश्वासवाक्यं ददाति।

38. णवरि अ विहीसणजलाहअच्छिणा वाणराहिवेण णहअरो।
पासम्मि धणुसहाओ दिट्ठो कअपेसणो दसाणणतणओ।।

[अनन्तरं च विभीषणजलाहताक्षेण वानराधिपेन नभश्चरः।
पार्श्वे धनुःसहायो दृष्टः कृतप्रेषणो दशाननतनयः।।]

Thereupon Sugrīva, whose eyes were spinkled with consecrated water by Vibhīṣana, saw the demon, the son of

[18] This word and पात्रीकृतः have been restored from *SC*.

Rāvaṇa,[19] as he stood close at hand, armed with his bow, having performed the task assigned to him.

K and Kula read *ṇisiaro* for *ṇahaaro* = नभश्चरः (R).

39. तो रोसतुलिअपव्वअसहसुद्धाइअपहाविओ सुग्गीओ।
लङ्कं भअविवलाअं अहिलेऊण णवरं ठिओ रअणिअरम्।।

[ततो रोषतुलितपर्वतसहसोद्धावितप्रधावितः सुग्रीवः।
लङ्कां भयविपलायितमभिलीय केवलं स्थितो रजनीचरम्।।]

Wrathfully lifting up a mountain, Sugrīva sprang up all of sudden and rushed headlong, and halted only after he had chased the demon to Laṅkā as he ran away in fear.

K and MY read अतिनीय for *ahileūṇa* = अभिलीय (R). MY says *aiṇeūṇa* अतिनीय। रजनिचरं लङ्कामतिनीय केवलं स्थितः। न तु क्षणमपि विलम्ब्येत्यर्थः। R says रजनीचरमिन्द्रजितं लङ्कामभिलीय प्रापव्य केवलं स्थितः।

Kula says ततो रोषेण तुलितपर्वतः, क्षणमपि ऊर्ध्वायित उत्थितः, (प्रधावितश्च) सुग्रीवो भयविपलायितं रजनिचरं मेघनादं लङ्कामतिलीय अनन्तरं स्थितः। If Kula's अतिलीय is a mistake for अतिनीय, his reading is same as that of K and MY. *SC* has *ahiṇeūṇa* (अभिनीय)। K, like Kula, has अथ स्थितः, i.e. *ṇavari a ṭhio*, for *ṇavaraṁ ṭhio* = केवलं स्थितः (R). *SC* text has *ṇavara-ṭṭhio* = केवलं स्थितः (*chāyā*).

R says रोषेण तुलितपर्वत उत्तोलितगिरिः सन सहसा उद्धावितः कृतोत्फालः तदनु प्रधावितः।

40. इन्दइणा विणिवेइअराहवणिहणसुहिओ णिसाअरणाहो।
आसाइअजणअसुआसमागमोवाअणिव्वुओ ऊससिओ।।

[इन्द्रजिता विनिवेदितराघवनिधनसुखितो निशाचरनाथः।
आसादितजनकसुतासमागमोपायनिर्वृत उच्छ्वसितः।।]

Gratified at the destruction of the scions of Raghu, as reported by Indrajit, Rāvaṇa cheered up, delighted to have found a means of winning Sītā.

Kula has उल्लासितः for *ūsasio* (उच्छ्वसितः), but it might be a rendering rather than a variant. Kula like R says इन्द्रजिता विनिवेदितेन राघवनिधनेन सुखितो निशाचरनाथः। *SC* takes वि separately — इन्द्रजितापि निवेदितेन, etc.

---

[19] I.e. Indrajit.

41\. अह णिसिअरीहि दहमुहवअणाणिअदिट्ठसरसखणवेहव्वा।
मुक्कक्कन्दविसंठुलदरविलविअमुच्छिआ कआ जणअसुआ।।

[अथ निशिचरीभिर्दशमुखवचनानीतदृष्टसरसक्षणवैधव्या।
मुक्ताक्रन्दविसंष्ठुलदरविलपितमूर्छिता कृता जनकसुता।।]

Thereupon brought to the battlefield by the female demons by Rāvaṇa's command, Sītā witnessed the momentary widowhood[20] that had just befallen her. Beside herself, she wept aloud and swooned away after mourning a while.

MY and Kula read *sarasa diṭṭha* for *diṭṭha*° (R).

MY says दशमुखवचनेन युद्धभुवमानीता सरसदृष्टक्षणवैधव्या चेति विग्रहः। Kula says सरसमभिनवं दृष्टं क्षणं वैधव्यं यया सा जनकसुता। R says सरसं तात्कालिकं क्षणं व्याप्य वैधव्यम्।

42\. तो गअमोहुम्मिल्लो पेच्छन्तो राहवो सुमित्तातणअम्।
परिदेविउं पउत्तो तक्खणपब्भट्ठसअलसीआदुक्खो।।

[ततो गतमोहोन्मीलः प्रेक्ष्यमाणो राघवः सुमित्रातनयम्।
परिदेवितुं प्रवृत्तस्तत्क्षणप्रभ्रष्टसकलसीतादुःखः।।]

Opening his eyes as he regained consciousness, Rāma beheld Lakṣmaṇa and began to lament, forgetting at the moment all his grief for Sītā.

R reads *pabbhaṭṭha*, and says प्रभ्रष्टं विस्मृतं सकलं सीतादुःखं येन। K has प्रमुषित, and Kula प्रस्मृत। MY says प्रस्मृत विस्मृतेत्यर्थः। *SC* (text) and manuscript C of Goldschmidt have *pamhaṭṭha* = प्रमुषित (*SC chāyā*). Manuscript B of MY seems to have *pamhu*°[21] Hemacandra 4.258 says *pamhuṭṭho* प्रमृष्टः प्रमुषितो वा। Cf. Extracts on 6.12.

Kula says उन्मीलितः प्रबुद्धः।

43\. जस्स सअलं तिहुअणं आरुहइ धणुम्मि संसअं आरूढे।
सो वि हओ सोमित्ती णत्थि जए जं ण एइ विहिपरिणामो।।

[यस्य सकलं त्रिभुवनमारोहति धनुषि संशयमारूढे।
सोऽपि हतः सौमित्रिर्नास्ति जगति यं नैति विधिपरिणामः।।]

---

[20] Momentary because Rāma was soon delivered from the serpent arrows, as described below.

[21] The Prākṛt word is missing in the other manuscript.

Even Lakṣmaṇa hath passed away. All the three worlds seemed to be in peril when his bow was strung. None there is in the world whom the sequal of fate doth not reach.

K and Kula read गतः (*gaö*) for *haö* = हतः (R). Kula says गतः अतीतः।

R reads *ṇatthi jae* (नास्ति जगति)। K and MY read जनः (*jaṇo*) for *jae*. Kula reads मन्ये, i.e. *maṇe*. Cf. *SC* (text) and R on 5.20. Hemacandra 2.206, where the line is quoted, has *vaṇe* for *maṇe* in the sense of संभावन–संभाव्यते एतदित्यर्थः।

MY says यस्य धनुषि आरूढे सज्जीकृते त्रैलोक्यं प्राणसंशयमारोहतीत्यन्वयः। नास्ति जन इत्यत्र स इति शेषः। Kula says अतो मन्ये विधिपरिणामो दैवविपाकः यं न ऐति स नास्ति। R says जगति यं विधेरदृष्टस्य परिणामो नैति नागच्छति। *SC* says धनुषि आरूढे आरोपितमौर्वीके।

44. अहवा अं कअकज्जो मज्झ कए मुक्कजीविओ सोमित्ती।
णिप्फलवूढभुअभरो णवर मए च्चेअ लहुइओ अप्पाणो।।

[अथवायं कृतकार्यो मम कृते मुक्तजीवितः सौमित्रिः।
निष्फलव्यूढभुजभरः केवलं मयैव लघूकृत आत्मा।।]

"Or having sacrificed his life for my sake, Lakṣmaṇa hath achieved his task. I alone have humiliated myself, carrying the burden of my arms in vain."

K reads कृतेन for *kae* = कृते (R), and गत for *mukka* = मुक्त (R). MY agrees with K as he says *majjha kaeṇa* मम कृतेन। Kula agrees with R.

MY says *imo* असौ। He seems to read *aha va imo* for *aha vāaṁ* = अथवायम् (R and Kula). Kula says अथवा मम कृते मदर्थं मुक्तजीवितोऽयं सौमित्रिः कृतकार्यः कर्तव्यं कृतमनेनेत्यर्थः।

45. अह जम्पइ सुग्गीवं महुरं उच्छाहदाविअपरिच्छेअम्।
वअणं सहसोवत्थिअमरणावत्थाववट्ठविअगम्भीरम्।।

[अथ जल्पति सुग्रीवं मधुरमुत्साहदर्शितपरिच्छेदम्।
वचनं सहसोपस्थितमरणावस्थाव्यवस्थापितगाम्भीर्यम्।।]

He then spoke to Sugrīva sweet words that showed his appreciation of the latter's martial zeal,[22] and were dignified

[22] See Mādhava in Extracts.

even in the mortal predicament that had suddenly arrived.

Kula says उत्साहस्य दर्शितः परिच्छेदः अवधिः यत्र। तत्क्षणोपस्थितायां मरणावस्थायां व्यवस्थापितं गाम्भीर्यं यत्र तद्वचनं मधुरं मनोहरं सुग्रीवं जल्पति। R says उत्साहेन दर्शितः परिच्छेदो लक्ष्मणेन सहानुमरणे निश्चयो यत्र। वक्तव्यभागपरिच्छेद इति वा। *SC* says उत्साहेन दर्शितः परिच्छेदो रावणवधरूपनिष्पत्तिर्येन।

MY says उत्साह इति सुग्रीवसमरव्यापारानुरूपस्य उत्साहस्य स्वात्मना परिच्छेदो ज्ञानं दर्शितो येन तत् तथा। Manuscript A has . . . व्यापाररूपस्य उत्साहस्य।

46. णिव्वूढं धीर तुमे इमो वि उअहुत्तभुअबलो कइलोओ।
कम्मं इमेण वि कअं जअणिव्वडिअजसदुक्करं मारुइणा।।

[निर्व्यूढं धीर त्वयायमप्युपभुक्तभुजबलः कपिलोकः।
कर्मानेनापि कृतं जगन्निर्वलितयशो दुष्करं मारुतिना।।]

"Wise one, thou hast achieved thy task. These apes, too, have exerted the power of their arms. Yonder Hanumat hath also accomplished an arduous deed of conspicuous renown in the world.

Kula says त्वया निर्व्यूढं यत् प्रतिज्ञातं तत् कृतम्। My says त्वया यत् कर्तव्यं तत् सर्वं निर्व्यूढम्। असावपि कपिलोको रिपुबलभञ्जनात् उपभुक्तभुजबलः।

K and Kula read उपयुक्त for *uahutta* = उपभुक्त (MY and R). Kula says उपयुक्तभुजबलः कृतविक्रमोचितसमरव्यापारः कपिलोकः।

K and MY read *kajjaṁ* for *kammaṁ* (R and Kula). Kula says अनेनापि मारुतिना जगतः पृथग्भूतम् असाधारणं यशो यत्र, तच्च तत् दुष्करं चेति तथाभूतं कर्म कृतम्।

MY reads यथा (*jaha*) for *jaa* = जगत् (R and Kula). MY says यथा अभिव्यक्तयशस्करतया दुष्करं स्यात् तथा अमुना मारुतिनापि कार्यं कृत। मित्यर्थः।

Kula reads वीर for धीर।

47. आबद्धबन्धुवेरं जं मे ण णिआ विभीसणं राअसिरी।
दुक्खेण एण अ महं अविहाविअबाणवेअणरसं हिअअम्।।

[आबद्धबन्धुवैरं यन्मया न नीता विभीषणं राजश्रीः।
दुःखेनैतेन च ममाविभावितबाणवेदनारसं हृदयम्।।]

I could not bring royal fortune to Vibhīṣaṇa who hath incurred the enmity of his kinsmen. Because of this sorrow, my heart doth not feel even the pain caused by these arrows.

K reads दुःखायते तेन मम for *dukkheṇa eṇa a mahaṁ* = दुःखेन एतेन च मम (R and Kula who has तेन)। MY's reading seems to be same as that of K as he says *dukkhāaī* दुःखायते। K and MY read मरण for बाण (R and Kula ?). Kula reads आरब्ध for आबद्ध।

48. ता वच्चसु मा मुज्झसु तुरिअं तेणेअ सेउबन्धेण तुमम्।
पेच्छसु बन्धववग्गं दुक्खं कालस्स जाणिउं परिणामम्॥

[तावद्व्रज मा मुह्य त्वरितं तेनैव सेतुबन्धेन त्वम्।
प्रेक्षस्व बान्धववर्गं दुःखं कालस्य ज्ञात्वा परिणामम्॥]

So lose not heart. Depart quickly by that very causeway, and see your kinsfolk. Hard it is to know the working of fate."

MY and Kula *pratīka* has *taṁ* for *tā* = तावत् (R). Kula says ततस्तस्मात्। K and MY read *pariṇāmo* for *pariṇāmaṁ* (R).

MY says यस्मात् त्वया कृत्यं सर्वं कृतं, दैवात् पुनरीदृशः परिणामः, अतो न प्राणाः त्वया परित्याज्याः, अपि तु स्वदेशस्वबान्धवाश्च द्रष्टव्याः। दुःखं दुष्करमित्यर्थः।

Kula also seems to read *pariṇāmo*. He says दुःखं कालस्य (?) विलासो[23] ज्ञातुमशक्यमित्यर्थः। *SC* says शक्यं श्वमांसादिभिरिति[24] क्षुत् प्रतिहन्तुमिति यत् . . . इति प्राञ्चः (e.g. K and probably Kula)। नव्यास्तु (e.g. R) प्राकृते क्त्वा-तुम्-प्रत्यययोरेकरूपतया वैकल्पिकत्वात् कालस्य परिणामं विरसं ज्ञात्वा मा मुह्य, . . . बान्धववर्गं प्रेक्षस्व दुःखं दुःखितमिति बन्धुवर्गविशेषणं वेत्याहुः। R says कालस्य परिणामं दुःखं दुःखहेतुं ज्ञात्वा। For the construction दुःखं कालस्य परिणामो ज्ञातुम् found in K, MY and probably Kula cf. 1.9. (निर्वोढुं भवति दुष्करं काव्यकथा)।

49. तो तिव्वरोसलङ्घिअविहुआणणदुक्खधरिअबाहुप्पीडो।
रहुवइणो पडिवअणं भणइ अदाऊण वाणरे पवअवई॥

[ततस्तीव्ररोषलङ्घितविधुताननदुःखधृतबाष्पोत्पीडः।
रघुपतेः प्रतिवचनं भणत्यदत्त्वा वानरान्प्लवगपतिः॥]

Thereupon the lord of apes,[25] choked with rage, and checking his tears with an effort as he shook his face, addressed the apes, without answering Rāma.

---

[23] This seems to stand for परिणामः।

[24] This should be श्वमांसादिभिरपि। See काव्यालंकारसूत्रवृत्ति of Vāmana 5.2.23.

[25] Sugrīva.

K, MY and Kula *pratīka* has *aha* (अथ) for *to* = ततः (R). Our copy of Kula has *muha* which is obviously a mistake. *SC* mentions *aha* as a variant.

50. वच्चह लक्खणसहिअं णवपल्लवरइअवीरसअणत्थरणम्।
पावेह वाणरउरिं अविहाविअबाणवेअणं रहुणाहम्।।

[व्रजत लक्ष्मणसहितं नवपल्लवरचितवीरशयनास्तरणम्।
प्रापयत वानरपुरीमविभावितबाणवेदनं रघुनाथम्।।]

"Go, and carry Rāma along with Lakṣmaṇa to the city of the apes[26] as he reclines on a hero's bed, made of fresh leaves, without feeling the pain caused by the arrows.

SC says वीरशय्यापदेन युद्धाभिहतस्य वीरस्य निषदनाय या शय्या साभिधीयते। R says वीरशयने आस्तरणं यस्य तम्।

51. अहअं पि विज्जुपडणाइरित्तसंपाअगहिअपव्विद्धधणुम्।
अद्धोहरिआसाइअवलिअभुअक्खित्तमोडिअगआविहलम्।।

[अहमपि विद्युत्पतनातिरिक्तसंपातगृहीतप्रवृद्धधनुषम्।
अर्धावहृतासादितवलितभुजाक्षिप्तमोटितगदाविह्वलम्।।]

For my part I will seize Rāvaṇa's bow with a pounce swifter than a flash a lightning, and throw it away; and as his mace is about to descend on me[27] I will seize and snatch it from his hand, twisted by me, and make him helpless by breaking it to pieces.

K and MY read आकारित for *āsāia* = आसादित (R and Kula).

MY says विद्युत्पतनातिरिक्तेन संपातेन गृहीतं क्षिप्तं च धनुर्यस्य तम्। अर्धोद्धूरितया, आहूतया, परावर्तितात् भुजादाक्षिप्तया, ततो मोटितया च गदया विह्वलं निश्चेष्टम्। अत्राहूतत्वं नाम यावदाच्छेदयोग्यसमयं व्यापारप्रतिरोधनम्। एवंभूतं करिष्यामि दशमुखमित्यागामिना सम्बन्धः। For the reading *āāria* (आकारित) cf. MY on 13.42 for *oharia* cf. My on 13.55.

Kula reads *vajja* for *vijju*. He says वज्रपतनातिरिक्तेन संपातेन संमुखगमनेन गृहीतं प्रविद्धं क्षिप्तं धनुर्यस्य तम्। अर्धावहृतासादितात् स्तोकव्यापारितप्रासात, वलितादपवृत्तात् (?) भुजादाक्षिप्तया, मोटितया गदया विह्वलं किंकर्तव्यमूढम्। Kula quotation in *SC* has वलितात् अपवर्जितात्। R says अर्धेन अर्धभागेन

[26] Kiṣkindhā

[27] Literally, half brought down.

अवहृतया मदुपरि अवपातितया अथ तदैव मयासादितया करेण धृतया तदनु वलितादामोट्य वक्रीकृतात् रावणस्य भुजादाक्षिप्तया अतिक्रम्य गृहीतया पश्चात् मोटितया भग्नया गदया विह्वलम्।

52. खन्धद्धन्तोवाहिअकरजुअलोलुग्गचन्दहासक्खग्गम्।
अक्कन्तचलणताडिअदलिअरहाहोमुहोसरन्तपहरणम्।।

[स्कन्धार्धान्तापवाहितकरयुगलावरुग्णचन्द्रहासखड्गम्।
आक्रान्तचरणताडितदलितरथाधोमुखापसरत्प्रहरणम्।।]

I will break his *candrahāsa* sword with my hands even as it is plunged into my shoulder, while his weapons with tumble out of his chariot, grabbed, kicked and smashed by me.

MY *pratīka* has *khandhatthamia*. He says स्कन्धास्तमितो हृतश्च चन्द्रहासाख्यः खड्गो मध्ये वितीर्णेन चरणेन मूलाग्रग्राहिभ्यां हस्ताभ्यामवभग्नो यस्य तम्। MY's reading might be *khandhatthamia-hia-majjha-caraṇa-hatthobhagga-candahāsa-khaggaṁ*. K's readings are uncertain. See Goldschmidt's footnote *adloc*.

R and Kula read *khandhaddhantovāhia-kara-jualolugga-candahāsa-kkhaggaṁ* except that Kula reads *obhagga* for *olugga* = अवरुग्ण (R). Kula says (स्कन्धार्धान्ते अर्थात् मदीये *SC*) स्कन्धैकदेशे अवगाहितो विधूतः, करयुगलेन (अर्थात् मदीयेन *SC*) अवभग्नः चन्द्रहासनामा खड्गो यस्य। R says स्कन्धस्य अर्धान्ते अपवाहितः पातितः।

In the second line K and MY read *valia* for *dalia*. MY says प्रथममुत्प्लुतावपतितात्, चरणेन ताडितादत एव वलितादवनमितपार्श्वात् रथात्, etc. Kula says आक्रान्तात्, चरणताडितात्, भग्नात् (i.e. दलितात्) रथात्[28] अधोमुखानि अपसरन्ति प्रहरणानि यस्य तम्। *SC* says आक्रान्तेन दत्तभरेण चरणेन ताडितः सन् दलितो यो रथस्तस्मात्। R says अर्थात् मयैव आक्रान्तादधिष्ठितात्।

53. भग्गपुरिल्लविसंठुलभुअजुअलुक्खुडिअसेसणिप्फलबाहुम्।
वज्जणिहहत्थणिवडन्तदिण्णदढमुट्ठिभिण्णवच्छद्धन्तम्।।

[भग्नपुरोगविसंष्ठुलभुजयुगलोत्खण्डितशेषनिष्फलबाहुम्।
वज्रनिभहस्तनिपतद्दत्तदृढमुष्टिभिन्नवक्षोर्धान्तम्।।]

After his front arms are broken and rendered powerless by me, I will tear off his remaining unavailing arms;[29] and split

---

[28] Our copy has मुखात्!

[29] He had twenty of them.

his chest with a strong and heavy punch,[30] emanating like thunder from my hand.

K, and MY read *°kkhalia* (स्खलित) for *(u)kkhuḍia* = उत्खण्डित (R). Kula reads *°kkhavia*, cf. *SC* text. K, MY and Kula read *garua* for *diṇṇa* (R) in the second line.

MY says *purilla* पुरोगत। भग्नतया विसंष्ठुलेन पुरोगतभुजयुगलेन स्खलिता अपवृत्ताश्च अत एव निष्फलाश्च शेषबाहवो यत्र तम्। वज्रनिभाभिः संघशो निपतन्तीभिः गुर्वीभिः दृढाभिः मुष्टिभिः भिन्नवक्षोऽर्धान्तमित्यर्थः।[31] MY seems to explain *hattha* as संघशः। *Deśīnāmamālā* 8.59 gives the word in the sense of शीघ्र।

Kula says भग्नं . . . यत् भुजयुगलं तेन (हेतुना *SC*) क्षयिता व्याहताः शेषा निष्फला बाहवो यस्य। वज्रनिभस्य (हस्तस्य) निपतता गुरुकेण दृढमुष्टिना भिन्नो वक्षोऽर्धान्तो[32] यस्य तम्। *SC* says वज्रनिभं यथा स्यात् तथा हस्तात् निपतता गुरुकेण मुष्टिना।

54. भुअणिव्वालिअकड्ढिअखुडिअक्केक्कविसरन्तपव्विद्धसिरम्।
णिप्फलसीआसंधिअणक्खुक्खुडिअहिअअं करेमि दहमुहम्।।
(अन्त्यकुलअम्)

[भुजनिर्वालितकृष्टखण्डितैकैकविसरत्प्रवृद्धशिरसम्।
निष्फलसीतासंहितनखोत्खण्डितहृदयं करोमि दशमुखम्।।]
(अन्त्यकुलकम्)

With my hands I will part, pull and sever each of his groaning heads from the body, and dash it down; and with my nails tear out his heart, attached to Sītā in vain.[33]

K and MY *pratīka* has *dhua* for *bhua* (R and Kula). K and Kula read *virasanta* for *visaranta* (MY and R).

MY says *ṇivvāḍia* पृथक्कृत। *pavviddha* प्रविद्ध। धुतेभ्यः शिरोऽन्तरेभ्यः पृथक्कृतमाकृष्टं, त्रुटितं, चैकमेकं विसरच्च, विक्षिप्तं शिरो यस्य तम्।

Kula says भुजाभ्यां पृथक्कृतानि, आकृष्टानि, खण्डितानि, प्रत्येकं रसन्ति आर्तनादं कुर्वन्ति, प्रविद्धानि[34] निक्षिप्तानि शिरासि (यस्य)। निष्फलं . . .

30 Literally, fist.

31 छिन्न . . . B.

32 Our copy has this in neut.

33 Verses 51-54 form a *kulaka*.

34 Our copy has प्रवृत्वानि।

सीतागतमनोरथं नखैः खण्डितं हृदयं यस्य। Kula seems to read *ṇakkha-kkhuḍia* for *ṇakkhu°*. R says नखैरुत्खण्डितम्।

R construes *pavviddha* as प्रवृद्ध। He says विसरन्ति भूमौ पतन्ति प्रवृद्धान्युपचितानि शिरांसि यस्य तम्।

55. इअ अज्जं चेअ मए णिहअम्मि दसाणणे णिआ किक्किन्धम्।
अणुमरिहिइ व मरन्तं दच्छिहि व जिअन्तराहवं जणअसुआ।।

[इत्यद्यैव मया निहते दशानने नीता किष्किन्धाम्।
अनुमरिष्यति वा म्रियमाणं द्रक्ष्यति वा जीवद्राघवं जनकसुता।।]

After Rāvaṇa is thus killed by me even today, Sītā, taken to Kiṣkindhā, shall either see Rāma alive, or die after he is dead."

My says *dacchihi*[35] द्रक्ष्यति। *jīaṁ*[36] *va* जीवन्ते वा। R reads *va jianta-(rāhavaṁ)* = वा जीवद्(राघवम्)। Kula reads जीवितं वा। He seems to read *jīaṁ va* like MY.

SC text has *dacchii* for *dacchihi*.

56. विसहरबाण त्ति इमे विहीसणेण विणिवारिए सुग्गीए।
आढत्तो चिन्तेउं मन्तं हिअएण गारुडं रहुणाओ।।

[विषधरबाणा इतीमे विभीषणेन विनिवारिते सुग्रीवे।
आरब्धश्चिन्तयितुं मन्त्रं हृदयेन गारुडं रघुनाथः।।]

When Sugrīva was held back by Vibhīṣana, saying: "These are serpent arrows", Rāma began to meditate on the mystic formula sacred to Garuḍa.[37]

MY reads *atthaṁ* (अस्रम्) for *mantaṁ* (R and Kula). Kula has हृदये (*hiaammi*) for *hiaeṇa*.

57. णवरि अ सहसुच्छिप्पन्तसाअरद्धन्तधुव्वमाणसुवेलम्।
जाअं खरवाआहअकिरन्तरक्खसकलेवरं धरणिअलम्।।

[अनन्तरं च सहसोत्क्षिप्यमाणसागरार्धान्तधूयमानसुवेलम्।
जातं खरवाताहतकीर्यमाणराक्षसकलेवरं धरणीतलम्।।]

---

[35] B adds अ।

[36] A has *jiaṁ*.

[37] The mythical bird with a human face who destroys serpents and carries Viṣṇu on his back.

Thereupon the Suvela mountain was washed by a portion of the sea stirred up all of a sudden; and the corpses of the demons were scattered by a violent gale.[38]

K and MY read *parinta* for *kiranta* = कीर्यमाण (R).

MY says *dhuvvamāṇa* धाव्यमान। R says दोधूयमानः कम्प्यमानो, धाव्यमानः क्षल्यमानो वा सुवेलो यत्र तादृशम्। MY says *parinta* परियत्। सहसोच्चलता सागरेण धाव्यमानसुवेलं, प्रचण्डपवनानीयमानराक्षसकलेवरं च भूतलं जातमित्यर्थः।

R says खरेण . . . वातेन कीर्यमाणमितस्ततः प्रेर्यमाणं राक्षसानां कलेवरं यत्र तत्। Kula says खरवातेनाहतानि क्षिप्तानि प्रेरितानि त्यक्तजीवितानि राक्षसां कलेवराणि यत्र तथाभूतं धरातलं जातम्। Kula's reading is uncertain, but the manuscript reading of *SC* text is *paritta* which might be a mistake for *parinta* (K and MY) for *kiranta* (R).

58–59. पेच्छइ अ कणअपेहुणबहलुज्जोअपडिसारिअमहातिमिरम्।
णवपिञ्छमनुअपम्हं थिरपित्थिणिहित्तमहुमहासणमग्गम्।।

दुव्वारवासवाउहघाअविमुक्केक्कपिञ्छपाअडवच्छम्।
रामो पाआलच्छिअकण्ठवलन्तट्ठिओरअधरं गरुडम्।।
(जुग्गअम्)

[प्रेक्षते च कनकपिच्छबहलोद्द्योतप्रतिसारितमहातिमिरम्।
नवपिच्छमृदुकपक्ष्माणं स्थिरपृष्ठनिहितमधुमथनासनमार्गम्।।

दुर्वारवासवायुधघातविमुक्तैकपक्षप्रकटवक्षसम्।
रामः पातालाञ्चितकण्ठवलत्स्थितोरगधरं गरुडम्।।]
(युग्मकम्)

Rāma behold Garuḍa. The darkness of the night was dispelled by the pervasive brilliance of his golden feathers. The imprint of Viṣṇu's seat on his firm back was plain to view, being stripped of the down; while the breast was clearly visible with a feather lost under the impact of the irresistible thunderbolt of Indra;[39] and he held a serpent, dragged out of the nether regions, and twined round his neck.

---

[38] The verse describes the advent of Garuḍa, the flapping of whose wings troubles the sea and produces a gale.

[39] A reference to the story of Garuḍa's flight with Indra and the other gods after he had carried off the closely guarded jar of nectar, which the gods eventually got back by conciliating him.

K and Kula read निशा for महा। K, MY and Kula read हृतपिञ्छ-पक्ष्मप्रकटं for *nava-piñcha-maüa-pamhaṁ* = नवपिच्छमृदुकपक्ष्माणम् (R).

MY says पृष्ठे स्थिरनिहितमधुमथनावकाशो हृतपक्ष्मभिः, प्रकटो यस्य तम्। K, MY and Kula seem to read *hia-piñcha-pamha-pāaḍa°*, but MY appears to read *mahumahaṇa-oāsaṁ* for *mahumahāsaṇa-maggaṁ*.

Kula says प्रेक्षते कनकमयस्य पक्षस्य बहलोद्द्योतेन प्रतिसारितनिशातिमिरम् उत्सारितरात्र्यन्धकारम्। घर्षणात् हृतपिञ्छपक्ष्मत्वेन[40] प्रकटश्च स्थिरे पृष्ठे निहितो मधुमथनस्य आसनमार्गो यस्मिन् तं गरुडमिति योज्यम्।

SC has *pecchaṇa* for *pehuṇa* (पिच्छ R)। *SC* says पेच्छणः पक्षे देशी।

MY reads *pāālajjia* = पातालार्जित। This is also the reading of K. R reads *pāālañchia* and says पातालादञ्चितः आकृष्टः।

Kula says पादाकृष्ट(कण्ठं) वलमान(?)स्थितमुरगं धारयन्तं गरुडं रामः प्रेक्षते चेति। Kula seems to read *pāāiñchia*. This is also the manuscript reading of *SC* text. See editor's fn. Hemacandra 4.187 gives *āiñchai* in the sense of कर्षति। He gives *añcai* also in the same sense. Cf. R above. Manuscript C of Goldschmidt has *lañcia*.

MY says वासवायुधघातविमुक्तः वज्रघातेन विगलितः।

60. तो कअरामपणामे गरुडे ओवइअसमुहसंठिअदिट्ठे।
दोह्ण वि मुक्कसरीरा ण विणज्जइ ते कहिं गआ सरणिवहा।।

[ततः कृतरामप्रणामे गरुडेऽवपतितसंमुखसंस्थितदृष्टे।
द्वयोरपि मुक्तशरीरा न विज्ञायते ते कुत्र गता शरनिवहाः।।]

Thereupon as Garuḍa bowed to Rāma, and was beheld by him as he alighted on the ground and stood before him, the serpent arrows left the bodies of both Rāma and Lakṣmaṇa. None knew whither they were gone.

K and MY read निष्ठित (*ṇiṭṭhia*) for *saṁṭhia* = संस्थित (R). MY says संमुखनिष्ठितदृष्टे संमुखावस्थिते दृष्टे इत्यर्थः। Kula's reading is uncertain. He says संमुखस्थितदृष्टे।

61. अह सरबन्धविमुक्को विणआतणओवऊहणक्खअरहिओ।
अप्पाहिअत्थमन्तो जाओ गअगरुडदारुणो रहुणाहो।।

---

[40] Our copy read कृत for हृत as it often does. *SC* also has कृत, but it does not give any meaning.

[अथ शरबन्धविमुक्तो विनतातनयोपगूहनक्षतरहितः।
अध्यापितास्त्रमन्त्रो जातो गतगरुडदारुणो रघुनाथः।।]

Delivered from the grip of the arrows, Rāma was healed as he embraced Garuḍa. Instructed by the latter in the mystic formula that was a weapon against serpents, he attained irresistible strength after Garuḍa had taken his leave.

The verse is not found in Kula and *SC*.

R reads *appāhiattha-manto* = अध्यापितास्त्रमन्त्रः। K reads आभाषितव्यशान्तः। Goldschmidt's suggestion that आभाषितव्य stands for *appāhiavva* is corroborated by My who, however, reads *avvāhiavvasanto* rendered as व्याहृतेन प्रशान्तः।[41] Hemacandra 4.180 gives *appāhai* as an equivalent of संदिशति which also suits the sense. See Extracts on 10.74, 75.

MY says गतगरुडदारुणः गतेन गरुडेन दारुणः दुःसहः गरुडापगमे परैः दुःसहवीर्यो जात इत्यर्थः।

62. अह सरबन्धविमुक्के सोऊण णिसाअराहिवो रहुणाहे।
आअअगरुडासङ्को धुम्मक्खम्मि सअलं णिमेइ रणभरम्।।

[अथ शरबन्धविमुक्तौ श्रुत्वा निशाचराधिपो रघुनाथौ।
आगतगरुडाशङ्को धूम्राक्षे सकलं नियोजयति रणभरम्।।]

Thereupon hearing that the scions of Raghu were rid of the arrows, Rāvaṇa who apprehended danger from Garuḍa entrusted Dhūmrākṣa with entire conduct of the war.

K and Kula read *rahu-taṇae* (रघुतनयौ) for °*ṇāhe* (°नाथौ) found in R.

MY says *ṇimei* न्याधात्। K and *SC chāyā* have निदधाति। Kula says निमिनोति निदिशति।[42] R renders it as नियोजयति।

63. सो रोसेण रहेण व उच्छाहेण व णिसाअरबलेण समम्।
णीइ भुअं व पहरिसं वहमाणो विक्कमं व वेरावन्धम्।।

---

[41] B has अव्याहृतेन which is a scribal error, MY's *avvāhiavva* seems to be a mistake for *appā*°. In his gloss on 10.74 he says *appāhijjaï* व्याह्रियत, while K has आभाष्यते स्म। In 10.75 MY explains *appāhento* as व्याहरन्।

[42] Our copy has निदशति।

[स रोषेण रथेनेवोत्साहेनेव निशाचरबलेन समम्।
निरैति भुजमिव प्रहर्षं वहमानो विक्रममिव वैराबन्धम्।।]

He sallied forth, prompted by rage, just as he was carried along by his chariot. He was imbued with zeal, just as he was accompanied by the host of demons. He kept up his spirits just as he held his banner aloft; and carried his weapons, just as he harboured rancour against the enemy.

K and MY read ध्वजम् (*dhaaṁ*) for *bhuaṁ* = भुजम् (R). *SC* has *dhaaṁ*, and this might be Kula's reading also, though our copy has रुद्धम् which is corrupt.

Kula and MY have *paharaṇaṁ* for *vikkamaṁ* (R).

MY says यथा रथेन युद्धभुवं नीयते तथा रोषेणापि। यथा चोत्साहः प्राणसंशयेऽपि एनं न जहाति तथा युद्धशिरसि सहायभूतं राक्षसबलमपि। ध्वजो यथा स्यात् साधारणं चिह्नं तद्वत् प्रहर्षोऽपि। यथा रिपुवधार्थमायुधमुपादत्ते तथा बन्धुवधजनितं वैरमपि इत्येषामुपमानोपमेयभावोऽनुसंधेयः। R says यथा विक्रमं तथा वैराबन्धमपि वहमान इति सर्वत्र सहोपमा।

64. तो सो रक्खसणिवहो सह धुम्मक्खेण साअरद्धन्तणिहो।
वडवामुहाणलस्स व संचरणपहम्मि मारुअसुअस्स ठिओ।।

[ततः स राक्षसनिवहः सह धूम्राक्षेण सागरार्धान्तनिभः।
वडवामुखानलस्येव संचरणपथे मारुतसुतस्य स्थितः।।]

As the host of demons, resembling a stretch of sea, confronted Hanumat along with Dhūmrākṣa, it seemed to come face to face with the submarine fire.[43]

SC (text) has वलवा for वडवा। Similarly, it reads गरुल for गरुड in verses 59 and 62. Verse numbers differ somewhat in *SC*. See printed text.

R says संचरणपथे संमुखे।

65. अह दारुणावसाणे कइरक्खससेण्णवइअरम्मि पअत्ते।
संभारिअक्खणिहणो ओत्थरइ सरेहिं मारुइं धुम्मक्खो।।

[अथ दारुणावसाने कपिराक्षससैन्यव्यतिकरे प्रवृत्ते।
संस्मृताक्षनिधनोऽवस्तृणाति शरैर्मारुतिं धूम्राक्षः।।]

---

[43] The black colour of the demons is contrasted with the red hair of Hanumat.

As the fatal encounter between the hosts of demons and apes began Dhūmrākṣa, reminded of Akṣa's[44] death, covered Hanumat with arrows.

MY says सैन्यव्यतिकरे सैन्ययोमिथःसंमेलने युद्ध इति यावत्। He and R render *saṁbhāria* as संस्मृत। Kula has संस्मारित।

MY says दारुणं घोरमवसानं विनिपातो यत्र तस्मिन्। R says दारुणमवसानं यस्य।

66. तो तस्स सरणिघाए रोमन्तरलग्गणिप्फले धुअमाणो।
अक्कमणमोडिअरहो हिअधुम्मक्खधणुसंठिओ हसइ कई।।

[ततस्तस्य शरनिघातान्रोमान्तरलग्ननिष्फलान्धुन्वानः।
आक्रमणमोटितरथो हृतधूम्राक्षधनुःसंस्थितो हसति कपिः।।]

Thereafter the ape as he shook off the ineffectual arrows, stuck fast in the hair on his body, swooped down on Dhūmrākṣa's chariot and smashed it; snatched his bow from him, and leaning thereon, mocked at the demon.

Kula says शरनिघातान् बाणसमूहान्। MY says रोमान्तरलग्नेत्यनेन शराणां भूयस्त्वेऽपि कुण्ठत्वं द्योत्यते। धूम्राक्षशरवर्षमगणयित्वैव तद्रथमवपतनरभसेनैव भंक्त्वा तत्क्षणात् तद्धनुराच्छिद्य पूर्ववदाकाशस्थो हनुमान् जहासेत्यर्थः। Kula says हृतधूम्राक्षधनुः संस्थितः (सम्यक्स्थितः *SC*) हसति कपिः। R says हृतमाच्छिद्य गृहीतं यत् धूम्राक्षस्य धनुः तत्र संस्थितः[45] हसति।

67. भग्गो भुअम्मिं फलिहो वच्छुच्छलिअदलिअं ण दट्ठं मुसलम्।
धुम्मक्खरोसमुक्कं पवअस्स जहिं तहिं विराइ पहरणम्।।

[भग्नो भुजे परिघो वक्षउच्छ्वलितदलितं न दृष्टं मुसलम्।
धूम्राक्षरोषमुक्तं प्लवगस्य यत्र तत्र विशीर्यति प्रहरणम्।।]

The club broke on Hanumat's arm; and the mace, rebounding from his breast, was shattered and seen no more. The weapons wielded by Dhūmrākṣa in his wrath, flew in pieces wherever they fell on the body of the ape.

Goldschmidt and *SC* (text) read *iṭṭhaṁ* (दृष्टम्)। N.S. edition has *daṭṭhaṁ*.

---

[44] Rāvaṇa's son killed Hanumat during the burning of Laṅkā.

[45] *Dhaṇu-saṁṭhia* seems to be an expression like *dhaṇu ṇisaṇṇa* used in *Gāthāsaptaśatī* 2.16, Gaṅgādhara says in his commentary — धनुषि निषण्णाः क्षितितलनिहिताटनीकं धनुरवलम्ब्य स्थिताः। See N.S. edn. 1889. This idiom occurs in Bhāravi 14, 37 : निषण्णमापत्प्रतिकारकारणे शरासने।

MY says *virāi* व्यलीयत। Kula has विशीर्यते।

68–69. तो दीहवामकरअलपडिवण्णावेढणोणअगलुद्देसम्।
रुम्भन्तजीवणिग्गमवच्छब्भन्तरभमन्तसीहणिणाअम्।।

खणवावारिविसंठुलगलन्तपहरणपलम्बिओहअहत्थम्।
कुणइ पभञ्जणतणओ उद्धुट्ठिअमुक्कजीविअं धुम्मक्खम्।।
(जुग्गअम्)

[ततो दीर्घवामकरतलप्रतिपन्नावेष्टनावनतगलोद्देशम्।
रुध्यमानजीवनिर्गमवक्षोभ्यन्तरभ्रमत्सिंहनिनादम्।।

क्षणव्यापारिविसंष्ठुलगलत्प्रहरणप्रलम्बितोभयहस्तम्।
करोति प्रभञ्जनतनय ऊर्ध्वोत्थितमुक्तजीवितं धूम्राक्षम्।।]
(युग्मकम्)

The son of the Wind God[46] then slew Dhūmrākṣa even as the latter stood erect, having pressed down his neck with the outstretched left hand. A roar like that of a lion, vibrating within the demon's breast, died away as it issued by degrees; while both his hands, stirring for a moment, became languid and drooped with the weapons slipping out of them.

K, Kula and MY read आपीडन for *āveḍhaṇa* = आवेष्टन (R). Kula says ततो दीर्घवामकरतलप्रतिपन्नेन आपीडनेन अवनतगलोद्देशम्। MY says दीर्घत्वं प्रसारितत्वम्। अनादरात् वामेनैव प्रसारितेन करतलेन निर्वर्तितात् आपीडनात् अवनतो (?) गलप्रदेशो (यस्य तम्)। My seems to read *ṇivvatta* for *paḍivaṇṇa*.

K and *SC* text read क्षीयमाणतलिननिर्गत (*jhijjanta-taliṇa-ṇiggaa*) for *rumbhanta-jiva-ṇiggama* = रुध्यमानजीवनिर्गम found in R. MY's reading appears to be same as that of K as he has अल्पनिर्गत। The Prākr̥t equivalent is corrupt in our copy, but it might be *taṇua-ṇiggaa*. Kula also says क्षीयमाणः तनुनिर्गतः वक्षसोऽभ्यन्तरे भ्रमन् सिंहनादो यस्य तम्। R says कण्ठस्य मोटित्वात् रुध्यमानो जीवनिर्गमस्तेन हेतुना वक्षोऽभ्यन्तरे भ्रमन् सिंहनिनादो यस्य तम्।

Kula reads व्यापृत, and MY व्यापारित for *vāvāri* = व्यापारिन् found in R. Manuscript C of Goldschmidt has *vāvaria*, while *SC* text has

[46] Hanumat.

vāvaḍia. Kula says क्षणं व्यापृतौ, . . . गलत्प्रहरणौ, प्रलम्बितौ उभौ हस्तौ यस्य। MY says क्षणं व्यापारितौ, पुनः परवशौ, गलदायुधौ, प्रचलितौ (?) चोभौ हस्तौ यस्य तम्।

K, MY and Kula read *uddha-ṭṭhia* for °*ddhu*° (R). MY says ऊर्ध्वस्थितदशायामेव मुक्तजीवितं न तु पतितदशायामित्यर्थः। R says ऊर्ध्वमुत्थितं गतं सत् मुक्तं त्यक्तं जीवितं येन तादृशम्।

70. अह पडिए धुम्मक्खे हअसेसम्मि अ गए णिसाअरसेण्णे।
दहमुहसमुहाणत्तं णिन्तं पेच्छइ अकम्पणं पवणसुओ।।

[अथ पतिते धूम्राक्षे हतशेषे च गते निशाचरसैन्ये।
दशमुखसंमुखाज्ञप्तं निर्यन्तं प्रेक्षतेऽकम्पनं पवनसुतः।।]

When Dhūmrākṣa fell, and the surviving *rākṣasa* troops withdrew, Hanumat saw Akampana coming out of Laṅkā, directly commanded by Rāvaṇa.

Kula reads निहते (*ṇihae*) for *paḍie* (पतिते)। K reads आयान्तम् (*entaṁ*) for *ṇintaṁ* = निर्यन्तम् R; निर्यान्तम् (Kula).

MY says दशमुखसंमुखाज्ञप्तमिति समरप्रेषणलाभाय स्वयमेव संमुखस्थिततया दशमुखेन प्रेषितमित्यर्थः।

71. तं पि विइण्णोरत्थलवीसत्थोहरिअणिट्ठिआउहणिवहम्।
ओसुम्भइ हणुमन्तो एक्केक्कक्खुडिअविप्पइण्णावअवम्।।

[तमपि वितीर्णोरःस्थलविश्वस्तावहृतनिष्ठितायुधनिवहम्।
अवपातयति हनूमानेकैकखण्डितविप्रकीर्णावयवम्।।]

Hanumat slew him too, tearing asunder his limbs one by one, and scattering them about; while he destroyed the weapons confidently brought down by the demon on his proffered breast.

MY says *ṇiṭṭhia* निष्ठित समापितेति यावत्।

R says वितीर्णं प्रहारायाग्रे कृत्वा दत्तं यदुरःस्थलं हनूमतेत्यर्थात् तत्र। Kula says विकीर्णे प्रसारिते (उरःस्थले) विश्वस्तमवहृतो व्यापारितो, निष्ठितो नष्ट (?) आयुधनिवहो यस्य तम्। प्रत्यकं खण्डितो वि(प्र)कीर्णः अवयवो (यस्य तं) हनूमान् पातयति[47]। R says निष्ठितः शतखण्डीभूय विनष्टः।

---

[47] Our copy has पतति। Besides, विकीर्णे is from *SC*. विभिन्नैः in our copy is corrupt.

72. अह दहमुहसंदिट्ठो हणुमन्ताघाअसमतुलग्गप्फिडिओ।
पडिओ णीलस्स मुहे अलद्धसमरसुहदूमिअस्स पहत्थो।।

[अथ दशमुखसंदिष्टो हनूमदाघातसमतुलाग्रस्फेटितः।
पतितो नीलस्य मुखेऽलब्धसमरसुखदुःखितस्य प्रहस्तः।।]

Thereafter ordered by Rāvaṇa to fight, Prahasta, who had escaped from a trial of strength with Hanumat in single combat, chanced to come face to face with Nīla,[48] who was unhappy because he had not had the pleasure of fighting

My says आघातः युद्धम्। समतुलाग्रं समप्रतिद्वन्द्वम्। तेन हनूमता सह युद्धे द्वन्द्वात् भ्रष्टः। अथवा हनूमता स्वस्य आघाते[49] वधे प्राप्ते तत्क्षणं भ्रष्ट इत्यर्थः। In the alternative explanation *sama-tulagga* is rendered as तत्क्षणम्। Cf. MY on 7.39, 6.23. R says हनूमत्कृतादाघातात् समतुलाग्रेण काकतालीयसंवादसाम्येन दैवात् स्फेटितो बहिर्भूतः प्रहस्तो नाम राक्षसः। Cf. Muda on 4.27.

Kula says अथ दशमुखेन संदिष्टः, हनूमदाघात एव समतुलाग्रं परीक्षार्थं समीकृततुलाग्रसदृशं, तत्रारूढस्य संशयास्पदत्वात्, तस्मात् स्फिटितो भ्रष्टः[50] . . . अलब्धसमरसुखत्वेन व्यथितस्य नीलस्य मुखे प्रहस्तः पतितः।

Śrīnivāsa's explanation quoted by *SC* is far-fetched — हनूमदाघातसमात् तुलाग्रात् दैवात् भ्रष्टः। यथा हनूमत्कृताघातात् तथा दैवात् निजभागधेयादपि स्खलित इत्यर्थः।

73. णवरि अ पत्थाणे च्चिअ बाणो कालाअसो पहत्थविमुक्को।
पडिओ णीलस्स उरे वणपडिभिण्णरुहिरुग्गमेण पिसुणिओ।।

[अनन्तरं च प्रस्थान एव बाणः कालायसः प्रहस्तविमुक्तः।
पतितो नीलस्योरसि व्रणप्रतिभिन्नरुधिरोद्गमेन पिशुनितः।।]

Thereupon as Nīla rushed at Prahasta an iron arrow, discharged by the latter, hit the former's bosom, and marked by the blood spurting out from the wound.

K and Kula read प्रस्थानसमम् (*patthāṇa-samaṁ*) for *patthāṇe ccia* = प्रस्थाने एव (R).

---

[48] One of the leaders of the apes.

[49] स्वाघाते B.

[50] Partly corrected from quotation in *SC* where केचित् refers to Kula.

Kula says अनन्तरं प्रस्थानसमं गमनसमकालं प्रहस्तेन मुक्तः कालायसः कृष्णलौहघटितो बाणः नीलस्योरसि पतितः समानवर्णतया दुर्लक्षः व्रणात् प्रतिभिन्नेन गलितेन रुधिरोद्गमेन पिशुनितः सूचितः।

74. वेओवत्तिअविडवं मुअइ कई वि सुरहत्थिपरिमलसुरहिम्।
गइमग्गलग्गभमलं पडिसोत्तपसारिअंसुअं कप्पदुमम्।।

[वेगापवर्तितविटपं मुञ्चति कपिरपि सुरहस्तिपरिमलसुरभिम्।
गतिमार्गलग्नभ्रमरं प्रतिस्रोतःप्रसारितांशुकं कल्पद्रुमम्।।]

The ape, too, hurled at Prahasta a *kalpa* tree, fragrant with the ichor of the celestial elephants that rubbed their shoulders against it; with the bees following in its wake, and branches bent back by the speed, and scarves streaming backwards (in the wind).[51]

K reads प्रतिपथ (*paḍivantha*) for *paḍisotta* = प्रतिस्रोतः (R and Kula ?).

Kula says वेगापवर्तितविटपं[52] वेगेन पश्चादावर्जितशाखं (?), सुरहस्तिनः परिमलेन सुरगजस्य मदकण्डूकषणेन (?) सुरभिम्, अत एव गतिमार्गेण लग्नभ्रमरं, प्रतिस्रोतोगतं (?) विपरीतं प्रसारितांशुकं कल्पद्रुमं नीलो (?)मुञ्चति। R says प्रतिस्रोतसा पश्चाद्वर्त्मना प्रसारितमंशुकं वस्त्रं यस्य। वेगमारुतेन इत्यर्थात्। SC says प्रतिस्रोतोगतानि विपरीतप्रसारितानि अंशुकानि यस्य।

75. वोलन्तजलहरस्स व तो से आसारजललवत्थवअणिहो।
आगममग्गम्मि ठिओ धुअविडवक्खलिअमोत्तिआफलणिवहो।।

[व्यतिक्रामज्जलधरस्येव ततोऽस्यासारजललवस्तबकनिभः।
आगममार्गे स्थितो धुतविटपस्खलितमुक्ताफलनिवहः।।]

All along the track of the tree as it came pearls dropped from the swaying branches, resembling drops of rain from a passing cloud.

SC text has *bolenta* for *volanta* (K, R and Kula) = व्यतिक्रामत्। Goldschmidt reads *bolanta*.

R reads *thavaa* (स्तबक) in the first line. K and *SC* text read *chea* (छेद)। Kula has बिन्दु। *SC* says जललवानां छेदनिभो बिन्दुसदृशः। Usually

---

[51] Cf. 9.25 and 82 where white scarves are described as hanging from the *kalpa* creepers, explained as branches of the all-giving *kalpa* trees.

[52] *SC* has अववर्तित।

K has बिन्दु for R's *thavaa* leading to the reading *theva*. See notes on 1.40 and 15.43.

K reads *mottia-pphala* (*SC* text also) for *mottiā-phala* = मुक्ताफल (R). Kula reads *mottia-dala*. K and Kula read प्रकर: (*paaro*) for *ṇivaho* (R). Kula reads खण्डित (*khuḍia*, cf. *SC* text) for *khalia* = स्खलित।

Kula says ततस्तस्य कल्पपादपस्य . . . आगमनपथे व्यतिक्रामतो जलधरस्येव आसारजललवानाम् उद्गलितबिन्दुसदृश:, धुतेभ्य: विटपेभ्य: खण्डित: च्युतो मौक्तिकदलप्रकर: (i.e. *mottia-dala-ppaaro*) स्थित:।

76. तो तस्स भुअविमुक्को भग्गो वणभरिअमोत्तिअप्फलवअरो।
भज्जन्तविडवविअलिअसिअंसुआवीअपहररुधिरम्मि उरे।।

[ततस्तस्य भुजविमुक्तो भग्नो व्रणभृतमौक्तिकफलप्रकर:।
भज्यमानविटपविगलितसितांशुकापीतप्रहाररुधिरे उरसि।।]

The tree, hurled by Nīla's arms, crashed on Prahasta's bosom, filling the wounds with pearls; while the flow of blood caused by the impact was absorbed by the white scarves slipping off the broken branches.[53]

Kula reads *bhaa-vimukke* for *bhua-vimukko* = भुजविमुक्त:। He reads °मौक्तिकदलप्रकर: in the locative for °*mottia-pphala-vaaro* = °मौक्तिकफलप्रकर:।

Kula says स कल्पद्रुम: तस्य प्रहस्तस्य भयविमुक्ते भयरहिते, भज्यमानेभ्यो विटपेभ्यो विगलितै: वृष्टै: सितांशुकैरापीतप्रहाररुधिरे, व्रणेषु भृतो मौक्तिकदलप्रकरो यत्र तस्मिन् उरसि भग्न:।[54]

MY says सितांशुकापीत सितांशुकचूषित (शोषित A)।

77. समअं वञ्चेइ सरे थएइ समअं कई दुमेहिं णहअलम्।
समअं तेण विमुक्को चउद्दिसं पाअडो सिलासंघाओ।।

[समं वञ्चयति शरान्स्थगयति समं कपिर्द्रुमैर्नभस्तलम्।
समकं तेन विमुक्तश्चतुर्दिशं प्रकट: शिलासंघात:।।]

The ape evaded Prahasta's arrows, and covered the sky with trees all at once; while at the same time the boulders hurled

[53] See verse 74.

[54] Several words have been corrected from *SC*.

by him appeared in the four quarters of the sky.

R and Kula read *pāaḍo* (प्रकट:)। MY has *vāvaḍo* rendered as व्यावृत: (B)[55].

78. विअलन्तदुमच्छेआ सरघाअदलन्तविअलिअसिलाणिवहा।
दीसन्ति दलिअपव्वअवोच्छिज्जन्तोज्झरा णहअलुद्देसा।।

विगलद्दुमच्छेदा: शरघातदलद्विगलितशिलानिवहा:।
दृश्यन्ते दलितपर्वतव्यवच्छिद्यमाननिर्झरा नभस्तलोद्देशा:।।]

The regions of the sky were seen to fill with crumbling boulders split by the arrows, and falling fragments of severed trees, and cascades cut-off from the mountains riven asunder.[56]

Kula reads विघटित (*vihaḍia*, cf. *SC* text) for *vialia* = विगलित (R). Manuscript C of Goldschmidt has *vihalia*.

Kula says शरघातै: दलन्तो विदीर्यन्तो विघटिता: शिलानिवहा येषु। दलितेभ्य: पर्वतेभ्यो (व्यव)च्छिद्यमाना निर्झरा येषु ते तथाभूता नभ:स्थलोद्देशा दृश्यन्ते।

79. गिरिधाउरअक्खउरो अंसविपल्हत्थबहकेसरणिवहो।
संझाअवविच्छुरिओ सजलो व्व घणो णहम्मि दीसइ णीलो।।

[गिरिधातुरज:कलुषोऽसविपर्यस्तबहलकेसरनिवह:।
संध्यातपविच्छुरित: सजल इव घनो नभसि दृश्यते नील:।।]

Nīla appeared in the sky, with his body coloured by the dust of the red earth of the mountains (hurled by him), and the shaggy mass of his hair scattered over his shoulders; he looked like a rain-cloud[57] suffused with the glow of the evening sky.

Kuaüra is rendered as मिश्रकलुष by Kula. R says गैरिकरजोभि: कलुष: कर्बुरित:।

80. णवरि अ गअणद्धन्ते ओवडणक्खित्तधणुणिअत्तत्थिमिओ।
तह धरिओ विअ दीसइ पढमविमुक्केहि सरसमूहेहि कई।।

---

[55] A is corrupt and has व्याप्नुवता। B adds प्रावृत:।

[56] The verse describes how the trees, stones and mountains hurled by Nīla were cut up by Prahasta's arrows.

[57] There is a hint at the literal meaning of his name Nīla.

[अनन्तरं च गगनार्धान्तेऽवपतनाक्षिप्तधनुर्निवृत्तस्तिमितः।
तथा धृत इव दृश्यते प्रथमविमुक्तैः शरसमूहैः कपिः॥]

The ape then swooped down on Prahasta's bow and snatched it from him; and as he returned and stood still in the sky, he seemed to be held up by the arrows discharged before by the demon.

MY says अवपतनाक्षिप्तधनुर्भूत्वा पुनर्निवृत्तस्थित इत्यर्थः।

Kula says अनन्तरं च गगनोद्देशे अवपतनेन छिन्नधनुः (आच्छिन्न° ?) निवृत्तस्तिमितः अपसृत(?)निश्चलश्च, तथा प्रथमविमुक्तैः शरसमूहैः धूत (धृत ?) इव कपिः नीलो दृश्यते।

R and MY have धृतः (*dhario*). According to Goldschmidt, K (*chāyā*) also has धृत, but the commentary has छादित which points to *vario* = वृतः found in *SC* text and *chāyā*.

81. अह णिसिअरेण मुसलं णीलस्स ललाटवट्टपच्चुप्फलिअम्।
मज्झम्मि धरेन्तरवं समुहागअतुरिअवञ्चिअं पडिवण्णम्॥

[अथ निशिचरेण मुशलं नीलस्य ललाटपट्टप्रत्युत्फलितम्।
मध्ये ध्रियमाणरवं संमुखागतत्वरितवञ्चितं प्रतिपन्नम्॥]

The club, which Prahasta next hurled at Nīla, rebounded from the latter's forehead, and was caught by the demon midway, with a roar, quickly evading it as it came towards him.[58]

SC text has *ṇaḍāla* for ललाट (R text).

K and Kula read *mutta* for *vaṭṭa* = पट्ट (R). K and MY read *paccupphiḍiaṁ* = प्रत्युद्भ्रष्टम् for *paccupphaliaṁ* = प्रत्युत्फलितम् (R and Kula).

Kula reads भज्यमान (*bhajjanta*, cf. *SC* text) for *majjhammi* = मध्ये (R and MY). Kula and MY read *dharanta* explained differently for *dharenta* = ध्रियमाण (R).

MY says *dharanta-ravaṁ* ध्रियमाणरवम्। संमुखागतत्वरितवञ्चितं मुसलं मध्ये प्रतिपन्नं गृहीतमित्यर्थः।

Kula says अथ निशाचरेण प्रहस्तेन नीलस्य करमुक्तं (ललाटे मुक्तं ? cf. *SC*) सत् प्रत्युत्फलितं प्रतीपीभूय उत्पतितं भज्यमानस्य (धरान्तस्य) पर्वतैकदेशस्येव रवो यस्य तत् तथाभूतं, संमुखागतं त्वरितवञ्चितम् अङ्गीकृत्य शीघ्रपरिहृतं (मुसलं) प्रतिपन्नं गृहीतम्। R says नीलस्य ललाटपट्टात् प्रत्युत्फलितम्।

[58] I.e. to avoid being hit by his own weapon.

SC says श्रीनिवासस्तु वज्रेण अन्तो नाशो यस्य एवंभूतस्य धरस्य अन्तः स्वरूपं समरवमित्याह, i.e. he reads *vajjanta-dharanta-ravaṁ* for *bhajjanta-dharanta°* (Kula).

82. गेण्हइ अ जलणतणओ सुवेलसिहरद्धलग्गमेहच्छाअम्।
विअडपहत्थोरत्थलसमबित्थारकढिणत्तणं कसणसिलम्।।

[गृह्णाति च ज्वलनतनयः सुवेलशिखरार्धलग्नमेघच्छायाम्।
विकटप्रहस्तोरःस्थलसमविस्तारकठिनत्वां कृष्णशिलाम्।।]

Thereupon the son of the Fire God[59] took up a black rock, resembling a cloud resting upon a peak of the Suvela, and broad and hard as Prahasta's massive chest.

Kula says सुवेलस्य शिखरार्धे मग्नस्य (लग्नस्य) मेघस्येव छाया यस्याः . . . तां कृष्णशिलां ज्वलनतनयो नीलो गृह्णाति च।

83. दूरसमुप्पइएण अ णीलेण सिलाअलोत्थअम्मि दिणअरे।
जाओ णहम्मि दिअसो तक्खणबद्धतिमिरा महिअलम्मि णिसा।।

[दूरसमुत्पतितेन च नीलेन शिलातलावस्तृते दिनकरे।
जातो नभसि दिवसस्तत्क्षणबद्धतिमिरा महीतले निशा।।]

As Nīla sprang high into the air, and shut out the sun with the rock, it was day in the sky and at the same moment murky night on the earth.

Kula seems to say (शिलातलेन) अवस्थगिते समाच्छादिते दिनकरे। He appears to read *otthaie* for *otthaammi* (अवस्तृते) found in R and *SC* text and *chāyā*. *SC* commentary has अवस्थगिते like Kula. For *atthaie* cf. 11.59.

MY says दिवसो नभसि जातः नभस्येव जात इत्यर्थः।

84. अह णीलस्स पहत्थो रणाणुराएण सहिअगाढप्पहरो।
घाअब्भन्तरभिण्णो गलन्तजीअरुहिरो गओ धरणिअलम्।।

[अथ नीलस्य प्रहस्तो रणानुरागेण सोढगाढप्रहारः।
घाताभ्यन्तरभिन्नो गलज्जीवरुधिरो गतो धरणितलम्।।]

Having endured Nīla's powerful blow[60] by virtue of his

[59] Nīla.

[60] I.e. the impact of the rock hurled by Nīla.

martial zeal, Prahasta, shattered by the shock[61] resulting from the injury, became unconscious and sank to the ground.

R reads *ghāabbhantara-bhiṇṇo galanta-jīa-ruhiro gaö dharaṇi-alaṁ* = घाताभ्यन्तरभिन्नो गलज्जीवरुधिरो गतो धरणितलम्। K and Kula seem to read *ghāabbhantara-saṁkhoha-bhiṇṇa-galia-hiaö gaö*, etc. This reading is found also in *SC* text.

Kula says अथ नीलस्य प्रहस्तो रणानुरागेण सोढगाढप्रहार:, घातस्य अभ्यन्तरे संक्षोभेण पीडाभरेण भिन्नं विदीर्णं गलितं व्यपगतं हृदयं वक्षो मनश्च यस्य स तथाभूतो धरणीतलं गत:।

MY's reading appears to be same as that of K and Kula as he says गलितहृदयो विसंज्ञ इत्यर्थ:।

R says घातेन शिलाभिघातेन अभ्यन्तरे भिन्न: चूर्णो बहि: क्षताभावात्। तत एव च गलत् बहिर्भवत् जीव: प्राणस्तद्रूपं रुधिरं यस्य तादृक्।

इअ सिरिपवरसेणविरइए कालिदासकए दहमुहवहे महाकव्वे
चउदहो आसासओ समत्तो।

[इति श्रीप्रवरसेनविरचिते कालिदासकृते दशमुखवधे महाकाव्ये
चतुर्दश आश्वासक: समाप्त:।]

---

[61] Literally internal disturbance. The reading of Kṛṣṇa and Kulanātha is followed. According to Rāmadāsa's reading (see Extracts): Prahasta, shattered within by the impact, sank to the ground as his life-blood oozed away.

पञ्चदश आश्वासकः
Fifteenth Āśvāsakaḥ

1. अह णिहअम्मि पहत्थे बन्धुवहामरिसणिन्तबाहुप्पीडो।
चलिओ सिहिपच्चग्गअहुंकारभरेन्तदसदिसो दहवअणो।।

[अथ निहते प्रहस्ते बन्धुवधामर्षनिर्यद्बाष्पोत्पीडः।
चलितः शिखिप्रत्युद्गतहुंकारभ्रियमाणदशदिग्दशवदनः।।]

When Prahasta was killed, Rāvaṇa, shedding tears in a rage at the killing of his kinsmen, sallied forth as he filled the ten directions with a roar that seemed to be preceded by a burst of flame.

K says अथ प्रहस्ते निहते बन्धूनां वधादमर्षाच्च निर्यद्बाष्पपूरो रावणः शिखिना अग्निना प्रत्युद्गतेन पुरस्कृतेन हुङ्कारेण दशभिर्मुखैः कृतेन पूर्यमाणदिङ्मुखो भूत्वा चलितः युद्धार्थमुत्थितः। MY says शिखिना प्रत्युद्गमनं च पातगोचरे अग्निजनकत्वम्।

2. तह कुविएण पहसिअं करालमुहकन्दराभरेन्तदशदिशम्।
जह से भअतुण्हिक्को भवणक्खम्भेसु परिअणो वि णिलुक्को।।

[तथा कुपितेन प्रहसितं करालमुखकन्दराभ्रियमाणदशदिशम्।
यथास्य भयतूष्णीको भवनस्तम्भेषु परिजनोऽपि निलुकितः।।]

Indignant he broke into a loud laugh, filling, as it were, the ten directions with his terrible cavernous mouths, in such a manner that his attendants, speechless with fear, hid behind the pillars of the palace.

K reads तथा च कुपितेन हसितं in the first line. He says कुपितेन तेन भयङ्कराभिः मुखकन्दराभिः पूर्यमाणदशाशं यथा तथा हसितं च। कथमिति चेत्–तस्य परिजनो यथा भयेन तूष्णींभूतो भवनस्तम्भेषु तिरोबभूव।

MY says *ṇiluggo* (*ṇilukko* ?) निलीनः छन्न इति यावत्। A has *ṇilluko*. K (*chāyā*) has निलीनः। R (*chāyā*) has निलुकितः।

3. तो रक्खसपरिवारं णिअपाअभरोणमन्तपच्छिमतडिमम्।
सारहिणा रुब्भन्तं चडुलतुरङ्गमधअं रहं आरूढो।।

[ततो राक्षसपरिवारं निजपादभरावनमत्पश्चिमतडिमम्।
सारथिना रुध्यमानं चटुलतुरङ्गमध्वजं रथमारूढः।।]

He mounted a chariot surrounded by the demons, weighing the rear down with his feet:[1] it was held fast by the charioteer as the horses chafed and the banners fluttered.

K seems to read भरभुग्न for *pāa-bhara* in the first line. He reads सारथिसंरुध्यमानं (MY and Kula also) for *sārahiṇā rubbhantaṁ* (R).

K says ततो रावणो राक्षसपरिवृतं, स्वदेहस्य भारेण कुटिलितनमत्पश्चिमतलं पुरस्तुरङ्गबहुलतया रथस्य पश्चिमभाग एवारोहणयोग्य:, सारथिना धार्यमाणं, चटुलतुरङ्गध्वजं रथमारूढ:।

My says *ṇisuḍhāvia* अवपातित। His reading is possibly *paa-bhara-ṇisuḍhāvia* for *pāa-bharoṇamanta* = पादभरावनमत् (R). He says *sārubbhantaṁ* संरुध्यमानम्। He remarks पश्चिमतलिमभागेनारोहणनियमात् वेगातिशयाच्च विशेषणानि समर्थनीयानि।

4. हुंकारेण सहाए खुहिअमहाकलअलेण लङ्कामज्झे।
पुरसेण्णकलअलेण अ णाओ चलिओ त्ति वाणरेहि दहमुहो।।

[हुंकारेण सभायां क्षुभितमहाकलकलेन लङ्कामध्ये।
पूर्णसैन्यकलकलेन च ज्ञातश्चलित इति वानरैर्दशमुख:।।]

The apes knew from Rāvaṇa's roar that he was in the court; from the loud voices of the excited courtiers (following him); that he was at the centre of Laṅkā; and from the noise of the troops in the city that he had left for the battlefield.

K MY and Kula read सभा (*sahā*) for महा° (R) in the first line. K reads पुरि for पुर; MY seems to read अरि। Kula's reading seems to be पुरी (*puri⁰*), cf. *SC* text.

K says तत्तदुद्देशजृम्भमाणेन तेन तेन शब्देन रावण: तत्र तत्र चलित इति वानरैर्ज्ञातम्। पुरीति सप्तम्यन्तं पदम्। सभायां कृतेन रावणस्य हुङ्कारेण तस्या: चलित इति ज्ञात: तत: क्षुभिताया: सभाया आस्थानजनसमूहस्य परितश्चलितस्य कलकलेन लङ्कामध्यं गत इति। तत: पुरि सर्वस्या सैन्यस्य कलकलेन पुनश्चलित इति ज्ञात इति क्रम:।

MY says सभायां वर्तत इति वानरै: हुङ्कारेण ज्ञात:। लङ्कामध्ये राज भवनाङ्गने वर्तत इति क्षुभितसभाकलकलेन। चलित इति अरिसैन्यकलकलेन चेत्यर्थ:। (Manuscript A has आदिसैन्य)।

Kula has हलहलेन for *kalaaleṇa*. For the reading हलहल see extracts

[1] I.e. he entered the chariot by the rear entrance.

on 12.87. See also verse 33 below. Kula says रोषगर्भेण सभायां हुङ्कारेण, क्षुभितायाः सभायाः प्रचलितायाः हलहलेन तारतम्येन लङ्कामध्ये, पुर्याः पुरनिवासिजनस्य सैन्यस्य च कलकलेन च दशमुखः चलित इति वानरैः ज्ञातः। *SC* says पुरीस्थितानां सैन्यानां कलकलेन।

5. णवरि अ मुहणिवहोवरि दुक्खपहुत्तधवलाअवत्तच्छाओ।
णिग्गन्तूण पुरीओ भञ्जइ भग्गरणमच्छरं कइसेण्णम्।।

[अनन्तरं च मुखनिवहोपरि दुःखप्रभूतधवलातपत्रच्छायः।
निर्गम्य पुरीतो भनक्ति भग्नरणमत्सरं कपिसैन्यम्।।]

Thereafter having gone out of the city, with his white parasol hardly sufficing to shelter the cluster of his heads, he put the host of apes to flight, with their will to fight broken.

K says अथ मुखनिवहस्य उपरि कृच्छ्रात् पर्याप्तधवलातपत्रच्छायः। अनेन मुखानां विकासातिशय उक्तः MY says दुष्प्रभूतः (दुःखप्र° B) कृच्छ्रेण पर्याप्तः। He reads *bhindai* for *bhañjai*. K says एवंभूतो लङ्काया निर्गत्य तत्क्षणमेव भग्नरणसंनाहं (भग्नरणमत्सरं *chāyā*) कपिसैन्यं दर्शनेनैव भनक्ति बभञ्ज। *SC* says मत्सरः शत्रुजिगीषा।

6. तो मुहमेत्तवलन्ता पच्छिमकेसरसडाहअग्गक्खन्धा।
भग्गाणुमग्गलग्गा पेच्छन्ति दसाणणं पवंगमणिवहा।।

[ततो मुखमात्रवलमानाः पश्चिमकेशरसटाहताग्रस्कन्धाः।
भग्नानुमार्गलग्नाः प्रेक्षन्ते दशाननं प्लवङ्गमनिवहाः।।]

The apes just turned the face round, with the hair at the back touching the top of their shoulders, and saw Rāvaṇa chasing them as they fled.

K read महा for *agga* (R and Kula) K, Kula and MY read *laggaṁ* for *laggā* (R).

K says रावणदर्शनेन भयात् पलायनपराः मुखमात्रेण वलमानाः परावृत्ताः, पश्चिमाभिः केसरसटाभिराहतमहास्कन्धाः कपिनिवहा भग्नानामनुमार्गे पृष्ठतो लग्नं रावणमपश्यन्। MY says भग्नानां स्वेषामनुमार्गलग्नं कपयः प्रत्येकमपश्यन्नित्यर्थः।

7. तो ते भिण्णपअट्टे दहवअणक्कन्तदिण्णविद्दविअपए।
पम्हट्ठजहाभणिए भणइ समुप्पण्णरणभए जलणसुओ।।

[ततस्तान्भिन्नप्रवृत्तान्दशवदनाक्रान्तदत्तविद्रवितपदान्।
प्रभ्रष्टयथाभणितान्भणति समुत्पन्नरणभयाज्ज्वलनसुतः।।]

Thereupon the son of the Fire God[2] said unto them as they scattered and took to their heels, being attacked by Rāvaṇa, forgetting their plighted word, and afraid to fight:

K reads आक्रान्ति for *akkanta* = आक्रान्त।

K says ततो ज्वलनसुतो नीलः दशवदनस्य आक्रान्त्या अभिभवेन दत्तविद्रुतपदान् कृतपलायनपदन्यासान् भिन्नप्रवृत्तान् भिन्नप्रवृत्तीन्, अथवा पूर्वस्थितिं भित्त्वा प्रवर्तमानान्, विस्मृतप्रतिज्ञावचनान्, समुत्पन्नरणभयान् तानुवाच।

MY says *bhiṇṇa-paatte* भिन्नप्रयत्नान्। *diṇṇa-viddavia-pae* दत्तविद्रावितपदान् कृतपलायनपदानित्यर्थः। R says विद्रवितं शीघ्रं विसंष्ठुलं वा।

Kula says भिन्नप्रवृत्तान् इतस्ततो विद्रुतान्। दशवदनेन आक्रान्तत्वात् आसादित्वात् दत्तं न्यस्तं विद्रुतं स्खलितं पदं येषां (तान्)। प्रमृष्टं (?) प्रस्मृतं तथाभणितं प्र(ति)ज्ञातरावणयुद्धं यैस्तान्। K (*chāyā*) has प्रमुषितयथाभणितान्। R has प्रभ्रष्ट explained as प्रस्मृत, which gives *pabbhaṭṭha* for *pamhaṭṭha*. Cf. Notes on 14.42.

8. मा मुञ्चह समरधुरं एस समुक्खित्तमलअसिहरद्धन्तो।
जस्स कएण पडाअह तं चिअ वो हरइ जीविअं पवअवई।।

[मा मुञ्चत समरधुरामेष समुत्क्षिप्तमलयशिखरार्धान्तः।
यस्य कृतेन पलायध्वं तदेव वो हरति जीवितं प्लवगपतिः।।]

"Do not abandon the burden of war. Yonder lord of the apes[3] that hath lifted up a section of a Malaya peak will rob ye of the very life for whose sake ye are taking to flight."

K reads शैल (*sela*) for *malaa* (R and Kula) K (*chāyā*) has यस्य कृतेन पलायध्वे तदेव वो हरति जीवितं प्लवगपतिः।

9. सीआहिअहिअएण अ अह सो त्ति दसाणणेण सारहिसिट्ठो।
ण वि तह रामो त्ति चिरं जह तीअ पिओ त्ति सबहुमाणं दिट्ठो।।

[सीताहितहृदयेन चाथ स इति दशाननेन सारथिशिष्टः।
नापि तथा राम इति चिरं यथा तस्याः प्रिय इति सबहुमानं दृष्टः।।]

With his heart bewitched by Sītā, Rāvaṇa long looked at Rāma with high esteem, when pointed out by his charioteer, not so much because he was Rāma as because he was her beloved.

---

[2] Nīla, one of the leaders of the apes.

[3] Sugrīva.

K has this verse after 6. It does not occur in Kula. K reads स्फुटं for चिरं। He says सीताहृतहृदयेन सीतया हृतमनसा रावणेन। R says सीताहितहृदयेन सीतायामाहितचित्तेन।

10. अह रामसराहिअओ पवएहि परंमुहोहसिज्जन्तरहो।
छिण्णपडिआअवत्तो लङ्काहिमुहो गओ णिसाअरणाहो।।

[अथ रामशराभिहतः प्लवगैः पराङ्मुखोपहस्यमानरथः।
छिन्नपतितातपत्रो लङ्काभिमुखो गतो निशाचरनाथः।।]

Hit by Rāma's arrows, the lord of the demons moved towards Laṅkā, with his royal parasol torn and fallen, and the apes making fun of his chariot as it turned back.

K reads *bhiṇṇa* for *chiṇṇa* (R and Kula) in the second line. He says पराङ्मुखत्वात् वानरैरपहस्यमानरथ इति योज्यम्। अन्यत् स्पष्टम्। MY's readings are different. He says *paraṁmuhoharijjantaraho* पराङ्मुखोपह्रियमाणरथः (B has पराङ्मुखाप . . .)। *laṁkā-hutto* लङ्काभिमुखः। Kula takes *paraṁmuho* separately, and says पराङ्मुखः प्लवगैः हन्यमानरथः (i.e. *haṇijjantaraho*).

11. तो तेण लघुइअजसं पत्तविणासेण मुक्कसोडीरपअम्।
पडिबोहणं अआले सुहोवसुत्तस्स कुम्भअण्णस्स कअम्।।

[ततस्तेन लघूकृतयशः प्राप्तविनाशेन मुक्तशौटीर्यपदम्।
प्रतिबोधनमकाले सुखोपसुप्तस्य कुम्भकर्णस्य कृतम्।।]

Faced with ruin, he prematurely woke Kumbhakarṇa who was fast asleep, abandoning reliance on his own strength; and lowering his high renown.

K and Kula read धुरं for *paaṁ* = पदं (R) in the first line. K reads प्रसुप्त (i.e. °*ppasutta*) for *uvasutta* = उपसुप्त (R and Kula).

K says ततः प्राप्तविनाशेन आसन्नविनाशेन अनेन रावणेन सुखप्रसुप्तस्य कुम्भकर्णस्य अकाले प्रतिबोधनं लघूकृतयशो यथा, मुक्तसामर्थ्यधुरं च यथा कृतम्। अकाले तस्य प्रबोधनात् यशश्च लघूकृतं स्वसामर्थ्यधुरा च विमुक्ताभूदित्यर्थः। Kula says मुक्ता शौटीर्यस्य धूः यथा स्यात् तथा। K (*chāyā*) has शौण्डीर्य। K *pratīka* has to *ṇeṇa* for *to teṇa* (R and Kula).

MY says प्राप्तविनाशेन। विनाशः पलायनम्।

12. सो वि अ जम्भाअन्तो अआलपडिबोहगरुइअसिरद्धन्तो।
णीइ हसिऊण सुइरं लहुअं सोऊण रामवहसंदेसम्।।

[सोऽपि च जृम्भायमाणोऽकालप्रतिबोधगुरूकृतशिरोर्धान्तः।
निरैति हसित्वा सुचिरं लघुकं श्रुत्वा रामवधसंदेशम्।।]

Kumbhakarṇa yawned, his head heavy because of the premature waking, and sallied out after a long laugh on hearing the trivial command to slay Rāma.

K explains शिरोऽर्धान्त as शिरःप्रदेश।

13. ओच्छुण्णरइरहवहो जाओ देहस्स से कणअपाआरो।
ऊरुपएसालग्गो दरखलिओ व्व तवणिज्जराअपरिअरो।।

[आक्रान्तरविरथपथो जातो देहस्यास्य कनकप्राकारः।
ऊरुप्रदेशालग्नो दरस्खलित इव तपनीयरागपरिकरः।।]

The golden wall of Laṅkā that seemed to touch the track of the Sun's chariot came up to the region of his thighs, and looked like a golden girdle that had slightly slipped off his waist.

K *pratīka* has *avacuṇṇa*, but *chāyā* has अवक्षुण्ण। MY has *occhuṇṇa* आक्रान्त। Kula says अवक्षुण्णो भग्नः। K, MY and Kula read *galio* for *khalio* (R).

K says परिकरशब्देन परिधानीयमुच्यते। राज्ञः परिकरो राजपरिकरः। तपनीयरागपरिकर इति वा। तपनीयवर्णः परिकर इत्यर्थः। MY says तपनीयरागपरिकरः कनकरञ्जितसिचयः। रविपथमाक्रामन्नपि प्राकारः कुम्भकर्णस्योरुदघ्नतया ईषत्स्रस्तं कनकरञ्जितं परिधानमिवालक्ष्यतेत्यर्थः। Kula says सुवर्णांशुकस्य परिकर इव वेष्ट इव जातः। He seems to read *tavaṇijja-vāsa-pariaro* for °*rāa*°. Cf. *SC* text. *SC chāyā* has तपनीयवासःपरिकरः।

R remarks परिकरो मेखलावत् त्रिके निबध्यत इति समाचारः। स तु सुप्तोत्थितस्य शिथिलीभवत्येवेति ध्वनिः।

14. लङ्घिअपाआरस्स अ तो से विवलाअमाणमअरप(क्क)ग्गाहा।
जाणुप्पमाणसलिला जाआ फडिहागआ समुद्दद्धन्ता।।

[लङ्घितप्राकारस्य च ततोऽस्य विपलायमानमकरप्रग्राहाः।
जानुप्रमाणसलिला जाताः परिखागताः समुद्रार्धान्ताः।।]

When he stepped over the wall, the waters of the sea entering the moat[4] reached only his knees, with the crocodiles and sea lions taking to flight.

vivalāa in the first line (see Goldschmidt's edition) is rendered as विपलायित (K and Kula). Kula has जानुप्रसारमलिना: for *jāṇu-ppamāṇa-salila*. MY says परिखागता: समुद्रार्धान्ता इति समुद्रं यावत् निखाते भूभागे समुद्रा एव परिखा भवन्तीति यावत्।

15. तो तं पेच्छन्त च्चिअ पच्छाहुत्ता णिअत्तरणवावारा।
हत्थपडन्तधराहरविसमक्कन्ता पडाइआ कइणिवहा।।

[ततस्तं पश्यन्त एव पश्चादभिमुखा निवृत्तरणव्यापारा:।
हस्तपतद्धराधरविषमाक्रान्ता: पलायिता: कपिनिवहा:।।]

As soon as the apes saw him they turned their backs, ceasing to fight, and ran away, impeded by the mountains dropping from their hands.

K and MY read मार्गाभिमुखा: (probably *maggaahuttā*) for *pacchāhuttā* = पश्चादभिमुखा: (R). K says पराङ्मुखा: इत्यर्थ:। शेषं स्पष्टार्थम्। Kula's reading is same as that of K and MY, but he construes it differently. See below. K, MY and Kula read प्रधाविता: (*pahāviā*) for *paḍāiā* = पलायिता: (R). Kula reads विमुक्त (*vimukka*) for *ṇiatta* (निवृत्त)।

MY says स्वकरेभ्यो निपतद्भि: गिरिभिरेव स्वयमाक्रान्ता यथागत- मार्गाभिमुखा: सर्वेऽपि कपय: प्रधावितुमारब्धा इत्यर्थ:। Kula says मार्गकेषु (*SC* adds अन्वेषकेषु अभिमुखा: प्रष्ठग्राहिषु दत्तपृष्ठा:)। *SC* text has *maggaahuttā*[5], which is Kula's reading.

16–17. अह सेलेहि तरूहि अ फलिहेहि अ मोग्गरेहि हन्तूण दढम्।
दढदण्डाउहमग्गणमुसलेहि खणेण वाणरबलं सअलम्।।

[अथ शैलैस्तरुभिश्च परिघैश्च मुद्गरैर्हत्वा दृढम्।
दृढदण्डायुधमार्गणमुशलै: क्षणेन वानरबलं सकलम्।।]

---

[4] I.e. the most reached as far as the sea letting in the waters of the ocean.

[5] The manuscript of *SC* has *maggāhuttā* marginally, according to the editor manuscript C of Goldschmidt also has this reading. The word as given in *DN* 6.111 is *magga* in the sense of पश्चात्। R on *Setu* 1.51 explains *maggāṇugao* as मार्गो रामस्य पश्चात् तमनुगत: and says मार्गशब्द: पश्चादर्थे निपातित:।

तो पवआइ गआइं तुरआइ अ रक्खसाइ लोहिअमत्तो।
रामसराघाअधुओ णिअअबले परबले पअत्तो खत्तुम्।।

[ततः प्लवगान्गजांस्तुरगांश्च राक्षसांल्लोहितमन्तः।
रामशराघातधुतो निजकबले परबले प्रवृत्तः खादितुम्।।]

After he had violently attacked the entire host of apes in a moment with mountains, trees, clubs and maces as well as strong pikes, arrows and heavy sticks, he, being harassed by Rāma's arrows and mad with blood, began to devour the apes as well as the elephants, horses and the demons, in both the armies, his own and that of the enemy.[6]

The verses are not found in K, MY and Kula found in R and *SC*. The latter shows slight variations and remarks एतत् पद्यद्वयं केनापि टीकाकारेण न धृतमिति।

18. चिरजुज्झिअस्स तो से दोएह वि रामधणुणिग्गअसराहिहआ।
पढमं धरणीअ भुआ पच्छा छेअरुहिरोज्झरा पल्हत्था।।

[चिरयोधितस्य ततोऽस्य द्वावपि रामधनुर्निर्गतशराभिहतौ।
प्रथमं धरण्यां भुजौ पश्चाच्छेदरुधिरनिर्झराः पर्यस्ताः।।]

After he had fought for a long while, both his arms, severed by Rāma's arrows, fell to the ground, followed by streams of blood spouting from the wounds.

K says चिरयुद्धस्य चिरं कृतयुद्धस्य। अन्यत् सुबोधम्। MY says चिरयोधितस्य (R also) चिरं कृतयुद्धस्येति यावत्। *doṇṇa vi* द्वावपि। छेदानन्तरं रुधिरागमे (रुधिरोद्गमे A) प्राप्ते भुजपतनात् पश्चाद्भावकथनं रामस्य लघुहस्तताद्योतनार्थम्।

19. एक्को रुद्धणइमुहो अणुवेलं णिवडिओ सुवेलो व्व भुओ।
साअरलद्धत्थामो बीओ से बीअसेउबन्ध व्व ठिओ।।

[एको रुद्धनदीमुखोऽनुवेलं निपतितः सुवेल इव भुजः।
सागरलब्धस्थामा द्वितीयो द्वितीयसेतुबन्ध इव स्थितः।।]

One of his arms lay on the seashore, like the Suvela, blocking

[6] The authenticity of the verses is doubtful. They are found only in Rāmadāsa. It may also be noted that the poem describes only the apes as fighting with trees and mountains as their weapons.

the mouths of the rivers; while the other lay motionless across the sea, like another causeway.

K (*chāyā*) has सागरलब्धस्थामा (°*tthāmo*) like R. He says अनुवेलम् अनुसमुद्रतीरम्। अन्यत् स्पष्टम्। MY says आक्रान्तवेलाभ्यर्णतया द्वितीयसुवेलबुद्धिमेको बाहुरकरोत्। द्वितीयस्तु तत्रालब्धावकाशतया सीमन्तितसागरस्थितो द्वितीयसेतु-भ्रान्तिमजनयदित्यर्थः। एकस्मिन् भुजे वेलोद्देशे पतिते द्वितीयस्य जलधावेव पतनं वेलायामनवकाशादिति तात्पर्यम्।

Kula says सागर लब्धस्थाघो द्वितीयो भुजः। He reads *thāha* for *thāma* (स्थानम्) as in 8.40 (*sāara-laddha-tthāhaṁ*), where he says सागरे लब्धः स्थाघो येन तं धराधरम्। R says *ad loc.* सागरे लब्धः स्थाघो (मूलं) येन तम्। लब्धसागरमूल यं यं धराधरम्।

20. आअण्णकड्ढिएण अ तो से चक्कलिअसिहिसिहेण रणमुहे।
रहुवइसरेण तुङ्गं चक्केण व राहुणो सिरं उक्खुडिअम्।।

[आकर्णकृष्टेन च ततोऽस्य चक्रलितशिखिशिखेन रणमुखे।
रघुपतिशरेण तुङ्गं चक्रेणेव राहोः शिर उत्खण्डितम्।।]

His lofty head was then struck off in the course of the fight by Rāma's arrow, drawn up to the ear, and encircled by flames, even as Rāhu's head was severed by (Viṣṇu's *sudarśana*) wheel.[7]

K (*chāyā*) renders *cakkalia* as चक्रीकृत, and has उत्त्रुटितम् for *ukkhuḍiaṁ*. Hemacandra 4.116 gives *khuḍai, tuḍai, tuṭṭai*, etc. as equivalents of तुड् meaning तोडन। R has उत्खण्डितम्।

21. गअणुण्णएण तेण अ पवणभरेन्तमुहकन्दरामुहलेण।
छिण्णपडिएण वि कओ चउत्थतुङ्गसिहरुग्गमो व्व तिऊडो।।

[गगनोन्नतेन तेन च पवनभ्रियमाणमुखकन्दरामुखरेण।
छिन्नपतितेनापि कृतश्चतुर्थतुङ्गशिखरोद्गम इव त्रिकूटः।।]

And the head, high as the sky, even though severed and fallen, and rumbling as the wind filled the cavernous mouth, seemed to provide the three-peaked Suvela with the fourth lofty summit.

K and MY read *bhiṇṇa* for *chiṇṇa* (R and Kula). K reads जातः (*jāo*) for *vi kao* = अपि कृतः। Kula seems to read च (*a*) for *vi*.

[7] Cf. *Naiṣadhacarita*, 4.64-66.

22. पडिए अ कुम्भअण्णे दूरपलाअदरभग्गपक्कग्गाहो।
देहभरन्तुच्छङ्गो पब्बालेइ वडवामुहं मअरहरो।।

[पतिते च कुम्भकर्णे दूरपलायितदरभग्नप्रग्राहः।
देहभ्रियमाणोत्सङ्गः प्लावयते वडवामुखं मकरगृहः।।]

When Kumbhakarṇa fell, the sea as his body filled its expanse flowed over the submarine fire,[8] with the sea monsters fleeing far afield, overcome by fear.

K and MY read रुग्ण for *bhagga* भग्न (R). MY says *daralugga* ईषद्रुगण। K (*chāyā*) has प्लावयति। MY has *pavvālei* प्राप्लावयत्। K (*chāyā*) has पक्वग्राहः (*pakkhaggāho*) rendered by R as प्रग्राहः जलसिंहः। Kula seems to explain the word as समर्था ग्राहा जलहस्तिनः। *Deśīnāmamālā* 6.64 has *pakkha* in the sense of दृप्त and समर्थ, but in 6.23 gives *pakkaggāha* in the sense of मकर।

SC explains *dara-bhagga* as भयभग्न। Kula is corrupt *SC*, however, says दूरं पलायिता विलीना इति कुलनाथः।

23. तो कुम्भअण्णणिहणं सोऊण दसाणणो पहत्थब्भहिअम्।
रोसाअवरज्जन्तं पुणो वि हसिऊण धुणइ मुहसंघाअम्।।

[ततः कुम्भकर्णनिधनं श्रुत्वा दशाननः प्रहस्ताभ्यधिकाम्।
रोषातपरज्यमानं पुनरपि हसित्वा धुनोति मुखसंघातम्।।]

Hearing of the death of Kumbhakarṇa, more grievous than that of Prahasta, Rāvaṇa once more broke into a laugh,[9] and shook his faces as they flamed with wrath.

K, MY and Kula *pratīka* has *aha* for *to* = ततः (R). K (*chāyā*) has रोषेण भ्रियमाणः for *rosāava-rajjantaṁ* = रोषातपरज्यमानम् (R and probably Kula).

K says प्रहस्ताभ्यधिकम्। शेषः सुबोधः। MY says प्रहस्ताभ्यधिकं प्रहस्तमरणाभ्यधिकम्।

24. णिन्तस्स अ तं वेलं अमरिसपरिवड्ढिअस्स भवणुच्छङ्गे।
खम्मन्तरवित्थारा ते च्चिअ वच्छत्थलस्स से ण पहुत्ता।।

---

[8] The rise in the sea level is fancied as flooding the submarine fire which is usually described as consuming the waters. Cf. 8.98.

[9] Cf. verse 2.

[निर्यतश्च तद्वेलायाममर्षपरिवर्धितस्य भवनोत्सङ्गे।
स्तम्भान्तरविस्तारास्त एव वक्षःस्थलस्यास्य न प्रभूताः।।]

As he went out at that hour the gaps between the pillars of the palace were not wide enough for his chest swelling with wrath.

K says तां वेलां तस्यां वेलायां निर्गच्छत इत्यर्थः। अन्यत् स्पष्टम्। MY says पूर्व एव स्तम्भान्तरविस्ताराः रोषपरिवर्धितस्य वक्षसो न पर्याप्ता इत्यन्वयः। Kula says स्तम्भानाम् अन्तरविस्तारा महान्तोऽन्तरालदेशाः त एव पूर्वं सुखनिर्गमा एव वक्षःस्थलस्य न प्रभूता निर्गमोचिता इत्यर्थः।

25. दरणिग्गअस्स णवरि अ उग्घाडिअवच्छभरिअभवणुच्छङ्गो।
जाणुपडिउट्ठिओ से जम्पइ हसिऊण मेहणाओ त्ति सुओ।।

[दरनिर्गतस्यान्तरं च उद्घाटितवक्षोभृतभवनोत्सङ्गः।
जानुपतितोत्थितोऽस्य जल्पति हसित्वा मेघनाद इति सुतः।।]

When he had almost gone out, his son Meghanāda went down on his knees, and said with a smile as he rose, filling, as it were, the interior of the palace with his high and wide[10] bosom.

K reads ऋज्वायत (*ujjāaa*) for *ugghāḍia* = उद्घाटित = प्रकाशित (R). MY reads ऋज्वागत। See below.

K says अथ किञ्चित् निर्गतस्य तस्य मेघनाद इति सुत्त इन्द्रजित् जानुभ्यां निपत्य उत्थितः, ऋजुना अवक्रेण उन्नतेन आयतेन च वक्षसा पूरितभवनाभ्यन्तरो हसित्वा जल्पति स्म। Kula says जानुना पतितस्थितः (*paḍiaṭṭhio* for *paḍiü°*).

MY says *ujjāgaa* ऋज्वागतश्च, वक्षोभृतभवनोत्सङ्गश्चेति विग्रहः। Kula also reads *ujjāgaa*, but explains it differently — ऊर्जागतेन बलपूर्णेन वक्षसा भूतभवनोत्सङ्गः।

26. णिम्माविअम्मि कज्जे साहसगरुए वि अप्पण च्चिअ गुरुणा।
पुत्तेण पुत्तसरिसं पुत्तप्फरिसं ण पाविओ होइ पिआ।।

[निर्मितेऽपि कार्ये साहसगुरुकेऽपि आत्मनैव गुरुणा।
पुत्रेण पुत्रसदृशं पुत्रस्पर्शं न प्रापितो भवति पिता।।]

"When a father accomplishes a deed, esteemed for its

---

[10] Kṛṣṇa's reading is followed. See Extracts.

boldness, by his own effort, the son cannot afford him the joy of embracing a worthy son.[11]

K, MY and Kula *pratīka* has *ṇimmāṇiammi* (निर्मिते K and MY) for *ṇimmāviammi* (R). K and MY read पुत्रैः for *putteṇa* in the second line. They and Kula read *garuammi* for *garue vi* = गुरुकेऽपि (R).

K is not well preserved here. He says साहसेन बलात्कारादिना गुरुणि कार्ये एवं . . . पित्रा निर्मिते सति पुत्रैः तिष्ठद्भिः पुत्रसदृशं पुत्रैः यादृशः (?) स्पर्शः स्यात् तथाविधं पुत्रस्पर्शं पिता न प्रापितः स्यात्। पुत्रसदृशं पुत्रकार्यमिति . . .[12] सत्पुत्राणाम् अनुरूपं पितुः पुत्रेषु स्पर्शमित्यर्थः।

R says गुरुके लोकैरादृते।

MY says निर्मिते साहसगुरुणि कार्ये सरसफलादौ गुरुणात्मनैव उपयुक्ते सति पुत्रैः कर्तुमुचितं पुत्रस्पर्शसुखं पुत्रैः न प्रापितः पिता। नूनमपि (नूनमिति A) स्यादित्यर्थः। यदि पितुः पुत्रेषु स्नेहस्तदा सुखातिशयहेतुनामीदृशानां कार्याणां प्रसक्तौ तेषु नियोजनमेव कार्यमिति तात्पर्यम्।[13] MY seems to read *ṇūṇa* (नूनम्) for *hoi* in the second line. Cf. 5.6 *SC* says पुत्रेण पुत्रसदृशं पुत्रस्योचितं पुत्रस्पर्शं पिता प्रापितो न भवति। कृतकार्यागतस्य पुत्रस्यालिङ्गनेन स्पर्शजन्यसुखं पुत्रेण पिता प्रापितो भवतीत्यर्थः।

27. कीस ममम्मि धरेन्ते माणुसमेत्तस्स दहरहसुअस्स कए।
इअ णीसि अप्पण च्चिअ लहुअन्तो अम्ह रक्खसउलस्स जसम्।।

[किमिति मयि ध्रियमाणे मानुषमात्रस्य दशरथसुतस्य कृते।
इति निरैषि आत्मनैव लघूकुर्वन्मम राक्षसकुलस्य यशः।।]

While I am alive, why art thou thus sallying out thyself, lowering the prestige of our *rākṣasa* race, because of a mere mortal, a son of Daśaratha?

K reads श्वसति for *dharente* = ध्रियमाणे (R and Kula). K and MY read *ṇīha* (निर्याथ) for *ṇīsi* = निर्यासि (Kula), निरैषि (R). K and MY read *lahuantā* in the plural for *lahuanto* (R and Kula).

K says मयि श्वसति जीवति मानुषमात्रस्य रामस्य कृते कस्मात् आत्मनैव एवं

[11] I.e. when a father does a heroic deed instead of allowing his son to do it the latter is deprived of the opportunity to prove his worth by achieving something of which the father can be proud.

[12] Manuscript has कार्याणां here.

[13] A reads तेषु नियोज्य गमनं कार्यमिति . . .।

निर्गच्छथ निर्याथ (*chāyā*)। अस्माकं राक्षसवंशस्य यशो लघूकुर्वाणाः (लघयन्तः *chāyā*)। अस्माकं कुलस्येति वक्तव्ये राक्षसशब्दः प्रसिद्धिहेतो प्रयुक्तः।

MY says *kīsa* कस्मात्। Kula says ध्रियमाणे अवतिष्ठमाने। इत्येवम् अस्माकं राक्षसकुलस्य यशो (लघू)कुर्वन्।

28. उक्खअभुअंगरअणं णिसुढिअणन्दणवणं पलोटिअसेलम्।
अप्पाणं व ण आणसि समं समत्थस्स तिहुअणस्स भरसहम्।।

[उत्खातभुजंगरत्नं निपातितनन्दनवनं प्रलोटितशैलम्।
आत्मानं वा न जानासि समं समस्तस्य त्रिभुवनस्य भरसहम्।।]

Or perhaps thou dost not know thyself to be capable of withstanding all the three worlds together, thou that hadst forced out gem embedded in Ananta's hood, devastated the Nandana garden, and turned round the Kailāsa mountain.[14]

K and MY read *āṇaha* (जानीथ) for *āṇasi* = जानासि। They read *mamaṁ* for समं (R and Kula). K (*chāyā*) has त्रिभुवनस्य समस्तस्य भरसहम्।

K says उत्खातभुजङ्गफणरत्नम्। अनेन पातालविजय उक्तः। भग्ननन्दनवनम् इत्यनेन स्वर्गजय उक्तः। प्रलोठितशैलम् इत्यनेन भूमण्डलविमर्दनम्। एवं त्रिभुवनस्य भरसहं त्रिभुवनस्य धारणे समर्थम्। अथवा परिभवितुमुद्यतस्य त्रिभुवनस्य गौरवसहं माम् आत्मानं भवन्तमिव (न) जानीथ किम् इति शेषः। MY says युष्मत्सदृशं मामद्यापि न जानीथेत्यर्थः।

Kula and R have निपातितनन्दनवनम्। Kula says प्रलोटितः(?) पर्यासितः शैलः कैलासो येन तम्। R (*chāyā*) has प्रलोटित, but commentary says प्रलोठितः परिवर्तितः। Kula says सममेककालम्।

29. किं णिहणेमि रणमुहे सरेक्कसोसविअसाअरं रहुणाहम्।
ओ सत्त वि अज्जं चिअ वलन्तवडवामुहे मलेमि समुद्दे।।

[किं निहन्मि रणमुखे शरैकशोषितसागरं रघुनाथम्।
उत सप्ताप्यद्यैव वलद्वडवामुखान्मृद्नामि समुद्रान्।।]

Shall I kill Rāma in the forefront of the battle, who hath but dried up a single ocean with his arrows,[15] or overwhelm

[14] The serpent Ananta who supports the earth, the Nandana garden and the Kailāsa mountain stand respectively for the nether regions, heaven and the earth.

[15] A reference to the conflagration of the sea described in canto V.

even today all the seven oceans, with the submarine fire rolling in them?"

K reads रघुतनयम् for *rahuṇāhaṁ* (R and Kula). K (*chāyā*) has वलमान–वडवामुखान्। He says स्पष्टोऽर्थः। MY says रामस्यापदानभूतम् एकसागरशोषणं किं सप्तसागरशोषणेन अतिशाययेयम् उत तस्यैव वधेन चेति तात्पर्यम्। MY has *ṇihaṇammi* for *ṇihaṇemi* (निहन्मि)।

30-31. इअ विण्णविअदहमुहो पच्छिमसारहिकरट्ठविअसीसक्को।
आबद्धकवअमन्थरपअविक्कमभरणमन्तकित्थअतडिमम्।।
धअसिहरट्ठिअजलहरमुच्चन्तासणिपडिप्फलिअसूरकरम्।
समरतुरिओ विलग्गइ रहं सुआसण्णरामधणुणिग्घोसो।।
(जुग्गअम्)

[इति विज्ञापितदशमुखः पश्चिमसारथिकरस्थायिशीर्षकः।
आबद्धकवचमन्थरपदविक्रमभरनमद्विस्तृततडिमम्।।
ध्वजशिखरस्थितजलधरमुच्यमानाशनिप्रतिफलितसूरकरम्।
समरत्वरितो विलसति रथं श्रुतासन्नरामधनुर्निर्घोषः।।
(युग्मकम्)

Having thus addressed Rāvaṇa, Meghanāda, hasting to the battle as he heard the sound of Rāma's bow close at hand, mounted his chariot, after he had placed his helmet in the hand of the charioteer in the rear. The spacious back floor bent under his heavy footsteps as he entered the vehicle[16] in full armour; while the rays of the sun were reflected in the flashes of lightning emitted by the clouds setting on the top of the banner.

K and MY read निर्गम for *vikkama* (R and Kula) in the second line.

K says एवं ज्ञापित (दशमुखः) इन्द्रजित् – रथस्य पुरस्तात् पृष्ठतश्च तुरङ्गा युज्यन्ते। तत्र पश्चिमतुरङ्गवाहकः सारथिः पश्चिमसारथिः। तस्य करे प्रागेव स्थापितशिरस्त्राणं, शीर्षकमिति शिरस्त्रपर्यायः आबद्धकवचभरत्वात् मन्थरेण गौरवात् मन्देन पदनिर्गमेन पदक्षेपेण नमद्विस्तृततलम् (°तलिमम् *chāyā*)। उत्तरत्र सम्बन्धः।

It will be seen that K reads *sīsakkaṁ* for °*sīsakko* (R and Kula) in the first line. Kula says पश्चिमस्य पृष्ठस्थितसारथेः करे (?) स्थापितं

[16] See verse 3.

शिरस्त्रं येन स मेघनादः। R says पश्चिमेन पश्चाद्वर्तिना सारथिना करे स्थापितं शीर्षकं शिरस्त्राणं यस्य स तथा।

MY says *sīsakkaṁ* शिरस्त्राणम्। पश्चिमे तलिमे कवचमाबध्य मन्थरपदं निर्गच्छतोऽस्य भरेण पश्चिमतलिममेव यथा नमेत् तथाभूतमित्यर्थः। R says भरेण गौरवेण नमत् . . . विस्तृतं तडिमं पश्चाद्वर्तिभित्तिभागो यस्य तम्। Kula says विक्रमस्य पादन्यासस्य भरेण। तलिमं (?) कुट्टिमम्।

K reads पात्यमान (see MY below) for *muccanta* = मुच्यमान (R and Kula)

K says ध्वजशिखरस्थितेन मेघेन पात्यमानायामशनौ प्रतिफलितरविकिरणं रथं श्रुतासन्नरामधनुर्निनादः अतएव समरत्वरित आरोहति स्म।

MY says *sumbhanta* अवपात्यमान। Kula says ध्वजशिखरे स्थितेन जलधरेण मुच्यमानासु अशनिषु प्रतिफलिताः संक्रान्ताः सूर्यकारा यत्र तम्।

32. इअ वारिअदहवअणो दहवअणाणत्तिविलइउक्खित्तभरो।
णीइ रहं आरूढो रक्खसपरिवारिओ दसाणणतणओ।।

[इति वारितदशवदनो दशवदनाज्ञप्तिविलगितोक्षिप्तभरः।
निरेति रथमारूढो राक्षसपरिवारितो दशाननतनयः।।]

Meghanāda who thus kept Rāvaṇa back from fight, and accepted at his behest the burden imposed on him, went out in his chariot, surrounded by the demons.

K *pratīka* has *aha* (अथ) for *ia* (इति)। K (*chāyā*) has दशवदनाज्ञप्तिविलगितोत्क्षिप्तधुरः। K commentary says दशवदनस्याज्ञप्त्या समारोपितोन्नतकार्यभरः। शेषं सुबोधम्। MY says निवारितदशवदनः, निवारणं च रणोद्योगात्। *SC* says विगलिता गृहीता स्वीकृतेत्यर्थः, उत्क्षिप्ता उपरिनिहिता (धूः) समरभारो येनेति लोकनाथः। *SC* text has °धुरो for °भरो।

33. जो दहमुहग्गदारे तुरिअपहाविअरहस्स जो णअरिमुहे।
खोहेन्तस्स कइबलं सो च्चिअ वेओ अ से पअत्तहलहलो।।

[यो दशमुखाग्रद्वारे त्वरितप्रधावितरथस्य यो नगरीमुखे।
क्षोभयतः कपिबलस एव वेगश्चास्य प्रवृत्तहलहलः।।]

As his chariot sped along his speed, throwing the enemy into confusion, was the same at the front door of Rāvaṇa's palace and at the city portal as when he assailed the host of apes.

K reads रणे for *a se* (चास्य), and कलकल for हलहल। He says निर्गच्छतस्तस्य दशमुखभवनाग्रद्वारे रावणभवनस्य बहिर्द्वारे यो वेग: प्रवृत्त:, त्वरितचोदितरथस्य तस्य नगरद्वारे यो वेग:, सहसा रणभुवं गत्वा कपिबलं क्षोभयत: तस्य स एव वेग: प्रवृत्तकलकलोऽभूत्। अनेन तस्य गमन-शैघ्र्यातिशय उक्त:। R says वेग: कीदृक्-प्रवृत्तो हलहल: क्षोभविशेषो यस्मात् विपक्षाणामित्यर्थात्। शब्दोऽयं देशी। MY seems to read कलकल like K. He says तस्य कपिबलक्षोभेषु (क्षोभणेषु A) एक एव प्रवृत्तहर्षरवो वेग: प्रावर्तत। न तु विरम्येत्यर्थ:।

Verses 32 and 33 are missing in our copy of Kula.

34. अह रामबद्धलक्खो पढमुद्धाइअपवंगमक्खविअबलो।
वाणरजोहेहि समं जलणसुएण वरिओ दसाणणतणओ।।

[अथ रामबद्धलक्ष्य: प्रथमोद्धावितत्प्लवङ्गमक्षपितबल:।
वानरयोधै: समं ज्वलनसुतेन वृतो दशाननतनय:।।]

Meghanāda who hit the mark in battle had his troops destroyed by the apes that rushed forward first, and was confronted[17] by Nīla together with the chief warriors among the apes.

K, MY and Kula read समरलब्धलक्ष: for *rāma-baddha-lakkho* (R). K and MY read *dhario* for *vario* = वृत: (R and Kula).

K says प्रागेव समरे नागास्त्रप्रयोगे लब्धलक्ष इन्द्रजित् प्रथमोत्थापितप्लवङ्गक्षपितबल: प्रथममेवोत्थापितै: कपिभि: ध्वंसितसैन्य:। अन्यत् स्पष्टम्।

R says प्रथमोद्धावितमग्रेकृतवेगम् अतएव प्लवङ्गमै: क्षपितं नाशितं बलं यस्य स तथा। ये पुर: समागता: ते कपिभि: हता इत्यर्थ:। Kula says प्रथममुद्धावितानां प्लवङ्गानां क्षपितं (?) बलं सैन्यं येन (स) दशाननतनय: वानरयोधै: समं ज्वलनसुतेन नीलेन वृत: प्रतीष्ट:। MY songs समरेषु अमोघविक्रमो, नासीरप्रधावितै: कपिभि: निवारितसैन्य:, कपियोधसहितेन नीलेन निवारितोऽभूदित्यर्थ:। MY seems to read *vāria* for °*kkhavia* (क्षपित); and *dhario* like K whose *chāyā* has धारित:।

35. णीलेण गण्डसेलं दिविएण दुमं सिलाअलं मारुइणा।
दारेइ सरेहि समं णलेण मुक्कं च मलअसिहरक्खण्डम्।।

[नीलेन गण्डशैलं द्विविदेन द्रुमं शिलातलं मारुतिना।
दारयति शरै: समं नलेन मुक्तं च मलयशिखरखण्डम्।।]

[17] Literally, chosen (as adversary).

He pierced with his arrows the rock and the tree and the boulder and the section of a Malaya peak, all at once, which was hurled at him respectively by Nīla, Dvivida, Hanumat and Nala.

K says निगदव्याख्यातमेतत्। Kula reads *vārei* for *dārei* (दारयति)। He says वारयति निराकरोति।

36. तो भग्गपवअसेण्णं णिउम्भिलाहुत्तसच्चविअपत्थाणम्।
वारेह मेहणाअं विभीसणेण भणिओ सुमित्तातणओ।।

[ततो भग्नप्लवगसैन्यं निकुम्भिलाभिमुखसत्यापितप्रस्थानम्।
वारयत मेघनादं विभीषणेन भणितः सुमित्रातनयः।।]

Thereupon counselled by Vibhīṣana, Lakṣmaṇa checked Meghanāda who had routed the host of apes, and was seen to proceed to the shrine of Nikumbhilā.[18]

K, MY and Kula read *vārei* (वारयति) for *vāreha* = वारयत् (R).

K says निष्कुम्भिला (*chāyā* also) नाम भद्रकाली। सा राक्षसानामभीष्टार्थप्रदेति प्रसिद्धा। प्लवङ्गान् विजित्य निकुम्भिलायतनाभिमुखलक्षितप्रयाणम् इन्द्रजितं विभीषणेन कथितवृत्तान्तः सौमित्रिः। वारयामासेति। K (*chāyā*) renders *saccavia* as सत्यापित। Kula has सत्यीकृतं दृष्टम्। R says सत्यापितं स्थिरीकृतं प्रस्थानं येन तं मेघनादं वारयत।

MY says विक्रमामोघत्वसिद्धये निकुम्भिलाख्यचण्डिकाभिमुखं लक्षीकृतपथं मेघनादं तत्प्रवेशात् प्रागेव विभीषणोक्तः सौमित्रिः न्यवारयदित्यर्थः। Manuscript A has निकुम्भिका। R says निकुम्भिला नाम यज्ञस्थानम्।

37. तो माआहि सरेहि अ सेलेहि अ जुज्झिअस्स रक्खससरिसम्।
सोमित्तिणा णिसुद्धं पिआमहत्थेण मेहणाअस्स सिरम्।।

[ततो मायाभिः शरैश्च शल्यैश्च युद्धस्य राक्षससदृशम्।
सौमित्रिणा निपातितं पितामहास्त्रेण मेघनादस्य शिरः।।]

Lakṣmaṇa struck off Meghanāda's head with the weapon sacred to Brahmā, after he had fought with magic arts as well as arrows and darts in a manner worthy of a demon.

K says स्पष्टोऽर्थः। K (*chāyā*) renders *selehi* as शैलैः। R has शल्यैः Cf. Assamese *śel* (lance). MY says *jujjhiassa* योधितवतः (युद्धस्य K and R; युद्धं कृतवतः Kula)।

[18] To worship for victory.

38. सोऊण इन्दइवहं मुअइ सरोसं दसाणणो वाहजलम्।
अब्भुत्तियदीवाणं णिवडइ तुप्पं व तक्खणं सहुआसम्।।

[श्रुत्वा इन्द्रजिद्वधं मुञ्चति सरोषं दशाननो बाष्पजलम्।
अभ्युत्तेजितदीपानां निर्बलति घृतमिव तत्क्षणं सहुताशम्।।]

Hearing that Indrajīt was slain, Rāvaṇa shed tears in anger that dripped at the moment, like the clarified butter of lighted lamps, touched by the flame.

The verse is not found in K and MY. Goldschmidt and N.S. text read *ṇivaḍai tuppaṁ va*, but R's reading, as pointed out by the former, is *ṇivvalai ghaam va* (निर्वलति पृथग्भूय पतति . . . घृतमिव R commentary)। Kula on the second line is somewhat corrupt, but he has तैलं[19] for *tuppaṁ* = घृतम्।

39. णिहए अ मेहणाए परिअत्तन्तेण तक्खणं चिअ विहिणा।
रोसविसाएहि समं हत्थेहि व दोहि आहदो दहवअणो।।

[निहते च मेघनादे परिवर्तमानेन तत्क्षणमेव विधिना।
रोषविषादाभ्यां समं हस्ताभ्यामिव द्वाभ्यामाहतो दशवदनः।।]

When Meghanāda was killed, Fate, turning adverse on the instant, smote Rāvaṇa with grief and despair at the same time, as if with both hands.

K *pratīka* has *suddhe* (पतिते *chāyā*) for *ṇihae* = निहते (R and Kula). K commentary has हते। MY *pratīka* has *paḍie* (पतिते)। K, MY and Kula have शोक (*soa*) for *rosa* (R). MY says परिवर्तमानेन पराङ्मुखीभवतेति यावत्। अत्र शोकः पुत्रव्यसनजात्मनः पीडा। विषादस्तु कार्यावसादजेति विभागः।

40. णीसेसणिहअबन्धू तो सो एक्को वि बहुभुआदुप्पेच्छो।
भीषणमुहसंघाओ रक्खसलोओ व्व णिग्गओ दहवअणो।।

[निःशेषनिहतबन्धुस्ततः स एकोऽपि बहुभुजादुष्प्रेक्ष्यः।
भीषणमुखसंघातो राक्षसलोक इव निर्गतो दशवदनः।।]

Even though left alone, with all kinsmen killed, Rāvaṇa who had a terrible cluster of faces, and formidable with his many arms, went out like a multitude of demons.

---

[19] (अभ्युत्तेजितानाम्) उत्कर्षि(त)दशानां (दीपानां) तत्क्षणं निपतितं तैलमिव Kula's reading might be *paḍiaṁ ṇehaṁ va*. *SC* text has *valaī siṇeha vva*.

MY says बन्धूनां निःशेषहततया एकाकित्वेऽपि भुजमुखबाहुल्यात् सकलबन्धुसहित इव लक्ष्यमाणो विनिर्गत इत्यर्थः।

K says अयमर्थः कालिदासेनापि उक्त –

भुजमूर्धोरुबाहुल्यादेकोऽपि धनदानुजः।
ददृशे ह्ययथापूर्वो मातृवंश इव स्थितः।। — *Raghu.* 12.88.

41–42. णवरि अ पवणपणोल्लिअकसणपलाआदरन्धआरिअसूरम्।
परिणअमत्तेरावणमअपव्वालिअतुरंगकेसरभारम्।।

चक्कमलमइलिओअरधअवडपुसिअससिबिम्बपच्छिमभाअम्।
धणअगआभङ्गुग्गअसिहिजालालुङ्खिअं रहं आरूढो।।
(जुग्गअम्)

[अनन्तरं च पवनप्रणोदितकृष्णपताकादरान्धकारितसूरम्।
परिणतमत्तैरावणमदप्लावितुरङ्गकेसरभारम्।।

चक्रमलमलिनितोदरध्वजपटप्रोञ्छितशशिबिम्बपश्चिमभागम्।
धनदगदाभङ्गोद्गतशिखिज्वालाकलुषितं रथमारूढः।।]
(युग्मकम्)

He then mounted his chariot that partly obscured the sun with its sable banners swayed by the wind. The heavy mane of the horses was drenched with the ichor of the furious Airāvata elephant when it had hit the car with its tusks (in the fight with Indra).

The reverse side of the lunar orb, soiled by the rust on the wheels, was wiped clean by the banners;[20] and the vehicle was scorched by the flames that had shot up when Kubera's mace hit it and broke (during his combat with Rāvaṇa).

K reads दरावच्छादितसूर्यकरम् (*chāyā*) for *darandhaāriasūraṁ* = दरान्धकारितसूरम् (R and probably Kula). K's reading seems to be *darocchaia-sūra-araṁ*. MY's reading appears to be about the same. He says ईषदवस्थगितसूर्यम्[21]। Manuscript C of Goldschmidt has *dara-thaia-sūra-araṁ*.

K says अनन्तरं पवनप्रणुन्नया कृष्णवर्णया पताकया दरच्छादितरविकिरणं, परिणतस्य दन्तप्रहारं कुर्वतो मत्तस्यैरावतस्य मदजलक्षालिततुरङ्गकेसरभारम्। उत्तरत्र सम्बन्धः।

---

20 I.e., during the aerial journeys of Rāvaṇa.

21 This is incomplete. सूर्यम् should be सूर्यकरम्। The Prākṛta equivalent is corrupt in the manuscripts, but *darocchaïa* appears in B

K says रथस्य नभसि मार्गवशादुपेते तुङ्गप्रदेशारोहणावरोहणे सति आरोहणसमये रथस्य चक्रगतेन मलेन मलिनितोदरः चन्द्रस्य पश्चिमभागः, पुनरवरोहणे तस्य ध्वजपटेन उन्मृष्टो निरस्तमलो भवति यस्येति बहुव्रीहिः। धनदेन सह युद्धे तस्य गदाताडनेनोद्गतया दहनज्वालया तप्तं रथमारूढः।

MY says अत्र रथचक्रेण चन्द्रमालिन्यं कुरुते, ध्वजपटेन मालिन्यमपाकुरुत इति द्वन्द्वमपि विवक्षितम्। *ālumbia* (*āluṁkhia* ?) उपतप्त। स्पृष्टेति वा। Manuscript A has *ālaṁghia*. Kula is corrupt, but he has स्पृष्ट (*SC* also). *SC* text has *ālaṁghia*. R explains *āluṁkhia* as कलुषित। See also R on 1.21. Hemacandra 4.182, 208 gives *āluṁkhai* in the sense of स्पृशति and दहति।

43. दट्ठूण अ तं णिन्तं पीआ मङ्गलमणाहि रअणिअरीहिं।
अत्तो च्चिअ उप्पण्णा तेहिं च्चिअ लोअणेहि बाहत्थबआ।।

[दृपा च तं निर्यान्तं पीता मङ्गलमनोभी रजनीचरीभिः।
अत एवोत्पन्नास्ताभ्यामेव लोचनाभ्यां बाष्पस्तबकाः।।]

When they saw him sally out, the *rākṣasa* women, wishing him well, choked back their tears with the very eyes from which they had issued.[22]

K and Kula[23] read बाष्पबिन्दवः for *bāha-tthavaā* = बाष्पस्तबकाः (R). Their reading is *theva* for *thavaa*. See extracts on 1.40. Cf. *SC* text. *SC* says थेव-शब्दो बिन्दुवचनो देशीय[24]।

K says निर्गच्छन्तं रावणं दृपा राक्षसीभिर्दयिताभिः बाष्पबिन्दवो लोचनैः पीता अन्तर्निरूढाः। प्रथमं शोकावेगात् यत एव येभ्यो निर्गताः तैरेव नयनैः पीताः। कथंभूताभिः-मङ्गलमनोभिः भर्तुर्मङ्गले मनांसि यासां ताभिः।

44. तो तेण करअलट्ठिअसेलोज्झरसलिलणिव्वरिअवच्छअडम्।
दट्ठीहि अ बाणेहि अ तुलिअं जाइ लहुअं पवंगमसेण्णम्।।

[ततस्तेन करतलस्थितशैलनिर्झरसलिलनिर्वृतवक्षःस्थलम्।
दृष्टिमिश्च बाणैश्च तुलितं याति लघुतां प्लवङ्गमसैन्यम्।।]

The host of apes, unsteady by nature, whose chests were

---

[22] Tears at the moment of departure were regarded as a bad omen.

[23] Kula manuscript here jumbles up the verses. After the beginning of the gloss on verse 43 appear verses 50-57, followed by the concluding portion of verse 43. After this come verses 44-49.

[24] This remark is from Kula's gloss which is here mutilated.

cooled by the cascades on the mountains held in their hands, was appraised by him with his eyes as well as his arrows.[25]

K and MY *pratīka* has *to ṇeṇa* for *to teṇa* (R and *SC* text). K (*chāyā*) has ततोऽनेन, but commentary has तेन (Kula also). Hemacandra 3.70, who quotes the beginning of the verse, has *ṇeṇa* and explains it as तेन।

K and Kula read निर्वापित (*ṇivvavia*) for *ṇivvaria* (R) = निर्वृत explained as शीतलित।

K says ततस्तेन जात्या लघुकं वानरसैन्यं दृष्टिभिश्च बाणैश्च तुलितं प्लवङ्गजात्या लघुत्वात् दृष्टिभिरवज्ञातं, बाणैः मुक्तैः तुलितम् अधःकृतम्। कथंभूतम् – करतलगृहीतानां शैलानां निर्झरैः पतद्भिः निर्वापितं शमितान्तस्तापं वक्षस्तटं यस्य तत्। अन्तस्तापश्च रावणदर्शनसंभवः।

SC says जात्या कुलेन स्वभावेन वा लघुकं सारशून्यं, संकटदर्शनादेव विस्मृतपराक्रमं वा।

MY says भयात् करतलस्थितशैलविक्षेपेऽपि जातिलघुतया शिथिलोद्यमं कपिबलं दृष्टिभिः बाणैश्च सारतस्तुलितमभूदित्यर्थः। Kula also says जातिलघुकं प्लवङ्गमसैन्यम्। The rest is corrupt.[26] R's construction is *jāi lahuaṁ* (याति लघुताम्)। He says प्रथमं दर्शनेनैव ज्ञातं कपिबलमिदं मदुपमर्दं न सहिष्यते चरमं शरत्यागे निर्धारितमिति तुलितपदार्थः। सांमुख्ये सति क्षुब्धं शरत्यागे सति क्षुब्धतरमभूदिति लघुतापदार्थः।

For *tulia* cf. notes on 2.37. तुलित means weighed, estimated, gauged, ascertained, etc. The word is also used in Pāli in the same sense. See *PTS Dictionary sub voce* which cites *Therīgāthā* 153 where the word is explained as परिच्छिन्न in the commentary. K's explanation of तुलित as अवज्ञात, अधःकृत is however supported by its use in Māgha 15.30, 61 where Mallinātha explains it as अवधूत, तिरस्कृत, अवधीरित। Vallabha in Māgha 15.61 (68 in Kashmir edn.) explains it as परिच्छिन्न।

45. पासावडिअम्मि वि से विहीसणे पवअसेण्णकअपरिवारे।
दीणो त्ति सोअरो त्ति अ अमरिसरससंधिओ वि उल्लइ सरो।।

---

[25] I.e. he judged the fighting qualities of the apes by observing them closely and assailing them with his arrows. According to Kṛṣṇa, he looked at them with contempt and overpowered them with his arrows.

[26] *SC* says दृष्टिपातैश्चबाणैश्च तुलितं परिकल्पितमिति कुलनाथः। Here परिकल्पितं is a mistake for परिकलितं। See Kula on 2.37.

[पार्श्वापतितेऽप्यस्य विभीषणे प्लवगसैन्यकृतपरिवारे।
दीन इति सोदर इति चामर्षरससंहितोऽप्युल्ललति शरः।।]

Even though Vibhīṣaṇa, surrounded by the host of apes, confronted him, his arrow, wrathfully joined to the bow, became unsteady, because Vibhīṣana was humble, and was his brother.

K, MY and Kula *pratīka* has *pantha* for *pāsa* = पार्श्व (R). K and possibly Kula have वश for रस (R) in the second line.

K says विभीषणे अभिमुखमार्गमापतिते सत्यपि (पथि आपतितेऽपि *chāyā*) रावणस्य अमर्षवशात् धनुषि संहितोऽपि शरः असौ दीनः बन्धुवर्गपरित्यागात् कपिबलपरिवृतत्वाच्च, क्षीणं[27] इति च, सोदर इति च मन्यमानस्य शर उल्ललति शिथिलीबभूव। अनेन तस्य माहात्म्यं भ्रातृस्नेहगौरवं च दर्शितम्। MY says शरपथापतिते दीन इति उदरभरणपर इति उल्ललति स्खलतीत्यर्थः। The reading of K, MY and Kula, i.e. *panthāvaḍia* (cf. *SC* text) is found also in *Setu* 6.34.

46. विसहिअपढमप्पहरो णवरि अ रोसेण संधिउब्भडबाणो।
इन्दासणीअ व दुमो सत्तीअ उरम्मि लक्खणो णिब्भिण्णो।।

[विसोढप्रथमप्रहारोऽनन्तरं च रोषेण संहितोद्भटबाणः।
इन्द्राशन्येव द्रुमः शक्त्योरसि लक्ष्मणो निर्भिन्नः।।]

Thereafter Lakṣmaṇa, who had endured the initial assault, and joined a formidable arrow to his bow, was pierced by Rāvaṇa in the chest with a lance, even as a tree is riven by the thunderbolt of Indra.

K and MY read प्रथमप्रहारमहितः (*paḍhama-ppahāra-mahio*) for *visahia-paḍhama-ppaharo* = विसोढप्रथमप्रहारः (R and Kula). K and Kula read तेन धनुः° (*teṇa* or *ṇeṇa dhaṇu*°) for *roseṇa* (R).

K says युद्धेषु प्रथमप्रहारेण महितो वीरैः पूजितः, अतएव धनुषि संहितविभीषणशरः (संहितोद्भटबाणः *chāyā*) लक्ष्मणः तेन रावणेन शक्त्या आयुधविशेषेण उरसि भिन्नः इन्द्रस्याशन्या वृक्ष इव प्रहतः।

MY says प्रथमप्रहारमहितः प्रथमेव शत्रुं प्रहृत्यातएव पूजितस्थितः। Kula has धनुषि संहितोत्कटबाणः।

---

[27] This seems to be a mistake.

47. सो वि अ पवणसुआणिअधराहरोसहिविइण्णजीअब्भहिओ।
तह संधिअचावसरो णिसाअरेहि सह जुज्झिउं आढत्तो।।

[सोऽपि च पवनसुतानीतधराधरौषधिवितीर्णजीवाभ्यधिक:।
तथा संहितचापशरो निशाचरैः सह योद्धुमारब्धः।।]

He was given a new lease of life by the plants of a mountain that was brought over by Hanumat, and began to fight with the demons, equipped with bow and arrows as before.

K and Kula read अभ्युदय (*obbhuaa*) for *abbhahia* = अभ्यधिक (R).

K says स लक्ष्मणश्च पवनसुतेनानीतस्य गिरेरोषधिभिः मृतसञ्जीवनी प्रभृतिभिः दत्तजीविताभ्युदयः[28] (वितीर्णजीवाभ्युदयः *chāyā*) तथैव पूर्ववत् संहितशरचापो भूत्वा राक्षसैः सह योद्धुमारब्धः।

Kula reads स एव (*so ccia*) for *so vi a* (सोऽपि च)।

48–50. अह रामो वि णिअच्छइ तुरअखुरप्पहरविहलजलहरवट्ठम्।
ठिअवज्जहरालम्बिअकणअद्धअक्खम्भणिम्महन्तपरिमलम्।।

वामभुअगहिअपग्गहमाअलिभरणमिअदीहरधुरादण्डम्।
भिज्जन्तमेहसीहरतण्णाओणअणिसण्णचामरपम्हम्।।

ससिणिहसतुसारोल्लिअरविअरवसुआअधअवडसिहद्धन्तम्।
उण्णअपच्छिमतडिमं णिवडन्तं खअवइं व सग्गाहि रहम्।।

(कुलअम्)

[अथ रामोऽपि निर्ध्यायति तुरगखुरप्रहारविह्वलजलधरपृष्ठम्।
स्थितवज्रधरालम्बितकनकध्वजस्तम्भनिर्यत्परिमलम्।।]

वामभुजगृहीतप्रग्रहमातलिभरनमितदीर्घधुरादण्डम्।
भिद्यमानमेघशीकरार्द्रावनतनिषण्णचामरपक्ष्माणम्।।

शशिनिघर्षतुषारार्द्रितरविकरशुष्कध्वजपटशिखार्धान्तम्।
उन्नतपश्चिमतडिमं निपतन्तं खगपतिमिव स्वर्गैरित्थम्।।]

Rāma then beheld a chariot descending from heaven, like the king of birds (Garuḍa), with the rear projecting upward. The surface of the clouds was ruffled by the impact of the

[28] Kula is here corrupt. Our copy has दत्तजीवितमुदयः। *SC* has दत्तजीविताभ्युदयः।

hooves of the horses; and the golden flag staff emitted a sweet smell because Indra used to stand leaning against it.

The long yoke bent with the weight of Mātali as he held the reins in his left hand; and the hair of the *cāmara* whisks[29] was smooth and close, being drenched with the spray of the scattered clouds; while the crest of the banner, moistened by frost as it rubbed against the moon, was dried by the rays of the sun.[30]

K reads विषम् for *vihala* = विह्वल (R). He says अथ रामः तुरगखुरप्रहारैः विषमीकृतजलधरपृष्ठभागं, स्थितेन विश्रम्य स्थितेन वज्रधरेणालम्बितात् कनकध्वजस्तम्भात् निर्वमत्परिमलं निर्गच्छन्महेन्द्रशरीराङ्गरागपरिमलं रथमित्युत्तरेण सम्बन्धः। MY says युद्धार्थमवस्थितेन वज्रधरेणालम्बितत्वात् तदङ्गगतकस्तूरिका-संस्पृष्टात् ध्वजस्तम्भात् निर्यत्परिमलम्। R says स्थितेन वज्रधरेण आलम्बितात् पृष्ठेनावष्टब्धात्।(48)

Kula has भिन्न for विह्वल। He says तुरगानां खुरप्रहारैः भिन्नजलधरपृष्ठम्।

K and MY read तुण्ड for दण्ड (R). K says वामकरेण गृहीततुरङ्गरज्जोः मातलेः स्थितस्य देहस्य (भरेण) नमितं दीर्घतरं[31] धूस्तुण्डं रथस्य मुखप्रदेशे धूः धुरा तस्याः तुण्डोऽग्रो यस्य तम्। धूः स्याद् यानमुखे भारे इति वैजयन्ती। चक्रनेमिभिः भिद्यमानानां मेघानां शीकरैरार्द्रत्वात् अवनतानि . . .[32] रोषाणि यस्य तम्। उत्तरत्र सम्बन्धः।(49)

MY says *dīhara-dhurā-tuṇḍaṁ* दीर्घधूस्तुण्डं दीर्घतरयुग्यदारुमुखमित्यर्थः। B has दीर्घयुग्य।

K says शशिनः चक्राभिहतस्य चन्द्रस्य निकषणभवेन तुषारेण प्रथममार्द्रीकृतः, ततो रविकिरणैः शोषितो ध्वजपटार्धान्तो यस्य तम्। अवतरणवशात् उन्नतपश्चिमतलं (°तलिमं *chāyā*) स्वर्गात् गरुडमिव निपतन्तं हिरण्मयं रथमपश्यत्। MY says आकारतो गरुडमिवेति वर्णयतः कवेस्तस्यैव भगवद्वहनशक्तता चेत्यभिप्रायः।

Kula reads सितार्धान्तम् (*siaddhantaṁ*) for *siha°* (शिखार्धान्तम्) He says ध्वजपटैः सितार्धान्तं धवलैकदेशम्। R says शशिनो निघर्षे सति तदीयतुषारैरार्द्रीकृतः पश्चात् तदधोवर्तिनो रवेः करैः शुष्को ध्वजपटस्य शिखा अग्रं तदर्धान्तो यत्र तम्।(50)

---

[29] See 13-66.

[30] The chariot belonged to Indra, Mātali being his charioteer.

[31] Manuscript has निमितदीर्घतरं।

[32] R says अवनतानि सन्ति निषण्णानि मिथो मिलितानि चामराणां पक्ष्माणि यत्र।

51. तो रामो माअडिणा पढमदराभासणुम्मुहपसण्णमुहो।
तिअसबहुमाणगरुअं दूरअरोणामिआणणेण पणमिओ।।

[ततो रामो मातलिना प्रथमदराभाषणोन्मुखप्रसन्नमुखः।
त्रिदशबहुमानगुरुकं दूरतरावनमिताननेन प्रणतः।।]

As Rāma was about to greet him first with a cheerful countenance Mātali, profoundly inclining his head, bowed to him reverently, conveying the high esteem of the gods.

K, MY and Kula read प्रथमतर for *paḍhama-dara* = प्रथमदर (R).

K says मातलेराभाषणात् प्रथमतरमेव आभाषणार्थमुन्मुखमुन्नतं प्रसन्नं मुखं यस्य स रामः अत्यन्तमवनमिताननेन मातलिना त्रिदशबहुमानगुरुकं त्रिदशानां देवानां रामविषयेण बहुमानेन गुरु यथा भवति तथा प्रणतः नमस्कृतः।

MY says उन्मुख उद्युक्तः। पूर्वभाषणोद्युक्तं च प्रसन्नं च मुखं यस्येति वा, पूर्वभाषणोद्युक्तः प्रसन्नमुखश्चेति वा विग्रहः। त्रिदशबहुमानगुरु त्रिदशानां प्रमाणप्रकारादपि[33] उपचारातिशयवत् यथा स्यात् तथा। न पुनर्मानुषोचितमित्यर्थः।

Kula says प्रथमतराभाषणाय उन्मुखं सादरं प्रसन्नं मुखं यस्य स रामः He reads त्रिदशपति (*tiasa-vai*) for *tiasa-bahu°*.

R explains प्रथमदर . . . as प्राथमिके कुशलप्रश्नादिरूपे किंचिदाभाषणे उन्मुखं सत् प्रसन्नं मुखं यस्य सः।

52. देइ अ रहपुञ्जइअं उहअकरक्खिवणपाअडिअवित्थारम्।
कवअं तिहुअणवइणो अब्भन्तरलग्गणिम्महन्तपरिमलम्।।

[ददाति च रथपुञ्जितमुभयकरक्षेपणप्रकटितविस्तारम्।
कवचं त्रिभुवनपतेरभ्यन्तरलग्ननिर्यत्परिमलम्।।]

He presented Rāma with the armour of Indra, the lord of the three worlds, which lay massive in the chariot. Its great size was revealed when both its arms were raised;[34] while the perfumed inside emitted fragrance.

K, MY and Kula read करोत्क्षेपण for *kara-kkhivaṇa* = करक्षेपण (R).

K says स्पष्टोऽर्थः। MY has *avaha* for *uhaa* (उभय)। Cf. Hemacandra 2.138. MY says *karukkhivaṇa* करोत्क्षेपण। त्रिभुवनपतेरिति महेन्द्रस्य।

---

[33] B has प्रमाणादपि।

[34] For lifting it from the chariot.

ṇimmahanta निर्यत् (निर्वमत् *chāyā*)। पूर्वं रथे पुञ्जितस्थितं पश्चादुभयकरोत्क्षेपण-प्रकटितविस्तारं तदेव . . . इन्द्रस्य कवचं रामाय प्रादादित्यर्थः।

53. तं च कवअं सुराहिवसव्वङ्गपहुत्तलोअणसुहप्फरिसम्।
सीआविरहोलुग्गे जाअं थोअसिढिलं रहुवइस्स उरे।।

[तच्च कवचं सुराधिपसर्वाङ्गप्रभूतलोचनसुखस्पर्शम्।
सीताविरहावरुग्णे जातं स्तोकशिथिलं रघुपतेरुरसि।।]

That armour, soft on the inside for Indra's eyes pervading his limbs, proved to be slightly loose on Rāma's bosom wasted by the grief of separation from Sītā.

K says सुराधिपस्य सर्वाङ्गेषु प्रभूतैः लोचनैः करणभूतैः सुखस्पर्शम् इन्द्रस्य लोचनानां सर्वाङ्गव्यापित्वात् तदनुकूलमृदुस्पर्शमित्यर्थः। तत् कवचं रामस्य सीतावियोगादवरुग्णे कृशे उरसि स्तोकशिथिलम् अल्पं शिथिलं जातम्। अनेन राघवस्य देवेन्द्रस्य च शरीरयोः समानप्रमाणत्वमुक्तम्। सीताविरहकार्श्यं न चेत् पर्याप्तं कवचं भवेदिति। MY says सुराधिपस्य सहस्रसंख्यतया सर्वाङ्गपर्याप्तानां लोचनानां कृते सुखस्पर्शनिमित्तमित्यर्थः।

54. महिअलमोइण्णेण अ सुरवइहत्थपरिमाससइदुल्ललिअम्।
आरूढस्स रहं से कवअं सव्वङ्गिअं कअं माअडिणा।।

[महीतलमवतीर्णेन च सुरपतिहस्तपरिमर्षसदादुर्ललितम्।
आरूढस्य रथमस्य कवचं सर्वाङ्गिकं कृतं मातलिना।।]

When Rāma mounted the chariot, Mātali, alighting on the ground, enveloped the former's body in the armour that had always been fondly touched by Indra's hands.

K reads महीतलपरिष्ठितेन for *mahi-alamoiṇṇeṇa* = महीतलमवतीर्णेन (R and Kula). He says रथमारूढस्य तस्य वक्षःस्थलगतं कवचं महीतलस्थितेन परिजनवत् अधस्तात् स्थितेन मातलिना तस्य सर्वाङ्गिकं सर्वाङ्गव्यापि कृतं च। कीदृशम्–सुरपतेः हस्तस्पर्शात् सदा दुर्ललितं गर्वितम्।

MY says *parimāsa* परिमर्श। *savvaṁgiaṁ* सर्वाङ्गीणं सर्वाङ्गव्याप्तमित्यर्थः। R says सुरपतेर्हस्ताभ्यां परिमर्षेण रजोमार्जनादिना व्यापारेण दुर्ललितं स्नेहपात्रीकृतम्। Kula says दुर्ललितं सुकुमारत्वात् असकृत स्पृष्टम्।

55. तो णीलरविसुराहिं समल्लिओ राहवं सुमित्तातणओ।
भणइ धरणीअ तक्खणविलइअधणुगब्भिणं णिमेऊण करम्।।

[ततो नीलरविसुताभ्यां समन्वितो राघवं सुमित्रातनयः।
भणति धरण्यां तत्क्षणविलगितधनुर्गर्भितं निवेश्य करम्॥]

Thereupon Lakṣmaṇa, approaching Rāma with Nīla and Sugrīva, spoke to him as he placed on the ground his hand which held the bow just taken up by him.[35]

K says ततो नीलसुग्रीवाभ्यां सह राघवमाश्रितो लक्ष्मणः तत्क्षणगृहीतधनुर्गर्भितं करं धरण्यां निधाय प्रणम्य भणति स्म।

MY says *samallio* प्राप्तः। नीलसुग्रीवाभ्यां सह समुपगतो[36] लक्ष्मणो धनुर्गर्भितमेव करं भूमौ विन्यस्याभणदिति। अत्र करं धरण्यां निमित्येति प्रणामप्रकारो दर्शितः।[37] Kula renders *samallio* as समन्वितः like R (समाश्रितः K *chāyā*)। R says नीलसुग्रीवाभ्यां समन्वितः सुमित्रातनयः . . . राघवं भणति।

56. वीसमउ तुम्ह चावं अडणिमुहप्फिडिअसिढिलजीआबन्धम्।
अइरा पेच्छ विराअं ममम्मि णीले व्व रविसुए व्व दहमुहम्॥

[विश्राम्यतु तव चापमटनिमुखस्फेटितशिखिलज्याबन्धम्।
अचिरात्पश्य विशीर्णं मयि नीले वा रविसुते वा दशमुखम्॥]

"Sire, let thy bow be at rest with the string detached from the ends and loose. Behold Rāvaṇa destroyed before long by Nīla or Sugrīva or myself.

K, MY and Kula read प्रभो मीलतु युष्मद्धनुः for *vīsamaü tumha cāvaṁ* = विश्राम्यतु तव चापम् (R). Their reading seems to be *pahu millaü tumha dhaṇuṁ*. Cf. *SC* text.

K says हे प्रभो युष्मद्धनुः अटनिमुखात् भ्रष्टशिथिलज्याबन्धं भूत्वा मीलतु युद्धसंनाहमपहाय निषीदतु। अचिरात् रावणं मयि नीले वा सुग्रीवे वा विलीनं पश्य।

MY says *pahu* प्रभो। *millaü* मीलतु निर्व्यापारी भवतु। *virāaṁ* विलीनं हतम्। युष्माकं धनुः कोटितः शिथिलज्याबन्धं भूत्वा निमीलतु। अस्मासु अन्यतमेन हन्यमानो दशमुखस्त्वया केवलं निरीक्षितव्यः।

Phiḍia is rendered as स्फेटित = उत्तारित by R; भ्रष्ट (K). R renders *virāa* as विशीर्ण।

---

[35] This was a manner of obeisance customary among warriors as pointed out by some of the commentators.

[36] समुपागतः A.

[37] *SC* says गृहीतास्त्रं पाणिं भूमौ निवेश्य प्रणम्यात्मनिवेदनं वीराणां स्वभावः।

57. गरुअम्मि कुणसु कोवं लहुए दहमुहवहम्मि मुअसु अमरिसम्।
तुङ्गं तटं णिसुम्मइ ण अ णइवप्पं समत्थलिं व वणगओ।।

[गुरौ कुरुष्व कोपं लघौ दशमुखवधे मुञ्चामर्षम्।
तुङ्गं तटं निपातयति न च नदीवप्रं समस्थलीं वा वनगजः।।]

Indulge in wrath in a matter that is weighty. Renounce vengeful persistence in the easy task of slaying Rāvaṇa. As elephant of the gods batters a lofty hillside down, but not a riverbank or the level ground.

K and MY read समुच्छ्रितमपि सुरगजः for *sama-tthaliṁ va vaṇa-gac* = समस्थलीं वा वनगजः। (R). Their reading seems to be *samūsiaṁ vi sura-gao*. K says गुरुणि कार्ये कोपं कुरु। लघुनि रावणवधे अमर्षं मुञ्च। सुरगजः तुङ्गं गिरितटं निपातयति। समुच्छ्रितमपि नदीतटं (नदीवप्रं *chāyā*) न निपातयति। K *chāyā* has न खलु (*ṇa hu*) for *ṇa a* (न च) in the second line.

MY says गुरौ वधे इति शेषः निमित्तसप्तमी चेयम्। *ṇisubbhai* (for *ṇisumbhai*) अवपातयति। सुरगजो हि उच्छ्रितमपि नदीकूलं न निपातयति। अपि तु तुङ्गगिरिशिखरमित्यर्थः। पूर्वं हीनतरो रावणस्त्वया न प्रतिद्वन्द्वीकर्तव्य इत्युक्तम्।

Kula is corrupt, but he reads *sura-gao*, as he has ऐरावतः। He seems to read *sama-tthaliṁ* like R, as सम appears in his gloss. *SC* says वप्रो मृत्कूट इति कुलनाथः।

58. पज्जत्तस्स समत्थं दहिउं अद्धच्छिपेच्छिएण वि तिउरम्।
रहुवइ किं व ण सुव्वइ आणत्ती तिणअणस्स तिअसेहि कआ।।

[पर्याप्तस्य समस्तं दग्धुमर्धाक्षिप्रेक्षितेनापि त्रिपुरम्।
रघुपते किं वा न श्रृणोषि आज्ञाप्तिस्त्रिनयनस्य त्रिदृशैः कृता।।]

Is it not reported,[38] O lord of the Raghus, that even though Śiva was capable of burning all the three cities of the demons by a mere glance, it was the gods who carried out his command?"[39]

K, MY and Kula read *pulaieṇa* (see below) for *pecchieṇa* = प्रेक्षितेन (R). K and MY read *tihuaṇaṁ* for *vi tiüraṁ* = अपि त्रिपुरम् (R and Kula).

[38] Literally heard.

[39] I.e. destroyed the cities under his command.

K says अर्धलोचनविलोकनेन (विलोकितेन *chāyā*) नयनस्यापाङ्गविलो- कनेनैव समस्तं त्रिभुवनं दुग्धुं पर्याप्तस्य त्रिनयनस्य त्रिपुरदहनस्य साधनसंपादनात् आज्ञा (त्रिदशैः कृता) किं न श्रूयते। तस्मादस्मानेव रावणवेधे नियुङ्क्ष्वेति वाक्यशेषः। K (*chāyā*) has किमिव न श्रूयते आज्ञप्तिस्त्रिनयनस्य त्रिदशैः कृता। Kula says किं वा न श्रूयते।

MY says *samattaṁ* (for °*tthaṁ* R) समस्तम्। *addhacchi-pulaieṇa* अर्धाक्षिप्रलोकितेन (Kula also).

59. तो दहवअणालोअणरोसुग्गअसेअलङ्घिअणिलाडअडो।
पुलइअणीलरविसुओ पणअं पडिभणइ लक्खणं रहुणाहो।।

[ततो दशवदनालोकनरोषोद्गतस्वेदलङ्घितललाटतटः।
प्रलोकितनीलरविसुतः प्रणतं प्रतिभणति लक्ष्मणं रघुनाथः।।]

Rāma, his forehead covered with sweat in his wrath at the sight of Rāvaṇa, looked at Nīla and Sugrīva; and replied to Lakṣmaṇa as he bowed to him.

K (*chāyā*) has विलोकितनीलरविसुतः। He says स्पष्टोऽर्थः। R and Kula have प्रलोकित। MY says *paṇaaṁ* प्रणतम्, but manuscript B has *vaaṇaṁ* वचनम्।

60. णिव्वूढजम्पिआणं आसङ्घइ तुम्ह ववसिअं मह हिअअम्।
किं उण भरो व्व होहिइ सअं अणिट्ठविअदहमुहो मज्झ भुओ।।

[निर्व्यूढजल्पितानामध्यवस्यति युष्माकं व्यवसितं मम हृदयम्।
किं पुनर्भर इव भविष्यति स्वयमनिष्ठापितदशमुखो मम भुजः।।]

"My heart is confident of the success of your endeavour, because you have fulfilled your promises. But my arm will be as a burden to me if it fails to destroy Rāvaṇa by its own effort.

K and probably MY read समरभारम् for *jampiāṇaṁ* = जल्पितानाम् (R and Kula). They read नाशङ्कते for *āsaṅghai* = अध्यवस्यति (R); आशंसति = संप्रत्येति, अवधारयति वा (*SC*). Kula is here corrupt.

K says युष्मद्व्यवसितं व्यवसाय एव व्यवसितं युष्मदध्यवसितं निर्व्यूढसमरभारमित्यत्र मम हृदयं न शङ्कते (नाशङ्कते chāyā) न संशेते। अथवा युष्मदध्यवसितमर्थान्तरं निर्व्यूढसमरभारमेव स्यात्। किं पुनः किंतु स्वयमेवानिष्ठापितदशसुखः अविध्वंसितरावणो मम भुजः भर इव भविष्यति। MY says मम हृदयं बह्वपदानदर्शनादेव त्वद्व्यवसायनिर्वहणं प्रति न संशेते।

Kula says निर्व्यूढं जल्पितं प्रतिज्ञातं यैस्तेषां युष्माकम्। R says मम हृदयं निर्व्यूढजल्पितानां निर्वाहितस्वप्रतिज्ञानां युष्माकं व्यवसितं कर्म अध्यवस्यति सिद्धत्वेन जानातीत्यर्थः।

61. कुम्भस्स पहत्थस्स अ दूसह णिहणेण इन्दइस्स अ समरे।
दसकण्ठं मुहवडिअं केसरिणो वणगअं व मा हरह महम्।।
[कुम्भस्य प्रहस्तस्य च तुष्यत निधनेनेन्द्रजितश्च समरे।
दशकण्ठं मुखपतितं केसरिणो वनगजमिव मा हरत मम।।]

Content yourselves with having slain Kumbha, Prahasta and Indrajit[40] in battle. Snatch not Rāvaṇa away who hath chanced to come face to face with me, like a wild elephant falling a prey to a lion's jaws."

K says वानराधिराजस्तावत् बलवत्तरं कुम्भं हतवान्। नीलश्च प्रहस्तं जघान। त्वमपीन्द्रजितमवधीः। एवं यूयमेकैकैः अपदानैः तुष्यत। मम् मुखे पतितं रावणं मा हरत मापकर्षत। केसरिणः पुरोगतं वनगजमिव।

MY says *tūsaha* (for *dūsaha* found in R) तुष्यत्।

62. ताण अ कहं पअत्तं वोच्छिन्दन्तस्स दहमुहस्स रणमुहे।
उम्मूलिउं पअत्तो अग्गक्खन्धम्मि कइबलं सरणिवहो।।
[तेषां च कथां प्रवृत्तां व्यवच्छिन्दतो दशमुखस्य रणमुखे।
उन्मूलयितुं प्रवृत्तोऽग्रस्कन्धे कपिबलं शरनिवहः।।]

Rāvaṇa's arrows, as if interrupting their talk that was in progress, began to overwhelm the host of apes in the front ranks in the battle.

K and MY read व्युच्छिन्दन्निव for *vocchindantassa* = व्यवच्छिन्दतो (R). Kula has व्यवच्छिन्दन्निव। MY says *vocchindanto vva* व्युच्छिन्दन्निव व्युच्छेदकरणाभिसन्धिनेति यावत्। Kula explains it as समापयन्निव।

MY reads *oaggiuṁ* for *ummūliuṁ* = उन्मूलयितुम् (R), and explains it as अभिभवितुम् found in K (*chāyā*) also. K says नात्र दुर्बोधमस्ति। Kula has अवकल्पितुमाक्षन्दितुम्, but is corrupt. If he reads अववल्गितुम्, his reading is same as that of K and MY. *SC* text has *ovaggīuṁ* rendered as आक्रमितुम्।

[40] Killed respectively by Sugrīva, Nīla and Lakṣmaṇa.

63. तो दोण्ह वि समसारं बाणवहप्फिडिअतिअसपेक्खिज्जन्तम्।
एक्कअरमरणगरुअं जाअं रामस्स दहमुहस्स अ जुज्झम्।।

[ततो द्वयोरपि समसारं बाणपथस्फेटितत्रिदशप्रेक्ष्यमाणम्।
एकतरमरणगुरुकं जातं रामस्य दशमुखस्य च युद्धम्।।]

Thereupon ensued the combat between Rāma and Rāvaṇa, marked by equal valour, and momentous because of the certain death of one of them, and watched by the gods, keeping out of range of the arrows.

K and Kula read रावणस्य for *dahamuhassa*. K (*chāyā*) has बाणपरिभ्रष्ट K says . . . द्वयोरपि समसारं सदृशवीर्योत्कर्षं, बाणपथादपगतैः देवैः दृश्यमानमेकतरस्य द्वयोरन्यतस्य मरणात् गुरुकं महत् युद्धं जातम्। R says बाणपथस्फेटिता बाणपातभिया बहिर्भूतस्थिताः। Kula says बाणपथात् स्फेटितैरपगतैः।

64. तो कड्ढिऊण चावं कुण्डलमणिकिरणघडिअजीआबन्धम्।
मुक्को रामस्स उरे पढमं हअबन्धुणा दहमुहेण सरो।।

[ततः कृष्ट्वा चापं कुण्डलमणिकिरणघटितज्याबन्धम्।
मुक्तो रामस्योरसि प्रथमं हतबन्धुना दशमुखेन शरः।।]

Rāvaṇa whose kinsmen had been slain first shot an arrow at Rāma's bosom, having drawn the bow in such a manner that the string glistened with the lustre of the jewels of his earrings.[41]

K *chāyā* has करमिलत् (*kara-milanta*) for किरणघडिअ = °घटित (R). Kula has °मिलित। K says रावणेन चापं कुण्डलमणिकिरणमिलज्ज्याबन्धं यथा आकृष्य, i.e. आकर्णमाकृष्य (MY), रामस्योरसि शरः प्रथमं मुक्तः। Kula says आकर्णाकर्षणात् कुण्डलमणीनां किरणैः मिलितज्याबन्धं चापं कृपा।

65. वेअपडिएण तेण अ तह धीरो वि परिकम्पिओ रहुणाहो।
अप्पाणणिव्विसेसं सअलं जह णेण कम्पिअं तेल्लोक्कम्।।

[वेगपतितेन तेन च तथा धीरोऽपि परिकम्पितो रघुनाथः।
आत्मनिर्विशेषं सकलं यथानेन कम्पितं त्रैलोक्यम्।।]

Even though firm, Rāma was shaken by that arrow as it swiftly descended on his bosom, in such a way that because of this all the three worlds, inseparable from him, were shaken like himself.[42]

---

41 I.e. he drew the bow up to the ear.

42 Rāma is identified with Viṣṇu comprising the universe in himself.

K says उरसि वेगपतितेन तेन शरेण रामश्च धीरोऽपि अप्रकम्प्योऽपि तथा प्रकम्पितः। कथम्-अनेन कम्पेन हेतुना सकलं त्रैलोक्यमात्मनो निर्विशेषं यथा परिकम्पितम्। R says वस्तुतस्तु आत्मनो निर्विशेषमभिन्नमात्मस्वरूपं त्रैलोक्यं कम्पितम्।

66. रहुणाहस्स वि बाणो अणुपरिवाडिघडिअप्फुडिअकेऊरम्।
दहवअणभुअणिहाअं तालवणक्खन्धपरिअएण अइगओ।।

[रघुनाथस्यापि बाणोऽनुपरिपाटिघटितस्फुटितकेयूरम्।
दशवदनभुजनिघातं तालवनस्कन्धपरिचयेनातिगतः।।]

Rāma's arrow in its turn pierced through the cluster of Rāvaṇa's arms, hitting the armlets breaking them in succession, by virtue of the skill gained by him in piercing the trunks of the (seven) palms in a grove.[43]

K and Kula read *milia* for *ghaḍia* (R). K and MY read *phiḍia* for *phuḍia* = स्फुटित (R). K and MY read *sāla-duma* for *tāla-vaṇa* (R and Kula). Kula reads स्तम्भ (*khambha*) for *khandha* (स्कन्ध)। He reads स्फटिक (*phaliha*) for *phuḍia* (see above).

K says रामस्यापि शरो रावणस्य पार्श्वे पतन् भुजपरम्परामनुपरिपाटि, परिपाटिरनुक्रमः, परिपाटिमनुबध्य मिलितभ्रष्टानि केयूराणि यथा भवन्ति तथा, पूर्वं सप्तसालस्कन्ध-भेदपरिचयेन अतिगतः भित्त्वा अतिक्रान्ताः। *malia-pphiḍia* इति वा पाठः। मृदितभ्रष्टमित्यर्थः[44]।

MY says *phiḍia* भ्रष्ट। अतिगतः भित्त्वा गतः। प्रागेव सालस्कन्धपरम्पराभेदनाभ्यासेन रावणस्य दश भुजानपि भित्त्वैव असक्तौ गत इत्यर्थः। Kula says अनुपरिपाट्या यथाक्रमम्। He has अभिगतः for अतिगतः, and says तालवनस्तम्भानां परिचयेन पूर्वानुभवेन अभिगतः विद्ध्वा निष्क्रान्तः।

R says अनुपरिपाट्यानुक्रमेण घटिता एकाभिमुख्येन स्थिताः, अथ च स्फुटिता बाणेनैव विद्धाः केयूरा यस्मिन् तमित्यङ्गदस्थान एव भुजानभिनदित्याशयः।

67. अण्णं संधिअबाणं रहसाअड्ढिअणिराअवट्ठं अण्णम्।
समअं रक्खसवइणो अण्णं सरलहुइओअरं होइ धणुम्।।

[अन्यत्संहितबाणं रभसाकृष्टनिरायतपृष्ठमन्यत्।
समं राक्षसपतेरन्यल्लघुकृतोदरं भवति धनुः।।]

---

[43] Reference to the story of his piercing seven palm trees at the same time.

[44] Our copy has मिलितभ्रष्टम्, but *malia* is मृदित।

(Of the bows in the several hands) of Rāvaṇa, one had the arrow fixed; another, drawn with force, was bent backward;[45] and another rid of the arrow, all at once.[46]

K reads आकर्षणनमत् for *āaḍḍhia-ṇirāa* = आकृष्टनिरायत (R and Kula).

K says रावणस्य वामभुजेषु एकं चापं संहितशरमभूत्। शरं संधाय रभसाकर्षणात् नमत्पृष्ठमन्यत्। अन्यत् धनुः मुक्तशरत्वात् लघूकृतोदरमभूत्। एवं सममेव ददृशे। Kula says अन्यत् शरलघुकृतोदरं मुक्तशरं समं युगपदेव रावणस्य धनुर्भवति।

MY says अन्यदत्र अन्यदन्यदिति वीप्सा द्रष्टव्या। तेन धनुषामुक्तन्यायेन त्र्यवस्थत्वेऽपि दशसंख्यत्वाविरोधः। Kula follows the same line of interpretation. R explains अन्यत् as अन्यावस्थम्, and takes the epithets to denote different aspects of the same bow. He says राक्षसपतेर्धनुः सममेकदैव भवति। कीदृशम् – संहितबाणं सत् अन्यत् अन्यावस्थं समकोटिद्वयत्वात्। रभसेनाकृष्टत्वात् निरायतपृष्ठमुत्थापितपृष्ठं सदन्यत् कोटिद्वयनमनात्। . . . इति संधानाकर्षणत्यागानामेककालिकत्वेन शिक्षाकौशलमुक्तम्। *SC* says निरायतमदीर्घम्; "contracted" (M. Williams). The word means also "stretched out", and *ṇirāa* is often used in the sense of "long" in the poem.

68. सइसंधिअणिन्तसरं अवङ्गदेससइलग्गजीवाबन्धम्।
दीसइ सइमुक्कसरं सइमण्डलिअविअडोअरं रामधणुम्।।

[सदासंहितनिर्यच्छरमपाङ्गदेशसदालग्रज्याबन्धम्।
दृश्यते सदामुक्तशरं सदामण्डलितविकटोदरं रामधनुः।।]

Rāma's bow was seen with the arrows continuously fixed and issuing forth, and the string constantly adhering to the corner of the eye;[47] while it gave forth a continuous sound, and appeared to be curved and empty all of time.

K and Kula read मुक्तरवम् for *mukka-saraṁ* (R). K says स्पष्टोऽर्थः। MY says एकस्यापि रामधनुषो युगपत् शरसंधानाकर्षणमोक्षणैः त्र्यवस्थत्वं

---

[45] Literally, had the back stretched. Rāmadāsa calls this *utthāpita*. Cf. Gk. *palintonos*, an epithet of the bow, *stretched back; bent backward*, i.e. the opposite way to that in which it was drawn. See Liddell and Scott: *Greek-English Lexicon* (the abridged edn. and the new edn. by Jones) and Bailly, *Dict. Grec-Fr. sub voce*. When used of the unstrung bow, it might refer to a curved bow of the Scythian type. Cf. *Odyssey* XXI.11, ed. Stanford with commentary, 1958.

[46] As Rāvaṇa had ten arms on each side, several bows were in action at the same time. For another explanation, see Extracts.

[47] I.e. the bow was drawn up to the ear, which is the usual phrase.

वेगवशाददृश्यतेत्यर्थः। Kula says सदा संहिता निर्यान्तः शरा यस्मात्। . . . सदा मुक्तो रवो येन। सदा मण्डलितं विकटं विशालम् (?) उदरं यस्य तत् तथाभूतं रामधनुर्दृश्यते। R says सदा मण्डलितं मण्डलाकारं सत् विकटोदरं तुच्छोदरं त्यक्तशरत्वात्।

69. वामो पसारिअ च्चिअ दाहिणहत्थो अवङ्गदेसणिवडिओ।
चावेसु अ तह णिमिआ ताणं दीसन्ति अन्तरालेसु सरा।।

[वामः प्रसारित एव दक्षिणहस्तोऽपाङ्गदेशनिपतितः।
चापयोश्च तथा नियोजितास्तयोर्दृश्यतेऽन्तरालेषु शराः।।]

The left hand remained outstretched,[48] and the right stuck to the corner of the eye;[49] yet the arrows, joined to their bows, were seen in the intervening space between them.[50]

K reads निगलितः (*chāyā*) for *ṇivaḍio* = निपतितः (R and Kula). *SC* text has *ṇialio* = निगडितः (*chāyā*).

K says तयोः वामो हस्तः प्रसारित एव ददृशे। दक्षिणहस्तः शराकर्षणं कुर्वन् अपाङ्गदेशे (नि)गलितः लग्नः। चापयोश्च शरास्तथा निहिताः। एवं हस्ताश्च शराश्च लाघवातिशयात् एककरोपस्थिताः। तथापि तयोरन्तरालप्रदेशेषु अन्योन्यं मुक्ताः शरा दृश्यन्ते स्म। शराणां संधानाकर्षणविसर्गाः कथंचिदपि नोपलक्षिता इत्यर्थः।

MY says भुजाश्च चापानि च शराश्च लाघवातिशयेन निर्व्यापारवत् एकरूपा अलक्ष्यन्त। तथापि तयोरन्तरालदेशः शरनिरन्तरोऽदृश्यतेत्यर्थः।

Kula says चापेषु तथा मिलिताः संहिताः (शराः)। His reading might be *miliā* for *ṇimiā* (निहिताः K; नियोजिताः R)। It is possible, however, that K reads *ṇihiā*. Cf. 2.19; 13.85.

70. दहमुहविसज्जिएण अ सरेण सीआविओअसइसंतत्तम्।
हिअअं अमुक्कधीरं णिहाअभिण्णं पि राहवेण ण णाअम्।।

[दशमुखविसृष्टेन च शरेण सीतावियोगसदासंतप्तम्।
हृदयममुक्तधैर्यं निघातभिन्नमपि राघवेण न ज्ञातम्।।]

Rāma was unaware even when his heart was violently pierced

---

[48] I.e. gripped the bow.

[49] While drawing the bow.

[50] I.e. the speed with which the arrows were discharged made it difficult to distinguish the movements of the hands which seemed to remain motionless.

by an arrow discharged by Rāvaṇa, because it was in anguish, being consumed by the grief of separation from Sītā.

K and Kula read जनकतनयावियोगप्रतप्तम् for *sīā-vioa-sai-saṁtattaṁ* = सीतावियोगसदासंतप्तम् (R). K, Kula and MY read अमुक्तवेदनम् for *amukka-dhīraṁ* = अमुक्तधैर्यम् (R).

K says सीतावियोगदुःखेन प्रतप्तम्, अतएवामुक्तवेदनं रामस्य हृदयं रावणमुक्तेन शरेण निघातात् प्रहारात् भिन्नमपि तेन न ज्ञातम्।

MY says *amukka-viaṇaṁ* अमुक्तवेदनम्। He explains *ṇihāa* as निखात (for निघात), and says रावणशरेण गाढभिन्नमपि स्वहृदयं सीतावियोगवेदनातिशयानुबन्धात् रामेण न ज्ञातमित्यर्थः। R says निघातः संघट्टविशेषः। Kula says गुरुप्रहारेण भिन्नमपि।

MY reads *pavvantaṁ* explained as क्लान्तम् for *saṁtattaṁ*. Cf. Hemacandra 4.18 — म्लेर्वा–पव्वायौ–वाइ पव्वायइ मिलाइ।

71. रहुणाहपेसिएण अ सरेण समुहागअस्स रक्खसवइणो।
भिण्णो णिडालवट्टो ण अ से फुडभिउडिविरअणा विद्दविआ।।

[रघुनाथप्रेषितेन च शरेण संमुखागतस्य राक्षसपतेः।
भिन्नं ललाटपृष्ठं न चास्य स्फुटभ्रुकुटिविरचना विद्राविता।।]

An arrow shot by Rāma pierced Rāvaṇa's forehead as he stepped forward, but failed to dispel his clearly visible frown.

K (*chāyā*)has ललाटपट्टः (Kula also) in the second line. He says सुबोधोऽर्थः।

72. तो से मुच्छाविहलो लोहिअणीसन्दभरिअलोअणणिवहो।
वारंवारपअट्टो भमिओ बाहुसिहरेसु मुहसंघाओ।।

[ततोऽस्य मूर्च्छाविह्वलो लोहितनिःस्यन्दभृतलोचननिवहः।
वारंवारप्रवृत्तो भ्रमितो बाहुशिखरेषु मुखसंघातः।।]

The cluster of his faces, drooping in a swoon, with the eyes streaming with blood, tossed on his shoulders again and again.

K *pratīka* has *to mucchā*. He reads ततो मूर्च्छागममुकुलः[51] for *to se mucchā-vihalo* = ततोऽस्य मूर्च्छाविह्वलः (R). Kula has ततस्तस्य मूर्च्छया

[51] Explained as मूर्छागमेन मुकुलो मुकुलिताकारः।

मृदुकः[52], i.e. *to se mucchā-maüo*. K seems to read *to mucchāgama-maülo*. He reads प्रलुठितः (*paloṭṭo*) for *paaṭṭo* = प्रवृत्तः (R). Kula's gloss is here incomplete. *SC* text has *paloṭṭo*.

K says ततो रावणस्य मुखसंघातः मूर्च्छागमेन मुकुलो मुकुलिताकारः, रुधिरनिष्यन्दघूर्णन्नयननिवहः (लोहितनिष्यन्दभरितलोचननिवहः *chāyā*) सन् बाहुशिखरेषु पर्यायेण लुठितः (प्रलुठित *chāyā*) भ्रान्तः। Kula explains लोहित as रुधिर।

73. तो गअमोहुम्मिल्लो णअणहुआसणपइत्तपत्तणपम्हम्।
मुअइ सरोसाअड्ढिअबिइअमुहावङ्गमिलिअपुङ्खं बाणम्।।

[ततो गतमोहोन्मीलो नयनहुताशनप्रदीप्तपत्रणापक्ष्माणम्।
मुञ्चति सरोषाकृष्टद्वितीयमुखापाङ्गमिलितपुङ्खं बाणम्।।]

Thereafter regaining consciousness at the end of the swoon, he let fly an arrow, wrathfully drawn, with the feathered shaft touching the eye-corner of his second face,[53] and the tips of the feathers burnt by the fire issuing from his eyes.

K reads निवह for *pamha* = पक्ष्मन् (R and Kula). K says स्पष्टोऽर्थः। K (*chāyā*) has ततः गतमोहोन्मीलितो नयनहुताशनप्रदीप्तपत्रनिवहम्। . . . बाणम्।। R says पत्रणा पुङ्खः तस्य पक्ष्माण्यग्राणि (रोमाणि Kula) *SC* says पत्रणायाः पक्ष्मरचनायाः पक्ष्माणि। Kula says उन्मीलितः प्रबुद्धः। R explains *ummilla* as उन्मीलितनयन।

74. तो सो खआणलणिहो किरणसहस्सेहि णिब्भरेन्तदसदिसो।
रहुवइसरराहुमुहे पन्थद्धे सूरमण्डलो व्व णिउड्डो।।

[ततः स क्षयानलनिभः किरणसहस्रैर्निर्भ्रियमाणदशदिक्।
रघुपतिशरराहुमुखे पथ्यर्धे सूरमण्डलमिव निमग्नः।।]

But that arrow, filling the ten directions with thousands of rays, and resembling the fire of the epoch of destruction, merged midway in an arrow of Rāma, as does the orb of the sun in the jaws of Rāhu.

The verse is not found in K and MY. Kula says निमग्नो नष्टः। *SC* text has *ṇiuṇṇo* for *ṇiuḍḍo* = निमग्नः (R). Further, it reads *pakkhante* (पक्षान्ते) for *panthaddhe* (पथ्यर्धे) i.e. अर्धे पथि found in R. *SC* says

---

[52] *SC* remarks मूर्छया विह्वलः। पाठान्तरे मृदुको हस्तादिस्पन्दशून्य इति लोकनाथः।

[53] I.e. the arrow was drawn to the furthest limit.

पक्षान्त इत्यनेन अकालग्रहोत्पातसूचनात् संनिहितो रावणविनाशः सूचित इति श्रीनिवासः।
The corresponding reading is missing in our copy of Kula.

75. रहुणाहो वि सधीरं उक्करिसेऊण अग्गहत्थेण सरम्।
आसण्ण लाइअव्वं पेच्छइ फुल्लकमलाअरं व दहमुहम्॥

[रघुनाथोऽपि सधैर्यमुत्कृष्याग्रहस्तेन शरम्।
आसन्ने लवितव्यं प्रेक्षते फुल्लकमलाकरमिव दशमुखम्॥]

Meanwhile Rāma steadily drew an arrow from the quiver, and observed Rāvaṇa, as if he were a lotus pool in bloom whose flowers[54] were to be cut before long.

K says रामोऽपि शरं सधैर्यं तूणीरात् उत्कृष्य आसन्ने संनिकर्षे शीघ्रमेव लवितव्यं छेत्तव्यं रावणं रावणस्य मुखसमूहमित्यर्थः फुल्लं कमलाकरमिवापश्यत्।

MY says *ukkariseūṇa* उत्कृष्य। *āsaṇṇa-lāiavvaṁ* आसन्नलाव्यम्। Kula says संनिहितच्छेदनम्। He takes *lāiavva* as a noun.

76. रामो संधेइ सरं विभीसणन्तेण वलइ रक्खसलच्छी।
दहमुहविणासपिसुणं फुरइ अ सीताइ तक्खणं वामच्छम्॥

[रामः संदधाति शरं विभीषणान्तेन वलति राक्षसलक्ष्मीः।
दशमुखविनाशपिशुनं स्फुरति च सीतायास्तत्क्षणं वामाक्षि॥]

As Rāma joined the arrow to his bow the Fortune of the demons turned towards Vibhīṣaṇa;[55] while at the same moment Sītā's left eye twitched,[56] presaging the destruction of Rāvaṇa.

K says उत्कृष्टं शरं रामः संदधाति धनुषि संदधे। तेन रावणवधं निश्चित्य राक्षसश्रीः विभीषणान्तेन विभीषणसमीपेन विभीषणं प्रति वलते रावणसकाशात् परावर्तते स्म, etc. MY says अन्तशब्दः पार्श्ववाची। He reads *vihīsaṇa* for *vibhīṣaṇa*.

77. वामं णिसिअरणअणं रहुवइणो दाहिणं च फुन्दइ णअणम्।
बन्धुवहरज्जपिसुणं पप्फुरइ विहीसणस्स लोअणजुअलम्॥

[वामं निशिचरनयनं रघुपतेर्दक्षिणं च स्पन्दते नयनम्।
बन्धुवधराज्यपिशुनं प्रस्फुरति बिभीषणस्य लोचनयुगलम्॥]

---

[54] Rāvaṇa's heads are likened to the flowers.

[55] Rāvaṇa's successor on the throne of Laṅkā.

[56] Considered lucky for a woman.

The left eye of Rāvaṇa twitched as did the right eye of Rāma; while both eyes of Vibhīṣaṇa throbbed, betokening the slaying of a kinsman[57] and his own acquisition of a kingdom.[58]

The verse is not found in K, MY and Kula.

78. वच्छभरन्तुच्छङ्गे संधिअबाणे धणुम्मि कड्ढिज्जन्ते।
रामसरपत्तणेहि व उप्पुसिआ सुरवहूण बाहत्थबआ।।

[वक्षोभ्रियमाणोत्सङ्गे संहितबाणे धनुषि कृष्यमाणे।
रामशरपत्रणैरिव उत्प्रोञ्छिताः सुरवधूनां बाष्पस्तबकाः।।]

As Rāma drew his bow, with the arrow fixed, filling the curve with his chest, the tears of the nymphs seemed to be wiped away by the feathers of the arrow.[59]

K and MY read वर्धितरभसनिनादे for *vaccha-bharantucchaṅge* = वक्षोभ्रियमाणोत्सङ्गे (R and Kula). K reads बिन्दवः for *thavaā* = स्तबकाः (R and Kula). See 15.43 above.

K says वर्धितरभसनिनादे प्रवृद्धाकर्षणरभसनादे धनुषि रामेण कृष्यमाणे सति कृष्यमाणस्य रामस्य शरस्य पत्रैरिव सुरवधूनां बाष्पबिन्दव इवोन्मृष्टाः। MY says रामेण संहितशरे धनुषि कृष्यमाणे तारध्वनिश्रवणादेव सुरबन्दीनां रावणविनाशनिश्चयात् अश्रुणि तत्क्षणात् व्यरमन् इति तात्पर्यम्।

Kula says वक्षसा विततेन हेतुना तेन भ्रियमाणोत्सङ्गे विस्तार्यमाणमध्ये, संहितबाणे धनुषि कृष्यमाणे, etc. R says रामशरस्य पत्रणं पुङ्खवर्तिपक्षाः तैरिव उत्प्रोञ्छिताः (Kula also) मार्जिताः। Kula also has पत्रण (*pattaṇa*) rendered as पत्र by K (*chāyā* and commentary).

79. णवरि अ सो रहुवइणा वारं वारेण चन्दहासच्छिण्णो।
एक्केण सरेण लुओ एक्कमुहो दहमुहस्स मुहसंघाओ।।

[अनन्तरं च स रघुपतिना वारं वारं चन्द्रहासच्छिन्नः।
एकेन शरेण लून एकमुखो दशमुखस्य मुखसंघातः।।]

Thereafter the cluster of Rāvaṇa's heads, which he once struck off one by one with his *candrahāsa* sword,[60] was severed all at once by Rāma with a single arrow.

---

[57] I.e. Rāvaṇa.

[58] The twitching of the right eye is lucky and that of the left eye unlucky for a man.

[59] I.e. the impending death of Rāvaṇa assured them of the end of their captivity.

[60] While worshipping Śiva with the exception of the tenth head. Cf. 6.17.

K says स्पष्टोऽर्थः। MY says यो हि दशमुखस्य मुखसंघातः चन्द्रहासेनैकेन पर्यायशः छिन्नः स एवैकेन रामशरेण युगपदेव छिन्न इत्यर्थः। Kula says वारंवारेण क्रमशः, and explains एकमुखः as एकच्छेदमार्गः। R says एकं मुखमुपक्रमो यस्य स एकोपक्रमः सन् लूनः। एकदैव छिन्न इत्यर्थः।

80. अविहत्तकण्ठगरुओ छिन्नो वि दसाणणस्स होइ भअअरो।
धरणिअलुत्तिण्णस्स व णिअअच्छेअपडिउट्ठिओ मुहणिवहो।।

[अविभक्तकण्ठगुरुकश्छिन्नोऽपि दशाननस्य भवति भयंकरः।
धरणितलोत्तीर्णस्येव निजकच्छेदप्रत्युत्थितो मुखनिवहः।।]

The cluster of Rāvaṇa's heads, massive with the necks undivided, looked terrible, even though severed from the body, as if they had grown again from the cuts while he emerged from below the earth.[61]

K reads सुविभक्त for *avihatta* = अविभक्त (R and Kula). K and probably MY read परिसंस्थितः for *paḍiuṭṭhio* = प्रत्युत्थितः (R).

K says रामशरेण युगपतं छिन्नः सुविभक्तै कण्ठैः छिन्नशेषैः कण्ठप्रदेशैः गुरः, भुवि पतित्वा निजच्छेदैः परिसंस्थितो जीवदवस्थायामिव भुवि स्थितो मुखनिवहः छिन्नोऽपि भयङ्करोऽभूत्। कथमिति चेत् मामया भूयो धरणितलोत्तीर्णस्येव पातालात् धरणितलं भित्त्वा उत्तीर्णस्येव दृश्यमानस्य रावणस्य। राक्षसानामसुराणां च पातालनिवासित्वं प्रसिद्धम्।

असुरा दानवा दैत्या दैतेयाः सुरशत्रवः।
पूर्वदेवाः शुक्रशिष्याः पातालनिलयाः स्मृताः।। इति हलायुधः।

MY says निजच्छेदमार्गेण प्रथिव्यां प्रतिष्ठितः अस्य मुखसंघातः पूर्वतो निर्विशेषतया पातालादुत्पतनशङ्कामकरोदित्यर्थः।

Kula says अविभक्तैः स्कन्धेन सह छिन्नत्वात् अपृथग्भूतैः कण्ठैः गुरुकः अपधधृष्यः, छिन्नोऽपि दशमुखस्य मुखनिवहो निजकेन छेदेन (छेद)स्थानेन पतितः धरणीतलात् उत्तीर्णस्येव धरणीतलं भित्त्वा निर्गतस्येव भयङ्करो भवति। Kula's reading might be पतितस्थितः (*paḍia-ṭṭhio*), Cf. *SC* text, for *paḍiu°* (R). See above. *SC* says निजच्छेदेन पतितस्थितः छेदानुरूपेण पङ्क्तीभूय पतित इत्यर्थः। R says निजकच्छेदेभ्यः प्रत्युत्थित इव पूर्ववत् पुनरुत्पन्न इव।

81. तस्स हअस्स रणमुहे रक्खसणाहस्स अहिमुहं अप्पाणो।
दसहि वि मुहेहि समअं सिहाकरालो व्व हुअवहो णिक्कन्तो।।

[61] Translation follows Rāmadāsa's reading. According to Kulanātha's reading, looked terrible, even though severed, as they lay on the ground along the line of the cut, as if he had emerged, etc. See Extracts.

[तस्य हतस्य रणमुखे राक्षसनाथस्याभिमुखमात्मा।
दशभिरपि मुखैः समं शिखाकराल इव हुतवहो निष्क्रान्तः।।]

The soul of the lord of the demons, slain as he confronted the enemy in battle, departed through his ten mouths at the same moment, as if it were fire bursting into a blaze.

K says रणमुखे तस्य रावणस्य आत्मा जीवात्मा शिखाकरालोऽग्निरिव सर्वेषामभिमुखं प्रत्यक्षमेव दशमभिरपि मुखैः निष्क्रान्तः। Kula says शिखाभिः करालो महान् हुतवह इव। R says करालः सच्छिद्रो दन्तुरो वा। Kula says तस्य राक्षसनाथस्य अभिमुखं रणमुखे हतस्य . . . सममेककालम् . . .।

82. अह णिहअम्मि दहमुहे ऊससिअम्मि अ समन्तओ तेह्लोके।
वअणम्मि अ उप्पुसिआ भिउडी ओआरिअं च रामेण धणुम्।।

[अथ निहते दशमुखे उच्छ्वसिते च समन्ततस्त्रैलोक्ये।
वदने वोत्प्रोञ्छिताभ्रकुटिरवतारितं च रामेण धनुः।।]

When Rāvaṇa was slain, and the three worlds heaved a sigh of relief all around, the frown disappeared from Rāma's brow, and his bow was unstrung.

K reads समस्ते (i.e. *samattammi*) for *samantao* (R and Kula).

K says अथ रावणे निहते त्रैलोक्ये चोच्छवसिते रामस्य वदने भ्रकुटिरुन्मृष्टा। रामेण चापं चावतारितम् अवरोपितमौर्वीकं कृतम।

Kula seems to read *samuppusiā* for *a uppusiā* as he has समुत्प्रोञ्छिता।

83. णिद्दअबन्धुप्पित्था जाणन्ती विक्कमं णिसाअरवइणो।
माअ त्ति परिगणेन्ती ण मुअइ णिअहं पि रावणं राअसिरी।।

[निर्दयबन्धूद्विग्ना जानती विक्रमं निशाचरपतेः।
मायेति परिगणयन्ती न मुञ्चति निहतमपि रावणं राजश्रीः।।]

Royal Fortune, distressed on account of her cruel friend,[62] did not forsake Rāvaṇa even when killed regarding his death as an illusion because she knew the might of the lord of the demons.[63]

The verse is not found in K and probably MY. The latter on verse 81 says गाथाचतुष्टयं स्फुट्म। The next verse he explains is 86.

[62] I.e. Rāvaṇa, because he left her suddenly.

[63] I.e. Rāvaṇa looked majestic in his death.

84. ताहे विभीसणस्स वि अन्तोहिअअम्मि बन्धुणेहुप्पण्णो।
दासरहिणो वि पुरओ मुक्को च्चिअ लोअणेहि बाहत्थवओ।।

[तदा विभीषणस्याप्यन्तर्हृदये बन्धुस्नेहोत्पन्नः।
दाशरथेरपि पुरतो मुक्त एव लोचनाभ्यां बाष्पस्तबकः।।]

At the moment, even in the presence of Rāma, tears welled up in Vibhīṣaṇa's eyes, because of the affection for his brother[64] in the inmost recesses of his heart.

K reads विभीषणेन चाशून्यहृदयेन for *vibhīsaṇassa vi antohiaammi* = विभीषणस्य अन्तर्हृदये (R and Kula). K and Kula(?) read बाष्पबिन्दवः for *bāha-tthavao* = बाष्पस्तबकः। (R). See 15.43 above. *SC* text has *bāha-tthevā* = ⁰बिन्दवः।

K says तदानीमशून्यहृदयेन च। हेतौ तृतीया। धैर्यात् कथंचित् अशून्यहृदयत्वेन हेतुना अविनष्टसंज्ञत्वेन इत्यर्थः। सुबोधमन्यत।

85. णिहअम्मि अ दहवअणे विहीसणो णिन्दिआमरत्तणसद्दो।
परिदेविउं पउत्तो मरणसमब्भहिअदुक्खदिण्णाआसो।।

[निहते च दशवदने विभीषणो निन्दितामरत्वशब्दः।
परिदेवितुं प्रवृत्तो मरणसमभ्यधिकदुःखदत्तायासः।।]

When Rāvaṇa was slain, Vibhīṣaṇa began to lament, decrying his immortality,[65] being racked by anguish greater than death.

K (*chāyā*) has अथ निहते दशमुखे for *ṇihaammi a dahā-vaaṇe* (R and Kula).

K says रावणे भ्रातरि हते विभीषणो निन्दितामरत्वशब्दः, वरप्रदानसमये ब्रह्मा विभीषणाय प्रसादात् अमरत्वं दत्तवानिति प्रसिद्धम्, तस्मात् भ्रातरि हते सति आत्मनो मरणाभावात् निन्दतीत्यर्थः। मरणादपि अभ्यधिकेन दुःखेन दत्तायासं यथा परिदेवितुमारब्धः। K (*chāyā*) has दत्तायासः।

86. जो च्चिअ जेऊण जमं दिट्ठो इच्छासुहं तुमे जमलोओ।
दीसिहिसि कह णु पत्थिव इण्हिं तं चेअ सेसजणसामण्णम्।।

[य एव जित्वा यमं दृष्ट इच्छासुखं त्वया यमलोकः।
द्रक्ष्यसि कथं नु पार्थिव इदानीं तमेव शेषजनसामान्यम्।।]

---

[64] Literally, kinsman.

[65] A boon granted to Vibhīṣana by Brahmā, now appearing to be burdensome as it prevented death from ending his sorrow.

"In common with all other beings, how wilt thou now, O king, visit the selfsame realm of Yama that thou hadst visited at will by conquering the latter?[66]

K says स्पष्टोऽर्थः। In K (*chāyā*) *jo ccia* is rendered as यत एव। R has य एव। In the second line K (*chāyā*) has पार्थिव कथम् (i.e. *patthiva kahaṁ*) for *kaha ṇu patthiva* (R). Kula also has only कथम् like K, and says तमेव यमलोकमिदानीं कथम् 'अशेष'जनसामान्यं द्रक्ष्यसि। Kula seems to read *saala* (सकल) for *sesa* like manuscript C of Goldschmidt.

MY reads *dicchihisi* (द्रक्ष्यसि) for *dīsihisi* (R). Manuscript B of MY has *dasihisi* which seems to be a mistake for *dīsi°*. *SC* text has *dacchihisi*. MY and *SC* texts have *eṇhiṁ* for *i°* (इदानीम्)।

87. एक्केण रक्खसाहिव पुव्वं अवहीरिओवएसेण वि ते।
समणिहणेण रणमुहे पडिमुक्कं णवर कुम्भअण्णेण तुहम्।।

[एकेन राक्षसाधिप पूर्वमवधीरितोपदेशेनापि ते।
समनिधनेन रणमुखे प्रतिमुक्तं केवलं कुम्भकर्णेन तव।।]

Lord of the demons, having fallen with thee in battle, Kumbhakarṇa alone hath requited his obligation to thee, even though thou hadst despised his counsel before?[67]

K reads निहतेन रणमुखे पुनः for *sama-ṇihaṇeṇa raṇamuhe* = समनिधनेन रणमुखे (R and Kula). He reads अनुसदृशम् (*aṇusarisaṁ*) and कृतम्। (*kaaṁ*) for *paḍimukkaṁ* (प्रतिमुक्तम्) and *tuhaṁ* (तव) found in R and Kula.

K says हे राक्षसाधिप ते त्वया अवधीरितोपदेशेन। अहं च कुम्भकर्णश्च त्वयावधीरितोपदेशौ जातौ। त्वया हृता रामपत्नी पुनस्तस्मै प्रदीयतामित्युपदिशन् अहं च कुम्भकर्णश्च त्वया पूर्वमवज्ञातौ। ततोऽहं भवन्तं परित्यज्य राममाश्रितः। त्वयावधीरितोपदेशेनापि त्वामपरित्यज्यरणमुखे निहतेन कुम्भकर्णेन एकेन केवलमनुसदृशं कृतम्। भ्रातृस्नेहसदृशं कृतम्। मया तु नृशंसमनुष्ठितमित्यर्थः।

MY says पूर्वं हितमुपदिशन्नपि त्वयावधीरितः कुम्भकर्ण एक एव त्वदर्थं रणे मुक्तजीवितो यशः कृतवानित्यर्थः।

Kula says त्वया पूर्वमधुतहितोपदेशेनापि तेन कुम्भकर्णेन केवलं रणःमुखे समनिधनेन

---

[66] I.e. the conqueror of the god of death will now visit the latter's kingdom like all other mortals.

[67] Kumbhakarṇa had advised Rāvaṇa to return Sītā to Rāma.

समकालप्राप्तनिधनेन तव प्रतिमुक्तं सुकृतं शोधितमित्यर्थः। Kula seems to read *avahua-hiovaesena* (अवधुतहितोपदेशेन) for *avahīro*° (अवधीरितोपदेशेन)[68]।

R says ते तव अवधीरित उपदेशो येन। पूर्वं प्रतिक्षिप्तभवदाज्ञेनापि स्वतन्त्रत्वात्।

88. पत्थिव तुमं मुअन्तो समसुहदुक्खेहि बन्धवेहि अमुक्कम।
जइ हं धम्मपहाणो धम्मपहाणाण को गणिज्जउ पुरओ।।

[पार्थिव त्वां मुञ्चन्समसुखदुःखैर्बान्धवैरमुक्तम्।
यद्यहं धर्मप्रधानोऽधर्मप्रधानानां को गण्यतां पुरतः।।]

If I am pious, I who forsook thee, unforsaken by thy other kinsmen who shared thy joys and sorrows, then, O king, who should be counted first among the impious?"

K reads *gaṇijai* (गण्यते) for *gaṇijjaü* = गण्यताम् (R and Kula).

K says समसुखदुःखैः बान्धवैः सर्वैः अमुक्तं त्वां मुञ्चन् अहं धर्मप्रधानो यदि धर्म एव प्रधानं यस्य स तथा स्यां यदि अधर्मप्रधानानां मध्ये पूर्वं को गण्यते। जगति अधार्मिकाणामग्रणीरहमेव हि गणनीय इत्यर्थः।

MY says *haṁ* अहम्। *tumaṁ* त्वाम्। *ahamma-pahāṇāṇa (adhamma*° A) अधर्मप्रधानानाम्। *purao* पुरतः प्रथमत इति यावत्। समदुःखसुखेषु बन्धुषु अमुञ्चत्सु त्वां पितृतुल्यं मुञ्चन् अहं कथं धर्मप्रधान इत्यर्थः। It will be seen that MY reads *adhamma*° or *ahamma*° for *dhamma*°, like manuscript C of Goldschmidt, but it violates the metre. The sense, however, requires it; and the other commentaries appear to construe *dhamma-pahāṇāṇa* as *(a)dhamma*° (अधर्मप्रधानानाम्)। It may be noted that manuscript A of MY actually reads *adhamma-pahuṇāṇa*[69] (for °*pahāṇāṇa*), which suits the metre, but *pahuṇa* does not give प्रधान। There is a *deśī* word *pahaṇa*[70] in the sense of कुल (*D N* 6.5) which is not suitable either. *SC* text has *adhamma-pavaṇāṇa* (अधर्मप्रवणानां) which looks like an attempt to avoid the metrical difficulty, but mars the antithesis between धर्मप्रधान and अधर्मप्रधान्।

---

[68] Cf. *SC* text which, however, has *avahaa* (अवहत)।

[69] Our copy has °*ṇāṇāṁ* which is a scribal error.

[70] K and Muda in their gloss on 36 construe *chāā-vahaṇa* as छायाप्रधान Muda explains the form *pahaṇa* by referring the word प्रधान to the उत्खात group metioned by Hemacandra 1.67 (*ukkhāa, ukkhaa*, etc.) but प्रधान is not included in that group.

89. आहासइ अ रहुवइं मरणसमोब्भहिअरुद्धबाहुप्पीडो।
बन्धुवहागअदुक्खो गिम्हुम्हासुक्खणइमुहो व्व महिहरो।।

[आभाषते च रघुपतिं मरणसमभ्यधिकरुद्धबाष्पोत्पीडः।
बन्धुवधागतदुःखो ग्रीष्मोष्मशुष्कनदीमुख इव महीधरः।।]

Sorrowing over the killing of his kinsmen, Vibhīṣaṇa spoke to Rāma as he checked his oncoming tears with an effort more unbearable than death, like unto a mountain whose streams were dried by the summer's heat.

90. पहु वीसज्जेहि महं ता दहमुहकुम्भअण्णचलणणिवडिओ।
पच्छा परलोअगअं छिवामि सीसम्मि मेहणाअं च सुअम्।।

[प्रभो विसृज मां तावद्दशमुखकुम्भकर्णचरणनिपतितः।
पश्चात्परलोकगतं स्पृशामि शीर्षे मेघनादं च सुतम्।।]

Sire, vouchsafe me leave to touch the head of the child Meghanāda that is dead, after I have fallen at the feet of Kumbhakarṇa and Rāvaṇa.

The verses are not found in K and MY. Kula has विसर्जय माम् in verse 90. R has विसृज।

91. महिअलपडिअविसंठुलहीसणविलावजाआणुअम्पेण।
रामेण वि पवणसुओ आणत्तो रक्खसाहिवइसक्कारे।।

[महीतलपतितविसंष्ठुलविभीषणविलापजातानुकम्पेन।
रामेणापि पवनसुत आज्ञप्तो राक्षसाधिपतिसंस्कारे।।]

Moved to pity by Vibhīṣaṇa's lament as he lay on the ground, distracted with grief, Rāma ordered Hanumat to perform the funeral rites for the lord of the demons.

K reads दत्तमन्युस्तम्भम् for *jāāṇuampeṇa* = जातानुकम्पेन (R). Kula has दत्तानुकम्पेन। K reads आज्ञप्तः (*āṇatto*) for *pavaṇa-suo* (R); and आरब्धः (*āḍhatto*) for *āṇatto* = आज्ञप्तः (R and Kula). K reads संस्कारः (MY also) for (*sakkāre* = संस्कारे (R). Kula's reading is same as R's, but he says सत्कारे अग्निदाने।[71]

K says महीतलपतितविसंस्थुलस्य विभीषणस्य विलापैः दत्तः कृतः रामस्य

[71] Some words are missing in Kula's gloss in the verse.

मन्युस्तम्भः कोपप्रशमो यथा भवति तथा रामेणापि आज्ञप्तः रावणस्य अन्त्यः संस्कार आरब्धः। Kula says विसंष्ठुलस्य व्याकुलस्य विभीषणस्य विलापेन।

MY's readings appear to be same as those of K. He says विभीषणादिषु भयादप्रार्थयमानेषु अपि अस्य संस्कारो रामेण स्वयमेवाज्ञापित इत्यर्थः। Manuscript A of MY gives सत्कार as the equivalent of *sakkāra*. Cf. Kula above.

92. णिहअम्मि अ दहवअणे आसंघन्तेण जणअतणआलम्भम्।
सुग्गीवेण वि दिट्ठो पच्चुबआरस्स साअरस्स व अन्तो।।

[निहते च दशवदनेऽध्यवस्यता जनकतनयालम्भम्।
सुग्रीवेणापि दृष्टः प्रत्युपकारस्य सागरस्येवान्तः।।]

Rāvaṇa having been slain, Sugrīva, confident of the recovery of Sītā, saw the end of his services in return for Rāma's kindness, just as he had seen the further shore of the ocean.

K says रावणे हते रामस्य सीतालाभोऽवश्यमेव सिद्ध इति विश्वसता सुग्रीवेण। MY says *āsaṁghanteṇa* आशंसमानेन निश्चिन्वता।

93. काऊण अ सुरकज्जं रहुवइवीसज्जिएण कइअणपुरओ।
जलहरगुप्पन्तधओ सग्गाहिमुहो रहो कओ माअडिणा।।

[कृत्वा च सुरकार्यं रघुपतिविसृष्टेन कपिजनपुरतः।
जलधरव्याकुलायमानध्वजः स्वर्गाभिमुखो रथः कृतो मातलिना।।]

Having completed his mission on behalf of the gods, Mātali, permitted by Rāma in the presence of the apes, turned his chariot towards heaven, with the banner fluttering amidst the clouds.

K reads रघुतनय for *rahuvai* (R and Kula). This shows that he reads *visajjieṇa* for *vī°* (R). K and MY read नीतः (*ṇio*) for *kao* = कृतः (R and Kula). K (*chāyā*) has जलधरयुक्तध्वजपटः for *jalahara-guppanta-dhao* found in R and Kula (गुप्यमान Kula; व्याकुलायमान R)। K does not explain the verse, and says स्पष्टम्।

94. घेत्तूण जणअतणअं कञ्चणलट्ठिं व हुअवहम्मि विसुद्धम्।
पत्तो पुरिं रहुवई काउं भरहस्स सप्फलं अणुराअम्।।

[गृहीत्वा जनकतनयां काञ्चनयष्टिमिव हुतवहे विशुद्धाम्।
प्राप्तः पुरीं रघुपतिः कर्तुं भरतस्य सफलमनुरागम्।।]

Taking with him Sītā, purified in the fire like a bar of gold, Rāma reached the city (of Ayodhyā) to crown Bharata's devotion to him with glory.

K has गृहीत्वा च जनकसुताम् for *ghettūṇa jaṇaa-taṇaaṁ* (R and Kula).

95. एत्थ समप्पइ एअं सीआलम्भेण जणिअरामब्भुअअम्।
रावणवह त्ति कव्वं अणुराअङ्कं समत्थजणणिव्वेसम्।।

[अत्र समाप्यते एतत्सीतालम्भेन जनितरामाभ्युदयम्।
रावणवध इति काव्यमनुरागाङ्कं समस्तजननिर्द्वेषम्।।]

Here ends the poem "The Slaying of Rāvaṇa", marked with the word *anurāga* (at the end of each canto). It rejoices the heart because of the recovery of Sītā, and is delightful to those who appreciate poetry.[72]

K, MY and Kula read हृदय (*hiaa*) for राम (R) in the first line. K reads सतृष्णसुख (*saaṇha-suha*) for *samattha-jaṇa* = समस्तजन (R).

K says रामस्य सीतालाभेन अभिषेकोत्सवादपि अभ्यधिकेन जनितहृदयाभ्युदयं जनितरामहृदयाभ्युदयम्, अनुरागशब्दैरुच्छ्वासान्तेषु अङ्कितम्, सतृष्णानां सुखं सुखकरो निर्वेशः अनुभवो यस्य, 'निर्वेशः संमूर्च्छने स्यात् कर्मभृत्युपभोगयोः' इति वैजयन्ती, रावणवध इत्येतत् काव्यमत्रैव समाप्यते। नातः परं वक्ष्यत इत्यर्थः।

Kula says सकर्णानां सुखहेतुः निवेशः (निर्वेशः ?) अनुभवः[73] यस्य तत् तथा। He seems to read *saaṇṇa-suha*. MY's reading appears to be same as Kula's. He says श्रोत्रवतां[74] कृतप्रबन्धांशमात्रेणैव सुखहेतुत्वात् हृदयोद्वेजनाजनकत्वाच्च इत्यर्थः। सीतालाभावसानिकतया हृदयोत्सवहेतुत्वाच्च इत्यर्थः। (अत्रैव समाप्यते)।

R (MY also) explains *ṇivvesa* as निर्द्वेषः। R says समस्तजनस्य द्वेषशून्यं सीतारामसम्बन्धित्वेन अनुरक्तसर्वजनमित्यर्थः। Cf. MY above — हृदयोद्वेजनाजनक।

इअ सिरिपवरसेणविरइए कालिदासकए दहमुहवहे महाकव्वे
पञ्च(न्द)रहो आसासओ समत्तो।

[इति श्रीप्रवरसेनविरचिते कालिदासकृते दशमुखवधे महाकाव्ये
पञ्चदश आश्वासकः समाप्तः।]

---

[72] Literally, those who have a (good) ear (for poetry). The reading followed is *saaṇṇa*. See Extracts.

[73] Our copy has अनुतनो, but the sense is clear from K's gloss.

[74] Corresponds to सकर्णानाम् which is the reading of Kula manuscripts A of MY has श्रोत्रवतां कवीनां प्रबन्धांशमात्रेणैव, etc.

Appendix

I

As pointed out in the Introduction, section V, the south Indian recension of the *Setubandha* contains some verses which are not found in Rāmadāsa. Four of these verses are, however, found also in Kulanātha, showing that they are common to the south Indian and Bengal recensions. They are included in the, text accompanying the *Setutattvacandrikā* commentary compiled in Bengal at a later date, and reproduced below with extracts from the commentaries.

The verse numbers are those of the Calcutta edition of the *Rāvaṇavaha-mahākāvyam* with the above-mentioned commentary.

गरुए वि समर-कज्जे विअसन्ते च्चिअ रसं लहन्ति समत्था।
बद्ध-प्फलम्मि कुसुमे वोलीणो होई महुअराण अवसरो।। 3.6

K *pratīka* has *guruammi*. He says गुरुणि समरकार्ये विकसत्येव रसं लभन्ते समर्थाः रसं विजयसुखास्वादं लभन्ते। अत्रोदाहरणमाह–कुसुमे बद्धफले जातफले सति मधुकराणामवसरो मधुपानामवकाशः अतिक्रान्तो भवतीति तद्वत् अन्यैः सेवकैः निर्वर्तितप्राये सति कार्ये समर्थानां पराक्रमावसरोऽतिक्रान्तः स्यादिति यावत्। Kula's gloss on the verse is anonymously reproduced in *SC*.

जलण–प्पहाणुविद्धं आवत-भमन्त-पव्वअ-दुमालग्गं।
संबद्ध-रअण-पुप्फं फुरइ फुरन्त-प्पहं पवाल-किसलअं।। 5.49

K says आवर्तेषु भ्रमतां पर्वतानां द्रुमेषु आलग्नं, ज्वलनप्रभयानुविद्धं, संबद्धरत्नपुष्पं, स्फुरत्प्रभं प्रवालकिसलयं विद्रुमकिसलयं स्फुरति स्म। रत्नं मौक्तिकं, तदेव वृक्षाणां पुष्पमिवासीत्। विद्रुम एव किसलयमभूत। इदं विशेष्यपदम्।

Kula says ज्वलनप्रभया तुल्यवर्णयानुविद्धं सत् स्फुरत्प्रभं स्फुरति राजते।

बाणोसारिअ–सलिला थोउब्भिज्जन्त–पाअडिअ–सिप्पि–उडा।
विअसन्ति विअसिआअव–वसुआअन्त–मणि–गब्भिणा पुलिण–वहा।। – 5.72

K seems to read *thoöbhijjanta* for *thoübhhi°* in the first line. He says स्तोकमीषत् अवभिद्यमानो विदीर्यमाणः प्रकटितः शक्तिपुटो यत्र। अन्यत् स्पष्टम्। MY says *vasuāanta* शुष्यत्। *gabbhiṇā* गर्भिताः। पुलिनानां विकासो जलक्षयात् विस्तारः। Kula has स्तोकोद्भिद्यमानप्रकटितशक्तिपुटाः।

आइद्ध-महिहर-णिहं उअहि-जल-पलोट्ट-मेह-अड-पब्भारं।
पडइ व पुरओहुत्तं टङ्क-च्छिण्णं व सेउ-बन्धस्स णहं।। 8.58

This is Kula's reading of the verse. The south Indian commentators read the second line differently. K (*chāyā*) has पततीव पुरतोऽभिमुखं टङ्कच्छेदे सेतुबन्धस्य मुखम्। Kula's gloss on the verse is missing in our copy. *SC* says सेतुबन्धस्य पुरतोऽभिमुखं टङ्कच्छिन्नमिव नभः पतति। टङ्कः पाषाणदारणे इति नभसः पाषाणसादृश्यं समाहितं टङ्करूपेण सेतुना छिन्नं यत् पुरोऽभिमुखं पततीवेत्यर्थः। . . . उदधिजलपर्यस्ता मेघतटप्राग्भारा अर्थात् गिरिशिखरप्रेरिता यस्मात्। एतेन मेघानां टङ्कच्छिन्नस्य नभसोऽवयवसाम्यमुक्तम्। . . . प्रक्षिप्तमहीधरनिभं नभ इत्यर्थः।

K says टङ्कः पाषाणभेदनः। आविद्धधहीधरनिभं पृथग्विभिन्नपर्वतनिभं समुद्रजले प्रलुठितं मेघतटजालं पर्वतैः सह पतितमेघजालं विरराजेत्यध्याहार्यम्। अत्रोत्प्रेक्ष्यते—सेतुं विरचयतो विश्वकर्मतनयस्य टङ्कच्छेदे पर्वतघटनार्थे टङ्कच्छेदे पर्वतघटनार्यं टङ्कच्छेदे सति पुरोमुखं सेतुबन्धस्य मुखमपतदिवेति। मुखशब्देन पर्वतखण्ड उच्यते। MY says उदधिजले प्रलुठितो मेघतटप्राग्भारो यत्र तत्तथा। आविद्धः रभसक्षिप्तः[1] महीधरो यस्य तदाविद्धमहीधरम्, तत्सदृशमेवंभूतं सेतुबन्धस्य मुखं टङ्कच्छेदे सति पुरतोऽभिमुखमपतदिवेति वासितक्षणच्छेदमन्वभूदिवेत्यर्थः। Deva reads मुखे for मुखम् and says . . . मेघतटप्राग्भारं सेतुबन्धस्य मुखे यः टङ्कच्छेदः पाषाणसन्धिः तस्मिन् विवरे पततीव।

II

Extracts from the commentary of Kṛṣṇadāsa.

1.1. नमतेत्यनेन तावत् समस्तप्रपञ्चव्यतिरिक्तरूपस्य भगवतो मधुमथनस्यासाधारणेन प्रपञ्चव्यतिरिक्तरूपेण निर्देशः क्रियते। . . . अथवा पञ्चापि भूतानि मधुमथनस्यैव रूपाणीति भवन्ति। तत्र तावदवर्धिततुङ्गमित्यनेन मधुमथनस्य गगनरूपत्वमुक्तम्। . . . गगनं ह्यवर्धितमहत्त्वं भवति, मधुमथनोऽपि तथेति। अविसारितविस्तृतमित्यनेन देवस्य पृथिवीरूपतोक्ता पृथिवी केनाप्यविसारितविस्तृता, मधुमथनोऽपि व्याप्तः। अनवनतगम्भीरमित्यनेन सलिलात्मकता। सलिलं ह्युद्धतगम्भीरं च भवति, मधुमथनोऽपि तथा। यदप्यज्ञातपरमार्थप्रकटत्वं पृथिव्यादिषु सर्वेषु भूतेषु अप्यविशिष्टं तथापि तेषु विशेषगुणाभिघानात् अनेनास्य तेजोरूपत्वमुक्तं, मधुमथनोऽपि तथा। किं मधुमथनस्य भूतानि रूपाणि दृश्यन्ते इति चेत् भूतारब्धत्वेन दृष्टस्यापि जगतो मधुमथनमयत्वेन प्रदर्शनायेति।

2.1. अथ रामः समुद्रमपश्यत् स्वकार्यस्य यौवनमिव स्थितमिति। सुग्रीवस्य सख्यादारभ्य सीताधिगमनं यावत् रामस्य कार्यं तत् समुद्रदर्शनात् प्रागचिरजातं शैशव इव वर्तते। समुद्रदर्शनादारभ्य तत्संबन्धं यावत् यौवन इव द्वितीयावस्थायाम् अतः समुद्रो यौवनत्वेन वर्तते। यौवने वर्तमानस्य पुरुषस्य दोषशतानि भवन्ति। तथा समुद्रसंबन्धितया

1 विक्षिप्तः A.

स्थितस्य तरुणरूपस्य कार्यस्य प्रतिबन्धकदोषशतानि भवन्ति। तेन चटुलत्वादियुक्तत्वेन समुद्रो यौवनत्वेन वर्ण्यते इति। समुद्रो हि चटुलस्तिमितिमिंगिलादिभिर्दोषशतैर्दुःखेनातिक्रमितव्यः। सारभूतेनामृतरसेन गुरुः। यौवनमपि चपलेन पुरुषेण युक्तं कामेनार्थक्षयादिभिर्दोषशतैर्युक्तममृतरसायमानेन कामस्य भोगादिसारेण युक्तं चेति। कस्यांचित् प्रतिहतौ सत्यां रामस्य रघुतनयादिभिर्व्यवहारो भवति। अन्यत्र रघुनाथरामादिभिरिति।

2.8. बहुशो वेलामतिक्रम्य तरङ्गैर्महीमप्याप्लाव्य निवर्तमानं समुद्रमिति। पार्श्वस्थिता वेला मही च समुद्रस्य भार्ये इव। तदा महीपार्श्वं गच्छन्तं समुद्रं मध्येमार्गे वेलालिङ्गति। तयालिङ्ग्य मुक्ते पश्चात् स्वपार्श्वमागते तरङ्गकरैरात्मानं स्प्रष्टुमारब्धे समुद्रे असहमाना मही धुतवनराजिकरतला भवति। तथा कुपितायामिव मह्यां सत्यां समुद्रोऽपि भयेनैव त्वरितमपसर्पति। आशयेव[2] पुनरुपसर्पति। पुनस्तस्मिन् आगते मही पूर्वमिव भवति। अथाप्यभिमतपुरुषस्पर्शागतेन रसेनार्द्रा भवतीति मह्यां स्त्रीत्वनिर्वाहाय मलयमहेन्द्रस्तनीत्युक्तम्।

2.16. उद्धतेन पुरुषेण प्रथमं प्रतिहतत्वात् प्रतिनिवृत्तगतिभिः, तस्मिन् अन्तः प्रविष्टे त्वरितनिवृत्ताभिः नदीभिः अन्वीयमानं[3] समुद्रमिति। स्त्रियो हि झटिति पुरुषेणानुगम्यमानाः स्वयं पराङ्मुख्यो भवन्ति। पश्चात्तस्मिन् उपेक्ष्य गते अनुशयविलोलास्तस्य गृहं स्वयमेवाभिसरन्ति। एवं समुद्रेण यदाभिलीना अभिगतास्तदा पराङ्मुख्योऽभूवन् नद्यः। स यदा स्पृष्ट्वा तत्रालब्धसुखोऽपसृतस्तदा अनुशयविलोलाभिरिव वेपमाननिवृत्तप्रस्थिताभिर्नदीभिः समुद्रोऽन्वीयमानमार्ग इति।

4.23. विषादादयो हि धैर्यादीनि नियतं नाशयन्ति। एवं वयःपरिणामोऽपि यत् गृहीतपक्षो नियतं नाशयति तत् किमुच्यतां न किंचिदपीत्यर्थः।

7.50. जले मज्जन्तः प्राणिनो हि नासाप्रविष्टजला भ्रियन्ते। तथा सति मज्जन्तो गजाः स्वनासारूपं करं जलाप्रवेशायोद्धरन्ति।

III

An extract from the Rāmadṛṣṭi fragment:

1.1. अप्रलघुपरिश्लक्ष्णम्-एवमुक्तनीत्या प्रलघुकम्। लघुरल्पः, अल्पेऽपि स्याल्लघुरित्यमरः, तदन्यमनल्पमपि परिश्लक्ष्णं सूक्ष्मम्। आकाशादपि अतीव प्रतनुकमिति भावः। यदुक्तं बृहद्वासिष्ठे–

गगनाङ्गादपि स्वच्छे शून्ये तस्मिन् परे पदे।
कथं सन्ति सरिन्मेरुसमुद्रगगनादयः॥

2 Citation in Devarāta has आशयेन।

3 Citation in Devarāta has पुनः प्रविश्यमानं।

इति व्याप्तत्वेऽपि सूक्ष्मत्वादेव नोपलब्धिविषय इति भावः नन्वेवं तर्हि एवंभूतस्यात्मानोऽस्तित्वे किं प्रमाणमित्याह–अज्ञातपरमार्थप्रकटमज्ञातपरमार्थम् उक्तनीत्या अननुभूतयाथार्थ्यमपि प्रकटं प्रकाशं सर्वेषामपि प्राणिनामहमिति स्वसंवेदनसिद्धमिति भावः। यदाहुः –

गोपालकुम्भदासीनामप्यसौ प्रकटः सदा।
रुद्रोपनिषदप्येवं स्तौति सर्वात्मकं शिवम्।।

इति सर्वेषामपि संवेदनसिद्धत्वमेवात्मनोऽस्तित्वे प्रमाणमिति भावः। अत्र एवमीश्वरस्य प्रकटत्वे सति कथं प्राणिनां संसारित्वमिति शङ्कायाः नावसरः अज्ञातपरमार्थ इत्युक्तादेव हेतोरिति। . . .

अत्र पञ्चभिर्विशेषणैः साक्षात् सत्यज्ञानादिलक्षणमनन्तानन्दसागरं निष्कलं परमात्मानं प्रतिपाद्य पुनर्मधुमथनशब्देन तद्विवर्तभूतं रामाद्यवतार- निदानभूतं–

अस्त्यनन्तविलासात्मा सर्वगः सर्वसंश्रयः।
चिदाकाशोऽपि नाशात्मा प्रदीपः सर्ववस्तुषु।।

स्पन्दास्पन्दसमाकारस्ततो विष्णुरजायत।
स्पन्दमानरसापूरात् तरङ्गः सागरादिव।।

इत्यादिना बृहद्वासिष्ठे प्रतिपादितं विष्णुतत्त्वमुच्यते।